Get these PostScript® Cookbook Routines on disk.

Only $19.95*

The PostScript routines used to generate the figures in this *Reference Guide,* as discussed in the Cookbook Section, are now available on disk, along with additional interesting and useful PostScript programs. Please send $19.95 (U.S.) check or money order, or charge to your Visa or MasterCard. Fill in the required information below, and send this card to:

> Cheshire Group
> P.O. Box 2103
> Menlo Park, CA 94026

Disk Format::   Macintosh   ☐

             IBM-PC   3.5″   ☐

             IBM-PC low density   5.25″   ☐

Name: _____ Daytime phone: _____

Address: _____

City: _____ State: _____ Zip: _____

If charging to your credit card:

Type: Visa ☐   MasterCard ☐
Number:
(please be sure to include all digits)

Expiration Date:
Signature: Date:

*California residents add 6½% sales tax. For export orders, add $5.00 (U.S.) shipping and handling.

Cheshire Group
P.O. Box 2103
Menlo Park, CA 94026-2103

PhoenixPage™

Please start my complimentary subscription to Phoenix Publications: Phoenix Report and Phoenix Bulletin.

Name: _____

Title: _____

Company/Institution: _____

Address: _____

_____

Telephone: _____

FAX: _____

Check which best describes you:

☐ Application/Software Developer

☐ End-User/Student

☐ OEM

☐ Other

If you're an OEM, would you like to receive more information about our PhoenixPage/PostScript Language Compatible interpreter?

☐ Yes　☐ No

Would you like a Phoenix Account Manager to contact you to discuss our PhoenixPage?

☐ Yes　☐ No

Which PostScript application packages do you currently use? Check all that apply.

☐ Ventura Publisher　☐ GEM

☐ PageMaker　☐ AutoCAD

☐ Illustrator　☐ MacDraw

☐ Freehand　☐ MacPaint

☐ Micrografx Designer　☐ Quark Express

☐ Micrografx Graph Plus　☐ Others

☐ Harvard Graphics　☐

Rate your proficiency in using the PostScript language.

1	2	3	4	5
None	Limited	Competent	Very Good	Expert

Do you currently own a PostScript-compatible printer?

☐ Yes　Make/Model: _____

☐ No

Would you like to receive information for PhoenixPage authorized PostScript-compatible printers?

☐ Yes　☐ No

Thank you for your response.
(Please fold in half and tape to close.)

Phoenix Technologies Ltd., 846 University Avenue, Norwood, MA 02062-3950, (617) 551-4000
Telex (710) 345-0199　FAX (617) 551-3750

Phoenix Technologies Ltd.
Attn: PhoenixPage
846 University Ave
Norwood, MA 02062-3950

PostScript Programmer's Reference Guide

Featuring PhoenixPage

David Holzgang

Scott, Foresman and Company
Glenview, Illinois   London

Library of Congress Cataloging-in-Publication Data

Holzgang, David, A.
    PostScript programmer's reference guide.

    Includes index.
    1. PostScript (Computer program language) I. Title.
QA76.73.P67H64 1989   005.13′3   89-6176
ISBN 0-673-38574-4

1 2 3 4 5 6 MVN 94 93 92 91 90 89

ISBN 0-673-38574-4

Scott, Foresman professional books are available for bulk sales at quantity discounts. For information, please contact Marketing Manager, Professional Books Group, Scott, Foresman and Company, 1900 East Lake Avenue, Glenview, IL 60025.

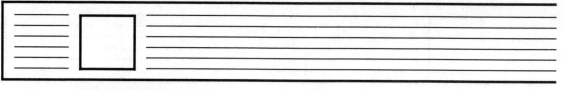

Foreword

There is no question that the PostScript™ language, designed by Adobe Systems® in 1982 to be a page description standard for electronic printing devices, has been instrumental in the ongoing desktop publishing revolution. However, for technology to be accepted as an industry standard, it must satisfy three basic criteria: it must be valued by its market because it provides a real solution; it must be an open standard in the public domain; and, lastly, it must be well-documented.

Bolstered by its device-independent design and total integration of text and graphics, PostScript provided the industry a functional solution at a critical time. In addition, Adobe's placement of the language's definition in the public domain reinforced PostScript as a modern industry standard page description language.

The final criterion, however – a complete and centralized PostScript reference manual – has, until now, been unavailable to the market. Adobe's original "Red" and "Blue" books, the *PostScript Language Reference Manual* and the *PostScript Language Tutorial and Cookbook,* do not address the full range of PostScript operators. Consequently, peripheral manufacturers, independent software developers, and end users have been faced with acquiring a diverse collection of manuals, supplements, and specifications in order to fully utilize the extensive number of recently developed operators and device-dependent extensions.

That's why Phoenix Technologies has endorsed the development of this book. This comprehensive PostScript reference guide includes a complete compilation of PostScript language operators and features. The book represents to PostScript what the Kernighan and Ritchie guide is to C and the Microsoft® BASIC™ manual is to BASIC: the definitive explanation and de facto reference to the programming language.

Since 1979, Phoenix has specialized in monitoring emerging industry standards and developing the system software necessary to embrace those standards. Phoenix is best known for its work in the personal computer arena, having helped over 100 manufacturers enter and profit in the industry.

Phoenix has expanded its compatibility engineering focus beyond the realm of personal computers to develop PhoenixPage, a flexible, modular solution for page description device manufacturers. Appendix D of this book describes some optionally available PhoenixPage enhancements and defines the full suite of PhoenixPage device-specific PostScript extensions.

I sincerely believe that this comprehensive reference guide will enhance your ability to master the PostScript language as no other manual has done before it.

Neil Colvin

Contents

Note: subtitles shown in author's original table of contents will appear on the opening pages of the respective part, section, or chapter.

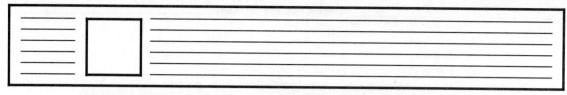

Introduction and Overview

This book is a guide to understanding and using the PostScript page-description language. PostScript was designed and developed by Adobe Systems, Incorporated, as a general-purpose programming language within which a large number of graphics operations are defined. The PostScript language, as you will see in this book, combines basic programming operations and powerful graphic operators that you can use to create and print complex pages of text and graphics.

WHAT IS POSTSCRIPT?

PostScript is a *page-description* language. That means that it has been designed specifically to communicate a description of a printable document from a computer-based composition system to a raster-output display device, which might be a printer, a typesetter, or a screen display. This description is an *object-oriented* description; it describes pages as a series of abstract graphic objects rather than describing them at a detailed, device-limited level.

PostScript is imbedded in an interpreter program that generally runs in an independent output device, such as a laser printer. The interpreter program (or, simply, the *interpreter* translates PostScript operations and data into device-specific codes and controls the output device to generate the graphics being described on the page. The interpreter processes each element – a name, string, array, number, or whatever – that is presented to it completely before it proceeds to the next element. You will learn all about these *syntactic objects* in the following chapters as we discuss the PostScript language, its syntax, and its operators.

This introduction will show you how to use this book, which was set up to help you understand the PostScript language. The first section introduces you to the PostScript language and discusses how to "think in PostScript." Because PostScript embodies many new concepts, particularly those concerned with graphics and page structure, you will want to understand some of the unique characteristics that give PostScript its distinct flavor before you start reading about the language itself.

The second section of the chapter deals with the purpose of the book and the structure that has been used to support that purpose. PostScript is a rich and complex language, and as for any such language, there are several ways to present language information. This section sets out in some detail the objectives that this book is designed to meet and relates those to the reader's expected needs and background.

THINKING IN POSTSCRIPT

PostScript represents a new and exciting way of creating complex pages of output that include both graphics and text. PostScript treats letters as graphic objects, that is, as shapes to be painted onto the output page. Moreover, PostScript provides features and operations that will allow you to control the precise rendering of text and graphics in ways that are not possible with traditional typesetting and printing technologies. You can stretch, bend, shade, and clip letters, using their shapes as graphic elements to create interesting (sometimes even bizarre) effects.

One of the principal advantages of PostScript is its ability to represent the potential range of output on raster devices in a high-level, device-independent way. Graphics artists have come to realize that here is a new, effective tool available to them, one that can both do the old tasks well, reducing the repetitive portion to a minimum, and provide scope for new, innovative approaches that were not feasible before. Its power has been enhanced by the development and acceptance of electronic page-composition systems that use Post-Script as their link to the individual devices, thus greatly expanding the potential for high-quality output. To appreciate the potential range of opportunities embodied in these applications, you need to understand PostScript's unusual capabilities as a computer language.

Preview of the PostScript Language

The PostScript language possesses distinctive characteristics that are important from the viewpoints of PostScript user and programmer alike. It is both a programming language and a page-description language, and its special characteristics derive directly from this dual nature. It is

- Interpreted
- Device-independent
- Graphically powerful
- Page-oriented

These characteristics are important qualities for you to understand before you begin the process of working in PostScript.

INTERPRETED

To begin with, PostScript is an interpreted language, like BASIC or APL. This means that PostScript operators are understood and acted upon by another program, the *interpreter*, which generally resides in the controller of the output device (laser printer, type-setter, etc.). Use of an interpreter provides both advantages and disadvantages to the programmer. On the plus side, it allows definition of many program requirements as the commands are being executed, which provides both flexibility and sensitivity to the current state of the output and the output device. It also allows for immediate feedback, error recognition, and command execution, which makes interpreted languages easier to debug and correct.

However, there are some negatives to an interpreted language as well. In particular, because the interpreter is itself a program, an additional layer of software is being executed. This can slow things down. In PostScript's case, this loss is usually not great, since the interpreter is running by itself in the output device and doesn't take up the resources of your computer.

Interpreted languages do not, in themselves, impose any specific structure on a program. So PostScript does not place any required structure on a document description – the PostScript equivalent of a program. This can be a negative point if the programmer doesn't impose a clear structure on himself. Generally, attention to such requirements and the self-discipline to enforce them comes only with some experience in the language.

PostScript has already established a recommended structure and approach, which are presented fully in Part III, Appendix A. Use of these conventions is not required for creation of successful PostScript page descriptions (programs), but following them makes clear to yourself and others what each part of the program is doing, so that programs can be easily compared and modified.

DYNAMIC

Because PostScript is an interpreted language, it is able to provide feedback to the programmer or the PostScript application. This feedback is particularily valuable in determining the current state of the execution environment – for example, whether a certain font is currently loaded and available. This is one sense in which the PostScript language is dynamic.

It is also dynamic in a different sense. PostScript page descriptions can be defined and modified as they are created by definition of new operations from the basic set of graphic and procedural operators. This dynamic process, also a function of the interpreter, makes PostScript significantly more powerful than traditional page description mechanisms.

DEVICE-INDEPENDENT

One of PostScript's great strengths is that it is independent of any specific output device. The basic set of PostScript operators are designed to be appropriate to the general class of raster-output devices upon which the language can be implemented. It is the interpreter's problem to adjust and convert PostScript commands to the specific device's requirements. On the other hand, where there is a need for specific, device-dependent information in order to construct a page or an image, PostScript has the capability to do that as well.

This freedom from the constraints of a specific output engine provides two major benefits to the PostScript programmer. First, you can generally remain unaware of the specific requirement of the output device. Second, a page described in PostScript can be proofed on one device and then produced on another with no modification of commands or operators. This means that pages can be proofed, corrected, and reset very quickly by use of a convenient, relatively inexpensive output device, such as a laser printer; but they can also be generated for final printing output on a typesetting machine once the proof and correction cycle have been completed. In this way, you gain the benefits of automated processing and quick turnaround while still having the quality of output available only from the high dot-density devices. It is this benefit that has created much of the excitement about "desktop publishing" in the business community.

GRAPHIC POWER

PostScript is especially designed for the creation and manipulation of graphic objects. This orientation toward graphics is such a major component of the language that probably the best way to think of PostScript is as a method of drawing electronically. PostScript also provides powerful primitive operators, such as **scale** and **rotate,** which can be combined in many ways to produce dramatic and surprising output.

This flexibility makes PostScript the language of choice for serious work, particularly work that combines text and graphics on a page. Where other languages or mechanisms are impediments to combining text and graphics, PostScript makes it easy and natural. This facility in combining the two modes derives in a large measure from PostScript's approach to text. Within PostScript, the individual characters in text are themselves treated as graphic objects that can be positioned, scaled, and rotated as required.

PAGE DESCRIPTION

Finally, PostScript is a page description language. A raster-output device typically prepares a page or unit of output at a time by setting each point on the page to a precise value. For black-and-white output, these points, or pixels, are set to either zero or one, representing either black or white. The page description is therefore a complete map of these values for the entire surface to be output – usually a full page, but sometimes less because of hardware limitations.

There are fundamental drawbacks to the pixel-by-pixel method of page description. Three of these issues stand out as particularly undesirable from the user's viewpoint:

- The description is particular to a specific device. It can represent only one array of values for a given page, even though different devices (of differing resolution or format) may require different values to represent the same page.
- The full description of a page is inevitably large. It requires one value for every addressable point on the page. For a typical laser output device, for example, this comes to more than 7,200,000 values per page.
- The mathematical process of deciding which points get what values for representation of a given object (called scan conversion) requires a substantial amount of computation and can be most efficiently carried out in a dedicated processor that has been optimized for this task.

PostScript provides a mechanism for description of a page of graphic objects rather than a page of pixels. It does this by using powerful primitive operators which correspond in a relatively natural way to how users ordinarily handle graphics. These operators can then be combined to produce a wide range of complex output.

BOOK PURPOSE AND STRUCTURE

The purpose of this book is to provide a complete reference for the PostScript language with all currently defined PostScript operators, including both the general-purpose operators and a sample of the most common device-specific operators. PostScript is, as has been said repeatedly, an extremely powerful language. Unfortunately, the power of a computer language is generally directly related to its complexity, and PostScript is no exception. PostScript is not inherently difficult to use; it is only unfamiliar and complex. This book will help the PostScript programmer by incorporating, in one place, both a description of the language from a theoretical and practical viewpoint and a complete discussion of the PostScript operators.

Purpose

This section of the chapter sets up the objectives that this book is intended to satisfy and also discusses the reciprocal requirements you'll need in order to gain the maximum advantage from its explanations and examples. There is more to these objectives than you might at first expect. No single book can adequately explore and discuss the complete range of PostScript operations. The objectives that are discussed here, therefore, represent the criteria that were initially used to determine what subjects would be included and in what order and depth they would be covered. In a similar way, the discussion of requirements tells you what is not covered and why.

OBJECTIVES

At the broadest level, the goal of this book has already been stated: to provide a complete reference guide to the PostScript language. This statement, however, is too expansive to provide much guidance for the construction of a satisfactory work. Therefore, three more specific objectives have been defined and are arranged according to their priority as follows:

1. The first objective is to present a clear and comprehensive overview of the PostScript language, both of its structure and its operations. The intention is to explore every aspect of the PostScript language, showing the concepts behind the language, the relationship of the operators that implement the concepts, and the precise description of all the current PostScript operators, both those that are general-purpose and those that are device-specific in their requirements and operations.

    The desire for comprehensive coverage of PostScript operations naturally creates some problems. Not all PostScript devices have all of the PostScript operations available within their version of the interpreter; for example, only a few devices have implemented composite fonts or color operations. Nevertheless, these operations have been included here, both the concepts and the operators, for two reasons. First, because these operations will become more common and widespread as new versions of the PostScript interpreter are available to replace or upgrade older versions. Second, because these new extensions to the language are of compelling interest to the practicing programmer, who must design and implement procedures that can work in many environments.

2. The second objective is to describe the PostScript language operators from a programmer's viewpoint. This includes not only the basic descriptions of the operators, but also examples and programming tips where appropriate. All of the general operators that are defined for use in any version of the PostScript interpreter are included here, along with an overview of the device-specific operators and examples of many of the most common of these.

3. The last objective, but by no means the least important one, is to provide a convenient reference volume for the working PostScript programmer. Clarity of organization, comprehensive coverage, and a straightforward reference structure are used here to allow you to return easily to the information that you require while you are programming. The alphabetical operator reference, for example, includes the type of the operator to allow you to quickly look up all associated operators in the type cross-reference.

Obviously these objectives are intertwined so closely that each supports and involves both of the others. And the book does not distinguish each objective but, like any good reference text, tries to incorporate all of them indistinguishably. In this way, you will learn both the PostScript language and its individual operators in a coherent and unified way. In addition, you will be able to keep returning to this book for reference and advice as you continue to program in PostScript.

REQUIREMENTS

Besides setting objectives for a book, there also has to be some vision of the type of reader that is going to use the book. This vision of a typical reader forms the basis for this discussion of requirements. Note that there is nothing restrictive here; there are no prerequisites for making effective use of the book. This is an explanation of where the book will expect that you already know or can work out what needs to be done rather than need to be given a long explanation.

To begin with, you should have some familiarity with the PostScript language. A language reference, by its nature, must include all variations and types in the language being described. Therefore it is not always possible to explain language sytax and use in the way that one would choose to introduce the language to a new user. This language reference contains a great amount of detail and many working examples, both in the operator reference (Part I, Section C) and in the Cookbook section (Part II); in all cases, the presumption is made that the reader can understand ordinary PostScript notation and use without too much explanation.

You should also have some patience and willingness to read and explore the language definitions and concepts before beginning your work. This book is not intended as a tutorial on the PostScript language; it therefore is not organized in a way to tutor you through the concepts. Instead, it is organized in a reference fashion so that you can easily find specific information on any aspect of the language: concepts, operator use, or operator definitions. Also, by definition, a language reference must present and discuss *all* of the language, not just the most commonly used operations. We have tried here to place all the operations, even the least-often used, into a secure and coherent framework, so that you, as a programmer, will know both when and why to use them.

One thing that is not covered here is general computer concepts. Although I try to define precisely all terms that are intrinsic or even related to PostScript, there are certainly a number of concepts that apply to computer operations and computer languages generally that are left undefined – your understanding of what a file is and what a computer language does is taken for granted.

Structure

The book follows a regular pattern that grows naturally out of the objectives that we discussed above. It is organized in two major divisions, besides this introduction. The first division (Part I) covers the PostScript language in depth. This part, entitled "Language Reference," contains a detailed description of the concepts and syntax of the PostScript language and the operators that implement the language. This part comprises the major part of the book. The second major divison is the Cookbook (Part II), which contains a variety of PostScript programs that show you in actual practice how the language is used to create figures that include both text and graphics.

POSTSCRIPT LANGUAGE REFERENCE—PART I

"Language Reference" (Part I) is itself divided into three sections. The first is a discussion of the concepts behind the PostScript language. The chapters in this section discuss the language structure, operations, and graphic and text processing in a general manner, without discussing the actual PostScript operators that implement these concepts. This is done to provide you with a clear view of the structure of the PostScript language and how these concepts fit together to create a flexible and powerful vehicle for graphics processing.

The second section of "Language Reference" is a discussion of the PostScript language operations. Here the concepts that were discussed in the first section are given body, as it were, by the actual PostScript operations that carry out the processes of creating marks on the output page. The operators are presented here without too much detailed information but instead are discussed in context of what they are supposed to do and how they work together to create the output page. These chapters discuss the operators within the language, grouped into natural sets that allow you to see the relative difference between similar operators and how they are intended to be used.

The third section of "Language Reference" is the detailed description of all of the PostScript language operators. The general operators are described first, in alphabetical order, as an easy reference for anyone looking up the exact requirements and results of a given operator. Many of the definitions also contain short examples that illustrate the effects of the operator. After the general operators, there is a discussion of device-specific operators, along with comprehensive definitions for the most common ones, covering both server operations and system parameters. Finally, all the operators are listed again by type, which provides a quick reference for programmers to similar operators.

COOKBOOK—PART II

Besides theory and discussion, a programmer needs some concrete examples to illustrate the concepts of a language. This book provides a short but realistic set of cookbook routines that allow you to see the PostScript language in action. These routines are real, working PostScript, being the actual PostScript programs that have been used to generate the figures that illustrate this book.

The Cookbook is divided into two sections. The first presents the common support routines that are used by all the figure programs. They illustrate one of the basic activities of PostScript programming, in which a programmer builds a library of routines that can be used to generate common graphic elements and solve common graphic and text processing requirements for a given project or, sometimes, for general recurring use. The second section of the Cookbook presents the figures themselves, complete programs that use the common routines, as well as some specialized ones to create the exact figures used in the book.

DEVICE USE

All of the work in this book, both text and examples, relies on generic PostScript features and is not tied to any specific implementation of PostScript in any specific device. Any exercise or example should execute correctly on any PostScript-equipped device, and the concepts and techniques that you will learn are as applicable to a typesetter as they are to a laser printer.

The work in the book is based solely on PostScript. There is no use of any language or program other than PostScript in this book. That means that you can complete all of the examples using only a PostScript-equipped device and a terminal, if necessary. Note that this would be an impossible request if PostScript were not a perfectly good general-purpose language as well as a specialized one.

Language Reference

Language Concepts

– a discussion of the basic concepts that underlie page description languages in general and PostScript in particular.

This section of the book discusses the general concepts that are basic to the PostScript language, while the next section will discuss specific language operations. These concepts provide an overview of how a page-description language defines and manipulates a page as a working unit and how you should think about pages and associated structures as you work in the language. A programmer's ability to produce compact, efficient and maintainable programs is, in my opinion, directly related to how clearly that programmer understands the fundamental structure of the language being used. PostScript is the page-description language of choice because its powerful and elegant features for handling integrated text and graphics on a page have been designed into the language, not added on as afterthoughts.

This discussion of language concepts is itself divided into five chapters, moving progressively through the language structure from the more general and basic concepts to the most specific. The first chapter discusses the structure of the language and covers the simple but vital issues of language notation and syntax. It presents the basic building blocks of PostScript, the operators that function as "verbs" for PostScript programs, outlining the general types of operators and how they work. This is important because all of the functions of PostScript are implemented through the operators, and discussion and examination of the set of PostScript operators, in one way or another, makes up the majority of this book. The chapter continues with a discussion of stack and dictionary processing, which are the twin engines that are used by the interpreter to accomplish many of its processing tasks. An understanding of these concepts leads naturally to a discussion of the flow within a PostScript program and the methods provided in the language to change and control that flow. These are the features that set PostScript apart from any other page-description mechanism, making it a full-featured programming language. As in any programming language, certain conventions provide the self-discipline necessary to producing efficient and maintainable code; the final portion of the chapter gives you an overview of these conventions for the PostScript language and their effect on processing PostScript page descriptions.

The second chapter deals entirely with the functioning of the PostScript interpreter. The interpreter is the software that parses and executes the PostScript instructions that it receives, and it makes the actual marks onto the output device. The interpreter understands and operates on a variety of PostScript objects; the first sections of the chapter are devoted to describing the complete set of PostScript objects and their attributes and how each of these objects is handled by the interpreter when that object is presented for execution. The chapter continues with a discussion of the shared responsibilities for resource management between the application program and the interpreter. This is a serious issue because an important part of PostScript coding is to manage the resources, such as virtual memory, carefully and correctly. The chapter ends with a discussion of the various operating modes of the interpreter and how you can use them.

The third and fourth chapters discuss PostScript graphic operations, first in a general manner and then in more concrete terms. The third chapter deals entirely with the structure of a PostScript page. Since PostScript is a "page-description" language, the structure of a page is an important component in the basic concepts of the language. One major benefit of PostScript is that it provides a device-independent description of complex pages, which is done by using a standard set of page structures that are independent of any specific device. These structures cover the measurement and coordinate systems that are used on the page and the process of adjusting from one coordinate system to another. These same techniques are also applied to map the device-independent descriptions into the requirements of a specific output engine. The fourth chapter then takes up these general page structure concepts and discusses how they are applied in the PostScript language to produce graphic images on a page. The chapter deals first with the simple issues of drawing lines, selecting regions on the page, and painting those regions – the basic graphic operations. Then the discussion becomes more complex, exploring the issues of halftone processing, color processing, color models; and, finally, representing and controlling arbitrary sampled images within the PostScript application. The chapter ends with a short general discussion of the issues of device setup and control.

The fifth, and last, chapter in this section deals entirely with the narrow issue of text and fonts. This issue is vital since much of the output created by applications is text, so the manner in which a page-description language handles text is an important factor in how easily and effectively it can be used. PostScript adopts a flexible yet efficient approach that treats text characters as graphic objects and allows use of character images both as text and as graphic design elements without distinction. This powerful conceptual approach would fail, however, if it were not backed by an effort to ensure that common processing problems would be handled with reasonable speed. This chapter discusses the overall design of PostScript fonts and the font machinery, as well as the special characteristics that speed up font processing. There are discussions of font measurements and how fonts are used to map character codes from the computer, which are essentially numbers, into the character shapes that are shown on the output page. Appropriately, the chapter (and the section) ends with a discussion of composite fonts, which extend the previous concepts to allow virtually unlimited mappings of codes into character shapes; composite fonts are especially suited to solving the problem of handling oriental alphabets, but they are equally appropriate for certain types of more ordinary concerns.

Language Structure

The PostScript language is a full-featured programming language that has special facilities for construction and display of graphics on certain types of output devices. At the same time, it is a page-description language of remarkable power and generality with full programming features. These are the two complementary approaches to thinking about the structure of PostScript that are both useful to a programmer. This chapter focuses on those basic elements of the language that are related to programming and program structure. The following chapters take up the view of PostScript as a page-description language. Both views are correct and important; they are just different ways to look at the same language.

As a programming language, PostScript has a complete set of general-purpose operators that allow you to solve any type of programming problem. The language has simple but well-defined notation and syntax, which are easy to read and understand once you become familiar with them. There are few special symbols and no reserved words in the language, and the execution flow is straightforward. In all, the PostScript language provides both a simple structure and a rich environment for programming.

This chapter presents the basic structural aspects of the PostScript language. You will learn how to read PostScript and how it is organized internally. There are sections on the use and operation of stacks and dictionaries, essential features of PostScript operations. There is also a discussion of the basic forms of program execution control provided by the language. All of these areas are part of PostScript's essential structure.

The PostScript language itself does not impose many structural restraints on a program. However, as is true in all forms of programming, certain conventions exist regarding both local program structure and overall document processing that should be observed for best results. This chapter also examines some of these issues to give you an overview and a guide to the correct structure that will allow your programs to be easily transportable and work correctly in a wide variety of PostScript environments.

These language features are taken up first, not because they are more important than the other fundamental concepts of graphics creation and manipulation, but because it is essential that you, as a programmer, can read and follow the language in the succeeding chapters and sections of the book. Therefore this chapter forms a basis for reading and understanding the further chapters, which generally assume that you will be already familiar with the syntax and notation of the PostScript language.

1.1 NOTATION

First, begin by looking at the basic structure of PostScript code and how that is written. PostScript is a language made up of operators, operands, and results. The operators in PostScript are like verbs in a sentence: they take some action. Each operator performs a single function, although sometimes that function can be quite complex. In order to take the desired action, many operators require information or data as input; this required input information is called *operands* in PostScript. Similarly, many operators return some information or value as a *result*. Complex functions can be accomplished by linking multiple operators up, one after another.

A major distinctive quality of PostScript code is that the operands precede the operator that they belong to. Thus, where you would most naturally say 'add 1 and 2' or write '1 plus 2', PostScript requires the format '1 2 add'. This form of notation is called *postfix notation* and is a little disconcerting at first. However, it has several advantages in construction of procedures and in passing results on to other operators as operands; you will find it quite natural once you become familiar with it.

Character Set

All the elements of the PostScript language are composed of the standard ASCII character set. In fact, a PostScript program can be completely specified using only the printable subset of the complete ASCII set, plus the characters space, tab, and newline (return or linefeed). This subset of the complete ASCII character set is called the *recommended character set*. Nothing within the language prevents using characters outside that subset, but if you do use such characters, you must be aware that they may cause problems during handling, transmission, and storage on some systems.

The space and the associated characters of tab and newline are *white space characters*. That is, they are treated in the same manner when in a program sequence, unless they are within a string or a comment. White space characters are used in PostScript to separate syntactical units from one another. Therefore you can use many spaces or continue statements onto a new line in any situation where you might otherwise use a single space – for example, to separate operands from each other or from an operator. All white space characters are treated as identical, and multiple white space characters following one another are treated as a single character. The only exception to this rule is in strings and comments, where each of the white space characters has specific (and different) effects, as described below.

Certain syntactical units in PostScript require that some characters be reserved to mark them off in a program. These characters are called *special characters* because they have a special meaning to the interpreter. These characters and their meanings are as follows:

Character(s)	Functions(s)
'(' and ')'	begin and end a string
'<' and '>'	begin and end a hexadecimal string
'/'	begins a name literal
'[' and ']'	begin and end an array
'{' and '}'	begin and end a procedure
'%'	begins a comment

Any of these characters causes special processing to take place and, therefore, automatically ends the preceding syntactical unit. Unlike the postfix notation for operators and their operands, these characters precede the units that they define and are never included in the units that went before.

Number Representation

PostScript has both real and integer numbers, and numbers in PostScript can be represented in a variety of ways. Integers are generally represented by a set of decimal numeric digits with no decimal point but possibly including a sign, such as:

$$1 \qquad 213 \qquad -24 \qquad +18$$

However, every PostScript implementation has a maximum integer value that it can represent, and any value greater than that maximum is automatically converted into a real number.

Real numbers are generally represented as a sequence of decimal digits, including a decimal point and possibly containing a sign as well, such as:

$$1.0 \qquad -45.2322 \qquad +18.5$$

Note that even integer values, such as 1.0, are considered to be and are stored as real numbers if they contain a decimal point. Real numbers may also be represented in exponential form by using an 'E' or 'e' to indicate the exponential form of the number. Exponential real numbers are formed in two portions. The first portion is an ordinary real or integer number, while the second portion is the *exponent*, which consists of the 'e' (or 'E') and an integer value, such as:

    1.25e2   1E−2   0.234e15

Integers may also be represented in *radix* format. In this format, numbers take the form *base#number*, where the *base* is a decimal integer in the range 2 to 36. The *number* is an unsigned integer interpreted according to the value of *base* and consists of digits from 0 to *base−1*, with digits greater than 9 being represented by alphabetic characters 'a' (or 'A') through 'z' (or 'Z'). The resulting number is converted into an ordinary integer value. This notation is designed for specification of numbers in alternate bases, such as octal and hexadecimal, which are often convenient representations for numbers.

Strings

PostScript uses strings to store and manipulate sets of characters primarily for output purposes. A string in PostScript is any sequence of characters contained between the *string delimiters* '(' and ')'. A string begins with the first occurrence of '(' and ends with the first ')' that is not matched by a preceding '('. Within a string, the only special characters are '(', ')', and '\' (backslash). A string may contain multiple occurrences of the parentheses characters without ending the string as long as the parentheses balance. All of the following are correct strings:

    (This is a typical use of a string)
    (This string extends
        over two lines)
    (Characters like %( ){ } are not special within a string)

Notice in this last example that paired parentheses, as mentioned earlier, are acceptable within the string.

The special backslash character '\' is used as an escape character within the string. With it, you can specify a variety of special circumstances within the string. The character immediately following the backslash determines the exact interpretation and action, as follows:

\b   backspace

\f   formfeed

\n   linefeed or newline

\r   carriage return

\t   horizontal tab

\ \	single backslash
\(	left parenthesis
\)	right parenthesis
newline	no character – both are ignored

This last (a backslash followed by a newline or carriage return) is used to combine several lines of input into one string, like this:

    (This is one string\
    broken into several lines\
    for input purposes)

which results in the following string internally:

    (This is one string broken into several lines for input purposes)

In addition, there is a special format of the backslash escape character that is used to include any arbitrary character within the string, as follows:

ddd   ASCII character represented by code *ddd* (octal)

This format allows you to include any character code from 0 to 255 in a string, such as:

    (This is a tilde \176 and a yen sign \245)

The *ddd* may consist of one to three octal digits. This technique allows you to specify characters outside of the recommended character set by using characters that are themselves within the recommended character set and thus avoids many problems of storage and transmission that are associated with using characters outside of that set.

A *hexadecimal string* is a special form of string that is bracketed by the characters '<' and '>'. This form of string is used to represent characters as hexadecimal (base 16) values. The only valid characters within a hexadecimal string are the characters '0' to '9' and 'a' (or 'A') to 'f' (or 'F'), which represent the hexadecimal digits, and white space characters, which are ignored. Since the ASCII characters are represented by code values from 0 to 255, it requires two hexadecimal digits to represent one character. For example, the string <61736b> is the same as the character string (ask), and the string <31 35 39> is the same as the character string (159). Note that the white space characters in the second example are not included within the string as they would be in a normal string representation. If you wish to include a space in a hexadecimal string, you must specifically code it as the space character, <20>. Generally, hexadecimal strings are not used to represent normal character data but are used to store and transmit information that is in binary format, such as scanned image data.

Names

Any sequence of characters that are not special or white space characters and that cannot be interpreted as a number (as described above) are considered to be a *name*. PostScript uses names in the ordinary way, to reference objects or groups of objects. The special character '/' (slash) is used to distinguish ordinary, or *executable*, names from *literal* names. A literal name, commonly referred to as a *name literal*, is any ordinary name preceded by a '/'. A full discussion of the distinction between literal and executable names is presented in Section A2.3.

Arrays and Procedures

Arrays are PostScript objects that are collections of other objects. They are delimited by the special characters '[' and ']' (square brackets), which serve to tell the interpreter that the objects within the square brackets should be formed into a single object. A *procedure* is a special form of array, also called an *executable array*, which is delimited by the characters '{' and '}' (braces, or curly brackets) rather than by square brackets. Processing of arrays and procedures is discussed more fully in Section A2.4.

Comments

Like all computer languages, PostScript provides a notation for comments. A comment is a portion of a program that is not intended to be processed in the ordinary fashion but is intended to annotate the program to provide information or explanation to a human reader. In PostScript, comments begin with any occurrence of the character '%' that is not inside a string, and they end with the next newline. You may put any characters between these two delimiters, including special characters and white space characters other than a newline. Comments are completely invisible to the PostScript language and have the same effect as a single white space character. An example of a comment would be:

```
1 2 add        % adds two numbers, 1 and 2
```

1.2 OPERATOR TYPES

PostScript operators can be grouped in several ways. One of the most common distinctions is to group operators by the type of action that they perform. This approach is very helpful in organizing the operators conceptually, in learning the operators, and in finding operators that perform tasks complementary to a given operator.

PostScript has more than 250 individual operators, but all these can be broadly divided into four categories: operators that deal with PostScript objects, operators that deal with

PostScript pages, operators that deal with PostScript programs, and operators that deal with PostScript devices. Each of these categories can be further subdivided into several groups for additional usefulness. Sections B and C of Part I of the book are primarily concerned with specific operator information, including discussion of groups of operators and of individual operators. In particular, Section C3 presents a complete list of all PostScript operators organized by groups. What follows is a brief overview of the operator types and groups.

Object Operators

These operators deal with each of the varieties of PostScript objects. Generally, they allow construction and manipulation of various types of objects. Types of objects within this category are as follows:

Array	Dictionary	Mathematical
Conversion	File	String

The *Array* operators create and access both standard and packed PostScript arrays. The *Dictionary* and *String* operators each create and access objects of their respective types. (We will discuss dictionary formation and use shortly.) The *File* operators access PostScript files, but creation, naming, and control of files are dependent upon the environment in which the PostScript interpreter is running, so that the action and even the existence of certain file operators may depend on the specific device. The *Mathematical* operators provide a standard set of mathematical operations to be used on numbers, which are created and represented as discussed above. Finally, the *Conversion* operators provide a method of changing between certain types of objects and of altering the characteristics of objects.

Page Operators

These operators deal with the ways of placing marks onto a page of output. For convenience, I have also included here operators that create and manipulate PostScript fonts, since they are intimately related to producing text output on a page. The groups of operators within this category are as follows:

Font	Painting
Graphics	Path

The *Font* operators provide the means to create and change PostScript fonts and also include those operators that produce text output on the page. The *Graphics* operators are those that set and report the variables that control a variety of important features in the PostScript graphics environment as well as those that can save and restore that environment as a whole. This group also includes those operators that deal with conversion from one color representation model to another and with the specific application of color functions in the page environment. The *Path* operators provide tools to create paths on the page, while the *Painting* operators provide the means to convert those paths into visible shapes.

Program Operators

These operators deal with controlling execution of PostScript code or setting up and manipulating PostScript operands. In addition, I have included in this category those operators that fall into the Miscellaneous group. The groups of operators within this category are as follows:

Boolean   Miscellaneous

Control   Stack

The *Boolean* operators include all the operators that test or set conditions. The *Control* operators change the order of execution of PostScript statements, usually based on some supplied operand that often may be the result of one of the Boolean tests. The *Stack* operators control the placement and ordering of objects on the operand stack (we will discuss stack operations and use in Section B). Finally, the *Miscellaneous* group of operators covers those functions that are related to PostScript programs but not included elsewhere.

Device Control Operators

These operators deal with controlling the output device and setting up or changing the PostScript coordinate system, either from one state of the page to another or between the page and the output device. The groups of operators within this category are as follows:

Coordinates   Font Cache   System

Device   Memory

The *Coordinates* group of operators provides methods of changing coordinate systems, both within the page framework and between the page and the output device. It also includes operators to map points from one coordinate system to another. The Device group is composed of operators that set up the output device and display output on it. The *System* group is related to the Device group in that it consists of operators that are specific to each PostScript device; for example, operators that allow selection of device features, such as paper size and paper tray or manual feed. The *Font Cache* group of operators controls the status and use of the font-caching mechanism. This is related to the font access and use mechanism but is quite distinct in purpose and execution. Complete details of font cache storage and results are given in Section A5.3. The last group in this category is the *Memory* group. This contains operators to manage PostScript's virtual memory resources, a very vital function which is treated much more extensively in the next chapter in Section A2.5.

It should be made clear that these categories are not rigid. PostScript operators were designed to perform functions; their categorization is done after the fact, after they have been defined. This categorization is intended to help you understand and use the operators but is not intrinsic to their definition. With that in mind, feel free to restructure this list in any way that will help you use the operators.

1.3   STACK OPERATIONS

One of the most notable characteristics of the PostScript language is that it works through a series of stacks. These stacks are areas of internal memory that hold items to be referenced by the PostScript interpreter. PostScript maintains and uses four distinct stacks:

- execution stack
- dictionary stack
- graphics state stack
- operand stack

All of these stacks are accessed and managed independently of one another. However, they share a common design and a common structural approach. Basically, if you understand how one stack works, you will understand how all of them work.

These stacks are push-down, pop-up stacks that hold various PostScript objects and states. They may also be described as last-in, first-out (LIFO) stacks, but the push-down, pop-up terminology may be easier to visualize. Whatever image or analogy you choose to use, however, there are several points to keep in mind about PostScript stacks. First, only the top item on the stack is generally accessible; nothing beneath it can be reached without removing or replacing the top item. Second, motion up the stack is automatic; that is, when the top item is removed,the item below automatically becomes the top item and all items lower down in the stack move up one. Finally, use of the stack mechanism provides PostScript with some powerful methods for performing its work, but it also requires attention and management. For that reason, the PostScript language includes a variety of operators that help you control and manage such information as you are responsible for on each of the stacks.

The *execution stack* is the major exception to the rule that the programmer must manage the stack contents. This stack is directly under the control of the PostScript interpreter;

it can only be interrogated by ordinary operators. The execution stack contains executable objects, normally procedures and files, that are in partial stages of execution. At any point during the execution of a PostScript program, this stack represents the *call stack* of the program. Whenever the interpreter interrupts execution of one object in order to execute some other object, the suspended object is pushed onto the execution stack. As the interpreter finishes execution of each object, it pops it from the execution stack and then resumes execution of the next object on the stack.

The *dictionary stack* and the *graphics state stack* are special stacks that are controlled by specific PostScript operators. The dictionary stack holds only dictionary objects; its operation is fully discussed in the next section of this chapter. The graphics state stack contains complete copies of the graphics state at a particular point in time. It is managed and used entirely by the program to aid in the process of controlling the graphics environment for PostScript operations. Both these stacks have particular importance for programming in PostScript.

The last stack, the *operand stack,* is the most commonly used stack in PostScript and the stack that has the most direct access and effect on user programs. As its name implies, this stack contains the operands that are required for the execution of PostScript operators, and it also receives the results of those operations. Like the other PostScript stacks, it is a push-down, pop-up stack. This stack is so commonly referenced and widely used that it is the stack that is meant when we say "the stack."

Each of these stacks has a maximum number of objects that it can hold. This limit depends on the specific implementation of PostScript that is available in the device and on the characteristics of the device itself. Any attempt to push an item onto a stack that is at its maximum capacity or to pop an item from a stack that is empty (or at its minimum size) will result in an error.

1.4 DICTIONARY OPERATIONS

The PostScript language makes extensive use of dictionary mechanisms to implement all of its processing functions. Like stacks, dictionaries are an essential part of the structure of the PostScript language. Neither of these concepts is difficult to understand or to use; however, the structure and use of stacks is more common in computer languages than the use of dictionaries. However, the dictionary concept is quite familiar to all of us from use of language dictionaries in ordinary reading and writing; the basic idea is no different in PostScript.

A dictionary for a language is a book that associates words of the language with their definitions. A PostScript dictionary is no different in concept; it is a table that associates a name, or *key,* with a *value.* More precisely, a PostScript dictionary associates any two PostScript objects: a key, which is usually but not necessarily a name literal; and any second PostScript object as the value. As you have probably guessed, the dictionary mechanism is how you can associate names with procedures or values in order to construct PostScript programs.

Although keys in a PostScript dictionary are usually names (and many PostScript implementations are designed to work optimally when they are), nevertheless any Post-Script object except the null object may be a key in a dictionary. Using a string as a key will result in the string being converted into a name object through the use of ordinary PostScript operations. Generally, as you will discover later, PostScript treats strings as equivalent to names in most circumstances.

Dictionary Structure

PostScript maintains a dictionary stack, as mentioned above, that holds all the currently available dictionaries. These dictionaries contain the keys for those objects in virtual memory that are available to the program without any explicit dictionary reference. Dictionaries can be created by a PostScript program and added to or removed from the dictionary stack at will. In all cases, the topmost dictionary is called the *current dictionary*.

The dictionary stack always contains at least two dictionaries that are built into the interpreter and are an essential part of the PostScript language. These are called the *systemdict* and the *userdict*. The **systemdict** is always the bottom dictionary on the dictionary stack, and it is the dictionary that associates PostScript operator names (the ones defined in Section C of Part I) with their built-in actions. The **userdict** is above the systemdict, and it contains all the code that is intended to be modified by programs as well as certain support procedures and other variables. In many cases, definitions added by PostScript programs will also be enrolled here. These two dictionaries are always the two bottom-most entries on the dictionary stack, and neither can be popped off; any attempt to do so will cause an error.

Dictionary Functions

There are three main methods of enrolling and retrieving key-value pairs in a dictionary. First, there are special operators that will access any specific dictionary, which must be supplied as an operand. Second, there are operators that access the current dictionary implicitly. Third, the interpreter accesses the dictionary stack to store and retrieve information. When the interpreter accesses the dictionary stack, it retrieves information in a consistent fashion by looking up a key first in the current dictionary. If the key is not found there, it continues to search down through the dictionary stack until it finds the key and retrieves the associated value or exhausts the stack.

1.5 PROGRAM CONTROL

Since PostScript is a full-featured programming language, it naturally contains mechanisms for changing the order of execution of operations. Some mechanism of this type is essential for any type of programming. However, PostScript does not provide any traditional "go to" or branch operator, nor does it have any statement labels or numbers to branch to. Because of this, we may say that PostScript is, in this sense, an example of a "structured" language.

Procedure Flow Control

Instead of branching, the PostScript language provides a variety of operators that perform procedures repeatedly or perform them based on a particular condition. PostScript also provides a set of logical operators that allow you to create, combine, and test conditions. By using these facilities, a PostScript program can construct any kind of procedural variation to accomplish a variety of complex tasks. The issue is to think of a program as a set of processes rather than as one complex flow.

The PostScript operators that control program execution can be divided into three groups:

- operators that execute a procedure repeatedly
- operators that execute a procedure conditionally, based on a test of an external object
- operators that control the state of execution, such as are used by the interpreter itself

These groups are somewhat arbitrary, but they provide a useful breakdown of how PostScript programs control execution. The first two groups are quite common both in PostScript coding and as a feature in structured programming, which we will discuss next. There is a more extensive discussion of these groups of operators, including discussion of individual operators within each group, in Section B2.1.

Structured Control Mechanisms

PostScript provides an excellent mechanism for structured programming. *Structured programming* is a method of developing program logic according to a specific set of rules that provide maximum readabilty and logical clarity. While any extensive discussion of structured programming is not appropriate for this book, a short review of the principles will aid you in seeing how you can adapt these techniques to your PostScript programs. One main rule of structured programming is that programs should use only three methods to control and alter program execution. These three methods are sequential control structure, loop control structure, and if-then-else control structure. Each of these structures is used as necessary to form a group of procedural statements into a complete process that both conforms to certain structural requirements and performs only a single logical function. This approach makes the code easy to read and easy to understand and modify.

The sequential control structure simply follows the normal way of executing one instruction after another, just as the computer does automatically. The loop control structure provides the ability to perform a procedure repeatedly and therefore conforms more or less closely to the first group of operators described above. The if-then-else control structure is a conditional execution mechanism, again following the second group of operators described above. As you can see, PostScript provides an excellent set of tools for producing structured code.

1.6   PROGRAM STRUCTURE

Besides program control, there are additional issues of program structure that are important. The PostScript language in particular requires some consideration of these issues, since it imposes almost no natural structure. Nevertheless, there are compelling advantages in establishing and following some structural conventions while doing PostScript programming. Your programs will be clearer – easier to read and understand.

Besides these general benefits, there are some additional benefits in following a published standard for overall program structure. First, your program will be able to work with a variety of document management programs in a wide variety of environments. This is particularly important in networked environments, where several users may share one or more output devices. However, it can even be important in the single-user environment, because many application programs can only provide automated support, such as downloading fonts, when the program being generated follows a structural standard. Second, when you follow the structural conventions, your programs will have a common structural base with other PostScript programs that follow those conventions. As a result, you may be able to share code and images. In fact, the EPS file format, which allows importation and display of PostScript images within applications that generate PostScript output, is based on just such common structures.

The important point to remember here is that the PostScript interpreter simply processes a program as a series of tokens. There are no reserved words and only a limited number of special characters in the PostScript language. Thus the PostScript interpreter does not impose any particular program structure. The only requirement is the obvious necessity to make sure variables and procedures are defined and accessible before you try to use them.

Important Qualities

Before we discuss specific recommendations for program structure, it would be helpful to establish what qualities or characteristics we are trying to produce by using conventions. In this way, you can see why the structure was developed and how it will help you if you use it.

The first and perhaps the primary reason for imposing a certain structure on Post-Script programs is to insure page independence. Each page of output that is produced by the program should be independent of all other pages of the document and not depend on results or conditions produced by any previous processing. Since PostScript is a page-description language, most PostScript programs produce documents consisting of multiple pages on an output device. Each page of that output, as it is created by the interpreter in raster memory, should not depend on anything that was done by or output on any preceding pages. Unless the pages are independent units, individual pages cannot be proofed and printed separately; changing or maintaining individual pages will be quite difficult. In the same way, it would make impossible some of the useful things that document management programs can do, such as print selected pages or reverse the order of printing for correctly collated output (as is necessary for some output devices). Finally, the most important reason for page independence is to ensure that no unintended and undesired remnants from any previous page carry forward and ruin the current page output.

A second and equally important quality is to establish a common structure with other PostScript programs. Use of common structures allows you to integrate pieces from several programs into a new program. This commonality is the basis for Encapsulated PostScript files (EPSF), which allow PostScript graphics to be created by one application and used in another. Common structure also benefits the programmer. It allows you to understand new code more quickly and handle it more confidently. Programs that follow the structure are easier to modify initially and to maintain subsequently. All of these benefits follow from the same basic reasons: common structures allow you to identify problems quickly and precisely and to confine a process to a specific place in the program.

Basic Program Structure

A straightforward, standard structure is published and recommended for all PostScript programs, which helps to achieve these important benefits. The complete details of this structure and how to implement it are presented in Part III, Appendix A. This structure has four basic components: header, prologue, script, and trailer. Each of these components performs an important function in establishing the complete program structure.

These four sections – header, prologue, script, and trailer – are defined in a correctly structured PostScript program in that order. The header and trailer segments are positioned at the beginning and end of the program respectively and are devoted primarily to providing specific global information about the program contained between them. The most important point about these sections is that, from the viewpoint of the PostScript interpreter, they consist of comments only and do not contain any executable PostScript code. The single exception to this is that the trailer section may contain executable code that performs cleanup functions, such as restoring the operand or dictionary stacks to their original state; such code must apply to the document as a whole and not to any individual page. The prologue and script, on the other hand, consist primarily of procedure definitions and executable code that are used by the interpreter to generate the actual output.

The *header* section contains two types of information. The first covers data regarding the creation of the file. This consists of information such as who created the document, when it was created, how it should be routed, and so forth, and is useful both in a networked environment and for sharing encapsulated files. The second type of data provided in the header is resource information, such as fonts required, whether the file uses multiple colors, and so on. This information is of particular use to document management and utility software, such as the Adobe Systems Separator™ product.

The *prologue* in a PostScript program contains procedures, named variables, and constants that will be used throughout the remainder of the program. The prologue will generally have been written by a programmer to provide specific functions and will then be included as a part of each document that requires it. In some cases, the prologue for a group of programs is loaded separately and kept internally by the interpreter for reference by many subsequent documents. In either case, the prologue will usually be relatively complex, with a variety of variables and nested procedures defined in it. The *script* defines specific elements to be produced on the output pages in terms of the procedures and variables created in the prologue, along with operands for these procedures as required. Each page description should depend only on the prologue and should be independent of any other page description. This is intended to fulfill one of our major conditions for program structure: independence. The intention is that each page can be fully created using only the prologue and the description for that page. When the prologue and script are well-crafted, the script portion of the program will generally be short and quite repetitive, using the same set of powerful procedures over and over to create the output.

This distinction between prologue and script is probably the most important one that you can make about program structure in PostScript. When you follow this convention, each section has its own unique responsibilities. The prologue contains all the required procedures and definitions and should never contain any code that makes marks on the output page. The script contains no procedure or variable definitions other than definitions that update a named variable. It contains only executable code and operand data. The two sections match one another like a lock and a key, each supplying what is missing in the other to ensure the correct operation of the whole.

The *trailer* contains cleanup information that ends the program. This is also the place for document information that could not be easily generated for the header section. This facility is provided for application programs that are generating PostScript output directly and would therefore otherwise have a problem providing the required document information in the header. For example, one of the required data items in the header is a list of fonts that are used within the document. This information is particularly important if the document requires that special, non-resident fonts be downloaded to the output device prior to printing. If the PostScript output is being directly output by an application, however, the application may not know at the beginning of the document what fonts are used within the document. In this case, the structural conventions allow the program to defer this information to the trailer of the document. A more complete discussion of these issues is presented in the next section; and a complete description of the document structuring conventions is given in Part III, Appendix A, "Structure Conventions."

Document Structure

In order to provide the necessary global information for structure, PostScript has established specific formats for items to be included in each of the defined segments: header, prologue, script, and trailer. It is important to keep in mind that none of these structural conventions are enforced, or even recognized, by the PostScript interpreter. There are other applications and utility programs that do recognize and use all or some of this data and that do require these specific formats; but the PostScript interpreter is not one of them.

Also, the specific content and format of these structuring conventions is subject to change. It is unlikely that whatever you do will become obsolete or unrecognized, however; what is more likely and, indeed, has happened in the past is that the structure will be enriched to provide additional information in support of new processes or issues. For example, the structuring conventions now have extended support for four-color printing that was not present originally.

The rationale for all these structural conventions is that applications such as document managers, spoolers, and other document utilites should be able to process and even reorder pages if necessary without actually understanding or executing the PostScript code. In addition, these conventions should not affect operation of the PostScript interpreter itself. The requirement, then, is for a method of indicating structure that will be easily identifiable for utility processing but transparent to the interpreter.

PostScript meets this objective by using a special form of comment to indicate the sectional divisions within a program and to provide the requisite structure. You have already been introduced to the form that comments take in a PostScript program in Section A1.1. The standard PostScript comment begins with a '%' and ends with a new line. Structural information within a PostScript program is provided in lines that begin with the characters '%%' or '%!' and end with a new line. As you can readily see, such lines are treated by the interpreter as comment lines and are ignored; however, because the lines begin with this special combination of characters, they can be easily distinguished and analyzed by any utility program that requires their information to work on a PostScript document. They are also immediately evident to any person reading the code.

A PostScript program does not have to implement all these structural conventions in order to meet the requirements above. A program is said to be *conforming* if it implements any proper subset of the conventions. Therefore you need only use those conventions that are appropriate and consistent with the task or operation at hand. However, in order to be a conforming program, a document must use those conventions that it does implement in the correct manner and according to the required syntax and conventions. Any program that does not follow these conventions is said to be *non-conforming*.

The document structuring conventions fall into three distinct types, covering three separate areas:

- structure comments
- resource requirements
- query conventions

Each of these conventions addresses specific requirements that may be present in a given document processing environment.

The *structure comments* are used to delimit the various parts of a PostScript document. These comments break the PostScript program into the segments described above, and they also provide two additional types of information. The first is document and page setup information. This includes information relating to output routing, network addressing, and similar issues. As a group, these may be considered management concerns, which may affect the document as a unit, individual pages within the document, or both. The second type of information is page or document markup information that delimits sections of the document that may require special processing or handling. This kind of markup is particularly important for certain segments of the document, such as included procedure set or fonts, that may have to be removed or ignored in certain environments.

The *resource requirements* are a type of comment that may occur anywhere within a document but most often occur in the header. They specify output device resources that are necessary to correctly produce the document but which are not included with the document. Such resources might include fonts, procedure sets, or files that need to be accessed separately to create the final document output. These comments also specify any external requirements for output device resources or paper requirements that are necessary for correct or satisfactory output.

The *query conventions* actually cover an entire class of special PostScript programs. Such programs use PostScript operators to query the output device as to certain state or status conditions and report the result to the application or person that initiated the query. Most of these operators are device-specific and are covered in Part I, Section C2. Generally, PostScript programs that make such queries should do nothing else and should be entirely distinct from other jobs in order to work correctly in spooler or networked environments. All of these structural conventions are presented in detail in Appendix A of Part III. The discussion there provides exact format and syntax information representing the most recent available data. The appendix also provides examples of the use of various kinds of structural information. The discussion here has been aimed at presenting a general overview of program and document structure in the PostScript programming environment.

Interpreter Operations

The PostScript interpreter is one of the important features of the PostScript language. The nature of PostScript objects and the syntax of PostScript statements are both formed by the action of the PostScript interpreter. The interpreter provides features and facilities that are absent from other, compiled languages and that, moreover, are invaluable in describing pages of output that include both text and graphics. Understanding how the interpreter operates and how it works with the language provides a programmer with valuable insight into PostScript programming requirements.

This chapter discusses the operation of the PostScript interpreter in detail. The chapter begins with a discussion of the basic operation of the interpreter. This leads naturally into an extended discussion of the PostScript objects that are fundamental to interpreter operations. The nature and attributes of objects is also related to the language structure discussed in Chapter 1. In particular, the chapter presents all the distinct types of objects and tells what action the interpreter takes for each type as that type is executed.

In fact, the remainder of the chapter focuses on execution processing by the interpreter. How the interpreter executes objects is just one of several important execution considerations. Others include how the interpreter creates objects through tokenization of PostScript input, how the interpreter manages its internal and external resources, and how it behaves in its several modes of operation.

This chapter complements the previous chapter on language structure, since the structure of the PostScript language is directly and intimately related to the fact that the language is processed by an interpreter. Although the two pieces are closely interwoven, the issues and features of each have been separated here to provide a clearer picture of the method of conceptual organization. This is something like the study of anatomy, where you might discuss first the skeletal structure of the body and then the musculature. In a real body, the muscles and the bones touch and interact at virtually every vital point, but it is useful and enlightening to consider each separately. In the same way, you will not be surprised that the action of the interpreter and the structure of the language interact at many vital points, even though we will discuss them separately for clarity.

2.1 INTERPRETER FUNCTIONS

The PostScript interpreter is the program that executes the PostScript language according to the syntax and rules set out in this chapter and the previous one. The interpreter processes a series of entities called PostScript *objects*, which are formed according to the rules set out below. By manipulating these objects, the interpreter carries out the programmed actions and generates the output pages as defined by the PostScript page description program.

The interpreter carries out its actions by executing a sequence of objects. Some objects, such as strings or numbers, are ordinarily considered operands or data. Other objects, such as operators or procedures, are ordinarily considered parts of programs. However the interpreter treats all objects according to the same rules and does not make this rather artificial distinction between program and data objects. In this, PostScript differs from most other computer languages, which require a clear delineation between programs and data.

The action taken by the interpreter depends on the type, attributes, and value of the object being executed. For example, objects of the type "integer" are executed by being pushed onto the operand stack, which was discussed earlier in Section A1.3, while operator objects are executed by performing a built-in action as defined for each operator in Section C.

Fundamentally, the interpreter gets the objects it executes from two sources. First, a character stream or file may be scanned according to the syntactical rules of the PostScript language to produce new objects. As each object is formed by the scanning process, it is immediately executed according to its type, attributes, and value. The character stream being scanned may come from an external source, such as a file or over a communication channel, or it may come from a string object that has been previously stored in PostScript memory. Second, the interpreter may execute previously stored objects. These objects are stored in procedures, which are executable forms of arrays.

The most important point to remember about the PostScript interpreter is that its sole function is to execute a sequence of PostScript objects. The nature of these objects, their attributes, and what it means to execute an object are the subjects of the next three subdivisions of this chapter.

2.2 OBJECT CLASSIFICATION

Everything in a PostScript program, including data and procedures, is stored in the form of objects. Objects are created by the scanning process and then executed by the interpreter. Objects are also created, manipulated, and consumed by the PostScript operators.

Each object has certain qualities that define it precisely and distinguish it from all other active PostScript objects. These are its *type*, its *attributes*, and its *value*. Typically, a PostScript object is a fixed size and contains within itself the definition of its type and attributes. Certain types of operators also contain their own values; others contain pointers to the places where the values are stored. The important point to notice here is that the type and attributes of a PostScript object are properties of the object itself and not of where it is stored, how it is named, or how it is used.

Object Type

The PostScript language has 14 distinct types of objects that fall into four major groups, as follows:

Numeric	Nominal	Composite	Special
integer	name	string	mark
real	operator	dictionary	null
boolean	file	array	save
		packedarray	fontID

All the syntactic elements that are recognized by the PostScript interpreter belong to one of these types. The PostScript interpreter can interrogate objects to determine their type; when it does so, the type is reported back as one of the type names listed above or as an abbreviation of the type name, with the suffix 'type' appended to the name or abbreviation; for example, an integer object would report its type as 'integertype'.

As with the earlier discussion of operator categories, the grouping of objects presented here is intended for learning and organizational purposes only. The group names do not reflect rigid categories, and they are not understood by the interpreter. Nor is the assignment of specific types to groups a precise division but is rather intended to make reference and discussion of common characteristics easier. The types of objects, on the other hand, are quite precise, are defined and implemented by the interpreter, and represent real and important differences in how objects are stored and executed.

Simple and Composite Objects

The first and most basic distinction between objects is the difference between simple objects and composite objects. Most PostScript objects are *simple objects*. These are objects that contain all their characteristics (type, attributes, and value) within themselves. In this case, the value is an intrinsic part of the object and cannot be distinguished. This seems reasonable enough, since you would be very surprised if the object *123* were the same as the object *123456*. The important point here is that simple objects have no internal structure that is discernable to the PostScript language.

Objects of the types *string, dictionary, array,* and *packedarray,* on the other hand, are defined as *composite objects*. Each type of composite object has an internal substructure that is accessible within the PostScript language by means of certain operators. In particular, the value of a composite object is stored separately from the object itself, and composite objects may share a value. Thus, for example, there may be two strings (123) and (123456) where the initial segment (123) is shared, even though the two objects are distinct and may even have different attributes.

Perhaps a short example will clarify this.

```
/ST (123456) def

ST 0 3 getinterval        ⇒        (123)

1 65 put

ST                        ⇒        (1A3456)
```

In this example, we first define a string 'ST' that is equal to (123456). Next we select a subsection of that string, using the **getinterval** operator, which leaves the substring on the operand stack. We use the **put** operator to modify the middle element of this substring from the initial value of (2) to the value of (A) – which has a decimal ASCII value of 65. Then we recall the previous string, 'ST', from memory and see that the value in the stored string has been changed. This happens because both strings are composite objects, and the original string that we stored shares values with the subsequent substring that is created and modified within this little program.

The major effect of this distinction between simple and composite objects lies in the characteristic mentioned above: that composite objects may share a value. Because of this, duplication of a composite object does not generally result in a new value even when a new object is created. Therefore, any change to the value of one object will also be reflected in all other composite objects that share that value. This is a matter of extreme importance in PostScript programming. The semantic distinction used here is to call the normal process of making one composite object out of another "duplication," with the understanding that this means that the source object and resulting object will share the value; while the process of "copying" a composite object will, in fact, create a new composite object with a new value – even if that value is identical to the value of the original object. This distinction arises from the PostScript operators involved, since the **dup** (or duplication) operator and the **copy** operator behave in exactly these ways. In all cases, however, the operator definitions provided in Section C distinguish carefully between the duplication and copying of composite objects.

Numeric Objects

The PostScript language supports two types of numeric objects: *integer* and *real*. In the last chapter, we discussed how the PostScript language represents numbers; here, we are discussing how the PostScript interpreter stores and executes numeric objects. Integer objects consist only of integer numbers that fall between certain implementation-defined limits. Real objects consist of real numbers within a wider range of limits. As discussed before, a real number may have an integer value; for example, the value '1.0' is a real object in PostScript. The same value would be represented as '1' if it were an integer object. Real numbers are generally implemented internally as floating-point numbers and therefore are subject to specific precision limits. Both types of numbers may be intermixed freely in PostScript code, except for those cases where an operand of a specific numeric type is required by an operator. Where that requirement exists, it is clearly set out in the operator description in Section C.

Although *boolean* objects are not strictly numbers, we have included them in this general group for easy reference. A boolean object has only two possible values: *true* and *false*. These objects are produced as indicators of the final result of a comparison or the state of some action. In addition, the values *true* and *false* are separately defined for easy access. Boolean values are equivalent to '0' and '1' and are often referred to in that way; and, indeed, many computer languages use binary numbers to represent true and false. However, in the PostScript language, these are distinct objects with their individual type; they are not numbers.

Nominal Objects

Three types of PostScript objects can be thought of as names or variants of names; these are name objects, operator objects, and file objects.

A *name object* is an indivisible symbol uniquely defined by a sequence of characters. Names serve as identifiers for variables, procedures, and so forth. Although they are constructed out of and referenced by a sequence of characters, names are simple objects and are not a string of characters. The individual characters that make up the name are not accessible as individual characters; they must be taken as a whole to determine the name.

Although a name is not a string, one can be formed out of a string or turned into a string by using appropriate operators. For this reason, the interpreter imposes no restriction on what characters can be used in a name; however, as discussed in the previous chapter, the language has specific requirements for names.

Names have several important characteristics. First, they must be unique. Any specific sequence of characters defines one, and only one, name object. Second, they do not have a value in the same sense that they do in other programming languages. Names in PostScript are associated with values through the dictionary mechanism. Finally, names are equal only if the corresponding characters in both names are identical. That means that upper-and lower case letters are distinct, so that the names 'A' and 'a' are not the same.

Operator objects represent built-in actions taken by the PostScript interpreter when the operator is encountered. Operators are accessed by the interpreter through their names, but operators are not their names. Rather, they are distinct objects that invoke a specific action when executed. Actually, PostScript operator objects are associated with their names in the system dictionary, *systemdict*, and are normally retrieved by the interpreter as the value part of a key-value pairing in that dictionary. The name of the operator is, of course, the key to the operator object stored in *systemdict*.

Operator names are distinct from the operators themselves and are not special or reserved in any way. Therefore it is perfectly possible for a PostScript program to redefine any given operator name in a dictionary higher on the dictionary stack than *systemdict* and change the action taken when that name is executed by the interpreter. This book, for convenience, will discuss operators as though they were synonymous with their names; for example, it will refer to the *add* operator. Although this will be quite clear, you should understand that this is a shorthand reference for the longer, but more accurate, statement, "the operator object that is referenced by the name *add* in *systemdict*."

A *file object* is a stream of characters that can be written to or read from in order to transfer information between the PostScript interpreter and its environment. Somewhat like operators, files are referred to by a name; the exact structure and meaning of the name depends on the device in which the interpreter is running. However, the file object is not its name; it represents the underlying, associated file.

The PostScript interpreter recognizes and uses a standard input file and a standard output file. The standard input file is generally the source of programs, commands, and data for the PostScript interpreter; the standard output file generally receives usual PostScript messages and other output not destined for the page device, especially error and status messages. Many PostScript programs run quite satisfactorily by simply accessing the standard files through the interpreter. When these methods are not sufficient, however, PostScript provides a full set of file operators that, among other things, allow you to open a file (the action that creates the file object) and to process the stream of characters that is the file in various ways. In environments that support richer file structures, the PostScript language has additonal operators for controlling and processing file data. See Section B2.2 for a complete discussion of file operators and their actions.

Although a file object is a simple object, it behaves in a manner similar to composite objects in that all copies of a file with the same name refer to the same underlying stream of characters. If a file object has an effect on the underlying file stream, such as closing or repositioning the file, all file objects that share that stream of data are equally affected.

Special Objects

PostScript also has four special objects that each exist to serve a specific purpose. All of these special objects are simple objects.

The *null* object is a special object used by the PostScript interpreter to fill empty or uninitialized positions in composite objects when they are created. There is only one value of type null; the name *null* is associated with this object in *systemdict*. Most operators will raise an error if they are given a null value as an operand.

The *mark* object is a special object used by the PostScript interpreter to mark a position on the operand stack. There is only one value of type mark; the names *mark* and [are associated with this object in *systemdict*. The use of the mark object is fully covered in the discussion of arrays in Section B2.2.

The *save* object is a special object that is created by the interpreter to store the current state of virtual memory and restore it upon request at some later point in processing. There may be many save objects available at any given time, with each one representing the state of virtual memory at a specific point in time. The creation and use of save objects is discussed more fully in Section A2.5.

The *fontID* object is a special object used in the construction of PostScript fonts. Note that these objects are not, in themselves, fonts; they are simply one of a number of objects that are normally associated with PostScript fonts. A complete description of font processing is presented in Chapter 5 of this section.

String Objects

The remaining four types of objects are all varieties of composite objects. We have already discussed the difference between simple and composite objects. Now we will discuss each of the types of composite objects individually.

A *string* is a composite object that consists of a set of *character codes,* which must be integer values in the range 0 to 255. The elements of strings are not actually integer values, but all the operators that handle string elements return and accept ordinary integer values in the range specified above.

String objects are conventionally used to store character data for text output. However, neither the PostScript interpreter nor the PostScript language requires that a string conform to any particular character encoding scheme or that it conform to any particular 'character' syntax. The result is that virtually any form of data can be contained within a string object, including arbitrary binary data.

Individual elements in a string can be accessed by means of an integer index. A PostScript string is indexed from 0, so that a string with n elements (characters) will have index values of 0 to $n-1$. The interpreter monitors all accesses to a string and will issue an error if any attempt is made to access outside of the valid index range.

Remember that a string is a composite object and that duplicating a string shares the value of the string between the old and the new object. In the same way, selecting a substring of a string shares values with a portion of the original string.

Array Objects

There are two types of objects that fall into the class of array objects. These are ordinary arrays and packed arrays. The major difference between these two types of arrays is how the data within them is stored; this difference in storage also creates some minor differences in accessing and creating each type. Because the two types are so similar, we will describe the basic array object first and then discuss packed arrays as a special case.

An *array* is a one-dimensional collection of PostScript objects accessed by a numeric index. Like so many PostScript concepts, and unlike most computer languages, arrays in PostScript do not have to contain all objects of the same or similar types. The elements of an array can be any PostScript object, including a heterogeneous mixture of numbers, strings, dictionaries, or other arrays. Although PostScript provides only one-dimensional arrays, multidimensional arrays can be easily constructed by nesting arrays within arrays to any arbitrary depth.

Procedures are a special form of array. When the interpreter creates a procedure, both the type and access are identical to an ordinary array; the difference is that procedures have the executable attribute, while ordinary arrays have the literal attribute. These attributes and the distinction between procedures and arrays are discussed more fully in the next section.

All PostScript arrays are indexed from 0, so that an array with n elements will have index values of 0 to $n-1$. The interpreter monitors all accesses to an array and will issue an error if any attempt is made to access outside of the valid index range.

Like all composite objects, an array shares values with any duplicate. Also, if a new array is created out of a subinterval of an array, that new array shares values with the original array in that subinterval.

A packed array object has a different type than an ordinary array object, but in most aspects it is identical to an ordinary array. In particular, there are operators – often the identical operators – to perform all the usual actions on an array: to extract elements or a particular subinterval, to enumerate the elements of the array, and so on. Individual elements within a packed array are ordinary PostScript objects, and creation of a new array out of a subinterval of a packed array results in a packed array.

As we said earlier, the major difference between ordinary arrays and packed arrays is in how the information in the array is stored. Packed arrays are primarily intended for storage and execution of procedures. They are particularly useful for this since procedures do not ordinarily need to be accessed or treated as data storage but rather are simply executed. Data is stored in a packed array in a way that typically saves 50 to 75 percent of the storage space that would be required for the equivalent ordinary array. However, packed arrays are not confined to procedures; like other arrays, packed arrays can contain any arbitrary PostScript objects.

The differences between packed arrays and ordinary arrays are as follows:

- Packed arrays are always read-only; you cannot store any data into a packed array once it has been created.
- Accessing an arbitrary element of a packed array by using its index can be quite slow; however, sequential access, as is done by the interpreter when executing a procedure, is about as fast as accessing an ordinary array sequentially.
- It is possible to copy a packed array to an ordinary array, that is, to create a new, unpacked array that does not share values with the original, packed array but contains the identical information.

Packed arrays are created in two ways. First, the interpreter can be instructed that all new, executable arrays (procedures) that are constructed shall be in the packed format.

This is done by setting a global variable, which will be discussed in Section B1.3. Second, a packed array can be explicitly created out of any arbitrary collection of objects (like any other array) by using certain PostScript operators.

Dictionary Objects

The last type of composite objects are *dictionary objects*. Dictionary objects are simply PostScript dictionaries and are accessed and manipulated as we discussed in the first chapter, in Section A1.4. Although it sounds a bit bizarre, since a dictionary is a composite object, any duplication of the dictionary will result in another dictionary that shares the values in the original dictionary. Therefore if you alter a definition (that is, the value half of a key-value pair) or add a definition in the new dictionary, you will alter or add to the old dictionary as well. This is of particular importance in handling PostScript fonts; we will cover this issue in more detail in Section B3.3.

2.3   OBJECT ATTRIBUTES

Besides type, there are some additional attributes that are also intrinsic to an object, which will be discussed in this section. These attributes affect the object's behavior when it is executed by the interpreter, or when certain operations are performed on it. However, the object's attributes have no effect when the object is treated simply as data by the interpreter; for example, two numbers that have equal values will always compare equal, regardless of their attributes.

With the exception of the dictionary object, the attributes of objects are part of the objects themselves and not part of the value of the object. Every object has certain attributes, and those attributes, while they can be changed by applying the appropriate operators to the object, can never be divorced from the object itself. Therefore two composite objects can share values but have different attributes. For dictionaries, however, the access attribute is a property of the value of the dictionary, and so dictionaries that share values share the access attribute as well.

Literal and Executable Attributes

Every object is either *literal* or *executable*. This attribute is used when the interpreter attempts to execute an object. If the object has the *literal* attribute, executing the object simply treats it like data and pushes it onto the operand stack. If the object has the *executable* attribute set, on the other hand, the interpreter will execute the object. The effect of executing the object differs according to the type of the object. Executing some types of objects, such as numbers, simply means pushing them onto the operand stack.

For those types of objects, there is no effective difference between having the literal or the executable attribute set. Other types of objects, such as arrays, behave quite differently if executed. See the next section, A2.4, for a complete discussion of what it means to execute each type of object.

Each PostScript object has either a literal or an executable attribute. This distinction has certain implications, as discussed in Section A1.1. First of all, all numbers, both integer and real, and all strings are created with the literal attribute. Names are literal if they are preceded by the special character '/', and executable otherwise. Arrays that are enclosed by the characters '[' and ']' are literal arrays, with the elements of the array being the objects enclosed by the delimiters. Executable arrays are called procedures, and are enclosed by the characters '{' and '}'.

Access Attributes

Certain objects have another attribute as well. Composite objects (strings, arrays and dictionaries) and file objects have an *access* attribute. The access attribute governs what actions may be performed on the value of an object. Other objects do not have this attribute because they do not have any internal structure that is visible or accessible to a PostScript program.

There are four possible levels of access: *unlimited, read-only, execute-only,* and *none,* in increasing order of restriction. Most objects are created with unlimited access; only packed array objects are created with read-only access, as described earlier. For an object with unlimited access, all PostScript operations that are defined on that object are allowed. An object with read-only access may not have its value modified (or written to, in the case of a file), but it still may be read or executed. An object with execute-only access may not be either modified or read, but it may still be executed by the intepreter. Finally, an object that allows no access may not be operated on in any ordinary way by a PostScript program. This form of access is primarily reserved for internal operations within the interpreter that are not of any interest to a PostScript application and are not documented here.

All this may not be quite clear at first review. Suppose that you have defined a procedure, such as {1 2 add}, which is an executable array. With unlimited access, you could modify an element of that procedure after it was defined; for example, by replacing the **add** with **sub** (for subtract). With read-only access, you could not modify elements of the procedure, but you could still retrieve them; for example, you could extract the integer 2 from the procedure. With execute-only access, you could not extract any individual element of the procedure, but you could still execute it to give the result '3'. If the procedure were made no-access, then you could not even execute it to get the result.

These two sets of attributes (literal vs. executable, and access) are entirely independent and are set and controlled separately. Although some combinations of the two are clearly not reasonable – for example, a literal array with the execute-only attribute – they are nevertheless possible.

2.4 EXECUTION PROCESSING

Now that we have covered language syntax and examined the various types of PostScript objects, we can proceed to a more complete discussion of how the PostScript interpreter performs execution processing. To begin with, the interpreter takes a stream of characters, which may come from an external source, such as a file or over a communications channel, or which may have been stored internally as a string, and processes this stream according to the rules of the PostScript language to create a series of tokens. For programming purposes, we may consider a token to be a PostScript object, although the exact scanning process used by any given interpreter implementation may result in one or more tokens being assembled to construct a single object. The object is then processed by the interpreter.

Generally, the interpreter processes an object by executing that object. However, when the interpreter encounters the begin-procedure delimiter, '{', it does not execute the resulting procedure object but instead stores the object as an executable array on the operand stack. This is known as *deferred execution,* which will be discussed in more detail below.

There are two points to notice about this process. First, the interpreter does not have any notion of a "program." It processes a sequence of PostScript objects whose execution of course, may have – indeed, most often will have – side results of adding objects to PostScript memory or making marks on an output device. Nevertheless, the interpreter itself does not have any notion of these events, nor does it maintain any global construct to represent some complete entity that can be thought of as a "program." Indeed, it has no notion of when it begins or ends a specific segment of processing, and no segment or object has any permanent existence in the interpreter.

Second, the process of constructing objects, called *tokenization,* is separate and distinguishable from the process of execution. This is important because of the issue of immediate or deferred execution mentioned above. It is also an important distinction because the process of tokenization need not be done in this fashion for all implementations of PostScript. In particular, the Display PostScript™ system from Adobe Systems sometimes uses binary tokens to speed PostScript processing for interactive display.

Immediate Execution

The normal process for the PostScript interpreter is to execute an object as soon as that object is presented to the interpreter. The objects being executed may come from a variety of sources. The nature of the source is immaterial; in every case, the interpreter performs in an identical manner.

Now, look at an example of a series of objects that are presented to the PostScript interpreter for processing. Consider this sequence:

```
4 2 add 72 mul
```

It adds the numbers '4' and '2' and then multiplies the result by the number '72'. The interpreter first gets the numeric object 4 and executes that, which is done by pushing the '4' onto the operand stack. Next it processes the '2' in the same way. Then the interpreter is presented with the name 'add'. This is an executable name (since it is not preceded by the special character '/') and so the interpreter executes this name by looking it up in the current dictionary stack. This name is associated in *systemdict* with the operator object that performs addition of two numbers. This operator object is retrieved from *systemdict* and executed, which has the result of removing the two values '4' and '2' from the operand stack and replacing them with the result, '6'. Notice here that the interpreter suspended processing of the input stream presented above while it executed the action called for by the operator. Now processing of the input stream continues by pushing the numeric object '72' onto the operand stack. Finally, the name 'mul' is looked up, as described above, and the operator that multiplies two operands from the stack is executed, which consumes the two numbers on the operand stack and returns the result, '432', there. The process described here represents immediate execution of PostScript objects.

Deferred Execution

Most PostScript objects are executed by the interpreter as soon as they are recognized. There are two objects, however, whose execution is not immediate but is delayed until they are recalled by the interpreter. This process is called *deferred execution,* and the two types of objects are 1) procedures, executable arrays bracketed by the special characters '{'and '}', and 2) name literals, names that are preceded by the special character '/'. In both cases, the interpreter handles these objects in a special, and similar, way.

A *name literal,* as you may remember from the discussion in Section A1.1, is any valid PostScript name preceded by the special character '/'. When the interpreter constructs a name literal from the input stream, it gives it the literal attribute, and therefore, when that name literal is executed, it is simply pushed onto the operand stack, as it does to any object that has the literal attribute. Where an ordinary name (which has the executable attribute) would be executed, as described above, by looking the name up in the dictionary stack, a name literal is executed simply by pushing it onto the operand stack. This is deferred execution for names.

Deferred execution for procedures is somewhat different. When the interpreter encounters the special character '{' in the input stream, it constructs an executable array from the objects that follow until it receives the matching, ending '}'. This array has the executable attribute; indeed, the only thing that distinguishes an ordinary array from a procedure is whether the array has the literal attribute, in which case it is an ordinary array, or the executable attribute, which makes it a procedure. The interpreter goes on to distinguish two methods of executing procedures. If it encounters the procedure directly, the procedure is treated as data and pushed onto the operand stack; in other words, the execution of the procedure is deferred. If the procedure is encountered indirectly, however – for example, by being retrieved from a dictionary – then it is executed in the ordinary way, by executing the objects that make up the procedure (the normal form of execution for arrays).

Next, consider a variant of the earlier example to illustrate these points. Consider this sequence:

```
/inch { 72 mul } def

4 2 add inch
```

Informally, this sequence defines a procedure, "inch," in the current dictionary and then uses it to convert the result of adding 4 and 2 to a new value. More precisely, the interpreter first encounters the name literal '/inch', which is executed by pushing it onto the operand stack, as described above. Then it encounters the procedure '{ 72 mul }'. The procedure here is encountered directly, so the interpreter treats it as data and pushes it onto the operand stack also. Now the interpreter encounters the operator name 'def', which performs the action of taking two objects from the operand stack and enrolling them as a key-value pair in the current dictionary. That means that the procedure that was placed on the stack earlier is now placed into the current dictionary as a value associated with the key '/inch'. Next the interpreter processes the objects '4', '2', and 'add', as we discussed above, to give the result '6'. The next object is the name 'inch'; this is not a name literal, since it is no longer preceded by a '/'; therefore the interpreter looks up the name in the current dictionary stack and retrieves the procedure associated with that name, '{ 72 mul }'. This time, the procedure has been encountered indirectly, and therefore the elements of the procedure are executed in order, resulting in placing the value '72' on the operand stack and then multiplying the two numbers on the stack, giving the exact result obtained by the earlier sequence, '432'.

It is very important to understand the issue of immediate versus deferred execution, especially as it concerns procedures. Luckily, the concept, although important, is easily grasped and falls naturally in with our intuitive ideas of how procedures are handled. Any other methods of setting up procedure definitions or handling these elements would surely be less intuitive and more confusing. This processing of procedures corresponds to their typical and natural use in PostScript programming. A procedure that is encountered directly by the interpreter is generally part of a construct, such as a definition or a conditional processing structure, and is not intended for immediate execution. On the other hand, if a procedure is encountered indirectly – by dictionary lookup, for example – it is generally intended to be executed immediately. In addition, the PostScript language has operators and facilities to override these assumptions should it be necessary.

Execution by Type

This section describes the action that is taken by the interpreter to execute each type of object. Remember that every object that has the literal attribute is executed by pushing it onto the operand stack; the following discussion applies only to objects that have the executable attribute.

The majority of PostScript objects behave the same way whether they are treated as data or executed: in either case, they are simply pushed onto the operand stack. This is true for numeric objects (integer, real, and boolean types), for mark, save, and fontID objects, and for dictionary objects. For all of these types of objects, the distinction between the literal and executable attribute is meaningless in practice, since the action taken is the same with either attribute setting.

An executable array or packed array object is a procedure. A procedure is pushed onto the operand stack if it is encountered directly by the interpreter. However, if a procedure is encountered indirectly, as a result of executing some other object, then it is said to be *called* instead of executed. When the interpreter calls a procedure, it places the procedure on the execution stack and then executes each element of the procedure in turn. When it is done, it removes the procedure from the execution stack and resumes processing where it left off.

An executable name object is looked up in the current dictionary stack, and the associated value is retrieved and executed. More precisely, the interpreter searches the dictionary stack, beginning with the topmost (or current) dictionary, looking for the name as a key in each dictionary. When it finds the name as a key value, it retrieves the value associated with that key in this dictionary and executes the associated value. It executes the value by examining the object's type and attributes and performs the appropriate functions as defined in this section of the chapter. In particular, if the retrieved value is a procedure, the procedure is called as described above. If the name is not present in any dictionary on the dictionary stack, the interpreter raises an error.

An executable operator causes the interpreter to perform the appropriate built-in action for that operator as defined in Section C of Part I.

An executable string is placed on the execution stack and then used as a source of characters to be tokenized and interpreted according to the PostScript language syntax. When all the characters in the string are exhausted, the string is popped from the execution stack.

An executable file is also treated as a source stream of characters for the PostScript interpreter. In this case, the process continues until end-of-file is reached, at which point the file object is removed from the execution stack.

There also is an executable null object. This is simply the normal null object with the executable attribute. Execution of a null object results in no processing taking place; specifically, nothing is placed on either the execution or operand stacks. In this way, the executable null is a true no-operation, since it has no discernable effects on the state of the interpreter.

Error Processing

A variety of errors can occur during processing a PostScript object. Some errors are detected by the interpreter, such as an overflow of a PostScript stack; others are detected during the execution of one of the built-in PostScript procedures, such as an operand of an incorrect type. However the error condition is detected, the resulting error is handled in a uniform fashion.

Error processing is done by the interpreter itself using standard PostScript methods and mechanisms. This is of major importance to the PostScript programmer because it means that all error processing can be modified as desired or required.

Each error condition that can occur in PostScript has an individual name. These names are entries into a special dictionary called *errordict* that is defined in *systemdict*. The value associated with the name is the procedure that is followed by the interpreter when the named error occurs. A complete list of PostScript error names and their causes is provided in Section C, "Operator Reference."

When an error is detected, the interpreter first restores the operand stack to the condition it was in at the beginning of execution of the current object. Then it pushes the current object onto the execution stack. Finally, the interpreter looks up the name of the error in *errordict* and executes the associated procedure which is expected to handle the error condition. All PostScript errors have default handling procedures that do something reasonable; usually, they report the error and terminate execution of the program. A more detailed description of error handling is provided in Section B2.3.

2.5 RESOURCE MANAGEMENT

One of the key functions performed within the interpreter is management of PostScript resources. This primarily means managing the memory within the PostScript device, although it may also include management of files and disk space in some devices. For our purposes here, we are primarily concerned with management of memory.

PostScript memory is the address space within the device where the PostScript interpreter is running that is accessible to objects in PostScript programs. This memory is referred to as "virtual memory" in PostScript because it may not have any direct relationship to the physical computer memory. The use of the word *virtual* is intended to emphasize that the description and management of memory from the viewpoint of the PostScript application or programmer may not have any relation to the actual handling of computer storage by the operating system (if one exists) or by the output device.

Virtual Memory

The virtual memory that is available to the interpreter is used primarily for storage of composite objects. As discussed earlier in Section A2.2, composite objects are objects whose value is stored separately from the object itself. Or, looked at from another point of view, composite objects have a value that consists of a collection of other objects. These collections are what consumes virtual memory.

The virtual memory that we are discussing here is not all the memory used by the interpreter; in particular, virtual memory is not the memory used for the PostScript stacks or other internal mechanisms within the interpreter. The operand, execution, and dictionary stacks can best be thought of, in this context, as working storage for PostScript objects and for the interpreter itself. Virtual memory is all the memory that can be reached by PostScript objects, that is, the memory that is accessible to objects that store or reference other objects.

Dynamic and Static Environments

Virtual memory is a valuable and limited resource, and the management of this resource is an important feature of PostScript programming. The PostScript language does not have any operators that allow a program to explicitly discard objects or remove their values. Once a composite object is created, it will continue to occupy virtual memory resources even after it has been "consumed" by the interpreter and there is no longer any direct method of retrieving it or making reference to it.

Most PostScript interpreters run in an environment where they are creating a single page of output at a time. In these circumstances, the interpreter also does not provide any "garbage collection" mechanism to retrieve memory no longer referenced by composite objects. In this environment, it is the responsibility of the PostScript program to manage the virtual memory resources that it uses.

There are PostScript environments, such as Display PostScript™, where multiple pages are being created and displayed. In such dynamic environments, it is generally not reasonable for a PostScript program to exercise as much control over virtual memory as it does in the more static, single-page environments. In such cases, the particular implementation of the PostScript interpreter may provide "garbage collection" to reclaim virtual memory resources that are no longer needed by the program.

Resource Recovery

In order to effectively manage virtual memory, the PostScript language provides two operators, **save** and **restore.** These operators allow a PostScript program to explicitly save a snapshot of the exact contents of virtual memory at a specific point in time and then to restore virtual memory to that saved snapshot at some subsequent point during processing. This has the effect of reclaiming all virtual memory that had been used by objects between the time the saved state was created and the time it is restored.

Let's consider an example to help clarify this issue. Suppose a sequence of commands (which we may call a program for convenience) is being processed in the normal fashion by the interpreter. At some convenient point, such as the beginning of a page, the program creates a snapshot of virtual memory by executing the appropriate PostScript operators. Then the program creates a page or pages of output. During this process, it generates and uses a number of composite objects: procedures, strings, and so on. At some later point, usually after a complete page of output has been generated, the program restores the snapshot of memory it took previously. When it does so, all the composite objects that were created in the meantime disappear, because they did not exist at the time that the snapshot was taken. The net result is that the memory consumed by those objects is again available for use by the program. This is how PostScript programs manage virtual memory.

An appropriate and recommended approach to using this snapshot facility is to take a snapshot of virtual memory at the beginning of creating a page of output and then restore it at the end. Besides recovering the virtual memory used by that page description, this process has the additional benefit of encapsulating each page, so that effects produced on one page cannot carry over onto any subsequent page. This, if you recall, was one of the desirable qualities of page description that we discussed earlier, in Section A1.6. Use of this approach is an important feature of the recommended PostScript program structure.

There are several reasons why this approach is particularly valuable for programs that are primarily engaged in creating page output – as most PostScript programs are. First, as we have just seen, this approach insures that the pages are independent of one another and therefore cannot produce unwanted and unintended results. In fact, this point is so important that this same mechanism – using snapshots of virtual memory – is how the interpreter itself provides separation between successive page descriptions or files.

Second, as described earlier, this approach preserves the maximum virtual memory for use by each page unit in succession. This can be very important if you are creating large or complex pages, which intrinsically will use substantial amounts of virtual memory resources. Finally, page descriptions typically have a significant amount of internal structure, such as individual pages or major segments within a page. These internal structures may have a requirement to modify dictionaries, arrays, and other data for some purpose that is entirely confined to the structure itself. The snapshot mechanism is an ideal method to ensure that local changes, such as these, are entirely confined to the structure that creates and uses them and that the original conditions that existed when the structure was started are exactly restored upon completion. The snapshot method is much easier to use and more efficient than any attempt to restore the conditions individually could possibly be.

2.6 MODES OF OPERATION

The PostScript interpreter provides several modes of operation. Each of the modes of operation has a particular use, and not all modes are necessarily present in every implementation. You must consult the documentation that accompanies your PostScript device to determine which modes are available on that device.

Every PostScript interpreter has a batch processing mode. This is the normal mode of operation for most interpreters and the mode that is most used by PostScript applications. In normal batch operation, the interpreter cycles repeatedly through a series of steps designed to sequentially process PostScript applications, or *jobs,* as they are conventionally called. A typical sequence of steps would be as follows: First, the interpreter sets up a clean execution environment for the job, including a clean copy of virtual memory. Then it executes the job by interpreting the standard input file, which usually represents one of several communications channels available on the device. When the file being processed reaches an end-of-file condition or when an error occurs, the interpreter cleans up after the job by restoring all the stacks to their initial state and restoring virtual memory to its initial state in preparation for the next job.

In this operation, the main function of the interpreter is as a *server* to execute PostScript programs that are transmitted to it over a communications channel. These programs are generally being executed in order to create marks on an output page which can then be printed. However, programs are not in any way limited to these operations. They may perform other tasks, such as accounting for job statistics or resetting certain parameters on the device, which do not create page output. Generally, any valid sequence of PostScript operations may be carried out in a batch job.

Interactive Mode

Many PostScript interpreters also support an interactive mode of operation. In the interactive mode, the interpreter prepares itself as it would for an ordinary batch job, creating a new copy of virtual memory and so on, and then executes a special internal PostScript routine to enter the interactive mode.

The interactive mode allows a user to interact directly with the PostScript interpreter in the device, generally by using a terminal as an input and output device and transmitting commands and receiving results over a communications channel. This mode provides some facilities to aid this process, such as limited editing capabilities, a ready prompt, and so on.

There are two ways you can change the interpreter into the interactive mode. First, you can directly execute the internal PostScript routine that performs the interactive function by executing the built-in PostScript routine **executive;** this implements interactive processing in the interpreter by sending that command over the communications line to the interpreter. Once you do that, the interpreter is placed in the interactive mode and begins to respond appropriately. The second way to enter the interactive mode is to set the mode externally, usually by a switch or through a control panel. When you do that, the interpreter automatically enters the interactive mode. Actually, the two methods come to the same thing, since changing the external switch simply executes the **executive** procedure.

The interactive mode continues until you transmit an end-of-file over the communications line, or until the PostScript **quit** operator is invoked, or until the external switch is reset to some other mode setting. From this you can see that the interactive mode is really just another job to the interpreter, although, of course, it's one that will run indefinitely if desired. In particular, typical PostScript errors and forms of interrupt other than the end-of-file simply abort processing of the current statement in the interactive mode rather than terminate the job as they would in the batch mode.

Emulation Modes

In addition to the batch and interactive modes, most PostScript interpreters provide one or more emulation modes. In these modes, the PostScript interpreter mimics, or *emulates,* the processing characteristics of some other device, usually some form of printer output device. In this mode, the output device running the PostScript interpreter can be connected to another device in place of the emulated device, where it both appears to be and functions like that device.

Emulation modes vary from device to device, and you will have to consult the documentation for your device to tell what emulation modes are available and how they operate. Generally, such modes are of little interest to the PostScript programmer, since they typically disable all PostScript intelligence in order to ensure that the emulation is successful.

Page Structure

Languages such as PostScript are called page-description languages because they deal with and generate output in structured pieces that can conveniently be considered as pages. Not all PostScript output is a full page; indeed, one of the most powerful PostScript features is the ability to imbed one unit, or "page", of graphics within another. Nevertheless, it is both convenient and generally correct to consider output units as pages.

The discussion that follows will continually refer to output units that are created by PostScript programs as pages. You should understand that this does not refer to a physical page of some specified dimensions that is output onto a specific medium. Instead, it refers to the general output unit created by the program. In many cases – perhaps in most cases – these two will be identical; the output unit will be exactly one physical page as produced on the output device. But the first concept to understand is that they need not be identical; there may be many "pages" of programming on one physical output page. The concept of a "page," then, is a metaphor that provides a powerful and useful visualization of the output being created within your program.

In other programming languages, the programs created and the output they generate are not usually designed to be thought of in units. Instead, the traditional application treats input and output as a continuous stream of characters or records. Any further output structure is supplied by the programmer, generally with some effort and loss of generality. A page-description language, on the other hand, forms pages of output naturally, without placing much burden on the programmer. Streams of output data are appropriate for lists, for the type of report that you might consider "typical computer output." The page format, on the other hand, is more natural for forms, artwork, financial statements, and any output that requires the integration of text and graphics.

3.1 PAGE DESCRIPTIONS

Describing output as pages comes particularly naturally to certain types of output devices, such as laser printers. These devices and others such as dot-matrix printers (which are not page-oriented) are all part of a general class of output devices called *raster output devices*. These devices are all characterized by having a number of dots that are activated or made visible in order to make an image. Television, which is the original raster output device, uses an electron beam to light up small dots of phosphor on the screen that are formed into images. Any method of creating dots will work just as well, and each category of devices has its own method. Essentially, the image is made up by filling an area with a series of dots. On some devices, the dots themselves can be made shades of light or dark to create shading; on other devices, the dots are only present or absent, and alternative techniques are used to create shades of gray or color. The most important thing about these devices, however, is that there is no completely solid area; all shapes, including lines, are rendered by filling them in with dots.

Not surprisingly, there are both advantages and disadvantages in using dots to represent images. The advantage is that dots can be used to represent any graphic shape, whether it be type, line art, or images. The disadvantage is that, since there are no continuous lines, all objects must be ragged and uneven at the finest and smallest level. Luckily, the human eye compensates to some degree for this effect and makes smoothly outlined shapes out of these dotted areas if the dots are close enough together.

Device Resolution

Each dot on a raster output device represents one picture element, or *pixel*. Although pixels are commonly referred to as dots, they may actually be square or oval or any other shape that is convenient and appropriate for the device. Pixels may also be any size, large or small, and devices are often classified by the size of their pixels; this classification is called *device resolution*. The closer together the pixels are, the higher the resolution and the better the device is at fooling the eye.

Resolution is measured by the number of dots or pixels in a given unit area. Most often, device resolution is identical in both vertical and horizontal directions; in such cases, resolution is usually given in *dots per inch*, or *dpi*. However, some devices have different resolutions in each direction; in such cases, each resolution must be expressed separately, for example, as 240 by 300 dpi.

The devices with the lowest resolution are typically terminal screens, which have a resolution of 50 to 100 dpi, with 72 dpi being one of the most common resolutions. Dot-matrix printers have slightly higher resolutions, ranging between 100 and 200 dpi. Most page printers, such as laser printers, ink-jet printers, and so on, have resolutions of 300 to 600 dpi. High-resolution devices, such as typesetting machines, have resolutions ranging from 1000 to 2500 dpi, and some very high-resolution devices have even more dots per inch.

Obviously, the higher the device resolution, the more information is required to define the image being created, and the greater is the demand on the system resources. As a result, such devices are more expensive to acquire and operate, but they create the highest quality output. On medium- and high-resolution devices, the eye generally cannot distinguish individual dots, although on devices with resolutions of 600 dpi or less, it may be able to discern a difference in shape or alignment of a single pixel.

Scan Conversion

Even on devices of the highest resolution, however, the issue of how to define the boundary of an image is an important one. The defining process is called *scan conversion*. It is probably the single task that consumes the most processing resources within the PostScript interpreter. Accurate scan conversion is most essential for letter shapes, because quick recognition of text characters is important for ease of reading. From a mathematical description of any graphical object, such as a square or a circle or a type character, this process determines what pixels must be activated and what values they must have to make the output the best rendition of the object.

Scan conversion of any graphical object essentially is the process of determining which pixels lie inside the shape and which lie outside and then setting the values of the pixels accordingly. Since it would be most unusual if the edge of an object lay exactly along a line of pixels, some technique is required to determine how to set the edges to give the most regular appearance. This process is exactly the same, no matter what the nature of the graphic; even type shapes are handled in exactly this way.

Page Output Methods

Obviously, one method of producing pages of output would be to generate a complete set of pixel values for a page and then send that to the device. This approach, however, has several drawbacks. First, the number of pixels per page is quite large, as you may easily calculate by multiplying the number of square inches per page by the number of pixels per square inch; at 300 dpi, this comes to something like 8.4 million pixel values for a typical 8 1/2-by-11-inch page. The values increase for larger page sizes and make even more dramatic jumps for higher-resolution devices; moreover, each pixel value may be represented by one to eight bits of data. Storing and transmitting such large data streams is very cumbersome and time-consuming. Second, this set of data is very dependent upon the device being used. Even two devices of the same resolution will often not have identical pixel maps for a page because of scanning systems or addressing methods or some other device-dependent attribute. Finally, the process of scan conversion requires a significant amount of computing resources. Trying to perform this task on a host computer, rather than in a special-purpose device, removes resources from the application software and often results in noticeable degradation in performance. Overall, therefore, this approach is not a very satisfying solution to the problem of page description.

All of these problems can be met by using a general purpose, high-level page description language, such as PostScript. Page descriptions can be produced in standard character streams or as binary tokens, as described in the previous chapters. This is much more compact than the pixel-by-pixel description that would otherwise be used. In addition, the description of the page does not become larger when used for higher-resolution devices. Such independent page descriptions can be processed separately, often within the output device itself, thus freeing the host for more productive work and allowing faster processing since the facilities within the device can be customized to speed the scan-conversion process. Finally, because the language is high-level, the page descriptions are not tied to any one device and can be easily modified to produce new pages.

Producing a page of output using a page description language, then, becomes a two-step process. First, the application or programmer that is designing the page describes the page in a way that is independent of the device, using the facilities of the language. Then that description is processed by a separate program that controls a specific raster-output device and converts the description into a pixel rendition of the desired page. Notice that these two steps do not have to happen immediately, one after the other, or even take place in the same device. The page description may be stored or transmitted with no loss of generality, and its processing is performed entirely asynchronously from the process that generated it.

Static and Dynamic Page Descriptions

Page description languages, however, differ in their approach to page production and in their generality and utility. The most important dimension of these differences is in whether the language provides static or dynamic formats for pages. A *static format* is one that uses some fixed set of defined operations to format a page. These operations are often done by use of "control codes" that specify some specific action to be taken at a given point on the page. For example, a specific control code might request a change to italic printing, and another might request a change in print spacing. The limitations of this approach are obvious, since the codes are designed to implement the capabilities of a certain device or class of devices. The net result is that this approach generates more and more codes and more and more specialized usage over time as the capabilities of devices increase. Such coding structures are generally created, and thought of, as a part of the data that they help define and display.

A *dynamic format,* on the other hand, is not limited in these ways. It implements a general set of operators, which can be extended to include new operations by combining old ones. The precise action attached to any given operator may not be completely known until the actual time of processing. Such a format is better thought of as a program than as data. Typically, a page description that is completely dynamic will implement programming language features such as procedure definitions, loops, and variables. PostScript is such a dynamic page-description language.

A PostScript page description implements a large number of dynamic features. It provides a set of graphics operators that can be combined in many ways to generate beautiful and unusual pages. It has a full set of language features that allow variable definition, dynamic program control, and interpreted flexibility. Furthermore, it has facilities to access and use device information for those pages that require an intimate connection to device characteristics to produce certain effects.

In order to implement this dynamic concept of a page, the PostScript language uses a conceptual model of a page of output and defines a series of general graphic operations on that model that allow it to create images of any sort for output. The remainder of this chapter is devoted to discussion of the PostScript page structure.

3.2 PAGE STRUCTURE

PostScript maintains a simple conceptual model of a "page" as a two-dimensional space. Images are rendered onto the "page" by placing "marks" in selected areas. These marks may be made visible in any one of several ways, and they may represent characters, filled or outlined shapes, or halftone representations of images. The marks may be colored or black and white, and they may be shaded in any degree allowed by the output mechanism. The marks are always opaque, so that the last image on a page overlays any previous marks that are underneath it. Any element on a page may be cropped or transformed as it is painted onto the page. Finally, once a page reaches the desired state, it may be rendered onto an output device.

Conceptually, all these operations follow a natural model of a brush or pen creating images on a page of paper. Even though the "page" is an electronic construct, and the "marks" are represented by binary digits, the concept remains the same. The major difference is that, in PostScript, the path that is generated onto the page is invisible until some specific action is taken to "mark" it. Even this has its natural analogy, as an artist might use a light pencil to define a path before inking it. The important point here is that the PostScript concept and the operations on that page follow a natural and comprehensible model.

PostScript begins its work on an ideal "page," which is independent of any specific device. This is called the *current page* and is the two-dimensional space where PostScript makes its marks. When PostScript begins, the current page is blank – that is, free from any marks or paths. Marks are made on a page by "pencilling" in a path and then "painting" it, using appropriate PostScript operators. These processes are discussed in the next chapter.

Graphics State

In addition to the parameters that define the current page, PostScript maintains a series of additional parameters that define the current state of the color being used, the size of a line and the shape of the joins and ends of a line, and the current type style, for example. All these parameters, taken together, make up what is called the *current graphics state*.

PostScript maintains the current graphics state on the graphics stack. This mechanism gives the programmer complete control of the parameters within the current graphics state and the ability to modify them and restore them at will. This ease of control is one of the major virtues of the PostScript language.

3.3   MEASUREMENT AND COORDINATES

As described earlier, PostScript pages are two-dimensional spaces that exist to hold the graphic objects created by the PostScript operators. This space holds the paths, points, and marks that make up the individual graphic objects. As you might expect, these paths and points are specified on a PostScript page in terms of a rectilinear coordinate system. Such a system fits naturally into the PostScript page structure, using two coordinates to specify any given point on a page. These two coordinates are conventionally represented as x and y, with the x axis being the horizontal axis, and the y axis running vertically, at right angles to x. In this way, any point on the page can be specified by two numbers, (x, y), which give its position from the *origin*, the point $(0, 0)$. By the same process, any path can be specified as a mathematical curve, and points can be defined as being inside or outside the curve according to some rule, which allows painting a figure with a given color or gray value. This coordinate system defines the *user space*.

Default User Space

In order to use this coordinate system, we must be able to define precisely where on a page a given set of (x, y) points places us. In order to do that, we need to define three things:

1. The location of the origin: the point $(0, 0)$. The origin of a PostScript page is at the *bottom left corner* of the page.
2. The directions of the x axis and the y axis. The x axis on a PostScript page extends horizontally, with the positive x direction to the right of the origin. The y axis on a page extends vertically, with the positive y direction going up the page.
3. The scale, or unit of measure, along these axes. The standard PostScript unit measure is $1/72$ inch. That means that 1 unit of motion on a PostScript page moves $1/72$ inch on the page image.

If you are unfamiliar with printing measures, the choice of $1/72$ inch may seem somewhat strange and arbitrary. Actually, $1/72$ inch is almost exactly a printer's *point*, which is fractionally larger than $1/72$ inch. Thus this choice for the scale of PostScript coordinates makes units on a PostScript page equivalent to point measures in normal printing processes. You should also notice that this choice of axes and origin makes every point on the normal page identifiable by a positive pair of (x, y) coordinate values.

This set of conventions now precisely identifies every point in the user space, using coordinates that are both easy and natural to use for printing and graphics composition. This set of coordinates and conventions is called the *default user space*.

You may find this set of conventions a little difficult at first. For one thing, it seems in some ways more natural to think of the upper left-hand corner of the page as the origin, and to have the positive y axis extend down the page, rather than up. The system used here, however, corresponds to the more traditional and usual mathematical practice and makes many mathematical tools readily available for working on paths and objects. In any case, PostScript provides the means to readjust these (and most other) conventions if you find it necessary; once you have a little experience with this system, you will usually find working with it quite easy and natural.

3.4 DEVICE SPACE

The default user space has no direct connection to the specific output device. It represents ideal coordinates and measures that always retain a fixed relationship to the current page.

Each individual output device has its own measure and coordinate system. Typically, an output device will use a measure that corresponds to the device resolution and will have some set of coordinates dictated by the motion of the output page through the device imaging system. This device coordinate system is known as the *device space*.

The PostScript interpreter provides a method for transforming the default coordinates into the coordinates that are used by the device. This process is normally transparent to the PostScript application and need not be considered in using PostScript operators. However, a program does have the ability to access the device space and determine device coordinates if required for special purposes. You should be clear, however, that most PostScript programs, whether coded by hand or generated by an application, do not need to be concerned with device space. This freedom is a major contribution toward the device independence that is so important in PostScript.

Device-Specific Concerns

The major issues that may ordinarily occur in relation to device space occur in the related areas of scan conversion and device resolution. As mentioned earlier, on devices of low and medium resolution, the human eye can often discern a difference in the relative position or size of a single pixel. In these cases, it is often necessary for a PostScript application to make adjustments to graphics based on the characteristics of the device. This is called *tuning* and is especially important when dealing with character shapes and text output at sizes where the device resolution is a significant fraction of the size of the text characters.

Although the exact nature of this tuning must inevitably depend on the exact circumstances of the application, you should be aware that PostScript provides the means to handle such concerns within the language and without sacrificing device independence. There are operators that allow conversion of coordinates and paths into the device space for precise alignment without compromising the ability of the program to run on all PostScript-equipped devices. Such features also contribute to the device-independent nature of the PostScript language, which we value so highly.

3.5 COORDINATE TRANSFORMATIONS

PostScript performs this conversion from one coordinate system to another by means of a mathematical process called *coordinate transformation*. This is a generalized mathematical process that changes points or distances in one coordinate system into another coordinate system by means of a *transformation matrix*. Every PostScript device comes with a built-in transformation matrix that is stored in the current graphics state and specifies how to transform user coordinates into device coordinates for that device. This matrix is called the *current transformation matrix*.

The elements of the matrix actually specify the coefficients of a pair of linear equations in x and y that specify how to derive a new, transformed x and y. This is simply a convenient mathematical representation of the more natural and familiar concepts of geometric transformations, such as rotation, translation, or scaling of coordinate systems. Most of the PostScript operators that implement these changes are organized according to this geometric model.

The form of transformation used most often does not replace the current transformation matrix but rather modifies it. In this way, the mapping from the user space to the device space is preserved, but with the addition of some new feature. The best way to visualize this is to think of the operators changing the user space coordinate system in a sequence of transformations, with the last transformation always being the one from user space to device space.

User Space Transformations

Such transformations have many uses. The simplest are the coordinate transformations that affect the entire page. These might be a change in measure from points to inches, for example, or a translation and rotation of the coordinates to print graphics in the landscape mode (sideways) rather than in the portrait mode. Basically, any change in the coordinate structure that is useful can be accomplished using these facilities.

A more interesting use for these operations is to *encapsulate* individual graphics or portions of a page of output within their own coordinate system. By doing this, the graphic can be moved, scaled, or otherwise transformed independently of its internal coordinates. In this fashion, the graphic element is decoupled from its actual location on the page. This ability to move and transform properly formed graphics is the basis of PostScript's ability to imbed page descriptions within one another.

Matrix Representation

Understanding the structure and use of the actual PostScript coordinate operators, which are described generally in the next section (Section B) and defined precisely in Section C, requires that you understand something about how matrices are constructed and used to represent coordinate systems. Naturally, there is not enough room here for a complete discussion of these issues, but a short explanation is essential. The important thing for you to understand from this discussion is not how the mathematics works but rather how these matrices represent the more accessible and intuitive geometric transformations.

A two-dimensional linear transformation is mathematically described by a 3×3 matrix as follows:

$$\begin{array}{ccc} a & b & 0 \\ c & d & 0 \\ t_x & t_y & 1 \end{array}$$

which represents the coefficients of the pair of linear equations:

$$x' = ax + cy + t_x$$
$$y' = bx + dy + t_y$$

which provide the actual transformation from a pair of coordinates (x, y) into the new coordinates (x', y'). This matrix is represented in the PostScript language as a six-element array as follows:

$$[\, a\ b\ c\ d\ t_x\ t_y\,]$$

since the third column of the matrix is always constant.

The most common geometric transformations are expressed quite naturally in this format. For example, the general formula for a translation of the origin to a new point (t_x, t_y) is given by the matrix

$$\begin{array}{ccc} 1 & 0 & 0 \\ 0 & 1 & 0 \\ t_x & t_y & 1 \end{array}$$

which is written in the PostScript array format as

$$[\, 1\ 0\ 0\ 1\ t_x\ t_y\,]$$

Therefore, if you want to translate the origin to a new point whose coordinates are at the point (100, 200) in the current coordinate system, you would require an array that looks like this:

[1 0 0 1 100 200]

Figure A3.1 shows you an example of a translation of a graphic object. Similarly, scaling the coordinates by a factor s_x in the x dimension and s_y in the y dimension is done by the matrix

$$\begin{matrix} s_x & 0 & 0 \\ 0 & s_y & 0 \\ 0 & 0 & 1 \end{matrix}$$

which is written in the PostScript array format as

[s_x 0 0 s_y 0 0]

Again, as a concrete example, let us suppose that the current transformation matrix is the default and you want to scale the units in PostScript to 1 inch horizontally and 1/2 inch vertically, you would require the following array:

[72 0 0 36 0 0]

since 72 units in the default coordinates of 1/72 inch would be 1 inch, and 36 units would be 1/2 inch. Figure A3.2 shows you an example of a uniformly scaled graphic object.

Figure A3.1 Translated Graphic

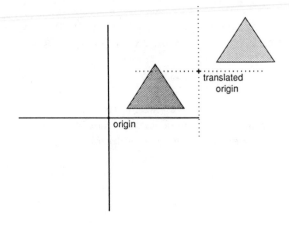

Figure A3.2 Scaled Graphic

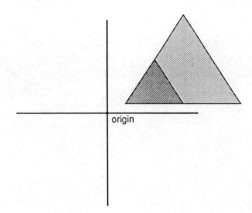

A simple rotation of the coordinates counterclockwise through an angle, θ, without moving the location of the origin, is done by the following matrix

$\cos\theta$	$\sin\theta$	0
$-\sin\theta$	$\cos\theta$	0
0	0	0

which, once again, is represented by the PostScript array

[$\cos\theta$ $\sin\theta$ $-\sin\theta$ $\cos\theta$ 0 0]

Suppose that you want to rotate the coordinates to a new position 30 degrees counterclockwise from the current orientation. Then you would require the array

[.866 .5 − .5 .866 0 0]

since the sine of 30 degrees is .5 and the cosine is .866. Figure A3.3 shows you an example of a rotated graphic object.

Any desired transformation can be accomplished by using these and other transformations performed in some specific order. An important property of describing these transformations by matrices in this fashion is that any sequence of operations can be *concatenated* into a single matrix representation. For example, translation to the point (100, 200) followed by a 30-degree rotation would result in the matrix

.866	.5	0
− .5	.866	0
100	200	1

and in a PostScript array that looks like

[.866 .5 − .5 .866 100 200]

Figure A3.3 Rotated Graphic

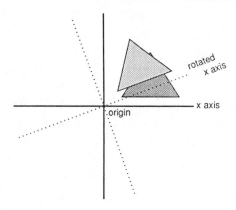

which performs both operations at once. This process of concatenation is based on the mathematical process of matrix multiplication and produces the same result as applying each of the desired transformations in succession. In this way, any combination of transformations can be accomplished by one matrix. It is this matrix that is stored as the current transformation matrix (CTM) in the graphics state.

It is sometimes necessary to perform the reverse operation and translate device coordinates into user coordinates. This requires the mathematical process of *inverting* the CTM. However, matrix inversion is not as clean and well-defined as concatenation. In particular, it is possible to attempt to invert a matrix that will give undefined results. This can happen, for example, if all the values a, b, c, and d are zero. Geometrically, such a matrix transforms all points in user space into a fixed point in device space. Therefore, any attempt to reverse the process yields an undefined result, since the reverse mapping translates a single point into many points. Such transformations are not useful, and generally happen through errors in PostScript operations; the transformation described above, for example, would be created by scaling by 0.

The fact that these types of errors can occur, however, should warn you against accessing the current transformation matrix (CTM) directly. The ordinary PostScript operators that perform these coordinate transformations do so by concatenating the CTM with a matrix, as described above, to generate a new CTM. This process insulates you as a programmer from most of the serious problems that you might otherwise face if you directly work with the CTM. In general, it is not good programming practice to change the CTM by replacing it; you should use the concatenation operations, which will normally be the best alternative for programming purposes.

4

Drawing Operations

Having discussed how a PostScript page is defined and produced, we now will proceed to the more interesting aspect of how PostScript produces graphic objects on that page. This chapter, therefore, presents a discussion of PostScript drawing operations.

Besides being a general-purpose language, PostScript implements a large number of operators that are specifically designed to create and paint graphic objects. We have already discussed how PostScript measures pages and uses coordinates as a means of reference. PostScript also uses these same coordinates as the source for the mathematical representation of arbitrary graphic objects. The basic method of creating graphic objects is quite straightforward. PostScript operators are used to define an arbitrary path that makes up the object. Then the path is painted in some fashion to make it visible. This process continues until all the graphics on the page have been drawn. Finally the entire page image, containing all the objects, is rendered onto a physical output page. We will now examine this process in detail.

4.1 PATHS AND FIGURES

The first step in the process of creating a graphic object is to create the path that defines the object. This path is actually a mathematical equation that defines the points that lie along the path. A path may be used to draw a line or mark out a region of the page that can be used as a clipping region. Often the path will be used to form the edges of an object, which can then be painted in a variety of ways. PostScript uses this path concept as an integral element of all its graphic operations.

A path is composed of straight line segments and curved line segments. These segments may be connected or discrete, and they may intersect in any way. The path may have any shape, may be closed or open, and may consist of multiple, independent sub-paths.

In other words, there really is no constraint on the shape or size of a path. Paths are represented by internal data structures that are not directly accessible as a specific Post-Script object; however, a path is created and can be read back using standard PostScript operations.

Path Construction

When the interpreter begins to operate on the first page, the page is entirely empty; there are no marks on it and there are no paths defined for it. Paths are created on the current page by sequential application of *path construction operators*. The path, once created, can be used to define an area to be painted, using one of the painting operators that we will discuss in Section A4.3. Alternatively, it can be read back and processed in a variety of ways. The path can be erased directly by specific action to start a new path or indirectly by using the path as a control for certain painting operations.

Current Path

In all of this, "the path" has been referred to as an individual and independent thing; and so it is. PostScript maintains a *current path* as a part of the current graphics state. The path construction operators add new segments to the current path or otherwise modify it, and the painting operators implicitly use the current path to define regions of the page for their operation.

A path is started by erasing any existing path structures and initializing the path; at this point, no path exists, and the current path is said to be *empty*. Then segments are created and added to the path by the path construction operators. A segment may consist of a single point, a line, or an arbitrary curve. The path may be built up of segments created in any sequence; however, the sequence of the segments is significant. In particular, one segment is said to be *connected* to another if the second segment is created immediately after the first and starts at the point that ended the first segment. Nonconsecutive segments that simply intersect, even at endpoints, are not connected.

A *subpath* is a series of connected segments. The current path is made up of one or more disconnected subpaths. A subpath may define a segment that explicitly returns to its starting point; such a subpath is said to be *closed*. Any subpath that is not closed is *open*. As with the concept of connecting segments, a subpath is not closed even if the end point of its final segment lies directly over the starting point of its first segment. The closure of a subpath must be done explicitly.

The points used to define the current path are all defined in the current coordinate system in user space. As each point is placed onto the page, the interpreter transforms the coordinates in user space into device space and positions the points accordingly. In this way, changes to the CTM do not affect previously defined and placed portions of the current path.

The last point in the current path is the *current point*. This is the endpoint of the last segment defined as a part of the current path. If the current path is empty, the current point is undefined. Most operators that add a segment to the current path start at the current point; if the current point is undefined, they will raise an error.

Clipping Path

The current graphics state also includes a *clipping path*. This is a path that defines the area or region of the page where the painting operators have an effect. Basically, areas within the clipping path can be affected by the painting operators, and areas that fall outside that boundary cannot be painted. Since PostScript can only output images that have been painted, you can see that any object or portion of an object that falls outside the clipping path will never appear on the output page. The clipping path conceptually behaves like a stencil or a mask, allowing marks onto the current page inside the areas defined and keeping them off the current page outside.

The clipping path can be concatenated with the current path to define a new clipping path that is the intersection of the two paths. The clipping path may be reduced, but never enlarged, by these methods.

Storage Limits

Although there is no intrinsic limit on the form or shape of a path, nor any limit on the number of subpaths that may form a path, every point that defines the current path must exist simultaneously in virtual memory. This doesn't mean every point on the path, just the ones that define the path. For example, a rectangle is defined by its four corner points. Nevertheless, if there are many complex subpaths to the current path, it is possible that all the necessary points will not fit in memory. There is a limit on the number of segments that a path may have. Also, there may be several paths that exist at the same time: the current path, the clipping path, and any paths related to previous graphics states that are still on the graphics state stack. Segments of all of these paths consume virtual memory. The total of the number of segments that may exist at any one point in time is dependent on the device and the implementation. You should check the documentation provided with your device for these limits.

In ordinary programming, it is unlikely that you will ever exceed these limits. The most important rule to follow to help avoid exceeding this limit is to construct separate objects on the page out of separate paths that are used and then erased. It is quite possible to exceed this limit if you attempt to create an entire page of complex graphics as a single path.

Positioning

PostScript operators that change position on the page fall into two classes. The first class are those operators that create lines on the page; as the line is created, the current point is changed to the end of the segment. All the operators that define lines – straight or curved – move the current point to the end of the line on completion of the operation. The second class are those operators that simply reposition the current point. In this case, there are no path segments created from the original point to the new point by the movement. This is also the process that you use to set the current point initially.

Remember that creating a path on a page does not, by itself, make marks on the page. Marks are produced only by application of painting operators to the current path. Normally, a graphic object is defined as a path or part of a path, and then the painting operators are applied to the path to make the shape; and the entire process is repeated until the page is filled with the desired set of graphics.

PostScript operations support two distinct types of motion: absolute and relative. *Absolute motion* is motion to a specific point in user space, as defined by the actual coordinates of the point that is desired. *Relative motion* is motion in relation to the current point, where the absolute coordinates of the destination point are not provided, but instead the coordinates for the destination are provided as displacements in user space from the current point. All paths begin with absolute motion; since relative motion is performed in relation to the current point, a current point (and the associated current path) must already exist before the motion is initiated.

4.2 PAINTING

Once a region or object has been constructed on the current page by specifying a path that describes it, it then must be made visible by painting that path in one of a variety of ways provided by the PostScript operators. There are two basic methods of making objects visible: by outlining them, or by filling them, or both. In either case, the object is made visible using the *current color,* which is an independent parameter set in the current graphic state. The current color may be black, a shade of gray, or an arbitrary color. The methods of defining colors are discussed in Section A4.5.

When an object is outlined, the current path is turned into a visible line. Each subpath of the current path is treated separately. The color of the line is determined by the current color; the size and other characteristics of the line are also controlled by certain parameters set in the current graphics state. The characteristics of a line that are controlled from the current graphics state are the following: line cap, line join, and miter limit. The *line cap* defines how an open end of the path is treated. Generally, the open end of a line – that is, an end that does not connect to another line – is cut off at the endpoint with a straight end. However, it is possible to define a line end that is round or that extends beyond the endpoint by a distance proportional to the width of the line.

See the description of the **setlinecap** operator in Section C1 for samples of each type of cap. The *line join* specifies how path segments that are connected join together. Lines may be connected by joins that are mitered, rounded, or beveled. See the description of the **setlinejoin** operator in Section C1 for samples of each type. Remember that segments that simply cross or intersect are not joined. In particular, paths that are not closed properly will have their line ends finished with the appropriate line cap rather than a join even if the ends overlap. Finally, if the lines are joined by an angled join (called a mitered join), there is a control to prevent the angle formed by the joined lines from becoming unacceptably large. This parameter is called the *miter limit*.

The other method of making an object visible is by filling it with the current color. Again, the current path defines the limits of the color application. In this case, however, the color is not applied along the path, as it is in outlining, but is instead applied to all points inside the path. All subpaths of the current path are treated uniformly; if the subpaths are disconnected, their inside points are taken together to determine what points get colored. If any subpaths are open, they are implicitly closed before color is applied. This is a particularly important point for programming. You may find what appear to be closed figures that have not been specifically closed; very often the program will be taking advantage of this implicit action to finish the construction, knowing that the area is going to be filled with paint rather than outlined.

Inside Rules

This raises the interesting question of how the interpreter determines which points are inside and which outside the current path. For a simple shape – a circle or a rectangle, for example – this determination is relatively easy. For more complex figures, however, particularly where the current path consists of multiple, independent subpaths, this process may be quite complex and unintuitive. As a result, the PostScript interpreter implements two separate rules for determining inside and outside points from the current path. The different rules are accessed by choosing different versions of the painting operators to apply color.

Both rules work in a similar conceptual fashion. A point is determined to be inside or outside a path by drawing an imaginary ray from the point toward infinity and counting how many times the ray crosses the path. The direction of the ray is taken to eliminate confusing situations such as the ray running parallel to the path. The *non-zero winding number rule* begins the count at zero and adds one every time the path crosses the ray from left to right and subtracts one every time the path crosses from right to left. After counting all the crossings, a result of zero indicates that the point is outside the path, while any other result indicates that the point is inside the path. Figure A4.1 shows the results of the non-zero winding number rule on two moderately complex paths: a five-pointed star and two concentric circles.

Figure A4.1 Examples of non-zero winding number rule

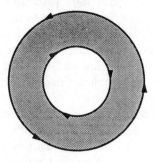

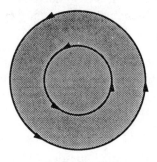

In both cases, the shaded area indicates the points recognized by PostScript as being inside the figures. As you see, the points you would expect to be inside the star are, in fact, inside. The concentric circles, however, present a different result depending on the direction of the path, as indicated by the arrows. For the first set, the two circles are drawn in the same direction, and so all points "inside" both circles are inside the figure. For the second set, the circles have been drawn in opposite directions, and so the crossing rule determines that points "inside" the smaller circle are not inside the figure.

The alternative is the *even-odd* rule. This performs the counting process in a similar way, except that one is added to the count every time the path crosses the ray in any direction. Again, after counting all the crossings, the point is judged inside the path if the resulting count is odd and outside if the result is even. For simple paths, the two rules yield identical results. Figure A4.2 shows the result of the even-odd rule applied to the same complex path shown using the non-zero winding number rule in Figure A4.1.

In both of these figures, points that were "inside" under the non-zero winding number rule are now considered "outside." Again, the shaded area shows the inside points as determined by the interpreter using the even-odd rule.

The non-zero winding number rule provides more intuitive results, as shown by the figures, and is more versatile. It is the default rule used by the PostScript interpreter. The even-odd rule, however, is used by some other graphics systems and is provided for compatibility with them; it also can be used to create some interesting special effects.

4.3 HALFTONES

One issue that must be addressed in any form of image processing is how to represent gray values on a device that has only black dots. This is often done in printing by using larger and smaller dots of ink to represent darker and lighter shades over the space of the entire image.

The PostScript interpreter uses a similar method to achieve the same result on those output devices that have only full black pixels (for example, a laser printer). In the case of raster output devices, the size of the dot cannot be changed; instead, a set of dots may be grouped into a cluster and changed proportionally to represent darker and lighter shades. This process in known as *halftoning*. A similar technique is used for creating full-color images on devices that have primary-color pixels that can only be turned on or off. That process is discussed in more detail in the next section (A4.4) of this chapter.

The halftoning process consists of defining a pattern, or *halftone screen,* that determines groups of pixels. The halftone screen is defined by establishing a uniform square grid of *halftone cells* over the device array. Each pixel on the output page belongs to one cell; a cell typically will consist of many pixels. The grid has a *frequency,* that is, a number of cells per unit area, and an *angle,* which is the orientation of the lines of grid cells relative to the device coordinate system. The number of pixels per cell is determined by dividing the resolution of the device by the grid frequency, with some adjustment for the screen

Figure A4.2 Examples under the even-odd rule

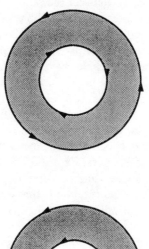

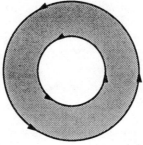

angle. As an example, a 300-dpi laser printer, using a screen with a frequency of 60 lines per inch – screens are usually defined in *lines* – at a screen angle of 0 degrees, will have cells with 5 pixels on each side, or 25 pixels in all. Since the arrangement of pixels is fixed for any given output device, screens of the same frequency but different angles may differ somewhat in the number of pixels per cell. Dividing the resolution by the frequency gives a good approximation of the pixels per cell for most programming purposes.

You should also note that not every combination of frequency and angle is available on each device. This occurs because the halftone machinery must create cells that will mesh together smoothly when applied over the entire area to be used and not show where one row of cells begins and another ends. This process, known as *tiling,* is limited by the physical device that is being used. For this reason, it can happen that you may request a particular frequency and angle from the halftone machinery and get only an approximation of your request. The values actually used are the closest values to the requested values that still provide correct tiling.

All parameters of the halftone screen, including the size and orientation of the halftone cells, are defined in device space; they are unaffected by the current transformation matrix. This property is essential to ensure that adjacent areas treated by halftone techniques don't show "seams" where they join. A PostScript program that defines a screen must know the resolution of the output device and the orientation of the device coordinates in order to properly set the screen. Very often, the best choice of screen parameters depends on specific device characteristics, such as pixel shape or the overlap between pixels. If a screen is not set correctly, often unwanted patterns or other unwanted effects appear in the output. All PostScript devices have a default screen established that provides good results for a wide range of conditions.

Each cell of the halftone screen may be made to approximate any shade of gray by turning some percentage of the pixels within the cell black and turning the remaining pixels white. The gray level produced within the cell is a number between 0 and 1, which is determined by the ratio of the number of pixels that are white to the total number of pixels in the cell. As you can readily see, a cell with n pixels can have at most $n+1$ gray levels. This tells you, as a programmer, that on any given device, with any given screen function, there are an integer number of gray values. Therefore, any given gray percentage will map into one of these integral values, and gray values that are "close" may map into the same integral value. This feature is particularly noticeable on low-resolution devices, where the number of pixels per spot cannot be very high.

Spot Function

As the pixels in a cell are changed from all white to all black (or vice versa, depending on the device), there needs to be some rule for choosing which pixels are to be turned on. In particular, consider the case where the cell is changing from one gray value to another, and the process, explained above, determines that an additional pixel must be turned black. The interpreter must establish some rule that chooses the pixel to be changed.

This rule is called the *spot function*, and it specifies the order in which pixels are changed-from white to black to accommodate varying values of gray.

There are some rules that this function must follow. In particular, if any spot is black at one gray level, it must remain black for all increasingly dark gray levels. Similarly, if one pixel is white for a given gray level, it must remain white for all increasingly light gray levels. The spot function defines the order of pixel changes in an indirect way that minimizes the interaction with the screen frequency and angle. This is done by having the spot function provide an ordering value for each pixel within the cell. The actual values returned by the spot function are not important; it is the relation of the values that are used to determine which pixels get turned on or off. In this process, the spot function provides the ordering value, and the interpreter determines how many pixels must be set on (or off) to achieve the desired gray value. Then the pixel with the lowest spot values are turned white (or, conversely, the pixels with the highest values are made black) until the desired number of pixels has been changed.

There are a variety of simple spot functions. For one example, you can define a spot function in which the values returned for a given pixel within the spot get lower the further the pixel is located from the center of the cell. This type of spot function produces a "dot screen," where the black pixels cluster around the center of the cell within a circle that gets larger as the percentage of black increases. This process is very similar to the use of larger and smaller dots in the printing process. Another example would be a spot function that returns a value for a pixel based on the pixel's distance from a line through the center of the cell, with pixels closer to the line getting higher values; such a function is called a "line screen." Remember, however, that any PostScript program that defines its own halftone screen or spot function becomes intimately tied to a particular device and loses its portability.

Transfer Function

In addition to the spot function, the PostScript interpreter defines a *transfer function*, which allows the interpreter or the PostScript program to correct gray values for the fact that some devices, along with human eyes, do not have a linear response to gray. That is, if you make a series of squares, each filled with pixels darkened in a direct ratio to the gray value, the eye will perceive some shades as closer to black or white than the percentage of pixels would indicate. The transfer function compensates for this by mapping one number between 0 and 1 into another number between 0 and 1. In this way, the interpreter can change a user gray value into a device gray value that will accurately represent the percentage as perceived by the eye. For example, the eye may perceive a square with one half of the pixels black and the other half white as being (say) 60 percent gray; and, conversely, perceive a square with 42 percent of the pixels set to black as 50 percent gray. The transfer function provides a method to transfer the user value of 50 percent into a device value of 42 percent, a user value of 60 percent into a device value of 50 percent, and so on.

A transfer function may also be used to provide certain special effects. For example, a transfer function that reversed the value from 0 to 1 uniformly would enable a program to produce an image like a photographic negative, with white areas turned black and vice versa. Other transfer functions might be defined to enhance or reduce contrast of an image.

4.4 COLOR PROCESSING

The PostScript language provides support for all types of color processing. The process of producing color output, as opposed to black-and-white output, introduces several new conditions and criteria that must be addressed. This entire subject is quite complex and not necessarily applicable for typical PostScript programming unless you have a color output device available or are printing color separations. Even in these cases, it may not be necessary that you understand in detail how color is produced and controlled in the PostScript environment. For these reasons, you may wish to skim this section of the book on first reading. In particular, if the processes of color generation and color printing are not familiar to you, the following discussion may be a little terse for best comprehension on first reading.

PostScript provides only a few operations that generate color and images (which will be discussed in the next section), but those operations are both powerful and complex. Also, many aspects of these operations are quite dependent upon characteristics of the devices themselves; in particular, for color processing the device will use either additive or subtractive color generation. For each PostScript device, a set of default procedures and operation interactions is established by the interpreter at device setup. Generally, these defaults will provide good color and image processing on that device for a wide range of conditions; these defaults should be modified only after careful consideration and only when you understand the processes involved.

Color Models

There are two methods of producing full color images for the human eye. These two methods differ essentially in whether the perception of color is produced by colored light being generated or light being absorbed. The first case is called the *additive color model* and is the process that occurs when the three primary color components, *red, green,* and *blue light,* are combined to produce the full color spectrum. When such a device is transmitting no light, it is black, and when it is transmitting all three color components at full intensity, it is transmitting white light. This is the process used on television screens, for example, and on computer monitors. The second case is called *subtractive color* and is essentially the inverse of the first. In this case, an object's perceived color is determined by the amount of red, green, or blue light it absorbs. When all three color components are absorbed completely, the object appears black, and when none of them are absorbed, the object appears white. This is the process that is used to produce color illustrations in books or magazines, and it is also the process used to produce color output on printers.

For subtractive color, the primary shades become the inverse of the primary colors of the additive spectrum: that is, *cyan,* which absorbs red light and therefore reflects only green and blue; *magenta,* which absorbs green light; and *yellow,* which absorbs blue light. When printing full-color images, it has been determined through long experience that blacks and grays are rendered more accurately if a fourth color component is added to these three: *black,* which absorbs all colors and therefore reflects no light at all. This is required because it often happens in printing that a black area or an area that has some black component in it cannot be faithfully rendered by combining the primary pigments. For example, if you mix equal amounts of cyan, yellow, and magenta inks on a press, the result is not black, as a black ink would be, but rather a dark brown. Therefore, true black ink or pigment is often added to make the colors truer to the viewer's eye. In this fashion, using four colored inks, a printing output device can produce accurate full-color reproductions of images.

As discussed before, the PostScript interpreter places marks on the page with a color determined by the current color parameter in the graphics state. The PostScript language provides support for any arbitrary color; black, white, and shades of gray are simply special cases. In addition, the language allows specification of the color according to several different color representation schemes. You should remember, however, that the vast majority of PostScript devices offer only black and white or, at best, shades of gray and are not full color devices. Even on black-and-white devices, however, it is possible to create and make proof copies of *color separations* that can be used in the printing process to produce full color images.

RGB Color Model

The first color scheme that can be used to specify a color to the interpreter is the *red-green-blue,* or RGB, model. As you might suspect, in this model the levels of the primary additive colors, red, green, and blue, are each specified and their combination is the current color in the current graphics state. To specify the current color, a program must provide three numeric values, one each for red, green, and blue; these numbers represent the intensity of the primary color within the derived color. The numbers perform essentially in the same fashion as the gray level, ranging from 0 to 1, with 0 being no component of this primary color and 1 indicating maximum intensity. If the intensities of all three primary colors are identical – that is, the number that specifies each color is the same – then the derived color is gray with its intensity equal to the common color value; if the intensities are different, then a color is output as defined by the component values. As expected, if all the intensities are 0, no color is produced and the spot is black. If all the intensities are 1, then white is produced. In all this, the model follows what you would intuitively expect.

As an alternative to the red-green-blue model, PostScript also implements a *hue-saturation-brightness,* or HSB, model of color. This model also uses three values between 0 and 1: one value for the hue of the color, placed around a color wheel or spectrum, where 0 indicates pure red, 1/3 indicates pure green, and 2/3 indicates pure blue, returning to pure red at 1; one value for the saturation of the color, essentially the depth or richness of the color, with 0 being no saturation and 1 being maximum saturation; and one value for the brightness of the color, with 0 being black (no brightness) and 1 being maximum brightness. There is a published standard (the NTSC video standard) that converts from the RGB to the HSB model and vice versa. Quite honestly, I am not aware of any application or system that employs the HSB model. It is presented here for reference only and because it is supported by the PostScript interpreter.

CMYK Color Model

Both of these models are additive color models. They specify what color of light or lights must be mixed to produce a specific color. In addition, PostScript implements a subtractive color model, the *cyan-magenta-yellow-black* model. Actually, this model can be used in one of two ways: with or without the black component. As stated previously, the black component is added to the usual color printing process in order to improve color rendition. If an output device does not support all four color components, the subtractive model may be used with only the three primary pigments.

The easiest way to understand and describe the CMYK color model is to think of colors being made up of inks, rather than light. Thus any given color is a blend of four inks, like colors on a palette. The CMYK model takes four numbers (three, if only CMY is being used), to define the amount of each of the four colors in the derived color. As before, the numeric value is between 0 and 1, but in this case, the 0 value represents no ink and the 1 represents full ink.

There is a straightforward conversion process from the RGB color model to the CMY colors. Since cyan is the absence of red light, a value of 1 for the cyan component of a color is equivalent to no red light, or 0 for the red value. The same inverse conversion is true for the other two color components. The result is a conversion table as follows:

cyan	=	1.0 – red
magenta	=	1.0 – green
yellow	=	1.0 – blue

This is a nice, clear conversion, except that it leaves us without a value for the black component of the CMYK color model. There is a similar relationship between the gray value stored by the interpreter and the black component, as follows:

black	=	1.0 – gray

This, however, is not quite sufficient to determine the black component, since a color specified in the RGB model may not have any specific gray value set.

Black Generation and Undercolor Removal

Generally, the amount of black that needs to be generated to make a good color rendition for printing has a direct relationship to the percentages of cyan, magenta, and yellow being used on the color. Typically, a *black generation function* is created within the interpreter to create a black component value based on the cyan, magenta, and yellow values. Since equal amounts of CMY equal a black component, the minimum value of the three colors is used as an operand to drive the black generation requirement. The black generation function is a PostScript function that provides a black component value based on the data passed to it; both the operand and the result must be numbers between 0 and 1. This value is made use of only in those cases where the color has been specified in three components (RGB or HSB) and is being output onto a four-color device.

When the black component is added to the equation for the derived color, the interpreter must compensate for the sudden intrusion of the black ink onto the picture. This process is called *undercolor removal,* and, as its name implies, it removes some portion of the cyan, magenta, and yellow inks from the image. It does this by adjusting these three values by an amount related to the new black component. It may adjust the ink levels to exactly match the amount of black ink, or it may not adjust the levels at all, or it might even increase the levels if required. The undercolor removal function also returns a value between 0 and 1 for each color; this is the amount to be subtracted from the value for each of the three process inks. As with black generation, this process is used only for colors specified in a three-color model being used on a four-color output device.

Spot Color

There is one additional issue that we should discuss regarding color handling and color models. In the real world of printing, using actual inks on paper, it is possible to call for an exact color that is represented by a particular ink. In this case, the image being rendered does not conform to any of the color models discussed above. The color is specified as a single color rather than in terms of components in a general model.

This process is clearly not used on raster-output devices. However, if a raster-output device is being used to prepare an image to be transferred onto a printing system, some accommodation must be made for this process. The first accommodation is done by expressing an equivalent color value for the custom color in terms of the color model being used (RGB or CMYK). This is not provided explicitly in the PostScript language but can be done by defining a special graphics control structure to map black, or black equivalent values from the color functions, into a custom color. The second accommodation can be done by providing special structural information within the file to aid external service programs in processing the output images correctly.

4.5 IMAGE CONSTRUCTION

PostScript also has a capability to accept, process, and output sampled images of all kinds. A *sampled image,* which we will just call an "image," is a rectangular array of values, with each value representing some color and the whole array comprising a representation of some scene or object. The values may be generated artificially, as they are in a computer graphic, or they may be a representation of some natural scene such as you would get on a television or video display device.

An image in PostScript is described by a sequence of values obtained by scanning the image in some organized fashion. Usually the scanning process is done by dividing the image into rows or columns and assigning a value to each element as it is processed, with each element becoming a pixel on the output image. There may be one, three, or four values assigned to each element in a row or column; representing either one gray value or three or four color values, depending on the scanning technique and the color model. Color images may be scanned in either by providing multiple values – one for each color component – for each element as it is scanned or by making multiple passes over the scanned image, providing one set of values for each component on each pass. The PostScript language supports any of these options.

Each value is represented internally by one, two, four, or eight bits of data, providing up to 256 shades of gray or any color component. Devices that use eight-bit data representations for each pixel are called *full gray-scale devices;* on such devices, no halftoning technique is necessary or provided. Devices that have one bit per pixel are *binary devices;* such devices always require halftoning to provides shades of gray or color tints. Devices with intermediate numbers of bits per pixel use a combination of varying intensity and halftoning to represent the complete range of grays or colors.

Image Processing

The properties of an image are entirely distinct from those of the raster-output device upon which it is to be displayed, but they are similar in character. Images have an orientation, based on the scanning orientation; a resolution, based on the resolution of the scanning device; a scanning order, based on whether the scan was done by rows or columns; and so on. All of these parameters must be transformed properly into the necessary form for use by the output device. PostScript provides controls for all these parameters. Generally, the PostScript graphics machinery tries to render the image as accurately as possible, using sampling and halftoning as appropriate, subject to the limitations of the given output device.

There are four data items that must be supplied in order to allow the PostScript interpreter to render an image correctly:

1. Source image format: width of the image in number of rows; height of the image in number of columns; and number of bits per sample element.

2. The image data values: consisting of a stream of binary data that is *width* × *height* × *bits / sample* bits long.

3. The transformation matrix from the image coordinates to the user coordinates for mapping the image into the user space correctly and also for defining the shape and size of the user region that is to accommodate the image.

4. The mapping of the color values in the image into the color values in the printed output.

Coordinate Transformation

Each image is produced by the PostScript image operators within its own coordinate system. This system mimics the default PostScript user coordinates, with the origin (0, 0) in the bottom left corner of the image, the *x* coordinates ranging from 0 to *width,* and the *y* coordinates ranging from 0 to *height*. Thus the image is contained in a rectangle that is *height* high by *width* wide, with each sample value occupying one unit square in the image coordinate system.

In addition, the PostScript graphics machinery assumes that the sample values to fill the image rectangle are presented in rows, from left to right, and that the rows are filled from bottom to top. In this format, the first sample data value fills the position (0, 0), the next fills (1, 0), and so on until the entire bottom row is filled. Then the next row up is filled, beginning with position (0, 1), then (1, 1), and so on.

These assumptions are not rigid. The actual scanning order and representation can be mapped into this coordinate system by the use of the usual coordinate transformation matrices. This default coordinate system is called *image space*. At this point, you should notice that we are dealing with three separate coordinate structures: image space, user space, and device space.

Once the image is loaded into the graphics machinery, then it may be mapped into user space. This is necessary in order to place and size the final output image correctly. (The assumption here is that the conversion from user space to device space will be the same for the image as for the rest of the page; if that were not correct, it would be easy enough to encapsulate the image on a "page" by itself and then map that "page" into the final output.) It would, of course, be possible to write a single transformation matrix that would take the image from the image space to the final position and scale in user coordinates. However, that is somewhat difficult to visualize and to program. An easier technique is to map the image space into a unit square at the page origin and then position and scale that unit square as desired.

In this process, the first step is to map the image coordinates into a square with corners of (0, 0), (0,1), (1, 1), and (1, 0). Then, as a second step, this unit square is mapped into the desired output region on the page, using ordinary PostScript translation and scaling techniques. In this way the entire image is correctly transformed into the region set aside for it on the output page. Exact details and procedures for this process are discussed more fully in Section B3.3.

Fast-path Processing

There is a set of special circumstances in which the process or rendering of sampled images is speeded up considerably; this is known as *fast-path processing*. Under these circumstances, the sampled image is rendered directly into device space, bypassing the sampling and halftoning mechanisms described in the previous sections. The conditions under which fast-path processing will occur are as follows:

- The image is binary; that is, it has one bit per sample element.
- The resolution of the image and the resolution of the device are identical. In other words, the combination of the image matrix and the current transformation matrix in user space results in a transformation matrix that has one unit in image space equal to one unit in device space.
- The image space coordinate system and the device coordinate system are aligned so that the *x*-axis and the *y*-axis of the image are either parallel or perpendicular to the corresponding device axis. This provides a total of eight different image orientations that are eligible for fast-path processing.

This set of conditions is often satisfied when images are scanned into a PostScript system. For example, printing an image on a typical 300 dpi laser printer would require that the image be scanned in at 300 dpi, that the image be scanned as binary values, and that the image be scanned with coordinates either parallel to the device in any orientation or rotated at 90 degrees to the device coordinates. For most images, the coordinate condition will be satisfied if the image is being presented (as most images would be) right-side-up and undistorted.

It may seem that fast-path processing violates the device-independence that is so important in PostScript. However, if you consider for a moment, you will see that this is not the case. The fast-path is determined by the interpreter for the device; if the image does not qualify for fast-path processing, it is handled by the general image processing mechanisms and is still rendered with equal fidelity, if at a significantly slower pace. You should also note that not all implementations of the PostScript interpreter support all the above conditions; in particular, earlier versions have more stringent conditions for the relation of the coordinates. In these cases, as in other cases that do not satisfy the conditions, the general image processing mechanism will handle the process to produce correct results without any concern on the part of the programmer.

Masks

PostScript also supports a special variety of binary image, called a *mask,* that behaves in the opposite manner to the typical image. An ordinary image, as described in the preceding sections, places marks on a page in the current color, using either actual color or gray values or using halftoning techniques to produce equivalent results. In either case, the image completely covers any object that is under it, as do all PostScript graphics.

A mask, on the other hand, provides a special control over where on the output page marks can be applied. The best way to think of this is to imagine pouring ink, in the current color, over a stencil (the mask) with one hole for each pixel. The mask provides a set of binary values that define where the ink is to be applied, with a 0 value indicating that no paint is to be applied and a 1 indicating that paint is to be applied (or vice-versa – the exact meaning of the binary values is under program control). Any pixel that is not inked retains its previous value and is not obscured by the mask over it as it would be if the image were rendered normally.

This mask process is most often used to render characters that are defined in fonts as bitmaps; however, the process can be used for any graphic image and can be used to create a variety of special effects. When this technique is used with character forms, there are some special issues and precautions that need to be considered. These are discussed in more detail in Section B3.4.

4.6 DEVICE SETUP AND CONTROL

As you can see from the discussions above, the PostScript graphics machinery has to establish a set of default values for a wide variety of functions that depend on and are related to the specific output device being used. These include functions that establish things like halftone screens, color transfer functions, and gray scale transformations, as well as the simpler issues of transformations from user space to device space, and so on.

Establishment of these functions and values in the graphics state is performed by a series of device setup operations. Default versions of these operations are defined for each device individually and are performed automatically when the device is powered on or reset. The general strategy in PostScript device setup assures that the default versions provide good to excellent results over a wide range of conditions. Where setup options exist, changes may often be specified by some straightforward change to a specific parameter; for example, many devices support several page sizes, which can be easily changed from the default value by setting a single parameter.

All these setup operations are available to the PostScript program through special operators. While it would be most unusual for a PostScript program to need to set these functions explicitly, it is nevertheless possible to do so for production of special effects or to handle non-standard conditions or output requirements. You should note that specific invocation of the setup operations ties the page description that contains them directly to specific output device characteristics and reduces or eliminates the possiblity of true device independence. For this reason, when such techniques are used, they should be grouped together and invoked as close to the page display command as possible. This keeps the device-dependent code in one place and will help during maintenance and modification.

5

Text Operations

The PostScript language generates text and characters using the identical mechanisms that it uses for all other graphics. It is therefore important to present the general view of PostScript graphic operations before discussing text operations. PostScript does, however, provide many special operations that work with text and characters in order to speed up and simplify text operations. This chapter will cover these operations in detail.

Before you begin to explore character generation and the organization of characters into fonts, however, it would be useful to discuss type as a graphic object. At first thought, it may seem strange that PostScript treats characters in the same way as it treats circles or rectangles; or you may suppose that this convention was adopted by the PostScript language as a convenience to allow easy representation of both kinds of objects on a single page. Actually, consideration of characters as graphics is both the oldest and the most accurate way to think about them.

All characters began thousands of years ago as ideograms, each of which expressed a complete word or concept. The Chinese language and the languages that use Chinese characters in writing, such as Japanese, still retain that system to a large extent. These characters actually were little pictures, which, over time, became more and more abstract. As alphabets were developed, characters still were small works of art, whether lettered carefully onto a parchment by medieval scribes or carved elegantly into a monument by stonemasons. When printing began, letters were formed in imitation of a scribe's calligraphy. Through modern times, the letters of the alphabet have been worked and reworked into forms with certain common design characteristics known as *typefaces,* wherein each character retains its ancient shape and yet maintains a subtle similarity of style and feel. In all these forms, the shape of characters has remained one of the key graphic elements, instantly recognizable and still capable of remarkable diversity.

The precise shape of each character in a beautiful typeface is indeed a small but perfect work of art. It has the qualities of beauty and utility combined in perfect proportion. Because a typeface has a specific job to perform, it must fulfill certain utilitarian values. It must be easy to recognize and easy to read; it often provides a certain stress or emphasis as well. Each typeface is designed to meet these special and restrictive design criteria in a certain page setting or design format. The selection of a good typeface is an important part of page makeup and graphic design.

Therefore it is not surprising that PostScript places a lot of emphasis on the issue of type. Handling such a demanding task well is a good test of graphic operations. By the same token, considering type as a graphic object provides the ultimate in accuracy and flexibility. It is precisely the limitations of non-PostScript output devices that force them to treat type differently from other graphic objects.

5.1   TYPE ORGANIZATION

There are several traditional dimensions to type organization. To begin with, type is traditionally organized as fonts. A *font* is a set of type, a complete collection of upper- and lowercase characters and punctuation in a single style and size. A font, therefore, gives a specific form and size to each letter and character as it is printed or displayed.

Fonts are often themselves grouped by design, or *typeface*. Most collections of fonts within a typeface offer a complete range of type styles and sizes that can be combined to preserve a certain design while allowing flexibility in page makeup. Such a collection of fonts, all with a common typeface, is called a *font family*. You should notice here that, properly speaking, a font has only one design, style, and size. Very often, the word "font" is used as a shorthand for what we have here defined as a font family. Generally, such a shorthand is perfectly clear, and we will continue to use this convention so long as it is clear from the context whether we are referring to a single size and style of type or are referring to a family.

Font families can themselves be grouped by different design characteristics. The most common grouping divides font families into three groups. The first group is called *serif* fonts. These are fonts where the characters are formed with short lines that finish off the major strokes of the letters. These strokes imitate and recall the characteristic effect of a chisel on stone, and therefore, serif fonts are generally used to give a more traditional look to a block of text. The second group is composed of the *sans-serif* fonts. As you might guess, characters in these fonts do not have serif lines; instead, the major strokes of the characters finish off cleanly. Sans-serif fonts have a more modern, cleaner appearance, and are used when design of a text block calls for this feeling. Finally, there is a group of fonts that do not easily fall into either of the previous groups. Such fonts often have some finish to the major strokes on certain characters, which gives them some of the look – if not the feeling – of a serif type. An example of this group is the Courier font, which is a common office typewriter font and is also implemented as a font family in all PostScript output devices.

Font Styles

Fonts within a font family generally also provide a variety of styles for output. The most common font styles are *italic*, in which the letters slope to the right to provide a sort of handwritten effect, and *bold*, in which the letters are made heavier and darker to make them stand out. There are also a wide variety of additional styles for any given typeface: condensed, extended, oblique, and others. In some cases, some styles may replace or substitute for others; for example, oblique is often used as a substitute for italic. Your font supplier will provide information regarding the exact variety of styles available for a given family and the differences between the styles.

Differences in styles and typefaces are used in documents for one or several of three reasons. To begin with, fonts are used for legibility. This may seem obvious, but it is an often overlooked or unacknowledged issue in the selection and use of type. If you take the trouble to print something, it is generally done so it can be read and understood with a minimum of strain – so that he who runs, may read, as the saying goes. Many fonts have been designed with exactly this requirement in mind and provide clear, readable characters that assist in conveying the message that is embodied in the text. Fonts are also used to improve the quality of the finished output. Typeset output provides both eye appeal and impact.

These differences are also used to provide emphasis and create certain design effects. Sometimes considerations of design are at odds with the requirements of legibility and clarity; use of old-fashioned gothic lettering or fancy script styles in block text would be an example of such a clash. Often, however, emphasis is provided by the use of different type styles and sizes within the same typeface, which avoids most of the problems. A common use of these techniques is to distinguish certain types of information within text; thus, for example, we have the conventional use of italics for book titles in a text block.

Font Sizes

Besides coming in different typefaces and styles, characters can be produced in varying sizes. Every character in a font has certain height and width. The width of characters is called *pitch*. In some fonts, all characters have the same pitch; such fonts are called *monospaced fonts*. For most fonts, however, each character has a distinct width; such fonts are called *proportional fonts*. Fixed pitch fonts are very often associated with typewriter-style output, since most typewriters cannot produce proportional spacing of letters. The Courier font, for example, is a monospaced font.

In a proportional font, the width of each character is carefully designed as a part of the overall shape. In traditional fonts, these widths are individually crafted to enhance the aesthetic appeal of the letters both in certain combinations and as a block. Proportions that are simply generated by mathematical ratios often lose this aesthetic quality when actually seen by the eye; arriving at the most pleasing proportions is a process involving equal measures of judgement and experience. One of the major advantages in using traditional fonts is that you have the benefit of many other people's craftmanship.

Font height is also a consideration. In general, font height and width are connected by the *font metrics,* which are a series of measurements for each character in a font. The characters in a font are normally set along a straight line called the *baseline.* The part of a lowercase letter such as 'p' or 'y' that extends below the baseline is called the descender, while the part that extends above the body height of a lowercase letter such as 'k' or 't' is called an ascender, or riser. Font size is measured in *points,* which is the same measure used in the default PostScript coordinate structure discussed previously. You will remember that a point is 1/72 inch, so that type that is 36 points will be about 1/2 inch in height. More precisely, the font size is the distance that must exist between the baselines of successive lines of type if the ascenders of the bottom line are not to overlap the descenders of the upper line. Therefore, font height is measured from the top of the ascenders on tall letters to the bottom of the descenders on letters that go below the baseline. Thus, for example, 36 point type will measure almost 1/2 inch from the top of a 'k' to the bottom of a 'p'. Smaller point sizes indicate smaller type, with 4- or 5-point type being about the limit of legibility for most people. The PostScript language itself has no limitation on the size of type; you may specify any size that can be stored and printed on your device.

5.2 FONT CONVERSION

Typefaces were originally designed for printing applications; and, in such applications, type is rendered as a solid line of ink. Type on a raster-output device is rendered as a series of dots, as are all other graphic objects. The scan conversion process applies to type as well as to any other graphic, but its accuracy is probably more essential and more visible in handling type than in converting almost any other object. Type is very familiar to our eyes, letters are very complex shapes, and distortions or distractions in character shapes or positioning are extremely distracting. For all these reasons, correct scan conversion of type is an important feature of PostScript processing.

Producing letter shapes can be done in several ways. The simplest method is to use preformed letter shapes. In this method, the shape of the letter is usually cut out of some masking material, and a beam of light or electrons is passed through the mask corresponding to the desired letter. This method is fast but very limited since there must be a different physical mask for every shape and size of type. Type placement and orientation are also limited to those provided by the mask. The best way to think of this method of reproducing letter shapes is to think of the type ball on a typewriter, which also uses preformed characters.

As an improvement on that technique, some printers load fonts in which the character shapes have already been changed into dots. In this case, any shape may be generated, and several different combinations of placement and orientation are usually available. The choice of pixels for each character may be adjusted, by eye if necessary, to provide the most aesthetically satisfying shape for the precise size being designed. However, some of the same limitations apply. The font may be scaled in size, but only with a significant loss in quality if the scaling process moves far from the original size. Such fonts are called *bitmapped fonts* because each character in each font is predrawn as a bitmapped image. In addition, bitmapped fonts are, at best, limited to devices with a single resolution. Clearly, the selection of pixels changes as the device resolution changes.

Finally, letter shapes may be drawn as outlines, using general graphic techniques, and then scaled or rotated as desired before being transformed into pixels and positioned onto the output. This is the general technique adopted by the PostScript language. This method offers the benefits of complete generality in positioning, sizing, and orientation. The conversion from the letter outline to the pixel version will be at least as good as the scan conversion process that is implemented for general filling of shapes, thus allowing easy and accurate scaling and rotation of characters. The major drawback to using outline processing for fonts is the time required to generate the pixel patterns from the outlines.

In traditional, hand-set lead type, individual letters were crafted at each point size to maintain the look and feel that the designer of the typeface had created. This might mean, for example, that the stroke widths or relative size of certain characters would be subtly adjusted as the type size changed. This adjustment process is known as *font tuning*. Precise adjustments of the sort provided by lead type cannot, obviously, be provided on any typeface that is composed of little dots instead of lines. Nevertheless, certain adjustments can be, and are, made to improve the quality of the typeface. For bitmapped fonts, such adjustments are made by hand for the single point size being designed; of course, these adjustments are of no use at any different point size. For outline fonts, font tuning is generally provided by creating special rules that adjust the scan conversion process. The time of concern is when the size of the pixels on the output device is a significant fraction of the size of the type being printed. For laser printers, for example, smaller point sizes, up to about 9 or 10 points, will be improved by this process. Since no tuning algorithm can make up for a poor outline, it is important that the PostScript fonts start from high quality outline definitions. Once a good outline is produced, then tuning can make the best possible representation out of it. For typesetting devices, where the pixel size is 1/1000 inch or smaller, such tuning is irrelevant; the pixels are so much smaller than even the smallest point size that only the quality of the outline has any influence on what you see.

5.3 PROCESSING CONSIDERATIONS

Since speed of processing is one of the major concerns in using outline fonts, designers of PostScript interpreters have come up with several approaches that increase the effective speed of the interpreter in placing text images on output. Many of these processing improvements are internal to the interpreter, and some of them are proprietary in nature. One of them, however, is both commonly used and, to a limited extent, controllable from within the PostScript application. This is the processing of caching characters once they are converted into pixel images.

The *font cache* is a defined data structure accessible to the PostScript interpreter where images of characters can be stored. Generally, the font cache consists of a fixed region of internal memory, although, in some implementations, the font cache may also take advantage of external storage. As characters from the current font are converted into pixels and placed onto an output page, the images are also stored in the font cache, including the character metric information and the device pixel arrays. When a character is requested for output, the interpreter checks the font cache and, if it finds the character in the cache, uses the image that is stored there, thus saving the processing required to convert the outline to the image. Typically, the process of retrieving a character from the cache is on the order of 1000 times faster than recreating the image from the outline description. The size of the font cache is implementation dependent, but typically it is large enough to accommodate all the characters in most page descriptions.

The font cache does not retain any information regarding the current color as it affects the character images; it only remembers which pixels were on and which were off. For this reason, certain operations are not allowed within the procedures that create character images, since the resulting output must not have any internal color component. This subject is discussed more fully in Section B3.3.

For the most part, the operation of the font cache is automatic and not anything to be concerned about. The first principle of using the cache is simply to realize its existence and understand that using characters that have been cached is significantly faster than converting characters. Since large blocks of text will often reuse identical characters, the more text you output, the more the printing process speeds up, within certain parameters. The second principle of using the cache is to understand these parameters, which govern how the interpreter stores and retrieves characters from the cache.

The interpreter determines which characters being requested are the same as characters currently in the cache by examining the following criteria:

- the character itself
- the current font
- the current point size
- the current transformation matrix (CTM)

Let us examine each of these in turn to see how they might affect your application processing. To begin with, the use of the actual character is certainly straightforward and unexceptional – you couldn't use an 'a' for a 'b', for example. The current font is checked by the fontID or FID, described more fully below. If you reencode a font, as discussed below, you must also rename the font and regenerate the fontID; the interpreter treats it as a change as complete as that from Times Roman to Helvetica, even if you have simply added a single character to the font.

Since the font cache saves images, any change in point size clearly requires new images. However, changes to the CTM may not be so evident. If you have changed the transformation from user space to device space, you have altered, in some way, the actual pixels that must be set on or off to render the image of a given character; for this reason, any change to the CTM requires a new set of images to be cached, even if the other three elements remain the same.

The action of the font cache is governed by certain parameters that establish guidelines for characters that will be stored in the cache. To begin with, there is an upper limit on the size of characters that are cached. Since larger characters require more storage for their associated pixel arrays on the one hand, and, on the other hand, since large characters are not used frequently on a page, characters larger than a certain limit are never cached but are always reimaged instead. In more recent implementations of PostScript, a lower limit is also established. All characters that are smaller than the lower limit are stored in the font cache unchanged; characters above the upper limit are never stored; and characters between the lower and the upper limit are stored in a compressed format, which is faster to decode than the outline format but more compact than the full device-pixel array.

As is usual in PostScript graphic operations, default limits are established for each device that provide an optimum balance between speed and efficiency based on the cache storage available, the device requirements, and a typical mix of standard page descriptions as output. However, these limits are accessible from the PostScript application and can be changed if necessary. Just remember that there are several interacting components in this process, and therefore you should have a clear idea of what you are changing and why you are changing it and how this is going to affect the other processing components before you make any changes.

Idle-Time Font Conversion

While the interpreter is between jobs, that is, when it has finished processing one job and is waiting for the first character of the next job, it occupies itself by converting a standard set of characters into images and storing the results in the font cache. This process is known as *idle-time font scan-conversion*. Idle-time font scan-conversion is intended to provide faster execution than would otherwise be possible for documents that use characters from the standard, preconverted set and to do so at no real additional cost since the processing is performed between jobs.

Each device has a default set of fonts and parts of fonts that are included in the idle-time font scan-conversion process. This list is controllable by the interpreter and can be accessed and changed if necessary. In addition, in many PostScript implementations, certain fonts are prescanned and made permanently resident in read-only memory for extremely fast access. Consult your printer documentation for a list of fonts (if any) that fall into either of these two categories.

5.4 METHODS OF ORGANIZATION

A PostScript font is a dictionary that defines the shapes for each character in a given typeface and style. In this sense, a PostScript font differs from both definitions of a font given above; it is not a complete font family, since it has only one style, but it does provide information for all sizes of the typeface. For here on, the word "font" will mean a PostScript font.

A font is implemented as a dictionary that contains a variety of information that describes the font, including the precise descriptions of the routines that generate each character. For most fonts, this will be the outlines; however, the PostScript font machinery will accommodate bitmapped fonts as well as the superior outline fonts. The definition of a character is done by executing the procedures provided in the font dictionary that use PostScript graphics operators to generate the character image.

A font specifies the shape of each character in one standard size. The standard size is one unit, which would be 1 point in the default user coordinates. This is too small to be useful directly, but the font machinery can easily be used to transform the characters within a font into any desired size and orientation. The font exists, as it were, in its own graphic space and has its own set of *character coordinates* that are independent of the user coordinates. These character coordinates can be scaled, rotated, or otherwise transformed in the same fashion as the user coordinates can be, without changing the user coordinate system. Of course, changes to the user coordinate system have the same effect on character output as they would on any other graphic object. Thus, for example, if the user coordinates were scaled so that the unit measure were 1 inch, then the default size of type would be 1 inch instead of 1 point. However, a font can be scaled to 1 inch (72 points) by transforming the character coordinates without altering the user coordinates.

Dictionary Structure

A font dictionary is an ordinary PostScript dictionary that is required to have a certain set of key-value pairs defined in it. Some of the key-value pairs must be present in a properly formed PostScript font dictionary, while others are optional and user-definable. The following table lists the keys that are required in any PostScript font dictionary, with associated values that must be the type of object shown in the table and contain the information described next to the key.

Key	Type	Information
Encoding	array	An array with 256 elements; normally, the elements are names associated with the character glyphs (shapes), and these elements are accessed by using the character codes as indexes into the array.
FontBBox	array	A four-element array that defines two pairs of x, y coordinates that represent the lower left and upper right corners of the font-

bounding box in the character coordinate system. The font-bounding box is the smallest rectangle that would enclose all the characters of the font if they were printed on top of one another with the character origins in the same point. The font-bounding box is used to provide font size information for caching and clipping operations; if any part of any character falls outside the defined bounding box, you may get incorrect results. If all four components of the **FontBBox** are zero, the bounding box information is ignored.

FID	fontID	A special entry that is required by the font machinery and is generated and maintained by the PostScript interpreter.
FontMatrix	array	A standard six-element transformation matrix that maps the character coordinates into user coordinates. Characters are usually defined in their own independent coordinate system. The **FontMatrix** maps this character coordinate system into a one-unit square in the user coordinate system. When the font is called for use, it is normally scaled or otherwise transformed to map into the desired size and orientation. That process concatenates the new transformation with the **FontMatrix** to yield the correctly transformed font.
FontType	integer	An integer value that indicates where to find the character descriptions and how these are represented. A value of *3* indicates a user-generated font; a value of *0* indicates a composite font (see the next section for a complete discussion of composite fonts). Any other value is either undefined or implementation-dependent.

In addition to the required information described above, there is additional information that is provided or may be provided for PostScript built-in fonts, as follows:

Key	Type	Information
CharStrings	dictionary	This dictionary associates character names (as defined in the **Encoding** array) with the glyph descriptions, generally stored in strings with a protected, proprietary format. This dictionary is required for certain **FontTypes**.
FontInfo	dictionary	This dictionary contains indicative data regarding the font. The specific contents are described below.
FontName	name	The font's name as it would be used for access within a PostScript program. This information is for the applicant's use

only; it is not used by the font machinery. An example would be '/Times-Roman'.

Metrics	dictionary	This is an optional dictionary that associates the name of characters (as defined in the **Encoding** array) with character metric information. The possible values in this dictionary are defined and explained in Section A5.6. When this dictionary is present, the values in it override the metrics that are encoded as part of the character definitions.

PaintType   integer   An integer value that indicates how the characters in a font are to be painted onto the output. The possible values are as follows:

0 The character descriptions are to be filled.

1 The character descriptions are to be stroked.

2 The character descriptions, which are designed to be filled, are to be outlined instead.

3 The character descriptions are responsible for controlling their own painting process.

Generally, changing the value of **PaintType** for a font will not give acceptable results. The only change that you should consider is from 0 (filled) to 2 (outlined).

Private   dictionary   This is a dictionary that contains protected and proprietary information about a font.

StrokeWidth   number   This is the stroke width, in character coordinate units, for outlined fonts (**PaintType** 2). This field is not initially present in the font dictionary; it must be added if you change the **PaintType** from 0 to 2.

UniqueID   integer   This is an identification integer that uniquely identifies this font. That is, every font or every different version of the same font, even if there is only a minor difference, should have a different value of this entry. The only exception is for changes that only affect the **Encoding** array; such changes do not require a new **UniqueID.** This entry is not necessarily present in every font; when present, it is used by the font machinery to speed up the caching process. Every **UniqueID**, if it exists, must be a unique 24-bit number, and the font creator is responsible for the ensuring this.

The **UniqueID** entry plays an important role in creation of the **FID** for a font, and therefore, directly affects the font cache operation. To understand this, you need to know that the PostScript font machinery uses the following components to generate a **FID**:

1. The **FontType** entry in the font dictionary.
2. The **UniqueID** entry in the font dictionary, or a created value if no entry exists.
3. The **PaintType** entry in the font dictionary.

As you can see, this means that each **FontType** has its own independent space of numbers for **UniqueID**. In addition, each **PaintType** also creats a new series of **UniqueID** numbers. Since the **FID** is used to determine the matching values for caching characters, changes to a font's **UniqueID** or **PaintType** will generate a new font.

In addition to these entries, user-created fonts must also provide a **BuildChar** entry. The **BuildChar** entry is associated with a PostScript procedure that takes the character code of the character to be created and builds the character pixel outline from that code, using the arrays and procedures defined in the font dictionary. When the PostScript interpreter goes to display a character from a user-defined font, it first looks in the font cache to see if the character is there already. If it is not, the interpreter calls the **Build-Char** procedure defined in the font dictionary to create the character. Depending on the procedures implemented in **BuildChar,** the resulting character may or may not be placed into the font cache before it is placed onto the output. The decision to cache a character shape is controlled by the **BuildChar** procedure for the user-defined font and the standard caching parameters, both of which can be controlled by the PostScript application.

The **FontInfo** dictionary contains a variety of information that may be used by the application. This information is for reference only and is not used by the font machinery. It has the following format:

Key	Type	Information
FamilyName	string	This string provides the family name of the font. For example, 'Helvetica'.
FullName	string	This string provides the full text name of the font. For example, 'Helvetica-BoldOblique'.
isFixedPitch	boolean	This is a boolean value that is *true* if the font is a fixed-pitch (or monospaced) font and *false* otherwise.
ItalicAngle	number	This is the angle in degrees of the dominant vertical strokes of the font, measured counterclockwise from true vertical. As a result, the **ItalicAngle** values for most italic or oblique fonts are negative numbers, since the fonts slope to the right (clockwise) rather than to the left. For example, the **ItalicAngle** value for the Helvetica-Oblique font is -12 (degrees).

Notice	string	This string gives the trademark or copyright information for the font, if applicable.
UnderlinePosition	number	This gives the distance from the baseline to the underline stroke in units of the character coordinate system.
UnderlineThickness	number	This gives the thickness of the underline stroke in units of the character coordinate system.
version	string	This string contains the version number of the font in the format 0.0.
Weight	string	This string gives the 'weight' of the font strokes; for example, Bold, Medium, Light, and so on. Note that this is a descriptive string value, and not a number.

A font dictionary is created by, and remains accessible to, ordinary PostScript operations. In addition, there are certain special font operators that access and use the font dictionaries.

Once a font is created, with all the necessary information in its dictionaries – as you have noticed, the font information is a dictionary that contains several other layers of dictionaries within itself – it must still be made available to the interpreter. This is done by maintaining all the currently available font dictionaries in a separate dictionary called the **FontDirectory**. The **FontDirectory** is itself a dictionary, where the keys are the font names, each one the same name reported by the **FontName** entry in the font itself; and the associated values are the font dictionaries. Remember that, although the name in the **FontDirectory** should be the same as the name reported and stored in the **FontName** field, there is no intrinsic connection between the two.

Encoding Fonts

Standard PostScript fonts use an ingenious encoding scheme to provide complete flexibility for producing character shapes from font descriptions. We have referred earlier to the dictionary entries that support this process. Now we shall examine the process itself in detail.

Characters in strings are represented by hexadecimal codes from 0 to 255. The translation from any individual code into a character glyph is not directly part of the font itself but is governed by the **Encoding** array. The entries in the **Encoding** array can be retrieved using the character code as an index; this provides the name of the character. This name is then used as a key into the **CharStrings** dictionary, which associates the actual glyph information with the name.

The names of characters are ordinary PostScript names and conform to all the usual name rules. The general run of alphabetic characters have name literals that consist of the character itself; for example '/A' or '/b'. Numbers have their usual names, such as

'/one' or '/two'. Common punctuation has the names you would expect, such as '/comma' or '/semicolon'. Accented letters and the less usual punctuation are named with words that suggest the character; for example '/ntilde' for a lowercase 'n' with a tilde accent over it, '/Egrave' for an uppercase 'E' with a grave accent, or '/braceleft' for the character '{'.

This flexibility in changing character codes to glyphs has two special values. First, it permits text that is encoded in other manners than the standard ASCII (e.g., EBCDIC) to be printed easily. Second, it allows an application to specify how characters outside of the standard encoding are to be encoded. Most fonts, for example, provide a wide variety of accented characters that are necessary for languages other than English. There are also ligatures and other little-used but still essential shapes. Not all of these can be fitted into the 256 places in the standard encoding; but, by the same token, not all would typically be used on a single page. Changing the **Encoding** array is one way to access these characters easily and efficiently.

Note that the **Encoding** array must be exactly 256 entries long to provide for each possible character code that may become an index value. When a position in the **Encoding** is not needed, it must be filled with the special name '/.notdef'. Attempting to print a character code that maps into a '/.notdef' will have no effect on the output and no side effects within PostScript. The encoding vector used as a default by most PostScript fonts is called the **StandardEncoding** and is described in Part III, Appendix B.

5.5 FONT METRICS

It has already been mentioned that characters in PostScript are defined in their own independent coordinate system, known as the *character coordinate system*. The origin, point $(0, 0)$, for the character coordinates, is the *reference point* for the character and is the point within the character coodinates that corresponds to the current point when the character is displayed on output. The line connecting the reference points of successive characters as they are displayed forms the baseline of the line of text, as shown in Figure A5.1.

The *character width* is the distance from the origin of one character to the origin where the next character would be placed when printing successive characters, as in a word. This value is a relative displacement from the current character origin defined by an x and a y component. Generally, characters in most Indo-European alphabets have a positive x component and a 0 y component. However, other alphabets have such features as negative x components, for languages that read right-to-left, and non-zero y components, for vertical writing.

The *bounding box* of a character is the smallest rectangle, oriented in alignment with the character coordinate axes, that will just enclose the shape of the entire character. The bounding box is defined by two points, the lower left and upper right corners of the box, given in character coordinates. The *left side bearing* is the distance from the character origin to the left edge of the bounding box, measured in character coordinates. The left side

Figure A5.1 Character metric information

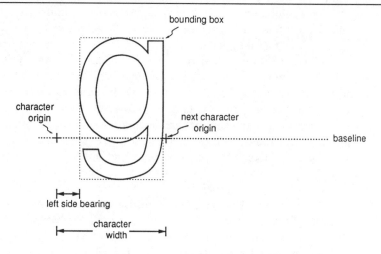

bearing for any character may be negative if that character extends to the left of the character origin. PostScript built-in fonts are designed so that the left side bearing of a character can be adjusted independently of the other character metrics. In this way, a character's bounding box can be shifted relative to the character origin.

Measurement Access

Font metric information can be obtained from within a PostScript application in a variety of ways. The width of any character string is easily available through standard PostScript operations, while the left side bearing and bounding box information can be generated on an individual character basis. In addition, the **FontBBox** entry in the font dictionary (described above) gives the global value of the bounding box that encompasses all characters in the font.

Font metrics can also be modified within a PostScript application by adjusting the values in the **Metrics** dictionary within the font dictionary. As we saw in the earlier discussion of font dictionaries, the **Metrics** dictionary is an optional dictionary that provides additional metric information for individual characters. The keys in the dictionary are the character names, as provided by the **Encoding** array. The values may take any one of three formats:

- a single number, indicating a new x value for the character width. The y value is assumed to be zero.

- an array of two numbers in which the first number indicates the new left side bearing and the second indicates a new *x* character width; in both cases, the *y* component is assumed to be zero.
- an array of four numbers in which the first pair of numbers are the *x* and *y* component values for the vector that gives the left side bearing, and the second pair of numbers are the *x* and *y* components of the character width vector.

Font metric information is also provided to external applications by *font metric files*. These files can be used by external applications, such as word processing programs, that are generating PostScript page descriptions to determine the widths of characters and strings for purposes such as line justification and so on. In addition, kerning information for adjusting character pairs is available.

Writing Mode

Character metrics are used to specify where a character shape will be placed relative to the current point, which is done by making the character origin correspond to the current point, and to determine where the current point will be moved to after the character is printed, which is done by adding the character width to the character origin to determine the new current point.

This system allows for characters within a font to be printed in any of the usual orientations: right to left, left to right, and top to bottom – all by changing the character width vector as described above. However, in some languages, both horizontal and vertical writing are used. In this case, it is inefficient to provide a complete new font just to change from horizontal to vertical writing; in particular, it would be a waste of font cache resources since the characters are exactly identical bitmaps. To solve this problem, recent PostScript implementations have included a *writing mode* indicator. This was done by adding an entry to the font dictionary, **WMode,** that has the value *0* to indicate that the characters are to be placed horizontally and a value of *1* to indicate that the characters are to be placed vertically.

In this format, two sets of metrics are associated with each character to allow for either horizontal or vertical writing. Figures A5.2a and A5.2b illustrate the relationship between the two sets of metrics.

The first diagram indicates the ordinary character metrics and the relationship of the character width vector, *w0*, to the change from the character origin, *origin 0*, to the new current point. This is the same mechanism that we described above. The character bounding box is represented by the two points, *ll* (for lower left) and *ur* (for upper right), which are specified in the character coordinates based on *origin 0*.

The second diagram shows the character width vector, *w1*, that defines the new current point based on a vertical writing mode and the vertical character origin, *origin 1*. As you see, the character has not changed position; only the position of the new current point, defined after the character is output, has changed to reflect the new writing mode.

Figure A5.2a and b Writing modes and relationship

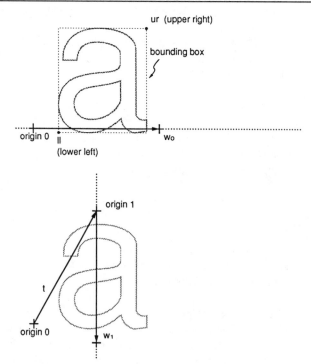

The third diagram shows the transformation vector, *t,* that defines the position of *origin 1* relative to *origin 0*. In this way, character metrics do not have to change; the character bounding box is simply redefined from the original coordinates based on *origin 0* to new coordinates based on *origin 1*. In this way, any character can be imaged either horizontally or vertically by changing the writing mode for the font.

When **WMode** is defined for a font, the **Metrics** entry in the font dictionary applies only to writing mode 0. An additional entry is defined to modify the metrics in writing mode 1, as follows:

Metrics2 This is a dictionary, similar to the **Metrics** entry, whose keys are the character names. The associated value is an array with four elements that provide *x* and *y* components for new vectors *w1* and *t* for the given character. These revised definitions are used only in writing mode 1.

There is one final way to alter the font metric information, and it is available only (to the best of my knowledge) in interpreters that implement **WMode**, although the feature applies equally to both writing modes of a font. This is an optional font dictionary entry that defines a procedure to alter character metrics after the ordinary font metric information has been applied, as follows:

CDevProc   This optional procedure is called by the font machinery after the character metrics have been applied and after any modifications provided by **Metrics** or **Metrics2** have been added, but immediately before **setcachedevice2** is called to establish the character metrics. There are eleven operands on the operand stack at the call to the procedure: the ten required by **setcachedevice2** and the character name (as a name literal) on the top of the stack. The procedure should use this information to change the character metrics as is necessary and return the desired ten operands for **setcachedevice2**, which is then called by the font machinery.

Where **Metrics** and **Metrics2** provide individual modification for characters within a given font, the **CDevProc** provides a global method for modifying font metrics based on the metric data already defined for a character. Such a procedure can be used to alter the metrics of a proportional font to become monospaced, for example, or to alter the metrics of one base font to match those of others being used together as one composite font.

5.6 COMPOSITE FONTS

The standard encoding mechanism that we have just described provides for up to 256 characters to be available in any font at one time. Although the **CharStrings** dictionary may provide more than 256 entries, the **Encoding** array has a maximum of only 256 positions. Of course, these positions correspond to the 256 possible character codes that are available for indexing, and therefore a normal font using a single 8-bit character code as an index cannot represent more than 256 characters at a time.

Since the ordinary Roman alphabet consists of 26 letters and 10 numbers, you may be wondering why this discussion is necessary. Even adding together all the upper- and lowercase letters, punctuation marks, and various accented characters, 256 possible characters seems quite adequate. Not all languages, however, use the Roman alphabet; and several of the non-Roman alphabets contain significantly more letters or variants of letters than our alphabet does. The worst case are those languages that use or have adapted the Chinese method of writing, such as Japanese. But Japan is one of the most important commercial markets, so some method had to be developed to provide access to a complete set of standard Japanese characters for output. Japanese publishers had previously settled on a standard set of about 7,000 signs (or characters, in our nomenclature) that provide a good working basis for quality written communications. The task then is to provide an encoding scheme that will allow the display of strings using codes that select one of these 7,000 (or more) characters.

Clearly, the first problem is how to create sufficient character codes to represent the 7,000 possible characters. The Japanese, having already faced this issue in working with computer representation of their language, have developed several different approaches that solve the problem. Any encoding structure that is designed to extend the normal processing mechanism described above must allow for and support these several different approaches to character representation.

This problem is solved by an extension to the basic font handling mechanism that allows the creation and processing of hierarchical *composite fonts* that allow access to a virtually unlimited set of characters by using a variety of character coding schemes, including one that is user-defined. The standard PostScript fonts described above are called *base fonts*. These fonts contain the actual character descriptions that are accessed to display characters on the output device.

Composite fonts are a hierarchical collection of base fonts. The font at the top of the hierarchy is called the *root font*. Fonts at lower levels of the hierarchy are called *descendent fonts*. Descendent fonts may be either composite fonts or base fonts, as required to represent the correct character structure. Composite fonts are designed to provide an algorithm to map elements of character strings into graphic shapes drawn from the base fonts within the hierarchy; this algorithm is called the *font mapping*.

Dictionary Entries

In order to implement this process, composite fonts have some different entries in the font dictionary than base fonts have; they also have different definitions for some existing entries in the dictionary. The font dictionary for a composite font has the following entries.

Key	Type	Information
Encoding	array	An array of integers. During font operations, the mapping algorithm extracts a number from the string being displayed that selects one element of this array. The value selected is used as an index into the **FDepVector** (described below), which selects a descendent font.
FontType	integer	A value of 0 indicates a composite font. Any other value indicates a base font.
FMapType	integer	This integer indicates the nature of the mapping algorithm that will be used to interpret the sequence of bytes from the string being displayed. The mapping algorithm first determines a font number that is used as an index into the **Encoding** array; then it determines a character code that is used as an index into the selected font.

The following algorithms are presently available and are selected by using the **FMapType** value shown:

2 Two bytes are extracted from the string. The most significant 8 bits (the high-order byte) are used to determine the font number, and the remaining 8 bits (the low-order byte) are used to select the character code. This is referred to as '8/8 mapping'.

3 One byte is extracted from the string. If it is equal to the escape character as defined by the **EscChar** entry (described below), the next byte is the font number, and subsequent bytes are character codes for the selected font. If the first byte of a string is not an escape character, font *0* is selected by default.

4 A single byte is extracted from the string. The most significant bit selects one of two fonts, and the remaining 7 bits are the character code and select the character within that font. This is referred to as '1/7 mapping'.

5 Two bytes are extracted from the string. The most significant 9 bits select the font number, and the remaining 7 bits are the character code for the selected font. This is referred to as '9/7 mapping'.

6 This is a user-defined mapping structure. In this type, the **SubsVector** string is used to specify the mapping algorithm. The number of bytes extracted from the string is determined by the value of the first byte of the **SubsVector** string. The remaining values in the string determine a series of consecutive numeric ranges that are used to control the mapping from the string into the font number and character code. See the description of the **SubsVector** below for further information.

FontMatrix array   This array has the same format and function in a composite font that it has in a base font.

FDepVector array   This is an array of font dictionaries. A The integer value that is extracted from the **Encoding** array is used as an index into this array, and the corresponding font dictionary is selected. If the selected font is a base font, a character will be selected from it using the character code provided by the font- mapping algorithm. If the font is a composite font, then that font's mapping algorithm is executed as described in the next part of the chapter.

The following entries are optional, but will usually be present in composite fonts.

Key	Type	Information
WMode	integer	This integer has possible values of *0* or *1* and indicates which writing mode will be used for the descendent fonts. A value of *0* indicates that the character metrics for writing mode zero (horizontal writing) are to be used, and a value of *1* indicates that the metrics for writing mode 1 (vertical writing) are to be used. Note that the writing mode of a root font overrides the modes of all descendent fonts; in this way, a single base font may be used with many composite fonts, whether they are writing mode 0 or 1.
PrefEnc	array	This array is normally the same as one or more of the entries in the **Encoding** arrays of the descendent fonts. If this array is present, the descendent fonts whose *Encoding* is listed here will be processed more quickly. If this entry is not present, the PostScript font machinery will create a default, null entry.

The following entry is required for a composite font with **FMapType** equal to 3 (escape encoding).

Key	Type	Information
EscChar	integer	This integer defines the escape-code value that is used for fonts with an **FMapType** of 3. If it is not provided by the application, 0 the PostScript font machinery inserts a default value of $8{\textcircled{©}}337$ (the standard ASCII escape character).

The following entry is required for a composite font with an **FMapType** equal to 6 (user-defined mapping).

Key	Type	Information
SubsVector	string	This string controls the mapping algorithm for composite fonts with an **FMapType** of *6* (user-defined mapping). A The first byte of the **SubsVector** string specifies the number of bytes to be extracted from the display string for each call to the mapping algorithm. A value of *0* indicates that one byte is extracted; a value of *1* indicates that two bytes are to be extracted. The remaining bytes in the **SubsVector** string define a series of consecutive numeric ranges. The first range, *range 0*, begins with the value 0 and contains *i* values, where *i* is the value of the second byte in the **SubsVector** string. Each succeeding byte in the **SubsVector** string gives the number of values that are included in the next range.

A value of 0 in this part of the **SubsVector** string is taken to mean that the next range consists of 256 values. The **SubsVector** entry is required if the **FMapType** is 6; if it is not present, the font machinery will not use the font and will issue an error.

This can be made somewhat clearer by an example. Suppose that you want to implement the 1/7 mapping; this accesses a single byte at a time and divides the possible values into two groups: one ranging from 0 to 127 (hexadecimal 00 to 7f) and the second ranging from 128 to 255 (hexadecimal 80 to ff). In the terms of the **SubsVector**, that yields a string with the following value: '<00 80 80>'. The '<' and '>' delimiters, you will recall, indicate that the enclosed string is in hexadecimal. The first byte of the string is '00', indicating that one byte is to be extracted each time. The second value, '80', indicates that the first hexadecimal 80 character codes, with values '00' to '7f', are the be used against the font in the **FDepVector** that is pointed to by the second value in the **Encoding** array. Since the maximum value for any one-byte code is 'ff', this arrangement fully defines the possible ranges of values.

By convention, if the last value range extends to the maximum possible value (as it does here), then it can be left out of the string. In other words, the string '<00 80>' will produce identical results to the string given above. However, I strongly recommend that you specify the complete range in the string; it makes reading and debugging easier and more obvious.

Nesting Composite Fonts

Descendent fonts of composite fonts may themselves be composite fonts. This arrangement is called *nesting* composite fonts. Arbitrary nesting is allowed for composite fonts, subject to two restrictions. First, the parent font of a font with escape code mapping must itself use escape code mapping. However, the descendent fonts of a font with escape code mapping may use any mapping. Second, the maximum nesting depth is 5 levels. The mapping algorithms also nest according to the following rules:

1. If the descendent font that is selected by a font with any non-escape code mapping (that is, the **FMapType** is not equal to 3) is itself a composite font, then the second part of the value extracted from the string being displayed is reused as the first part using the descendent's mapping algorithm.
2. If the descendent font that is selected uses escape code mapping (that is, has an **FMapType** equal to 3), then the **EscChar** of the root font overrides the **EscChar** of the selected descendent font.
3. An escape code followed by a byte that is not an escape code causes the mapping algorithm to descend the font tree toward the base fonts. An escape code followed by another escape code cause the algorithm to ascend the font tree toward the root font. (Remember that logical tree structures, unlike real trees, grow upside down, with the root at the top and the branches at the bottom).

Section B

Language Operation

– a discussion of specific language features and
implementation.

This section of the book discusses the specific operations that are basic to the PostScript language. You learned, in the previous section, the concepts behind the power of Post-Script. In this section you will look at the specific operators that are used to implement the language concepts. The discussion in this section revolves around how to use these operators in a general way; specific information on operator requirements, operands, and results is presented in the next section.

This section is divided into three chapters. The first chapter presents the stack and dictionary operators that form the backbone of PostScript programming. Because these operators are so essential, they are presented separately from all the other operators. The chapter begins by looking at stack operations and how objects are placed onto and popped off the stack. Then it discusses the operators that control, count, or redistribute stack objects – one part of the entire subject of correct sequence of operands in the PostScript language. Next you'll look at dictionary operators. Much of the dictionary operation is automatic, and you'll learn how dictionaries are normally referenced and placed into use. The final subsection of the chapter deals with when and how certain definition operations happen and how you can control this process to speed up your PostScript processing.

The second chapter presents all the general-purpose PostScript operators. This chapter is divided into three subsections, each covering one major group of the general purpose operators. The first discusses operators that affect the sequence of operation within a Post-Script program. These are the sequence-control operators and their companion relational and boolean operators. The second subsection is something of a catch-all; it contains descriptions of the mathematical operators, the string and array operators, the operators that allow you to test and change the type and attributes of objects, and those file operators that are common to all PostScript devices. The third subsection of the chapter discusses the issues of interpreter and device control and the operators that report and control that behavior. It also contains an extensive discussion of the ordinary PostScript error processing and how it can be modified to provide custom error reporting and handling.

The third chapter presents the operators at the heart of PostScript – the graphics operators. Because PostScript is a graphics language, quite a number of issues are taken up in this chapter. The chapter begins with a section on the operators that provide controls for individual elements within the graphics state, and the operators that handle coordinate transformations. It also deals with the process of saving the graphics state on the graphics state stack and restoring it again. The next subsection deals with the process of creating figures and the operators that are used to make the current path. These are also the primary means to create and control a clipping path, and that process is discussed here. After the path is constructed, it is necessary to paint it to make it visible on the output. The next portion of the chapter deals with the operators that do that, beginning with the simplest. Then it discusses the operators that implement halftones and image processing in black and white; and it ends with a discussion of the same considerations applied to color output. The last part of the chapter deals with the important issue of font selection and display. This begins with a discussion of the operators that are normally used for text processing, presented in the natural sequence of use. Then you'll look at some of the alternative methods of defining fonts and how you may go about writing your own fonts, either by using certain information from an existing font or by creating a new font from the beginning. The chapter concludes with a short discussion on composite fonts, the use of composite fonts, particularly for printing in non-roman alphabets, and the special operators that are available for processing with composite fonts.

1

Stack and Dictionary Functions

As you saw in Section A, PostScript relies on two mechanisms very heavily to provide processing power and flexibility. These two are stack and dictionary operations. PostScript operates through the use of several push-down, pop-up stacks: the executive stack, the dictionary stack, the graphics state stack, and, most importantly, the operand stack. The executive stack is, for most purposes, unable to be accessed directly from a PostScript program. Control and use of the graphics state stack will be discussed in Chapter 3 of this section (B3) with the other graphics operators. This chapter (B1) will deal with using and controlling the dictionary and operand stacks.

In addition to using stacks, the PostScript interpreter uses dictionaries for many purposes. The two most important uses of dictionaries in PostScript are 1) as a definition mechanism for processing operators and procedures and 2) as a vehicle for storing and accessing font information. The first of these operations will be discussed in this chapter. This is what may be thought of as 'ordinary dictionary processing' in PostScript. All of the operators and operations in this category are equally applicable to font dictionaries as well as to ordinary dictionary objects; however, they do not use the font dictionaries as font references. The operators that specifically deal with accessing and using fonts are described in Section B3.3 (Chapter 3.3 of this section).

1.1 STACK OPERATORS

The operand stack, as you recall, provides the input and output mechanism for PostScript operators. There are essentially two methods of using the operand stack. The first is to take actions that have the effect of pushing objects onto the stack and popping them off. The second is to manipulate the stack directly by the use of certain PostScript operators. Both uses will be discussed here.

Most objects get put onto the stack, or 'pushed', when they are executed. Execution of PostScript objects was described in Section A2.4. In addition, objects that are stored in dictionaries can be placed onto the stack by using the load or get operators, which will be presented in more detail later along with dictionary operations. Placing objects on the stack is important, because the stack is the source of operands for PostScript operators. Whenever you want to perform some action in PostScript, you need to execute either an operator or a collection of operators stored as a procedure. Here you'll begin with the simplest case – a single operator; later, in Chapters B2 and B3, you'll find the creation and use of procedures presented in more detail. In any case, most PostScript operators require data – earlier defined as *operands* – in order to function. You remember that operands for PostScript operators precede the operator itself; so the correct presentation to add the two numbers 20 and 30 together would look like this: '20 30 add'. This method of writing PostScript actually represents the following sequence of actions. The number '20' is received over a communication channel, is tokenized, and then is presented to the interpreter, which executes it. Execution of a number means pushing it onto the operand stack. Graphically, you might envision the operand stack as a series of positions, with the newest on top and the oldest on the bottom; and each new item moves all the older ones down by one position. Using such an analogy, it looks something like Figure B1.1 at this point:

Next the interpreter encounters the number '30' (after the same process of reception and so on) and executes that. Now there are two numbers on the stack, with '30' on top and '20' underneath, and the stack looks like Figure B1.2.

Now the interpreter receives the name 'add' – notice that I did not say the operator 'add'. At this point, the interpreter doesn't know 'add' from 'pyrzqxgl'; a name is just a name. The interpreter executes the name by looking it up in the dictionary stack (as discussed earlier in Section A2.4). When it does so, it finds the operator 'add' stored in *systemdict* associated with the name 'add' – assuming that you have not redefined the operator name another dictionary in the meantime – and and executes the operator. The operator looks on the operand stack for two operands to be added together and finds '30' and '20'. It pops these from the stack, adds them together, and pushes the result, '50', back onto the operand stack. The operand stack now looks like Figure B1.3

This is a simple example of how the operand stack works in practice. You can now see why PostScript statements are written as they are; they are presented to you in the

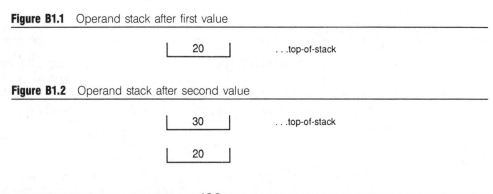

Figure B1.1 Operand stack after first value

| 20 | . . .top-of-stack

Figure B1.2 Operand stack after second value

| 30 | . . .top-of-stack

| 20 |

Figure B1.3 Operand stack after 'add'

| 50 | . . .top-of-stack

same way that the interpreter reads them: left to right, with each object executed as it is read. Now you understand why it is so important to know the language concepts and syntax before you begin working with PostScript statements – once you know them, you can envision how these processes are carried out.

Operand Sequence

Once objects are on the stack, they can be manipulated in several ways. One of the most common is to resequence the objects. This is often necessary because various PostScript operators expect their operands in a certain sequence, and, although the data exists on the operand stack, it is not yet in a correct order. A short example may make this clearer.

Suppose that you want to subtract the product of two numbers, say 4 and 5, from a third number, say 30. Using the PostScript operators **mul** (for multiply) and **sub** (for subtract), you might think to write the following PostScript code to get the desired result:

4 5 **mul** 30 **sub**

However, this would give you the incorrect result of −10, since the **sub** operator subtracts the second, or top, number on the stack from the first, or bottommost, number. In this case, the number you want to subtract is below the number you want to subtract it from. Therefore you need to simply resequence the operand stack to get the correct result. This can be done by switching the two operands using the **exch** (exchange) operator, as follows:

4 5 **mul** 30 **exch sub**

which gives the correct result. This example illustrates why you sometimes need to resequence the operand stack.

Objects already on the operand stack can be resequenced by the **exch** operator, which, as you just saw, swaps the two top objects on the stack, and by the **roll** operator, which moves more than one object. It is also possible to duplicate either all items or just selected items on the stack. The **dup** operator simply duplicates the top object; the **index** operator duplicates a selected object, one chosen by an index operand, onto the top of the stack; and the **copy** operator will duplicate any number of objects from the top of the stack. Finally, it is possible to place a *mark* object on the stack by executing the **mark** or the [operators and use that as a marker for various types of stack procedures. This is most useful when you don't know the exact number of items you must work with; in such cases, a mark can keep a place on the stack and allows easy processing of variable length groups. The number of objects in the stack above the mark can then be determined using the **counttomark** operator.

Objects are removed from the stack in basically the same two ways as they are put on the stack, 1) indirectly, as a byproduct of operator fuctioning and 2) directly, by invoking stack operators. The indirect manner is illustrated by the short example above. There, the two operands, '20' and '30', were removed from the operand stack as a byproduct of the **add** processing. The PostScript operators generally consume their operands and return results or nothing to the stack; they very seldom leave the operands untouched on the top of the stack. The direct removal of objects is done by two operators: **pop** removes the top object from the stack and discards it, and **clear** removes all objects from the stack and discards them. If the objects on the stack have been delimited by a *mark*, then they can also be cleared by the **cleartomark** operator.

1.2   DICTIONARY OPERATORS

Before you begin looking at the various operators that work with dictionaries, it's a good idea to briefly review how the PostScript interpreter uses and accesses dictionaries. This material was more fully presented in Section A1.4.

The PostScript interpreter maintains a *dictionary stack* that is used for most access and storage purposes; this is called the *current dictionary context*. The interpreter looks up name objects in the current dictionary context, comparing the name to the *keys* in the dictionary and retrieving the *values* for processing. The order of dictionary access is from the top of the dictionary stack to the bottom. The dictionary on the top of the stack is called the *current dictionary* and can be directly placed on the operand stack for reference by the **currentdict** operator. The dictionary stack always contains at least two dictionaries: *userdict* and *systemdict,* with *userdict* on top of *systemdict*.

Two sets of operations are performed on PostScript dictionaries. First, a few operators control and manipulate the dictionary stack; second, a number of operators add, change, and otherwise manipulate the objects stored in the dictionaries. The latter operations may be further subdivided into two groups: the operators that access a specific dictionary (which usually must be supplied as an operand) and those that operate in the current dictionary context.

The operators that deal with dictionary creation and operation of the dictionary stack begin, logically enough, with the **dict** operator, which allows you to create a new dictionary. You can test the maximum capacity of a dictionary by using the **maxlength** operator, and you can find out how many entries exist currently by using the **length** operator. In both cases, the desired dictionary must be explictly referenced, generally by executing its name, which is associated with an operator that pushes a duplicate of the dictionary onto the operand stack. Once on the operand stack, a dictionary may be added to the dictionary stack, thus becoming part of the current dictionary context, by invoking the

begin operator. When you're finished with the dictionary, it can be removed from the dictionary stack by executing the operator **end,** which pops the current dictionary, removing it from the current dictionary context (that is, making it unavailable for reference), and makes the dictionary immediately beneath it the new current dictionary. However, neither the *userdict* nor the *systemdict* can be removed from the dictionary stack under any circumstances; any attempt to do so raises the error **dictstackunderflow.**

Dictionary Reference

The operators that work with specific dictionary references have a certain special virtue: the dictionaries that you reference with them do not have to be on the dictionary stack and so are not part of the current dictionary context. Using these operators, you can manipulate the contents of dictionaries without necessarily changing the current context. The **copy** operator allows you to copy one dictionary into another, empty dictionary. Notice that this provides a true copy, not a duplicate; that is, the dictionary that is output does not share values with the input dictionary. However, if there are any composite objects defined in the dictionaries, those objects will share values. Look back at Section A2.2 for a discussion of simple and composite objects and the difference between copying and duplication. The **get** and **put** operators allow you to retrieve and store objects into a specific dictionary by providing both the dictionary and the key. The **known** operator allows you to test whether a specific key is in a given dictionary without fear of raising an error. Finally, the **forall** operator enumerates all the elements of a dictionary in an arbitrary order and allows you to perform any desired processing on each one.

Several of these operators (**get, put, copy,** and **forall**) perform essentially the same functions on other composite objects. The exact processing that is performed is dependent on the type of operand that is presented to the operator when it executes. Such operators are called *polymorphic* operators, and they will discussed again, in their other roles, together with general operators in Chapter 4 later in this section.

The most common operators that work with dictionaries are those that execute within the current dictionary context. These operators do not require a specific dictionary reference as an operand; they simply work with the dictionaries on the dictionary stack. All of these operators perform in the same fashion as the interpreter itself, searching the dictionary stack from the top down to find or insert a key-value pair. Without doubt, the most common dictionary operator is the **def** operator, which defines a new key-value pair by adding it to the current dictionary. Such definitions are created by **def** and retrieved by the ordinary processing of the interpreter, which retrieves a key and processes a value as described earlier. Values can also be retrieved and inserted using the operators **load** and **store,** which search for a specified key within the current dictionary context. Finally, the **where** operator provides a means to look up a key within the current context and determine both whether the key exists and, if it does exist, what dictionary it is defined in.

1.3 DEFINITION CONTROL

In ordinary PostScript processing, all definition and name lookup follows the same processing cycle. Key-value pairs are defined in the current dictionary context using the operators discussed above, and the most common use of these definitions occurs when the interpreter receives a name object, which it then looks up within the current context, extracts the value associated with the name as a key, and executes the value. If the value itself contains additional names, then these are looked up in turn as they are encountered in execution.

PostScript procedures are essentially constructed in this fashion. You remember (from Section A1) that procedures are executable arrays of PostScript operators. Procedures are defined, like other PostScript objects, by associating the executable array (the value) with a name literal (the key) in a dictionary. Inevitably, a large part of most procedures consists of names of operators and of other procedures, and, when these are executed, the interpreter looks up each name in turn as described earlier.

It is possible to alter this process somewhat at the time you define a procedure in order to provide two important benefits – speedier processing and an assurance that the procedure will access the correct operator definitions. That last comment may seem a strange point, so it will be discussed in more detail.

Early and Late Binding

As you already know, when the interpreter looks up a name, it looks it up in the current dictionary context. You also may remember from previous discussions that there are effectively no reserved words in PostScript; in particular, the names associated with operators in *systemdict* are not reserved or protected in any way. This presents some potential problems for the PostScript programmer, in that it is possible for the operator names to be redefined before a procedure is executed, thus changing the action of the procedure when it is executed. This happens because the interpreter, when it looks up the names during execution of the procedure in the current dictionary context, finds the redefined name before it encounters the original definition. Let me hasten to emphasize that this is not an ordinary occurrence. It can happen only if your application or some related application redefines an operator name for some reason.

This chance can, however, be avoided if you perform a **bind** operation on the procedure before you define it. The **bind** operator looks up all the operators in the procedure and replaces their names with the actual operator itself – that is, with the value that is associated with that operator name in *systemdict*. Once this is done, any changed definition for the procedure name will have no effect, because the interpreter will not encounter a name but instead will encounter the operator value itself when it executes the procedure. This **bind** operation also speeds up the processing, since the interpreter is saved one complete cycle of looking up the operator names in *systemdict* and then executing them every time the procedure is executed. This can result in significant increases in processing speed if the procedure is executed often. This increase in efficiency is the primary reason to bind procedures.

The **bind** has no drawbacks for redefined operators either; if you have redefined an operator prior to issuing the **bind,** the name is not replaced and the interpreter will process the name in the ordinary way as it executes the procedure. This is done by effectively testing the type of each name when the **bind** is executing; if the name represents an *operatortype,* it is replaced; but if it is any other type, it is left alone. Therefore a program may redefine the **showpage** operator, for example, and be certain that any subsequent procedures that call that operator name will not inadvertently substitute the actual operator and possibly cause disastrous results when the program is included in another PostScript program. Use of the **bind** operator is good PostScript programming practice, for the reasons mentioned above. This practice of binding procedures before they are defined is known as *early binding,* the normal PostScript practice is known as *late binding* because the mapping from the names to the operators is left until the moment the procedure is executed. In addition, procedures that have had the value substituted for the operator names are called *tightly bound* because no process intervenes between the procedure and its actual execution.

Immediately Evaluated Names

A similar process can be applied to names as well as to operators. In the case of names, it is necessary to use a special form of name literal called an *immediately evaluated name.* An immediately evaluated name is any name preceded by two slash characters with no intervening space, like this: //name. When the interpreter encounters such a name, it immediately looks up the name in the current dictionary context and substitutes the value associated with it for the name itself. The name must be defined in the current context or an **undefined** error is raised.

You can see how similar this is to the process when **bind** is used. Moreover, the purpose of using the immediately evaluated name and the **bind** operator is the same: namely, to tightly bind procedures to their component parts, whether those parts are operators, procedures, or other variables. There are, however, several differences. The first is perhaps the most obvious, but it still needs to be emphasized. The **bind** works only on names that refer to operators, and it works automatically on any procedure when you invoke it. The immediately evaluated name, on the other hand, is a special form of name that must be specifically included in the procedure when you code it and that will then always be executed for that name.

The second difference is a bit more subtle but of more concern to a programmer. This is the distinction between procedures that are encountered indirectly by the interpreter and those that it encounters directly. Procedures that are encountered indirectly are looked up and executed, as described in Section A2.4, while procedures that are encountered directly are simply pushed onto the operand stack. Therefore, in order to get the desired results, you may have to make additional changes to your procedures as illustrated by the program fragments below.

Suppose that you define two procedures as follows:

```
/ first        { 1 2 add } def
/ second       { 2 3 mul } def
```

and then you combine both these into a third procedure as follows:

```
/ third        { first second div } def
```

If you now execute the procedure 'third', you will get the expected result of 0.5, since the interpreter will encounter the two procedures 'first' and 'second' indirectly (while executing the procedure 'third') and will execute them. Of course, you can modify the procedure 'third' by the simple fact of redefining one of the components, like this:

```
/ first        { 10 20 add } def
```

and now if you execute 'third' you get a new result of 5.0.

However, you might have attempted to avoid this result–caused by the redefinition of 'first'–by using the immediately executed names. Then you would, most likely, rewrite 'third' as follows:

```
/ third        { // first // second div } def
```

Unfortunately, although that's certainly the obvious thought, it doesn't work. The reason lies in the interpreter's handling of procedures. The sequence above results in the following code being stored:

```
/ third        { {1 2 add} {2 3 mul} div } def
```

which looks correct but, once you examine it, clearly won't execute correctly. Unlike the preceding case, the interpreter here encounters the procedure objects directly and therefore pushes them onto the operand stack instead of executing them. The net result is that the **div** operator has two procedure operands rather than the necessary two numeric operands and complains by raising the **typecheck** error. This problem can be solved in several ways, most notably by inserting an **exec** operator after each of the immediately evaluated names; but, as you see from this example, the simple expedient of replacing procedure names with immediately evaluated names will not work.

Global and Local Definition

Dictionary control can be used in a variety of ways when you are programming in Post-Script. One of the most useful and most common is to create a working dictionary within your application and use that dictionary exclusively throughout the program. This provides safety because it controls the current dictionary and hence ensures that your procedure definitions are the first available in the current dictionary context. It also helps you manage your memory resources by including all your composite objects and their definitions in one place. The control of the current dictionary in this way, moreover, has an additional benefit that often goes unnoticed.

When you create a dictionary and make it the current dictionary by placing it onto the dictionary stack with a **begin,** you know that the definitions that you make into this dictionary will be accessed before those in any other dictionary beneath it on the dictionary stack. However, the previous definitions don't go away; they are simply masked from use in the current dictionary context. This allows you to create global and local variables, as you choose, simply by changing dictionaries in the current context.

The process proceeds like this. The global variables are defined in a dictionary that is available on the dictionary stack to the all the procedures that you define. Then, for those cases where you want to define local variables, you define a new dictionary, place it onto the dictionary stack, and store the local variables in it. All the global definitions that you have not redefined locally still remain accessible, while your local definitions supersede any global ones. When you are done with the local definitions, you pop the dictionary by using the **end** command, which discards the local definitions and reinstates the previously masked global variables.

Procedures and Programs

Procedures form the basic building blocks for PostScript programs. As stated earlier in Section A1.6, the general format for PostScript programs is the *prologue* and *script* format. When a PostScript program follows this structure, all the procedure definitions are located in the prologue; and all the actual execution of these procedures takes place in the script, where the data for use by the procedures is stored.

This structure is easily implemented by using a private dictionary, as described above, for storage of the prologue. In this fashion, the procedure definitions in the prologue are carefully segregated from any other procedures that may be, or have already been, defined. The prologue can be stored into its own dictionary, and the script, when it begins to execute, can start using that dictionary by invoking it with the PostScript **begin** operator. When the processing is complete, the trailer portion of the program should perform cleanup, which will include executing the matching **end** operator to remove the private dictionary from the dictionary stack.

General Functions

This chapter deals with the general PostScript operators. This includes all operators that are not stack or dictionary operators, which were covered in the last chapter, and are not graphics operators, which will be covered in the next chapter.

That leaves a lot of ground, some of which is not easily categorized. In this chapter, you will look at the operators that provide program control and change the sequence of operations. These operators are particularly important because they make PostScript into a full programming language. You will also examine those operators called – for want of a better category name – general operators. That simple label covers the mathematical operators, the operators that work on strings and arrays, the operators that deal with types and attributes and with conversion among the forms of PostScript objects, and the operators that provide general file functions. Finally you will examine those operators that control the interpreter itself and those that provide error handling and device management.

This is certainly a large range of functions. Please remember that the discussion here is only an overview intended to provide some context for the use of the operators without becoming too slowed down by detailed explanations. For a complete description of any operator, see the operator definitions in Sections C1 and C2. Detailed study and understanding are particularly important before using the operators that govern the interpreter and the device itself, since errors in these areas can be potentially disastrous.

2.1 SEQUENCE OPERATORS

The first set of operators that you will examine are those operators that change the sequence of execution within a PostScript program. As discussed in Section A1.5, operators that control the sequence of execution can be roughly divided into three categories. The first category contains operators that execute a procedure repeatedly. In PostScript, the first operator in this category is the **loop** operator, which does exactly what you would expect – it takes a procedure as an operand and executes it continuously. The execution is stopped by executing an **exit** operator from within the procedure. The **repeat** operator executes a procedure a given number of times. The **for** operator also executes a procedure a given number of times, but it also passes the controlling numeric variable to the procedure for use as an operand as it is being executed. Also in this category are a number of operators that enumerate elements in various PostScript objects. The most common of these is the **forall** operator, which will take any composite object (array, string, or dictionary) and read out every element within the object, executing a given procedure for each element and passing the element to the procedure as an operand. This is a most efficient method of listing or processing the elements of a composite object. Two variants on **forall** are provided for processing other types of objects that are not generally accessible. The **pathforall** operator enumerates the elements of the current path, and the **filenameforall** enumerates the files on an external device (if one is defined and attached). All of these operators may have their normal execution terminated early if the procedure being executed itself executes an **exit** operator, but only the **loop** operator will never terminate of its own accord. Also, in all cases, the procedure to be executed is provided as an operand to the operator described above, sometimes along with other necessary control operands.

The second category of sequence control operators are those that execute a procedure conditionally. In PostScript, such processing is done based on the state of a boolean object, which is passed to the operator as an operand. The most straightforward of these operators is the **if** operator, which executes a procedure if the boolean operand is *true* and does not execute it if the boolean is *false*. A slightly more complex approach is provided by the **ifelse** operator, which takes two procedures and executes one if the boolean is *true* and the other if the boolean is *false*. In this same category we may place the **exec** operator, which does not take any boolean operand but simply and unconditionally executes any object that is presented to it. Notice that, unlike all the other operators discussed here, **exec** will execute any object, not just a procedure.

The third category are those operators that control the state of execution. In PostScript, this really is one set of two related operators that can be used to establish the execution environment and to exit from it once it has been established. These two operators are **stopped** and **stop.** The **stopped** operator establishes the execution environment for a given operand, which may be a procedure, an executable string, or a filestream. It executes these in the standard way, in this aspect behaving exactly like **the exec** operator. However, the **stopped** context (as it is referred to) also monitors the execution. If the operand finishes execution normally, **stopped** returns a boolean value *false* to the operand stack as a result, and processing continues with the next sequential instruction. However, the procedure can communicate an abnormal condition by executing the **stop** operator within itself. In that case, the **stopped** operator recognizes the abnormal termination of the procedure and returns the boolean value *true* to the operand stack. In this way, subsequent processing can determine whether the procedure executed by **stopped** completed normally or not and take whatever action is appropriate. Since the default PostScript error procedures execute a **stop,** they can also trap errors that occur during processing.

These operators provide an effective and appropriate method for PostScript programs to control the execution of procedures and to trap errors or other premature terminations of processing. They allow programs to retain control of the processing and provide error recovery, where appropriate, or graceful termination of the procedure. In fact, this is exactly the process that is used by the interpreter itself, which executes each PostScript application within a **stopped** context and then, if any error or abnormal condition arises, can regain control in order to provide standard error handling.

Relational and Boolean Operators

As you have just seen, several of these sequence-control operators require an external boolean object as an operand to control their processing. PostScript provides a complete set of relational testing and boolean manipulation operators to create the necessary values for these controls. The relational operators, as you would expect, will test any pair of operands for equality, using the **eq** operator, or for inequality, using the **ne** operator. The definition of equality depends on the types of the objects being compared. The objects do not necessarily have to be of the same type; for example, strings can be compared to name literals, and real numbers can be compared to integers, with correct results.

Comparison of dictionaries and arrays, however, is somewhat ambiguous. Remember that these are composite objects and that duplicate composite objects share values. Dictionaries and arrays are judged equal if, and only if, they share all values, that is, if the two objects being compared are duplicates of one another. Comparison of nonduplicate arrays or dictionaries will always result in an unequal result even if the contents of the two objects are exactly equal. Thus you can have the rather unnerving experience illustrated in the following example:

[1 2 3] [1 2 3] eq   ⇒   false

In this case, the example creates two distinct arrays that have identical components; however, because the arrays are not duplicates of one another, they compare *false* when tested for equality.

There is one exception to this rule regarding comparison of arrays, and it is illustrated in the following example:

[ ] [ ] eq   ⇒   true

Here, you are comparing two empty, or *null*, arrays. These arrays always compare equal, so you can test for an empty array successfully, even though you cannot test directly for equal contents in other arrays.

Strings, on the other hand, even though they are also composite objects, do compare in the natural way. Two strings are equal if they have the same length and each of their elements are equal; the strings do not have to share values. Therefore the equivalent test to the example above provides an expected response, as follows:

(asdfg) (asdfg) eq   ⇒   true

because the two strings, although distinct, have identical lengths and elements.

Although any objects may be tested for equality, only numbers and strings can be tested for other relations, such as greater than or less than. This restriction is really quite reasonable, because defining these relations for other types of objects would be quite difficult and somewhat arbitrary. Inequality relations for numbers are quite well-defined, and PostScript numbers of both real and integer types and in all formats may be freely mixed in these relational tests. Inequality for strings is done along the same lines, by testing the character codes as numbers and ordering the strings accordingly. If two strings are of unequal length and are identical for the length of the shorter string, the longer string is always greater. However, if two strings are of unequal length but are not identical for the length of the shorter string, the comparison is made up to the point of inequality and the decision is made on the difference at that point. Thus a string of 100 blanks will be less than a string that consists of the single character (a), as it should be.

PostScript also has a complete set of boolean operators that combine various types of boolean values to generate a result. Thus there is an **and**, which combines two boolean operands; an **or** that is non-exclusive, meaning that only two *false* operands give a *false* result; an exclusive or, **xor**, meaning that two *true* operands also give a *false* result; and a **not** operator that reverses the value of its boolean operand.

These same operators can be used on integer numbers, which are treated as binary numbers or bit strings. As bit strings, the numbers can have the same logical operations performed on them in bitwise fashion, taking '0' as the equivalent of 'false' and '1' as the equivalent of 'true.' The **not** operator, when applied to an integer, returns the one's complement of the number in binary representation.

2.2   GENERAL OPERATORS

In this part of the chapter, we will examine all the operators that, for want of a better description, might be called general operators. These operators provide much of the non-graphics power of the PostScript language, and they have an important place in the programming lexicon of every PostScript programmer.

The operators cover a wide range of functions, and the groups have little in common. Since they are also the operators that are most like the common functions implemented in a wide variety of programming languages, each of the groups can be simply presented without much preliminary discussion.

Mathematical Operators

PostScript implements a basic set of mathematical operations. For the obvious reason that the PostScript language is devoted to marking pages of output, the selection of mathematical operators includes several that may seem a bit exotic. However the requirements for each will become quite apparent.

First of all, there are the simple, basic arithmetic operations: **add**, **sub** for subtract, **mul** for multiply, and **div** for divide. Because PostScript operators that require numeric operands often require that those operands be integer, there is also a variant of division, **idiv,** that produces only an integer result. For the other arithmetic operators, the type of the operands determines the type of the result.

There are also some more sophisticated arithmetic operators. The **mod** operator provides a type of *modulo* processing, returning the remainder that is left when two integer operands are divided into one another. The **neg** operator reverses the sign of the operand, while the **abs** operator returns the absolute value. The operators **ceiling** and **floor** return the next integer value greater than or equal to and less than or equal to the operand, respectively. As you would expect, the **round** operator rounds to the nearest integer, with values of .5 and greater being rounded up. The **truncate,** on the other hand, simply removes and discards the fractional part of the number without, however, changing the type.

There are several exponential operators. The first is **exp,** which raises a base operand value to an exponential power, where the exponent value is also an operand. On a simpler note, you can take a square root of any positive number by using the **sqrt** operator. In this same category, there are also two logarithmic operators whose names follow standard mathematical conventions: **log** for the logarithm of any number to the base 10, and **ln** for the natural logarithm (using the base e).

There are three trigonometric operators as well. These operators are useful because PostScript provides a wide variety of graphic operations, many of which can be most easily performed by using trigonometric functions. PostScript implements **sin** and **cos,** which take an angle as an operand and return the sine and cosine, respectively, of the angle. There is one inverse trigonometric function, **atan** or arc tangent. This takes the x and y coordinate distances as operands and returns the angle that is created by these two values. Figures B2.1 and B2.2 illustrate the connection between the x and y values and the resulting angle.

Figure B2.1   Arc tangent in the first quadrant

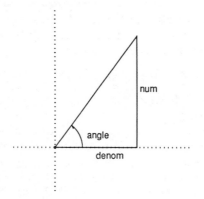

Figure B2.2 Arc tangent in the second quadrant

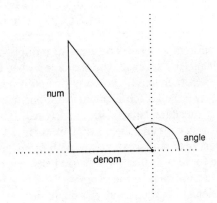

As you can see, determination of the angle defined by the arc tangent of the two coordinates is quite useful. In addition, by using various trigonometric identities, these three operators provide all that is necessary to calculate any possible relationship.

Finally, there are several operators that provide a pseudo-random number facility. It is a 'pseudo' random number because you can control its behavior to some extent. The **rand** operator returns a pseudo-random integer number as a result. You can use the **rrand** number to return the current random number 'seed', which is the value that controls the next random number generated; because the next number is controlled, the number generated is not truly random. The seed value can be given to the **srand** operator and will cause the next number generated by **rand** to be identical to the number generated at any previous time that the seed was the same. In this way, it is possible to generate a repeatable sequence of random numbers.

String and Array Operators

There are a variety of operators that handle string and array composite objects. Because these types of objects are generally similar, the same operators are often equally valid on both types of objects. To begin with, each of these objects has a special operator that creates an empty version of the object: **array** for arrays, and **string** for strings. In each case, you must provide a length operand to tell the operator what size the empty object should be. 'Empty', in the case of an array, means filled with null objects; in the case of a string, it means filled with binary zeros.

You remember that composite objects have an internal structure, or elements, that are accessible to a PostScript program. In all cases, the elements in an array or string are accessed by providing an index value. All the elements are indexed from *0* to *n−1,* assuming that the array or string has *n* elements. The **length** operator returns the number of elements in the object as an integer value. The **get** operator retrieves a given element from the object, and the **put** operator will replace a given element, overwriting the previous element. In a similar fashion, **getinterval** retrieves a subsection of the given object, which is determined by a starting position and a number of elements to be retrieved; **putinterval** stores a subsection in the same way. Since these are composite objects, remember that the subsection that is returned is a duplicate of the object and shares the value of the original. Any changes you make to either part will be reflected in the other.

On the other hand, the **copy** operator will make an independent copy of a given object, transferring each element from one array or string into another. The resulting copy does not share values with the original. If the **copy** is applied to an array, however, and that array contains objects that are themselves composite objects, then those composite objects may still share values with other duplicates of themselves. Along the same lines, the **forall** operator extracts each element of the array or string in turn and applies a procedure operand to the element. In this way, you can perform arbitrary processing on each element of the array or string in turn, without worrying about indices and length of the object.

There are also certain operators that apply to only one or the other of these objects. These operators supply functions that are not common to the composite structure of the objects but rather are specific to the particular nature of each type. For strings, these are several operators that search strings for certain elements or groups of elements. The most basic of these is the **search** operator, which searches a given string for the first occurrence of a substring that matches a given group of characters. The **anchorsearch** operator provides the same facility but limits the matching process to the initial characters of the given string. Finally, the **token** operator takes a given string and breaks it up according to PostScript syntax, returning the first complete PostScript object that can be constructed out of the string. All these operators function in a similar way, returning a boolean object as a last result so that you can test to see if the operation was successful. They also return the remainder of the operand string after processing so that you can continue processing later, if desired.

For array processing, there are also certain special operators that provide specific functions not applicable to strings. The foremost of these are the paired operators, **[** and **]**, which produce an array object out of whatever objects are enclosed by them. The **[** pushes a mark object onto the stack, and the subsequent **]** takes everything on the stack down to the mark and includes it in a new array object. There is also the **aload** operator, which takes an array as an operand and places all the elements individually onto the operand stack, followed by the original array itself. This is a useful method of breaking an array into its component elements for further processing. The reverse process is performed by the **astore** operator. This operator takes a given array, which may or may not be empty, on the top of the operand stack and stores as many objects into the array as are required to fill it, using whatever objects are beneath it on the stack. Obviously, there must be enough objects on the stack to fill the array, otherwise an error results.

Type, Attribute, and Conversion Operators

Every PostScript object is of a certain type and has certain attibutes, as pointed out earlier in the book. The PostScript language provides a variety of operators that allow testing of object types and conversion, within certain limits, from one type of object to another and that allow testing and conversion of an object's attributes.

The first operator in this category is the **type** operator, which can be applied to any object and will return that object's type as a result. Then there are the operators that perform conversions from one type of object to another. The most commonly used of these is the **cvs** operator, which will convert any object into a string representation of that object. This is used so often because most types of PostScript objects – for example, all types of numbers – cannot be directly output onto a page; they must be converted into string representation first. Because of the utility of this process, PostScript provides an additional operator, **cvrs,** that specifically converts numbers into the correct string value in any base. Although **cvs** accepts any type of object for conversion, certain types of objects do not have any normal string equivalent; in such cases, **cvs** returns a standard response of '– nostringval –'.

There are also operators that proceed in the reverse direction. Both **cvi** and **cvr** will accept string operands and convert them into integer and real numbers, respectively. These two operators also will take a numeric operand and convert it to the given type. In the case of a real number supplied as an operand to **cvi,** this also includes truncation of any fractional portion of the number. Finally, the **cvn** operator will transform a string operand into a name object.

There is also a set of operators that deal with the attributes of PostScript objects. To begin with, every PostScript object is either *literal* or *executable.* The **xcheck** operator will test for the executable attribute and return a boolean result to indicate the current setting. Since this is essentially a binary quality, only one test is required; any object that is not executable is literal by definition. The **cvx** operator converts any operand object to executable and the **cvlit** converts to literal; both operators do not care what the current state of the operand is and apply equally to objects that already have the desired attribute and to those that do not.

In addition to the literal / executable attribute, every PostScript composite object has an *access* attribute, which controls the ability of general programs to read or modify the object and its elements. The access attribute provides four progressively restrictive levels: write access, which is the least restrictive; read-only access; execute-only access; and no access whatsoever. Two operators test access levels, and three set levels. Write access can be tested by the **wcheck** operator, which returns a boolean result showing whether write access is allowed for the operand or not. Read-only access is tested similarly, by the operator **rcheck.** There are no explicit tests for execute-only and no access. The current access level of an object can be reduced but never increased. Therefore, if an object allows write access, it can be reduced to read-only by the **readonly** operator and further reduced by the **executeonly** operator. Finally, it is possible to use the **noaccess** operator to remove an object from all access; however, such objects are intended for internal use only and are useless to most PostScript applications.

General File Operators

A *file* in PostScript is a finite stream of characters that is terminated by an end-of-file marker. Such streams may be permanently resident on some external device, such as an external disk, or they may be transmitted over a communication channel. Files are the means by which the PostScript interpreter receives the objects that it processes and are also its means of communicating back to the external environment.

Files are generally classified into two types. An *input* file is a source of characters that can be read and processed by the interpreter or by a PostScript application. An *output* file is a place where the interpreter or an application can write characters. A PostScript file is represented by a file object. File objects can be accessed by name, using the **file** operator detailed below. The precise syntax and structure of a valid file name depend on the operating environment in which the interpreter is running. Every PostScript interpreter, however, implements certain standard files and file names, as follows:

%stdin   the standard PostScript input file; generally, the source of the currently executing application.

%stdout   the standard PostScript output file; generally, the recipient of messages and other communications generated by the application.

%stderr   the standard error file; used by the interpreter to report certain types of errors and, in most implementations, identical to the standard output file.

Remember that these names are strings and, like all strings, must be enclosed in parentheses; therefore the '%' that is part of the name is not mistaken by the interpreter as a comment. The standard files are usually associated with one of the communications channels. See Section C2.1 for a more extensive discussion of communications channels and their controls.

All PostScript interpreters provide some general file operations that use these standard files. In addition, some PostScript devices have types of external file storage. We will discuss only the general file operators here; the operators that support external devices are presented and discussed in Section C2.1.

Most PostScript file operators require a file object as an operand. To provide that file object, you must use the **file** operator, which takes a file name (in string form) and an access mode (also a string) and returns the matching file object for further processing. The word 'file' in the rest of this section will mean a file object, such as is returned by the **file** operator. The **file** operator also makes the given file available for access; in effect, it opens the file. A file can be explicitly closed by using the **close** operator, and a file's current availablity is tested and reported by the **status** operator.

Files can be read and written in the usual way by using the **read** and **write** operators, which access a single character at a time. In addition, there are some special modes of accessing files. The **readstring** and **writestring** operators use a defined string as a controlling variable, filling the string or writing it as a continuous set of characters.

The **readhexstring** and **writehexstring** provide a variation on this process by reading and writing only valid hexadecimal characters in the string. This limitation can be very useful when you're reading or transmitting certain types of data. In addition, there is a **readline** operator that will read to the next *newline* character in the input stream; and the **token** operator, which you met earlier in the discussion of strings, can also be applied to files to read the next valid PostScript object according to the syntax rules. All exception processing, including handling end-of-file conditions, is provided by all the file operators on a uniform basis. If an end-of-file is encountered during a read operation before the requested item is read, the operation is terminated, the file is closed, and a boolean value is returned on the operand stack as an explicit end-of-file indication. Any attempt to read from a file that is already closed, whether closed explicitly by the **close** operator or implicitly by an end-of-file condition, results in identical handling as described above. All other exceptional conditions during a read or a write raise the **ioerror** error condition.

Because PostScript treats files as streams of characters, you can use several operators to control the filestream buffers. The **flushfile** operator sends any buffered characters to the given file immediately rather than waiting for the buffer to fill. The **resetfile** operator discards any characters currently in the file buffers. The **flush** operator performs the same function as the **flushfile,** except that it always acts on the standard output file and so does not require a file operand.

PostScript provides several operators that transmit messages over the standard output file. The **print** operator delivers any string. The = and = = operators remove the topmost value on the operand stack and display it in string format on the output file. The **stack** and **pstack** operators perform a similar function, but for the entire contents of the stack, not just the top object, and they do not remove any object from the stack; in other words, they display the stack contents but do not disturb them.

This completes the overview and discussion of the general PostScript operators. As you have seen, they provide enormous flexibility and potential for processing power. As you work with them, you will be better able to appreciate their usefulness.

2.3   CONTROL OPERATORS

PostScript also provides operators to control the interpreter itself, to provide error recovery and handling, and to control the output device. Again, the operators presented here are all operators that are commonly defined in all versions of the PostScript interpreter.

Interpreter Management

The operators that are classified under interpreter management fall into two groups: virtual memory management and font cache management. Section A2.5 presented, in general terms, the requirements and advantages of correct management of virtual memory resources. Here we will just review the concepts behind virtual memory management and the operators that implement that management.

You remember that all composite objects consume virtual memory and that, under ordinary processing modes, PostScript does not provide any method for recovering the virtual memory used by these objects, even when they are no longer needed. Memory recovery is provided by saving the state of virtual memory at a given point in time by using a **save** operator and then restoring it to that saved state at some subsequent point in processing by invoking the **restore** operator, thus discarding all composite objects that were created in the meantime and recovering the virtual memory that they had used. The operator **save** is usually issued at the start of any application processing, and a matching **restore** is done at the end. In addition, in multipage documents, a **save** and **restore** are commonly placed around each individual page description, thus ensuring that each page does not interfere with the subsequent pages and that the maximum amount of virtual memory is available for each page. PostScript also provides a **vmstatus** operator that will report the current state and availability of virtual memory. The results are placed onto the operand stack, where they can be reported over an output link by using the standard file operations or can be used for control purposes.

The general process of font caching was discussed earlier in Section A5.3. The font cache is special storage where the interpreter keeps bitmaps of characters that have already been used, in order to speed up the process of reprinting those characters. Since the font cache memory is a limited resource, there must be some rules regarding its use. The general rule is that characters are stored in the font cache until it is full, at which time the memory occupied by the characters that have remained unreferenced the longest is reused. In addition to this simple rule, certain restrictions on the persistence and inclusion of characters in the font cache are provided. Generally, these rules are established for each device and should not be changed. However, it is possible to access and adjust them if required.

The **setcachelimit** and **setcacheparams** operators establish upper bounds for characters that are included in the font cache and, in the case of **setcacheparams,** also establish a boundary for a compressed format of storage. These same parameters are reported by the **currentcacheparams** operator; and these, along with some additional information on the cache status, are also reported by the **cachestatus** operator. If you create your own fonts, you will also have to use the **setcachedevice** or **setcachedevice2** operators to set up the information necessary for your characters to be included in the caching process; by the same token, you can opt out of the process by using the **setcharwidth** operator when making your own characters.

Error Handling

The general concepts of how PostScript provides error processing were discussed earlier in Section A2.4. Briefly, every PostScript error has a name, and whenever an error is discovered, either directly by the PostScript interpreter or indirectly through the execution of an operator, the name of the resulting error is looked up in a special dictionary, *error-dict,* and the procedure associated with the name is executed. These procedures are known collectively as the *default error handlers.*

All the default error handlers operate in a similar fashion. They record certain information regarding the state of the interpreter at the time of the error in a special dictionary, **$error,** and then they execute the equivalent of a **stop.** When the interpreter executes a PostScript application, it does so within a **stopped** context; and therefore it regains control when the default error handler executes the **stop.** This assumes, of course, that the user program has not established a **stopped** context of its own. If it has, control returns to it at this point instead of reverting to the interpreter. Otherwise, at this point, the interpreter executes the procedure **handleerror,** which prints selected items from the **$error** dictionary onto the standard output file.

The **$error** dictionary will contain the following elements when it is filled in by an error procedure:

Key	Type	Value
command	any	the name of the operator or other object that was being executed when the error occurred.
errorname	name	the name of the error that was reported; this is also the name of the error handler that was executed to fill in these items.
newerror	boolean	set to *true* to show that an error has occurred; the **handleerror** procedure resets this to *false.*
estack	array	an array containing the entire contents of the execution stack at the time the error occurred, in the same form that would be returned by the **execstack** operator.
dstack	array	an array containing the entire contents of the dictionary stack at the time the error occurred, in the same form that would be returned by the **dictstack** operator.
ostack	array	an array containing the entire contents of the operand stack just prior to the occurrence of the error, in the same form that would be generated by applying an **astore** with an array that was exactly the size of the operand stack.

Since this error processing is done entirely using PostScript features, it is possible for an application program to redefine the standard error processing to provide special handling if desired. The standard processing can be changed in two distinct ways to accomplish different objectives. First, the error reporting mechanism can be changed by redefining the **handleerror** procedure in *errordict.* You might do this to report additional information from the **$error** dictionary, for example, or to print the error message instead of reporting it over the standard output file. This latter change can be extremely useful in certain shared or networked environments, where the error messages get lost or redirected incorrectly. Second, an application may change how any individual error is handled by redefining the default error handler for that error in *errordict*. This can be useful, for example, when testing particular forms of procedures where certain types of errors may occur (or may even be forced) and where you want to control the results from that error. There is no intrinsic limit on what you may choose to do in an error handler; from the interpreter's view, an error handler is just another PostScript program.

Device Management

Most of the PostScript operators that deal directly with the output device are, naturally enough, device-dependent and as such are covered in Section C2, which lists both the functions of device-specific operators and their exact syntax. There are, however, a few operators that are not device-specific and yet deal with the management of the device and its output. These few operators are described here.

Although there are only a few operators in this group, one of them is both common and important. The **showpage** operator takes the images that have been created by a PostScript program in raster memory and transfers them to the output page. The **showpage** operator is the standard method of transferring all the graphic and text images that have been accumulated on the current page to the output device to be placed on a physical page. After completing this transfer, the **showpage** operator also erases the current page, so that no marks are left on it, and partially resets the graphic state, so that the next page to be created starts from a standard condition.

There is also a **copypage** operator, which generates an output page in the same manner as the **showpage** but does not erase the image on the current page and does not reset the graphic state. This operator is primarily useful in debugging a PostScript application and is intended to be used when additional image data is going to be added to the image already created on the current page. For many reasons, primarily having to do with the performance of the output device, **copypage** should be used only when necessary and never in a production application. In particular, it is not necessary to use **copypage** to generate multiple copies of an output page. It is much more efficient and correct to set the variable **#copies** to the desired number of copies. In fact, the **#copies** variable can be used with **copypage** as well as **showpage** – for example, if you are debugging an application that generates multiple copies.

3

Graphics Functions

This chapter deals with the PostScript graphics operators. Since PostScript is designed as a page-description language, these operators form the core of the unique processing power of the language. Here you will find the operations that provide the ability to draw, fill, and image graphic elements onto a page, as well as the special operators that provide text handling.

The chapter is divided into four segments. The first segment discusses the operators that control the graphics state in various ways. Essentially, these break up into two mechanisms: operators that control coordinate transformations and operators that set or report components of the graphics state. The second deals with the general process of constructing or controlling the current path. Such operations are the first steps in producing visible output on a page. The third segment discusses the painting operators that produce the actual marks on the page, including the operators that process sampled data and provide color support. The fourth segment presents the operators that manage fonts and process text output. These four segments represent rough, and rather arbitrary, divisions of operators that are used together to produce the output page; these divisions are intended primarily as a convenient method for organizing the data rather than representing any natural distinction in programming or approach. In actual use, some operators out of each group are essential for successful processing.

3.1 GRAPHICS CONTROL OPERATORS

As mentioned above, the operators that control the graphics state can be divided into two groups: those that control the current transformation matrix (CTM) and those that control any other aspects of the current graphics state. As described in Section A3.3, a variety of operations affect the CTM, because changes to the CTM represent a method of reshaping the graphic objects in user space as well as providing a mapping from the user coordinate system into the device coordinates.

Coordinate Transformation

The operators that have the effect of changing the user coordinate system are, naturally enough, the ones most commonly used in PostScript programming. The **translate** operator effectively moves the origin of the current user coordinate system to a new point, so that the new origin – the point (0, 0) – is set at the point whose coordinates in the old coordinate system are given as an operand to **translate.** As an example, the PostScript statement

> 72 144 **translate**

would move the origin of the user coordinate system to the point (72, 144) in the current coordinates; after the transformation the point (0, 0) would be the same physical point previously described by the coordinates (72, 144).

The user coordinates can also be rotated around their current origin by the **rotate** operator. **rotate** is given an angle as an operand, with positive angles representing counterclockwise rotation. To complete this set of usual changes, the measure on the user coordinate system can be changed using the **scale** operator. The measure, which is the length of one unit, can be changed separately on each coordinate axis by **scale,** which takes one operand as a scale factor for each axis. The scale factor is the amount each unit of the current coordinate system is multiplied by in the new coordinate system. Thus, for example, the effect of the PostScript statement

> 2 4 **scale**

is to multiply each unit on the current x axis by a factor of 2 and to multiply each unit on the y axis by a factor of 4. This results in nonuniform measures, as we discussed before; in this case, for example, a square in the user coordinate system will be represented on the output by a rectangle twice as high as it is wide.

In addition to these "standard" transformations, any possible transformation can be applied to the CTM by using the **concat** operator. This takes a new transformation matrix, formed according to the requirements given in Section A3.5, and concatenates it with the existing CTM to generate a new CTM that incorporates both the old transformation and the new one. Each of the simpler transformation operators actually prepares a transformation matrix and concatenates it in this fashion. Generally, it is not appropriate to replace the CTM, because this makes it impossible to transform the resulting figure by a simple mapping at the beginning of the program, as is normally done by programs that imbed PostScript figures within other pages of output. In addition, there is the possibility of introducing errors into the mapping from the user coordinates to the device coordinates.

All of these transformations can be applied to an arbitrary matrix rather than to the CTM by providing a matrix operand in addition to the other operands that are required for each transformation. The only exception to this is the **concat** operator; to apply an arbitrary transformation, which is defined by one matrix, to another matrix requires the special **concatmatrix** operator. In all cases where the transformation is applied to another matrix, there is no effect on the CTM whatever.

Coordinate Mapping and Control

In addition to the coordinate transformations, there are operators that provide mapping from the current user coordinates to device coordinates and vice versa. This allows a Post-Script application to transform any set of user coordinates into device coordinates and back again, using the CTM as the guide. Such an action effectively mimics the process that the interpreter is going to take when it maps a path or graphic image from the user space into device space, and it provides some user control over the process.

The basic process of mapping from user coordinates to device coordinates is done by the **transform** operator. This operator takes a pair of *x,y* coordinates in user space and maps them into the matching coordinates in device space, using the CTM. The reverse of this process is provided by the **itransform** operator, which provides the *inverse transformation* operation by mapping a pair of *x,y* coordinates in device space into the equivalent user coordinates. There is also a variation on this process, called *delta transformation,* that maps a distance value as given by an *x,y* pair of values into another distance value. The **dtransform** operator provides this mapping from user to device coordinates, and the **idtransform** provides the reverse.

As in the coordinate transformation operators, each of these operators has a variant that takes an arbitrary matrix as an operand and applies the same function to that matrix instead of applying it to the CTM. In this case, of course, none of these operators change either the CTM or the matrix operand, anyway; the difference is that in one case you are mapping from user coordinates to device coordinates using the CTM, and in the other you are mapping from one set of arbitrary coordinates to another, and the results cannot necessarily be related to either the user or the device coordinate systems.

In addition to these mapping functions, PostScript provides operators that aid the programmer in handling the sort of matrices that are associated with coordinate transformations. The **matrix** operator requires no operands and provides an identity matrix as a result. The identity matrix, as you may remember, is a six-element array in the form [1 0 0 1 0 0]. This is very useful for working with many of the other operators, as it provides a known base as a starting point. A related operator is **identmatrix**, which takes an existing matrix and fills it with an identity matrix. The **currentmatrix** operator fills a matrix operand with the current value of the CTM. **defaultmatrix** fills a matrix operand with the default CTM that maps from the default user coordinate system into the device coordinate system, while the **initmatrix** operator sets that matrix as the CTM, effectively resetting the CTM to what it is when the device is powered on. Finally, there is a **setmatrix** operator, which allows an application to set the CTM directly, without the usual concatenation. However, this is intended for setup operations and should never be necessary for ordinary PostScript applications.

Graphics State

The CTM, although important, is only one of many elements in the current graphics state. A complete list of the components of the current graphics state are given below.

Parameter	Type	Value
CTM	array	the current transformation matrix, which provides a mapping from the user coordinates to device coordinates. This can be modified by various PostScript operators as described above. The default value maps the default user coordinates (described in Section A3.3) into the output device coordinates.
color	(internal)	the current color, which is used during painting operations. This may be set and reported using any one of several color models, including black and white (*current gray*) or an actual color value.
path	(internal)	the current path as defined by path construction operators. The initial value is an empty path.
point	2 numbers	the current point, which is the endpoint of the current path. The initial value is undefined.
clipping path	(internal)	the current clipping path, which defines the area on the output page where marks will appear. The initial value is the path that outlines the page size set for the output device, so that the complete printable area of the page is available.
font	dictionary	the current font, which defines the source and shape of text characters on the output device. This is in the form of a font dictionary. The initial value is device-dependent, and for most devices, it is undefined.
line width	number	the thickness of the line produced by the **stroke** operator in user coordinate units. The initial value is 1.
line cap	integer	an integer code that defines the method of finishing open segments of the current path when they are rendered by **stroke**. The possible values and the results are shown under the **setlinecap** operator. The initial value results in square, butt caps.
line join	integer	an integer code that defines the shape of the line at the point where two line segments join. The possible values and the results are shown under the **setlinejoin** operator. The initial value results in mitered joins.

miter limit number a number that defines the maximum length of mitered joins. The number defines the minimum size of a mitered join and so defines the maximum angle at which a mitered join becomes a bevel join. The method of calculation of this number and the results are described under the **setmiterlimit** operator. The initial value results in the change from mitered to bevel joins occurring when line segments join at an angle of about 11 degrees or less.

flatness number a number that defines the degree of accuracy (or the smoothness) of curves on the output device. All curves are rendered as a series of straight lines that approximates the actual curve. This number controls how closely the curve is approximated by specifying the maximum distance, in device pixels, that the straight-line approximation can deviate from the actual curve. Smaller numbers give closer approximations. The initial value is 1.0.

dash pattern (several) defines the dash pattern that will be used when a line is rendered by the **stroke** operator. A full discussion of the correct settings and results of the parameter are described under the **setdash** operator. The initial value of this parameter results in a solid line.

halftone screen (several) a collection of PostScript objects that define the parameters of the current halftone screen. The precise set of parameters and their results are described under the **setscreen** operator. The initial value for this is device-dependent.

transfer procedure the current transfer function, which is a procedure that maps user gray levels into device gray levels. The initial value of this function is device-dependent.

device (internal) an internal set of data that defines the current output device and its characteristics. The initial value is device-dependent.

All these parameters can be both set and recalled by the appropriate PostScript operators. For example, the current point is reported by the **currentpoint** operator and set by the **moveto** operator (and certain other operators, as mentioned above). Most of these parameters, however, are reported by an operator that begins **current . . .** , followed by the name of the desired parameter, and are reset by an operator that begins **set . . . .** Thus you can use **currentlinecap** to report the value of the current line cap and the **setlinecap** operator to change it. Similarly for **setlinewidth, currentlinewidth, setflat** and **current-flat,** and so on. The list of these operators is provided in the listing of operators by type in Section C3; and, of course, they are also listed alphabetically in Section C1.

Graphics Management

Besides all these operators that control and report the various components of the graphics state, there are three more operators that allow control over the graphics state stack itself. These operators allow an application to reset the graphics state to a previous version without specifically resetting individual parameters. This is a very useful feature and one of the most common methods of controlling the execution environment for an application or for any part of an application.

The current graphics state is saved on the graphics state stack by executing a **gsave** operator. The most recently saved graphics state, that is, the one on the top of the graphics state stack, is made the current graphics state by executing the **grestore** operator. Note the difference here between these operators and the more general **save, restore** processing. The **save** operator produces a save object on the operand stack; the **gsave** automatically saves the current state on a special stack. The **restore** restores a specific, previously-saved state, which need not be the most recently saved. The **grestore,** on the other hand, always restores the graphics state on the top of the stack; there is no way to select a specific, previously-saved state. The single partial exception to this rule is the **grestoreall** operator. This restores either the first graphic state on the stack that was saved by a **save** operation or the bottommost one, whichever comes first. In this case, all saved graphics states above the restored state are ignored and discarded.

3.2   FIGURE OPERATORS

These are the operators that create, add to, or control the current path. The current path and related concepts were discussed in Section A4.1. The current path is maintained in the current graphics state and controls the marks that are placed onto the page by the painting operators. The best and easiest method of presenting the path construction operators is probably to take them in normal order of use.

Every new page starts with a new path. The **showpage** operator automatically removes any previous path information, as do several of the painting operators. However, because a path is invisible, it is important to have some way to ensure that there are no extraneous pieces of the path inadvertently remaining on a page when you need to start fresh. PostScript provides a **newpath** operator that clears away any remaining path information and makes the current path empty. Once the current path is empty, the first thing that has to be done is to establish an initial point in a new current path. This is normally done with a **moveto** operator, which sets the current point at the coordinates given as operands. This establishes the starting point for the current path.

You can then add straight line segments to the current path by using the **lineto** operator, which adds a straight line from the current point to a given point, or by using the **rlineto** operator, which adds a straight line from the current point to a point described by a position relative to the current point.

Curved arcs, which are portions of circles, can be added by using the **arc** or **arcn** operators, which draw their arcs in the counterclockwise or clockwise direction, respectively. These two operators alone, among the operators that add segments to the current path, do not require a current point when they are executed. If a current point does not exist, they establish it at the beginning of the arc; if the current point does exist, they add a straight line segment from the current point to the starting point of the arc. Another way to append an arc to the current path is by using the **arcto** operator. This takes a pair of point coordinates and a radius value as operands and creates an arc with the given radius that is tangent to the lines defined from the current point to the first point given as an operand and from that point to the second point.

You can also add segments that are general curves, that is, that are not arcs of circles, by using the **curveto** operator. **curveto** adds a Bezier cubic section to the current path, beginning at the current point. Like the **lineto** operator, the **curveto** operator has a counterpart in the **rcurveto** operator, which performs the same functions but uses coordinates measured relative to the current point rather than fixed coordinates. The relative movement operators (**rmoveto, rlineto**, and **rcurveto**) are particularly useful in situations where you want to create a graphic element that is not fixed to any specific coordinate position.

Finally, you can close an open subpath of the current path by issuing the **closepath** operator. This has two results. First, it automatically appends a straight line segment from the current point to the starting point of the current open subpath, which normally will be the point specified in the last **moveto** or **rmoveto**. Second, when it completes the path, it fills in the two line segments with a line join that ensures that the corner of the figure is correctly formed. This is, generally speaking, always the proper way to complete a figure.

There are also a group of operators that work with or control the entire current path. The **flattenpath** operator converts curved line segments in the current path to straight lines. The precision of the approximation is governed by the *flatness* parameter of the current graphics state. The **pathbbox** operator returns the bounding box coordinates, that is, the coordinates of the lower left and upper right corners of a box that completely encloses the current path. This can be particularly useful for calculating the bounding box information necessary for Encapsulated PostScript format (EPSF) output. The **reversepath** operator reverses the direction of the current path without otherwise changing it. The **strokepath** operator returns the outline for the image that would be created if the current path were imaged using the **stroke** operator, as described below. A similar effect can be obtained for a string of text by using the **charpath** operator.

Clipping

PostScript also defines a clipping path in the current graphics state. Once a path has been constructed, using the path operators described above, that path can be made a clipping path that defines the area within which marks will be applied to the current page. A new path is joined to the current clipping path by the **clip** operator, and the intersection of those two paths becomes the new clipping path. The interior of the current clipping path defines the clipping region, and only marks that fall within the clipping region will show on the page. The new clipping region cannot be larger than the old one—that is why, as stated above, the new clipping path is the intersection of the previous clipping path and the current path. The clipping path can, however, be reset to the default value for the device by using the **initclip** operator. Since the clipping region is formed from the interior points of a region defined by the current clipping path, whether any given point is in the interior is calculated by the usual non-zero winding number rule. To invoke the alternate, even-odd rule for a clipping region, you can use the **eoclip** operator.

3.3 PAINTING OPERATORS

The path construction operators define a current path, but they do not make it visible. That is done by the painting operators, which take the graphic objects that have been created by the other operators and render them into raster memory in the output device, thus producing marks on the output page. The most basic, and most commonly used, painting operators are **stroke** and **fill**, which will be discussed in more detail in a moment. A more sophisticated type of black-and-white painting result is provided by the **image** and **imagemask** operators, while equivalent color processing is done by the **colorimage** operator. These types of paint application are also discussed in this section. Finally, there are a variety of character operators that paint text shapes that are discussed next in this chapter.

The **stroke** operator renders the current path as a line of some thickness. Each segment of the current path, whether straight or curved, is represented by a line centered on the path for that segment. All aspects of how the line is handled are controlled by parameters in the current graphics state. The thickness of the line is set by the *linewidth* parameter in the current graphics state; the line is stroked in the current color; the form of the joins and line caps are set by the *linejoin* and *linecap* parameters; and so on. A full listing of these parameters was provided earlier in this chapter (pages 130–131) as part of the discussion of the current graphics state.

As an alternative to stroking, the current path can be used to define a region to be filled with the current color. If the path consists of disconnected subpaths, all the interior points of all the subpaths are treated together. If any subpaths are open, they are implicitly closed (as though by a **closepath**) before being painted. This painting operation is normally carried out by the **fill** operator, which determines interior points to the current path using the non-zero winding number rule (the PostScript default rule; see Section A4.2); the **eofill** operator performs the same function using the even-odd rule.

Image Processing

Filling and stroking are the two most common methods of creating images on the output page; however, there are other methods that are used for black and white and for color image reproduction. In particular, the **image** operator provides a method for reproducing sampled images, either from external sources such as photographs or from synthetic images that are generated internally, in an effective and device-independent manner. A complete description of the concepts behind image processing is given in Section A4.5.

A sampled image (or just 'image') that is brought into a PostScript application, by whatever means, is rendered onto the output page by the **image** operator. The source image is read by the **image** operator by executing a PostScript procedure, passed to the operator as an operand, that has the responsibility to provide the image data from the source image. There need be no connection between the amount of input provided by this procedure and the natural dimensions of either the source or output images. In this fashion, it is possible to define any variety of procedures to supply the sample data, based on the nature of the source and the requirements of the output.

There is no requirement that all of the image data be present in the interpreter at one time. The data can be processed incrementally and may therefore come from any number of sources. One of the most common is to receive the data over a communications line, possibly the same one that is transmitting the program itself; or the data may be stored in a file and be retrieved from there. The image data could even be generated from within the input procedure itself, thus producing a type of synthetic image.

The **image** operator imposes a coordinate system on the source image data in order to provide some structure for reconstructing the image. The actual coordinate system and the scanning order used in the source image is not a consideration, since, whatever they may be, they can be mapped into the image coordinate system used by the **image** operator. This is done by the normal PostScript coordinate transformation processes.

Although this can be done within a single matrix—as can all linear coordinate transformations—it is best to do it in two steps. The first step transforms the user coordinates to map a unit square—that is, a square with corners at the points (0, 0), (1, 0), (1,1), and (0, 1)—into a space of the correct size and shape that is formed by the transformation operators. Thus, for example, suppose we have a rectangular source image with an aspect ratio (ratio of width to height) of 2:1, and we wish to place this image onto the output page in the region bounded by the points (100, 100), (400, 100), (400, 250), and (100, 250). This region preserves the same aspect ratio, since it is 300 units wide by 150 units high—the same 2:1 ratio. You can map the unit square into this region by using the following PostScript commands:

100 100 translate 300 150 scale

which provide the necessary transformation. Obviously any transformation could be used, rotating or otherwise changing the coordinate system. The only concern is that the aspect ratio must be preserved if you don't want to distort the image.

Next is the process of mapping the image coordinates into the unit square. This is done by a providing an appropriate transformation matrix as an operand to the **image** operator. Here is where the versions of the coordinate transformation operators that can be applied to a general matrix can be useful. The **image** operator default coordinates run from the bottom left corner of the sample to the top right corner, filling in the rows as you go up. If the source image was provided in this same sequence of samples and was 20 samples wide by 10 samples high, then the required matrix would be

[20 0 0 10 0 0]

and this matrix could be generated by the PostScript commands

20 10 **matrix scale**

Notice how the **matrix** operator is used to provide the necessary matrix operand so the **scale** operator does not interact with or change the CTM.

If you had the same image data, but it had been scanned from the top left corner to the bottom right (left to right and top to bottom is the usual format, in fact), the required matrix would be

[20 0 0 −10 0 10]

which maps the coordinates from the image into the unit square quite nicely. Notice that it maps the y axis in the necessary negative direction, since the image coordinates increase down the image while the default coordinates, like the PostScript defaults, increase up the image. Then the translation component is used to move the y axis origin to the top of the image. And thus the transformation is completed. A similar process can be used to map rotated images into the unit square and so on. Although this example is probably most easily done by simply writing it in as a matrix, as we just did, nevertheless it too can be generated by the following PostScript code:

20 −10 **matrix scale**
0 10 **matrix translate**
matrix concatmatrix

If only a portion of the image is desired, a clipping path can be defined and placed into use by executing the **clip** operator in the region prepared to receive the image data. In this way, the portion of the image that falls outside the clipping region will not leave any marks on the output page. As an example, suppose you again have the same sampled image but now wish to display it in a 100-unit square, cropping the left-hand half. Then, after performing the desired coordinate transformation, you could write

```
0          0 moveto
0          0.5 rlineto
0.5        0 rlineto
0          −0.5 rlineto
closepath
clip
```

This establishes a clipping region over the left-hand half of the unit square and will effectively crop the right half of the **image**.

Here, then, is a three-step process to bring image data into the PostScript application and then render it onto the output page with any desired revision to its shape:

1. Transform the user coordinates to map a unit square into the correct region for placement of the image.
2. Crop the image, if desired, by establishing a clipping path over the unit square.
3. Map the image coordinates into the unit square by using the required transformation matrix as an operand to **image**.

The masking process discussed earlier in Section A4.5, functions much like the imaging process. The main difference is that in masking the current color is applied through the mask, and any image data that is on the output page remains in place wherever the mask shields it. This function is provided by the **imagemask** operator, which for the most part takes similar operands to the **image** operator. In particular, it uses the same mechanisms to map its data into the output page.

Color Processing

As described in Section A4.4, PostScript supports three color models: the red-green-blue model, the hue-saturation-brightness model, and the cyan-magenta-yellow-black model. Each of these models can be used to set and to report the current color in the current graphics state.

Most PostScript output devices, however, are simply black and white, and the default PostScript color processing is black and white also. Actually, the normal PostScript model can most easily be thought of as working with white light. Then the amount of light or white to be applied to a page is determined by the **setgray** operator, which takes the percentage of white light as its operand: 1.0 being pure white, 0.0 being pure black, and 0.5 being half-and-half. So this model provides for an infinity of gray shades, from pure black to pure white and every shade in between, subject always to the limitations on the output device's ability to reproduce varying shades of gray, as you learned in Section A4.3. The current gray value in the graphics state is reported by the **currentgray** operator.

Two additional operators govern how gray shades are actually produced on output devices that are not full gray-scale devices. As discussed in Section A4.3, on such devices it is necessary to represent some or all gray values by a halftoning process, which makes use of two functions. The halftone screen defines both a screen and a spot function that together provide a method of representing gray values on devices that do not support a full range of grays. The parameters that determine the screen are established by the **setscreen** operator. Although the default screen values for a device, which are set during device initialization, generally provide good reproduction, it is possible for a PostScript application to make changes to these values for special processing effects by using the **setscreen** operator. In the same fashion, the transfer function for the device, which adjusts the actual gray levels to correspond to the visual perception of gray, can be modified if required by the **settransfer** operator. In both cases, successful use of these operators requires extensive knowledge of the device characteristics.

Color can be represented and used in PostScript applications even when the output device does not provide color output. In that case, the current color is translated into a shade of gray for output on the device; however, the components of the color are kept individually internally so that the image can be correctly rendered on either a color or a black-and-white device. The current color can be set in any of the color models by the **setrgbcolor, sethsbcolor,** or **setcmykcolor** operators. Similarly, the current color can be reported in any of the three color models as required; transformations are provided from one model to another to generate the same output.

In addition to setting the current color, PostScript provides several operators that allow setting various functions within the current graphics state that govern transfer of color images to the output device. These are all analogous to the similar black-and-white operators discussed above. A **setcolorscreen** function allows setting halftone screen parameters individually for each color component; also, a setcolortransfer provides the transfer functions for each color component. It is somewhat more likely that the color screens might need adjusting for a specific color output than that a gray value would need to be adjusted, because the interaction of the color screens on particular tints can cause unwanted patterns to appear. In any case, the ability to make any required adjustments is provided.

A **colorimage** operator can be used to transfer sampled images in color to the output page. The **colorimage** operator is a logical extension of the **image** operator to full-color processing. Mapping and other functions of the **image** operator remain the same for **colorimage**. However, the **colorimage** operator provides two formats for the procedure that supplies the data values for the sampled image. They are necessary because there are two possible methods of providing color data when the original image is sampled. In both cases, the source that produces the image data values must provide one sample for each spot in each of the color values, and which color values are used depends on the color model. For explanation here, we will use the red-green-blue model, but either of the other two models would work the same way.

The first method of providing the necessary sample values is to sample each color component separately. In such a case, the effect is similar to passing the image through the sampling process three (or four) times, with each pass generating one set of values. In this case, the **colorimage** operator must have one procedure for each color component. In the case of the red-green-blue model, there will be three procedures, with the first procedure providing the red values for **colorimage**, the second providing the green, and the third, the blue. These three procedures are each called in turn by **colorimage** and must each read a given amount of data for their color component and pass it on to the operator each time they are called. The amount of data that each produces must be the same for each cycle of calls, and the storage used by each one for its string of color values must be separate.

The second method produces a complete set of values for each sample in one string. This generally happens when the scanning device can provide all three (or four) values in one pass of the image. In this case, there is only one input procedure required for **colorimage** and the samples will be in a form something like this:

Bits / Sample	Data			
1	RGBRGBRG	BRGBRGBR	GBRGBRGB	RGBRGBRG ...
2	RRGGBBRR	GGBBRRGG	BBRRGGBB	RRGGBBRR ...
4	RRRRGGGG	BBBBRRRR	GGGGBBBB	RRRRGGGG ...
8	RRRRRRRR	GGGGGGGG	BBBBBBBB	RRRRRRRR ...

with bit values in each byte reading in normal fashion, from the high-order value on the left to low-order on the right and the bytes numbered from 0 on the left.

The **colorimage** operator uses a boolean operand to distinguish between these two forms. If the value is *true,* the operator expects data to be produced by multiple procedures; and if the value is *false,* then it expects to use a single procedure. In any case, however, the **colorimage** operator must have all the sample values for each spot as it is processing. The only question is whether the values are all interleaved within the sample data itself – in which case the single procedure is used; or the data is provided in discrete form – in which case the multiple procedures allow **colorimage** to perform the interleaving process internally.

When an application is preparing color output for four-color printing (and therefore using the cyan-magenta-yellow-black color model), it is often necessary to provide certain special processing to produce the correct color output. The functions required provide for black generation and undercolor removal as discussed in Section A4.4. PostScript provides two special operators to handle these processes: **setblackgeneration** and **setundercolorremoval.** The **setblackgeneration** procedure defines a PostScript procedure that generates a black component based on the values in the current color for the cyan, magenta, and yellow components. The **setundercolorremoval** defines a PostScript procedure that is given a color value between 0 and 1 as an operand and returns a new value in the range +1 to −1, to indicate the amount of decrease or increase in the color component. The equivalent reporting operators for each of these are **currentblackgeneration** and **current-undercolorremoval**.

All of these operators have significant requirements before you can use them successfully. The complete description of the operators and their operand requirements is given in Section C1. In addition, not all implementations of the PostScript interpreter provide full color processing, particularly implementations on black-and-white devices; consult your device documentation for information on whether these operations are available.

3.4 FONT OPERATORS

Most pages of output have a substantial amount of text on them. In fact, the ability to combine text and graphics in a natural way is one of the outstanding strengths of the PostScript language. It follows quite naturally, then, that handling text output is one of the more important tasks that the PostScript interpreter undertakes. In order to provide fast, flexible, and efficient processing for text within a document, PostScript implements a variety of specialized operators that deal with handling and output of character data. We refer to these collectively as font operators.

The font operators provide essentially two general functions. First, they transfer characters from strings to the output page using the current font dictionary; and, second, they select and manipulate the font dictionaries. All of these processes were discussed in Chapter A5. Here the focus is on the actual operators that implement these processes in their normal sequence of use – a natural approach to describing their function.

Font Use

To begin with, you must establish a current font in the current graphics state. The current font provides a set of character outlines in a specific size that is used whenever the interpreter is called on to produce text output. The first requirement is to select the character outlines, or font, that is desired. This is done by the **findfont** operator, which takes the name of the desired font as an operand and looks it up in the **FontDirectory** maintained by the interpreter. You will see a little further on how fonts become enrolled into the **FontDirectory.** If **findfont** finds a font in the **FontDirectory** whose key value matches the name given to it as an operand, it retrieves that font (actually a font dictionary) from the **FontDirectory** and returns it to the operand stack. If it does not find a matching key, it may take one of several error actions; usually, it will issue an error message and substitute another font. Next, the font must be created in the correct point size for the output. All PostScript built-in fonts are defined as one-point outlines to begin with and must be enlarged to the desired size before use. This is done by the **scalefont** operator, which takes a numeric operand specifying the desired point size along with the font to be scaled. It then creates a tranformation matrix that scales the font outlines to the correct size, stores the matrix into the font, and then returns the font to the operand stack. Finally, the **setfont** operator takes the font from the operand stack and makes it the current font in the graphics state.

In addition to the **scalefont** operator, there is a **makefont** operator that performs essentially the same function, except that you provide the desired tranformation matrix for **makefont** as an operand. This is especially useful if you want to generate characters that are not uniformly scaled, for example, that are more or less wide than they ordinarily would be for the point size defined. However, there are no intrinsic limitations on the matrix provided, and any arbitrary transformation can be used.

Once the current font is set, there are a variety of operators that are used to paint characters onto the output page. The most common of these is the **show** operator. The **show** takes a string of characters and uses the current font to paint each character on the output page, beginning at the current point and adjusting the current point after each character is painted by the width of the character as specified in the font metrics and modified by the point size. There are also several variants on **show** that provide special processing features while performing the same basic function of displaying a character string. The **ashow** operator adjusts the width of each character by a supplied value. The **widthshow** adjusts the width of a specific character by a supplied value. Both of these operators take a width operand as a pair of x and y values. They are primarily used for printing lines of text that are justified on both margins; the **ashow** is generally used to make small adjustments throughout the line of text, while the **widthshow** typically makes larger adjustments at an appropriate character, such as a space. It is possible to combine the effects of these two operators by using the **awidthshow** operator, which provides both services at once. Finally, the **kshow** operator allows an application to define an arbitrary procedure that is called between the printing of each character of the string. The name **kshow** stands for 'kern show'. It is intended to provide a means to adjust the spacing between certain pairs of characters, a process called *kerning* in regular typesetting. However, there is no restriction on what the procedure that is defined by **kshow** can do.

There are two more general font operators that provide various services for using fonts. The **currentfont** operator retrieves the current font from the graphics state and pushes it onto the operand stack for further processing. The **stringwidth** operator takes a string for an operand, like the **show** operator, and calculates the width of the string in the current font. That is, it returns the displacement value that would be applied if the string were shown on the page in the current font. This is especially useful for justification and centering, where the length of the printed string is an important piece of information for the calculations required.

Font Definition

Most of the fonts used by PostScript applications are already defined for the application and loaded into the device. Sometimes, however, it is necessary for a user to define a font for a special purpose. Such a font can be developed in one of two ways. A user may modify an existing font definition to provide certain new features, or a user may create an entirely new font.

In either case, the font must be defined as an ordinary PostScript dictionary with the correct and appropriate entries, as defined and discussed in Section A5.4. Once such a font dictionary has been created, it is loaded onto the operand stack. The **definefont** operator takes the name for the new font and the font dictionary off of the operand stack, checks the font for certain format requirements – for example, the necessary required entries – and, if it passes the checks, enrolls it in the **FontDirectory** under the given name.

The most common user-defined fonts are modifications of existing fonts with a specialized encoding vector. This process is also discussed in Section A5.4. Taking that as an example of defining a new font by using a previous one, you would follow these steps.

First you make a copy of the existing font that you wish to modify. Notice that this must be a new object, not a duplicate of the existing font. The best way to do this is to create a new dictionary and copy each element from the old dictionary into the new one except the **FID** entry, which is the internal information for each font and will be filled in by the **definefont** operator. Second, you replace those elements in the font that you want to change. In this example, that would mean replacing the **Encoding** entry whose associated value would normally be the **StandardEncoding** vector with a new encoding vector, which you might call 'NewEncoding'. Finally, use the **definefont** operator to enroll the new font dictionary with a new name in the **FontDirectory**. Now, you can use the normal **findfont, scalefont, setfont** sequence to retrieve the new font, and the normal operation of **show** will use the new encoding to select the characters to be shown.

It is also possible to use this same basic technique to modify the font metrics by redefining (or adding, if it isn't already present) the **Metrics** entry in the font dictionary. For a composite font, you may also change the font metrics by redefining the **CDevProc** for the font. Another common change would be to use outlined character shapes instead of filled ones by changing the **PaintType** of the font. All these changes can be done by redefining an existing font and enrolling it as a user-defined font.

Although quite a bit more complex, it is also possible to build a new, user-defined font from scratch. This is a more complex process because PostScript assumes that a font is reasonably well-behaved and because there is not much error recovery or correction possible from within the font machinery. Essentially, a user-defined font must behave pretty much like all other PostScript fonts in order to function correctly. In particular, a user-defined font must have the required key entries as explained in Section A5.4, it must have a **FontType** value of 3, and it must provide a special procedure named **BuildChar**.

The **BuildChar** procedure is the heart of this process. When the PostScript interpreter goes to print a character that has been selected out of a user-defined font, it first checks to see if the character is in the font cache. If not, it executes the font's **BuildChar** procedure, with the requested character code as an operand. The **BuildChar** must use this information to construct the desired character image. Typically, a **BuildChar** procedure will use the character code provided as an index into an array (similar to the **Encoding** array) that will provide the necessary procedures to set the character metrics, actually draw the character shape, and paint the character in some fashion. Obviously, the **Build-Char** may choose to do this by means of some mechanism similar to that of normal font construction, that is, by developing a dictionary of these procedures for each character (similar to the **CharStrings** dictionary) where the key is provided by the array that is indexed by the character code. However, any mechanism that accomplishes the task is generally acceptable.

The interpreter executes the **BuildChar** within a **gsave, grestore** pair, so that any changes made to the graphics state within the **BuildChar** will not affect subsequent processing. In addition, the interpreter concatenates the CTM for user space at the time the character is printed with the transformation matrix provided by the **FontMatrix** entry in the font definition, in order to generate a new CTM that is in place for the **BuildChar**. The origin of this space is the character origin in user space, and the CTM that is in place provides that the processes executed in character coordinates by **BuildChar** will translate correctly to the user space, so that the character will have correct size and orientation on the output page. Each call to **BuildChar** is therefore quite independent; the **Build-Char** should draw and paint the desired character in character coordinates, using (0, 0) as the character origin and treating the process as a new graphic object each time. The **BuildChar** procedures should start by setting a current point, then drawing the character and painting it, without being concerned about the final position of the path.

Before the character is actually drawn, procedures are required to establish the character metrics for the font machinery. This is done by executing one of three operators: **set-cachedevice, setcachedevice2,** or **setcharwidth.** The **setcachedevice** and **setcache-device2** operators establish both the character width and the necessary metric information for handling the process of putting the resulting bitmap into the font cache. If the character should not be cached for any reason, then the **setcharwidth** operator must be used to set the character width. This is the value that will be used to move from the present character origin to the next, and that is why the position of the current point at the end of a **BuildChar** procedure is not an issue. A complete description of each of these operators is provided in Section C1.

After using one of these required operators to define the character metrics, the **Build-Char** procedure can proceed to draw the character outline and paint it, using standard PostScript operators. After it does so, the font machinery transfers the resulting character image onto the page and also stores it into the font cache if the font cache metrics were defined for this character using **setcachedevice** or **setcachedevice2.** It also then moves the current point in user space to the position defined by the character metric information provided. This sets up the character origin for the next character to be displayed.

Composite Fonts

In addition to the standard font operators, there are a few operators that are designed to work with composite fonts. You will remember the discussion of composite font construction and use in Section A5.6 describing the hierarchical structure of composite font mappings. Because of this hierarchical structure, there must be some additional font operators for composite fonts.

The **setcachedevice2** operator is designed for use with character definitions in composite fonts. It provides width and cache information for both writing mode *0* (the normal horizontal writing mode) and writing mode *1* (vertical writing). There is also a **rootfont** operator that returns the root font in the current hierarchy, that is, the hierarchy that was established by the most recent **setfont**. The **findencoding** operator retrieves a specified encoding array. Also, a special character display operator called **cshow** takes a procedure and a string as operands and executes the procedure for each character in the string after executing the font mapping algorithm for the current font. During the execution of a **cshow,** the current font is the base font selected by the font mapping algorithm for the given character. The **cshow,** however, differs from the character painting operators like **show.** It does not image the character, and it does not update the current point. It is left to the procedure operand to take those actions if they are desired. After the execution of **cshow,** the current font is the same as when the processing started, and the current point is wherever it was set by the final invocation of the procedure operand.

Operator Reference

– a presentation of all general PostScript operators and selected device-dependent operators, listed alphabetically and by type.

This section lists all generally accessible PostScript operators alphabetically along with certain other procedures that are defined in a standard PostScript system. The other procedures are those that are executed and used in a fashion similar to operators, or they are support procedures, such as error-handling.

Because PostScript is a growing and dynamic environment, not all of the following operators are in every PostScript interpreter. In particular, the packed array operators and certain of the cache handling operators are implemented only in versions of the PostScript interpreter that are 25.0 or later. In the same way, the composite font handling operators, discussed earlier in Section A5.6, are implemented only on certain devices; the same is true of some of the color operators. All the operators that are not present in the standard versions of the PostScript interpreter – defined here as PostScript version 38.0, used in the Apple LaserWriter – are marked as shown in the operator reference:

*colorimage

The ultimate authority for what operators are present in your version of the interpreter is the controller manufacturer (generally, the name on the printer) and, secondarily, the source of the interpreter running in the controller. The utility files available for this book also give details of techniques for listing out the contents of the various dictionaries; you can use these techniques to list for yourself the operators that have been implemented in your version of the interpreter.

The operators have been divided into two sections: general operators and device-specific operators. This division represents a rough distinction between those operators that are not dependent on specific features of the device for their correct operation and those that are. For example, the definition and operation of an **add** or a **showpage** do not depend on the type of device that is being used, whereas the definition and use of **manualfeed** clearly depend on the availability of some method to feed a single sheet of paper (or whatever the output medium may be) into the output device. The general operators are presented in Section C1. The device-specific operators are presented in Section C2 along with a discussion of the device characteristics that are required for these operators to function correctly.

The listings are shown in a standard format, as follows:

operator

operand1 operand2 . . . **operator** result1 result2 . . .

A description of operator action and results.

EXAMPLE: where appropriate, one or more examples of use of the operator will be provided and discussed.
TYPE: the type of operator
ERRORS: list of possible error results from this operator
ASSOCIATED: list of related operators

In this format, *operand1, operand2,* . . . are the operands required by **operator** in the sequence in which they would normally be written in PostScript code; that is, *operand1* is at the *bottom* of the stack, *operand2* is above *operand1* on the stack, and so on. The results are listed in the same order, with *result1* being at the lowest position on the stack, *result2* above it, and so on. We will use the conventional symbol, '–' to indicate that no operand is required on the stack or that no result is left on the stack by the given operator. The symbol '|–' will indicate the bottom of the stack, that is, that there are no objects remaining on the stack below it.

If the conventional '–' is used as a result, that does not imply that the stack is empty on completion of the operation; it only states that the operator has added nothing to the contents of the stack and whatever objects were on the stack below the defined operands (if any) are still there. On the other hand, if the '|–' is shown as a result, there are no objects remaining on the stack below this symbol.

The examples are presented in three different formats that vary according to the requirements of the operator under discussion. The first format looks like this:

operand1 operand2 etc . . . operator $\Rightarrow$ result1 result2 etc . . .

In this format, the operands are written as they would be in an ordinary PostScript program, followed by the operator itself. The arrow, '$\Rightarrow$', indicates execution of the operator by the interpreter and divides the operator and its operands from the results left on the operand stack after execution. These results are in the sequence used above for the definition of the operator; namely, *result1* is on the bottom of the stack, *result2* is above it, and so on. This format is both compact and easy to read, as long as the sequence of operands or results is not misunderstood.

The second format provides information identical to that shown above, but in a more expanded and more graphic form. This format is used wherever there is a question of sequence of stack contents or operation. The format looks like this.

Stack in: (top operand)   operator   ⇒   Stack out: (top result)
        (etc . . .)   (etc . . .)
        (operand2)   (result2)
        (operand1)   (result1)

This format is used where a graphic depiction of the contents and sequence of operands or results and the condition of the stack seem important for complete understanding of the operator. The format shows the contents of the operand stack at the beginning of excution of the operator on the left, the operator itself in the center, and the results left on the stack on the right. The same indicator of interpreter action, '⇒', is used as in the previous example. The important feature here is that the stack contents, for both operands and results, follow the display presented by the interpreter itself (by the **pstack** operator, for example). For this reason, it seems the clearest way to display stack structure and contents for certain operators.

As you can see, the two formats translate directly into one another. The sole difference between these two formats is the presentation of the condition of the stack before and after the execution of the operator. The second format is more graphic but less compact; therefore, it is used only for operators where the graphic portrayal of the stack will significantly clarify the operator action.

The third format is quite different from the first two. In this format, you are presented with a series of PostScript statements that generate some result or output, which is shown in an accompanying figure. The series of statements are a form of small program in themselves and are used to generate output that illustrates the action of the operator under discussion. Very often, these also illustrate the requirements for setting up and using the operator. These small programs are complete in themselves regarding the action of the operator and the results depicted; as such, they can be entered directly into a PostScript interpreter as presented and will produce the result shown in the accompanying figure. However, they are not complete programs in that they generally do not have any of the normal and required housekeeping functions, and they do not have the necessary display commands to produce a page of output.

The TYPE shows the type of the operator under consideration according to the list of types presented earlier. If an operator falls into more than one type category – for example, **get** – all the types are listed; the type of the operand will determine the type of the operator in actual use. The list of errors presents all the error types that can be generated by this operator. The error messages are also listed in alphabetical sequence as part of the definitions in this section, for two reasons. First, the listing provides a convenient reference. Second, the errors are themselves PostScript procedures and can be accessed and redefined as required, as discussed in Section B2.3. The list of associated operators lists other operators that are related to the given operator in one way or another. This is particularly helpful when the operator referenced does not quite do what you need done.

A series of abbreviations for operands and results indicates their types and characteristics. In particular, descriptive names are used for required numbers, such as *angle* or *sum*. Unless otherwise stated, all numbers may be either integer or real. Also, for many operators that reference strings or arrays, the result returned to the top of the operand stack will be identical with the operand or a portion of one of the operands. In such cases, the identifier used on both sides of the operator listing will be identical (if the objects are identical) or have 'sub-' as a prefix to the result (if the result is a portion of the operand named). As an example, if the **getinterval** operator is applied to a string, the resulting return is a portion of the original string and is labeled 'substring' to indicate that fact.

The abbreviations or names used for both operands and results are, for the most part, self-explanatory. The list below shows the abbreviations that are used most often.

any	any valid PostScript object
array	any PostScript array
bool	a boolean value: either *true* or *false*
composite object	any PostScript composite object: an array, packed array, dictionary, or string
dict	a PostScript dictionary
file	a PostScript file object
font	a PostScript font
int	any integer number
key	a key entry into a PostScript dictionary
mark	a mark object
matrix	a six-element PostScript coordinate description or transformation matrix (see Section A, Chapter 3, "Page Structure," for a full discussion of the required elements).
num	any number (integer or real)
packedarray	any PostScript packed array
proc	a PostScript procedure
real	any real number
string	any PostScript string
value	an object associated with a key in a PostScript dictionary

General Operator Definitions

#copies

       −   **#copies**   int

is a PostScript variable that defines the number of copies of a page of output that are produced when a **showpage** operator is executed. This is not a PostScript operator itself but is a special variable defined in *userdict*.

    This variable can be redefined to alter the number of copies produced; this is the preferred method of producing multiple copies of the same page. By changing **#copies**, you allow the PostScript printing machinery to take maximum advantage of parallel operation and reproduction process. You can change the number of copies produced by all subsequent **showpage** operations by redefining the **#copies** variable to be the number of copies that you want output. The default value of **#copies** is 1 and is defined in *userdict*. You may redefine the variable by changing it in *userdict* or by redefining it in some other dictionary that is higher on the dictionary stack.

    EXAMPLE:

        #copies   ⇒   1

        /#copies 3 def

will cause the next **showpage** and all subsequent **showpage**s to create three copies of the page output.

TYPE:	Device
ERRORS:	stackoverflow
ASSOCIATED:	**showpage, banddevice, framedevice, userdict**

=

any	**=**	—

produces a string representation of *any* on the standard output file. The string representation is the one that is generated by applying the **cvs** operator to the object and then using the print operator to generate the output. The object is popped from the stack.

Generally, this operator does not produce very satisfactory results; it will display only certain types of data (numeric, string, name, operator, or boolean) and displays those without any indication of type (see Example 2 below). Any other type of object is displayed as '--nostringval--', which is the result of applying the **cvs** operator to the object. In most cases, you will prefer to use = = and its derivatives.

= is a built-in PostScript procedure; it is not an operator. In this context, the name '=' is in no way special, and it must be used just like any other PostScript procedure name – delimited by white space or special characters. The actual procedure can be retrieved from *systemdict* and examined if you desire.

EXAMPLE 1:

> Stack in: (asdfg)   =   ⇒   Stack out: —

and shows the result 'asdfg' on the system output file (see Section B2.2 for a discussion of system files).

EXAMPLE 2:

> Stack in: /name   =   ⇒   Stack out: —

and shows the result 'name' on the system output file. Note that this result cannot be distinguished from the result that you would get from using = on the string (name).

EXAMPLE 3:

> Stack in: [1 2 3]   =   ⇒   Stack out: —

and shows the result '--nostringval--' on the system output file.

TYPE:	File
ERRORS:	stackunderflow
ASSOCIATED:	==, **cvs, print, stack**

==

any	**==**	—

produces an edited string representation of *any* on the standard output file. The string is produced and then edited to indicate the type of object; for example, a string is represented delimited by ( ), an array is delimited by [ ], a name literal is displayed with a leading /, an operator is shown delimited by --, and so forth. The object is popped from the stack.

Generally, this operator produces the most satisfactory results for displays; it provides a correct and consistent representation of an object, and, more importantly, it allows you to distinguish types of objects by the output. Note also that the string, name, and array representations are in a form that can be reintroduced to the interpreter to generate the same object. In most cases, this will be your preferred display method for objects on the stack.

= = is a built-in PostScript procedure; it is not an operator. In this context, the name '==' is in no way special, and it must be used just like any other PostScript procedure name: delimited by white space or special characters.

EXAMPLE 1:

Stack in: (asdfg)   ==   ⇒   Stack out: –

and shows the result '(asdfg)' on the system output file (see Section B2.2 for a discussion of system files). This result differs from the output of =, since it includes the string delimiters '(' and ')'.

EXAMPLE 2:

Stack in: / name   ==   ⇒   Stack out: –

and shows the result '/name' on the system output file.

EXAMPLE 3:

Stack in: [1 2 3]   ==   ⇒   Stack out: –

and shows the result '[1 2 3]' on the system output file.

TYPE: File
ERRORS: stackunderflow
ASSOCIATED: =, **print, pstack**

[

–   [mark

pushes a mark object onto the stack. The mark object is a special PostScript object that indicates a position on the stack. All marks are identical, and the stack may contain many of them at once. In particular, the **mark** operator is a synonym for [.

Generally, the [operator is used to mark the beginning of a collection of PostScript objects that will be formed into an array by use of the] operator. This collection of objects need not be of any predetermined length, and so the mark is used as a delimiter for the array construction mechanism. See the discussion under the] operator and under the **mark** operator for further information.

EXAMPLE:

Stack in: −   [⇒   Stack out: −mark−

TYPE: Array
ERRORS: stackoverflow
ASSOCIATED: **], array, astore, mark**

]

creates a new array of $n+1$ objects out of the objects any_0 to any_n stored above the topmost *mark* on the stack. The objects and the mark are removed from the stack, and the objects are stored into the new *array* which is returned to the top of the stack.

It is common to think of the related operators, [and], as working like string delimiters, (and). However, the [operator simply pushes a mark onto the stack; it does not begin any special processing mode. Any objects following the mark are processed by the interpreter as they are presented; therefore the array generated by processing a subsequent] operator will contain the executed results of processing the objects presented, not necessarily the objects themselves. (see Example 2 below).

EXAMPLE 1:

Stack in: (asd)   ]   ⇒   Stack out: a three-element array;
          2   element 0 equals 1,
          1   element 1 equals 2,
          −mark−   and element 3 equals
                                                                    the string (asd).

Such an array is conventionally displayed by the PostScript interpreter and in written PostScript as [1 2 (asd)]; however, in this context, that has the potential to be somewhat confusing because the sequence to generate the 'Stack in' could also be written '[1 2 (asd)'. Actually, the −mark− on the stack can be generated by either the [or the **mark** operator interchangeably.

EXAMPLE 2:

Suppose that you present the interpreter with the following set of objects arranged in the ordinary order of writing PostScript: [1 2 add 3 4 mul]. As the interpreter processes this collection of objects, you will generate the following result:

Stack in: 12   ] $\Rightarrow$ Stack out: [3 12]
          3

that is, a two-element array consisting of the result of processing the elements on the stack that are generated by the commands within the delimiting brackets, in this case, 3 and 12. The point here is that the interpreter continues to process objects after a [operator in the ordinary way. Therefore, at the time of execution of the] operator, there are only two elements above the mark: the result of the operations '1 2 add' and '3 4 mul', as shown under 'Stack in' above. Thus you see that the [is in not a special character or delimiter (as '(' is for strings), and does not affect the operation of the interpreter.

TYPE: Array
ERRORS: unmatchedmark, VMerror
ASSOCIATED: **[, array, astore, mark**

abs

num1   **abs**   num2

returns the absolute value of *num1*. The absolute value is the value of *num1* without any sign; effectively **abs** changes negative numbers to positive ones. The type of *num2* is the same as the type of *num1*, unless *num1* is the maximum negative integer, in which case *num2* is real, since the 2's complement notation used by the PostScript interpreter to represent negative integers allows the storage of a negative integer that is one greater than the maximum positive integer.

EXAMPLE:

3.12 abs $\Rightarrow$ 3.12
−4.1 abs $\Rightarrow$ 4.1
4 abs $\Rightarrow$ 4   (an integertype result)

TYPE: Mathematical
ERRORS: stackunderflow, typecheck
ASSOCIATED: **mod, neg, floor, round**

add

num1 num2   **add**   sum

adds two numbers, *num1* and *num2,* together to give result *sum*. The type of *sum* depends on the type of *num1* and *num2*. If these are both integers, *sum* will be an integer type; otherwise, it will be a real number.

EXAMPLE:

2 4 add	$\Rightarrow$	6	(an integertype result)
2.0 4 add	$\Rightarrow$	6.0	(a realtype result)

TYPE: Mathematical
ERRORS: stackunderflow, typecheck, undefinedresult
ASSOCIATED: **div, idiv, mul, sub**

aload

array	**aload**	$a_0 \ldots a_n$ array
packedarray	**aload**	$a_0 \ldots a_n$ packedarray

successively pushes all $n+1$ elements of *array* or *packedarray* onto the operand stack, where $n+1$ is the number of elements in *array* or *packedarray,* and finally pushes the array itself.

This operator is a way of loading the individual elements of an array, in either packed or unpacked format, onto the operand stack.

EXAMPLE 1:

Stack in: [1 2 3]   aload $\Rightarrow$ Stack out: [1 2 3]
3
2
1

EXAMPLE 2:

Stack in: [(asd) [1 2 3] / name]   aload $\Rightarrow$ Stack out: [(asd) [1 2 3]
/ name]
/ name
[1 2 3]
(asd)

TYPE: Array
ERRORS: invalidaccess, stackunderflow, stackoverflow, typecheck
ASSOCIATED: **array, astore, get, getinterval**

anchorsearch

		if found:
string pattern	**anchorsearch**	suffix match true
		if not found:
		string false

determines if the intial part of *string* matches the string *pattern*. That is, that *string* is at least as long as *pattern* and the characters are identical. If the initial substring of *string* matches *pattern*, **anchorsearch** returns *string* in two pieces: *match*, which matches the *pattern*, and *suffix*, which is the remainder of *string*. Finally, it pushes the boolean value *true* onto the stack for testing. If the initial substring of *string* is not identical to *pattern*, **anchorsearch** returns the *string* unchanged and pushes *false* onto the stack.

Note that, in both cases, the output returned is part of the original string. Since strings are composite objects, any changes that use these parts of the string will also affect the original string representation. This remains true even if you redefine those parts of the string. (See the discussion of simple and composite objects in Section A2.2).

EXAMPLE 1:

Stack in: (asd)　　　anchorsearch　　⇒　　Stack out: true
　　　　　(asdfg)　　　　　　　　　　　　　　　　　　(asd)
　　　　　　　　　　　　　　　　　　　　　　　　　　(fg)

EXAMPLE 2:

Stack in: (sdf)　　　anchorsearch　　⇒　　Stack out: false
　　　　　(asdfg)　　　　　　　　　　　　　　　　　　(asdfg)

TYPE:	String
ERRORS:	invalidaccess, stackunderflow, stackoverflow, typecheck
ASSOCIATED:	**search, token**

and

　　　bool1 bool2　　**and**　　result

performs a logical **and** of *bool1* and *bool2* and returns the boolean value *result*.

EXAMPLES:

true	true	and	⇒	true
false	true	and	⇒	false
false	false	and	⇒	false

int1 mask   **and**   result

performs a bitwise **and** of the integers *int1* and *mask* and returns the integer value *result*. The result is a straight, bit-wise **and**, taking *int1* and the associated *mask* as simple bit representations; no character values are used, and the operands must be integers. The *mask* controls the value of *result*: where the *mask* has a bit set to 0, the *result* will always be 0; and where the *mask* has a bit set to 1, the *result* will have a bit value equal to the corresponding bit position in *int1*.

EXAMPLES:

2 1	and	$\Rightarrow$	0
3 1	and	$\Rightarrow$	1
8 4	and	$\Rightarrow$	0
3 10	and	$\Rightarrow$	2

TYPE: Logical
ERRORS: stackunderflow, typecheck
ASSOCIATED: **not, or, true, false, xor**

arc

x y rad ang_1 ang_2 **arc**   —

appends a counterclockwise circular arc to the current path. If a current point is defined, a straight line is appended to the current path from the current point to the beginning of the arc. The arc has the point (x, y) as a center, *rad* as a radius, and begins at the point defined by the vector that begins at (x, y) with length *rad* and forms an angle ang_1 with the positive x axis. The arc ends at the point defined by a similar vector that has the same beginning and length and forms an angle ang_2 with the positive x axis. The arc therefore forms the portion of the circle that has (x, y) as its center, *rad* as its radius, has an interior angle of $(ang_2 - ang_1)$ degrees, and begins at ang_1 degrees from the x axis.

If there is a current point, the **arc** operator draws a straight line from that point to the beginning point of the arc and then constructs the arc. If there is no current point, the arc begins at the point defined above. In either case, the current point at the end of the operation is the end point of the arc.

The operands must all be numeric, but there are no restrictions on value. Positive values for ang_1 and ang_2 represent angles measured counterclockwise from the positive x axis, while negative numbers represent angles measured clockwise from the same axis.

Remember, however, that the arc is always drawn in a counterclockwise direction. (See Example 3 below). The arc produced is circular in user space. If the user coordinates have been transformed, for example, by a **scale** or **rotate** operator, the resulting arc will be transformed in the same ways. In particular, if the user coordinates have been scaled nonuniformly so that x- and y-axis units of measure represent different distances, the arc produced will be elliptical when you print it on the device.

All curves that are generated in PostScript are, in fact, approximated to a high degree of accuracy using Bezier cubic curves, which are more fully described under the **curveto** operator. For all drawing purposes you can treat the curves generated by **arc** as circles. However, if you apply the **pathforall** operator to the current path after using an arc operator, you will not have the **arc** parameters returned to you, but rather you will get the equivalent **curveto** parameters (see Figure C1.1).

Figure C1.1   **arc** operator

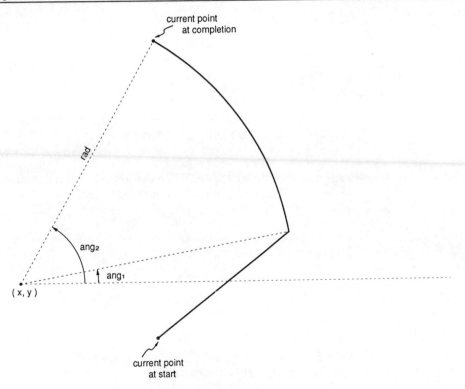

EXAMPLE 1:

```
newpath              % set for no current point
100 100 40 0 50 arc  %draw arc
stroke               %image the path for display
```

draws a simple arc and paints it.

EXAMPLE 2:

```
110 90 moveto        % set current point
100 100 40 0
50 arc               %draw arc preceded by straight line
stroke               %image the path for display
```

draws the same arc as EXAMPLE 1 but preceded by a straight line.

EXAMPLE 3:

```
newpath                % set for no current point
100 100 40 0 −50 arc   %draw arc
stroke                 %image the path for display
```

reverses ang_2 and then draws the arc. Note that the arc still is drawn in a counterclockwise direction and therefore paints all around the circle.

```
     TYPE:  Path
   ERRORS:  stackunderflow, typecheck, rangecheck
ASSOCIATED:  arcn, arcto, curveto
```

arcn

$x\ y\ rad\ ang_1\ ang_2$ **arcn** —

appends a clockwise circular arc to the current path. If a current point is defined, a straight line is appended to the current path from the current point to the beginning of the arc. In all respects, **arcn** behaves like **arc**, except that it draws in the opposite, or negative, direction (see Figure C1.2).

Figure C1.2 **arcn** operator

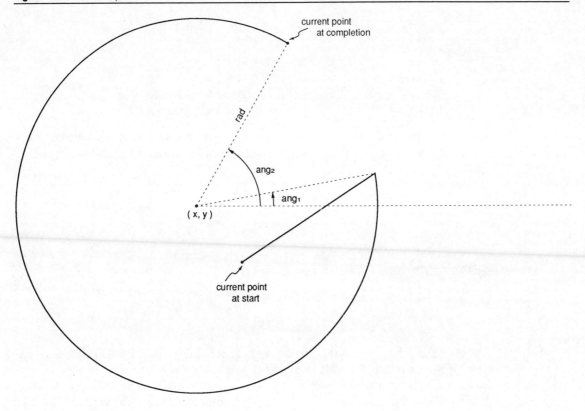

EXAMPLE 1:

        newpath   % set for no current point
        100 100 40 0 50 arcn   %draw arc in negative direction
        stroke   %image the path for display

draws a simple arc and paints it.

EXAMPLE 2:

        newpath   % set for no current point
        100 100 40 0 −50 arcn   %draw reverse arc
        stroke   %image the path for display

reverses ang_2 and then draws the arc. Note that the arc still is drawn in a clockwise direction. Compare this result with the output from Example 3 under the **arc** operator, above.

        TYPE: Path
        ERRORS: stackunderflow, typecheck, rangecheck
    ASSOCIATED: arc, arcto, curveto

arcto

    x_1 y_1 x_2 y_2 rad   **arcto** xt_1 yt_1 xt_2 yt_2

appends an arc of a circle to the current path, generally preceded by a straight line segment. If the current point is denoted as (x_0, y_0), the arc is constructed as a portion of the circle that is tangent to two lines: from (x_0, y_0), the current point, to (x_1, y_1) is called the *first tangent line;* and from (x_1, y_1) to (x_2, y_2), called the *second tangent line.* The two lines form a vee, and the circle whose center is at distance *rad* from the two lines. The circle touches the two lines at exactly two points: (xt_1, yt_1), which lies alongs the lines from (x_0, y_0), the current point, to (x_1, y_1); anbd the point (xt_2, yt_2), which lies along the line defined by (x_1, y_1) and (x_2, y_2), which fors the other side of the vee. Mathematically, a curve and a line are tangent if they touch at one, and only one, point. These two points, (xt_1, yt_1) and (xt_2, yt_2), are the tangent points of these two lines to the circle.

The circle has a radius *rad,* and its center is the only point that is located at a distance *rad* along a perpendicular to both tangent lines. The arc is drawn from the point (xt_1, yt_1) to the point (xt_2, yt_2). A straight line segment is drawn from the current point, (x_0, y_0), to the first tangent point, (xt_1, yt_1) unless the current point is identical to the first tangent point. If the current point is undefined, you will get the error **nocurrentpoint**. In this, **arcto** differs from **arc** and **arcn**, which will execute without a current point. At the completion of the operation, the current point is always (xt_2, yt_2).

If the three points, (x_0, y_0), (x_1, y_1), (x_2, y_2), all lie along the same line, then there is no circle that can be drawn that is tangent to both lines, because the point that should be the center of the circle is undefined. In this case, the **arcto** operator will generate the straight line from (x_0, y_0) to (x_1, y_1), and the arc is considered to have a 0 radius. Also, the two tangent points, (xt_1, yt_1) and (xt_2, yt_2), are identical and are exactly the same as (x_1, y_1).

The **arcto** operator returns the values of the two tangent points on the stack; these are for information only and are generally popped off the stack before execution of any further operations (see Figure C1.3).

Figure C1.3 The **arcto** operator

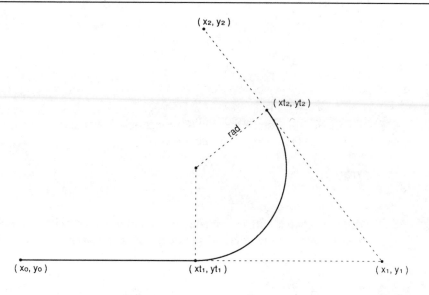

EXAMPLE 1:

100 80 moveto	% set current point
100 140 160 140 40 arcto	%draw arc
4 {pop} repeat	%throw away unnecessary coords
stroke	%image the path for display

draws a simple arc and paints it.

EXAMPLE 2:

100 80 moveto	%set current point
150 80 30 160 40 arcto	%draw arc
4 {pop} repeat	%throw away unnecessary coords
stroke	%image the path for display

draws an arc where the points that define the first tangent line and the second tangent line lie on different sides of the current point, thus creating an arc that curves back over the initial line segment.

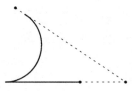

TYPE: Path
ERRORS: stackunderflow, typecheck, rangecheck, nocurrentpoint
ASSOCIATED: **arc, arcn, curveto**

array

    int   **array**   array

creates *array* that initially contains *int* null objects as entries. *int* must be a non-negative integer less than the device-dependent maximum array length.

EXAMPLE:

Stack in: 2 array   Stack out: [–null– –null–]

TYPE: Array
ERRORS: rangecheck, stackunderflow, typecheck, VMerror
ASSOCIATED: **[,], aload, astore, packedarray**

ashow

wx wy string   **ashow**   –

prints *string* in a similar way to the **show** operator, except that, during the printing process, **ashow** adds *wx* to the *x* width of each character and *wy* to the *y* width. This changes the effective spacing between characters, adjusting it by a fixed amount, *wx* and *wy*, for each character. The operands *wx* and *wy* are in the current user coordinates, not in character coordinates.

If the current font is a composite font, **ashow** prints the *string* using the appropriate mapping algorithm (see the discussion of composite fonts in Section A5.6) and raises the **rangecheck** error if the mapping of *string* is incomplete.

EXAMPLE:

/Helvetica findfont 20 scalefont setfont
100 100 moveto
(Normal spacing) show
100   65 moveto
4 0 (Wide spacing) ashow
100   10 moveto
2 4 (staircase) ashow

Normal spacing

Wide spacing

staircase

TYPE: Font
ERRORS: invalidaccess, invalidfont, nocurrentpoint, rangecheck, stackunder-
             flow, typecheck
ASSOCIATED: **show, kshow, widthshow, awidthshow**

astore

any_0 .. any_{n-1} array   **astore**   array

fills *array* with any_0 through any_{n-1}, where *array* has a length of *n*. The **astore** operator first removes *array* from the stack and determines its length, and then stores the *n* remaining operands from the stack into *array*, with the top of the stack becoming the last or n^{th} element in *array*, the next becoming the next-to-last element, and so on until all *n* positions have been filled. After all positions of *array* have been filled, it is returned to the stack.

This operator is a way of storing individual elements into an array and returning the filled array onto the operand stack. Note that **astore** does not work for packed arrays; instead you must use the **packedarray** operator.

EXAMPLE 1:

3 array	⇒	[–null– –null– –null–]
(as) 1 5 3 array astore	⇒	[(as) 1 5]

EXAMPLE 2:

/Test 3 array def		
(as) 1 5 Test astore	⇒	[(as) 1 5]

Note that *Test* has been effectively redefined, so that the array on the stack is, in fact, *Test* itself.

> TYPE: Array
> ERRORS: invalidaccess, stackunderflow, typecheck
> ASSOCIATED: **aload, array, packedarray, put, putinterval**

atan

> num denom   **atan**   angle

returns the angle whose tangent is *num* divided by *denom*. This function is commonly called the *arctangent* or *inverse tangent* of the result of the division. The resulting *angle* is between 0 and 360 degrees and is always a real number.

The sign of *num* and the sign of *denom* determine together what quadrant of the circle *angle* lies in. Although a complete discussion of the trigonometric relationships is beyond the scope of this book, Examples 2 and 3 give you examples of how the signs interact to generate the various angles. As a reminder, the tangent of 90 degrees (and all multiples of 90 degrees) is 0, while the tangent of 45 degrees (and all its multiples) is 1.

EXAMPLE 1:

72.654 1 atan	⇒	89.2114
72.654 10 atan	⇒	82.1631
72.654 100 atan	⇒	35.9999
72.654 1000 atan	⇒	4.15547

This example shows the effect of using the *denom* as a scale factor to generate different arctangents.

EXAMPLE 2:

1 1 atan	⇒	45.0
1 –1 atan	⇒	135.0

$$-1 \quad 1 \; \text{atan} \quad \Rightarrow \quad 315.0$$
$$-1 \quad -1 \; \text{atan} \quad \Rightarrow \quad 225.0$$

Notice that the signs have an individual effect; it is not the sign of the result of the division that counts. A negative *num* defines the resulting *angle* as being below the horizontal *x* axis, or greater than 180 degrees, while a negative *denom* defines the resulting *angle* as being across the vertical *y* axis, or between 90 and 270 degrees.

EXAMPLE 3:

$$1 \quad 0 \; \text{atan} \quad \Rightarrow \quad 90.0$$
$$0 \quad -1 \; \text{atan} \quad \Rightarrow \quad 180.0$$
$$0 \quad 1 \; \text{atan} \quad \Rightarrow \quad 0.0$$
$$-1 \quad 0 \; \text{atan} \quad \Rightarrow \quad 270.0$$

This example shows you the boundaries of the sectors defined by the positive and negative values of *num* and *denom*. You should also note that, although *denom* can be zero, both *num* and *denom* cannot be zero.

> TYPE: Mathematical
> ERRORS: stackunderflow, typecheck, undefinedresult
> ASSOCIATED: **sin, cos**

awidthshow

> cx cy char wx wy string   **awidthshow**   –

prints the characters in *string* in a manner similar to show but combines the effects of **ashow** and **widthshow**. Like **ashow**, the operation of **awidthshow** adds the distance *wx* to the *x* width of each character and *wy* to the *y* width after imaging each character. In addition, like **widthshow**, if the integer value of the character currently being imaged matches the integer value *char*, the values *cx* and *cy* are added to the current point after imaging the character and before imaging the next character.

If only base fonts are being used, *char* is an integer value between 0 and 255 that represents the character number in the current encoding of the character that is to be adjusted. If composite fonts are being used, the integer value of the character being shown is calculated in the following way. The font number, *f*, and the character code, *c*, that are selected by the font mapping algorithm are combined into a single integer number according to the the **FMapType** of the immediate parent of the selected base font using the following rule:

FMapType 2   the integer value is $(f \times 256) + c$.
FMapType 3   the integer value is $(f \times 256) + c$.
FMapType 4   the integer value is $(f \times 128) + c$.
FMapType 5   the integer value is $(f \times 128) + c$.
FMapType 6   the integer value is $(f \times 256) + c$.

EXAMPLE:

/Helvetica findfont 10 scalefont setfont
100 100 moveto
(Normal spacing) show
100   85 moveto
4 0 8#040 2 0 (Wide spacing) awidthshow

where 8#040 is the octal value in the standard encoding for a space character.

Normal spacing

W i d e   s p a c i n g

TYPE: Font
ERRORS: invalidaccess, invalidfont, nocurrentpoint, rangecheck, stackunder-
            flow, typecheck
ASSOCIATED: **show, kshow, widthshow, ashow**

banddevice

matrix width height proc   **banddevice**   —

installs a band buffer as the raster memory for an output device and sets certain parameters
for that device. Basically, a band device is one that paints a page of output by using a
series of of rectangular *bands* of pixels rather than painting an entire page, or *frame,* at
a time. A dot-matrix printer is an example of a band device, while most laser printers
are frame devices.

The **banddevice** operator is used to define important characteristics of a full page
of output. Each page is defined as being 8 × *width* pixels wide by *height* pixels high, with
the width and height being determined by the actual physical configuration of the output
device. The *matrix* operand is the default transformation matrix for the device and should
reflect the transformation necessary to map user coordinates into device coordinates. After
execution of **banddevice**, the *matrix* operand becomes the current transformation matrix
(CTM). Also, the current clipping path is determined and set by **banddevice** using the
operands *width, height,* and *matrix.*

The *proc* operand is a procedure that is executed every time a page is output on the
device, normally by the **showpage** operator. This procedure must create the page output. In a band device, this will include use of the **renderbands** operator and possibly
other device-dependent operations as well. See the description of **renderbands** for further information. In particular, *proc* is responsible for implemention of the **#copies**
parameter, which is described in more detail under **#copies** and **showpage**.

The **banddevice** operator is one of two operators (**banddevice** and **framedevice**) that
define types of raster output devices. If a device uses bands for output, then **banddevice**
and **renderbands** will be defined in the intepreter and **framedevice** will not be defined.

TYPE: Device
ERRORS: stackunderflow, typecheck
ASSOCIATED: **framedevice, nulldevice, renderbands, showpage**

begin

dict   **begin**   –

pushes *dict* onto the dictionary stack and makes it the current dictionary.

TYPE: Dictionary
ERRORS: dictstackoverflow, invalidaccess, stackunderflow, typecheck
ASSOCIATED: **end, dictstack, countdictstack**

bind

proc   **bind**   proc

replaces executable operator names in *proc* with the actual operators themselves. Every time that **bind** finds a name in *proc* that has type **operatortype**, it replaces the name with the operator object. If the name is a procedure – which will have the type **arraytype** – the name is not replaced.

The effect of **bind** on *proc* is to replace all operator names in *proc* with the actual operators. This has two main results. First, the interpreter will execute a procedure that has been bound faster than one that has not been bound, since it doesn't have to look up the operator names in the current dictionary stack. Secondly, and less importantly for most application programs, the use of **bind** "locks in" the value of the operator in the procedure. This means that if anyone should redefine the operator after the **bind** has been performed, the procedure will still execute correctly, using the expected operator.

You should note that any redefinition of an operator (for example, **showpage**) will automatically change the type from **operatortype** to **arraytype**, even if the redefinition is to the same operator and is itself bound. Therefore, it is safe to bind any procedure as long as all required redefinitions are performed before the definition of the given procedure.

EXAMPLE 1:

```
/T1 {showpage} bind def
/T2 {showpage} def
/showpage {} def
/T1 load            ⇒        {--showpage--}
/T2 load            ⇒        {showpage }
```

where '--operator--' is the conventional way that the interpreter displays operator objects. The net result of the above sequence is that execution of T1 will cause a **showpage** to occur, while execution of T2 will cause nothing to happen, since you have redefined **showpage** to a null procedure.

EXAMPLE 2:

```
/T1 {showpage} bind def
/T2 {showpage} def
/showpage {showpage} def
/T3 {showpage} bind def
/T1 load          ⇒          {--showpage--}
/T2 load          ⇒          {showpage }
/T3 load          ⇒          {showpage }
```

This illustrates the change that occurs in the bind operation once a redefinition has occurred. Procedure *T1* is still bound to the operator value, but procedures *T2* and *T3* carry the procedure definition. This happens even though *T3* has been bound and even though the procedure *showpage* is defined as the **showpage** operator. In other words, if you redefine the *showpage* procedure again, both *T2* and *T3* will be affected, while *T1* will remain unchanged.

EXAMPLE 3:

```
/lineTest
      { currentpoint exch 540 lt
               { pop }
               { 12 sub 72 exch moveto }
      ifelse
      }
bind def
```

This definition will bind all operators in the procedure *lineTest,* including **pop, sub, exch,** and **moveto,** the operators that are in the two procedures that are excuted by the **ifelse** conditional test. This illustrates that the **bind** operator does not distinguish levels of procedures within the procedure being bound. However, if we define the following procedure

```
/nextLine
      {12 sub 72 exch moveto } def
```

and substitute this for the previous false branch above, as follows:

```
/lineTest
      / currentpoint exch 540 lt
               { pop }
               { nextLine }
      ifelse
      }
bind def
```

then the procedure *nextLine* will not be bound, and this version of *lineTest* will execute more slowly than the first version.

TYPE: Miscellaneous
ERRORS: stackunderflow, typecheck
ASSOCIATED: **load, type**

bitshift

int shift   **bitshift**   result

shifts the binary representation of *int* to the left for *shift* bits and returns *result,* which is an integer. Bits shifted out are lost; bits shifted in are zero. If *shift* is negative, the shift is performed to the right. In all cases, both *int* and *shift* must be integers.

Bitshift operations are often used to perform the equivalent of multiplication and division. Use of a bitshift to perform division by a shift to the right using a negative *shift* value requires some special care, however. This operation will only produce an arithmetically correct result for positive values of *int,* since the sign bit will be shifted in for a negative *int*. This is necessary so that, in cases where a direct bitshift is intended, the high-order bit, which is used as the sign bit, will be correctly propagated.

EXAMPLE:

4	1 bitshift	$\Rightarrow$	8
−4	1 bitshift	$\Rightarrow$	−8
4	−1 bitshift	$\Rightarrow$	2
−4	−1 bitshift	$\Rightarrow$	2147483646

TYPE: Boolean
ERRORS: stackunderflow, typecheck
ASSOCIATED: **and, or, not, xor**

bytesavailable

file   **bytesavailable**   int

returns the number of bytes immediately available from *file*. The operator returns −1 if end-of-file has been reached or if the number of bytes is indeterminate for other reasons; for example, when running in the interactive mode, a **bytesavailable** query on the *%stdin* file will yield −1.

TYPE: File
ERRORS: ioerror, stackunderflow, typecheck
ASSOCIATED: **file, read**

cachestatus

—   **cachestatus**   bsize bmax msize mmax csize cmax blimit reports the measurements for current consumption and maximum limit of several types of font cache resources: bytes of bitmap storage (bsize and *bmax*); number of font/matrix combinations (msize and *mmax*); total number of cached characters (csize and *cmax*); and the limit on the number of bytes occupied by a single cached character (blimit). All these measurements, except *blimit*, are informational only; they cannot be changed by a PostScript program. The value for *blimit* can be changed by using the **setcachelimit** operator. See Section B3.3 for a full discussion of font cache use and management.

TYPE:	Font
ERRORS:	stackoverflow
ASSOCIATED:	**setcachelimit, setcacheparms**

ceiling

num1   **ceiling**   num2

returns the least integer value that is greater than or equal to *num1*. The type of *num2* is the same as the type of num1.

EXAMPLE:

4.2 ceiling	⇒	5.0	
−4.2 ceiling	⇒	−4.0	
5 ceiling	⇒	5	(an integertype result)

TYPE:	Mathematical
ERRORS:	stackunderflow, typecheck
ASSOCIATED:	**floor, round, truncate, cvi**

charpath

string bool   **charpath**   —

makes character path outlines for the characters in *string* as if it were shown at the current point using **show**. These outlines are added to the current path and form shapes suitable for general filling, stroking, or clipping. If *bool* is *true*, the resulting path is suitable for filling or clipping; if *bool* is *false*, the result is suitable for stroking. This distinction affects only stroked fonts (**PaintType** 1); when the current font is an outline font (**PaintType** 0 or 2), the results will be identical. Nevertheless, I recommend that you use *false* for results that you want to **stroke** and *true* otherwise; such code will work no matter what the font type.

The path created by the **charpath** operator is quite complex, and it is generally not good practice to use a long string or a very large point size when using this operator. Because of the complexity of character shapes, it is quite possible to get a **limitcheck** error if you attempt to do too much at once. Also, as long as any portion of the current path has been generated with a **charpath**, the **pathforall** operator is disabled.

If **charpath** is applied to a composite font, the font-mapping algorithm is invoked in the ordinary way to determine the character's path, and a **rangecheck** error will be raised if the mapping of *string* is incomplete.

EXAMPLE:

```
/Helvetica findfont 36 scalefont setfont
100 100 moveto
(SHOW) false charpath
stroke
```

SHOW

TYPE: Path
ERRORS: invalidaccess, limitcheck, rangecheck, nocurrentpoint, stackunderflow, typecheck
ASSOCIATED: **show, clip, pathbbox**

clear

|– any$_1$ . . . any$_n$ **clear** |–

pops all objects from the operand stack.

TYPE: Stack
ERRORS: (none)
ASSOCIATED: **count, pop, cleartomark**

cleartomark

mark obj$_1$ . . . obj$_n$ **cleartomark**   –

pops all objects from the operand stack above the first *mark* object on the stack. The *mark* is also popped from the stack. If there is no mark on the stack, **cleartomark** executes the **unmatchedmark** error.

TYPE: Stack
ERRORS: unmatchedmark
ASSOCIATED: **mark, clear, pop, counttomark**

clip

–   **clip**   –

intersects the inside of the current path with the inside of the current clipping path to produce a new, smaller current clipping path. The inside of the current path is determined by the non-zero winding number rule normally used by PostScript (see Section A4.2), while the inside of the current clipping path is determined by whatever rule was in effec-tat the time the path was created. Before determining the intersection, any open sub-paths of the current path are implicitly closed.

In general, the **clip** operation produces a new path, whose interior (as defined by the non-zero winding number rule) is all areas that were inside of both of the original paths – the current path and the current clipping path. By definition, therefore, the in-terior of the new clipping path (called the *clipping region*) will be smaller than or equal to the previous clipping region. There is no way to enlarge the clipping region except by using the **initclip** or **initgraphics** operators, which return the clipping region to its initial value. Generally, the correct way to move back to a larger clipping region is to use the **gsave** operator to save the current graphics state before setting a new clipping region and use the **grestore** operator to restore the graphics state after you use it. Since the current clipping path is a part of the graphics state, this has the effect of enlarging the clipping region by restoring the clipping path previously in use.

Note that **clip**, unlike some of the more common path operators such as **fill** and **stroke**, does not clear the current path. Therefore, unless a **newpath** operator has been explicitly invoked, operations that add segments to the current path may give unexpected results if used after a **clip** operation.

EXAMPLE:

```
100 100 moveto          %generate a rectangular path
100 130 lineto
160 130 lineto
160 100 lineto
closepath
clip                    %set as clipping region
gsave
    .2 setlinewidth
    stroke              %and also stroke it so we can see it
grestore
newpath
130 115 moveto
150 90 lineto
170 115 lineto
150 140 lineto
closepath
stroke
```

This example creates a rectangular path and sets it as a clipping region. It also strokes the path with a thin line to show the clipping region boundaries. Then it draws and strokes a diamond-shaped figure. As you expect, only the portions of the diamond that fall within the clipping region are shown on the output. (The dotted lines show the remainder of the diamond that lies outside of the clipping region.)

TYPE: Path
ERRORS: limitcheck
ASSOCIATED: **eoclip, clippath, initclip**

clippath

–   **clippath**   –

sets the current path to be identical to the current clipping path. This operator is useful for determining the exact extent of the current imageable area, which is the current clipping region.

EXAMPLE:

```
gsave
100 100 moveto          %generate a rectangular path
100 130 lineto
160 130 lineto
160 100 lineto
closepath
clip
/Helvetica findfont 12 scalefont setfont
110 110 moveto
(Clip this line) show
clippath
.2 setlinewidth
stroke
grestore
```

This example creates a rectangular path, uses it to set the current clipping region, and then sets a line of type that falls partially within and partially without the clipping region. Then it resets the current path to the current clipping path, using **clippath**, and strokes the path.

Clip this l

TYPE:	Path	
ERRORS:	(none)	
ASSOCIATED:	**clip, eoclip, initclip**	

closefile

file	**closefile**	—

closes *file*; that is, it breaks the association between the file object and the underlying file itself. If *file* is an output file, **closefile** performs a **flushfile** before closing the file in order to ensure that all data has been transmitted. The complete set of actions taken by **closefile** depends on the device and the device file structure.

TYPE:	File	
ERRORS:	ioerror, stackunderflow, typecheck	
ASSOCIATED:	**file, flushfile, read, status**	

closepath

—	**closepath**	—

closes the current subpath by appending a straight line segment from the current point to the starting point of the subpath – generally the point defined in the most recent **moveto**. If the current subpath is already closed or the current path is empty, **closepath** does nothing. In all cases, **closepath** terminates the current subpath. Any subsequent segments that are added to the current path will define a new subpath, even if it starts from the point that is the current point after the execution of **closepath**.

TYPE:	Path	
ERRORS:	limitcheck	
ASSOCIATED:	**fill, lineto, moveto, stroke**	

*colorimage

width height samp matrix		
proc$_1$ [... proc$_{ncolors}$]		
multiproc ncolors	**colorimage**	—

renders a sampled image with one, three, or four color components onto the current page. The first four operands, *width, height, samp,* and *matrix,* are identical in form and use the first four operands of the **image** operator. If there is more than one color component, the *samp* operand applies equally to all.

The number and use of the procedure operands depend on the last two operands: *multiproc* and *ncolors*. The *multiproc* operand is a boolean value that indicates the presence

* This operator is not present in PostScript version 38.0.

of multiple procedure operands and, by extension, multiple sources of color data; the *ncolors* operand is an integer that can have values of 1, 3, or 4 to show the number of color components represented in the sample data. If *ncolors* is 1, the image is black and white, and the sample values are levels of gray; this is exactly equivalent to an image processed by the **image** operator. If *ncolors* is 3, the sample values represent RGB color values, where high values indicate lighter shades. If *ncolors* is 4, the sample values represent CMYK color values, where high values indicate darker shades. On an output device that can produce four-color images, a CMYK color image will bypass the automatic generation of black and removal of the undercolors that is associated with an RGB color image.

When *multiproc* is *false*, it indicates that there is only one procedure operand and that the stream of color data contains combined coding for each of the colors as determined by *ncolors*. When *multiproc* is *true*, it indicates that there is one procedure operand for each color, where *ncolors* is the number of colors. Generally, each procedure will handle its own stream of color data. If *ncolors* is 1, there will only be a single input procedure ($proc_1$) whether *multiproc* is *true* or *false*.

The **colorimage** operator is a natural extension of the concepts and operation of the **image** operator to a full-color environment. As discussed above, the use of **image** is precisely identical to the use of **colorimage** with *ncolors* set equal to 1. The **colorimage** operator and the associated color procedures are only defined in those versions of the PostScript interpreter that support color operations. See Section A4.4 for a detailed description of color operations.

Use of the *colorimage* operator after **setcachedevice** within a **BuildChar** operation to create a character image is not allowed; an attempt to do so will raise the **undefined** error.

Programmers should note that errors in image processing, particularly in setting up or handling procedures, may cause the operator to lose control of the output device. If that happens, the output device may reset automatically, or it may require resetting manually before continuing operations. In either case, all page data is lost, and connection with the output device may have to be reestablished.

TYPE: Painting
ERRORS: invalidaccess, limitcheck, rangecheck, stackunderflow, typecheck, undefinedresult, undefined
ASSOCIATED: **image, imagemask**

concat

matrix   **concat**   –

concatenates *matrix* with the current transformation matrix, conventionally indicated as 'CTM'. The **concat** operator replaces the CTM by *matrix* × CTM. The effect is to define a new set of user coordinates, whose *x* and *y* values are related to the former user coordinates by transforming them by *matrix*. See Section A3.5 for a description of coordinate tranformations.

The operand *matrix* must be a six-element numeric array, or you will get the **type-check** error.

TYPE: Coordinate
ERRORS: stackunderflow, typecheck
ASSOCIATED: **concatmatrix, currentmatrix, matrix, setmatrix, scale, rotate, translate**

concatmatrix

matrix1 matrix2 matrix3   **concatmatrix**   matrix3

returns the result of multiplying *matrix1* by *matrix2* as *matrix3*. Note that *matrix3* must be on the stack prior to execution and that the operation of **concatmatrix** overlays all elements of *matrix3*. This operator does not access the CTM and has no effect on it.

TYPE: Coordinate
ERRORS: invalidaccess, stackunderflow, typecheck
ASSOCIATED: **concat, currentmatrix, matrix**

copy

array1   array2   **copy**   subarray2
or   *or*
string1 string2   substring2

copies all elements of *array1* or *string1* into *array2* or *string2*. The types of the two operands must be the same: either both must be arrays or both must be strings. The length of the second operand must be at least the length of the first; **copy** returns the changed elements of the second operand onto the stack as *subarray2* or *substring2*. If the second operand is longer than the first, the remaining values are unaffected by the **copy**. Unlike all other operations on composite objects, **copy** generates a new composite object from the old one by making copies of the values in the object; it does not just share values as you would after a **dup**, for example. However, **copy** performs this transfer of values only at the first level of the object. If the object itself contains composite objects (an array within an array, for example), those objects still share values with the original version of the object. See Section A2.2 for a discussion of simple and composite objects.

EXAMPLE:

/Array$_1$ [1 2 3 4] def
/Array$_2$ 5 array def
Array$_1$ Array$_2$ copy   ⇒   [1 2 3 4]
Array$_2$ ⇒   [1 2 3 4 –null–]

packedarray array2   **copy**   subarray2

copies all elements of *packedarray* into *array2*. Note that in this case *array2* cannot be a packed array; **copy** cannot copy into a packed array, since all packed arrays are read-only. However, **copy** will copy from a packed array, as it does here, into an ordinary array. The **length** of *array2* must be at least that of *packedarray;* **copy** returns the changed elements of *array2* onto the stack. If *array2* is longer than *packedarray,* the remaining values are not affected by the operation.

dict1 dict2   **copy**   dict2

copies all elements of *dict1* into *dict2*. The **length** of *dict2* must be 0; that is, *dict2* must be empty when the **copy** takes place; **copy** returns the revised *dict2* onto the stack. *dict2* must have a **maxlength** that is at least as great as the **length** of *dict1*. As before, **copy** produces a new composite object by copying the values in *dict1,* not just the object. However, **copy** performs this transfer of values only at the first level of *dict1*. If *dict1* itself contains composite objects (an array or a string, for example), those objects in *dict2* will still share values with the original version of the object in *dict1*. See Section A2.2 for a discussion of simple and composite objects.

$any_1 \ldots any_n \; int$ **copy** $any_1 \ldots any_n \; any_1 \ldots any_{int}$

when the top element on the operand stack is a non-negative integer *int,* **copy** pops *int* and then duplicates the top *int* elements of the operand stack.

EXAMPLE:

Stack in:	2	**copy**	$\Rightarrow$	Stack out:	4
	4				5
	5				4
	6				5
					6

TYPE:	Array, Dictionary, Stack, String
ERRORS:	invalidaccess, rangecheck, stackunderflow, stackoverflow, typecheck
ASSOCIATED:	**dup, get, put, length, maxlength**

copypage

—   **copypage**   —

outputs one copy of the current page onto the current output device without erasing the current page or changing the graphics state. In this, it differs from the more usual **showpage**, which clears the page and resets the graphic state after output.

The use of **copypage** should be confined to debugging PostScript programs or to unusual situations where incremental printing of pages is essential. The **copypage** operator has two fundamental drawbacks. First, it generally slows down the output device because it prevents parallel processing and the use of multiple frame buffers; for some fast printers, this slowdown may be especially severe. Second, use of **copypage** does not conform to the requirements of the 2.0 document-structuring conventions and makes a document containing it nonconforming. This can be of particular concern when working in a shared or networked environment.

If you want to generate multiple copies of a document, use the **#copies** parameter, which is discussed above. If you need to save the graphics state for reuse after printing, use the following sequence: **gsave showpage grestore.**

TYPE: Device
ERRORS: (none)
ASSOCIATED: **showpage, erasepage, initgraphics, #copies**

cos

angle **cos** real

returns the cosine of *angle,* which is taken as an angle in degrees. The cosine will always be a real number between 0 and 1.

EXAMPLE:

90 cos	⇒	0.0
360 cos	⇒	1.0
450 cos	⇒	0.0
60 cos	⇒	0.5
45 cos	⇒	0.707107
225 cos	⇒	− 0.707107

TYPE: Mathematical
ERRORS: stackunderflow, typecheck
ASSOCIATED: **atan, sin**

count

|− any$_1$ . . . any$_n$ **count** |− any$_1$ . . . any$_n$ n

counts the number of objects on the operand stack and returns that integer, *n,* to the top of the stack.

EXAMPLE:

Stack in: (asdfg)   count   Stack out: 2
/name   (asdfg)
|−   /name
                                           |−

TYPE: Stack
ERRORS: stackoverflow
ASSOCIATED: **countdictstack, countexecstack, counttomark**

countdictstack

—   **countdictstack**   int

counts the number of dictionaries on the dictionary stack and returns that integer, *int*, to the top of the operand stack. For a discussion of the names and operation of the Post-Script stacks, see Section A1.3.

TYPE: Dictionary
ERRORS: stackoverflow
ASSOCIATED: **count, dict, begin, end, length**

countexecstack

—   **countexecstack**   int

counts the number of objects on the execution stack and returns that integer, *int,* to the top of the operand stack. For a discussion of the names and operation of the PostScript stacks, see Section A1.3.

TYPE: Control
ERRORS: stackoverflow
ASSOCIATED: **count, execstack**

counttomark

mark obj_1 . . . obj_n **counttomark**   mark obj_1 . . . obj_n n

counts the number of objects on the operand stack above the first *mark* and returns that integer, *n,* to the top of the stack. The count does not include the *mark* itself.

EXAMPLE:

Stack in:	(asdfg)	counttomark	Stack out:	2
	/name			(asdfg)
	–mark–			/name
	[1 2]			–mark–
				[1 2]

TYPE: Stack
ERRORS: stackoverflow, unmatchedmark
ASSOCIATED: **mark, cleartomark, count**

*cshow

proc string   **cshow**   —

invokes *proc* once for each operation of the font-mapping algorithm on each character in *string*. The current font during the execution of *proc* is the base font that is ultimately selected by the font mapping algorithm, and the current point is the point at which the character being used would image; however, **cshow** does not image the character and does not update the current point, although *proc* may do both of these and probably would at least provide for imaging the character. There are three values on the stack when *proc* is invoked. These are 1) the character code of the character being processed, 2) the *x* value of the width vector for that character in user coordinates, and 3) the *y* value of the width vector for that character in user coordinates. The **cshow** operator does not remove these operands; the *proc* should consume them. When *proc* finishes execution, the original current font is restored.

The purpose of **cshow** is to provide careful positioning of each character while allowing you to make use of the mapping algorithm for composite fonts.

The **cshow** operator may be used with a base font. The mapping algorithm for a base font simply selects consecutive characters from *string*.

TYPE: Font
ERRORS: invalidaccess, invalidfont, stackunderflow, rangecheck, typecheck
ASSOCIATED: **show, currentfont, ashow, kshow**

*currentblackgeneration

—   **currentblackgeneration**   proc

returns the current black-generation procedure, *proc,* from the current graphics state. The black-generation procedure is defined only in those versions of the PostScript interpreter that support color operations. See Section A4.4 for a detailed description of color operations and also see the discussion of black generation under the **setblackgeneration** operator.

TYPE: Graphics
ERRORS: stackoverflow
ASSOCIATED: **setblackgeneration**

currentcacheparms

—   **currentcacheparms**   mark lower upper ...

returns the current cache parameters, *lower* and *upper,* on the operand stack, preceded by a *mark*. The *mark* is used because the number of cache parameters is variable; see the **setcacheparms** operator for more detail.

* This operator is not present in PostScript version 38.0.

TYPE: Font cache
ERRORS: stackoverflow
ASSOCIATED: **cachestatus, setcacheparms**

*currentcmykcolor

—   **currentcmykcolor**   cyan magenta yellow black

returns the four components of the current color parameter from the current graphics state according to the cyan-magenta-yellow-blackmodel. Each of these values is a number between 0 and 1 that indicates the percentage of cyan, magenta, yellow, and black in the current color. See the discussion under the **setcmykcolor** operator and in Section B3.3 for a more complete explanation.

TYPE: Graphics
ERRORS: stackoverflow
ASSOCIATED: **setgray, fill, show, stroke, currentgray, currenthsbcolor, currentrgbcolor**

*currentcolorscreen

—   **currentcolorscreen**   rfreq rangle rproc
                                                 gfreq gangle gproc
                                                 bfreq bangle bproc
                                                   grayfreq grayangle grayproc

returns the twelve color halftone screen components from the current graphics state. These color screen components are defined only in those versions of the PostScript interpreter that support color operations; other versions support only the gray components, which are accessed through the **currentscreen** operator. See Section A4.4 for a detailed description of color operations.

TYPE: Graphics
ERRORS: stackoverflow
ASSOCIATED: **setcolorscreen, currentscreen, setscreen**

*currentcolortransfer

—   **currentcolortransfer**   rproc gproc bproc grayproc

returns the four color transfer functions *rproc* for the red color component, *gproc* for the green color component, *bproc* for the blue color component, and *grayproc* for the black color component – that define the current color in the current graphics state. These color components are defined only in those versions of the PostScript interpreter that support

* This operator is not present in PostScript version 38.0.

color operations; other versions support only the gray component, which is accessed through the **currenttransfer** operator. See Section A4.4 for a detailed description of color operations.

> TYPE: Graphics
> ERRORS: stackoverflow
> ASSOCIATED: **setcolortransfer, currenttransfer, settransfer**

currentdash

> — **currentdash** array offset

returns the current dash setting from the current graphics state. The current dash pattern is defined by *array,* and the current dash phase, or offset, is defined by *offset.* See the discussion under the **setdash** operator for a more complete explanation of the values and use of *array* and *offset.*

> TYPE: Graphics
> ERRORS: stackoverflow
> ASSOCIATED: **setdash, stroke**

currentdict

> — **currentdict** dictionary

returns a duplicate of the current dictionary, the dictionary on the top of the dictionary stack, to the operand stack. Note that this does not affect the position or contents of the current dictionary on the dictionary stack. In particular, it does not remove the current dictionary from the dictionary stack; that action can be performed only by the **end** operator.

> TYPE: Dictionary
> ERRORS: stackoverflow
> ASSOCIATED: **begin, end, dictstack**

currentfile

> — **currentfile** file

returns the current file object. The current file is the file that the PostScript interpreter was most recently reading for program input. More specifically, **currentfile** searches down the execution stack for the first file object and returns that. If there is no file object on the execution stack, it returns an invalid file object. This should never happen in the execution of a PostScript application program.

The file normally returned by **currentfile** is the standard input file, *%stdin.* An important exception to this occurs when working in the interactive mode. In the interactive mode, the interpreter does not read the PostScript statements directly from *%stdin* but rather reads each edited statement from another file.

The **currentfile** operator is used primarily to read in data that has been included within the program file itself. This can be a very useful and valuable tool. At any point in time, the file is positioned at the end of the last PostScript token read by the interpreter. If the token was a name or a number, the file is positioned after the first whitespace character after the token; for all other types of tokens, the file is positioned after the last character of the token itself.

TYPE:	File
ERRORS:	stackoverflow
ASSOCIATED:	**file, read, run**

currentflat

—	**currentflat**	num

returns the current flatness parameter from the current graphics state. The current flatness parameter is a positive number which defines the precision with which curved lines are rendered on the output device. See the discussion under the **setflat** operator for a more complete explanation.

TYPE:	Graphics
ERRORS:	stackoverflow
ASSOCIATED:	**setflat, flattenpath**

currentfont

—	**currentfont**	font

returns the current font dictionary from the current graphics state. The current font dictionary is the font dictionary that was referenced by the most recent **setfont** and is the font that will be used for character operations. If composite fonts are being used, **currentfont** returns the root composite font which has been selected by the most recent **setfont**, unless it is used within **BuildChar** or **cshow** procedures. In those cases, **currentfont** returns the selected base font. See the discussion under the **setfont** operator for a more complete explanation.

TYPE:	Graphics
ERRORS:	stackoverflow
ASSOCIATED:	**setfont, rootfont, show, cshow**

currentgray

—	**currentgray**	num

returns the gray value of the current color parameter from the current graphics state. The gray value is a number between 0 and 1 that indicates the degree of light or white to be used when painting on the output device.

If color values are being used, the **currentgray** operator returns a weighted average of the components of the current color. See the discussion under the **setgray** operator for a more complete explanation.

TYPE: Graphics
ERRORS: stackoverflow
ASSOCIATED: **setgray, fill, show, stroke, currentcmykcolor, currenthsbcolor, currentrgbcolor**

currenthsbcolor

  — **currenthsbcolor** hue sat bright

returns the three components of the current color parameter from the current graphics state according to the hue-saturation-brightness model. Each of these values is a number between 0 and 1 that indicates the hue, saturation, and brightness of the current color. See the discussion under the **setgray** operator and in Section B3.3 for a more complete explanation.

TYPE: Graphics
ERRORS: stackoverflow
ASSOCIATED: **setgray, fill, show, stroke, currentgray, currentcmykcolor, currentrgbcolor**

currentlinecap

  — **currentlinecap** int

returns the current line cap parameter in the current graphics state. The current line cap parameter is an integer value, 0, 1, or 2, that defines the method of finishing the ends of line drawn on the output device. See the discussion under the **setlinecap** operator for a more complete explanation.

TYPE: Graphics
ERRORS: stackoverflow
ASSOCIATED: **setlinecap, stroke, currentlinejoin, setlinejoin**

currentlinejoin

  — **currentlinejoin** int

returns the current line join parameter in the current graphics state. The current line join parameter is an integer value, 0, 1, or 2, that defines the method of finishing the joins between lines drawn on the output device. See the discussion under the **setlinejoin** operator for a more complete explanation.

TYPE: Graphics
ERRORS: stackoverflow
ASSOCIATED: **setlinejoin, stroke, currentlinecap, setlinecap**

currentlinewidth

—   **currentlinewidth**   num

returns the current line width parameter in the current graphics state. The current line width parameter is the size in user coordinate units of the stroke produced when a line is drawn on the output device. See the discussion under the **setlinewidth** operator for a more complete explanation.

TYPE: Graphics
ERRORS: stackoverflow
ASSOCIATED: **setlinewidth, stroke**

currentmatrix

matrix   **currentmatrix**   matrix

replaces the value of *matrix* with a copy of the current transformation matrix (CTM) from the current graphics state. The current transformation matrix governs the mapping of user coordinates into device coordinates. See the discussion under **setmatrix** and in Section A3.5 for further information.

TYPE: Coordinate
ERRORS: stackoverflow
ASSOCIATED: **setmatrix, defaultmatrix, intimatrix, concat**

currentmiterlimit

—   **currentmiterlimit**   num

returns the current miter limit parameter in the current graphics state. The current miter limit parameter affects the shape of the corners produced when a line is drawn on the output device. See the discussion under the **setmiterlimit** operator for a more complete explanation.

TYPE: Graphics
ERRORS: stackoverflow
ASSOCIATED: **setmiterlimit, stroke**

currentpacking

—   **currentpacking**   bool

returns a boolean value that indicates whether array packing is currently in effect or not. See the discussion under the **setpacking** operator for a more complete explanation.

            TYPE: Array
      ERRORS: stackoverflow
ASSOCIATED: **setpacking, packedarray**

currentpoint

—   **currentpoint**   x y

returns the coordinates of the current point in the current graphics state as x and y. If there is no current point, the **currentpoint** operator executes the **nocurrentpoint** error.

     The coordinates of the current point that are returned by **currentpoint** are the coordinates of the point at the end of the current path as determined in the present set of user coordinates. If the current transformation matrix (CTM) has been changed since establishing the current point, the coordinates reported back by **currentpoint** will be different from the coordinates of the point when it was created. The coordinates reported will be those of the same point on the output device now transformed by the new CTM. See Example below.

EXAMPLE:

         100 100 moveto
         currentpoint $\Rightarrow$ 100.0 100.0
         100 100 translate
         currentpoint $\Rightarrow$ 0.0   0.0

            TYPE: Path
      ERRORS: nocurrentpoint, stackoverflow, undefinedresult
ASSOCIATED: **moveto, lineto, curveto, arc**

currentrgbcolor

—   **currentrgbcolor**   red green blue

returns the three components of the current color parameter from the current graphics state according to the red-green-blue model. Each of these values is a number between 0 and 1 that indicates the percentage of red, green, and blue in the current color. See the discussion under the **setrgbcolor** operator and in Section A4.4 for a more complete explanation.

TYPE: Graphics
ERRORS: stackoverflow
ASSOCIATED: **setgray, fill, show, stroke, currentgray, currentcmykcolor, currenthsbcolor**

currentscreen

—   **currentscreent**   freq angle proc

returns the three components of the current halftone screen from the current graphics state. See the discussion under the **setscreen** operator and in Section B3.1 for a more complete explanation.

If color operators are implemented in the interpreter, **currentscreen** returns only the halftone screen values for the black and white (gray) screen function. See the discussion under the **setcolorscreen** operator and in Section A4.4 for a detailed explanation of color operations.

TYPE: Graphics
ERRORS: stackoverflow
ASSOCIATED: **setscreen, currenttransfer, settransfer**

currenttransfer

—   **currenttransfert**   proc

returns the transfer procedure, *proc,* being used by the current graphics state. **proc** maps user gray values into device gray values. See the discussion under the **settransfer** operator and in Section B3.1 for a more complete explanation.

If color operators are implemented in the interpreter, **currenttransfer** returns only the gray transfer function. See the discussion under the **setcolortransfer** operator and in Section A4.4 for a detailed explanation of color operations.

TYPE: Graphics
ERRORS: stackoverflow
ASSOCIATED: **settransfer, currentcolortransfer, setcolortransfer, currentscreen, setscreen**

*currentundercolorremoval

—   **currentundercolorremoval**   proc

returns the current undercolor removal function from the current graphics state. See Section A4.4 for a complete discussion of color processing and printing.

* This operator is not present in PostScript version 38.0.

TYPE: Graphics
ERRORS: stackoverflow
ASSOCIATED: **setundercolorremoval**

curveto

dx_1 dy_1 dx_2 dy_2 ax_2 ay_2 **curveto**   —

adds a curved line segment, described by a pair of Bezier cubic equations, to the current path. The curve begins from the current point, which we will call the first *anchor point*, with coordinates (ax_1, ay_1), to the second anchor point, whose coordinates are (ax_2, ay_2). The shape of the curve between the two anchor points is governed by two additional points, called *direction points*, whose coordinates are (dx_1, dy_1) and (dx_2, dy_2), respectively. The entire curved line segment is contained within the box formed by the lines connecting these four points.

The curved segment is entirely defined by these four points. The curve begins at the first anchor point and is tangent to the line between the first anchor point and the first direction point. The curve ends at the second anchor point and is tangent to the line from the second direction point to the second anchor point at the second anchor point. The second anchor point, (ax_2, ay_2), becomes the new current point at the completion of the **curveto**. The length of the line from the first anchor point to the first direction point and the angle formed by that line and a straight line connecting the two anchor points govern the first part of the curve, while the length of the line from the second direction point to the second anchor point and the corresponding angle govern the last part of the curve (see Figure C1.4).

TYPE: Path
ERRORS: limitcheck, nocurrentpoint, stackunderflow, typecheck
ASSOCIATED: **lineto, moveto, arc, arcto**

cvi

num   **cvi**   int
or
string

converts a number, *num*, or a string that is equivalent to a number, *string*, into the integer value, *int*. The integer value is determined by truncating any fractional part of the operand, rounding the value toward zero. For a string operand, *string* is converted into a number according to PostScript syntax rules and then integer conversion is applied. If the string does not convert to a valid number, a **typecheck** error will result. An attempt to convert a real number that is beyond the integer range will result in a **rangecheck** error. The maximum integer values (positive and negative) are implementation-dependent.

Figure C1.4 curveto operator

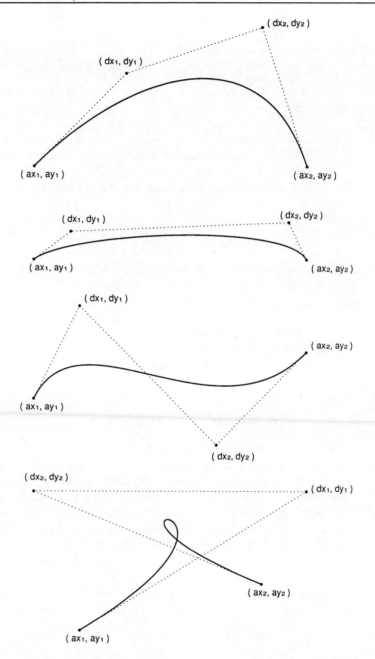

EXAMPLE:

12.7 cvi	⇒	12
− 12.7 cvi	⇒	− 12
8#40 cvi	⇒	32
3.35E1 cvi	⇒	33

Note that **cvi** will accept numeric values in any valid numeric format but returns a standard decimal integer.

> TYPE: Conversion
> ERRORS: invalidaccess, rangecheck, stackunderflow, syntaxerror, typecheck, undefinedresult
> ASSOCIATED: **ceiling, cvr, floor, round, truncate**

cvlit

> any   **cvlit**   any

converts the object *any* on the top of the operand stack to have the literal attribute. Note that this does not change the type of the object; it changes only the literal/executable attribute of that object to literal.

> TYPE: Conversion
> ERRORS: stackunderflow
> ASSOCIATED: **cvx, cvs, xcheck**

cvn

> string   **cvn**   name

converts the *string* operand to a PostScript *name* that is lexically identical to *string*. The resulting *name* will be executable if *string* was. The attempt to generate a name from a string that is longer than the maximum name length will result in a **rangecheck** error. The maximum allowed length of strings and names is implementation-dependent.

PostScript programmers should note that although any string may be given to **cvn** and converted to a name, this can result in creation of a name that has invalid characters in it, such as white-space characters or other special characters that normally cannot be included in names. Such names can be used, but they require a roundabout method for retrieval that is both cumbersome and tricky. It is recommended that you ensure that any strings that you convert to names in this way should have the correct form to be names; just remember that the interpreter isn't going to check this.

EXAMPLE:

(proc) cvn	⇒	/proc
(proc) cvx cvn	⇒	proc

which could then be executed by the **exec** operator.

TYPE: Conversion
ERRORS: invalidaccess, rangecheck, stackunderflow, typecheck
ASSOCIATED: **cvs, type**

cvr

num **cvr** real
or
string

converts a number, *num,* or a string that is equivalent to a number, *string,* into the real number, *real.* For a string operand, *string* is converted into a number according to Post-Script syntax rules, and then conversion is applied. If the string does not convert to a valid number, a **typecheck** error will result.

TYPE: Conversion
ERRORS: invalidaccess, rangecheck, stackunderflow, syntaxerror, typecheck, undefinedresult
ASSOCIATED: **cvi, cvs, cvrs**

cvrs

num base string **cvrs** substring

converts *num* into a string equivalent, according to the number system whose base number or radix is given by *base.* This is equivalent to performing two operations in succession: first, a conversion of *num* into a string object, then conversion of the string representation into the desired base. The string equivalent of *num* is stored in the beginning of *string,* overlaying anything that might have been there before, and the portion of *string* taken up by the new value is returned to the top of the operand stack as *substring.* Any remaining portion of string is unchanged.

If *num* is real, it is converted into an integer as though by application of **cvi.** The *base* operand must be an integer between 2 and 36. Digits greater than 9 are represented by letters between 'A' and 'Z'.

EXAMPLE:

255 8 3 string cvrs	⇒	(377)	% 255_{10} = 377_8
255 16 3 string cvrs	⇒	(FF)	% 255_{10} = FF_{16}

TYPE: Conversion
ERRORS: invalidaccess, rangecheck, stackunderflow, syntaxerror, typecheck, undefinedresult
ASSOCIATED: **cvi, cvr, cvs**

cvs

any string   **cvs**   substring

converts *any* arbitrary object into a string representation and stores the result in *string*, overwriting the initial portion. The portion of string taken up by the new value is returned to the top of the operand stack as *substring*, while the remaining portion of *string*, if any, remains unchanged.

If *any* is a number, **cvs** returns the string representation of that number. If *any* is a boolean, **cvs** returns the string 'true' or the string 'false'. If *any* is a string, **cvs** copies the contents of *any* into *string*. Note that this is a true copy, not a duplicate, and subsequent changes to *string* or *substring* (which are identical for the length of *substring*) will not affect the contents of *any*. If *any* is any other type of object, **cvs** returns the string '--nostringval--'.

EXAMPLE:

1 2 eq 5 string cvs	⇒	(false)
8#40 5 string cvs	⇒	(32)
mark 15 string cvs	⇒	(--nostringval--)

TYPE: Conversion
ERRORS: invalidaccess, rangecheck, stackunderflow, typecheck
ASSOCIATED: **copy, cvi, cvr, cvrs, string, type**

cvx

any   **cvx**   any

converts the object *any* on the top of the operand stack to have the executable attribute. Note that this does not change the type of the object; it changes only the literal / executable attribute of that object to executable.

TYPE: Conversion
ERRORS: stackunderflow
ASSOCIATED: **cvlit, xcheck**

def

key value   **def**   —

associates *key* with *value* in the current dictionary. If *key* already exists in the current dictionary, **def** simply replaces the old value with *value;* if *key* does not exist, **def** inserts a new *key, value* pair into the dictionary. If the dictionary does not have room for another pair, the **def** operation will return the **dictfull** error.

Generally, a key will be a name literal, but it is not restricted to this and can, in fact, be other types of objects. If *key* is a string, the interpreter will convert it to a name literal, the equivalent to applying the **cvn** operator, prior to storing the entry into the dictionary. Use of other types of objects as keys may, however, require unusual techniques for retrieval and processing and should be considered carefully before use.

EXAMPLE:

/index 1 def	%defines 'index' as = 1
/index 1 index add def	%defines 'index' as = 2

TYPE:	Dictionary
ERRORS:	dictfull, invalidaccess, limitcheck, stackunderflow, typecheck
ASSOCIATED:	**length, maxlength, store, put**

defaultmatrix

matrix   **defaultmatrix**   matrix

replaces the value of *matrix* with the default coordinate transformation matrix for the output device. Any values previously in *matrix* are overwritten.

TYPE:	Coordinate
ERRORS:	invalidaccess, rangecheck, stackunderflow, typecheck
ASSOCIATED:	**currentmatrix, initmatrix, setmatrix, concat**

definefont

key   font   **definefont**   font

registers *font* as a font dictionary associated with *key*, which is usually a name literal. **definefont** also creates an additional entry in the font dictionary, whose key is **FID** and whose value is an object of type fontID; *font* must be large enough to hold this additional entry. The *font* operand must also conform to the other format requirements of a well-formed font; see Section A5.4 for a discussion of required entries in a font dictionary.

The new font is registered in the global **FontDirectory** dictionary and can be retrieved by subsequent use of the **findfont** operator.

TYPE:	Font
ERRORS:	dictfull, invalidfont, stackunderflow, typecheck
ASSOCIATED:	**makefont, scalefont, setfont, FontDirectory**

dict

> int **dict** dict

creates an empty dictionary with a maximum capacity of *int* entries and places the created dictionary onto the operand stack. *int* must be a non-negative integer.

> TYPE: Dictionary
> ERRORS: rangecheck, stackunderflow, typecheck, VMerror
> ASSOCIATED: **begin, length, maxlength, end**

dictfull

> (error process)

occurs when the referenced dictionary, normally *currentdict,* is already full and a Post-Script operation attempts to store another object into it. A dictionary is full when its **length** and its **maxlength** are equal. A dictionary is created with a maximum capacity as specified by the integer operand passed to the **dict** operator. **dictfull** is actually a procedure stored in the *errordict* dictionary.

> TYPE: Error
> ASSOCIATED: **def, put, store, errordict**

dictstack

> array **dictstack** subarray

places all elements of the dictionary stack into *array,* overwriting the inital elements. The changed portion of *array* is returned to the operand stack as *subarray.* The bottom element of the dictionary stack, normally *systemdict,* becomes the first entry (entry 0) in *subarray,* and the top element becomes the last entry (entry n − 1), where there are n dictionaries on the dictionary stack. The dictionary stack itself is unchanged. The *array* operand must have at least n elements or the rangecheck error will occur.

> EXAMPLE:

> 5 array dictstack ⇒ [−dictionary− −dictionary−]

if only the two default dictionaries are on the dictionary stack. Notice that the dictionary objects themselves are returned; not their names.

> TYPE: Dictionary
> ERRORS: invalidaccess, rangecheck, stackunderflow, typecheck
> ASSOCIATED: **begin, end, countdictstack**

dictstackoverflow

(error process)

occurs when the dictionary stack already contains the maximum number of active dictionary entries, and a **begin** operation attempts to store another dictionary on it. The maximum capacity of the dictionary stack is implementation dependent. **dictstackoverflow** is actually a procedure stored in the *errordict* dictionary.

TYPE: Error
ASSOCIATED: **begin, end, errordict**

dictstackunderflow

(error process)

occurs when the dictionary stack contains the minimum number of active dictionary entries, *userdict* and *systemdict,* and an **end** operation attempts to remove a dictionary from it. It is impossibe to remove the two bottommost dictionaries, *userdict* and *systemdict,* from the stack. This condition usually occurs when there is a use of the **end** operator without a corresponding **begin**. **dictstackunderflow** is actually a procedure stored in the *errordict* dictionary.

TYPE: Error
ASSOCIATED: **begin, end, errordict**

div

num1 num2 **div** quotient

divides *num1* by *num2* giving result *quotient*. The *quotient* is always a real number. Use the **idiv** operator if it is necessary to produce an integer quotient.

EXAMPLE:

4.5 1.5 div $\Rightarrow$ 3.0
6 2 div $\Rightarrow$ 3.0

TYPE: Mathematical
ERRORS: stackunderflow, typecheck, undefinedresult
ASSOCIATED: **idiv, mul**

dtransform

ux uy **dtransform** dx dy

transforms the distance vector, (ux, uy), into device space using the current transformation matrix, (CTM), and returns the equivalent distance vector for the device onto the operand stack as (dx, dy). The transformation takes place without regard to the translation components (t_x, t_y) of the CTM; this type of transformation is known as a *delta transformation*. This makes the distance calculations without any reference to a position on the output page, in either user space or device space, and is used to determine how distances map from user space to device space.

EXAMPLE:

72 144 dtransform $\Rightarrow$ 300 −600

using the default transformation matrix for the LaserWriter. This means that a distance vector that has an *x* width of 72 and a *y* height of 144 in the user coordinate system has an equivalent *x* width of 300 and *y* height of −600 in device coordinates on the LaserWriter output device. This is exactly what we would expect, since 1 units at 1/72 inch (the default PostScript coordinate unit) is 4.1667 units at 1/300 inch (the device resolution of the LaserWriter), and therefore 72 PostScript units will be 300 device units, and 144 PostScript units will be 600 device units. The negative sign indicates that a positive distance in PostScript coordinates is a negative distance on the device – that is, the LaserWriter addresses increase as you proceed down the page.

dx dy matrix   **dtransform**   dx′ dy′

transforms the distance vector, (dx, dy), into device space using *matrix* as a transformation matrix (instead of the current CTM), and returns the equivalent distance vector after the transformation onto the operand stack as (dx', dy'). The transformation takes place without regard to the translation components (t_x, t_y) of *matrix*.

EXAMPLE:

3 4 [4 0 0 2 0 0] dtransform $\Rightarrow$ 12.0 8.0
3 4 [4 0 0 2 5 9] dtransform $\Rightarrow$ 12.0 8.0

This transforms the (dx, dy) pair (3, 4) onto a space that is scaled by a factor of 4 in the *x* direction and a factor of 2 in the *y* direction. Notice that changing the (t_x, t_y) components of the transformation matrix has no effect on the result.

TYPE: Coordinate
ERRORS: stackunderflow, typecheck
ASSOCIATED: **idtransform, transform, itransform**

dup

any   **dup**   any any

duplicates the topmost object on the operand stack. If the original *any* is a composite object, the duplicate returned to the top of the stack shares values with the original. See Section A2.2 for a complete discussion of simple and composite objects.

EXAMPLE:

Stack in: 12   dup   Stack out: 12
                                                 12

TYPE: Stack
ERRORS: stackoverflow, stackunderflow
ASSOCIATED: **copy, count, index, exch, roll**

echo

bool   **echo**   —

specifies whether the characters that are received from the standard input file are written to the standard output file during interactive mode operation. The normal (default) value for *bool* is *true*. The application and meaning of the **echo** operator depends to some extent on the operating environment. See Section B2.2 for a discussion of file operations and Section A2.6 for a discussion of the interactive mode.

TYPE: File
ERRORS: stackunderflow, typecheck
ASSOCIATED: **file, read, prompt**

end

—   **end**   —

pops the current dictionary off the dictionary stack and makes the dictionary that was immediately below it the new current dictionary.

TYPE: Dictionary
ERRORS: dictstackunderflow
ASSOCIATED: **begin, countdictstack, dictstack**

eoclip

—   eoclip   —

intersects the inside of the current path with the inside of the current clipping path to produce a new, smaller current clipping path. The inside of the current path is determined by the even-odd rule rather than the non-zero winding number rule normally used by PostScript (see Section A4.2), while the inside of the current clipping path is determined by whatever rule was in effect at the time the path was created. Before determining the intersection, any open subpaths of the current path are implicitly closed.

The only difference between **eoclip** and **clip** is the choice of a rule to determine what lies inside the current path. In all other respects, they are identical in operation.

TYPE: Path
ERRORS: limitcheck
ASSOCIATED: **clip, clippath, initclip, eofill**

eofill

–   **eofill**   –

paints the inside of the current path with the current color. The inside of the current path is determined by the even-odd rule rather than the non-zero winding number rule normally used by PostScript (see Section A4.2). The only difference between **eofill** and **fill** is the choice of a rule to determine what lies inside the current path. In all other respects, they are identical in operation.

TYPE: Paint
ERRORS: limitcheck
ASSOCIATED: **fill, eoclip**

eq

any1 any2   **eq**   bool

compares the top two objects on the operand stack, *any1* and *any2,* and returns the value *bool,* which is *true* if the objects are equal and *false* otherwise.

The definition of equality depends on the types of the objects being compared. Simple objects are equal if their types and values are equal. Numbers are equal if their mathematical values are equal, even if they are mixed integer and real types. Composite objects are equal if they are identical; also, strings are equal to other strings if their lengths and contents are equal. Strings and names are equal if they have the same sequence of characters, that is, if they transform into one another under the rules for the **cvs** and **cvn** operators. Other attributes of objects, such as the literal/executable and access attributes, are not taken directly into consideration for determining equality; however, the **invalidaccess** error can still be raised if you try to compare an object that you cannot access.

From a programming standpoint, **eq** can be freely used in a natural way, with one exception. If you compare composite objects other than strings (for example, arrays), they will be equal only if they are identical; that is, if the two composite objects share definitions of their values. If, however, they are separate objects, they will not be equal even if their types, lengths, and contents are equal. Therefore, for example, if you **copy** an array and then compare the results, you will get a *false* return. This can be the source of some suprising results.

EXAMPLE 1:

1 1.0 eq	⇒	true	%real and integer numbers
1 (1) eq	⇒	false	%strings and numbers
/a (a) eq	⇒	true	%names and strings

EXAMPLE 2:

/Array1 [1 2] def		%define an array
/Array2 Array1 def		%another array identical to Array1
Array1 Array2 eq	⇒	true

but if we change Array2 as follows:

/Array2	
Array1 2 array	
copy	%make a true copy of Array1
def	%and define Array2 as that copy

then we have the result:

Array1	⇒	[1 2]
Array2	⇒	[1 2]
eq	⇒	false

even though Array2 is an exact copy of Array1.

TYPE:	Boolean
ERRORS:	invalidaccess, stackunderflow
ASSOCIATED:	**true, false, ne, ge, gt, le, lt**

erasepage

     –   **erasepage**   –

erases the entire contents of the current page. The **erasepage** operator basically performs a **fill** of the entire page with a gray level of 1. This normally will be white, but it may have been changed by the **settransfer** operator. **erasepage** changes only the contents of raster memory and hence the output page; it does not affect the current graphics state, and it does not cause a page to be output on the output device.

The **showpage** operator automatically performs an **erasepage** after it outputs a page. Since **erasepage** will affect the entire page regardless of the current clipping path, it is normally not good programming practice to use it within a PostScript program; if you do, the page description will not be able to be included within another PostScript page. Therefore, use of the **erasepage** operator does not conform to the requirements of the 2.0 document structuring conventions and makes any document containing it non-conforming.

EXAMPLE:

clippath 1 setgray fill

This sequence of operations performs the same function that an **erasepage** does but does it in a conforming manner, since the execution of these operations will not erase the entire page unless the entire page is within the current clipping path.

TYPE: Painting
ERRORS: (none)
ASSOCIATED: **showpage, clippath, fill**

errordict

—   **errordict**   dict

returns the dictionary *dict*, which is the *errordict* dictionary. The *errordict* dictionary is a normal PostScript dictionary that is defined in *systemdict* and contains as keys all the PostScript error messages and as values all the procedures that handle the associated error condition. See Section B2.3 for a complete discussion of error handling.

TYPE: Dictionary
ERRORS: stackoverflow
ASSOCIATED: **systemdict, userdict, begin, end**

exch

any1 any2   **exch**   any2 any1

exchanges the two top objects on the operand stack to reverse their order.

EXAMPLE:

Stack in: (asd)   exch   Stack out: 123
            123   (asd)

TYPE: Stack
ERRORS: stackunderflow
ASSOCIATED: **dup roll, index, pop, clear**

exec

any   **exec**   —

immediately executes the object on the top of the operand stack. The effect of execution on an object depends on the object's type and its literal/executable attribute. To begin with, executing any object with the literal attribute will just cause it to be replaced on the operand stack. Executing an object with the executable attribute will cause different actions, depending on the type of the object. In particular, executing a procedure name causes the procedure to be invoked. See Section A2.3 for a complete discussion.

EXAMPLE 1:

(1 2 add) **exec** ⇒ (1 2 add)

since a string has the literal attribute.

(1 2 add) cvx **exec** ⇒ 3

Here the string's attribute is changed from literal to executable by using the **cvx** operator, yielding an executable PostScript statement.

EXAMPLE 2:

5 3 /mul **exec** ⇒ 5 3 /mul

since / mul is a name literal and has the literal attribute.

5 3 /mul cvx **exec** ⇒ 15

since the **cvx** operator changes the name literal *mul* to the name *mul;* then **exec** executes that name (which is an operator name) and results in placing the product of the two operands 5 and 3, 15, onto the stack.

EXAMPLE 3:

[1 2 3] **exec** ⇒ Stack out: [1 2 3]

but if you change attributes again, as follows:

[1 2 3] cvx ⇒ Stack out: {1 2 3 }
exec ⇒ Stack out: 3
                                         2
                                         1

since the effect of changing the array into an executable form is to make it a procedure. When you execute the procedure, the result is to push each element onto the stack individually.

TYPE: Control
ERRORS: invalidaccess, stackunderflow
ASSOCIATED: **xcheck, cvx, run**

execstack

array	**execstack**	subarray

places all the elements of the current execution stack into array, overwriting the initial elements. The changed portion of *array* is returned to the operand stack as *subarray*. The bottom element of the execution stack becomes the first entry (element 0) in *subarray* and the top element becomes the last entry in *subarray*, (element $n-1$) where n is the current depth of the execution stack. The execution stack itself is unchanged. The *array* operand must be large enough to contain all n elements of the execution stack, or a **range-check** error will occur.

TYPE:	Control
ERRORS:	invalidaccess, rangecheck, stackunderflow, typecheck
ASSOCIATED:	**countexecstack, exec**

execstackoverflow

(error process)

occurs when the execution stack has grown too large; procedure invocation is nested deeper than the interpreter allows. The maximum depth of the execution stack is implementation-dependent.

TYPE:	Error
ASSOCIATED:	**exec, countexecstack**

executeonly

array	**executeonly**	array
or		or
packedarray		packedarray
or		or
file		file
or		or
string		string

reduces the access attribute of the operand to execute-only. Any attempt to read or modify the object subsequent to this operation will raise the **invalidaccess** error; however, the object can still be executed by the interpreter, either in the ordinary course of processing or explicitly by the **exec** operator. When an object is processed by **executeonly**, only the object that is returned has its attribute changed. If other duplicates of the object exist and share values with the object, their attributes remain unchanged.

Notice that this can only reduce the access attribute, never increase it. Also, the access attribute (any/read only/execute only/no access) is not the same as the literal/executable attribute; see Section A2.3 for a complete discussion of object attributes.

TYPE: Conversion
ERRORS: invalidaccess, stackunderflow, typecheck
ASSOCIATED: **readonly, noaccess, rcheck, wcheck, xcheck**

executive

   –   **executive**   –

places the PostScript interpreter into the interactive access mode if the interpreter provides that mode of access. **executive** is not a PostScript operator itself but rather is a procedure, defined in the *userdict* dictionary, that uses PostScript operators and file operations to provide interactive access to the intepreter. See Section A2.6 for a discussion of the interactive access mode.

TYPE: File
ERRORS: (none)
ASSOCIATED: **file, run, echo, prompt**

exit

   –   **exit**   –

terminates execution of the currently active instance of a looping context. A looping context is a procedure that is repeatedly executed by using one of the control operators – **for, loop, repeat, forall, pathforall,** or **renderbands**. The **exit** operator clears the execution stack down to that operator and then resumes execution with the next object in normal sequence after that operator. **exit** does not affect the operand or dictionary stacks; anything that has been placed on either of those stacks during the execution of the procedure remains in place.

An **exit** operator cannot be used to terminate a procedure being executed by a **stopped** operator, and it cannot be used to terminate the execution of a **run** operator. Any attempt to do so causes the **invalidexit** error and remains within the context of the **run** or **stopped**. If an **exit** operator is encountered in normal processing outside the context of one of the looping operators enumerated above, it is interpreted as attempting to exit from the **stopped** context that encloses all normal PostScript operations, and it will raise the **invalidexit** error.

TYPE: Control
ERRORS: invalidexit
ASSOCIATED: **for, forall, loop, pathforall, renderbands, repeat, run, stop, stopped**

exp

base exponent		**exp**	real

raises *base* to the *exponent* power and returns the result *real*. The operands may be any numbers; however, a fractional *exponent* implies taking some root of *base*, and therefore is defined only for positive values of *base*.

EXAMPLE:

3.5	2	**exp**	⇒	12.25
12.25	.5	**exp**	⇒	3.5
10	−2	**exp**	⇒	0.01

TYPE: Mathematical
ERRORS: stackunderflow, typecheck, undefinedresult
ASSOCIATED: **log, ln, sqrt**

false

−	**false**	false

returns the boolean object *false*. **false** is not a PostScript operator; it is a name in *systemdict* associated with the boolean value.

TYPE: Boolean
ERRORS: stackoverflow
ASSOCIATED: **true, and, eq, not, or, xor**

file

filestring accessstring	**file**	file

returns the file object *file* that is identified by the file name *filestring* with access rights defined by *accessstring*. Conventions regarding file names, as presented to the operating system by *filestring*, and access specifications, as referenced by *accessstring*, are implementation-dependent. However, all PostScript interpreters provide certain standard files and access methods. There is also an implementation-dependent limit on the maximum number of files that can be open at one time.

Two of the standard files are the standard input file, '%stdin', and the standard output file, '%stdout'; these are the most commonly used standard files. Other standard files are described in Section B2.2, which discusses file access and handling. The two standard access modes that can be specified by *accessstring* are as follows:

r   defines an input file (read-only). In a PostScript system that provides permanent file storage, the file identified by *filestring* must already exist; if it doesn't, the **undefined-file** error is executed.

w   defines an output file (write-only). In a PostScript system that provides permanent file storage, the file identified by *filestring* will be overwritten if it already exists or created if it does not already exist.

In addition, other access modes, such as read-write, may be available in some environments.

   Once a file object has been created and associated with a file, it remains active and valid until the file is closed. A file may be closed in two ways: by executing a specific **closefile** operation or by reaching end-of-file while reading or executing the file. A file is also effectively closed by executing a **restore**, if the **file** operation that created the *file* was executed after the matching **save**.

EXAMPLE:

> (%stdout) (w) file   ⇒   file object for the standard
> (This is a test) write   output file

prints the string 'This is a test' on the output file. This sequence is equivalent to the PostScript statement:

> (This is a test) print

> TYPE: File
> ERRORS: invalidaccess, invalidfileaccess, limitcheck, stackunderflow, typecheck,
>   undefinedfilename
> ASSOCIATED: **closefile, currentfile, read, status, write**

fill

> —   **fill**   —

paints the inside of the current path with the current color. Any previous contents of that area are overpainted and obscured. The inside of the current path is determined by the non-zero winding number rule normally used by PostScript (see Section A4.2). Before painting, the **fill** operator closes any open subpaths of the current path; it then approximates any curved line segments on the current path with straight lines (see **setflat**).

   Completion of a **fill** makes the current path empty, as though by execution of a **newpath**. To preserve the current path after a **fill**, use **gsave**, **grestore** around the operator in the usual way. (See Example 2 below).

EXAMPLE 1:

> newpath
> 100 100 10 0 360 arc   ●
> fill

This example creates a simple circular path and fills it with the current color.

EXAMPLE 2:

```
newpath
100 100 10 0 360 arc
gsave
    .5 setgray
    fill
grestore
.5 setlinewidth
stroke
```

This example creates a simple circular path and both fills and strokes it by saving the current path.

TYPE:	Painting
ERRORS:	limitcheck
ASSOCIATED:	**clip, stroke, eofill, eoclip**

*findencoding

key   **findencoding**   array

obtains the encoding array from the font identified by *key* and returns it to the operand stack. If the encoding array specified by *key* does not exist or cannot be found, **findencoding** raises the **undefined** error. In environments where file operations are available, **findencoding** may attempt to access the encoding definition from a file.

TYPE:	Font
ERRORS:	stackunderflow, typecheck, undefined
ASSOCIATED:	**findfont**

findfont

key   **findfont**   font

obtains a font dictionary, *font,* that is associated with the *key* in the **FontDirectory** and places it on the operand stack. This is generally done as part of a **findfont, scalefont, setfont** sequence that establishes the font associated with *key* as the active font.

If *key* is not found, **findfont** takes action that is implementation-dependent. Most commonly, it will issue a message and substitute use of a default font, typically Courier. In an environment that supports such devices, it may attempt to find and load the font from an attached disk file. Alternatively, however, it may execute the error **invalidfont**.

Fonts are loaded into the **FontDictionary** in two ways. Some fonts are built into the output device and are, therefore, automatically enrolled in the **FontDictionary**.

* This operator is not present in PostScript version 38.0.

Otherwise, a font dictionary must be enrolled by using the **definefont** operator. See Section A5 for a complete discussion of font use.

findfont is not a PostScript operator but is rather a built-in procedure defined in *systemdict*. As such, it can be redefined by a PostScript program that needs to impement an alternative strategy for finding fonts.

> TYPE: Font
> ERRORS: invalidfont, stackunderflow, typecheck
> ASSOCIATED: **definefont, makefont, scalefont, setfont, FontDIrectory**

flattenpath

> —   **flattenpath**   —

replaces the current path with a new path in which all the curved line segments are approximated by straight lines. The **flattenpath** operator leaves any straight line segments within the current path unchanged.

The closeness of the approximation is determined by the flatness parameter in the current graphic state. See the **setflat** operator for a complete description.

If you attempt to flatten a very complex path, it is possible to exceed the maximum number of points that are allowed in a current path; to do so will raise the **limitcheck** error. This limit is implementation-dependent.

> TYPE: Path
> ERRORS: limitcheck
> ASSOCIATED: **setflat, currentflat, curveto, pathbbox**

floor

> num1   **floor**   num2

returns as *num2* the greatest integer value less than or equal to *num1*. The result, *num2*, is an integer type if *num1* is an integer and is a real type otherwise.

EXAMPLE:

2.75 floor	⇒	2.0
− 4.7 floor	⇒	− 5.0
5 floor	⇒	5 (an integertype)

> TYPE: Mathematical
> ERRORS: stackunderflow, typecheck
> ASSOCIATED: **abs, ceiling, cvi, round, truncate**

flush

—	**flush**	—

forces any characters stored in a buffer for the standard output file to be output immediately. Generally, any program that needs immediate output, such as an interactive program, should use the **flush** operator to ensure prompt transmission of output.

TYPE:	File
ERRORS:	ioerror
ASSOCIATED:	**closefile, flushfile, print**

flushfile

file	**flushfile**	—

If *file* is an output file, **flushfile** performs the same function for that file as **flush** performs for the standard output file; that is, **flushfile** causes any buffered characters to be sent immediately. Any program that needs immediate output on a file (other than the standard output file) should use the **flushfile** operator to insure prompt transmission of output.

If *file* is an input file, **flushfile** reads the file and discards all input until reaching an end-of-file. Such action is often appropriate for error recovery, and **flushfile** is used for that purpose within the PostScript control program itself.

TYPE:	File
ERRORS:	ioerror, stackunderflow, typecheck
ASSOCIATED:	**closefile, flush, read, write**

FontDirectory

—	**FontDirectory**	dict

returns the global directory of fonts as *dict*. This directory is an ordinary PostScript dictionary that associates font names with font dictionaries. Additional entries are placed into this dictionary by **definefont,** and names of fonts are looked up by **findfont**. In addition, the **FontDirectory** may be accessed explicitly by ordinary dictionary operators for inquiry and retrieval; however, entries may not be directly modified, since it is read-only. **FontDirectory** is not a PostScript operator but is rather a name defined in *systemdict* associated with the dictionary object.

While the **FontDirectory** contains all fonts that are currently accessible in PostScript virtual memory, it does not necessarily contain the names of all available fonts. In some environments it may be that a **findfont** operation can retrieve fonts not present in virtual memory, for example, by retrieving them from an external storage system.

TYPE:	Font
ERRORS:	stackoverflow
ASSOCIATED:	**definefont, findfont, StandardEncoding**

for

init incr limit proc   **for**   —

executes *proc* repeatedly and, at each execution, provides a variable number on the operand stack. This number, called a control variable, begins at *init* and has *incr* added to it at every repetition. The procedure *proc* is repeated until the control variable exceeds *limit*. The **for** operator expects *init*, *incr*, and *limit* to be numbers.

More precisely, **for** sets the control variable to *init* to begin. It then compares the control variable to *limit* to see if it exceeds *limit*. If *incr* is positive, the control variable exceeds *limit* if it is greater than *limit*; if *incr* is negative, the control variable exceeds *limit* if it is less than *limit*. If the control variable does exceed *limit*, *proc* is not executed, and the *for* processing is ended. If the condition is not met, **for** pushes the control variable onto the operand stack and executes *proc*. When *proc* finishes execution, **for** adds *incr* to the current value of the control variable and begins the cycle again. If *proc* executes the **exit** operator at any time, the **for** loop is terminated immediately.

Usually, *proc* is constructed to use the value present on the stack. However, in any case, *proc* must clear the value from the stack or the value will accumulate on the stack. The **for** operator does not remove the value from the stack.

EXAMPLE:

    1 2 8 { = =} for

returns the successive values of the control variable, 1 3 5 7, and prints them on the standard output file.

    1 −2 8 { = =} for

returns nothing, since the initial value is less than the limit and the increment is negative.

    1 −2 −8 { = =} for

returns the successive values of the control variable, 1 −1 −3 −5 −7, and prints them on the standard output file, as before.

TYPE:	Control
ERRORS:	invalidaccess, stackoverflow, stackunderflow, typecheck
ASSOCIATED:	**forall, loop, pathforall, repeat, exit**

forall

array proc   **forall**   —

or

packedarray proc

or

string proc

enumerates every element of the first operand and executes *proc* for each of those elements. The **forall** operator pushes an element from the first operand onto the operand stack and executes the procedure *proc,* beginning with element 0 and continuing sequentially until all elements have been used. The objects pushed onto the stack are the individual components of the first operand; in the case of a *string,* these are the numeric values of the characters that form the string, not one-character strings (see Example below).

Usually, *proc* is constructed to use the value present on the stack. However, in any case, *proc* must clear that value from the stack or it will accumulate there. The **forall** operator does not remove results from the stack.

EXAMPLE:

(asdf) { = =} forall

returns the ASCII character values, 95 115 100 102, and prints them on the standard output file.

[(a) 1 {1 2 add}] { = =} forall

returns the individual components of the array, (a) 1 {1 2 add}, and prints them. Notice that no execution of the elements has taken place.

dict proc   **forall**   —

enumerates every (key, value) pair in *dict,* pushing both elements onto the operand stack, and then executes *proc.* The elements of *dict* are placed onto the stack in the order of 1) key, 2) value; that is, the key is pushed onto the stack first, followed by the value. The order in which pairs are retrieved from *dict* is arbitrary and may change from one execution of *forall* to the next. If *proc* adds entries into *dict* during the execution of a forall, the entry may or may not be included in the enumeration.

Usually, *proc* is constructed to use the values present on the stack. However, in any case, *proc* must clear those values from the stack or they will accumulate there. The **forall** operator does not remove results from the stack.

TYPE: Control
ERRORS: invalidaccess, stackoverflow, stackunderflow, typecheck
ASSOCIATED: **for, loop, pathforall, repeat, exit**

framedevice

> matrix width height proc   **framedevice**   –

installs a frame buffer as the raster memory for an output device and sets certain parameters for that device. Basically, a frame device is one that paints an entire page, or *frame,* at a time.

The **framedevice** operator is used to define important characteristics of a full page of output. Each page is defined as being 8 × *width* pixels wide by *height* pixels high, with the width and height determined by the actual physical configuration of the output device. The *matrix* operand is the default transformation matrix for the device and should reflect the transformation necessary to map user coordinates into device coordinates. After execution of **framedevice**, the *matrix* operand becomes the current transformation matrix (CTM). Also, the current clipping path is determined and set by **framedevice** using the operands *width, height,* and *matrix.*

The *proc* operand is a procedure that is executed every time a page is output on the device, normally by the **showpage** operator. This procedure must create the page output. The procedure does this by executing special, device-dependent operators that are implementation-dependent. In addition, *proc* is responsible in most devices for implementation of the **#copies** parameter, which is described in more detail under **#copies** and **showpage**.

The **framedevice** operator is one of two operators (**bandevice** and **framedevice**) that define types of raster output devices. If a device uses frames for output, then **framedevice** will be defined in the interpreter, and **banddevice** and its associated operator, **render-bands**, will not be defined.

       TYPE: Device
    ERRORS: stackunderflow, typecheck
ASSOCIATED: **banddevice, nulldevice, showpage**

ge

> num1 num2   **ge**   bool
>   or
> string1 string2

compares the first operand to the second operand and returns the boolean value *true* if the first is greater than or equal to the second and *false* otherwise. If the operands are numeric, *num1* is compared mathematically with *num2*. If the operands are strings, *string1* is compared element by element with *string2*, taking the elements as numbers between 0 and 255. For all string comparisons, the first non-equal character determines the result; if one string is longer than the other and both are equal up to the length of the shorter string, the longer string is greater. If the operands are of different types, or if they are not strings or numbers, ge indictates a **typeerror**.

EXAMPLE:

1 − 12 ge	⇒	true
(abc) (abd) ge	⇒	false
(abc) (abc) ge	⇒	true
(abd) (abc) ge	⇒	true

as you expect.

(##) (##!) ge	⇒	false
(##!) (##) ge	⇒	true
(#$) (##!) ge	⇒	true

As discussed above, the longer string will always be greater if the two strings are equal up to the length of the shorter string.

> TYPE: Boolean
> ERRORS: invalidaccess, stackunderflow, typecheck
> ASSOCIATED: **eq, gt, le, lt, ne**

get

> array index
>   or
> packedarray index   **get**   any
>   or
> string index

looks up the *index* in *array, packedarray,* or *string* and returns the element identified by *index* (counting from zero). The *index* must be between 0 and $n-1$, where n is the number of elements in *array, packedarray,* or *string;* if not, **get** executes the error procedure **rangecheck**.

EXAMPLE:

[1 2 3 4] 2 get	⇒	3	
(asdfg) 2 get	⇒	100	%character 'd' = 100

> dict key   **get**   any

looks up the *key* in *dict* and returns the associated value. If *key* is not defined in *dict*, get executes the error procedure **undefined**.

EXAMPLE:

> statusdict **/**jobsource get   ⇒   (Appletalk)

gets the string value of the source of the current job from the *statusdict*. (In this case, the job was running on an Apple LaserWriter and the source of the job was the Appletalk network.) Notice here that *statusdict* is not on the dictionary stack; **get** has referenced it directly to retrieve the desired value.

TYPE:	Array, Dictionary, String
ERRORS:	invalidaccess, rangecheck, stackunderflow, typecheck, undefined
ASSOCIATED:	**getinterval, put, putinterval**

getinterval

array index count	**getinterval**	subarray
or		
packedarray index count		or
or		
string index count		substring

duplicates a section of the operand *array*, *packedarray*, or *string*, beginning at the element identified by *index* (counting from zero) and extending for *count* elements. The duplicated section is returned as *subarray* or *substring*, which shares values with the original operand. See Section A2.2 for a discussion of shared values and composite objects.

The operands *index* and *count* must be non-negative integers, and the sum *index* + *count* must be between 1 and *n*, where *n* is the number of elements in *array*, *packedarray*, or *string*; if not, **getinterval** executes the error procedure **rangecheck**.

EXAMPLE:

(ASDFG) 1 4 getinterval	⇒	(SDFG)
(ASDFG) 1 0 getinterval	⇒	( ) % a string with 0 elements
[1 2 3 4] 1 2 getinterval	⇒	[2 3]

TYPE:	Array, String
ERRORS:	invalidaccess, rangecheck, stackunderflow, typecheck
ASSOCIATED:	**get, put, putinterval**

grestore

–	**grestore**	–

restores the graphics state to the state that is on the top of the graphics state stack and pops the graphics state stack. This has the effect of eliminating all values in the current graphics state and restoring the graphics state to the same values that were in effect when the **gsave** that created the state on the top of the stack occurred.

The **grestore** operator is normally used in conjunction with the **gsave** operator to reset the graphics state and its associated values to some previous point in the processing. However, **grestore** can be used without a matching **gsave**. In that case, **grestore** restores the state at the top of the graphics state stack without popping the stack. The state at the top of graphics state stack will either be one produced by the last unmatched **save** or it will be the initial state of the system.

> TYPE: Graphics
> ERRORS: (none)
> ASSOCIATED: **gsave, grestoreall**

grestoreall

> –   **grestoreall**   –

restores the graphics state to the one created by the last unmatched **save**, popping all states on the stack that were produced by any **gsave** operations made after the **save**. If there is no state on the graphics state stack that was produced by an unmatched **save**, it restores the bottommost graphics state, leaving only that state on the graphics state stack.

> TYPE: Graphics
> ERRORS: (none)
> ASSOCIATED: **gsave, grestore**

gsave

> –   **gsave**   –

saves a copy of the current graphics state and all its associated values on the top of the graphics state stack. The saved state may be restored at a later point in the processing by a matching **grestore**.

The **save** operator performs an implicit **gsave**; and a state saved in this way may be restored by using **grestore** or **grestoreall**. This process differs from the normal restore in that the state saved by **save** is not popped from the stack, whereas a state saved by a **gsave** is. Notice the difference between **gsave** and **save** in these operations. The **gsave** operator does not return a save object to the operand stack as **save** does; it places its result directly onto the graphics state stack, where it will be restored in strict sequence by **grestore**.

> TYPE: Graphics
> ERRORS: limitcheck
> ASSOCIATED: **grestore, grestoreall**

gt

> num1 num2   **gt**   bool
>   or
> string1 string2

compares the first operand to the second operand and returns the boolean value *true* if the first is greater than the second and *false* otherwise. If the operands are numeric, *num1* is compared mathematically with *num2*. If the operands are strings, *string1* is compared element by element with *string2*, taking the elements as numbers between 0 and 255. For all string comparisons, the first non-equal character determines the result; if one string is longer than the other and both are equal up to the length of the shorter string, the longer string is greater. If the operands are of different types, or if they are not strings or numbers, **gt** indicates a **typeerror**.

EXAMPLE:

1 – 12 gt	⇒	true
(abc) (abd) gt	⇒	false
(abc) (abc) gt	⇒	false
(abd) (abc) gt	⇒	true

as you expect.

(zz) (zza) gt	⇒	false
(zza) (zz) gt	⇒	true
(zy) (zza) gt	⇒	true

As discussed above, the longer string will always be greater if the two strings are equal up to the length of the shorter string.

(A) (a) gt	⇒	false

since all comparisons are made on character numeric values; 'A' is '65', and 'a' is '97'.

> TYPE: Boolean
> ERRORS: invalidaccess, stackunderflow, typecheck
> ASSOCIATED: **eq, ge, le, lt, ne**

handleerror

(error processor)

is a procedure defined in *errordict* that is executed to report error messages and error information in a standard way. See Section A2.4 for a discussion of standard error handling and reporting.

Note that there is nothing special about **handleerror**; it is an ordinary PostScript procedure and can be redefined to provide additional or specialized handling of errors as required. **handleerror** is also defined in *systemdict;* the definition there simply retrieves and executes the procedure from *errordict*.

> TYPE: Error
> ASSOCIATED: **errordict, systemdict**

identmatrix

matrix   **identmatrix**   matrix

replaces the contents of *matrix* with the identity matrix [0.0 0.0 1.0 0.0 0.0]. The identity matrix is the matrix that transforms any coordinate into itself; that is, it makes no change to the coordinate.

          TYPE: Coordinates
    ERRORS: invalidaccess, stackunderflow, typecheck
ASSOCIATED: **matrix, currentmatrix, defaultmatrix, initmatrix**

idiv

int1 int2   **idiv**   result

divides *int1* by *int2* and returns the integer portion of the quotient as *result;* any remainder is discarded. Both operands must be integers, and the *result* is an integer.

From a programmer's point of view, the primary use for **idiv** is as an alternative to *div* when you want an integer result. The **div** operator always returns a *realtype* result, even when the operands are *integertype* and the result is an integer; and most mathematical operands will return a *realtype* result if any of the operands are *realtype*. So if you have any sequence of calculations that includes division and you require an *integertype* result, you will want to use **idiv**. An example of such a requirement is shown in Example 2.

Although there is no reason why **idiv** should not work correctly with real operands as well as integers, it is defined to require only integer operands. However, in some versions of the PostScript interpreter from Adobe Systems, it can be given real operands and, in fact, it does work correctly for cases where both operands are of the same type, that is, integer or real. But operands of different types may give incorrect or unexpected results without any error indication. For example, in the LaserWriter Version 38.0, any sequence of *integertype* divided by *realtype* gives a 0 result.

EXAMPLE 1:

      7 2 idiv   ⇒   3
      7 3 idiv   ⇒   2

EXAMPLE 2:

Suppose that you have constructed an array that contains pairs of data and wish to access the information within the array as pairs, using the first element of each pair as an index for storage into another array of data. This will require the use of **idiv** and might be done as follows:

```
/Store 5 array def                     % empty array
[ 2 /agrave 3 /egrave 4 /eacute ]      % source array
aload                                  % break into components
length 2 idiv                          % calculate pair length
{Store 3 1 roll put}                   % proc to put values into Store
repeat                                 % repeat pair length times
Store = =                              % display result
```

[–null– –null– /agrave /egrave /eacute]

The key here is calculation of the number of pairs in the source array; this provides the number of times to execute the **repeat** loop. However, **repeat** (like many other operators) requires an *integertype* as an operand. This requirement is satisfied by the use of **idiv** rather than **div** to calculate the index (the number of pairs) by dividing the length of the source array by 2.

TYPE: Mathematical
ERRORS: stackunderflow, typecheck, undefinedresult
ASSOCIATED: **div, add, cvi, mod**

idtransform

dx dy   **idtransform**   ux uy

transforms the distance vector, (dx, dy), in device coordinates into user coordinates, using the inverse of the current transformation matrix (CTM), and returns the new distance vector for the user coordinates to the operand stack as (ux, uy). The transformation takes place without regard to the translation components (t_x, t_y) of the CTM; this tranformation is called the *inverse delta transformation*. It is the inverse process to the **dtransform** operator, and, like that operator, provides distance calculations without any reference to a specific position in either device space or user space. The **idtransform** operator is used to determine how distances map from device space to user space.

EXAMPLE:

300 300 idtransform   ⇒   72.0 – 72.0

using the default transformation matrix for the Laserwriter. This means that a distance vector that has an x width of 300 units and a y height of 300 units on the Laserwriter has dimensions of 72 units and – 72 units in the default PostScript user coordinates, as you would expect. The negative sign on the y coordinate tells you that the Laserwriter y coordinates move in the opposite direction from the user coordinates.

dx' dy' matrix   **idtransform**   dx dy

transforms the distance matrix, (dx', dy') into user space using the inverse of *matrix* as a transformation matrix (instead of the inverse of the CTM), and returns the equivalent distance vector after the transformation as (dx, dy). The transformation takes place without respect to the translation components (t_x, t_y) of *matrix*.

EXAMPLE:

12 8 [4 0 0 2 0 0] idtransform	⇒	3.0 4.0
12 8 [4 0 0 2 5 8] idtransform	⇒	3.0 4.0

This transforms the distance vector (12, 8) in a coordinate system that has been scaled by a factor of 4 in the *x* direction and a factor of 2 in the *y* direction. Notice that changing the (t_x, t_y) components of the transformation matrix have no effect.

TYPE: Coordinate
ERRORS: stackunderflow, typecheck
ASSOCIATED: **dtransform, transform, itransform**

if

bool proc   **if**   —

executes *proc* if *bool* is *true;* otherwise, it pops both operands and does nothing. Although **if** leaves no results on the stack, *proc* may do so.

EXAMPLE:

4 4 eq { 2 3 add } if	⇒	5
4 3 eq { 2 3 add } if	⇒	—

TYPE: Control
ERRORS: invalidaccess, stackunderflow, typecheck
ASSOCIATED: **ifelse**

ifelse

bool proc1 proc2   **ifelse**   —

executes *proc1* if *bool* is *true* and executes *proc2* if *bool* is *false.* Although **ifelse** leaves no results on the stack, either procedure it executes may do so.

EXAMPLE:

4 4 eq {2 3 add} {2 3 sub} ifelse	⇒	5
4 5 eq {2 3 add} {2 3 sub} ifelse	⇒	− 1

TYPE: Control
ERRORS: invalidaccess, stackunderflow, typecheck
ASSOCIATED: **if**

image

width height samp matrix proc   **image**   –

renders a sampled image onto the current page. The image is produced by translating strings of data that are presented to the **image** operator as a binary representation of a sampled image. See Sections A4.5 and B3.3 for a more complete discussion of image handling and processing.

The sampled image consists of a rectangular array of sample points that exist in their own coordinate system. The coordinates of this rectangle follow the usual PostScript standard, with the point (0, 0) at the bottom left corner of the rectangle, the positive x axis extending to the right, and the positive y axis extending up the rectangle. This rectangle is defined to be *width* samples wide and *height* rows of samples tall. The top right corner of the image rectangle therefore has coordinates of $(width-1, height-1)$. Each sample point within the image rectangle consists of *samp* bits of data, where *samp* may be 1, 2, 4, or 8. The data is presented to the **image** operator as a string of character data that is interpreted as a series of binary integers, grouped according to *samp* to form the sample values. The string of character data is produced by *proc,* which may get the data from any source but must leave the data on the operand stack. **image** reads the sequence of bits on the stack and uses the values to fill the image rectangle, beginning at (0, 0) and continuing to $(1, 0) (2, 0)$ . . . $(width-1, 0) (0, 1)$ . . . $(width-1, 1) (0, 2)$ . . . and so on to $(width-1,$ $height-1)$, at which time all the sample points in the image rectangle are filled. If the number of values initially presented on the operand stack is not sufficient to fill the image rectangle, **image** calls *proc* repeatedly until enough values have been presented. However, if *proc* returns an empty string onto the stack, processing is terminated. If there are additional values on the operand stack after the image rectangle has been filled, they are ignored.

The user coordinate system is mapped into the image rectangle by *matrix,* which is a standard PostScript tranformation matrix. Note that the direction of this coordinate transformation is from user coordinates into image coordinates. This means, for example, that a translation of the origin (0, 0) to (10, 10) will move the user origin to the image coordinate position (10, 10), which has the effect of moving the rendered image to the position $(-10, -10)$ in user coordinates. This can be a source of some confusion.

Use of the *image* operator after **setcachedevice** within a **BuildChar** operation to create a character image is not allowed; an attempt to do so will raise the **undefined** error. However, the **imagemask** operator can be successfully used in the same context.

Programmers should note that errors within the **image** processing, particularly in setting up or handling *proc,* may cause the *image* operator to lose control of the output device. If that happens, the output device may reset automatically, or it may require resetting manually before continuing operations. In either case, all page data is lost, and connection with the output device may have to be reestablished.

EXAMPLE:

100 100 translate	% move user origin
72 72 scale	% scale image to 1-inch cube
16 16	% 16 samples wide by 16 rows high
2	% 2 bits for each sample
[16 0 0 16 0 0]	% mapped into unit square
{ <0f> }	% 4 samples of 2 bits each
image	% '00 00 11 11' repeated

produces a repeating pattern of eight pairs of bars, pairs of black bars (<00> <00>) alternating with pairs of white bars (<11> <11>).

TYPE:	Painting
ERRORS:	invalidaccess, stackunderflow, typecheck, undefinedresult, undefined
ASSOCIATED:	**imagemask**

imagemask

width height invert matrix proc   **imagemask**   —

renders an image onto the page, using the source data as a mask of 1-bit samples that governs where to apply paint (in the current color) to the page. See Section A4.5 for a more complete discussion of image handling and processing.

The source data consists of a rectangular array of sample points that exist in their own coordinate system. The coordinates and mapping of this rectangle into user coordinates follow the same system used by the **image** operator, and the operands *width, height,* and *matrix* all have the same functions. Since **imagemask** always uses one bit per sample, there is no need for an operand to control bits per sample; instead, the *invert* operand is a boolean value that governs the polarity of the mask. If *invert* is *true,* sample values of 1 allow paint to be applied to the page; values of 0 mask the page, leaving anything underneath them unchanged. If *invert* is false, the reverse applies, with values of 0 allowing paint to be applied and values of 1 becoming the mask.

As in the **image** operator, the procedure *proc* is required to provide the sample data to be processed by **imagemask**. The data is presented to the **image** operator as a string of character data that is interpreted as a series of binary integers that form the mask for processing. Note that the mask does not itself have a color; it works like a stencil or cutout to govern where on the image paint in the current color should be applied. Unlike the image operator, **imagemask** can be used after **setcachedevice** within a **BuildChar** operation to create a character image.

Programmers should note that errors within the **imagemask** processing, particularly in setting up or handling *proc*, may cause the *imagemask* operator to lose control of the output device. If that happens, the output device may reset automatically, or it may require resetting manually before continuing operations. In either case, all page data is lost, and connection with the output device may have to be reestablished.

EXAMPLE:

```
100 100 translate           % move graphic onto page
32 32 scale                 % scale to 1/2 inch
0 0 moveto                  % move to new origin
0 1.5 lineto 1.5 1.5 lineto % paint background
1.5 0 lineto closepath      % 1.5 unit square
.9 setgray fill             % and fill it with light gray
0 setgray                   % reset to black
.1 .1 translate             % move graphic onto background
8 14                        % sample is 8 bits wide by 14 high
false                       % zeros paint, ones don't
[8 0 0 14 0 0 ]             % map to unit square
{ <c0 f3 f3 f3 f3 f3 f3 f3
    f3 f3 93 c3 e3 f3 > }   % define bit-mapped 1
imagemask                   % and image it
```

The layout of the bit-mapped '1' used here is shown in Figure C1.5, page 222. As you can see, the image is arranged with the addressing beginning in one lower left corner and increasing upwards. The image is designed so that all positions with '0' values paint, while all positions with '1' values retain the color of the underlying image – in this case, a light-gray square. Notice how the bit-mapped image appears fitted to the square even though the non-paint portion of the image does not match the outline of the square.

TYPE: Painting
ERRORS: invalidaccess, stackunderflow, typecheck, undefinedresult
ASSOCIATED: **image**

Figure C1.5   bit map for **imagemask**

1	1	1	1	0	0	1	1	row 14 - hexadecimal 'f3'
1	1	1	0	0	0	1	1	row 13- hexadecimal 'e3'
1	1	0	0	0	0	1	1	row 12 - hexadecimal 'c3'
1	0	0	1	0	0	1	1	row 11- hexadecimal '93'
1	1	1	1	0	0	1	1	row 10 - hexadecimal 'f3'
1	1	1	1	0	0	1	1	row 09 - hexadecimal 'f3'
1	1	1	1	0	0	1	1	row 08 - hexadecimal 'f3'
1	1	1	1	0	0	1	1	row 07 - hexadecimal 'f3'
1	1	1	1	0	0	1	1	row 06 - hexadecimal 'f3'
1	1	1	1	0	0	1	1	row 05 - hexadecimal 'f3'
1	1	1	1	0	0	1	1	row 04 - hexadecimal 'f3'
1	1	1	1	0	0	1	1	row 03- hexadecimal 'f3'
1	1	1	1	0	0	1	1	row 02 - hexadecimal 'f3'
1	1	0	0	0	0	0	0	row 01 - hexadecimal 'c0'

index

$$\text{any}_n \ldots \text{any}_0 \ n \qquad \textbf{index} \qquad \text{any}_n \ldots \text{any}_0 \ \text{any}_n$$

uses the non-negative integer n as a pointer into the operand stack and retrieves the nth object on the stack, counting from the top element, 0. This object is duplicated on the top of the stack.

EXAMPLE:

Stack in: 3   (d)
       (a)   (a)
       (b)   (b)
       (c)   (c)
       (d)   (d)
       (e)   (e)

TYPE: Stack
ERRORS: rangecheck, stackunderflow, typecheck
ASSOCIATED: **copy, count, dup, roll**

initclip

—   **initclip**   —

replaces the clipping path in the current graphics state with the default clipping path for the current output device. This usually is the maximum imageable area for the device as established by the **framedevice** or **banddevice** operator.

Generally, use of **initclip** is not good PostScript programming practice. A page description that contains an **initclip** operator generally cannot be successfully included in another page description and its use does not conform to the requirements of the 2.0 document-structuring conventions.

TYPE: Path
ERRORS: (none)
ASSOCIATED: **clip, eoclip, initgraphics**

initgraphics

—   **initgraphics**   —

resets the most common variables in the graphics state to their initial, default values for the current output device. These variables are:

- current transformation matrix (default)
- current path (empty)
- current point (undefined)
- current clipping path (default)
- current color (black)
- current line width (one user coordinate unit)
- current dash (solid line)
- current line cap (butt ends)

- current line join (miter joins)
- current miter limit (10)

Each of these variables can also be individually reset by the appropriate operator.

The execution of **initgraphics** leaves other variables in the current graphics state unchanged, including current values for output device, font, flatness, the halftone screen, and the transfer function. Also, it does not affect the contents of raster memory for the device and therefore does not change anything already imaged onto the page.

Generally, use of **initgraphics** is not good PostScript programming practice. A page description that contains an **initgraphics** operator generally cannot be successfully included in another page description, and its use does not conform to the requirements of the 2.0 document-structuring conventions. If a page description needs to return to the graphic state at the beginning of its execution, it should explicitly save that state by using either a **gsave** or a **save**; it should then return to that saved state rather than assume that the default state was in effect initially.

TYPE: Graphics
ERRORS: (none)
ASSOCIATED: **gsave, grestore, grestoreall, save, restore**

initmatrix

—   **initmatrix**   —

restores the current transformation matrix (CTM) to the default matrix for the current output device. This matrix maps the default user coordinates into device coordinates and is the matrix established by the **framedevice** or **banddevice** operator.

Generally, use of **initmatrix** is not good PostScript programming practice. A page description that contains an **initmatrix** operator generally cannot be successfully included in another page description, and its use does not conform to the requirements of the 2.0 document-structuring conventions.

TYPE: Coordinate
ERRORS: (none)
ASSOCIATED: **defaultmatrix, currentmatrix, setmatrix**

interrupt

(error process)

processes an external interrupt to halt execution of a PostScript program. When the interpreter receives an interrupt request, it executes the procedure **interrupt,** which is defined in the dictionary *errordict,* in the same way as it would process an error. Execution of the **interrupt** occurs between execution of two successive objects being interpreted in normal sequence.

The exact cause and circumstances of an external interrupt are device-dependent. One typical example of an external interrupt is receipt of a control-C character over a serial communication channel, which allows a user to explicitly abort a PostScript process. Although **interrupt** is not precisely an error, it is a PostScript procedure that is stored in **errordict** and executed in the same manner as one of the error procedures. The default definition of **interrupt** executes a **stop** operator.

TYPE: Error
ASSOCIATED: **handleerror**

invalidaccess

(error process)

occurs when an attempt has been made to access a composite object or a file object in a way that violates the access attribute for that object. For example, an attempt has been made to store into a read-only object, or an access has been attempted to an object that has been given the noaccess attribute. This error is also executed if an attempt is made to execute the **pathforall** operator when the current path includes the results of a **charpath** operator.

TYPE: Error
ASSOCIATED: **executeonly, noaccess, rcheck, readonly, wcheck**

invalidexit

(error process)

occurs when an attempt has been made to execute an **exit** for which there is no dynamically enclosing looping context, as set up by one of the control operators **for, loop, repeat, forall, pathforall,** or **renderbands**. The error **invalidexit** also occurs when an attempt is made to exit from the **stopped** or **run** contexts.

TYPE: Error
ASSOCIATED: **exit, run, stopped**

invalidfileaccess

(error process)

occurs when the access string supplied to the **file** operator is unacceptable.

TYPE: Error
ASSOCIATED: **file**

invalidfont

(error process)

occurs when a PostScript font operator determines that a font dictionary is malformed in some way. The most common occurrences of **invalidfont** are caused by attempting to use **makefont** or **setfont** on an object that is not a well-formed font dictionary. In some PostScript implementations, this error may also be caused by presenting an invalid font name to the **findfont** operator.

TYPE:　　　Error
ASSOCIATED:　**definefont, findfont, makefont, setfont**

invalidrestore

(error process)

occurs when an attempt has been made to **restore** a saved state under invalid conditions. One or more of the dictionary, execution, or operand stacks contain composite objects that were created after the saved state being referenced was created by the **save** operator; these objects, therefore, would be referenceable but undefined if the **restore** were effective. Since the **restore** does not affect these stacks, the attempt to restore the saved state is invalid.

Generally, an **invalidrestore** is caused by incorrect stack manipulations and can be rectified by clearing the operand stack or popping the dictionary stack.

TYPE:　　　Error
ASSOCIATED:　**save, restore**

invertmatrix

matrix1 matrix2　　　**invertmatrix**　　　matrix2

replaces *matrix2* with the inverse of *matrix1*. If *matrix1* maps a coordinate value (x, y) into the new coordinate value (x', y'), then *matrix2* is the inverse of *matrix1* if it maps every (x', y') back into the correct (x, y).

It is possible to have matrices that have no valid inverse. Any attempt to apply the **invertmatrix** operator to such a matrix will raise the **undefinedresult** error. Generally, such matrices are only created by a program error, for example, by scaling both axes by 0.

TYPE:　　　Coordinate
ERRORS:　　invalidaccess, stackunderflow, typecheck, undefinedresult
ASSOCIATED:　**idtransform, itransform**

ioerror

(error process)

occurs when a processing error has occurred during execution of one of the file operators. The exact nature of such error conditions is implementation-dependent but typically will include detection of parity errors, checksum errors, or loss of communications during a file operation. The **ioerror** may also be raised by trying to write to a read-only file or trying to write to a file that is closed. Occurrence of an **ioerror** does not change a file's status to closed unless it occurs during **closefile**.

TYPE: Error
ASSOCIATED: **closefile, file, read, write**

itransform

dx dy   **itransform**   ux uy

transforms the device coordinates, (*dx, dy*), into user coordinates using the inverse of the current transformation matrix (CTM), and returns the new coordinates to the operand stack as (*ux, uy*). This transformation maps an absolute pair of coordinates in device space to matching coordinates in user space, and it is the inverse process to the **transform** operator.

EXAMPLE:

0 0 itransform   ⇒   18.0 784.32

using the default transformation matrix for the Laserwriter. This means that the origin for the LaserWriter is at coordinates (18, 784.32) in the default user coordinate system used in PostScript.

dx′ dy′ matrix   **itransform**   dx dy

transforms the coordinates, (*dx′, dy′*) into user space using the inverse of *matrix* as a transformation matrix (instead of the inverse of the CTM) and returns the equivalent coordinates after the transformation as (*dx, dy*).

EXAMPLE:

12 8 [4 0 0 2 0 0] itransform   ⇒   3.0 4.0
12 8 [4 0 0 2 4 2] itransform   ⇒   2.0 3.0

This transforms the position (12, 8) in a coordinate system that has been scaled by a factor of 4 in the *x* direction and a factor of 2 in the *y* direction. Notice that changing the (t_x, t_y) components of the transformation matrix by an appropriate displacement changes the resulting returned coordinates by an equivalent amount.

TYPE: Coordinate
ERRORS: stackunderflow, typecheck, undefinedresult
ASSOCIATED: **dtransform, idtransform, transform**

known

dict key   **known**   bool

searches the PostScript dictionary, *dict,* for an occurrence of *key* and returns the boolean value *true* if it is found and *false* otherwise. Notice that this explicitly references *dict,* which does not have to be on the dictionary stack but must be available through normal Post-Script lookup.

TYPE: Dictionary
ERRORS: invalidaccess, stackunderflow, typecheck
ASSOCIATED: **get, load, where**

kshow

proc string   **kshow**   —

prints *string* in a similar way to the **show** operator except that for every character in *string,* **kshow** invokes *proc* with two operands: the character currently being imaged and the following character. When **kshow** images the last character in string, it does not execute *proc,* since there is no following character.

When *proc* is invoked, there are two character codes on the operand stack as integers, and the current point has been updated to include the width of the character being imaged. Generally, *proc* will use these two codes to determine whether it wishes to alter the character spacing by adjustment of the current point. There is no restriction on *proc,* which may have any result, including altering the current graphics state. Any changes made within *proc* will persist throughout the execution of **kshow** and afterwards as well. In the same way, *proc* must remove the operands supplied by **kshow**, or they will remain on the stack.

The **kshow** operator is intended to provide for the kerning of character pairs in a string. *Kerning* is a process used in traditional typesetting to adjust the spacing between certain pairs of letters, such as 'A' and 'V', to achieve a visually more pleasing effect. However, **kshow** is not limited to such operations, and *proc* may take any action desired. Any attempt to apply **kshow** to a composite font will result in raising the **invalidfont** error.

EXAMPLE:

/Helvetica findfont 12 scalefont setfont
100 100 moveto   % move on page
(AVE) show   % ordinary show
100 85 moveto   % move to next line

```
{86 eq { − 1 0 rmoveto pop}
{pop}ifelse }                        % procedure for kerning
(AVE) kshow                          % kern 'A' and 'V'
```

This example shows the string (AVE) in the normal way and then shows it with a 2-point adjustment between the characters 'A' (code 65) and 'V' (code 86) to make them look more uniform.

AVE
AVE

TYPE:	Font
ERRORS:	invalidaccess, invalidfont, nocurrentpoint, stackunderflow, typecheck
ASSOCIATED:	**show, ashow, awidthshow, widthshow**

le

num1 num2	**le**	bool
or		
string1 string2		

compares the first operand to the second operand and returns the boolean value *true* if the first is less than or equal to the second and *false* otherwise. If the operands are numeric, *num1* is compared mathematically with *num2*. If the operands are strings, *string1* is compared element by element with *string2*, taking the elements as numbers between 0 and 255. For all string comparisons, the first non-equal character determines the result; if one string is longer than the other and both are equal up to the length of the shorter string, the shorter string is lesser. If the operands are of different types, or if they are not strings or numbers, **le** indictates a **typeerror**.

EXAMPLE:

−12 1 le	⇒	true
(abc) (abd) le	⇒	true
(abc) (abc) le	⇒	true
(abd) (abc) le	⇒	false

as you expect.

(##) (##!) le	⇒	true
(##!) (##) le	⇒	false
(#$) (##!) le	⇒	false

As discussed above, the longer string will always be greater if the two strings are equal up to the length of the shorter string.

(Z) (a) le   ⇒   true

since all comparisons are made on character numeric values, and 'Z' is '90' while 'a' is '97'.

        TYPE: Boolean
      ERRORS: invalidaccess, stackunderflow, typecheck
  ASSOCIATED: **eq, ge, gt, lt, ne**

length

            array   **length**   int
              or
        packedarray
              or
            string

returns *int* as the number of elements that make up the value of *array, packedarray,* or *string.*

EXAMPLE:

    (ASDFG) length   ⇒   5
    [0 1 5] length   ⇒   3

    dict   **length**   int

returns *int* as the current number of key-value pairs in *dict.*

EXAMPLE:

    /workdict 10 dict def
    workdict length   ⇒   0

since there are no entries in *workdict* even though it has been defined to hold 10 entries.

        TYPE: Array, Dictionary, String
      ERRORS: invalidaccess, stackunderflow, typecheck
  ASSOCIATED: **maxlength, array, dict, packedarray, string**

limitcheck

    (error process)

occurs when an implementation limit has been exceeded. These limits are different for each PostScript limitation but typically include exceeding the maximum number of open files, having too many items on the operand stack, or having a path that is too complex, that is, contains too many points.

TYPE: Error
ASSOCIATED: **closefile, file, read, write**

lineto

x y   **lineto**   —

appends a straight line segment to the current path, extending from the current point to the point defined by (x, y) in the current coordinates; and (x, y) becomes the new current point at the completion of the operation. The current point must be defined, or **lineto** raises the **nocurrentpoint** error.

EXAMPLE:

```
newpath              % make sure we start fresh
100 100 moveto       % create 1/2-inch horizontal line
136 100 lineto       % from (100, 100) to (136, 100)
stroke               % paint current path
```

TYPE: Path
ERRORS: limitcheck, nocurrentpoint, stackunderflow, typecheck
ASSOCIATED: **curveto, moveto, rlineto**

ln

num   **ln**   real

returns the natural logarithm of *num*. The natural logarithm is the logarithm to the base *e*.

TYPE: Mathematical
ERRORS: stackunderflow, typecheck, undefinedresult
ASSOCIATED: **log, exp**

load

key   **load**   value

searches for *key* in every dictionary on the dictionary stack, following the normal interpreter search order, and returns *value* that is associated with the first occurrence of *key*. If *key* is not found in any dictionary on the dictionary stack, **load** raises the **undefined** error.

    The **load** operator is used to retrieve a value associated with a key in the dictionary stack without executing it. If you simply name an object, the interpreter will look up that object and then execute it. If you **load** the object, it is not executed. For some object, such as strings or arrays, the distinction is insignificant, since executing these objects simply pushes them onto the stack. For others, such as procedures, however, the difference is crucial. If you retrieve a procedure in the ordinary way by naming it, you will execute the procedure; if you load the procedure, you will have it pushed on the stack without executing it.

EXAMPLE:

```
/Double {5 2 mul} def
Double                    ⇒        10
/Double load              ⇒        {5 2 mul}
```

TYPE:	Dictionary
ERRORS:	invalidaccess, stackunderflow, typecheck, undefined
ASSOCIATED:	**get, known, store, where**

log

num   **log**   real

returns the common logarithm of *num*. The common logarithm is the logarithm to the base *10*.

TYPE:	Mathematical
ERRORS:	stackunderflow, typecheck, undefinedresult
ASSOCIATED:	**ln, exp**

loop

proc   **loop**   —

executes *proc* continuously until *proc* terminates execution internally. The execution is generally ended by an **exit** operator and continues with the next statement after the **loop**. Execution is also ended if the *proc* invokes the **stop** operator, in which case it resumes after the enclosing **stopped** context. See the description of **stop** and **stopped** for more details.

If *proc* never executes an **exit** or a **stop** operator, the loop will continue to execute indefinitely until execution is broken by an external interrupt. See the **interrupt** operator for more details.

TYPE:	Control
ERRORS:	stackunderflow, typecheck
ASSOCIATED:	**exit, for, forall, repeat, stop**

lt

num1 num2   **lt**   bool
    or
string1 string2

compares the first operand to the second operand and returns the boolean value *true* if the first is strictly less than the second and *false* otherwise. If the operands are numeric, *num1* is compared mathematically with *num2*. If the operands are strings, *string1* is compared element by element with *string2*, taking the elements as numbers between 0 and 255. For all string comparisons, the first non-equal character determines the result; if one string is longer than the other and both are equal up to the length of the shorter string, the shorter string is lesser. If the operands are of different types, or if they are not strings or numbers, **lt** indicates a **typeerror**.

EXAMPLE:

– 12 1 lt	⇒	true
(abc) (abd) lt	⇒	true
(abc) (abc) lt	⇒	false
(abd) (abc) lt	⇒	false

as you expect.

     (##) (##!) lt   ⇒   true

As discussed above, the longer string will always be greater if the two strings are equal up to the length of the shorter string.

     (Z) (a) lt   ⇒   true

since all comparisons are made on character numeric values, and 'Z' is '90' while 'a' is '97'.

TYPE: Boolean
ERRORS: invalidaccess, stackunderflow, typecheck
ASSOCIATED: **eq, ge, gt, le, ne**

makefont

font matrix   **makefont**   newfont

applies *matrix* to *font*, and produces *newfont*, whose characters are transformed by the values in *matrix* when they are printed. The operator first creates a copy of *font*, then replaces the **FontMatrix** in the copy with the result of combining the original **FontMatrix** and *matrix*. The resulting *newfont* is returned to the stack.

     The essential operation of **makefont** is to change the character coordinates of a font in the same manner as **concat** modifies the user coordinates. Because of this, *matrix* has the same components and the same requirements as any other coordinate transformation matrix. This allows a programmer to modify the appearance of a font by changing the coordinates for display of the font without modifying of the entire coordinate system. The effect of the transformed coordinates is confined to the display of the font. If **makefont** is applied to a composite font, the transformation applies to each of the descendent fonts.

The **scalefont** operator is a special case of **makefont** that provides uniform scaling in both the x and y dimensions. Generally, a programmer will use **makefont** to provide non-uniform scaling for a font but otherwise will use it in the same place and in the same manner as a **scalefont** operator.

EXAMPLE:

```
/Times Roman findfont       % get font dictionary
[ 12 0 4.36764 12 0 0 ]     % set transformation matrix
makefont                    % 12 point 20° oblique font
setfont
100 100 moveto
(TIMES) show
```

This example uses the **makefont** operator to create a 12-point font whose letters are slanted at a 20-degree angle to the vertical. The third component of the transformation matrix specifies the angle of the letters as 12 times tangent 20 degrees.

TIMES

TYPE: Font
ERRORS: invalidfont, stackunderflow, typecheck
ASSOCIATED: **scalefont**

mark

—   **mark**   mark

pushes a mark object onto the stack. The mark object is a special PostScript object that indicates a position on the stack. All marks are identical, and the stack may contain many of them at once. The **mark** operator and the **[** operator are synonymous. See the discussion under the **[** operator for further information.

The **mark** operator is used to indicate a stack position for the beginning of a collection of PostScript objects. This collection need not be of any predetermined length, and so the mark is used as a delimiter for a processing or counting mechanism. The **countto-mark** and **cleartomark** operators can then be used within the process to provide access to the collection of objects on the stack.

The most common use of a mark object is to delimit a collection of objects to be made into an array. In that case, the **[** operator is most often used. See the description of the **]** operator for more detail.

EXAMPLE:

Stack in: –   **mark**   ⇒   Stack out: –mark–

TYPE: Array
ERRORS: stackoverflow
ASSOCIATED: **[,], array, cleartomark, counttomark**

matrix

–   **matrix**   matrix

generates an identity transformation matrix, *matrix*, and places it on the operand stack. The identity transformation matrix is a six-element array with the value [1.0 0.0 0.0 1.0 0.0 0.0]; if this array is applied to any coordinate matrix, the resulting transformation is identical to the original matrix.

The primary use of **matrix** in programming is to generate an empty transformation matrix for use with other coordinate transformation operators, such as **concat** and **concatmatrix**, which require a matrix operand for storage of the result.

EXAMPLE:

```
[ 12 0 0 12 0 0 ]
[ 1 0 .36397 1 0 0 ]
matrix
concatmatrix                ⇒        [ 12 0 4.36764 12 0 0 ]
```

This example uses **matrix** to provide a place for the result of concatenating a 12-point scale transformation matrix and a 20-degree shear transformation matrix. The resulting matrix replaces the identity matrix.

TYPE: Coordinate
ERRORS: stackoverflow
ASSOCIATED: **concat, concatmatrix, currentmatrix, defaultmatrix, identmatrix, initmatrix, setmatrix**

maxlength

dict   **maxlength**   int

returns *int* as the maximum number of key-value pairs that *dict* can hold, as defined by the **dict** operator that created *dict*.

The maximum length of a dictionary represents only what can be inserted; to find out how many key-value pairs are currently present in a dictionary, use the **length** operator.

EXAMPLE:

userdict maxlength	⇒	200
userdict length	⇒	34

Obviously, the values returned are system-dependent; these are typical values for a Laser-Writer system.

TYPE:	Dictionary
ERRORS:	invalidaccess, stackunderflow, typecheck
ASSOCIATED:	**dict, length**

mod

int1 int2   **mod**   remainder

returns the remainder of the division of *int1* by *int2*. The sign of *remainder* is the same as the sign of *int1*. Both operands must be integers, and the result is an integer.

EXAMPLE:

7	2 mod	⇒	1
7	4 mod	⇒	3
−7	4 mod	⇒	−3
−7	−4 mod	⇒	−3

TYPE:	Mathematical
ERRORS:	stackunderflow, typecheck, undefinedresult
ASSOCIATED:	**div, idiv**

moveto

x y   **moveto**   −

moves the current point to (*x, y*) and starts a new subpath of the current path in the current graphic state. **moveto** resets the current point without creating any additional line segments and without affecting any previously created line segments.

From a programmer's point of view, **moveto** simply establishes or resets the current point. Multiple, successive **moveto** operations simply change the current point; they do not add points to the current path. Since a point has no dimensions, single points cannot be painted. If you want to generate a dot (to represent a point), you must use something like the **arc** operator and fill the resulting circle, however small.

If a path already contains the maximum number of points, any attempt to add an additional point by using a **moveto** will raise the **limitcheck** error. The maximum number of points in a path is implementation-dependent.

TYPE: Path
ERRORS: limitcheck, stackunderflow, typecheck
ASSOCIATED: **rmoveto, arc, curveto, lineto**

mul

num1 num2   **mul**   product

multiplies *num1* by *num2*, giving result *product*. If both operands are integers, and the result is less than the maximum integer, the result will be an integer; otherwise, the result is a real.

EXAMPLE:

4 5 mul	$\Rightarrow$	20
4.0 5 mul	$\Rightarrow$	20.0
123456 dup mul	$\Rightarrow$	1.52414e+10
1.2e+4 2.344e+16 mul	$\Rightarrow$	2.8128e+20

TYPE: Mathematical
ERRORS: stackunderflow, typecheck, undefinedresult
ASSOCIATED: **add, div, idiv, mod, sub**

ne

any1 any2   ne   bool

compares the top two objects on the operand stack, *any1* and *any2*, and returns the value *bool*, which is *true* if the objects are not equal and *false* otherwise.

The definition of equality depends on the type of the objects being compared. The precise definition of what it means to say that objects are equal is fully discussed under the **eq** operator.

TYPE: Boolean
ERRORS: invalidaccess, stackunderflow
ASSOCIATED: **true, false, eq, ge, gt, le, lt**

neg

num   **neg**   −num

reverses the sign of *num*.

The **neg** operator is most often used in programming to change the sign of a variable number. This is necessary since the interpreter must retrieve the variable from the dictionary stack before it can become a negative. Simply placing a minus sign before a variable name will not work, since the variable is not turned into a numeric value until the interpreter looks it up in the dictionary stack. However, the **neg** operator can be placed after the variable name to give the same effect without an error.

EXAMPLE 1:

5 neg	$\Rightarrow$	-5
-5 neg	$\Rightarrow$	5

EXAMPLE 2:

/Five 5 def			%define a variable number
Five	$\Rightarrow$	5	
Five neg	$\Rightarrow$	-5	

TYPE: Mathematical
ERRORS: stackunderflow, typecheck
ASSOCIATED: **abs**

newpath

—   **newpath**   —

initializes the current path, making it empty and making the current point undefined.

TYPE: Path
ERRORS: (none)
ASSOCIATED: **closepath, stroke, fill, gsave**

noaccess

composite object	**noaccess**	composite object
or		or
file		file

changes the access attribute of *composite object* or *file* to allow no access of any kind. See the discussion of access attributes in Section A2.3.

The value of a no-access object or file cannot be obtained through the normal interpreter mechanisms, and this state is generally of no interest or use to a programmer.

For all composite objects except a dictionary, setting the no-access attribute for one object does not affect the access attributes for other composite objects that share the same values. For a dictionary, however, changing one copy to no-access will cause all other dictionary objects that share values with the given dictionary to also become no-access.

TYPE: Conversion
ERRORS: invalidaccess, stackunderflow, typecheck
ASSOCIATED: **executeonly, readonly, rcheck, wcheck**

nocurrentpoint

(error process)

occurs when an operator requires a current point but the current path is empty and, therefore, the current point is undefined. Generally, this can be solved by inserting an initial **moveto** to the desired location before the offending command.

TYPE: Error
ASSOCIATED: **moveto, curveto, lineto, rmoveto, show**

not

bool1   **not**   bool2

performs the logical negation of *bool1* and returns the boolean value *bool2*.

The **not** operator is most often used in programming to reverse the sign of a conditional test on some object for the purpose of providing the correct sequence for a control operator, such as **if**.

EXAMPLES:

Stack in: true   not   ⇒   Stack out: false
           false   not   ⇒   true

int1   **not**   int2

takes the bitwise complement of *int1* and returns the integer value *int2*. The result is a straight one's complement, taking *int1* as a simple bit representation and not as a character. The operand must be an integer.

TYPE: Logical
ERRORS: stackunderflow, typecheck
ASSOCIATED: **and, or, true, false, xor**

null

—   **null**   null

pushes a *null* object onto the stack. The null object is used as a place holder in arrays and on the stack; it is the only object that has the type *nulltype*, and has no value.

TYPE: Miscellaneous
ERRORS: stackoverflow
ASSOCIATED: **array, type**

nulldevice

—   **nulldevice**   —

installs the 'null device' as the default output device. The 'null device' behaves in all respects like a real, raster-output device except that it has no raster memory. Therefore, operators such as **stroke** and **fill** that make marks onto the page have no actual effect, and operators such as **showpage** produce no output. In all other ways, the 'null device' performs exactly the same functions as a real device, including setting the graphics state, invoking the font-handling machinery, and so on.

The **nulldevice** operator sets the default transformation matrix to the identity matrix. This may be changed by using the **setmatrix** operator to install the desired transformation matrix, thus allowing a program to simulate any particular output device coordinates. The font machinery supported by **nulldevice** includes the font cache, and characters that are referenced by a **show** operator will be placed into the font cache as usual, even though no output will be generated.

The **nulldevice** operator is primarily used in programming to exercise various capacities of the graphic state, such as placing characters into the font cache or performing complex path operations, without generating any marks on an output page. If **nulldevice** is used in this fashion, it should be surrounded by a matched pair of **gsave**, **grestore** operators to insure that the original device can be reinstalled when required.

> TYPE: Device
> ERRORS: (none)
> ASSOCIATED: **banddevice, framedevice**

or

bool1   bool2   **or**   result

performs a logical or of *bool1* and *bool2* and returns the boolean value *result*.

EXAMPLES:

true true	or	Stack out:	true
false true	or	⇒	true
false false	or	⇒	false

int1   mask   **or**   result

performs a bitwise inclusive or of *int1* and *mask* and returns the integer value *result*. The process is a straight, bit-wise inclusive or, taking the integer as a simple bit representation; both of the operands must be integers. The **or** is inclusive, so that if a bit is on in either operand, the matching bit in the result is also on.

EXAMPLES:

2	1	or	$\Rightarrow$	3
3	1	or	$\Rightarrow$	3
8	4	or	$\Rightarrow$	12
3	10	or	$\Rightarrow$	11

TYPE: Logical
ERRORS: stackunderflow, typecheck
ASSOCIATED: **and, not, true, false, xor**

packedarray

any_1 ... any_n n **packedarray** packedarray

creates *packedarray* out of the elements any_1 *through* any_n. The **packedarray** operator uses the first operand, *n* to determine the number of elements on the stack to be included in *packedarray* and then takes that number of elements from the stack and places them into *packedarray* as elements *0* to *n−1*. The operand *n* must be an integer, and there must be at least *n+1* items on the stack.

A packed array object has read-only access and has the type 'packedarraytype'; in other respects it can be used and accessed like an ordinary array. See Section A2.2 for a further discussion of packed arrays. Since packed arrays are not supported in all versions of PostScript, it is important to test for the availability of this facility before attempting to use it.

All arrays created by **packedarray** have the literal attribute; it cannot be used directly to create executable arrays (procedures). Procedures can be directly created in a packed form by using the **setpacking** operator, or they can be created out of packed arrays by using **cvx**.

EXAMPLE:

1 2 (asd) (efg)		% elements for array
4		% number of elements
packedarray	$\Rightarrow$	[1 2 (asd) (efg)]

Notice that the result is displayed like any array. If we continue with this result on the stack, we can test for a packed array as follows:

type	$\Rightarrow$	packedarray
(packedarray) eq	$\Rightarrow$	true

The only way to determine that the result is a packed array is by testing its type, as shown, or by attempting to change or store some element in it, which will raise the **invalidaccess** error.

TYPE: Array
ERRORS: rangecheck, stackunderflow, typecheck, VMerror
ASSOCIATED: **currentpacking, setpacking, [,], array**

pathbbox

— **pathbbox** llx lly urx ury

returns the bounding box of the current path in user coordinates. The bounding box is a rectangle with sides parallel to the *x* and *y* axes that contains all the points on the current path. It is described by the coordinates of two points: the lower left corner, (*llx, lly*), and the upper right corner, (*urx, ury*). These coordinates are real numbers that represent the corner points in the current user coordinates, which may not be the coordinates in effect when the path was constructed. If the current path is empty, the **pathbbox** operator raises the **nocurrentpoint** error (see Figure C1.6).

Figure C1.6 pathbbox operator

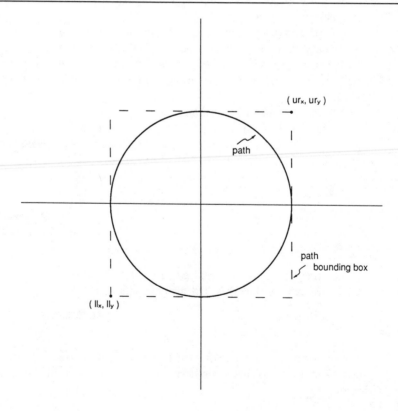

More exactly, **pathbbox** computes the current path in device coordinates and then maps those coordinates into user coordinates (as though using an **itransform**) with the inverse of the current transformation matrix. If the current path includes curved segments, the direction points for those segments as well as the anchor points (see the discussion under **curveto** for a fuller explantion of these points) are included within the bounding box rectangle, which may produce a larger bounding box than expected. This effect can be eliminated by first applying a **flattenpath** operator to the path.

EXAMPLE:

    100 150 10 0 360 arc
    [pathbox]   ⇒   [90.0 140.0 110.0 160.0]

which are the coordinates of the box that exactly encloses the circle generated by the **arc** operator, whose center is at the point (100, 150) with a radius of 10 points.

    100 150 10 0 360 arc
    100 150 translate
    [pathbbox]   ⇒   [− 10.0 − 10.0 10.0 10.0]

Even though the circle was created in one set of user coordinates, the bounding box that is returned is in the current user coordinates.

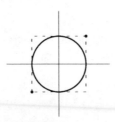

TYPE:	Path
ERRORS:	nocurrentpoint, stackoverflow
ASSOCIATED:	**clippath, flattenpath, newpath**

pathforall

    mvproc lnproc cvproc csproc   **pathforall**   −

enumerates all the elements of the current path, using the procedure operands, *mvproc, lnproc, cvproc,* and *csproc.* Each of these procedures applies to one or more types of segments that can be present in the current path and receives certain operands on the stack when it is called by **pathforall** as follows:

mvproc   receives (x, y) as operands; it applies to all segments generated by a **moveto** operation or an **rmoveto**, or to those generated by an implicit **moveto**, such as the first segment generated by an **arc** or **arcn** executed without any current point.

lnproc   receives (x, y) as operands; it applies to all segments generated by a **lineto** or an **rlineto**, or to those generated by an implicit **lineto** such as the first segment generated by an **arc** or **arcn** if there is a current point, or to the first segment generated by an **arcto**.

cvproc   receives six operands: $(dx1,\ dy1)$, $(dx2,\ dy2)$, $(ax2,\ ay2)$ on the operand stack; applies to all segments generated by a **curveto** or **rcurveto**, or to those generated by an implicit *curveto,* such as the circular segments generated by the **arc**, **arcn**, and **arcto** operators.

csproc   receives no operands; applies to all segments generated by a **closepath** operator.

The operands provided to the procedures are the point coordinates in user space of the operands that would be required for execution of the respective primary operator: **moveto**, **lineto**, **curveto**, or **closepath**. These coordinate operands will be the same as the coordinates used when the segments were created, unless the user coordinate system has been modified in the meantime. In all cases, the **pathforall** operator converts the device coordinates of the path into the user coordinates (as though using an **itransform**) with the inverse of the current transformation matrix.

If any portion of the current path was constructed using a **charpath** operator, execution of a **pathforall** will result in raising the **invalidaccess** error.

        TYPE: Path
     ERRORS: invalidaccess, stackoverflow, stackunderflow, typecheck
ASSOCIATED: **closepath, curveto, lineto, moveto**

pop

        any   pop   —

removes the top element from the operand stack.

    EXAMPLE:

    Stack in: (abc)   pop   Stack out: (def)
              (def)   1
              1   2
              2

and if you issue the **pop** again,

        pop $\Rightarrow$ 1 2

        TYPE: Stack
     ERRORS: stackunderflow
ASSOCIATED: **clear, =, ==**

print

string   **print**   –

writes *string* onto the standard output file. The **print** operator does not add a *newline* or any other character to *string* when it is sent.

Note that **print** is a file operator, similar to **writestring**, that works exclusively with the standard output file. It is primarily used in programming to generate text output for a host computer application or an interactive user. The **print** operator does not place characters onto an output page on the current device; only **show** and related operators do that.

TYPE: File
ERRORS: invalidaccess, stackunderflow, typecheck
ASSOCIATED: **=, ==, file, write, writehexstring, writestring**

prompt

–   **prompt**   –

produces the prompt that is displayed to the user during the interactive mode. The initial (default) definition of **prompt** produces the string 'PS>'. **prompt** is not a PostScript operator itself but rather is a procedure that is defined in the *userdict* dictionary that uses PostScript operators and file operations to generate the desired prompt string. See Section A2.6 for a discussion of the interactive mode.

TYPE: File
ERRORS: (none)
ASSOCIATED: **echo, executive**

pstack

|- any$_1$ . . . any$_n$ **pstack** |- any$_1$ . . . any$_n$

produces an edited string representation of all objects on the operand stack, *any*$_n$ through *any*$_1$, onto the standard output file. The edited string is generated for each *any* as though by application of the == operator; however, no stack contents are disturbed, and the stack is the same after the display as it was before.

The **pstack** operator is primarily used in programming to display the current contents of the stack during interactive work. It is the best method of display because it produces edited string representation and because it is nondestructive. Because **pstack** is nondestructive of the stack, it generates additional elements on the stack prior to display; for this reason, it is possible to overflow the stack during execution of a **pstack**.

TYPE: File
ERRORS: stackoverflow
ASSOCIATED: **=, ==, stack**

put

array index value	**put**	—
or		
string index value		

stores *value* into *array* or *string* at the position identified by *index* (counting from zero). *index* must be in the range 0 to $n-1$, where n is the number of elements in *array* or *string*.

EXAMPLE:

```
/Array [1 2 3 4 ] def
Array 2 (A) put
Array                          ⇒        [1 2 (A) 4 ]
```

Notice that **put** consumes the array as it inserts the element; the resulting new array does not remain on the stack.

```
/String (asdfg) def
String 2 65 put
String                         ⇒        (asAfg)
```

Notice that the character to be inserted into the string must be the numeric code of a character, that is, any number between 0 and 255.

dict key value	**put**	—

uses *key* and *value* and stores them as a key-value pair into *dict*. If *key* is already present in *dict,* its associated value is replaced by the new *value;* if it is not present, **put** creates a new entry.

EXAMPLE:

```
/workdict 5 dict def
workdict /String (string) put
workdict /String get              ⇒        (string)
workdict /String (newstring) put
workdict /String get              ⇒        (newstring)
```

Notice that there is still only one entry, *String* in *workdict,* and that *workdict* is referenced explicitly by both **get** and **put**; it does not have to be on the dictionary stack.

TYPE: Array, Dictionary, String
ERRORS: dictfull, invalidaccess, rangecheck, stackunderflow, typecheck
ASSOCIATED: **get, putinterval**

putinterval

array index array2   **putinterval**   –
or
string index string2

replaces a section of the operand *array* or *string,* beginning at the element identified by *index* (counting from zero), with the contents of *array2* or *string2*. The contents of *array2* or *string2* are retrieved as though by a **get** and each element is inserted into *array* or *string* as though by a **put**. Therefore the resulting **array** or *string* does not share values with *array2* or *string2*. However, in working with arrays, if any of the elements that are inserted are themselves composite objects, the new copy will share values with the original. See Section A2.2 for a discussion of shared values and composite objects.

The operand *index* must be a non-negative integer, and the sum *index* + the number of elements in *array2* or *string2* must be between 1 and *n*, where *n* is the number of elements in *array,* or *string;* if not, **putinterval** executes the error procedure **rangecheck**.

EXAMPLE:

```
/String (ASDFG) def
String 1 (4) putinterval
String                    ⇒       (A4DFG)
/Array [1 2 3 4 ] def
Array 1 [12 ] putinterval
Array                     ⇒       [1 12 3 4 ]
```

TYPE: Array, String
ERRORS: invalidaccess, rangecheck, stackunderflow, typecheck
ASSOCIATED: **get, put, getinterval**

quit

–   **quit**   –

terminates operation of the interpreter or of the current PostScript program. The **quit** operator as defined in *systemdict* terminates the interpreter; execution of this operator may also cause other consequences that are implementation-dependent. Examples of other actions are that the printer may reset and restart, or, where there is a separate operating system, control may be passed back to the operating system, and so on. The action of the **quit** operator is usually masked by a procedural definition of **quit** stored in *userdict,* which terminates the current PostScript program but not the interpreter itself.

In PostScript environments with a file system and an operating system, the PostScript interpreter will save a copy of virtual memory (VM) on the file system at the time a **quit** operator is executed and will reload that saved state from the file when it restarts.

TYPE:	Control
ERRORS:	(none)
ASSOCIATED:	**stop, start, interrupt**

rand

	rand	int
–		

generates a random integer within an implementation-defined range. The integer is generated by a pseudo-random number generator, whose state can be determined by the **rrand** operator and reset by the **srand** operator. Together, the three operators provide a complete set of facilities for handling random numbers.

TYPE:	Mathematical
ERRORS:	stackoverflow
ASSOCIATED:	**rrand, srand**

rangecheck

(error process)

occurs when a numeric operand is outside the range expected by the operator. One example of a range-check error is an index number larger than the size of an array or string that is used in any operator that accesses components of arrays or strings, such as **get** and **put**. Another example is the use of a negative number where a positive one is required, such as the stack access index required by the **index** operator. Operators that require a defined space as working storage, such as **cvs** or **dictstack**, may also execute this error if the available information exceeds the length of the operand provided as a storage area.

TYPE:	Error
ASSOCIATED:	**cvs, get, index, put, roll**

rcheck

composite object	**rcheck**	bool
or		
file		

tests the access attribute of the operand to see whether the operand is available to be read explicitly by PostScript operators – that is, whether the access attribute of the operand is either read-only or unlimited. If the object is available for read-access, it returns the boolean value *true;* it returns *false* otherwise.

TYPE: Conversion
ERRORS: stackunderflow, typecheck
ASSOCIATED: **executeonly, noaccess, readonly, wcheck**

rcurveto

rdx_1 rdy_1 rdx_2 rdy_2 rax_2 ray_2 rcurveto   —

adds a curved line segment, described by a pair of Bézier cubic equations, to the current path in the same manner as the **curveto** operator, except that the operands are relative to the current point rather than absolute coordinates. The curve begins from the current point, described here as the first *anchor point,* with coordinates (ax_1, ay_1), and extends to the second anchor point, whose coordinates are (ax_1+rax_2, ay_1+ray_2). In other words, the second anchor point is defined as the point that is at a distance (rax_2, ray_2) relative to the current point. The shape of the curve between the two anchor points is governed by two additional points, called *direction points,* whose coordinates are (ax_1+rdx_1, ay_1+rdy_1) and (ax_1+rdx_2, ay_1+rdy_2), respectively. The entire curved line segment is contained within the box formed by the lines connecting these four points. The second anchor point becomes the new current point at the completion of the rcurveto.

TYPE: Path
ERRORS: limitcheck, nocurrentpoint, stackunderflow, typecheck, undefinedresult
ASSOCIATED: **curveto, rlineto, rmoveto**

read

                               if not end-of-file:
file   **read**   byte true
                               if end-of-file
                               false

reads a single character from the designated *file* and returns it to the operand stack as an integer value. Then the **read** pushes the boolean value *true* to indicate that the action was successful. If the end-of-file is encountered before a character is read, **read** pushes the boolean value *false* to indicate end-of-file and closes the file. Any other result or error – for example, failure to complete the read because of a parity or checksum error – raises the **ioerror** condition.

Because **read** accesses only one character at a time, it is not generally the best way to deliver information to a PostScript program.

TYPE: File
ERRORS: invalidaccess, ioerror, stackoverflow, stackunderflow, typecheck
ASSOCIATED: **bytesavailable, readhexstring, readline, readstring, write**

readhexstring

file string   **readhexstring**   substring bool

reads characters from the designated *file* into *string* until all space in *string* is filled or until end-of-file. The characters are expected to be hexadecimal digits, '0' through '9' or 'A' (or 'a') through 'F' (or 'f'). Each successive pair of digits is taken as a single hexadecimal number that is translated into a character code, which is an integer in the range 0 to 255. These integer values are stored in successive positions in *string* until all positions are filled or an end-of-file indication is posted from *file*. The boolean result, *bool*, indicates whether the read terminated normally by filling the string—in which case it will be *true*; or whether end-of-file was encountered first—in which case it will be *false*. In either case, the result *substring* contains the valid characters that were read from the file.

The **readhexstring** operator ignores any characters read that are not hexadecimal digits, including file transmission code, spaces, newlines, and so on. Only valid hexadecimal digits are included in the resulting *substring*. For this reason, this is the preferred operator for reading and processing arbitrary binary data, such as might be generated by a scanned image. Any hexadecimal stream of data can be transmitted over a communications channel without any significant concern about file structure, communication control characters, or operating system limitations. This feature of the **readhexstring** operator makes it very useful in procedures associated with the **image** and **imagemask** operators, for example.

TYPE: File
ERRORS: invalidaccess, ioerror, rangecheck stackunderflow, typecheck
ASSOCIATED: **bytesavailable, read, readline, readstring, write**

readline

file string   **readline**   substring bool

reads characters from the designated *file* into *string* until a *newline* character (which indicates the end of a line) is received or until end-of-file. The characters read are stored in successive positions in *string* until the *newline* character is received or there is an end-of-file indication posted from *file*. The boolean result, *bool*, indicates whether the read terminated normally with a *newline*, in which case it will be *true*, or whether end-of-file was encountered first, in which case it will be *false*. In either case, the result *substring* contains the characters that were read from the file. The *newline* character is not stored in *string* and therefore is not included at the end of *substring*. If the **readline** operator reaches the end of *string* before it receives an *newline* character, it executes the **rangecheck** error and terminates processing.

TYPE: File
ERRORS: invalidaccess, ioerror, rangecheck, stackunderflow, typecheck
ASSOCIATED: **bytesavailable, read, readhexstring, readstring, write**

readonly

composite object   **readonly**   composite object
or   or
file   file

changes the access attribute of *composite object* or *file* to allow only read access. Access can only be reduced in this way, never increased; that is, if an object was already no-access, attempting to use the **readonly** operator will only result in an **invalidaccess** error. See the discussion of access attributes in Section A2.3.

The value of a read-only object or file cannot be modified through the normal interpreter operations; however, it can still be read by PostScript operators and executed by the interpreter.

For all composite objects except a dictionary, setting the read-only access attribute for one object does not affect the access attributes for other composite objects that share the same values. For a dictionary, however, changing one copy to read-only access will cause all other dictionary objects that share values with the given dictionary to also become read-only.

> TYPE: Conversion
> ERRORS: invalidaccess, stackunderflow, typecheck
> ASSOCIATED: **executeonly, noaccess, rcheck, wcheck**

readstring

file string   **readstring**   substring bool

reads characters from the designated *file* into *string* until all space in *string* is filled or until end-of-file. All characters are allowed and treated identically and are translated into a character code, which is an integer in the range 0 to 255. These integer values are stored in successive positions in *string* until all positions are filled or there is an end-of-file indication posted from *file*. The boolean result, *bool*, indicates whether the read terminated normally, by filling the string – in which case it will be *true;* or whether end-of-file was encountered first – in which case it will be *false.* In either case, the result *substring* contains the valid characters that were read from the file.

The **readstring** operator does not treat any characters as special; and, in particular, it does not provide any special processing for the *newline* character.

> TYPE: File
> ERRORS: invalidaccess, ioerror, rangecheck, stackunderflow, typecheck
> ASSOCIATED: **bytesavailable, read, readhexstring, readline, write**

renderbands

proc   **renderbands**   –

renders bands of raster data from raster memory to the current output device. The current output device must have been installed using the **banddevice** operator, and **renderbands** can only be called from the procedure installed by **banddevice**. Both the **renderbands** and **banddevice** operators are defined only in PostScript devices that use band buffers. See the discussion under **banddevice** for further information.

    renderbands divides the output page into rectangular arrays of pixels, or *bands*. The size of these bands depends on the characteristics of the output device and is implementation-dependent. The bands are then transferred to the band buffer, and the procedure *proc* is executed to transfer the band buffer to the physical output device. This generally requires specialized, device-dependent operators, which will be documented individually for each device.

TYPE: Device
ERRORS: stackunderflow, typecheck
ASSOCIATED: **banddevice, framedevice, nulldevice**

repeat

int proc   **repeat**   –

executes *proc int* times. The *int* operand must be a non-negative integer and may be 0, in which case **repeat** does not execute *proc* at all, and processing continues at the next command. The **repeat** operator removes both operands from the stack, but *proc* may leave values on the stack that will not be removed by the operation of repeat. In addition to the normal termination by executing *proc* the given number of times, **repeat** may be terminated at any earlier time by execution of an **exit** operator within *proc*.

EXAMPLE:

```
2 {2 3 add} repeat        ⇒        5 5
2 2 {3 add} repeat        ⇒        8
```

since the first execution leaves a result 5 on the stack.

```
[12 13 14 15 ]
aload
4 {pop} repeat        ⇒        12
```

since the **aload** leaves the matrix and the four values on the stack, and the **repeat** removes the top four objects.

TYPE: Control
ERRORS: invalidaccess, rangecheck, stackunderflow, typecheck
ASSOCIATED: **exit, for, forall, loop**

resetfile

    file   **resetfile**   –

resets the file by discarding all buffered characters that are associated with *file*. If *file* is an input file, **resetfile** discards any characters that have been received by the interpreter but not yet processed; if *file* is an output file, any characters that have been written but not yet transmitted are discarded.

    The **resetfile** operator may also have other effects that are implementation-dependent; for example, in some environments it may restart or reestablish communications over the communication channel in use. In any case, **resetfile** never waits for characters to be received or transmitted.

TYPE: File
ERRORS: stackunderflow, typecheck
ASSOCIATED: **file, closefile, flush, flushfile**

restore

    saveobj   **restore**   –

resets virtual memory (VM) to the state it was in when the *saveobj* was created by the **save** operator.

    The **restore** operator alters only the contents of VM; it does not alter the contents of the execution, dictionary, or operand stacks. However, if those stacks contain objects that consume VM that were created after the *saveobj* being restored, the **restore** will fail and raise the **invalidrestore** error. This occurs because the objects would still exist on the stacks and be notionally accessible, but the actual values would be removed by the **restore**. Such objects are composite objects, names, files, and save objects themselves. The graphics state stack is altered by the **restore**. The **restore** performs the equivalent of a **grestoreall** to reset the graphics state.

    restore can be called with any save object that is still valid, not just the most recent save object. In this, **save** and **restore** do not behave like **gsave** and **grestore**. If a *saveobj* is referenced by a **restore,** both it and all save objects created after it, if any, are invalidated. For this reason, any save object can be referenced only once. In addition, the graphic state stored by the save object is also removed from the graphics state stack.

TYPE: Memory
ERRORS: invalidrestore, stackunderflow, typecheck
ASSOCIATED: **save, gsave, grestore, grestoreall**

reversepath

−   **reversepath**   −

replaces the current path with a new version of the path that has all the segments of each subpath enumerated in reverse order. However, the order of individual subpaths within the current path is not changed.

EXAMPLE:

```
100 100 moveto
20 0 rlineto
100 115 moveto
10 −10 rlineto
10 10 rlineto
100 130 moveto
10 10 rlineto
10 −10 rlineto
```

draws three lines on the current path. The top line consists of one segment, while each of the bottom two lines consists of two segments. If these lines were enumerated, as if by **pathforall**, you would see the following segments:

```
moveto segment 100.0 100.0
lineto segment 120.0 100.0
moveto segment 100.0 115.0
lineto segment 110.0 105.0
lineto segment 120.0 115.0
moveto segment 100.0 130.0
lineto segment 110.0 140.0
lineto segment 120.0 130.0
```

Now suppose you create the same path and reverse it as follows:

```
100 100 moveto
20 0 rlineto
100 115 moveto
10 −10 rlineto
10 10 rlineto
100 130 moveto
10 10 rlineto
10 −10 rlineto
reversepath
```

which still draws the same three lines on the page, but gives the following result if enumerated:

```
moveto segment 120.0 100.0
lineto segment 100.0 100.0
moveto segment 120.0 115.0
lineto segment 110.0 105.0
lineto segment 100.0 115.0
moveto segment 120.0 130.0
lineto segment 110.0 140.0
lineto segment 100.0 130.0
```

The three lines are now each drawn in reverse, with the **moveto** going to the far end of the line and the **lineto** segments moving in the reverse direction. Notice, however, that the order of the lines remains the same: the first line created is still first, and so on. This illustrates the point that the order of the segments within a subpath is reversed, but the order of the subpaths remains the same. In this case, a move segment and one or more line segments form each of three independent subpaths.

TYPE: Path
ERRORS: (none)
ASSOCIATED: **pathforall**

rlineto

rx ry   **rlineto**   –

adds a straight line segment to the current path in the same manner as the **lineto** operator except that the operands are relative to the current point rather than absolute coordinates. The straight line segment extends from the current point, defined as (x_0, y_0), to the point (x_0+rx, y_0+ry); the point (x_0+rx, y_0+ry) becomes the new current point at the completion of the line construction.

TYPE: Path
ERRORS: limitcheck, nocurrentpoint, stackunderflow, typecheck
ASSOCIATED: **lineto, moveto, rcurveto, rmoveto**

rmoveto

rx ry   rmoveto   –

starts a new subpath of the current path by moving to a new current point defined by the operands (rx, ry), which are relative to the current point. If the current point is denoted by the coordinates (x_0, y_0), then the new current point after **rmoveto** will be the point (x_0+rx, y_0+ry).

There are two things to note when using **rmoveto** in programs. First, like **moveto**, the **rmoveto** does not construct a path segment between the current point and the new current point. The move simply replaces one current point with another. However, unlike **moveto**, it does require that the current point be defined, since the movement is defined relative to the current point. Any attempt to use **rmoveto** when the current path is empty will result in raising the **nocurrentpoint** error.

> TYPE: Path
> ERRORS: limitcheck, nocurrentpoint, stackunderflow, typecheck
> ASSOCIATED: **lineto, moveto, rcurveto, rlineto**

roll

$$\text{any}_{n-1} \ldots \text{any}_0 \ n \ int \qquad \textbf{roll} \qquad \text{any}_{int-1} \ldots \text{any}_0 \ \text{any}_{n-1} \ldots \text{any}_{int}$$

performs a circular shift of the contents of the operand stack. The top n objects on the stack after the two control operands n and int are shifted by amount int. A positive value of int indicates movement up the stack, that is, toward the top of the stack; a negative value indicates movement down the stack. The operand n must be a non-negative integer, and there must be at least n elements on the stack below the top two operands. The operand int must be an integer.

It is possible to have int greater than or equal to n. If int is equal to n, then the top n objects on the stack are rotated in a circular manner so that each object returns to its original position in the stack, like a toy train on a track. In this case, the operation has no effect. If int is greater than n, then **roll** continues this circular procession and rotates the objects on the stack around the loop until it has moved int times. The net result is the same as if int were divided by n and only the remainder of the division were used to control the move. This happens because each n rotations return the objects on the stack to their original positions and so the only effective motion on the stack is the value of int that is greater than some multiple of n. Mathematically, this is called int modulo n.

EXAMPLE:

Stack in:	2	roll	⇒	Stack out:	(b)
	4				(a)
	(d)				(d)
	(c)				(c)
	(b)				(z)
	(a)				
	(z)				

Stack in:	−1	roll	⇒	Stack out:	(a)
	4				(d)
	(d)				(c)

```
                (c)                                        (b)
                (b)                                        (z)
                (a)
                (z)
Stack in: 14          roll      ⇒      Stack out: (b)
           4                                        (a)
          (d)                                       (d)
          (c)                                       (c)
          (b)                                       (z)
          (a)
          (z)
```

which is identical to the result in the first example, since 14 mod 4 is 2 – that is, 14 divided by 4 has a remainder of 2.

TYPE: Stack
ERRORS: rangecheck, stackoverflow, stackunderflow, typecheck
ASSOCIATED: **copy, dup, exch, index, pop**

*rootfont

—   **rootfont**   font

returns the root composite font that has been selected by the most recent setfont. The **rootfont** operator will return the root composite font even when invoked from within a **BuildChar** or a **cshow**, at which time the **currentfont** operator would return the descendent base font.

This operator is defined only in versions of the interpreter that support composite fonts.

TYPE: Font
ERRORS: stackoverflow
ASSOCIATED: **currentfont, setfont**

rotate

angle   **rotate**   —

rotates the user coordinates around their origin by *angle*. If *angle* is positive, the user coordinates are rotated in a counterclockwise direction; and they are rotated in a clockwise direction if *angle* is negative. Precisely, **rotate** builds a temporary transformation matrix as follows: [cos θ sin θ − sin θ cos θ 0 0], where θ is *angle* in degrees, and concatenates

* This operator is not present in PostScript version 38.0.

it with the current transformation matrix (CTM) to give a new CTM. The position of the origin and the scale of the x and y axes are unchanged.

> angle matrix   **rotate**   matrix

adjusts the values in *matrix* by the transformation matrix described above: [$\cos \theta \sin \theta$ $-\sin \theta \cos \theta$ 0 0], where θ is *angle* in degrees, and returns the modified matrix back to the operand stack. No change is made to the CTM (see Figure C1.7).

See Section A3.3 for a complete discussion of PostScript coordinates and their matrix representation.

Figure C1.7   **rotate** operator

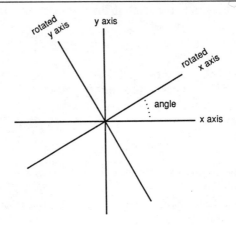

EXAMPLE:

> 30 matrix rotate $\Rightarrow$ [0.866025 0.5 −0.5 0.866025 0.0 0.0]

> TYPE: Coordinate
> ERRORS: invalidaccess, stackunderflow, typecheck
> ASSOCIATED: **concat, matrix, scale, translate**

round

> num1   **round**   num2

rounds *num1* to the nearest integer value, *num2*. If *num1* is equally close to its two nearest integers, the result is the greater of the two. The type of *num2* is the same as the type of *num1*. Generally, of course, they will be real numbers, since the result of rounding an integer is simply to return the same value.

EXAMPLE:

2.4 round	⇒	2.0
2 round	⇒	2
3.5 round	⇒	4.0
− 2.4 round	⇒	− 2.0
− 3.5 round	⇒	− 3.0

TYPE: Mathematical
ERRORS: stackunderflow, typecheck
ASSOCIATED: **ceiling, cvi, floor, truncate**

rrand

                    —   **rrand**   int

returns an integer value, *int,* that represents the current state of the pseudo-random number generator used by the interpreter. This *int* can be saved and later presented to the **srand** operator to reset the generator to the current position. If this is done, it will cause the sequence of numbers generated by successive calls to the rand operator to repeat. See the example under **srand** for more details.

TYPE: Mathematical
ERRORS: stackoverflow
ASSOCIATED: **rand, srand**

run

               filestring   **run**   —

executes the contents of the file identified by *filestring*. In this mode, the **run** operator interprets the incoming character stream as a PostScript program. **run** stops execution and closes the file when it either encounters an end-of-file character or when it is terminated from within the program, for example, by execution of a **stop**. The **run** context cannot be terminated by an **exit** operator; any attempt to do so results in an **invalidext** error.

Although **run** does not leave any results on the stack, the program that is executed by **run** may make any changes to any stack, some of which may persist after termination of execution.

TYPE: File
ERRORS: ioerror, limitcheck, stackunderflow, typecheck, undefinedresult
ASSOCIATED: **exec, file**

save

—   **save**   saveobj

creates a *saveobj* that preserves and represents the current state of virtual memory (VM). The **save** operator also saves the current graphics state stack by pushing a copy onto the graphics state stack in the same manner as a **gsave**.

   The state of virtual memory at the time of the **save** can later be restored by using a **restore** operator. See Section A2.5 for a description of virtual memory and the handling of **save** and **restore**. The graphics state that is preserved by a **save** is also restored when a **restore** is performed and can also be referenced by the **grestoreall** operator.

          TYPE: Memory
      ERRORS: limitcheck, stackoverflow
ASSOCIATED: **restore, gsave, grestoreall**

scale

sx sy   **scale**   —

scales the user coordinates around their origin by *sx* along the *x*-axis and *sy* along the *y*-axis. The net effect is to make 1 unit along the *x*-axis in the new coordinates the equivalent of *sx* units in the old coordinates, and 1 unit along the new *y*-axis equal to *sy* units along the old. Precisely, **scale** builds a temporary transformation matrix as follows: [sx 0 0 sy 0 0], and concatenates it with the current transformation matrix (CTM) to give a new CTM. The position of the origin and the orientation of the *x* and *y* axes are unchanged.

sx sy matrix   **scale**   matrix

adjusts the values in *matrix* by the transformation matrix described above, [sx 0 0 sy 0 0], and returns the modified matrix back to the operand stack. No change is made to the CTM. See Section A3.3 for a complete discussion of PostScript coordinates and their matrix representation.

      EXAMPLE:

          3 5 matrix scale   ⇒   [3 0 0 5 0 0]

          TYPE: Coordinate
      ERRORS: invalidaccess, stackunderflow, typecheck
ASSOCIATED: **concat, matrix, rotate, translate**

scalefont

font1 scale   **scalefont**   font2

scales *font1* by the scale factor *scale* to generate a new font, *font2,* whose characters are magnified equally along both axes when they are imaged. Precisely, the **scalefont** operator makes a copy of *font1* and creates a new **FontMatrix** by multiplying the old **Font-Matrix** by *scale*. This copy, with its new **FontMatrix,** is returned as *font2.*

The essential operation of **scalefont** is to change the character coordinates of a font in the same manner as **scale** modifies the user coordinates, except that **scalefont** provides only one scaling factor in both dimensions – essentially the equivalent of **scale** with *sx* equal to *sy*. This allows a programmer to modify the size of a font by changing the coordinates for display of the font without modifying the entire coordinate system. The effect of the transformed coordinates is confined to the display of the font. If **scalefont** is applied to a composite font, the transformation is also applied to each of the descendent fonts.

The **scalefont** operator is a special case of **makefont** that provides uniform scaling in both the *x* and *y* dimensions. A programmer must use **makefont** to provide nonuniform scaling for a font.

EXAMPLE:

```
/Times Roman findfont        % get font dictionary
12 scalefont                 % make a 12-point version
setfont
100 100 moveto
(TIMES) show
```

This example shows the ordinary use of **scalefont** to create a font of the desired size. The font dictionary for the Times Roman font is retrieved by the **findfont** operator and returned to the stack. Then the scale factor of 12 is pushed onto the stack and the **scalefont** is invoked. This changes the font's size as described above and returns a new font dictionary to the stack that has the correct size incorporated into its **FontMatrix.** This new font is then passed to the **setfont** operator, which makes it the current font.

TYPE: Font
ERRORS: invalidfont, stackunderflow, typecheck, undefined
ASSOCIATED: **findfont, makefont, setfont**

search

string   pattern **search**

if found:
    suffix match prefix true
if not found:
    string false

determines if any part of *string* matches the string *pattern,* that is, that *string* is at least as long as *pattern* and any sequence of characters within *string* is identical to *pattern.* If any substring of *string* matches *pattern,* **search** returns *string* in three pieces: *match,* which matches the *pattern; suffix,* which is the remainder of *string* after *match;* and *prefix,* which is the portion of *string* that occurs before *match.* Finally, it pushes the boolean value *true* onto the stack to indicate successful completion of the comparison. If no substring of *string* is identical to *pattern,* **search** returns the *string* unchanged and pushes *false* onto the stack.

Note that, in both cases, the output returned is part of the original string. Since strings are composite objects, any changes that use these parts of the string will also affect the original string representation. This remains true even if you redefine those parts of the string. (See the discussion of simple and composite objects in Section A2.2).

EXAMPLE 1:

Stack in: (sd)	**search**	⇒	Stack out: true
(asdfg)			(a)
			(sd)
			(fg)

EXAMPLE 2:

Stack in: (sdg)	**search**	⇒	Stack out: false
(asdfg)			(asdfg)

TYPE: String
ERRORS: invalidaccess, stackunderflow, stackoverflow, typecheck
ASSOCIATED: **anchorsearch, token**

*setblackgeneration

proc   **setblackgeneration**   —

sets the current black generation function in the current graphics state to *proc,* which must be a PostScript language procedure that accepts an operand in the range 0 to 1 and returns a result in the same range. The values supplied to *proc* represent the *cyan, magenta,* and *yellow* components of the current color, and the procedure maps the appropriate minimum of these values into a black component. This is an automatic process that is designed to aid the mapping of RGB color values into CMYK values. See Section A4.4 for a complete discussion of color operations.

The use of **setblackgeneration** after a **setcachedevice** operation within a **BuildChar** procedure is not allowed, because the font cache cannot preserve color information; an attempt to use it will result in raising the **undefined** error.

* This operator is not present in PostScript version 38.0.

For those PostScript devices that support color operations, the device setup procedures for the device provide a set of default adjustments for each color component that are carefully chosen to provide good results in a wide variety of circumstances. They should be changed (using **setblackgeneration** and **setundercolorremoval**) only after careful consideration and planning.

TYPE: Color
ERRORS: invalidaccess, stackunderflow, typecheck
ASSOCIATED: **currentblackgeneration, setundercolorremoval, currentundercolorremoval, setgray, setcmykcolor, setrgbcolor, currentgray, currentcmykcolor, currentrgbcolor**

setcachedevice

wx wy llx lly urx ury   **setcachedevice**   —

passes width and bounding box information for a character to the PostScript font machinery. The **setcachedevice** operator may be executed only within the context of a **BuildChar** procedure for a user-defined font. The **BuildChar** procedure first invokes **setcachedevice** to define the character width and bounding box and to tell the font machinery that the subsequent character is to be placed into the font cache, if possible. Then **BuildChar** invokes standard PostScript operators to define and paint the character.

After execution of a **setcachedevice** within a **BuildChar** procedure, the following operators are not permitted for the creation and painting of characters: **setgray, setcmykcolor, sethsbcolor, setrgbcolor, settransfer**, and **image**, and any other operators that change the current color. All these operators produce results that cannot be carried into the cache mechanism; if, therefore, these operators are required, the **BuildChar** must use the the operator **setcharwidth** instead of **setcachedevice**. However, the use of the **imagemask** operator is permitted. In any case, **BuildChar** must use either one of the **setcachedevice** operations or **setcharwidth** to establish the necessary character metrics when creating a character.

The operands for **setcachedevice** are all numeric values interpreted as coordinates in the character coordinate system. See Section A5.5 for a full discussion of character coordinates and metrics. The wx and wy operands give the width vector of the character; that is, the next character should normally begin in the position that is displaced by (wx, wy) from the current point. Generally, for roman alphabets, wy will always be 0. For devices that implement composite fonts, **setcachedevice** installs two sets of character metrics that are identical, so that characters will be positioned relative to the current point and change the current point in a way that is not dependent upon the writing mode.

The bounding box operands, *llx, lly, urx,* and *ury,* define the corners of a rectangle with the sides parallel to the character coordinate axes that completely encloses the marks placed on the page by executing the character definition and painting operations that follow. The values are exactly those that would be returned by applying the **pathbbox** operator to the path defined for the character. The bounding box information passed to the font machinery must be correct; any portion of a character that lies outside the bounding box will not image correctly.

TYPE:	Font Cache
ERRORS:	stackunderflow, typecheck, undefined
ASSOCIATED:	**cachestatus, setcachelimit, setcharwidth**

*setcachedevice2

w0x w0y llx lly urx ury

w1x w1y vx vy   **setcachedevice2**   –

passes character metric information for an individual character to the PostScript font machinery. The **setcachedevice2** operator may be executed only within the context of a **BuildChar** procedure for a user-defined font. The **BuildChar** procedure first invokes **setcachedevice2** to define the character metrics and to tell the font machinery that the subsequent character is to be placed into the font cache if possible. Then **BuildChar** invokes standard PostScript operators to define and paint the character.

The **setcachedevice2** operator is very similar to the **setcachedevice** operator and has the same requirements and limitations on operands and in execution. The **setcachedevice2** operator is designed to provide alternate metric information for characters that require different metrics when printed in both horizontal and vertical writing modes. The operands are all numeric values interpreted as coordinates in the character coordinate system. See Section A5.5 for a full discussion of character coordinates and metrics. This operator is defined only in versions of the interpreter that support composite fonts.

The *w0x* and *w0y* operands give the width vector of the character in writing mode *0;* that is, the next character should normally begin in the position that is displaced by (*wx, wy*) from the current point when characters are displayed horizontally. The bounding box operands, *llx, lly, urx* and *ury,* define the corners of a rectangle with the sides parallel to the character coordinate axes that completely encloses the marks placed on the page by executing the character definition and painting operations that follow. The operands *w1x* and *w1y* are the height vector of the character in writing mode *1;* that is, the next character should normally begin in the position that is displaced by (*w1x, w1y*) from the current point when characters are displayed horizontally. Finally, the *vx* and *vy* operands define the relation of the character origin in writing mode *0* to the origin in writing mode *1;* that is, the origin in mode *1* is displaced by (*vx, vy*) from the origin in mode *0.*

Both sets of metrics are installed with the character definition in the font. The appropriate metric is determined at the time of imaging the character by whether the base

---

* This operator is not present in PostScript version 38.0.

font that contains the character is a descendent of a composite font with writing mode *0* or one with mode *1*. The writing mode of the root composite font will always override that of all subsequent descendent fonts.

TYPE: Font Cache
ERRORS: stackunderflow, typecheck, undefined
ASSOCIATED: **cachestatus, setcachelimit, setcharwidth**

setcachelimit

num **setcachelimit** –

sets *num* as the maximum number of bytes that may be taken up by the bit map of a single cached character; this is the same as the *blimit* reported by the **cachestatus** operator. Any character whose bit map is larger than *num* is not included in the font cache but instead is recreated from its character description every time it's used. The size of a character, for these purposes, is determined by the bounding box information provided by the **setcachedevice** operator.

Changing **setcachelimit** affects only characters created after the change; it does not affect characters already in the cache. Greater values of *num* allow larger characters to be included in the cache but at the possible price of using up larger amounts of cache storage for each character, thereby limiting the total number of characters in the cache at any given time. Generally, the default value of **setcachelimit** has been carefully chosen to provide the best tradeoff in storage use and character size; therefore, changes to **setcachelimit** should be made only in unusual circumstances and after thorough consideration.

The maximum value of *num* depends on the output device; this value is usually the total size of the font cache (*bmax* as reported by the **cachestatus** operator). Clearly, under ordinary circumstances, the value of *num* should be some small fraction of *bmax*. In a LaserWriter running Adobe's PostScript interpreter, Version 38.0, these values are 12500 and 136064, respectively.

TYPE: Font Cache
ERRORS: limitcheck, rangecheck, stackunderflow, typecheck
ASSOCIATED: **cachestatus, setcachedevice, setcharwidth**

setcacheparams

mark lower upper **setcacheparams** –

sets the current cache parameters to the integer values on the operand stack that are above a *mark*. In present implementations, there are just two: *lower* and *upper*. The *mark* is used because the number of cache parameters is variable and may be changed in future implementations. **setcacheparams** reads the values and uses them as required, then clears the stack as if using a **cleartomark**.

The *upper* operand is the value *blimit* and is the same as the value accessible through the **setcachelimit** operator. This defines the maximum number of bytes that may be occupied by a single cached character.

The *lower* operand defines the threshold above which a character's array is stored in compressed form rather than as full pixel arrays. When the character's size exceeds *lower*, it is stored in compressed format in the cache and reconstituted when it is required. *lower* can be any non-negative integer; if it is zero, all characters are stored in compressed format. Compression can be disabled by setting *lower* to a value greater than *upper*.

The tradeoff is that although characters that are compressed take longer to convert and image onto the output page, their reduced storage requirements allow more characters to be stored in the font cache. All characters in the font cache, even in compressed format, are rendered substantially faster than characters that are not cached.

> TYPE: Font cache
> ERRORS: rangecheck, unmatchedmark
> ASSOCIATED: **cachestatus, currentcacheparams**

setcharwidth

> wx wy　　　　**setcharwidth**　　　　　–

performs a function similar to **setcachedevice**, but provides only character width information to the PostScript font machinery. The choice of this operator (instead of **setcachedevice**) to set character metrics implies that the character is not to be included in the font cache.

Because characters defined by **setcharwidth** do not go into the font cache, their definition and painting process may use the operators that are prohibited when using **setcachedevice**, namely, **setgray, setcmykcolor, sethsbcolor, setrgbcolor, settransfer, image**, and so on. Use of these operators can be important if you want to paint a character with a specific color or a specific gray level rather than letting it default to the current color as you would normally do.

> TYPE: Font cache
> ERRORS: stackunderflow, typecheck, undefined
> ASSOCIATED: **setcachedevice**

*setcmykcolor

> cyan magenta yellow black　　　　**setcmykcolor**　　　　–

sets the values *cyan*, *magenta*, *yellow*, and *black* as the four components that define the current color parameter in the current graphics state according to the cyan-magenta-yellow-black (CMYK) model. Each of these values is a number between 0 and 1 that indicates

* This operator is not present in PostScript version 38.0.

the percentage of cyan, magenta, yellow, and black in the current color. The current color is the color that is used for all subsequent painting operations, such as **fill** and **stroke**, on the current page.

Note that **setcmykcolor** bypasses processes of automatic black generation and undercolor removal. This operator and these processes are defined only in PostScript devices that support color operations. Use of **setgray** in this environment sets the *black* operand to 1.0 minus the value supplied to **setgray** and sets the other CMYK color component values to 0.0. See the discussion of color operations in Section A4.4 for a more complete explanation.

The use of **setcmykcolor** after a **setcachedevice** operation within a **BuildChar** procedure is not allowed, because the font cache cannot preserve color information; an attempt to use it will result in raising the **undefined** error.

TYPE: Color
ERRORS: stackunderflow, typecheck, undefined
ASSOCIATED: **setgray, sethsbcolor, setrgbcolor, currentgray, currenthsbcolor, currentrgbcolor**

*setcolorscreen

rfreq rangle rproc
gfreq gangle gproc
bfreq bangle bproc
grayfreq grayangle grayproc   **setcolorscreen**   —

sets the twelve color halftone screen components in the current graphics state. There is one complete set of screen definitions for each color component. The *freq* operands for each color component are real numbers that define the screen frequency for that component, which is measured in halftone cells per inch in device space. The *angle* operands are real numbers that specify the rotation angle of the halftone screen of each color component in relation to the device coordinate system. The *proc* operands define the *spot function* for each color component. These functions determine the order in which the pixels within a halftone cell are changed from no color to full color to generate shades of the desired color component. The red, green, and blue screens will have no effect on a black-and-white device; the gray screen will have no effect on a RGB or CMY (three-color) device, and none of the screens will have an effect on a device that uses a full gray scale (eight bits per pixel).

The **setcolorscreen** operator is a natural extension of the **setscreen** operator to full-color operations. It takes the same type of operands, each type repeated for each of the four color components. This operator and these color screen components are defined only in those versions of the PostScript interpreter that support color operations; other versions support only the gray components. See Section A4.4 for a detailed description of color operations.

* This operator is no present in PostScript version 38.0.

For those PostScript devices that support color operations, the device-setup procedures provide default halftone screens for each color component that are carefully chosen to provide good results in a wide variety of circumstances. They should be changed (using setcolorscreen) only after careful consideration and planning.

TYPE: Color
ERRORS: invalidaccess, limitcheck, rangecheck, stackunderflow, typecheck
ASSOCIATED: **currentcolorscreen, currentscreen, setscreen**

*setcolortransfer

rproc gproc bproc grayproc   **setcolortransfer**   –

sets the four color-transfer functions, *rproc* for the red color component, *gproc* for the green color component, *bproc* for the blue color component, and *grayproc* for the gray color component, that define the current color in the current graphics state.

Each *proc* defines a transfer procedure to be used by one component of the current color in the current graphics state. Each **proc** must be a PostScript procedure that is called with an operand between 0 and 1, which is the current value for the specific component in the graphics state, and returns a result that defines the same color component in device values. The current value of a color component is the value set by the **setrgbcolor** operator, adjusted by the **setblackgeneration** and the **setundercolorremoval** processes, or 1.0 minus the values set by **setcmykcolor**. In this way, *proc* maps user color values into device color values. These color components are defined only in those versions of the PostScript interpreter that support color operations; for example, red, green, and blue transfers will have no effect on a black-and-white device, while the gray transfer will have no effect on a RGB or CMY (three-color) device.

The use of **setcolortransfer** after a **setcachedevice** operation within a **BuildChar** procedure is not allowed, because the font cache cannot preserve color information; an attempt to use it will result in raising the undefined error.

The **setcolortransfer** operator is a natural extension of the **settransfer** operator to full-color operations. It takes the same type of operands, each type repeated for each of the four color components. This operator and these color transfer procedures are defined only in those versions of the PostScript interpreter that support color operations; other versions support only the gray procedure. See Section A4.4 for a detailed description of color operations.

For those PostScript devices that support color operations, the device-setup procedures provide a set of default transfers for each color component that are carefully chosen to provide good results in a wide variety of circumstances. They should be changed (using **setcolortransfer**) only after careful consideration and planning.

* This operator is not present in PostScript verion 38.0.

TYPE: Color
ERRORS: invalidaccess, stackunderflow, typecheck
ASSOCIATED: **currentcolortransfer, currenttransfer, settransfer**

setdash

array offset   **setdash**   —

sets the current dash setting in the current graphics state according to the *array* and *offset* operands. The current dash pattern is defined by *array,* and the current dash phase, or offset, is defined by *offset.* The current dash setting governs the type of line produced by subsequent executions of the **stroke** operator.

The *array* that governs the current dash pattern may be empty, in which case the line produced by **stroke** is a solid line, or it may consist of any number of non-negative integers, at least one of which must be greater than zero. These integer values measure distances along the current path in user coordinates. These distances alternate as measures of the length of a dash and the length of the next gap between dashes. The elements of *array* are used cyclically by stroke; when it reaches the end of the elements, it starts over again until the entire path has been stroked.

The *offset* operand is a number that defines the starting point of the dash pattern along the path; it may be considered the 'phase' of the pattern relative to the starting point of the path. Before applying the dash pattern to a path, **stroke** cycles *offset* distance through the dash pattern, adding each element of *array* until the total equals *offset.* Then **stroke** begins to paint from the beginning of the path, applying the dash pattern from the point that has been reached.

Multiple subpaths of the current path are treated individually, and the dash pattern and offset are applied independently to each one from its beginning.

EXAMPLE:

The following are not complete PostScript examples; instead, they simply show what the results of a **setdash** would be with the given *array* and *offset.*

[] 0 setdash	% solid line
[2] 1 setdash	% 1 dash – 2 gap – 2 dash . . .
[2] 3 setdash	% 1 gap – 2 dash – 2 gap . . .
[3] 1.5 setdash	% 1.5 dash – 3 gap – 3 dash . . .

Notice that the offset need not be integer.

```
[2 4 ]   0 setdash        % 2 dash – 4 gap – 2 dash . . .
[2 4 ] 10 setdash         % 2 gap – 2 dash – 4 gap . . .
```

since the offset cycles through the array distances as 2 (dash) + 4 (gap) + 2 (dash) + 2 (of the 4 gap) before starting the stroke, leaving a gap of 2 at the start of the path.

```
[2 4] – 2 setdash         % 4 dash – 4 gap – 2 dash – 4 gap . . .
```

Notice that the offset need not be positive; a negative offset adds that much solid line at the beginning of the path before the array pattern kicks in.

```
[2 4 3 6 ] 0 setdash           % 2 dash – 4 gap – 3 dash – 6 gap – 2 dash . . .
```

```
          TYPE:   Graphics
        ERRORS:   limitcheck, stackunderflow, typecheck
    ASSOCIATED:   currentdash, stroke
```

setflat

```
      num        setflat           –
```

sets *num* as the current flatness parameter in the current graphics state. The current flatness parameter is a positive number that defines the precision with which curved lines are rendered on the output device. The painting operators, **stroke**, **fill**, and **clip**, all approximate curved lines by using a series of straight line segments. The 'flatness' of the approximation is a measure of how close the straight lines are constrained to the actual curve value: the smaller the flatness, the closer the straight lines must be to the curve. The flatness parameter actually measures the maximum distance, in output device pixels, that the straight line approximation can vary from the true curve.

The flatness parameter can be any number within some defined range. On the Laser-Writer, this range is 0.2 to 100.0 The smaller values provide greater accuracy in matching the curve but at the expense of adding many additional points to the path and causing significantly more computation during the imaging process. A default value is established for each device and generally provides the best tradeoff between accuracy and computational efficiency; it should be modified (by using **setflat**) only with good reason.

If *num* falls outside of the defined range for setflat, it will be forced to the nearest value within the range without any error indication.

TYPE: Graphics
ERRORS: stackunderflow, typecheck
ASSOCIATED: **currentflat, flattenpath**

setfont

font   **setfont**   –

sets *font* as the current font dictionary in the current graphics state. The current font dictionary is the font dictionary that will be invoked by all subsequent operations that require a font definition to be used for character operations. *font* must be a well-formed font dictionary such as would be returned by a **findfont** operator.

If composite fonts are being used, **setfont** sets the root composite font that is used to establish the mapping for subsequent character operations. If the mapping algorithm so established is incomplete when it is subsequently invoked to handle a string, a **rangecheck** error will result.

TYPE: Graphics
ERRORS: stackunderflow, typecheck
ASSOCIATED: **currentfont, findfont, rootfont, show**

setgray

num   **setgray**   –

sets *num* as the gray value of the current color in the current graphics state. The gray value is a number between 0 and 1 that indicates the degree of light or white to be used when painting on the output device. The value of 1 corresponds to white, and the value 0 corresponds to black, with values in between indicating a corresponding percentage of white to produce intermediate shades of gray. The use of the **setgray** operator defines the current color to be black and white. The current color is the color that is used for all subsequent painting operations, such as **fill** and **stroke**, on the current page. See the discussion of gray scales and color operations in Sections A4.3 and A4.4 for a more complete explanation.

The use of **setgray** after a **setcachedevice** operation within a **BuildChar** procedure is not allowed, because the font cache cannot preserve color information; an attempt to use it will result in raising the **undefined** error.

TYPE: Graphics
ERRORS: stackunderflow, typecheck, undefined
ASSOCIATED: **currentgray, fill, show, stroke, setcmykcolor, sethsbcolor, setrgbcolor**

sethsbcolor

hue sat bright   **sethsbcolor**   —

sets the values *hue, sat,* and *bright* as the three components that define the current color parameter in the current graphics state according to the hue-saturation-brightness model. Each of these values is a number between 0 and 1 that indicates the hue, saturation, and brightness of the current color. The current color is the color that is used for all subsequent painting operations, such as **fill** and **stroke**, on the current page. See the discussion of color operations in Section A4.4 for a more complete explanation.

The use of **sethsbcolor** after a **setcachedevice** operation within a **BuildChar** procedure is not allowed, because the font cache cannot preserve color information; an attempt to use it will result in raising the undefined error.

TYPE: Graphics
ERRORS: stackunderflow, typecheck, undefined
ASSOCIATED: **currenthsbcolor, fill, show, stroke, setgray, setcmykcolor, setrgbcolor**

setlinecap

int   **setlinecap**   —

sets the current line cap parameter in the current graphics state. The current line cap parameter is an integer value, either 0, 1, or 2, that defines the method of finishing the ends of any line drawn on the output device. The three values correspond to the three methods of finishing the lines, as follows:

0   butt cap: the line is squared off at the endpoint of the path; no part of the line extends beyond the end of the path.

1   round cap: the line is finished with a semicircular arc centered around the endpoint with a radius equal to one-half the linewidth.

2   projecting square cap: the line is finished with a square end that projects beyond the endpoint by one-half the line width.

The 0 linecap is the default value. In Figure C1.8, the white interior line represents the path generated by the PostScript path construction operators, and the white dots represent the starting and ending points, respectively, of that path. The black area represents the path as stroked by the **stroke** operator when the line cap parameter is as indicated by the captions.

TYPE: Graphics
ERRORS: rangecheck, stackunderflow, typecheck
ASSOCIATED: **currentlinecap, stroke, currentlinejoin, setlinejoin**

Figure C1.8 **setlinecap** values

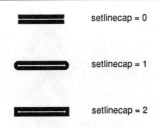

setlinecap = 0

setlinecap = 1

setlinecap = 2

setlinejoin

int   **setlinejoin**   —

sets *int* as the current line join parameter in the current graphics state. The current line join parameter is an integer value, either 0, 1, or 2, that defines the method of finishing the joins between lines drawn on the output device. The three values correspond to the three methods of joining lines, as follows:

0   miter join: the outer edges of each line are extended until they join in a point. If the point where the two outer edges meet extends more than a limiting amount from the point of the join, a bevel join is used instead. The limiting amount for the extension of the joined lines is controlled by the miter limit parameter, which is set by the **setmiterlimit** operator.

1   round join: a circle with a radius of one-half the line width, centered on the point of the join, is drawn and filled. If the line segments are quite short (less than one-half the line width), you may see a portion of the circle on the 'wrong side' of the lines.

2   bevel join: the two meeting lines are finished with butt caps, as described under the **setlinecap** operator, and a straight line is drawn from the outer edge of one line to the outer edge of the other. This triangular notch between the two ends is then filled in (see Figure C1.9).

Joins, in the sense used here, occur only when two line segments are connected because one is a continuation of the other or because they are deliberately joined, for example, by the **closepath** operator. If line segments happen to cross one another, they are not considered joined, and no special treatment is provided. Curved line segments are rendered by series of straight lines (see the **setflat** operator for more detail), and those straight line segments are joined with the current line join. Under typical settings of the flatness parameter, however, the join is undetectable.

Figure C1.9 setlinecap values

setlinejoin = 0

setlinejoin = 1

setlinejoin = 2

TYPE: Graphics
ERRORS: rangecheck, stackunderflow, typecheck
ASSOCIATED: **currentlinejoin, stroke, currentlinecap, setlinecap**

setlinewidth

num   **setlinewidth**   —

sets *num* as the current line width parameter in the current graphics state. The current line width parameter is the size in user coordinate units of the stroke produced when a line is drawn on the output device.

The **stroke** operator actually paints all points that are less than or equal to one-half of *num* units from the current path, thus generating a line that is *num* units wide and centered around the current path. The fact that the line extends equally on both sides of the path can be the cause of some surprising results if *num* is a large value.

The *num* operand can be any number; if a negative value is used, it is converted to its absolute value before being set. If *num* is zero, it is taken to be a line width of one device pixel, which is the smallest line that can be imaged. Since the size of a pixel is device-dependent, and since some devices cannot render a one-pixel line, using a zero *num* is not recommended.

TYPE: Graphics
ERRORS: stackunderflow, typecheck
ASSOCIATED: **currentlinewidth, stroke**

setmatrix

matrix   **setmatrix**   —

replaces the current transformation matrix (CTM) in the current graphics state with the value of *matrix*. The current transformation matrix governs the mapping of user coordinates into device coordinates, and **setmatrix** changes this without any reference to the previous value of the CTM. Since the default CTM is carefully chosen for each device, it is generally inappropriate for a PostScript program to change the CTM directly. The better way to introduce modifications to the CTM is by use of **concat** or one of the related transformation operators: **rotate, scale,** or **translate.**

> TYPE: Coordinate
> ERRORS: rangecheck, stackunderflow, typecheck
> ASSOCIATED: **currentmatrix, defaultmatrix, intimatrix, concat**

setmiterlimit

> num   **setmiterlimit**   –

sets *num* as the current miter limit parameter in the current graphics state. The current miter limit parameter is a number greater than or equal to 1 that determines the shape of the corners produced when miter joins have been specified in the **setlinejoin** operator. When miter joins have been specified, lines that join at a sharp angle will have a spike that extends well beyond the actual point of the join. The purpose of the miter limit parameter is to convert the corner produced at the join into a bevel when that spike becomes too long.

For any given join, the *miter length* is the distance from the intersection of the inner edges of the stroke for each line to the intersection of the outer edges of the stroke. As the angle at the join between the two line segments becomes smaller, the miter length becomes longer. The miter limit parameter, *num,* represents the maximum value for the ratio of *miter length* to *line width.* If that ratio exceeds *num,* the join is converted from a miter join to a bevel join.

The ratio represented by the miter limit is directly related to the angle between the line segments at the join by the following formulae:

$$num = \text{miter length} \mathbin{/} \text{line width} = cosecant \, (\theta \mathbin{/} 2)$$

where θ is the angle at the join between the two segments. This can be redefined in terms of PostScript operators by applying the trigonometric identity that the *cosecant* of an angle is equal to *1 / sine* of the angle, as in the alternative formula:

$$num = 1 \mathbin{/} sine \, (\theta \mathbin{/} 2)$$

A miter limit of 1 (the lower limit for *num*) will make every join into a bevel join, thus being essentially identical to setting the line join parameter to 2. A miter limit of 2.0 corresponds to a join angle of 60 degrees, while a miter limit of 2.6 will produce bevel joins at angles of 45 degrees and less. The normal default value for the miter limit is 10, which corresponds to a join angle of approximately 11.5 degrees.

> TYPE: Graphics
> ERRORS: rangecheck, stackunderflow, typecheck
> ASSOCIATED: **currentmiterlimit, setlinejoin, stroke**

setpacking

bool   **setpacking**   —

sets the array packing mode to *bool*. The array packing mode determines whether procedures are stored in packed or unpacked format as they are constructed by the interpreter. The value *true* indicates that procedures are to be packed; the value *false* indicates that they are to be stored unpacked.

The array packing mode affects only procedures, that is, executable arrays created by the interpreter when it encounters objects delimited by the '{' and '}' characters. Such arrays may be generated while processing an executable file or string, or during execution of the **token** operator. The mode setting never affects the creation of ordinary array objects, such as would be delimited by the '[' and ']' characters; packed versions of these arrays can be created by the **packedarray** operator.

The array packing mode persists until it is explicitly reset by execution of a new **setpacking** operator or until reset to a previous value by a **restore**. The default value for the array packing mode is *false*. Procedures that are created in one mode do not change when the mode is changed; if packed procedures are created, they will remain packed even after the array packing mode is reset.

A procedure that is generated as a packed array object has read-only access and has the type 'packedarraytype'; in other respects, it is used and accessed like an ordinary procedure. See Section A2.2 for a further discussion of packed arrays. Since packed arrays are not supported in all versions of PostScript, it is important to test for the availability of this facility before attempting to use it.

EXAMPLE:

```
systemdict / setpacking known
{ / PrevPack currentpacking def
true setpacking }
if
/ inch { 72 mul } def
% other procedures could be inserted here
systemdict / setpacking known
{ PrevPack setpacking }
if
```

This defines the procedure *inch* (and any following procedures) in packed form if the packing feature is available. If packing is not available, the definitions will still take effect as ordinary, unpacked procedures.

TYPE: Array
ERRORS: stackunderflow, typecheck
ASSOCIATED: **currentpacking, packedarray**

setrgbcolor

red green blue   **setrgbcolor**   –

sets the values *red, green,* and *blue* as the three components of the current color parameter from the current graphics state according to the red-green-blue model. Each of these values is a number between 0 and 1 that indicates the percentage of red, green, and blue in the current color. The current color is the color that is used for all subsequent painting operations, such as **fill** and **stroke**, on the current page. See the discussion of color operations in Section A4.4 for a more complete explanation.

The use of **setrgbcolor** after a **setcachedevice** operation within a **BuildChar** procedure is not allowed, because the font cache cannot preserve color information; an attempt to use it will result in raising the **undefined** error.

TYPE: Graphics
ERRORS: stackunderflow, typecheck
ASSOCIATED: **currentrgbcolor, fill, show, stroke, setgray, setcmykcolor, sethsbcolor**

setscreen

freq angle proc   **setscreen**   –

sets the values *freq, angle,* and *proc* as the three components of the current halftone screen from the current graphics state. The *freq* operand is a real number that determines the screen frequency in halftone cells per inch in device space. The *angle* operand is a real number that specifies the rotation angle of the halftone screen in relation to the device coordinate system. The proc operand defines a procedure known as the *spot function,* which determines the order in which the pixels within a halftone cell are changed from black to white to generate shades of grey. See Section A4.3 for additional information about halftone screens.

The device setup procedures for each device provide a default halftone screen that is carefully chosen to provide good results in a wide variety of circumstances. It should be changed (using setscreen) only after careful consideration and planning.

TYPE: Graphics
ERRORS: limitcheck, rangecheck, stackunderflow, typecheck
ASSOCIATED: **currentscreen, currenttransfer, settransfer**

settransfer

proc   **settransfer**   –

sets *proc* as the transfer procedure to be used by the current graphics state. **proc** is a PostScript procedure that is called with an operand between 0 and 1 (the current gray value in the graphics state) and returns a result between 0 and 1 (the percentage of pixels to be set to white). In this way, *proc* maps user gray values into device gray values.

The use of **settransfer** after a **setcachedevice** operation within a **BuildChar** procedure is not allowed, because the font cache cannot preserve color information; an attempt to use it will result in raising the **undefined** error.

TYPE: Graphics
ERRORS: stackoverflow
ASSOCIATED: **settransfer, currentscreen, setscreen**

*setundercolorremoval

proc **setundercolorremoval** –

sets the current undercolor removal procedure in the current graphics state to *proc,* which must be a PostScript language procedure that is called with an operand in the range 0 to 1 inclusive and which returns a value in the range −1 to 1 inclusive. This procedure maps the minimum values of *cyan, magenta,* and *yellow* color components of the current color into new values computed by subtracting the undercolor removal value returned by **setundercolorremoval** for each of these components. Therefore, if *proc* returns a negative value, the color increases by the resulting amount; for a positive value, the color decreases. This operator and these color adjustment procedures are defined only in those versions of the PostScript interpreter that support color operations. See Section A4.4 for a detailed description of color operations.

The use of **setundercolorremoval** after a **setcachedevice** operation within a **BuildChar** procedure is not allowed, because the font cache cannot preserve color information; an attempt to use it will result in raising the **undefined** error.

For those PostScript devices that support color operations, the device setup procedures provide a set of default adjustments for each color component that are carefully chosen to provide good results in a wide variety of circumstances. They should be changed (using **setblackgeneration** and **setundercolorremoval**) only after careful consideration and planning.

TYPE: Color
ERRORS: invalidaccess, stackunderflow, typecheck
ASSOCIATED: **currentundercolorremoval, currentblackgeneration, setblackgeneration, setcmykcolor, setrgbcolor, currentcmykcolor, currentrgbcolor**

* This operator is not present in the PostScript verion 38.0.

show

string   **show**   –

paints the characters that are elements of *string* on the current page at the current point using the current font. **show** requires that the current point be set before execution, as, for example, by a **moveto**; otherwise, the **nocurrentpoint** error occurs. The current font consists of a selected font family, font style, point size, and orientation as set by the most recent **setfont**, and it must be established before a **show**; otherwise an error (which may vary depending on conditions in the current graphic state) occurs. See Chapter A5 for a complete description of font structure and the font machinery.

If **show** is used with a composite font, the font-mapping algorithm selected for that font is invoked, and a **rangecheck** error will be raised if the mapping of *string* is incomplete.

TYPE:	Font
ERRORS:	invalidaccess, invalidfont, nocurrentpoint, rangecheck, stackunder-flow, typecheck, undefined
ASSOCIATED:	**ashow, awidthshow, charpath, cshow, kshow, widthshow, setfont**

showpage

–   **showpage**   –

produces the current page on the current output device, causing any marks that have been painted in the imageable area of the current page to appear on the output. **showpage** then resets the graphic state (as though by an **initgraphics** operation) and erases the current page (as though by an **erasepage**).

If the current output device produces physical output, **showpage** looks up the value of the **#copies** parameter, which must be a non-negative integer, and produces the number of output copies specified there. The **#copies** parameter is defined in *userdict* with a default value of 1. This value may be overridden by redefining it; see the description of **#copies** for more information.

The precise process that **showpage** uses to transfer marks from the current page to the output device is highly device-dependent. It is usually set by executing the **framedevice** or **banddevice** operator (as appropriate) to establish the device in the current graphic state.

TYPE:	Device
ERRORS:	(none)
ASSOCIATED:	**copypage, erasepage, initgraphics**

sin

angle	**sin**	real

returns the sine of *angle,* which is taken to be an angle in degrees. The sine will always be a real number between -1 and $+$.

EXAMPLE:

30 sin	$\Rightarrow$	0.5
45 sin	$\Rightarrow$	0.707107
90 sin	$\Rightarrow$	1.0
225 sin	$\Rightarrow$	-0.707107
450 sin	$\Rightarrow$	1.0

TYPE: Mathematical
ERRORS: stackunderflow, typecheck
ASSOCIATED: **atan, cos**

sqrt

num	**sqrt**	real

returns the square root of *num,* which must be a non-negative number.

EXAMPLE:

2 sqrt	$\Rightarrow$	1.41421
100 sqrt	$\Rightarrow$	10.0

TYPE: Mathematical
ERRORS: rangecheck, stackunderflow, typecheck
ASSOCIATED: **exp, ln, log**

srand

int	**srand**	—

takes the integer value, *int,* and initializes the current state of the pseudo-random number generator used by the interpreter to that number. Initializing the generator with a specific value of *int* will cause a reproducible sequence of numbers to be generated by successive calls to the **rand** operator.

EXAMPLE:

rrand	$\Rightarrow$	-2085328199
/Seed exch def		% save rrand value as Seed

rand	$\Rightarrow$	62155449
rand	$\Rightarrow$	546679431
rand	$\Rightarrow$	1530011492
Seed srand		% reset seed value
rand	$\Rightarrow$	62155449

TYPE: Mathematical
ERRORS: stackunderflow, typecheck
ASSOCIATED: **rand, rrand**

stack

$\vdash$ any$_1$ ... any$_n$ **stack** $\vdash$ any$_1$ ... any$_n$

produces a string representation of all objects on the operand stack, any_n through any_1, onto the standard output file. The string is generated for each any as though by application of the = operator; however, no stack contents are disturbed and the stack is the same after the display as it was before.

The **stack** operator generally does not produce as satisfactory a display of the stack as the **pstack** operator, since it uses a string similar to the one produced by the = operator rather than the more informative version produced by the = = operator. See the discussion of these two operators for an explanation of the differences between them. Because **stack** is non-destructive of the stack, it generates additional elements on the stack prior to display; for this reason, it is possible to overflow the stack during execution of a **stack**.

TYPE: File
ERRORS: stackoverflow
ASSOCIATED: **=, = =, pstack**

stackoverflow

(error process)

occurs when the number of operands on the operand stack exceeds the implementation-defined maximum number.

The interpreter creates a large array containing all the elements on the operand stack, clears the stack, and then pushes the array back on the stack before it invokes the **stackoverflow** error routine. If you wish to write your own error-handling routines, you may be able to make use of this for debugging. See Section B2.3 regarding customization of error processing.

TYPE: Error
ASSOCIATED: **count, clear, dup**

stackunderflow

(error process)

occurs when the interpreter attempts to remove an operand on the operand stack and the operand stack is already empty. This happens most often when some operator is executing and does not have all the required operands on the operand stack.

TYPE: Error
ASSOCIATED: **clear, pop, dup**

StandardEncoding

– **StandardEncoding** array

returns the standard PostScript encoding vector as *array*. This is a 256-element array that provides the names of the characters associated with each character code. It is normally accessed by the font machinery, using the character code as an index into the array. At the point of the array indexed by the code is found the name of the character that identifies the procedure that must be executed to draw the character. See Section A5.4 for a description of font-encoding arrays.

The **StandardEncoding** is not itself a PostScript operator; instead, it is a name in *systemdict* associated with the array object itself. This encoding array is the encoding used by most standard alphabetic PostScript fonts – but not by special fonts such as Symbol. The contents of the standard encoding are given in Appendix B.

TYPE: Font
ERRORS: stackoverflow
ASSOCIATED: **FontDirectory**

start

– **start** –

is the procedure executed by the PostScript interpreter when it first starts execution. After establishing the state of the virtual memory (possibly including restoring it from a state saved on an external medium), the interpreter executes **start** in the default dictionary context, that is, with only *userdict* and *systemdict* on the dictionary stack. **start** is not a PostScript operator but is a procedure defined in *userdict*. The precise definition and actions taken by **start** depend on the device that is being started. This procedure should never be invoked by an ordinary PostScript program.

TYPE: Control
ERRORS: (none)
ASSOCIATED: **quit, stop, interrupt**

status

file **status** bool

returns the boolean value *true* if *file* is still associated with an open file and returns *false* otherwise.

TYPE:	File
ERRORS:	stackunderflow, typecheck
ASSOCIATED:	**closefile, file, read, write**

statusdict

— **statusdict** dict

returns the dictionary *dict*, which is the *statusdict* dictionary. The *statusdict* dictionary is a normal PostScript dictionary that is defined in *systemdict;* it contains the definitions of PostScript operators and associated variables that provide support for printer-specific operations, such as paper handling, files, communications, and so on. See Section C2 for a complete discussion of *statusdict* operations and examples of typical printer-specific operators.

TYPE:	Dictionary
ERRORS:	stackoverflow
ASSOCIATED:	**errordict, systemdict, userdict**

stop

— **stop** —

terminates execution of the currently active instance of a stopped context, which is a procedure or other executable object invoked by a **stopped** operator. Precisely, **stop** pops the execution stack down to the level of the **stopped** operator, effectively terminating all processing within the invoked procedure, and then pushes the boolean value *true* onto the operand stack. This has the effect of changing the result from the **stopped** operator from the usual *false* to *true* and thus provides an indicator for subsequent processing that the procedure was terminated by a **stop** rather than finishing execution normally. See the example under the **stopped** operator.

    stop does not affect the operand, dictionary, or graphic state stacks. Any changes made to these stacks during execution of the stopped context persist after execution is terminated.

TYPE:	Control
ERRORS:	(none)
ASSOCIATED:	**exit, loop, stopped**

stopped

any   **stopped**   bool

executes *any*, which is usually a procedure or an executable file but may be any executable object. If *any* proceeds to normal completion, **stopped** returns *false* as the boolean result. If *any* is terminated prematurely by a **stop** operator, then **stopped** returns the boolean result *true*. Regardless of the method or condition at termination, execution resumes with the next sequential instruction.

The primary use of the **stopped** operator in PostScript programs is to provide a method to trap errors and other abnormal termination conditions and allow some form of error recovery if desired and appropriate. See Section A2.4 for a discussion of the error-handling mechanism.

EXAMPLE:

```
{ (this is a test \n) print (and another line \n) print }
stopped        ⇒        false
```

and displays the string 'this is a test' and then the string 'and another line' on the next line, followed by a newline character, on the standard output file.

```
{ (this is a test \n) print stop (and another line \n) print }
stopped        ⇒        true
```

and displays only the string 'this is a test', followed by a newline character. The difference between these two procedures is only that the second terminates with a **stop** operator prior to normal execution of the second **print** operator. As a result, the **stopped** operator returns *true* to indicate the abnormal end of execution.

TYPE: Control
ERRORS: stackunderflow
ASSOCIATED: **exit, loop, stop**

store

key value   **store**   —

searches the dictionary stack in the ordinary way, looking for a match to *key*. If a matching *key* is found in any dictionary on the stack, *value* replaces the old value associated with *key* in that dictionary. If no matching **key** is found, then **value** is associated with **key** and placed as a new entry in the current dictionary.

store is essentially a convenience operator for a sequence of PostScript instructions that would search for a dictionary that contained *key* and do a **put** into that dictionary, if found; otherwise, it would enroll *key* and *value* in the current dictionary.

EXAMPLE:

The following procedure can be defined to perform the same function as the **store**:

```
/eqStore
{ exch dup where {} {currentdict} ifelse
        3 1 roll exch put}
def
```

and the following two sequences produce identical results:

```
/Key (value) store
/Key (value) eqStore
```

TYPE:	Dictionary
ERRORS:	dictfull, invalidaccess, limitcheck, stackunderflow
ASSOCIATED:	**def, get, known, put, where**

string

int	**string**	string

creates a string with length *int* and initializes each element of the string with the binary value 0. The *int* operand must be a non-negative integer that is less than the implementation-defined maximum string length. If *int* is 0, an empty string is created.

TYPE:	String
ERRORS:	limitcheck, rangecheck, stackunderflow, typecheck, VMerror
ASSOCIATED:	**array, dict, length, type**

stringwidth

string	**stringwidth**	wx wy

calculates the cumulative change in the current point that would occur if **string** was printed in the current font by using **show**. The results, *wx* and *wy*, represent relative displacements, such as those used by an **rmoveto** operator. They are constructed by accumulating the widths of each character in *string*, taking into account the character widths, the point size, and the writing mode of the current font. See Section A5.5 for a discussion of font metrics. If **stringwidth** is used with a composite font, the font mapping algorithm for that font is invoked; a **rangecheck** error is raised if the mapping of string is incomplete.

During execution, the **stringwidth** operator may actually image some characters from *string* and place them in the font cache to determine the width components. However, it never makes any marks onto the output page.

The **stringwidth** operator is most often used to determine string lengths prior to printing for justification and centering algorithms. Examples of this use are given in the Cookbook routines in Part II.

TYPE: Font
ERRORS: invalidaccess, invalidfont, rangecheck, stackunderflow, typecheck
ASSOCIATED: **show, makefont, scalefont, setfont**

stroke

    –   **stroke**   –

paints a line defined by the current path, with a thickness given by the current linewidth as set by **setlinewidth,** and using the current color. The sides of the line are parallel to the current path, the join points are filled in according to the current line join parameter as defined by **setlinejoin,** and free ends of the path or subpaths are finished according to the current line cap parameter as set by **setlinecap.** Finally, the entire line is painted solid or dashed according to the current dash array and dash phase as set by **setdash.** The parameters that are in effect at the time **stroke** is executed govern the characteristics of the line.

stroke clears the current path at the end of its execution as though by executing a **newpath.** To preserve the path across a **stroke,** save the current path before executing the **stroke** by doing a **gsave** and then restore the path after execution with a **grestore.**

TYPE: Painting
ERRORS: limitcheck
ASSOCIATED: **setdash, setlinewidth, setlinecap, setlinejoin, setmiterlimit**

strokepath

    –   **strokepath**   –

replaces the current path with a new path that outlines the area that would be painted by applying **stroke** to the current path. The resulting path is suitable for most path operations, including using the **fill, clip,** and **pathbbox** operators. In general, however, it is not suitable for stroking, since the stroke-to-outline conversion may result in disconnected subpaths or interior segments.

TYPE: Path
ERRORS: limitcheck
ASSOCIATED: **charpath, clip, fill, pathbbox, stroke**

sub

num1 num2   **sub**   diff

subtracts *num2* from *num1*, giving result *diff*. The type of *diff* depends on the type of *num1* and *num2*. If both operands are integers and the result is within integer range, *diff* is an integer; otherwise, it is a real.

EXAMPLES:

4 2 sub	$\Rightarrow$	2	(an integertype result)
4.0 2 sub	$\Rightarrow$	2.0	(a realtype result)
4 −2 sub	$\Rightarrow$	6	

TYPE: Mathematical
ERRORS: stackunderflow, typecheck, undefinedresult
ASSOCIATED: **add, div, idiv, mod, mul**

syntaxerror

(error process)

occurs when the PostScript input scanner (or *tokenizer*) encounters program text that does not follow the syntax rules for PostScript. This can happen either during interpretation of an executable file or string or by specific invocation of the **token** operator. See Chapter A2 for a complete discussion of PostScript syntax requirements.

Since PostScript syntax is not generally rigorous, there are only a few occurrences that can cause a **syntaxerror**. The following are the most common:

- an opening string, hexadecimal string, array, or procedure bracket '(', '<,' '[', or '{' is not matched by a corresponding ending bracket before the end of the file or the string being interpreted.
- a closing string, hexadecimal string, array or procedure bracket, ')', '>', ']', or '}', has been encountered that was not preceded by a matching opening bracket.
- a character other than a valid hexadecimal digit or a white space character appears between hexadecimal string delimiters '<' and '>'. Valid hexadecimal digits are 1 to 9 and 'A' (or 'a') to 'F' (or 'f').

Poorly formed tokens, such as characters in a numeric value, are not flagged by the tokenizer; instead they are generally passed to the interpreter as name values (and, as such, may result in an **undefined** error when they are processed). Similarly, tokens that exceed implementation limits, such as strings that are too long or numeric values that are too large, are flagged by the interpreter with a **rangecheck** error.

TYPE: Error
ASSOCIATED: **file, token**

systemdict

       —   **systemdict**   dict

returns the dictionary object *dict,* which is the *systemdict* dictionary. The name *systemdict* is a key that is defined in *systemdict* itself and associated with the dictionary object. The dictionary contains the definitions of PostScript operators and associated variables that provide support for general operations, specifically those defined in this section of the book. See Section A1.4 for a complete discussion of *systemdict* operations.

          TYPE: Dictionary
      ERRORS: stackoverflow
ASSOCIATED: **errordict, statusdict, userdict**

timeout

       (error process)

occurs when the PostScript interpreter exceeds some implementation-defined time value. For example, the interpreter has been waiting for some external interrupt for a time greater than that defined as an implementation maximum.

     The PostScript language does not impose any inherent time limitations; however, most implementations have a variety of timeout parameters that are appropriate to the environment. Many of these values are stored in the *statusdict* and can be changed if necessary.

          TYPE: Error
ASSOCIATED: **statusdict**

token

                           if found:
     file   **token**   any true
                       if not found
                       false

reads characters from *file,* interpreting them according to the PostScript syntax rules, until it has constructed a complete PostScript object, which is then returned to the operand stack as result *any.* In this case, token returns the object as *any* and pushes the boolean value *true* to indicate successful completion. However, if **token** encounters end-of-file before it completes construction of a PostScript object, it pushes only the boolean value *false.*

                           if found:
    string   **token**   post any true
                       if not found:
                       false

reads characters from *string,* interpreting them according to the PostScript syntax rules, until it has constructed a complete PostScript object, which is then returned to the operand stack as result *any.* In this case, **token** first pushes *post,* which is the substring remaining after **token** has constructed its result, then returns the object as *any* and pushes the boolean value *true* to indicate successful completion. However, if **token** encounters the end of the string before it completes construction of a PostScript object, it pushes only the boolean value *false.*

In either case, *any* is a standard PostScript object. It may be simple, such as a number or a name, or composite, such as an array or string. It may have the literal attribute, such as an array, or the executable attribute, such as a procedure. **token** constructs an object in the same way that **exec** would, except that it places the object onto the operand stack rather than executing it.

All the characters that make up the object are removed from *file* or *string* by **token** and are consumed. **token** recognizes white-space and other special characters as part of its processing. White-space characters that occur before the object are consumed by **token**; white space characters after the object are also consumed unless the object is terminated by a special character, such as the string delimiter ')', the procedure delimiter '}', and so on. If an object is terminated by a delimiter that begins a new object, such as '(' or '{', **token** leaves the delimiter with the input sequence.

EXAMPLE 1:

      Stack in: ((sd)9 7(asdfg))   **token**   Stack out: true
                                                                    (sd)
                                                                    (9 7(asdfg))

EXAMPLE 2:

      Stack in: (9 7(asdfg))   **token**   Stack out: true
                                                                     9
                                                                     (7(asdfg))

EXAMPLE 3:

      Stack in: (7(asdfg))   **token**   Stack out: true
                                                                      7
                                                                     ((asdfg))

EXAMPLE 4:

      Stack in: ((asdfg))   **token**   Stack out: true
                                                                      (asdfg)
                                                                     ( )

EXAMPLE 5:

Stack in: ( )   **token**   Stack
                                             out: false

These examples show **token** applied repeatedly to a string, and they illustrate some of the rules mentioned above. Notice that **token** generally behaves pretty much as you would want and might expect.

TYPE: File, String
ERRORS: invalidaccess, ioerror, rangecheck, stackoverflow, stackunderflow, syntaxerror, typecheck, undefinedresult
ASSOCIATED: **anchorsearch, read, search**

transform

x y   **transform**   x′ y′

transforms the distance vector, (x, y), into device space using the current transformation matrix (CTM) and returns the equivalent distance vector for the device onto the operand stack as (x', y').

EXAMPLE:

100 100 transform   ⇒   2851.33 341.667

using the default transformation matrix for the LaserWriter. This means that the point on the user coordinate system (the current page) that has coordinates (100, 100) is translated into the point (341.667, 2851.33) on the device coordinates.

x y matrix   **transform**   x′ y′

transforms the position (x, y), into device space using *matrix* as a transformation matrix (instead of the current CTM), and returns the equivalent position after the transformation onto the operand stack as (x', y').

EXAMPLE:

3 4 [4 0 0 2 0 0] transform   ⇒   12.0   8.0
3 4 [4 0 0 2 5 9] transform   ⇒   17.0 17.0

This transforms the (x, y) pair (3, 4) onto a space that is scaled by a factor of 4 in the x direction and a factor of 2 in the y direction. Notice that changing the (t_x, t_y) components of the transformation matrix has the effect of translating the origin of the space and hence moving the output point by 5 units in the x direction and 9 units in the y direction.

TYPE: Coordinate
ERRORS: stackunderflow, typecheck
ASSOCIATED: **dtransform, idtransform, itransform**

translate

tx ty   **translate**   —

translates the current origin of the user coordinates to the point (tx, ty), which becomes the new origin. Precisely, **translate** builds a temporary transformation matrix as follows: [1 0 0 1 tx ty], where tx and ty are the translation coordinates in the current user coordinates, and concatenates it with the current transformation matrix (CTM) to give a new CTM. The orientation and the scale of the x and y axes are unchanged.

tx ty matrix   **translate**   matrix

adjusts the values in *matrix* by the transformation matrix described above, [1 0 0 1 tx ty], and returns the modified matrix back to the operand stack. No change is made to the CTM.

See Section A3.3 for a complete discussion of PostScript coordinates and their matrix representation.

EXAMPLE:

5 9 matrix translate   ⇒   [1.0 0.0 0.0 1.0 5.0 9.0]

TYPE: Coordinate
ERRORS: invalidaccess, stackunderflow, typecheck
ASSOCIATED: **concat, matrix, rotate, scale**

true

—   **true**   true

returns the boolean object *true*. **true** is not a PostScript operator; it is a name in *systemdict* associated with the boolean value.

TYPE: Boolean
ERRORS: stackoverflow
ASSOCIATED: **false, and, eq, not, or, xor**

truncate

num1   **truncate**   num2

truncates the value of *num1* toward zero by removing the fractional part. The type of *num2* is the same as the type of *num1*.

EXAMPLE:

4.2 truncate	$\Rightarrow$	4.0	
– 4.2 truncate	$\Rightarrow$	– 4.0	
5 truncate	$\Rightarrow$	5	(an integertype result)

TYPE: Mathematical
ERRORS: stackunderflow, typecheck
ASSOCIATED: **ceiling, floor, round, cvi**

type

any   **type**   typename

returns *typename,* which is a PostScript name object that specifies the type of *any.* Possible values for *typename* are:

arraytype	booleantype	dicttype
filetype	fonttype	integertype
marktype	nametype	nulltype
operator type	packedarraytype	realtype
savetype	stringtype	

See Section A2.2 for a full discussion of PostScript objects and their types. Note that the **fonttype** does not refer to a font dictionary, such as *Helvetica,* but rather refers to an object of type *fontID* as defined and discussed in Section A5.4. A PostScript font dictionary is indistinguishable from any other PostScript dictionary object, and application of **type** to a font dictionary returns the type *dicttype.*

The result returned, *typename,* has the executable attribute set and can be used as an index into a dictionary structure to provide specialized processing by type. This is done by creating a dictionary that associates a procedure to provide the desired processing with each type name on the dictionary stack and then executing the *typename* returned by the type operator.

TYPE: Conversion
ERRORS: stackunderflow
ASSOCIATED: **stackunderflow**

typecheck

(error process)

occurs when the type of some operand is not the type expected by the operator in question. This error, along with the **stackunderflow** error, is a common error in a PostScript program. Moreover, both of them generally are caused by the same root problem – incorrect stack handling: some operand is missing from the stack, operands are out of order, or some information has been incorrectly left on the stack.

TYPE: Error
ASSOCIATED: **type**

undefined

(error process)

occurs when a name used in a dictionary key cannot be found in the current dictionary context. If the PostScript operator limits examination to one dictionary (such as **get**), then the **undefined** refers only to that dictionary; if it looks at the entire dictionary stack, then **undefined** refers to the entire stack contents.

Some PostScript operators are disabled in certain contexts; for example, the **setgray** after **setcachedevice** within a BuildChar; any attempt to access these operators under the defined circumstances will also raise the **undefined** error.

TYPE: Error
ASSOCIATED: **exec, get, known, load, where**

undefinedfilename

(error process)

occurs when a string used as a name for a file or a **run** operator cannot be found or cannot be opened. The **undefinedfilename** error may also be raised if an attempt to access certain system files is made in invalid circumstances; these conditions are implementation-dependent.

TYPE: Error
ASSOCIATED: **file, run**

undefinedresult

(error process)

occurs when a numeric computation would produce an undefined result (such as division by zero) or one that cannot be represented as a PostScript number (such as the inverse transformation of a non-invertible matrix). One form of **undefinedresult** may be raised by numeric underflow and overflow conditions created by results that exceed specific implementation-defined limits on numeric values.

TYPE: Error
ASSOCIATED: **(none)**

unmatchedmark

(error process)

occurs when an operator expects a mark object on the operand stack but none is present.

TYPE: Error
ASSOCIATED: **[,], cacheparams, counttomark, cleartomark, mark**

unregistered

(error process)

occurs when an operator object has been executed for which the interpreter has no built-in process or procedure. This can never occur except as a result of an interpreter malfunction.

TYPE: Error
ASSOCIATED: (none)

userdict

—   **userdict**   dict

returns the dictionary *dict*, which is the *userdict* dictionary. The *userdict* dictionary is a normal PostScript dictionary that is defined in *systemdict;* it contains the definitions of common PostScript procedures and associated variables; it is also the *currentdict* when the PostScript interpreter begins processing a PostScript application. See Section A1.4 for a complete discussion of *userdict* operations.

TYPE: Dictionary
ERRORS: stackoverflow
ASSOCIATED: **errordict, statusdict, systemdict**

usertime

—   **usertime**   int

returns the value of a clock that increments one unit for every millisecond of execution time. This value has no relation to any external clock.

   usertime is primarily used as an interval counter or timer in much the same fashion as a stopwatch would be used. Note that the exact accuracy of this clock mechanism is entirely dependent upon the device environment.

TYPE: Miscellaneous
ERRORS: stackoverflow
ASSOCIATED: (none)

version

— **version** string

returns a string that identifies the version of the PostScript interpreter that is running in the current output device. The *string* is a version number only and does not provide any information about the type (name) of the device being used or the connection, and so on. Other device-specific operators are available to access such information. See the information on System Parameters in Section C2.2 for details.

TYPE: Miscellaneous
ERRORS: stackoverflow
ASSOCIATED: **jobname, printername, product, revision**

VMerror

(error process)

occurs when an error has occurred in handling or accessing the virtual memory (VM) of the output device. The most likely cause of this error is an attempt to create a new composite object (array, dictionary, packedarray, or string) that would exhaust or exceed VM resources if created.

The amount of virtual memory that is available to a PostScript application depends on several variables: the amount of real memory available to the device; the number and size of PostScript procedures that may have been loaded outside the current **save, restore** context; and the amount of auxiliary information (such as font definitions) that accompanies the application. One major area for investigation if a **VMerror** occurs is the application's use of memory management techniques, namely **save** and **restore**.

TYPE: Error
ASSOCIATED: **save, restore, vmstatus**

vmstatus

— **vmstatus** level used maximum

returns the current status of virtual memory resources (VM) in the current output device. The *limit* result is an integer value that tells the number of **save** operations that have not yet been matched by a **restore**. The next two results give information about the amount of virtual memory. *used* defines the amount of virtual memory that is currently in use, and *maximum* is the maximum available amount of VM. Both amounts are reported as integer values representing a number of eight-bit bytes of virtual memory. However, in some environments, the PostScript interpreter may be able to dynamically alter the value of *maximum* during execution by obtaining additional resources from the operating system.

Notice that the values returned by **vmstatus** are numbers (generally integers), and, as such, are simple objects that do not consume virtual memory. Therefore it is possible to use **vmstatus** even after getting a **VMerror** to discover exactly how much virtual memory is left for processing.

TYPE: Miscellaneous
ERRORS: stackoverflow
ASSOCIATED: **save, restore**

wcheck

composite object	**wcheck**	bool
or		
file		

tests the access attribute of the operand to see whether the operand is available to be written explicitly by PostScript operators – that is, whether the access attribute of the operand is unlimited. If the object is available for write-access, **wcheck** returns the boolean value *true* and returns *false* otherwise.

Note that a *packedarray* object will always return *false* to the **wcheck** operator, since packed arrays can only be read or executed, not written into.

TYPE: Conversion
ERRORS: stackunderflow, typecheck
ASSOCIATED: **executeonly, noaccess, rcheck, readonly**

where

		if found:
key	**where**	dict true
		if not found:
		false

searches the dictionary stack and returns the dictionary that contains an entry that is associated with *key,* if that dictionary exists on the dictionary stack. The search proceeds in the normal fashion down the dictionary stack. If **where** finds the *key* value, it pushes the dictionary object *dict* containing *key* onto the operand stack and then pushes the boolean value *true;* if the search proceeds through the entire dictionary stack with no match, **where** returns only the boolean value *false.*

TYPE: Dictionary
ERRORS: invalidaccess, stackoverflow, stackunderflow
ASSOCIATED: **get, known, put, load**

widthshow

cx cy char string   **widthshow**   –

prints the characters in *string* in a manner similar to show; but, in addition, if the integer value of the character currently being imaged matches the integer value *char,* the values *cx* and *cy* are added to the current point after imaging the character and before imaging the next character.

If only base fonts are being used, *char* is an integer value between 0 and 255 that represents the character number in the current encoding of the character that is to be adjusted. With base fonts, *char* is adjusted modulo 256 to fall in the range 0 to 255 if it is outside that range. If composite fonts are being used, the integer value of the character being shown is calculated in the following way. The font number, *f,* and the character code, *c,* that are selected by the font mapping algorithm are combined into a single integer number according to the **FMapType** of the immediate parent of the selected base font, using the following rule:

FMapType 2   the integer value is $(f \times 256) + c$.

FMapType 3   the integer value is $(f \times 256) + c$.

FMapType 4   the integer value is $(f \times 128) + c$.

FMapType 5   the integer value is $(f \times 128) + c$.

FMapType 6   the integer value is $(f \times 256) + c$.

EXAMPLE:

```
/Helvetica findfont 10 scalefont setfont
100 100 moveto
(Normal word spacing) show
100      85 moveto
4 0 8#040 (Wide word spacing) widthshow
```

where 8#040 is the octal value in the standard encoding for a space character.

Normal word spacing

Wide word spacing

TYPE: Font
ERRORS: invalidaccess, invalidfont, nocurrentpoint, rangecheck, stackunder-
           flow, typecheck
ASSOCIATED: **ashow, awidthshow, kshow, show**

write

> file byte   **write**   —

writes a single character, *byte,* to the designated *file.* The value of *byte* is an integer in the range 0 to 256; any value outside that range is reduced to the acceptable range by taking it modulo 256. If *file* is not a valid PostScript file or if any other error occurs, **write** raises the **ioerror** condition.

Because **write** accesses only one character at a time, it is not generally the best way to deliver information to a PostScript program.

> TYPE: File
> ERRORS: invalidaccess, ioerror, stackunderflow, typecheck
> ASSOCIATED: **bytesavailable, read, writehexstring, writestring**

writehexstring

> file string   **writehexstring**   —

writes characters from the designated *string* into *file* until all the characters in *string* are transmitted. The characters are transmitted as hexadecimal digits, '0' through '9' or 'A' (or 'a') through 'F' (or 'f'). Each successive character code, which is an integer in the range of 0 to 255, is transmitted as a pair of hexadecimal digits.

> TYPE: File
> ERRORS: invalidaccess, ioerror, stackunderflow, typecheck
> ASSOCIATED: **bytesavailable, read, write, writestring**

writestring

> file string   **writestring**   —

writes characters from the designated *string* into *file.* All characters are allowed and treated identically and are transmitted as character codes, which are integers in the range 0 to 255. The **writestring** operator does not treat any characters as special; and, in particular, it does not append any *newline* characters to a *string.*

> TYPE: File
> ERRORS: invalidaccess, ioerror, stackunderflow, typecheck
> ASSOCIATED: **bytesavailable, read, write, writehexstring**

xcheck

> any   **xcheck**   bool

tests whether *any* has the executable or literal attribute. **xcheck** returns *true* if *any* is executable and *false* otherwise. Note that this is not a test of the object's access attribute (unlimited; read-only; execute-only; no access). See Section A2.3 for a more detailed discussion of object characteristics.

```
      TYPE:    Conversion
    ERRORS:    stackunderflow
ASSOCIATED:    cvx, cvlit
```

xor

```
    bool1 bool2        xor        result
```

performs a logical 'exclusive or' of *bool1* and *bool2* and returns the boolean value *result*.

EXAMPLES:

```
true  true      xor      Stack out: false
false true      xor      ⇒         true
false false     xor      ⇒         false

int1 int2       xor         result
```

performs a bitwise exclusive or of *int1* and *int2* and returns the integer value *result*. The process is a straight, bit-wise exclusive or, taking the integers as simple bit representations; no character values are used and the operands must be integers. The or is exclusive, so that if matching bits are on in both operands, the result is off.

EXAMPLES:

```
2  1        xor     ⇒     3
3  1        xor     ⇒     2
8  4        xor     ⇒     12
3  10       xor     ⇒     9
```

```
      TYPE:    Logical
    ERRORS:    stackunderflow, typecheck
ASSOCIATED:    and, not, true, false, or
```

Device-Specific Operator Definitions

The previous chapter presented complete definitions for all the operators that are generally available in a PostScript environment. However, each PostScript device has a set of operators that relate to specific functions on that device. These operators are not defined in every PostScript device; they are usually defined only on devices that have the appropriate facility. However, all PostScript devices have some of these facilities, and the PostScript language approaches all of these requirements in an identical fashion. The following chapter discusses how the most common of these features are accessed and used and provides detailed operator descriptions for typical features. The operator list in this section is intended to be illustrative only; the precise set of operators available on any specific machine and their use are completely documented in the PostScript language supplement for that device.

These operators are stored in a special dictionary, *statusdict,* that is itself stored in *systemdict.* The *statusdict* is not normally accessible during application processing because it is not automatically placed on the dictionary stack. To access it, you must place it on the stack, which can be done with the following code: **statusdict begin**. After completing work on whatever parts of the *statusdict* you are working with, you should pop it from the dictionary stack by using the **end** operator. Alternatively, you can use the *get* and *put* operators to access and change values in **statusdict**.

This chapter lists typical entries contained in *statusdict.* These are operators or other PostScript objects (strings, numbers, and boolean values) that are specifically used for determining the status of the PostScript device. The format used to present these operators and objects is the same format that was used in the preceding chapter.

2.1 SERVER OPERATION

Section A2.6 discussed the normal operation of the PostScript interpreter as a server that processes PostScript jobs as they are presented. Many of the basic functions and parameters of this server processing are controllable by the user. This section of the chapter will deal with those aspects of server operation that are under user control; the next section of the chapter will discuss in detail the operators that control these functions or parameters.

Start Page

Many PostScript printers produce a startup page when they are powered on. Typically, the page shows information regarding the current setup of the device, such as the following: current communication channel, communications paramenters, fonts available, number of pages printed, printer identification, PostScript version, and so on. While the information on this page is useful, many users find it annoying, especially if they do not change any of these parameters under normal circumstances. Whether this page is produced or not is under the control of a PostScript parameter, **dostartpage**, which is a boolean value; as you might expect, setting it to *true* allows a startup page to be printed, while setting it to *false* inhibits the startup page. Often this page also demonstrates the positioning of the normal output page on the paper; complete details of the contents of the startup page will be given in the device manual.

Page Types

The PostScript interpreter executes in devices that support a wide variety of paper sizes. The interpreter provides built-in procedures that set up the device for those sizes of paper that are supported. Unlike the other status and device-dependent procedures, they are defined in *userdict*. These procedures are simply executed, as any other procedure would be; they take no operands and return no results.

The size of the page that can be produced on any device is a function of both the hardware and the software. The hardware imposes limits on the physical page size that can be handled and on the margins required by the printing engine for paper handling. The software limits things such as the amount of memory available for a page image. Together these determine the page sizes and types that can be actually printed by the device. On film recording devices, there may also be variants of these procedures that allow the user to set the direction of the page output relative to the device scan.

In all cases, these procedures define an imageable area on the given page size that is centered on the page. Width is measured along the x axis of the default coordinates, and height is measured along the y axis; in other words, most of the following pages print in portrait mode (with the paper fed along the short edge). The exact dimensions of the imageable area are device-dependent.

Page Type	Page Size
a4	An imageable area centered on a page 210 mm wide by 297 mm high. This is an ISO A4-size page.
b5	An imageable area centered on a page 182 mm wide by 257 mm high. This is the standard European B5-size paper.
ledger	An imageable area centered on a page 11 inches wide by 17 inches high.
legal	An imageable area centered on a page 8.5 inches wide by 14 inches high. This is the standard legal page size.
letter	An imageable area centered on a page 8.5 inches wide by 11 inches high. This is the American standard page and is usually the default setting for page size.
note	This selects a smaller imageable area than the standard page size by increasing the margins of the page according to the papertray installed. It is intended to save virtual memory for use by PostScript applications.
folio	An imageable area centered on a page 8.5 inches wide by 13 inches high. This is a standard folio sheet size.
quarto	An imageable area centered on a page 215 mm wide by 275 mm high. This is a standard quarto page.

In some devices, the interpreter can sense the size of the paper tray installed and performs the setup based on the tray that is in the device at startup. For those devices where it cannot sense the paper tray size or where there are multiple paper trays, a default tray and size are used. When paper tray sensing is available, the following procedures are defined (they may also be defined for compatibility in devices that do not have paper tray sensing). In all cases, however, the default value set by the interpreter can be overridden by executing one of these procedures or one of the page type procedures defined above within the application.

As you might expect, this whole area of setting page type and size is one area where there is the highest degree of variation among PostScript devices. This happens because each device provides slightly different paper paths and paper-handling facilities that distinguish it from other devices with the same or similar capabilities. And, in fact, this entire area of setting page sizes and controlling paper selection is of genuine concern to real-world users as they use a device every day, many times a day. However, from the PostScript programmer's viewpoint, this means that the operators that control and sense the paper size and related variables will generally be different from device to device. In addition, devices that record on film rather than output on paper have their own fairly extensive set of special operators that set and define the recording process. The bottom line here is if you need or want to use these parameters, do some homework first and discover how the output process works. In all cases, the device manual should spell out in some detail what operators are available and how they operate within the device environment.

Another source for this information is the *PostScript Printer Description* file (usually abbreviated as 'PPD'). This is a text file designed to be both read by humans and to be parsed by a program such as a document manager or an application. The file provides, in a rigorous format, access to device-specific features such as paper size, paper tray and output handling, and so on. A complete discussion of PostScript Printer Description file structure and use is available from Adobe Systems, the creators of the PostScript language, at the address given in Appendix A.

With that caution, here are some typical values for paper trays that are in use for devices that output onto paper.

Tray	Value
a4tray	Sets an a4 page type and selects the tray that is that size. This operator raises the **rangecheck** error if the correct tray and paper size are not installed.
b5tray	Sets a b5 page type and selects the tray that is that size. This operator raises the **rangecheck** error if the correct tray and paper size are not installed.
legaltray	Sets a legal page type and selects the tray that is that size. This operator raises the **rangecheck** error if the correct tray and paper size are not installed.
lettertray	Sets a letter page type and selects the tray that is that size. This operator raises the **rangecheck** error if the correct tray and paper size are not installed.

For all page types, the point (0, 0) will be the lower left-hand corner of the page in portrait orientation (when the long edge is the default y axis); however, the first imageable position typically will be inside the origin by some distance. That is, any attempt to print something at the origin is likely to lose some part of the image, depending on the exact imageable area and the page type.

Communication

PostScript devices have several paths to communicate with their *host* or supporting computer systems. Each of these paths, or *communication channels,* allow transmission of data to the PostScript device; depending on the characteristics of the channel, it may also allow communication from the PostScript device back to the host. The exact specifications and access methods for the channels that are available on any given device are fully described in the documentation that accompanies the device. Often, the setting and use of the communication channels involve switches or other external settings that are available on the device. However, we can discuss here the three most common communication channels (although not all of them will be present on every device), and we can discuss the Post-Script operations that allow the setting and recording of the communication parameters.

The three types of communications channels are 1) serial communications, 2) parallel communications, and 3) networked communications. In serial communications, one bit (binary digit) is transmitted at a time at speeds generally no greater than 9600 baud. In parallel communications, eight bits are transmitted simultaneously, with the result that effective transmission rates are much higher. Both of these forms of communication are designed to connect from a single host to a single device. In networked communications, multiple devices all communicate over shared lines, allowing several host devices to share use of an output device, such as a printer, and also allowing one host device to access several different output devices, using some form of naming scheme. For PostScript devices, AppleTalk is the most common network protocol; however, other forms of networked protocols may be supported in some devices.

Serial communications take place over one or more serial communications channels that are controlled by the interpreter. Sometimes, these channels can be set by using external switches or key-setting methods. Typically, however, all the parameters that control serial communications can also be set from within the interpreter. This is done by invoking the two operators, **setsccbatch** and **setsccinteractive,** where *scc* stands for *serial communications channel*. As you might guess, these two operators control the batch and the interactive settings respectively.

Serial communication is asynchronous, start-stop, with eight bits per character (where the high-order bit may or may not be significant), and with one start bit and two stop bits. The details of serial communications are governed by three parameters: channel selection, baud rate, and channel options. The channel selection applies to devices that have more than one serial communication channel. The baud rate sets the speed of transmission and may go as high as 57,500 baud, although 1200 and 9600 are more usual values. Obviously, the higher the baud rate, the faster the transmission of data will be. The options set additional communications parameters, such as the form of transmission control and the parity setting.

Transmission control is an important feature in serial communications. Transmission control governs how the host and the output device coordinate processing and transmission to insure that no data is lost. This is of primary importance when processing large files because, in such cases, the host must occasionally stop transmitting characters for a time while the output device processes the data that it has already received. Generally, there are two methods of transmission control: software control and hardware control. Under software control, the PostScript device sends a special character to notify the host that transmission should stop until the device is ready to continue processing; then it sends another special character to notify the host that it is again ready to receive data. The host may make use of the same special characters to control flow of information back from the device.

One of the most common forms of software flow control is the XON/XOFF protocol, which is generally supported in PostScript devices. The major drawback to this (or any other software-based flow control) is that both sides must have software that understand the protocol and will take appropriate action when the special characters appear. Also, the special characters themselves must never be used as ordinary data in the transmission.

The hardware flow control is somewhat different. In this case, the output device signals the host computer to pause transmission by adding or removing a voltage on a specific contact on the communication channel. When that is done, the host stops transmission until the opposite action is taken. The same kind of processing is available in the reverse direction, between the host and the device, by using another wire to carry the signal. Obviously this protocol does not require any special software on the host; moreover, it is very much in use in serial communications. The main drawback here is the same as it would be for any other protocol, namely, both devices must agree on a method of communication or you may lose data during transmission.

Serial communication on a PostScript device requires some special codes that allow certain actions to be taken; the special codes for transmission control are typical. A representative set follows, with the ASCII character codes shown in decimal:

Character	Code	Function
Control-C	3	interrupt; causes execution of the PostScript **interrupt** process. See the description of **interrupt** in Section C1.
Control-D	4	end-of-file
Control-Q	17	XON flow control character; start output (only if using XON/XOFF control)
Control-S	19	XOFF flow control character; stop output (only if using XON/XOFF control)
Control-T	20	status query; causes the interpreter to produce a one-line status message. See the description of status messages below.
Linefeed	10	end-of-line; this is the PostScript *newline* character, as described in Section A1.1. If both a Return (ASCII 13) and a Linefeed are received in succession, only one *newline* is passed on to the interpreter. Also, if a *newline* is written to the standard output file, it is converted into the two-character sequence: Return, Linefeed.
Return	13	end-of-line; translated into a PostScript *newline* (see above).

There is no way to pass these characters directly through the serial channel to the PostScript interpreter, nor is there any way to transmit ASCII characters with the high-order bit set (range 129-255) if the parity and transmission settings require that bit for communications. In this sense, then, the serial communications channel is not a fully transparent connection. However, as you remember, PostScript provides all features within the standard, low-range ASCII character set. Therefore, in ordinary processing, there is no difficulty; and there is no processing that cannot be accomplished by using correct Post-Script techniques over the serial communications channel.

Parallel communication, as mentioned above, sends one complete 8-bit byte with no parity check required. The special characters reserved for operations are the same as those listed above for serial communications, except that the XON/XOFF flow control characters are ignored and passed through to the interpreter. A parallel communication channel controls the flow of information by using a hardware method.

The parallel communications channel as seen by the host is generally an output-only channel. Since the PostScript interpreter provides a variety of messages, such as error messages, status reports, and possibly application-generated output, there needs to be some method of transmitting these back to the host. Some devices do allow bidirectional communication over a parallel port, most notably the IBM PS/2. Consult your hardware documentation for information. Where this is possible, using the parallel port for communication with your PostScript device may be the best choice. Where it is not available, however, there are other alternatives. Usually this is done by returning a message from the interpreter to the host over a serial channel. Although the host can send batch jobs to the interpreter without having two-way communications, it is a bad idea to use only one-way communications, because important error and status information may be lost.

Networked communications is always two-way, since a network allows all devices to send messages to one another with equal facility. The major programming concerns in networked environments are those of device names and correct program structure. The names of networked devices are important because they control the routing and reception of information within the network. Program structure is important because it allows the network to identify PostScript jobs and provide processing and document-handling services (if any are provided).

Timeouts

The PostScript interpreter also has a timeout facility that limits the amount of time that the server will remain in any of its various states. There are three timeout values that are of interest to the PostScript programmer; *job* timeout, *manualfeed* timeout, and *wait* timeout. All of these timeouts are set to default values at the start of a PostScript program, but an application can modify the values if desired by using appropriate operators, as defined in Section C2.2. In addition, the default values may be altered by using the **setdefaulttimeouts** operator, which permanently resets the default values.

The job timeout value, if non-zero, limits the total amount of time the job will execute. This protects against jobs that are in perpetual loops or that run for an excessive length of time. If the value is zero, there is no limit to how long the job can run; also note that the application program can reset the job timeout as often as desired while executing.

The manualfeed timeout, if non-zero, governs how long the server will wait for a piece of paper to be supplied in manual feed mode. On devices that provide a manual feed, the user can request that individual pieces of paper (or envelopes, transparency stock, labels, and so on) be supplied individually for output through a manual feed. The use of the manual feed is governed by the **manualfeed** boolean value defined in *statusdict;* if **manualfeed** is *true,* the server will request (in some fashion) that output paper be supplied in some non-standard fashion. If **manualfeed** is *false,* however, the normal access is used to supply the output medium. If no paper (or other output medium) is supplied within the time limit specified in *manualfeed timeout,* the job is aborted.

The wait timeout value, if non-zero, limits the time the server will wait for additional input for a job that is in progress. This limit is designed to prevent the server from being hung up by a loss of communication with the host or by an abnormal termination of the host application or communication program. Under ordinary circumstances, this will abort the current job in either batch or emulation modes; however, for obvious reasons, this parameter is disabled when the server is running in the interactive mode.

Status Queries

PostScript provides status query facilities that allow the host or user to determine something about the state and current processing status of the output device. The PostScript interpreter responds asynchronously to any status queries, processing them prior to continuing normal job execution. This allows document manager programs or other document processing applications to determine the current state of the printer at any point during the processing cycle. The actual implementation of the status query mechanism differs depending on the current communications channel, but the syntax and semantics of the queries and responses are the same in all cases.

A status response by the interpreter has a standard format that is intended to be read by an application if desired. It consists of one or more 'key: value' pairs of information, each separated from other pairs by a semicolon, ';'. An example of a typical status message is as follows:

%%[job: memo; status: printing; source: AppleTalk]%%

Note that the status message always begins with the sequence '%%[' and ends with the sequence ']%%'. This allows host document management software to parse such messages and respond or redirect them as appropriate.

The possible keys that are transmitted on a status message and the meanings of the associated values are as follows:

job   the name of the job, as stored in the **jobname** entry in *statusdict;* if the application has not stored a value in **jobname**, this key is omitted. See the description of **jobname** below.

status   what the interpreter is currently doing:
idle   no job in progress
busy   executing a PostScript program
waiting   awaiting additional I/O during processing
initializing   during startup
printing   paper in motion
printing test page   (self-explanatory)
PrinterError: reason   (where the *reason* may be a paper jam, no paper tray, and so on)

source   the source of the job the server is currently executing; the exact values depend on the communications channels available on the specific device. This field is omitted if the server is idle.

All other messages that are generated by the interpreter internally (as opposed to being generated by a PostScript application using the **print** operator) also use the same format as the status message. That is, they are sent as ordinary data over the current output communications channel in sequence with any other data being transmitted and are bracketed by the character strings '%%[' and ']%%'. These messages, and their meanings, are as follows:

%%[Error: *error;* OffendingCommand: *name*]%%

An error has been detected by the PostScript interpreter and the error processing has resulted in calling the standard error handler, **handleerror**. The *error* field gives the name of the error process originally invoked, such as **stackunderflow** or **typecheck**. The *name* field gives the name of the operator or procedure that was being executed at the time the error occurred. See Section A2.4.

%%[PrinterError: *reason*]%%

A problem has been detected involving the printing or paper-handling mechanism. Generally, such errors only occur during the actual printing process. The appropriate action for the server is normally to notify the user of the error and wait for it to be corrected; the exact action taken is determined by the **printererror** procedure in *statusdict*, which is one of the volatile parameters defined below.

%%[Flushing: rest of job (to EOF) will be ignored]%%

A previous error or other condition has occurred that prevents the interpreter from continuing to process the current job; the remainder of the current job is discarded. Any further input is discarded until an end-of-file indication (normally, a Control-D) is received.

%%[exitserver: permanent state may be changed]%%

> This message indicates that the currently operating PostScript application has successfully exited from the server's normal **save, restore** context and that it may now make changes to the persistent parameters stored in *statusdict* or may load procedures into virtual memory that will persist until power-off or reset occurs. See Section C2.2 for more information.

The advantage of having all these messages in a common format should be evident. They are equally intelligible to a human viewer and a document controller. However, they can be quite cryptic, particularly the '%%[Error: . . .' message. Since this reports only what the error was and not where it occurred, it generally is not of much use in debugging a program, particularly when the same operators occur over and over in a program.

2.2   SYSTEM PARAMETERS

Every PostScript device implements a fairly extensive set of parameters and procedures that control its behavior. These device-dependent parameters can be divided into two groups, based on whether the parameter retains its value or not when the device is powered off. Parameters that are maintained even when the power is off are stored in some form of non-volatile storage. All these parameters, operators, and procedures are stored in the *statusdict*, as described earlier.

Password Protection

Under normal conditions, the PostScript interpreter surrounds each job with a **save, restore** pair of operators that allow for control of error processing and recovery of virtual memory resources that are used within a job. There are reasons, however, when a PostScript job may wish to exit this normal process and be able to access virtual memory without being included within a **save, restore** context. Fundamentally, there are two times when this is necessary. The first is when a job wishes to load procedures or values into virtual memory that will not be erased at the end of the job. This is often done by certain application programs to avoid repeated transmission of identical information to the output device and thereby to speed up processing. The second is when a job wishes to change the non-volatile, or *persistent*, parameters in the *statusdict*, which is the case we are concerned with here.

In order to prevent a PostScript application from accidentally exiting the normal server routine, the access to this state is protected by a *system administrator password*. This password is a PostScript integer with a default value of zero. It can be changed by using the *setpassword* operator detailed below. However, changing the password should be undertaken with caution, because any change to the password will not only prevent unauthorized access to the persistent parameters but will also inhibit access for applications that load procedures outside of the ordinary server loop – which many of the most common Post-Script applications do.

To exit from the normal server loop, you must execute the following PostScript routine:

```
serverdict begin password exitserver
```

where *password* is the correct system adminstrator password. If the password is incorrect, the **exitserver** operator executes the error **PasswordIncorrect**, which immediately terminates execution. If the password is correct, **exitserver** responds with the message

```
%%[exitserver: permanent state may be changed]%%
```

which lets you know that the process has been successful. The interpreter then clears the stacks, and so forth, as though to process the next job, but does not perform another **save** as it would normally do. Note that, since a new job is starting, the user or application must never issue an **end** operator to match the original **serverdict begin**; you must use the exact command sequence detailed above to correctly and successfully exit the server loop. A user in the interactive mode will have to reenter the **executive** command at this point to restart interactive processing outside the server loop.

From this point to the next end-of-file, the PostScript application or user is allowed to access the *statusdict* and change persistent parameters. In addition, any changes made to values, any new objects created, and so on, will remain in memory until the PostScript device is reset or is powered off. This means that everything that is added at this time will remain in memory and be available to all subsequent jobs. Use of this process should be done carefully, since any objects added at this time consume resources that cannot be recovered by the normal **save**, **restore** process. That means that the amount of virtual memory that is available to application programs is reduced by the amount used during this process and cannot be recovered until the device is reset or powered off.

You should be aware that the server itself is not protected from harmful changes when it is in this state. This allows the server itself to be patched, should that be necessary. However, it also means that it is possible to make changes, in error, that cause serious server malfunctions.

Changing Persistent Parameters

With all that said, it's time to look at those parameters in *statusdict* that deal with persistent values. All the operators that deal with these values are stored in *statusdict* and are listed below. For the most part, the operators are listed alphabetically. However, many of these operators come in pairs, with one operator reporting the current value or status of the desired parameter and an associated operator setting a new value. In such cases, the pair of operators is presented in order by the name of the reporting operator, and the setting operator generally has the same name with **set** as a prefix – for example,

printername and **setprintername**. In any case, the operators are grouped in sets that associate related functions. They are presented in a format similar to the one used in the last chapter but with some exceptions to fit the unusual nature of these objects. First, the 'Associated' line is not present, because these operators are grouped together and generally have no association with other status parameters. Second, we have replaced the 'Type' information with a line labeled 'Value' that gives the typical default value for that parameter (if it is implemented in the device and if a standard value has any meaning for it). Finally, there are almost no examples of these operators since their device-dependent nature makes examples rather unreliable for general reference.

PERSISTENT PARAMETERS (in *statusdict*)

checkpassword

int **checkpassword** bool

returns *true* if *int* is equal to the current system administrator password. Otherwise waits for one second and returns *false*.

    VALUE: *password* 0, true
    ERRORS: stackunderflow, typecheck

old new **setpassword** bool

sets the system administrator password to *new* if the correct *old* password is provided. Both *old* and *new* must be PostScript integers. **setpassword** returns the boolean value *true* if the new password has been set correctly and returns *false* otherwise.

    ERRORS: stackunderflow, typecheck

defaultpageparams

    —   **defaultpageparams**   width height margin resolution

returns the default values for **pageparams**, which is defined in the listing of volatile parameters later on in this chapter. These are the values that will be set at power-on for the parameters that govern *width, height, margin,* and *resolution*. The default value for *margin* is the same as the value returned by **defaultmargin**. For a discussion of the effect of the **pageparams** parameter, see the volatile parameters below.

    VALUE: —device dependent—
    ERRORS: stackoverflow

width height margin resolution **setdefaultpageparams** —

sets the default values of the **pageparams** parameters *width, height, margin,* and *resolution,* all of which are integers.

> ERRORS: stackunderflow, typecheck

defaultpapertray

> – **defaultpapertray** tray

returns *tray,* which is the default tray number. In devices with more than one paper feed and therefore with more than one paper tray, this parameter determines the default tray that is used both to feed paper and to determine the page size parameters, if the device can sense the page size of the tray. See the previous discussion of page sizes and tray values in Section C2.1, "Server Operation," for more information.

> VALUE: 0 (usually the uppermost paper tray)
> ERRORS: stackoverflow

> tray **setdefaultpapertray** –

sets the default value for the paper tray to be used as a source of paper and to establish the page size parameters for the device at startup.

> ERRORS: rangecheck, stackunderflow, typecheck

defaulttimeouts

> – **defaulttimeouts** job manualfeed wait

returns the default values for the three timeout parameters, *job* timeout, *manualfeed* timeout, and the *wait* timeout. At the start of each job, the interpreter initializes these three timeouts to the values given by this operator. If a program wishes to change the timeout values while executing, it may change each one individually by using the **setjobtimeout** operator or by redefining the **manualfeed** or **waittimeout** values. See the definitions of these parameters in the list of volatile parameters further on in this chapter.

> VALUE: 0 60 30
> ERRORS: stackoverflow

> job manualfeed wait **setdefaulttimeouts** –

resets the default timeouts to the values *job, manualfeed,* and *wait.*

> ERRORS: invalidaccess, rangecheck, stackunderflow, typecheck

dostartpage

— **dostartpage** bool

returns the boolean value *true* if the device is set to produce a startup page and returns *false* otherwise.

VALUE: true
ERRORS: stackoverflow

bool **setdostartpage** —

sets *bool* as the controlling value to determine whether a startup page is produced at power-on; the value *true* produces the page, and the value *false* suppresses the page.

ERRORS: invalidaccess, stackunderflow, typecheck

dosysstart

— **dosysstart** bool

returns the boolean value *true* if the system is set to execute a default setup file at startup and returns *false* otherwise. The file name and location are device-dependent information.

VALUE: false
ERRORS: stackoverflow

bool **setdosysstart** —

sets *bool* as the controlling value to determine whether a standard startup file is executed at power-on; the value *true* executes the file, if it exists, and the value *false* does not execute the file. The name and location of the file are device-dependent.

ERRORS: invalidaccess, stackunderflow, typecheck

eescratch

index **eescratch** setting

returns the integer *setting*, which is the value of the parameter located at *index* in the scratch (unallocated) non-volatile memory storage of the device. The possible correct range for *index* depends on the amount of scratch memory that is allocated in the non-volatile storage and is device-dependent. *index* has an allowed range of 0 to 255, although values in that range that reflect actual states of parameters are device-dependent. The scratch portion of non-volatile memory is set aside to provide for storage of persistent parameters that were not designed into the device mechanism. For that reason, the meaning of each position selected by *index* is also device-dependent and will be provided by the device documentation.

VALUE: —device dependent—
ERRORS: rangecheck, stackoverflow, typecheck

index setting   **seteescratch**   —

sets the value *setting* into the position in scratch non-volatile memory selected by *index*.

ERRORS: invalidaccess, rangecheck, stackunderflow, typecheck

hardwareiomode

—   **hardwareiomode**   setting

returns the current hardware I/O mode coded as a PostScript integer, *setting*. The hardware I/O mode governs the method of communication between the interpreter and the controlling host, selecting one of the available communication channels. Possible values for *setting* are device-dependent.

VALUE: 0
ERRORS: rangecheck, stackoverflow, typecheck

setting   **sethardwareiomode**   —

sets the hardware I/O mode to the value *setting*, which must be a PostScript integer that codes the desired hardware interface mode for startup. A new value of *setting* does not take effect until the end of the current job.

ERRORS: rangecheck, stackunderflow, typecheck

idlefonts

—   **idlefonts**   mark font s_x s_y rot nchar . . .

returns a *mark* object, followed by up to 150 integers that represent the parameters controlling idle-time font scan conversion. The integers are presented in groups of 5 and specify the fonts and other characteristics of the characters that are scan-converted while the device is idle. The default result is an empty list, shown by only the *mark,* which indicates that the device-dependent default list is to be scan-converted. See the description of idle-time font scan conversion in Section A5.3.

The values of the results have the following meanings:

font   a font number (not a name) taken from the list of fonts built into the device. The complete set of built-in fonts is device-dependent, but typical values for the basic set of PostScript fonts are:

0   Courier

1   Courier-Bold

2   Courier-Oblique

3   Courier-BoldOblique

4   Times-Roman

5   Times-Bold

6   Times-Italic

7   Times-BoldItalic

8   Helvetica

9   Helvetica-Bold

10   Helvetica-Oblique

11   Helvetica-BoldOblique

12   Symbol

s_x
s_y the scaling factors in the x and y axes, multiplied by a factor of 10. That is, to provide 12-point scaling, you would use the value 120.

rot   the rotation angle of the font in 5-degree increments. That is, to rotate a font by 90 degrees, you would use the value 18 (since 18 times 5 equals 90).

nchars   the number of characters out of the standard 94 character set that are to be converted. A value of 52, for example, would include all the lower- and uppercase alphabetic characters in the font (or the equivalent positions in the Symbol font).

VALUE: mark
ERRORS: stackoverflow

mark font s_x s_y rot nchars . . .   **setidlefonts**   —

sets up to 150 integer values, taken as groups of five (*font, s_x, s_y, rot, nchars*) that define the character sets to be scan-converted during the device idle-time processing. The list must be preceded by a *mark* object, because the length of the list is variable. If the only operand is a *mark*, that indicates that the default set of characters for the device is to be scan-converted.

ERRORS: rangecheck, typecheck, unmatchedmark

margins

> —   **margins**   top left

returns the two margin adjustment parameters, *top* and *left*. The values *top* and *left* are integer numbers that give the adjustment to the top and left margins of the physical output page; that is, these are the values that control the positioning of the imageable area on the output page. Previously, we had said that the imageable area is centered on the output page; these adjustment values are provided to compensate for small irregularities in the centering of the imageable area. Note that these are not the margin settings for the output page, which are set by the appropriate page type procedures; these parameters are provided solely for correction of physical alignment problems at the time of device installation.

The values of *top* and *left* are integers that specify the distance to move each of the respective margins in units in device space; that is, one unit is one device pixel. The top margin is the margin that emerges from the output device first; a positive value of *top* increases the size of the margin, while a negative value decreases it. Similarly, a positive value of *left* widens the left margin, while a negative value makes it smaller.

> VALUE: 0 0
> ERRORS: stackoverflow

> top left   **setmargins**   —

sets the margin adjustment values for the top and left margins, respectively, to the integer values *top* and *left*.

> ERRORS: invalidaccess, rangecheck, stackunderflow, typecheck

pagecount

> —   **pagecount**   int

returns *int* as the number of pages that have been printed since the output device was built. There is no functional way to reset this number.

> ERRORS: stackoverflow

pagestackorder

> —   **pagestackorder**   bool

returns the boolean value *true* if output pages stack with the front of the second page facing the back of the first page, and so on, and returns *false* otherwise. This usually represents whether the device has face-up stacking for output, which would result in a value *false*, or has face-down stacking, which would result in a value *true*. This value is useful to document management software, which may be able to change the print order for a document in order to provide collated output based on testing this parameter. That is, if **pagestackorder** is *false,* a document manager may print documents that conform to the structuring conventions last page first, and so on, in order to produce output in the correct, collated sequence.

```
VALUE:    – device-dependent –
ERRORS:   stackunderflow, typecheck
```

bool   **setpagestackorder**   –

sets the value reported by the **pagestackorder** operator to the boolean value, *bool.* Note that this does not control the page order; it simply reports how the output is stacked. Since most devices cannot sense the correct stack order, it is up to the application or setup procedures to set this value correctly.

```
ERRORS:   stackoverflow
```

printername

string   **printername**   substring

returns *substring,* the name of the printer as defined to any external environment. The name value is inserted into the supplied *string* and overwrites the initial portion of the string. The *string* must be long enough to contain the name. There is generally a maximum size imposed on the name, and there may be restrictions, which will be device-dependent, on name format, character, etc.

```
VALUE:    device name
ERRORS:   invalidaccess, rangecheck, stackunderflow, typecheck
```

string   **setprintername**   –

sets *string* as the name of the printer as reported to communications channels, and as reported by the **printername** operator. The maximum length and the standard construction of the name are device-dependent.

```
ERRORS:   invalidaccess, rangecheck, stackunderflow, typecheck
```

ramsize

–   **ramsize**   int

returns *int,* which is the number of bytes of random-access memory (RAM) installed in the device.

```
VALUE:    device-dependent
ERRORS:   stackoverflow
```

sccbatch

channel   **sccbatch**   baud options

returns the current baud rate, *baud*, and the options setting *options* for the serial communications channel *channel* when that channel is in the batch mode. The maximum baud rate and the precise meaning of the options settings are device-dependent; however, both are PostScript integers. Typical values for *baud* range from *0*, which indicates that the channel is disabled, to *19,200*, although some channels may support even higher rates. The values for *option* encode a variety of parameters such as parity, flow control, stop bits, and number of data bits; the default value of *0* indicates the most common setting of the parameters. These parameters may be set independently for each serial communications channel that is available on the device. Which channel is reported is selected by the *channel* operand, which is also an integer.

VALUE: 9600   0
ERRORS: rangecheck, stackoverflow, stackunderflow, typecheck

channel baud options   **setsccbatch**   –

sets the communications parameters for the serial communication channel selected by *channel* to *baud* and *option* when the channel is in the batch mode. Setting a baud rate of *0* disables the serial communications channel, but it is usually not allowed to disable all the serial communications channels at one time. The new values for *baud* and *options* do not take effect until the end of the current job.

ERRORS: invalidaccess, rangecheck, stackunderflow, typecheck

sccinteractive

channel   **sccinteractive**   baud options

returns the current baud rate, *baud*, and the options setting *options* for the serial communications channel *channel* when that channel is in the interactive mode. The maximum baud rate and the precise meaning of the options settings are device-dependent; however, both are PostScript integers. Typical values for *baud* range from *0*, which indicates that the channel is disabled, to *19,200*, although some channels may support even higher rates. The values for *option* encode a variety of parameters such as parity, flow control, stop bits, and number of data bits; the default value of *0* indicates the most common setting of the parameters. These parameters may be set independently for each serial communications channel that is available on the device. Which channel is reported is selected by the *channel* operand, which is also an integer.

VALUE: 9600   0
ERRORS: rangecheck, stackoverflow, stackunderflow, typecheck

channel baud options   **setsccinteractive**   —

sets the communications parameters for the serial communication channel selected by *channel* to *baud* and *option* when the channel is in the interactive mode. Setting a baud rate of *0* disables the serial communications channel, but it is usually not allowed to disable all the serial communications channels at one time. The new values for *baud* and *options* do not take effect until the end of the current job.

ERRORS: invalidaccess, rangecheck, stackunderflow, typecheck

softwareiomode

—   **softwareiomode**   setting

returns the current software I/O mode coded as a PostScript integer, *setting*. The software I/O mode governs the interface between the interpreter and the controlling host, covering conditions such as startup in batch, interactive, or an emulation mode. Possible values for *setting* are device-dependent.

VALUE: —device dependent—
ERRORS: stackoverflow

setting   **setsoftwareiomode**   —

sets the software I/O mode to the value *setting,* which must be a PostScript integer that codes the desired software interface mode for startup. A new value of *setting* does not take effect until the end of the current job.

ERRORS: rangecheck, stackunderflow, typecheck

As we discussed above, accessing any of these operators that change non-volatile parameters (as distinguished from the operators that merely report the current setting) requires that you exit the server loop and supply the correct password. Generally these are the operators that begin with 'set . . . '; however, a complete list of these operators is as follows:

setdefaultpageparams	**setidlefonts**	**setsccinteractive**
setdostartpage	**seteescratch**	**setsoftwareiomode**
setdosysstart	**setpagestackorder**	**setsccbatch**
setdefaulttimeouts	**setprintername**	**setdefaultpapertray**
sethardwareiomode	**setmargins**	

Changing Volatile Parameters

PostScript also provides a series of parameters that do not persist beyond power-off or beyond the end of the current job; these are called *volatile* parameters. These parameters are operators and other PostScript variables (boolean values, numbers, strings, and so on) that are defined in *statusdict* in the ordinary way.

Like all other PostScript objects, except those persistent parameters that we discussed above which are stored in non-volatile memory, the values of the PostScript variables stored in *statusdict* generally do not persist beyond the end of a job. Therefore, if one of them, such as **manualfeed**, is modified by the current job, it is reset at the end of the job to the default value. Like other objects in virtual memory, however, an application can change a value for an entire working session on the device by exiting the server loop, as described earlier, and then changing the desired value. In that case, the change to the value persists until the device is powered off. In other words, if you change **manualfeed** to *true* inside an application, that value will apply only to the job that set it; if you exit the server loop first, the change will apply to the job that makes the change and all subsequent jobs until the device is powered off.

This distinction is of some importance. It is impossible to change the persistent parameters listed in the preceding section without exiting the server loop. However, it is possible, and indeed usually desirable, to change the volatile status parameters from within an ordinary job, simply by accessing the value through a *statusdict* reference as shown below. If you do change the volatile parameters outside the server loop, the changes will persist until the device is shut off; when the device is powered on again, the original default values will be set again.

Many of the volatile parameters are not PostScript operators at all but rather are simply ordinary PostScript objects. Such parameter values can be changed by merely redefining the value using ordinary PostScript operations. For example, the boolean value **manualfeed** can be set (or reset) to the value *true* simply by the sequence

```
statusdict / manualfeed true put
```

As you see, this requires no special operators or special access. For convenience, the data type of each volatile parameter is provided as part of the description and is indicated at the end of the listing.

VOLATILE PARAMETERS (in *statusdict*)

appletalktype

—	**appletalktype**	string

is the *string* that defines the type portion of the device's AppleTalk name according to the Name Binding Protocol. The default value will always be 'LaserWriter', even if the device is something other than a LaserWriter, since the Macintosh Print Manager assumes that all PostScript printers are of type 'LaserWriter'.

```
DATA TYPE:   string
    VALUE:   (LaserWriter)
   ERRORS:   rangecheck, stackoverflow, typecheck
```

duplex

—   **duplex**   bool

returns the boolean value *true* when the device is set up for duplex (two-sided) printing and returns the value *false* if the device is set up for simplex (one-sided) printing.

```
DATA TYPE:   operator
    VALUE:   false
   ERRORS:   stackoverflow
```

bool   **setduplex**   —

causes the device to select duplex (two-sided) printing if the value of *bool* is true and selects simplex (one-sided) printing if the value is *false*. In duplex printing, the device prints subsequent output pages on alternate sides of the paper. The first page and each subsequent odd **showpage** prints on the front of a page; the second page and each subsequent even **showpage** prints on the back.

```
   ERRORS:   stackunderflow, typecheck
```

jobname

—   **jobname**   string

is the *string* that defines the name of the currently executing job. If a PostScript program defines **jobname**, the status responses will include a 'job' field that will show *string* as part of the message. The *string* should not include characters that will conflict with the message format. See Section C2.1 for more information.

```
DATA TYPE:   string
    VALUE:   ( )
   ERRORS:   stackoverflow
```

jobsource

—   **jobsource**   string

is the *string* that defines the source of the current job, that is, what communication channel the job is transmitted over. See the discussion of status messages in Section C2.1. This value is set and maintained by the interpreter.

```
DATA TYPE:   string
    VALUE:   ( ) when the server is idle
   ERRORS:   stackoverflow
```

jobstate

—   jobstate   string

is the *string* that defines the status of the current job, that is, one of the status values defined for the status messages as discussed in Section C2.1. This value is set and maintained by the interpreter.

```
DATA TYPE:   string
    VALUE:   (idle) when the server is idle
   ERRORS:   stackoverflow
```

jobtimeout

—   jobtimeout   int

returns the integer *int,* which is the number of seconds remaining before job timeout will occur. A value of 0 indicates that the job will never timeout.

```
DATA TYPE:   operator
    VALUE:   0
   ERRORS:   stackoverflow
```

int   **setjobtimeout**   —

sets the timeout value for the job to *int* seconds. *int* must be a non-negative integer value that specifies the length of time until the job either completes processing or resets the job timeout value. If the job does not terminate or reset the job timeout value within *int* seconds, the interpreter executes the **timeout** error.

```
   ERRORS:   rangecheck, stackunderflow, typecheck
```

manualfeed

—   manualfeed   bool

is the boolean value *bool* that controls feed of the next output page. If the boolean value is *true,* the page is to be fed from the manual input; if *false,* it comes from the standard or default input.

DATA TYPE: boolean
VALUE: false
ERRORS: stackoverflow

manualfeedtimeout

– **manualfeedtimeout** int

is the integer value, *int,* that gives the number of seconds currently set for the interpreter to wait for a page to be inserted into the manual feed slot. If a page is not fed within *int* seconds, the interpreter sends a '%%[PrinterError: manual feed timeout]%%' message and aborts the request. The page image remains in raster memory and can still be reprinted. The value set for the manual feed timeout is only used if the device is in manual feed mode; that is, if **manualfeed** is *true.*

At the beginning of a job, the interpreter initializes **manualfeedtimeout** to the default value as reported by the **defaulttimeouts** operator. Notice that this is explicitly reset for every new job; even if the value was reset outside the server loop (by using **exitserver**) it will not persist to a new job.

DATA TYPE: integer
VALUE: 60
ERRORS: stackoverflow

papertray

– **papertray** int

is the integer value that determines which paper tray the next sheet of output will feed from. The possible values of *int* are device-dependent. This variable can be reset in two ways: by using the **setpapertray** operator, which is described below, or by redefining the value in *statusdict,* using ordinary PostScript operators (**get, put, def,** and so on). The difference is that redefining the value of **papertray** in *statusdict* simply selects the tray; using the operator **setpapertray** also makes other changes (see below).

DATA TYPE: integer
VALUE: the value set by **defaultpapertray**
ERRORS: stackoverflow

int **setpapertray** –

sets the paper tray selection mechanism to the tray represented by the integer, *int,* by redefining the variable **papertray**; it also sets the imageable area to the value appropriate to the size of that tray. Note that this operator changes the imageable area of the page and therefore should be invoked before any marks are made on the page. If you want only to select a different source for the paper and do not wish to change the imageable area of the device, the correct method is to redefine the parameter **papertray** directly rather than by using this operator.

DATA TYPE: operator
ERRORS: rangecheck, stackunderflow, typecheck

printererror

status tries   **printererror**   −

is a procedure that is executed if the output hardware reports an error during execution of a **showpage** or similar operation. The two operands are supplied by the server. The *status* operand is an integer that indicates the type or reason for the error report, such as 'out of paper', or 'no paper tray' or 'paper jam', or whatever status variables have been established for the device. The *tries* operand is the number of times that an error has occurred for this execution of the output operator. If the **printererror** procedure returns normally, the output operation is retried; if it terminates processing (by executing a **stop** operator), then the output processing is terminated but the output image remains in raster memory. In particular, if an error occurs and processing is terminated, the usual effects of a **showpage**, such as **erasepage** and **initgraphics,** do not take place.

The standard **printererror** procedure produces an error message in the format '%%[PrinterError: *reason*]%%', with the value of *reason* being based on the *status* value provided as an operand to the **printererror** procedure by the server. For most errors, the standard procedure will continue to try to print the page at intervals indefinitely.

DATA TYPE: operator
ERRORS: stackunderflow, typecheck

product

−   **product**   string

is the *string* that identifies the product name of the device. If you want to know what make and model of output device you are running on, this string provides the information.

DATA TYPE: integer
VALUE: −device dependent−
ERRORS: stackoverflow

revision

—	**revision**	integer

is the integer value, *int,* that designates the current revision level of the device-dependent portion of the PostScript interpreter. The complete identification of the current version of the PostScript interpreter that is running is given by the general operator **version.**

```
DATA TYPE:   integer
    VALUE:   —device dependent—
   ERRORS:   stackoverflow
```

waittimeout

—	**waittimeout**	int

is the integer value, *int,* that gives the number of seconds currently set for the interpreter to wait for additional input over the current communication channel. If additional input is not received from the host within *int* seconds, the interpreter executes the error procedure **timeout,** which normally terminates the job and flushes the input data stream to the next end-of-file. A PostScript application, however, may reset the value to any nonnegative integer by using ordinary PostScript operations. A value of 0 indicates that the timeout should never occur.

At the beginning of a job, the interpreter initializes **waittimeout** to the default value as reported by the **defaulttimeouts** operator. Notice that this is explicitly reset for every new job; even if the value was reset outside the server loop (by using **exitserver**) it will not persist to a new job. When executing in the interactive mode, however, the value of **waittimeout** is always set to 0, no matter what the default value is.

```
DATA TYPE:   integer
    VALUE:   30
   ERRORS:   stackoverflow
```

Remember that these are representative operators, not the actual set of operators for any device. Your specific device will have a different set of operators, which may include certain operators that are not mentioned here, and which almost certainly will not include all of the operators presented here. This list is intended to cover the more common operators that are often included in many devices with the same or similar requirements. The point here is that even though these operators do depend on facilities that vary from device to device, nevertheless the approach taken by the PostScript language has a common feeling and is consistent in presentation across many devices. The documentation supplied with your device is the correct source for a complete and definitive discussion of the device-specific operators and their use.

2.3 DISK OPERATIONS

Some PostScript devices have an external disk storage mechanism that is available to the PostScript interpreter either directly or through an operating system interface. For such devices, the PostScript interpreter defines a series of operations over and above those standard file operations that are always present. Some of these operators are defined in *systemdict,* and others are defined in the *statusdict.* For those that are in *statusdict,* as for all *statusdict* objects, you must explicitly access *statusdict* before you can use them.

External storage may also be implemented on devices other than an external disk; for example, some PostScript devices have external cartridge storage. Although the storage medium is different, the approach to handling the device and the operations defined are similar. As is true with all the device-dependent operators, a thorough reading of the manual that accompanies the device is your best guide to the correct syntax and use of the available operators.

Where an external file storage system is available, the PostScript interpreter commonly provides a simple set of operations that allow use of the system. Such file systems provide non-volatile and extended storage for the font cache, for virtual memory, and for font outline definitions; they also provide user-accessible file storage. Such a system is implemented on the premise that it is more secure than RAM storage but less secure than a full file system, which is backed up and controlled by an operating system. The assumption is that all information on the PostScript file system can be reconstructed from other forms of storage in a reasonable way. It is the user's responsibility to see that this is an accurate assumption. The file system maintains a file directory that enables the interpreter to look up any given file name. Typically, the file system is tested for correct operation at startup. If it fails the test, then all or part of the information previously contained in it may be erased, or the disk may be reinitialized.

Some file systems provide for automatic processing of a specially named or referenced job at power-on. Such jobs are stored on the file system and executed just like any other PostScript job when the device is powered on. When such facilities exist, special care must be taken to ensure that the jobs execute correctly and are correctly named. For obvious reasons, any error in such a startup job is particularly dangerous because there is often no good recovery method. Because these jobs are sensitive, access to the commands that access or record them are generally controlled in the same way that non-volatile parameter access is controlled, namely, it is necessary to exit the server loop before working with these files.

Font Extension

The one area that is most noticeable from a programming point of view in a device with a file system is that the **findfont** operator is no longer limited to fonts that are loaded into memory. In general PostScript processing, any font that is not currently accessible in the **FontDirectory** must be provided by downloading from the host before it can be used. When you have an external file system, this is no longer the case.

With an external file system, the **findfont** operator behaves somewhat differently than its normal operation as described earlier. When a font name is presented to the **findfont** operator, it first looks up the name in the **FontDirectory** as it normally would. If the font is found there, it is used, and processing continues in the ordinary way. If the font is not there, **findfont** initiates a search of the file system for a file with a name, structured from the requirements of the file system naming conventions and the font name. If the file is present, **findfont** executes that file, thereby loading the file into virtual memory (as though the file were downloaded at that point and **definefont** executed), registers the name in the **FontDirectory,** and presents the requested font dictionary on the operand stack. Obviously, if the file is not found, processing continues in the ordinary fashion.

As with any font that is loaded from an external medium, it is essential that the application monitor the use of resources, particularly virtual memory, and take the necessary steps to manage memory correctly by using **save** and **restore** at appropriate places in the program.

File Conventions

As indicated earlier, the file system that is implemented by the PostScript interpreter is not a full-featured one; in particular, it does not provide features such as access protection, hierarchical directory structures, and so on. In order to ensure correct access and operation, therefore, a user program must carefully follow a set of conventions, most particularly with regard to file names.

File names on the external device are case sensitive and generally have certain device specific limitations on length and format. PostScript uses what might be called a hierarchical naming structure, where the structure of the names indicates how the associated files fit into a complete hierarchical structure. For users with experience with MS-DOS or UNIX, it will seem very familiar; the difference is that the structure is simply a convention and is not supported or enforced by any operating system.

Disk-Based File Operators

We covered the standard PostScript file operators above, together with the general operators. Those PostScript devices that have hard disks attached also implement the following operators. Each operator indicates what dictionary it will be located in.

DISK-BASED FILE OPERATOR (mixed *statusdict* and *systemdict*)

deletefile

namestring **deletefile** —

deletes the file identified by *namestring* from the disk.

TYPE: External file
LOCATED IN: systemdict
ERRORS: ioerror, stackunderflow, typecheck, undefinedfilename

devdismount

namestring **devdismount** —

dismounts the device whose name is given by *namestring*. When a device is dismounted, it is no longer available to the PostScript interpreter for processing and may be removed or disconnected from the system. If the name given as *namestring* does not correspond to a valid device, the interpreter raises the **undefinedfilename** error.

TYPE: External file
LOCATED IN: systemdict
ERRORS: limitcheck, stackunderflow, typecheck, undefinedfilename

devmount

namestring **devmount** bool

returns the boolean value *true* if the device named by the *namestring* is mounted and available to the interpreter for processing; it returns *false* otherwise. For certain external devices, such as cartridges, it is necessary that the device be mounted before it can be used in ordinary PostScript processing. If the name given as *namestring* does not correspond to a valid device, the interpreter raises the **undefinedfilename** error.

TYPE: External file
LOCATED IN: systemdict
ERRORS: limitcheck, stackunderflow, typecheck, undefinedfilename

devstatus

namestring **devstatus** free size

returns the status information *free* and *size* for the device whose name is given by *namestring*. The interpretation of *free* and *status* are device-dependent; generally, they represent the amount of free storage and the total amount of storage on the device. If the name given as *namestring* does not correspond to a valid device, the interpreter raises the **undefinedfilename** error.

TYPE: External file
LOCATED IN: systemdict
ERRORS: limitcheck, stackunderflow, stackoverflow, typecheck, undefined-
filename

diskdriveparams

string **diskdriveparams** substring

returns the current disk drive parameters as a *substring* of the *string* operand, overwriting some portion of the initial value of *string*. The exact format and meaning of the returned parameters are device-dependent.

TYPE: External file
LOCATED IN: statusdict
ERRORS: rangecheck, stackunderflow, typecheck

diskonline

— **diskonline** bool

returns a boolean, *bool,* that indicates the availability of the external disk device. A value *true* indicates that the disk is attached and online, while *false* indicates that the disk is not online or not attached.

TYPE: External file
LOCATED IN: statusdict
ERRORS: stackoverflow

diskstatus

— **diskstatus** free total

returns the number of pages currently available in the file system as the integer value *free,* and the maximum number of pages as the integer value *total.* A page is 1024 bytes.

TYPE: External file
LOCATED IN: statusdict
ERRORS: stackoverflow

filenameforall

pattern proc string   **filenameforall**   –

searches the entire list of files in the file system directory for any names that match *pattern*. If it finds any files matching the *pattern*, **filenameforall** inserts the complete file name into *string* and executes *proc*, passing *string* to *proc* on the operand stack. *pattern* may contain wildcard characters: the character '*' matches any substring; and the character '?' matches any single character. The operand *string* must be long enough to contain the maximum allowable file name (currently 100 characters). As is true for the regular **forall** operator when handling dictionaries, **filenameforall** does not enumerate the files in any particular order, and any file names altered by *proc* may or may not be encountered during the execution of the operator.

TYPE: External file
LOCATED IN: systemdict
ERRORS: stackoverflow, stackunderflow, typecheck

initializedisk

pages action   **initializedisk**   –

initializes the file system and formats some or all of the disk. A value of *pages* equal to *0* selects the entire disk; any value of *pages* greater than 0 selects that number of pages to be formatted. A page is 1024 bytes. The value of *action* controls the events that occur, as follows:

0   the file system is initialized, but the disk is not formatted.

1   the disk is first formatted for the number of pages specified, and then the file system is initialized.

n   for n > 1, the disk is first formatted, then the disk surfaces are tested $n-1$ times to search for bad pages; and finally the file system is initialized.

TYPE: External file
LOCATED IN: statusdict
ERRORS: ioerror, rangecheck, stackunderflow, typecheck

renamefile

oldnamestring newnamestring   **renamefile**   –

renames the file specified by *oldnamestring* to the new name given by *newnamestring*.

```
          TYPE:    External file
    LOCATED IN:    systemdict
        ERRORS:    ioerror, stackunderflow, typecheck, undefinedfilename
```

setdiskdriveparams

paramstring   **setdiskdriveparams**   –

sets the disk drive parameters to the values given in *paramstring*. The exact format and meaning of the parameters are device-dependent.

```
          TYPE:    External file
    LOCATED IN:    statusdict
        ERRORS:    rangecheck, stackunderflow, typecheck
```

setuserdiskpercent

percent   **setuserdiskpercent**   –

takes the integer value *percent* and reserves that percentage of the file system disk storage for user files. The remainder of the disk is reserved for font cache, display buffers, file system overhead, and so on. This percentage may be set to any number, but values above 50 (50 percent) may degrade system performance. Optimum performance is generally achieved with values between 10 and 20 (10 and 20 percent). If the requested amount of space is not currently available, more room is obtained by eliminating the least-recently-used bitmaps in the font cache until sufficient room is made available.

```
          TYPE:    External file
    LOCATED IN:    statusdict
        ERRORS:    rangecheck, stackunderflow, typecheck
```

status

if file found:

namestring   **status**   pages bytes access creation true

if file not found:

false

returns the boolean value *false* if the file specified by *namestring* is not found on the file system directory; it returns a series of values that give file status information if the file does exist. The *pages* is the number of pages that have been allocated to the file, while *bytes* is the number of actual characters that have been written into the file. The result values *access* and *creation* are integer values that indicate the "time" of most recent access and of creation of the file. The notion of "time" in this case is not based on any external time or any calendar value; like the "time" value returned by the **usertime** operator, it is simply a monotonically increasing value, so that a lower number indicates an earlier "time" than a higher number, but nothing else.

Note that this version of the **status** operator is an extension of the standard version of **status** as defined in the *systemdict*. The behavior described here occurs when the operand presented to **status** is a stringtype and an external file system exists; the ordinary behavior of the **status** operator still applies when the operand is a file object.

TYPE:	External file
LOCATED IN:	systemdict
ERRORS:	stackoverflow, stackunderflow, typecheck

userdiskpercent

–   **userdiskpercent**   percent

returns the integer *percent* that represents the amount of disk space on the file system currently set aside for user files as a percentage of total file space. The default value for *percent* is 0.

TYPE:	External file
LOCATED IN:	statusdict
ERRORS:	stackoverflow

3

Operators by Type

3.1 ARRAY

$$- \quad [\quad mark$$

pushes a mark object onto the stack.

$$mark \ any_0 \ldots any_n \quad] \quad array$$

creates a new array of $n+1$ objects out of the objects any_0 to any_n stored above the topmost *mark* on the stack.

$$array \quad \textbf{aload} \quad a_0 .. a_n \ array$$
$$packedarray \quad \textbf{aload} \quad a_0 .. a_n \ packedarray$$

successively pushes all $n+1$ elements of *array* or *packedarray* onto the operand stack, where $n+1$ is the number of elements in *array* or *packedarray*, and finally pushes the array itself.

$$int \quad \textbf{array} \quad array$$

creates *array* that initially contains *int* null objects as entries.

$$any_0 .. any_n array \quad \textbf{aload} \quad array$$

fills *array* with any_0 through any_n, where *array* has a length of $n+1$.

$$array1 \ array2 \quad \textbf{copy} \quad subarray2$$
$$packedarray \ array2 \quad \textbf{copy} \quad subarray2$$

copies all elements of *array1* or *packedarray* into *array2*.

$$- \quad \textbf{currentpacking} \quad bool$$

returns a boolean value that indicates whether array packing is currently in effect or not.

array proc	**forall**	–	
packedarray proc	**forall**	–	

enumerates every element of the first operand and executes *proc* for each of those elements.

array index	**get**	any	
packedarray index	**get**	any	

looks up the *index* in *array* or *packedarray* and returns the element identified by *index* (counting from zero).

array index count	**getinterval**	subarray	
packedarray index count	**getinterval**	subarray	

duplicates a section of the operand *array* or *packedarray* beginning at the element identified by *index* (counting from zero) and extending for *count* elements.

array	**length**	int	
packedarray	**length**	int	

returns *int* as the number of elements that make up the value of *array* or *packedarray*.

–	**mark**	mark

pushes a mark object onto the stack.

any_1 . . . any_n n	**packedarray**	packedarray

creates *packedarray* out of the elements any_1 through any_n.

array index value	**put**	–

stores *value* into *array* at the position identified by *index* (counting from zero).

array1 index array2	**putinterval**	–

replaces a section of the operand *array1* beginning at the element identified by *index* (counting from zero) with the contents of *array2*.

bool	**setpacking**	–

sets the array packing mode to *bool*.

3.2 CONTROL

—	**countexecstack**	int

counts the number of objects on the execution stack and returns that integer, *int,* to the top of the operand stack.

any	**exec**	—

immediately executes the object on the top of the operand stack.

array	**execstack**	subarray

places all the elements of the current execution stack into *array,* overwriting the initial elements.

—	**exit**	—

terminates execution of the currently active instance of a looping context.

init incr limit proc	**for**	—

executes *proc* repeatedly and, at each execution, provides a variable number on the operand stack.

packedarray proc	**forall**	—
string proc	**forall**	—

enumerates every element of the first operand and executes *proc* for each of those elements.

bool proc	**if**	—

executes *proc* if *bool* is *true;* otherwise pops both operands and does nothing.

bool proc1 proc2	**ifelse**	—

executes *proc1* if *bool* is *true* and executes *proc2* if *bool* is *false.*

proc	**loop**	—

executes *proc* continuously until *proc* terminates execution internally.

—	**quit**	—

terminates operation of the interpreter or of the current PostScript program.

int proc   **repeat**   –

executes *proc int* times. The *int* operand must be a non-negative integer and may be 0, in which case **repeat** does not execute *proc* at all and processing continues at the next command.

–   **start**   –

is the procedure executed by the PostScript interpreter when it first starts execution.

–   **stop**   –

terminates execution of the currently active instance of a stopped context, which is a procedure or other executable object invoked by a **stopped** operator.

any   **stopped**   bool

executes *any*, which is usually a procedure or an executable file but may be any executable object.

3.3   CONVERSION

num   **cvi**   int
string   **cvi**   int

converts a number, *num*, or a string that is equivalent to a number, *string*, into the integer value, *int*.

any   **cvlit**   any

converts the object *any* on the top of the operand stack to have the literal attribute.

string   **cvn**   name

converts the *string* operand to a PostScript *name* that is lexically identical to *string*.

num   **cvr**   real
string   **cvr**   real

converts a number, *num*, or a string that is equivalent to a number, *string*, into the real number, *real*.

num base string   **cvrs**   substring

converts *num* into a string equivalent according to the number system whose base number or radix is given by *base*.

any string	**cvs**	substring

converts *any* arbitrary object into a string representation and stores the result in *string*, overwriting the initial portion.

any	**cvx**	any

converts the object *any* on the top of the operand stack to have the executable attribute.

array	**executeonly**	array
packedarray	**executeonly**	packedarray
file	**executeonly**	file
string	**executeonly**	string

reduces the access attribute of the operand to execute-only.

composite object	**noaccess**	composite object
file	**noaccess**	file

changes the access attribute of *composite object* or *file* to allow no access of any kind.

composite object	**rcheck**	bool
file	**rcheck**	bool

tests the access attribute of the operand to see whether the access attribute of the operand is either read-only or unlimited.

composite object	**readonly**	composite object
file	**readonly**	file

changes the access attribute of *composite object* or *file* to allow only read access.

any	**type**	typename

returns *typename*, which is a PostScript name object that specifies the type of *any*.

composite object	**wcheck**	bool
file	**wcheck**	bool

tests the access attribute of the operand to see whether the access attribute of the operand is unlimited.

any	**xcheck**	bool

tests whether *any* has the executable or literal attribute.

3.4 COORDINATES

matrix **concat** —

concatenates *matrix* with the CTM.

matrix1 matrix2 matrix3 **concatmatrix** matrix3

returns the result of multiplying *matrix1* by *matrix2* as *matrix3*.

matrix **currentmatrix** matrix

replaces the value of *matrix* with the current transformation matrix (CTM) from the current graphics state.

matrix **defaultmatrix** matrix

replaces the value of *matrix* with the default coordinate transformation matrix for the output device.

dx dy **dtransform** dx' dy'

transforms the distance vector, (dx, dy), into device space using the current transformation matrix (CTM), and returns the equivalent distance vector for the device onto the operand stack as (dx', dy').

dx dy matrix **dtransform** dx' dy'

transforms the distance vector, (dx, dy), using *matrix* as a transformation matrix, and returns the equivalent distance vector after the transformation onto the operand stack.

matrix **identmatrix** matrix

replaces the contents of *matrix* with the identity matrix [1.0 0.0 0.0 1.0 0.0 0.0].

dx dy **idtransform** ux uy

transforms the distance vector, (dx, dy), in device coordinates into user coordinates, using the inverse of the current transformation matrix (CTM), and returns the new distance vector for the user coordinates to the operand stack as (ux, uy).

dx′ dy′ matrix   **idtransform**   dx dy

transforms the distance matrix, (dx', dy') into user space using the inverse of *matrix* as a transformation matrix, and returns the equivalent distance vector after the transformation as (dx, dy).

—   **initmatrix**   —

restores the current transformation matrix (CTM) to the default matrix for the current output device.

matrix1 matrix2   **invertmatrix**   matrix2

replaces *matrix2* with the inverse of *matrix1*.

dx dy   **itransform**   ux uy

transforms the device coordinates, (dx, dy), into user coordinates using the inverse of the current transformation matrix (CTM), and returns the new coordinates to the operand stack as (ux, uy).

—   **matrix**   matrix

generates an identity transformation matrix, *matrix*, and places it on the operand stack.

angle   **rotate**   —

rotates the user coordinates around their origin by *angle*.

angle matrix   **rotate**   matrix

adjusts the values in *matrix* by the rotation transformation matrix and returns the modified matrix back to the operand stack. No change is made to the CTM.

sx sy   **scale**   —

scales the user coordinates around their origin by *sx* along the *x* axis and *sy* along the *y* axis.

sx sy matrix   **scale**   matrix

adjusts the values in *matrix* by the scaled transformation matrix and returns the modified matrix back to the operand stack. No change is made to the CTM.

matrix   **setmatrix**   —

replaces the current transformation matrix (CTM) in the current graphics state with the value of *matrix*.

x y   **transform**   x′ y′

transforms the distance vector, (x, y), into device space, using the current transformation matrix (CTM), and returns the equivalent distance vector for the device onto the operand stack as $(x′, y′)$.

x y matrix   **transform**   x′ y′

transforms the position (x, y), using *matrix* as a transformation matrix, and returns the equivalent position after the transformation onto the operand stack as $(x′, y′)$.

tx ty   **translate**   –

translates the current origin of the user coordinates to the point (tx, ty), which becomes the new origin.

tx ty matrix   **translate**   matrix

adjusts the values in *matrix* by the appropriate transformation matrix and returns the modified matrix back to the operand stack. No change is made to the CTM.

3.5 DEVICE

–   **#copies**   int

defines the number of copies of a page of output that are produced when a **showpage** operator is executed.

matrix width height proc   **banddevice**   –

installs a band buffer as the raster memory for an output device and sets certain parameters for that device.

–   **copypage**   –

outputs one copy of the current page onto the current output device without erasing the current page or changing the graphics state.

matrix width height proc   **framedevice**   –

installs a frame buffer as the raster memory for an output device and sets certain parameters for that device.

–   **nulldevice**   –

installs the 'null device' as the default output device.

proc   **renderbands**   −

renders bands of raster data from raster memory to the current output device.

−   **showpage**   −

produces the current page on the current output device, causing any marks that have been painted in the imageable area of the current page to appear on the output.

3.6 DICTIONARY

dict   **begin**   −

pushes *dict* onto the dictionary stack and makes it the current dictionary.

dict1 dict2   **copy**   dict2

copies all elements of *dict1* into *dict2*.

−   **countdictstack**   int

counts the number of dictionaries on the dictionary stack and returns that integer, *int*, to the top of the operand stack.

−   **currentdict**   dictionary

returns a duplicate of the current dictionary to the operand stack.

key value   **def**   −

associates *key* with *value* in the current dictionary.

int   **dict**   dict

creates an empty dictionary with a maximum capacity of *int* entries and places the created dictionary onto the operand stack.

array   **dictstack**   subarray

places all elements of the dictionary stack into *array*, overwriting the inital elements.

−   **end**   −

pops the current dictionary off the dictionary stack and makes the dictionary that was immediately below the current dictionary.

−   **errordict**   dict

returns the dictionary *dict*, which is the *errordict* dictionary.

dict proc **forall** –

enumerates every (key, value) pair in *dict*, pushing both elements onto the operand stack, and then executes *proc*.

dict key **get** any

looks up the *key* in *dict* and returns the associated value.

dict key **known** bool

searches the PostScript dictionary, *dict*, for an occurrence of *key* and returns the boolean value *true* if it is found and *false* otherwise.

dict **length** int

returns *int* as the current number of key-value pairs in *dict*.

key **load** value

searches for *key* in every dictionary on the dictionary stack and returns *value* that is associated with the first occurrence of *key*.

dict **maxlength** int

returns *int* as the maximum number of key-value pairs that *dict* can hold, as defined by the dict operator that created *dict*.

dict key value **put** –

uses *key* and *value* and stores them as a key-value pair into *dict*.

– **statusdict** dict

returns the dictionary *dict*, which is the *statusdict* dictionary.

key value **store** –

searches the dictionary stack in the ordinary way, looking for a match to *key*.

– **systemdict** dict

returns the dictionary *dict*, which is the *systemdict* dictionary.

– **userdict** dict

returns the dictionary *dict*, which is the *userdict* dictionary.

		if found:
key	**where**	dict true
		if not found:
		false

searches the dictionary stack and returns the dictionary that contains an entry that is associated with *key,* if that dictionary exists on the dictionary stack.

3.7 ERROR

dictfull   (error process)

occurs when the referenced dictionary is already full and a PostScript operation attempts to store another object into it.

dictstackoverflow   (error process)

occurs when the dictionary stack already contains the maximum number of active dictionary entries and a **begin** operation attempts to store another dictionary on it.

dictstackunderflow   (error process)

occurs when the dictionary stack contains the minimum number of active dictionary entries, *userdict* and *systemdict,* and an **end** operation attempts to remove a dictionary from it.

execstackoverflow   (error process)

occurs when the execution stack has grown too large; procedure invocation is nested deeper than the interpreter allows.

handleerror   (error processor)

is a procedure defined in *errordict* that is executed to report error messages and error information in a standard way.

interrupt   (error process)

processes an external interrupt to halt execution of a PostScript program.

invalidaccess   (error process)

occurs when an attempt has been made to access a composite object or a file object in a way that violates the access attribute for that object.

invalidexit   (error process)

occurs when an attempt has been made to execute an **exit** for which there is no dynamically enclosing looping context.

invalidfileaccess   (error process)

occurs when the access string supplied to the **file** operator is unacceptable.

invalidfont   (error process)

occurs when a PostScript font operator determines that a font dictionary is malformed in some way.

invalidrestore   (error process)

occurs when an attempt has been made to **restore** a saved state under invalid conditions.

ioerror   (error process)

occurs when a processing error has occurred during execution of one of the file operators.

limitcheck   (error process)

occurs when an implementation limit has been exceeded.

nocurrentpoint   (error process)

occurs when an operator requires a current point but the current path is empty and therefore the current point is undefined.

rangecheck   (error process)

occurs when a numeric operand is outside the range expected by the operator.

stackoverflow   (error process)

occurs when the number of operands on the operand stack exceeds the implementation-defined maximum number.

stackunderflow   (error process)

occurs when the interpreter attempts to remove an operand on the operand stack and the operand stack is already empty.

syntaxerror   (error process)

occurs when the PostScript input scanner (or *tokenizer*) encounters program text that does not follow the syntax rules for PostScript.

timeout   (error process)

occurs when the PostScript interpreter exceeds some implementation-defined time value.

typecheck   (error process)

occurs when the type of some operand is not the type expected by the operator in question.

undefined   (error process)

occurs when a name used in a dictionary key cannot be found in the current dictionary context.

undefinedfilename   (error process)

occurs when a string used as a name for a **file** or a **run** operator cannot be found or cannot be opened.

undefinedresult   (error process)

occurs when a numeric computation would produce an undefined result (such as division by zero) or one that cannot be represented as a PostScript number (such as the inverse transformation of a non-invertible matrix).

unmatchedmark   (error process)

occurs when an operator expects a mark object on the operand stack, but none is present.

unregistered   (error process)

occurs when an operator object has been executed for which the interpreter has no built-in process or procedure.

VMerror   (error process)

occurs when an error has occurred in handling or accessing the virtual memory (VM) of the output device.

3.8   FILE

any   **=**   −

produces a string representation of *any* on the standard output file.

any   **==**   −

produces an edited string representation of *any* on the standard output file.

file   **bytesavailable**   int

returns the number of bytes immediately available from *file*.

file   **closefile**   −

closes *file;* that is, breaks the association between the file object and the underlying file itself.

—   **currentfile**   file

returns the current file object.

bool   **echo**   —

specifies whether the characters that are received from the standard input file are written to the standard output file during interactive mode operation.

—   **executive**   —

places the PostScript interpreter into the interactive access mode, if the interpreter provides that mode of access.

filestring accessstring   **file**   file

returns the file object *file* that is identified by the file name *filestring* with access rights defined by *accessstring*.

—   **flush**   —

forces any characters stored in a buffer for the standard output file to be output immediately.

file   **flushfile**   —

If *file* is an output file, flushfile causes any buffered characters to be sent immediately. If *file* is an input file, flushfile reads the file and discards all input until it reaches end-of-file.

string   **print**   —

writes *string* onto the standard output file.

—   **prompt**   —

produces the prompt that is displayed to the user during the interactive mode.

|- any_1 ... any_n **pstack** |- any_1 ... any_n

produces an edited string representation of all objects on the operand stack, any_n through any_1, onto the standard output file.

file   **read**
if not end-of-file:
byte true
if end-of-file:
false

reads a single character from the designated *file* and returns it to the operand stack as an integer value.

file string   **readhexstring**   substring bool

reads characters from the designated *file* into *string* until all space in *string* is filled or until end-of-file.

file string   **readline**   substring bool

reads characters from the designated *file* into *string* until either a *newline* character (which indicates the end of a line) or until end-of-file is reached.

file string   **readstring**   substring bool

reads characters from the designated *file* into *string* until all space in *string* is filled or until end-of-file.

file   **resetfile**   —

resets the file by discarding all buffered characters that are associated with *file*.

filestring   **run**   —

executes the contents of the file identified by *filestring*.

|- any$_1$ . . . any$_n$ **stack** |- any$_1$ . . . any$_n$

produces a string representation of all objects on the operand stack, *any*$_n$ through *any*$_1$, onto the standard output file.

file   **status**   bool

returns the boolean value *true* if *file* is still associated with an open file and returns *false* otherwise.

if found:

file   **token**   any true

if not found:
false

reads characters from *file*, interpreting them according to the PostScript syntax rules, until it has constructed a complete PostScript object, which is returned to the operand stack as result *any*.

file byte   **write**   —

writes a single character, *byte*, to the designated *file*.

file string   **writehexstring**   —

writes characters from the designated *string* into *file* until all the characters in *string* are transmitted.

file string   **writestring**   —

writes characters from the designated *string* into *file.*

3.9 FONT

wx wy string   **ashow**   —

prints *string* in a similar way to the **show** operator, except that, during the printing process, **ashow** adds *wx* to the *x* width of each character and *wy* to the *y* width.

cx cy char wx wy string   **awidthshow**   —

prints the characters in *string* in a manner similar to **show** but combines the effects of **ashow** and **widthshow**.

—   **currentfont**   font

returns the current font dictionary from the current graphics state.

proc string   **cshow**   —

invokes *proc* once for each operation of the font mapping algorithm on each character in *string.*

key font   **definefont**   font

registers *font* as a font dictionary associated with *key,* which is usually a name literal.

key   **findencoding**   array

obtains the encoding array from the font identified by *key* and returns it to the operand stack.

key   **findfont**   font

obtains a font dictionary, *font,* that is associated with the *key* in the **FontDirectory** and places it on the operand stack.

—   **FontDirectory**   dict

returns the global directory of fonts as *dict.*

proc string   **kshow**   —

prints *string* in a similar way to the **show** operator, except that for every character in *string,* **kshow** invokes *proc.*

font matrix **makefont** newfont

applies *matrix* to *font* and produces *newfont*, whose characters are transformed by the values in *matrix* when they are printed.

— **rootfont** font

returns the root composite font that has been selected by the most recent **setfont**.

font1 scale **scalefont** font2

scales *font1* by the scale factor *scale* to generate a new font, *font2*, whose characters are magnified equally along both axes when they are imaged.

font **setfont** —

sets *font* as the current font dictionary in the current graphics state.

string **show** —

paints the characters that are elements of *string* on the current page at the current point using the current font.

— **StandardEncoding** array

returns the standard PostScript encoding vector as *array*.

string **stringwidth** wx wy

calculates the cumulative change in the current point that would occur if **string** was printed in the current font by using **show**.

cx cy char string **widthshow** —

prints the characters in *string* in a manner similar to **show**, but in addition, if the integer value of the character currently being imaged matches the integer value *char*, the values *cx* and *cy* are added to the current point after imaging the character and before imaging the next character.

3.10 FONT CACHE

— **cachestatus** bsize bmax msize mmax csize cmax blimit

reports the measurements for current consumption and maximum limit of several types of font cache resources.

— **currentcacheparms** mark lower upper

returns the curent cache parameters, *lower* and *upper,* on the operand stack, preceded by a *mark*.

wx wy llx lly urx ury   **setcachedevice**   —

passes width and bounding box information for a character to the PostScript font machinery.

w0x w0y llx lly urx ury   **setcachedevice**   —
w1x w1y vx vy   **setcachedevice2**   —

passes character metric information for an individual character to the PostScript font machinery.

num   **setcachelimit**   —

sets *num* as the maximum number of bytes that may be taken up by the bit-map of a single cached character.

mark lower upper   **setcacheparams**   —

sets the current cache parameters to the integer values on the operand stack that are above a *mark*.

wx wy   **setcharwidth**   —

performs a function similar to **setcachedevice** but provides only character width information to the PostScript font machinery.

3.11 GRAPHICS

—   **currentblackgeneration**   proc

returns the current black generation procedure, *proc*, from the current graphics state.

—   **currentcmykcolor**   cyan magenta yellow black

returns the four components of the current color parameter from the current graphics state according to the cyan-magenta-yellow-black model.

—   **currentcolorscreen**   rfreq rangle rproc gfreq
gangle gproc bfreq bangle
bproc grayfreq grayangle grayproc

returns the twelve color halftone screen components from the current graphics state.

—   **currentcolortransfer**   rproc gproc bproc grayproc

returns the four color transfer functions that define the current color in the current graphics state.

–   **currentdash**   array offset

returns the current dash setting from the current graphics state.

–   **currentflat**   num

returns the current flatness parameter from the current graphics state.

–   **currentfont**   font

returns the current font dictionary from the current graphics state.

–   **currentgray**   num

returns the gray value of the current color parameter from the current graphics state.

–   **currenthsbcolor**   hue sat bright

returns the three components of the current color parameter from the current graphics state according to the hue-saturation-brightness model.

–   **currentlinecap**   int

returns the current line cap parameter in the current graphics state.

–   **currentlinejoin**   int

returns the current line join parameter in the current graphics state.

–   **currentlinewidth**   num

returns the current line width parameter in the current graphics state.

–   **currentmiterlimit**   num

returns the current miter limit parameter in the current graphics state.

–   **currentpoint**   x y

returns the coordinates of the current point in the current graphics state as x and y.

–   **currentrgbcolor**   red green blue

returns the three components of the current color parameter from the current graphics state according to the red-green-blue model.

–   **currentscreen**   freq angle proc

returns the three components of the current halftone screen from the current graphics state.

–   **currenttransfert**   proc

returns the transfer procedure, *proc*, being used by the current graphics state.

—   **currentundercolorremoval**   proc

returns the current undercolor removal function from the current graphics state.

—   **grestore**   —

restores the graphics state to the state that is on the top of the graphics state stack and pops the graphics state stack.

—   **grestoreall**   —

restores the graphics state to the one created by the last unmatched **save**, popping all states on the stack that were produced by any **gsave** operations made after the **save**.

—   **gsave**   —

saves a copy of the current graphics state and all its associated values on the top of the graphics state stack.

—   **initgraphics**   —

resets the most common variables in the graphics state to their initial, default values for the current output device.

proc   **setblackgeneration**   —

sets the current black generation function in the current graphics state to *proc.*

cyan magenta yellow black   **setcmykcolor**   —

sets the values *cyan, magenta, yellow,* and *black* as the four components that define the current color parameter in the current graphics state according to the cyan-magenta-yellow-black (CMYK) model.

rfreq rangle rproc
gfreq gangle gproc
bfreq bangle bproc
grayfreq grayangle grayproc   **setcolorscreen**   —

sets the twelve color halftone screen components in the current graphics state.

rproc gproc bproc grayproc   **setcolortransfer**   —

sets the four color transfer functions that define the current color in the current graphics state.

array offset   **setdash**   —

sets the current dash setting in the current graphics state according to the *array* and *offset* operands.

num   **setflat**   –

sets *num* as the current flatness parameter in the current graphics state.

font   **setfont**   –

sets *font* as the current font dictionary in the current graphics state.

num   **setgray**   –

sets *num* as the gray value of the current color in the current graphics state.

hue sat bright   **sethsbcolor**   –

sets the values *hue, sat,* and *bright* as the three components that define the current color parameter in the current graphics state according to the hue-saturation-brightness model.

int   **setlinecap**   –

sets the current line cap parameter in the current graphics state.

int   **setlinejoin**   –

sets *int* as the current line join parameter in the current graphics state.

num   **setlinewidth**   –

sets *num* as the current line width parameter in the current graphics state.

num   **setmiterlimit**   –

sets *num* as the current miter limit parameter in the current graphics state.

red green blue   **setrgbcolor**   –

sets the values *red, green,* and *blue* as the three components of the current color parameter from the current graphics state according to the red-green-blue model.

freq angle proc   **setscreen**   –

sets the values *freq, angle,* and *proc* as the three components of the current halftone screen from the current graphics state.

proc   **settransfer**   –

sets *proc* as the transfer procedure to be used by the current graphics state.

proc   **setundercolorremoval**   –

sets the current undercolor removal procedure in the current graphics state to *proc.*

3.12 LOGICAL

> bool1 bool2   **and**   result

performs a logical and of *bool1* and *bool2* and returns the boolean value *result*.

> int shift   **bitshift**   result

shifts the binary representation of *int* to the left for *shift* bits and returns *result,* which is an integer.

> any1 any2   **eq**   bool

compares the top two objects on the operand stack, *any1* and *any2,* and returns the value *bool,* which is *true* if the objects are equal and returns *false* otherwise.

> —   **false**   false

returns the boolean object *false.*

> num1 num2   **ge**   bool
> string1 string   **ge**   bool

compares the first operand to the second operand and returns the boolean value *true* if the first is greater than or equal to the second and returns *false* otherwise.

> num1 num2   **gt**   bool
> string1 string2   **gt**   bool

compares the first operand to the second operand and returns the boolean value *true* if the first is greater than the second and returns *false* otherwise.

> num1 num2   **le**   bool
> string1 string2   **le**   bool

compares the first operand to the second operand and returns the boolean value *true* if the first is less than or equal to the second and returns *false* otherwise.

> num1 num2   **lt**   bool
> string1 string2   **lt**   bool

compares the first operand to the second operand and returns the boolean value *true* if the first is strictly less than the second and returns *false* otherwise.

any1 any2   **ne**   bool

compares the top two objects on the operand stack and returns the boolean value *true* if the objects are not equal and returns *false* otherwise.

bool1   **not**   bool2

performs the logical negation of *bool1* and returns the boolean value *bool2*.

bool1 bool2   **or**   result

performs a logical 'inclusive or' of *bool1* and *bool2* and returns the boolean value *result*.

–   **true**   true

returns the boolean object *true*.

bool1 bool2   **xor**   result

performs a logical 'exclusive or' of *bool1* and *bool2* and returns the boolean value *result*.

3.13   MATHEMATICAL

num1   **abs**   num2

returns the absolute value of *num1*.

num1 num2   **add**   sum

adds two numbers, *num1* and *num2*, together to give result *sum*.

num denom   **atan**   angle

returns the angle whose tangent is *num* divided by *denom*.

num1   **ceiling**   num2

returns the least integer value that is greater than or equal to *num1*. The type of *num2* is the same as the type of *num1*.

angle   **cos**   real

returns the cosine of *angle*, which is taken as an angle in degrees.

num1 num2   **div**   quotient

divides *num1* by *num2*, giving result *quotient*.

base exponent	**exp**	real	

raises *base* to the *exponent* power and returns the result *real.*

num1	**floor**	num2	

returns as *num2* the greatest integer value less than or equal to *num1.*

int1 int2	**idiv**	result	

divides *num1* by *num2* and returns the integer portion of the quotient as *result;* any remainder is discarded.

num	**ln**	real

returns the natural logarithm of *num.*

num	**log**	real

returns the common logarithm of *num.*

int1 int2	**mod**	remainder

returns the remainder of the division of *int1* by *int2.*

num1 num2	**mul**	product

multiplies *num1* by *num2,* giving result *product.*

num	**neg**	− num

reverses the sign of *num.*

−	**rand**	int

generates a random integer within an implementation-defined range.

num1	**round**	num2

rounds *num1* to the nearest integer value, *num2.*

−	**rrand**	int

returns an integer value, *int,* that represents the current state of the pseudo-random number generator used by the interpreter.

angle	**sin**	real

returns the sine of *angle,* which is taken to be an angle in degrees.

num	**sqrt**	real

returns the square root of *num,* which must be a non-negative number.

int **srand** –

takes the integer value, *int,* and initializes the current state of the pseudo-random number generator used by the interpreter to that number.

num1 num2 **sub** diff

subtracts *num2* from *num1,* giving result *diff.*

num1 **truncate** num2

truncates the value of *num1* toward zero by removing the fractional part.

3.14 MEMORY

saveobj **restore** –

resets virtual memory (VM) to the state it was in when the *saveobj* was created by the **save** operator.

– **save** saveobj

creates a *saveobj* that preserves and represents the current state of virtual memory (VM).

– **vmstatus** level used maximum

returns the current status of virtual memory resources (VM) in the current output device.

3.15 MISCELLANEOUS

proc **bind** proc

replaces executable operator names in *proc* with the actual operators themselves.

– **null** null

pushes a *null* object onto the stack.

– **usertime** int

returns the value of a clock that increments one unit for every millisecond of execution time.

– **version** string

returns a string that identifies the version of the PostScript interpreter that is running in the current output device.

3.16 PATH

x y rad ang1 ang2   **arc**   —

appends a counterclockwise circular arc to the current path.

x y rad ang1 ang2   **arcn**   —

appends a clockwise circular arc to the current path.

p1x p1y p2x p2y rad   **arcto**   t1x t1y t2x t2y

appends an arc of a circle to the current path, generally preceded by a straight line segment.

string bool   **charpath**   —

makes character path outlines for the characters in *string* as if it were shown at the current point using **show**.

—   **clip**   —

intersects the inside of the current path with the inside of the current clipping path to produce a new, smaller current clipping path.

—   **clippath**   —

sets the current path to be identical to the current clipping path.

—   **closepath**   —

closes the current subpath by appending a straight line segment from the current point to the starting point of the subpath.

d1x d1y d2x d2y a2x a2y   **curveto**   —

adds a curved line segment, described by a pair of Bezier cubic equations, to the current path.

—   **currentpoint**   x y

returns the coordinates of the current point in the current graphics state.

—   **eoclip**   —

intersects the inside of the current path with the inside of the current clipping path to produce a new, smaller current clipping path.

—   **flattenpath**   —

replaces the current path with a new path where all the curved line segments are approximated by straight lines.

— **initclip** —

replaces the clipping path in the current graphics state with the default clipping path for the current output device.

x y **lineto** —

appends a straight line segment to the current path, extending from the current point to the point defined by (x, y).

x y **moveto** —

moves the current point to (x, y) and starts a new subpath of the current path in the current graphic state.

— **newpath** —

initializes the current path, making it empty and making the current point undefined.

— **pathbbox** llx lly urx ury

returns the bounding box of the current path in user coordinates.

mvproc lnproc cvproc csproc **pathforall** —

enumerates all the elements of the current path, using the procedure operands, *mvproc, lnproc, cvproc,* and *csproc.*

rd1x rd1y rd2x rd2y ra2x ra2y **rcurveto** —

adds a curved line segment, described by a pair of Bezier cubic equations, to the current path in the same manner as the **curveto** operator, except that the operands are relative to the current point rather than absolute coordinates.

— **reversepath** —

replaces the current path with a new version of the path that has all the segments of each subpath enumerated in reverse order.

rx ry **rlineto** —

adds a straight line segment to the current path in the same manner as the **lineto** operator, except that the operands are relative to the current point rather than absolute coordinates.

rx ry **rmoveto** —

starts a new subpath of the current path by moving to a new current point defined by the operands (rx, ry) which are relative to the current point.

—   **strokepath**   —

replaces the current path with a new path that outlines the area that would be painted by applying **stroke** to the current path.

3.17   PAINTING

width height samp matrix proc$_1$
[. . . proc$_{ncolors}$]
multiproc ncolors   **colorimage**   —

renders a sampled image with one, three, or four color components onto the current page.

—   **eofill**   —

paints the inside of the current path with the current color.

—   **erasepage**   —

erases the entire contents of the current page.

—   **fill**   —

paints the inside of the current path with the current color.

width height samp matrix proc   **image**   —

renders a sampled image onto the current page.

width height invert matrix proc   **imagemask**   —

renders an image onto the page, using the source data as a mask of one-bit samples that governs where to apply paint (in the current color) to the page.

—   **stroke**   —

paints a line defined by the current path, of a thickness given by the current linewidth as set by **setlinewidth**, using the current color.

3.18   STRING

string target	**anchorsearch**	*if found:* post match true *if not found:* string false

determines if the intial part of *string* matches the string *target*.

string1 string2   **copy**   substring2

copies all elements of *string1* into *string2*.

string proc   **forall**   –

enumerates every element of the first operand and executes *proc* for each of those elements.

string index   **get**   any

looks up the *index* in *array, packedarray,* or *string* and returns the element identified by *index* (counting from zero).

string index count   **getinterval**   substring

duplicates a section of the operand *string,* beginning at the element identified by *index* (counting from zero) and extending for *count* elements.

string   **length**   int

returns *int* as the number of elements that make up the value of *string*.

string index value   **put**   –

stores *value* into *string* at the position identified by *index* (counting from zero).

string1 index string2   **putinterval**   –

replaces a section of the operand *string1* beginning at the element identified by *index* (counting from zero) with the contents of *string2*.

<pre>
                          if found:
string target   search   post match pre true
                          if not found:
                          string false
</pre>

determines if any part of *string* matches the string *target*.

int   **string**   string

creates a string with length *int* and initializes each element of the string with the binary value 0.

<pre>
                       if found
string   token   post any true
                       if not found:
                       false
</pre>

reads characters from *string*, interpreting them according to the PostScript syntax rules, until it has constructed a complete PostScript object, which is returned to the operand stack as result *any*.

3.19 STACK

$$|- \text{ any}_1 \ldots \text{ any}_n \quad \textbf{clear} \quad |-$$

pops all objects from the operand stack.

$$\text{mark obj}_1 \ldots \text{ obj}_n \quad \textbf{cleartomark} \quad -$$

pops all objects from the operand stack above the first *mark* object on the stack.

$$\text{any}_1 \ldots \text{ any}_n \text{ int} \quad \textbf{copy} \quad \text{any}_1 \ldots \text{ any}_n \text{ any}_1 \ldots \text{ any}_{int}$$

when the top element on the operand stack is a non-negative integer *int*, **copy** pops *int* and then duplicates the top *int* elements of the operand stack.

$$|- \text{ any}_1 \ldots \text{ any}_n \quad \textbf{count} \quad |- \text{ any}_1 \ldots \text{ any}_n \text{ n}$$

counts the number of objects on the operand stack and returns that integer, *n*, to the top of the stack.

$$\text{mark obj}_1 \ldots \text{ obj}_n \quad \textbf{counttomark} \quad \text{mark obj}_1 \ldots \text{ obj}_n \text{ n}$$

counts the number of objects on the operand stack above the first *mark* and returns that integer, *n* to the top of the stack.

$$\text{any} \quad \textbf{dup} \quad \text{any any}$$

duplicates the topmost object on the operand stack.

$$\text{any1 any2} \quad \textbf{exch} \quad \text{any2 any1}$$

exchanges the two top objects on the operand stack to reverse their order.

$$\text{any}_n \ldots \text{ any}_0 \text{ n} \quad \textbf{index} \quad \text{any}_n \ldots \text{ any}_0 \text{ any}_n$$

uses the non-negative integer *n* as a pointer into the operand stack and duplicates the nth object on the stack, counting from the top element as 0.

$$\text{any} \quad \textbf{pop} \quad -$$

removes the top element from the operand stack.

$$any_{n-1} \ldots any_0 \; n \; int \quad \textbf{roll} \quad any_{(int-1)} \ldots any_0 \; any_{n-1} \ldots any_{int}$$

performs a circular shift of the contents of the operand stack.

3.20 PERSISTENT DEVICE-SPECIFIC

This section provides a selection of the possible available device-specific operators that set or report values that persist even after the output device is turned off. Not all of these will be implemented in every device, and the correct use of many of these operators is password protected. See Section C3.2 for more information.

Many of the operators in this listing come as a set of two related operators, one that retrieves certain information or parameters, and an associated one that sets them. For convenience, both operators are listed together, alphabetically arranged according to the name of the first operator.

$$int \quad \textbf{checkpassword} \quad bool$$

returns *true* if *int* is equal to the current system administrator password.

$$old \; new \quad \textbf{setpassword} \quad bool$$

sets the system administrator password to *new* if the correct *old* password is provided.

$$- \quad \textbf{defaultpageparams} \quad width \; height \; margin \; resolution$$

returns the default values for pageparams, which is defined in the volatile parameters.

$$width \; height \; margin \; resolution \quad \textbf{setdefaultpageparams} \quad -$$

sets the default values of the **pageparams** parameters *width, height, margin,* and *resolution,* all of which are integers.

$$- \quad \textbf{defaultpapertray} \quad tray$$

returns *tray,* which the default tray number.

$$tray \quad \textbf{setdefaultpapertray} \quad -$$

sets the default value for the paper tray to be used as a source of paper and to establish the page size parameters for the device at startup.

— **defaulttimeouts** job manualfeed wait

returns the default values for the three timeout parameters, *job* timeout, *manualfeed* timeout, and the *wait* timeout.

job manualfeed wait **setdefaulttimeouts** —

resets the default timeouts to the values *job, manualfeed,* and *wait.*

— **dostartpage** bool

returns the boolean value *true* if the device is set to produce a startup page and returns *false* otherwise.

bool **setdostartpage** —

sets *bool* as the controlling value to determine whether a startup page is produced at power-on.

— **dosysstart** bool

returns the boolean value *true* if the system is set to execute a default setup file at startup and returns *false* otherwise.

bool **setdosystart** —

sets *bool* as the controlling value to determine whether a standard startup file is executed at power-on.

index **eescratch** setting

returns the integer *setting,* which is the value of the parameter located at *index* in the scratch (unallocated) non-volatile memory storage of the device.

index setting **seteescratch** —

sets the value *setting* into the position in scratch non-volatile memory selected by *index.*

— **hardwareiomode** setting

returns the current hardware I/O mode coded as a PostScript integer, *setting.*

setting   **sethardwareiomode**   –

sets the hardware I/O mode to the value *setting,* which must be a PostScript integer that codes the desired hardware interface mode for startup.

–   **idlefonts**   mark font s_x s_y rot nchar . . .

returns a *mark* object, followed by up to 150 integers that represent the parameters controlling idle-time font scan conversion.

mark font s_x s_y rot nchars . . .   **setidlefonts**   –

sets up to 150 integer values, taken as groups of five (font, s_x, s_y, rot, *nchars*) that define the character sets to be scan onverted during the device idle-time processing.

–   **margins**   top left

returns the two margin adjustment parameters, *top* and *left.*

top left   **setmargins**   –

sets the margin adjustment values for the top and left margins, respectively, to the integer values *top* and *left.*

–   **pagecount**   int

returns *int* as the number of pages that have been printed since the output device was built.

–   **pagestackorder**   bool

returns the boolean value *true* if output pages stack with the front of the second page facing the back of the first page, and so on, and returns *false* otherwise.

bool   **setpagestackorder**   –

sets the value reported by the **pagestackorder** operator to the boolean value, *bool.*

string   **printername**   substring

returns *substring,* the name of the printer as defined to any external environment.

string   **setprintername**   –

sets *string* as the name of the printer as reported to communications channels and as reported by the **printername** operator.

– **ramsize** int

returns *int*, which is the number of bytes of random-access memory (RAM) installed in the device.

channel **sccbatch** baud options

returns the current baud rate *baud* and the options setting *options* for the serial communications channel *channel* when that channel is in the batch mode.

channel baud options **setsccbatch** –

sets the communications parameters for the serial communication channel selected by *channel* to *baud* and *option* when the channel is in the batch mode.

channel **sccinteractive** baud options

returns the current baud rate *baud* and the options setting *options* for the serial communications channel *channel* when that channel is in the interactive mode.

channel baud options **setsccinteractive** –

sets the communications parameters for the serial communication channel selected by *channel* to *baud* and *option* when the channel is in the interactive mode.

– **softwareiomode** setting

returns the current software I/O mode coded as a PostScript integer, *setting.*

setting **setsoftwareiomode** –

sets the software I/O mode to the value *setting*, which must be a PostScript integer that codes the desired software interface mode for startup.

3.21   VOLATILE DEVICE-SPECIFIC

This section provides a selection of the possible available device-specific operators and other parameters that set or report values that last only for the duration of a job or (depending on the manner of setting) until the device is powered off. Many of these are not operators but are simple PostScript objects; if you are in doubt, consult the full operator listing in Section C3.2 or in your device manual. Not all of these will be implemented in every device.

Some of the operators in this listing come as a set of two related operators, one that retrieves certain information or parameters and an associated one that sets them. For convenience, both operators are listed together, alphabetically arranged according to the name of the first operator.

—   **appletalktype**   string

is the *string* that defines the type portion of the device's AppleTalk name according to the Name Binding Protocol.

—   **duplex**   bool

an operator that returns the boolean value that reports whether the device is set up for duplex (two-sided) printing.

bool   **setduplex**   —

the operator that causes the device to select duplex (two-sided) printing or not.

—   **jobname**   string

is the *string* that defines the name of the currently executing job.

—   **jobsource**   string

is the *string* that defines the source of the current job.

—   **jobstate**   string

is the *string* that defines the status of the current job.

—   **jobtimeout**   int

an operator that returns the integer *int,* which is the number of seconds remaining before job timeout will occur.

int **setjobtimeout** —

sets the timeout value for the job to *int* seconds.

— **manualfeed** bool

is the boolean value *bool* that controls feed of the next output page.

— **manualfeedtimeout** int

is the integer value, *int,* that gives the number of seconds currently set for the interpreter to wait for a page to be inserted into the manual feed slot.

— **papertray** int

is the integer value that determines which paper tray the next sheet of output will feed from.

int **setpapertray** —

is the operator that sets the paper tray selection mechanism to the tray represented by the integer, *int,* by redefining the variable **papertray**; it also sets the imageable area to the value appropriate to the size of that tray.

status tries **printererror** —

is a procedure that is executed if the output hardware reports an error during execution of a **showpage** or similar operation.

— **product** string

is the *string* that identifies the product name of the device.

— **revision** integer

is the integer value, *int,* that designates the current revision level of the device-dependent portion of the PostScript interpreter.

— **waittimeout** int

is the integer value, *int,* that gives the number of seconds currently set for the interpreter to wait for additional input over the current communication channel.

3.22 DISK FILE

These operators are defined only on devices that have external storage devices, such as cartridge storage or hard disk subsystems. As such, these too are device-specific operators, and the listing here is only a representative selection of common operators that are implemented in devices that have such external media. As always, your device documentation is the appropriate source for precise information.

Some of the operators in this listing come as a set of two related operators, one that retrieves certain information or parameters and an associated one that sets them. For convenience, both operators are listed together, alphabetically arranged according to the name of the first operator.

namestring **deletefile** –

deletes the file identified by *namestring* from the disk.

namestring **devmount** bool

returns a boolean value to indicate if the device named by the *namestring* is mounted and available.

namestring **devstatus** free size

returns the status information *free* and *size* for the device whose name is given by *namestring*.

namestring **devdismount** –

dismounts the device whose name is given by *namestring*.

string **diskdriveparams** substring

returns the current disk drive parameters as a *substring* of the *string* operand.

paramstring **setdiskdriveparams** –

sets the disk drive parameters to the values given in *paramstring*.

– **diskonline** bool

returns a boolean, *bool,* that indicates the availability of the external disk device. A value *true* indicates that the disk is attached and online, while *false* indicates that the disk is not online or not attached.

— **diskstatus** free total

returns the number of pages currently available in the file system as the integer value *free* and returns the maximum number of pages as the integer value *total*.

pattern proc string **filenameforall** —

searches the entire list of files in the file system directory for any names that match *pattern*.

pages action **initializedisk** —

initializes the file system and formats some or all of the disk.

oldnamestring newnamestring **renamefile** —

renames the file specified by *oldnamestring* to the new name given by *newnamestring*.

namestring **status** pages bytes access creation true
if file not found:
false

returns a series of values that give file status information if the file specified by *namestring* exists. An extension to the general status operator.

— **userdiskpercent** percent

returns the integer *percent* that represents the amount of disk space on the file system currently set aside for user files as a percentage of total file space.

percent **setuserdiskpercent** —

takes the integer value *percent* and reserves that percentage of the file system disk storage for user files.

Part II

Cookbook

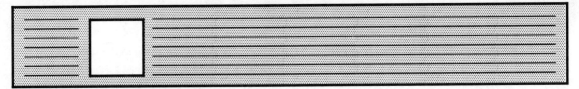

Cookbook

This part of the book presents a variety of PostScript programs that you can use for study, as examples for your own coding, or as useful routines to be copied. This cookbook is rather different from most language cookbooks in that the routines included here were not specifically designed to illustrate certain coding techniques or to solve certain coding problems. Instead, the routines presented here are a selection of the actual PostScript programs used in the production of the figures in the first sections of this book.

All the figures and examples in the book were produced in PostScript and required no further artwork or handling for inclusion. In itself, this is hardly unusual; today, many publications, both books and magazines, do similar work. What is different here is that you will see the actual code that was used to produce these illustrations as well as receive a short – but, I hope, enlightening – commentary on both the routines and the general scheme used to produce the set of figures. You have probably already noticed that the examples of various operators provided in the operator reference text in Part I, Section C, included the output of those examples. The code presented here is the code used to produce the figures that you have seen in the previous sections of the book. The code not only draws the figures but provides the labels and identification data as well.

By adopting a coordinated approach to these figures, as you will see, one can produce the complete set both quickly and efficiently by using a common library of procedures that provide reusable functions. As we said earlier, the PostScript language is a full-featured programming language and, as all full programming languages, offers a variety of ways to accomplish a single purpose. The procedures used here have been created with the purpose of illustrating an approach – or in some cases, alternative approaches – to solving common problems that arise in producing actual artwork. As you become more familiar with PostScript, you will be able to adapt these methods to accomplish your goals.

Obviously, it is not possible to teach PostScript programming and coding techniques within the confines of a series of short cookbook procedures such as these. I have assumed in all the discussion of the code presented in the following sections that you can read and understand basic PostScript code. Where the procedures seem complex or unusual, I have made some effort to explain the code; otherwise, I have not made comments on the actual coding methods. The same point is also applicable to the program structure and the over-all approach to the figures. In all cases, the procedures presented here generally follow good PostScript coding practice and will behave nicely in a shared environment.

Common Library Functions

The programs that draw the figures in this book use PostScript procedures that are divided into two pieces. The first and largest part is a common library of procedures that are used repeatedly in creating the figures. The procedures in the second part are specialized procedures that are provided for each figure, if required. This chapter focuses on those basic procedures that are common to all the figures. The following chapter presents each of the figure programs in turn, including any of the special procedures required by a specific figure. In order to follow the discussion of the figures, you will begin by examining the common procedures.

Like all good, maintainable code, these procedures and the associated programs follow certain conventions regarding naming and structure. For the most part, these are the structural conventions that have been established by Adobe Systems for PostScript programs as version 2.1 of the structuring conventions, which are described in detail in Part III, Appendix A. These set out global structural requirements for a conforming PostScript program. In addition, these procedures follow certain other conventions that you will find useful in programming. First, the names of variables begin with capital letters, while the names of procedures begin with small letters. This allows you to distinguish within a program at a glance the difference between a value, 'Average', and the procedure that calculates that value, 'average', for example. Full, descriptive names are used for most procedures and for variables where shorter names seem confusing or unclear. The extra overhead of transmission is not a major factor compared to the ease of debugging and maintenance. Where procedures or variables have two or more words in their names, I capitalize the subsequent words. Also, all multiline definitions are indented, from the name literal to the corresponding **def** operator, so you can easily perceive the scope of the definition. For the same reason, code contained within a **gsave**, **grestore** pair is indented.

Procedures also follow a common format. All procedure definitions begin with a short comment on the use of the procedure. The last two lines of the comment always give 1) any prerequisite definitions for procedures or variables that must be available when the procedure is executed and 2) the calling sequence of the procedure, using the same format used in the operator reference section of the book. Each procedure delimiter (the curly brace) is placed on a line by itself for ease in debugging. See Appendix C for a discussion of programming environment and debugging tools used to create these programs.

These procedures are all created and stored in a common dictionary called **PvtDict**. This provides two benefits. First, it allows you to control the scope of the procedure definitions and provides a clean, working copy of all the procedures at the start of each program. Second, it allows the preloading of these procedures into printer memory in order to save time and speed up execution, if desired. The code that defines **PvtDict** and encloses the procedures that are included in it is shown below. **PvtDict** is defined as a "Proc-Set" to allow it to conform to the structuring conventions and to provide a method for automatic inclusion in systems that have a document manager that understands PostScript structure and is capable of such processing decisions. The leading and trailing procedures to set up **PvtDict** are as follows:

```
%%BeginProcSet:PS_Pgr_Ref 0 0
% Copyright (C) 1988 Cheshire Group.
% All Rights Reserved.
% PostScript Programmer's Reference Guide.
%published by: Scott, Foresman and Company
/PvtDict 50 dict def
PvtDict begin

... routines inserted here ...


end
%%EndProcSet
```

The first procedure in the ProcSet is **setFonts**. This procedure defines the three fonts that will be used in the programs: the font for the labels, **LabelHelv**; the font for the titles, **TitleHelv**; and the font for the subscripts within the labels, **SubsHelv**. Each of these fonts is selected and defined at the desired size and then stored under the correct name for subsequent use. Notice that **SubsHelv** is a resized version of **LabelHelv**, since you want the subscripts to be the same font as the labels that they are part of, only somewhat smaller. To preserve the visual consistency while being used with the labels, the subscripts are scaled non-uniformly by using **makefont**. Finally, the procedure defines **IN** and **LL**, which are named variables that set the values for indentation and line leading, respectively, within multiline labels. The **setFonts** procedure is as follows:

```
/setFonts
    %setup all font dictionaries
    %    and indent + leading values
    %    for multi-line labels
    {
    /LabelHelv
        /Helvetica findfont
        10 scalefont
```

```
        def
        /TitleHelv
            /Helvetica findfont
            12 scalefont
        def
        /SubsHelv
            %font for subscripts
            %requires:  LabelHelv
            LabelHelv
            [.8 0 0 .6 0 0 ]
            makefont
        def
        /IN 14 def
        /LL -12 def
        }
    def
```

The next two routines are used to set subscripts within the labels. The design of these routines allows the strings that are to be used as labels to have an escape character within the string that defines all subsequent characters up to the next space character as a subscript – that is, a character to be set and shown in the subscript font rather than the label font. The escape character was arbitrarily chosen as binary 0; any character that does not occur naturally in label strings might have been used.

The basic subscripting mechanism is implemented in two pieces, as a master procedure and a support routine. This sort of code – a master procedure and one or more support routines – is quite typical of PostScript and many other computer languages, because it allows certain operations that will be performed repeatedly to be coded and tested separately. You will see this pattern again and again, both in the following procedures and in other PostScript code. In fact, the subscripting mechanism itself is called by the **label** and **label2** procedures, which use it instead of the **show** operator.

In this case, the support routine is called **subScript**. This routine saves the current graphics state, sets the subscript font, moves down a small distance to set the position for the subscript, and shows the subscript. The routine duplicates the subscript and measures it before showing it. This is necessary because the **gsave**, **grestore** pair that is required to preserve any font setting and current path segments also resets the current point. In this case, we want to set the new current point to the original current point plus the width of the string being shown for the subscript. Notice that this is not the point at completion of the **show**, since we moved down a small amount to position the subscript. The correct position is the previous current point plus the string width, without the downward movement. The coordinates from the **stringwidth** operator are placed onto the stack and are used by the **rmoveto** after the **grestore** has taken effect. The **SubScript** procedure is as follows:

```
/subScript
    %shows a subscript
    %requires:  SubsHelv
    {
    gsave
        SubsHelv setfont
        0 -.35 rmoveto
        dup stringwidth
        3 -1 roll
        show
    grestore
    rmoveto
    }
def
```

The master procedure, in this case, is the procedure **subsShow**, which takes a string and shows it – in the same way as the **show** operator – at the current point. The string is first examined for an escape code, which is \000 in the code shown but might be any uncommon character value. The **search** operator divides the string into segments, the length of which depends on whether the escape value is present or not, and it also leaves a boolean value on the top of the stack to indicate success or failure. This boolean is the argument for an **ifelse** operator, which executes one of two procedures depending on the **search** result. If no escape character is found, the string is simply rendered normally, using the **show** operator. If the escape character is found, the first part of the string is rendered normally, and then the **subScript** procedure is used to show the subscript. If more of the original string exists, the **subsShow** procedure is invoked recursively to print the remainder of the string.

Note the use of recursion here in printing the subscripted label information. Because PostScript is an interpreted language, using a procedure recursively is quite simple and requires no special handling. However, as in all self-referencing procedures, it is extremely important to thoroughly test the code to avoid creating an infinite loop during execution. The LaserTalk® environment used to develop these routines makes testing and debugging such routines quite easy; see Appendix C for a fuller discussion of the configuration and software used here. The **subsShow** procedure is as follows:

```
/subsShow
    %shows strings with subscripts
    %
    %requires:  subScript
    %called as: (str\0001) subsShow --
    {
```

```
(\000) search
    {
    show
    pop
    (\040) search
        {
        subScript
        show
        subsShow
        }
        { subScript }
    ifelse
    }
    { show }
ifelse
}
def
```

The next two procedures are **label** and **label2**, which are presented on page 380. These two procedures are designed to handle two different types of labels on the output figures. Both procedures have identical calling sequences and perform essentially the same functions. The only difference is that **label2** is designed to set point coordinates of the format (x_1, y_1) and does not provide for two lines in the label, while **label** does provide two label lines if desired and will not correctly set subscripted point coordinates.

The **label** procedure takes three operands. The first is the string that is to be set as the label; the next two are the displacements, relative to the current point, where the label string is to be placed. The string may have a *newline* (\n) character in it, in which case the label is set on two lines, with the second line indented by the value **IN** and the baseline for the second line set below the first by the line leading value **LL**. Both **IN** and **LL**, you will recall, were defined in the procedure **setFonts**. The procedure first saves the current graphics state in order to preserve current path information and then sets the label font and scans the label string for a newline character. If the newline is present, the first part of the label string is shown within a **gsave, grestore** to preserve the current point; then the current point is moved to the next line and indented; and the remainder of the string is shown. If no newline is present, the entire string is shown at the given location.

As noted above, the **label** procedure will not correctly set a subscripted point coordinate. This occurs because the **subsShow** procedure makes a subscript out of all the characters from the escape character to the next space; however, in a point coordinate, the subscript value is immediately followed by a comma. There are several ways to correct this problem, but since point coordinates are never printed on two lines, the easiest and clearest is to

create a second procedure, **label2,** modeled on **label,** that handles this problem. **label2**
divides a label string at the comma and shows each part of the string separately, with
subscripts if present. The **label** and **label2** procedures are as follows:

```
/label
    %procedure to set label information
    %   in two lines if desired
    %requires:  LabelHelv; subsShow
    %called as: (str) dx dy label --
    {
    gsave
        LabelHelv setfont
        rmoveto
        (\n) search
            {
            gsave
                subsShow
            grestore
            pop
            IN LL rmoveto
            subsShow
            }
            { subsShow }
        ifelse
    grestore
    }
def

/label2
    %procedure to set label information
    %   for subscripted point value
    %   (single line only)
    %requires:  LabelHelv; subsShow
    %called as: (str) dx dy label --
    {
    gsave
        LabelHelv setfont
        rmoveto
        (,) search
            {
            subsShow
            show
            subsShow
            }
            { subsShow }
        ifelse
    grestore
    }
def
```

In addition to label information, every figure must have a title to identify it. The **figureTitle** procedure and its support routine, **centerString**, define a common approach to providing this information. This procedure takes four operands: an x and y position on the page, where the titles are to be placed, and two title strings. The first title line is centered at the position provided by the x and y operands, while the second title line is centered beneath it. Notice here that the second line is offset beneath the first line by a fixed distance, rather than by using a variable as in spacing the label information above. Generally, where a value may be changed from time to time, or where it is used several times in several routines, it is better to define it as a variable and use the variable in procedures rather than to provide the value each time. Both methods are used here to show you the alternatives.

The centering process is performed by the support procedure **centerString**, which calculates the actual position required to center any given string. It takes only one operand: the string to be shown. It calculates the length of the string and then subtracts one-half of the length from the current point and uses this to reset the current point to the correct value to display the string, centered at the previous current point. Note that the routine does not save and restore the graphics state, since you want to change one component of the graphics state, namely the current point, to use in the calling routine. It is left to the master routine to provide such services, if required. The **figureTitle** procedure and its support routine, **centerString**, are as follows:

```
/centerString
    %centers arbitrary string at current point
    %called as: (str) centerString --
    {
    dup
    stringwidth
    pop
    2 div
    currentpoint
    3 -2 roll
    exch sub exch
    moveto
    }
def

/figureTitle
    %prints figure titles centered at given point
    %requires:  centerString; TitleHelv
    %called as: x y (title) (caption) figureTitle --
    {
    gsave
        TitleHelv setfont
        4 2 roll
        moveto
        gsave
```

```
            exch
            centerString
            show
        grestore
        currentpoint
        14 sub
        moveto
        centerString
        show
    grestore
    }
def
```

Now we begin a series of graphics procedures that generate useful graphic elements that are commonly used within the figures. The first of these are two procedures that draw dots on the page at the current point. The first procedure, called, appropriately enough, **dot**, creates a dot by drawing a filled circle whose radius is 1.5 times the current line width. This allows dots that are scaled to the lines upon which they are generally placed. For some cases, however, such a scaled dot would be too small to be seen. In such cases, we have a procedure, **fixedDot**, that generates a dot whose radius is 1.5 units. Such a dot can be used and will remain visible even when the line it appears on is very fine. Note that such a dot will be scaled to whatever the current unit value is; if you should require a dot of a fixed size, regardless of current scaling, you could use the **unitLine** function (described below) together with the **dot** procedure to give the desired result. The **dot** and **fixedDot** procedures are as follows:

```
/dot
    %procedure to draw a dot
    %
    %called as: -- dot --
    {
    gsave
        [] 0 setdash
        currentpoint
        newpath
        1.5 currentlinewidth mul
        0 360 arc
        fill
    grestore
    }
def

/fixedDot
    %procedure to draw a dot
    %   of fixed size (1.5 units)
    %called as: -- fixedDot --
    {
    gsave
```

```
                                 [] 0 setdash
                                 currentpoint
                                 newpath
                                 1.5 0 360 arc
                                 fill
                              grestore
                              }
                      def
```

Besides dots, many figures require crosses to mark points on the page. This is done here by the **crossHairs** procedure, which draws a crosshair of a selected length at the current point. It uses two supporting routines, **verticalBar** and **horizontalBar**, which each draw the vertical and horizontal components of the crosshairs, respectively. Both of these take the same length operand. Note that it would easily be possible to redefine the **crossHairs** procedure to take two operands if you wanted unequal horizontal and vertical arms. All of these routines save and restore the current graphics state, so that you can draw the crosshairs at any convenient point during the creation of a figure without worrying about the effect on the graphic element being drawn. The **crossHairs** procedure with supporting procedures is as follows:

```
/verticalBar
      %procedure to draw a vertical bar
      %    at current point
      %called as: length verticalBar --
      {
      gsave
          dup
          neg
          0 exch
          rmoveto
          2 mul
          0 exch
          rlineto
          stroke
      grestore
      }
  def

/horizontalBar
      %procedure to draw a horizontal bar
      %    at current point
      %called as: length horizontalBar --
      {
      gsave
          dup
          neg
          0
          rmoveto
```

```
            2 mul
            0
            rlineto
            stroke
        grestore
        }
    def


/crossHairs
    %procedure to draw crosshairs
    %    centered at current point
    %requires:  verticalBar; horizontalBar
    %called as: length crossHairs --
    {
    /L exch def
    gsave
        L verticalBar
        L horizontalBar
    grestore
    }
def
```

The next group of procedures provides lines that finish with arrowheads, which are often used in figures. All of these procedures use the support routine **arrowHead**. This routine produces an arrowhead whose size is scaled to the current line width. The tip of the arrowhead is at the current point, so that the arrowhead can be drawn at the end of any line or curve and will point to the correct position. The arrowhead is an isosceles triangle, with the point of the triangle pointing along the y axis; its base is four times the current line width; and its height is twice the base, or eight times the current line width. The triangle is drawn and then filled with 100 percent black. Since the arrowhead is always drawn in an upright position, it will be the responsibility of the calling procedure to orient the axes so that the arrowhead appears in the correct relation to the line that it will finish.

The first set of procedures draws a straight line from any point to any point and finishes the line with an arrowhead. The first procedure, **lineArrow**, takes the same coordinates as a **lineto** operator but does two additional things: it strokes the line (as well as creates the path) and it finishes the line with an arrowhead. These functions are enclosed in **gsave**, **grestore** pairs, so that **lineArrow** can be used in a fashion very similar to **lineto**: namely, the current point at the end of the operation is still at the end of the line. Note that this also leaves the straight line segment that you created as part of the current path.

The most interesting point in this code is the calculation of the rotation angle for the arrowhead. Remember that the **arrowHead** procedure draws the arrow pointing straight up; therefore, it is necessary to rotate the axes so that the y axis lies along the line that is being created. Once that is done, the arrowhead will be correctly positioned along the line. This can be done using the **atan** operator, which returns an angle, given an x and a y displacement. (See Figure B2.1 in Part I on page 118 and the associated discussion in the text for how **atan** works.) The x displacement is the difference between the x value of the current point and the x coordinate of the final point, and the y displacement is the difference between the y values. This, however, returns the angle between the x axis and the line; we want the angle between the y axis and the line, since the arrowhead is drawn along the y axis. That angle is 90 degrees minus the angle calculated above. Once the correct rotation angle is calculated, we leave it on the stack for later use and create the desired line segment in the current path. Then, after saving the graphics state (to preserve the line segment), we rotate the coordinate system and draw the arrowhead, finally restoring the graphics state. The last thing the procedure does is stroke the line segment. The set of procedures to draw arrowheads is as follows:

```
/arrowHead
    %draws an arrowhead
    %    whose tip is the current point
    %    4xlinewidth wide by 8xlinewidth long
    %    oriented pointing along y-axis
    %called as: -- arrowHead --
    {
    gsave
        currentpoint
        /W currentlinewidth def
        newpath
        moveto
        0 -8 W mul rmoveto
        -2 W mul 0 rmoveto
        4 W mul 0 rlineto
        -2 W mul 8 W mul rlineto
        closepath
        0 setgray
        fill
    grestore
    }
def

/lineArrow
    %procedure to draw a line to any point
    %    using same operands as 'lineto'
    %    but finish line with an arrowhead
    %requires:  arrowHead
    %called as: x2 y2 lineArrow --
    {
    /Y2 exch def
    /X2 exch def
    currentpoint
    Y2 exch sub
    exch
    X2 exch sub
    atan
```

```
90 sub
X2 Y2 lineto
gsave
    rotate
    arrowHead
grestore
gsave
    stroke
grestore
}
def
```

The **rlineArrow** procedure does the same thing as **lineArrow**, but it takes displacements as operands rather than absolute coordinates. This produces some small changes in the actual procedure, since it is no longer necessary to calculate the displacements, which are already provided by the operands. All that is required is that the operands be duplicated and then 1) used to calculate the rotation angle (as described above) and 2) passed on to the **rlineto** operator that draws the line segment, as follows:

```
/rlineArrow
    %procedure to draw a line to any point
    %   using same operands as 'rlineto'
    %   but finish line with an arrowhead
    %requires:  arrowHead
    %called as: dx2 dy2 rlineArrow --
    {
    2 copy
    exch atan
    90 sub
    3 1 roll
    rlineto
    gsave
        rotate
        arrowHead
    grestore
    gsave
        stroke
    grestore
    }
def
```

The next two groups of procedures provide the same basic output; the only difference is that one is the mirror image of the other. These are what I have called "curved arrows," lines that curve back upon themselves and then continue forward and end in an arrowhead. These are a common pointing device in many figures, as you have seen in previous sections of the book. Because the lines are mirror images, the discussion will first cover one of the sets of procedures in detail and then show the small differences that were necessary to provide the reverse image. The two different orientations are needed because you may want the line to curve either to the left or to the right of the base point, given the position of the label and the point to be illustrated.

The basic design of the line curves to the right, which gives positive values for all coordinates. The procedures and support routine that draw this version of the line are next. As with the straight line pointers described above, there are two versions of these procedures: one that uses actual coordinate values, called **curvedArrow**, and another that uses relative displacements, called **rcurvedArrow**. Both versions require an additional support procedure called **curvedBase** that draws the actual figure; however, **rcurvedArrow** invokes it indirectly by setting up coordinates and calling **curvedArrow**.

First we will examine the support routine, **curvedBase**. This routine draws a curved line whose base is at the origin (0, 0) and its end at the point (50, 200), with control points for the curve at (0, 200) and (50, 0). This produces a line that curves down and then back up to the right, while holding all points (both the points on the path and the control points) within a path bounding box of 0 0 50 200. The line is drawn with a relatively large line width of 5 units and finished with an arrowhead produced by the **arrowHead** routine described above. The large line width is used because the basic curved line drawn here needs to be much larger than the usual output, which would be scaled to the required dimensions in the figure in which it is to be used.

The **curvedArrow** procedure requires four operands: the x and y coordinates of the point where the base of the line is to be and the x and y coordinates of the point at the end of the line where the arrowhead is. To use the support routine, **curvedBase**, we need to do three things. First, the coordinate system must be translated, so that the origin is at the base of the line. Second, the coordinates must be rotated, so that the line points in the right direction. Third, the coordinates must be scaled, so that the line fits into the space designated for it. All of these can be accomplished with the four coordinate operands provided.

The design of the procedure is really quite simple and is based on the same bounding box principles that can be used to orient and scale EPSF objects. Drawn as described above, the basic figure has a bounding box whose lower left and upper right corners – this is the usual method of specifying a bounding box – are given by the coordinates (0, 0) and (50, 200); while the bounding box of the figure that you want to generate is given by the two points that are the operands of the procedure: (x_1, y_1) and (x_2, y_2). The first requirement can be taken care of by translating the coordinates to the point (x_1, y_1). The second requirement requires a little more computation. You need to calculate the angular difference between the orientation of the base figure generated by **curvedBase** and that of the desired figure. Now, in one sense, the base figure is oriented directly parallel to the y axis, since the base of the line and the arrowhead point straight along that axis. However, that doesn't allow you any way to calculate the change in orientation required here. Instead, take a diagonal line drawn from the lower left corner of the figure to the upper right corner and calculate the difference between the angle measured from the x axis to the diagonal on the base figure and the same angle measured on the desired output. You can calculate this because, in all cases, you have the coordinates of the lower left corner and the upper right corner as part of the bounding box. The actual angles are produced by the **atan** operator in the same manner as you saw before. Note that, since the lower left corner of the base figure is at the origin (0, 0) the coordinates of the upper right corner are also the x and y displacement values required by **atan**. The angle for the desired orientation is calculated first, then the angle for the base figure is calculated and subtracted from it. This provides a correct sign on the result to ensure that the rotation is in the correct direction.

The third requirement requires some more calculation and a little thought about how to do it. The scaling calculations are quite straightforward: you want to divide the desired height and width of the figure by the height and width of the base figure, 200 and 50 units respectively. The question is how to determine the desired height and width. You could, of course, subtract the original bounding box coordinates to generate these numbers, as you did earlier in the procedure. You could also have saved the results of those previous calculations as named variables in order to reuse them here. The **curved-Arrow** procedure adopts a different route to the same end. Remember that once the coordinates have been translated so that the lower left corner is the origin, the x coordinate of the upper right corner is identical to the width of the figure, while the y coordinate value is the height. You can use this fact to quickly determine the height and width values, once you know the coordinates of the upper right corner of the bounding box in the translated and rotated coordinate system. To determine that, use a simple PostScript trick. First, invoke the **translate** operator to change the coordinates of the upper right corner (as provided by the operands to the procedure) into device coordinates. These device coordinate values remain fixed at all times, regardless of how you adjust the user coordinates. Now perform the translation and rotation as described above, leaving the device coordinate values on the operand stack. When you are finished, you can change these absolute coordinates back into user coordinates in the new user coordinate system by means of the **itransform** operator. This gives you the desired coordinates of the upper right corner of the figure and hence the desired height and width values. Once these are available, you can perform the scaling operation, calculating first the height scale value and then the width scale value. The last thing is to draw the figure itself, using the **curvedBase** routine.

```
/curvedBase
    %procedure to create basic curved line+arrow
    %bounding box (procedure)
    %    -50 0 0 200
    %requires:  arrowHead
    %called as: -- curvedBase --
    {
    0 0 moveto
    0 200 50 0 50 200 curveto
    5 setlinewidth
    arrowHead
    stroke
    }
def
```

```
/curvedArrow
      %procedure to create curved line+arrowhead
      %    line curves right
      %requires:  curvedBase
      %called as: x1 y1 x2 y2  curvedArrow --
      %    where (x1, y1) is the base of the line
      %        and (x2, y2) is the tip of the arrow
      {
      /Y2 exch def
      /X2 exch def
      /Y1 exch def
      /X1 exch def
      gsave
            X2 Y2
            transform
            X1 Y1
            translate
            Y2 Y1 sub
            X2 X1 sub
            atan
            200 50 atan
            sub
            rotate
            itransform
            200 div exch
            50 div exch
            scale
            curvedBase
      grestore
      }
      def
```

The next procedure, **rcurveArrow**, is identical to **curveArrow** except that it takes displacements instead of absolute coordinates. In this case, the procedure converts the given displacement coordinates into absolute coordinates by a pair of **rmoveto** operators, stores the resulting current point coordinates onto the operand stack, and calls the **curveArrow** procedure. The only thing to notice here is the use of **grestore** and **gsave** in the middle of the procedure to return to the initial position before moving; the ordinary indentation notation was not used here because in this case it would obscure the way the operators are being used rather than clarify it. This is a good example of how to use structural conventions correctly. Conventions on indentation, capitalization, and so on are intended to clarify the working of a procedure; they should be used with some thought and care, not automatically or mechanically.

```
/rcurvedArrow
    %same as 'curvedArrow'
    %   but uses relative displacements
    %requires:  curvedArrow
    %called as: dx1 dy1 dx2 dy2  rcurvedArrow  --
    {
    gsave
        rmoveto
        currentpoint
        4 -2 roll
        grestore
        gsave
        rmoveto
        currentpoint
        4 -2 roll
        curvedArrow
    grestore
    }
    def
```

A set of procedures to produce a mirror image of the curved line and arrow of the preceding set is shown below. These procedures are exactly like the preceding ones, except that the origin is at the bottom right corner of the bounding box rather than the bottom left corner. In this graphic, the line begins at the bottom right corner and proceeds upward, curving down to the left and then back up to end at the upper left corner. Therefore, the bounding box for this graphic element is −50 0 0 200. The procedures, however, are essentially the same, with just a difference in sign on some calculations. The procedures to draw mirror-image pointing arrows are as follows:

```
/curvedRevBase
    %procedure to create basic curved line+arrow
    %bounding box (procedure)
    %   0 0 -50 200
    %requires:  arrowHead
    %called as: -- curvedRevBase --
    {
    0 0 moveto
    0 200 -50 0 -50 200 curveto
    5 setlinewidth
    arrowHead
    stroke
    }
    def
```

```
/curvedRevArrow
    %procedure to create curved line+arrowhead
    %   line curves left
    %requires:  curvedRevBase
    %called as: x1 y1 x2 y2  curvedRevArrow --
    %   where (x1, y1) is the base of the line
    %       and (x2, y2) is the tip of the arrow
    {
    /Y2 exch def
    /X2 exch def
    /Y1 exch def
    /X1 exch def
    gsave
        X2 Y2
        transform
        X1 Y1
        translate
        Y2 Y1 sub
        X2 X1 sub
        atan
        200 -50 atan
        sub
        rotate
        itransform
        200 div exch
        -50 div exch
        scale
        curvedRevBase
    grestore
    }
def

/rcurvedRevArrow
    %same as 'curvedRevArrow'
    %   but uses relative displacements
    %requires:  curvedRevArrow
    %called as: dx1 dy1 dx2 dy2  rcurvedArrow  --
    {
    gsave
        rmoveto
        currentpoint
        4 -2 roll
```

```
                        grestore
                        gsave
                        rmoveto
                        currentpoint
                        4 -2 roll
                        curvedRevArrow
                    grestore
                    }
             def
```

The last procedure is a bit unusual and also somewhat difficult to follow; however, it illustrates an effective use of certain PostScript operators and techniques to provide a useful routine. The need here is to be able to set line width independently of any scaling factor that has been applied to the user coordinates. As you know, if the user coordinates are scaled by a factor of 10, for example, then a 1-unit line width will print as 10 points wide. Sometimes this scaling is just fine, but other times you want to retain the line width as a fixed value, independent of any scaling. For such circumstances, you can use this **unitLine** procedure to set line width at a point value that is independent of the current user coordinate transformation.

The process itself is simple PostScript, although a bit complex in calculation. To begin with, you retrieve the current transformation matrix (CTM) and then the default transformation matrix. With both of these on the operand stack, calculate the inverse of the default matrix and multiply the CTM by the result. Think of the process this way: the CTM contains the current device scale factor – call it 'S' – which is the actual scaling factor multiplied by certain other factors that relate to the specific device. You take the default device matrix – call it 'D' – and calculate its inverse – '1/D' – and then multiply that times 'S' to give 'S/D'. The resulting matrix contains only the *x* and *y* scaling values. You then apply this matrix to the coordinates (1, 1), and perform an **idtransform**, which returns the inverse of the distance values associated with the unit vector according to the matrix that you just calculated. You need to use the distance transformation to ensure that any translation components are removed from the calculation. The result left on the operand stack is the inverse of the *y* scale factor on the top of the stack and the inverse of the *x* scale factor below it. Since the line width can be set only to a single value, whether the scale is uniform in both axes or not, you would arbitrarily discard the *y* value and multiply the inverse *x* value times your desired line width. This always yields a line width of the desired value. The **unitLine** procedure is as follows:

```
/unitLine
     %sequence to set linewidth to N
     %  even if CTM has been scaled
     %called as: N unitLine --
     {
     /N exch def
     matrix currentmatrix
     matrix defaultmatrix
     matrix invertmatrix
```

```
matrix concatmatrix
1 1
3 -1 roll
idtransform
pop
N mul
setlinewidth
}
def
```

This completes the review of the common routines that are used to generate the figures in the previous chapters. The next section will discuss the actual programs that use these procedures.

Figure Routines

This chapter presents a selection of the actual programs that produce the figures in the book. The programs are presented here in the same order that the figures appear in the book, although some programs generate more than one figure. Basically, where there was a high degree of commonality among the figures, and where the figures were able to fit on a single page, then one program was used to create a page of figures. The programs selected for inclusion here represent a variety of problems that naturally arise when creating figures of this nature. In some cases, they also represent alternative approaches to solving some of these problems.

2.1 COMMON PROGRAM STRUCTURE

Each of these programs follows a standard format as well as using the common set of routines described in the previous chapter. Before you explore each of these programs in detail, it would be a good idea to review their general structure, using the first program, shown in Figure II-2.1, as an example. This program generates three figures that are used to demonstrate coordinate transformations.

All these programs follow the structuring conventions established by Adobe Systems for their PostScript programs and published by them as the 2.0 Structuring Conventions. The exact contents and format of these conventions are given in detail in Appendix A of Part III. Here I will just briefly discuss some of these comments. The first line shows that these files all conform to the Adobe PostScript 2.0 structuring conventions, and, in addition, conform to the EPSF (Encapsulated PostScript Format) conventions at version 1.2. Also, in all cases, the **%%Title:** comment provides the page title for the figure or group of figures and allows you to match the program with the generated output – just look up that figure in the previous chapters. The **%%BoundingBox:** is always the same and represents the entire imageable area of a page on the Apple LaserWriter. This was done so that the entire page can be placed within another page, if desired, using the EPSF printing guidelines.

Figure II-2.1   Program for Figure A3.1

```
%!PS-Adobe-2.0 EPSF-1.2
%%Creator:Lasertalk(TM) 1.1
%%For:David A. Holzgang
%%Title:Figure A-3
%%CreationDate:9/3/88 9:34 AM
%%BoundingBox:18 8 593 784
%%DocumentFonts: Helvetica
%%DocumentNeededProcSet:PS_Pgr_Ref 0 0
%%EndComments
%%IncludeProcSet:PS_Pgr_Ref 0 0
%%EndProcSet
PvtDict begin
/triangle
    %procedure to draw a triangle
    %   with base along x-axis
    %called as: -- triangle --
    {
    0 0 moveto
    8 0 lineto
    4 6 lineto
    closepath
    gsave
        fill
    grestore
    gsave
        .4 unitLine
        0 setgray
        stroke
    grestore
    newpath
    }
def
end

%%EndProlog
%%BeginSetup
/PvtDict where
    {  pop PvtDict begin}
    { (Error - PvtDict not loaded!!)
        print flush
        stop
    }
ifelse
/_Save_One save def
setFonts
%%EndSetup
```

Figure II-2.1 *continued*

```
%Do first figure
%    example of translation
gsave
    180 640 translate
    1 unitLine
    0 0 moveto
    dot
    100 crossHairs
    (origin) 5 -10 label
    gsave
        20 10 translate
        .55 setgray
        8 8 scale
        triangle
    grestore
    100 50 translate
    0 0 moveto
    dot
    [.5 4 ] 0 setdash
    70 crossHairs
    (translated\norigin) 5 -10 label
    gsave
        20 10 translate
        .85 setgray
        8 8 scale
        [] 0 setdash
        triangle
    grestore
grestore
%Position first figure title
300 550
(Figure A-3.1)
(Translated graphic)
figureTitle

%Do second figure
%    example of scaling
newpath
gsave
    180 400 translate
    1 unitLine
    0 0 moveto
    dot
```

Figure II-2.1 *continued*

```
                100 crossHairs
                (origin) 5 -10 label
                20 10 translate
                gsave
                    .85 setgray
                    16 16 scale
                    triangle
                grestore
                gsave
                    .55 setgray
                    8 8 scale
                    triangle
                grestore
            grestore
            %Position second figure title
            300 300
            (Figure A-3.2)
            (Scaled graphic)
            figureTitle

            %Do third figure
            %   example of rotation
            newpath
            gsave
                300 150 translate
            1 unitLine
            0 0 moveto
            dot
            (origin) 5 -10 label
            gsave
                100 crossHairs
                (x axis) 103 -2 label
                20 10 translate
                .55 setgray
                8 8 scale
                triangle
            grestore
            20 rotate
            [.5 4 ] 0 setdash
            100 crossHairs
            (rotated\nx axis) 103 5 label
            gsave
```

Figure II-2.1 *continued*

```
                    20 10 translate
                    .85 setgray
                    8 8 scale
                    [] 0 setdash
                    triangle
                grestore
            grestore
            %Position third figure title
            300 40
            (Figure A-3.3)
            (Rotated graphic)
            figureTitle
            %%Trailer
            _Save_One restore
            end
            %now show output
            showpage
```

The **%%DocumentNeededProcSet:** and the **%%IncludeProcSet:** comments indicate the requirement for and placement of the PvtDict routines and procedures discussed before. These comments allow document management software to properly control printer setup and manage printer resources – if you have such software. If not, these comments are informational only. Here you can assume that all downloading, or including of these common procedures, is done manually. There are essentially two methods that you can use to provide access to **PvtDict**, which contains all the common procedures. First, you could include a copy of the dictionary definition and all the included procedures in each program after the **%%IncludeProcSet:** comment and before the **%%EndProcSet**. This is completely acceptable and is, in fact, probably the best and most efficient method of handling such requirements if you are going to print only one or two programs. The second alternative is to download the **PvtDict** separately. If you do this, you must ensure that the programs that run afterwards can access the dictionary. This is most commonly done by loading the dictionary outside the server loop, thus ensuring that it remains in the printer memory until the printer is reset and is not purged at the end of the job. That is done by placing the following two lines of code before the ProcSet definition:

```
serverdict begin
0 exitserver
```

where '0' is the required password to exit the server loop. (See the discussion of persistent parameters and server operations in Part I, Section C2.2). If you are running in the interactive mode, you can simply download the ProcSet at the beginning of your session and then work with the programs individually. Since an interactive session is a single 'job' as viewed by the interpreter, the definitions will remain accessible as long as you are running in this mode. Note, however, that in this case you must either provide your own **save**, **restore** processing around each program, or you must anticipate that all the auxiliary procedures and variables that are used in each program are going to continue to consume virtual memory for the length of the run. In fact **PvtDict**, as defined above, is large enough to accommdate all definitions in all the programs.

After the **%%EndProcSet** comment, any special procedures required by the individual figure are defined and placed into **PvtDict**. In normal processing – that is, not in interactive mode – these procedures will be defined in **PvtDict** only for the length of the job. This section of code is followed by the **%%EndProlog** comment, which delimits the prologue from the script portion of the document. Remember that the intention is that no processing is to be performed in the prologue; all processing is to be done in the script.

The script begins with a setup section that establishes certain common circumstances for the execution of the program. First, you'll check for the existence of **PvtDict** and place it onto the dictionary stack if it is available. Since the programs will not execute correctly if it isn't present, the alternative procedure simply aborts the job after an error message. If it is present, then the procedure saves the current state of virtual memory, following good PostScript practice. This allows you to return to the base state for your program at any time that it may be required; in particular, it allows each page or section of a document to be independent. Finally, as part of the setup, you'll execute the **set-Fonts** procedure to establish the correct fonts and define the two global variables, IN and LL.

Each program also terminates in a standard way. The end of the program begins with the **%%Trailer** comment. Then the saved state is restored and **PvtDict** popped from the dictionary stack. These commands must be given in the reverse order of their execution in the setup, since the saved state was defined in **PvtDict** itself and would not be available if the dictionary were not on the dictionary stack. The last action in the program is to show the page produced by the script. If you are going to use this file as an EPSF file, of course you would have to disable the **showpage** before you placed and executed the file.

The Program for Figures A3.1, A3.2, and A3.3

Now you are ready to examine each of the figures individually. The first program produces the three figures A3.1, A3.2, and A3.3 on pages 60, 61, and 62, respectively, and is listed in Figure II-2.1 on pages 395 through 398. It is designed to demonstrate the effects of the basic coordinate transformations on the placement of a graphic object. It uses one special procedure, **triangle**, which draws an isosceles triangle of a fixed size, with its base along the x axis and the left corner at the origin. The triangle is both stroked and filled, the stroke done in black and the fill done in the current color. The page of output is divided roughly into thirds, giving three areas 8.5 inches wide by 3.67 inches high, with one figure on each third of the page. The first figure, A3.1, is placed on the top of the page, using a **translate** command. Then the origin for the figure is displayed by using the **crossHairs** procedure, and a dot is placed to indicate the origin, along with a label. Then the first version of the triangle is placed at a small distance from the origin and filled with a medium gray.

After producing the first triangle, the coordinate origin is moved to a new location. Here the coordinate axes are again drawn and labeled, this time with a dashed line to distinguish them from the original axes on the figure. Another triangle is drawn at the same distance from the newly translated origin and filled in light gray. Note that the label for the translated origin uses the two-line feature of the **label** procedure. The program makes extensive use of **gsave** and **grestore** to ensure that the graphics state is maintained correctly. In particular, you see that each of the figures are individually enclosed so that translation, rotation, and scaling can be performed on each segment without any effect on the others. Finally, the figure is titled at the bottom of the first third of the page.

The second figure, A3.2, shows two overlapping triangles, one twice as large as the other. The larger and lighter of the two is produced first, since you want it to be covered by the smaller in order to illustrate the scaling principle. Remember that print density and color have no effect on PostScript output; only the painting order determines what shows on the page. Therefore, if you don't want the lighter and larger figure to completely obliterate the smaller, you have to paint them in this order. The figure ends with a title, placed at the bottom of the middle third of the page.

The third figure, A3.3, shows the effects of rotation of coordinates on placement of figures. Again, the figure begins with the basic triangle, which is placed in the same relative position to the origin as in the first figure. The axes and the origin are labeled as before. Then the coordinates are rotated by 20 degrees, and the new coordinate axes are drawn in as dashed lines and labeled. The second triangle is produced at the same point, relative to the transformed coordinates, as the first triangle. The figure ends with the title, placed at the bottom of the page.

The Program for Figure A4.1

Next we examine the program that generates Figure A4.1, page 68, and is listed in Figure II-2.2. This is a more demanding example, since this program was designed to demonstrate the different handling of paths under the **fill** and **eofill** operators. In order to do so, it was necessary to draw concentric circles in the same direction and in opposite directions. This program uses the default, non-zero winding number rule for filling the figures; the associated program that generates Figure A4.2 uses the alternate even-odd rule. These programs are virtually identical; therefore, only the first one is presented here.

As before, the program begins with several support procedures. The program is structured so that each of the example figures is produced by one procedure. The first two examples are each composed of two concentric circles, identical except that in one case the circles are drawn in the same direction, while in the other case they are drawn in reverse directions. The final example consists of a single five-pointed star, for which the direction of the path does not have any effect.

Figure II-2.2   Program for Figure A4.1

```
%!PS-Adobe-2.0 EPSF-1.2
%%Creator:Lasertalk(TM) 1.1
%%For:David A. Holzgang
%%Title:Figure A-4.1
%%CreationDate:8/29/88 7:42 AM
%%BoundingBox:18 8 593 784
%%DocumentFonts: Helvetica
%%DocumentNeededProcSet:PS_Pgr_Ref 0 0
%%EndComments
%%IncludeProcSet:PS_Pgr_Ref 0 0
PvtDict begin
/concentRevCirc
    {
    0 0 25 360 0 arcn
    0 0 50 0 360 arc
    .65 setgray
    myfill
    0 setgray
    0 0 25 360 240 arcn
    gsave
        240 rotate
        180 rotate
        arrowHead
    grestore
    0 0 25 240 120 arcn
    gsave
        120 rotate
        180 rotate
        arrowHead
    grestore
    0 0 25 120 0 arcn
    gsave
        180 rotate
        arrowHead
    grestore
    gsave
        stroke
    grestore
    25 0 rmoveto
    0 0 50 0 120 arc
    gsave
        120 rotate
        arrowHead
    grestore
    0 0 50 120 240 arc
    gsave
```

Figure II-2.2 *continued*

```
              240 rotate
              arrowHead
        grestore
        0 0 50 240 360 arc
        gsave
              arrowHead
        grestore
        gsave
              stroke
        grestore
        }
def

/concentFwdCirc
        {
        0 0 25 0 360 arc
        0 0 50 0 360 arc
        .65 setgray
        myfill
        0 setgray
        0 0 25 0 120 arc
        gsave
              120 rotate
              arrowHead
        grestore
        0 0 25 120 240 arc
        gsave
              240 rotate
              arrowHead
        grestore
        0 0 25 240 360 arc
        gsave
              arrowHead
        grestore
        gsave
              stroke
        grestore
        25 0 rmoveto
        0 0 50 0 120 arc
        gsave
              120 rotate
              arrowHead
        grestore
        0 0 50 120 240 arc
        gsave
```

Figure II-2.2   *continued*

```
                                    240 rotate
                                    arrowHead
                            grestore
                            0 0 50 240 360 arc
                            gsave
                                    arrowHead
                            grestore
                            gsave
                                    stroke
                            grestore
                            }
                    def

                    /star+arrow
                        {
                        gsave
                            0 0 moveto
                            30 0 rlineto
                            36 rotate
                            -30 0 rlineto
                            36 rotate
                            30 0 rlineto
                            36 rotate
                            -30 0 rlineto
                            36 rotate
                            30 0 rlineto
                            .65 setgray
                            myfill
                        grestore
                        gsave
                            0 0 moveto
                            20 0 rlineto
                            arrowFwdStar
                            10 0 rlineto
                            36 rotate
                            -20 0 rlineto
                            arrowRevStar
                            -10 0 rlineto
                            36 rotate
                            20 0 rlineto
                            arrowFwdStar
                            10 0 rlineto
                            36 rotate
                            -20 0 rlineto
                            arrowRevStar
                            -10 0 rlineto
```

Figure II-2.2 *continued*

```
                          36 rotate
                          20 0 rlineto
                          arrowFwdStar
                          closepath
                          .3 setlinewidth
                          stroke
                     grestore
                     }
        def

        /arrowFwdStar
            {
            currentpoint
            gsave
                newpath
                moveto
                -90 rotate
                -.5 0 rmoveto
                1 0 rlineto
                -.5 2 rlineto
                closepath
                0 setgray
                fill
            grestore
            }
        def

        /arrowRevStar
            {
            currentpoint
            gsave
                newpath
                moveto
                90 rotate
                -.5 0 rmoveto
                1 0 rlineto
                -.5 2 rlineto
                closepath
                0 setgray
                fill
            grestore
            }
        def
        end
```

Figure II-2.2 *continued*

```
%%EndProlog
%%BeginSetup
/PvtDict where
    {  pop PvtDict begin}
    { (Error - PvtDict not loaded!!)
        print flush
        stop
    }
ifelse
/_Save_One save def
setFonts
%%EndSetup
%test fill and eofill versions
% of concentric circles
%
%presumes that all functions are loaded
%    into a working dictionary
%first define fill function
/myfill {fill} def
%then do reverse circles
gsave
    300 660 translate
    1.5 1.5 scale
    concentRevCirc
grestore
%then do forward circles
gsave
    300 450 translate
    1.5 1.5 scale
    concentFwdCirc
grestore
%finally do star
%
gsave
    220 200 translate
    5 5 scale
star+arrow
grestore
250 50
(Figure A-4.1)
(Examples of non-zero winding number rule)
figureTitle
%%Trailer
_Save_One restore
end
%now show output
showpage
```

The two sets of concentric circles are produced by the procedures **concentRevCirc** and **concentFwdCirc. The concentRevCirc** produces concentric circles whose paths have been drawn in opposite directions, while **concentFwdCirc** produces concentric circles that have been drawn in the same direction. There is nothing very difficult about either of these procedures. Each procedure first generates and fills the concentric circles, then goes back and draws the outline of each circle with arrowheads pointing in the direction of the path. The fill process is done indirectly, by invoking a procedure called **myfill**, which is defined at the beginning of the script to be either **fill** or **eofill**, depending on which figure is being presented. As before, the arrowheads must be rotated into the correct position to show the direction in line with the curve of the path. To do this, the path itself is created in segments and the arrowhead is rotated to match the path. When the path is being drawn in a positive (counterclockwise) direction, this is done simply by rotating the arrowhead the same amount as the terminal angle for the arc segment. Actually, **concentRevCirc** does not rotate the arrowheads for the negative (clockwise) direction directly to the desired orientation, but rotates first to the positive orientation and then reverses the arrowhead with an additional 180-degree rotation.

The procedure that draws the five-pointed star, **star + arrow**, requires two support routines to draw the arrowheads along the lines. In this case, the arrowheads are included in separate routines that each draw the arrowhead, independent of the line width, along the x axis – pointing in the positive x direction in the case of **arrowFwdStar** and in the negative x direction in the case of **arrowRevStar**. The **star + arrow** procedure itself follows the same basic format as the two circle procedures; namely, it creates the figure and fills it first, then returns and strokes the figure while adding the arrowheads along the strokes. Some calculation and a little trigonometry show us that the interior angle at the end of each arm of the star is 36 degrees – one-fifth of 180 degrees. Therefore we rotate the axes by 36 degrees after stroking each arm of the star and return in the opposite direction to draw the next arm. When stroking each arm, we stop two-thirds of the distance along the arm to place the arrowhead, using the positive or negative orientation appropriate to the direction of the path.

The program itself is very straightforward. It first defines the type of fill to be used in the figures. Next, it simply moves to the correct location for placement of each of the figure elements, scales the element to an appropriate size – which is determined empirically – and then invokes the correct procedure. It ends by placing the titles on the bottom of the page as usual.

The Program for Figure A5.1

This section presents the program that generates Figure A5.1 on page 94; it is shown in the listing in Figure II-2.3. This is a relatively long and complex program, because it is doing quite a number of labels and figure elements. Let us look at them in turn, beginning with the special procedures and routines that are used in this program. Essentially there is one special procedure used here, **letterBbox**, that requires two additional

Figure II-2.3   Program for Figure A5.1

```
%!PS-Adobe-2.0 EPSF-1.2
%%Creator:Lasertalk(TM) 1.1
%%For:David A. Holzgang
%%Title:Figure A-5.1
%%CreationDate:9/4/88 8:42 PM
%%BoundingBox:18 8 593 784
%%DocumentFonts: Helvetica
%%DocumentNeededProcSet:PS_Pgr_Ref 0 0
%%EndComments
%%IncludeProcSet:PS_Pgr_Ref 0 0
PvtDict begin
/width
    %procedure to calculate the width of a bounding box
    %   used with bounding box array
    %called as: [array] width w
    {
    dup
    2 get
    exch
    0 get
    sub
    }
def

/height
    %procedure to calculate the height of a bounding box
    %   used with bounding box array
    %called as: [array] height h
    {
    dup
    3 get
    exch
    1 get
    sub
    }
def

/letterBbox
    %sequence to produce bounding box
    %   given bbox array
    %requires:  width; height
    %called as: [array] letterBbox --
    {
    gsave
```

Figure II-2.3 *continued*

```
                      aload
                      dup
                      width
                      /W exch def
                      height
                      /H exch def
                      .2 unitLine
                      moveto
                      dot
                      moveto
                      [1 2 ] 0 setdash
                      0 H rlineto
                      W 0 rlineto
                      0 H neg rlineto
                      closepath
                      stroke
                 grestore
                 }
            def
            end

            %%EndProlog
            %%BeginSetup
            /PvtDict where
                { pop PvtDict begin}
                { (Error - PvtDict not loaded!!)
                    print flush
                    stop
                }
            ifelse
            /_Save_One save def
            setFonts
            %%EndSetup
            %draw character and its bounding box
            250 350 moveto
            /Helvetica findfont
            200 scalefont
            setfont
            gsave
                (g) false charpath
                gsave
                    stroke
                grestore
                flattenpath
                [ pathbbox ]
                /BBox exch def
                BBox letterBbox
```

Figure II-2.3 *continued*

```
grestore
%draw baseline and labels:
%   character origin; next character origin;
%   bounding box; baseline
%do baseline
gsave
    -40 0 rmoveto
    320 0 rlineto
    (baseline) 5 -2 label
    [1 2 ] 0 setdash
    stroke
grestore
-20 0 rmoveto
%note that we have distorted the actual character origin
%   by 20 points for visibility
/CO currentpoint 2 array astore def
5 crossHairs
-15 14 -5 5 rcurvedArrow
(character\norigin) -45 30 label
(g) stringwidth
rmoveto
10 0 rmoveto
%note that we have distorted the actual next character origin
%   by 10 points for visibility
/NCO currentpoint 2 array astore def
5 crossHairs
25 14 2 2 rcurvedRevArrow
(next character\norigin) 17 20 label
365 470 351 458 curvedRevArrow
365 470 moveto
(bounding box) -10 5 label
%draw width and bearing vector labels
%   first left side bearing
CO aload pop
60 sub
moveto
10 0 rmoveto
-10 0 rlineArrow
5 verticalBar
10 0 rmoveto
BBox 0 get
currentpoint exch pop
lineArrow
5 verticalBar
(left side bearing) -37 -14 label
%   then character width
```

Figure II-2.3 *continued*

```
CO aload pop
100 sub
moveto
40 0 rmoveto
-40 0 rlineArrow
5 verticalBar
NCO aload pop
100 sub
moveto
-40 0 rmoveto
40 0 rlineArrow
5 verticalBar
(character\nwidth) -80 4.5 label

%Position figure title
320 200
(Figure A-5.1)
(Character metrics)
figureTitle
%%Trailer
_Save_One restore
end
%now show output
showpage
```

support routines, **width** and **height**. The two support routines are easy to comprehend: they each take two elements from a bounding box array, which has the standard format [ll_x ll_y ur_x ur_y], and calculate either the width of the bounding box by taking the difference between the x values or, alternatively, the height by taking the difference in the y values. The procedure **letterBbox** itself draws a dotted outline along the rectangle defined by the bounding box coordinates, with dots at the lower left and upper right corners, which are the points that define the box.

The body of the program begins by drawing the outline of a character 'g'; then it flattens the path that defines the character to minimize all extraneous points (such as off-the-path direction points that have been used to define the curves of the letter); and it finally converts the flattened path into a bounding box for the path that outlines the letter, using **pathbbox**. This provides the bounding box array that is used by **letterBbox**. After the letter and bounding box are established, you proceed to show the x axis as a baseline. This is presented as a simple dashed line, followed by the label 'baseline'. Next the program draws the character origin and the next character origin, using the **crossHairs** procedure to mark the points, since dots are harder to see for such work. Both the character origin and the next character origin are displaced away from their actual position to allow the character metrics to be fully visible. They are also saved by the program as **CO** and

NCO respectively, since they will subsequently be required to position the line displays for the left side bearing and the character width, as you will see. Finally, each is labeled and pointed to using the common procedures that you noted above. After all this, the bounding box label is placed near the upper right corner of the box, with a curved arrow.

With that all done, you still need to draw the two lines that show the left side bearing and the character width. Each of these is done in a similar manner, with vertical bars at the ends and with lines that end in arrows to show the actual width values. The character origin and the ll_x component from the bounding box are used to define the two end points for the left side bearing in the x axis, while the y axis is set to an arbitrary 60 points below the baseline. Then the character width is is drawn, again using the character origin and the next character origin to define the position for the vertical bars at the ends of the line, while the line itself is displaced 100 points below the character baseline. Because the left side bearing line is small, the label for that line is placed beneath it, while the label for the character width is placed on two lines between the two vertical bars. Finally, the figure is titled in the usual fashion and printed.

The Program for Figures B1.1, B1.2, and B1.3

The program that generates the three figures on pages 106 and 107 is shown in Figure II-2.4 and discussed in this section. It is not as complex as several of the previous programs. This program is used to illustrate the contents of the operand stack and draws three instances of the stack contents onto one page. Like the first program that we discussed, this program does its display by dividing the page into thirds and showing one instance in each third.

The one departure from the previous programs is in the mechanism for determining whether **PvtDict** is correctly available. In the previous programs, we tested for **PvtDict** by using the **where** operator. This searches the entire dictionary stack for the key, or name, provided and returns the dictionary and the boolean value 'true' to the stack if the key is found. The procedure that is executed for the 'true' condition, therefore, pops off the unwanted dictionary and establishes **PvtDict** as the current dictionary. This program illustrates an alternative approach. Here you load the current dictionary onto the operand stack and test whether **PvtDict** is loaded in it. The result is a simple boolean value that tells whether the given key is present or absent in the given dictionary. If it is, you continue, as before, by making **PvtDict** the current dictionary. If not, you use the same process as in the previous test to abort the program. The only difference between these two procedures lies in the use of **known** or **where**. The **where** operator searches the entire dictionary stack, but it returns an additional, and unnecessary, result in the form of a dictionary. The **known** operator, on the other hand, returns only the desired boolean result but will scan only one given dictionary. In this case, you would reasonably expect that **PvtDict** is defined in the current dictionary if it is defined at all. Therefore you test only the current dictionary, making the assumption that **PvtDict** is not available if it isn't known there. So this is simply an alternative method to provide the same check function; it is used here to illustrate another approach to the problem.

Figure II-2.4 Program for Figures B1.1, B1.2, and B1.3

```
%!PS-Adobe-2.0 EPSF-1.2
%%Creator:Lasertalk(TM) 1.1
%%For:David A. Holzgang
%%Title:Figure B-1
%%CreationDate:9/4/88 7:38 AM
%%BoundingBox:18 8 593 784
%%DocumentFonts: Helvetica
%%DocumentNeededProcSet:PS_Pgr_Ref 0 0
%%EndComments
%%IncludeProcSet:PS_Pgr_Ref 0 0
%%EndProcSet
PvtDict begin
/stack
    %procedure to display a string
    %    within a box
    %    to represent the operand stack
    %requires:  TitleHelv; centerString
    %called as: (str) stack --
    {
    gsave
        1 unitLine
        currentpoint translate
        0 15 moveto
        0 0 lineto
        70 0 lineto
        70 15 lineto
        stroke
        TitleHelv setfont
        35 5 moveto
        centerString
        show
    grestore
    }
def
end

%%EndProlog
%%BeginSetup
currentdict /PvtDict known
    { PvtDict begin}
    { (Error - PvtDict not loaded!!)
        print flush
        stop
    }
ifelse
/_Save_One save def
```

Figure II-2.4 *continued*

```
setFonts
%%EndSetup
%Do first figure
%    one operand on stack
250 650 moveto
(20) stack
(. . .top-of-stack) 120 5 label
%Position first figure title
300 600
(Figure B-1.1)
(Operand Stack with 1 operand)
figureTitle

%Do second figure
%    second operand on stack
newpath
250 460 moveto
(30) stack
(. . .top-of-stack) 120 5 label
0 -35 rmoveto
(20) stack
%Position second figure title
300 380
(Figure B-1.2)
(Operand stack with 2 operands)
figureTitle

%Do third figure
%    result on stack
newp ath
250 200 moveto
(50) stack
(. . .top-of-stack) 120 5 label
%Position third figure title
300 150
(Figure B-1.3)
(Operand stack with result)
figureTitle
%%Trailer
_Save_One restore
end
%now show output
showpage
```

The program begins with a special procedure, **stack**, that provides most of the effort required to illustrate a stack representation. This procedure draws a shallow, U-shaped figure to represent a stack position and centers a string, which represents the contents of the stack position, within the figure. The procedure requires two of the support mechanisms from the common **PvtDict** in this process, using **centerString** to calculate where the string operand should be placed and using **TitleHelv** as the font for showing it.

Once this procedure has been defined, it is quite easy to follow the remainder of the program. Each of the stack elements is drawn in its appropriate one-third of the page, with the label 'top-of-stack' placed next to the first stack element. In this case, the elements shown are all two-digit numbers, but the routines used here could be used to display any type of stack contents. This is an example of how to make routines that are more general rather than tailored only to the immediate situation.

The Program for Figure C1.1

Figure C1.1, page 157, is an illustration for the arc operator; the program that generates it is shown in Figure II-2.5. This program does not require any special support procedures; it simply produces a standard output from the desired operator and then labels the resulting figure with the tools that have already been built in **PvtDict**. This, of course, was the main reason for generating **PvtDict** and its associated procedures in the first place.

The manner in which the program begins is the reverse of that in the previous programs in that the title for the page is produced before the image itself is created. This is done, as the comment in the program observes, to allow you to translate the coordinate system without worrying about restoring it. Of course, it would not be difficult to enclose the image portion of the program in a **gsave**, **grestore** pair, which would preserve the coordinates. Here, however, the only purpose of such action would be so you can properly position the figure label; it seems easier and better to accomplish the same effect by simply setting the title first.

After the title is set, you can begin work on the figure itself. In this case, the actual arc is the last thing generated, as you will see. However, you'll make use of the **arc** operator several times throughout the program to generate curves for labeling and illustration purposes. The program begins by translating the coordinates to position the coordinate axis on the page for the best and clearest placement; then it sets the line width at 1.2 points to emphasize the actual arc that will constitute the figure. The first requirement of the figure is to generate the dotted lines that extend from the center of the arc to each of the end points. The first **gsave**, **grestore** segment contains the code to do this. This code segment begins by setting the dash factor for the line; then it moves to the desired center of the arc—in this case, the point (110, 120) in the translated coordinates. This point is labeled with the same operand names as are used in the operator reference, a fixed-size dot is placed at this point for reference, and then the **arc** operator is invoked with the same parameters that will be used later for the figure. This draws a straight line from the current point, which has been set to the center point of the arc, to the point that

Figure II-2.5 Program for Figure C1.1

```
%!PS-Adobe-2.0 EPSF-1.2
%%Creator:Lasertalk(TM) 1.1
%%For:David A. Holzgang
%%Title:Figure C-1.1
%%CreationDate:8/27/88 8:16 AM
%%BoundingBox:18 8 593 784
%%DocumentFonts: Helvetica
%%DocumentNeededProcSet:PS_Pgr_Ref 0 0
%%EndComments
%%IncludeProcSet:PS_Pgr_Ref 0 0
%%EndProlog
%%BeginSetup
/PvtDict where
    {  pop PvtDict begin}
    { (Error - PvtDict not loaded!!)
        print flush
        stop
    }
ifelse
/_Save_One save def
setFonts
%%EndSetup
%procedure to generate figure
%    to illustrate arc operator
%do title first before translate for image
300 150
(Figure C-1.1)
(arc operator)
figureTitle
%now for arc
0 200 translate
1.2 setlinewidth
gsave
    [2 3] 0 setdash
    .1 setlinewidth
    110 120 moveto
    (( x, y )) -10 -12
    label
    fixedDot
    gsave
        110 120 300 10 60 arc
        closepath
        stroke
    grestore
    1000 0 rlineto
    stroke
```

Figure II-2.5 *continued*

```
grestore
gsave
    .5 setlinewidth
    110 120 85 0 10 arc
    gsave
        5 rotate
        1.5 1.5 scale
        arrowHead
    grestore
    (ang\0001) 10 -10 label
    stroke
        110 120 70 0 60 arc
        gsave
            55 rotate
            1.5 1.5 scale
            arrowHead
        grestore
        (ang\0002) 30 -25 label
        stroke
grestore
gsave
    110 120 translate
    60 rotate
    0 0 moveto
    (rad) 150 4 label
grestore
260 60 moveto
(current point\n at start)
-28 -30 label
-18 -20 0 -4 rcurvedArrow
dot
110 120 300 10 60 arc
dot
(current point\n at completion)
15 20 label
22 16 2 4 rcurvedRevArrow
stroke
%%Trailer
_Save_One restore
end
%now show output
showpage
```

begins the desired arc, then draws the arc itself. The **closepath** operator draws a straight line segment back to the center of the arc. Then this entire path is stroked with the thin, dotted line that you defined earlier. This looks like a pie segment; however, you will later stroke over the outer arc with the final, heavier solid line, leaving only the dotted lines pointing to each endpoint of the arc.

Next the program creates the labels and lines to show each of the angles that delimit the **arc** operation. First you produce the line that represents the smaller angle, again using the **arc** operator and a 10-degree angle to define the line. The line terminates with an arrowhead, which is drawn 1.5 times normal size to compensate for the smaller line width and is rotated by an amount 5 degrees less than the angle being marked for correct placement. This degree of rotation is determined empirically. Finally, a label is made for the first arc, located below and to the right of the end point of the arrowhead. Then the second, larger angle is done is the same way. Notice that the rotation of the arrowhead is again 5 degrees less than the angle being marked.

The next label to be added to the figure is that for the radius of the arc. This is placed along the outer dotted line that connects the center of the arc and the end point at completion. It is placed by moving back to the center point, rotating the axes through 60 degrees to match the arc, and then moving out along the positive x axis and slightly up.

Now you'll begin the actual example figure itself. First, the program moves to a point off the direct line of the arc in order to illustrate the feature of the **arc** operator that inserts an optional straight line segment. Once positioned at the correct point, a label is provided to show this as the initial current point. Then the arc itself is created and stroked, using the larger line width set earlier in the program. The last thing is to add the final label, which shows the current point at the end of the operation.

The Program for Figure C1.5

The program for Figure C1.5 on page 222 is very similar to the program that generates Figure A5.1, which we discussed earlier. This program is designed to illustrate the **pathbbox** operator itself, whereas before we used the **pathbbox** as a means to the end of showing the character bounding box. In this illustration, the figure constructed is a very simple circle, and the **pathbbox** is used to outline the bounding box and label the critical lower-left and upper-right corners that define the box. The text of the program is given in Figure II-2.6.

The major feature of the program is the **bBox** procedure, which, like the **letterBbox** procedure we discussed in the earlier example, takes the bounding box array and uses it to draw, stroke, and, in this case, label the bounding box. This special procedure is not a generalized procedure, as you will note, since it assumes that the bounding box is a square rather than the more general rectangle. In this instance, of course, we have created a path that will deliberately generate a square as a bounding box, and therefore we can save ourselves some extraneous calculations. However, a look back at the **letterBbox** procedure will show you how one could modify this procedure to provide processing for the more general case.

Figure II-2.6   Program for Figure C1.5

```
%!PS-Adobe-2.0 EPSF-1.2
%%Creator:Lasertalk(TM) 1.1
%%For:David A. Holzgang
%%Title:Figure C-1.5
%%CreationDate:8/29/88 4:37 PM
%%BoundingBox:18 8 593 784
%%DocumentFonts: Helvetica
%%DocumentNeededProcSet:PS_Pgr_Ref 0 0
%%EndComments
%%IncludeProcSet:PS_Pgr_Ref 0 0
PvtDict begin
%sequence to produce bounding box
%    given array
%called as: [ array ] bBox --
/bBox
    {
    aload
    dup 2 get exch 0 get sub
    /W exch def
    .5 unitLine
    moveto
    gsave
        1 unitLine
        dot
        currentlinewidth
        dup scale
        (( ur\000x, ur\000y )) -5 10 label2
    grestore
    moveto
    gsave
        1 unitLine
        dot
        currentlinewidth
        dup scale
        (( ll\000x, ll\000y )) -25 -12 label2
    grestore
    [1 2 ] 0 setdash
    0 W rlineto
    W 0 rlineto
    0 W neg rlineto
    closepath
    stroke
    }
def
end
```

Figure II-2.6 *continued*

```
%%EndProlog
%%BeginSetup
/PvtDict where
    {   pop PvtDict begin}
    { (Error - PvtDict not loaded!!)
        print flush
        stop
    }
ifelse
/_Save_One save def
setFonts
%%EndSetup
%examples for pathbbox
% now produce examples
%
gsave
    320 375 translate
    10 10 scale
    newpath
    1 unitLine
    0 0 10 0 360 arc
    gsave
        stroke
    grestore
    [ pathbbox ]
    bBox
    [] 0 setdash
    0 0 moveto
    20 crossHairs
grestore
%now add labels
360 440 380 450 curvedArrow
355 430 moveto
(path) 0 0 label
435 310 422 297 curvedRevArrow
435 310 moveto
(path\nbounding box) -5 7 label
%Position figure title
320 150
(Figure C-1.5)
(pathbbox operator)
figureTitle
%%Trailer
_Save_One restore
end
%now show output
showpage
```

The procedure itself begins by exploding the array operand into its components as well as using the array for calculating the width (which, in this case, is the height as well) of the bounding box. The width calculation consumes the array element on the stack, leaving the individual coordinate values. The top two are those of the upper right corner of the box – remember that the values are stored on the stack in reverse order – and so the first action is to move there and paint a dot, along with the necessary label information. Then you return to the lower left corner in the same fashion and label it. The last thing is for the procedure to actually draw the box itself, using a dashed line to outline the square that it has computed.

The program itself begins by translating to the center of the page and setting a scale value so the entire figure will fill a major portion of the screen. Then it draws the circle, centered at the origin, and uses the **pathbbox** operator to generate the necessary bounding box array for the **bBox** procedure. Once the bounding box is drawn, labeled, and stroked, the procedure adds a set of x and y axes to provide some placement of the figure on the PostScript page. It then provides labels and pointers for the path and the bounding box. The coordinate offsets for positioning these labels was provided by empirical testing; unfortunately, there are no formulas for this kind of work. The last thing in the program is, as usual, the figure label.

The Program for Figure C1.7

The program that is used to generate Figure C1.7, page 258, is shown in Figure II-2.7, the last example in this cookbook. It is also, in some respects, the easiest. It is included here to illustrate using overlapping gray values and some of the possible uses of different procedures that we have already defined.

As in the earlier Figure II-2.5, this program does not require any special support procedures. The program is designed to illustrate the three varieties of line caps, each produced by the interpreter according to the setting of the **linecap** value in the current graphic state. Each of the three possible values is illustrated by stroking a large, thick line segment, using the appropriate linecap parameter.

The major issue here is creating and displaying a small white line within the thick black one to demonstrate the actual coordinate values used for the larger line. The program will produce three lines, one below the other, and each will be the identically the same as the others except for its linecap value. The lines are organized in order by the line cap value, so the first line corresponds to a line cap of 0, the second to a value of 1, and the third to a value of 2. The line is made 50 units long and 10 units wide, so that the line and the cap are quite visible, extending 5 points on either side of the basic line. After each line is stroked, the program sets the current color to white, sets the line width to a very small value, and returns to the starting point of the line. There it draws a small dot at the current point, creates a line the same length as the first line, and draws another dot. The line is then stroked in white to give the desired effect. Remember that the last thing stroked always overlays anything underneath it on the page, even if the

Figure II-2.7   Program for Figure C1.7

```
%!PS-Adobe-2.0 EPSF-1.2
%%Creator:Lasertalk(TM) 1.1
%%For:David A. Holzgang
%%Title:Figure C-1.7
%%CreationDate:9/2/88 9:18 AM
%%BoundingBox:18 8 593 784
%%DocumentFonts: Helvetica
%%DocumentNeededProcSet:PS_Pgr_Ref 0 0
%%EndComments
%%IncludeProcSet:PS_Pgr_Ref 0 0
%%EndProlog
%%BeginSetup
/PvtDict where
    {  pop PvtDict begin}
    { (Error - PvtDict not loaded!!)
       print flush
       stop
    }
ifelse
/_Save_One save def
setFonts
%%EndSetup
%figure for setlinecap
%start processing
%now do simple butt cap
100 500 moveto
gsave
    50 0 rlineto
    10 setlinewidth
    0 setlinecap
    0 setgray
    stroke
grestore
gsave
    .5 setlinewidth
    1 setgray
    dot 50 0 rlineto dot
    stroke
grestore
(setlinecap = 0) 80 -2 label
%second figure - round cap
100 450 moveto
gsave
```

Figure II-2.7 *continued*

```
                    50 0 rlineto
                    10 setlinewidth
                    1 setlinecap
                    0 setgray
                    stroke
              grestore
              gsave
                    .5 setlinewidth
                    1 setgray
                    dot 50 0 rlineto dot
                    stroke
              grestore
              (setlinecap = 1) 80 -2 label
              %third figure - round cap
              100 400 moveto
              gsave
                    50 0 rlineto
                    10 setlinewidth
                    2 setlinecap
                    0 setgray
                    stroke
              grestore
              gsave
                    .5 setlinewidth
                    1 setgray
                    dot 50 0 rlineto dot
                    stroke
              grestore
              (setlinecap = 2) 80 -2 label
              %Position figure title
              250 330
              (Figure C-1.7)
              (setlinecap values)
              figureTitle
              %%Trailer
              _Save_One restore
              end
              %now show output
              showpage
```

last one is small and light, while the first is large and dark. And so it appears here, as expected. The line is finished with a label telling what the line cap value is for this illustration.

The figure continues with the next two lines, each using the same pattern but changing the line cap value. As you review this program, notice how easily the three segments might have been drawn by one procedure that was called with one or two operands (depending on how you wanted to structure the process) and used repeatedly.

This ends the cookbook routines for you to use. All of these techniques are available and useful in various circumstances. One of the most important skills for you to develop as a PostScript programmer is to be able to determine which techniques are most appropriate to your specific problem. I hope these examples of actual PostScript code, being used in a working environment, are of some help in that process.

Appendixes

Appendix A

Structure Conventions

This appendix explains both the original PostScript structuring conventions, which were version number 1.0, and the revised document structure conventions released by Adobe Systems in January, 1987. These conventions were given version number 2.0, and they both revise and extend the original structuring conventions. Subsequent minor revisions have brought the conventions up to version 2.1 as of January, 1989.

If you follow the original conventions, you will automatically satisfy the requirements of the new 2.1 conventions. However, there are many new extensions to the original version that allow new facilities and expand old ones substantially. If you require these extensions, you should add the new conventions that implement them.

These 2.1 conventions are primarily designed to improve handling of PostScript documents in multi-user, networked environments. They provide facilities that allow a class of programs, including print spoolers, device servers, and other postprocessors – known collectively as *document managers* – to manage printer resources efficiently and to process PostScript documents effectively in such environments.

The conventions generally allow complete cooperation between document managers at all levels and allow PostScript document descriptions to be created and printed to make maximum use of network facilities. The conventions are an external structure, neither imposed by the interpreter nor checked by it. They rely on the cooperation of the document creation functions to implement as much or as little of specific conventions as are required and appropriate.

To aid in this process, Adobe Systems, the creator of the PostScript language, has defined a printer description (PPD) file format that provides printer-specific information in a standard format for use by document managers. The format of a PPD file is available from Adobe Systems if you require it (see address below). The information contained in these files works in conjunction with the information provided by the structuring conventions to provide a mechanism for specification and use of printer features and functions.

Because so many of these new conventions rely on site-specific information, there will not be extensive discussion regarding many of the new comments in this appendix.

If you are working in an environment that implements these conventions, there will be full documentation available from your network administrator regarding supported features and correct usage. If you are the network administrator and are trying to implement these conventions in a network, you can obtain a complete description of the 2.1 (or later) conventions from:

Adobe Systems
P.O. Box 7900
Mountain View, CA 94039

1.1 COMMENT CONVENTIONS

There are three types of structural comments defined in the 2.1 conventions. These are as follows:

- Structure Comments
- Resource Requirements
- Query Conventions

The Structure Comments are used to define various structural components of a PostScript document. These will generally include a header, prologue, script, and trailer; they may include information regarding page breaks. Note that all the version 1.0 conventions fall under this category.

The Resource Requirements are comments that define exactly what resources are required within a PostScript document that have not been included within the text of the document itself and that indicate by their placement where in the document these resources are required. These may include fonts, procedures (in the form of specific prologue information), and files. The requirements may also be device-specific, or they may be application- or environment-dependent, such as specific forms, paper colors, or collating order.

The Query Conventions are used to delimit PostScript programs that inquire regarding specific resource availability. These queries cannot be included within a conforming document, because they compromise the ability of document managers to process such programs. Therefore they must be handled independently and can then provide valuable information for a PostScript programmer or application.

Recommended Structure

PostScript recommends following a straightforward, standard structure that is implemented by using a set of Structural Comments. There are four basic components in the recommended structure: header, prologue, script, and trailer. Each of the components plays an important role in establishing the overall structure in a PostScript program.

There are four sections required in a properly structured PostScript program: header, prologue, script, and trailer. The header and trailer segments of the PostScript program are primarily devoted to providing certain global information about the program contained between them. The most important point about the header and trailer sections is that, from the viewpoint of the PostScript interpreter, they consist of comments only and do not contain any executable PostScript code.

The *header* section contains two types of information. The first type of information is what might be termed "creation data." This information covers who created the document, when it was created, and so on, and is primarily required in a networked environment for routing and other identification purposes. The second type of information contained in the header is document information covering the fonts used and so on and is primarily oriented toward use by utility programs.

The *prologue* contains procedures and named variables and constants that will be used throughout the rest of the document. The prologue will generally have been written by a programmer and then will be included as the first part of every document (or script) that requires it. The prologue will usually be relatively complex, with a variety of variables and nested procedures defined within it. The prologue should contain only procedure and variable definitions; it should not contain any code that changes the state of the page or the device, and, in particular, it should not contain any code that results in marks on the output page. The *script* describes the specific elements to be produced on the output pages in terms of procedures and variables defined in the prologue, along with operand data as required. Each page description is expected to depend only on the prologue and to be independent of all the other pages. The intention here is that it should be possible to produce any page correctly, given only the prologue and the description of that specific page. When the process is done well, each page description within the script will be relatively short and probably quite repetitive, using the same procedures over and over.

Finally, there is a *trailer,* which contains cleanup information. This is a place for document information that couldn't be easily generated in the header sections. This facility is provided for application programs that are directly generating PostScript output and can't easily provide all the required document information in the header. For example, one of the required data items in the header is a list of fonts used in the document. This information is particularly important if the document requires nonstandard fonts that need to be downloaded to the printer prior to processing the document. If the PostScript output is being created by an application, however, it may be quite difficult to generate this information in the header before the document itself has been created. The structural conventions therefore allow that the font information can be deferred to the end of the document and put in the trailer section. You will see how this works when each of the sections and their contents are discussed in detail below.

So you see that a PostScript program that follows the recommended structure will consist of four elements. The first two are a header and a trailer that provide certain global information and enclose the entire PostScript document. The document description portion contains the remaining two parts of the structure: a prologue that contains procedures and global variables and a script that actually describes each of the pages to be output. These four sections will always be presented within the program in the following sequence:

Header

Prologue

Script

Trailer

Besides dividing your PostScript program into these four sections, there is another practice you should follow in the script portion of the program to ensure page independence. Every PostScript program that generates a printable document should maintain its own indicators of the current status of the PostScript document output. When the document crosses a major structural boundary, such as a page, the PostScript program should take steps to ensure that the new page is independent of all preceding pages and does not interfere with any subsequent ones. This can most easily be accomplished by invoking the two PostScript operators, **save** and **restore**. These operators are more fully described in Part I, Section C, "Operator Reference."

Specific Format

In order to provide the necessary global information for structure, PostScript has established specific formats for items to be included in the header, trailer, and script portions of a PostScript program. You should also understand that these specific format conventions may be subject to change.

The requirement, then, is for a method of indicating structure in a PostScript program that is easily identifiable but that will be transparent to the interpreter. This objective is met by using a special form of comment to indicate sections and to provide structural information within a PostScript program. You have already been introduced to comments in a PostScript program. The standard PostScript comment begins with the character '%' and ends with a newline. Structural information in a PostScript program is contained in lines that begin with the characters '%%' or '%!' and end with a newline. As you can immediately see, such lines will be treated by the PostScript interpreter as comment lines and hence ignored. However, because the lines of structural information begin with this combination of special characters, they can be distinguished from ordinary comment lines by any utility or other application program that needs the information to work on a PostScript document.

Now we are ready to discuss the exact format of the structural comments. Note that you must enter these comments exactly as shown; they are not like the regular PostScript comments, which are free-form. These comments must begin with '%%', and these two characters are followed by a keyword. There is no space between the '%%' and the keyword.

As in all PostScript commands, upper- and lowercase letters are distinct, so you must enter keywords exactly as shown. In comments that require data, the keyword is followed by a ':' and again there are no spaces. There may be one or more data values whose exact interpretation depends on the keyword. The first value is separated from the ':' by one space, and each subsequent value is separated from the following value by one space. A newline must appear immediately after the last value or after the keyword if there is no data.

With this new set of conventions, PostScript has a new definition of a *conforming* page description. Previously, there existed a concept of a minimally conforming PostScript document. This was a page description that did not implement the complete set of PostScript conventions but nevertheless provided a certain minimum of structural information. Now, a conforming program is one that implements any proper subset of the document conventions. In other words, there are no longer any specific comments that must exist in a PostScript document in order for it to conform to the 2.1 standards. However, there is still a certain constraint on PostScript programs, namely, that any PostScript document that does use the conventions shall use them in a manner consistent with the standard usage as described below. In particular, this implies that certain system-level PostScript operators must not be employed within a conforming program. It also implies the reverse, that a conforming document will provide the required structural information where appropriate.

There are some general constraints that apply to any conforming PostScript document. The first one is that the document be divided into a prologue and script and that there be no code that makes marks on the output page in the prologue and no procedural definitions in the script. In particular, this means that the prologue section of the document should be able to be downloaded separately into the printer if desired. The second is that the **%%Page** comment (described in more detail below), if used, shall apply only to pages that are independent of all other pages in the script, that is, to pages that can be output using the information in the prologue and in the specific page description alone. The third is that the lines in the document description shall not exceed 256 characters in length. This is not a PostScript limitation, but it is a limitation in many document processing and handling systems. If a comment must extend over more than one line, the 2.1 conventions provide a new facility for continuation comments. These comments shall continue on the next line after the keyword, on a line beginning with the string %%+. An example might be where there are a number of fonts to be used within a document. This could be recorded as in the following example:

```
%%Document Fonts: Helvetica Helvetica-Bold Helvetica-Narrow
%%+ Helvetica-BoldOblique Symbol Times-Roman
%%+ Times-Italic Times-BoldItalic
```

Finally, there are certain constraints on PostScript operations that must be followed within a conforming document. The first of these is that the **showpage** operator shall be used outside of a **save**, **restore** pair that surrounds a page. This is required to ensure that redefinition of **showpage**, which may be required in some complex environments, will work correctly. The second is that the PostScript program avoid use of certain operations, such as those listed in Figure III-A1.

Figure III-A1 Operations to avoid in conforming programs

banddevice	copypage	erasepage	exitserver
framedevice	grestoreall	initclip	initgraphics
initmatrix	nulldevice	quit	setdevice
setmatrix	setsccbatch	setscreen	settransfer
setcolortransfer			

1.2 STRUCTURE COMMENTS

The document structuring conventions are designed to allow document managers that are running in a networked environment to understand and, to some extent, manipulate document descriptions. Such handling will inevitably be installation-specific in most cases. Ideally, applications that produce document descriptions in such an environment should be able to compose a document without any consideration of available resources and be able to rely on the document manager in the network to provide the necessary resources or provide the user with reasonable alternatives.

There are two ways to approach this ideal; neither excludes the other, but they represent somewhat different philosophies toward document preparation. In the first case, the document description relies on the document manager to generate or otherwise provide all necessary resources. In this case, the document description contains only structural and resource information that indicates a requirement for a certain resource. In the second case, the document description provides all the required resources itself but delimits the resource-specific code with appropriate structural comments so that a document manager, if one exists, could remove these sections and substitute others as required.

Here is a simple example that may make this a bit clearer. Suppose you have generated a document that is intended to use a certain unusual font. If you are running on a dedicated printer, this represents no problem: you have either installed the font or you can download the font before you print the document. However, if you are running in a networked environment, there is a problem. You do not know whether the font is available, for several reasons: you may not know which printer your document will print on, or you may not know when your document will print. In any case, you need to be sure that the font required is provided for your document.

In a dedicated environment, you would query the **FontDirectory** and determine whether the font was already loaded; if not, you would download the font and then print. In a network, such interaction with the printer is not feasible. Instead you may use one of the two methods outlined above. First, you could simply indicate the need for this special font through the use of the established conventions as described below, relying on the document manager to perform the necessary query and download functions. Alternatively, your document itself could include the required font download instructions and thereby ensure that the font was on the correct printer at the required time. However, this makes the document take longer to transmit and possibly longer to execute. If you do use the second method, you want to delimit the font information using the appropriate conventions so that a document manager could remove or reprocess the document for more efficient execution. These two cases indicate the two alternative methods of handling resource-specific requirements.

The important point here is that, whichever method is chosen, there is a way to determine from the document structure in a consistent manner what functions need to be or can be performed on the document without altering the desired result. To implement both of these alternative approaches, the 2.1 Structuring Conventions contain a large number of new comments that represent *BEGIN* and *END* pairs of comments that delimit printer-specific elements within a document. Similarly, the entire set of Requirement Conventions is newly developed to provide a mechanism for a document to request some resource (such as a font) or some device-specific feature (such as alternate paper) by the use of *INCLUDE* comments.

There are three types of structure comments that make up the full set of Adobe 2.1 Structuring Conventions. These are

- Header Comments: These occur only once in a document; as the name implies, they are placed before any executable PostScript code in the document.
- Body Comments: These may appear anywhere inside a document and generally delimit use of specific features or ingredients that are used in the document.
- Page Comments: These are similar to header comments, in that they appear before each script page to define the page-level structure. They will occur before each page. The trailer delimiter is part of the page comments, as it marks the end of the last page of output.

Header Comments

All PostScript programs that conform to these structuring conventions must begin with a comment line that starts with the characters '%!'. This has certain advantages in some specific environments (such as UNIX); you'll know if you are working in such an environment. In the typical micro-based environment, there is no advantage to following this recommendation if you're not going to follow the other structural conventions. In a conforming program, this first line gives information regarding the structuring of the program, and is called the *version identifier*. Its format is as follows:

%!PS-Adobe-2.0

This version identifier comment is identical in use to the similar 1.0 comment, except for the revision in version number. Note that the version identifier remains at 2.0 for documents adding the 2.1 comments.

There is a new feature added to this comment; it may now contain one of three *keywords* following the 2.0. These keywords indicate to a document manager that the following document belongs to certain special classes of documents, so that it can change modes of processing, if required. These keywords are:

EPSF   This indicates that the following file is in a special format, known as "encapsulated PostScript." Such files primarily produce illustrations, and the format is designed to allow them to be included easily in other documents. The EPSF keyword can be followed by a version number.

Query   This indicates that the entire job that follows consists of PostScript query commands. This is discussed below in the section on Query Comments.

ExitServer   This indicates a job that will modify the persistent information in PostScript by issuing an **exitserver** operator.

The *header* comments proper begin immediately after the version identifier and end with **%%EndComments** or with any line that doesn't begin with '%%'. Where specific information can be postponed to the trailer section, as described earlier, the appropriate header keyword must be followed by the value (**atend**) instead of the data value or values described below.

The following comments are identical in use to the 1.0 comments of the same name.

%%Title: title

gives the title of the document. This can be any text and is terminated only by a newline. The title is used for identifying documents; in some environments, this might be a file name, or it might be formatted to be machine-readable.

%%Creator: name

the name of the person, user, or program (or maybe all of the above) who generated the PostScript document. This may be different from the person or user designated to receive the document, which may be designated by the **%%For** comment (see below). The name consists of any arbitrary text, terminated by a newline.

%%CreationDate: text

gives the date and time of the creation of the document. There is no specific format for this information; all that is expected is that the text will be readable as a date and a time by humans. Generally, this will come from the system in whatever the standard system format may be.

%%For: userid

this is the identification of the person or user who gets the output; if this comment is absent, the output destination is presumed to be the same as the **%%Creator**.

%%Pages: number [page order]

this is a non-negative, decimal integer that represents the number of pages expected to be produced on the output device. If no pages will be output, the number 0 should be inserted. The optional page order argument is provided to allow document managers to reorder pages if appropriate. Allowable values are −*1*, indicating that the document pages have been produced in **descending** (last page to first page) order; *1*, indicating that the document pages are in **ascending** (first page to last page) order; and *0*, indicating a special order. The *0* value indicates that the pages are in some defined order that must not be altered by the document manager; for example, signature order. In the absence of a page order value, the document manager may, at its option, reorder pages within the document; however, if the *0* value is present, it must respect the existing page sequence and not alter it. This comment also can be deferred to the trailer section by use of (**atend**).

%%BoundingBox: llx lly urx ury

this gives the dimensions of the box that bounds all the marks on a PostScript page. If the PostScript program produces more than one page, this is the largest box that bounds any page. The values are the x and y coordinates of the lower left and upper right corners of the page given in the default user coordinate system. This comment may be deferred to the trailer section by use of (**atend**). This comment is required for EPSF files.

%%DocumentFonts: font font font . . .

lists the fonts used in the document by their PostScript names. This comment can be deferred to a trailer by use of the (**atend**) specification.

%%EndComments

this comment explicitly ends the header section of the PostScript program. It is not required, since any line that does not begin with the characters '%%' or '%!' will also automatically terminate the header, as explained above.

There are a series of new header comments that have been added, as follows:

%%Routing: text

This comment provides information about how to route a document in a networked environment. The contents and format are system- and site-dependent.

%%Requirements: keyword keyword . . .

This comment contains keywords that define document requirements for specific physical features on a printer, such as duplex printing, collating, color printing, and so on. The nature and precise meaning of the keywords will be site-specific.

%%ProofMode: keyword

This comment contains a keyword that defines the action taken by a document manager when it discovers a lack of resources for printing a document or when it discovers an error within a document. There are three keywords currently defined, as follows:

TrustMe
Substitute
NotifyMe

These keywords define messages to the document manager. If it discovers errors in the document, or finds that the requested resources, such as certain fonts or certain paper sizes, for example, are not available, then these messages tell what action the author wishes to be taken.

The **TrustMe** message tells the document manager that the author has additional information regarding the state of the system, network, or device, and wishes the document printed regardless of the conditions noted. The assumption is the the document author has taken care of the condition, no matter what that may be. Obviously, such an instruction should only be used when you don't mind having the output even with an error.

The **Substitute** message tells the document manager to make the best substitution that is available to it, and continue processing. This is should be the default, and will usually result in a close approximation of the desired output. In this mode, the document manager may, for example, substitute fonts when requested fonts are not available, or may scale pages to compensate for a missing paper size.

The **NotifyMe** message asks the document manager to not continue processing if there is an error or resource lack, but instead to notify the originator or sender of the document. This would be appropriate, for example, where the cost of processing or outputting the document is high, and an unsatisfactory page is not an acceptable alternative.

These messages apply to errors and resource lacks discovered by the document manager itself, and are not passed on the interpreter. If an error occurs during processing a document, the normal PostScript error handling mechanisms will deal with it, independently of this convention.

%%DocumentNeededFonts: fontname fontname . . .

This comment, if used, lists fonts that are required within the document and are not contained within it. These fonts would presumably be downloaded by the document manager prior to execution of the document. It is assumed that there will be corresponding **%%IncludeFont** directives for each font listed here.

%%DocumentSuppliedFonts: fontname fontname . . .

This comment provides a list of all the fonts that are provided within the document description itself. It is assumed that there will be at least one **%%BeginFont** and **%%EndFont** pair of comments within the document for each font listed here.

Note two things about these conventions. First, the **%%DocumentNeeded** and the **%%DocumentSupplied** comments are complementary, since fonts that are included will not be provided by the document manager and vice versa. There are several more pairs of comments in the header that follow this same format and have essentially the same meaning. There is a difference between the two comments, however, in that **%%DocumentNeeded** is essential if the corresponding **%%Include** is used, but the **%%DocumentSupplied** comment is optional. Second, not all fonts used in the document need to be listed in either of these comments, since it is possible that the document uses only fonts that are already loaded and available in the printer (as our own examples do).

There are a series of similar comments, which we will list here without additional discussion.

%%DocumentNeededProcSets: name version revision . . .
%%DocumentSuppliedProcSets: name version revision . . .
%%DocumentNeededFiles: filename filename . . .
%%DocumentSuppliedFiles: filename filename . . .

These comments have the same format and perform the same function for procedure sets and files that the preceding ones had for fonts. They also have corresponding **%%Include** and **%%Begin** and **%%End** comments associated with them.

With the release of Illustrator 88 by Adobe Systems in May of 1988, some additional header comments that support color processing and color handling in a document have been added. These comments are not required for most documents; however, if you are using color in your document, they may be essential to provide post-processing by service programs like Adobe's Separator (which can produce four-color separations from a color-encoded file). A full discussion of color printing and handling is beyond the scope of this appendix. The comments required for this type of color processing are presented here without much explanation; if you need further explanation consult the documentation that is available from your device manufacturer or software supplier.

All of these comments are placed in the document header. The following are the color header comments.

%%ColorUsage: Black&White
or
%%ColorUsage: Color

This comment allows you to specify whether the document uses only black ink (Black&White) or whether it uses all four process colors (Color). Note that these are specific names and must be used this way; also, (**atend**) is allowed for this comment.

%%DocumentProcessColors: name . . .
%%+ name . . .

where *name* can be Cyan, Magenta, Yellow or Black. The document is expected to use just the process inks specified. If this comment does not appear, the document is expected to use all four process colors. The (**atend**) specification is allowed.

The following comments allow you to specify how custom colors are defined and used within a document. We will not discuss here the use and handling of custom colors, but you should have some knowledge of color printing requirements and color usage before you use these comments.

%%DocumentCustomColors: string

If this comment is absent, the document is presumed to use no custom colors. The *string* may be any name that describes the custom color except for (Process Cyan), (Process Magenta), (Process Yellow), or (Process Black), which are reserved for application use; for example, it might be 'PMS 284 Yellow', or some other standard color nomenclature. The (**atend**) specification is allowed.

%%GreyCustomColor: gray string
%%RGBCustomColor: red green blue string
%%HSBCustomColor: hue saturation brightness string
%%CMYKCustomColor: cyan magenta yellow black string

All of these comments define a custom color's process color approximation. All of them can be continued in the usual fashion, and the (**atend**) specification is allowed.

Finally, there are a series of document level requirements that can be included in the header. These are mostly self-explanatory, and are as follows:

%%DocumentPaperSizes: sizename sizename . . .
%%DocumentPaperForms: formname formname . . .
%%DocumentPaperColors: colorname colorname . . .
%%DocumentPaperWeights: integer integer
%%DocumentPrinterRequired: networkname productname
    [version] [revision] . . .

Body Comments

The body comments break up the executable portion of a PostScript program into the prologue and the individual pages of the script. If a utility program acts on a structured PostScript program, it must respect these markers and keep the structure intact as it operates on the program text. In particular, it must retain the prologue at the beginning (since the pages in the script portion depend upon it), and it must retain any trailer information at the end.

The *prologue* begins with the first line of the PostScript program that does not begin with the characters '%%' or '%!', or it begins with the first line after the **%%EndComments** statement that terminates the header section. The only comment in the prologue is:

%%EndProlog

which explicitly terminates the prologue section of the PostScript program. This comment is required in minimally conforming programs.

Body comments may appear anywhere in a document and are designed to provide structural information about the organization of the document. In particular, many body comments are designed to match related information provided in the Header Comments section.

%%BeginSetup
%%EndSetup

This pair of comments delimits information that performs device setup functions. This comment is unusual because it must come immediately after the prologue, that is, after the **%%EndProlog** comment. It forms the first part of the script, before any page output is generated.

%%BeginDocument: name [version] [type]
%%EndDocument

These comments delimit an entire document file when it is included within another document description.

%%BeginFont: fontname [printername]
%%EndFont

These comments delimit a downloaded font that is included within a document. The optional *printername* is intended for use in networked environments where fonts may be tied to certain printers by license or other registration arrangements.

%%BeginProcSet: name version revision
%%EndProcSet

%%BeginFile: filename
%%EndFile

These comments delimit procedure sets and files contained within the document.

%%BeginBinary: bytecount
%%EndBinary

These comments delimit binary information included within a page description (such as data for the **image** operator). They are provided because binary data can cause severe difficulties for a document manager during processing.

%%BeginPaperSize: sizename
%%EndPaperSize

These comments delimit code that invokes procedures to set a particular paper size.

%%BeginFeature: featuretype [option]
%%EndFeature

These comments delimit code that invokes specific printer features as defined and described in the printer PPD file (see definition of PPD files above). The *featuretype* must correspond exactly to one of the keywords in the PPD file.

%%BeginExitServer: password
%%EndExitServer

These comments delimit code that exits the normal server loop and installs procedures or other code into the PostScript memory for retention beyond the end-of-job. This was discussed in Part I, Section C2.1. If used, the job should begin with the **ExitServer** keyword in the version identifier comment. See discussion of keywords for the version identifier, above.

Page Comments

The *script* begins with the first line of the PostScript program following the 'EndProlog'. The following comments are placed in the script code to mark page boundaries and to provide page information. These page-level comments are all self-explanatory; they mirror at the page level the information discussed above at a document level. They are as follows:

%%Page: label number

marks the beginning of an individual page within the document. The *label* and the *number* identify the page according to two methods. The *label* value is a text string that gives the page identification according to the document's internal numbering or labeling scheme. For example, this might be page ix of the introduction or page 2-4 (meaning the fourth page of chapter 2, for example). The *number,* on the other hand, is a positive integer that gives the position of this page within the normal document output. This number begins at 1 and runs through *n* for an *n*-page document. This information is intended to be useful to utility programs; using this information, they can retrieve pages by either the internal page descriptions, i.e., "pages 2–4 through 2–9," or they can retrieve pages by position, i.e., "the last 10 pages." It also allows pages to be handled in nonsequential order, for example, to produce pages in folio order for bookbinding.

%%PageFonts: font font font . . .

This comment lists the fonts required on the current page. These will be a subset of the fonts listed in the **%%DocumentFonts** header. Generally, this comment is only useful when many fonts are used in a document and you (or an application or utility program) need to manage the fonts at the output device on a page level. This usually happens when the number of fonts in a document exceeds the memory capacity of the output device.

%%PageFiles: filename filename filename . . .
%%PageBoundingBox: llx lly urx ury

%%PageProcessColors: keyword keyword . . .
%%PageCustom Colors: string

%%BeginPageSetup
%%EndPageSetup

%%BeginObject: [name] [code]
%%EndObject

This last pair of comments delimits individual graphic elements on a page in circumstances where it is useful or necessary for the document manager to extract or recognize such portions of a page.

The end of the last page of the script marks the beginning of the trailer processing, which begins with the comment:

%%Trailer

which ends the script portion of the program and marks the beginning of the trailer section (if any). Any non-comment PostScript commands that follow this comment are presumed to be cleanup or otherwise not part of the page output.

The *trailer* section begins immediately after the **%%Trailer** comment that terminates the script. The trailer section consists of cleanup procedures, such as restoring the state of the printer, removing dictionaries used during processing from the dictionary stack, and so on, as well as information that has been deferred from the header section by use of the (**atend**) parameter.

The order of the header and trailer comments is not generally significant. It becomes important only if there is more than one comment with the same keyword. In that case, the data from the *first* header with the duplicated keyword is retained and used; for a trailer, the data is taken from the *last* keyword. This allows a utility program to modify the header and trailer information by simply placing the new header at the front of the PostScript program – after the version identifier, of course – and placing a new trailer at the end of the program, without having to delete any of the previous structural data. Remember, however, that the trailer data will be used only if there is a header with the same keyword and the (**atend**) data specification.

1.3 RESOURCE REQUIREMENTS

These comments may occur anywhere In a document, and they indicate that the named resource is required and should be included in the document at the point where the comment is encountered. It is essential that no resource request occur in the body of the document unless a corresponding comment indicating the requirement has been included in the header section.

These comments all form a matching set with previously discussed header comments, and so further discussion here is kept to a minimum. The resource requirement comments are as follows:

%%IncludeFont: fontname
%%IncludeProcSet: name version revision
%%IncludeFile: filename
%%ExecuteFile: filename

This comment has the same function as the **%%IncludeFile** comment, but indicates that the requested file is an executable page description, rather than (for example) a prologue. Essentially this means that the probably contains at least one **showpage** operator.

%%ChangeFont: fontname
%%PaperForm: formname
%%PaperColor: colorname
%%PaperWeight: integer
%%PaperSize: sizename
%%Feature: featuretype [option]
%%EOF

This last comment is used to request that the document manager transmit an end-of-file indication to the PostScript printer in circumstances where the application itself cannot imbed such a character in a file.

1.4   QUERY CONVENTIONS

A *query* is defined as any PostScript program that will generate some response back to the originator across the communications channel that links the host and the output device. Examples of operators that would qualify under this definition are = = and **pstack**. The query conventions defined in the 2.1 convention set are designed to allow applications to determine the status of certain resources before generation of a page description.

All the query comments consist of a *BEGIN, END* pair of comments with keywords indicating the type of query performed by the code contained in the comments. For all the comments, the *END* comment includes a *default value,* which the document manager will return to the application as a response if it cannot understand or does not support the given query. This default value is entirely dependent upon the application.

The possible queries are as follows:

%!PS-Adobe-2.0 Query

This form of the version identifier comment indicates that what follows is a query program rather than a page description. All queries, to be fully transparent in a network environment, should be sent as separate jobs.

%%?BeginQuery: identifier
%%?EndQuery: default

%%?BeginPrinterQuery
%%?EndPrinterQuery: default

%%?BeginVMStatus
%%?EndVMStatus: default

%%?BeginFeatureQuery: featuretype option
%%?EndFeatureQuery: default

%%?BeginFileQuery: filename
%%?EndFileQuery: default

%%?BeginFontQuery: fontname fontname . . .
%%?EndFontQuery: default

%%?BeginFontListQuery
%%?EndFontListQuery

%%?BeginProcSetQuery: name version revision
%%?EndProcSetQuery: default

These sets each have specific application, most of which should be obvious to you by now. The set **%%?BeginQuery** and **%%?EndQuery** are the only ones that do not have a specific meaning; they are provided for installations who need to define installation-specific queries and can now do so using this method.

Appendix B

Standard Font Construction

This appendix provides information on the structure of standard PostScript fonts. A complete discussion of font construction and use is given in sections I-A5.4 and I-B3.3. Each PostScript font has a set of charaters that it can represent, which are given in the **Char-Strings** dictionary within the font; and each character is mapped into the **CharStrings** dictionary by the **Encoding** array in the font. This appendix provides a look at both the standard encoding and the characters that are available for text fonts and for the Symbol font that are installed in all PostScript printers.

Figures III-B1.1 and III-B1.2 present the **Encoding** arrays for standard text fonts and for the Symbol font respectively. The tables are organized to show the octal value of the character as an index and the associated character in the matching box. Octal codes are used because these are easily inserted into PostScript strings and are the most common way of identifying uncommon characters with strings. The octal code is constructed with the high-order two digits running vertically along the left side and the low-order digit running along the top. Empty spaces are unused by the standard encodings. The first 32 characters and the last character are shaded to remind you that these positions, although not used by the encoding, are used in the standard ASCII encoding for transmission control.

Figure III-B1.3 shows the standard ASCII control character values for the first 31 positions along with those charcters that are specifically recognized by the PostScript interpreter. The control codes indicated for the PostScript values are those that can be produced by the keyboard. Rememeber that all PostScript characters can be inserted into strings and printed using only characters between octal 40 (decimal 32), the space, and octal 177 (decimal 127). Such characters never have the high-order position within the byte set on and so are completely transparent to most networking and transmission protocols. The last character, octal 377 or hexadecimal 'FF', is often used as a marker within transmisssions, since all bits of the character are on.

Figure III-B2.1 and III-B2.2 list the standard encoding arrays for text fonts (**StandardEncoding**) and for the Symbol font (**SymbolEncoding**). The figure shows the array position in both decimal and octal values along with the corresponding character and the character name. Remember that the character name is the method used to access the procedure that draws the character in the **CharStrings** dictionary associated with the font. All values not shown correspond to the empty spaces in the previous tables; within the actual array, each of these positions is filled with the special name '\.notdef', which corresponds to a null procedure in the **CharStrings** dictionary.

Figures III-B3.1 and III-B3.2 present the complete listings of the **CharStrings** dictionary for standard text fonts and for the Symbol font, sorted by character name. This shows the possible range of characters that can be accessed within a given font. Characters that are included in the standard encoding for the font show the octal code that corresponds to the character in the **Encoding** vector; characters that are unencoded in standard fonts are shown with a '−'.

Figure III-B1.1 Table of Standard Text Encoding

octal code	*--0*	*--1*	*--2*	*--3*	*--4*	*--5*	*--6*	*--7*
\00-								
\01-								
\02-								
\03-								
\04-		!	"	#	$	%	&	’
\05-	(	)	*	+	,	-	.	/
\06-	0	1	2	3	4	5	6	7
\07-	8	9	:	;	<	=	>	?
\10-	@	A	B	C	D	E	F	G
\11-	H	I	J	K	L	M	N	O
\12-	P	Q	R	S	T	U	V	W
\13-	X	Y	Z	[	\	]	^	_
\14-	‘	a	b	c	d	e	f	g
\15-	h	i	j	k	l	m	n	o
\16-	p	q	r	s	t	u	v	w
\17-	x	y	z	{	|	}	~	
\20-								
\21-								
\22-								
\23-								
\24-		¡	¢	£	⁄	¥	ƒ	§
\25-	¤	'	“	«	‹	›	ﬁ	ﬂ
\26-		–	†	‡	·		¶	•
\27-	‚	„	”	»	…	‰		¿
\30-		`	´	ˆ	˜	¯	˘	˙
\31-	¨		˚	¸		˝	˛	ˇ
\32-	—							
\33-								
\34-		Æ		ª				
\35-	Ł	Ø	Œ	º				
\36-		æ				ı		
\37-	ł	ø	œ	ß				

Figure III-B1.2   Table of Symbol Encoding

octal code	--0	--1	--2	--3	--4	--5	--6	--7
\00-								
\01-								
\02-								
\03-								
\04-		!	∀	#	∃	%	&	∋
\05-	(	)	*	+	,	−	.	/
\06-	0	1	2	3	4	5	6	7
\07-	8	9	:	;	<	=	>	?
\10-	≅	Α	Β	Χ	Δ	Ε	Φ	Γ
\11-	Η	Ι	ϑ	Κ	Λ	Μ	Ν	Ο
\12-	Π	Θ	Ρ	Σ	Τ	Υ	ς	Ω
\13-	Ξ	Ψ	Ζ	[	∴	]	⊥	_
\14-	‾	α	β	χ	δ	ε	φ	γ
\15-	η	ι	φ	κ	λ	μ	ν	ο
\16-	π	θ	ρ	σ	τ	υ	ϖ	ω
\17-	ξ	ψ	ζ	{	|	}	~	
\20-								
\21-								
\22-								
\23-								
\24-		ϒ	′	≤	⁄	∞	ƒ	♣
\25-	♦	♥	♠	↔	←	↑	→	↓
\26-	°	±	″	≥	×	∝	∂	•
\27-	÷	≠	≡	≈	…	|	—	↵
\30-	ℵ	ℑ	ℜ	℘	⊗	⊕	∅	∩
\31-	∪	⊃	⊇	⊄	⊂	⊆	∈	∉
\32-	∠	∇	®	©	™	∏	√	·
\33-	¬	∧	∨	⇔	⇐	⇑	⇒	⇓
\34-	◊	®	⟨	©	™	Σ	⎛	⎜
\35-	⎝	⎡	⎢	⎣	⎧	⎨	⎩	⎪
\36-		⟩	⌠	⎞	⎟	⎠	⎞	⎟
\37-	⎞	⎤	⎥	⎦	⎫	⎬	⎭	

Figure III-B1.3 Standard ASCII Control Characters

decimal code	octal code	ASCII name	
0	\000	/NUL	
1	\001	/SOH	
2	\002	/STX	
3	\003	/ETX	also PostScript interrupt: Control-C
4	\004	/EOT	also PostScript end-of-file: Control-D
5	\005	/ENQ	
6	\006	/ACK	
7	\007	/BEL	
8	\010	/BS	
9	\011	/HT	
10	\012	/LF	PostScript end-of-line: Line-feed
11	\013	/VT	
12	\014	/FF	
13	\015	/CR	PostScript end-of-line: Return
14	\016	/SO	
15	\017	/SI	
16	\020	/DLE	
17	\021	/DC1	also XON flow control: Control-Q
18	\022	/DC2	
19	\023	/DC3	also XOFF flow control: Control-S
20	\024	/DC4	also PostScript status query: Control-T
21	\025	/NAK	
22	\026	/SYN	
23	\027	/ETB	
24	\030	/CAN	
25	\031	/EM	
26	\032	/SUB	
27	\033	/ESC	
28	\034	/FS	
29	\035	/GS	
30	\036	/RS	
31	\037	/US	

Figure III-B2.1 Listing of StandardEncoding

decimal	octal	char	name	decimal	octal	char	name
32	\040		space	51	\063	3	three
33	\041	!	exclam	52	\064	4	four
34	\042	"	quotedbl	53	\065	5	five
35	\043	#	numbersign	54	\066	6	six
36	\044	$	dollar	55	\067	7	seven
37	\045	%	percent	56	\070	8	eight
38	\046	&	ampersand	57	\071	9	nine
39	\047	'	quoteright	58	\072	:	colon
40	\050	(	parenleft	59	\073	;	semicolon
41	\051	)	parenright	60	\074	<	less
42	\052	*	asterisk	61	\075	=	equal
43	\053	+	plus	62	\076	>	greater
44	\054	,	comma	63	\077	?	question
45	\055	-	hyphen	64	\100	@	at
46	\056	.	period	65	\101	A	A
47	\057	/	slash	66	\102	B	B
48	\060	0	zero	67	\103	C	C
49	\061	1	one	68	\104	D	D
50	\062	2	two	69	\105	E	E

Figure III-B2.1 *continued*

decimal	octal	char	name		decimal	octal	char	name
70	\106	F	F		126	\176	~	asciitilde
71	\107	G	G		161	\241	¡	exclamdown
72	\110	H	H		162	\242	¢	cent
73	\111	I	I		163	\243	£	sterling
74	\112	J	J		164	\244	/	fraction
75	\113	K	K		165	\245	¥	yen
76	\114	L	L		166	\246	ƒ	florin
77	\115	M	M		167	\247	§	section
78	\116	N	N		168	\250	¤	currency
79	\117	O	O		169	\251	'	quotesingle
80	\120	P	P		170	\252	"	quotedblleft
81	\121	Q	Q		171	\253	«	guillemotleft
82	\122	R	R		172	\254	‹	guilsinglleft
83	\123	S	S		173	\255	›	guilsinglright
84	\124	T	T		174	\256	fi	fi
85	\125	U	U		175	\257	fl	fl
86	\126	V	V		177	\261	–	endash
87	\127	W	W		178	\262	†	dagger
88	\130	X	X		179	\263	‡	daggerdbl
89	\131	Y	Y		180	\264	·	periodcentered
90	\132	Z	Z		182	\266	¶	paragraph
91	\133	[	bracketleft		183	\267	•	bullet
92	\134	\	backslash		184	\270	‚	quotesinglbase
93	\135	]	bracketright		185	\271	„	quotedblbase
94	\136	^	asciicircum		186	\272	"	quotedblright
95	\137	_	underscore		187	\273	»	guillemotright
96	\140	`	quoteleft		188	\274	…	ellipsis
97	\141	a	a		189	\275	‰	perthousand
98	\142	b	b		191	\277	¿	questiondown
99	\143	c	c		193	\301	`	grave
100	\144	d	d		194	\302	´	acute
101	\145	e	e		195	\303	^	circumflex
102	\146	f	f		196	\304	~	tilde
103	\147	g	g		197	\305	¯	macron
104	\150	h	h		198	\306	˘	breve
105	\151	i	i		199	\307	·	dotaccent
106	\152	j	j		200	\310	¨	dieresis
107	\153	k	k		202	\312	°	ring
108	\154	l	l		203	\313	¸	cedilla
109	\155	m	m		205	\315	˝	hungarumlaut
110	\156	n	n		206	\316	˛	ogonek
111	\157	o	o		207	\317	ˇ	caron
112	\160	p	p		208	\320	—	emdash
113	\161	q	q		225	\341	Æ	AE
114	\162	r	r		227	\343	ª	ordfeminine
115	\163	s	s		232	\350	Ł	Lslash
116	\164	t	t		233	\351	Ø	Oslash
117	\165	u	u		234	\352	Œ	OE
118	\166	v	v		235	\353	º	ordmasculine
119	\167	w	w		241	\361	æ	ae
120	\170	x	x		245	\365	ı	dotlessi
121	\171	y	y		248	\370	ł	lslash
122	\172	z	z		249	\371	ø	oslash
123	\173	{	braceleft		250	\372	œ	oe
124	\174	|	bar		251	\373	ß	germandbls
125	\175	}	braceright					

Figure III-B2.2 Listing of SymbolEncoding

decimal	octal	char	name	decimal	octal	char	name
32	\040		space	91	\133	[	bracketleft
33	\041	!	exclam	92	\134	∴	therefore
34	\042	∀	universal	93	\135	]	bracketright
35	\043	#	numbersign	94	\136	⊥	perpendicular
36	\044	∃	existential	95	\137	_	underscore
37	\045	%	percent	96	\140	‾	radicalex
38	\046	&	ampersand	97	\141	α	alpha
39	\047	∋	suchthat	98	\142	β	beta
40	\050	(	parenleft	99	\143	χ	chi
41	\051	)	parenright	100	\144	δ	delta
42	\052	*	asteriskmath	101	\145	ε	epsilon
43	\053	+	plus	102	\146	φ	phi
44	\054	,	comma	103	\147	γ	gamma
45	\055	−	minus	104	\150	η	eta
46	\056	.	period	105	\151	ι	iota
47	\057	/	slash	106	\152	φ	phi1
48	\060	0	zero	107	\153	κ	kappa
49	\061	1	one	108	\154	λ	lambda
50	\062	2	two	109	\155	μ	mu
51	\063	3	three	110	\156	ν	nu
52	\064	4	four	111	\157	o	omicron
53	\065	5	five	112	\160	π	pi
54	\066	6	six	113	\161	θ	theta
55	\067	7	seven	114	\162	ρ	rho
56	\070	8	eight	115	\163	σ	sigma
57	\071	9	nine	116	\164	τ	tau
58	\072	:	colon	117	\165	υ	upsilon
59	\073	;	semicolon	118	\166	ϖ	omega1
60	\074	<	less	119	\167	ω	omega
61	\075	=	equal	120	\170	ξ	xi
62	\076	>	greater	121	\171	ψ	psi
63	\077	?	question	122	\172	ζ	zeta
64	\100	≅	congruent	123	\173	{	braceleft
65	\101	A	Alpha	124	\174	|	bar
66	\102	B	Beta	125	\175	}	braceright
67	\103	X	Chi	126	\176	~	similar
68	\104	Δ	Delta	161	\241	Υ	Upsilon1
69	\105	E	Epsilon	162	\242	′	minute
70	\106	Φ	Phi	163	\243	≤	lessequal
71	\107	Γ	Gamma	164	\244	⁄	fraction
72	\110	H	Eta	165	\245	∞	infinity
73	\111	I	Iota	166	\246	ƒ	florin
74	\112	ϑ	theta1	167	\247	♣	club
75	\113	K	Kappa	168	\250	♦	diamond
76	\114	Λ	Lambda	169	\251	♥	heart
77	\115	M	Mu	170	\252	♠	spade
78	\116	N	Nu	171	\253	↔	arrowboth
79	\117	O	Omicron	172	\254	←	arrowleft
80	\120	Π	Pi	173	\255	↑	arrowup
81	\121	Θ	Theta	174	\256	→	arrowright
82	\122	P	Rho	175	\257	↓	arrowdown
83	\123	Σ	Sigma	176	\260	°	degree
84	\124	T	Tau	177	\261	±	plusminus
85	\125	Y	Upsilon	178	\262	″	second
86	\126	ς	sigma1	179	\263	≥	greaterequal
87	\127	Ω	Omega	180	\264	×	multiply
88	\130	Ξ	Xi	181	\265	∝	proportional
89	\131	Ψ	Psi	182	\266	∂	partialdiff
90	\132	Z	Zeta	183	\267	•	bullet

Figure III-B2.2 *continued*

decimal	octal	char	name
184	\270	÷	divide
185	\271	≠	notequal
186	\272	≡	equivalence
187	\273	≈	approxequal
188	\274	...	ellipsis
189	\275			arrowvertex
190	\276	—	arrowhorizex
191	\277	⌐	carriagereturn
192	\300	ℵ	aleph
193	\301	ℑ	Ifraktur
194	\302	ℜ	Rfraktur
195	\303	℘	weierstrass
196	\304	⊗	circlemultiply
197	\305	⊕	circleplus
198	\306	∅	emptyset
199	\307	∩	intersection
200	\310	∪	union
201	\311	⊃	propersuperset
202	\312	⊇	reflexsuperset
203	\313	⊄	notsubset
204	\314	⊂	propersubset
205	\315	⊆	reflexsubset
206	\316	∈	element
207	\317	∉	notelement
208	\320	∠	angle
209	\321	∇	gradient
210	\322	®	registerserif
211	\323	©	copyrightserif
212	\324	™	trademarkserif
213	\325	∏	product
214	\326	√	radical
215	\327	·	dotmath
216	\330	¬	logicalnot
217	\331	∧	logicaland
218	\332	∨	logicalor
219	\333	⇔	arrowdblboth
220	\334	⇐	arrowdblleft
221	\335	⇑	arrowdblup
222	\336	⇒	arrowdblright
223	\337	⇓	arrowdbldown

decimal	octal	char	name
224	\340	◊	lozenge
225	\341	⟨	angleleft
226	\342	®	registersans
227	\343	©	copyrightsans
228	\344	™	trademarksans
229	\345	Σ	summation
230	\346	⌠	parenlefttp
231	\347			parenleftex
232	\350	⌡	parenleftbt
233	\351	⌈	bracketlefttp
234	\352			bracketleftex
235	\353	⌊	bracketleftbt
236	\354	⌠	bracelefttp
237	\355	{	braceleftmid
238	\356	⌡	braceleftbt
239	\357			braceex
240	\360	●	apple
241	\361	⟩	angleright
242	\362	⌠	integral
243	\363	⌠	integraltp
244	\364			integralex
245	\365	⌡	integralbt
246	\366	⌉	parenrighttp
247	\367			parenrightex
248	\370	⌋	parenrightbt
249	\371	⌉	bracketrighttp
250	\372			bracketrightex
251	\373	⌋	bracketrightbt
252	\374	}	bracerighttp
253	\375	}	bracerightmid
254	\376	}	bracerightbt

Note:
The apple symbol (octal code \360)
  may not be encoded in non-Apple devices.

Figure III-B3.1 Display for Times-Roman Sorted List of CharStrings

char	octal	name	char	octal	name	char	octal	name
A	\101	A	P	\120	P	•	\267	bullet
Æ	\341	AE	Q	\121	Q	c	\143	c
Á	—	Aacute	R	\122	R	ˇ	\317	caron
Â	—	Acircumflex	S	\123	S	ç	—	ccedilla
Ä	—	Adieresis	Š	—	Scaron	,	\313	cedilla
À	—	Agrave	T	\124	T	¢	\242	cent
Å	—	Aring	U	\125	U	ˆ	\303	circumflex
Ã	—	Atilde	Ú	—	Uacute	:	\072	colon
B	\102	B	Û	—	Ucircumflex	,	\054	comma
C	\103	C	Ü	—	Udieresis	©	—	copyright
Ç	—	Ccedilla	Ù	—	Ugrave	¤	\250	currency
D	\104	D	V	\126	V	d	\144	d
E	\105	E	W	\127	W	†	\262	dagger
É	—	Eacute	X	\130	X	‡	\263	daggerdbl
Ê	—	Ecircumflex	Y	\131	Y	¨	\310	dieresis
Ë	—	Edieresis	Ÿ	—	Ydieresis	$	\044	dollar
È	—	Egrave	Z	\132	Z	˙	\307	dotaccent
F	\106	F	Ž	—	Zcaron	ı	\365	dotlessi
G	\107	G	a	\141	a	e	\145	e
H	\110	H	á	—	aacute	é	—	eacute
I	\111	I	â	—	acircumflex	ê	—	ecircumflex
Í	—	Iacute	´	\302	acute	ĕ	—	edieresis
Î	—	Icircumflex	ä	—	adieresis	è	—	egrave
Ï	—	Idieresis	æ	\361	ae	8	\070	eight
Ì	—	Igrave	à	—	agrave	…	\274	ellipsis
J	\112	J	&	\046	ampersand	—	\320	emdash
K	\113	K	å	—	aring	–	\261	endash
L	\114	L	^	\136	asciicircum	=	\075	equal
Ł	\350	Lslash	~	\176	asciitilde	!	\041	exclam
M	\115	M	*	\052	asterisk	¡	\241	exclamdown
N	\116	N	@	\100	at	f	\146	f
Ñ	—	Ntilde	ã	—	atilde	fi	\256	fi
O	\117	O	b	\142	b	5	\065	five
Œ	\352	OE	\	\134	backslash	fl	\257	fl
Ó	—	Oacute	|	\174	bar	ƒ	\246	florin
Ô	—	Ocircumflex	{	\173	braceleft	4	\064	four
Ö	—	Odieresis	}	\175	braceright	/	\244	fraction
Ò	—	Ograve	[	\133	bracketleft	g	\147	g
Ø	\351	Oslash	]	\135	bracketright	ß	\373	germandbls
Õ	—	Otilde	ˇ	\306	breve	`	\301	grave

Figure III-B3.1 *continued*

char	octal	name	char	octal	name	char	octal	name
>	\076	greater	œ	\372	oe	°	\312	ring
«	\253	guillemotleft	.	\316	ogonek	s	\163	s
»	\273	guillemotright	ò	—	ograve	š	—	scaron
‹	\254	guilsinglleft	1	\061	one	§	\247	section
›	\255	guilsinglright	ª	\343	ordfeminine	;	\073	semicolon
h	\150	h	º	\353	ordmasculine	7	\067	seven
˝	\315	hungarumlaut	ø	\371	oslash	6	\066	six
-	\055	hyphen	õ	—	otilde	/	\057	slash
i	\151	i	p	\160	p		\040	space
í	—	iacute	¶	\266	paragraph	£	\243	sterling
î	—	icircumflex	(	\050	parenleft	t	\164	t
ï	—	idieresis	)	\051	parenright	3	\063	three
ì	—	igrave	%	\045	percent	˜	\304	tilde
j	\152	j	.	\056	period	™	—	trademark
k	\153	k	·	\264	periodcentered	2	\062	two
l	\154	l	‰	\275	perthousand	u	\165	u
<	\074	less	+	\053	plus	ú	—	uacute
¬	—	logicalnot	q	\161	q	û	—	ucircumflex
ł	\370	lslash	?	\077	question	ü	—	udieresis
m	\155	m	¿	\277	questiondown	ù	—	ugrave
¯	\305	macron	"	\042	quotedbl	_	\137	underscore
—	—	minus	„	\271	quotedblbase	v	\166	v
n	\156	n	“	\252	quotedblleft	w	\167	w
9	\071	nine	”	\272	quotedblright	x	\170	x
ñ	—	ntilde	‘	\140	quoteleft	y	\171	y
#	\043	numbersign	’	\047	quoteright	ÿ	—	ydieresis
o	\157	o	‚	\270	quotesinglbase	¥	\245	yen
ó	—	oacute	'	\251	quotesingle	z	\172	z
ô	—	ocircumflex	r	\162	r	ž	—	zcaron
ŏ	—	odieresis	®	—	registered	0	\060	zero

Figure III-B3.2 Display for Symbol Sorted List of CharStrings

char	octal	name	char	octal	name	char	octal	name
A	\101	Alpha	⟩	\361	angleright	⌋	\373	bracketrightbt
B	\102	Beta	🍎	\360	apple	⎪	\372	bracketrightex
X	\103	Chi	≈	\273	approxequal	⌉	\371	bracketrighttp
Δ	\104	Delta	↔	\253	arrowboth	•	\267	bullet
E	\105	Epsilon	⇔	\333	arrowdblboth	⌐	\277	carriagereturn
H	\110	Eta	⇓	\337	arrowdbldown	χ	\143	chi
Γ	\107	Gamma	⇐	\334	arrowdblleft	⊗	\304	circlemultiply
ℑ	\301	Ifraktur	⇒	\336	arrowdblright	⊕	\305	circleplus
I	\111	Iota	⇑	\335	arrowdblup	♣	\247	club
K	\113	Kappa	↓	\257	arrowdown	:	\072	colon
Λ	\114	Lambda	—	\276	arrowhorizex	,	\054	comma
M	\115	Mu	←	\254	arrowleft	≅	\100	congruent
N	\116	Nu	→	\256	arrowright	©	\343	copyrightsans
Ω	\127	Omega	↑	\255	arrowup	©	\323	copyrightserif
O	\117	Omicron			\275	arrowvertex	°	\260	degree
Φ	\106	Phi	*	\052	asteriskmath	δ	\144	delta
Π	\120	Pi	|	\174	bar	♦	\250	diamond
Ψ	\131	Psi	β	\142	beta	+	\270	divide
ℜ	\302	Rfraktur			\357	braceex	·	\327	dotmath
P	\122	Rho	{	\173	braceleft	8	\070	eight
Σ	\123	Sigma	⎩	\356	braceleftbt	∈	\316	element
T	\124	Tau	⎨	\355	braceleftmid	...	\274	ellipsis
Θ	\121	Theta	⎧	\354	bracelefttp	∅	\306	emptyset
Υ	\125	Upsilon	}	\175	braceright	ε	\145	epsilon
ϒ	\241	Upsilon1	⎭	\376	bracerightbt	=	\075	equal
Ξ	\130	Xi	⎬	\375	bracerightmid	≡	\272	equivalence
Z	\132	Zeta	⎫	\374	bracerighttp	η	\150	eta
ℵ	\300	aleph	[	\133	bracketleft	!	\041	exclam
α	\141	alpha	⎣	\353	bracketleftbt	∃	\044	existential
&	\046	ampersand	⎢	\352	bracketleftex	5	\065	five
∠	\320	angle	⎡	\351	bracketlefttp	ƒ	\246	florin
⟨	\341	angleleft	]	\135	bracketright	4	\064	four

Figure III-B3.2 *continued*

char	octal	name	char	octal	name	char	octal	name
⁄	\244	fraction	ω	\167	omega	®	\342	registersans
γ	\147	gamma	ϖ	\166	omega1	®	\322	registerserif
∇	\321	gradient	o	\157	omicron	ρ	\162	rho
>	\076	greater	1	\061	one	″	\262	second
≥	\263	greaterequal	(	\050	parenleft	;	\073	semicolon
♥	\251	heart	⎛	\350	parenleftbt	7	\067	seven
∞	\245	infinity	⎜	\347	parenleftex	σ	\163	sigma
∫	\362	integral	⎛	\346	parenlefttp	ς	\126	sigma1
⌡	\365	integralbt	)	\051	parenright	~	\176	similar
⎮	\364	integralex	⎞	\370	parenrightbt	6	\066	six
⌠	\363	integraltp	⎟	\367	parenrightex	⁄	\057	slash
∩	\307	intersection	⎞	\366	parenrighttp		\040	space
ι	\151	iota	∂	\266	partialdiff	♠	\252	spade
κ	\153	kappa	%	\045	percent	϶	\047	suchthat
λ	\154	lambda	.	\056	period	Σ	\345	summation
<	\074	less	⊥	\136	perpendicular	τ	\164	tau
≤	\243	lessequal	φ	\146	phi	∴	\134	therefore
∧	\331	logicaland	ϕ	\152	phi1	θ	\161	theta
¬	\330	logicalnot	π	\160	pi	ϑ	\112	theta1
∨	\332	logicalor	+	\053	plus	3	\063	three
◊	\340	lozenge	±	\261	plusminus	™	\344	trademarksans
−	\055	minus	∏	\325	product	™	\324	trademarkserif
′	\242	minute	⊂	\314	propersubset	2	\062	two
μ	\155	mu	⊃	\311	propersuperset	_	\137	underscore
×	\264	multiply	∝	\265	proportional	∪	\310	union
9	\071	nine	ψ	\171	psi	∀	\042	universal
∉	\317	notelement	?	\077	question	υ	\165	upsilon
≠	\271	notequal	√	\326	radical	℘	\303	weierstrass
⊄	\313	notsubset	‾	\140	radicalex	ξ	\170	xi
ν	\156	nu	⊆	\315	reflexsubset	0	\060	zero
#	\043	numbersign	⊇	\312	reflexsuperset	ζ	\172	zeta

Notes:
Unlike the text fonts, the SYMBOL font contains no unencoded characters.
The apple symbol (octal code \360) may not be encoded in non-Apple devices.

Appendix C

Programming Environment

This appendix provides a brief summary of the programming environment that was used to create and test the PostScript programs used in this book to produce the figures and develop the cookbook – which are, to a large extent, the same materials – and to test error conditions and output for the PostScript general operators. This information is provided for several reasons. First, so you can reproduce it if you want. Second, to give you, as a programmer, some ideas for your own programming setup. Finally, to provide identification of the precise conditions that were used in this process, to eliminate possible problems with versions or features, and to provide some idea of the range of PostScript environments.

The majority of program and operator testing was done using a Macintosh SE and an Apple LaserWriter running Adobe's PostScript language interpreter, version 38.0. This is one of the most common configurations available, so it seemed a good choice for testing and for programming. The Macintosh has System version 4.2 and Finder version 6.0. The programming and testing were done using the interactive mode of the PostScript interpreter, using the Lasertalk ® PostScript programming environment. This was an enormous help, since Lasertalk allows a PostScript programmer to immediately see stack and dictionary changes and has a Preview mode for viewing graphics before they are printed; it provides, as well, a substantial amount of on-line help information. I myself did the testing, development, and debugging, with the exception of some operator tests that were performed by Randy Adams, President of Emerald City Software and creator of Lasertalk, for the purposes of checking and confirming my results.

Many of the operator functions and error reporting, along with some of the programs, were also tested on a QMS PS810, running PostScript version 47.0. This provided a check for those variations that were the results of errors or anomalies in a single version of the PostScript interpreter. Some of the processing and testing were also done using a Zenith Data Systems 386 computer, running MS-DOS 3.21 and Windows 386. Here, too, Lasertalk/PC was used for a programming environment, connected to the LaserWriter by a serial port at 9600 baud. This resulted in a simple transition from the Macintosh to the MS-DOS and an easy way to check the correctness of certain programs when the Macintosh wasn't available.

Device-dependent operators were derived by dictionary printouts from a variety of PostScript devices, including the following: Apple LaserWriter (version 38.0) and Laser-Writer Plus (version 42.2), Texas Instruments Omnilaser™ 2106 (version 45.0), QMS PS-800+ (version 47.0), Agfa P400PS (version 42.0), and Linotronic 100 (versions 38.0 and 42.0). In most cases, these and other devices were not used as test vehicles but were used simply to provide a listing of the operators in the **systemdict**, **errordict**, and **status-dict** dictionaries. These lists were then cross-referenced to provide the selection of device-dependent operators presented in the text; generally, only device operators that appeared in several of the printers were included. Of course, the complete listing of all the device-dependent features of these printers – or any others, for that matter – is presented in the PostScript language supplement that is available for each device from the printer manufac-turer. As a programmer, you should see this supplement as your primary guide to the availability and use of the features that are installed on any specific printing device, and you can use the PPD file for automated access to these features; the discussion in the text will have provided you with the general understanding to make the best and most effec-tive use of this information.

The information on the PhoenixPage controller was provided by Phoenix Technolo-gies and tested on a prerelease version of its software made available at its Cambridge, Massachusetts, and Scott Valley, California, offices. In addition to the testing that I did personally, some of the testing was carried out by Phoenix technical personnel at my request.

For programmers not familiar with the Lasertalk PostScript programming environ-ment, further information can be obtained by writing Emerald City Software at the ad-dress below:

Emerald City Software
P.O. Box 2103
Menlo Park, CA 94026
(415) 324-8080

Appendix D

PhoenixPage

This appendix describes the PhoenixPage control system and discusses it in relation to the PostScript language. PhoenixPage was developed by Phoenix Technologies and includes a page description language interpreter that is compatible with the PostScript page description language described in the body of this book. This appendix provides an overview of the PhoenixPage design philosophy and a detailed review of the special characteristics of the PhoenixPage interpreter that provides PostScript language compatibility. It includes sections on the PhoenixPage design structure, its font handling capabilities, differences from the PostScript language described in this book, and a selection of device-dependent operators that are unique to PhoenixPage.

1.1 PHOENIXPAGE DESIGN

PhoenixPage includes a page description language interpreter developed by Phoenix Technologies and licensed to a variety of printer manufacturers for use in their output devices. It is designed to provide fast, efficient page descriptions that are operationally compatible with the PostScript page description language described in this book. But before we discuss the characteristics of the PhoenixPage interpreter, we need to discuss what "operationally compatible" means for you, as a programmer.

PostScript Compatibility

PhoenixPage is designed to be operationally compatible with the PostScript language. That means that page descriptions that have been created according to the standard PostScript language rules – as presented in this book, for example – can be executed on a PhoenixPage output device with no further changes. The output from such page descriptions will be equivalent, but not necessarily identical at the pixel level, to the output produced by such descriptions on a PostScript device, using the standard Adobe Systems PostScript interpreter. *Equivalent output* means that graphic images have the same shape, placement, and structure as they would have on a standard PostScript output device with the same resolution. Text output has the same character measurements, which means that lines of text break at the same points and that individual characters can be precisely substituted for graphic effects and so on; however, the precise shape (or outline) of the characters may differ.

As we have noted several times throughout this book, PostScript is a dynamic and growing environment. For obvious reasons, any language that attempts to provide complete functional equivalence to the PostScript language must choose some fixed version of the language to match. PhoenixPage version 1.0 is designed to match the PostScript language version 38.0 as implemented in the Apple LaserWriter Plus, with a few exceptions. These exceptions, which mostly have to do with anomalies in the version 38.0 PostScript implementation, are fully documented below. In most cases, PhoenixPage has simply adopted corrections implemented in later versions of the PostScript interpreter.

From a programmer's point of view, PhoenixPage generally provides the same features, operations, and functionality as the PostScript language described in the body of this book. Other than the anomalies mentioned above, due to corrections or adjustments to the version 38.0 PostScript, PhoenixPage generally provides additional functionality, a superset of that provided in the base PostScript language. This is most noticeable in the additional functions, described below, that are available in the interactive mode of the interpreter.

The PhoenixPage Design Approach

PhoenixPage uses a flexible design approach that adopts a modular architecture to enhance compatibility and performance. The result provides complete PostScript language compatibility along with the ability to emulate other page description languages and printer emulations. PhoenixPage itself is divided into two distinct but interlocked layers of software, the Printer Language Interpreter (PLI) and the Page Description Interface (PDI), that provide this functionality. The PLI layer provides the language interpretation capabilities that emulate the PostScript language, and it may include interpreters for other page description languages or other printer emulations as well. The PDI layer provides control of the imaging functions in the hardware and font management, and it also uses Phoenix's preprocessed font outlines for generating characters. This proprietary font-processing algorithm enables fast scaling and scan conversion from highly compressed font outlines. This layer also provides the hardware interfaces required for handling color processing or other special processing requirements.

1.2 PHOENIXPAGE REVIEW

Since PhoenixPage has been designed to be functionally compatible with the PostScript language, almost everything that we have said in the body of this book about PostScript is equally applicable to PhoenixPage. In particular, all the information about interpreter functions, operator definitions, and even device-dependent operators can be used with PhoenixPage as well as in any other device compatible with the PostScript language. This section of the appendix discusses and reviews those few areas where PhoenixPage operations differ from the programming of other devices that implement the PostScript language.

Font Handling

Font management and font handling are probably the most notable areas where you, as a programmer, will see a major difference between a device supporting PhoenixPage and one that supports standard PostScript as implemented by Adobe Systems. We have already mentioned one of the major differences between the PhoenixPage interpreter and the basic Adobe PostScript language interpreter: PhoenixPage uses a preprocessed outline technology to store and render fonts. Adobe Systems' interpreters use a proprietary font outline technology that, for legal and practical reasons, has not been copied in PhoenixPage. Instead, Phoenix Technologies has developed its own font technology to provide high quality and quick access to character renditions.

Another major difference between the PhoenixPage interpreter and the Adobe PostScript interpreter lies in the use of Adobe fonts. As mentioned above, all Adobe Systems PostScript language interpreters use font technology supplied by, and proprietary to, Adobe Systems. Fonts supplied by Adobe Systems use this technology and therefore cannot be used on any non-Adobe device. Any attempt to add Adobe fonts to any non-Adobe interpreter, whether PhoenixPage or any other, is likely to result in incorrect output and, generally, a major execution error. PhoenixPage itself uses font outlines supplied by Bitstream, but any fonts, whether supplied by Bitstream or another font vendor, that use standard PostScript definitions – that is, that do not use proprietary encoding techniques – can be used in PhoenixPage devices.

You may wonder why this problem arises. To a programmer, this is an interesting area for discussion. The problem arises because the human eye can see differences in character shapes at small point sizes on low- and medium-resolution (72 dpi to about 400 dpi) devices. In the original type design and setting process, where lead characters were used to set a line of type, characters at each point size were handcrafted with subtly different stroke weights to provide the correct, eye-appealing quality that the type designer had in mind. Thus, in 6-point type, the bowl of an 'a' for example, might be constructed with a thinner line, proportionally, than would be used at 16 points, in order to ensure that the center of the letter didn't fill in with ink and look too dark. By the same token, it is necessary to adjust the scan-conversion process for type outlines on raster output devices to prevent a similar problem from occurring when printing on devices where the dots used are large enough to be noticeable to the eye. In raster printing technology, such corrections are called "hints." Because Adobe Systems uses a proprietary "hint" technology that is imbedded into the fonts, its fonts do not print correctly with any non-Adobe interpreter.

If, in the future, Adobe Systems licenses its fonts, or if the outline format could be decoded without violation of the proprietary nature of the font encoding, then it would be possible to use these fonts, without the hints, on printers or other output devices that are otherwise compatible with the PostScript language.

The PhoenixPage interpreter currently provides resident, preprocessed font outlines designed by Bitstream. These fonts are equivalent to the resident fonts that are provided in an Adobe PostScript interpreter. These preprocessed outline fonts use their own "hints," supplied by Bitstream. The following is a table of the families of Bitstream fonts that will be used if a PostScript program requests the Adobe font family listed. This translation is automatic and transparent to the PostScript program.

Adobe font family	Bitstream font family
Times	Dutch 801
Courier	Courier
Helvetica	Swiss 721
Symbol	Symbol
Palatino	Zapf Calligraphic
Avant Garde	ITC Avant Garde
Bookman	ITC Bookman
Helvetica Narrow	Swiss 712
New Century Schoolbook	Century Schoolbook

In other words, if you execute a **findfont** operator using one of the Adobe names listed above, you automatically get the equivalent Bitstream font list next to it. These fonts are identical to the corresponding Adobe fonts in character width and height, but are not necessarily identical in outline. The net result is that all lines of type set in one font will match those set in the corresponding one – they will occupy the same space and break at the same point – so that justification and hyphenation routines in an application will work correctly for either. However, since the character outlines are not exactly the same, use of characters as graphic elements may not translate correctly from one application to another. If you are using character shapes as elements in a complex graphic design with other elements, it will be best if you deliberately choose the font you want rather than allow the transformation described above to take place. Also be sure to use the correct screen font to match the font that you are working with. Even if you are not doing graphic composition, it is better to use the proper Bitstream screen fonts while working with your document, so that your document composition will accurately reflect the final output. These screen fonts are available from Bitstream or from your PhoenixPage printer vendor. In addition, you should be aware that the Courier font provided by Bitstream is an outline font, whereas the Adobe version is a stroked font. This has no effect when the font is filled, as it normally would be, but may have some effect if you are using the **charpath** operator with Courier font characters.

General Operator Differences

The first set of differences between the PhoenixPage interpreter and the Adobe PostScript interpreter are not properly differences at all, but rather corrections to errors or discrepancies in operation between various versions of the PostScript interpreter. In most cases, PhoenixPage adopts the latest, corrected action that is implemented in any PostScript printer – generally, the action adopted in PostScript version 42.2 for the Apple Laser-Writer Plus. Programmers may wish to note these discrepancies, since they may affect processing in other, earlier versions of PostScript, such as the common version 38.0, implemented in many models of Apple LaserWriter and LaserWriter Plus. These exceptions are also discussed in the general operator reference section under the individual operator name.

The first exception is in the **idiv** operator. In early versions of PostScript, this operator does not correctly check for *realtype* operands; and it returns incorrect values for integer operands rather than raising the **typecheck** error as it should. Both PostScript versions (42.2 and later) and PhoenixPage correctly check for *realtype* operands.

In early versions of PostScript, the internal translation from rgb color values to hsb color values is incorrect. For example, in version 38.0, a set of rgb values of red: 1, green: 0, and blue: 0 returns hue: 0.000735187, saturation: 1.0, and brightness 0.301961 instead of the correct values, hue: 1.0, saturation: 1.0, and brightness: 1.0. Both PostScript (versions 42.2 and later) and PhoenixPage return the correct values.

Only in the LaserWriter version 38.0 (so far as I can tell) does the sequence of commands **0 array [ ] eq** return a *false* result under certain circumstances. This should always be *true*, and does not appear to fail on PostScript versions 42.2 or later or in PhoenixPage.

In addition to these corrected errors, there is a difference in processing between Post-Script version 38.0 and later versions in handling objects that have been processed with the **noaccess** operator. Consider the following sequence of commands.

[1 2] cvx noaccess xcheck

This creates a literal array containing the two integer elements, 1 and 2, changes the literal/executable attribute of that array from literal to executable, and then sets the access attribute to forbid any access – write, read, or execute. It then, finally, tests for the executable attribute – which, remember, is distinct from the access attribute. The Laser-Writer version 38.0 returns a value of *false*, since the **noaccess** resets the literal/executable attribute to literal. This is reasonable, but not strictly in accordance with the separation of the two attributes. PostScript (versions 42.2 and later) and PhoenixPage do not change the literal/executable attribute and so will return the pedantically correct but confusing result *true*, even though any attempt to execute the resulting array will raise the **invalidaccess** error. Be aware, however, that in the later PostScript versions and in PhoenixPage there is no easy way to test for **noaccess** objects; the only test that I know of is to try to modify some attribute and then test to see if the modification was successful: if yes, the object can be accessed; if not, the object is **noaccess**.

There is an additional problem with the Adobe PostScript interpreter, uncorrected in any version that I am aware of. This involves path processing with the **reversepath** operator after execution of a **closepath**. The **closepath** leaves the current point at the start of the current subpath, and any subsequent path operations start from that point. A subsequent **reversepath**, however, does not correctly reconstruct the created path. Consider the following sequence of commands:

```
100 100 moveto
100 0 rlineto
0 100 rlineto
−100 0 rlineto
closepath
−20 0 rlineto
stroke
```

This short program draws a square, using the **closepath** to finish the last side of the square, then adds a short straight-line segment to the left of the base of the square. If you execute the program with the addition of a **reversepath** operator just before the **stroke**, however, the additional segment added to the subpath after the **closepath** is missing. The same program, without the additional line, correctly produces a square whether stroked after a **reversepath** or not. Use of a **pathforall** operator in place of the **stroke** shows that the path, after the **reversepath**, is reversed incorrectly, by placement of a **moveto** without the corresponding **lineto**. This anomaly can be the source of inconsistent behavior. PhoenixPage correctly reverses the path by following the **moveto** with a **lineto** that draws a line to the terminating point of the **closepath** after this sequence of operations.

As mentioned in the discussion of the **clippath** operator, not all paths that are used for clipping can be stroked. Because PhoenixPage uses different internal mechanisms to represent paths than PostScript interpreters do, paths that may be successfully stroked in one environment may fail in the other.

PhoenixPage provides a font cache for bitmaps of characters only; it does not support compressed character formats as mentioned in the text. The use of the **setcacheparams** operator must be modified accordingly.

Interactive Mode Differences

In addition to the general operator differences, PhoenixPage provides a number of enhancements available during interactive mode operation. These allow a PostScript programmer to recall lines of code previously sent to the interpreter and to edit and retransmit these lines. This can be a tremendously useful feature when working in the interactive environment.

There are three major features that have been added to PhoenixPage. All of these features support the interactive mode, which is entered by executing the PostScript operator **executive** as described in Part I, Section A2.6. First, all executive mode statements are internally numbered. This number may be displayed as a part of the prompt displayed by the interactive mode. This is used in the default interactive mode prompt, which is the string 'PPS*n*>', where *n* is the current statement number as described below. Second, this default prompt can be reset to any value and can include a variety of special strings. Third, the executive mode keeps a statement history, so that previously entered statements up to a settable maximum value can be retrieved, edited, and reexecuted. These three new features are described in detail as follows.

1. Interactive mode statement numbering

This numbering is used in the statement history and the settable prompt string features described below. Statements are numbered from the beginning of interpreter start-up, not from the execution of the **executive** operator; therefore, exiting and reentering the interactive mode will not reset the statement numbers. Statement numbers can be retrieved by the use of a new operator, **statementnumber**, and they are displayed as part of the default prompt string. For further discussion of this feature, see item 2 below.

–	**statementnumber**	int

returns the number of the last statement entered, as maintained in the interpreter. Note that, in the interactive mode, this number is the number of the statement that invoked the **statementnumber** operator itself.

2. Settable prompt string

The prompt string displayed in the interactive mode can now be set by an application by setting the new **promptstring** variable, in *userdict*. This variable can be set to any string, using the ordinary **def** operations; however, there are some special strings that can be included within the new *promptstring* that expand to provide additional information for the interactive mode. These strings are as follows:

%> expands the '>' in the prompt string to be displayed the number of times that **executive** has been called. This can occur because PostScript allows complete recursion. Therefore, it is possible to execute the **executive** operator from the interactive mode. Using this expandable string element will allow you to see immediately how many times the **executive** operator has been called. For example, suppose on the first invocation of **executive** you get the following string:

'PPS>'. Now you set the string to the value 'PPS%>'. If you execute the **executive** operator again, the prompt string will now show 'PPS>>', and so on, with the number of '>' characters displayed equal to the number of times **executive** has been started.

%v   expands to the maximum VM size.

%u   expands to the size of VM currently in use.

%#   expands to the current statement number.

3. **Interactive mode statement history**
The interpreter will maintain a history of statements entered in the interactive mode, up to some user-defined limit. The limit can be set, as described below, to any value – subject only to the limitations of memory available. The default value is 20 statements. This history is accessible by calling two procedures that are newly available in *systemdict*: **History**, and !. These two procedures provide access to a new dictionary, **historydict**.

Both of these procedures perform essentially the same function, differing only in where they return their result. The **History** procedure returns results to the operand stack, while the ! procedure displays results after the interactive prompt. In either case, the procedure is called with an integer operand. If the integer is positive, it is interpreted as a statement number, and that statement number is displayed. If the number is negative, it is interpreted as a displacement from the current statement, and the selected statement is displayed. Thus, for example, the sequence '35 History' calls statement 35 back and places it onto the operand stack; while the sequence '−1 History' retrieves the last statement entered onto the stack, and '−2 History' brings back the statement before the last statement; and so on. Similarly, the sequence '35 !' would return a copy of statement 35, placing it after the interactive prompt. Since the line terminator (carriage return or linefeed) is not part of the statement history, the line appears after the prompt as though it were typed in again and can be edited in the usual ways before being reexecuted. If the numeric operand references a statement outside of the number of statements saved, all the statements that are currently saved are displayed. If the current limit of statements saved is 20 (the default limit), then the sequence '−21 History' would result in displaying all the currently saved statements.

Although this facility is very useful, it is possible to disable the history facility. This must be done outside the server loop, because **historydict** is read-only during ordinary processing. Once you have exited the server, you can set the boolean value **dohistory** to *false* to stop the history function. You can also set other variables to increase or decrease the number of statements of history that are saved. See the documentation that accompanies your device for precise details.

PhoenixPage Device-Specific Operators

Operators that pertain to specific devices are, almost inevitably, one place where different versions of the PostScript language differ, whether the versions come from the same supplier or from different suppliers. Because PhoenixPage is implemented on devices that, in some cases, have unique physical characteristics, there are some device-specific operators that exist only in PhoenixPage. In all cases, the PhoenixPage device operators follow the same form and use the same types of conventions as other PostScript device-specific operators. A selection of the PhoenixPage operators that work with specific devices are listed below in the same format that we used in Part I, Section C.

duplex

—   **duplex**   bool

returns the boolean value *true* when the device is set up for duplex (two-sided) printing and returns the value *false* if the device is set up for simplex (one-sided) printing. This operator is identical to the one used in some Adobe Systems PostScript devices.

```
DATA TYPE:   operator
   VALUE:    false
   ERRORS:   stackoverflow
```

bool   **setduplex**   —

causes the device to select duplex (two-sided) printing if the value of *bool* is true and to select simplex (one-sided) printing if the value is *false*. In duplex printing, the device prints subsequent output pages on alternate sides of the paper. The first and each subsequent odd **showpage** prints on the front of a page, while the second and each subsequent even **showpage** prints on the back. This is identical to the operator used in some Adobe Systems PostScript devices.

```
ERRORS:   stackunderflow, typecheck
```

—   **defaultduplex**   bool

returns the boolean value *true* when the default state of the device is set up for duplex (two-sided) printing and returns the value *false* if the default setup is for simplex (one-sided) printing.

```
ERRORS:   stackoverflow
```

bool   **setdefaultduplex**   —

causes the device to select duplex (two-sided) printing as the default value after a reset or at power-on if the value of *bool* is true and to select simplex (one-sided) printing if the value is *false*. This value is a persistent parameter and must therefore be set outside of the server loop. See Part I, Section C2.2 for details of server loop operation.

>   ERRORS: stackunderflow, typecheck

jogoutput

>   —   **jogoutput**   —

causes the output tray to be joggled if it is currently not being joggled, or vice versa. Jogging the output tray refers to shifting the output tray approximately half an inch at the end of each job in order to distinguish the output of one job from another.

>   DATA TYPE: operator
>   ERRORS: (none)

inputtray

>   —   **inputtray**   tray

returns the integer value *tray*, which is the current number of the input tray.

>   DATA TYPE: operator
>   VALUE: 1
>   ERRORS: stackoverflow

>   tray   **setinputtray**   —

causes the device to select *tray* as the current input tray. The maximum value of *tray* is device-dependent.

>   ERRORS: rangecheck, stackunderflow, typecheck

>   —   **defaultinputtray**   tray

returns the integer value *tray*, which is the default tray number used at startup or after a reset operation.

>   ERRORS: stackoverflow

>   tray   **setdefaultinputtray**   —

causes the device to select tray number *tray* as the default input tray. This value is a persistent parameter and must therefore be set outside the server loop. See Part I, Section C2.2 for details of server loop operation.

>   ERRORS: rangecheck, stackunderflow, typecheck

linkinputtray

–   **linkinputtray**   bool

returns the boolean value *true* when the device uses an alternate tray for input if the currently selected tray is empty or unavailable; it returns the value *false* if it does not.

```
DATA TYPE:   operator
    VALUE:   true
   ERRORS:   stackoverflow
```

bool   **setlinkinputtray**   –

causes the device to automatically link to another input tray when the selected tray is unavailable if the value of *bool* is true, and not if set to *false*.

```
   ERRORS:   stackunderflow, typecheck
```

–   **defaultlinkinputtray**   bool

returns the boolean value *true* when the default state of the device is to use an alternate tray for input if the currently selected tray is empty or unavailable; it returns the value *false* if the default is to not use an alternate tray.

```
   ERRORS:   stackoverflow
```

bool   **setdefaultlinkinputtray**   –

causes the device to default to automatically link to another input tray when the selected tray is unavailable if the value of *bool* is true, and not if set to *false*. This value is a persistent parameter and must therefore be set outside the server loop. See Part I, Section C2.2 for details of server loop operation.

```
   ERRORS:   rangecheck, stackunderflow, typecheck
```

outputtray

–   **outputtray**   tray

returns the integer value *tray*, which is the current number of the output tray.

```
DATA TYPE:   operator
    VALUE:   1
   ERRORS:   stackoverflow
```

tray   **setoutputtray**   —

causes the device to select *tray* as the current output tray. The maximum value of *tray* is device-dependent.

    ERRORS: rangecheck, stackunderflow, typecheck

—   **defaultoutputtray**   tray

returns the integer value *tray*, which is the default tray number used at startup or after a reset operation.

    ERRORS: stackoverflow

tray   **setdefaultoutputtray**   —

causes the device to select tray number *tray* as the default output tray. This value is a persistent parameter and must therefore be set outside the server loop. See Part I, Section C2.2 for details of server loop operation.

    ERRORS: rangecheck, stackunderflow, typecheck

tumble

—   **tumble**   bool

returns the boolean value *true* when the device is set up for duplex (two-sided) printing and the second side of sheets are printed head-to-toe with the first side. It returns the value *false* otherwise. The **tumble** operator is used only if duplex printing is in effect; it is ignored otherwise.

    DATA TYPE: operator
       VALUE: false
      ERRORS: stackoverflow

bool   **settumble**   —

causes the device to select head-to-toe printing if the value of *bool* is true and to select head-to-head printing if the value is *false*. In duplex printing, the device prints subsequent output pages on alternate sides of the paper. Normal procedure is to print reverse sides so that the head (top) of each page is at the same edge of the paper; if you wish to print the head of the second page reversed from the front page, you may set tumble to *true*.

    ERRORS: stackunderflow, typecheck

—   **defaulttumble**   bool

returns the boolean value *true* when the default state of the device is set up for head-to-toe printing and returns the value *false* if the default setup is for head-to-head printing.

ERRORS: stackoverflow

bool   **setdefaulttumble**   —

causes the device to select head-to-toe printing as the default value after a reset or at power-on if the value of *bool* is true and to select head-to-head printing if the value is *false*. This value is a persistent parameter and must therefore be set outside the server loop. See Part I, Section C2.2 for details of server loop operation.

ERRORS: stackunderflow, typecheck

Index

Alphabetical Index

*TO THE STUDENT: A Study Guide for this textbook is available through your college bookstore under the title **Study Guide for Managerial Accounting** by Geraldine Dominiak and Joseph Louderback. The **Study Guide** can help you with course material by acting as a tutorial, review, and study aid. If the **Study Guide** is not in stock, ask the bookstore manager to order a copy for you.*

LEO ING
682-7876

MANAGERIAL ACCOUNTING

THE KENT SERIES IN ACCOUNTING

AlHashim and Arpan, *INTERNATIONAL DIMENSIONS OF ACCOUNTING, Second Edition*

Austin, *BIG GAME COMPANY: A COMPUTERIZED AUDITING PRACTICE SET*

Bainbridge, *DRILLMASTER: A COMPUTERIZED TUTORIAL TO ACCOMPANY PRINCIPLES OF ACCOUNTING*

Bayes and Nash, *CASES IN ACCOUNTING INFORMATION SYSTEMS*

Bazley, Nikolai, Grove, *FINANCIAL ACCOUNTING: CONCEPTS AND USES, Second Edition*

Bierman, Dyckman, Hilton, *COST ACCOUNTING: CONCEPTS AND MANAGERIAL APPLICATIONS*

Bryan, *PRINCIPLES OF ACCOUNTING PROBLEMS USING LOTUS 1-2-3*

Bryan, *INTERMEDIATE ACCOUNTING PROBLEMS USING LOTUS 1-2-3*

Diamond, Flamholtz, Flamholtz, *FINANCIAL ACCOUNTING, Second Edition*

Dominiak and Louderback, *MANAGERIAL ACCOUNTING, Sixth Edition*

Flamholtz, Flamholtz, Diamond, *PRINCIPLES OF ACCOUNTING*

Evans, Taylor, Holzmann, *INTERNATIONAL ACCOUNTING AND REPORTING*

Flesher, Kreiser, Flesher, *INTRODUCTION TO FINANCIAL ACCOUNTING*

Gelinas, Oram, Wiggins, *ACCOUNTING INFORMATION SYSTEMS*

Gibson, *FINANCIAL STATEMENT ANALYSIS: USING FINANCIAL ACCOUNTING INFORMATION, Fourth Edition*

Gibson and Frishkoff, *CASES IN FINANCIAL REPORTING, Second Edition*

Hansen, *MANAGEMENT ACCOUNTING*

Henke, *ACCOUNTING FOR NONPROFIT ORGANIZATIONS, Fifth Edition*

Henke, *INTRODUCTION TO NONPROFIT ORGANIZATION ACCOUNTING, Third Edition*

Henke and Spoede, *COST ACCOUNTING AND MANAGERIAL USE OF ACCOUNTING DATA*

Hirsch, *ADVANCED MANAGEMENT ACCOUNTING*

Hirsch and Louderback, *COST ACCOUNTING: ACCUMULATION, ANALYSIS, AND USE, Second Edition*

Hudson, *COST ACCOUNTING PROBLEMS USING LOTUS 1-2-3*

KENT/BENTLEY JOURNAL OF ACCOUNTING AND COMPUTERS, Volume VI

Marshall, Misiewicz, Parker, *PROGRAMMED GUIDE TO TAX RESEARCH, Fourth Edition*

Nash, *ACCOUNTING INFORMATION SYSTEMS, Second Edition*

Nikolai and Bazley, *FINANCIAL ACCOUNTING, Third Edition*

Nikolai and Bazley, *INTERMEDIATE ACCOUNTING, Fifth Edition*

Nikolai, Bazley, Stallman, *PRINCIPLES OF ACCOUNTING, Third Edition*

Ochi and Hughes, *ACCOUNTING WITH LOTUS 1-2-3*

Pearson and Stiner, *A REVIEW OF THE ACCOUNTING CYCLE FOR THE IBM PC*

Porter and Perry, *EDP: CONTROLS AND AUDITING, Fifth Edition*

Stiner and Pearson, *MANAGERIAL ACCOUNTING PROBLEMS FOR THE IBM PC*

Thomas, Ward, Henke, *AUDITING: THEORY AND PRACTICE, Third Edition*

Thompson and Brady, *ESSENTIAL CPA LAW REVIEW, Seventh Edition*

Ulmer, *LOTUS 1-2-3 APPLICATIONS FOR MANAGEMENT ACCOUNTING*

Vaccaro, *ACCOUNTANTS' GENERAL LEDGER*

Verreault and Verreault, *COST ACCOUNTING APPLICATIONS AND EXTENSIONS USING LOTUS 1-2-3*

Verreault and Verreault, *MANAGERIAL ACCOUNTING APPLICATIONS AND EXTENSION USING LOTUS 1-2-3, Second Edition*

Wallace, *AUDITING, Second Edition*

Weiss and Raun, *MCGEE: A COMPUTERIZED ACCOUNTING INFORMATION SYSTEM*

Wolk, Francis, Tearney, *ACCOUNTING THEORY: A CONCEPTUAL AND INSTITUTIONAL APPROACH, Second Edition*

Wolk, Gerber, Porter, *MANAGEMENT ACCOUNTING: PLANNING AND CONTROL*

SIXTH EDITION

MANAGERIAL ACCOUNTING

GERALDINE F. DOMINIAK
Texas Christian University

JOSEPH G. LOUDERBACK III
Clemson University

PWS-KENT PUBLISHING COMPANY ▪ *Boston*

PWS-KENT
Publishing Company

20 Park Plaza
Boston, Massachusetts 02116

PWS-KENT Publishing Company is a division of Wadsworth, Inc.

Material from Uniform CPA Examination Questions and Unofficial Answers, copyright © 1980, 1979, 1973, 1971, 1970, 1969, 1966, 1959, 1958 by the American Institute of Certified Public Accountants, Inc., is reprinted (or adapted) with permission.
Material from the Certificate in Management Accounting Examinations, copyright © 1988, 1984–1982, 1979, 1976, 1973, 1972 by the National Association of Accountants, is reprinted (or adapted) with permission.

Library of Congress Cataloging-in-Publication Data

Dominiak, Geraldine, F.
    Managerial accounting / Geraldine F. Dominiak, Joseph G. Louderback III. — 6th ed.
        p. 864   cm. — (The Kent series in accounting)
    Includes index.
    ISBN 0–534–91959–6
    1. Managerial accounting.   I. Louderback, Joseph G.   II. Title.
III. Series
HF5657.4.D66   1990   90-44390
658.15—dc20   CIP

Printed in the United States of America
91 92 93 94 95—10 9 8 7 6 5 4 3 2 1

International Student Edition ISBN 0-534-98371-5

Sponsoring Editor: Al Bruckner
Editorial Assistant: Kelle Karshick
Production Editor: S. London
Manufacturing Coordinator: Marcia A. Locke
Production Management: Hockett Editorial Service
Interior Illustrator: Ken Urban
Cover Designer: Adapted from a design by Nancy Lindgren, photograph by Greg Bowl
Typesetter: Bi-Comp, Incorporated
Cover Printer: John P. Pow Company, Inc.
Printer and Binder: R. R. Donnelley & Sons

BRIEF CONTENTS

CONTENTS

4   ADDITIONAL ASPECTS OF VOLUME-COST-PROFIT ANALYSIS   108

7   FINANCIAL BUDGETING   252

8 CAPITAL BUDGETING, PART I 295

9   CAPITAL BUDGETING, PART II   329

PART THREE   CONTROL AND PERFORMANCE EVALUATION   373

10   RESPONSIBILITY ACCOUNTING   375

12 CONTROL AND EVALUATION OF COST CENTERS   485

PART FOUR   PRODUCT COSTING   535

15 PROCESS COSTING AND THE COST ACCOUNTING CYCLE   633

PART FIVE   SPECIAL TOPICS   679

18   *ANALYZING FINANCIAL STATEMENTS*   *763*

APPENDIX: TIME VALUE OF MONEY 804

INDEX 819

PREFACE

This book is designed for an introductory course in managerial accounting. Though we wrote the book with the undergraduate student in mind, we have had many reports of its successful use in both graduate and management development courses. One reason is that the wide variety of assignment material allows instructors to select assignments consistent with their students' backgrounds.

The book emphasizes the *uses* of managerial accounting information. It is therefore appropriate not only for accounting majors but also for nonaccounting business majors (in marketing, management, finance, etc.), and majors in nonbusiness areas such as engineering, mathematics, and the physical sciences. Our desire to reach a broad audience is consistent with enrollment trends in managerial accounting courses.

We make few assumptions about the reader's background knowledge. We assume a reader has had one or two terms of financial accounting or a working exposure to basic financial statements. But from a limited accounting background we expect only that a reader has some understanding of the most basic principles on which financial statements are based. The journal-entry/T-account framework appears only in Chapter 15 and is not, with the exception of that chapter, critical to understanding the concepts being presented.

Most discussions in the book focus on the functions of management: planning, decision making, controlling, and performance evaluation. This emphasis is apparent even in the chapters on product costing (Chapters 13–15), a topic that accounting textbooks seldom discuss with the nonaccountant in mind. Thus, those chapters approach product costing from the standpoint of analyzing results under different costing systems, rather than concentrating on cost-accumulation procedures or the accounting problems related to those procedures.

Our objectives in this edition remain essentially the same as those for the first five editions:

1. To present clearly and understandably the most important conceptual and practical aspects of managerial accounting;
2. To order the material in a way that allows the reader to build from elementary concepts to more complex topics and thus to integrate and expand early understanding;

3. To show students some of the interrelationships between managerial accounting and several other courses required in a normal business curriculum;

4. To show the reader, through discussion, illustration, and assignment material, what seems to us the almost infinite number of applications of managerial accounting principles to decision making in economic entities of all types (including personal decisions);

5. To encourage the reader to recognize that *people,* not entities, make decisions and are responsible for the results of those decisions.

We use several means to achieve these objectives. First, we use examples and illustrations liberally. Sometimes we introduce an important concept by means of an example; sometimes we try to give meaning to a rather abstract concept by immediately concentrating on an illustration. Second, we proceed through the text (and its increasingly complex concepts) in a building-block fashion. Thus, we begin with the principles of cost behavior and volume-cost-profit analysis, which underlie virtually all of managerial accounting, and use this basis to approach the more complex problems encountered in decision making, comprehensive budgeting, responsibility accounting, and product costing. A reader will see the continued reliance on previously developed concepts by the regularity of references to earlier chapters. Our frequent text references to the concepts, research, and practices of other business disciplines are intended both to encourage further study and to remind the reader that decision making requires an integration of knowledge from many areas.

The applicability of managerial accounting concepts to a wide variety of economic entities is most obvious in sections of the text that specifically refer to nonbusiness situations. But both the examples used in other parts of the text and the decision situations posed in assignment material also reflect our efforts to demonstrate the opportunities for using managerial accounting concepts in a nonbusiness context.

We regularly draw attention to the qualitative and difficult-to-quantify aspects of a topic. As part of the qualitative considerations, we discuss behavioral problems and point out the implications of such problems. We raise these qualitative issues to emphasize that decisions are made by individuals with beliefs and feelings. From the attention given to these issues, we also expect readers to recognize that accounting data provide relevant information but do not dictate courses of action.

Throughout the book we emphasize that decisions are made on the basis of estimates and that some factors important to a decision are difficult to quantify. Our intentions are to underscore (1) the presence of the manager's constant companion, uncertainty, and (2) the importance of recognizing all the available alternatives and all the factors relevant to each alternative. Both the text and many of the problems—especially those appearing relatively late in the assignment material—emphasize that a major problem in managing any enterprise is determining the right questions to ask and, concomitantly, what kinds of information to seek. In our opinion, students should learn that real-world problems do not present themselves in the form of schedules to be filled in and manipulated. Indeed, sometimes a manager's most difficult task is to discern, from the mass of economic activity taking place all around, exactly what the problem is that requires investigation and resolution.

PLAN OF THE BOOK

We organized this book to emphasize the fundamental importance of cost behavior patterns to all aspects of managerial decision making. After an introductory chapter, Part One, Volume-Cost-Profit Analysis and Decision Making, consists of four chapters that are intended to help the student develop a clear and firm grasp of the basic implications and applications of this fundamental issue. These chapters introduce different types of cost behavior, the reasons for such behavior, a tool for using information about behavior (volume-cost-profit analysis), and the basic analytical approaches used for making short-term decisions.

Part Two, Budgeting, treats operating, financial, and capital budgeting in four chapters. Chapter 6 concentrates on operating budgets, building on the material in Part One and introducing, on a more formal basis, behavioral considerations. Chapter 7 deals with financial budgeting, including cash budgets and pro forma balance sheets, and considers the special problems of budgeting for not-for-profit entities. Chapter 8 introduces capital budgeting; it considers income taxes, but deals only with relatively straightforward decisions involving acquiring new assets. Chapter 9 addresses more complex decisions, such as those involving the replacement of assets, and a few aspects of the Accelerated Cost Recovery System. Understanding Chapters 8 and 9 requires understanding the concepts of present value analysis. An Appendix offers a basic discussion and illustrations of present value analysis, with the emphasis on understanding relationships, and without mathematical development of present value factors.

Part Three integrates the topics of control and performance evaluation. Chapter 10 introduces responsibility accounting, alternative organizational structures, and cost allocation, emphasizing the behavioral aspects of these topics. Chapter 11 treats divisional performance evaluation—again, emphasizing behavioral issues. Chapter 12 discusses standard variable costs and variance analysis to evaluate cost centers.

Part Four consists of three chapters on product costing. These chapters emphasize the uses of product-cost information and analysis of reports prepared under different product-costing methods. Chapter 13 introduces the general ideas of cost flows, absorption costing, and predetermined overhead rates; both actual and normal costing are illustrated in a job-order context. Building on the standard cost concepts of Chapter 12 and absorption costing ideas of Chapter 13, Chapter 14 develops the idea of a standard fixed cost per unit and contrasts absorption and variable costing. Chapter 15 completes the product-costing coverage by introducing the special problems of a process-costing situation and illustrating the flows of costs through accounts. (An Appendix to Chapter 15 illustrates the first-in-first-out cost-flow assumption under process costing.)

NEW FEATURES

1. The most comprehensive change reflected in this edition is the integration of the terminology and techniques of the just-in-time philosophy and the new manufacturing environment. These ideas are incorporated throughout the book consistent with its overall plan, so that almost every chapter in Parts One through Four is affected. Some of the more extensive changes are:

    a. Chapter 1 introduces and contrasts the conventional and advanced environments.

    b. Chapters 2 and 3 use the new terminology in an expanded discussion of the importance of identifying the activity driving a cost.

    c. Chapters 4 and 10 give added attention to the importance of the traceability of costs. The discussion of allocated costs in Chapter 10 has been revised and expanded.

    d. The chapters on budgeting (Chapters 6 through 9) consider the effects of the new environment on inventory policies.

    e. The discussions of absorption costing and overhead application in Chapters 13 and 14 reinforce the importance of identifying cost drivers and illustrate the use of multiple bases for applying overhead.

    f. Chapter 15 includes an illustration of backflush costing as an example of the impact of a JIT environment on the cost accounting cycle.

    The assignment material in various chapters has been revised or expanded to reflect the integration described above. In addition, we have incorporated in the text the reported experiences of some companies that have adopted advanced manufacturing techniques.

2. We simplified and refined the discussion in Chapter 3 on the relationships between cost classification schemes and managerial actions.

3. The Appendix to Chapter 10 now includes the reciprocal method, as well as the step-down method, of allocating costs of service departments.

4. To reflect the increasing interest in a global perspective on business, Chapter 11 includes a section on the problems of performance evaluation and transfer prices in multinational companies.

5. Chapter 17 conforms with the pronouncement of the Financial Accounting Standards Board (Statement Number 95) on the cash flow statement.

6. About one-third of the assignment material is new or revised, and the total number of assignment items is slightly higher than in the fifth edition. Revisions and additions appear, for the most part, among exercises and the earlier problems.

ASSIGNMENT MATERIAL

One of the strongest features of this book is the assignment material, because of its integration with the text, its volume, and its variety with respect to degree of difficulty and economic entities. Users of previous editions have told us that these factors make it possible to teach this course, and the individual topics therein, at various levels of difficulty. Users cite the same factors as facilitating successful offerings of the course to students with widely different backgrounds and in a variety of time frames. (Comments in the Instructor's Manual aid in judicious choice of assignment items to accommodate different objectives.)

End-of-chapter material includes questions for discussion, exercises, problems, and cases. There are no review questions that can be answered by referring to a sentence or two in the chapter. Discussion questions are designed to increase students' understanding of concepts, and many have no clearly correct answers. Exercises are usually short and cover basic applications of one or two key concepts. Problems tend to be longer than exercises, and are more challenging, sometimes contain irrelevant information, and often ask the student to state reservations about whatever solutions are proposed. Both exercises and problems are generally arranged in order of increasing difficulty.

Cases normally contain less information than is needed to develop a single solution, our intention being to emphasize this inconvenient characteristic of real-life situations. For most cases, the student must propose an analytical approach appropriate to the available, relevant information. Cases, and the later problems, require the student to determine what principles are relevant and how those principles apply in a given situation. That is, these assignments are designed to encourage the student to think, since a manager must do so.

ALTERNATIVE CHAPTER SEQUENCING

The text contains more material than is needed for a one-term course, and we expect most users to omit one or more chapters. Several users have found alternative sequencing to be practical. We recommend, however, that whatever chapters are used be covered in the order presented. The text does offer considerable flexibility in the order of coverage.

Chapters in Part Four are the most likely candidates for omission or alternative sequencing. Chapters 17 and 18, on cash flows and financial analysis, are primarily for students whose financial accounting backgrounds did not include these topics. These chapters contain only a few, noncritical references to earlier chapters. Accordingly, either one or both of these chapters can be taken up at any time or omitted entirely.

Chapter 16, which discusses several quantitative methods of analysis, can be covered separately at any time after Chapter 12. Or, individual segments of that chapter can be assigned in conjunction with earlier chapters. The section on statistical decision theory has illustrations that use materials from Chapters 6, 8, and 12. The illustrations, while concentrating on applying the quantitative methods, draw on topics discussed in these earlier chapters. [The concept of expected value can be introduced as early as Chapter 5.] The section on inventory control models is particularly relevant to Chapter 6, which covers production and purchases budgets. The linear programming section extends the material in Chapter 5 on alternative uses of limited resources. Similarly, the section on learning curves can supplement the discussion in Chapter 3 on cost prediction methods.

Instructors desiring an earlier and greater emphasis on product costing can move to Chapters 12 through 15 after Chapter 5. Moving to Chapter 12 after Chapter 4 (or even after Chapter 3) is possible if additional time is given to the early discussion of indirect/common costs. (Note that giving early emphasis to product costing requires incorporating Chapter 12 in the coverage of that topic rather than as part of the study of responsibility accounting, because some understanding of standard costs is assumed in Chapters 14 and 15.) Some users increase the time available to cover product costing by omitting Chapters 10 and 11. Alternatively, some users omit all product-costing material, or omit all or parts of Chapter 14 and 15.

Chapter 4 can be omitted without loss of continuity. It is also possible to omit one or both chapters on capital budgeting (Chapters 8 and 9) without serious loss of continuity, and some users have taken these options.

The Appendix dealing with present values was designed to be used with Chapters 8 and 9 on capital budgeting. It assumes no previous exposure to the general idea of the time value of money, but those who have had such exposure are likely to find this material useful for review.

SUPPLEMENTARY MATERIAL

An **Instructor's Manual** contains suggested time allocations for alternative course lengths and chapter sequencing, additional comments on assignment materials, and further descriptions of teaching supplements such as Lotus templates. For each chapter, it provides a brief statement of the topical coverage, suggestions of assignment items for coverage of basic concepts, and a brief commentary about concepts or approaches that students find difficult to understand.

The **Test Bank** contains true-false and multiple-choice questions, and short problems. A Computerized Test Bank is also available on 3½-inch and 5¼-inch PC disks.

The **Solutions Manual** contains solutions for all assignment material and suggested times for completing assignments. It also provides notes to the instructor regarding class use of the material. These notes offer (1) alternative approaches for arriving at solutions; (2) suggestions for eliciting class discussion; and (3) suggestions for expanding individual assignments to cover new issues, pursuing existing issues in more depth, or highlighting relationships between managerial accounting concepts and concepts studied in other business disciplines.

A list of *check figures* for at least some parts of virtually every exercise, problem, and case is available in quantity from the publisher. In addition, *transparencies* are available upon adoption for all solutions and some text illustrations. There is also a set of Lotus 1-2-3® templates for various assignments.

The **Study Guide** is designed to help students obtain full value from the study of this text. This supplement, which offers key statements to use as guides in reading the chapters, includes not only objective questions but also a variety of short and medium-length problems (solutions included) to test understanding. The final section of the Guide for each chapter identifies those concepts, practices, or approaches that cause the most difficulty or greatest misunderstanding for students.

ACKNOWLEDGMENTS

We wish to thank the many instructors and students whose comments and suggestions have helped us significantly in the preparation of all six editions of this book. In particular, we want to thank the reviewers of the first five editions, plus the reviewers of the revised material for the sixth edition:

Robert Boylan
Rensselaer Polytechnic Institute

Don E. Collins
Franklin University

Alfreda Dobyianski
Sam Houston State University

Daniel Elnathan
University of Southern California

Michael Fetters
Babson College

Maurice L. Hirsch, Jr.
Southern Illinois University at
Edwardsville

James T. Hood
Northeast Louisiana University

Philip Jagolinzer
University of Southern Maine

Wayne Johnson
Bowling Green State University

Bernard T. Kaylor
Northeast Louisiana University

Dayal Kiringoda
University of Akron

Robert Koehler
The Pennsylvania State University

Eugene Laughlin
Kansas State University

Donald Lucy
Millersville University of
Pennsylvania

W. E. McTeer
Texas A&I University

Thomas A. Morrison
University of Connecticut

Denis T. Raihall
Drexel University

John M. Ruble
Bradley University

Robert Ruland
Northeastern University

Stephen Senge
Western Washington University

Ken Sinclair
Lehigh University

Don Stone
University of Massachusetts
at Amherst

Jeannette Sylvestre
University of South Alabama

Judith Webb
University of Montana

David Weiner
University of San Francisco

Special thanks for their insightful comments and suggestions go to Arnold Barkman, Bill Ferrara, Sanoa Hensley, and Donald Lucy.

We also express our appreciation to the American Institute of Certified Public Accountants and National Association of Accountants for their generous permission to use problems adapted from past CPA and CMA examinations, respectively.

Finally, we thank our respective institutions, and our colleagues at those institutions, without whom the development of this volume, in its current and prior editions, would have been a much less pleasant task.

Geraldine F. Dominiak
Joseph G. Louderback

CHAPTER *1*

INTRODUCTION

Accountants develop and communicate much of the economic information used by people interested in businesses and other economic organizations. One important aspect of the accountant's function is providing information to external parties, such as creditors, stockholders, and governmental agencies. This aspect is **financial accounting. Managerial accounting** is meeting the information needs of internal parties, the organization's managers.

Managers make decisions about acquiring and using economic resources and need information to help them make those decisions. Managerial accounting deals with much of that information, as well as with some of the techniques managers use in performing their jobs. No reasonably concise definition of managerial accounting captures all of its aspects. The subject is constantly changing to adapt to technological changes, changes in managers' needs, and new approaches to other functional areas of business—marketing, production, finance, organizational behavior, and management. Managerial accounting is an indispensable part of the system that provides information to managers—the people whose decisions and actions determine the success or failure of an organization.

Managerial accounting obviously applies to businesses, for it deals with economic information, and businesses seek profits and other economic goals. Managerial accounting also applies to organizations that do not seek profits—government units, universities, hospitals, churches—because those organizations, like businesses, use economic resources to meet their objectives. Hence, an understanding of the concepts of managerial accounting is important to managers in any organization. In this book we do not assume that you plan to major in accounting or to become an accountant. We assume only that you are interested in managing and are familiar with the basic components of financial statements.

FUNCTIONS OF MANAGEMENT

Two important functions of management are planning and control. The **planning function** is the process of setting goals and developing ways to achieve them. It includes the important process of budgeting. **Budgeting** is the relating of goals to the specific means for achieving them. For example, if a goal is a particular level of profit, the budgeting process requires determining what machinery, cash, labor force, and other resources will be needed to achieve that goal and how to acquire the necessary amount of each resource.

Managing requires **decision making,** which we view as a subfunction of planning. A plan for a year, for example, requires decisions about what products or services to sell, and at what prices, as well as about what machinery to acquire, how many people to hire, whether to borrow money or issue stock, and so on.

Often, the planning process uses an important managerial method—**management by objectives.** A management-by-objectives program, in its simplest form, requires that managers set objectives and then try to achieve them. On occasion, the objectives of various units within the firm may conflict, and the managerial accountant may gather relevant information to help resolve the conflict. For example, the sales manager might want increased production of a particular product to meet a sales objective. The production manager might argue that it would be prohibitively expensive—preventing him or her from meeting cost and production objectives—to shift production away from other products to meet this request. The managerial accountant might analyze the effects of the changed production schedule and recommend what to do.

Control is determining whether goals are being met, and if not, what can be done. What changes might we make to achieve existing goals? Should we change the existing goals? Implicit in control is **performance evaluation**—managers reviewing the accomplishments of their subordinates and weighing them against standards. Many such evaluations use managerial accounting information.

The size of most modern corporations precludes close contact among persons who are several levels apart in the organizational hierarchy. Even in relatively small companies, managers are not likely to exercise constant oversight of the activities of their subordinates. The principle of **management by exception** helps managers to control operations. Applying this principle, managers rely on reports to keep informed. The reports reduce the need for minute-by-minute, physical supervision and allow managers time to perform their other functions. If reports show that results are not in accordance with plans—that is, if there are exceptions—investigation and action might follow. Thus, accounting reports partially substitute for managers' personal supervision of activities.

TYPES OF MANAGERS

It is common practice to distinguish between *line* and *staff* functions in an organization. The manager of a **line function** is concerned with the primary operating activities of the firm—usually, acquiring and selling a physical product or performing a service. A staff manager manages a department that serves other departments. For example, financial managers are concerned with obtaining sufficient cash to keep operations running smoothly. The manager of the legal department advises other managers regarding the legal ramifications of actions.

Accounting is a **staff function,** with the managerial accountant providing information to other managers. The information can relate to financial statements, tax problems, dealings with governmental authorities, and other matters. The managerial accountant, like other staff managers, often recommends courses of action to those using the information. But neither the managerial accountant, nor any other staff manager, can impose recommendations on line managers. Nevertheless, because of their expertise, staff managers can influence decisions. In fact, in some organizations "management accountants have votes on some line decisions, and, on certain decisions, their prior approval is sought."[1] Staff managers, like all managers, must also make decisions about the activities in their own departments.

MANAGERIAL ACCOUNTING AND FUNCTIONS OF MANAGEMENT

Managers require information to plan and control adequately. The managerial accountant is the primary, though not the only, provider of information. Such information includes the prices of materials, wages paid to employees, rents on leased facilities or equipment, costs of fringe benefits, and various taxes. Managers also use information originating outside the firm. For example, statistics on the state of the economy are helpful in forecasting sales; studies of patterns of population growth are relevant to decisions about locations for new stores, warehouses, or manufacturing plants; statistics on the state of the industry, or industries, in which a company operates are useful in forecasting both sales and related expenses.

Planning and Budgeting

Without careful planning, goals are achieved only by accident. Managerial accounting is closely interwoven in planning both because it provides information for decision making and because the entire budgeting process is developed around accounting-related reports.

If a firm sets a target profit for a year, it must also determine how to reach that target. For example, what products are to be sold at what prices? The managerial accountant develops data that help managers identify the more profitable products. Often, the managerial accountant is asked to determine the effects of alternative prices and selling efforts. (What will profit be if we cut prices 5% and

---

[1] Gerald H. Lander, James R. Holmes, Manuel A. Tipgos, and Marc J. Wallace, Jr., *Profile of the Management Accountant* (New York: National Association of Accountants, 1983), 10.

increase volume 15%? Would spending $250,000 on advertising, or offering a 10% sales commission, be wise if it led to a 20% increase in sales?)

As part of the budgeting process, managerial accountants prepare budgeted (forecasted) financial statements, often called **pro forma statements.** Among the most important is the budget of cash receipts and disbursements. Forecasts of cash requirements are used by the finance department to determine whether borrowing will be necessary. The *management* of cash is extremely critical; more companies fail because they run out of cash as a result of inadequate planning than because they are unable to make a profit. Making profits and maintaining adequate cash are two very different things, and managers must understand that success in one does not necessarily mean success in the other.

Decision Making

Much of the information provided by managerial accountants is used in decision making, which is, as we stated earlier, an important part of the planning process. Some decision making is carried on continually. For example, managers must decide daily or weekly how many units of a product to buy or make, or how much advertising to place in specific newspapers or on specific radio stations. Often, they also must decide what prices to set for products or services. Timeliness is critical for reports that are needed for such decisions. It is equally important that the information in the reports be relevant to the decision at hand. A sales manager needs, among other data, information about product costs and margins, trends of sales, and inventories. That same manager probably does not need detailed information about the cost to make a particular product. On the other hand, the production manager *does* need detailed information about product costs, so that reports to production managers might show 20 or more categories of costs.

Some decisions are made at relatively infrequent intervals, such as whether to build a new factory, buy a new warehouse, introduce a new product line, or enter a foreign market. Developing the information managers need to help them make such decisions usually requires that the managerial accountant do special analyses. The data for such analyses are probably not readily available in the needed form. The managerial accountant determines what data are needed, presents those data in an understandable way, and explains the analysis to the managers making the decisions.

Managerial accountants assist managers in making decisions not only by providing information, but also by employing analytical techniques that help managers understand the implications of a decision. For example, managerial accountants can often tell managers how many units of a new product they must sell to earn some desired profit or what cost savings are necessary to justify buying new machinery. We discuss many of these techniques in this book.

Although managers use accounting data extensively as they make decisions, such data do not *answer* the questions that managers face. *People* make decisions, and people bring to decision making their experience, values, and knowledge which often cannot be incorporated into quantitative analyses. An action that seems best based on an analysis of the accounting data might not be taken because of some factor not captured in those data. For example, because the managers of a firm want the company to maintain technological leadership, they might launch a new product that is expected to be unprofitable. Quantifying the benefits of such leadership is not easy. It is unlikely that such a quantification would be included in the managerial accountant's analysis of the desirability of bringing out the new product. It is, however, quite likely that a report of that analysis would include a comment about the inability to quantify such benefits. That is, reports from managerial accountants are very likely to recognize factors whose financial implications are not incorporated in the reports.

Controlling

For many managers, the most common contact with managerial accounting information comes through **control reports,** reports detailing costs incurred by the managers and their subordinates and usually relating those costs to budgeted costs. Managers use such reports to determine whether some aspect of their areas of responsibility requires special attention and perhaps corrective action. The use of control reports follows the principle of management by exception. As a rule, when budgeted and actual results are very close, the manager will conclude that operations are going according to plan and that no special investigation is needed. When significant differences between budgeted and actual results arise, a manager will usually investigate to determine what is going wrong and, possibly, which subordinates might need help.

Control reports do not tell managers what to do. The fact that actual results differ greatly from planned results does not tell managers why the results differed. Control reports provide feedback to help managers determine where attention might be required; they do not tell managers how to correct any problems that might exist.

Control reports should be timely and relevant. A manager might receive one report daily, another weekly, and others monthly, the frequency depending on the manager's position. The closer the manager is to actual operations, the more frequent the reports. For example, some factory foremen and other such supervisors receive daily reports on production and costs, but higher-level managers need production reports at less frequent intervals.

Advances in computers and in the ability to store and retrieve large amounts of information have sometimes been accompanied by an unfortunate side effect called *information overload*. Some managers receive far more information than they can possibly use. One of the challenges in managerial accounting is to develop ways to determine what information is relevant for particular managers, summarize the information, and present it in a usable form. The general manager of a factory employing 500 people cannot effectively use weekly reports showing the actual amounts incurred for 800 cost categories. The general manager could, however, use a report showing which costs differed significantly from their budgeted amounts.

Evaluating

Evaluating and controlling are very closely related. Managers are usually evaluated partly on the basis of how well they control their operations: whether they achieve budgeted sales volume, meet budgeted cost levels, or produce budgeted quantities of product. Because the topmost managers of today's large organizations are far removed from day-to-day activities, they rely on the information reported by management accountants about the performance of subordinate managers.

Developing suitable measures of performance for a given manager can be difficult. For example, if sales managers are evaluated on the basis of total sales dollars, they might concentrate on obtaining the highest dollar sales without regard to the profitability of the items sold, and the result might be very high sales volume but a very low overall profit. Similarly, if production managers are evaluated based on whether they meet budgeted costs, they might be tempted to ignore the quality of the product, postpone preventive maintenance, or take other actions that harm the firm in the long run. Selecting appropriate measures of performance is of constant concern to both managers and managerial accountants.

Illustration

Figure 1-1 diagrams some managerial processes and related accounting activities. Usually the topmost level of management sets overall objectives that are then formalized into profit plans. Objectives such as 10% growth in sales, 12% growth in profits over the next three or five years, a 20% return on total investment, and a 35% return on stockholders' equity can be put into profit plans. Other objectives, such as those related to product quality, pollution abatement, and employee satisfaction cannot be described formally in profit plans but must be taken into account in developing those plans. For example, factory managers might estimate that a pollution abatement program will add 3% to manufacturing costs. This increase will affect the achievement of profit goals.

Managers set broad objectives and strategies, then make detailed plans to realize them. What new products can we introduce? What can existing products contribute to future profits and sales? What will foreign competitors do? Can some of our products be marketed more widely? Should we stress overseas operations or pay more attention to domestic business? Strategic and tactical questions like these and others are thrashed out, and planning is then based on the company's strengths and weaknesses and the opportunities and threats that it faces. Such plans are expressed in budgets and pro forma financial statements.

Having established plans that are consistent with the broad objectives of the firm, managers implement these designs. They direct research programs on new products, advertising, and other sales efforts, add plant capacity to meet anticipated demand, and fill requirements for workers, managers, and other personnel. Many results of these actions show up within the framework of the accounting system. The results of sales efforts show up as revenues, while the firm's

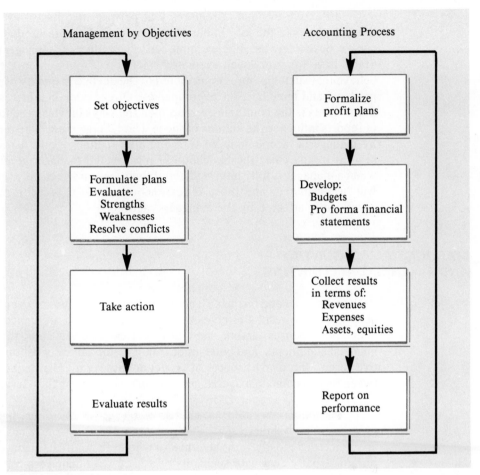

Figure 1-1   Management and Accounting

efforts show up as expenses and assets. The financing aspects of the various efforts are reflected in equities—long-term debt, common stock issuances, and increases in retained earnings.

In Figure 1-1 we have shown the boxes labeled "Take action" and "Evaluate results" as independent, but there is usually continual feedback. The most recent results are evaluated quickly so that corrective action can be taken if necessary. Evaluations of results can also lead to reconsideration of the original objectives or of the plans formulated to meet the objectives. Thus, the cycle shown rarely runs a complete course without any modifications. Plans and budgets are not static; managers change them continually.

Periodically, the results of management decisions, in the form of formal financial statements, are distributed outside the firm. But periodic reporting does not change the continuous nature of the process of managing the firm. Indeed, by the time periodic reports have been prepared and distributed, managers have already made more plans and decisions.

Effective evaluation requires that performance measures capture the essential aspects of the job. Failure to do so can be counterproductive to the company's best interests. For example, many production managers in the United States have for years been evaluated solely on output and cost. Some observers believe that such measures contributed to the decline in quality of many American products and have hurt those companies. Of considerable interest to managerial accountants is the continuing research on the ways in which the form and content of reports influence the actions of those who receive them. The reports developed by managerial accountants should continue to improve as a result of such research. In any case, the likelihood of misdirected managerial efforts is reduced when a manager is fully informed about the bases on which his or her performance will be evaluated, and those bases encompass all aspects of the firm that are significantly affected by the managers' actions.

MANAGERIAL ACCOUNTING AND FINANCIAL ACCOUNTING

Both managerial and financial accounting deal with economic events. Both require quantifying the results of economic activity, and both are concerned with revenues and expenses, assets, liabilities, and cash flows. Both, therefore, involve financial statements, and both suffer from the difficulties of capturing, in quantitative terms, the many aspects of an economic event. The major differences between financial and managerial accounting arise because they serve different audiences.

Financial accounting serves persons outside the firm, such as creditors, customers, government units, and investors. Hence, financial accounting reports are concerned mostly with the firm as a whole. In contrast, managerial accounting reports usually deal with segments of a firm, with managers getting information related to their own responsibilities rather than to the entire firm.

The different audiences for financial accounting and managerial accounting information use information for different purposes. Creditors and investors use information to decide whether or not to extend credit to the firm, whether to buy, sell, or hold its stock. (In Chapter 18 we describe some of the steps taken by these individuals as they analyze information about the firm.) Individuals inside the firm use accounting information to make decisions such as which of several products to sell, whether to issue bonds or stock, which employees to reward for good performance, and what prices to charge.

The classification schemes used in managerial accounting reports usually differ from those used in financial accounting reports. In financial accounting, costs are usually classified by the *object* of the expense (salaries, taxes, rent, repairs) or by the *function* of the expense (cost of goods sold, selling expenses, administrative expenses, financing expenses). In contrast, reports for managerial accounting purposes often follow a cost classification scheme based on the *behavior* of costs, separating costs that change when activity levels change, from costs that do not change regardless of the level of activity. Some managerial accounting reports concentrate on the concepts of *responsibility* and *controllability*, so that costs are classified according to whether or not a particular manager is responsible for the cost and can control it. These classification schemes of managerial accounting (behavior, responsibility, and controllability) underlie much of the material in this book and are critical to almost all aspects of planning, control, and evaluation.

Information in financial accounting reports might also differ in source and nature from that in managerial accounting reports. Financial accounting reports are developed from the basic accounting system, which is designed to capture data about completed transactions. Some managerial accounting reports incorporate information not contained in the normal accounting system and related primarily to future transactions, or even to alternatives to past transactions. For example, financial accounting reports (obtainable from the normal accounting system) may include depreciation for a particular building. A managerial accounting report might include, instead, the rent that would have to be paid for the building if it were not owned (information not obtainable from the normal accounting system).

To a great extent, managerial accounting reports are specifically designed for a particular user or a particular decision, whereas financial accounting reports are general purpose reports. For this reason, a particular cost may appear on one internal report and not on another; the cost might be relevant for some internal decisions and not for others. We can illustrate this point with an example from everyday life. Suppose you own a car and pay $450 for insurance per year. That cost is part of the total cost of owning the car, but it is irrelevant if you are trying to determine how much it will cost to take a 200-mile trip. Because you pay the same $450 for insurance whether you take the trip or not, you can ignore it in determining the cost of the trip. The phrase "different costs for different purposes" describes this characteristic of managerial accounting.

Some have suggested that financial and managerial accounting information differ in that the former is historical while the latter is more concerned with the future. Although many items in financial statements incorporate expectations (e.g., estimated useful life and residual value in the computation of depreciation, estimated warranty work to be done on items sold, and so on), financial accounting reports concentrate more on the results of past decisions. Internal reports to managers, on the other hand, very often concentrate on what is likely to happen in the future.

Managerial accounting has no restrictions such as the generally accepted accounting principles that govern financial accounting. For managerial purposes, relevance is the important concern, and the managerial accountant responds to specific information requirements. For example, market price or replacement cost or some other measure will be used in a managerial accounting report if it will help the manager make a better decision. Such alternatives are usually not allowed in financial accounting.

In summary, managerial accounting is different from financial accounting in purpose, orientation, and constraints. In addition, as we noted earlier, there is a difference in the timing and timeliness aspects of internal and external reporting. Formal financial statements are prepared less often than reports for managers and therefore include information that is less current than that received by managers.

ADVANCED MANUFACTURING

Although managerial accounting deals with all types of economic enterprises, a significant number of them are manufacturers. One of the driving forces behind many recent developments in managerial accounting is profound changes in manufacturing. At various points throughout this text we use the terms **new manufacturing environment,** or, more often, **advanced manufacturing,** to describe such developments. To help you better understand these references we discuss those changes and some of their implications in this introductory chapter.

Conventional Manufacturing: Its Background and Its Problems

Practices that have come to be called conventional manufacturing originated in conditions facing U.S. manufacturing firms for more than two decades after World War II. American companies were the unchallenged world leaders in manufacturing. They had huge leads in product quality, in capacity, and in distribution facilities, and it is only a slight exaggeration to say that they could sell nearly anything they made. Production was the critical activity.

In this environment, many U.S. manufacturers adopted practices that reflected a ''just-in-case'' philosophy. As insurance against production delays caused by defects in components or the unavailability of materials, companies routinely purchased more than required to meet production needs. (They inspected all incoming shipments, though they often adopted sophisticated statistical techniques to cope with this growing task.) To avoid production shortfalls caused by manufacturing errors (or by delays because of defects in materials), firms scheduled production earlier, and in quantities greater, than required to meet shipping schedules. As a result, **lead time** or **cycle time**—the period that begins with the arrival of materials and ends with shipment of a finished unit—extended well beyond the time required for the manufacturing process alone. (A product that could be manufactured in a day or two might have a lead time of one, two, or even three months.)

Not surprisingly, there were costs associated with these manufacturing practices. The resulting high inventories of materials and finished units increased the risk of spoilage and obsolescence, as well as the costs of storage, insurance, financing, and handling. Inspecting more incoming materials and more finished units was also costly. Inevitably, prices rose to cover the increased costs. An unfortunate outcome of striving to meet output requirements on a timely basis was that waste, scrap, and the reworking of defective units came to be thought of as normal. Such an attitude did not encourage high quality and may even have discouraged quality-control efforts. Thus, practices that might have been wise *if* quality was suspect often contributed to lowering quality.

Philosophies and practices that characterize the new manufacturing environment surfaced as overseas companies began to compete with U.S. manufacturers. In searching for a competitive edge, attention centered on the weaknesses of conventional manufacturing practices, particularly declines in quality and high inventories. The term often used to describe a manufacturing environment that would eliminate those weaknesses is just-in-time manufacturing.

Just-in-Time Manufacturing

Just-in-time (JIT) manufacturing is a philosophy that focuses not just on meeting shipping dates, but on efficiency and quality in meeting commitments. One major aspect of this philosophy is to increase customer satisfaction by reducing lead time. (Have you ever been told you must wait two months for something you are ready to order? A commitment to reducing cycle time was thought important enough at IBM to be mentioned by the chairman of its Board of Directors at an annual stockholders meeting.) Advocates of the JIT philosophy are concerned with techniques to ensure a smooth and rapid flow of materials and products.

The term "just in time" refers to one way of characterizing the goals of such techniques. Under ideal conditions purchased materials and components arrive just in time to be used, partly assembled units arrive at work stations just in time for the next step in production, and finished units emerge from production at the shipping date requested by the customer. Of course, the ideal conditions are virtually impossible to achieve, but they serve as goals against which to measure progress, and that progress has been dramatic in many cases. As examples, some factories receive deliveries of some items several times a day, and some have eliminated loading docks in favor of entrances allowing trucks to deliver materials directly to work stations. (One company, Allen-Bradley, reports that its "factory within a factory" can take an order one day, produce the required units, and ship the order the following day, with only a small amount of material, and no finished or unfinished units, on hand at the end of day.[2]) Progress toward achieving the goals means a shortened lead time, as well as reduced inventories and inventory costs.

The JIT philosophy is concerned with all aspects of cycle time, not just inventory reduction. So managers continually scrutinize each step in the production process itself, trying to determine which cost-producing and time-consuming activities add value to the final product and which do not. For example, some managers see the moving of partially finished units from one work station to another as a non-value-adding activity. Hence, work stations in a JIT environment are often adjacent, rather than being spread throughout a factory, so that as much work as possible is done in a small cluster of machinery and workers, called a manufacturing cell. Coupling the use of cells with reduced needs for space to store inventories of various types, JIT operations use less space than conventional operations. Figure 1-2 on page 12 illustrates production flows in a conventional operation and a JIT operation.

In their efforts to reduce production time, JIT managers have also put more emphasis on reducing *set-up time,* the time required to change over from making

---

[2] Robert A. Howell and Stephen R. Soucy, "Cost Accounting in the New Manufacturing Environment," *Management Accounting,* August 1987, 5.

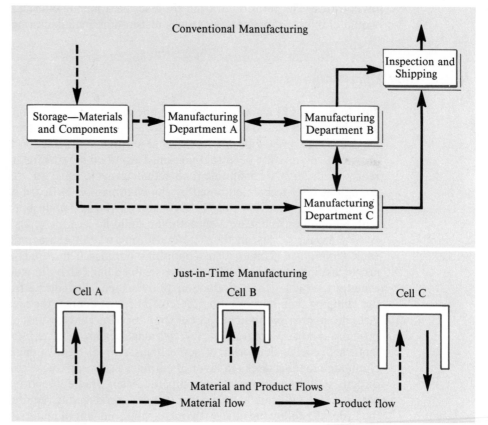

Figure 1-2   Material and Product Flows

one product to another. The term *flexible manufacturing systems* describes a JIT environment where set-up time is particularly critical and customers demand quick responses to orders (perhaps to prevent obsolescence or spoilage). For example, some modern plants for the manufacture of wearing apparel, which often has a high risk of obsolescence, can make and ship an order of ten pairs of bermuda shorts, in various sizes, colors, and patterns, within 24 hours of receiving the order. A manufacturer's ability to achieve flexible manufacturing depends partly on the available technology. But the goal of a flexible manufacturing system is to produce by units, rather than by batches.

Of course, the condition most critical to the success of JIT operations is total quality control. If there are virtually no inventories of purchased materials and components of finished units, everything received must be without defects that could delay production, and manufacturing errors leading to defective units cannot be tolerated. Several practices have evolved to achieve this condition, which is often referred to as *zero defects*. For example, JIT companies stop inspecting incoming shipments when assured that a supplier is providing components of the desired quality, and simply stop buying from suppliers who do not meet that standard. Similarly, JIT companies pinpoint problems by inspecting units throughout the production process instead of only at a few points. Moreover, to reduce costs and increase quality, JIT manufacturers emphasize that quality must be designed into products, rather than inspected into them.

The following schedule contrasts JIT and conventional manufacturing.

JIT Manufacturing	*Conventional Manufacturing*
1. Manufacturing cells concentrating on one product	Departments working on all products
2. Multiskilled workers	Single-skilled workers
3. Small batches, smooth flows	Large batches, erratic flows
4. Total quality control	Some defects seen as inevitable
5. Short production cycle	Long production cycle
6. Zero or trivial inventories	Large inventories held as buffers
7. Daily delivery of materials and components	Large deliveries
8. Relentless search to improve, eliminate all waste	Achieve acceptable performance

ACTIVITIES OF MANAGERIAL ACCOUNTANTS

As we stated at the start of the chapter, accountants within an organization perform functions related to both financial and managerial accounting. We concentrate here on those aspects of the internal accountant's activities that involve serving the needs of internal information users. Some of the major activities of managerial accountants are: (1) aiding in the design of the firm's information system; (2) gathering data; (3) ensuring that the system is performing according to plan; (4) undertaking special analyses for management; (5) interpreting accounting data based on the particular requirements of the manager in a given situation.

The information system of the firm must meet the needs of all individuals within the firm who require information for the performance of their jobs. For example, managers responsible for the sales of a particular product might need weekly sales reports for each territory. Their supervisor, who also supervises other managers, might need a weekly report for a group of products. The chief sales executive might want monthly reports of sales by product groups and sales territories. The managerial accountant must ensure that the system meets these varying needs.

The actual recording of transactions in journals and ledgers is usually done by computer. The accountant is responsible for supervising the gathering of data and for monitoring the system, making sure it is functioning as intended. The accountant must also make sure that the output of the information system is understood and used appropriately. Suppose that a particular report was designed for the sales manager to help identify sales trends by geographic area and that the report has subsequently been used as the basis for computing commissions to salespeople. The report is inappropriate for this second use if it fails to reflect customer returns on which no commissions should be paid.

Special analyses are required when managers consider nonroutine actions. In some cases, such as the possibility of building a new plant, relevant data might not be available in a form that enables managers to decide on the best course of action. Accountants must develop relevant information to serve such special purposes.

Finally, the accountant frequently explains accounting data and reports to other managers. Perhaps a manager is unable to understand a report. Or the data in a report might not be appropriate for the manager's particular purpose. The latter situation indicates that some change in the system might be appropriate.

Managerial accountants have gained status in recent years as their activities have become concerned more with analysis of the firm's operations and less with the problems of recording and computing costs of products. The National Association of Accountants, the principal organization of managerial accountants in the United States, has instituted a program to provide certification for managerial accountants. The **Certified Management Accountant** (CMA) examination was first given in 1972. Nearly 9,000 people successfully completed the examination by the end of 1989. A listing of the required subject areas in the CMA examination indicates the breadth of knowledge expected of the professional managerial accountant. The examination consists of the following five parts: Economics and Business Finance; Organization and Behavior, Including Ethical Considerations; Public Reporting Standards, Auditing and Taxes; Periodic Reporting for Internal and External Purposes; and Decision Analysis, Including Modeling and Information Systems. NAA has also promulgated a code of ethics for management accountants.

Further evidence of the increasing importance and status of managerial accountants appeared in an article on 3M, which is the second most admired corporation in America in a *Fortune* magazine study. At 3M, divisional controllers are seen as "business advisors and financial consultants who are part of the operating/decision-making team."[3] This attitude was not prevalent 20 years ago. Controllers and other management accountants were then viewed as "bean counters" whose only purpose was to harass operating managers with trifling reports.

SUMMARY

Managerial accounting and financial accounting both deal with economic events and reports about them. But the two areas of accounting differ in many ways, primarily because they serve different audiences. Managerial accounting serves internal managers in organizations. In businesses, managers in sales, production, finance, and accounting, and top executives use accounting data for planning and control, including decision making and performance evaluation. Managers of not-for-profit organizations perform many of these same functions and use much of the same accounting data as managers in businesses.

As you study managerial accounting, you will be introduced to some of the activities managers carry out in several areas of a business firm or other economic organization. Some

[3] Kathy Williams, "The Magic of 3M, Management Accounting Excellence," *Management Accounting,* February 1986, 20–27.

managerial accounting concept or type of report is related to almost every area of managerial activity, and managerial accounting draws heavily on the concepts from related business disciplines. Changes in the manufacturing environment are prompting changes in managerial accounting as well as in related disciplines.

KEY TERMS

advanced manufacturing	line function
budgeting	management by exception
Certified Management Accountant	management by objectives
control function	performance evaluation
control reports	planning function
cycle time	pro forma statement
decision making	staff function
just-in-time manufacturing	

ASSIGNMENT MATERIAL

Questions for Discussion

1-1 *Everyday planning and control* For each of the following activities, find an analogy to the planning and control process described in the chapter. Describe the process to be undertaken in these activities and compare with the process described in the chapter.

(a) Taking a course in college, including preparation and study, taking examinations, and evaluating test results.

(b) Taking a long automobile trip.

(c) Decorating your own room or apartment.

(d) Coaching an athletic team.

1-2 *Financial versus managerial accounting information* The chapter illustrates that financial and managerial accounting overlap to some extent, but that managerial accounting uses information not normally used in financial accounting. For financial accounting purposes, the information needed about a particular automobile is its cost, its expected useful life, its residual value at the end of that life, and the method of depreciation to be applied. What other information about a particular business automobile might be important for managerial accounting purposes?

1-3 *Who needs financial accounting?* The chapter points out that differences between financial and managerial accounting relate to differences in the decisions made by managers and those made by parties external to the firm. If managerial accounting is supposed to serve the information needs of managers, why should managers know and understand financial accounting?

Problems

1-4   **Review of financial statement preparation**   Following is the balance sheet for Illustrative Company as of December 31, 19X4 and selected information relating to activities in 19X5.

Illustrative Company
Balance Sheet
as of December 31, 19X4

Assets

Current assets:		
Cash	$ 10,000	
Accounts receivable	40,000	
Inventory	65,000	
Total current assets		$115,000
Property, plant, and equipment:		
Cost	250,000	
Less: Accumulated depreciation	100,000	
Net		150,000
Total assets		$265,000

Equities

Current liabilities:		
Accounts payable	$ 10,000	
Taxes payable	12,000	
Total current liabilities		$ 22,000
Long-term debt:		
Bonds payable, 7%, due 19X8		100,000
Total liabilities		122,000
Stockholders' equity:		
Common stock, no par value, 10,000 shares		
issued and outstanding	90,000	
Retained earnings	53,000	
Total stockholders' equity		143,000
Total equities		$265,000

During 19X5 the following events occurred.
(a) Sales on account were $350,000.
(b) Collections on receivables were $360,000.
(c) Credit purchases of inventory were $180,000.
(d) Cost of goods sold was $150,000.
(e) Payments to suppliers for inventory were $165,000.
(f) Cash paid for operating expenses was $80,000; interest on bonds was also paid.
(g) Plant and equipment were bought for $70,000 cash.
(h) Taxes payable at December 31, 19X4, were paid.
(i) Depreciation expense was $30,000.
(j) Income taxes are 40% of income before taxes. No payments were made on 19X5 taxes in 19X5.
(k) A dividend of $10,000 was declared and paid.

Required
1. Prepare an income statement for Illustrative Company for 19X5.
2. Prepare a balance sheet for Illustrative Company as of December 31, 19X5.

1-5 ***Review of the cash flow statement***   Using the information from 1-4, prepare a cash flow statement for 19X5 for Illustrative Company.

1-6 ***Review of financial statement preparation***   Below is the balance sheet for Example Company as of December 31, 19X4, followed by selected information relating to activities in 19X5.

Example Company
Balance Sheet
as of December 31, 19X4

Assets

Current assets:		
Cash	$ 20,000	
Accounts receivable	50,000	
Inventory	120,000	
Prepaid expenses	8,000	
Total current assets		$198,000
Property, plant, and equipment:		
Cost	350,000	
Less: Accumulated depreciation	130,000	
Net		220,000
Total assets		$418,000

Equities

Current liabilities:		
Accounts payable	$ 40,000	
Taxes payable	25,000	
Accrued expenses	12,000	
Total current liabilities		$ 77,000
Long-term liabilities:		
Bonds payable, 6%, due 19X7		200,000
Total liabilities		277,000
Stockholders' equity:		
Common stock, $10 par value, 5,000		
shares issued and outstanding	50,000	
Retained earnings	91,000	
Total stockholders' equity		141,000
Total equities		$418,000

Other data relating to activities in 19X5 were as follows.
(a) Sales on account were $480,000.
(b) Collections on accounts receivable were $430,000.
(c) Credit purchases of goods for resale were $220,000.
(d) Cost of goods sold was $240,000.
(e) Payments of accounts payable were $210,000.

(f) Interest expense on bonds payable was paid in cash.

(g) Prepaid expenses at the beginning of the year expired and new prepayments in the amount of $6,000 were made in 19X5.

(h) Accrued taxes payable at the beginning of the year were paid.

(i) Accrued expenses payable are for wages and salaries. Total cash payments for wages and salaries during 19X5 were $95,000. At the end of 19X5, $7,000 was owed to employees.

(j) Other cash payments for expenses during 19X5 were $65,000, not including the $6,000 prepayments in (g).

(k) Common stock was sold for $40,000 (4,000 shares).

(l) Plant and equipment were purchased for $30,000 cash.

(m) Depreciation expense was $40,000.

(n) The income tax rate is 40%. Income taxes for 19X5 were unpaid at year end.

(o) A dividend of $5,000 was declared and paid.

Required

1. Prepare an income statement for Example Company for 19X5.
2. Prepare a balance sheet for Example Company as of December 31, 19X5.

1-7 *Review of the cash flow statement*   Using the information from 1-6, prepare a cash flow statement for 19X5 for Example Company.

1-8 *Different costs for different purposes*   Suppose you are going to drive home this weekend, a round trip of 180 miles. Your car gets 30 miles per gallon of gas and you expect gas to cost $0.80 per gallon. Insurance and depreciation are $1,000 per year. You usually drive 10,000 miles per year. A friend asks you to take her along. She lives a block from your home.

Required

1. What are the costs of taking your friend along, as opposed to going by yourself?
2. Suppose now that you are not planning on going home. Your friend asks for a ride and you are willing to go. What are the costs of going, as opposed to not going?

VOLUME-COST-PROFIT ANALYSIS AND DECISION MAKING

The first part of this book discusses the most basic principles of decision making, the principles of volume-cost-profit analysis. These principles underlie the chapters in Part One and most of the material in the rest of the book. Much planning and decision making depends on classifying costs according to their behavior. An understanding of cost behavior is essential if a manager is to have the best information for making rational decisions.

The principles and techniques developed in this section are discussed and illustrated primarily in a business context. But nearly all are applicable to not-for-profit economic entities, such as hospitals, universities, charitable institutions, and government units.

CHAPTER 2

PROFIT PLANNING

Companies must earn profits to stay in business. Managers want to take actions that will increase profitability and therefore need to predict how their actions will affect profits. (For example, what will happen to profits if increasing promotional efforts by $250,000 increases sales by 50,000 units?) Managers are also concerned with questions such as: How many units must we sell to earn $50,000? What selling price should we set? Should we hire another salesperson? Would staying open another two hours each day be profitable?

In reports prepared for external use, costs are normally grouped according to the functional areas of business: production (cost of goods sold); marketing (selling expenses); administration (general and administrative expenses); and financing (interest expense).[1] A functional classification does not provide the information necessary to predict what is likely to happen to costs and profits if circumstances change, and a manager must plan for change and take actions to make changes.

Volume-cost-profit analysis helps managers to plan for change and to answer questions such as those posed above. **Volume-cost-profit (VCP) analysis** is a method for analyzing the relationships among volume, costs, and profits.[2] Managers use these relationships to plan, budget, and make decisions. The first step in

---

[1] Other terms you may encounter that mean essentially the same thing as VCP analysis are *cost-volume-profit analysis, breakeven analysis,* and *profit-volume analysis.*

[2] In financial accounting the term *cost* denotes the initial expenditure or incurrence of a liability. *Expense* denotes expired costs—costs assigned to the income statement for a period of time. Since *cost* is the more general term, we shall generally use it to refer to both expired and unexpired costs.

VCP analysis is classifying costs according to behavior. Classifying costs according to behavior is distinctive to managerial use of accounting information.

COST BEHAVIOR

We classify a cost as either fixed or variable, according to whether the *total* amount of the cost changes as activity changes. *Activity* is a general term denoting anything that the company does; examples of activity include units of product sold or produced, hours worked, invoices prepared, and parts inspected. *Volume* is, for most purposes, virtually synonymous with activity, and we use both terms throughout this book. In this chapter we use sales as the measure of volume and classify costs either as fixed or as variable with sales. Not all costs fall into these categories; other measures of activity are often important. We consider these in Chapter 3.

Variable Costs

A **variable cost** changes, in total, in direct proportion to changes in volume. To illustrate this concept, let us consider Ted's Threads, a retail store.

Ted buys shirts for $9.80 each from a wholesaler and sells them for $20 each. He also incurs a $0.20 cost for wrapping materials for each shirt sold. The monthly rent for Ted's store is 10% of his sales. At a selling price of $20 per shirt, the cost of rent is $2 per shirt ($20 × 10%). For now, we shall assume, unrealistically, that he has no other costs.

There is a difference between the rent and the other two costs. The per-unit cost of rent changes if Ted changes his selling price, while the per-unit amounts of the other two costs do not. But all three costs vary with the volume of sales. That is, they are incurred each time a shirt is sold, and the *total* of each increases or decreases in proportion to changes in sales. For our purposes, we can treat these three costs as a single variable cost of $12 per shirt ($9.80 + $0.20 + $2.00).

Suppose that in the month of April Ted sells 750 shirts. His income statement is

Ted's Threads
Income Statement for April

Sales (750 units × $20)	$15,000
Variable costs (750 × $12)	9,000
Income	$ 6,000

Suppose that Ted sells 751 shirts in May. What will his income be? Instead of preparing a whole new income statement, you could find the additional income from the sale of one more shirt and add it to the income for 750 shirts. This added income is $20 − $12 = $8. Ted's income will be $6,008.

Contribution Margin

Contribution margin is the difference between selling price per unit and variable cost per unit. (The term is also often used to denote *total contribution margin,* the difference between total sales and total variable costs.) In some cases it is useful and convenient to express contribution margin as a percentage. The **contribution margin percentage** is per-unit contribution margin divided by selling price, or total contribution margin divided by total sales dollars.

The term *contribution* is used because what is left from a sale after variable costs are covered *contributes* to covering other costs and producing profit. In Ted's case, contribution margin per unit is $8 ($20 − $12) and contribution margin percentage is 40% ($8/$20).

If all costs are variable, as in Ted's case, income equals total contribution margin and can be computed by multiplying either per-unit contribution by the number of units sold, or contribution margin percentage by total sales dollars. Thus, even without preparing an income statement you could compute Ted's income from selling 750 shirts as $6,000 ($8 × 750). Moreover, with knowledge of the contribution margin, you know that income increases by $8 when sales increase by one unit, to 751. What will Ted's income be if he sells only 749 shirts in June? Ted will earn $5,992 ($8 × 749).

Fixed Costs

Fixed costs remain the same in *total* over a wide range of volume. Suppose that Ted spends $4,800 per month to pay a salesperson and to rent display counters, cash registers, and other equipment. These costs will be the same whether he sells 600 or 800 shirts, and they might even be the same if he sells no shirts at all.

We can determine total costs as

Total costs = fixed costs + (variable cost per unit × unit volume)

As you can see, fixed costs are a part of total cost but are the same regardless of volume. The following income statements for Ted's Threads show the effects of his fixed costs.

Ted's Threads
Income Statements at Various Sales Levels

	749 Units	750 Units	751 Units
Sales	$14,980	$15,000	$15,020
Variable costs	8,988	9,000	9,012
Contribution margin	5,992	6,000	6,008
Fixed costs	4,800	4,800	4,800
Income	$ 1,192	$ 1,200	$ 1,208

Notice that the $8 difference in contribution margin at 749, 750, and 751 units is also the difference in incomes for those levels. Fixed costs do not change the usefulness of contribution margin per unit in predicting income. When a firm has both variable and fixed costs, income can be predicted by multiplying per-unit contribution margin by unit sales and then subtracting total fixed costs.

Thus, to calculate Ted's income for sales of 800 shirts, we can multiply the $8 contribution margin by 800 shirts. This gives total contribution margin of $6,400, and when we subtract fixed costs of $4,800, we find income of $1,600. We could also determine total contribution at that level of sales by multiplying sales of $16,000 (800 × $20) by the 40% contribution margin percentage, giving $6,400. Again, income is total contribution margin minus fixed costs.

An important use of VCP analysis is to help managers predict how income will *change* if sales change. If Ted wonders what will happen to his income if sales increase by 50 shirts per month, VCP analysis can tell him that income will increase by $400, the 50-shirt increase multiplied by the $8 per-shirt contribution margin. The $400 change in income can also be determined by computing the increase in sales revenue (50 units × $20 = $1,000) and multiplying by the contribution margin percentage of 40%. Note that the increase in income is $400 no matter what the current level of sales.

Emphasis on Expectations

At this early stage we are dealing with a simplified case, looking at the costs in a single period (a month, a quarter, or perhaps a year) and predicting costs and income for the following period. The point is that we are dealing with the future, not the past. It is unreasonable to expect either per-unit variable costs or total fixed costs to remain the same month after month, or year after year. There are many reasons why total fixed costs, per-unit variable costs, and selling prices can change.

Inflation is a major cause of changes in both fixed and variable costs. Suppliers might raise their prices. Lessors might raise rents. Salaries might rise, and so on. Profit planning must take into account *expected* changes in costs. VCP analysis does not assume that costs remain constant over time; the analysis is based on expectations. Thus, if Ted expected the price that he pays for shirts to go up by $0.80 next month, he would use $10.60 (instead of $9.80) in his planning for next month.   *9.80 + .80*

Because of inflation, or for other reasons, managers might change selling prices. For example, because he expects an increase in the price he pays for shirts, Ted might raise his price to $21. (Of course, an increase in his selling price will also increase Ted's per-unit cost for rent, so Ted would use both the new price and the new variable costs in his plans.)

The emphasis on expectations is also important because managers can themselves change some of their costs. Ted could hire another employee at a monthly salary, increasing his fixed costs, or he could advertise (also increasing fixed costs). In a more complex firm, many cost changes are the result of managerial actions. A large company could increase (or decrease) its office staff or change its level of spending on such items as travel and employee training. Thus, fixed costs might change from one period to the next without any change in the nature of those costs (as not varying with the level of activity). For planning purposes, managers predict fixed costs based on what they *expect* for the coming period.

As a general rule, managers can change some fixed costs more easily than they can change per-unit variable costs (and, hence, total variable costs), especially over short periods of time (more about this in Chapter 3). Some accountants, therefore, use the term **nonvariable costs** instead of *fixed costs*. Their point is that fixed costs are not fixed in the sense that they cannot be changed, but rather that, unlike per-unit variable costs, fixed costs do not *automatically* change when volume changes. We call such costs *fixed* because that term is more common, and the term is best thought of as describing those costs that do not change with changes in volume. Regardless of terminology, the emphasis in planning is on expectations. If actual conditions (selling prices, prices from suppliers, etc.) do not coincide with expectations, or if managers later change decisions, there will be differences between actual and predicted costs and profit. Such differences between actuality and expectations are inherent in business but do not reduce the need to plan.

Income Statement Formats – Financial Accounting and Contribution Margin

You have probably noticed that the format used for income statements in this chapter differs from that used in financial accounting. As stated earlier, in financial accounting, costs are usually classified by function or by object. The income statements in Exhibit 2-1 highlight the differences between the two approaches.

Exhibit 2-1
Comparison of Income Statements Using the Financial Accounting and the Contribution Margin Approaches

Financial Accounting Format		Contribution Margin Format	
Sales	$15,000	Sales	$15,000
Cost of sales (750 × $9.80)	7,350	Variable costs:	
		Cost of shirts (750 × $9.80)	7,350
Gross profit	7,650	Wrapping (750 × $0.20)	150
		Store rent (750 × $2, or 10% of $15,000)	1,500
		Total	9,000
Operating expenses:			
Wrapping (750 × $0.20)	150	Contribution margin	6,000
Store rent (750 × $2, or 10% of $15,000)	1,500		
Salary and equipment rent	4,800	Fixed costs:	
Total operating expenses	6,450	Salary and equipment rent	4,800
Income	$ 1,200	Income	$ 1,200

Notice that the sales and income figures are the same under both approaches, but the costs are classified in different ways. The statements are for a month when Ted sells 750 shirts.

The obvious differences between the statements are in terminology and the placement of the costs of store rent and wrapping materials. The principal difference is that a manager who receives a statement in the financial accounting format must first rearrange the costs to perform VCP analysis. The financial accounting format does not permit a manager to predict how a change in sales volume affects profit because it tells little about cost behavior. One unfortunate result is the tendency of some managers to treat fixed costs as if they were variable and to use average total cost per unit for planning. You should see that, because total fixed costs remain the same at different levels of activity, the *average* fixed cost per unit changes whenever volume changes. Thus, the average fixed cost per unit when Ted sells 750 units is $6.40 ($4,800/750), while the average when he sells 800 units is $6 ($4,800/800). The **average total cost per unit,** then, depends on the level of activity, with the average total per-unit cost for Ted being $18.40 ($6.40 fixed plus $12 variable) when he sells 750 units, and $18 ($6 fixed plus $12 variable) when he sells 800 units.

Failing to recognize that average total per-unit cost changes as volume changes can create problems when a manager attempts—unwisely—to use averages to predict future costs. You cannot use the average total per-unit cost for one level of activity to predict total costs at another level.

To illustrate this point, suppose Ted tries to use the $18.40 average total cost per unit (at a volume of 750 shirts) to predict total costs at a volume of 800 shirts. He would predict costs of $14,720 ($18.40 × 800 shirts). But Ted's income statements at volumes of 750 and 800 shirts are

	750 Shirts	800 Shirts
Sales	$15,000	$16,000
Variable costs	9,000	9,600
Contribution margin	6,000	6,400
Fixed costs	4,800	4,800
Income	$ 1,200	$ 1,600
Average cost per unit	$ 18.40	$ 18
Profit per unit	$ 1.60	$ 2

Total costs at a volume of 800 shirts are $14,400 ($9,600 + $4,800). What *appears* to be additional profit per unit at the higher level of activity is simply the result of spreading the fixed costs over a larger number of units. The behavior of Ted's costs has not changed at all; variable costs remain at 60% of sales ($12 per unit) and fixed costs remain at $4,800. Using average total cost per unit to predict total costs is appropriate *only if all costs are variable.*

In the preceding example, notice that income *as a percentage of sales* (called **return on sales,** or **ROS**) differs at the two levels of volume. At sales of 750 units, income is 8% of sales, while at sales of 800 units, income is 10% of sales. Perhaps the most common mistake managers make is to use the ROS percentage at one level of volume to predict income at another volume level. The earlier discussion of fixed costs showed that if a company has *any* fixed costs, its income, as a percentage of sales, increases as volume increases. Additionally, the percentage increase in income is greater than the percentage increase in sales. In the income statements just shown, a mere 6⅔% increase in sales ($1,000/$15,000) produced a 33⅓% increase in income (from $1,200 to $1,600).

RELEVANT RANGE

We have already stated that per-unit variable costs and total fixed costs might not remain the same over several periods. Neither can we expect per-unit variable costs and total fixed costs to be the same at all possible levels of activity. That is, the per-unit variable cost and total fixed cost can be expected to behave as we predict only over some limited range of volume.

For example, Ted might be able to handle the store with only one helper as long as he sells no more than, say, 900 shirts per month. At some point around that level of sales, he will have to hire additional help. If he pays a new employee a commission on each shirt sold, his variable cost per unit will increase; if he pays the new employee a salary, his fixed costs will increase. It is also possible that if Ted sells a great many shirts he will get a discount on the purchase price, thus reducing his per-unit variable costs.

An important assumption underlying VCP analysis is that the firm will operate within a **relevant range,** a range of volume over which it can reasonably expect selling price, per-unit variable cost, and total fixed costs to be constant.[3] Firms usually have several relevant ranges and cannot use the same value of each factor (price, per-unit variable cost, total fixed costs) at all levels of volume. For planning purposes, managers forecast the approximate range of activity and use the costs they believe will hold within that range.

A special case of operating outside the relevant range occurs when a business shuts down for a short period. A firm that closes for a week or a month would find its total costs for that period to be less than its normal total fixed costs. For instance, a company closing for a month would turn out the lights, not heat the building at the normal temperature, and probably not advertise. The company might also lay off salaried employees. Thus, it is not appropriate to interpret *fixed costs* as the costs that the firm would incur at zero volume. Rather, fixed costs are better thought of as the planned costs that will not change in total as volume changes *within the relevant range*. The relevant range is a range of volume over which price, fixed costs in total, and variable costs per unit are expected to remain the same.

VOLUME-COST-PROFIT GRAPH

Figure 2-1 gives a graphical representation of the VCP picture for Ted's Threads. At any volume, the vertical distance between total costs and fixed costs is total variable costs at that volume. The revenue line shows total sales dollars at any

---

[3] The problem of changing selling prices is considered in Chapter 4.

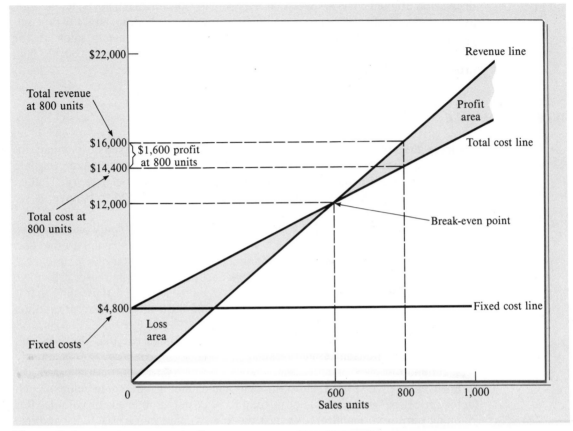

Figure 2-1   Volume-Cost-Profit Chart

volume and is simply the selling price per unit multiplied by the level of unit volume.

Although we have extended the lines on the graph far to the right and to the vertical axis on the left, it is not usually legitimate to do so because of the relevant range. In Ted's case, as suggested earlier, fixed costs would be less than $4,800 if the store were closed for the month (zero volume), and either per-unit variable or total fixed costs, or both, are likely to change if volume exceeds 900 shirts per month. Thus, we extend the lines to zero volume and beyond 900 shirts primarily to make it easier to read the graph.

The graph highlights an important point. As long as price exceeds variable cost (contribution margin is positive), selling more units will benefit the firm, either by increasing profits or by *decreasing losses*. Thus, the firm might well be better off to stay open and incur losses than to shut down and incur larger losses. Such is often the case with *seasonal* businesses. For example, many firms operating in summer resort areas *expect* losses during the winter. Similarly, toy companies expect losses after the Christmas season. Many seasonal businesses continue to operate in the off-season because they recognize that the contribution margin from the additional, though lower, sales reduces their losses. Chapter 3 considers this point in more detail.

The graph brings to a manager's attention a particularly important point—the point where total revenues equal total costs. This is the **break-even point**—the point at which profits are zero. When a firm operates above the break-even point it makes profits; below that point, it shows losses. At any volume, the vertical distance between the revenue line and the total cost line is the amount of profit or loss (shaded areas) at that volume.

Knowing the break-even point is useful for many purposes. Managers of not-for-profit organizations frequently seek to break even, or show only a small profit or loss, on some of their activities. For a business firm, breaking even is the first step in the pursuit of profits. We can derive an equation to find this point by using relationships we already know. We know that profit equals total sales minus total variable costs minus total fixed costs. That is,

$$\begin{array}{ccc}\text{Total} & \text{total} & \text{total} \\ \text{sales} & -\ \text{variable} & -\ \text{fixed} = \text{profit} \\ \text{dollars} & \text{costs} & \text{costs}\end{array}$$

Using Q to denote the quantity of units sold, we can restate the formula as

$$\left(\begin{array}{c}\text{Per-unit} \\ \text{selling} \times Q \\ \text{price}\end{array}\right) - \left(\begin{array}{c}\text{per-unit} \\ \text{variable} \times Q \\ \text{cost}\end{array}\right) - \begin{array}{c}\text{total} \\ \text{fixed} = \text{profit} \\ \text{costs}\end{array}$$

Knowing that selling price minus variable cost per unit equals contribution margin per unit, we can combine the first two components, add fixed costs to both sides, and get

$$\left(\begin{array}{c}\text{Contribution} \\ \text{margin} \times Q \\ \text{per unit}\end{array}\right) = \begin{array}{c}\text{total} \\ \text{fixed} + \text{profit} \\ \text{costs}\end{array}$$

Since we are looking for the break-even point (where profit is *zero*), the profit term drops out. Now we can solve for Q (the break-even point in units) by dividing both sides by contribution margin per unit, producing

$$\begin{array}{c}Q\ \text{(break-even} \\ \text{sales in units)}\end{array} = \frac{\text{total fixed costs}}{\text{contribution margin per unit}}$$

We can interpret this formula as saying "How many units must we sell to cover fixed costs of $4,800, if each unit contributes $8 to cover those fixed costs?" Applying this formula to Ted's case reveals a break-even point of 600 shirts.

$$\begin{array}{c}\text{Break-even sales} \\ \text{in units}\end{array} = \frac{\$4,800}{\$20 - \$12} = \frac{\$4,800}{\$8} = 600\ \text{shirts}$$

Both the graph in Figure 2-1 and the break-even formula derived above show sales in units. We could just as well use another measure of sales volume, sales dollars.[4] It is sometimes more convenient to work with the contribution margin percentage, in which case contribution margin percentage replaces per-

---

[4] Of course, we could calculate break-even sales dollars by multiplying the break-even sales in units by the selling price. The answer is $12,000 (600 × $20).

unit contribution margin in the break-even calculation and the result is break-even sales dollars. The following equation shows this alternative applied to Ted's situation.

$$\text{Break-even sales in dollars} = \frac{\text{total fixed costs}}{\text{contribution margin percentage}} = \frac{\$4,800}{40\%} = \$12,000$$

We can interpret this version of the break-even formula as saying: "How many dollars of sales does it take to cover fixed costs of $4,800, *given* that each sales dollar yields $0.40 of contribution margin (the 40% contribution margin percentage)?" The units required to break even are still 600 ($12,000/$20 selling price per unit), and both formulas give the same answer for the break-even point, 600 units or $12,000.

The contribution-margin-percentage approach is especially useful to companies that sell several products. For instance, managers of a department store that sells thousands of items find it awkward to work with unit sales. (It makes little sense to speak of sales of 12,500,000 units when the units are as diverse as handkerchiefs, shoes, refrigerators, and television sets.) They prefer to work with sales dollars because their experience allows them to interpret numbers such as $4,000,000 of sales. Chapter 4 discusses multiproduct companies in more detail. For a single-product company, either of the ways of stating contribution margin (and of determining the break-even point) can be used, the choice depending on computational convenience.

Firms that provide services, rather than goods, often charge their clients for the hours that they work. CPA firms, law firms, and consulting firms are examples. For these firms, chargeable hours (the number of hours worked that are chargeable to client business) is an appropriate and useful measure of volume, and works well as the horizontal axis of a VCP graph.

ACHIEVING TARGET PROFITS

The break-even point is of interest, but managers of profit-seeking organizations are also concerned with meeting a desired or **target profit.** The target could be expressed as an absolute dollar amount or as an ROS percentage. The technique for determining the volume needed to achieve a target profit is a simple variation of the break-even case. The break-even point tells you what sales are required to make no profit and incur no loss; by incorporating into the analysis the amount or rate of profit desired, we can determine the sales volume required to achieve that profit.

Target Dollar Profit

In break-even calculations we found the number of units or the sales dollars required to provide total contribution margin equal to total fixed costs. Finding the volume required to achieve a target profit is essentially the same thing. We now want to know what sales are required, in units or dollars, to earn total contribution margin equal to the *sum* of total fixed costs and the target profit.

Suppose Ted wishes to earn a profit of $2,000 per month. How many shirts must he sell? We know that total contribution margin must be equal to fixed costs of $4,800 for Ted to break even. Hence, to achieve a profit of $2,000, total contribution margin must be $2,000 greater than fixed costs, or $6,800. To achieve total contribution margin of $6,800 when the contribution margin per unit is $8 ($20 − $12), he must sell a total of 850 units. Expressed in general terms

$$\left(\begin{array}{c}\text{Sales, in units,} \\ \text{to achieve} \\ \text{target profit}\end{array} \times \begin{array}{c}\text{contribution} \\ \text{margin} \\ \text{per unit}\end{array}\right) - \begin{array}{c}\text{fixed} \\ \text{costs}\end{array} = \begin{array}{c}\text{target} \\ \text{profit}\end{array}$$

Restating this equation to solve for the needed level of sales yields

$$\frac{\text{Sales, in units, to}}{\text{achieve target profit}} = \frac{\text{fixed costs + target profit}}{\text{contribution margin per unit}}$$

Applying this formula in Ted's case, we have

$$\frac{\text{Sales, in units, to}}{\text{achieve target profit}} = \frac{\$4,800 + \$2,000}{\$20 - \$12} = \frac{\$6,800}{\$8} = 850 \text{ units}$$

Notice that the numerator of the formula is the total contribution margin required to earn the target profit. It consists of the $4,800 contribution margin required for break-even plus the $2,000 contribution margin required for the target profit.

The same technique applies if we work with contribution margin percentage rather than per-unit contribution margin. Substituting the contribution margin percentage in the above formula, and recognizing that the switch to a percentage yields sales dollars rather than sales in units, the formula is

$$\frac{\text{Sales, in dollars, to}}{\text{achieve target profit}} = \frac{\text{fixed costs + target profit}}{\text{contribution margin percentage}}$$

Applying the formula to Ted's situation yields required sales of $17,000.

$$\frac{\text{Sales, in dollars, to}}{\text{achieve target profit}} = \frac{\$4,800 + \$2,000}{40\%} = \frac{\$6,800}{40\%} = \$17,000$$

Once again, the answer is the same regardless of approach. Target sales in units are 850 units, whether computed directly or as a result of the computation of target sales dollars ($17,000/$20), and target sales in dollars are $17,000 (850 × $20).

Target Return on Sales

Occasionally, managers state their profit target as an ROS (ROS = profit divided by sales). Managers with such a profit target are saying that their desired dollar profit varies with sales.

Suppose that Ted wishes to earn a 15% ROS. We know that his variable costs are already 60% of sales ($12/$20). Therefore, 75% of his sales go to variable costs and profit, leaving 25% to cover fixed costs. We use a variation of the break-even formula based on contribution margin percentage to find target sales.

$$\text{Sales, in dollars, to achieve target ROS} = \frac{\text{fixed costs}}{\text{contribution margin percentage} - \text{target ROS}}$$

To achieve a target ROS of 15% Ted needs sales of

$$\text{Sales, in dollars, to achieve target ROS} = \frac{\$4,800}{40\% - 15\%} = \frac{\$4,800}{25\%} = \$19,200$$

Again, note that because Ted needs 75% of sales for variable costs and profit, 25% is left to cover fixed costs. Ted's income statement shows that logic.

Sales	$19,200	100%
Variable costs (60% of sales)	11,520	60%
Contribution margin	7,680	40%
Fixed costs	4,800	25%
Income (equal to 15% × $19,200)	$ 2,880	15%

Warning: Don't forget that the percentages of fixed costs and profit to sales are valid *only* at this volume. To achieve sales of $19,200, Ted has to sell 960 shirts ($19,200/$20).

We could also translate Ted's goal of a 15% ROS into a $3 profit per shirt ($20 × 15%). Subtracting the variable costs of $12 *and* the $3 profit from the $20 selling price leaves $5 to cover fixed costs. In a variation of the basic break-even formula (fixed costs/contribution margin), we could determine the sales volume needed for a target 15% ROS as 960 units ($4,800/$5). Note that this answer agrees with the one computed earlier.

Changing Plans

The concepts of contribution margin, break-even analysis, and target profit are useful when managers are contemplating some change in plans in the hope of increasing profits. A typical example is an increase in advertising, with the expectation of increased sales.

It should be clear that the advertising does not increase profits by the increase in units sold multiplied by the per-unit contribution margin. Why? Although *total contribution margin* increases by that amount, total fixed costs also increase by the cost of the advertising. Thus, the change in profit is the change in total contribution margin *minus* the change in fixed costs.

Consider a firm with a per-unit contribution margin of $10 and a $50,000 proposed advertising campaign that is expected to increase sales by 4,000 units. Total contribution margin will increase by $40,000 (4,000 × $10), but fixed costs will be $50,000 higher, so that profit will be $10,000 less than it would have been without the extra advertising. Using the break-even formula and the concept of contribution margin, we can determine that it will take a sales increase of 5,000 units just to cover the increase in fixed costs ($50,000 fixed costs/$10 per-unit contribution margin). Total profit will increase only if the advertising can increase sales by more than 5,000 units.

The preceding analysis does not require knowing the sales that the firm expected without the advertising campaign. That is, it does not matter whether sales expected without the additional advertising were 0, 50,000, or 2,000,000 units; as long as the increase in volume is greater than 5,000 units, taking the proposed action increases profits over what they would have been.

TARGET SELLING PRICES

We can also use VCP analysis to determine the selling price to charge to earn a target profit *given* expected unit sales. The technique for determining a target selling price requires separating *variable* costs into those that are constant amounts per unit and those that are a constant percentage of selling price. There are three possibilities: (1) all variable costs are a constant amount per unit; (2) all variable costs are a constant percentage of selling price; and (3) variable costs are a mixture of the two types. Only the first and third of these possibilities are realistic, so we limit our discussion to those situations.

Variable Costs as a Constant Per-Unit Amount

Because the task of determining target selling price is simpler when, in contrast to Ted's case, all variable costs are a constant amount per unit, we present this technique first. Consider another retailer, Joan's Jeans. Its per-unit variable costs are $12, none of which depends on selling price, and its monthly fixed costs are $4,800. Suppose Joan wishes to earn $1,500 per month and believes she can sell 900 pairs of jeans. What price must she charge?

It is easiest to answer this question by building an income statement from the bottom up. Start with the required profit of $1,500, add the $4,800 of fixed costs, and arrive at a total required contribution margin of $6,300. At a volume of 900 units, Joan's total variable costs are $10,800 ($12 × 900). The following is Joan's income statement as far as we know it.

Joan's Jeans
Income Statement at Volume of 900 Units

Sales	$?
Variable costs ($12 × 900)	10,800
Contribution margin	6,300
Fixed costs	4,800
Income	$ 1,500

Sales must be $17,100, the amount necessary to provide $6,300 of contribution margin when variable costs are $10,800. The unit selling price has to be $19 ($17,100/900 units).

Another approach is to determine the desired contribution margin per unit—by dividing the total required contribution margin by unit volume ($6,300/900 = $7 in Joan's case)—and add that amount to the per-unit variable cost to arrive at the required selling price. Adding the $7 to the $12 per-unit variable cost yields, again, a price of $19.

Of course, a manager's analysis does not end with determining a required selling price. Suppose that Joan set a target profit of $6,000 per month on expected sales of 900 units. The required selling price would be $24. (Prove this for yourself.) If other stores sell similar jeans for $20, monthly sales of 900 units at $24 are probably unachievable. The analysis gives only the price required to reach a particular profit goal and does not mean that the assumed sales volume could be realized at that price.

Mixture of Variable Costs

For a firm whose variable costs are mixed—some being a constant amount per unit and others a constant percentage of selling price—the required price is determined most easily by using a formula. To illustrate, let's return to Ted's Threads.

Assume that Ted's target, like Joan's, is $1,500 per month and that he expects to sell 900 shirts. Remember that Ted's variable costs are $9.80 to purchase a shirt and $0.20 for wrapping material, plus rent at 10% of sales. Thus, his per-unit variable cost is $10 plus 10% of selling price. Instead of preparing an income statement, you can use a formula that describes an income statement.

$$\text{Sales} - \quad \text{variable costs} \quad - \text{fixed costs} = \text{profit}$$
$$S - [(900 \times \$10) + 10\%S] - \quad \$4,800 \quad = \$1,500$$
$$S - \quad \$9,000 - 10\%S \quad - \quad \$4,800 \quad = \$1,500$$
$$90\%S = \$15,300$$
$$S = \$17,000$$

Dividing the required sales of $17,000 by the expected volume of 900 shirts yields a target price of $18.89 (rounded).

Again, whatever the basis used for setting a target profit, the manager must then ask: Is the assumed sales volume likely to be achieved at the calculated selling price? VCP analysis cannot answer this question.

TARGET COSTING

Some companies, especially foreign ones, are now using a planning technique called target costing, which is almost the reverse of target pricing. They use the technique to help them decide whether to enter a new market or bring out a new product. The usual sequence is to estimate costs and volume, set a target profit, and then determine a target price. The essence of **target costing** is to determine how much the company can spend to manufacture and market a product, given a target profit. That is, the price and volume are estimated first, then the costs. The idea of target costing arose because, as noted earlier, the usual sequence often results in a price that is so high that the estimated volume is unachievable. Proponents of target costing argue that its use increases the involvement of manufacturing, designing, and engineering people in planning because they have a cost to aim at, and will be encouraged to be creative in reaching the target cost.

Analytically, the technique simply requires solving the basic VCP equation for total cost, variable cost, or fixed cost. For instance, if the managers agree on a target profit of $300,000 and that unit volume of 100,000 is achievable at a $20 price, the total allowable cost is

Revenue (100,000 × $20)	$2,000,000
Target profit	300,000
Total allowable cost	$1,700,000

If there is good reason to expect total fixed costs to be $1,200,000, the total variable costs can be $500,000, or $5 per unit. The $5 then, along with the $1,200,000 fixed cost, becomes an objective for the managers responsible for designing and manufacturing the product. Note, however, that as with target pricing, the answer given by the analysis might not be achievable. The managers responsible for manufacturing might be unsuccessful in reaching the target cost objective. In such cases the top managers might decide against introducing the new product or entering the new market. But they might also choose to reexamine their profit target and estimates of price and volume. For example, reconsideration of the profit target is more likely when the new product (or market) is one the managers believe especially important for, say, the company's reputation as an innovator, or for pursuing a long-range strategy.

ASSUMPTIONS AND LIMITATIONS OF VCP ANALYSIS

We have already mentioned some of the conditions necessary for VCP analysis to give useful predictions. First, sales volume must be within the relevant range. Second, it must be possible to graph both revenues and total costs as straight, rather than curved, lines. (To review, this second requirement means that selling price, per-unit variable cost, and total fixed costs must be constant throughout the relevant range.) We introduce two other assumptions here, but we discuss them in detail in later chapters.

First, VCP analysis assumes either (1) that the company sells only one product or (2) that the sales of each product in a multiproduct company are a constant percentage of total sales. The term **sales mix** is used to describe the percentage of each product's sales to total sales. If there is a change in sales mix, there is a possibility that the contribution margin percentage will change. Chapter 4 discusses multiproduct VCP analysis.

The second assumption is relevant only to manufacturing companies. It does not affect merchandising and service companies. To apply VCP analysis to a manufacturing firm, *production must equal sales*. Because of certain requirements of financial accounting (and tax laws) for manufacturing companies, income reported for financial accounting (or tax) purposes usually does not agree with income predicted by VCP analysis. Chapter 13 explains how those requirements cause differences between reported income and income predictions using VCP analysis.

Our primary examples, Ted's Threads, and its counterpart, Joan's Jeans, are relatively simple operations compared with most companies today. Bigger, more diverse companies are more difficult to analyze. Yet VCP analysis is a tool that can be and *is* used, in various forms, by managers of the largest and most complex organizations.

SUMMARY

Volume-cost-profit analysis is critical to planning and requires classifying costs by behavior. A cost is either fixed or variable depending on whether the total amount of the cost changes as activity changes. Contribution margin, the difference between price and variable cost, is important in VCP analysis. Contribution margin can be expressed as a per-unit amount, a total, or a percentage of selling price. The critical points in the chapter are the recognition of the fixed/variable cost classification scheme, the analytical value of this classification, and the usefulness of contribution margin.

Volume-cost-profit analysis can answer such questions as: What profits are earned at different levels of sales? What sales are needed to earn a particular profit? What are the effects of changes in selling prices? What price must we charge to earn a particular profit?

The usefulness of VCP analysis depends on estimates of revenue and cost behavior within relevant ranges of volume and over short periods. Managers can, with varying degrees of ease, change both costs and prices. Hence, VCP analysis is based on managers' estimates about conditions in the future, not those prevailing in the past. A VCP graph presents a single set of conditions that managers expect. The graph is a rough gauge of VCP relationships.

Volume-cost-profit analysis is valuable in planning, selecting alternatives, analyzing results, and incorporating new information into plans.

KEY TERMS

average total cost per unit	relevant range
break-even point	return on sales (ROS)
contribution margin	sales mix
contribution margin percentage	target costing
cost behavior	target profit
fixed costs	variable costs
nonvariable costs	volume-cost-profit (VCP) analysis

8. 625 units. Income will not be affected as long as the contribution margin from the additional units sold is sufficient to offset the expenditure for advertising. Hence, we need only determine what additional sales will produce contribution margin sufficient to cover the cost of the advertising. Because contribution margin per unit is $8, the number of units needed to cover the $5,000 advertising campaign is $5,000/$8 or 625 units. (Note that the current level of sales is irrelevant to the decision of whether or not to undertake the advertising campaign. As long as the campaign will increase sales by 625 units, Glassman will be neither better nor worse off than it would have been without it.)

9. (a) 12,500 units. The contribution margin per unit remains at $8 ($18 selling price − $10 variable cost) and the fixed costs remain at $100,000. Hence, the break-even point, in units, remains the same as before, or 12,500 units ($100,000/$8).

   (b) $225,000. Although the number of *units* to break even remains the same, the total sales in dollars must change in order to break even. One approach is simply to multiply the break-even sales in units by the selling price per unit (12,500 × $18 = $225,000). Another approach is to divide the fixed costs of $100,000 by the new contribution margin percentage of 44.44% ($8/$18).

This review problem has emphasized the possibility of changes in the structure of costs and selling prices. Managers must be alert for changes from outside (for example, a supplier raising prices) and should understand their effects on profits. Additionally, managers can analyze changes that they propose to see if they will increase profits. Part 8 of this problem gave an important practical example: an increase in a fixed cost was expected to lead to some increase in volume. If the marketing manager believes that the added cost will generate additional sales in excess of 625 units, the proposal for additional advertising would be wise.

APPENDIX: INCOME TAXES AND PROFIT PLANNING

Income taxes are a cost of doing business and should be considered, as should all costs, in the planning process. Income taxes are based on the amount of income before taxes. For our purposes, it is reasonable to assume that income taxes are a constant percentage of income before taxes. In most large corporations, this assumption is reasonable, but we hasten to point out that the tax law is exceedingly complex, not all businesses are incorporated, and that generalizations are risky.

Income taxes must be considered if managers seek an *after-tax* target profit. An after-tax target requires a revision of the basic target-profit formula. The revision requires converting the after-tax target profit to a pretax profit, which is computed by dividing the after-tax target profit by the quantity 1 minus the income tax rate. For example, suppose Ted wants to earn an after-tax profit of $2,100 and his tax rate is 30%. (We already know that his fixed costs are $4,800 and that his contribution margin percentage is 40%.)

To earn $2,100 after taxes, Ted must earn $3,000 before taxes ($2,100/ 70%). Of the pretax income of $3,000, $900 goes to the government ($3,000 × 30%), leaving $2,100 ($3,000 − $900). Accordingly, we use the basic formula for calculating the volume needed to earn a target profit as follows:

$$\text{Sales to achieve target after-tax profit} = \frac{\text{fixed costs} + \dfrac{\text{after-tax profit}}{1 - \text{tax rate}}}{\text{contribution margin percentage}}$$

or

contribution margin per unit

For a $2,100 profit after taxes, solving for sales dollars gives

$$\text{Sales} = \frac{\$4,800 + \dfrac{\$2,100}{70\%}}{40\%}$$

$$= \frac{\$4,800 + \$3,000}{40\%} = \frac{\$7,800}{40\%}$$

$$= \$19,500$$

We could calculate the unit sales required by dividing the $8 contribution margin per unit into the $7,800 (fixed costs plus required pretax profit), giving an answer of 975 shirts. The principle involved in planning for income taxes is quite similar to that of contribution margin. Contribution margin is the amount, or percentage, left over after covering variable costs. After-tax income is the amount left over after paying income taxes.

ASSIGNMENT MATERIAL

Questions for Discussion

2-1 VCP assumptions   You have been trying to convince a friend to use VCP analysis in planning her business, a clothing store. She has come up with the following objections to using the analysis and asks you to explain how to overcome them, if possible.

1. Inflation makes it likely that she will have to pay successively higher prices for the utilities, clothing she buys, the salaries she pays employees, and other operating costs. In addition, she will raise her selling prices as her costs rise. Therefore, she cannot use the current prices and costs to plan operations.
2. She sometimes advertises heavily, sometimes lightly. Because she can alter advertising cost almost at will, she wonders how you can treat it as fixed.
3. On occasion, she must sell clothes at greatly reduced prices to make room for new merchandise. Therefore, the percentage of the purchase price to the selling price is not always constant, and she is unsure whether that can be worked into the analysis.

Required: Respond to these objections.

2-2 Misconceptions about VCP analysis   A classmate is having trouble with VCP analysis and asks for your help. He has the following questions.

1. "How can VCP analysis work when you really don't know what's going to happen? You might have to change your selling price. Your suppliers might

change their prices. You might not sell the number of units you need to sell in order to earn a target profit. All sorts of things can happen that will invalidate your calculations."

2. "When I took economics, I learned that the higher the price, the less you sell. So how can you draw a straight revenue line?"

3. "I don't see how you can say that some costs are fixed. I'll accept depreciation and a few others, but salaries can be raised or lowered easily, your insurance premiums can go up or down, you can spend more or less on advertising, travel, and all sorts of other elements that you would call fixed."

Required: Answer your classmate's questions.

2-3 Will Sears' stockholders understand?   The following statement appeared in the Sears, Roebuck and Co. report to stockholders for the first quarter of a recent year.

Traditional buying patterns in the merchandise business generally result in the lowest sales of the year in the first quarter, producing a relatively high ratio of fixed costs to sales and lower ratio of income to sales.

Discuss this statement in relation to the concepts introduced in Chapter 2 and the traditional, late-January "white sales" at most department stores.

Exercises

2-4 Income statements and VCP analysis   Each of the following cases is independent of the others.

	Case		
	1	2	3
Unit selling price	$10	$20	$40
Unit variable cost	$8	$8	$20
Total fixed costs	$80,000	$500,000	$450,000
Unit volume	60,000	50,000	20,000

Required

1. Prepare an income statement for each case using the contribution margin format.

2. Determine the break-even point for case 1 in (a) units and (b) sales dollars.

3. For case 3, determine the (a) unit volume and (b) dollar volume required to earn a 10% return on sales.

4. For case 1, determine the price that the company must charge to double the profit you determined in item 1, still selling 60,000 units.

2-5 Income statements and VCP analysis   Each of the following cases is independent of the others.

	Case		
	1	2	3
Sales	$200,000	$800,000	$400,000
Variable cost percentage	60%	40%	30%
Total fixed costs	$ 60,000	$450,000	$300,000

Required
1. Prepare an income statement for each case using the contribution margin format.
2. Determine the break-even point in sales dollars for case 1.
3. For case 2, determine the dollar volume required to double the profit you determined in item 1.
4. For case 3, determine the dollar volume required to earn a 10% return on sales.

2-6 Income statements and VCP analysis, with taxes (related to Appendix)   Use the data from 2-4 for this assignment. Also assume a 30% income tax rate.

Required
1. Prepare income statements for cases 1 and 2.
2. For case 1, determine the (a) unit volume and (b) dollar volume required to double the after-tax profit you determined in item 1.
3. For case 2, determine the selling price that will double the before-tax profit at the original volume.

2-7 Income statements and VCP analysis with taxes (related to Appendix)   Use the data from 2-5 for this assignment. Also assume a 40% income tax rate.

Required
1. Prepare income statements for cases 1 and 2.
2. For cases 1 and 2, determine the dollar volume required to double the after-tax profit you determined in item 1.

2-8 Basic VCP analysis   Sea-Crest Company sells frozen fish dinners to supermarkets for $30 per case. Variable cost is $12 per case and annual fixed costs are $600,000.

Required
1. Determine the break-even point in (a) units and (b) dollars.
2. Determine the volume required to earn a $120,000 profit in (a) units and (b) dollars.
3. Determine the volume required to earn a 15% return on sales in (a) units and (b) dollars.
4. If Sea-Crest can sell 30,000 cases, what price would it have to charge to earn a $100,000 profit?
5. Redo item 4 assuming that the variable cost of $12 consists of $9 related to the case and a 10% commission on sales ($3 per case at the $30 price).

2-9 Basic VCP relationships, with income taxes (related to Appendix)   In one of its factories, M&J Company manufactures a single type of water pump sold to auto parts dealers throughout the country. M&J sells the pump for $30. Variable costs are $12 and annual fixed costs are $2,000,000. The tax rate is 40%.

Required
1. Determine the volume required to earn a $300,000 after-tax profit in (a) units and (b) dollars.
2. If M&J can sell 150,000 pumps, what price would it have to charge to earn a $300,000 after-tax profit?
3. Redo item 2 assuming that the variable cost of $12 consists of $10.50 for manufacturing and a 5% commission on sales ($1.50 per pump at the $30 price).

2-10 *Relationships among variables* Fill in the blanks for each of the following independent situations.

Case	(a) Selling Price per Unit	(b) Variable Cost Percentage	(c) Number of Units Sold	(d) Contribution Margin	(e) Fixed Costs	(f) Income (Loss)
1.	$80	—	4,000	$80,000	—	($10,000)
2.	40	70%	—	—	$60,000	12,000
3.	25	—	15,000	—	25,000	50,000
4.	—	60	15,000	—	22,000	8,000

2-11 *Relationships among variables* Fill in the blanks for each of the following independent situations.

	1	2	3	4
Selling price per unit	$ 5	—	$ 25	—
Variable cost per unit	$ 3	$ 6	$ 19	$ 6
Number of units sold	—	4,000	—	1,000
Total contribution margin	$4,000	$16,000	—	$2,000
Total fixed costs	$1,500	$ 8,000	$1,200	—
Income	—	—	$3,000	$1,200

2-12 *VCP graph* The graph on page 44 portrays the operations of Richmond Company.

Required: Using the graph, determine the following.
1. Sales dollars at the break-even point.
2. Fixed costs at 4,500 units sold.
3. Total variable costs at 4,000 units sold.
4. Variable cost per unit at 2,000 units sold.
5. Variable cost per unit at 5,000 units sold.
6. Selling price per unit.
7. Total contribution margin at 3,000 units sold.
8. Profit (loss) at sales of 3,000 units.
9. Profit (loss) at sales of 5,000 units.
10. Break-even sales, in units, if fixed costs were to increase by $500.

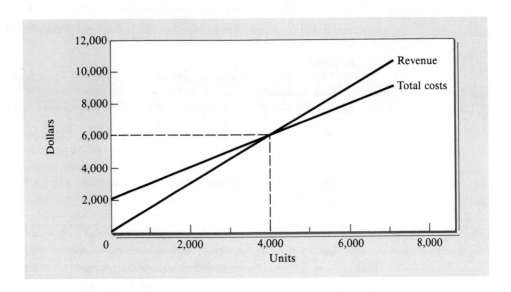

2-13 Graphs of cost behavior The graphs below depict the behavior of costs in relation to volume.

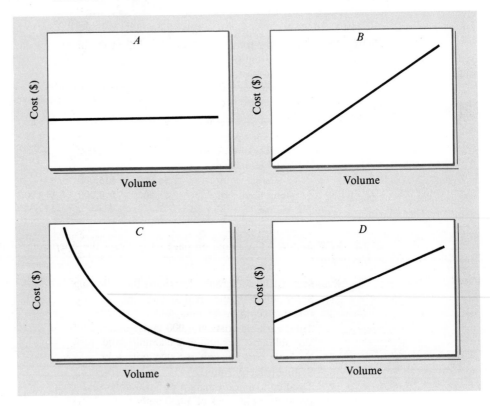

Required: Fill in the blanks using the letters from the graphs (A–D). One letter may be the answer to more than one question.

1. Which graph shows the behavior of total variable costs? _____
2. Which graph shows the behavior of total fixed costs? _____
3. Which graph shows the behavior of variable costs per unit? _____
4. Which graph shows the behavior of fixed costs per unit? _____
5. Which graph shows the behavior of total costs? _____

2-14 VCP chart   The chart below portrays the operations of Weyand Company.

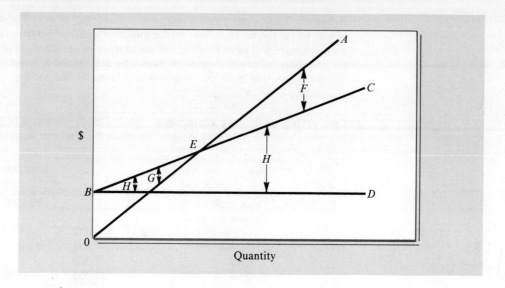

Required: Fill in the blanks with the appropriate letter(s) from the chart. You may have to indicate additions or subtractions.
1. Revenue line   _____
2. Variable costs   _____
3. Fixed costs   _____
4. Profit area   _____
5. Loss area   _____
6. Total cost line   _____
7. Break-even point   _____
8. Contribution margin   _____

2-15 VCP graph, analysis of changes   You have prepared a VCP graph for NMA Shoes. It reflects the following expectations.

Selling price	$50
Unit variable cost	$30
Total fixed costs	$400,000

NMA's managers are wondering what the effects will be on operations if some changes take place, either by management decision or by some outside force such as the prices charged by a supplier. The following specific changes are the most likely possibilities.

a. An increase in the selling price resulting from less-than-expected competition
b. An increase in unit variable cost arising from a decision to use more expensive leather in the shoes
c. An increase in total fixed costs accompanied by a decrease in unit variable cost from introducing labor-saving machinery
d. A decrease in the number of units expected to be sold
e. An increase in the selling price combined with an increase in unit variable cost resulting from a decision to increase the quality of the product

Required: Treat each change independently of the others. For each, state the effects on (a) the revenue line, (b) the total cost line, and (c) the break-even point. Some changes will have no effect on one or more of the items. In at least one case, the effect on the break-even point cannot be determined without additional information. Note that both the intercept and slope of the total cost line could be affected by a set of changes.

2-16 **Converting an income statement** Sandy Goode, president of SG Enterprises, has given you the following income statement for a recent month.

Sales		$250,000
Cost of goods sold		150,000
Gross profit		100,000
Operating expenses:		
Salaries and commissions	$42,000	
Utilities	11,200	
Rent	13,300	
Other	23,000	89,500
Profit		$ 10,500

SG sells one product, an exercise glove, at $20 per pair. Cost of goods sold is variable. A 10% sales commission, included in salaries and commissions, is the only other variable cost. Goode tells you that the income statement is not helpful, for she cannot determine such things as the break-even point or the price that will achieve a target profit.

Required
1. Redo the income statement using the contribution margin format.
2. Determine the break-even point in (a) units and (b) dollars.
3. Determine the price that would give a $15,000 profit at 12,500 units. The cost of the product is a constant $12 per unit.

2-17 **Target costing** Managers of TNC Enterprises are thinking about a new product in the industrial electronics area. TNC has considerable technical expertise in the field but has never entered the segment of the market in which the new product would compete. Before writing specifications for performance, the managers want to determine what costs are allowable. They estimate sales of 200,000 units per year at a $100 selling price. They also want a profit of $6,000,000.

Required
1. Determine the total costs that TNC can incur and meet its profit objective.
2. Suppose that the designers, engineers, and manufacturing managers estimate

that annual fixed costs will be about $9,000,000 per year. Find the maximum per-unit variable cost that TNC can incur and meet its profit objective.

2-18 ***Profit planning*** Tinney Company, a wholesaler of jeans, had the following income statement in 19X5.

Sales (40,000 pairs at $15)		$600,000
Cost of sales		300,000
Gross margin		300,000
Selling expenses	$150,000	
Administrative expenses	90,000	240,000
Income		$ 60,000

Mr. Tinney informs you that the only variable costs are cost of sales and $2 per-unit selling costs. All administrative expenses are fixed. In planning for the coming year, 19X6, Mr. Tinney expects his selling price to remain constant, with unit volume increasing by 20%. He also forecasts the following changes in costs.

Variable costs:	
Cost of goods sold	up $0.50 per unit
Selling costs	up $0.10 per unit
Fixed costs:	
Selling costs	up $10,000
Administrative costs	up $15,000

Required
1. Prepare an income statement for 19X6 using the contribution margin format and assuming that all forecasts are met.
2. Determine the number of units that Tinney will have to sell in 19X6 to earn the same profit it did in 19X5.
3. If 19X6 volume is 48,000 units, what selling price will earn $60,000? All variable costs are constant per unit.

2-19 ***Basic income taxes (related to Appendix)*** Mayes Company is introducing an electronic printer that will sell for $140. Unit variable manufacturing cost is $92, and Mayes pays a 10% sales commission. Fixed costs for the printer are $250,000 per year. The tax rate is 40%.

Required
1. Determine the profit after taxes that Mayes would earn selling 12,000 printers.
2. Determine the number of units that Mayes has to sell to earn an after-tax profit of $120,000.
3. Determine the price that Mayes has to charge to earn a $180,000 pretax profit selling 11,000 units.

2-20 ***Changes in contribution margin*** Mr. Pahl, owner of Jeantown, a specialty clothing store, asks you for some advice. Last year, his business had the following income statement.

Sales (10,000 units at $20)	$200,000
Variable costs	100,000
Contribution margin	100,000
Fixed costs	50,000
Income	$ 50,000

Mr. Pahl expects variable costs to increase to $11 per unit in the coming year.

Required
1. Determine the volume that Mr. Pahl needs to earn $50,000 in the coming year.
2. Mr. Pahl decides to increase his selling price so that he can earn $50,000 next year with the same unit volume he had last year. (a) What price will achieve that objective? (b) What dollar sales will he have?
3. Suppose now that Mr. Pahl raises his price so that the contribution margin percentage is the same as it was last year. (a) What price will he set? (b) What dollar volume will give a $50,000 profit? (c) What is the unit volume?

2-21 **Pricing and return on sales**   Rogers Construction Company builds steel structures for commercial and industrial customers. The buildings are of various shapes and sizes, with the average price being $30 per square foot and the average variable cost $18 per square foot. Annual fixed costs are $5,000,000.

Required: Answer each of the following items independently.
1. Determine the volume that will give Rogers a 20% return on sales in (a) sales dollars and (b) square feet of construction.
2. If Rogers can sell 600,000 square feet of construction in the coming year, what selling price will give a $400,000 profit?
3. If Rogers can sell 600,000 square feet of construction in the coming year at $30, how high could variable cost per square foot rise and still allow Rogers to earn a $280,000 profit?
4. If variable cost increases to $21 per square foot and Rogers can sell 500,000 square feet, what price will give a $280,000 profit?

Problems

2-22 **Per-unit data**   The controller of Walker Company provides the following per-unit analysis, based on a volume of 50,000 units.

Selling price		$20
Variable costs	$8	
Fixed costs	7	
Total costs		15
Profit		$ 5

Required: Answer each of the following questions independently of the others.
1. What total profit does Walker expect to earn?
2. What total profit should the company earn at 60,000 units?

3. What is its break-even point in units?
4. Walker's managers expect to increase volume to 55,000 units by spending an additional $40,000 on salaries for more salespeople. What total profit will Walker earn?
5. The managers expect to sell 60,000 units and want a $310,000 profit. What price per unit must the firm charge? Variable costs are constant per unit.
6. Redo item 5 assuming that the variable cost of $8 consists of a $6 purchase price and a 10% sales commission ($2 at the $20 price).

2-23 **VCP analysis for a CPA firm** Bret McConnell, a certified public accountant, has estimated the following fixed costs of operation for the coming year.

Office salaries	$42,000
Rent, utilities	21,000
Other	14,000
Total	$77,000

There are no variable costs as McConnell currently plans operations. He charges clients $60 per hour for his time.

Required
1. How many hours must McConnell work to earn a profit of $50,000?
2. McConnell is thinking about hiring one or two senior accounting majors from a local university for $8 per hour to do some routine work for his clients. He expects each to work about 300 hours, but about 30 of those hours (training and temporary idle time) will not be chargeable to clients. McConnell wants each student to provide at least $3,000 profit. What hourly rate must he charge for their time to achieve his objective?

2-24 **Pricing decision – nursery school** The Board of Directors of First Community Church is considering opening a nursery school. Members of the board agree that the school, which would be open to all children, should operate within $100 of the break-even point.

The school would be open for nine months each year, with two classes, one in the morning and one in the afternoon. The treasurer prepares an analysis of the expected costs of operating the school, based on conversations with members of other churches that run similar programs.

Salaries—teacher and assistant	$16,400 for nine months
Utilities	$800 for nine months
Miscellaneous operating costs	$300 for nine months
Supplies, paper, paint	$2 per child per month
Snacks, cookies, juice	$4 per child per month

The best estimate of enrollment is 20 children in each of the two classes, which is all that the teacher and assistant can handle and still achieve the quality that the board feels is essential.

Required

1. Determine the monthly fee per child that would have to be charged for the school to break even (round to nearest dollar) with its maximum enrollment.
2. If the monthly fee is $60, what is the break-even point in enrollment?

2-25 **Relationships**   Answer the following questions, considering each situation independently. You may not be able to answer the questions in the order they are asked.

1. A firm earns $40,000 selling 50,000 units at $5 per unit. Its fixed costs are $180,000.
    (a) What are variable costs per unit?
    (b) What is total contribution margin?
    (c) What would income be if sales increased by 5,000 units?
2. A firm has return on sales of 10%, income of $30,000, selling price of $10, and a contribution margin of 30%.
    (a) What are fixed costs?
    (b) What are variable costs per unit?
    (c) What are sales in units?
    (d) What are sales in dollars?
3. A firm has return on sales of 15% at sales of $300,000. Its fixed costs are $75,000, and variable costs are $6 per unit.
    (a) What are sales in units?
    (b) What is contribution margin per unit?
    (c) What is income?

2-26 **Sensitivity of variables**   Cranston Jellies expects the following results in 19X5.

Planned sales in cases—19X5	40,000
Selling price	$20
Variable costs	$14
Total fixed costs	$200,000

Required: Answer the following questions, considering each independently.

1. Which of the following would reduce planned profit the most:
    (a) A 10% decrease in selling price?
    (b) A 10% increase per case in variable costs?
    (c) A 10% increase in fixed costs?
    (d) A 10% decrease in sales volume?
2. Which of the following would increase planned profit the most:
    (a) A 10% increase in selling price?
    (b) A 10% decrease per case in variable costs?
    (c) A 10% increase in sales volume?
    (d) A 10% decrease in fixed costs?
3. If the selling price declined by 10%, how many cases would have to be sold to achieve the planned profit?
4. If the selling price increased by 20%, by how much could variable cost per case increase and the planned profit be achieved?

2-27 **VCP analysis – changes in variables**   During two recent months the Thompson Company had the following income statements.

	March	April
Sales	$200,000	$216,000
Variable costs	130,000	120,600
Contribution margin	70,000	95,400
Fixed costs	40,000	40,000
Income	$ 30,000	$ 55,400

You learn that the price of the product Thompson sells generally changes each month, though its purchase cost is stable at $11 per unit. The only other variable cost is a 10% commission paid on all sales.

Required: Determine the selling price, unit volume, and variable cost per unit in each of the two months.

2-28 **VCP analysis on new business** Some managers of Harter Enterprises, a medium-sized manufacturer of dress gloves, want to branch out from the company's traditional business into exercise gloves. Doing so requires leasing additional equipment for $550,000 per year. Other fixed costs associated with the new venture, including new personnel, advertising, and promotion are estimated at $380,000 annually.

The variable cost of the new glove is expected to be about $7 per pair and the selling price about $15 per pair. The managers are reluctant to try the new gloves unless they can be fairly confident of earning $150,000.

Required
1. Determine how many pairs Harter must sell to earn the target profit on the new gloves.
2. The marketing people believe that unit sales will be 115,000 units. What selling price will yield the target profit at that volume?
3. Suppose again that 115,000 units is the best estimate of volume and that Harter will stick with the $15 price. How much must Harter reduce the expected variable cost to meet the profit target?

2-29 **VCP analysis for a hospital** The administrator of the Caldwell Memorial Hospital is considering methods of providing X-ray treatments to patients. The hospital now refers about 160 patients per month to a nearby private clinic, and each treatment costs the patient $35. If the hospital provides the treatment, it will have to rent a machine for $1,600 per month and hire a technician for $2,400 per month. Variable costs are $5 per treatment.

Required
1. The administrator is considering charging the same fee as the clinic. By how much will the hospital increase its income if it provides the service?
2. How much must the hospital charge to break even on the treatments?

2-30 **VCP in a service business** Microprog develops microcomputer programs to customer order, primarily for business applications. The company charges its customers $40 per hour for programming time. The managers are planning operations for the coming year and develop the following estimates.

Total estimated chargeable hours	80,000
Total fixed costs, salaries, rent, etc.	$1,750,000

Microprog employs 15 full-time programmers at an average salary of $30,000. These salaries are included in the cost figure given above. Each programmer works about 2,000 chargeable hours per year. The company does not wish to hire additional programmers, but rather wants to use free-lancers to meet demand. Free-lancers charge an average of $25 per hour.

Required
1. If the company meets its goal of 80,000 chargeable hours, what profit will it earn?
2. How many chargeable hours must it obtain from free-lancers, in addition to the hours its full-time programmers work, to earn a $300,000 profit?

2-31 **Developing VCP information**   The manager of Sans Flavour Food Store, a franchise operation, is confused by the income statements he has received from his accountant. He asks you to help him with them. He is especially concerned that his return on sales dropped much more than sales from April to May.

	April	May
Sales	$100,000	$80,000
Cost of sales	40,000	32,000
Gross profit	60,000	48,000
Operating expenses:		
Rent	1,200	1,200
Salaries, wages, commissions	34,500	30,500
Insurance	1,100	1,100
Supplies	2,000	1,600
Utilities	1,500	1,500
Miscellaneous expenses	6,000	6,000
Total operating expenses	46,300	41,900
Income	$ 13,700	$ 6,100
Return on sales	13.7%	7.6%

The manager informs you that the salaries, wages, and commissions account includes the salaries of several clerks and himself, as well as commissions. All salespeople earn commissions of 20% of sales. Supplies are primarily wrapping paper and tape and vary directly with sales. The manager had expected the $20,000 decline in sales, but expected income of $10,960, 13.7% of expected sales. He is now concerned that income will continue to be 7.6% of sales.

Required: Prepare income statements using the contribution margin format for April and May, and explain to the manager the advantages of this alternative format.

2-32 **New market area**   Whizzer Toy Company has just finished analyzing its cost and sales picture for 19X6.

Planned selling price	$40
Variable costs per unit	$32
Total fixed costs	$320,000
Planned sales volume	50,000 units

Required: Answer the following questions, considering each independently.
1. What is the break-even point in units?
2. Sales volume is 10% higher than planned. What is the break-even point?
3. If the company wants to increase profit by $30,000 over what it would earn at the planned sales volume, by how many units must sales increase?
4. Suppose the company could sell 15,000 units in a foreign country where it has no sales at this time. It needs a $40,000 advertising campaign to achieve these sales. The price (in the foreign country only) is to be $36. Additional shipping costs of $1 per unit will be incurred. Would the venture be profitable?
5. The preceding question indicates that this would be the first time the company tried to sell in the particular foreign country. What is the importance of the statement that the sales be made in another country?

2-33 *Changes in operations* Bart Packard operates the 15th Street Parking Lot, leasing the lot from the owner at $12,000 per month plus 10% of sales. Packard is thinking about staying open until midnight. He now closes at 7:00 P.M. Keeping the lot open requires paying an additional $800 per week to attendants. Increases in utilities and insurance will be another $100 per week. The lot must pay a 5% city tax on its total revenue. The parking charge is $0.80 per hour.

Required
1. Suppose that Packard expects additional business amounting to 2,000 hours per week. Should he stay open until midnight?
2. How much additional business, stated in hours, does Packard need to break even on the additional hours of operation?

2-34 *Converting income statement to contribution margin basis* Clarkston Manufacturing Company has been profitable over the past few quarters and the top managers are taking steps to continue the increased profitability. The most recent quarterly income statement appears below. All amounts are in thousands.

Sales		$3,882.6
Cost of sales:		
Materials and parts	$763.3	
Labor	588.1	
Fringe benefits	69.0	
Repairs and maintenance	322.1	
Depreciation	189.2	
Supplies	56.1	
Power	118.6	
Miscellaneous	47.8	2,154.2
Gross margin		1,728.4
Operating expenses:		
Sales salaries and commissions	$489.2	
Sales expenses	112.7	
Advertising	377.4	
Administrative expenses	541.3	1,520.6
Income before taxes		$ 207.8
Unit volume		415.3

The controller is concerned about the format of the income statement, which has been in use for several years. The controller is relatively new to the job and prefers income statements that use the contribution margin format. After talks with the relevant managers, she determines the following.

	Variable Amount per Unit	Quarterly Fixed Amount
Materials and parts	$1.838	$ 0
Labor	1.416	0
Fringe benefits	0.166	0
Repairs and maintenance	0.323	188.0
Depreciation	0.000	189.2
Supplies	0.135	0
Power	0.131	64.2
Miscellaneous	0.032	34.5
Sales salaries and commissions	0.789	161.5
Sales expenses	0.124	61.2
Advertising	0.000	377.4
Administrative expenses	0.022	532.2

Required
1. Prepare a new income statement using the contribution margin format.
2. Comment on the differences between your statement and the one above. For example, what decisions are easier, or more difficult, to make with your statement?

2-35 **Unit costs**   Carl Murphy owns a chain of shoe stores. He recently opened a store in a shopping mall and was not pleased with the results for the first month.

Sales		$80,000
Cost of sales		40,000
Gross margin		40,000
Salaries and wages	$23,000	
Utilities, insurance, rent	3,500	
Commissions at 15% of sales	12,000	38,500
Profit		$ 1,500

Noting that sales were 4,000 pairs at an average price of $20, Murphy calculates the per-pair cost at $19.625 ($78,500/4,000), leaving only a $0.375 profit per pair. He did expect sales to rise to 5,000 pairs at an average price of $20 over the next month or two, but he figured that profit would increase only to about $1,875 (5,000 × $0.375), which was still not adequate.

Murphy asks for your advice, and, in response to your questions, says that even with the increase in sales there will be no need for additional salaried personnel and that utilities, insurance, and rent will remain about the same. The cost of sales percentage will also remain at 50%.

Required: Prepare an income statement based on sales of 5,000 pairs of shoes. If profit is different from Mr. Murphy's estimate, explain the fallacy in his reasoning.

2-36 ***VCP analysis and break-even pricing — municipal operation***   Gardendale operates a municipal trash collection service. Analyses of costs indicate that monthly fixed cost is $15,000 and variable cost is about $0.80 per pickup per customer. The city collects trash in the business district 12 times a month and in the residential districts four times a month. The difference in frequency results from the much larger volume of trash in the business district. There are 250 businesses and 1,500 residences served by trash collection.

Required
1. The city manager is aware that other cities charge business customers $20 per month and residential customers $6 per month. What profit or loss would the operation generate at these prices?
2. The city manager would like to break even or show a small profit on trash collection. She believes it fair to charge businesses three times as much as residences because the businesses get three times as much service. What monthly prices would make the operation break even?

2-37 ***VCP analysis for a service business***   Walker Associates is a market research firm. Companies come to it asking for various types of studies regarding consumers' preferences, and Walker develops a plan for the study. If the company approves the plan, Walker does the job.

   Walker's business involves interviewing people near supermarkets, drugstores, and department stores. Walker hires part-timers to do the interviews for $9 per hour and pays such expenses as mileage and meals. These expenses average $11 per day per person. Each person works about six hours per day. Fixed costs associated with Walker's operation consist largely of salaries to the permanent staff. These, along with rent and utilities, total $400,000 per year.

   Walker wants to develop a pricing policy based on an hourly rate, that is, charging the client company an amount per hour that Walker's part-time employees spend interviewing.

Required
1. Walker's managers expect enough business to require about 10,000 six-hour days of interviewing. What hourly charge will give a $75,000 profit?
2. Suppose that Walker sets the charge at $17 per hour. How many six-hour days must it achieve to earn a $75,000 profit?
3. Walker is considering using full-time, salaried interviewers rather than part-time people. What are some of the implications of such a change?

2-38 ***Alternative cost behavior — a movie company (continued in Chapters 3 and 4)***   Blockbusters Incorporated, a leading producer of movies, is currently negotiating with Sky Kirkwalker, the biggest box-office attraction in the movie industry, to star in *War Trek*, a science fiction film. For a starring role, Sky normally receives a salary of $1,500,000 plus 5% of the receipts-to-the-producer. (The producer normally receives 40% of the total paid admissions wherever the movie is shown.) However, Sky is quite optimistic about the prospects for *Trek* and has expressed some interest in a special contract that would give him only 25% of his normal salary but increase his portion of the receipts-to-the-producer to 20%. Other than Sky's pay, costs of producing the picture are expected to be $2,500,000.

Required: Answer the following questions, calling the alternative compensation schemes N (for the normal contract) and S (for the special contract).

1. What are the break-even receipts-to-the-producer under each of the compensation schemes?
2. If total paid admissions in theaters are expected to be $14,000,000, what will be the income to the producer under compensation schemes N and S?
3. At what level of receipts-to-the-producer would Sky earn the same total income under compensation schemes N and S?

2-39 ***Conversion of income statement to contribution margin basis*** The following income statement is prepared by the controller of Wassenich Company. Materials and labor are variable costs of manufacturing the product.

Wassenich Company
Income Statement for 19X4

Sales (10,000 units)		$120,000
Cost of goods sold:		
Materials	$30,000	
Labor	35,000	
Other manufacturing costs:		
Variable	16,000	
Fixed	14,000	95,000
Gross profit		25,000
Selling and administrative expenses:		
Variable	9,000	
Fixed	22,000	31,000
Loss		($ 6,000)

Required
1. Prepare a new income statement using the contribution margin format.
2. What is the break-even point in units?
3. The president believes that spending an additional $7,000 on advertising will increase sales by 4,000 units. His son, the general manager, says that would be silly because the firm is losing enough already. Is the son right?

2-40 ***Occupancy rate as measure of volume*** Norman Motels is a chain operating in small cities throughout the Midwest. Its most relevant measure of volume is the occupancy rate, the percentage of available rooms rented to guests. Monthly revenue is $100,000 per percentage point of occupancy. (For example, at 40% occupancy, revenue is $4,000,000.) Contribution margin is 70%, monthly fixed costs $4,200,000.

Required
1. Find the monthly break-even point in (a) dollars and (b) occupancy rate.
2. Determine Norman's profit at a 75% occupancy rate.
3. Determine the occupancy rate Norman needs to earn $700,000 per month.
4. Determine whether Norman should increase advertising $100,000 per month if doing so increases the occupancy rate by two percentage points.

2-41 ***Assumptions of VCP analysis*** Last year you were engaged as a consultant to Thompson Products Company and prepared some analyses of its VCP relationships. Among your findings was that the contribution margin percentage was 40% at the planned selling price of $20. The firm expected to sell 10,000, which you estimated would yield a $46,000 income. You told Mr. Thompson, the owner, that profit would change at the rate of $0.40 per $1 change in sales.

Mr. Thompson has just called to tell you that the results did not come out as you had said they would. The firm earned $63,200 on sales of $226,800. Variable costs per unit were incurred as expected, as were total fixed costs. Mr. Thompson was very pleased at the results. However, he asks you why profit did not increase by 40% of the added sales volume of $26,800, but rather by somewhat more.

Required
1. Prepare an income statement for the year, based on the actual results.
2. Determine (a) the number of units sold and (b) the selling price per unit.
3. Tell Mr. Thompson why the results were not as you had forecast.

Cases

2-42 A concessionaire Ralph Newkirk is considering a bid for the hot dog and soft drink concession at the 14 football games for the season. There will be seven college games and seven professional games. Average attendance at college games is 20,000, at professional games, 50,000. Ralph estimates that he sells one hot dog and one soft drink for each two persons attending a game.

Revenue and cost data are as follows.

	Hot Dogs	Soft Drinks
Selling price	$0.50	$0.30
Variable costs:		
Hot dog	0.080	
Roll	0.040	
Mustard, onion, etc.	0.005	
Soft drink and ice		0.125

In addition, salespeople earn a 15% commission on all sales. Fixed costs per game are $4,000 for rentals of heating, cooking, mixing, and cooling equipment.

The stadium management requests that bids be made in the form of royalties on sales. The highest percentage of sales bid will win the contract.

Required
1. What percentage of sales can Ralph pay as royalty to the stadium and earn $20,000 for the season? (Round to nearest one tenth of a percentage point.)
2. If Ralph bids 12% of sales, what income can he expect if operations go according to plan? (Is this consistent with your answer in item 1?)
3. Assuming a royalty of 12% of sales, what is Ralph's break-even point for the season, based on total attendance?
4. What kinds of information does Ralph need if he is also deciding to bid for the concession at baseball games at the same stadium?
5. Ralph has forecast attendance for football games. He then learns that the star quarterback of the local professional team will retire before the coming season. What effect does this information have on Ralph's planning?

2-43 **Soccer camp**   Since Jean Longhurst has been head soccer coach at Oldberne College, she has enjoyed considerable success. Longhurst has coached at summer camps for children and now is considering a summer camp for Oldberne. The college would provide room and board for the campers at a price (see below) and would also take 10% of revenue. Longhurst asks you for advice. You say that some of the important factors are setting a price, estimating enrollment, and estimating costs. After a few weeks, Longhurst returns with the following information, gathered from various sources.

Average enrollment	90 campers
Average price for one-week camp	$ 190
Costs:	
Food, charged by college	$ 50 per camper
Insurance and T-shirts	$ 12 per camper
Room rent charged by college	$ 15 per camper
Coaches' salaries	$ 450 per coach
Brochures, mailing, miscellaneous	$2,800 total

Longhurst also says that other camps have typically employed one coach for each 15 campers, excluding the director (Longhurst in this case). One problem is that you generally need to engage the coaches before you know the enrollment, although it is usually possible to find one or two at the last minute. It is, however, necessary to engage some of the coaches early so that you can use their names in brochures. Furthermore, while the enrollment and price given above are averages, there is wide variation, with enrollments ranging from 40 to 120 and prices ranging from $160 to $230. As might be expected, the better-known camps have higher enrollments at higher prices, but they also pay better, as high as $800 per week for a well-known coach. Longhurst will keep the profits and suffer the losses, and so wants to be fairly confident before proceeding.

Required
1. If Longhurst hires enough coaches to meet the average enrollment and achieves all of the averages given above, what will her profit be?
2. If she wants to earn $4,000 and expects 100 campers, what price must she set?
3. The college offers to take over the cost of brochures, mailing, and miscellaneous ($2,800 estimated) in exchange for a higher share of the revenue. If Longhurst achieves the results from item 1 (meets the averages), what percentage of revenue will she be able to pay the college and earn the same profit expected in item 1?
4. What advantages and disadvantages are there to Longhurst and to the college of the proposed arrangement?

CHAPTER 3

ANALYZING COST BEHAVIOR

In Chapter 2 we assumed we knew how much cost was variable and how much was fixed. In real life, costs do not come with labels describing their behavior, so each cost must be studied to *determine* its behavior. Some costs do not vary with sales, but with some other activity. For example, costs of materials and labor to manufacture a product vary with production, while the cost of sending sales invoices to customers varies with the number of sales orders. Some costs do not follow the strict fixed-variable pattern but rather exhibit a combination of both patterns. An example is the cost of water, which typically includes a minimum payment for being connected to the water system plus a charge that varies with the volume of water used.

A major portion of this chapter focuses on methods used to determine how costs behave. The final section of the chapter examines the issue of cost structure and explores the efforts that managers make to balance fixed and variable costs in order to produce a desired level of profit.

OBJECTIVES OF ANALYZING COSTS

To do their jobs, managers must understand the behavior of costs. As we showed in Chapter 2, managers need that understanding in order to plan. For example, to plan income for a future period, they must be able to predict costs for that period.

Similarly, managers want good estimates of variable cost so that they can compute contribution margin, an important factor in decision making.

Managers must also understand cost behavior to fulfill their controlling function. In order to predict and control a cost, they need to know what activity *causes* the cost to rise and fall and the level of that causal activity. For instance, some companies have found that a number of costs rise when they add new types of parts and components to their products. (New parts mean new vendors or suppliers to be evaluated, new inventory records to be kept, and perhaps more inspection of incoming shipments.) The term commonly used to describe causal activities is **cost drivers.** Cost analysis, then, is also important because of the role it plays in *cost management,* the manager's ongoing tasks of monitoring and controlling costs and cost drivers.

DETERMINING COST BEHAVIOR

There are several ways to determine the behavior of costs. The methods range from simple to sophisticated. Each method has advantages and disadvantages, and managers in most companies use more than one method.

A simple, yet sometimes effective method of classifying the behavior of a cost is *account analysis,* in which the manager decides how to classify a cost by knowing its name. For instance, costs such as rent, depreciation, salaries, and advertising are generally thought to be fixed costs. Account analysis only works for a few costs, but might even give erroneous results for those costs. For example, we show below a situation in which rent, normally a fixed cost, is partly variable.

Another widely used method of ascertaining cost behavior is the *engineering approach,* which is used successfully to determine per-unit variable costs in manufacturing firms. For example, engineers study the material and labor requirements of products and related operations, then make per-unit estimates of costs that should vary with production. The engineering approach is not as successful for nonmanufacturing costs.

Sometimes analysis indicates that a particular cost is strictly fixed or strictly variable; perhaps more often, the analysis suggests that a cost is mixed. A **mixed** (or **semivariable**) cost has both a fixed component and a variable component. For example, Ted's Threads pays rent at 10% of sales. If Ted's lease called for a fixed monthly rent *plus* 10% of sales, the rent would be a mixed cost. Figure 3-1 shows the behavior of a mixed cost; the pattern corresponds to that of total costs when there are both fixed and variable costs.

Neither account analysis nor the engineering study works well when applied to costs likely to be mixed. The methods discussed in the remainder of this section have proved useful in analyzing mixed costs.

To aid the presentation of the remaining methods, let us turn again to Ted's Threads. Suppose Ted employs a person part-time, at $6 per hour, to help with the store. Each month, the person works about 10 to 15 hours doing routine tasks like tagging merchandise, filling out forms for ordering merchandise, and keeping

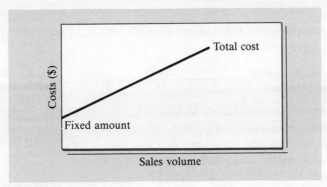

Figure 3-1   Mixed Cost Behavior

some records. This person also comes in when Ted expects to need help to wait on customers because he expects sales to be relatively heavy.

The cost of employing the part-time person, wages expense, varies perfectly with the number of hours worked, but not with sales. The behavior of the total cost is mixed. There is a fixed component because the person works about 10 to 15 hours per month regardless of sales volume. There is also a variable component, because the person works more hours when sales are expected to be high than when they are expected to be low. If Ted wants to predict the wage cost he can expect to incur in some future period, he must find the fixed and variable components of this mixed cost.

High-Low Method

A relatively unsophisticated yet widely used method of estimating the components of a mixed cost is the **high-low method,** or **two-point method.** This method uses two past levels of volume and the amounts of the cost incurred at those volumes. The high and low points of the name are the highest and lowest levels of activity (as opposed to the highest and lowest costs) within the relevant range. To find the variable component of the cost, we divide the difference in cost at the two levels by the difference in volume of the cost-driving activity. The formula for finding the variable cost factor in a mixed cost is

$$\frac{\text{Variable cost component}}{\text{in mixed cost}} = \frac{\text{cost at high volume} - \text{cost at low volume}}{\text{high volume} - \text{low volume}}$$

Assume that Ted has found the following wages at the extremes of his relevant range of sales of $5,000 and $18,000.

	High	Low	Difference
Sales	$18,000	$5,000	$13,000
Wages for part-time help	$ 408	$ 148	$ 260

Costs

Wages were $260 higher when sales were $13,000 higher. So, wages increased at a rate of $0.02 per sales dollar ($260/$13,000), or 2% of sales dollars. Applying the formula to Ted's situation,

$$\frac{\text{Variable cost}}{\text{component}} = \frac{\$408 - \$148}{\$18,000 - \$5,000} = \frac{\$260}{\$13,000} = \frac{\$0.02 \text{ or } 2\% \text{ of}}{\text{sales dollars}}$$

Because the total cost at *any* volume equals total variable cost at that volume plus total fixed cost, the fixed component of the total cost equals the difference between the total cost and the total variable cost at that volume. In formula notation this becomes, using the high volume

$$\begin{array}{l} \text{Fixed cost} \\ \text{component of} \\ \text{mixed cost} \end{array} = \begin{array}{l} \text{total cost} \\ \text{at} \\ \text{high volume} \end{array} - \left(\begin{array}{l} \text{high} \\ \text{volume} \\ \text{in units} \end{array} \times \begin{array}{l} \text{variable cost per} \\ \text{unit of} \\ \text{volume} \end{array} \right)$$

or

$$= \begin{array}{l} \text{total cost} \\ \text{at} \\ \text{high volume} \end{array} - \left(\begin{array}{l} \text{high} \\ \text{volume} \\ \text{in dollars} \end{array} \times \begin{array}{l} \text{variable cost} \\ \text{percentage per} \\ \text{sales dollar} \end{array} \right)$$

At sales of $5,000, total cost is $148 and the variable portion is $100 ($5,000 × 2%), so the fixed component is $48 ($148 − $100). We get the same answer by subtracting the $360 variable portion at sales of $18,000 ($18,000 × 2%) from the total cost of $408 at that volume ($408 − $360 = $48 fixed cost). The formula that Ted can use to predict his total wage cost is then: Total cost = $48 + (2% × sales).

The rationale for the high-low method is this: Because variable costs (the dependent variable) change proportionately with changes in volume (the independent variable), the change in total cost between two volumes is the result of the change in total variable cost. Therefore, when you divide the change in cost by the change in volume, you are finding the rate of change in cost per unit of volume. In this case, we knew that sales influenced the cost and we used sales dollars to measure the volume of that activity. In other situations, we might find that production, unit sales, or some other type of activity best describes what causes the cost to change. In general, the problem for the cost analyst is to find the activity that drives the cost.

At this point we remind you that the volume levels used when applying the high-low method must be within the relevant range if the resulting cost prediction formula is to be useful. (Remember from Chapter 2 that the relevant range is that over which per-unit variable cost and total fixed cost can be expected to remain constant.) The high-low method has some serious disadvantages, which will become clearer as we discuss the next method of analyzing costs.

Scatter-Diagram Method

Like the high-low method, the **scatter-diagram** (or **graphical**) **method,** requires cost and volume data from prior periods, and derives an equation based on those data. The first step is to plot points that represent total cost at various levels of activity within the relevant range. The dots in Figure 3-2 show the wage cost Ted incurred at various levels of sales. Step two is to draw a line as close to all the points as possible. (Figure 3-2 shows such a line.) The placement and slope of the line are matters of judgment; the manager "eyeballs" the data and fits the line visually.

Once you have drawn the line, you find the fixed and variable components of the cost in the following manner. The fixed component is simply that point at which the line hits the vertical axis, $72 in this case. (Notice that the $72 found by this method is close to the employee's wages for the 10 to 15 hours worked every month on nonsales tasks.) To find the variable component, determine the *total* cost at some point on the line and subtract the fixed cost to obtain the total variable cost at that level of volume. Then, divide total variable cost by the level of volume associated with that point. For example, in Figure 3-2, the total cost is $252 at a sales volume of $10,000. Of that total cost, $72 is fixed cost, so total variable cost is $180. Dividing the total variable costs of $180 by sales volume of $10,000 yields $0.018, which is the variable cost per dollar of sales. Thus, the scatter-diagram method gives Ted the following formula to predict his total wage cost: Total cost = $72 + 1.8% of sales.

We have now used two methods to develop a formula to predict Ted's wage cost. Which method or formula should he use? For two reasons, the scatter-diagram method is generally preferable. First, because it relies on only two observations, the high-low method carries the risk that the resulting prediction formula will be unduly influenced by a random oddity or unusual event occurring in one of the time periods used and will therefore be inaccurate. By using more observations, the formula developed with the scatter-diagram method is less influenced by

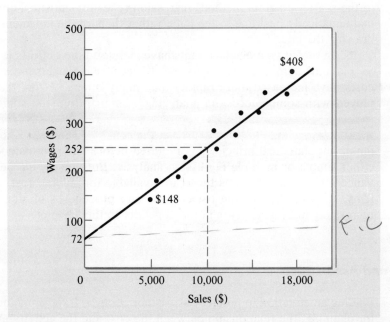

Figure 3-2   Scatter Diagram

such events and oddities and therefore more accurate. The second advantage of the scatter-diagram method is its visual aspect. By looking at the plotting of costs at various levels of volume of a particular activity, a manager will get some idea of how closely the cost follows changes in the selected activity. This issue is discussed in more detail later.

Whichever formula Ted uses, note that he cannot expect to predict his wage costs exactly. The number of points on the scatter diagram that do *not* fall on the line suggests that differences can be expected, but can you explain why? Remember that Ted calls in his part-time person when he expects sales to be heavy. Anticipating a big selling day, Ted might ask the employee to work some extra hours; if sales are less than expected, the actual wage cost will be greater than that predicted using the actual level of sales. Thus, differences can be caused by Ted's inability to predict accurately the heavy sales periods when additional help will be needed. Ted can reduce the differences and better manage this cost if he can improve his ability to predict daily, or perhaps weekly, sales.

Regression Method

A more sophisticated method for estimating the fixed and variable components of a mixed cost is **regression analysis** (or just **regression**). Like the two methods already discussed, this statistical method uses cost and volume data from prior periods and provides an equation of the form: Total cost = fixed cost + (variable cost per unit of activity × level of activity). But in contrast to the high-low method, regression uses all available observations, not just two. And in contrast to the scatter-diagram method, regression relies on statistical concepts to fit the mathematically best line to the data, rather than on the judgment of the manager drawing the line.

In recent years, accountants have increased their efforts to find techniques for planning administrative costs, partly because managers have noted that such costs have increased more rapidly than many others. A tool that has been employed with some success in analyzing administrative and some other costs is *multiple regression analysis*—a variation of regression analysis that uses two or more independent variables to predict the behavior of a cost. Knowledge of some important statistical principles is required before you can understand and apply either simple or multiple regression analysis. But you should be aware that advanced techniques such as these are available for solving cost estimation problems. A discussion of the basic terms and procedures of simple and multiple regression analysis appears in the appendix to this chapter.

Correlation and Association

Finding an equation to predict costs is not enough. If the equation is to be useful for planning, the relationship between the cost and the activity measure must be fairly close. The closeness of the relationship is called **correlation** or **association**.

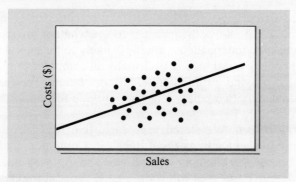

Figure 3-3   Scatter Diagram of Invoice Preparation Costs Plotted Against Sales Dollars

Consider, for example, the costs of preparing invoices to bill customers. Figure 3-3 is a scatter diagram relating the total costs of a firm's billing department to sales dollars. It shows a wide spread of costs around the cost-prediction line, which means that using sales dollars to predict the cost of invoice preparation is unlikely to be successful. (A moment of thought about the facts should suggest some reasons why this might be so. Does it necessarily take more time or more people to prepare an invoice for $100,000 than one for $10,000?) Some other measure of activity might give better results.

Figure 3-4 shows invoice preparation costs plotted against another activity, the number of sales orders processed. Because it is common to prepare one invoice for each sales order, and because individual sales orders are likely to vary in dollar value, it is not surprising that the total cost for invoice preparation appears to vary more closely with the number of sales orders than with the dollar sales volume represented by the orders. Finding this better correlated activity measure can be important for cost management as well as cost prediction. For example, with this information on the cost driver, managers can investigate whether salespersons write separate sales orders for reasons not related to servicing the customer. They might then try to develop procedures that will reduce the number of orders written (and the processing costs) without affecting customer satisfaction.

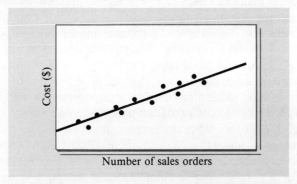

Figure 3-4   Scatter Diagram of Invoice Preparation Costs Plotted Against Sales Orders

As stated earlier, the visual aspect of the scatter-diagram method is an important advantage; it allows the manager to see whether the particular activity measure chosen as the independent variable is likely to be a good predictor of the value of the dependent variable (cost). Virtually all computer programs for regression analysis also provide information about correlation. The high-low method, because it includes only two points, does not provide this important information.

Spurious Correlation   We stated very early that one purpose in analyzing costs is to determine *what* activity drives the cost. Computers make it possible to analyze many, many combinations of cost and activity very quickly. It is quite possible that computer analyses will show a good correlation between a cost and an activity even though no causal relationship exists. Such a correlation is called *spurious* and can present problems for the unwary. For example, electric utility companies can have a relatively high correlation between the number of kilowatt hours they generate and the cost of outside maintenance (cutting the grass, landscaping, and so on). There is no way that outside maintenance costs are driven by producing electric power (or vice versa), so why the high correlation? Both electric power output and outside maintenance are highest in the summer; both are also low in the winter. The logical reason for the high correlation is that both depend on another factor: the weather. Because both are related to that factor, they appear to be related to each other. The key, then, in seeking a relationship that will provide useful predictions and enhance cost management is to question high correlations that seem to have no causal basis. The measure of activity used to predict a cost must make sense.

PROBLEMS AND PITFALLS
OF COST BEHAVIOR ANALYSIS

The common thread in the high-low, scatter-diagram, and regression methods is that they all use past (historical) information about both the dependent variable (the cost to be predicted) and the independent variable (the measure of activity). Though easy to gather, historical information should be used carefully, because formulas based on historical data can give useful predictions only if conditions that prevailed in the past will also prevail in the future. For example, observations from months before a company installed new machinery are suspect because having the new machinery probably changed the cost structure. Similarly, the usefulness of a formula for predicting electricity cost is reduced if rates have changed since the observations were collected. (The cure in the latter example is to develop the equation using electricity consumption in kilowatt hours, and then apply the *expected* rates to the predicted use of kilowatt hours.)

The usefulness of a cost-prediction formula can also be reduced if nonrepresentative data are included in its development. (Apart from observations outside the relevant range, an example of a nonrepresentative observation is cost and volume data for a period when a company used temporary, and less efficient, workers.) Formulas developed using nonrepresentative data can lead to major misestimates of costs. Hence, managers should apply the cost estimation methods we have discussed only after they review and understand the operating conditions under which cost and volume data were gathered. Because the plotting phase of the scatter-diagram method tends to highlight out-of-line points, managers often do such plotting even when they plan to use regression analysis to develop the prediction formula. If there is, say, one out-of-line observation (called an *outlier*), it can often be ignored.

A final note of caution. Regardless of the method used to derive the cost prediction formula, the predictions depend for their validity on observations within the particular range of volumes over which the observations were gathered. Hence, some skepticism should be associated with predictions for activity levels outside that range.

The next section deals with a fairly common cost-behavior pattern that might be revealed by either a scatter diagram or a study of the contract covering the acquisition of the good or service.

STEP-VARIABLE COSTS

Figure 3-5 shows a pattern of cost behavior that fits neither the fixed-variable classification scheme nor the pattern of a typical mixed cost. A cost exhibiting such behavior is commonly called a **step-variable cost.** It is fixed over a range of volume, then jumps to a new level and remains fixed at that level until the next jump. The width of the range of volume over which the cost remains fixed varies with the particular cost. Most often, step-variable costs exist because of the indivisibility of resources; that is, many resources cannot be acquired in infinitely divisible increments. For instance, suppose a manager establishes a policy of having one production supervisor for every 20 workers, or one inventory clerk for every 1,000 items of inventory. The firm cannot add fractional supervisors or inventory clerks to maintain the established balance as individual workers and inventory items are added. Or consider that an airline can only make a flight or not; it cannot use fractions of planes to provide exactly as many seats as passen-

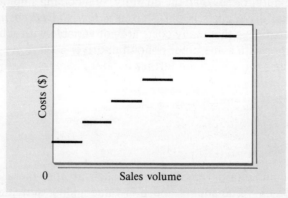

Figure 3-5   Step-Variable Cost

gers demand. In greater or lesser degree, all companies are confronted with step-variable costs.

How should a firm plan step-variable costs? Should the relevant range consist of only the segments over which the cost is fixed? Or should the cost be planned as if it were variable, even though this will result in predictions that seldom equal actual costs? The approach usually adopted is to treat them either as mixed, or as entirely variable (as opposed to fixed). Actual costs regularly differ from cost predictions using either of these alternatives. Step-variable costs are particularly troublesome to predict and manage when, as in the examples of production supervisors and inventory clerks, the point at which the cost jumps is a matter of managerial choice. Is one supervisor per 20 workers the best decision? Should a supervisor be added and responsibilities reshuffled when some available supervisors are responsible for more than 20 people, only when all have at least 20 people, or perhaps when the average span of responsibility is, say, 18 people?

It is also difficult to predict and manage step-variable costs if managers fail to identify the activity driving the cost. The activity is not incorporated in the prediction formula nor, therefore, is it carefully monitored and controlled. Isolating the activity that drives a step-variable cost is often difficult because many such costs do not change in direct proportion to short-term changes in activity, but are likely to respond to changes in activity over longer periods.

A simple tool that has proved useful in determining what drives step-variable costs is interviewing—asking managers what is likely to happen to particular costs, given specific actions. For instance, the purchasing manager can probably suggest the increase in workload that would follow the introduction of a new product that requires parts not used in any other products. Using such parts requires evaluating new vendors, establishing testing procedures, doing paperwork, and so on. The new parts may also require additional personnel in purchasing, and perhaps in receiving and inspection. Many companies have reported success in controlling some types of step-variable costs only after they recognized the cost-driving activity and so were able to concentrate on reducing the level of that activity. For example, companies that have worked closely with suppliers to achieve a high level of quality in purchased materials have been able to reduce inspection and rework costs after recognizing that those costs were driven by the quality, rather than the quantity, of incoming shipments. Identifying the activities that drive costs is one step in *activity-based costing*. The idea of activity-based costing is that many costs are not variable with sales or production volume, but rather with some other nonoutput driver such as we have mentioned above. We discuss this technique further in later chapters.

Value-Adding and Non-Value-Adding Costs

In advanced manufacturing environments (such as JIT) there is an important distinction between value-adding and non-value-adding activities and costs. A value-adding activity (and its cost) is one that is necessary to manufacture the product, while a non-value-adding activity (and its cost) is not necessary. Examples of non-value-adding activities and costs include moving semifinished product from one work station to another, rework of defective units, and separate inspection at the end of production. JIT companies therefore organize manufacturing cells to minimize moving semifinished goods, make units right the first time to eliminate rework, and inspect each unit as it progresses so that no separate final inspection is necessary.

Non-value-adding costs are the focus of attention, with the ultimate objective to eliminate all of them. Of course, such an objective can never be met. There will always have to be *some* movement of semifinished goods, or of workers, but the ideal serves as a long-term goal toward which the company can strive.

COST CLASSIFICATIONS AND MANAGERIAL ACTIONS

Understanding cost behavior goes beyond developing cost prediction formulas. Managers have learned that planning—particularly in its subfunction, decision making—requires that they understand how their actions affect cost behavior. At a minimum, managers must recognize that behavior patterns can be dictated by planning decisions. For example, many companies *plan,* or budget, to incur such fixed costs as advertising, employee training, and research and development, at some percentage of sales. Such costs then, if plotted, *appear* to be variable, but it is managerial action that creates that appearance. In this section we discuss three cost classification schemes that contribute to managers' understanding of the relationships between their actions and their costs.

Committed and Discretionary Fixed Costs

Recall from Chapter 2 that our use of the term "fixed" to describe a cost does not imply that the cost cannot be changed, only that it is nonvariable. Because some fixed costs can be changed more easily and quickly than others, it is sometimes useful to classify them using this criterion. Fixed costs that can be quickly altered by managerial action are called **discretionary costs.** Both the current incurrence and the current amount of such costs are subject to decisions by current managers. Advertising is an example of a discretionary fixed cost. (Ted probably decides each month whether to advertise and how much to spend.) Fixed costs that cannot be changed fairly rapidly by decisions of current managers are **committed costs,** so called to express the idea that managers have made some prior commitment. Depreciation is an example of a committed fixed cost. Like many committed fixed costs, depreciation arises from past managerial decisions—sometimes made several years ago—and cannot be changed without disposing of the asset to which it applies. (Ted's rent is probably determined by a lease agreement signed when he opened the store at its current location.)

It is not always possible to tell whether a cost is committed or discretionary just by knowing what the cost is (rent, salaries, research and development, and so on). For example, suppose part of the cost of research and development is depreciation and property taxes on a building used only by the research and development department, and the remainder is salaries for associated personnel. Regardless of its use, the depreciation and property taxes are committed as long as the firm owns the building. Some costs are on the borderline between committed and discretionary in the sense that a past decision committed the firm to incurring the cost but did not dictate its level. Referring to the earlier example, a decision to carry on research and development activities implies a commitment to incur *some* salary cost for employees fulfilling that purpose, but management can exercise discretion over the number of such employees and the level of their salaries. On a broader scale, the very existence of the company embodies a commitment to employ people to manage it. But to a great extent the number and compensation of those people are subject to the discretion of current managers.

Necessary versus Unnecessary   Do not misinterpret the discretionary-committed classification as distinguishing between unnecessary and necessary costs, respectively. Advertising is a discretionary fixed cost, but *some* type of advertising—a sign, a Yellow-Pages listing, whatever—is probably necessary for most every enterprise. Similarly, depreciation is a committed fixed cost; yet most enterprises could probably operate successfully without one or more of several cash registers, telephone lines, or display racks. Unfortunately, discretionary costs tend to be the first cut in cost-reduction programs. Such cuts reflect a misunderstanding of the classification. Consider the long-run effect of cutting the following discretionary costs: research and product development; management training programs; programs to upgrade worker skills; advertising; and maintenance.

Research and product development are crucial to the success of companies in such high-technology fields as pharmaceuticals, computers, aircraft, and some consumer products. Reducing expenditures for personnel development can lead to reduced morale, high turnover, and lessened productivity. A decline in advertising can influence buyer-recognition of the company's name and, hence, weaken prospects for future acceptance of new products. Deferring routine maintenance might result in high repair costs, as well as interruptions of production when machines finally break down.

Managers treat discretionary and committed fixed costs differently when analyzing day-to-day operations. We have already noted that, perhaps unwisely, discretionary costs are often the first targets of cost-reduction programs. Recognizing that little, if anything, can be done to change committed costs over short periods, managers are often inclined to watch committed costs less closely than they do discretionary costs. It should be obvious, however, that failure to monitor committed costs can also prove unwise, if only because every commitment that begins must have an end and so must be evaluated for its continuing importance.

Avoidable and Unavoidable Costs

Another useful subdivision of fixed costs hinges on whether the company could avoid the cost by dropping or curtailing some activity. The amount by which a cost can be reduced is **avoidable,** the amount that cannot be reduced is **unavoidable.** Thus, the ideas of avoidability and unavoidability apply only when a decision is at hand: avoidable if we do what?

At first glance, the avoidable-unavoidable categories might seem to parallel the discretionary-committed categories. This is sometimes so, but there can be significant exceptions, and determining whether or not a cost is avoidable typically requires a case-by-case analysis. Consider the following monthly income statement for a regional sales office of a large company. Upper-level management expects the results to continue about the same indefinitely.

Sales		$100,000
Variable costs		80,000
Contribution margin		20,000
Fixed costs:		
Salaries	$15,000	
Rent	1,000	
Other fixed costs	7,000	22,000
Loss		($ 2,000)

Despite the expectation of continued losses, there may be compelling reasons for keeping this particular sales office open. For example, the managers might believe that the firm's reputation requires having offices in certain geographical areas and that closing this office could hurt that reputation. That is, policy considerations might override financial concerns.

Policy issues aside, a decision about the future of the office requires more information about the fixed costs. First, note that the rent and certainly *some* salaries are committed costs because the company cannot have an office without having space and some people. Nevertheless, some of the committed costs might be unavoidable *if the company were to close the office.* Perhaps all or some salaries can be avoided if the firm lets the people go, or if it can use them elsewhere and thus avoid having to hire others. However, suppose that the entire $15,000 is salaries of salespeople who have contracts stating that they cannot be transferred and that they must receive their $15,000 whether or not they work. In that case, the $15,000 is unavoidable: The salespeople cannot be used elsewhere, nor can they be let go. Thus, even if the rent and other fixed costs could be avoided by closing the office, it is better to keep the office open and lose only $2,000 than to close it and still have to pay $15,000.

The managers would study the rent in the same way. In all likelihood, there is a lease on the office so that the firm cannot move out immediately upon making a decision to close the office. If the lease runs for another year and the firm cannot find anyone to move in and take over the lease, the firm has to pay the $1,000 monthly rent for one more year and the cost is unavoidable until a year has passed. Again, it is better to keep the office open and lose $2,000 than to close it and still pay $12,000. In general, then, the question is not whether the office is unprofitable but whether or not the unavoidable fixed costs are greater than the loss incurred by keeping the office open.

Direct and Indirect (Common) Costs

In some of the same situations where a manager wants to determine whether a cost is avoidable or unavoidable, a refinement of our basic cost classification scheme is often useful. Costs may be classified as direct or indirect.

A **direct cost,** also called a **separable cost,** is incurred specifically because of a particular activity of the firm, like a product, product line, or geographical area. (All costs are direct to *some* activity, if only to the activity represented by the company as a whole.) An **indirect cost,** also called a **common** or **joint cost,** does not relate to one specific activity, but rather to several.

Variable costs are direct to their associated product. Some fixed costs are direct to particular products or other activities, and some are not. Consider a company that makes many models of lawnmowers. One department in the factory does some work on every model. The fixed costs of that department are direct to the lawnmower business as a whole, but not to any particular model. As another example, salaries of salespeople who cover particular geographical regions are direct to those regions. But if the salespeople sell several products, their salaries are indirect to each of the products. Thus, to classify a cost as direct or indirect, it is necessary first to specify the activity in which the manager is interested.

Direct costs are usually avoidable, although there certainly can be exceptions. If a company rents a sales office and the lease has ten years to run, the rent is direct to the office, but is unavoidable. Indirect costs are generally unavoidable; by definition, they are incurred to support two or more activities, so they will continue to be incurred if only one of the activities is discontinued. Even here, though, the individual circumstances determine the classification. Consider a large company with six major production departments in a single factory building. Dropping one department could enable the company to reduce such indirect costs as those of operating the payroll and personnel functions, even though no one person in either of those departments works exclusively on the production department being dropped. Thus, some portion of the indirect cost is avoidable.

MANUFACTURING COSTS

A manufacturer must make its products and incur manufacturing costs, before it sells them. For this reason, the behavioral classification of manufacturing costs for planning purposes generally rests on whether the costs are fixed or variable in relation to the volume of production. Note the importance of cost planning for a company in an industry where production must be undertaken several months before a peak selling season. The toy industry is a good example.

A typical manufacturing firm has three general types of manufacturing costs: raw materials, direct labor, and manufacturing overhead. The cost of **raw materials** (sometimes called **direct materials** or simply **materials**), the materials and goods that the firm buys and transforms into its products (steel, wood, etc.), normally varies with the volume of production. Also included in this category are manufactured parts and components, although they have been through some manufacturing process already. The cost of **direct labor** (those employees who work *directly* on the product) is also normally variable with the volume of production. **Manufacturing overhead** (which consists of all production costs other than materials and direct labor) includes costs that might be fixed, variable, or mixed. Some examples of manufacturing overhead are

Wages of materials handlers (workers who move materials from one area to another)

Salaries of supervisors

Maintenance and repair costs for work performed on machinery and equipment used to make products

Wages of workers assigned responsibility for the storage and control of materials

Heat, light, and other power costs associated with the production areas

Depreciation and property taxes on factory buildings and factory machinery

Salary and office expenses of the manager (and subordinate personnel) responsible for production

From this brief listing of some manufacturing overhead costs you should see that *total* manufacturing overhead will be a mixed cost, with some variable component and some fixed component. Like its individual elements, total manufacturing overhead can be analyzed into its fixed and variable components using one or more of the methods discussed earlier in this chapter.

In a multiproduct firm it is not usually possible to relate the behavior of manufacturing overhead to a broad measure of output such as the number of units produced. A company that makes, for example, refrigerators, ovens, and toasters does not expect each type of manufacturing overhead cost to vary with the total number of units produced because the units are so different. (Making a toaster does not give rise to as much overhead as does making a refrigerator.) Managers usually try to relate manufacturing overhead to some *input* factor in the production process, such as number of hours worked by direct laborers or the number of machine hours. The variable component of overhead cost per unit of product is then found by multiplying the variable overhead rate by the number of hours a unit of product requires.

For example, a manager has found that total manufacturing overhead is well described by the equation

$$\text{Total cost} = \$40,000 + (\$3 \times \text{machine hours})$$

Suppose further that a toaster requires 1 machine hour, a refrigerator requires 20 hours. The variable manufacturing overhead for each product is as follows.

	Toaster	Refrigerator
Machine hours	1	20
Variable overhead per machine hour	$3	$ 3
Variable manufacturing overhead per unit	$3	$60

The manager adds the variable overhead to the direct labor and material cost to get the total variable manufacturing cost for each type of product.

The managers in a manufacturing firm often face a problem when analyzing cost behavior so as to apply VCP analysis. For financial accounting purposes, manufacturing firms must calculate cost of goods sold using fixed manufacturing costs. From Chapter 2 you know that per-unit fixed costs are of little use in planning (because they are different at every level of volume). Hence, to analyze the cost structure of the manufacturing firm requires eliminating the effect of fixed costs from the per-unit manufacturing costs computed for financial accounting purposes. That task can become extremely complicated, and we defer a complete discussion of it to Chapters 13, 14, and 15. At this point, we shall simply show how a manufacturer calculates the per-unit cost of product and prepares its income statement.

Assume the following data for MFG Manufacturing Company. MFG makes a single product. It produced 25,000 units and sold them all at $20 per unit. There was no beginning inventory.

Total variable manufacturing cost per unit	$ 6
Total variable manufacturing cost (25,000 × $6)	$150,000
Total fixed manufacturing overhead	$200,000
Total manufacturing costs	$350,000
Variable selling expenses per unit	$ 2
Total fixed selling and administrative expenses	$ 60,000

Fixed manufacturing cost per unit is $8 ($200,000/25,000), so the total manufacturing cost per unit is $14, $6 variable plus $8 fixed. (The total cost per unit could also be determined by dividing the $350,000 total manufacturing cost by 25,000 units.) Accordingly, Cost of Goods Sold will be $14 per unit on the income statement.

MFG's income statement, for financial reporting purposes, appears on the left side of Exhibit 3-1, along with one prepared using the contribution margin approach for comparison. The incomes shown under the two approaches are the same, but the contribution margin format allows the manager to understand the firm's cost structure and facilitates the use of VCP analysis. For these reasons, the contribution margin format is often used in reports prepared for managers even when such managers also receive copies of the reports prepared for persons outside the firm.

Exhibit 3-1
MFG Manufacturing Company Income Statements for the Year

Financial Accounting Format		Contribution Margin Format		
Sales (25,000 × $20)	$500,000	Sales (25,000 × $20)		$500,000
Cost of sales (25,000 × $14)[a]	350,000	Variable costs:		
		Manufacturing		
Gross margin	150,000	(25,000 × $6)	$150,000	
		Selling (25,000 × $2)	50,000	
Selling and administrative expenses[b]	110,000			200,000
		Contribution margin		300,000
		Fixed costs:		
		Manufacturing	200,000	
		Selling and administrative	60,000	
				260,000
Income	$ 40,000	Income		$ 40,000

[a]Variable cost of $6 per unit + fixed cost of $8 per unit ($200,000/25,000 units) = $14 manufacturing cost per unit.
[b]Variable cost of $2 per unit + fixed cost of $60,000 = $110,000.

COST STRUCTURE AND MANAGERIAL ATTITUDES

Businesses can operate in different ways. A company can use a great deal of labor and little machinery or vice versa. Salespeople might be on salary, commission, or a combination of the two. When making choices, managers must consider the effects of their decisions on the cost structure—the relative proportions of fixed and variable costs. For example, a company might take on higher fixed costs to reduce variable costs and thereby increase contribution margin. (Automation does exactly that.) Such an action increases potential profitability, but it also increases risk. The break-even point will probably increase, and if volume drops, profits will fall more rapidly with the higher contribution margin.

Suppose the managers of Benson Company have decided to introduce a new product. They expect to sell 20,000 units at $10. They can make the product using either of two manufacturing processes. Process A uses a great deal of labor and has variable costs of $7 per unit and annual fixed costs of $40,000. Process B uses more machinery, with unit variable costs of $4 and annual fixed costs of $95,000. Given these estimates, Process B yields more profit, as shown in the following income statement.

	Process A	Process B
Sales (20,000 × $10)	$200,000	$200,000
Variable costs at $7 and $4	140,000	80,000
Contribution margin at $3 and $6	60,000	120,000
Fixed costs	40,000	95,000
Profit	$ 20,000	$ 25,000

If the managers were certain that the numbers were correct, they would choose Process B. However, the numbers are estimates. The managers should therefore do some additional analysis before deciding which process to use. One item of interest is the break-even point for each process:

Breakeven

Process A: $40,000/$3 = 13,333 units

Process B: $95,000/$6 = 15,833 units

Process B has higher fixed costs than Process A and is therefore riskier. Process B's higher break-even point is one indication of its greater risk. Using Process A, the company might experience a greater fall in volume before it begins to show losses on the new product. Managers often express risk by referring to the margin of safety.

Margin of Safety

MOS
— Exp - BE

The decline in volume from the expected level of sales to the break-even point is called the **margin of safety (MOS).** As the name suggests, the MOS measures the extent to which sales must fall before the situation becomes unprofitable. The MOS can be expressed as a unit amount, dollar amount, or percentage. In our example, the MOS for Process A is 6,667 units (20,000 expected − 13,333 break-even), or $66,670 (6,667 units at $10 each), or 33.3% (6,667/20,000). For Process B it is 4,167 units (20,000 − 15,833), $41,670 (4,167 units at $10), or 20.8% (4,167/20,000). Generally, the higher the MOS, the lower the risk. Our example involved computing the MOS for a single product, but the concept can also be applied to an entire company or to a group of products.

Indifference Point

I.P

A tool that helps managers to choose between alternative cost structures is the indifference point. The **indifference point** is the level of volume at which total costs, and hence profits, are the same under both cost structures. If the company operated at that level of volume, it would not matter which alternative it used because income would be the same either way.

We calculate the indifference point by setting up an equation where each side represents total cost under one of the alternatives. (If selling price is the same under both alternatives, profits will be the same when total costs are the same.) At unit volumes below the indifference point, Process A gives higher profits, while at volumes above the indifference point, Process B is more profitable. The indifference point for Benson's new product is 18,333 units, calculated as follows, with Q equal to unit volume.

Total Cost for Process A		Total Cost for Process B
Fixed cost + variable cost		Fixed cost + variable cost
$40,000 + $7Q	=	$95,000 + $4Q
$3Q	=	$55,000
Q	=	18,333 (rounded)

At volumes below 18,333 units, Process A gives lower costs and higher profits; above 18,333 units, Process B gives higher profits.

The line $3Q = $55,000 gives a clue to the tradeoff between the alternatives: the company is gaining $3 per unit in reduced variable costs by increasing fixed costs $55,000. The indifference point shows that the firm needs 18,333 units to make the tradeoff desirable, only 1,667 units (or 8%) below the estimated volume of 20,000. If Benson's managers believe there is a high likelihood that volume will be lower than their estimate of 20,000 units, they might decide to use Process A.

Figure 3-6 shows Benson's choices in a variation of the usual VCP graph from Chapter 2. As in Chapter 2, the axes represent volume and dollars. Each line represents profit at each level of volume for the associated alternative. Notice that the line for each process begins at a negative point equal to fixed costs for that process and crosses zero at the break-even point for that process. Where profit is the same under both alternatives, the two lines cross. This form of the graph is especially useful in examining alternatives because it reduces the number of lines needed to represent an alternative.

There is no correct or incorrect answer for Benson's managers in their choice of a cost structure. Analytical tools such as the indifference point and the VCP graph can help them evaluate alternatives, but the decision depends on their attitudes about risk and return. If they want to avoid risk, they will choose Process A, foregoing the potential for higher profits from Process B. If they are venturesome, they will probably be willing to take some risk for the potentially higher returns and choose Process B.

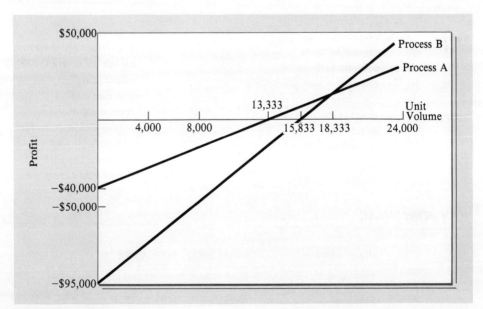

Figure 3-6   Benson's Alternatives

SUMMARY

Costs do not always fit into fixed or variable classifications, and not all variable costs are variable with sales. Some costs are mixed and contain both fixed and variable elements. Step-variable costs are fixed over small ranges of activity but at different levels for different ranges. Some manufacturing costs vary with the number of units manufactured, some selling costs vary with the number of orders placed by customers, and so on. It is not always easy to find an appropriate measure of activity for planning a given cost, but finding critical relationships is important to the manager both for planning and for cost management. Scatter diagrams, high-low estimates, and regression analysis are useful tools for analyzing cost behavior but must be used with care. Actual costs will differ from planned costs, and predictions of cost behavior based on a single measure of volume might be inaccurate.

There are several other classifications of costs: discretionary or committed; avoidable or unavoidable; direct or indirect. Discretionary fixed costs can be changed on relatively short notice. Committed fixed costs cannot be changed quickly. In general, only future levels of committed costs can be affected by present management.

Classifying costs as avoidable or unavoidable relates to specific decisions, such as closing an office. Direct costs relate to a specific activity, while indirect, or common, costs benefit more than one activity. Generally speaking, direct costs other than committed fixed costs are avoidable, and indirect costs unavoidable if the activity is stopped.

Within limits, managers can control the relative proportions of fixed and variable costs in the cost structure. The indifference point, expected sales, the potential for variations from expectations, and the managers' attitudes toward risk-return relationships are some of the factors that influence decisions in planning cost structure.

KEY TERMS

avoidable costs	indirect cost
committed costs	manufacturing overhead
common (joint) cost	margin of safety (MOS)
correlation and association	mixed cost
cost driver	raw materials
direct (separable) cost	regression analysis
direct labor	scatter-diagram method
discretionary cost	semivariable cost
high-low method	step-variable cost
indifference point	unavoidable costs

KEY FORMULAS

Margin of safety	= current sales − break-even sales
Total costs	= fixed costs + (variable cost per unit of sales × number of units sold)
Total costs	= fixed costs + (variable cost as % of sales × dollars of sales)

$$\frac{\text{Variable cost component}}{\text{in mixed cost}} = \frac{\text{cost at high volume} - \text{cost at low volume}}{\text{high volume} - \text{low volume}}$$

$$\frac{\text{Fixed cost component}}{\text{in mixed cost}} = \frac{\text{total cost at}}{\text{high volume}} - (\text{high volume} \times \text{variable cost factor})$$

REVIEW PROBLEM

Swanboy Company had the following income statement in 19X2.

Sales (100,000 units at $6)	$600,000
Variable costs (100,000 units at $3.60)	360,000
Contribution margin (100,000 units at $2.40)	240,000
Fixed costs	180,000
Income	$ 60,000

Required
1. Swanboy expects sales of 110,000 units for the next several years. The firm currently rents machinery that can be returned to its owner at any time. If the machinery is returned, the firm will save $20,000 in fixed costs per year. However, variable costs will increase to $3.80 per unit.
   (a) What are the break-even points under the current and the alternative cost structures?
   (b) At what level of volume is total profit the same whether or not Swanboy continues to rent the machinery? (That is, what is the indifference point?)
   (c) Would it be wise for the firm to stop renting the machinery?
2. Swanboy operates several stores in a single city. One of the stores is expected to show the following annual results for the next few years.

Sales (10,000 units)		$60,000
Variable costs		36,000
Contribution margin		24,000
Fixed costs:		
Salaries	$15,500	
Rent	6,000	
Insurance and utilities	2,000	
Miscellaneous	3,000	26,500
Income (Loss)		($ 2,500)

The firm has a ten year lease on the space occupied by the store, and the lease cannot be canceled. Determine the change that would occur in the firm's total profit if the store were closed.

Answer to Review Problem

1. (a) This part is a review of Chapter 2 but provides information of use in item c. Current contribution margin is given at $2.40. Proposed contribution margin, if the machinery is not rented, is $2.20 ($6.00 − $3.80). Break-even points are:

Current break-even = $180,000/$2.40 = 75,000 units

Proposed break-even = $160,000/$2.20 = 72,727 units (rounded)

(b) 100,000 units

Total Costs, Proposed Structure	=	*Total Costs, Current Structure*
$160,000 + $3.80Q	=	$180,000 + $3.60Q
$0.20Q	=	$20,000
Q	=	100,000 units

(c) At the expected volume of 110,000 units, the current structure—renting the machinery—is the better alternative because the indifference point is less than 110,000. Another way to reach this conclusion is to prepare income statements, which show that profit is $2,000 higher under the current structure.

	Current Arrangement		*Proposed Arrangement*	
Sales (110,000 units × $6)	$660,000		$660,000	
Variable costs	396,000	($3.60/unit)	418,000	($3.80/unit)
Contribution margin	264,000	($2.40/unit)	242,000	($2.20/unit)
Fixed costs	180,000		160,000	
Profit	$ 84,000		$ 82,000	

Another way to determine the effect is to determine whether the decrease in contribution margin would be more than the decrease in fixed costs. At 110,000 units the firm loses $22,000 in contribution margin (110,000 × $0.20) if it stops using the machinery. This is $2,000 more than the $20,000 saving in fixed costs.

Beyond the indifference point (100,000 units), the structure with the higher contribution margin—the current structure—produces the higher profit. Of course, the managers still should assess their confidence in the volume estimate of 110,000 units. If a realistic estimate of volume is something less than 100,000 units, the firm would be better off not renting the equipment.

2. Considering only the facts as given, total profit would drop by at least $3,500 per year. The $6,000 rent is unavoidable; it would not be eliminated if the store were closed. That is, the loss for the store would be $6,000 if it were closed, compared with the current loss of $2,500, because there would be *no* revenues and thus no contribution margin. Even if the store were closed, the loss might exceed $6,000 if, as part of the rental agreement, the firm were required to insure the premises, or if there were some type of fixed-term employment agreement with the store's manager such that he or she could not be transferred to another location.

APPENDIX: REGRESSION ANALYSIS

Regression analysis fits a mathematically precise line to a set of data. The procedures for developing a regression equation manually are laborious. However, many computer programs are available for doing regression analysis, and even some advanced hand calculators can be used to reduce the number of required computations.

Although regression analysis has many uses, our interest here is in determining cost behavior—finding the fixed and variable components of a cost given a measure of activity with which the cost is thought to be associated. Regression analysis gives an equation for predicting costs. The first step in regression analysis is to decide what measure of activity to use—sales dollars, production in units, number of sales invoices prepared, hours worked by direct laborers, number of inventory parts stocked.

This appendix discusses two basic techniques, simple and multiple regression. Simple regression provides the equation that best describes the relationship between one dependent variable and one independent variable. With multiple regression we develop the equation that best describes the relationship between one dependent variable and two or more independent variables.

Simple Regression

Developing a regression equation requires the solving of two equations simultaneously. These equations, which are given below, are called the **normal equations.**

$$(1) \quad \Sigma XY = \Sigma Xa + b\Sigma X^2$$

$$(2) \quad \Sigma Y \;\; = na + b\Sigma X$$

where

X = measure of volume

Y = cost

a = fixed cost

b = variable cost per unit

n = number of observations

Σ = sum of (e.g., ΣX^2 = sum of the squares of the volumes)

The letter Y is used to designate the *dependent variable,* the one that we are trying to predict. The letter X is used to designate the *independent variable,* the one that we believe affects, or drives, the dependent variable. In our applications, Y will usually be a cost or group of costs such as factory overhead, and X will be some measure of activity, such as production in units, sales in units or dollars, labor hours worked, or sales invoices processed.

We shall use the following data to illustrate the procedures of regression analysis. In this example, the cost is monthly factory operating cost and the activity is machine hours used during the month. (Both are in thousands.)

Machine Hours	Overhead Cost
110	$660
120	685
90	620
80	595
130	670
125	665
135	710
130	695
105	650
100	630

The schedule below gives the values required for the normal equations.

	X	Y	X^2	XY
	110	$ 660	12,100	72,600
	120	685	14,400	82,200
	90	620	8,100	55,800
	80	595	6,400	47,600
	130	670	16,900	87,100
	125	665	15,625	83,125
	135	710	18,225	95,850
	130	695	16,900	90,350
	105	650	11,025	68,250
	100	630	10,000	63,000
Totals	1,125	$6,580	129,675	745,875

Substituting the appropriate values in the normal equations gives

(1) $745,875 = 1,125a + 129,675b$

(2) $6,580 = 10a + 1,125b$

With two equations and two unknowns, we can solve the equations in several ways. Perhaps the simplest is to solve for b first by eliminating a. To do so, we multiply equation (1) by 10 (the coefficient of a in equation (2)), and equation (2) by 1,125 (the coefficient of a in equation (1)). This gives

(1) $7,458,750 = 11,250a + 1,296,750b$

(2) $7,402,500 = 11,250a + 1,265,625b$

Subtracting equation (2) from equation (1) gives

$$56,250 = 31,125b$$

$$b = \$1.8072$$

The value of b, \$1.8072, is the slope of the regression equation—the variable component of the cost.

We can now substitute the value of b in either equation and solve for a. Substituting \$1.8072 for b in equation (2) we get

$$(2)\ \ 6,580 = 10a + (\$1.8072 \times 1,125)$$

$$a = \$454.69$$

The value for a, the fixed component of the cost, is \$454.69 thousand. The formula for total cost is then

$$\text{Total factory overhead cost} = \$454,690 + (\$1.8072 \times \text{machine hours})$$

Correlation and the Standard Error

Because managers use the regression equation and the estimates of a and b, they want to have some idea about the accuracy of the predictions. There are several measures of goodness of fit, how well the regression line fits the data, that suggest to managers how good their predictions are likely to be. The two measures we discuss are the **coefficient of determination,** often called r^2 and the **standard error of the estimate.**

The coefficient of determination is a measure of how well the regression line accounts for the changes in Y, the dependent variable. It can have values from zero through 1. The value is the percentage of the variation in Y that is "explained" by the movement of X. A value of 1 means that the regression line is perfect: all points fall on it. A value near zero means that the values of Y are randomly scattered with no relationship to the values of X. Figure 3-7 shows two cases.

Using machine hours as the independent variable, it is clearly easier to predict Cost A than Cost B. Perhaps you could better predict Cost B using some other measure of activity, or perhaps Cost B is not driven by any activity, but is just random.

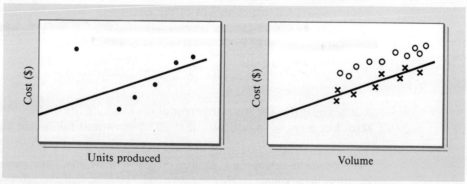

Figure 3-7   High and Low Correlations

The coefficient of determination is calculated in the following way.

$$r^2 = 1 - \frac{\Sigma(Y - Y_c)^2}{\Sigma(Y - \overline{Y})^2}$$

The differences, $Y - Y_c$ are the differences between the actual values of Y and those predicted by the regression equation. The differences, $Y - \overline{Y}$ are the differences between the actual values of Y and the mean, or average of the values of Y. (The differences are squared for reasons that we shall not discuss here.) Roughly speaking, if you had no values for X and had to predict Y using only the past values of Y, your best prediction is the average of previous costs. The variation around that mean is the denominator of the equation. The numerator of the equation is the unexplained variation, which is zero if the regression line were perfect and all observations fell on it. The schedule below shows the calculations.

Y_c	Y	$(Y - Y_c)^2$	$(Y - \overline{Y})^2$
653.482	660	42.484	4
671.554	685	180.795	729
617.338	620	7.086	1444
599.266	595	18.199	3969
689.626	670	385.180	144
680.590	665	243.048	49
698.662	710	128.550	2704
689.626	695	28.880	1369
644.446	650	30.847	64
635.410	630	29.268	784
		1,094.337	11,260

For our data,

$$r^2 = 1 - (1,094.337/11,260) = .9028$$

The result indicates a good fit of the line to the data, so predictions using the regression equation should be good. Again, however, we have only ten observations to keep down the calculations. Using more observations, say 20 to 30, would make us more confident of the equation.

The standard error of the estimate (S_e) is a measure of the variation around the regression line as is shown by its calculation.[1]

$$S_e = \sqrt{\frac{\Sigma(Y - Y_c)^2}{n - 2}}$$

The lower the standard error of the estimate, the better. A standard error of zero, like an r^2 of 1, indicates that all observations fall on the regression line.

---

[1] The divisor is actually the number of observations minus the number of coefficients estimated in the equation. We estimate a and b here. In multiple regression, we could have four or more coefficients and the divisor would decrease accordingly.

In our case,

$$S_e = \sqrt{\frac{\$1,094.337}{8}}$$

$$= \$11.696 \text{ thousand}$$

Statistical theory tells us that roughly 68% of the actual values of cost lie within one standard error of their predicted values, about 95% within two standard errors.[2] With the standard error of $11,696 here, about 68% of the time actual cost will be within $11,696 of its predicted value, and within $23,392 (2 × $11,696) about 95% of the time. Assuming a cost prediction at the average of $658,000, 95% of the time actual cost should differ by no more than 3.6% ($23,392/$658,000). Thus, the standard error of the estimate, like r^2, suggests a good fit of the regression line to the data.

Multiple Regression

In many cases, more than one activity drives a cost. Multiple regression analysis is a technique for developing a prediction equation using more than one independent variable.

In a modern business, many costs depend on more than one activity. The cost of heating a factory depends both on the number of hours it is open and on the outside temperature. Shipping costs depend on both the weight of the goods and the distance over which they must travel. As indicated in the chapter, the costs to prepare invoices to customers are affected not only by the number of sales orders received but also by the number of items covered by each sales order.

A multiple regression equation has the following general form.

$$Y = a + b_1X_1 + b_2X_2 + b_3X_3 \ldots b_nX_n$$

where

Y = the dependent variable to be predicted

$X_1 \ldots X_n$ = the values of the various independent variables influencing the value of Y

$b_1 \ldots b_n$ = the coefficients of the various independent variables

a = the fixed component (as in simple regression)

Suppose the manager of a factory that makes a number of different products has requested an analysis of manufacturing overhead costs. The managerial accountant, working in conjunction with a statistician, came up with the following analysis.

---

[2] The following is very rough, but is given to illustrate the principle of the standard error of the estimate. The actual intervals within which predicted costs are likely to fall are wider than the standard error of the estimate.

Fixed component of manufacturing overhead cost	$32,500 per month ($a$)
Variable components (independent variables):	
Direct labor hours (X_1)	$2.40 per hour ($b_1$)
Machine-hours (X_2)	$1.80 per hour ($b_2$)
Weight of materials put into production (X_3)	$0.30 per pound ($b_3$)

Using statistical techniques, the description of which is beyond the scope of this text, the accountant and the statistical consultant have found that variations in three variables (direct labor hours, machine-hours, and weight of material processed) better describe variations in total overhead costs than do variations in any one or combination of two such variables. Such a conclusion is reasonable when one considers that many overhead costs (fringe benefits, for example) are related to labor time, that some (like power, supplies, and lubricants) are readily associated with machine time, and that still others (like materials handling and storekeeping costs) depend on the quantity of materials being used.

Suppose, now, that the factory manager expects the following activity in the coming month.

Direct labor hours	20,000
Machine-hours	15,000
Pounds of material processed	70,000

The manager could predict total manufacturing overhead of $128,500.

Total
manufacturing = $32,500 + ($2.40 × 20,000) + ($1.80 × 15,000) + ($0.30 × 70,000)
overhead

= $32,500 +	$48,000	+	$27,000	+	$21,000
fixed	variable with		variable with		variable with
cost	direct labor		machine-hours		pounds of
	hours				material

The cautions associated with simple regression discussed in the chapter also apply here, plus one more. In multiple regression analysis, there is an assumption that the independent variables are not correlated *with each other*. In our example, for instance, it is important to know whether direct labor hours and machine-hours (or some other combination of the three independent variables) are closely associated. If two (or more) of the independent variables are highly correlated, the results of multiple regression analysis must be used with care and the underlying statistical problems must be understood. You will study such problems in depth in your statistics courses.

A multiple regression equation also has a coefficient of determination and a standard error of the estimate, but the calculations are somewhat different than they are for simple regression and we shall omit them.

In summary, when using either simple or multiple regression analysis, you must understand the statistical principles that underlie these approaches. Critical to the production of useful results under either approach is the need for the observations to be representative of conditions expected to prevail during the period for which predictions are being made.

ASSIGNMENT MATERIAL

Questions for Discussion

3-1 **Cost classification** Indicate whether each of the following items of cost is likely to be discretionary or committed. If in doubt, describe the circumstances under which the cost would fall into one or the other category. If the cost is mixed, consider only the fixed portion.
(a) Straight-line depreciation on building.
(b) Sum-of-years'-digits depreciation on a machine.
(c) Salaries of salespeople.
(d) Salaries of president and vice-presidents for production, sales, and finance.
(e) Fees for consultants on long-range planning.
(f) Utilities for factory—heating and lighting.
(g) Management development costs—costs of attending seminars, training programs, etc.

3-2 **High-low method** The controller of your firm recommends the following approach to estimating the fixed and variable components of manufacturing overhead costs such as supervision, indirect labor, and supplies.

Estimate the total cost that the firm would incur if it shut down, and treat that amount as fixed cost. Then estimate the total cost if the firm worked at 100% of capacity, stated in machine hours. Divide the difference in the two cost figures by the difference in machine hours and treat that as the variable component.

Required: Comment on the procedure. Would the formula derived from it work well for the firm if it normally operated between 75% and 90% of capacity?

3-3 **Take or pay contract** Boulder Chemical Company has a contract that requires it to buy 100,000 tons of a raw material each month. The material is perishable, and if Boulder cannot sell the products that use the material, the unused material must be discarded. In most firms, raw materials costs are variable. Is that so in this case?

3-4 **Committed fixed costs** Analyze each of the following statements, explaining what is wrong with it.
(a) The controller tells you that the units-of-production method is used for depreciation of machinery and that depreciation is therefore a variable cost, not a committed fixed cost.
(b) The same controller tells you that, since the firm nearly always operates at full capacity, all fixed costs cannot be reduced and are therefore committed.
(c) A sales manager tells you that the firm cannot operate without salespeople and that therefore salespeople's salaries are committed fixed costs.
(d) Another controller says that if committed costs are those necessarily incurred because the firm is in business, there are no such costs because the firm could reduce its costs to zero by simply closing up.

3-5 **Cost classification** Melton Company sells a variety of industrial products. It operates eight regional sales offices. State whether each of the following costs is likely to be (a) avoidable or unavoidable and (b) direct or indirect to the South-Central office.
(a) Salaries of salespeople in the South-Central region.
(b) Rent on the South-Central office. The lease has five years left.
(c) Rent on equipment used in the South-Central regional office. The equipment can be returned with one week's notice.
(d) Salaries of the national vice-president for sales and her staff.
(e) National advertising.
(f) Travel expenses of salespeople working in the South-Central region.

3-6 **Cost classification** Talley Industries makes small fiberglass boats. It has two production departments, the Forming Department and the Finishing Department. State whether each of the following costs is likely to be (a) avoidable or unavoidable and (b) direct or indirect to the Forming Department.
(a) Wages of workers in the Forming Department.
(b) Property taxes on the factory building.
(c) Depreciation on machinery used only in the Forming Department.
(d) Salaries of the plant controller and her staff.
(e) Salary of the Forming Department manager.
(f) Wages of maintenance workers who take care of all machinery in the factory.

Exercises

3-7 **Accuracy of predictions** The scatter diagrams below show two costs plotted against production. Which cost can you predict and plan for more easily? Explain.

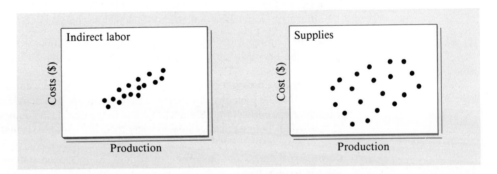

3-8 **Mixed costs** The president of Gorman Company has asked you to develop a behavioral classification for indirect labor cost. You have the following data from two recent months.

Direct Labor Hours	Indirect Labor Cost
19,000	$47,600
27,000	60,800

Required: Compute the fixed and variable portions of indirect labor cost based on direct labor hours.

3-9 **Margin of safety** Trivia Inc. plans to market a new electronic game. The game will sell for $120, and Trivia expects to sell 11,000 units. Per-unit variable manufacturing cost is $82. The only other variable cost is a 15% sales commission. Fixed costs for the game are $160,000.

Required: Compute the margin of safety at the expected sales volume.

3-10 **Alternative VCP graph (extension of 3-9)** The managers of Trivia Inc. have determined that the game could also be brought out using a different combination of production and marketing strategies. The alternative strategies would reduce per-unit variable manufacturing cost to $71, but annual fixed costs would increase to $175,000 and the sales commission would be raised to 20%.

Required: In a VCP graph like the one on page 77, plot the results of the two alternatives that Trivia is considering.

3-11 **Indifference point** Travelco sells a particular piece of soft-sided luggage, for $60. Unit variable cost is $34, and monthly fixed costs are $60,000. A combination of changes in the way Travelco produces and sells this product could reduce per-unit variable cost to $30 but would increase monthly fixed costs to $84,000.

Required
1. Determine the monthly break-even points under the two available alternatives.
2. Determine the indifference point of the two alternatives.

3-12 **Cost behavior** A study of office supplies used in the regional sales offices of a large manufacturer shows that the cost is mixed. A record of sales and corresponding supply costs in one of the offices is as follows.

Monthly Sales	Cost of Supplies
$43,000	$2,164
48,000	2,486
34,000	2,115
52,000	2,521
37,000	2,315
38,000	2,464
45,000	2,728
56,000	2,984
50,000	2,652

Required: Determine the variable cost percentage of sales and the fixed costs using the high-low point method.

3-13 **Revenue and cost analysis — high-low method** The controller of your firm, a retail store, is attempting to develop VCP relationships to be used for planning and control. He is not sure how this might be done and asks your assistance. He has prepared two income statements from monthly data.

	October	November
Sales	$50,000	$60,000
Cost of goods sold	30,000	36,000
Gross profit	20,000	24,000
Operating expenses:		
Selling expenses	7,400	7,700
Administrative expenses	6,200	6,400
Total expenses	13,600	14,100
Income	$ 6,400	$ 9,900

Required
1. Determine the fixed and variable components of cost of goods sold, selling expenses, and administrative expenses.
2. Prepare a contribution margin income statement based on sales of $70,000.

3-14 Explaining regression analysis (related to Appendix) The controller of ARCON, Inc. has received the following regression results from the industrial engineering department.

$$Y = \$89,234 + \$0.8765X, \ r^2 = .6781, \ S_e = \$9,289$$

$$Y = \text{monthly manufacturing supplies cost, } X = \text{machine hours}$$

The data were collected in a range of 30,000 to 50,000 monthly machine hours for the company's only plant. The controller wants your assistance in explaining these results to a group of managers.

Required: Explain the meaning and significance of each of the items in the regression results.

3-15 Interpretation of scatter diagram The graph below depicts the costs experienced by Magma Enterprises.

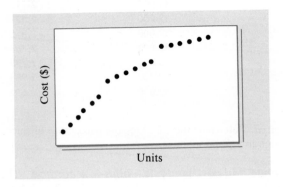

Required
1. Give some possible reasons for the observed behavior of costs.
2. How would you plan for costs that exhibited this type of behavior?

3-16 High-low method for manufacturing company The chief accountant of Blackman Industries prepared the following income statements.

	June	July
Sales	$420,000	$450,000
Cost of sales	226,000	235,000
Gross margin	194,000	215,000
Selling and administrative expenses	105,000	108,000
Income before taxes	$ 89,000	$107,000

Blackman produces a single product.

Required
1. Determine the fixed and variable components of cost of sales and of selling and administrative expenses.
2. Prepare income statements for June and July using the contribution-margin format. Comment on the differences between the statements above and the ones that you prepared.

3-17 Cost structure Ben Skove, production manager of SKE Company, is trying to decide which of two machines to rent. He needs a machine to sand the surfaces of a picnic table that SKE manufactures. Data related to the two alternatives are

	Hand-Fed Machine	Automatic Machine
Annual rental payments	$ 14,000	$ 36,000
Other annual fixed costs	100,000	110,000

Skove expects variable cost per table to be $34 using the hand-fed machine and $27 using the automatic machine. He also expects annual volume of about 3,000 tables.

Required
1. Determine the total annual cost to make 3,000 tables with each machine.
2. Determine the annual volume of tables at which total manufacturing cost is the same for each machine.
3. Which machine would you select?

3-18 Using per-unit data Nimmer Company expects the following per-unit results at a volume of 80,000 units.

Sales		$4.00
Variable costs	$1.40	
Fixed costs	2.25	3.65
Profit		$0.35

Required: Answer the following questions independently of one another.
1. How many units must the company sell to earn a profit of $80,000?
2. If Nimmer could sell 60,000 units, what selling price will yield a $60,000 profit?

3. Nimmer can undertake an advertising campaign for $6,000. Volume will increase by 3,000 units at the $4 selling price. By how much and in which direction (increase or decrease) will the company's profit change if it takes the action?

3-19 **Percentage income statement** The president of Fillmore Industries has developed the following income statement showing expected percentage results at sales of $800,000.

Sales	100%
Cost of sales	60%
Gross margin	40%
Other expenses	30%
Income	10%

The president tells you that cost of sales is all variable and that the only other variable cost is commissions, which are 10% of sales.

Required
1. Determine the profit that the company expects to earn.
2. Determine the break-even point and the margin of safety.
3. If sales are $700,000, what will profit be?
4. The president wants a $120,000 profit. Expected unit volume is the same as for the statement above. By what percentage must the company increase its selling price to achieve the goal? Assume the *per-unit* cost of sales remains constant.

3-20 **Cost behavior graphs (AICPA adapted)** Graphs and descriptions of cost elements are given opposite. For each description, select the letter of the graph that best shows the behavior of the cost. Graphs may be used more than once. The zero point for each graph is the intersection of the horizontal and vertical axes. The vertical axis represents *total* cost for the described cost and the horizontal axis represents production in units. Be prepared to discuss any assumptions you might have to make in selecting your answers.
1. Depreciation of equipment, using the units-of-production method.
2. Electricity bill, a flat charge plus a variable cost after a certain number of kilowatt-hours are used.
3. City water bill, computed as follows:

First 1,000,000 gallons or less	$1,000 flat fee
Next 10,000 gallons	0.003 per gallon used
Next 10,000 gallons	0.006 per gallon used
Next 10,000 gallons	0.009 per gallon used
etc., etc., etc.	

4. Cost of lubricant for machines, where cost per unit decreases with each pound of lubricant used (for example, if one pound is used, the cost is $10.00;

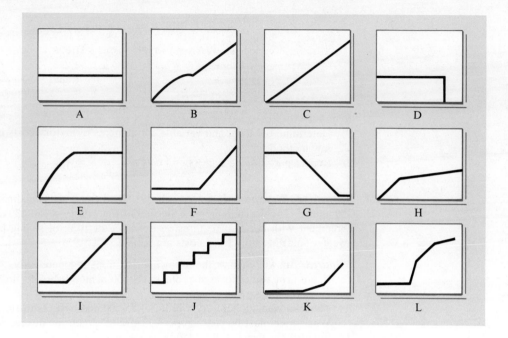

if two pounds are used, the cost is $19.98; if three pounds are used, the cost is $29.94; with a minimum cost per pound of $9.25).

5. Depreciation of equipment, using the straight-line method.
6. Rent for a factory building donated by the city, where the agreement calls for a fixed-fee payment unless 200,000 person-hours are worked, in which case no rent need be paid.
7. Salaries of repairpeople, where one repairperson is needed for every 1,000 hours of machine-time or less (i.e., 0 to 1,000 hours requires one repairperson, 1,001 to 2,000 hours requires two repairpeople, etc.).
8. Federal unemployment compensation taxes, where the labor force is constant in number throughout the year and the average annual wage is $16,000. The tax is levied only on the first $8,500 earned by each employee.
9. Rent for production machinery, computed as follows:

First 10,000 hours of use	$20,000 flat fee
Next 2,000 hours of use	$1.90 per hour
Next 2,000 hours of use	$1.80 per hour
Next 2,000 hours of use	$1.70 per hour
etc., etc., etc.	

10. Rent for a factory building donated by the county, where the agreement calls for rent of $100,000 less $1 for each hour laborers worked in excess of 200,000 hours, but a minimum rental payment of $20,000 is required.

3-21 Cost behavior—regression analysis (related to Appendix) The following data have been collected for the purpose of determining the behavior of factory costs.

Month	Units Produced	Factory Costs
January	112	$1,820
February	154	2,296
March	98	1,568

Required
1. Determine the fixed and variable components of factory costs using the high-low method.
2. Repeat part 1 using regression analysis.

3-22 ***Target profits and unit prices***   Tina's Handicrafts sells handmade sweaters at $50 apiece. The firm acquires the sweaters from Ms. Posey at $30 apiece, but the agreement with her also requires an extra fee of 10% (of selling price) for each sweater sold. Monthly fixed costs are $3,000.

Required: Answer each of the following questions independently.
1. If the firm wants to earn profit of $3,000 a month before taxes, how many sweaters must it sell?
2. The firm wants a before-tax profit of $5,000 and expects to sell 500 sweaters. What price must be charged per sweater to obtain the desired level of profit?
3. Suppose the firm is selling 450 sweaters per month at $50 and making a before-tax profit of $3,750. Ms. Posey offers to renegotiate the buying agreement so that there would be a charge of $24 per sweater plus a 20% (based on selling price) fee per sweater sold. How many sweaters must the firm sell under the new agreement to earn the same $3,750 in before-tax profits?

3-23 ***Profit improvement alternatives***   Below is the income statement for Meriwether Company for 19X6.

Sales (100,000 × $10)	$1,000,000
Variable costs (100,000 × $7)	700,000
Contribution margin	300,000
Fixed costs	250,000
Profit	$ 50,000

Leslie Meriwether, president of the company, was not happy with the 19X6 results and stated that a profit of $100,000 was a reasonable target for 19X7. She instructed the controller to analyze each component of the statement separately and determine the change in each component that would allow the firm to earn the target profit of $100,000. (For example, what change in per-unit selling price would produce the target profit if sales volume, fixed costs, and per-unit variable costs remained constant; or what change in sales volume would be needed, assuming that prices and costs did not change?)

Required: Comply with Meriwether's request.

Problems

3-24 **Interpretation of data** Your assistant used the scatter diagram below to separate maintenance expenses into the fixed and variable components. She derived the
following equation: Monthly total cost = $350 + ($0.80 × machine-hours), which is
represented by the line drawn on the diagram.

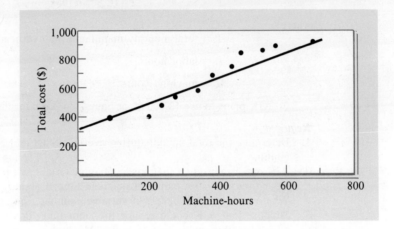

Required: Comment on the way in which your assistant fitted the line to the data
and make an alternative recommendation.

3-25 **Activity-based cost analysis** The controller of the Wellcome Plant of RKD
Industries has been analyzing costs of support departments to identify the major
cost drivers and seek ways to reduce costs. He has just finished analyzing the costs
and activity of the Production Scheduling Department. The schedulers determine
when particular products will be made, what machinery will be used, and how large
the batch will be. Scheduling has come under increasing pressure as the number of
products the plant manufactures has increased. The controller has assembled the
following information regarding scheduling costs and the number of different products being made. All amounts are in thousands.

Quarter	Number of Products	Costs of Production Scheduling Department
19X6 Q4	5.2	$93.0
19X6 Q3	5.2	84.0
19X6 Q2	4.2	83.8
19X6 Q1	4.1	82.3
19X5 Q4	4.0	75.1
19X5 Q3	3.2	74.0
19X5 Q2	3.2	67.0
19X5 Q1	2.7	66.0

Required: Analyze the Scheduling Department costs using a scatter diagram or regression analysis. Comment on the usefulness of the results for pursuing cost reduction?

3-26 *Multiple regression analysis (related to Appendix)*   Your boss at AJK Company has just handed you the following results of a regression analysis.

$$Y = \$32,450 + \$2.44L + \$1.10M$$

where

Y = total monthly manufacturing overhead cost

L = labor hours

M = machine hours

AJK plans to use 12,000 labor hours and 2,000 machine-hours next month.

Required
1. Determine the total manufacturing overhead cost that AJK should incur next month.
2. AJK makes a product that has $3.50 in material cost. It requires two hours of labor time and 30 minutes of machine time. Laborers earn $7.50 per hour. What is the product's per-unit variable manufacturing cost?
3. Suppose that AJK could reduce the labor time for the product described in item 2 by 30 minutes, to 1.50 hours. Machine time will remain the same. By how much would the per-unit variable manufacturing cost fall?

3-27 *Understanding regression results (related to Appendix)*   The controller of the Cromwell Plant of TAYCO Enterprises has the following regression results prepared by the plant's statistician.

$$Y = \$57,528 + \$2.3561X, \ r^2 = .8243, \ S_e = \$11.356$$

Y = monthly power cost, X = machine hours

The results are based on the past 30 months of operations during which monthly machine hours ranged from 80,000 to 140,000. The controller wants you to explain the results to some of her staff.

Required
1. If the plant will work 100,000 machine hours next month, what is the predicted power cost?
2. If the plant shuts down next month, should power cost be $57,528?
3. The company is considering a new product that requires 45 machine hours per batch of 100 units. What is the variable cost of power for the product?
4. How close are your predictions of power costs likely to be to the actual results? For example, can you state the range within which actual cost should be some specified percentage of the time?
5. Can you tell whether this equation is the best available to predict power costs?

3-28 *Changes in cost structure*   Manfred Company makes a product with variable production costs of $8.30 per unit. The production manager has been approached by a salesperson from a machinery maker who offers a machine for rent for five years on a noncancelable lease at $24,000 per year. The production manager expects to save $0.60 per unit in variable manufacturing costs using the machine.

Required

1. Determine the annual unit production that would make renting the machine and continuing with current operations yield the same profit to the firm.
2. Suppose that the expected volume is 70,000 units per year. Determine the change in annual profit if the firm were to rent the machine.
3. Would you be more likely or less likely to rent the machine if the lease were cancelable at your option rather than noncancelable for a five-year period? Explain your answer.

3-29 **Review problem, including income taxes, Chapters 2 and 3 (continued in Chapter 4)** After reviewing its cost structure (variable costs of $7.50 per unit and monthly fixed costs of $60,000) and potential market, Forecast Company established what it considered to be a reasonable selling price. The company expected to sell 50,000 units per month and planned its monthly results as follows.

Sales	$500,000
Variable costs	375,000
Contribution margin	125,000
Fixed costs	60,000
Income before taxes	65,000 100%
Income taxes (at 40%)	26,000 40
Net income	$ 39,000 60

Required: On the basis of the preceding information, answer the following questions independently. Items with an asterisk involve income taxes.

1. What selling price did the company establish?
2. What is contribution margin per unit?
3. What is the break-even point in units?
4. If the company determined that a particular advertising campaign had a high probability of increasing sales by 4,000 units, how much could it pay for such a campaign without reducing its planned profits?
5. If the company wants a $50,000 before-tax profit, how many units must it sell?
6. If the company wanted a 10% before-tax return on sales, what level of sales, in dollars, does it need?
*7. If the company wants a $45,000 after-tax profit, how many units must it sell?
*8. If the company wants an after-tax return on sales of 9%, how many units must it sell?
*9. If the company wants an after-tax profit of $45,000 on its expected sales volume of 50,000 units, what price must it charge?
10. If the company wants a before-tax return on sales of 16% given its expected sales volume of 50,000 units, what price must it charge?
11. The company is considering offering its salespeople a 5% commission on sales. What would the total sales, in dollars, have to be in order to implement the commission plan and still earn the planned pretax income of $65,000?

3-30 **Cost formula, high-low method** The owner of Bed and Bath Boutique regularly uses part-time help in addition to the full-time employees. Some minimum of part-time help is needed for miscellaneous chores and the owner arranges for additional hours based on estimates of sales for the following week. The following is a record of the wages paid to part-time employees at recent monthly sales volumes.

Sales	Wages Paid to Part-Time Help
$ 9,600	$ 874
2,000	600
6,400	730
17,000	1,260
18,000	1,350
12,800	1,030
15,000	1,362
5,000	675
11,000	960

The owner considers these months to be relatively normal except that in the month with volume of $2,000, the Boutique was closed for about two weeks for repainting and the installation of new carpeting.

Required: Determine the variable cost rate and fixed costs using the high-low method.

3-31   *Fixed costs in decision making*   Warren Keith owns a restaurant in a suburb of a large city. The restaurant does not do very much business during August, and Keith is considering closing down and taking a vacation for the month. He develops the following income statement based on planned operations for August.

Sales		$24,860
Cost of sales		9,740
Gross margin		15,120
Wages to part-time help	$4,500	
Utilities	1,500	
Rent on building	1,500	
Depreciation on fixtures	750	
Supplies and miscellaneous	6,250	14,500
Income		$ 620

Keith believes it is not worthwhile to stay open unless he can net at least $2,000 for the month. He works hard when the restaurant is open and believes that he deserves at least that much to compensate him for the work he does.

He also tells you that if he closes, he will have to pay a minimum utility bill of $350. Supplies and miscellaneous expenses are fixed, but these fixed costs will fall to zero if he closed.

Required: Advise Mr. Keith about the desirability of staying open for August.

3-32 *Cost structure* Shelly Cooper owns a beauty parlor. She has some space and wants to install a tanning bed. Her estimates below are based on observations and discussions with knowledgeable people.

Annual volume, $\frac{1}{2}$ hour sessions	800
Price per session	$6.00
Variable cost per session, mostly electricity	$0.80

Shelly can lease a suitable bed from a manufacturer for $2,000 per year. She can also lease one for $1,200 per year plus $1.50 per half hour of use. The beds have instruments to verify use. There are no other fixed costs.

Required
1. Suppose that Shelly leases the bed for $2,000.
    (a) Determine the expected profit from the bed.
    (b) What is break-even volume in number of sessions?
2. Redo item 1 assuming that Shelly elects the other lease option.
3. Which lease arrangement would you prefer?

3-33 *Alternative cost structures — a movie company (continuation of 2-38)*
Lois Lane, the president of Blockbusters Incorporated, has reviewed the preliminary analysis of the two contract alternatives and wishes to give further consideration to the arrangements with Kirkwalker. Kirkwalker's agent is also having second thoughts about the alternatives and is wondering what is best for his client.

Required: Answer the following questions.
1. If total paid admissions are expected to be between $9 and $10 million, which compensation scheme is best for (a) Blockbusters and (b) Kirkwalker? (*Hint:* Refer to your answers in 2-38 regarding break-even points.)
2. If total paid admissions are expected to be about $20 million, which scheme is better for (a) Blockbusters and (b) Kirkwalker?

3-34 *Regression analysis (related to Appendix)* Your new assistant has just handed you the following results of a regression analysis.

$$\text{Factory overhead} = \$262,203 + (\$13.19 \times \text{units produced})$$

You are surprised because your company makes several models of lawnmowers and you had not thought it possible to express factory overhead so simply. Your assistant assures you that the results are correct, giving you the following data.

Month	Units Produced	Factory Overhead
January	1,700	$260,000
February	1,100	280,000
March	2,800	300,000
April	2,300	260,000
May	2,000	360,000
June	1,800	320,000
July	2,400	320,000
August	2,000	200,000
September	2,100	300,000

Required: Comment on your assistant's results. You may assume the mathematical accuracy of your assistant's work.

3-35 **Alternative VCP graph**   Below are data for three alternatives being considered by the managers of Sanders Company. Each represents a particular strategy for one of its products. The differences result from alternatives such as salaries versus commissions and different levels of product quality, advertising, and promotion.

Alternative	Price	Variable Cost	Fixed Costs
1	$20	$12	$180,000
2	$20	$ 8	$240,000
3	$18	$10	$120,000

When evaluating alternative strategies, the firm's managers prefer the alternative graphical approach presented on page 77. It represents a graph with Alternative 1 already plotted.

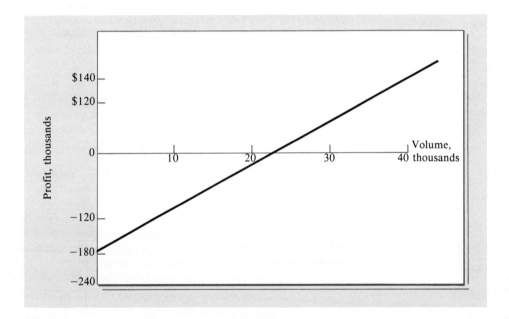

Required
1. Plot the profit lines for alternatives 2 and 3.
2. What general conclusions can you draw from the completed graph? Could you select the best alternative based on the graphical results?

3-36 **Changes in costs**   Stoneham Company manufactures a complete line of toiletries. The average selling price per case is $20 and cost data appear below.

Variable costs per case:	
Materials	$4.00
Labor	2.00
Other variable costs	2.00
Total variable costs	$8.00
Annual fixed costs:	
Manufacturing	$1,500,000
Selling and administrative	$2,500,000

Art Stoneham, the president, expects to sell 350,000 cases in the coming year. After gathering the above data, Stoneham learned that material costs will increase by 25% because of shortages.

Required

1. Determine the profit that Stoneham expected before the increase in material prices.
2. Given the increase in material costs, determine the price that Stoneham has to charge to earn the profit you calculated in item 1.
3. Suppose that Stoneham decided to raise the price enough to maintain the same contribution margin percentage it had before the cost increase.
   (a) Determine the price.
   (b) Would Stoneham earn more or less than your answer to item 2 if it charged that price and sold 350,000 cases?

3-37 Cost drivers, activity-based analysis   The controller of the Summerton Division of KPL Industries was concerned that costs of some departments normally thought to be fixed had been rising over the past few years. The purchasing department had come in for special review because its costs had been rising rapidly. The purchasing manager argued that the division's increasing number of products and of component parts had strained his resources. The division's products are similar, but product designers use parts that differ in size or other characteristics. Purchasing is responsible for finding and evaluating vendors, inspecting incoming shipments, reordering parts when needed, and other tasks associated with managing component parts.

The controller developed the following data related to quarterly costs of the purchasing department and the number of different component parts used in the division's products (not the total number of parts put into products). All amounts are in thousands.

Quarter	Number of Parts	Purchasing Department Costs
19X6 Q4	14.2	$123.1
19X6 Q3	14.1	115.1
19X6 Q2	12.8	111.7
19X6 Q1	11.0	109.0
19X5 Q4	10.9	106.7
19X5 Q3	10.8	106.6
19X5 Q2	10.1	104.6
19X5 Q1	10.1	100.1

Required: Analyze the Purchasing Department's costs using a scatter diagram or regression analysis. What do your results tell about cost reduction?

3-38 **Negative fixed costs**   The managers of Kooper Company have observed the following costs and activity.

Month	Direct Labor Hours	Overhead Costs
1	2,200	$3,590
2	2,500	4,210
3	2,800	4,830
4	2,300	3,780
5	3,100	5,400
6	3,200	5,650

Required
1. Find the fixed and variable components of overhead costs using either a scatter diagram or regression analysis.
2. Does the pattern make sense to you? Is it possible to have negative fixed costs? Can you suggest an explanation?
3. How would you handle the negative fixed cost for planning purposes?

3-39 **Cost structures and average costs**   At a dinner meeting of a local association of company accountants, the following conversation took place.

Ruth Hifixed: "My firm has enormous fixed costs, and volume is our critical problem. My cost per unit is now $6, at 100,000 units, but if I could get 200,000 units, cost per unit would drop to $4. My selling price is also too low, only $6."

Jim Lofixed: "You are lucky. My cost per unit is $5 at 200,000 units, but we can't produce any more than 200,000. At least we're now better off than we were when sales were 80,000 units. At that volume we lost $0.50 per unit at our $6 price. We kept the same selling price at all volumes."

Required
1. Compute the profit earned by each firm at its current level of sales.
2. Determine fixed costs, variable cost per unit, and contribution margin per unit for each firm.
3. Compute the break-even point for each firm.
4. Which firm earns more at 150,000 units?
5. Which firm earns more at 100,000 units?

3-40 **Cost classification**   Halton's Flower Shop buys and sells floral arrangements. The average selling price is $25, and average purchase cost is $5. Weekly fixed costs are $4,000. Because the arrangements are perishable, the shop cannot sell any units after they have been in inventory for one week. The shop must order a full week's supply at one time.

Mr. Halton, the owner, would like to earn $1,000 per week from the business. A friend has explained VCP analysis to him and made the following calculation.

$$\text{Unit volume required for \$1,000 profit} = \frac{\$4,000 + \$1,000}{\$25 - \$5}$$

$$= 250 \text{ arrangements}$$

Required
1. Is the above equation correct in the sense that if Mr. Halton *orders* 250 arrangements per week, he will earn $1,000? Why or why not?
2. Is the purchase cost fixed or variable? Explain.
3. Can you tell Mr. Halton how many arrangements he must sell to earn $1,000 if he purchases 300? If he purchases 400?

3-41 **Cost estimation — service business** William Jarvis operates his own firm of Certified Public Accountants. For planning purposes, he is interested in developing information about the cost structure of the firm. At times, he hires part-time employees, usually accounting majors from the nearby university.

The best measure of activity for the firm is chargeable hours, the number of hours that employees work on client business, and for which the firm charges the clients at hourly rates. Jarvis has the following data regarding wages of part-time employees from recent months.

Total Chargeable Hours	Part-Time Wages
3,000	$3,000
3,500	3,100
2,800	2,990
3,200	3,090
4,800	5,400
5,200	6,180
5,600	6,900

Required: Plot the data on a scatter diagram and comment on the results. Can Mr. Jarvis use your results for planning? What reasons might there be for the pattern that you observe?

3-42 **Labor policies — cost behavior** In conversation with the president of Hirsch Industries, you hear the following: "We employ 40 skilled workers and guarantee them 80 hours of work per month even if production doesn't keep them busy. When we crank up production beyond a 40-hour week for all of our employees, we work overtime and pay $6 per hour instead of the usual $4. Each of our workers produces two units of product per hour."

Required
1. Determine the firm's total labor cost at the following monthly volumes of production in units. Assume that a month has four weeks.
   (a) 5,000
   (b) 6,000
   (c) 7,000
   (d) 10,000
   (e) 14,000
   (f) 16,000

2. Graph the firm's labor costs, with clearly marked points on the horizontal axis for the volumes where the cost behavior changes.
3. What is the range, if any, over which labor cost per unit behaves like a true variable cost?

3-43   *Understanding regression results (related to Appendix)* Your assistant in the Cost Management Office has just brought in some regression results sent over by the plant's operations analysis group. The group tried several regressions to analyze power costs. The first equation used direct labor hours as the independent variable.

$$Y = \$182,938 + \$0.5612X, \ r^2 = .2691, \ S_e = \$79,982$$

$$Y = \text{monthly power costs}, \ X = \text{labor hours}$$

The second equation used machine hours as the independent variable.

$$Y = \$61,122 + \$1.4651X, \ r^2 = .7314, \ S_e = \$8,982$$

$$Y = \text{monthly power costs}, \ X = \text{machine hours}$$

The number of labor hours per month runs between 15,000 and 25,000. The number of machine hours between 70,000 and 125,000, depending on the mix of products being made.

The controller has requested that your office do a study to help her planning and you are to discuss the results with her shortly.

Required: Make a recommendation for the controller. Justify your recommendation.

3-44   *Margin of safety* Nelson Wallet Company is considering two new wallets for introduction during the coming year. Because of a lack of capacity, only one will be brought out. Data are given below.

	Model 440	Model 1200
Expected sales	$200,000	$250,000
Expected contribution margin	60,000 (30%)	150,000 (60%)
Expected fixed costs—for production, advertising, promotion, etc.	39,000	120,000
Expected annual profit	$ 21,000	$ 30,000

Required
1. Determine the margins of safety for each wallet, in dollars and as percentages of expected sales.
2. Suppose that the firm is relatively conservative; its top managers do not like to take significant risks unless the potential profits are extremely high. Which wallet would you recommend be introduced? Why?

3-45   *VCP analysis for an airline* Icarus Airlines flies a number of routes in the southwestern United States. The firm owns six airplanes, each of which can hold 150 passengers. All routes are about the same distance, and all fares are $66 one way. The line is obligated to provide 250 flights per month. Each flight costs $4,000 for gasoline, crew salaries, and so on. Variable costs per passenger are $6, to cover a meal and a head tax imposed for each passenger at every airport to which Icarus flies. Other costs, all fixed, are $130,000 per month.

Required
1. How many passengers must Icarus carry on its 250 flights in order to earn a $70,000 per month profit? What percentage of capacity is this number?
2. If the firm could cut its flights to 200 per month, how many passengers are required to earn $70,000 per month? What percentage of capacity does this number represent (using 200 flights as capacity)?
3. Is the $4,000 cost per flight fixed or variable?
4. What is the chief problem faced by a firm with this type of cost structure?

3-46 Promotional campaign Ajax Publishers sells magazine subscriptions. Its managers are considering a large promotional campaign in which it will award prizes of $10,000,000. Other costs associated with the campaign appear below.

Television time	$ 4,400,000
Fee to Fred Mahon, TV spokesman	700,000
Mailing	5,300,000
Total	$10,400,000

Ajax plans to mail 20,000,000 packages containing entry blanks and forms for subscribing to magazines. Ajax receives 25% of total subscription revenue. Experience indicates that about 15% of those receiving a package take out one or more subscriptions. The average subscription revenue from a respondent is $35.

Required
1. What profit will Ajax earn if the campaign meets all expectations?
2. What is the break-even point for the campaign expressed as a response rate, assuming that each respondent orders $35 in magazine subscriptions?

3-47 Calculating contribution margin percentage Bell Company has a 25% margin of safety. Its after-tax return on sales is 6%, and its tax rate is 40%.

Required
1. Determine Bell's contribution margin percentage.
2. Assuming that current sales are $120,000, determine total fixed costs.

3-48 Committed versus discretionary cost Gladack Company makes a number of products and uses a great deal of machinery. A new product this coming year will require the acquisition of a new machine. The machine can only be leased, not purchased. There are two alternative leasing arrangements: (1) a month-to-month lease that can be canceled on 30-days' notice by either Gladack or the lessor, at a monthly rental of $6,000, and (2) a five-year noncancelable lease at $5,200 per month. The new product is expected to have a life of five years, during which annual revenues will be $250,000, annual variable costs $100,000. There are no new fixed costs other than the lease payments. The president is concerned that the five-year lease removes a great deal of flexibility: if the product does not pan out as expected, the company is stuck with the machine and there are no other uses for it. He does, however, like the idea of saving $800 per month.

Required

1. Are the rentals, under each alternative, discretionary or committed fixed costs?
2. Why would the president hesitate between the choices? What could happen to make him regret choosing (a) the five-year lease? (b) the month-to-month lease?
3. Suppose Gladack takes the monthly lease option. It is now the end of the fourth year, and management expects the sales of the product will be $90,000 in year five, evenly spread over the year. Should the firm use the machine for the fifth year?
4. Answer item 3 again assuming that the firm had signed the five-year lease.

3-49 **Loss per unit** A firm had a loss of $3 *per unit* when sales were 40,000 units. When sales were 50,000 units, the firm had a loss of $1.60 *per unit*.

Required

1. Determine contribution margin per unit.
2. Determine fixed costs.
3. Determine the break-even point in units.

3-50 **VCP analysis — measures of volume** Acme Foam Rubber Company buys large pieces of foam rubber (called "loaves") and cuts them into small pieces that are used in seat cushions and other products. A loaf contains 5,000 board feet of foam rubber (a "board foot" is one foot square and one inch thick), of which 10% becomes scrap during the process of cutting up the loaf. A loaf costs $700, including freight, and the firm is currently processing 100 loaves per month.

The firm charges $0.22 per board foot for its good output, $0.07 per board foot for the scrap. Variable costs of cutting the loaf are $100, for labor and power to run the cutting machines. Fixed costs are $18,000 per month.

The president of the firm has asked for your assistance in developing VCP relationships.

Required

1. Determine the firm's income when it processes 100 loaves per month.
2. Determine the firm's break-even point expressed as number of loaves processed.
3. The president tells you that your analyses in items 1 and 2 are not what he had in mind. He says that he is accustomed to thinking in terms of board feet of good output sold. He would like to know how many board feet he would have to sell to earn $6,000 per month. Determine the firm's contribution margin per board foot of good output sold and sales required to earn $6,000 per month.

Cases

3-51 **Measures of volume** The controller of Throckton Company has been to a seminar on VCP analysis and wants to use some of the techniques she learned. She gives you the following data and asks that you analyze each cost into its fixed and variable components. She plans to use the information for profit planning. You prepare the following schedules of costs and measures of activity for the previous 6 months.

Sales	Labor Hours	Production Costs	Selling Expenses	Administrative Expenses
$12,000	500	$ 9,100	$3,250	$3,200
10,000	700	11,000	2,980	3,300
21,000	1,200	14,300	4,130	4,100
30,000	1,300	15,300	4,950	4,500
33,000	900	11,980	5,370.	4,300
35,000	800	11,200	5,560	4,800

Required: Analyze the cost behavior patterns in accordance with the request of the controller. Indicate weaknesses and suggest possible improvement.

3-52 **Cost structure** Wink Company manufactures replacement parts for automobiles and sells them to distributors in the northeastern United States. The president wants to begin selling in the Southeast but is uncertain how to expand most profitably. Two alternatives have been selected for final consideration. Under the first, Wink would use the services of independent sales representatives who sell to distributors for a 15% commission. This plan would increase the clerical costs at the company's central office by $20,000 per year. Under the second alternative, Wink would hire its own salespeople to work on straight salary. It is estimated that salaries for salespeople would be $100,000 per year; additionally, an office would be opened in the region and cost $25,000 per year to operate.

Variable cost on parts is now 35%. The president is uncertain about demand in the Southeast and asks that you analyze profitability under both plans at various volumes. He selects $500,000, $700,000, $1,000,000, and $1,200,000 as the sales volumes to be used for comparison.

Required: Choose an alternative and defend your choice. Identify the nonquantified factors that are related to the alternatives.

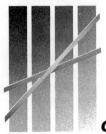

CHAPTER 4

ADDITIONAL ASPECTS
OF VOLUME-COST-PROFIT
ANALYSIS

This chapter treats some problems of VCP analysis that we have not yet discussed, with special attention to multiple-product firms. VCP analysis is a powerful planning tool, but planned and actual results can differ. A difference between planned and actual results is called a **variance.** This chapter illustrates techniques for analyzing variances. Chapter 12 continues the discussion. Finally, we discuss the use of VCP analysis in the special context of not-for-profit entities.

ANALYZING RESULTS

Income depends on several factors, two of which are selling price and unit sales. Planned and actual results rarely coincide, often because of one or both of those factors. To plan and evaluate previous decisions, managers need to know the sources of variances. For example, if a sales manager orders a 10% price cut and volume increases by 15%, was the decision wise? The technique discussed here helps to answer such questions.

The analytical approach in this chapter concentrates on variances in contribution margin, specifically those that arise because of differences between (1) planned and actual sales volume and (2) planned and actual selling prices. The same approach can be used to analyze differences between actual and planned gross margin (sales minus cost of goods sold). In addition, managers often use the analysis to explain differences between the actual results of two periods, such as the current and the prior month. Of course, planned and actual contribution margin can differ because of changes in variable costs. Cost analysis requires a full chapter and we leave it to Chapter 12. The analyses we do here are nevertheless important and provide useful information for planning and control.

Suppose Horton Company expected to sell 20,000 units at $20 and incur unit variable costs of $12. Horton actually sold 21,000 units at $19. These results and the differences appear below.

	Actual	Planned	Difference
Units sold	21,000	20,000	1,000
Sales	$399,000	$400,000	$ 1,000
Variable costs	252,000	240,000	12,000
Contribution margin	$147,000	$160,000	$13,000

We want to explain the $13,000 difference between planned and actual contribution margin. Total revenues were $1,000 less than planned, while total variable costs were $12,000 more than planned. But notice that actual variable cost per unit was $12 ($252,000/21,000), so the difference in total variable costs is due to the increase in volume.

Two factors caused the difference between planned and actual contribution margin: a variance in selling price and a variance in sales volume. To isolate the effect of each factor, we hold one of them (price or volume) constant and look at the effect of the change in the other. One simple way to do this is to prepare a statement that shows what would have happened if the firm had sold the actual volume, but at the planned price.

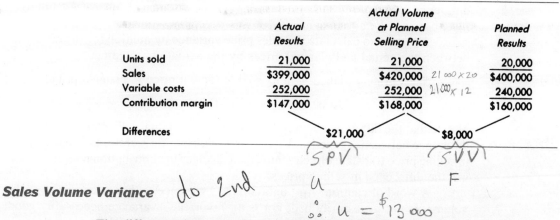

	Actual Results	Actual Volume at Planned Selling Price		Planned Results
Units sold	21,000	21,000		20,000
Sales	$399,000	$420,000	21 000 × 20	$400,000
Variable costs	252,000	252,000	21,000 × 12	240,000
Contribution margin	$147,000	$168,000		$160,000
Differences		$21,000	$8,000	

SPV   SVV
                 F

Sales Volume Variance   do 2nd   u

∴ u = $13,000

The difference between planned contribution margin ($160,000) and contribution margin if the actual sales volume had been achieved at the planned selling price ($168,000) is $8,000. That difference is called the **sales volume variance.** Had Horton been able to sell 21,000 units *and* maintain its selling price at $20 it would have earned $8,000 more than planned, which is the 1,000 additional units sold times the $8 planned contribution margin per unit. Thus, the sales volume variance can also be computed as

$$\begin{array}{l}\text{Sales volume} \\ \text{variance}\end{array} = \begin{array}{l}\text{planned} \\ \text{contribution} \\ \text{margin per unit}\end{array} \times \left(\begin{array}{l}\text{actual sales,} \\ \text{in units}\end{array} - \begin{array}{l}\text{planned sales,} \\ \text{in units}\end{array} \right)$$

$$\$8,000 \qquad = \$8 \qquad\qquad \times (21,000 - 20,000)$$

If a firm sells more units than planned, the variance is favorable. If fewer units are sold than was planned, the variance is unfavorable. In this example, the variance is favorable. Again, please notice that we are holding unit variable cost constant because we want to determine the effect on total contribution margin of selling more (or fewer) units than planned. Holding selling price constant also holds contribution margin per unit constant.

Even if unit variable cost changed, we would still use the planned unit variable cost for this analysis, because we want to isolate the effects of sales volume *apart* from changes in variable costs or selling prices. Now we can look at the variance in total contribution margin that is attributable only to the difference between the planned and actual selling price.

Sales Price Variance

As you know, a change in selling price changes unit contribution margin by the same amount and in the same direction. The difference between the $168,000 contribution margin that would have been earned if the $20 price had been maintained and the actual contribution of $147,000 is caused by a variance in selling price. Horton sold its product for $19, or $1 less than planned. This $21,000 difference is called the **sales price variance.** The variance in this case is unfavorable, because the actual selling price was less than planned.

We can also calculate the sales price variance by multiplying the difference between the actual and planned prices by the actual unit volume.

$$\text{Sales price variance} = \text{units sold} \times (\text{actual price} - \text{planned price})$$

$$\$21,000 = 21,000 \qquad \times (\$19 - \$20)$$

Notice that the difference between the planned and actual selling prices is also the difference between planned and actual unit contribution margin. Because changes in selling price translate directly into equal changes in contribution margin, we can use the difference in selling prices.

A word of caution. An "unfavorable" variance, either sales price or sales volume, is not necessarily bad, nor is a "favorable" variance necessarily good. Managers might deliberately reduce price to sell more units. The *total* variance in contribution margin is more important than either variance taken separately. Pricing policy is discussed in more detail later in the chapter. Managers might reduce prices because competitors are reducing theirs, and failing to respond might result in a severe drop in volume. It is also important to know whether conditions were as expected when the original plans were developed. For instance, suppose the planned volume was based on forecasts of rapid growth for the industry and that growth failed to materialize. The company probably could not meet its planned volume, but the managers are not at fault because they cannot control industry sales. (The managers are responsible for accepting the inaccurate forecast, however.)

MULTIPLE PRODUCTS

Chapter 2 stated that VCP analysis assumes either a single product or a constant sales mix. (Recall that **sales mix** is the percentage of each product to total sales.) The reason for the assumption is that if the products have widely differing contribution margins, and if the mix changes, the company's contribution margin percentage will change and results could be much different from those predicted. Multiple-product firms can easily use VCP analysis for each individual product or for groups of products where the contribution margins (per-unit or percentage) are about equal. They can also use VCP analysis where contributions differ greatly, provided that the sales mix remains constant.

A constant sales mix is not unrealistic. There are several reasons why firms have the same sales mix over several periods. For example, some products are sold and used together so that their sales are associated (tables and chairs, cups and saucers, wallpaper and paste). In other cases, although the products are not always sold together, they are used together, so that the sales of one influence the sales of the other (e.g., cameras and film and gasoline and motor oil). Such products are called **complementary products.**

Even when there is no apparent relationship among the products, the sales mix might still remain fairly constant. For example, a department store might consistently derive 40% of its sales from clothing, 25% from furniture and housewares, and 35% from its other departments. These percentages might be relatively constant over time despite the absence of obvious causes. Where sales mix is predictable, VCP analysis uses a weighted-average contribution margin.

Weighted-Average Contribution Margin Percentage

As its name suggests, a **weighted-average contribution margin percentage** is the overall contribution margin percentage. It consists of the individual products' percentages weighted by their relative sales. The weighted-average contribution margin percentage is used just as we use the contribution margin percentage for a single product.

Suppose that Ted of Ted's Threads is expanding his business. He is now selling shirts, shoes, and jeans. His fixed costs are now $30,000 per month because he has added employees and moved to a larger store. Data for the individual products appear below.

	Shirts	Shoes	Jeans
Selling price	$20	$50	$30
Variable cost	12	20	15
Contribution margin	$ 8	$30	$15
Contribution margin percentage	40%	60%	50%
Percentage in sales mix	60%	10%	30%

given → (handwritten annotation at "Percentage in sales mix" row) *given* (handwritten annotation at right)

The percentages shown for sales mix are the proportions of total sales dollars coming from each product. (Note that these percentages must add to 100 percent.)

Ted still has the same questions he had in Chapter 2: What is the break-even point? What sales are required to achieve a particular profit target? If Ted were studying one product, he might well work with either dollars or units. With multiple products, it might be more convenient, and simpler, to work with sales dollars so long as he is looking at the business as a whole. In that case, Ted would measure volume by sales dollars instead of units, using the weighted-average contribution margin percentage.

We can calculate the weighted-average contribution margin percentage in several ways. The most obvious way is to prepare an income statement, such as the one below, which assumes total sales of $100,000 and the expected sales mix.

(handwritten: $3000 \times VC (\$12)$ and $60000 \div SP (20) = 3000 \times VC (\$12)$)

	Shirts	Shoes	Jeans	Total	Percentage of Sales
Sales	$60,000	$10,000	$30,000	$100,000	100%
Variable costs	36,000	4,000	15,000	55,000	55%
Contribution margin	$24,000	$ 6,000	$15,000	45,000	45%
Total fixed costs				30,000	
Profit				$ 15,000	

The weighted-average contribution margin percentage is 45%.

You can always prepare an income statement to find the weighted-average contribution margin percentage. A more direct way is to multiply the contribution margin percentage for each product by its percentage in the sales mix and add the results. This calculation appears below.

	Shirts	Shoes	Jeans	Total
Contribution margin percentage	40%	60%	50%	
Percentage in sales mix	60%	10%	30%	100%
Weighted average	24% +	6% +	15% =	45%

Let's look at the logic of this calculation. With the 60%, 10%, 30% sales mix, the *average* sales dollar is composed of $0.60 from shirts, $0.10 from shoes, and $0.30 from jeans. The $0.60 sales from shirts provides $0.24 in contribution margin because the contribution margin on shirts is 40%. *That* is the 24% in the shirts column. Similarly, the $0.30 sales of jeans in the average sales dollar provides $0.15 contribution margin because the rate on jeans is 50%. The following schedule shows the calculations in dollars.

	Shirts	Shoes	Jeans	Total
Average sales dollar	$0.60	$0.10	$0.30	$1.00
Contribution margin percentage	40%	60%	50%	
Contribution margin	$0.24 +	$0.06 +	$0.15	$0.45

Because the average sales dollar yields $0.45 in contribution margin, the weighted-average contribution margin percentage is 45%.

Using the 45% weighted-average contribution margin percentage, Ted can now do the same analyses he did in Chapter 2. His break-even point is $66,667; $30,000 fixed costs divided by 45% weighted-average contribution margin percentage. To earn a $20,000 target profit requires sales of $111,111 [($30,000 + $20,000)/45%].

Changes in Sales Mix

Sales mix is very important when the contribution margin percentages differ greatly among products. (If all products have the same contribution margin percentages, that percentage *is* the weighted-average contribution margin percentage.) Suppose that Ted sees a trend that is likely to change his sales mix to 40% shirts, 30% shoes, and 30% jeans (a shift from shirts to shoes). His new weighted-average contribution margin percentage is 49%, an increase of four percentage points.

	Shirts	Shoes	Jeans	Total
Contribution margin percentage	40%	60%	50%	
Percentage in sales mix	40%	30%	30%	100%
Weighted average	16% +	18% +	15% =	49%

[handwritten in right margin:]
BE = 30 000 / .49
= $61 224
∴ Lower BE
∴∴ Better
due to Higher WA CM.

Figure 4-1 (page 114) shows Ted's VCP chart. Note that the horizontal axis shows sales in dollars rather than in units because we are working with contribution margin percentage. The chart shows two total cost lines to represent two sales mixes. The dotted line shows the 55% variable cost percentage, which holds when the weighted-average contribution margin percentage is 45% (as originally computed when the sales mix was 60% shirts, 10% shoes, and 30% jeans). The solid total cost line uses a 51% variable cost percentage, which holds when the

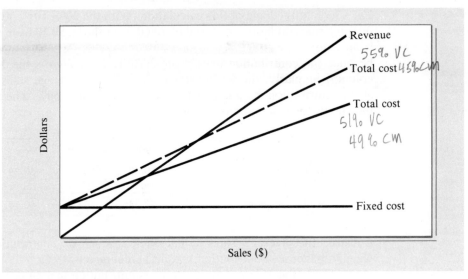

Figure 4-1   VCP Chart for Ted's Threads

weighted-average contribution margin is 49% (the second computation, when the sales mix was 40% shirts, 30% shoes, and 30% jeans).

The break-even point is lower and profits are higher, at any level of sales, when contribution margin is 49% than when it is 45%. *Other things equal,* a richer sales mix—one with a higher contribution margin percentage—is better, which explains why managers routinely try to enrich mix. Note, however, that enriching the mix might make other things unequal. Increasing advertising or promotional effort to enrich mix increases fixed costs. In such cases, the indifference analysis described in Chapter 3 can prove helpful.

Weighted-Average Contribution Margin per Unit (CM Per Unit)

Some multiple-product companies use units, rather than dollars, to measure volume. For instance, managers of an automobile manufacturer usually talk about the number of cars sold, rather than dollars of sales. (They are concerned, of course, about dollar sales, but most of the analyses they perform use units—cars—instead of dollars.) Similarly, managers of service businesses, such as CPA firms, law firms, and consulting firms, discuss their sales volume in terms of chargeable hours, the hours that personnel spend on client business. Like cars, chargeable hours is a measure of unit volume.

Such companies could calculate weighted-average contribution margin percentages, but they often find it more useful to calculate a weighted-average contribution margin per unit. Consider the following data for Corbin Company, a manufacturer of three models of desks.

	President	Senior VP	Junior VP
Selling price	$1,000	$800	$500
Unit variable cost	600	500	300
Unit contribution margin	$ 400	$300	$200
Percentage in mix, in units	20%	30%	50%

The **weighted-average contribution margin per unit** is calculated in basically the same way as the weighted-average contribution margin percentage. The per-unit contribution margin of each product (in *dollars,* not as a *percentage*) is multiplied by its percentage in the sales mix.

	President	Senior VP	Junior VP	Total
Unit contribution margin	$400	$300	$200	
Mix percentage, in units	20%	30%	50%	
Weighted-average unit contribution margin	$ 80 +	$ 90 +	$100	= $270

So long as the sales mix holds, managers can use the weighted-average unit contribution margin of $270 just as they would if the company made a single product. Thus, if Corbin's fixed costs are $500,000, its break-even point is about 1,852 desks (fixed costs of $500,000 divided by the weighted-average per-unit contribution margin of $270). To show that the per-unit calculation works, suppose that Corbin sells 1,000 desks in the expected mix. Its income statement, through contribution margin, is

	President	Senior VP	Junior VP	Total
Sales in units	200	300	500	1,000
Sales	$200,000	$240,000	$250,000	$690,000
Variable costs	120,000	150,000	150,000	420,000
Contribution margin	$ 80,000	$ 90,000	$100,000	$270,000

Total contribution margin is $270,000, which is exactly $270 times 1,000 total units. We might also note that the weighted-average contribution margin percentage is about 39.1% ($270,000/$690,000). Corbin's managers could use either form of contribution margin to do their analyses.

Overall Planning

Historical trends often provide clues to the expected sales mix, and managers can use the weighted-average contribution margin for planning. As suggested above, managers can also take actions to influence the sales mix. For example, they might undertake special advertising campaigns or sales promotions aimed at one product. They can also encourage salespeople to concentrate on certain products, either through direct instructions or special commissions. Of course, if some products are complementary, as we discussed earlier, managers should not adopt strategies to influe ce the volume of one product, unless they have considered the effects on sales of complementary products.

Before proposing a program that could influence sales mix, a manager needs to know price and cost data for each product. These data give the manager some idea of profitability by product and how the sales mix might be better. Managers often study sales and cost data for various products and evaluate alternative strategies by assuming different mixes of sales. *Simulation* is a technique used in this type of study. Simulation is a computer-assisted process by which a manager inputs sets of assumptions about sales mix and other factors, and the computer calculates the profit for each combination. Alternative assumptions could relate to different selling prices, variable costs, and sales mixes.

In planning sales mix, managers should continually evaluate individual products or product lines. A **product line** is a group of similar products. An example is a hair care line, consisting of shampoos, conditioners, colorings, creams, tonics, and restorers. In many cases, managers will treat the entire line as a single ''product.'' There are many reasons for taking this simplified approach for analytical purposes.

First, the products might have such similar contribution margin percentages that little is gained by examining them individually. Planning does, after all, involve estimates; moreover, minor differences that may result from grouping products with slightly different contribution margins are not likely to affect decisions. Another reason is that the sheer number of products might make analyzing them individually very difficult and time consuming.

A third reason for grouping products relates to the level of the manager for whom an analysis is being prepared. Different managers make different decisions and therefore need different kinds of information. The president of a full-line department store never looks at the sales and cost details for every product stocked by the store. A lower-level manager—say the one in charge of sporting goods—does, however, look at individual products in that line. That manager is concerned about each product and makes decisions about adding and dropping individual products. The president, however, is more concerned with the product line as a whole and makes decisions about adding or dropping entire departments.

An important factor in analyzing either an individual product or a product line is an understanding of the nature of the fixed costs associated with that product or line. The next section applies principles from Chapter 3 to multi-product companies.

Fixed Costs and Multiple-Product Firms

Chapter 3 introduced the concepts of committed/discretionary, direct/indirect, and avoidable/unavoidable fixed costs. These concepts are important in evaluating products, product lines, geographical areas, and other activities, or segments, of a company. The classification of a particular cost depends on the segment. Nationwide advertising (for example, on network television) for a product line is discretionary, avoidable, and direct to the line. But the cost is indirect and unavoidable to any particular geographical region. Thus, so long as the company advertises nationally, there is no discretionary component to this cost from the standpoint of any geographical region. Similarly, regional advertising promoting several product lines is discretionary, direct, and avoidable to the region, but indirect and unavoidable to any single line.

The importance of a particular classification, such as direct or avoidable, depends on the purpose of the analysis. If a manager is trying to decide whether to drop a segment (drop a product or line, stop selling in a particular region), the important issue is whether a cost is avoidable. If the manager is assessing a segment's profitability, then avoidability is important, but it is also important to know whether a cost is direct or indirect. Decisions to drop segments are multifaceted and are discussed in detail in Chapter 5. Our focus here is on developing information that will help managers to evaluate segments.

Exhibit 4-1 (page 118) shows a segmented income statement with two important subtotals: **short-term margin** and **long-term margin.** Generally speaking, a segment with a negative short-term margin is unprofitable. A segment with a negative long-term margin is not profitable in the long-term, and it might be wise for the company to liquidate it gradually by not renewing the commitments represented by direct, committed fixed costs.

Exhibit 4-1 shows that Sundries has a $120,000 short-term margin. This means that Davis's total profit would fall by $120,000 if it dropped Sundries *and* if there were no effects on the other lines. But as Sundries has a relatively low long-term margin, Davis might be wise to phase it out by not renewing the commitments that underlie the direct, committed fixed costs. Davis should consider substituting another line for Sundries.

It is important to trace as much cost as possible to segments because that makes the analysis of product profitability much better. If little cost is directly traceable to products, they will probably all look very profitable, making it difficult to distinguish among them. IBM seeks to identify as much fixed overhead as possible with specific products, calling its practice *direct charging*. One thing that makes this tracing possible in some plants is that assembly lines are dedicated to one product, so that there is relatively little use of common facilities.[1]

Increasing the traceability of costs is one of the advantages of JIT manufacturing, especially of the use of cells that specialize in one product. The more work done on each product in a dedicated area, the more the traceable cost. Because the people in the cells do the inspection, the materials-handling, and much of the required maintenance, there is less factory-wide cost for these support activities. Were these support activities done by centrally managed departments, much of their cost would be common to production departments and products.

[1] Robert H. Kelder, "Era of Cost Accounting Changes," in *Cost Accounting, Robotics, and the New Manufacturing Environment,* ed. Robert Capettini and Donald K. Clancy (Sarasota, FL.: American Accounting Association, 1987), 3.18.

Exhibit 4-1
Davis Department Store
Product-Line Income Statement for 19X5
(thousands of dollars)

	Clothing	Housewares	Sundries	Total
Sales	$2,400	$1,800	$1,300	$5,500
Variable costs:				
Cost of goods sold	1,050	900	910	2,860
Commissions	240	180	130	550
Other variable costs	150	120	90	360
Total variable costs	1,440	1,200	1,130	3,770
Contribution margin	960	600	170	1,730
Avoidable fixed costs:				
Salaries and expenses of				
department managers	80	65	40	185
Other	30	15	10	55
Total avoidable fixed costs	110	80	50	240
Short-term product margin	850	520	120	1,490
Direct committed fixed costs:				
Depreciation on fixtures	80	40	35	155
Other	45	30	20	95
Total direct committed fixed costs	125	70	55	250
Long-term margin	$ 725	$ 450	$ 65	1,240
Common fixed costs:				
Rent on store				250
Salaries of administrative staff				365
Utilities				130
Other				300
Total common fixed costs				1,045
Profit				$ 195

PRICE-VOLUME RELATIONSHIPS

We have assumed that selling price was constant, or changed only by managerial action. We also briefly discussed whether a company could sell a given volume of product at a given price. It is, of course, true that a company can sell more units at a lower price than it can at a higher price. This price-volume relationship is reflected in the **law of demand,** which states that as prices increase the quantity sold decreases, and vice versa. In most realistic situations, there is *some* price-volume interdependence and managers must recognize such interdependence in developing their plans.

Consider a company that currently sells 10,000 units of product at $15 per unit. Variable costs are $10 per unit. The sales manager believes that if the price were increased to $16, volume would fall to 9,000 units. The firm can evaluate its alternatives by considering only contribution margin. The existing price yields $50,000 of contribution margin ($5 × 10,000), whereas the proposed price is expected to yield $54,000 ($6 × 9,000). If fixed costs stay the same, the $16 price increases income by $4,000.

VOLUME-COST-PROFIT ANALYSIS IN NOT-FOR-PROFIT ENTITIES

The term *not-for-profit entities* encompasses many kinds of economic entities, including governmental units, universities, churches, charitable organizations such as the Red Cross and American Cancer Society, and clubs and fraternal groups. We prefer the term *not-for-profit* in preference to *nonprofit* because the former term better describes the intent of such organizations. (Many business firms turn out to be "nonprofit," but not by choice!)

Income is one measure of how well a business is doing. Although profit is not the only objective of a business firm (survival, growth, product quality, good corporate citizenship are others), earning profits sufficient to attract capital investment is necessary to its survival. How then is VCP analysis relevant to entities that do not intend to earn profits?

First, many not-for-profit entities do try to earn profits, or at least to break even, on some of their activities. College bookstores and food services often operate profitably and help to defray other costs of the college. Municipalities run parking lots or utilities that operate at a profit. When a not-for-profit entity operates a service that benefits only a portion of the members, it might try to break even on that service. For instance, not everyone in a city will use a municipal golf course. The city's elected officials might believe that the course should "pay its own way" and, therefore, require that the prices charged provide enough revenue to cover the costs.

Second, not-for-profit entities must often choose from among alternative ways to accomplish some task. Making these choices requires an understanding of cost behavior. For instance, a city can do its own trash collection or contract the task to a private firm. If the outside firm charges on the basis of the volume of trash collected, the cost is variable. If the city has its own trucks and personnel, a large portion of the costs is fixed. Recognizing the implications of the different types of behavior, city officials need information about the likely volumes of trash, including estimates about probable growth in volume.

The examples mentioned so far are relatively straightforward applications of cost analysis or VCP analysis. As a rule, however, the major activities of not-for-profit entities are not amenable to such straightforward applications because there is often no objective way to determine the value of the services—there is no revenue. Of course, not-for-profit entities do get revenues—taxes, donations, tuition—but not necessarily from the specific services that they provide. Cities have police forces, but the people do not pay for this service on the basis of use; they pay for it in taxes that also support the other activities of the government.

Despite the difficulties associated with measuring the results of the activities of not-for-profit entities, some evaluations of results are always being made. Essentially, not-for-profit entities are concerned with analyzing the benefits and costs of activities, not so much with the revenues, costs, and profits. Accordingly, they use **benefit-cost analysis.**

Benefit-Cost Analysis

Many actions taken by not-for-profit entities are based on analyses that incorporate some kind of monetary measurement of both benefits and costs. For instance, governmental studies relating to the construction of a new dam are likely to include not only construction costs but also estimates of benefits from flood control and recreational opportunities. Opponents of the dam might offer an alternative analysis that measures the benefits using different assumptions, attempts to quantify the cost of displacing people who live near the dam site, and states that the proposed dam would do irreparable, unquantifiable harm to various species of wildlife. The parties will dispute each other's figures on quantified points and argue about how to evaluate the unquantified ones.

In other situations, especially those relating to ongoing activities such as public education or police and fire protection, it might be even more difficult to measure benefits and costs. Most people believe that a better-educated citizen is more beneficial to a community than one less well educated. But how much more beneficial? Is the difference between the income taxes that the two would pay a reasonable measure, or, perhaps, the difference between their incomes?

As a practical matter, many public service problems of this type have been approached by the responsible decision makers in one of two basic ways:

1. Decide on the amount of money to spend on a particular activity and concentrate on getting the most benefit from that level of expenditure.
2. Decide on the level of service to be provided and concentrate on providing that level of service at the most reasonable cost.

As an example of the first approach, a city council might decide to spend $500,000 on police protection. The chief of police then decides how best to spend the allotted money. Should the chief increase the number of patrol cars and cut down on police officers walking beats, or the reverse? Should the department send officers to training programs on advanced crime-fighting techniques, and if so, how many officers and which programs? Unfortunately, establishing the level of expenditure does not avoid the problems of measuring the benefits of public services. The chief must find ways to measure the benefits from alternative plans to provide police protection. Meanwhile, the council must decide whether the city is getting its money's worth, which means finding ways to measure the accomplishments for the fixed expenditure. Often, the measures selected are difficult to interpret. Were the funds well spent if the number of arrests increased? (Not necessarily, because arrests for minor offenses count as much as ones for major crimes.) Are the funds being better used this year if the crime rate has dropped? (Possibly, but many factors besides the quality and quantity of the police force affect the level of crime.)

The second approach—deciding first on the level of service and then trying to achieve that level at reasonable cost—presents many of the same problems as the first. For example, a state legislature might decide that all high school graduates should have the opportunity to attend college whether or not they can afford it. A number of alternatives, with differing costs, are available. Should there be branches of the state university in large population centers? Should the state establish community colleges to prepare students for work at senior colleges? Might it be better to provide money for tuition assistance directly to the students, who could use the funds to attend a college of their choice? (Should the fundable choices include private colleges? Colleges outside the state?) How does one evaluate whether the stated level of service has been provided at reasonable cost? Choosing among the alternatives involves not only determining the costs but also developing some measures of the benefits of each alternative. Thus, trying to achieve a specified level of service at a reasonable cost does not entirely avoid the problems of measuring the benefits of a public service or evaluating the performance of that service.

In sum, analyzing public service activities is exceedingly difficult because of the lack of objective, unarguable measures of services and performance. Analyzing costs, especially if one is trying to determine whether or not money is spent wisely, is also difficult, but usually less so. The problems are not limited to not-for-profit entities. Business firms spend a great deal of money on employee training, research and development, and on other activities where the benefits are not readily measurable in monetary terms. Finding ways to make useful measurements is a constant concern of managers and a goal of much research in universities, business, and government.

SUMMARY

The techniques of VCP analysis are helpful in analyzing the results of operations. Differences between planned and achieved contribution margin and income may be attributed to differences in volume, price, and mix. Managers then concentrate on those products or strategies (pricing, promotion, etc.) that can be expected to yield the best results. Managers also use contribution margin information to identify profitable products.

Multiproduct companies need to compute a weighted-average contribution margin to do VCP analysis. This computation requires information about the sales mix, stated either in dollars or units, as well as price and cost data.

Not-for-profit entities use benefit-cost analysis, a counterpart of VCP analysis. It is difficult to define and measure benefits deriving from a particular expenditure in a not-for-profit entity. Despite these difficulties, more and more managers in such entities are finding that adaptations of the concepts of managerial accounting can be helpful in their organizations.

KEY TERMS

benefit-cost analysis
complementary products
law of demand
long term margin
product line
sales mix

sales price variance
sales volume variance
short-term margin
weighted-average contribution margin percentage
weighted-average contribution margin per unit

KEY FORMULAS

$$\text{Sales volume variance} = \text{planned contribution margin per unit} \times \left(\text{actual sales, in units} - \text{planned sales, in units} \right)$$

$$\text{Sales price variance} = \text{units sold} \times (\text{actual price} - \text{planned price})$$

REVIEW PROBLEM

Data on the three types of can openers that are sold by McMichael Company are given below. Monthly fixed costs are $90,000.

	Regular	Deluxe	Super
Selling price	$2.00	$3.00	$5.00
Variable costs	1.20	1.50	2.00
Contribution margin	$ .80	$1.50	$3.00
Contribution margin percentage	40%	50%	60%

Required: Consider each part independently.
1. Suppose the sales mix in *dollars* is Regular, 60%; Deluxe, 30%; and Super, 10%.
   (a) Determine the weighted-average contribution margin percentage and the monthly sales to break even.
   (b) Determine how many units of each model are sold at the break-even point.
   (c) Prepare an income statement by product line for sales of $250,000. Assume that, of the $90,000 fixed costs, avoidable fixed costs for each model are $10,000 and direct committed fixed costs are $5,000, $7,000, and $3,000 for the Regular, Deluxe, and Super models, respectively.
2. Suppose now that the sales mix in *units* is Regular, 50%; Deluxe, 30%; and Super, 20%.
   (a) Determine the weighted-average contribution margin per unit.
   (b) Determine the total sales dollars required to earn $26,000 profit per month.
3. Suppose that in one month the firm expected to sell 40,000 Regular openers at $2 each.

It actually sold 42,000, but the average selling price was $1.85. Compute the sales price variance and sales volume variance.

Answer to Review Problem

1. (a) The weighted-average contribution margin percentage is 45%, computed as follows:

	Regular	Deluxe	Super	Total
Contribution margin percentage	40%	50%	60%	
multiplied by sales mix percentage	60%	30%	10%	
equals				
contribution margin per sales dollar	24% +	15% +	6% =	45%

The sales required to break even are $200,000 per month (fixed costs of $90,000/45%).

(b) Sales are 60,000 units, 20,000 units, and 4,000 units of the Regular, Deluxe, and Super models, respectively. Unit sales for each model are computed by multiplying the sales mix percentage by total sales, to get dollar sales for each model, and then dividing by the selling price per unit.

Regular: ($200,000 × 60% = $120,000)/$2 = 60,000 units

Deluxe: ($200,000 × 30% = $ 60,000)/$3 = 20,000 units

Super: ($200,000 × 10% = $ 20,000)/$5 = 4,000 units

(c)

	Regular	Deluxe	Super	Total
Sales[a]	$150,000	$75,000	$25,000	$250,000
Variable costs[b]	90,000	37,500	10,000	137,500
Contribution margin	60,000	37,500	15,000	112,500
Avoidable fixed costs	10,000	10,000	10,000	30,000
Short-term margin	50,000	27,500	5,000	82,500
Direct committed fixed costs	5,000	7,000	3,000	15,000
Long-term margin	$ 45,000	$20,500	$ 2,000	67,500
Common fixed costs				45,000
Income				$ 22,500

[a] Based on the stated sales mix of 60%, 30%, and 10%. $250,000 × 60% = $150,000; $250,000 × 30% = $75,000; $250,000 × 10% ≈ $25,000.
[b] These figures can be determined by using the variable cost percentages, which are 60%, 50%, and 40% (all are 1 − contribution margin percentages). Or, the number of units of each product can be determined by dividing sales for the product by selling price per unit as given in the problem. Then, the results are multiplied by variable cost per unit as given in the problem. For example, sales of the Regular model are 75,000 units ($150,000/$2). Variable costs are given as $1.20 per unit, so such costs would be $90,000 for 75,000 units ($1.20 × 75,000).

2. (a) The weighted-average contribution margin per unit is $1.45.

	Regular	Deluxe	Super	Total
Unit contribution margin	$0.80	$1.50	$3.00	
Sales mix, percentage in units	50%	30%	20%	
Weighted-average contribution margin	$0.40 + $0.45 + $0.60 = $1.45			

(b) Unit sales required for $26,000 profit, computed using the target profit formula from Chapter 2, are 80,000 units [(fixed costs of $90,000 + target profit of $26,000)/$1.45 weighted-average contribution per unit]. Dollar sales are computed by using the sales mix to determine the number of units sold of each type and then multiplying by the selling price per unit.

Regular:	(80,000 × 50% = 40,000 units) × $2	=	$ 80,000
Deluxe:	(80,000 × 30% = 24,000 units) × $3	=	72,000
Super:	(80,000 × 20% = 16,000 units) × $5	=	80,000
Total			$232,000

3. Because of the way in which the information is given, the easiest way to solve the problem is to deal with only the price and volume differences, as follows.

Sales price variance
= quantity sold × (actual price − planned price)
= 42,000 × ($1.85 − $2.00)
= 42,000 × (−$0.15)
= $6,300 unfavorable (unfavorable because actual price was lower than planned)

Sales volume variance
= planned contribution margin × (actual volume − planned volume)
= $0.80 × (42,000 − 40,000)
= $0.80 × 2,000
= $1,600 favorable (favorable because actual volume was greater than planned)

Alternatively, we could prepare the following schedule, similar to the one on page 109.

	Actual Results	Actual Volume at Planned Selling Price	Planned Results
Sales	$77,700 (42,000 × $1.85)	$84,000 (42,000 × $2)	$80,000
Variable costs	50,400 (42,000 × $1.20)	50,400 (42,000 × $1.20)	48,000
Contribution margin	$27,300 (42,000 × $0.65)	$33,600 (42,000 × $0.80)	$32,000

$6,300 unfavorable sales price variance

$1,600 favorable sales volume variance

ASSIGNMENT MATERIAL

Questions for Discussion

4-1 **Price determination – postal service** What do you think is the major problem in determining prices to be charged for the various classes of mail handled by the postal service?

4-2 **VCP chart** Explain how preparation of a VCP graph differs between (a) a firm that sells only one product and (b) one that sells several products.

4-3 **Unit costs and governmental performance** The manager of a medium-sized city was quoted as saying that trash collection service in her city was better than that in many neighboring cities because the unit cost was lower. The unit cost was the total cost of collections divided by the number of tons collected. Does having a low unit cost mean that the city is doing a good job?

Exercises

4-4 **Basic variance analysis** Tartan Mills expected to sell 30,000 of its Style 105 knit sweaters at $30 each. It actually sold 29,000 at $29. Variable cost is $14 per sweater.

Required
1. Determine the sales volume variance.
2. Determine the sales price variance.

4-5 **Basic sales mix** The general manager of Lo-Price Grocery Stores was reviewing the following data. Fixed costs are $680,000 per month.

	Produce	Meat/Dairy	Canned Goods
Contribution margin percentage	40%	35%	30%
Sales mix percentage, in dollars	30%	20%	50%

Required
1. Determine the weighted-average contribution margin percentage.
2. Determine the break-even sales volume per month.
3. Determine the sales necessary to earn $90,000.

4-6 **Improving sales mix** Davis Exterminating Company performs a wide variety of pest control services. George Davis, the owner, has been examining the following forecasts for 19X6.

Type of Service	Expected Dollar Volume for 19X6	Contribution Margin Percentage
Termites	$120,000	60%
Lawn pests	90,000	50%
Interior pests	90,000	70%

Total fixed costs are expected to be $140,000 in 19X6.

Required

1. What is the weighted-average contribution margin percentage?
2. What profit should Davis earn?
3. The actual sales mix turned out to be 30% termites, 30% lawn pests, and 40% interior pests. Total actual sales were $300,000 and total fixed costs were $140,000. Determine (a) the actual weighted-average contribution margin percentage and (b) profit.

4-7 Relationships Bruton Syrup sold 11,000 cases of Light Maple. It had a $3,000 unfavorable sales volume variance and a $3,300 favorable sales price variance. It had a budgeted selling price of $10 and variable cost of $7.

Required

1. Determine the number of cases that Bruton had budgeted to sell.
2. Determine the actual price per case that Bruton received.
3. Determine Bruton's budgeted and actual contribution margins.

4-8 Price and volume variances Klaxton Company makes large plastic wastebaskets. Planned results for March were as follows.

Sales (30,000 units)	$210,000
Variable costs	75,000
Contribution margin	$135,000

Actual results were as follows.

Sales	$212,350
Variable costs	77,500
Contribution margin	$134,850

Variable costs were incurred as expected, per unit.

Required

1. How many wastebaskets did the firm sell?
2. What was the actual selling price?
3. What were the volume variance and price variance?

4-9 Product line income statements Campus Laundromat is two years old. Sales have been $3,000 per week, contribution margin is 75% of sales, and weekly fixed costs are $1,200. Jill Owens, its owner, recently began to sell beer and also installed stereo equipment. She is now selling 800 bottles per week at $0.80 each. Variable cost is $0.30 per bottle. Additional fixed costs associated with the beer and stereo equipment are $300 per week. The laundry business has also increased to $3,600 per week. Jill's accountant has prepared the following income statement.

	Beer	Laundry	Total
Sales	$640	$3,600	$4,240
Variable costs	240	900	1,140
Contribution margin	400	2,700	3,100
Fixed costs	380	1,120	1,500
Income	$ 20	$1,580	$1,600

The accountant assigned the $300 fixed costs added by the beer business to beer. He also allocated $80 in building rent, light, and heat to beer, based on the relative space occupied by the bar and the laundry equipment.

Required
1. Prepare an income statement for Jill's business before she sold beer.
2. Prepare a new product-line income statement for Jill's business after she started selling beer. Show the $300 fixed costs as direct to beer and the original $1,200 as direct to the laundry business.
3. Does the income statement you prepared for item 2 better show the results of the two lines? Why or why not?

4-10 Basic sales mix Allen Cosmetics makes two facial creams, Allergy-free and Cleansaway. Data are as follows.

	Allergy-Free	Cleansaway
Price per jar	$10	$8
Variable cost per jar	$ 5	$2

Monthly fixed costs are $90,000.

Required
1. If the sales mix in dollars is 60% for Allergy-free and 40% for Cleansaway, what is the weighted-average contribution margin percentage? What dollar sales are needed to earn a profit of $30,000 per month?
2. If the sales mix is 50% for each product in units, what is the weighted-average unit contribution margin? What unit sales are needed to earn $30,000 per month?
3. Suppose that the firm is operating at the level of sales that you calculated in item 1, earning a $30,000 monthly profit. The sales manager believes that it is possible to persuade customers to switch to Cleansaway from Allergy-free by increasing advertising expenses. He thinks that $6,000 additional monthly advertising would change the mix to 40% for Allergy-free and 60% for Cleansaway. Total dollar sales will not change, only the mix. What effect would the campaign have on profit?

4-11 Weighted-average contribution margin Blue-Room Products sells three types of simulated brass soap dishes, the Necessary, the Frill, and the Luxury. Detailed selling price and cost data for the products appear below.

	Necessary	Frill	Luxury
Selling price	$10	$20	$25
Variable cost	$ 4	$12	50% of selling price

Fixed costs for these products are $286,000.

Required
1. If the company has a choice of selling one more unit of any one of its products, which product should it choose to sell one more unit of?
2. If the company could sell $1,000 more of any one of its products, which product should it choose?

3. Assume that the sales dollar volume of the company is distributed 40% from Necessary, 20% from Frill, and 40% from Luxury.
    a. What is the weighted-average contribution margin percentage?
    b. What is the break-even point for the company in sales dollars?
    c. At the break-even point, how many units of Luxury are sold?
4. Assume, instead, that the company's sales in *units* are 40% for Necessary, 20% for Frill, and 40% for Luxury.
    a. What is the weighted-average unit contribution margin?
    b. What is the break-even point in units?
    c. At the break-even point, how many units of Luxury would be sold?

4-12 ***Variance analysis***   The controller of MHA Inc. is examining the following budgeted and actual income statements for its principal product for 19X5. All amounts are in thousands of dollars.

	Budget	Actual
Sales	$4,800.0	$4,967.2
Variable costs	1,680.0	1,780.8
Contribution margin	$3,120.0	$3,186.4

The budgeted unit selling price is $8.00. Actual unit volume is 6% over budget, but the actual selling price is below budget. Per-unit variable costs are incurred as budgeted.

Required: Determine the sales price variance and sales volume variance.

4-13 ***Pricing policy – public service***   Speebus, the city-owned bus service of Middleville, charges $0.75 for all rides. The city has many retired citizens, whose incomes are generally lower than those of working citizens. A member of the city council has proposed that Speebus reduce its fares for persons over 65 to $0.40.
    At the present time, about 1,200,000 rides per month are made on Speebus buses, about 30% of which are by citizens over 65. Buses are rarely crowded. The councilman estimates that the decrease in fares to older persons would increase their use of the bus service by 50%. The number of other users would remain the same. Even with the expected increase in riders, buses would rarely be crowded.

Required
1. How much will it cost per month for Speebus to reduce fares to riders over 65?
2. Suppose that the bus service is breaking even. By how much would regular fares have to increase to get back to break-even if the reduction is granted?

4-14 ***Product profitability and mix***   The sales manager of Worthem Company has been looking at the following extracts from the monthly marketing plan for the coming year. Worthem distributes scented bath oils.

	Paree	Enchanté	Whisper
Selling price	$20	$16	$8
Variable cost	6	4	4
Contribution margin	$14	$12	$4
Expected monthly volume, in bottles	5,000	12,000	16,000

Required
1. Determine which product is most profitable (a) per unit sold and (b) per dollar sold.
2. The sales manager would like to achieve a better mix and believes that an advertising campaign could result in buyers of 3,000 of the bottles of Enchanté switching to Paree and buyers of 8,000 of the bottles of Whisper switching to Paree. The campaign would cost $70,000 per month. Determine whether Worthem should undertake the campaign.

4-15 *Price-volume relationships* Watson Brothers manufactures two models of shelving. The standard model sells for $20 and has variable costs of $7. The deluxe model sells for $50 and has variable costs of $35. Unit volume for each model is 8,000 per month. The sales manager believes that a 10% price reduction for either model would increase its unit volume by 25%. Referring to the following schedule, which shows that sales of the deluxe model would increase more than those of the standard model, he suggests reducing the price for the deluxe model.

	Standard Model	Deluxe Model
Sales after reduction:		
10,000 × $18	$180,000	
10,000 × $45		$450,000
Current sales:		
8,000 × $20	160,000	
8,000 × $50		400,000
Increase in sales	$ 20,000	$ 50,000

Required
1. Determine the total contribution margin that each model currently earns.
2. Determine the total contribution margin that each model would earn after the proposed price reduction.
3. Would you reduce the price of either model?

4-16 *Pricing to break even* The Student Senate at Western University sponsors programs for students and faculty. Among them is a monthly movie in an auditorium that holds 3,200 people. The movies selected would not ordinarily be shown in the one theater in the small town in which the university is located, and attendance at the university showings is high. A one-evening showing is invariably sold out. When shown on two evenings, attendance at each showing averages 2,375.

Movies are rented at a cost of $2,400 for one showing, $3,200 for two showings. Other fixed costs per showing are $600, and variable costs are $0.40 per person for chair rentals, tickets, and miscellaneous items. The Senate wants to break even for the year on the movie program.

Required
1. Determine the prices that must be charged so that the Senate can break even on the movie showings for the year assuming (a) one showing of each movie and (b) two showings of each movie.
2. Make a recommendation to the Senate regarding the number of times a movie should be shown, explaining the factors that influenced your decision.

4-17 Market share   MBT Company produces and sells consumer products. It recently hired a new vice president for sales who is a great believer in increasing the market share of a product. One of his first proposals was to reduce the price of Kleenbrite, a toothpaste that had a 15% share of the total market of 2,000,000 tubes.

The current price is $1.60 per tube, variable costs $0.50. The new vice president reduced the price by $0.10, and Kleenbrite increased its share of the market to 16% of the 2,000,000 tube market.

Required
1. Was reducing the price to gain market share a wise move? Show separately the effects of the change in price and the change in volume.
2. What share of the market did Kleenbrite need to achieve in order to justify the $0.10 price reduction?
3. Suppose that the firm could increase the market share of Kleenbrite at the $1.60 price by increasing advertising and promotion expenses. What additional expenditures would MBT be able to make to increase market share by one percentage point without reducing its overall profit?

4-18 Variances from plans (extension of 3-29)   Competitive pressures late in February prompted the managers of Forecast Company to reduce its selling price for March to $9.80. Per-unit variable costs, total fixed costs, and income tax rates continued to behave as planned, and total variable costs for March were $420,000.

Required
1. How many units were sold in March?
2. What was the total contribution margin for March?
3. Was the March sales volume variance favorable or unfavorable?
4. What was the sales volume variance?
5. Was the March sales price variance favorable or unfavorable?
6. What was the sales price variance?
7. What net income did the company earn in March?

4-19 Product profitability   Wrynn Company sells three kinds of tobacco jars. The controller has prepared the following analysis of profitability of each of the jars.

	Flavorsaver	Shagholder	Burleykeeper
Selling price	$5.00	$8.00	$11.00
Variable costs	2.00	4.00	6.40
Fixed costs	3.00	3.00	3.00
Total costs	5.00	7.00	9.40
Profit	—	$1.00	$ 1.60
Profit percentage to selling price	0%	12.5%	14.5%
Annual volume	22,000	15,000	13,000

The firm has total fixed costs of $150,000 per year. The controller obtained the fixed cost per unit figure of $3 by dividing $150,000 by 50,000 units (22,000 + 15,000 + 13,000). On the basis of her analysis, the controller suggests that the Flavorsaver model be discontinued if a more profitable substitute can be found.

This conclusion upsets the sales manager, who has planned a $10,000 promotional campaign for Flavorsavers. He has estimated that the $10,000 expenditure on any product would increase its volume by 25%. Sales of the other products would be unaffected, as would existing fixed costs.

Required: Determine which product should be selected for the special promotion.

4-20 ***Variances in a service business*** Earl Torgeson, the managing partner of Torgeson, Watts, and Gold, Certified Public Accountants, is comparing planned and actual results for 19X1. Because all employees are on salary, there are no variable costs associated with chargeable hours (hours worked on client business).

	Planned			Actual		
Employee Category	Hourly Rate	Total Hours	Revenue	Hourly Rate	Total Hours	Revenue
Junior staff	$20	40,000	$800,000	$19	38,000	$722,000
Senior staff	40	12,000	480,000	38	13,000	494,000

Required: For each category, determine the price (rate) and volume variances.

Problems

4-21 ***Segmented income statements – costs of activities*** Claxton Industries makes three principal product lines: sporting goods, housewares, and hardware. The company has suffered reduced profitability in the past few quarters, and the top managers have taken a number of actions to try to improve the situation. The most recent quarterly income statement, segmented by product line, appears below. Common fixed costs are allocated to the lines based on relative sales or labor content.

Claxton Industries
Income Statement, Second Quarter, 19X9
(in thousands of dollars)

	Total	Sporting Goods	Housewares	Hardware
Sales	$3,337.0	$650.0	$921.0	$1,766.0
Cost of sales	1,928.8	357.3	545.7	1,025.8
Gross margin	1,408.2	292.7	375.3	740.2
Operating expenses:				
Selling expenses	787.6	157.1	225.9	404.6
Administrative expenses	514.6	94.2	135.6	284.8
Total operating expenses	1,302.2	251.3	361.5	689.4
Income before taxes	$ 106.0	$ 41.4	$ 13.8	$ 50.8

The managers are still not happy with the 3.2% return on sales, but the $106 thousand pretax profit was a bit higher than the previous quarter's profit. The consensus of the managers is that they should concentrate on sporting goods and hardware because their ROS's are higher than that of housewares so that additional sales of sporting goods and hardware will be more profitable. One manager even wants to ignore housewares because its ROS was only 1.5%. "If we only keep a cent and a half from a dollar's sales, why even bother with it?"

When asked to confirm the judgments about relative profitabilities, the controller points out that some common costs are allocated to the product lines and that some distortions might result from those allocations. She has therefore asked her assistant to prepare an alternative income statement without making allocations. The assistant's analysis of Claxton's cost structure reveals the following, dollars in thousands.

Variable Costs, Percentage of Sales	Sporting Goods	Housewares	Hardware
Cost of sales	28.00%	32.00%	35.00%
Selling expenses	2.00%	1.50%	1.80%
Administrative expenses	0.90%	0.70%	2.00%
Direct Fixed Costs			
Cost of sales	$158	$141	$197
Selling expenses	56	87	133
Administrative expenses	13	22	43

The assistant evaluates the costs by examining the activities that generate them. For example, she finds that sporting goods require relatively more attention from manufacturing support personnel, such as engineers, than hardware and so is assigned relatively higher direct fixed manufacturing costs. By the same token, hardware consumes considerably more relative administrative time than sporting goods, giving it relatively more direct cost.

Required
1. Prepare a new segmented income statement using the assistant's findings.
2. Comment on the differences between your statement and the one above. For example, what decisions are easier, or more difficult, to make with your statement?

4-22 **Costs and profits per unit**   Managers of Hylman Company, which manufactures a packaged beverage-sweetener, have been trying to decide what price to charge for the product next year. One manager has come up with the following analysis.

		Likely Results	
Price per Case	Case Volume	Average Total Per-Case Cost	Per-Case Gross Margin
$260	60,000	$225.00	$35.00
$250	70,000	$218.00	$32.00
$240	80,000	$212.75	$27.25

"It seems to me," the manager says, "that we should go with the $260 price, since the per-case gross margin is highest at that price."

Required: Determine the price that yields the highest total profit to the firm.

4-23 **VCP analysis – product mix** Happy Times Brewery produces and sells two grades of beer: regular and premium. Premium sells for $6.50 per case, regular for $4.20. Variable brewing costs per case are $3.10 (premium) and $2.05 (regular). Sales of regular beer, in cases, are double those of premium. Fixed brewing costs are $90,000 monthly and fixed selling and administrative costs are $75,000 monthly. The only variable cost besides variable brewing costs is a 10% sales commission.

Required
1. Compute the break-even point in total cases per month.
2. How many cases of each kind of beer are sold at break-even?
3. The brewery is now selling about 90,000 cases per month. The advertising manager believes that sales of premium beer could be increased by 20% if an extensive advertising campaign were undertaken. The campaign would cost $4,000 per month. However, sales of regular beer are expected to fall by about 5% because some customers now buying the regular grade would merely switch to premium. Should the campaign be undertaken?
4. If the campaign were undertaken, what is the weighted-average unit contribution margin?
5. What is the new break-even point in unit sales?

4-24 **Pricing a product** Watson Camera Company makes cameras and film. The firm is introducing a new camera this year, the Super-90. It has variable costs of $20 per unit. Associated fixed costs are $2,000,000 per year for production, advertising, and administration. The sales manager of Watson believes that if the camera is priced at $40, about 250,000 units per year will be sold. If the price is $50, about 200,000 units per year would be sold.

Required
1. Determine which price would yield the higher profit.
2. Suppose that for each camera sold the firm also sells eight packages of film per year. Film sells for $6 per package, and the variable cost is $1.20 per package. Would this information affect your analysis in part 1?

4-25 **Pricing decision and average costs** The sales manager for Markham Pen Company has been trying to decide what price to charge for a pen the firm is introducing this year. His staff has prepared a research report that indicates the following price-volume relationships.

Price	Volume (millions)
$3.25	1.6 units
3.10	1.8
2.95	2.0
2.80	2.2
2.65	2.4

The variable cost per pen is $1.50, and total annual fixed costs are estimated at $1.5 million. The sales manager believes that any product should be priced at 150% of total cost. He decides to use 2.2 million units as the volume to determine the average unit cost and computes the cost at $2.182 per pen. He intends to set the price at $3.25.

Required
1. Assuming that the predictions of the staff are correct, determine what profit would be earned if the pen is priced at $3.25.
2. Again assuming the correctness of the staff's predictions, determine which price would yield the highest profit.
3. Suggest what might be wrong with the sales manager's method of setting prices.

4-26 Product profitability Immediately on graduation from State University, Jan Wilks took the position of assistant controller with Crow Clothing Company. The controller has given her the following information based on expected operations for the coming year.

	T-Shirts	Sweatshirts	Jeans
Selling price	$6	$15	$20
Variable costs	3	6	12
Contribution margin	$3	$ 9	$ 8
Sales mix percentage, in dollar sales	40%	40%	20%

Total fixed costs are $840,000.

Required
1. The marketing manager believes that the company could increase sales of any of the three products by one unit for each $4 in additional advertising expenditures. Which product would it be most profitable to advertise?
2. Determine the weighted-average contribution margin percentage.
3. Determine the break-even point.
4. The president wants a profit of $210,000. Determine the sales dollars needed to achieve this goal.
5. After extensive discussions with the sales manager and marketing department, the controller believes that the sales mix will probably change to 20%, 30%, and 50% for T-shirts, sweatshirts, and jeans, respectively.
   (a) Determine the new break-even point.
   (b) Determine the sales needed to earn $210,000.

4-27 Sales promotion Sales of pizza and beer at Bob's Pizza & Pub have been averaging about $3,000 per week. The weighted-average contribution margin is 60% and weekly fixed costs are $1,200. To attract more business, Bob has hired a local band to play on Saturday nights. The band charges $450 per night. Other costs associated with having the band are $60 per night. Bob charges each person a $1 entry fee when the band is playing. Sales on Saturday nights had been about $600 before the band was hired. Since Bob hired the band, Saturday night attendance has averaged 300 people.

Required
1. Determine the income or loss attributable to having the band. For the moment, ignore the effects that the band might have had on sales of pizza and beer.
2. Determine the increase in sales of pizza and beer that Bob needs to maintain his weekly income at the same level it was before he hired the band.
3. Sales of beer and pizza on Saturday nights actually increased to $1,100, raising total weekly sales to $3,500. Determine the overall effect on Bob's weekly income of hiring the band.
4. Item 3 stated that the entire increase in weekly sales came on Saturday nights. Suppose that weekly sales increased by $500, but that $300 of the increase came on Saturday nights and $200 on other nights. Would your analysis from item 3 still hold? Why or why not?

4-28 **_Product-line report_** Karen Bell is president of Bell & Company, which distributes consumer products to supermarkets. Ms. Bell has been trying to analyze the profitability of her lines. She has available the following information.

Line	Annual Sales	Gross Profit Percentage	Direct Fixed Costs
Paper products	$2,000,000	30%	$110,000
Detergents	1,200,000	40%	150,000

The only variable cost, besides cost of goods sold, is a 10% commission paid on all sales. Bell incurs $350,000 in fixed costs that are common to both lines. All direct fixed costs listed above are discretionary.

Required: Answer each item independently.
1. Prepare an income statement using the format shown in Exhibit 4-1.
2. Ms. Bell believes that she could increase the volume of either line by 10% by increasing promotion of the line by $30,000. Which, if either, line should she select? She cannot select both.
3. Ms. Bell believes that she could increase the volume of either line by 10% if she raised the commission rate on that line to 12%. Which, if either, line should she select? She cannot select both.
4. How does the report format you used for item 1 provide better information than would an income statement showing only combined results for the two lines?

4-29 **_Sales interdependencies (AICPA adapted)_** Breezway Company operates a resort complex on an offshore island. The complex consists of a 100-room hotel, shops, a restaurant, and recreational facilities. Mr. Blenem, manager of the complex, has asked for your assistance in planning the coming year's operations. He is particularly concerned about the level of profits the firm is likely to earn.

Your conversation with Mr. Blenem reveals that he expects the hotel to be 80% occupied during the 300-day season that it is open. All rooms rent for $40 per day for any number of persons. In virtually all cases, two persons occupy a room. Mr. Blenem also tells you that past experience, which he believes is an accurate guide to the future, indicates that each person staying at the hotel spends $10 per day in the shops, $20 in the restaurant. There are no charges for use of the recreational facilities. All sales in the shops and restaurant are made to guests of the hotel, which is isolated from the only large town on the island.

After talking with Mr. Blenem, you obtain the following data from the firm's controller.

	Shops	Restaurant
Variable costs, as a percentage of sales dollars:		
Cost of goods sold	40%	30%
Supplies	10	15
Other	5	5

For the hotel, variable costs are $6 per day per occupied room, for cleaning, laundry, and utilities. Fixed costs for the complex are $1,200,000 per year.

Required
1. Prepare an income statement for the coming year based on the information given.
2. Mr. Blenem tells you he believes that the occupancy rate would increase to 90% if the room rate were reduced to $35 per day. Determine the effect on planned income if the rate were reduced.

4-30 *Variance analysis — brain teaser* Mack Bolend, controller of AMH Industries, received the following budgeted and actual income statements for one of its major products for a recent month. Not having time to analyze them, he requests that you determine why the company did not achieve its budgeted results. All dollar amounts are in thousands.

	Budget	Actual
Sales	$2,350.0	$2,197.8
Variable costs	1,527.5	1,405.3
Contribution margin	$ 822.5	$ 792.5

Per-unit variable costs were incurred as budgeted.

Required: Determine the sales price variance and sales volume variance.

4-31 *Product profitability and pricing* Jackson Confections makes three flavors of jelly: grape, strawberry, and peach. Price and cost data are as follows.

	Grape	Strawberry	Peach
Selling price per case	$10	$12	$14
Variable cost per case	6	9	7

Monthly fixed costs are $250,000.

Required
1. The sales mix, in dollars, is 40%, 40%, 20% for grape, strawberry, and peach jelly, respectively. Determine the sales dollars that will yield a monthly profit of $50,000.

2. The president would like to earn $50,000 on sales of $800,000. He proposes to do this by increasing the price of strawberry jelly. He expects the mix to remain the same after the price of strawberry jelly increases. What price must Jackson charge for strawberry jelly to achieve the president's goal?

4-32 **Product line reporting, activity analysis** Kelly Company is a retail store specializing in men's clothing. The firm has three major product lines: suits, sport clothes, and accessories. The most recent monthly income statement is given below.

Kelly Company
Income Statement for April 19X7
(thousands of dollars)

Sales		$800.0
Cost of sales		572.0
Gross profit		228.0
Operating expenses:		
Commissions	$48.0	
Salaries	71.4	
Rent	21.4	
Shipping and delivery	15.2	
Insurance	14.0	
Miscellaneous	20.8	190.8
Income before taxes		$ 37.2

The president wants a product-line income statement. She gives you the following additional data:
1. The sales mix in April was 30% suits, 50% sport clothes, and 20% accessories, expressed in dollars of total sales.
2. The cost of sales percentages are 80% for suits, 75% for sport clothes, and 50% for accessories.
3. Sales commissions are 6% for all product lines.
4. Each product line is the responsibility of a separate manager, and each manager has a small staff. The salaries that are directly related to each product line are $12,000 for suits, $8,000 for sport clothes, and $5,200 for accessories. These salaries are avoidable. All other salaries are common to the three lines.
5. Rent is for both office and warehouse space, all of which is in a single building.
6. Shipping and delivery costs are for operating expenses and depreciation on the firm's three trucks. Each truck serves a particular geographical area and delivers all three product lines.
7. Insurance includes a $6,000 fixed amount for basic liability coverage. The rest is for coverage of merchandise at the rate of one percent of the selling price of the average inventory on hand during the month. In April the average inventories at selling prices were equal to sales for each product line.
8. Miscellaneous expenses are committed, but direct. The amounts are $6,000 to suits, $8,800 to sport clothes, and $6,000 to accessories.

Required: Prepare an income statement by product, using the format shown in Exhibit 4-1.

4-33 **Product profitability**   Messorman Company produces three models of pen and pencil sets, regular, silver, and gold. Price and cost data are as follows.

	Regular	Silver	Gold
Selling price	$10	$20	$30
Variable costs	6	8	15

Monthly fixed costs are $200,000.

Required
1. Which model is most profitable per unit sold?
2. Which model is most profitable per dollar of sales?
3. Suppose the sales mix in dollars is 40% Regular, 20% Silver, and 40% Gold.
   (a) What is the weighted-average contribution margin?
   (b) What is the monthly break-even point?
   (c) What sales volume is necessary to earn a profit of $30,000 per month?
4. Suppose the sales mix in dollars is 30% Regular, 30% Silver, and 40% Gold.
   (a) What is the break-even point?
   (b) What sales volume is necessary to earn $30,000 per month?
5. Suppose that the sales mix in units is 40% Regular, 20% Silver, and 40% Gold.
   (a) What is the weighted-average unit contribution margin?
   (b) What is the break-even point in total units?
   (c) How many total units must Messorman sell to earn $30,000 per month?

4-34 **What is profitability?**   Kimbell Company sells three products. Data are

	Product		
	A	B	C
Selling price	$30	$50	$100
Variable cost	20	25	60
Contribution margin	$10	$25	$ 40
Annual unit volume	50,000	10,000	5,000

Required
1. Rank the products in order of profitability as measured by (a) total annual profit, (b) profitability per unit sold, and (c) profitability per dollar of sales.
2. Explain what the rankings mean and how Kimbell's managers might use the information.

4-35 **Product line income statements**   The president of Mifflan Tool Company has just received the firm's income statement for January 19X8. He is puzzled because you had told him last year, when working as a consultant to the firm, that sales of $500,000 should produce a profit of about $46,500 before income taxes.

Mifflan Tool Company
Income Statement for January 19X8

Sales		$500,000
Cost of sales		307,500
Gross profit		192,500
Operating expenses:		
Rent	$40,000	
Salaries	70,000	
Shipping and delivery	23,000	
Other expenses	30,000	163,000
Income before taxes		$ 29,500

The firm sells three lines of power tools, and your analysis assumed the following sales mix in dollars: saws, 30%; drills, 20%; and sanders, 50%. The actual mix in dollars in January was 40%, 30%, 30%. The firm does not manufacture its products. Cost of sales and shipping and delivery are variable costs. All others are fixed. Data per unit for each product are

	Saws	Drills	Sanders
Selling price	$50	$20	$40
Cost of sales	30	15	20
Shipping and delivery	2	1	2
Total variable costs	32	16	22
Contribution margin	$18	$ 4	$18

None of the fixed costs is directly associated with any particular product line. All costs were incurred as expected, per unit for variable costs, in total for fixed costs. Selling prices were as expected.

Required
1. Prepare a new income statement by product, based on actual results in January. Show both gross profit and contribution margin for each product.
2. Prepare an income statement by product for January, assuming that the expected sales mix had been achieved.
3. Explain the reasons for the differences between the two statements.

4-36 **_Revenue variances for an airline_**   Big Sky Airline had planned for $22 million revenue in March, expecting a 60% load factor (percentage of seat-miles occupied). Actual revenue was $22.5 million. The load factor was 66%. Variable cost per seat-mile is negligible.

Required: Determine the difference between planned and actual revenue attributable to (a) price and (b) volume (load factor). Round to the nearest $100,000.

4-37 **_Decision making for student programs_**   The Speaker Committee at a large university invites distinguished persons to address students, faculty, and members of the public. Students and faculty are admitted free; members of the public pay $2. Students and faculty must pick up tickets in advance; any tickets left on the day of the speech are sold to the public. The speaker program is expected to break even for the year.

The committee is trying to decide whether to invite Marvin Gardens, a noted environmentalist, or Cayuga Waters, a famous industrialist. One student member of the committee argues that Marvin Gardens is an ideal speaker. His fee is $800. The student states that the auditorium, which holds 2,000 people, will be almost completely filled with students and faculty if Garden speaks. He believes that only about 500 tickets would be available to members of the public and that all available tickets could be sold. One of the other members, an administrative officer of the university, says that Waters would be a better speaker. She estimates that only 500 students and faculty would show up, leaving 1,500 tickets to be bought by the public. These tickets could easily be sold to the public, she believes. Waters charges a fee of $2,000.

Required

1. Assuming that both committee members are correct in their assessments of demand for tickets, which speaker would be more profitable?
2. What other factors should be considered in reaching a decision?
3. What do you recommend?

4-38 Cost analysis in a university The School of Management at State University currently has 500 students and 25 faculty members. The school has only juniors and seniors who take all their courses in the school, an average of five courses per semester. The school offers 75 sections per semester, with each faculty member teaching three sections.

Following are the data for the number of sections, average number of students per section, and "student-sections," which is the total number of enrollments in all sections. Since 500 students take five courses each semester, there are 2,500 student-sections.

Number of Sections	×	Average Enrollment	×	Student- Sections
20		20		400
30		35		1,050
25		42		1,050
75				2,500

The university's administration is considering increasing the enrollment in the School of Management to 1,000 students. One university officer objects that the cost would be prohibitive. He states that faculty salaries are now $950,000 per year and would double if enrollment were to double because twice the number of faculty now teaching would be required.

Another officer points out that it would not be necessary to double the size of the faculty because the sizes of sections could be increased, although university policy is that no more than 45 students be enrolled in a single section.

You are assigned the task of determining the additional cost of faculty salaries required to support enrollment of 1,000 students. You estimate that demand for the classes now averaging 20 students per section is such that each section would go up to 25 students if enrollment went to 1,000. All other sections would be increased to the 45-student maximum. A faculty member would be hired for each three sections per semester added, at a salary of $30,000 per year.

Required

1. How many sections are needed if enrollment increases to 1,000 students? (*Hint:* Because 1,000 students will take five courses per semester, you must account for 5,000 individual enrollments.)
2. How much additional cost will be incurred for faculty salaries?
3. After you performed the analysis in items 1 and 2, the chancellor of the university became concerned about the large class sizes. She asks you to redo the analysis of required additional faculty salaries assuming that only 40 sections would hold 45 students, 20 would still hold 25 students, and the rest would have a maximum of 36 students.

4-39 *Multiple products—movie company (continuation of 2-38 and 3-33)*
Both the producing company and prospective star have given further thought to the contract terms and concluded that some provision probably should be made for revenues to be earned from contracts authorizing showings of the movie on television. After lengthy negotiations, Kirkwalker's agent proposed the following terms: (a) a payment of $1,000,000, plus (b) 15% of the receipts-to-the-producer from theater admissions, plus (c) 10% of the revenues from sales of television rights. Blockbusters' negotiating team leaves the negotiations to study the potential effect of the new offer.

A study of past productions indicates that the producer can expect revenues from sales of television rights to be approximately one eighth (12.5%) of producer's revenues from theater admissions. Ms. Lane is pleased with the opportunity to lower the fixed-payment part of the contract but is concerned about the magnitudes of the two off-the-top percentages.

Required

1. At what level of receipts-to-the-producer will Blockbusters break even under the new contract proposal?
2. Considering the additional information about the sale of television rights, at what level of receipts-to-the-producer will Blockbusters break even under Kirkwalker's normal contract terms ($1,500,000 plus 5% of the producer's receipts)?
3. Assume that, because of Blockbusters' delay in accepting the contract offer, Kirkwalker's agent decides that his client should also receive a percentage of the revenues Blockbusters will derive from the sale of screening rights in foreign countries, which revenues typically amount to 10% of domestic receipts. If the agent proposes a 5% "cut" of those revenues for Kirkwalker, what is the break-even point for Blockbusters Incorporated?

4-40 *Interrelationships between products* Rapidcal Company manufactures hand-held calculators. The industry is highly competitive and pricing is critical to sales volume. Warren James, sales manager of Rapidcal, has been trying to set a price for a model that the firm will introduce shortly. The new model, the RC-89, is somewhat more sophisticated than the RC-63, which has been successful in recent years. The RC-63 now sells at retail for $20, of which 30% goes to the dealer, 70% to Rapidcal. Variable costs for the RC-63 are $8 per unit. The variable costs for the RC-89, exclusive of dealer share, are $18 per unit.

James is especially concerned about the effects on sales of RC-63 following the introduction of the RC-89. He believes that if the RC-89 is priced at $44 retail, there would be no loss in sales of the RC-63. However, if the RC-89 were sold at $42, he thinks that some people will buy the RC-89 instead of buying the RC-63. At the $44 price, James expects sales of 150,000 RC-89s per year. For each $2 price cut for RC-89s, sales would increase by about 30,000 units, but about 40% of the increased sales of RC-89 would be at the expense of sales of the RC-63. At any price for the RC-89, Rapidcal receives 70%, the retailer 30%.

Also, James believes that a $38 retail price is rock-bottom for the RC-89. He therefore instructs you to determine the effects on the income of the firm of pricing the RC-89 at $44, $42, $40, and $38.

Required: Comply with the sales manager's request and determine the price that should be set for the RC-89.

4-41   ***Multiple products (extension of 3-29)***   The planned data for Forecast Company, as shown in 3-29, represent the combined plans for three products: a platter, a cup, and a saucer. The expected sales mix of the three products, in sales dollars, is 40%, 30%, and 30%, for the platter, cup, and saucer, respectively.

Required
1. What are the expected sales, in dollars, for each product?
2. If the contribution margin percentage for cups is 10% and that for saucers is 30%, what is the contribution margin percentage for platters?
3. The normal sales mix is one platter for every two cup-and-saucer sets, and the planned results reflect that mix. If the expected sales of 50,000 units counts each platter, cup, and saucer as a separate unit, what are the planned selling prices and per-unit variable costs for each of the three products?
4. Assume that the actual sales for April were $450,000 and that the sales mix, in dollars, was 60% platters and 20% each for cups and saucers.
    (a) What was the actual total contribution margin earned for April?
    (b) What was the actual weighted-average contribution margin percentage for April?
5. B. J. Douglas, sales manager for Forecast Company, considers the April results to be unusual and not likely to be repeated. That is, she believes that sales and cost data reflected in the original plans are appropriate as long as there are no changes in costs or selling prices. But she is convinced that the price of plates (in relation to those charged for the other two products) is too high and not in the firm's best interest. Accordingly, she has developed several plans for improving sales, all involving price reductions for plates. These plans, together with Douglas's best estimates of their effects on sales, are summarized below.

Plan A: Reduce the price of a plate to $19. Douglas estimates that unit sales of plates will increase by 10% and that the price reduction will have no effect on the sales of the other two products.

Plan B: Reduce the price of a plate to $16. Douglas estimates that unit sales of plates will increase 20% and that the price reduction will result in more customers buying cups and saucers so that three of each of the other products will be sold for every plate sold.

Plan C: Reduce the price of a plate to $18. Douglas estimates that unit sales of plates will increase 20% and that the present sales mix of two cups and two saucers sold for every plate sold will not change.

Which, if any, of the proposed plans should be adopted?

4-42 *Personnel policies and decisions* Patterson Company operates a chain of hardware stores in a metropolitan area. Each store has a manager, several salespeople, and a clerk or two. The vice president has reviewed the performance of each store and is considering closing the Middleton store. The income statement shows the following for 19X8 and future results are expected to be about the same.

Middleton Store
Income Statement for 19X8

Sales		$500,000
Cost of sales	$350,000	
Salaries	85,000	
Commissions, 10% of sales	50,000	
Rent on building	20,000	
Rent on store equipment	4,000	
Miscellaneous expenses	7,000	516,000
Net loss		($ 16,000)

If Patterson closes the Middleton store, it will transfer all personnel to other stores. The firm is opening several new stores and needs to hire additional people even if the ones from the Middleton store are transferred. The miscellaneous expenses are fixed, but avoidable if the store is closed. If the store closes, none of its former business would go to any of the existing stores.

Required
1. Assume that the leases on building and equipment have 12 years to run. Patterson has no other use for the building and equipment and could not sublease them to another firm. Determine whether the firm should close the store.
2. Assume now that the leases are month-to-month and can be canceled at any time. Determine whether the store should be closed.
3. Assume that the leases are unavoidable, as in item 1. However, suppose now that the Middleton store has been losing business because the firm has two newer stores relatively close by. The vice president believes that closing the Middleton store will increase total sales in its other stores by $80,000 per year. Cost of sales and commissions, as percentages of sales dollars, are the same in all stores. Fixed costs in the other stores would not be affected by the increases in sales. Determine whether the Middleton store should be closed.

4-43 *Line of business reporting (CMA adapted)* Riparian Company produces and sells three products. Each is sold domestically and in foreign countries. The foreign market has been disappointing to management because of poor operating results, as evidenced by the income statement for the first quarter of 19X8.

	Total	Domestic	Foreign
Sales	$1,300,000	$1,000,000	$300,000
Cost of goods sold	1,010,000	775,000	235,000
Gross profit	290,000	225,000	65,000
Selling expenses	105,000	60,000	45,000
Administrative expenses	52,000	40,000	12,000
	157,000	100,000	57,000
Income	$ 133,000	$ 125,000	$ 8,000

Management decided a year ago to enter the foreign market because of excess capacity, but is now unsure whether to continue devoting time and effort to developing it. The following information has been gathered for consideration of the alternatives that management has identified.

	Products		
	A	B	C
Sales:			
Domestic	$400,000	$300,000	$300,000
Foreign	100,000	100,000	100,000
Variable manufacturing costs (percentage of sales)	60%	70%	60%
Variable selling expenses (percentage of sales)	3%	2%	2%

Of the $190,000 total fixed manufacturing costs, $30,000, $40,000, and $70,000 are direct to products A, B, and C, respectively. These amounts are not avoidable in the short-term. Additionally, $90,000 in fixed manufacturing costs are direct to the domestic market, $20,000 to the foreign market. These amounts are also unavoidable.

All administrative expenses are fixed and common to the three products and to the two markets. Fixed selling expenses are separable and avoidable by market. Some $40,000 of fixed selling expenses are direct to products, and also avoidable. The percentages of the $40,000 applicable to each product are 30% to A, 30% to B, and 40% to C.

Management believes that if the foreign market were dropped, sales in the domestic market could be increased by $200,000. The increase would be divided 40%, 40%, 20% among products A, B, and C, respectively.

Management also believes that a new product, D, could be introduced by the end of the current year. The product would replace product C and would increase fixed costs by $30,000 per quarter.

Required

1. Prepare an income statement for the quarter by product, using the format of Exhibit 4-1.
2. Prepare an income statement for the quarter by market, using the format of Exhibit 4-1.
3. Determine whether the foreign market should be dropped.
4. Assume that the foreign market would not be dropped. Determine the mini-

mum quarterly contribution margin that product D would have to produce in order to make its introduction desirable.

4-44 Price and volume variances (AICPA adapted)   Bay City Gas Company supplies liquefied natural gas to residential customers. Below are the results, both planned and actual, for the month of November 19X7. Although he knows that the price of gas per 1,000 cubic feet drops with increases in purchases by a customer, the operations manager is having difficulty in interpreting the report.

	Planned	Actual	Difference
Number of customers	26,000	28,000	2,000
Sales in thousands of cubic feet	520,000	532,000	12,000
Revenue	$1,300,000	$1,356,600	$56,600
Variable costs	$ 416,000	$ 425,600	($ 9,600)

Required: Compute the sales price variance and sales volume variance.

4-45 Sales strategies   Nova Company sells cosmetics through door-to-door salespeople who receive 25% commissions. Nova's national sales manager has been evaluating alternative selling strategies for the coming season. She is trying to decide whether any products should be discounted in price by 30%, receive increased promotional efforts, or be left alone. She is now considering four products, data for which are given below.

	Mascara	Eyeliner	Lipstick	Cologne
Normal selling price	$2.50	$2.20	$2.00	$12.00
Variable cost	0.90	1.00	0.80	5.00
Contribution margin	$1.60	$1.20	$1.20	$ 7.00
Expected volumes:				
Without discount or special				
promotion (units)	800,000	750,000	2,000,000	200,000
With 30% discount	1,650,000	1,350,000	3,200,000	380,000
With special promotion	950,000	920,000	2,150,000	240,000

If the special promotion is chosen for a particular product, its price and variable cost will remain the same. Additional fixed costs are $200,000 for each product selected, primarily for advertising and incentive payments to salespeople.

If a product is selected for a 30% price cut, variable costs will remain the same, per unit, because Nova pays sales commissions on the basis of the normal selling price even during such special sales.

Required
1. For each product, determine which of the following should be done: reduce price, do a special promotion, or do nothing.
2. Discuss some additional factors that might influence the sales manager's decisions about each product.

4-46 VCP for a hospital – patient-days   The administrator of Brookwood Memorial Hospital has developed the following estimate of costs.

Total annual cost = $39,000,000 + ($28 × P1) + ($40 × P2)

where

$$P1 = \text{patient-days on medical wards}$$
$$P2 = \text{patient-days on surgical wards}$$

A *patient-day* is one patient occupying a bed for one day. The administrator expects contribution margins, other than from room charges, to be about $25 per day from each medical patient and $60 per day from each surgical patient. These come from pharmacy, blood bank, operating room charges, and other such sources.

Required

1. Suppose that patient-days on medical wards generally run twice the number of those on surgical wards. The room charges are tentatively set at $75 per day for medical patients, $100 for surgical patients. How many patient-days must the hospital achieve to break even?

2. Suppose now that the administrator forecasts 250,000 medical patient-days and 150,000 surgical patient-days. He wants to set room rates so that the hospital breaks even and also wants each type of patient-day to provide the same dollar contribution margin. What room rates will achieve these objectives? (The $25 and $60 miscellaneous contributions should be included in determining the contribution margins from room charges.)

3. Repeat item 2 assuming that the administrator wants both types of patient-day to provide the same contribution margin percentage.

4-47 **Comprehensive review of Chapters 2, 3, and 4**   Tacky Company makes three products and sells them in about the same mix each month. Below are income statements for two recent months.

Tacky Company Income Statements
(in thousands of dollars)

	April	May
Sales	$80	$60
Costs	60	52
Income	$20	$ 8

Selling price and cost data by product are as follows.

	A	B	C
Selling price	$20	$10	$5
Variable costs	8	3	3
Contribution margin	$12	$ 7	$2
Contribution margin percentage	60%	70%	40%
Percentage of total sales dollars (mix)	40%	40%	20%

Required

1. Using the income statements for April and May, find total fixed cost and variable cost as a percentage of sales dollars.
2. Determine the break-even point in sales dollars.
3. Which product is most profitable per unit sold?
4. Which product is most profitable per dollar of sales?

5. What sales dollars are needed to earn $35,000 per month, and how many units of each product will be sold at that sales level if the usual mix is maintained?
6. The sales manager believes that he could increase sales of C by 10,000 units per month if more attention were devoted to it and less to B. Sales of B would fall by 2,000 units per month. What change in income would occur if this action were taken?
7. June sales were $100,000 with a mix of 40% A, 30% B, and 30% C. What was income?
8. July sales were $90,000 and income was $22,000.
   (a) What was the contribution margin percentage?
   (b) Which product would you think was sold in a higher proportion than in the usual mix?
9. Suppose the firm is currently selling 6,000 units of C. Because this is the least profitable product, management believes it should be dropped from the mix. If C is dropped, it is expected that sales of B would remain the same and those of A would rise. By how much would sales of A have to rise to maintain the same total income?

4-48 **Segmented income statements, activity analysis** Vic Kemp, executive vice president of Taylor, Inc., is examining the most recent monthly income statements, which are segmented by geographical area. Taylor, a distributor of products used by paper manufacturers, began operations in the western part of the United States 20 years ago and expanded into the southern and eastern markets only a year ago. Taylor does not manufacture its products, but rather buys them for resale to its customers.

Because Taylor has a good reputation and strong product lines, it has done well in the new markets, or at least Kemp thinks it has. The company has relatively few people and other assets in the market areas, mostly salespeople. The bulk of expenses are incurred at the home offices in Corvallis, Oregon.

Taylor, Inc.
Income Statement, October 19X9
(in thousands of dollars)

	Total	Eastern	Southern	Western
Sales	$2,896.0	$589.0	$752.0	$1,555.0
Cost of sales	1,231.9	200.3	300.8	730.8
Gross margin	1,664.1	388.7	451.2	824.2
Selling expenses:				
Salaries and commissions	754.2	156.2	192.6	405.4
Shipping and warehousing	187.3	43.2	67.1	77.0
Other selling expenses	84.5	12.1	27.6	44.8
Total selling expenses	1,026.0	211.5	287.3	527.2
Administrative expenses:				
Salaries	147.2	42.6	36.8	67.8
Building occupancy	61.7	22.7	26.5	12.5
Other	56.1	12.3	22.1	21.7
Total administrative expenses	265.0	77.6	85.4	102.0
Total operating expenses	1,291.0	289.1	372.7	629.2
Income before taxes	$ 373.1	$ 99.6	$ 78.5	$ 195.0

Kemp is happy with the results in the new territories, but at the same time mistrusts them, not really knowing how the statements are prepared. Kemp is also concerned that the push into the new territories has caused managers to neglect the western territory, which seems to be slipping from past levels of profitability. He is quite concerned that the income statements do not give him the kind of information he needs to make judgments and decisions. He has asked the chief accountant for an explanation of the income statements, but to little avail. The chief accountant usually puts him off by saying that it is very complicated and that he does not have the time to explain every number.

Taylor's chief accountant has been allocating costs to the markets using a set of formulas based on relative sales volume in both unit and dollar terms. No one else quite knows how he prepares the statements. Kemp finally goes to the controller and asks for a special study to help him get the information he feels he needs. The controller has been concerned with the allocation methods for some time and has collected the following information based on analyses of the activities in each territory.

Variable Costs, Percentage of Sales	Eastern	Southern	Western
Cost of sales	34.00%	40.00%	47.00%
Selling expenses	14.00%	13.00%	16.00%
Administrative expenses	0.00%	0.00%	0.00%
Direct Fixed Costs			
Cost of sales	$ 0	$ 0	$ 0
Selling expenses	152	155	207
Administrative expenses	9	12	19

The controller explains that she has developed the information by analyzing the cost driving activities associated with each category. For instance, the eastern territory has relatively heavy direct fixed selling expenses for several reasons. First, there are more established competitors in that region, and new customers are harder to cultivate. Second, shipping costs tend to be higher because orders from the east are smaller than those from the other regions, thus losing economies of large shipments. Other reasons contribute to the differences between the activity-based direct costs and the costs as allocated in the income statement above.

Required
1. Prepare a segmented income statement using the contribution margin format. Work with totals only for selling expenses and administrative expenses. Ignore the individual components of those cost categories.
2. Tell Mr. Kemp how each territory is doing.

4-49 Comprehensive problem on VCP analysis   You are presented with the following information about Gammon Sales Company, based on plans for the year 19X1.

Sales ($1 per unit)		$100,000
Variable costs:		
Cost of goods sold	$67,000	
Other operating costs	15,000	
Total		82,000
Contribution margin		18,000
Fixed costs		13,140
Planned income before taxes		$ 4,860

Required

1. What is Gammon's break-even sales volume?
2. The company's officers have analyzed anticipated cash flows for the year and have determined that it could afford to spend $3,600 on a special advertising campaign. They are not sure, however, that the expenditure would be worthwhile. What is the break-even point if the campaign is undertaken?
3. If, as a result of the advertising campaign, the number of units sold could be expected to increase in an amount equal to the change in the break-even point in units, would the campaign be financially advisable? Explain.
4. Assume that Gammon has decided not to undertake the advertising campaign and is looking for other ways to improve the financial outlook for 19X1. The purchasing agent determines that there is a supplier (other than the one with which the company now deals) that will allow the company to buy at a price 10% below the anticipated purchase price. The sales manager believes that the new supplier does not provide a product of equal quality, and he estimates that sales volume will decrease by about 15% if the new supplier were used. The controller has determined that the switch in suppliers will necessitate minor changes in the administrative procedures, which will increase fixed costs by approximately $1,000. Would the change of suppliers be wise? Explain your answer with supporting computations.
5. Are there some qualitative considerations that might influence the decision on the change in suppliers?
6. After further investigation, you determine that Gammon has not one but three separate products in its line, each of which has the same selling price. The planned activity for 19X1 in more detail is as follows.

	Product			
	1	2	3	Total
Sales ($1 per unit)	$50,000	$30,000	$20,000	$100,000
Variable costs:				
Cost of goods sold	30,000	21,000	16,000	67,000
Other operating costs	7,500	4,500	3,000	15,000
Total	37,500	25,500	19,000	82,000
Contribution margin	$12,500	$ 4,500	$ 1,000	18,000
Fixed costs				13,140
Planned income before taxes				$ 4,860

Gammon has decided not to dilute the impact of a special advertising campaign by trying to promote more than one product. Which product should the company probably choose to promote in the $3,600 advertising campaign? Explain.

7. The company has found an alternative supplier for each of its products. Each supplier is willing to sell to the company at a price 10% lower than is currently being paid. In each case, however, the product from the new supplier will probably reduce the total sales of that product by 15%. However, the company can change suppliers for only one of the products at a time. Ignoring any qualitative considerations, decide for which product, if any, Gammon should change suppliers. Support your answer.

8. Assume that Gammon's directors decide to postpone the advertising campaign and continue doing business with current suppliers. At the end of 19X1, despite sales of $110,000, income before taxes was only $360. Analysis of sales by product showed the following.

Sales of Product 1	$ 30,000
Sales of Product 2	20,000
Sales of Product 3	60,000
Total	$110,000

These results surprised the board of directors because operating managers assured the directors that variable and fixed costs had behaved exactly as expected and sales were in excess of the forecast. Explain the reason or reasons for the disappointing results.

4-50 **Explaining revenue differences for a motel** Great Eastern Inns, a large motel chain, had revenue of $60 million in 19X5, operating at a 70% occupancy rate. In 19X6, Great Eastern raised its room rates by 5%, and its occupancy rate fell to 65%. Variable costs are negligible.

Required
1. Determine Great Eastern's revenue for 19X6.
2. Determine how much of the difference in revenue, from 19X5 to 19X6, is attributable to (a) room rates and (b) room occupancy. You can treat 19X5 in the same way you usually do "planned results," and 19X6 as you do "actual results." Round to the nearest $100,000.

Cases

4-51 **Product mix, profit planning, taxes** Michael Monte, the new assistant controller of Remley Company, has prepared a VCP analysis for the firm based on sales of the firm's three products from 19X7. He will present the analysis to a group of managers later in the week. Data per unit are given below.

	Products		
	101	102	103
Selling price	$3.50	$4.00	$5.00
Variable costs	1.50	3.00	2.00
Contribution margin	$2.00	$1.00	$3.00

On the basis of the sales mix in 19X7, Michael believed that of every ten units sold, four would be 101s, four 102s, and two 103s. Total fixed costs were predicted to be $90,000. Total sales were expected to be 100,000 units, based on a projection of trends in recent years, and Michael had prepared the following planned income statement for the year 19X8.

	101	102	103	Total
Sales	$140,000	$160,000	$100,000	$400,000
Variable costs	60,000	120,000	40,000	220,000
Contribution margin	$ 80,000	$ 40,000	$ 60,000	180,000
Fixed costs				90,000
Income before tax				90,000
Income taxes (40%)				36,000
Net Income				$ 54,000

At the meeting, Michael demonstrated that his analysis could be used to predict changes in profits that would be expected to follow changes in sales. As an example he said that the break-even point for the firm is $200,000 in sales, because the contribution margin percentage is 45% and fixed costs are $90,000. He showed the other managers that target profits can also be computed, although the presence of income taxes makes it a bit more complicated than computing the break-even point. He said that if an after-tax profit figure were desired, it was necessary to divide it by 60%, the percentage of net income to income before taxes. The resulting before-tax profit could be added to fixed costs and the sum divided by 45%. Thus, the sales required for profits of $90,000 are about $533,300, since before-tax profits have to be $150,000, and ($90,000 + $150,000)/45% is $533,333.

Some of the managers were becoming restless as Michael explained his analysis. Finally, the production manager said that it was all very interesting, but irrelevant. She told the group that labor costs, which are 50% of variable costs, would increase by 20% under a new union contract.

The controller said that he was somewhat disappointed with Michael's analysis because it had failed to provide for a $40,000 dividend to stockholders that the president of the firm had said should be a target. The firm has a policy of not allowing dividends to be more than one-third of after-tax profits. The controller had thought that Michael would incorporate the desired dividend into his analysis to show the other managers what had to be done to meet the president's goal.

As the managers began to mumble among themselves about the irrelevance of the analysis, the sales manager announced that the assumed sales mix was no good. He said, "I don't know how this will affect the analysis, but we expect that each product will be sold in equal amounts during this coming year. The demand for 103s is increasing substantially."

Slapping her forehead, the production manager commented that she had forgotten that the firm was going to rent some additional equipment to increase production of 103s. The rental would be $10,000 per year. She wondered what effect that news would have on Michael's figures.

As he left the meeting, Michael chastised himself for not having obtained more information before going in and looking like a fool.

Required: Prepare a new analysis for Remley, incorporating the goals and changed assumptions learned at the meeting. Show the sales necessary to (a) break even and (b) meet the profit required to pay the $40,000 dividend without violating the firm's dividend policy.

4-52   *Explaining territorial differences* Barkman Company sells various types of jams and jellies all across the country. The following income statement shows results for two territories for a recent month, in thousands of dollars.

	Northwest	Southeast
Sales	$2,800	$2,400
Variable costs	840	600
Contribution margin	1,960	1,800
Fixed costs, discretionary	920	920
Territory income	$1,040	$ 880

Variable costs per case are the same in both territories. The territorial managers have wide discretion over setting prices and incurring advertising and promotion expenses.

Required: Compare the pricing strategies of the managers of the territories. Show why the Northwest territory is more profitable than the Southeast.

4-53   *Variance analysis (CMA adapted)* Handler Company distributes two power tools to hardware stores: a heavy-duty hand drill and a table saw. Handler buys the tools from a manufacturer that attaches the Handler label to them.

The 19X4 planned and actual results appear below. The plan was adopted in late 19X3 based on Handler's estimates of market share for each tool. During the first quarter of 19X4 it seemed likely that the total market for the tools would be 10% less than Handler had estimated. In an attempt to prevent planned unit sales from declining by 10%, Handler's managers instituted a marketing program consisting of price reductions and increased advertising. The table saw was emphasized over the drill in this program.

Handler Company
Income Statement for 19X4
(all data in thousands)

	Drill		Table Saw		Total	
	Plan	Actual	Plan	Actual	Plan	Actual
Unit sales	120	86	80	74	200	160
Revenue	$7,200	$5,074	$9,600	$8,510	$16,800	$13,584
Variable costs	6,000	4,300	6,400	5,920	12,400	10,220
Contribution margin	$1,200	$ 774	$3,200	$2,590	4,400	3,364
Unallocated costs:						
Selling					1,000	1,000
Advertising					1,000	1,060
Administration					400	406
Total unallocated costs					2,400	2,466
Income					$ 2,000	$ 898

Required

1. For each product, determine the sales price variance and sales volume variance.
2. Was the marketing program (price reductions and increased advertising) successful?

CHAPTER 5

SHORT-TERM DECISIONS AND ACCOUNTING INFORMATION

Making decisions is choosing from among alternatives. Even continuing to do what you have been doing is a decision, if there is some other alternative available. (When there are no alternatives, there is no decision because you have no choice.) Should we raise the price of our product? Should we drop a particular product? Should we add a new product? Should we compensate salespeople by salary (a fixed cost) or by commission (a variable cost)? Should we make a component in our factory or buy it? Managers are continually concerned about such sets of alternatives.

Another critical characteristic of decisions is that they relate to future actions: they cannot be made retroactively. (You cannot decide in August, after the price of a particular stock has increased, to buy that stock the previous February.) There are two important implications of this characteristic. First, because managers must base their decisions on estimates, a decision is not necessarily bad just because some unpredictable change in circumstances caused results to differ markedly from expectations. Second, managers can never be *sure* that a particular decision was wise, because it is impossible to know what would have happened if they had selected different courses of action. But managers can have a reasonable degree of confidence if the decision is based on the best available information, *and* if they understand the significance of the information.

The focus of this chapter is short-term decisions; Chapters 8 and 9 treat long-term decisions. The distinction between these two types of decisions is sometimes hazy. Most managers and accountants consider a decision to be short-term if it involves a period of one year or less. The cutoff is arbitrary but commonly used. The basic principles that apply to short-term decisions also apply to long-term ones, but long-term decisions require some additional considerations. Perhaps a better distinction between short- and long-term decisions is that the former do not require large capital investments. For this reason, short-term decisions are more easily reversible than long-term ones. (You can almost always change prices or the method of compensating salespeople, but you cannot so simply sell a factory or even a large piece of equipment.) In general, the long-term decisions discussed in later chapters require the commitment of money for a fairly long period.

One final matter before we proceed. Almost every decision has both quantitative and qualitative aspects, and managers must understand both. In this chapter we often mention qualitative issues associated with specific decisions, but our analytical approaches concentrate on the quantitative, economic aspects. In many cases, qualitative considerations might even override quantitative factors, and managers will select an alternative that is not as economically sound as others because of company policy or a belief that an action just isn't right for the firm. To take one example, some manufacturers of name-brand products sell unlabeled products to discount stores. Such business can be profitable, but some firms do not accept it because their managers believe that the firm's reputation for quality could suffer if people learned that discount stores were carrying the merchandise under another name. Such managers cannot be called wrong. But it is critical that they be aware of the costs, in the form of lost profits. The techniques described in this chapter help them to determine what such a policy is costing.

THE CRITERION FOR SHORT-TERM DECISIONS

The economic criterion for making short-term decisions is simple: *Take the action that you expect will give the highest income (or least loss) to the firm.* Applying this rule is not always simple, and two subrules might be helpful:

1. The only revenues and costs that are *relevant* in decision making are the expected future revenues and costs that will *differ* among the choices that are available. These are called **differential revenues** and **costs,** or **incremental revenues** and **costs.**
2. Revenues and costs that have already been earned or incurred are *irrelevant* in making decisions. Their only use is that they might aid in predicting future revenues and costs.

Differential (Incremental) Revenues and Costs

The term *differential* is more inclusive than *incremental*. The latter term suggests increases, and some decisions result in decreases in both revenues and costs. But the terms used are not as important as what they denote. Differential costs are *avoidable* costs, which we introduced briefly in Chapters 3 and 4. If the firm can change a cost by taking one action as opposed to another, the cost is avoidable and therefore differential. Suppose a firm could save $50,000 in salaries and other fixed costs if it stopped selling a product in a particular geographical region. The $50,000 is avoidable (differential) because it will be incurred if the firm continues to sell in the region and will not be incurred if it stops selling in that region. Of course, the company will lose revenue if it discontinues sales in the region. Hence, the lost revenue is differential in a decision to stop selling in the region.

Sunk Costs and Opportunity Costs

The emphasis on differential revenues and costs gives rise to two other, related concepts: *sunk costs* and *opportunity costs*. A **sunk cost** is one that has already been incurred and therefore will be the same no matter which alternative a manager selects. Sunk costs are *never* relevant for decision making because they are not differential.

Suppose a company has spent $500,000 developing a new product. Problems have arisen and the managers must now decide whether or not to market it. The $500,000 is irrelevant to the decision because it is not differential; that is, the cost will be the same whether or not the firm markets the product. Similarly, depreciation on a machine is irrelevant in deciding which products to make with that machine. *All* historical costs, whether original cost or book value (cost minus accumulated depreciation), are sunk costs.

Even though the historical cost of a resource is sunk, it can have a cost for decision-making purposes. If a resource can be used in more than one way, it has an opportunity cost. In general terms, an **opportunity cost** is the benefit lost by taking one action as opposed to another. The "other" action is the best alternative available other than the one being contemplated.

Suppose PPF Company owns a warehouse and can either use it to store products or rent it to another company for $8,000 per year. Using the space for storage requires that PPF forego the opportunity to rent it, which means that there *is* a difference to PPF if it chooses to take one action rather than another. When PPF considers any action that requires using the space for storage, the relevant cost of the space is its opportunity cost, the $8,000 rent PPF will not collect. What if PPF would have to pay $1,000 per year for a license to rent the warehouse? The opportunity cost of using the space for storage falls to $7,000, the net sacrifice that PPF makes by foregoing the rental opportunity.

As another example, suppose PPF owns a machine that it can use to produce either of two products, X and Y. The products require the same amount of machine time, but the contribution margin of X is greater than that of Y. When PPF considers a decision to use the machine to produce X, the cost of using the machine is its opportunity cost, the contribution margin sacrificed by not using it to produce Y. If PPF is considering using the machine to produce Y, the cost is the contribution margin sacrificed by not using it to produce X. As you can see, opportunity cost depends on what action is being considered.

The example described in the next section incorporates the concepts of differential revenues and costs, sunk costs, and opportunity costs. As you read, be on the lookout for examples of these concepts.

Basic Example

Walters Company manufactures clothing. From an earlier production run, it has 5,000 shirts that it cannot sell through normal channels. The cost to manufacture these shirts was $17,000. A chain store approaches Walters with an offer to buy the shirts for $12,000. The president says he'd rather throw out the shirts than sell them at a loss of $5,000 ($17,000 manufacturing costs − $12,000 revenue). Is he correct? He is not; the chain's offer should be accepted.

If there is no likelihood of getting a better offer, Walters has two alternatives: (1) throw the shirts away and (2) sell them to the chain. Throwing the shirts away yields no revenue and requires no additional costs. The chain's offer should be accepted because the difference in profit is $12,000. The differential revenues and costs for selling to the chain as opposed to throwing out the shirts are shown below.

Sell to Chain Rather than Throw Shirts Away	
Differential revenues	$12,000
Differential costs	0
Profit	$12,000

The opportunity cost of throwing the shirts away is $12,000, the benefit you lose by not taking the best available alternative course of action. What is the opportunity cost of using the shirts for the sale to the chain? Nothing, because Walters would obtain no benefit from taking that alternative, which is to throw the shirts away. Thus, opportunity cost depends on which alternative is being considered.

But what of the $17,000 cost to make the shirts? You understand the concepts of differential and sunk costs if you saw that the $17,000 is sunk. That cost has already been incurred and will not change regardless of which alternative is chosen. True, Walters will have a $5,000 loss if it sells the shirts to the chain ($17,000 − $12,000). But if the shirts are simply thrown out, Walters will have a loss of $17,000. (Note that Walters is better off selling the shirts for $12,000, whether the cost to manufacture them was $2,000, $17,000, or even $50,000.)

Let us now add another alternative: Another chain store has offered to pay $20,000 for the shirts provided that Walters puts on two more pockets and dyes them a different color. The production manager estimates the incremental cost to do the work at $5,000. The president isn't happy about this alternative either, because the total cost ($17,000 + $5,000) is greater than the $20,000 offer.

Three alternatives are now available, but because we already know that the as-is sale is preferable to throwing the shirts away, we need only compare the new alternative with the as-is sale. Which of those two alternatives should Walters choose? It should do the work and sell the shirts for $20,000. To support Walters' selection of this alternative, consider the differential revenues and costs.

	Rework and Sell, Rather than Sell As Is
Differential revenues ($20,000 − $12,000)	$8,000
Differential costs ($5,000 − $0)	5,000
Differential profit	$3,000

Walters would be $3,000 better off by reworking the shirts rather than selling them as is.

What is the opportunity cost of an as-is sale of the shirts? The best available alternative is the rework option, which has a profit of $15,000 ($20,000 revenue minus $5,000 cost). So, the opportunity cost of selling the shirts as is is the $15,000 profit sacrificed by not using them for the rework option. If the opportunity cost is incorporated into the analysis of the option to sell the shirts as is, the analysis will show a $3,000 loss from selecting that option (revenues are $12,000 and costs are $15,000).

What is the opportunity cost of accepting the rework offer? It is $12,000, the benefit lost by foregoing the opportunity to sell the shirts without reworking. Incorporating opportunity cost into the analysis of the rework option, the revenues will still be $20,000, but the costs will be $17,000 ($5,000 for the extra work *plus* the $12,000 opportunity cost of the shirts), so the analysis will show a $3,000 profit for the rework option. Thus, comparing the two alternatives *after* considering opportunity cost results in the same choice: Accept the rework option because its $3,000 profit is preferable to the $3,000 loss from selling the shirts as is.

Note that, as before, the $17,000 cost of manufacturing the shirts is irrelevant. To emphasize the irrelevance of this sunk cost, consider the firm's income statement for each of the alternatives.

	Throw Out Shirts	Sell Shirts for $12,000	Rework Shirts
Revenues	$ 0	$12,000	$20,000
Costs:			
Manufacturing	(17,000)	(17,000)	(17,000)
Rework			(5,000)
Profit (loss)	($17,000)	($ 5,000)	($ 2,000)

D.P $3,000

The $2,000 loss is the lowest of the three, which confirms the results of the differential analyses. The loss incurred by selling the shirts as is is $12,000 less than that from throwing them out, which is equal to the $12,000 differential profit shown in the first analysis. The $2,000 loss reported for reworking the shirts is $3,000 less than the loss from the as-is sale, which is equal to the $3,000 differential profit we found when comparing those choices.

The unchanged fact is that Walters has on hand 5,000 shirts that were manufactured at a cost of $17,000. But now assume that the shirts can be sold at regular prices. Walters will then have to produce similar shirts to meet future sales if it sells the on-hand shirts now. The production manager says that the cost of manufacturing 5,000 shirts has risen to $20,000. A discount outlet offers Walters $18,000 for the shirts on hand. What should the firm do under these conditions? The key to the analysis is to understand that, *whatever* Walters decides to do, it needs to have 5,000 shirts available for the expected future sale at the regular price. (Everything that happens after that point, including the expected regular sales, will be the same no matter what Walters decides to do about the 5,000 shirts now on hand.)

There are two alternatives. First, Walters can hold the shirts until they can be sold at regular prices, which is to say it can choose to "do nothing." If Walters chooses that alternative, it receives no revenues and incurs no costs between now and the time the shirts are needed for regular sales, for a net of zero. Second, Walters can sell the shirts now and make others to meet regular sales needs. If this alternative is chosen, Walters receives $18,000 revenue and incurs a cost of $20,000 (to produce the shirts needed for regular sales), for a loss of $2,000. The better choice is to "do nothing"; Walters will be $2,000 better off by choosing that action.

The opportunity cost of choosing to sell the shirts now is $20,000, the cost of replacing them later. This is their value because selling them now requires replacing them at a $20,000 cost. Opportunity cost is replacement cost in some situations. In our previous examples, it was always a selling price (less additional costs to complete).

DEVELOPING RELEVANT INFORMATION

Managers make many decisions that affect a relatively small segment of the company: a product, a product line, a factory, even a single component of a finished product. Often, the segment (individual activity) that managers are reviewing for possible change is not large enough to warrant separate reporting.

For example, consider a company that makes office equipment. It might make several models each of typewriters, calculators, and copiers, sell them in several countries to different types of customers (businesses, hospitals, governmental agencies, etc.), and operate several factories, some of which make only one product or line and others of which make several products. Normal accounting reports might not show information by model of product, by region, by type of customer, and by factory.

An existing accounting report, such as the product-line income statement illustrated in Chapter 4 (page 118), is a good base from which to analyze a product line (because it highlights avoidable costs). But information in past accounting reports is of interest only if it helps you to predict the future. Other sources are often more important. Engineers provide information about materials needs and labor requirements for a new product. From the marketing department come estimates of future sales of a product. Thus, even the availability of a regular accounting report on the segment for which some change is contemplated does not mean that the report contains the information needed for making a decision about that change.

The widespread availability and use of computers make it easier to develop some types of information, like the number of units of a particular product sold in each region to each type of customer. But a computer cannot determine the effect of, say, dropping a particular model. Chapter 4 pointed out some of the problems of determining whether or not costs are avoidable. Making these determinations requires a great deal of work and close cooperation between the managerial accountant and other managers.

For example, consider the office equipment company described above. Suppose salespeople are paid salaries, concentrate on specific types of customers, *and* sell all of the firm's products. Neither sales salaries nor travel costs are avoidable costs in analyzing a particular *model* of copier; if a model is dropped the salespeople will still call on the same customers. On the other hand, some sales salaries and related expenses might well be avoidable if the segment is a particular type of customer. Similarly, if salespeople cover specific geographical regions, their salaries and other expenses are avoidable in a segment analysis by region.

The most important point about decisions relating to segments is that the analyses will differ with the decisions. There are no magic formulas for identifying the costs and revenues relevant to decisions; costs avoidable, and therefore differential, when one segment is under review might be unavoidable when looking at a different segment. *In general, the smaller the segment the less the avoidable cost.* Avoidable costs of a model of typewriter sold in a particular region are probably limited to the variable costs of producing that model. Those associated with the entire line of typewriters in the same region include variable production costs and perhaps some selling expenses. Some fixed manufacturing costs might also be saved, especially if typewriters sold in that region are made in a factory that does not make other product lines, but even that conclusion depends on the specific circumstances of that plant. As the segment under study expands to, say, an entire product line, more and more costs become avoidable.

Allocated Costs

The task of identifying the costs relevant to a particular decision is often complicated by the accounting practice of allocating common costs to segments. For example, firms regularly allocate fixed manufacturing costs to units of product, because they are required to do so for financial accounting and tax purposes. For reasons discussed in Chapter 10, cost allocations are often incorporated into internal reports that serve as a starting point for decision making.

Earlier in this chapter we emphasized that the basis for decision making was information about the future. We showed, in Chapter 2, that per-unit fixed costs—the result of allocations—are not useful in predicting future costs. Hence, they are not relevant for decision making. By definition, common costs are unavoidable to individual segments to which they are common. Allocating such costs to individual segments does not make the allocated amount avoidable in the future. Hence, for making decisions about a segment, common costs allocated to that segment are not relevant; the only relevant costs are those that will change (be differential) if a firm chooses one course of action rather than another.

Although common costs are by definition not avoidable, it is sometimes possible to reduce common costs if a large enough segment is eliminated. For example, suppose that each of the 20 employees of a payroll department works on the payrolls of all six factories that the company operates. The salaries of all of the employees in the payroll department are then common to the six factories. But if one large factory closes, the payroll department might be able to reassign work and people, reducing the staff to 17 or 18. This is part of analyzing costs in an activity framework, activity-based costing. Again, analyzing costs for decisions requires very careful attention to the specific situation. Nonetheless, when you see the term *allocated costs,* there is a strong presumption that the cost is unavoidable.

The appearance of allocated costs on segment reports raises an important point about providing information within a firm. An information system must provide data for preparing financial statements, completing tax and other government forms, and making decisions. The system is usually designed around the needs of financial accounting and taxation, because the specific information required for these purposes is well-known and is needed regularly. Because the information system and resulting segment reports serve several purposes, a manager using such reports should take care to include only relevant costs in analyzing a particular decision.

The remainder of this chapter is devoted to typical examples of short-term decisions. Although the situations appear to be quite different, the same principle applies to all: Find the most profitable alternative by analyzing the differential revenues and costs. In some cases, it will be relatively easy to determine the differentials and choose among the alternatives. In others, you might find it easier to make your choice by preparing complete income statements for the alternatives. But the two approaches should lead to the same decision.

TYPICAL SHORT-TERM DECISIONS

Dropping a Segment

As noted before in this chapter, there are many ways to segment a firm. Determining the best mix of segments is a continual problem for managers, who frequently have to decide whether to drop a segment or replace it with another. Consider the following income statement for a recent month for the Moorehead Department Store. Its managers expect these results to continue for the foreseeable future.

	Clothing	Appliances	Housewares	Total
Sales	$40,000	$30,000	$15,000	$85,000
Variable costs	22,000	14,000	11,000	47,000
Contribution margin	18,000	16,000	4,000	38,000
Fixed costs:				
Avoidable	(4,000)	(3,000)	(1,500)	(8,500)
Common, allocated on sales dollars	(8,000)	(6,000)	(3,000)	(17,000)
Profit (loss)	$ 6,000	$ 7,000	($ 500)	$12,500

The income statement has been prepared after a careful analysis of cost drivers. That analysis shows how much cost the company could probably avoid if it dropped each of the segments. Some of these avoidable costs are direct, some are indirect. The latter represent the savings from reductions in activities such as payroll that are common to all segments. Dropping a segment is qualitatively different from reducing its volume. Reducing volume will not always save fixed costs, but eliminating the segment almost certainly will. Identifying cost drivers is critical to evaluating the effects of eliminating the segment.

Suppose a manager decided that the housewares line should be dropped because it shows a loss. Is that the right decision? You are correct if you object to the decision because you see that Moorehead would lose $4,000 contribution margin while saving only $1,500 in avoidable fixed costs. The common costs allocated to the segments will not change. Hence, dropping the houseware line will reduce total profit by $2,500 ($4,000 lost contribution margin—$1,500 in fixed cost savings). Of course, the decision should be made only after considering *all* the alternatives. For example, if Moorehead dropped housewares it most likely could use the freed-up space in some other way, such as to expand another department or even to rent to another company.

You already know that Moorehead would lose $2,500 if it dropped housewares and did nothing else. Suppose that the space now devoted to housewares could be rented to another company. Because dropping the housewares line would reduce profit by $2,500, it would take at least $2,500 in rental income to offset that loss. That is, the opportunity cost of using the space to sell housewares is the rental income foregone if the firm continues to sell housewares.

Let us examine a more complicated alternative. Suppose that Moorehead could substitute a shoe department, using the same space. Suppose further that the shoe department is expected to generate revenues of $20,000, with variable costs of $8,000 and avoidable fixed costs of $3,000. An income statement incorporating the estimates for the shoe department appears on page 163. Note that we have identified the short-term margin (contribution margin less avoidable fixed costs) for each segment and did not allocate the common costs. This is different from the format shown before.

	Clothing	Appliances	Shoes	Total
Sales	$40,000	$30,000	$20,000	$90,000
Variable costs	22,000	14,000	8,000	44,000
Contribution margin	18,000	16,000	12,000	46,000
Avoidable fixed costs	4,000	3,000	3,000	10,000
Short-term margin	$14,000	$13,000	$ 9,000	36,000
Common costs, unallocated				17,000
Income				$19,000

The statement shows that dropping housewares and adding shoes will increase total profit by $6,500 ($19,000 − $12,500). The same conclusion is given by the following differential analysis.

Differential contribution margin ($12,000 − $4,000)	$8,000
Differential avoidable fixed costs ($3,000 − $1,500)	(1,500)
Difference in profit, favoring shoes	$6,500

We must emphasize that this analysis depends on the assumption that the space now devoted to housewares would be used for shoes. If the store had enough space to accommodate both lines and had no other alternatives, it would be wise to add shoes to the existing lines.

Finally, we remind you that reports prepared for one purpose might not be usable for another, and that costs carrying a label in one kind of report might well warrant some other label in a report prepared for some other purpose.

Complementary Effects and Loss Leaders

The preceding examples did not include the possibility that dropping or adding a product (or product line) might affect the sales of continuing lines. However, as we noted in the discussion of sales mix (Chapter 4), a change in the sales of one product might be accompanied by a change in the sales of another. When there is such a relationship, we say that a decision about the one product will have **complementary effects;** that is, the sales of some products will be affected by the sales of one or more other products.

Let us return to the case of the Moorehead Department Store, whose managers are considering dropping housewares and adding shoes. Moorehead's managers might believe that a complementary relationship exists between shoes and clothing, such that selling shoes will increase clothing sales because people coming to shop for shoes are also likely to buy clothing. The managers might also believe that a complementary relationship exists between housewares and appliances, because people coming to shop for housewares look at and buy appliances at the same time. Often, marketing studies of shopping habits can help to quantify the effects of suspected complementary relationships.

Suppose that Moorehead's managers, after reviewing available studies, believe that appliance sales will drop 10% and clothing sales will increase 5% if they substitute shoes for housewares. Assume further that avoidable fixed costs are expected to remain constant in the two continuing areas (appliances and clothing). Should the substitution be made? The following schedule, which concentrates on differential revenues and costs shows that the substitution is still wise.

Increase in profit from substituting shoes for hardware (from page 163)	$6,500
Complementary effects:	
Increase in profit from clothing (5% × $18,000 contribution margin)	900
Decrease in profit from appliances (10% × $16,000 contribution margin)	(1,600)
Net increase in profit	$5,800

The advantage of the substitution is less than computed earlier ($5,800 versus $6,500), but the substitution is still profitable.

A particularly interesting case of complementary effects is the **loss leader,** a product or line that shows a negative profit in the sense that its contribution margin does not cover its avoidable fixed costs. In an extreme case, the product might even have a negative contribution margin! If the complementary effects between the loss leader and the firm's other products are large enough, even such an extreme pricing policy could be beneficial.

Consider the manager of a local pizza parlor who is dismayed by a lack of business at lunchtime. He attributes this to the specials of competing restaurants and is eager to change the situation. He has prepared the following income statement, based on a normal week, for the 11:00 A.M. to 2:00 P.M. period. The costs shown are all incremental.

	Pizza	Beverages	Total
Sales (200 pizzas @ $1.80)	$360	$100	$460
Variable costs	120	40	160
Contribution margin	$240	$ 60	300
Part-time employee salaries			80
Income			$220

He is thinking about offering with each pizza all the free beverages a customer can drink. He believes that the offer could double his lunchtime pizza sales. On the basis of his experience and judgment, he anticipates that beverage consumption will increase to two and one-half times the present level. To take care of the additional business, he estimates that he will have to hire additional part-time help at an additional cost of $40 per week. There will be no revenue from beverages, but there will be costs, so he will obviously lose money on beverages. Can he gain enough on the sales of pizza to offset the loss? Using his estimates of the effects of the special (which are the best information available), he can prepare the following expected income statement for the lunchtime period.

	Pizza	Beverages	Total
Sales	$720	$ 0	$720
Variable costs	240[a]	100[b]	340
Contribution margin	$480	($100)	380
Part-time employee salaries			120
Income			$260

(2.5 × 40) (handwritten)

[a] Variable costs computed at the same rate as before, one-third or 33⅓% of selling price.
[b] Variable costs computed as two and one-half times the previous costs.

Beverages show a *negative* contribution margin, yet total profits increase by $40 per week ($260 − $220) if expectations about increased sales are realized.

The potential for complementary effects is more obvious in some cases than in others. For example, one can readily see the relationship between sales of gasoline and motor oil. But the loss-leader rationale is behind many low prices that are expected to encourage sales of products that are not complementary. Examples are supermarket offers of extremely inexpensive name-brand items in return for a newspaper coupon and the sale of well-known products for a few pennies to any customer purchasing a specific dollar amount of other merchandise.

Emphasizing the total profit picture is important in evaluating any product. A product that is selling at a loss (that is, negative contribution or product margin) might be so essential to the sales of other products that it should not be dropped. A manager contemplating the elimination of a specific product should consider the potential for complementary effects.

Make-or-Buy Decisions

Most manufactured products contain components that are assembled into a finished unit. Many of these components can be bought from an outside supplier or made by the assembling firm. Several qualitative factors must be considered when deciding whether to purchase or make a component. Will the quality of purchased components be as good as the firm can achieve? Will the supplier meet delivery commitments? Will the supplier who quotes a low price now raise it once he thinks that you are a captive customer? The make-or-buy decision is especially important in an advanced manufacturing environment. A just-in-time manufacturer is extremely concerned with quality and delivery schedules and will not buy a component unless both are guaranteed. Such a company will make a component, even at a cost disadvantage, rather than risk compromising quality or delivery schedules.

The quantitative factors are the differential costs to make and to buy. XYZ Company now makes a component. A manager has prepared the following estimates of costs at the expected volume of 20,000 units.

Materials at $2 per unit	$ 40,000
Direct labor at $5 per unit	100,000
Variable overhead at $3 per unit	60,000
Allocated fixed overhead (building depreciation, heat and light, etc.)	120,000
Total costs	$320,000

An outside supplier offers to supply the component at $14 per unit or $280,000 for 20,000 units. Should the offer be accepted?

We first need to determine whether there are alternative uses of the space and equipment now used to make the component. If there is no alternative use, then the analysis is quite straightforward. Because XYZ will sell the same quantity of product whether the component is made internally or purchased from an outside supplier, there are no differential revenues. Hence, the decision depends on which alternative results in the lower cost. The fixed costs that are now being allocated to making the component will not change if the component is bought from the outside supplier. Hence, they are not relevant. The following schedule focuses on the relevant costs for each available course of action.

the $20 000 are sunk costs

	Decisions	
	Make	Buy
Materials	$ 40,000	0
Direct labor	100,000	0
Variable overhead	60,000	0
Purchase price	0	$280,000
Total	$200,000	$280,000

The firm saves $80,000 by making the component. Note that we could include the fixed overhead of $120,000 under *both* alternatives, in which case the $80,000 advantage of making still holds. Of course, if XYZ could actually reduce fixed costs by outside purchase of the component, the cost that could be avoided should be part of the total cost of making the component internally.

The firm is better off making the component unless it can obtain more than $80,000 by using the space and equipment in some other way. The firm needs to earn at least $80,000 from an alternative use in order to induce it to buy outside. You could say that XYZ should use the available space and equipment to make the component until some other opportunity arises such that the opportunity cost—the benefit to be gained by using the space and equipment for that other purpose—exceeds the $80,000 cost savings available by using the resources to make the component. Such a benefit could come from renting the space and equipment or using them to make a product that would bring more than $80,000 in incremental profit.

Joint Products

When a single manufacturing process invariably produces two or more separate products, the products are called **joint products.** The process that makes the joint products is called a **joint process.** Refining crude petroleum yields a number of products, such as gasoline, various grades of oil, and kerosene. Processing cattle results in hides, hoofs, various cuts of meat, and other items (fat, organs, lips). Some joint products are quite valuable; some have little or no value. Some can be sold just as they emerge from the joint process or can be processed further. For example, a meat packer might sell hides to a tanner, or if it has the expertise and the facilities, it could tan the hides and make shoes, gloves, and other products.

Manufacturers of joint products must decide whether to sell them at the **split-off point**—the point at which they emerge from the joint process—or to process them further. This decision cannot be based on the total costs of the individual final products or even on the total variable costs. To produce *any* of the joint products, the firm must undertake the joint process, incurring all the costs to perform that process. For example, a meatpacker might pay $300 per animal. This cost does not relate to particular cuts of meat, to hides, or to by-products. To get *any* of those products, the packer must buy the entire animal. The $300 varies with the number of animals entering the joint process, but it cannot be identified with any specific cut of meat or even with all cuts of meat yielded by the joint process. Hence, the costs incurred prior to split-off are irrelevant in determining whether the joint products should be sold immediately or processed further. The costs of the joint process are relevant only in determining whether that process should be carried on at all. In determining whether to sell a product at the split-off point or process it further, *all* costs—fixed and variable—incurred prior to the split-off are sunk.

Consider the following example. A chemical company makes two products, Alpha and Omega, in a joint process. Each 1,000 pounds of material yields 600 pounds of Alpha and 400 pounds of Omega. Both Alpha and Omega can be sold at the split-off point or processed further. Selling price and cost data per batch (1,000 pounds of raw material) are given below.

	Alpha	*Omega*
Selling price at split-off	$1,200 ($2 per pound)	$1,600 ($4 per pound)
Selling price after additional processing	$3,600 ($6 per pound)	$2,000 ($5 per pound)
Costs of additional processing, all variable	$900 ($1.50 per pound)	$500 ($1.25 per pound)

What should be done with each product? We can analyze the results of both alternatives for each product. Alpha is analyzed as follows:

	Decision on Alpha	
	Sell at Split-Off	Process Further
Sales value	$1,200	$3,600
Incremental cost	0	900
Incremental profit	$1,200	$2,700

Alpha should be processed further because profit will be $1,500 higher ($2,700 − $1,200). We can reach the same conclusion by examining just the revenues and costs that differ by processing Alpha further.

Differential revenue ($3,600 − $1,200)	$2,400
Differential costs	900
Profit	$1,500

Similar analysis reveals that Omega should be sold at split-off, not processed further.

Differential revenues ($2,000 − $1,600)	$400
Differential costs	500
Loss	($100)

$5 x 1000 lbs

The firm would be $100 worse off if it processed Omega further.

The preceding analytical approaches are appropriate when all incremental costs of additional processing are variable. However, when the additional processing requires fixed costs, a slightly different approach is necessary. Let us assume that further processing Alpha requires avoidable fixed costs of $10,000 per month and that the company usually processes ten batches per month. Note that the $10,000 is *joint* to all pounds of Alpha further processed during the month and hence cannot be identified with any one batch. The monthly output of Alpha is 6,000 pounds (10 × 600 pounds per batch). The analysis shown below indicates that the firm should still process Alpha beyond split-off.

	Decision on Alpha	
	Sell at Split-Off	Process Further
Sales: 10 × $1,200 per batch	$12,000	
10 × $3,600 per batch		$ 36,000
Incremental costs:		
Variable (10 × $900 per batch)		(9,000)
Fixed and avoidable		(10,000)
Incremental profit	$12,000	$ 17,000

The $24,000 additional revenue from processing further ($36,000 − $12,000) is greater than the additional costs of further processing ($19,000). There is a $5,000 difference in profit in favor of a decision to process Alpha beyond the split-off point. Another way to look at the decision is to say that the opportunity cost of processing further is the $12,000 given up by not selling at split-off. Including the opportunity cost among the other costs of the decision to process further gives total costs of $31,000 ($9,000 + $10,000 + $12,000). Subtracting $31,000 from $36,000 revenue also gives the $5,000 advantage.

One final word of caution. Segment reports commonly allocate the costs of a joint process among the various joint products. Such allocated costs are, as stated earlier, irrelevant to decision making on the individual segments and should accordingly be ignored in analyses of the joint products.

The joint products case exemplifies a critical point made earlier: the relevance or irrelevance of a cost depends on the specific decision at hand. The variable costs of the joint process are relevant in deciding whether to operate that process at all. But they are irrelevant in deciding whether to sell a given joint product at the split-off point or to process it further. Thus, a cost can be relevant for one decision, irrelevant for others. Therefore, the managerial accountant must understand just what decisions managers are trying to make when they call for information. The accountant cannot respond to the question "What does it cost?" without knowing why the manager wants the answer to that question.

Special Orders

Manufacturing companies often make products to be sold under their own brand names, as well as nearly identical products that are sold at lower prices under the brand names of chain stores (called *house brands*). The manufacturer normally sells to chains at lower prices than to dealers who sell the products under the manufacturer's brand name. Manufacturers also sometimes accept special, one-time orders at lower prices than usual.

The planned income statement on page 170 is for Griffith Company. Griffith has just been approached by a chain store that wants to buy 20,000 units at $10 each. Griffith could hire enough workers to produce a total of 100,000 units. The variable portion of selling, general, and administrative expenses is $12,000 for sales commissions, but commissions would not have to be paid on the 20,000-unit special order. The president is hesitant to accept the order, even though sufficient capacity is available. He sees that average manufacturing costs are $13 per unit ($780,000/60,000) and that the $10 per-unit price is below this average cost.

Avg. cost doesn't matter

Griffith Company, Planned Income Statement		
	Per Unit	Total
Sales (60,000 units)	$15	$900,000
Manufacturing costs:		
Materials	4	$240,000
Direct labor	3	180,000
Overhead (one-third variable)	6	360,000
Total	13	780,000
Gross margin		120,000
Selling, general, and administrative expenses		80,000
Operating income		$ 40,000

As always, only the differential elements should be considered in making a decision.

	Per Unit	Total	
Differential revenues (20,000 units)	$10		$200,000
Differential costs:			
Materials	4	$80,000	
Direct labor	3	60,000	
Variable overhead	2	40,000	180,000
Profit			$ 20,000

Accepting the special order increases income by $20,000; therefore, Griffith should accept it.

In this example, the only differential costs were variable manufacturing costs. In another situation there could be variable selling, general, and administrative expenses on the special order, and those variable costs should be included in the analysis. Where the special order requires a large increase in production, additional fixed costs might be incurred. Those costs, too, should be incorporated in the analysis.

Special orders, either one-shot or continuing (like the house-brand arrangement mentioned above), require careful study. Of major importance is the potential effect of the special order on sales at regular prices. For instance, an appliance manufacturer agreeing to supply a discount chain with 100,000 washing machines might find that its sales to regular dealers fall because some customers buy from the discount chain instead of from regular dealers. Or, a firm accepting a special order might find that its sales at regular prices could have been higher than originally thought, but that it cannot fill these more profitable orders because the special order has brought it to full use of its manufacturing capacity. In either case, the potential for lost sales should be incorporated into the analysis of the special order. We can illustrate the problem of lost sales, and a basic approach for dealing with it, by continuing the example of Griffith Company.

Suppose that because of a shortage of labor Griffith can produce only 75,000 units, rather than the 100,000 units stated earlier. If Griffith accepts the special order, it will not be able to fill orders for 5,000 units at the regular price (capacity of 75,000 − 20,000 units on the special order leaves capacity for 55,000 units at the regular price, 5,000 units less than the 60,000 expected). We could prepare a new income statement reflecting these facts, or we could simply calculate the lost contribution margin from the 5,000 units and compare it with the $20,000 profit expected on the special order. The more direct, differential analysis is shown below.

Profit from special order (previously calculated)		$20,000
Lost contribution margin on regular sales:		
Selling price	$ 15.00	
Variable manufacturing cost ($4 + $3 + $2)	(9.00)	
Commissions ($12,000/60,000)	(0.20)	
Unit contribution margin on regular sales	$ 5.80	
Lost sales volume, in units	5,000	
Lost contribution margin		29,000
Net loss from accepting special order		($ 9,000)

Under the revised conditions, the special order is not profitable.

If there were no capacity constraint, but the managers of Griffith believed the firm would lose *some* sales at the regular price through customers buying from the chain, they could at least determine the sales that the firm could lose before the special order became unprofitable. The special order generates $20,000 incremental profit considered in isolation. At a $5.80 unit contribution margin for normal sales, Griffith could lose sales of up to 3,448 units ($20,000/$5.80) at the regular price before accepting the order would hurt overall profits. The question then becomes whether the managers believe that actual lost sales are likely to approach this critical number. Such an estimate is often very difficult because it involves predicting the responses of customers.

Because managers view special-order decisions as short term, they focus on variable costs when quoting a price. Many managers do understand, however, that these decisions can have long-term consequences. For example, a company might accept so much private branding that it must acquire additional manufacturing capacity to meet the continuing growth of its regular sales. Another long-term effect of accepting special orders has to do with the company's prospects for survival, because it cannot continue indefinitely without covering *all* of its costs. Hence, when quoting prices for special orders, managers must consider their cost structures. A firm with relatively high variable costs and relatively low fixed costs is able to quote a price closer to variable cost than can a firm with the opposite cost structure. Such structural differences are likely to exist between a traditional manufacturer (higher variable costs) and one that has adopted the techniques of just-in-time operations (higher fixed costs).

Even when managers know that the difference between the price and the variable costs of a special order should depend on the firm's cost structure, they must still decide what contribution margin is adequate. For a firm in which variable costs predominate, the contribution from a special order must be sufficient to allow for errors in computing or forecasting variable costs. (A 3% underestimate in a $49 variable cost for an order with a $50 price would change the contribution margin from positive to negative.) Where fixed costs predominate, the managers' determination of an adequate contribution margin must consider all special orders rather than a single order, lest the contribution from all orders and regular business still be insufficient to cover fixed costs. Unfortunately, there are no rules for determining an adequate contribution margin for a single special-order opportunity.

Factors in Limited Supply

In the special-order example, Griffith's production was limited to 75,000 units because of a shortage of labor. A shortage of some other factor, such as space, machine time, or some critical material might also restrict operations. The term *constraint* is often used to describe a shortage of an input factor.

A firm with two or more products faces the additional problem of deciding how to use the limited quantity of the constraining factor. Consider Neal Company, which makes a desk tray and a box for computer diskettes. Neal can sell all it can make of either product. Both products require processing on a machine that can operate only 100 hours per week. Data relating to these two products appear below.

	Desk Tray	Diskette Box
Selling price	$10	$ 6
Variable cost	6	4
Contribution margin	$ 4	$ 2
Number of units that can be made per machine-hour	60	150

Looking only at contribution margin, Neal's managers will conclude that it should make trays, each of which brings twice the contribution margin of a diskette box. However, Neal can make (and sell) more boxes than trays. If the managers are to make the best possible use of the available machine time, they must consider both the difference in contribution margin and the difference in the production demands on the scarce input factor, machine time. Two approaches are available to combine these differences. The first approach compares total contribution margin from the products over some specific period, such as a week (100 machine hours available).

	Desk Tray	Diskette Box
Maximum weekly production		
(60 × 100)	6,000	
(150 × 100)		15,000
Contribution margin per unit	$ 4	$ 2
Total weekly contribution margin	$24,000	$30,000

The analysis shows that producing boxes is the more profitable use of the machine time. (You should see that the same answer follows whether the period used for the analysis is an hour, a day, a week, or a month.)

The second approach also shows differences in contribution margin but concentrates on a unit of the scarce input. That is, the second approach determines the *contribution margin per unit of the scarce factor*. In Neal's case, the scarce factor is machine time, so the analysis, shown below, compares contribution per machine hour.

	Desk Tray	Diskette Box
Number of units that can be made per machine-hour	60	150
Contribution margin per unit	$ 4	$ 2
Contribution margin per hour	$240	$300

The second analysis, like the first, shows that it is more profitable to produce boxes; boxes contribute more than trays, *per hour of machine time used*. Using a term introduced in this chapter, we can say that the opportunity cost of using an hour of machine time making trays is the $300 you give up by not using that hour to make boxes. (If the machine time could be used to make some third product, say a drawer organizer, the opportunity cost of choosing to make that product is $300, the benefit gained from the best available alternative use of the limited resource.)

Information derived from the preceding analyses can be useful for decisions about product pricing as well as about the use of available facilities. For example, suppose Neal is considering raising the price of its desk tray. You already know that producing diskette boxes is the more profitable use of the available machine time. What price must Neal charge for the desk tray to make using machine time for it as profitable as using the time to make boxes? The contribution margins per machine-hour have to be equal, which means that the margin for making trays has to be $300 per hour. Since Neal can make 60 trays per hour, the contribution per tray has to be $5 ($300/60). From Chapter 2 we know that adding the $5 desired margin to the $6 variable cost per tray gives a required selling price of $11 per tray. At that price, devoting machine time to making trays yields the same contribution margin as spending the time making boxes.

At the start of the example we stated that Neal could sell all that it could produce of either product. Even if that were not so, the preceding analyses are important in deciding how to use the limited supply of machine hours. Suppose that Neal could sell only 9,000 boxes per week (though it could make 15,000). The previous analyses show that Neal should make as many boxes as it can sell and devote the remaining hours of machine time to making trays. Thus, Neal should spend 60 hours of machine time making boxes (9,000 boxes/150 boxes per hour) and use the remaining 40 hours (100 − 60) making trays.

The importance of understanding cost and contribution margin data when evaluating the effects of constraints, was recently illustrated in an article in *Management Accounting*.[1] A plant of the very successful Latex Division of GenCorp Polymer Products faced a problem in analyzing product profitability because it had reached capacity and was unable to supply the demand for all of its products. The constraining factor was the capacity of reactors, vessels in which the ingredients for each product are cooked. Any product can be made in any reactor, but the reactors differ in size, and the time required to process a product depends on the size of the reactor. Hence, a product's contribution margin per unit of processing time, and any ranking of product profitability based on such a contribution, would only apply to reactors of a particular size. The managers wanted to choose products independent of the reactor size, so they selected a single size reactor and stated the processing time for each product in *relative* terms (calling the result "product standard processing time"). These standardized times were incorporated into a measure called the Product Profit Velocity (PPV), which was used to analyze product profitability. The measure is calculated below (materials and freight-out are the only variable costs).

$$\text{PPV} = \frac{\text{Revenue per}}{\text{Reactor run}} - \frac{\text{Materials and}}{\text{Freight-out}} = \frac{\text{Contribution}}{\text{Margin}} \Big/ \frac{\text{Product standard}}{\text{processing time}}$$

The products were then ranked, and the lower-ranked products were cut back when capacity was reached. Because of concerns about customer ill-will, the plant manager chose to increase prices rather than drop lower-ranking products. The rankings were also used to highlight products to study for ways to reduce costs (for example, by changing the material mix).

This section suggests analytical approaches for making decisions when the firm faces a single constraint. Chapter 16 extends the analysis to situations where there are two or more constraints.

A Word of Caution

The approaches that we have presented have many things in common, including the need for the manager to understand VCP relationships and the concepts of

[1] Gary B. Frank, Steven A. Fisher, and Allen R. Wilkie, "Linking Cost to Price and Profit," *Management Accounting* (June 1989), 22–26.

common/joint and avoidable/unavoidable costs. But perhaps the most important commonality is that each approach requires the manager, and hence the managerial accountant, to use estimates. There are estimates of future sales volumes, future costs, future cost savings, lost sales, and so on.

Estimates about the future are not certainties. Managers often say that the only thing they can be certain about is the uncertainty of the future and of the information used in decision making. We discuss some formal methods of dealing with uncertainty in Chapter 16, and the typical collegiate program of study presents those and other methods in courses in statistics and management science. At this point in your study of decision making and the use of accounting information, you should recognize the extent to which estimates, and the associated uncertainties, influence the decision-making process.

DECISION MAKING UNDER ENVIRONMENTAL CONSTRAINTS

The United States has laws that managers must be aware of when deciding among various courses of action. Antitrust laws forbid actions that might substantially reduce competition. Environmental protection laws restrict actions that could harm wildlife or increase pollution. At various times controls on wages and prices have restricted price increases. We shall limit our discussion to the major law dealing with pricing practices.

The Robinson-Patman Act forbids charging different prices to different customers *unless* there are intrinsic cost differences in serving the different customers; in other words, this act forbids discriminatory pricing. The Federal Trade Commission is the regulatory agency responsible for enforcing the act. The passing of the act was partially stimulated by the practice of selling to large customers (say, grocery chains) at lower prices than to corner grocery stores, enabling the large chains to charge their customers lower prices and endangering the existence of smaller firms. The act does not, of course, forbid charging different prices for different goods. Thus, to ensure compliance with the law, manufacturers who sell private brands usually modify the items offered for private branding.

As a general rule, the law does not accept differences in manufacturing costs as justification for differences in prices for the same product. For example, the Federal Trade Commission (FTC) will not permit a firm to justify lower prices to some customers on the grounds that the incremental cost of production is less than the average cost, including fixed costs. The FTC's position is that, because fixed costs relate to all products, the manufacturing cost of all units of the same product is the same. However, differences in distribution costs can be used to justify price differences. In the special order discussed on page 170, there were no sales commissions. This could be used as a defense against a suit for discrimination. In another situation, a company might justify price differences by showing that larger orders require fewer deliveries, and hence lower delivery costs. If a suit alleging price discrimination is filed, the managerial accountant will usually help prepare evidence for the defense.

SUMMARY

Managerial accountants supply information for short-term decision making. The essential quantitative factors influencing such decisions are differential revenues and costs, including opportunity costs. Costs and revenues that will be the same whatever action is taken can be ignored. Historical costs are sunk, and are irrelevant for current decisions because they cannot be changed by some current action. Avoidable fixed costs are relevant. Whether a cost is relevant to a particular decision does not always depend on whether the cost is variable or fixed.

Typical examples of short-term decisions are whether to drop a product or product line; whether to produce a component internally or purchase it from an outside supplier; whether to further process joint products; whether to accept a special order; and how best to use the limited supply of some critical input factor.

As a general rule, the action that is expected to result in the highest income for the firm should be pursued. This decision rule considers only the quantifiable factors in a given situation. In most decisions, there will be some factors that can have monetary effects but for which no reliable estimates can be made. Still other factors, such as a company policy prohibiting certain types of products, may not lend themselves to quantification at all. These qualitative factors should not be ignored.

KEY TERMS

allocated cost	joint products
complementary effects	loss leader
differential revenue and cost	opportunity cost
incremental revenue and cost	split-off point
joint (common) cost	sunk cost
joint process	

REVIEW PROBLEM

Andrews Company makes three products. Below are revenue and cost data for a typical month.

| | Product | | | |
	X	Y	Z	Total
Sales	$300	$500	$800	$1,600
Variable costs	100	200	400	700
Contribution margin	200	300	400	900
Fixed costs:				
Avoidable	80	100	120	300
Common, allocated on sales dollar basis	60	100	160	320
Total fixed costs	140	200	280	620
Profit	$ 60	$100	$120	$ 280

Required: Answer each of the following questions independently.

1. If product X were dropped, what will total profit be?

2. Andrews is considering a new product P, to take the place of X. Product P will sell for $7 per unit, have variable costs of $5 per unit, and have avoidable fixed costs of $130. How many units of P would have to be sold to maintain the existing income of $280?

3. The firm charges $10 per unit for product Z. One customer has offered to buy 40 units of Z per month at $8 per unit. Fixed costs in total and variable costs per unit would not be affected by the sale. Andrews has the capacity to produce 110 units of Z per month. If Andrews accepts the offer, what will its total monthly income be?

4. Closer analysis reveals that X, Y, and Z are joint products of a single raw material and are all now being processed beyond the split-off point. The cost of the joint process, including raw material, is the $320 joint allocated fixed cost. All other costs are incurred to process the three products beyond the split-off point. If the sales values of X, Y, and Z are $110, $220, and $230, respectively, at split-off, could Andrews increase its profits by selling one or more products at split-off? If so, which product or products should be sold at split-off and what will the increase in total profit be?

5. Unit sales of X and Z are 100 and 200, respectively. Both products are made on a single machine that has a limited capacity. The machine can make five units of X per hour, or eight units of Z.

   (a) Assuming that all units made of either product can be sold, should Andrews continue to make both products? If not, which product should it make?

   (b) Assuming that the machine is being operated at its capacity of 45 hours per month, what will happen to monthly profits if the firm makes only the more profitable product as determined in part (a)? Give the dollar increase in profits. (*Hint:* Remember that if only one product is made, the firm will save the avoidable fixed costs on the product that it drops.)

Answer to Review Problem

1. $160. Andrews would lose the contribution margin from the sale of X but would save the $80 avoidable fixed costs. Net reduction in profit is $120 ($200 − $80), which should be subtracted from current profit of $280 to arrive at $160. The $120 drop is the incremental profit on X.

2. 125 units. To achieve the same profit, the new product must provide the same incremental profit that is lost by discontinuing the sale of X. Incremental profit from X is $120 (see item 1). The sale of P must provide contribution margin sufficient to cover both the new avoidable fixed costs and the $120 profit. Since the new fixed costs are $130, the contribution margin needed is $250 ($130 fixed costs plus the desired profit). P carries a contribution margin of $2 per unit ($7 − $5), so a total of 125 units ($250/$2) have to be sold.

3. $350. It is important to see that if this special order is accepted, the company will have to curtail its regular sales at the regular price. Capacity is 110 units and planned sales are 80 units ($800/$10 selling price). If 40 units are sold to the new customer, regular sales will be cut by 10 units. The analysis might proceed as follows.

Gain from contribution margin on special order ($8 − $5ª) × 40 units	$120
Lost contribution margin because of loss of sales of 10 units at regular price	
($10 − $5ª) × 10 units	50
Gain on special order	70
Planned profit	280
New monthly income	$350

ª Variable cost per unit ($400/80 units = $5 per unit).

4. The firm could increase its profits by $20 per month by selling product Y at split-off, as shown by the following analysis.

	X	Y	Z
Sales with further processing	$300	$500	$800
Additional processing costs:			
Variable costs	100	200	400
Avoidable fixed costs	80	100	120
Total additional processing costs	180	300	520
Profit if further processed	120	200	280
Split-off values	110	220	230
Advantage (disadvantage) of further processing	$ 10	($ 20)	$ 50

5. (a) The company should concentrate on product Z rather than product X. This can be shown even without knowing the number of hours available; the contribution margin per hour of machine time spent on product Z is the higher.

	X	Z
Contribution margin per unit	$2 ($200/100)	$2 ($400/200)
Units that can be made in 1 hour	5	8
Contribution margin per hour	$10	$16

As long as the company can sell all the units it makes of either product, total contribution margin will be greater by making only product Z.

(b) Profit will increase by $200. The analysis involves both contribution margin and incremental profit. If the firm used its capacity of 45 hours to produce only Z, it could make 360 units of Z (45 × 8), which would bring total contribution margin of $720 (360 × $2 per unit). This is an increase of $320 ($720 − $400 contribution margin already anticipated). However, Andrews loses the current *incremental profit* from product X, which is $120 (see item 1). Thus, if the firm concentrated on product Z it would gain $200 ($320 additional contribution margin from Z − $120 incremental profit lost from not producing X).

ASSIGNMENT MATERIAL

Questions for Discussion

5-1 **"Where do you start?"** One of your classmates, who believes that he thoroughly understands the principle of incremental costs, placed the following advertisement in the school paper.

Wanted—Ride to Linville

I will pay all of the extra costs involved in taking me to Linville. Call Bob at 555-6202.

Linville is 1,200 miles from the university. Did your classmate make a mistake in wording the advertisement the way he did?

5-2   *Cost analysis*   While standing in line to use a telephone, you hear the following part of a conversation. "No dear, I'm going to play golf today." (Pause) "Look, sweetie, I know it costs $6 for a caddy and $3 for drinks after the round, but it really does get cheaper the more I play. Look, the club dues are $1,000 per year, so if I play 50 times it costs, ah, let's see, $29 per round. But if I play 100 times it only costs, um, just a second, yeah, about $19 per round." (Pause) "I knew you'd understand, see you at dinner, bye." How did the golfer figure the cost per round? Comment on her analysis.

5-3   *The generous management*   Several years ago, a leading newspaper ran an advertisement for itself. The advertisement stated that the paper, which cost the customer $0.40, cost the publisher $0.53 for paper, $0.09 for printers' labor, $0.05 for ink, $0.15 for salaries of editorial employees (reporters, editors, etc.), and $0.18 for other operating expenses such as executives' salaries, rent, depreciation, and taxes. Thus, the opportunity to buy a paper for $0.40 that had a cost of $1.00 was presented as a great bargain. Is the buyer actually paying less than cost? What assumptions did you make to arrive at your answer? How can the management be so generous to its readers?

5-4   *Pricing policy*   At Washington National Airport you enter the departure area of an airline just before a flight to Los Angeles is to take off. The plane is about 80% full, and the regular fare for the flight is $300. You have neither a ticket nor a reservation for the flight, but you offer to pay $50 to take the flight. Assume there are no variable costs associated with the number of passengers. Do you think the airline would accept your offer? Explain.

5-5   *Unit costs*   The B-2, or Stealth bomber, was much in the news in 1989, partly because of its cost. The consensus seemed to be that buying 132 of the aircraft would cost $70 billion, or about $530 million per plane. At that time the total cost already incurred for development and a couple of prototypes was about $23 billion, which is included in the $70 billion total cost. Opponents of the program argued that we could not afford to spend $530 million for each aircraft, while proponents said that the amount already spent was wasted unless we did produce the bomber.

Required: Would it have cost $530 million per plane to continue the program? If not, what is your estimate of the future per-plane cost if 132 are built? Assume that the $70 billion figure holds.

Exercises

5-6   *Special order*   Watt, Inc. manufactures lamps and expects to sell 350,000 units in 19X0 at a price of $21 per unit. Planned per-unit manufacturing costs at that level of production are as follows.

Variable manufacturing costs	$9
Fixed manufacturing costs	$5

Early in 19X0, a new customer approaches Watt offering to buy 28,000 lamps at $11 each. Watt can produce additional units with no change in fixed manufacturing cost or per-unit variable cost. The only additional fixed cost for this order is for packing and shipping, estimated at $2,200.

Required: Determine the effect of accepting the special order on planned profit for the year. Assume that filling the special order will not affect regular sales.

5-7 Joint products   Rox Company produces two families of chemicals, orides and octines. The production phase of each chemical group begins with a joint process. Below are production, sales and cost data for the products that result from each 100-gallon batch of materials going through the joint process that produces orides.

	Boride	Doride	Foride
Gallons produced	40	50	10
Selling price per gallon at the split-off point	$ 6	$ 5	$ 0
Selling price per gallon after further processing	$10	$ 9	$ 4
Per-gallon variable cost of further processing	$ 5	$ 2	$ 3

Required: Determine which of the joint products should be sold at the split-off point and which should be processed further.

5-8 Joint products (extension of 5-7)   Rox normally processes 120,000 gallons of oride mixture per month. You have determined that, in addition to the variable costs of the additional processing of boride, doride, and foride, there are monthly fixed costs associated with such added processing, as listed below.

	Boride	Doride	Foride
Avoidable fixed costs of additional processing	$40,000	$55,000	$20,000
Unavoidable fixed costs of additional processing, allocated	$25,000	$60,000	$ 4,000

Required
1. Does the information about the fixed costs of additional processing of the joint products change your answer as to whether any of those products should be processed after the split-off point?
2. Assume that Rox takes the most profitable course of action with respect to each of the joint oride products. Ignoring the costs of the joint process, what will be the total monthly profit from orides?

5-9 Product selection – capacity constraint   Winston Company makes three products, all of which require the use of a special machine. Only 200 hours of machine time are available per month. Data for the three products are as follows.

	Gadgets	Supergadgets	Colossalgadgets
Selling price	$12	$16	$20
Variable cost	8	10	11
Contribution margin	$ 4	$ 6	$ 9
Machine time required in minutes	4	10	12

Winston can sell as much of any product as it can produce.

Required
1. If all products required the same amount of machine time, which product should be made?
2. Given the capacity constraint, determine which product should be made and the total monthly contribution margin that would be earned if only that product were made.
3. How much would the selling price of the next most profitable (per machine-hour) product have to rise to be as profitable, per machine-hour, as the product that you selected in item 2?

5-10 Dropping a segment Colbert Company expects the following results for the coming year.

	Hats	Belts	Jeans	Total
Sales	$100,000	$150,000	$470,000	$720,000
Variable costs	$ 52,000	$ 50,000	$190,000	$292,000
Fixed costs	80,000	50,000	240,000	370,000
Total costs	132,000	100,000	430,000	662,000
Profit (loss)	($ 32,000)	$ 50,000	$ 40,000	$ 58,000

Required: Answer each of the following questions independently.
1. Suppose that all fixed costs are allocated based on the floor space each segment occupies and are all unavoidable. What will total profit be if Colbert drops the hat segment?
2. Suppose that $55,000 of the fixed costs shown for the hat segment are avoidable. What will the firm's total profit be if Colbert drops the hat segment?
3. Suppose that Colbert could avoid $55,000 in fixed costs by dropping the hat segment (as in item 2). However, the managers believe that if they do drop hats, sales of each of the other lines will fall by 5%. What will profit be if Colbert drops hats and loses 5% of the sales of each of the other segments?

5-11 Make or buy GFA Company is introducing a new product. The managers are trying to decide whether to make one of its components, part #A-3, or to buy it from an outside supplier. Making the part internally requires using some available machinery that has no other use and no resale value. The space that would be used to make the part also has no alternative use.

The outside supplier will sell the part for $5 per unit. An estimate of costs to make the part appears below.

	Cost to Make Part #A-3
Materials	$1.50
Direct labor	2.00
Variable manufacturing overhead	.50
Fixed manufacturing overhead	2.50
Total cost	$6.50

The above estimate reflects anticipated volume of 10,000 units of the part. The fixed manufacturing overhead consists of depreciation on the machinery and a share of the costs of the factory (heat, light, building depreciation, etc.) based on the floor space that manufacturing the part would occupy.

Required: Determine whether GFA should make or buy part #A-3.

5-12 **Special order** Devio Company produces high-quality golf balls. A chain of sporting goods stores would like to buy 25,000 dozen balls at $15 per dozen. The chain would sell the balls for $20, which is $5 less than usually charged by dealers who stock the balls. The chain would obliterate the Devio name so that customers would not be able to tell who had made the balls.

Devio can produce 200,000 dozen balls per year. Planned results for the coming year, without considering the order from the chain, are given below.

Sales (150,000 dozen at $18 per dozen)	$2,700,000
Cost of goods sold	1,110,000
Gross profit	1,590,000
Selling and administrative expenses, all fixed	600,000
Income	$ 990,000

Cost of goods sold contains variable costs of $7 per dozen balls. The rest of the cost is fixed.

Required
1. Determine whether Devio should accept the order.
2. Might your answer to item 1 change if the Devio name were to appear on the balls sold in the chain stores?

5-13 **Short-term decisions** Nickolai Company expects the following results in 19X5.

	Product A	Product B	Total
Sales	$500	$300	$800
Variable costs	200	150	350
Contribution margin	300	150	450
Fixed costs	150	90	240
Profit	$150	$ 60	$210

Fixed costs, all unavoidable, are allocated based on relative sales dollars.

Required: Answer each question independently, unless otherwise told.
1. The managers are considering increasing advertising for product B by $18. They expect to achieve a 30% increase in volume for product B with no change in selling price, but some of that increase will be at the expense of product A. Sales of A are expected to decline by 5%. What will the firm's total profit be if it takes the action?
2. What is the maximum percentage decline in volume of product A that would leave the action in item 1 just barely desirable?
3. The firm is considering dropping product B and replacing it with product C. Introducing product C would increase total fixed costs by $24. Its contribution margin percentage is 40%. What dollar sales of product C are needed to maintain the original profit of $210?

5-14 Analyzing data for decisions   The expected results for the coming year for Porter Company, which manufactures two lines of products, appear below, in thousands of dollars.

	Kitchenwares	Officewares	Total
Sales	$3,300	$2,700	$6,000
Variable costs	1,650	810	2,460
Contribution margin	1,650	1,890	3,540
Avoidable fixed costs	650	1,300	1,950
Incremental profit	$1,000	$ 590	1,590
Common, unavoidable fixed costs			900
Profit			$ 690

Required: Suppose that Porter uses the same production facilities for both products. Demand is such that the firm could sell $500,000 more of either product line but it would have to reduce output and sales of the other line by the same amount. Which line should the firm make more of and what is the effect on total profit?

5-15 Changing product lines (extension of 5-14)   Referring to the data in 5-14, suppose Porter could introduce a new line that is much more profitable than either of the existing ones. To introduce the new line, however, Porter must drop one of the existing lines entirely. The other line—the one not dropped—will continue as originally planned. Which line should Porter drop?

5-16 Joint products   TAB Company produces four joint products at a joint cost of $80,000. All products are currently processed beyond the split-off point, and the final products are sold as follows.

Products	Sales	Additional Processing Costs
M	$260,000	$170,000
N	110,000	80,000
O	45,000	40,000
P	30,000	25,000

The firm could sell the products at the split-off point for the following amounts: M, $80,000; N, $50,000; O, $15,000; and P, zero.

Required
1. Determine which products the firm should sell at the split-off point.
2. Determine what TAB's profit would be if it took the most profitable action with respect to each of its products.

5-17 Dropping a product – complementary effects Kaiser Face Care Company makes three products in the same factory. Revenue and cost data for a typical month are given below, in thousands.

		Product		
	Razors	After-Shave	Shaving Cream	Total
Sales	$400	$600	$400	$1,400
Variable costs	300	240	120	660
Contribution margin	100	360	280	740
Fixed costs				
Avoidable	120	150	70	340
Unavoidable, allocated on basis of relative sales dollars	80	120	80	280
Total fixed costs	200	270	150	620
Income (loss)	($100)	$ 90	$130	$ 120

Required
1. Determine total income if razors were dropped from the product line.
2. Suppose that if razors were dropped, the sales of after-shave would decline by 20% and those of shaving cream by 10%. Determine income for the firm if razors were dropped.

5-18 Inventory values James Company has 300 pounds of a chemical compound called bysol, bought at $3.20 per pound several months ago. Bysol now costs $3.80 per pound. The firm could sell it for $3.50 per pound (shipping costs account for the $0.30 difference between the cost to buy and the selling price).

Required: Answer each of the following questions independently.
1. Suppose the firm has stopped making the product for which it used bysol and will sell it or use it to make a special order. The special order has a price of $2,000. Incremental costs, excluding the bysol, are $900. What is the relevant cost of using the bysol in the special order? Should the firm accept the order?
2. Suppose the firm has alternative uses for bysol so that if it accepts the special order it will have to buy more for its regular production. What is the relevant cost of using the bysol in the special order? Should the firm accept the order?

5-19 Make or buy (AICPA adapted) MTZ Company manufactures 10,000 units of part Z-101 annually, using the part in one of its products. The controller has collected the following data related to the part.

Materials	$ 20,000
Direct labor	55,000
Variable overhead	45,000
Fixed overhead	70,000
Total costs	$190,000

Vortan Company has offered to supply the part for $18 per unit. If MTZ accepts the offer, it will be able to rent some of the facilities it devotes to making the part to another firm for $15,000 annually and will also be able to reduce its fixed overhead costs by $40,000.

Required
1. Should MTZ accept the offer based on the available information?
2. What is the maximum price that MTZ is willing to pay for the part—the price that would give it the same income it would have if it continued making it?
3. Assuming the $18 price from Vortan, at what annual unit volume will MTZ earn the same income making the part as it would buying it?

5-20 *Joint products* Grevel Company slaughters cattle, processing the meat, hides, and bones. The hides are tanned and sold to leather manufacturers. The bones are made into buttons and other sundries. In a typical month, about 3,000 cattle are processed. An income statement for such a month follows, in thousands of dollars.

	Totals	Meat	Hides	Bones
Sales	$500	$300	$120	$80
Cost of cattle[a]	300	180	72	48
Gross profit	200	120	48	32
Additional processing costs, avoidable	80[b]	40[b]	20[b]	20[b]
Allocated costs[c]	60[b]	30[b]	15[b]	15[b]
Income (loss)	$ 60	$ 50	$ 13	($ 3)

[a] Allocated on the basis of relative sales value (60% of sales).
[b] Deduction.
[c] Allocated on the basis of additional processing costs, all unavoidable.

Required
1. Is the firm losing money by processing the bones into buttons and sundry items?
2. A tanner has offered to buy the hides as they come off the cattle for $7 each. He contends that income from hides would be $21,000 if hides were sold directly to him (3,000 hides × $7). Should his offer be accepted?
3. If the bones could be sold without further processing, how much would have to be received per month to keep total profits the same as they are now?

5-21 *Opportunity cost pricing* Boyett Company makes three products. Data are as follows.

	Product		
	Wallet	Belt	Hat
Current selling price	$10	$15	$25
Variable cost	3	6	10
Contribution margin	$ 7	$ 9	$15
Machine time required, in minutes	15	10	20

Boyett has 40,000 minutes of machine time available per week. It can sell all of any of the three products that it can make.

Required
1. Determine which product the firm should make.
2. Determine the selling prices that the firm would have to charge for each of the other two products to make them equally profitable per minute of machine time as the one you selected in item 1.

5-22 **Comprehensive review of short-term decisions** The data below relate to the planned operations of Kimble Company before considering the changes described later.

	Product		
	Chair	Table	Sofa
Selling price	$ 120	$ 400	$ 600
Variable costs	40	160	360
Fixed costs	30	120	180
Total costs	70	280	540
Profit per unit	$ 50	$ 120	$ 60
Annual volume	8,000	3,000	4,000

All fixed costs are direct, but unavoidable.

Required: Answer each of the following items independently of the others unless otherwise instructed.
1. What is total profit expected to be?
2. What will happen to profit if the company drops sofas?
3. What will happen to profit if the company drops chairs, but is able to shift the facilities to making more sofas so that volume of sofas increases to 7,000 units? (Total fixed costs remain constant.)
4. Variable cost per sofa includes $60 for parts that the company now buys outside. The company could make the parts at a variable cost of $45. It would also have to increase fixed costs by $35,000 annually. What would happen to profit if the company took the proposed action?
5. The company has received a special order for 1,000 tables at $250. There is sufficient capacity to make the units, and sales at the regular price would not be affected. What will happen to profit if the firm accepts the order?

6. Repeat item 5 assuming now that the order is for 1,500 tables and that capacity is limited to 4,000 tables.

5-23 **Using per-unit data**   The managers of Ferrara Company expect the following per-unit results at a volume of 200,000 units.

Sales		$10
Variable costs	$6	
Fixed costs	3	9
Profit		$ 1

Required: Answer each of the following parts independently of the others.

1. The company has the opportunity to sell 20,000 units to a chain store for $8 each. The managers expect that sales at the regular price will drop by about 8,000 units as some customers will buy from the chain store instead of from the regular outlets. What will happen to the company's profit if it accepts the order?

2. Of the total unit variable cost of $6, $2.80 is for a part that the company now buys from an outside supplier. The company could make the part for $2.25 variable cost plus $100,000 per year fixed costs for renting additional machinery. What will happen to annual profit if it makes the part?

3. The company is considering a new model to replace the existing product. The new model has a $6 unit variable cost and the same total fixed costs as the existing product. The new model has expected sales of 100,000 units per year. At what selling price per unit will the new model give the same total profit as the existing one?

Problems

5-24 **Product pricing – off-peak hours**   Marie Angelo, owner of Gino's Pizzeria, is considering a luncheon special to increase business during the slow time from 11:00 A.M. to 1:00 P.M. on weekdays. For $2.20 on any weekday, she will give a customer all the pizza he or she can eat. Marie has prepared the following data for weekly business during those hours.

	Pizza	Beverages	Total
Sales (average pizza price, $2.80)	$420	$84	$504
Variable costs	120	24	144
Contribution margin	$300	$60	360
Avoidable fixed costs—wages of students hired			180
Current incremental profit, lunch period			$180

She estimates that at the special price she will serve about 300 pizzas per week to about 250 customers. (Some customers will eat more than one pizza, given the lower price.) She also anticipates that variable costs per unit will be about 20%

higher because people will want more toppings than they now order. Beverage sales will bear the same relationship to the number of customers that they do now when each customer eats one pizza. The increase in the number of customers will entail an increase in personnel during the hours of the special, increasing wage cost by 15%.

Required: Evaluate the monetary effects of the proposed luncheon special.

5-25 **Just-in-time, costs of activities**   Racine Machinery recently began to change one of its plants to a just-in-time operation. So far, it has set up one manufacturing cell to make a product that had formerly been made in large batches. The following analysis of April operations for the cell was disappointing to the controller who had expected dramatic improvements with JIT.

Operations for April	
Units Produced	20,000
Costs:	
Materials	$ 55,000
Labor	67,000
Overhead	35,000
Total	$157,000
Per-unit	$7.85

The overhead cost shown is mostly allocated costs. Roughly $9,000 is incremental, avoidable cost. The per-unit cost to manufacture the product under the old system follows.

Materials	$2.90
Labor	2.80
Overhead	1.80
Total	$7.50

Overhead is based on 22,000 units and is 40% variable, 60% fixed at that level. Under the old system, quality control was weak so that the company had to produce about 22,000 units to obtain 20,000 good units. With the JIT cell, workers do their own inspection during production, and only 20,000 total units are produced to obtain 20,000 good units.

Under the old system, manufacturing the product required the following people in addition to direct laborers. The costs given include fringe benefits such as health insurance.

Two inspectors, each earning $2,000 per month
One production scheduler earning $2,500 per month
Two maintenance people each earning $1,800 per month

Since Racine set up the cell, it reassigned the people described above. It also reassigned other support personnel who had worked on the product. The other support people earned about $11,000 per month, including fringes.

Required: Determine the incremental cost to produce 20,000 good units in a month under the old method and using the JIT cell.

5-26 ***Car pool*** You and your neighbor carpool to work, driving on alternate days. A colleague at work has injured his hand and will not be able to drive for the next three months. He inquires about riding with you and your neighbor. He could ride a bus for $2 per day and offers to pay you a "fair price."

From your house it is a 10-mile round trip to work. If you pick up your injured colleague, the round trip is 14 miles. Last year, your car cost you the following for 15,000 miles. (Your neighbor's car cost the same for the same number of miles.)

Gasoline and oil	$1,350
Maintenance	450
New tires (life of 30,000 miles)	300
Insurance and registration	600
Decline in market value	3,000
Total	$5,700

Required
1. Quote a daily price to your colleague that seems fair to you.
2. If you were your colleague, what would you say is a fair price?

5-27 ***Sales premiums*** Mrs. Nelson's Coffee Company has been experiencing difficulties in achieving sales goals because of increased competition. The sales manager has proposed the following to stimulate sales: The firm will place a coupon in each one-pound can of coffee. A customer who returns ten coupons will receive merchandise that costs the firm $1. In addition, mailing and handling costs will be $0.20 for each $1 of merchandise. The sales manager expects an increase in sales of about 50,000 one-pound cans per month and further predicts that only about 40% of the coupons will be redeemed. The firm currently sells 350,000 one-pound cans per month at $1.50, with variable costs being $0.90.

Required: Should the firm adopt the plan?

5-28 ***Joint products – changes in mix*** Brewer Company makes three products in a joint process. The process is set up to yield the following quantities of each product from ten pounds of raw material: Nyron, three pounds; Xylon, three pounds; and Krylon, four pounds. Each product can be further processed; price and cost data are given below.

	Nyron	Xylon	Krylon
Selling price at split-off, per pound	$2	$4	$ 6
Additional processing costs, per pound	$1	$3	$ 8
Selling price after additional processing, per pound	$8	$6	$12

Required
1. Determine which products the firm should sell at split-off.
2. Assume that Brewer is now operating in accordance with your answer to item

1. Suppose that by changing the production process the firm could get eight pounds of Nyron and one pound each of Xylon and Krylon from ten pounds of raw material. There would be additional costs of $60,000 per month to process the raw material. The firm generally processes 100,000 pounds of raw material each month. Should Brewer change the process?

3. At what level of output per month, expressed in pounds of raw material processed, would Brewer have the same income under the existing process and under the changed process as described in item 2?

5-29 Hours of operation   Bronson Book Store is normally open 12 hours per day, six days per week. As an experiment, the owner kept the store open for six hours one Sunday and had sales of $750. The payroll was $110.

In an effort to determine whether it was worthwhile to stay open on Sundays, the owner collected the following additional information on annual results.

Sales		$361,400
Cost of sales		162,700
Gross margin		198,700
Operating expenses:		
Salaries	$88,300	
Rent	36,000	
Utilities	11,500	
Insurance	6,500	
Other	17,200	159,500
Profit		$ 39,200

Doing a few calculations, the owner came up with $511 as the estimated daily cost of operations, exclusive of cost of sales. He therefore concluded that about $930 in sales was necessary to justify staying open.

Required
1. Try to determine just what calculations the owner made to get his figures of $511 and $930.
2. With the information available, does it appear profitable to stay open Sundays?
3. What other information would you wish to get before making a final decision?

5-30 Special order — alternative volumes   Woolen Products Company makes heavy outdoor shirts. Data relating to the coming year's planned operations appear below.

Sales (230,000 shirts)	$4,140,000
Cost of sales	2,760,000
Gross profit	1,380,000
Selling and administrative expenses	805,000
Income	$ 575,000

The factory has capacity to make 250,000 shirts per year. Fixed costs included in cost of goods sold are $690,000. The only variable selling, general, and administrative expenses are a 10% sales commission and a $0.50 per shirt licensing fee paid to the designer.

A chain store manager has approached the sales manager of Woolen Products offering to buy 15,000 shirts at $14 per shirt. These shirts would be sold in areas where Woolen's shirts are not now sold. The sales manager believes that accepting the offer would result in a loss because the average total cost of a shirt is $15.50 [($2,760,000 + $805,000)/230,000]. He feels that even though sales commissions would not be paid on the order, a loss would still result.

Required
1. Determine whether the company should accept the offer.
2. Suppose that the order was for 40,000 shirts instead of 15,000. What would the firm's income be if it accepted the order?
3. Assuming the same facts as in item 1, what is the lowest price that the firm could accept and still earn $575,000?
4. How many sales at the regular price could the company lose before it became profitable to accept the order in part 2?

5-31 **Make or buy** Christensen Appliance Company is bringing out a new washing machine. The machine requires a type of electric motor not used for the current line of products. The purchasing manager has received a bid of $29 per motor from Wright Motor Company for any number the firm would need. Delivery is guaranteed within two weeks after order.

Christensen's production manager believes the firm could make the motor by extensively converting an existing model. Additional space and machinery would be required if the firm were to make the motors. The firm currently leases, for $39,600 per year, space that could be used to make the motors. However, the space is now used to store vital materials, so the firm would have to lease additional space in an adjacent building to store the materials. That space could be rented for $48,000 per year. It is suitable for storage, but not for converting the motors. The equipment needed to convert the motors could be rented for $45,000 per year.

The treasurer has developed the following unit costs based on the expected demand of 18,000 units per year.

Materials	$11.80
Direct labor	10.60
Rent for space	2.20
Machinery rental	2.50
Other overhead	8.20
Total cost	$35.30

The "other overhead" figure includes $5.40 in fixed overhead that would be allocated to conversion of the motors.

Required
1. Determine whether the motors should be bought or made.
2. Determine the volume of motors at which Christensen would show the same total income whether it bought or made the motors.

3. Suppose that the firm had decided to make the motors, however wisely or unwisely according to your analysis in item 1. One-year contracts have been signed for the additional space and for the equipment. These contracts cannot be canceled. Determine the price that Wright Motor would have to offer Christensen to induce it to buy the motors.

5-32 Dropping a product – opportunity costs Grothe Company has three product lines. Data for the coming year's operations that reflect the managers' best estimates appear below.

	Cabinets	Shelves	Bureaus
Sales	$450,000	$320,000	$200,000
Variable costs	200,000	180,000	125,000
Contribution margin	250,000	140,000	75,000
Avoidable fixed costs	110,000	60,000	40,000
Product margin	$140,000	$ 80,000	$ 35,000
Investment in receivables and inventories	$350,000	$300,000	$320,000

Unallocated joint costs total $130,000 and plant and equipment is $560,000.

The managers are not happy with the expected results of the bureau line and are considering dropping it. If they did so, the firm could recover the investment in receivables and inventory related to the line and pay off debt of $320,000 that bears 14% interest.

Required: Determine whether the firm should drop the bureau line.

5-33 Joint process (extension of 5-8) Rox's production manager for orides is following the advice you gave in your answer to 5-8. The vice president of manufacturing is satisfied with the results but is now wondering whether Rox should continue competing in the oride market. The controller has provided the following information about the joint process that is the first phase in producing the chemicals in the oride family.

Variable costs per 100 gallon batch	$ 180
Monthly fixed costs:	
Avoidable	$92,000
Unavoidable	$50,000

Required: Assume that Rox has no alternative uses for the facilities now devoted to operating the joint process that starts the production of orides. Determine whether the firm should continue to operate the joint process.

5-34 Salesperson's time as scarce resource Lombard Company sells to both wholesalers and retailers. The firm has 30 salespeople and cannot easily increase the size of the sales force. An analysis has shown that a salesperson's call on a wholesale customer yields an average order of $400, on a retailer $180. However, prices to wholesalers are 20% less than those to retailers. Cost of goods sold (all variable) is 60% of prices charged to retailers, 75% of prices charged to wholesalers. A salesperson can call on 7 wholesalers or 12 retailers per day. (The greater number of retailers reduces travel time between calls.)

Required
1. Should salespeople concentrate on wholesalers or retailers? Provide an analysis based on one salesperson for one week showing the difference.
2. What other factors require consideration?

5-35 *Special order — capacity limitation* Weston Tire Company has been approached by a large chain store that offers to buy 80,000 tires at $17. Delivery must be made within 30 days. Weston can produce 320,000 tires per month and has an inventory of 10,000 tires on hand. Expected sales at regular prices for the coming month are 300,000 tires. The sales manager believes that about 60% of sales lost during the month would be made up in later months. Price and cost data are as follows.

Selling price		$24
Variable costs:		
Production	$12	
Selling	3	15
Contribution margin		$ 9

Variable selling costs on the special order are $2 per unit.

Required
1. Determine whether the firm should accept the special order.
2. Determine the lowest price Weston could charge on the special order and not reduce its income.
3. Suppose now that the chain offers to buy 50,000 tires per month at $17. The offer is for an entire year. Expected sales are 300,000 tires per month without considering the special order. Assume also that there is no beginning inventory and that any sales lost during the year would *not* be made up in the following year. Determine whether the offer should be accepted and determine the lowest price that Weston could accept.

5-36 *Special orders and qualitative factors* Robinson Company has had a reputation for high-quality phonograph products for many years. The firm is owned by descendants of its founder, Allan Robinson, and continues the policy of producing and selling only high-quality, high-priced stereo components.

Recently James Giselle, president of a chain of discount stores, proposed that Robinson make and sell him a cheaper line of components than it currently produces. Giselle knows that Robinson has excess capacity and that many other firms produce lower-quality lines for sale in discount stores. Giselle believes that buyers will become aware that Robinson makes the components even though the Robinson name will not appear on them. Giselle tries to convince the management that its only potential for growth lies in the private-brand field, because Robinson now sells only to devoted aficionados who would not settle for less than Robinson components.

Giselle proposes that Robinson sell to the chain at 60% of its current selling price to other outlets. Variable costs are now about 60% of normal selling price but would be reduced by 20% per unit if the cheaper components were made. The first-year order is to be $1,260,000, for which Robinson has enough excess capacity.

Required
1. Evaluate the monetary effects of the proposed deal.
2. How would you evaluate qualitative factors such as the attitudes of the management and the family owners and the reputation of the firm?

5-37 *Cost of being your own boss* Martha and Jim Crain own a leather goods store in a large city. Their most recent year's income statement showed the following results.

Sales		$123,000
Cost of sales		55,000
Gross profit		68,000
Other expenses:		
Rent (monthly lease)	$3,600	
Utilities	2,450	
Advertising	1,000	
Supplies	700	
Insurance	250	
Licenses and fees	380	
Miscellaneous	720	
		10,000
Income		$ 58,000

In discussing the results, Martha said that it was nice to own your own business and not have to work for someone else, and Jim agreed. He commented that he had been earning $25,000 per year before the store had been opened and that she had been earning $32,000. She replied that their hours were much longer working in the store than in their previous jobs. "Of course," she went on, "we have $50,000 invested in the business, which is a lot, but we also don't have to fight the traffic to get there."

Required: Assume that the Crains could sell the business for $50,000, invest the proceeds at 12% interest, and go back to their former jobs. Should they do so?

5-38 *Pricing policy and excess capacity* Electric utilities face several problems in achieving optimal use of their facilities. First, because electricity cannot be stored economically, utilities must be able to generate enough electricity to meet demand at all times. Second, the use of electricity is seasonal, especially in warmer climates where air conditioning produces high-peak requirements in the summer months.

Executives of Southern Electric Company are evaluating a proposal by the sales manager to offer discounts on electrical service to customers who will use electrical heating equipment. The controller has amassed the following data at the request of the sales manager.

Current generating capacity—monthly	20 million kilowatt-hours (kwh)
kwh sold—typical winter month	7 million
kwh sold—typical summer month	18 million
Price per 1,000 kwh	$35
Variable cost per 1,000 kwh	$19

The proposal is to reduce the price of electricity to $29 per 1,000 kwh if the customer uses electrical heating equipment. It is anticipated that about 5 million additional kwh per month could be sold in the winter, a total of about 22 million additional hours per year. Total annual sales are now 120 million kwh. Users expected to convert to electrical heating now consume a total of about 30 million kwh per year. Sales to customers currently using electrical heating equipment, who would also qualify for the discount, are about 10 million kwh per year.

Required: Evaluate the monetary effects of the proposed decision.

5-39 **Processing decisions**   Ayers Sawmill buys pine logs and saws them into boards of two grades, A and B. The grade is determined by factors such as the number of knotholes and quality of the grain. Bark and sawdust also emerge from the sawing operation. Each log usually produces, by volume, about 35% A-grade boards, 55% B-grade boards, and 10% bark and shavings. Charles Ayers, the owner, has just received the income statement for a typical month's operations. Ayers expects much the same results in the foreseeable future.

	Total	Grade A	Grade B	Bark/Shavings
Sales	$80,000	$36,000	$41,000	$3,000
Costs:				
Logs	$42,000	$14,700	$23,100	$4,200
Sawing	17,000	5,950	9,350	1,700
Trimming	3,200	2,340	860	
Sanding	7,700	4,320	3,380	
Shipping	4,500	1,550	2,430	520
Total costs	74,400	28,860	39,120	6,420
Income (loss)	$ 5,600	$ 7,140	$ 1,880	$(3,420)

Sawing costs include wages, depreciation, and other nonitemized costs of running the sawmill. The cost of logs and of sawing are allocated based on volume (35%, 55%, 10%). Trimming, sanding, and shipping costs are direct and avoidable. Ayers was disturbed at the results. He told an employee, "The bark and shavings are really hurting me. I might as well throw the stuff out rather than sell it."

Required
1. Tell Ayers whether he should continue selling bark and shavings or throw it out. Explain the reasons for your decision.
2. A chain of lawn and garden stores has offered to buy Ayers's output of bark and shavings if Ayers will grind it into mulch. The grinding would cost about $1,500 per month for wages and equipment rental. The chain will pick the

mulch up at the mill, so Ayers will not incur shipping costs. What monthly revenue does Ayers need to make it profitable to do the grinding?

3. A furniture manufacturer has approached Ayers with an offer to buy all of the sawmill's output of grade B lumber for $30,000 per month as it comes out of the sawing operation. Ayers would not have to trim or sand the lumber. Shipping costs would be $1,200. Determine whether Ayers should accept the offer.

5-40 Evaluating a decision—costs of activities   Six months ago the marketing manager of Arcon Company approved the sale of sizable quantities of the company's principal product to a chain store in a geographical region where the company's products are not currently sold. The sales were made monthly. The sales manager recently asked the controller for an analysis of the business to see whether it should be renewed for another six months as the chain wants to do. The controller prepares the following income statement related to the special order.

Sales	$320,000
Cost of sales	247,000
Gross margin	73,000
Operating expenses	61,000
Profit	$ 12,000

The controller concludes that a $12,000 profit over six months is not enough to justify the added time and effort, as well as the risk of being unable to supply regular customers. Although the company has not operated at capacity during the period, it has come close on occasion.

The sales manager is surprised at the results and asks for more information. The controller provides the following additional data regarding the income statement.

(a) Cost of sales includes the following.

Materials	$ 86,000
Labor	41,000
Overhead, 60% variable	120,000
Total	$247,000

(b) Operating expenses:

Sales salaries	$ 27,000
Clerical	12,000
Other	22,000
Total	$ 61,000

The sales manager is confused about some items and receives the following additional explanation. The sales salaries are for the time of a sales representative who services the account. The representative spends about 80% of her time on the account, and the $27,000 is 80% of her six-month salary. The clerical costs are for a part-time clerk who works exclusively on this account. The bulk of the "other" category is a $16,000 administrative charge. This charge, equal to 5% of sales, is levied on all products to cover administrative expenses of the company. The remaining $6,000 are all incremental costs of various activities as estimated by the controller.

The sales manager seeks your help in understanding the statement and evaluating the order. He is confused and wonders whether to bother discussing renewal of the arrangement.

Required: Prepare a new income statement that will assist the sales manager in evaluating the business.

5-41 ***Relevant range*** The president of Ipswick Company has received an offer to purchase 20,000 of the tables made by his firm. The offer is to be filled any time during the coming year, and the offer price per table is $60. The planned income statement for the year without this order is as follows.

Sales (45,000 tables at $100)		$4,500,000
Cost of goods sold:		
Materials	$ 900,000	
Direct labor	810,000	
Overhead	1,340,000	
Total cost of goods sold		3,050,000
Gross profit		1,450,000
Selling, general, and administrative expenses		1,220,000
Income		$ 230,000

The president believes that the order should be rejected because the price is below average production cost of $67.78 per table. He asks you to check the matter further because he knows that some costs are fixed and would not be affected by the special order.

In your analysis you find that $800,000 in overhead is fixed and that a 10% commission is the only variable selling, general, and administrative expense.

Required: Answer the following questions, considering each situation separately.
1. Assume the relevant range for the firm is between 30,000 and 70,000 tables, that existing sales would not be affected, and that the 10% sales commission would not have to be paid on the special order. What effect would there be on income if the order were accepted? Should it be accepted?
2. The relevant range is the same as in item 1, and existing sales would be unaffected, but the 10% sales commission would have to be paid. Should the order be accepted?
3. The relevant range is now 30,000 to 55,000 tables. If the special order is accepted, sales at regular prices would fall to 35,000 units. The 10% sales commission would not be paid on the special order. Should the order be accepted?
4. The relevant range is the same as in item 3, but production could be increased to meet the special order as well as regular planned sales. For all units produced above 55,000, labor cost per unit and per-unit variable overhead would

be 20% higher than planned. Fixed production overhead would increase by $47,000. No sales commission would be paid on the order, and other selling, general, and administrative expenses would remain the same as planned. Should the order be accepted?

5-42 **Value of new products – effects on sales of other products**   Jackman's Grocery is a medium-sized operation in a suburb of a large city. Joe Jackman, the owner, is contemplating the addition of a department to sell either hardware or beer and wine. He has talked to owners of several similar stores and has reached the following conclusions.

1. A hardware department would generate sales of $40,000 per year with a gross profit of 60%. No other variable costs would be added. Fixed costs added would be $12,000. Sales of groceries would increase 5% because of increased traffic through the store.

2. A beer and wine department would generate sales of $60,000 per year with gross profit of 40%. No other variable costs would be added, and additional fixed costs would be $18,000. Sales of groceries would increase by 8%.

The income statement for a typical year for grocery sales alone is as follows.

Sales	$600,000
Cost of goods sold (variable)	240,000
Gross profit	360,000
Other variable costs	120,000
Contribution margin	240,000
Fixed costs	140,000
Income	$100,000

Required
1. Ignore the effects on sales of groceries for the moment. Compute the change in income that would result from adding (a) the hardware department and (b) the beer and wine department.
2. Recompute the effects on income of adding each department, considering the effects on sales of groceries. Which department should be added and why?
3. What can be learned from this problem?

5-43 **Special orders – effects on existing sales**   Hunt Company makes high-quality calculators that are sold only by department stores and office equipment dealers. A large discount chain has offered to buy 30,000 calculators this year at an average price of $30. The income statement expected for the coming year shows the following without considering the special order.

Sales (90,000 units at average price of $50)	$4,500,000
Variable production costs (average of $20)	1,800,000
Contribution margin	2,700,000
Fixed costs (production and selling, general, and administrative)	2,200,000
Income	$ 500,000

The 30,000 units to be bought by the chain are in the same mix as Hunt currently sells. The firm has the capacity to produce 140,000 units per year.

Required
1. Should the order be accepted if there would be no effect on regular sales?
2. Suppose that accepting the order will result in a 10% decline in sales at regular prices because some current customers would recognize the chain store's product and make their purchases at the lower price. The sales mix would remain unchanged. Should the special order be accepted?
3. By how much could sales at regular prices decline before it became unprofitable to accept the order?
4. Assuming the same facts as in item 2, what other factors should be considered before the order is accepted?

5-44   *Alternative uses of product (CMA adapted)*   So-Clean Corporation manufactures a variety of cleaning compounds and solutions for both industrial and household use. Some of its products share ingredients and some can be refined into others.

Grit 337 is a coarse, industrial cleaning powder that sells for $2.00 per pound and has variable costs of $1.60 per pound, all for manufacturing costs. The firm currently uses a portion of Grit 337 in making a silver polish that sells for $4.00 per jar. Each jar requires one quarter pound of Grit 337. Other variable production costs for the silver polish are $2.50 per jar and variable selling expenses are $0.30 per jar. Monthly avoidable fixed costs of making the silver polish are $5,600.

Required
1. Assuming that the firm cannot sell all of the Grit 337 it can produce, how many jars of silver polish must it sell monthly to justify continuing to sell it?
2. Suppose now that the firm can sell all of the Grit 337 that it can make. How many jars of silver polish must the firm sell per month to justify further processing Grit 337 into silver polish?

5-45   *Services of an athlete – jumping leagues*   The Fort Bluff Titans of the Cross Continental Football League have been approached by Flinger Johnson, the star quarterback of the Snidely Whips, a team in the other major football league—the Nationwide Football League. Johnson is unhappy with his current salary and wants to jump leagues if a satisfactory arrangement can be made. His contract has run out, so he is free to negotiate with the opposing league.

The owner of the Titans believes that acquiring Johnson would be a boon to attendance, estimating that he would be worth 10,000 additional admissions in every game he played. No team in the Cross Continental League comes close to filling its stadium, and even with Johnson there would be no sellouts. There are six teams in the league, each playing each of the others twice, for a total of ten games. Each team plays every opponent once at home and once away. Tickets sell for $10 per game and variable costs are about $2 per ticket. The home team collects $7 per admission, the visiting team $3. The home team pays the variable costs.

Required
1. What is the additional annual income to the Titans that would be attributable to acquiring Johnson?
2. What is the additional annual income to *all* teams in the Cross Continental League?

3. Why is it necessary to state that there would be no sellouts even if Johnson were playing? If there were, how would it affect your analysis?
4. Suppose that Johnson demands $500,000. Should the Titans meet his demand?
5. Suppose that the other teams in the league agree to pay part of Johnson's salary. How much could each team pay without reducing its profits below the current level? (Include the Titans and each of the other five teams.)
6. Johnson is now being paid $300,000 per year. Suppose that the teams in the Nationwide League decide to try to keep Johnson. The member teams estimate that if Johnson jumps, 8,000 admissions will be lost for each game in which he would have played. Ticket prices are $12, with $2 variable costs, and each team plays 12 games.
   (a) How much would the total profits of the teams in the league fall if Johnson did jump leagues?
   (b) How much of a raise could be given to Johnson to yield the same total profit that would be earned if he jumped leagues?
   (c) Assume the same facts except that each team has 50% of its games sold out. There are usually 3,000 more requests for tickets than seats available for the sellouts. If Johnson were to jump, the total number of requests for tickets per game in which his old team plays would drop by 8,000. How would this additional information affect your analysis?

5-46 Product processing Taylor Plywood company makes wall paneling used in homes and offices. The firm buys walnut logs and processes them into thin sheets of veneer that are glued to sheets of plywood to make the paneling. The firm makes plywood from various kinds of wood. Taylor has enough capacity to make 1,000,000 square feet of veneer per month and 1,200,000 square feet of plywood. Capacity in the gluing operation is 1,300,000 square feet per month.

At the present time the firm can sell its paneling for $178 per 1,000 square feet. Veneer and plywood can be sold separately for $74 and $81, respectively, per 1,000 square feet. Cost data developed by the controller are given below, per 1,000 square feet.

	Plywood	Veneer	Paneling
Materials	$18	$16	$ 34
Direct labor	25	20	55
Overhead	32	29	93
Total	$75	$65	$182

The figures shown for paneling are cumulative. They are the sums of the costs of veneer and plywood plus the additional costs associated with the gluing operation. Thus, no new materials are added in the gluing operation because the paneling cost for materials is equal to the sum of the veneer and plywood costs for materials. Direct labor in the gluing operation is $10 per 1,000 square feet, $55 total minus $25 for plywood operation and $20 for veneer operation.

The controller stated that Taylor should stop making paneling because it is unprofitable, and instead make and sell veneer and plywood.

You learn that the overhead figures given on page 200 contain both fixed and variable overhead. The variable portion of overhead is 80% of direct labor cost. All fixed overhead is unavoidable.

Required
1. Determine how much of each product should be produced and sold.
2. Determine what the firm should do if the price of paneling drops to $164 per 1,000 square feet.
3. Assume that paneling can be sold for $178 and veneer for $74, as in item 1. At what price for plywood would Taylor earn the same profit selling all of its plywood and veneer separately as it would combining them into paneling?
4. Assume the prices in item 1. Suppose Taylor could increase capacity in any operation by renting equipment on a month-to-month lease. Determine the maximum monthly cost the firm could incur to increase capacity by 100,000 square feet in each of the three operations, considered independently.

5-47 **Special order (CMA adapted)** Anchor Company manufactures jewelry cases. The firm is currently operating at 80% of its capacity of 7,500 direct labor hours per month. Its sales manager has been looking for special orders to increase the use of capacity. JCL Company has offered to buy 10,000 cases at $7.50 per case provided that delivery is within two months. Per-case cost data for the order are as follows.

Materials	$2.50
Direct labor (½ hour at $6)	3.00
Manufacturing overhead	2.00
Total unit cost	$7.50

Variable overhead is $1.50 per direct labor hour and the firm allocates fixed manufacturing overhead to units of product based on their direct labor time. Without the order, Anchor has enough business to operate at 6,000 direct labor hours (7,500 × 80%) in each of the next two months. The normal selling price of the jewelry case is $10.50. JCL would put its own label on the case.

The production manager is concerned about the labor time that 10,000 cases require. She cannot schedule more than 7,500 labor hours per month because Anchor has a policy against overtime. Thus, the firm will have to reduce some regular-price sales of the jewelry case if it accepts the order. JCL will not take fewer than 10,000 cases.

Required
1. Determine whether or not Anchor should accept the order.
2. Determine the price per case for the order that would make Anchor indifferent between accepting and rejecting the order (the price that would give Anchor the same profit under both alternatives).

5-48 **Processing decision** Most beef bought in stores comes from cattle that have been fattened on feedlots. A feedlot is an area consisting mainly of pens and barns in which cattle are closely packed and fed diets designed to increase their weight rapidly. The cattle are bought from ranchers when they weigh about 500 pounds, at a cost of $260, including freight. After the cattle are fattened, their selling price is $0.50 per pound and the buyer pays the freight.

The average animal gains weight in the pattern shown below.

First month	140 pounds
Second month	130
Third month	120
Fourth month	100
Total potential gain	490 pounds

For each month that an animal is on the feedlot, it eats $52 worth of feed. The lot can hold 5,000 head of cattle at a time.

Required

1. Assume that there is a shortage of animals available for fattening. The lot is only able to buy 600 head per month. Determine the number of months that each animal should be kept on the lot before being sold.
2. Suppose the supply of animals is very high so that the lot is operating at full capacity. Determine the number of months each animal should be kept.

Cases

5-49   *Peanuts for peanuts* *

The Time: Hopefully never, but then everybody knows the outcome of wishful thinking.

The Scene: A small neighborhood diner in a small New Jersey town about 25 miles from New York City. The operator-owner, Mr. Joseph Madison, is preparing to open for the day. He has just placed a shiny new rack holding brightly colored bags of peanuts on the far end of the counter. As he stands back to admire his new peanut rack, his brother-in-law, Harry, a self-styled efficiency expert, enters from the back door.

Harry. Morning Joe. What're you looking so pleased about?

Joe. I jus' put up my new peanut rack—the one I tole you about the other night.

Harry. Joe, you told me that you were going to put in these peanuts because some people asked for them. But I've been thinking about it and I wonder if you realize what this rack of peanuts is costing you.

Joe. It ain't gonna cost. Gonna be a profit. Sure, I hadda pay $25 for a fancy rack to hol' the bags, but the peanuts cost 6¢ a bag and I sell 'em for 10¢. I figger I can sell 50 bags a week to start. It'll take twelve and a ha'f weeks to cover the cost of the rack and after that I make a clear profit of 4¢ a bag. The more I sell, the more I make.

Harry (shaking his finger at Joe). That is an antiquated and completely unrealistic approach. Fortunately, modern accounting procedures permit a more accurate picture which reveals the complexities involved.

---

* Used with the permission of Rex H. Anderson, Senior Vice-President, INA Reinsurance Company.

Joe. Huh?

Harry. To be precise, those peanuts must be integrated into your entire operation and be allocated their appropriate share of business overhead. They must share a proportionate part of your expenditures for rent, heat, light, equipment depreciation, decorating, salaries for waitresses, cook . . .

Joe. The cook? What's he gotta do wit' the peanuts? He don't even know I got 'em yet.

Harry. Look, Joe. The cook is in the kitchen; the kitchen prepares the food; the food is what brings people in; and while they're in, they ask to buy peanuts. That's why you must charge a portion of the cook's wages, as well as a part of your own salary to peanut sales. Since you talked to me I've worked it all out. This sheet contains a carefully calculated cost analysis which clearly indicates that the peanut operation should pay exactly $1,278 per year toward these general overhead costs.

Joe (unbelieving). The peanuts? $1,278 a year for overhead? That's nuts!

Harry. It's really a little more than that. You also spend money each week to have the windows washed, to have the place swept out in the mornings, to keep soap in the washroom and provide free cokes to the police. That raises the actual total to $1,313 per year.

Joe (thoughtfully). But the peanut salesman said I'd make money—put 'em on the end of the counter, he said—and get 4¢ a bag profit.

Harry (with a sniff). He's not an accountant; and remember, he wanted to sell you something. Do you actually know what the portion of the counter occupied by the peanut rack is worth to you?

Joe. Sure. It ain't worth nuttin'. No stool there—just a dead spot at the end.

Harry. The modern cost picture permits no dead spots. Your counter contains 60 square feet and your counter business grosses $15,000 a year. Consequently, the square foot of space occupied by the peanut rack is worth $250 per year. Since you have taken that area away from general counter use, you must charge the value of the space to the occupant. That's called opportunity cost.

Joe. You mean I gotta add $250 a year more to the peanuts?

Harry. Right. That raises their share of the general operating costs to $1,563 per year. Now then, if you sell 50 bags of peanuts per week, these allocated costs will amount to 60¢ per bag.

Joe (incredulously). What?

Harry. Obviously, to that must be added your purchase price of 6¢ a bag, which brings the total to 66¢. So you see, by selling peanuts at 10¢ per bag, you are losing 56¢ on every sale.

Joe. Something's crazy!!

Harry. Not at all. Here are the figures. They prove your peanut operation just can't stand on its own feet.

Joe (brightening). Suppose I sell lotsa peanuts—1,000 bags a week mebbe, 'stead of 50?

Harry (tolerantly). No. Joe, you just don't understand the problem. If the volume of peanut sales increased, your operating costs will go up—you'll have to handle more bags, with more time, more general overhead, more everything. The basic principle of accounting is firm on that subject: "The bigger the operation the more general overhead costs must be allocated." No, increasing the volume of sales won't help.

Joe. Okay, You so smart, you tell me what I gotta do.

Harry (condescendingly now). Well—you could first reduce operating expenses.

Joe. Yeah? How?

Harry. You might take smaller space in an older building with cheaper rent. Maybe cut salaries. Wash the windows biweekly. Have the floor swept only on Thursdays. Remove the soap from the washrooms. Cut out the cokes for the cops. This will help you decrease the square-foot value of the counter. For example, if you can cut your expenses 50%, that will reduce the amount allocated to peanuts from $1,563 down to $781.50 per year, reducing the cost to 36¢ per bag.

Joe. That's better?

Harry. Much, much better. Of course, even then you'd lose 26¢ per bag if you charged only 10¢. Therefore, you must also raise your selling price. If you want a net profit of 4¢ per bag, you would have to charge 40¢.

(Harry is looking very confident, now, but Joe appears flabbergasted.)

Joe. You mean even after I cut operating costs 50%, I still gotta charge 40¢ for a 10¢ bag of peanuts? Nobody's that nuts about nuts! Who'd buy 'em?

Harry. That's a secondary consideration. The point is, at 40¢, you'd be selling at a price based upon a true and proper evaluation of your then reduced costs.

(Joe does not look convinced; then, he brightens.)

Joe. Look! I gotta better idea. Why don't I jus' throw the nuts out—so I lost $25 on the rack. I'm outa this nutsy business and no more grief.

(Harry is shaking his head vigorously.)

Harry. Joe, it just isn't that simple. You are in the peanut business! The minute you throw those peanuts out, you are adding $1,563 of annual overhead to the rest of your operation. Joe—be realistic—can you afford to do that?

Joe (by now completely crushed). It's unbelievable! Last week I wuz makin' money. Now I'm in trouble—jus' becuz I think peanuts onna counter is gonna bring me some extra profit. Jus' becuz I believe 50 bags of peanuts a week is easy.

Harry (by now smiling and satisfied that his brother-in-law will not be so quick to argue with him in the future). That is the reason for modern cost studies, Joe—to dispel those false illusions.

Curtain falls.

Required
1. Who's nuts?
2. Evaluate the position(s) expounded by Harry.

5-50   ***Dropping a segment***   Tom Johnson, owner of Johnson's Drugstore, is opposed to smoking and wants to drop the tobacco counter from the store. He has determined from industry statistics and opinions of other drugstore managers that the tobacco counter creates a good deal of other business because many people who come in just for cigarettes, cigars, and pipe tobacco buy other articles. Moreover, some people will go elsewhere for drugs and sundries if they know that tobacco is not being sold.

The manager estimates that sales of drugs would drop by 5% and sundries by 10% if the tobacco counter were removed. The space now occupied by the tobacco counter would be devoted to greeting cards, which Johnson does not now sell. Estimated annual sales for greeting cards are $8,000, with cost of sales of $3,000.

If the tobacco counter is dropped, one clerk earning $4,000 could be dropped. But a pharmacist would have to handle the greeting card sales which would result in a further drop in drug sales of 2% (from the current level).

Carrying costs of the inventory of greeting cards are expected to be about $300 less per year than those associated with tobacco products.

The manager has asked you to advise him in this decision. He has provided you with an income statement for the coming year showing his expectations if tobacco products are retained.

Johnson's Drugstore
Expected Income Statement for the Coming Year

	Tobacco	Drugs	Sundries	Total
Sales	$27,000	$120,000	$33,000	$180,000
Cost of goods sold	9,000	50,000	11,000	70,000
Gross profit	18,000	70,000	22,000	110,000
Operating expenses:				
Salaries	6,700	36,000	7,300	50,000
Occupancy costs (rent, utilities, maintenance, etc.)	3,000	7,000	4,000	14,000
Miscellaneous	1,500	6,700	1,800	10,000
Total operating expenses	11,200	49,700	13,100	74,000
Income before taxes	$ 6,800	$ 20,300	$ 8,900	$ 36,000

You learn that occupancy costs are allocated to each product group based on percentages of space occupied for display of those products. These costs will not change in total if greeting cards are substituted for tobacco. The manager's salary, $18,000, is arbitrarily allocated to departments and included in the salaries amount in the income statement. Miscellaneous expenses are allocated based on relative sales volume and would be unaffected by the change except for the cost of carrying inventory.

Required: Comment on the cost to Mr. Johnson of implementing his convictions about smoking.

5-51   Alternative uses of space   Several years ago the Star Department Store began leasing space to Clothes Horse, Inc., a chain of boutiques specializing in high-priced women's clothing and accessories. The boutiques are usually separate stores in shopping centers, but the management of Clothes Horse wished to experiment with an operation in a department store and Star was willing, as the space was not then needed for its own operations.

Clothes Horse pays Star a monthly rental of $3,000 plus 5% of its gross sales, and the arrangement has been profitable for both parties. Star pays all electricity, gas, and other costs of occupancy, which are negligible when considered incrementally because the space would have to be lighted and heated anyway. The lease is about to expire, and Clothes Horse is eager to renew it for another year on the same terms. However, some of Star's department heads have indicated a desire to take over the operation of the boutique, and others have requested the use of the space to expand their selling areas.

After reviewing all the requests, Ron Stein and Bill Rausch, Star's executive vice president and general manager, respectively, have narrowed the range of choices to the following: (1) renew the lease with Clothes Horse; (2) keep the boutique, but place it under the women's wear department head, Margot Miller; (3) use the space to expand the shoe department, which is located next to the boutique.

The boutique had total sales of $400,000 in the first ten months of the current year, and the monthly rate is expected to double for the last two months, which come at the height of the Christmas season. Stein and Rausch expect a 10% increase in sales in the coming year if Clothes Horse continues to operate the boutique. Ms. Miller has presented the following expected income statement for the coming year, which she believes she could achieve if she took over the operation of the boutique.

Sales		$380,000
Cost of sales		171,000
Gross profit		209,000
Salaries	$75,000	
Advertising and promotion	14,000	
Supplies	7,000	
Miscellaneous	8,000	
		104,000
Profit		$105,000

Mr. Stein commented that Ms. Miller is generally too optimistic and that her estimate of sales volume was probably about 10% too high. He noted that she had provided for fewer salespeople than were employed by Clothes Horse and that the somewhat reduced level of service would not help business. He felt that expenses other than cost of sales would probably be about as she had estimated, even at the lower volume that he thought would be achieved.

The manager of the shoe department believed that if the space were used to expand his department his sales would increase by about $200,000 with a gross profit rate of 45%. He would need to add one salesperson, who would work on a 10% commission, like the other employees in that department. Virtually all other store employees work on salary, not commission.

Rausch and Stein both brought up the subject of traffic through the store and both agreed that traffic had increased since Clothes Horse opened the boutique. They were uncertain about the effects of the increased traffic on sales in the store's own departments, and so Rausch said that he would investigate the matter.

Rausch instructed several of his assistants to interview people in the store, particularly in the boutique, regarding their shopping habits. Several days later, the results were in, and he went to Stein's office to discuss them. The following major conclusions were contained in the reports Rausch had received.

1. About 40% of sales made in the boutique are to people who come especially to shop there. These people have to walk through parts of the store to get to the boutique and spend about 20% as much in the store as they do in the boutique.
2. The remainder of the boutique's sales are to people who come for other reasons. Many drop in on their way in or out of the store; some plan to shop in the

store's other departments as well as in the boutique. These people spend about twice as much in the store's own departments as they do in the boutique.

After a discussion lasting nearly an hour, Stein and Rausch decided that the people who came in especially to shop in the boutique would not patronize the store at all if Clothes Horse did not operate it. The executives believed that only the popularity of the Clothes Horse name induced these people to come in.

Of the other group, they believed that about 10% of the patronage would be lost if Clothes Horse did not operate the boutique. This loss of sales would be spread fairly evenly throughout the store. The average gross profit rate in the store is 45%, and other variable costs are an additional 8% of sales.

Required: Determine the best course of action for the store.

PART TWO

BUDGETING

Economic enterprises engage in a myriad of activities. These activities require not only planning but also coordination of plans. We explore the relationships among those activities in this part.

The comprehensive budget is a tool to make planning effective, and provides a means for monitoring whether activities are going according to plan. In a formal and integrated way, the budget captures and reflects the results of planning decisions, from decisions about product mix and cost structure, to those about dividends and major new investments.

Both VCP analysis and knowledge of cost behavior are important in budgeting for the relatively near future—the coming year. Those concepts are also important in analyzing the potential of longer-term projects, the expenditures for which might have to be made in the near future. In addition, some of the principles from financial accounting are important in budgeting because a comprehensive budget includes financial statements normally prepared for external reporting.

Budgeting is more than a technical or mechanical exercise. Because it is people who plan and people who act (according to or contrary to plans), the ways that budgets are developed and used can affect people's behavior and vice versa. In this part we introduce some behavioral problems entailed in the budgeting process. A more comprehensive treatment of these problems is given in Part Three.

OPERATIONAL BUDGETING

The functional areas of a business (marketing, production, purchasing, finance) are interdependent and must work in harmony to achieve profit goals. The production department must make enough units for marketing to achieve its sales objectives. But it must not overproduce because having too much inventory causes excessive costs for storage, insurance, taxes, and interest. For the same reason, the purchasing manager must not overpurchase, yet must ensure that enough material is available to meet production schedules. The finance department must make cash available for paying for material, labor, and other operating costs, as well as for dividends, acquisitions of assets, and debt repayments. But the timing and magnitude of those cash needs depends on the plans of other managers.

The overall plans of the business, then, must be so specified that the manager of each functional area knows what must be done to ensure smooth performance for other areas and for the firm as a whole. Firms use comprehensive budgets to coordinate all of these activities.

COMPREHENSIVE BUDGETS

A **comprehensive budget** is a set of financial statements and other schedules showing the *expected,* or pro forma, results for a future period. A comprehensive budget normally contains an income statement, a balance sheet, a statement of cash receipts and disbursements, and schedules of production, purchases, and fixed asset acquisitions. The budget package might have other components, depending on the needs of the firm.

Comprehensive budgeting uses the principles of VCP analysis. It requires careful studies of cost behavior patterns, and the income statements you developed for VCP analysis and short-term decision making are very similar to budgeted income statements. But budgeting involves more than VCP analysis. For instance, budgeting cash collections requires both predicting sales *and* estimating the pattern of cash collections (how much do we collect within 30 days? within 60 days?). Predicted cash collections from sales combine with cash receipts from planned borrowing to become a cash receipts budget.

Comprehensive budgeting is also more complex than VCP analysis because a change in a single assumption affects the whole set of budgets, not just one or a few items in an income statement. For example, changing the forecasted sales for a particular month affects not only cost of sales, other variable costs, and profit, but also the plans for purchasing the items to be sold, and the timing and amounts of expected cash receipts, payments for purchases, and perhaps even the loans that must be negotiated.

All levels of management are involved in putting together some part of the interrelated statements and schedules that make up the comprehensive budget. However, individual managers deal only with segments of the total package, and the degree of detail in the schedules they use varies with the breadth of the manager's responsibilities. Thus, while top managers are interested in overall results, the production manager might deal only with schedules of production data. In general, most managers have budgets showing what is expected of *them*—what objectives *they* are to achieve and at what costs.

Budgets and Planning

The comprehensive budget is conspicuous evidence that a firm has a formal and overall plan, in contrast to an intuitive approach to operations. A major benefit of formal planning is that it requires explicit statements not only of objectives (such as sales volume and profit) but also of the means required to achieve those objectives. Some of the objectives initially considered feasible may prove not so in light of the budget. Suppose the budget specifies high sales in the early part of the year. When the production manager tries to plan production on the basis of the initial sales budget, he or she may recognize that productive capacity is insufficient to meet budgeted level of sales. Or perhaps the financial manager will see that sufficient production and inventory to meet the budgeted level of sales are possible *only* if the firm obtains a great deal of short-term financing. If securing the necessary financing is undesirable (or even impossible), the budgets have to be modified to be consistent with the amount of cash available.

Figure 6-1 shows how the budgeting process coordinates the financial statements and other schedules into a comprehensive system. Chapter 5 shows that decision making, which is considered part of the overall planning process, relies on estimates about future results under alternative courses of action. Budgeting is related to decision making in that managers consider the status quo as one alternative and compare it with possible alternatives (such as special orders). In making

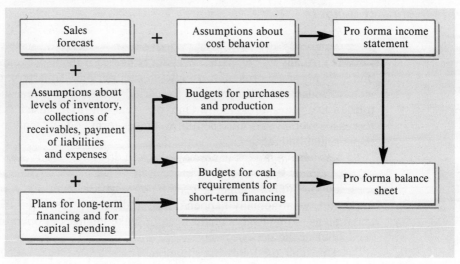

Figure 6-1   Relationships Among Financial Statements in Budgeting

their short-term decisions, managers can use the information in carefully prepared budgets as a baseline for determining incremental revenues and costs. Moreover, the comprehensive budget incorporates the current effects of plans for long-term financing and for acquisitions of major assets. The development of those long-term plans, and the related decision making, are discussed in Chapters 7, 8, and 9.

Budgets and Control

Budgets express targets or goals; actual results express achievements. Thus, a comparison of budgeted and actual results is a basis for evaluating performance and helps control future operations. Corrective action can be taken to eliminate problems that show up in the comparisons.

The preceding statements are oversimplified but fair statements of the role of budgets in control and performance evaluation. Actual performance is best judged by comparison with expected, rather than past, performance. This is true if expectations are reasonable, carefully formulated, and based on all available information. Using past performance to judge current performance is inappropriate because circumstances change. Moreover, comparisons with past performance cannot reveal whether current performance is as good as it should have been. Improvement over past results is desirable, but it is more important to know if the improvement has been as great as it could have been. (A student who gets a 38 on one examination and a 42 on the next has improved, but is still not performing adequately.)

The budgeting process incorporates all the managerial functions that we have associated with managerial accounting. Planning, control, decision making, and performance evaluation are integrated in the budgeting cycle.

Organization of Budgets

Budgets usually cover specific periods, such as a month, a year, or a five-year period. Virtually all companies prepare budgets for the fiscal year, and the annual budget is normally broken down into shorter periods—quarters, months, or even weeks. Budgets are also prepared for periods longer than a year, usually for three, four, or five years, broken down into one-year units. Because it is more difficult to forecast several years into the future, longer-term budgets tend to be less detailed than annual budgets.

An annual budget is normally broken down into shorter periods for several reasons. First, it is easier for managers to monitor progress toward meeting the goals in the annual budget if benchmarks are available during the year. More important, what actually happens is often different from even the most sophisticated plans, so managers might need to make changes in operating plans for the remainder of the period.

Consider the following situation. The sales manager sees that actual sales for the first month of the year are higher than budgeted. Even with the flexibility provided by a true JIT environment, she must try to determine whether the additional sales in this month will be offset by lower sales later, or whether the high sales are an indication that the *total* expectations were too low. Suppose she concludes that sales for the rest of the first quarter, or even for the year, will be in excess of budgeted amounts. If the *original* production plan for future months is followed, inventory will be less than budgeted at the end of the first month and shortages may develop. The sales manager might then want to have production increased to meet the expected increases in sales. An increase in production means acquiring greater quantities of materials and perhaps hiring more employees, actions that involve other managers. Changes in plans—such as increased production—will go more smoothly and more effectively if the need for them is recognized well in advance of the point at which a crisis develops.

Even if the sales manager concludes that sales for the full year will not be materially greater than budgeted, the higher-than-expected sales in the first month could mean that inventory will be lower than budgeted. It might then be necessary to plan a temporary increase in production sufficient to maintain the desired level of inventory. Thus, whether sales in excess of expectations are a temporary or a longer-lasting phenomenon, new plans must be made, with implications for production and cash flows.

Seasonal businesses must make or buy large quantities of goods in advance of the selling season, thus creating a need for funds prior to the receipt of cash from customers. But even without seasonality, cash requirements vary over the year because some costs fluctuate throughout the year. For example, property taxes can normally be paid in two installments, some insurance premiums are due only annually, interest payments might be required quarterly, semiannually, or annually, and dividends are seldom paid monthly. (It makes a big difference whether a $100,000 payment for taxes or dividends must be made in January or July, because the funds must be available when the payment falls due.) Cash budgets are an important part of the total budget package, and budgets prepared for the year as a whole fail to reveal these irregular funds requirements and so are not useful for monthly planning.

Continuous Budgets   Most managers like to have plans for at least a year in advance. If budgets are prepared only for fiscal years, as the year goes by the period for which a budget is available will shorten until the budget for the next year is prepared. To alleviate this problem some firms use **continuous budgets,** which add a budget for a month (or quarter) as one of these periods goes by. Thus, there is a 12-month budget at all times. Managers are then kept aware of the needs for the next 12 months, regardless of the time of the year.

Project Budgets   Some kinds of budgets are not oriented to time periods but to stages in completing specific projects. For example, a firm building a new plant will have a time schedule (finish the exterior by June, the interior by November, begin production by March). The periods selected, which may be of unequal length, depend on the project and are of no importance in themselves. The focus is on completing each stage of the project. Of course project budgets have implications for periodic budgeting because cash expenditures for projects must be incorporated in the cash budget.

Capital Budgets   Virtually all firms prepare budgets of expenditures for fixed assets, often for many years into the future. These are called **capital budgets.** Expenditures from these budgets must be incorporated into the cash budgets for the appropriate periods. Chapters 8 and 9 treat capital budgets in detail.

Developing
the Comprehensive Budget

The development of the comprehensive budget begins well in advance. This is necessary because initial expectations must often be revised for reasons already discussed. In many companies, the earliest discussions of prospects for the coming year focus on some overall goal relating to profit or growth (such as a 10% increase in income, a 2% increase in return on sales or on assets, a 15% increase in sales, or perhaps a 2 point increase in market share). That is, some budgets are, at least at the outset, driven by some desired result. But whatever the initial concerns, in every case the budget for the coming period begins with a sales forecast, because expected sales determine production requirements, needs for labor, for material and other operating costs, cash flows, and financing requirements. The ways in which each of these various elements are related depend on managerial policies (how much inventory to keep, what credit terms to offer to customers) and operating characteristics (costs, production time).

You are already familiar with the preparation of income statements based on sales forecasts and cost behavior. With minor exceptions, preparing a budgeted income statement is an extension of VCP analysis. Other budgets, especially the pro forma balance sheet and statement of cash flows, present some technical difficulties because of the leads and lags involved. For example, revenue is generally *recorded* at the point of sale, though cash may not be collected for some time after the sale. Cost of goods sold is recognized when revenue is recorded. But the costs to purchase or produce the inventory are incurred before the sale. Liabilities are recorded as they are incurred, but cash payments may be delayed for varying periods. These leads and lags give rise to the critical technical problems in comprehensive budgeting.

In the remainder of this chapter we discuss and illustrate sales forecasts, purchases budgets, and expense budgets. These budgets are usually called **operating budgets.** In Chapter 7 we complete the process by considering **financial budgets** (pro forma balance sheet and cash budget).

SALES FORECASTING

The sales forecast is critical to budgeting because virtually everything else depends on it. Firms use many methods to forecast sales. Not all firms can use all of the methods we discuss, but most firms can use one or more.

Indicator Methods

The sales of many industries are closely associated with some factor in the economy. Sales of long-lasting consumer goods (cars, washing machines, furniture, etc.) generally correlate well with indicators of economic activity like the Gross National Product and personal income. Sales of baby food are associated with the number of births, housing units with the formation of new households. A firm in such an industry might first use the economic indicator to predict total sales for the industry and then forecast its own sales by estimating its share of the total market. Both scatter diagrams and regression analysis are widely used in forecasting sales, just as they are in predicting costs.

Sales in many industries depend to a great extent on sales of some other industries. Makers of cans and bottles look at forecasts for sales of beer and soft drinks. Steel companies and tire companies keep abreast of developments affecting the auto industry. In these situations, too, a firm tries to develop a forecast for its industry and then for itself, but the indicator is a forecast from *another* industry.

To use an indicator for sales forecasting, the indicator itself must be predictable. Suppose you have observed over time that the sales in your industry correlate well with Gross National Product. You can use GNP to predict industry sales (and then your sales) only if you can obtain a prediction of GNP. Thus, once the relationships have been determined as well as possible (probably using regression equations) *and* a forecast of the indicator is available, the relationships can be used to forecast sales for the industry or firm.

The scatter diagram in Figure 6-2 shows the number of automobiles sold plotted against per capita income (PCI). See if you can develop an equation of the form: Auto sales = constant + (PCI × ?). If per capita income is forecast to be $4,800 for the coming year, what do you forecast for automobile sales? If your firm makes parts for automobiles, what could you do with your forecast of auto sales?

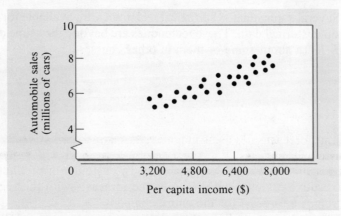

Figure 6-2   Automobile Sales and Per Capita Income

A line fitted to the points would hit the vertical axis at about 4 million cars. The slope is about 0.5 million cars per $1,000 in per capita income. The line would be at about 5.5 million cars at $3,200, 7.9 million at $8,000, a difference in cars of 2.4 million for a $4,800 difference in income. Thus, car sales might be expected to rise about 500 (2.4 million cars/$4,800 change in income) for each rise of $1 in per capita income. At $4,800 per capita income, sales would be forecast as follows: 4 million + (500 × $4,800) = 4 million + 2.4 million = 6.4 million cars.

Sometimes managers can obtain predictions of their industry's sales directly. Many trade associations publish studies that provide guidance in sales forecasting. For example, an association of appliance dealers might conduct studies to determine what kinds of appliances are likely to sell, and in what quantities. A study for the purpose of forecasting the sales of washing machines could take into account the overall economic outlook, previous sales of washing machines, the average age of machines currently in use (to see whether replacements will be significant), and the forecasts for new housing units. Although the study would not indicate how these factors affect the sales of any single dealer, each dealer has a picture of what is likely to happen to industry sales and can apply it to his or her own sales forecasts.

Historical Analysis

Some firms analyze their sales of previous years and project the trend to arrive at a forecast. Thus, if sales have been rising at 10% per year, the firm will start with a forecast based on last year's sales plus 10%. This is only a start. Are there factors that suggest higher or lower sales? Were last year's sales abnormally high or low because of a strike, unusual weather conditions (ice cream, beer, golf balls, and many other products sell better in hot weather)? Are there discernible changes in taste that could affect our sales? The past can be used for guidance on what might happen, but differences in conditions can cause the future to differ from the past.

Several sophisticated statistical techniques are available for making predictions from historical data. These techniques are beyond the scope of this book, but you may learn about some of them in other courses.

Judgmental Methods

Some firms forecast sales using judgment based on experience with the company's customers and products. Each regional sales manager will, in consultation with the sales staff, estimate sales in that area, by customer or product line. The chief sales executive reviews and discusses the forecasts with the regional managers and develops a forecast for the entire company.

The analysis underlying these judgment-based forecasts follows the lines of the other methods described here, but is less formal. Instead of using regression analysis or some other mathematical tool, the manager will rely on his or her experience and personal perceptions of changing circumstances to develop a forecast of the prospects for the industry and for the firm. For example, the manager may notice several newspaper and magazine articles about the decreasing length of the work week and reason that people will have increased leisure time. If the firm's products are used for leisure-time activities, the manager is likely to correctly forecast increased sales for the industry and for the firm.

Which Method to Use

The applicability of any of the methods discussed depends on the characteristics of the firm. Most firms use a combination of methods. Forecasts using judgmental methods alone might reflect unwarranted optimism of the sales manager and sales force. For some firms, there may be no reliable—or predictable—indicators. Even where indicators are available and used, there is danger in relying on them to the exclusion of other factors. (Current conditions may differ from those in force when the relationships among the indicators and the sales of the firm or industry were first developed.) Successful forecasting results from combining sound and experienced business judgment with the judicious use of quantitative tools.

Whatever methods are used to forecast, the sales budget for the firm as a whole is likely to evolve from several forecasts made on a smaller scale. The original forecasts may be by individual product or product line, by geographical area, by department, or by some combination of these. The scope of the original forecasts and the methods used depend on the organization of the firm.

Expected Values and Forecasting

As just indicated, several managers are usually involved in preparing the sales forecast. Some firms might generate several forecasts by using different indicators or methods. When different methods are used, or different persons are preparing forecasts, the resulting forecasts are likely to differ. Even a single manager might come up with several forecasts based on different assumptions and judgments about conditions in the coming period. In such cases, the concept of expected value is sometimes used to reach a single forecast figure to use in budgeting.

To determine an **expected value,** managers assign probabilities to each alternative forecast. The probabilities reflect the managers' judgments of the likelihood of each forecast actually coming about. For example, suppose the vice president for sales and the regional managers believe there is a 30% probability of sales being $4,500,000 next year, a 50% probability that they will be $5,000,000, and a 20% probability that they will be $6,000,000. The following schedule shows the calculation of the expected value of $5,050,000.

(1) Forecast	(2) Assigned Probability	(1) × (2) Expected Value
$4,500,000	0.30	$1,350,000
5,000,000	0.50	2,500,000
6,000,000	0.20	1,200,000
Expected value	1.00	$5,050,000

The probabilities must add up to 1, or 100%, because there must be *some* value for sales. The vice president would use the $5,050,000 expected value in the budget but would recognize that sales could run from $4,500,000 to $6,000,000. He or she would monitor actual results and be prepared to revise the budget if conditions warranted. (Although we have introduced the expected-value concept in connection with sales forecasting, the concept also applies to budgeting costs.)

In most cases, probability assignments are based on the manager's judgment and experience, sometimes refined by other statistical techniques. The probabilities are, therefore, said to be *subjective:* different managers might assign different probabilities. As with any managerial tool, the quality of the final information or decision rests heavily on the quality of the manager's judgment.

Interim Period Forecasts

The forecasting methods discussed apply to sales forecasts of three distinct types: (1) annual forecasts, (2) longer-term forecasts (three to five years), and (3) quarterly or monthly forecasts. Once a forecast for the year has been approved as a basis for planning, it is necessary to break it down into shorter periods, called *interim periods*.

Often the data used to forecast annual sales (economic indicators, sales for other industries) are already broken down by quarters. In such cases, the manager can base quarterly forecasts on the same indicator used for the annual forecast. Many firms have developed other reliable ways for breaking down annual forecasts. For example, their experience may show that consistent percentages of yearly sales occur in particular quarters or months (15% of annual sales are concentrated in March, 40% in the first quarter, and so on).

Whatever the methods used to develop the sales forecast, and whatever the length of the forecast period, managers revise budgets when they obtain more information. A budget is a plan, not a straitjacket; changing it in the face of changing conditions is sound practice.

EXPENSE BUDGETS

Each manager is responsible for specific tasks and expenses. Hence, each manager should have a **budget allowance** stating the acceptable limits for expenses the manager may incur in accomplishing his or her assigned tasks.

There are two general ways to develop budget allowances. One approach sets the budget for a particular cost at a single amount without considering the level of activity. An allowance set this way is called a **static budget.** This approach is used with fixed costs. The other approach sets a variable, or **flexible budget allowance,** based on volume of activity. Budgets are set in this fashion for variable costs and mixed costs.

Budget allowances for committed costs can generally be set by referring to existing obligations (because costs to be incurred have largely been set by actions already taken). Discretionary cost allowances are generally set by managerial policy. For example, a flexible budget allowance would be appropriate if it is the firm's policy to spend an amount equal to some percentage of sales on advertising, research and development, bonuses, and other discretionary costs. The manager responsible for controlling the discretionary cost will participate with higher management in determining the amount to be allowed. (Some problems relating to the budgeting of discretionary costs are discussed later in the chapter.)

Alternative Measures of Activity

As indicated in Chapter 3, the amount of a particular cost may vary with some activity other than sales. The amounts originally budgeted for such costs, and the subsequent flexible budget allowances, must be based on the activity determined to be the best in predicting the amounts of the cost in question.

The most obvious example of a manager needing an activity other than sales to predict costs is the production manager. The production budget for the period must be related to production activity rather than sales. Whether units are sold or not, the cost to make them is incurred at the time of production. Unless, as in an ideal JIT company, production exactly coincides with sales shipments, the production manager incurs costs before they become expenses in the income statement. Hence, the budget allowance for production costs is some fixed amount *plus* the variable costs of production times the number of units produced.

Suppose a department manager and his superior have agreed on the following flexible budget allowances for the listed components of factory overhead in the department.

Cost	Fixed Amount per Month	Variable Amount per Hour of Direct Labor
Indirect labor	$1,200	$0.50
Supplies	200	0.40
Maintenance	2,400	0.10
Depreciation	1,200	0
Miscellaneous	700	0.05
Total	$5,700	$1.05

Suppose further that 1,000 direct labor hours are budgeted for the coming month. The original budget allowances for the month will be determined and reported as in the first column of Exhibit 6-1. Budgeted amounts for each cost element are computed by using the following formula

$$\begin{array}{l}\text{Flexible} \\ \text{budget} \\ \text{allowance}\end{array} = \begin{array}{l}\text{fixed cost} \\ \text{per month}\end{array} + \left(\begin{array}{l}\text{direct} \\ \text{labor} \\ \text{hours}\end{array} \times \begin{array}{l}\text{variable} \\ \text{cost per} \\ \text{hour}\end{array}\right)$$

For example, the budget amount for indirect labor is computed as $1,200 + (1,000 × $0.50) or $1,700. This exhibit is actually the beginning of a performance report that will be completed later when actual labor hours are known.

The budget allowances for 1,000 hours represent expected costs *only* for 1,000 hours. If actual hours are higher (or lower), the production manager should be expected to incur more (or less) cost. That is the idea of flexible budgets: to give the manager a budget allowance based on the actual level of activity.

Suppose the department actually works 1,300 hours. The manager should have a *revised* budget allowance for each cost element, taking into consideration the higher production. For example, for indirect labor, the flexible budget allowance for the month would now be $1,850 [$1,200 + (1,300 hours × $0.50)]. In Exhibit 6-2, we have completed the performance report by inserting the flexible

Exhibit 6-1
Production Performance Report

Month __March__   Department __Mixing__
Manager __E. Jones__

	Budget Allowances			
	Budgeted Hours	Actual Hours	Actual Costs Incurred	Variance
Direct labor hours	1,000			
Indirect labor	$1,700			
Supplies	600			
Maintenance	2,500			
Depreciation	1,200			
Miscellaneous	750			
Total	$6,750			

Exhibit 6-2

Production Performance Report

Month __March__   Department __Mixing__
Manager __E. Jones__

| | Budget Allowances | | (Assumed) | Variance |
	Budgeted Hours	Actual Hours	Actual Costs Incurred	Favorable (Unfavorable)
Direct labor hours	1,000	1,300		
Indirect labor	$1,700	$1,850	$1,870	($20)
Supplies	600	720	705	15
Maintenance	2,500	2,530	2,470	60
Depreciation	1,200	1,200	1,200	—
Miscellaneous	750	765	780	(15)
Total	$6,750	$7,065	$7,025	$40

budget allowances for the achieved level of production, inserted some assumed actual costs, and computed a variance between the *revised* budget and the actual costs. When actual costs are less than the budget allowance, the variance is *favorable;* when the reverse is true, the variance is *unfavorable*. Hence, the variances for supplies, maintenance, and total costs were favorable. In Chapter 12 we discuss methods for analyzing variances.

Of course, careful cost analysis may show that a cost varies with some activity other than sales, or labor hours, or production. A budget allowance must be established based on *whatever* variable is determined to have a predictable relationship with actual cost. In many cases, important cost-driving activities are not related directly to production volume. For example, significant costs are often associated with activities such as the number of vendors from whom the company buys materials and components, the number of employees in a department, the number of different types of products manufactured, or the number of design changes made to a product. The analytical methods discussed in Chapter 3 help managers identify activities that are useful for budgeting purposes.

Budgeting Discretionary Costs

Establishing budget allowances for discretionary costs presents some of the most difficult problems in budgeting because no one really knows the optimal amount to spend on most discretionary activities. What *is* optimal spending for employee development? for improving current products? for research on potential products?

Expenditures for discretionary items seldom produce immediately measurable output. Research and development activities might not show results for several years, and the same is true for employee training. In some cases, budgets for discretionary items are related to some variable input factor, such as the number of employees being given training or the number of products being studied by research scientists and engineers. (But, note that the number of employees to be trained or products to be studied is also a matter of managerial choice for which there is no right answer.) In some cases, a manager might be able to specify, at least qualitatively, what benefits could come from a particular level of spending on a discretionary item. For example, the data processing manager might be able to say that leasing a certain software package would speed customer billing by one or two days. (Getting bills out quicker could mean that payments would come in sooner. But there remains the question whether the benefits of speeded up collections—the opportunity cost of money tied up in accounts receivable—exceed the cost of leasing the software package.)

Because optimal levels of spending on discretionary items cannot be determined, budget allowances for them are often set through negotiations between the affected managers and the budget director, or perhaps between those managers and upper levels of management. In many instances, budgets for these areas are established by specific policy decisions of top management. "We shall increase spending on research and development by 10% per year for the next five years" is an example of such a policy statement. Such a statement is likely to be the result of top managers having set a particular goal for the firm, such as the goal to be an innovator in the industry. Whatever the goal accepted by top management, it is important that the managers of the affected areas understand the reason behind a stated policy, so that those managers authorize actions (and the related expenditures) consistent with the goal.

BUDGETING AND HUMAN BEHAVIOR

Budgeting necessarily entails behavioral problems. These problems include the following: conflicting views, imposed budgets, budgets as checkup devices, and unwise adherence to budgets.

Conflicts

We can illustrate the problem of conflicts in budgeting by considering a matter of importance to almost any firm—inventory policy. The sales manager wants inventory to be as high as possible because it is easier to make sales if the goods are available immediately to the customer. The financial manager wants low inventories because of the costs associated with having inventory (storage, insurance, taxes, interest, and so on). In a manufacturing firm, the production manager is not interested in inventory per se, but in production. He or she wants steady production, no interruptions for rush orders, and no unplanned overtime, because these conditions minimize the costs of production. Thus, three managers have different views on the desirable level of inventory. Each will be evaluated by reference to how well the individual does his or her job, so each has an interest in the firm's inventory policy. In a conventional manufacturing environment, the conflict is resolved with great difficulty, if at all, and the managerial accountant might be called in to determine the best level of inventory for the firm. Note that a manufacturing firm committed by its top management to the just-in-time philosophy has already established a policy or goal for the level of its materials and finished products: little or none. The firm-wide commitment to this common goal not only drops the financial manager's concerns from the conflict, but also encourages the other managers to work together to achieve the maximum sales at the minimum cost.

Imposed Budgets

From the many assumptions stated in this chapter, you may have gotten the impression that cost levels, production levels, and so on are determined rather mechanically. This is seldom the case. Actual cost levels are determined by how well managers and workers perform their assigned jobs. Unfortunately, it is not uncommon for higher levels of management to *set* performance standards for the individuals below them. When such is the case, the standards are said to be imposed, and serious behavioral problems can arise (or be avoided) depending on the managers' attitudes.

Some managers believe that performance standards should be set very high (budgeted costs very low)—so high that almost no one could be expected to meet the budget. This position is sometimes justified on the grounds that it "keeps people on their toes" and is based on the assumption that people will slacken performance if they can easily meet a budget. Other managers say that budgets should be achievable given a good, but not exceptional, performance.

Significant problems can result from the imposition of unachievable (unrealistic) budgets. Managers can become discouraged and feel no commitment to achieving budgeted goals. They may act in ways that *seem* to help achieve goals (such as scrimping on preventive maintenance to achieve lower costs in the short run). But the actions taken may well be harmful in the longer run (when machinery breaks down and production must be halted altogether).

A major problem with imposed budgets is that they are often useless for planning, when planning is one of a budget's primary purposes. Consider, for example, the implications of setting unrealistically high sales goals. Based on those goals, production plans will be made, including perhaps commitments for materials and the hiring and training of factory workers. Based on sales goals, production plans, and inventory policies, storage areas for inventory will be acquired. Based on sales goals, cash receipts will be planned, and the firm will estimate and perhaps negotiate certain amounts of short-term financing.[1] Now what if the sales goals are not realized? Inventory will be higher than expected, and additional space may have to be contracted for at unfavorable rates. Cash receipts will not materialize as planned, and additional short-term financing may have to be negotiated on terms unfavorable to the firm. If subsequent production schedules are adjusted to bring them into line with lower sales and to reduce

---

[1] One of the advantages of the cash portion of the comprehensive budget is that it allows the firm to identify financing needs before they occur, so the managers have time to seek the best financing sources. More on this in Chapter 7.

inventory, employee relations may suffer as workers are laid off, and relations with suppliers may be harmed as delays in delivery of materials are requested.

We could say that, at their worst, unrealistic budgets can have serious financial effects on the firm. At the very least, unrealistic budgets will probably be ignored.

It is possible, of course, for imposed budgets to reflect achievable, realistic performance goals. There are, however, at least two reasons to adopt a budgeting approach that involves participation in standard-setting by the individuals expected to meet those standards. First, managers can never be as knowledgeable about the costs to perform specific tasks as are the persons actually performing them. Second, a considerable body of empirical evidence suggests that allowing individuals a say in their expected levels of performance is conducive to better performance than when those individuals are not consulted. While the managers, including top-level managers, must take the final responsibility for establishing goals, their methods of arriving at those goals can have a significant effect on the performance of individuals affected by those goals.

Budgets as "Checkup" Devices

Behavioral problems do not arise solely because of the procedure followed for developing budget allowances. Comparisons of budgeted and actual results and subsequent evaluation of performance also introduce difficulties. In ideal circumstances managers use actual results to evaluate their own performance, to evaluate the performance of others, and to correct elements of the operations that seem to be out of control. The budget serves as a feedback device; it lets managers know the results of their actions. Having seen that something is wrong, they can take steps to correct it.

Unfortunately, budgets are often used more for checking up on managers; that is, the feedback function is ignored. Where this is the case, managers are constantly looking over their shoulders and trying to think of ways to explain unfavorable results. The time spent on thinking of ways to defend the results could be more profitably used to plan and control operations. Some evaluation of performance is necessary, but the budget ought not to be perceived as a club to be held over the heads of managers. More attention is given to behavioral problems of performance evaluation in Chapters 10, 11, and 12.

Unwise Adherence to Budgets

As we said earlier, the budget sets limits on cost incurrence, allowances beyond which managers are not expected to go. When budgeted amounts are viewed as strict limits on spending, they may cause managers to spend either too little or too much. For example, there are times when exceeding the budget benefits the firm. Suppose a sales manager believes that a visit to several important customers or potential customers will result in greatly increased sales. If taking the trip will result in exceeding the travel budget, he or she will be reluctant to authorize the visit.

At the other extreme, a manager who has kept costs well under the budget might be tempted to spend frivolously so that expenditures will reach the budgeted level. The manager may fear that the budget for the following year will be cut because of the lower costs for the current year. Not wishing to be given a lower budget next year, the manager might take an undesirable action—authorize an unnecessary trip—in order to protect personal interests.

Because the activities carried on in a typical company are interrelated, managerial actions influenced by budget concerns in one area are likely to affect the actions taken by managers in other areas. A recently reported example of this interrelationship involved a manufacturing foreman who was running a machine under his supervision at 50% of its rated capacity.[2] Asked why, he said that the machine needed new bearings and would produce only scrap if run faster. The foreman's request for maintenance had been ignored for several months because the maintenance foreman had been controlling *his* costs by not replacing employees who left, and that practice had been going on for several years.

ILLUSTRATION OF A COMPREHENSIVE BUDGET   (Pro forma)

We illustrate the preparation of a comprehensive budget by working with Cross Company, a retailing firm. The illustration will be done in two parts. In this chapter we prepare the sales forecast, purchases budget, and tentative pro forma income statement. In Chapter 7 we prepare the cash budget, which requires some of the data in the budgets developed here. We shall then see how the operating and financial budgets are related, especially how the results in the tentative cash budget could induce the managers to look again at the operating budgets and possibly make changes in them. The example uses dollar amounts that are unrealistically small because we want to avoid long and arduous computations.

The managers of Cross Company are developing its comprehensive budget for the first six months of 19X4. As the first step, they have developed the following sales budget, which extends to August 19X4. (As we shall see shortly, a firm must budget sales beyond the six-month period in order to complete the purchases budget for June.)

Month	Sales Budget	Month	Sales Budget
Jan.	$ 400	May	$1,200
Feb.	600	June	800
Mar.	800	July	700
Apr.	1,000	Aug.	800

[2] Robert D'Amore, "Just-in-Time Systems," in *Cost Accounting, Robotics, and the New Manufacturing Environment,* ed. Robert Capettini and Donald K. Clancy (Sarasota, Fl.: American Accounting Association, 1987).

Sales are obviously seasonal; they increase through May and then drop off, with May sales budgeted at three times those of January.

Budgeted Income Statement

First, we develop a budgeted or pro forma income statement. To do so, additional assumptions are necessary, and we shall assume that the managers of Cross have decided that the following assumptions about cost behavior will provide a good basis for planning.

Cost of goods sold will be 60% of sales dollars.
Other variable costs will be 15% of sales.
Total fixed costs will be $240, of which $120 is depreciation expense.

With this information we can develop the budgeted income statements for the six months, as shown in Exhibit 6-3.

Separate income statements for each month are not needed; a statement for the six-month period will suffice. However, the other budgets have to be broken down by month, and the monthly income statements will facilitate the preparation of those budgets.

Purchases Budget

Our next step is to determine what inventory level is considered desirable. As we have already suggested, this determination can be extremely complex. We assume here that the interested managers agreed that inventory should be kept at a level of

Exhibit 6-3
Cross Company
Budgeted Income Statements, for the Six Months Ending June 30, 19X4

	Jan.	Feb.	Mar.	Apr.	May	June	Six-Month Period
Sales	$400	$600	$800	$1,000	$1,200	$800	$4,800
Cost of goods sold (60% of sales)	240	360	480	600	720	480	2,880
Gross profit	160	240	320	400	480	320	1,920
Other variable costs (15% of sales)	60	90	120	150	180	120	720
Contribution margin	100	150	200	250	300	200	1,200
Fixed costs (depreciation, rent, etc.)	40	40	40	40	40	40	240
Income	$ 60	$110	$160	$ 210	$ 260	$160	$ 960

two months' budgeted sales. That is, the managers have adopted an *inventory policy* requiring that at the end of each month the firm should have on hand enough inventory to cover the sales of the following two months. An inventory policy related to expected sales levels is in keeping with the fact that a firm stocks in anticipation of sales. Hence, if sales are expected to increase in the next period, inventory should also increase.

You should recognize that as you move from budgeting sales to budgeting inventory and purchases you must also move from considering selling prices to considering costs. (Remember that inventory is carried at cost.) We can determine purchasing requirements for the six months by using the general formula for cost of goods sold (from financial accounting):

$$\frac{\text{Cost of}}{\text{goods sold}} = \frac{\text{beginning}}{\text{inventory}} + \text{purchases} - \frac{\text{ending}}{\text{inventory}}$$

Adding ending inventory and subtracting beginning inventory from both sides, we obtain

$$\text{Purchases} = \frac{\text{cost of}}{\text{goods sold}} + \frac{\text{ending}}{\text{inventory}} - \frac{\text{beginning}}{\text{inventory}}$$

Exhibit 6-4 shows the purchases budget by month for the period. Note that the sum of the cost of sales for two consecutive months is the inventory required at the beginning of that two-month period. For example, the inventory required at the end of January ($840) is the sum of the cost of sales for February ($360) and March ($480). The circled items show the derivations of the ending inventory for January and April. Note also that the ending inventory in one month *is* the beginning inventory in the following month.

The total requirement for any one month is the amount needed to cover that month's sales plus what the company has determined must be on hand at the end of that month. The total requirement can be met from two sources: goods already on hand (beginning inventory) and purchases during the month. Thus,

Exhibit 6-4
Purchases Budget for the Six Months Ending June 30, 19X4

	Jan.	Feb.	Mar.	Apr.	May	June	Six Months
Cost of sales for month (Exhibit 6-3)	$ 240	$ 360 + $ 480	$ 600	$ 720 + $ 480			$2,880
Ending inventory required	840	1,080	1,320	1,200	900[a]	900[b]	900
Total requirements	1,080	1,440	1,800	1,800	1,620	1,380	3,780
Beginning inventory	600[c]	840	1,080	1,320	1,200	900	600
Purchases required	$ 480	$ 600	$ 720	$ 480	$ 420	$ 480	$3,180

[a]June and July cost of sales, 60% × ($800 + $700).
[b]July and August cost of sales, 60% × ($700 + $800).
[c]Inventory at January 1 is assumed to be consistent with company policy.

purchase requirements are total requirements less beginning inventory. Work through the budget to be sure you understand the calculations.

The rows for cost of sales and purchases add across to the totals, but the inventory rows and total requirements row do not. The beginning inventory in the total column is the beginning inventory for the six-month period. The ending inventory is the required ending inventory for the last month being budgeted. The final column is the result you would obtain if you were budgeting *only* for the six-month period as a whole. The ending inventory balance, derived as part of the purchases budget, will appear on the June 30 pro forma balance sheet. As you will see in Chapter 7, the purchases budget is also important in preparing the cash budget.

PURCHASES BUDGET – A MANUFACTURING FIRM

Just as a retailer must budget purchases to meet sales goals and adhere to inventory policy, so a manufacturer must budget production in keeping with expected sales and inventory policy. That is, the manufacturer must *produce* sufficient units to meet the sales goals, while the retailer must *purchase* those units. Moreover, the manufacturer must purchase sufficient materials to meet production goals. Thus, both types of firms must plan purchases, and the basic idea of such planning is the same. But developing the final budget is somewhat more complex for the manufacturer because such a firm must first develop a budget for production in units before developing a purchases budget in dollars. Units must be used first because both variable and fixed costs are associated with the production process, and the presence of the latter makes the use of dollars difficult without an intermediate budget in units.

Suppose that Brandon Company, a conventional manufacturer, wishes to keep an inventory of the firm's product equal to the budgeted sales for the following two months (much like the retailer in the earlier example). Brandon's managers have gathered the following budgeted data for 19X8.

Units of product on hand at December 31, 19X7			200 units
Pounds of material on hand, December 31, 19X7			3,000 pounds
Budgeted sales for the next five months:			
January	120 units	April	280 units
February	180 units	May	336 units
March	240 units		
Variable costs of production per unit:			
Materials (8 lbs. at $0.50)			$4.00
Labor			3.00
Manufacturing overhead:			
Fringe benefits			0.40
Power			0.30
Supplies			0.30
Total			$8.00

Fixed costs of production per month:	
Rent of machinery	$ 400
Supervisory salaries	600
Insurance	100
Managerial salaries	800
Total	$1,900

Brandon has identified its costs as variable or fixed, as did the retailer. But for Brandon, the variable production costs will vary with the number of units produced, not with the number of units sold. A production budget shows the number of units that must be produced each period to meet sales and inventory requirements. Brandon's budget appears in Exhibit 6-5. Note that even though a sales forecast is available for the first five months of 19X8, we can prepare a production budget for only the first three months. This is true because the firm's inventory policy for finished units is based on the expected sales for the following two months, and we do not know the expected sales beyond May.

Unless it is committed to the just-in-time philosophy, a manufacturing firm rarely buys its materials only as they are needed for production. A conventional manufacturer usually has a policy regarding how much material should be on hand, just as it has a policy about a desired inventory of finished units. Referring to the original data, we see that the $4 material cost per unit of product consists of eight pounds of material at $0.50 per pound. Let us assume further that Brandon's managers desire to keep a ᵣ terials inventory equal to 150% of the coming month's budgeted production needs. (In a conventional manufacturing environment it is reasonable to set the inventory policy for materials based on production, not on sales, because materials are needed when the product is made, not when it is sold.)

Exhibit 6-6 shows a budget for materials purchases in January and February. Brandon's inventory policy for materials makes it impossible to budget purchases for March because such purchases depend on an unknown, the budgeted production for April. This example offers further evidence of the problem that

Exhibit 6-5
Production Budget for the Three Months Ended March 31, 19X4
(in units)

	Jan.	Feb.	Mar.	Three Months
Expected sales	120	180	240	540
Ending inventory required	420	520	616	616
Total units required	540	700	856	1,156
Beginning inventory	200	420	520	200
Required production	340	280	336	956

Exhibit 6-6
Purchases Budget—Materials,
January and February, 19X4

	January	February	March
Budgeted production (from Exhibit 6-5)	340	280	336
Needed for current production (budgeted production × 8)	2,720	2,240	2,688
Ending inventory, 150% of coming month's production needs (280 × 8 × 1.5) and (336 × 8 × 1.5)	3,360	4,032	?
Total pounds of material needed	6,080	6,272	
Beginning inventory	3,000	3,360	
Required purchases, in pounds	3,080	2,912	
Required purchases at $0.50	$1,540	$1,456	

lead times can create, and of the need for planning if the firm is to operate efficiently.

In a retailing firm, the purchases budget is important in developing a cash budget, because the payments for purchased units are not likely to be made at exactly the time of purchase. In a manufacturing firm, both the production and the materials purchases budgets are important for the budgeting of cash, because payments for materials purchases are not likely to be required at the same time as the payments for other costs associated with production. The development of a cash budget, one of the most important of the schedules included in a comprehensive budget, is discussed in detail in Chapter 7.

SUMMARY

Comprehensive budgeting is vital to effective planning and control. The comprehensive budget is the major near-term planning document developed by the firm and consists of a set of financial statements and other schedules showing the expected results for a future period. The development of a comprehensive budget formalizes management objectives and helps coordinate the many activities performed within a single firm.

Sales forecasting is critical to the budgeting process because the sales budget drives all other budgets. Several approaches are used for forecasting sales. The approach adopted depends on the reliability of available data, the nature of the product, and the experience and sophistication of the managers. The sales forecast and assumptions about cost behavior and inventory policy are used to prepare the purchases and expense budgets and a pro forma income statement. Flexible budget allowances are recommended for most types of costs because they are useful in identifying problems that require managerial action and in evaluating performance. In a manufacturing firm, the production budget is the equivalent of the purchases budget in a retailing firm. The production budget is the basis for determining the purchases budget of a manufacturer.

The budgeting process entails numerous behavioral problems, which can be particularly severe if managers do not participate in the development of the budget, or if budget goals are perceived as unachievable.

KEY TERMS

budget allowance	flexible budget allowance
capital budget	operating budgets
comprehensive budget	production budget
continuous budget	purchases budget
expected value	sales forecast
expense budget	static budget
financial budgets	

KEY FORMULAS

$$\text{Budgeted purchases}^a = \text{cost of current sales} + \text{desired ending inventory} - \text{beginning inventory}$$

$$\text{Budgeted production, in units} = \text{units needed for current sales} + \text{desired ending inventory} - \text{beginning inventory}$$

a For budgeting purchases in a manufacturing firm, "cost of current sales" becomes "cost of units of materials needed for current production."

REVIEW PROBLEM

Using the following data for Exempli Company, prepare a budgeted income statement and a purchases budget in units and dollars for January 19X4.

Budgeted sales for January	5,000 units at $20	$100,000
Budgeted sales for February	6,000 units at $20	$120,000
Cost data:		
Purchase price of product		$5 per unit
Commission to salespeople		10% of sales
Depreciation		$2,000 per month
Other operating expenses		$40,000 per month plus 5% of sales

Exempli's policy is to maintain inventory at 150% of the coming month's sales requirements. Inventory at December 31, 19X3, is $30,000 (6,000 units at $5), which is less than budgeted.

Answer to Review Problem

Budgeted Income Statement for January 19X4

Sales		$100,000
Cost of sales (5,000 units at $5)		25,000
Gross profit		75,000
Variable costs:		
Commissions (10% × $100,000)	$10,000	
Variable operating expenses (5% × $100,000)	5,000	15,000
Contribution margin		60,000
Fixed costs:		
Depreciation	2,000	
Other operating expenses	40,000	42,000
Income		$ 18,000

Purchases Budget for January 19X4

	Units	Dollars
Cost of sales	5,000	$25,000
Desired ending inventory (6,000 × 150%)	9,000	45,000
Total requirements	14,000	70,000
Beginning inventory	6,000	30,000
Purchases required for the month	8,000	$40,000

ASSIGNMENT MATERIAL

Questions for Discussion

6-1 **"Why bother with budgets?"** Evaluate the following statement: "I suppose budgets are fine for firms that can plan ahead, but I can't. Things are too uncertain for me to make plans. And besides, I have to spend my time looking after day-to-day operations and trying to figure out what is wrong."

6-2 **Expense budgeting** What are the major factors in setting budgeted amounts for the following?
(a) Commissions to salespeople
(b) Electricity
(c) Taxes on land and buildings
(d) Taxes on personal property (physical assets other than land and buildings)
(e) Charitable contributions
(f) Office salaries

6-3   *Sales forecasting — effects of external events*   Indicate what effect, if any, each of the following events would have on the sales forecast that you have already prepared. Explain your reasoning.

(a)   Your firm makes building materials. The federal government just announced a new program to assist low-income families to buy their own homes.

(b)   Your firm makes toys. The government announces that the economic outlook is better than had been thought. Personal income is likely to increase and unemployment decrease.

(c)   You make parts for the automobile industry. A strike against your major customer is announced by the head of the union.

(d)   You process baby food. The number of marriages is expected to drop sharply because of poor economic conditions.

(e)   You make heating and air conditioning equipment. The prices of electricity, heating oil, and natural gas are expected to rise rapidly.

(f)   You make insulation for houses and other buildings. The prices of electricity, heating oil, and natural gas are expected to rise rapidly.

(g)   Your firm publishes college textbooks. Recent statistics show that the numbers of high school seniors and juniors have fallen off from previous years.

(h)   Your firm makes plumbing pipe from copper. The major source of copper is Chile, which has just gone to war with one of its neighbors.

6-4   *Budget requests*   Some organizations follow the practice of cutting all budget requests by some set percentage, ignoring the merits of the specific requests. For example, the total budget for each department might be reduced by 5%, or each line item in each department reduced by 5%. Explain how this practice could be beneficial. Is there any way in which this practice could be harmful?

6-5   *Six months is already too long*   The owner of a retail store told his controller: "Seems pretty silly to me to make budgets for more than a month or two in advance. You make a purchases budget based on a sales forecast and an inventory policy. Ha! Inventory policies are fine; but you know as well as I do that a month's sales are never exactly what we have forecast, so within a month our actual inventory is different from the budget. All the time we spend putting together budgets for more than two months in advance is a waste." How would you respond to the owner's comments?

6-6   *Sales forecasting — value of indicators*   The following conversation took place between two company presidents.

Grant: "We hired a consultant to help us with our sales forecasting and he has really done a good job. As you know, we make ballpoint pen refills, and he found that our sales are very closely correlated with sales of refillable pens from four months previous. He says that four months seems to be the average life of the cartridges used in most pens. Of course, we don't make pens, but our refills fit the pens that nearly every firm makes."

Harrison: We've done the same thing. Our major product is baby bottles, and our consultant found that the number of bottles we sell is very closely related to the number of births about a month later. People seem to buy bottles about a month before the baby is born."

Required: Determine which firm seems to be in the better position to forecast its sales. Explain your answer.

6-7 *What's happening here?* Jack Rolland, the assistant to the controller of Upton Company, was looking at the following report for the marketing department. Upton's fiscal year ends December 31.

		Expenditures Through	
Cost Category	Annual Budget	November	December
Salaries	$240,000	$220,000	$240,000
Travel	36,000	24,000	36,000
Other	96,000	87,000	96,000

Rolland said to you: "I wonder why Cal [the marketing department manager] waited so long to spend his travel money. Maybe a lot of his business is concentrated in December."

Required: Tell Rolland why you think Cal spent his travel budget the way he did.

Exercises

6-8 *Purchases budget (continued in 6-9 and Chapter 7)* Gentry Sporting Goods has the following sales budget.

May	$220,000
June	250,000

Gentry's cost of sales is 60%. Its policy is to have inventory equal to budgeted sales needs for the following month. Gentry began May with inventory of $90,000.

Required: Prepare a purchases budget for May.

6-9 *Budgeted income statement (continuation of 6-8, continued in Chapter 7)* Gentry's variable costs other than cost of sales are 10% of sales, and its monthly fixed costs are $20,000, including $4,000 depreciation.

Required: Prepare budgeted income statements for May and for June.

6-10 *Budgeted income statement and purchases budget (continued in Chapter 7)* Jordan Clothing has the following sales forecast for the first four months of 19X9.

January	$210,000
February	240,000
March	230,000
April	260,000

Jordan's cost of sales is 70% of sales. Its fixed costs are $20,000 per month. Jordan maintains inventory at 150% of the coming month's budgeted sales requirements and has $220,000 inventory at January 1.

Required

1. Prepare a budgeted income statement for the first three months of 19X9, total only, not by month.
2. Prepare a purchases budget for the first three months of 19X9, in total and by month.

6-11 Budgeted income statement and purchases budget (continued in Chapter 7)   The following data relate to the operations of Thomas Company, a retail store.

Sales Forecast—19X4

January	$ 80,000
February	90,000
March	120,000
April	160,000

1. Cost of sales is 40% of sales. Other variable costs are 10% of sales.
2. Inventory is maintained at twice budgeted sales requirements for the following month. The beginning inventory is $64,000.
3. Fixed costs are $40,000 per month.

Required

1. Prepare a budgeted income statement for the first quarter of 19X4. (Do not prepare separate statements for each month.)
2. Prepare a purchases budget, by month, for the first quarter.

6-12 Budgeting manpower and costs   Kramwer Company has established a policy of having a foreman for every nine workers; whenever the number of foremen divided into the number of workers is greater than nine, a foreman is hired. The firm is expanding output and has budgeted production in units as follows.

January	4,800	April	6,800
February	5,400	May	7,300
March	6,100	June	7,500

A production worker can produce 100 units per month. Both workers and foremen are hired at the beginning of the month in which they are to be added. Workers are paid $1,500 per month, foremen, $2,800.

Required: Prepare a budget of requirements for workers and for foremen, by month, in number and dollar cost.

6-13 Purchases budget—units and dollars   Warner Company expects the following unit sales.

	Feb.	Mar.	Apr.	May	June
Sales	1,900	2,200	2,300	2,100	1,700

The firm maintains inventory equal to budgeted sales for the following two months. The beginning inventory is 3,700 units. Each unit costs $4.

Required
1. Prepare purchases budgets for as many months as you can in (a) units and (b) in dollars.
2. Explain why you had to stop where you did.

6-14 Budgeted income statements Weinstock Building Supply operates a chain of lumberyards in a large metropolitan area. The sales manager has retained a prominent economist to develop sales forecasting methods to enable the firm to plan better. The economist, for a substantial fee, has developed the following equation that he says will forecast sales quite well based on past patterns of behavior.

$$\text{Monthly sales in dollars} = \$136,000 + \left(\$0.052 \times \frac{\text{dollar value of building}}{\text{permits issued in prior month}} \right)$$

The sales manager asks your advice. He shows you the following data regarding building permits. The forecasts were developed by the Association of Builders in the area and have generally been accurate.

March	$3,000,000 (actual)
April	4,750,000 (forecast)
May	6,900,000 (forecast)
June	7,100,000 (forecast)

It is now April 3, and the sales manager would like forecasts of sales and income for as many months as you can prepare. He also states that cost of goods sold, which is all variable, is 45% of sales. Other variable costs are 8% of sales, and fixed costs are $140,000 per month.

Required: Prepare budgeted income statements for as many months as you can, given the data available. Round to the nearest $100.

6-15 Flexible budget and variances Adams Company makes a single product. Materials for a unit of the product cost $4, labor is $3, and manufacturing overhead is $20,000 per month fixed, plus $5 per unit variable (with production). In one month, production was 18,000 units and costs incurred were as follows: materials, $71,800; labor, $56,100; variable overhead, $89,000; and fixed overhead, $20,000.

Required
1. Prepare a flexible expense budget formula.
2. What should costs have been to produce 18,000 units? (Consider each element of cost separately.)
3. What were the variances between actual and budgeted costs?

6-16 **Expected values** You have received the following data from the marketing department, regarding the expected unit sales of a new type of coffee maker that your company will introduce in a few months.

Sales	Probability
30,000	0.20
35,000	0.50
42,000	0.20
50,000	0.10

Required: Determine the expected value of sales.

6-17 **Flexible and static budgets** You have just become the supervisor of the grinding department of GHJ Company. The production manager has been concerned about the use of supplies in your department and has, after discussions with you, come up with the following monthly budget formula

Budgeted supplies expense = $13,400 + ($1.85 × units produced)

Your department was budgeted to produce 10,000 units in April, giving a budget allowance of $31,900. You actually produced 11,500 units and incurred $33,950 in supplies expense. The production manager attached a note to your monthly report saying that you needed to get better control of supplies because you exceeded the budget by $2,050 ($33,950 − $31,900).

Required: Show that you actually did control supplies expense in April and point out the mistake that the production manager made.

Problems

6-18 **Production budget** StillWare Pottery manufactures various products. It has the following sales budget, in sets, for its Mexicali line of dishes: April, 20,000; May, 25,000; and June, 28,000. It keeps its inventory at twice the coming month's budgeted sales. At April 1, its inventory is expected to be 42,000 sets.

Required: Prepare production budgets for April and for May.

6-19 **Purchases budget (extension of 6-18)** The manufacturing of one set of StillWare's Mexicali dishes requires 12 pounds of material that costs $2.50 per pound. StillWare keeps its inventory of materials at 150% of the coming month's budgeted production. At the beginning of April, StillWare expects to have 540,000 pounds of material on hand.

Required: Prepare a materials purchases budget for April in (a) pounds and (b) dollars.

6-20 **JIT Manufacturing (extension of 6-18 and 6-19)** StillWare Pottery is considering the adoption of just-in-time and flexible manufacturing principles. Some of its managers have studied other companies and believe that StillWare can implement some aspects of JIT now. They believe the company could very quickly cut its finished goods inventory to a constant 800 sets of Mexicali dishes and its materials inventory to a two day supply (1/15th of a month). They believe that later on the company can achieve even greater reductions, with zero inventories the objective.

Required
1. Prepare production budgets for April and May, and a purchases budget for April. Assume also that April's beginning inventories conform to the new policies.
2. What advantages do you see in reducing inventory as indicated here?

6-21 **Budgeting production and purchases** The production manager of Cram Company wishes to maintain an inventory of materials equal to budgeted production needs for the next two months. Each unit of product takes five pounds of material. Inventory of finished goods is usually maintained at 150% of the following month's budgeted sales. The sales budget for the first five months of the coming year, given in units, is as follows.

January	14,000	April	18,000
February	12,000	May	21,000
March	15,000		

As of December 31, there were 120,000 pounds of material on hand and 21,000 units of finished product.

Required: Prepare budgets of production and purchases of materials in units and pounds, respectively, for as many months as possible.

6-22 **JIT manufacturing (extension of 6-21)** Cram Company's managers have begun to use some principles of just-in-time manufacturing. They have been able to reduce finished goods inventory to a ten-day supply (one-third of the coming month's budgeted sales requirements) and materials inventory to a three-day supply (one-tenth of the coming month's budgeted production). Inventories at August 31 reflect these policies. The sales budget for the coming few months, in units, is: September 14,000; October, 15,000; November, 15,500; December, 16,000.

Required: Prepare budgets of production and purchases of materials for as many months as you can. (Round all items to the nearest hundred units or pounds.) Comment on the differences between these budgets and those in the preceding assignment and on the advantages of the JIT operation.

6-23 **Production and purchases budgets** Bordan Products makes sets of plastic kitchen containers. For one of its lines it has the following sales forecast for the first four months of 19X8: January, 1,800; February, 2,200; March, 1,900; and April, 1,800. Company policy is to keep inventory of finished sets equal to budgeted sales for the following two months. Each set requires five pounds of material that costs $0.60 per pound. Bordan maintains materials inventory at 150% of the following month's production requirements. At December 31, 19X7, Bordan has 4,200 sets of finished containers and 10,500 pounds of materials.

Required
1. Prepare a production budget for January and for February.
2. Prepare a purchases budget for January in (a) units and (b) dollars.

6-24 **Relationships**   The following income statement relates to Habib Company operations for April. No change in inventories is planned.

Sales (900 units at $50)		$45,000
Variable costs:		
Materials ($5 per unit)	$4,500	
Labor ($7 per unit)	6,300	
Overhead—manufacturing ($4 unit)	3,600	
Selling expenses ($2 per unit)	1,800	16,200
Contribution margin		28,800
Fixed costs:		
Manufacturing	8,000	
Selling and administrative	9,600	17,600
Income		$11,200

Required: Fill in the blanks.

1. Budgeted production for April is _____ units.
2. Total variable manufacturing costs for April are $_____ .
3. The sale of an additional 10 units would increase income by $_____ .
4. Total costs and expenses if 920 units were sold would be $_____ .
5. Break-even volume in units is _____ .
6. If variable manufacturing costs increased by $2 per unit, income at 900 units
   sold would be $_____ .
7. If fixed costs increased by $2,400, and the firm wanted income of $11,200, sales
   in units would have to be _____ .
8. If ending inventory were to be 20 units higher than beginning inventory, manufacturing costs incurred during the period would be $_____ .

6-25 **Multiple materials – manufacturing firm**   Williams Company expects the
following sales by month, in units, for the first five months of 19X9.

	January	February	March	April	May
Budgeted sales	1,500	1,800	1,900	2,500	1,900

The company's one product, the Tow, requires two raw materials: Tics and Tacs.
Each Tow requires three Tics and two Tacs. Williams follows the policy of having
finished goods equal to 50% of budgeted sales for the following two months. Raw
material inventories are maintained at 150% of budgeted production needs for the
coming month. All inventories at December 31, 19X8, reflect these policies.

Required

1. Prepare a production budget for Tows for as many months as you can.
2. Prepare purchases budgets for Tics and Tacs for as many months as you can.

6-26 **Smoothing production**   Maynard Company makes bathing suits, with its sales
falling heavily in the April–June period, as shown by the sales budget opposite (in
thousands of units).

	January	February	March	April	May	June
Sales	100	100	110	160	200	250

The firm's normal inventory policy has been to have a two-month supply of finished product. The production manager has criticized the policy because it requires wide swings in production, which add to costs. He estimates that per-unit variable manufacturing cost is $3 higher than normal for each unit produced in excess of 180,000 units per month. Maynard's treasurer is concerned that increasing production in the early months of the year would lead to high costs of carrying inventory. He estimates that it costs the firm $0.80 per unit per month in ending inventory, consisting of insurance, financing, and handling costs. He emphasizes that these costs are incremental.

All of the managers agree that the firm should have 450,000 units on hand by the end of April. The production manager wants to spread the required production equally over the four months, while the treasurer believes that the firm should stick to its current policy unless it turns out to be costlier.

Required
1. Prepare a budget of production for January through April following the firm's current policy. Inventory at January 1 is 200,000 units.
2. Prepare a production budget using the production manager's preference.
3. Determine which budget gives lower costs.

6-27 *Relationships among sales and production budgets* Partially completed sales and production budgets for Firmin Company are shown below. The firm maintains an inventory equal to 150% of the budgeted sales for the coming month. Fill in the blanks.

Sales Budget in Units

Jan.	Feb.	Mar.	Apr.	May	June	July
3,000	3,400	——	——	——	5,800	——

Production Budget (in units)

	Jan.	Feb.	Mar.	Apr.	May	June
Ending inventory	——	6,300	——	——	8,700	——
Sales	3,000	——	——	——	——	5,800
Total requirements	——	——	——	13,900	——	——
Beginning inventory	——	5,100	——	6,900	——	——
Production	3,600	——	——	7,000	——	5,200

2. Prepare new reports showing in the budget columns the amounts of cost that you would expect to be incurred given the actual production achieved. Use the same format as is shown above.

6-28 *Preparing flexible budgets* As a new assistant to the controller of GHJ Company, you have been assigned the task of preparing a set of flexible budget allowances for overhead costs. You have the following data available.

Cost	Variable Amount per Direct Labor Hour	Fixed Amount
Supplies	$0.70	$17,000
Repairs	0.12	9,200
Power	1.10	15,600
Depreciation		18,800

Supervision, the only other overhead item, is a step-variable cost. It is expected to be $7,000 at 10,000 direct labor hours and to rise by $1,000 for each additional 1,000 direct labor hours.

Required: Prepare a schedule showing the budgeted amount of each cost element, and of total budgeted overhead cost, at 10,000, 12,000, and 14,000 direct labor hours.

6-29 *Budgeted income statements – expected values* Burke Company is preparing its comprehensive budget for 19X7. The sales manager has said that he does not wish to pin down a single estimate of sales, but would prefer to give three forecasts, along with his estimates of the probabilities he attaches to them.

Sales Forecast	Probability
$ 500,000	0.6
800,000	0.3
1,000,000	0.1

Variable costs are 60% of sales and total fixed costs are budgeted at $250,000.

Required
1. Prepare budgeted income statements based on each of the three forecasts.
2. Prepare a budgeted income statement based on the expected value of sales.

6-30 *Budgeting in a CPA firm* Donald Ebit is a certified public accountant practicing in a large city. He employs two staff accountants and two clerical workers. He pays the four employees a total of $6,100 per month. His other expenses, all fixed, for such items as rent, utilities, subscriptions, stationery, and postage are $3,400 per month.

Public accounting is, for most firms, highly seasonal, with about four months (January through April) that are extremely busy, eight months of less activity.

The most relevant measure of volume in a CPA firm is charged hours—the hours worked on client business for which the clients are charged. Mr. Ebit expects his two staff accountants to work an average of 120 charged hours each month during the eight slower months, and 200 hours each per month during the January–April busy season. Clerical personnel work about 600 charged hours each per year, and Mr. Ebit works about 1,400. For both the clerical personnel and Mr. Ebit, approximately 40% of their charged hours fall in the four-month busy season.

Mr. Ebit charges his clients $50 per hour for his time, $25 for the time of a staff accountant, and $10 for the time of clerical personnel.

Required: Prepare a budget of revenues and expenses for a year for Mr. Ebit's firm. Separate the budgets for the periods January–April and May–December.

6-31 *Sales forecasting – scatter diagram and regression* Ridley Carpet Company has engaged you as a consultant to help in its sales forecasting. After a long discussion with Robert Ridley, president of the firm, you develop the following data.

Year	Housing Units Built (in thousands)	Sales of Ridley Company (in thousands)
19X1	1,300	$2,440
19X2	1,400	2,610
19X3	1,900	3,380
19X4	1,500	2,760
19X5	2,000	3,520
19X6	1,600	2,875

Required
1. Develop an equation to be used to forecast sales for Ridley Company. Use a scatter diagram and regression analysis.
2. Mr. Ridley has learned that housing units to be built in 19X7 will be about 1.8 million. What is your forecast for Ridley's sales? Are you relatively confident about your forecast? Why or why not?

6-32 *Comprehensive budget (continued in Chapter 7)* The managers of Calco Products Company have been developing information for the comprehensive budget for the coming year. They have decided to use the following estimates and policies for planning.

Sales forecast, in units:	
January	20,000
February	24,000
March	30,000
April	25,000
May	22,000
Selling price	$30 per unit
Material cost	$8 per unit of product
Direct labor and variable overhead	$6 per unit of product
Variable selling expenses	$2 per unit sold
Fixed manufacturing costs	$120,000 per month
Fixed S, G, & A expenses	$60,000 per month

The managers plan to keep inventory of finished goods equal to budgeted sales for the following two months, and inventory of materials equal to twice budgeted production for the coming month. The December 31 inventories are: finished goods, 35,000 units; materials, 66,000 units (one unit of material per unit of product).

Required
1. Prepare budgeted income statements for January, February, and the two-month period, using the contribution margin format.
2. Prepare production budgets for January, for February, and for March.
3. Prepare purchases budgets for materials for January and for February.

6-33 **Budgeting for a hospital (AICPA adapted)** The administrator of Taylor Memorial Hospital, Dr. Gale, has asked for your assistance in preparing the budget for 19X7, which he must present at the next meeting of the hospital's board of trustees. The hospital obtains its revenues through two types of charges: charges for use of a hospital room and charges for use of the operating room. The use of the basic rooms depends on whether the patient undergoes surgery during the stay in the hospital. Estimated data as to the types of patients and the related room requirements for 19X7 are as follows:

Type of Patient	Total Expected	Average Stay in Days	Percentages Selecting Kinds of Rooms		
			Private	Semiprivate	Ward
Surgical	2,400	10	15%	75%	10%
Medical only	2,100	8	10%	60%	30%

Basic room charges are $50, $40, and $30 for private, semiprivate, and ward, respectively.

Charges for use of the operating room are a function of the length of the operation and the number of persons required to be involved in the operation. The charge is $0.15 per man-minute. (A man-minute is one person for one minute; if an operation requires three persons for 40 minutes, there would be a charge for 120 man-minutes at $0.15 per man-minute, or $18.) Based on past experience the following is a breakdown of the types of operations to be performed.

Type of Operation	Number of Operations	Average Number of Minutes per Operation	Average Number of Persons Required
Minor	1,200	30	4
Major—abdominal	400	90	6
Major—other	800	120	8
	2,400		

Required
1. Prepare a schedule of budgeted revenues from room charges by type of patient and type of room.
2. Prepare a schedule of budgeted revenues from operating room charges by type of operation.

6-34 **Inventory policy – carrying costs** The managers for production, sales, and finance of the Steele Company are discussing production and inventory policies.

The sales manager would like the firm to stock more units in inventory. The production manager is willing to do so. The financial manager argues that the cost of storing, insuring, and financing the additional inventory would be prohibitive; it costs the firm $4 per month per unit to cover these costs and they are variable with the number of units on hand.

The sales manager believes that if inventory were increased by 5,000 units, sales would be 2,000 units per month higher. Contribution margin per unit is $7.

Required
1. What is the value (per month) of the additional sales that would be generated by the increased inventory?
2. What additional monthly costs are associated with carrying the additional 5,000 units in inventory?
3. What decision should be made regarding production and inventory?

6-35 *Flexible budget, multiple drivers* The controller of Ames Industries has analyzed the costs of the Linden Plant. She comes up with the following cost drivers. Data are quarterly.

	Fixed Component	Variable Component	Cost Driver
Inspection	$ 72,500	$120.00	Shipments
Maintenance	61,200	2.40	Machine hours
Data processing	9,700	0.25	Transactions
Purchasing	63,600	180.00	Number of vendors
Other	278,800	2.20	Labor hours

Some of these costs are step-variable, so the variable components do not apply to small changes in activity, but only to relatively large movements. You may assume for this assignment that all changes are large.

Required: Develop flexible budget allowances for each element of cost, and for total cost, for the following two cases.

	Case	
	A	B
Shipments	110	75
Machine hours	15,000	22,000
Transactions	220,000	360,000
Number of vendors	120	40
Labor hours	7,000	11,000

6-36 *Flexible and static budget* Wilkinson Company prepares budgets for each month. Budgeted amounts, along with actual results, are shown in reports that are circulated to the managers whose operations are being reported on *and* to their superiors. Excerpts from the report of the latest two months for one production department are given on page 246.

	April			May		
	Budget	Actual	Variance	Budget	Actual	Variance
Production in units	8,000	7,000	1,000	10,000	10,500	(500)
Costs:						
Material	$16,000	$14,600	$1,400	$20,000	$20,800	($800)
Direct labor	24,000	21,600	2,400	30,000	31,300	(1,300)
Indirect labor	4,000	3,900	100	5,000	5,300	(300)
Power	7,000	6,700	300	8,000	8,400	(400)
Maintenance	5,200	4,700	500	6,000	6,200	(200)
Supplies and other	4,600	4,580	20	5,000	5,050	(50)
Total costs	$60,800	$56,080	$4,720	$74,000	$77,050	($3,050)

Required

1. Using the budgeted amounts, determine the fixed and variable components of each cost.
2. Comment on the desirability of Wilkinson's method of providing information to its managers.

6-37 Manufacturing cost budget Horton Company makes a variety of household products, usually in about the same mix. On the average, each unit requires $3 in materials and $2 in variable manufacturing overhead. Direct labor averages $4 per unit up to 100,000 units per month. Direct labor rises to $6 per unit for units over 100,000, because of overtime premium. The remainder of manufacturing overhead is step-variable, with the following pattern.

Monthly Unit Production	Other Costs
Up to 100,000	$230,000
100,001–120,000	245,000
120,001–140,000	275,000

The pattern of these costs reflects increased supervision, utilities, and other costs associated with operating beyond the normal eight-hour day.
Budgeted unit production for the next few months is

March	90,000
April	115,000
May	130,000
June	105,000
Total	440,000

Required

1. Prepare budgets for manufacturing costs for each month, and in total.
2. What would total production costs be for the four-month period if the company could equalize production at 110,000 units per month?
3. If the company needs only to produce 440,000 units for the entire four-month

period, how should it produce by month to obtain the lowest possible total production cost?

4. What reasons might there be for the company to stick to the original monthly production budget despite its higher costs?

6-38 *Preparation of flexible budget – high-low, scatter diagram, and regression analysis* Hensley Company has used flexible budgets for some years and is now reviewing the rate it uses to budget utility costs. The following data have been collected.

Month	Direct Labor Hours	Utility Costs
1	7,000	$22,000
2	8,200	24,700
3	9,100	26,700
4	8,600	25,800
5	7,800	23,800
6	7,300	23,000

Required

1. Estimate the variable utility rate per direct labor hour using the following:
   (a) the high-low method
   (b) the scatter-diagram method
   (c) regression analysis
2. Prepare a formula for budgeting utility costs.

6-39 *Indicators for sales forecasting* The following economic indicators and other data might be useful in forecasting sales for certain kinds of firms: income per capita, population, car sales, and rate of unemployment.

For each of the types of firms listed below, state which, if any, of the listed indicators you think would be relevant in forecasting sales. Indicate briefly why you think each indicator is relevant or irrelevant.

(a) food company
(b) maker of outboard motors
(c) home construction firm
(d) tire maker
(e) textbook company
(f) jewelry maker
(g) maker of nonprescription drugs

6-40 *Budgeting and behavior* Rydell Company sets sales budgets for its salespeople, who are evaluated by reference to whether they achieve budgeted sales. The budget is expressed in total dollars of sales and is $200,000 per salesperson for the first quarter of 19X3. The firm makes two products, for which price and cost data are given below.

	Wiffers	Trogs
Selling price	$10	$15
Variable costs	4	10
Contribution margin	$ 6	$ 5

During the first quarter of 19X3, all salespeople met the $200,000 sales budget. Wiffers are a new product that the firm's president thinks should become a big seller, while Trogs are the standard model that has been popular for some years. The products are sold to different kinds of customers; the customers who have been buying Trogs for years are not expected to buy Wiffers. Customers for Wiffers must be sought out by the salespeople and convinced of the high quality of the product. The $200,000 budgeted sales per person is a fairly high goal, but is attainable.

Required
1. Which product should salespeople stress?
2. Under the circumstances described, which product do you think sold most?
3. If your answers to items 1 and 2 conflict, what changes would you suggest for the firm's budgeting process?

6-41 **Production and purchases budgets – units and dollars** Drummond Company manufactures several products, including a frying pan with a wooden handle. The sales forecasts for the frying pan for the next five months are given below, in units.

	April	May	June	July	August
Budgeted sales	2,500	3,100	2,800	3,500	2,400

Each frying pan requires a blank sheet of iron that Drummond buys from a single supplier and molds into the appropriate shape. The handles are purchased in ready-to-use condition from another supplier. The firm's policy is to keep finished goods inventory at twice the coming month's budgeted sales, blank iron sheets at budgeted production requirements for the coming two months, and handles at budgeted production requirements for the coming month.

Each sheet of blank iron is made into one frying pan and costs $2. Handles cost $0.40. Labor costs for shaping the iron and putting on a handle are $1.50 and variable manufacturing overhead costs are $0.80. Fixed manufacturing costs are $4,500 per month.

At the end of March the firm expects to have the following inventories.

Finished pans	5,300
Blank iron sheets	5,600
Handles	4,600

Required
1. Prepare production budgets for April through July, by month, in units and in dollar costs.
2. Prepare purchases budgets in units and dollars for blank iron sheets and handles for April and for May.

6-42 **Conflicts in policy** Timmons Fashions has the following sales budget, in units, for its best-selling line of women's wear.

January	65,000	April	60,000
February	90,000	May	100,000
March	60,000	June	80,000

Timmons manufactures the line in a single plant. Because of union agreements and employment policies, the only feasible amounts of monthly production are 72,000 and 90,000 for a four-day week and five-day week, respectively.

Timmons's policy is to keep inventory of at least 15,000 units at the end of each month to serve as a buffer in case of slow deliveries by suppliers or other problems that could lead to lost sales. Storage is limited, such that having inventory greater than 40,000 units results in abnormally high costs. The inventory at January 1 is 20,000 units.

Required: Develop a production budget for the six months. If you cannot keep inventory within the limits stated, be prepared to defend the reasoning you used in making your selection.

6-43 *Budgeting administrative expenses* The controller of Kaufman Company has asked you to prepare a flexible budget for costs in the purchasing department. It has been determined that the typists in the department can type about 100 lines per hour and the average purchase order has 10 lines. Typists are paid $4 per hour and work a 35-hour week. When there is not enough typing to keep them busy, the typists file and perform other work. Order clerks prepare the purchase orders to be typed. They are paid $6 per hour for a 35-hour week and generally take 20 minutes to prepare an order for typing. They also work at other tasks when purchase orders are slack. The purchasing agent is paid $300 per week. Supplies, stationery, and so on average $0.40 per purchase order.

Required

1. If normal volume in the purchasing department is 800 orders per week, how many order clerks and typists are required?
2. Based on your answer to item 1, how much slack time do clerks and typists have available to perform other duties?
3. If salaries for clerks and typists, and costs for supplies and stationery are to be budgeted as variable costs, what is the flexible budget formula?
4. What variance from the budget would you expect if 800 orders were processed during one week? (Use the data for personnel requirements developed in item 1.)
5. What is the capacity of the purchasing department given the personnel requirement derived in item 1?
6. What is the flexible budget formula if the personnel requirements in item 1 are treated as fixed costs?

6-44 *Sales forecasting, budgeted income, and budgeted production (continued in Chapter 7)* Richards Company manufactures ignition systems used in automobile engines. The firm has developed a forecasting tool that has been successful in predicting sales for the firm. Written in equation form, sales = 80,000 + (0.009 × automobile sales). This coming year's automobile sales are expected to be 8,000,000.

Each system contains material costing $5. Direct labor is $10 per unit and variable manufacturing overhead is $12. Besides the variable manufacturing cost, there are commissions to salespeople of 10% of dollar sales. The system sells for $80 per unit. Fixed costs of manufacturing are $1,200,000 per year; fixed selling and administrative expenses are $1,800,000 per year. Both are incurred evenly over the year.

Sales are seasonal; about 60% of sales are in the first six months of the fiscal year, which begins June 1. The sales forecast for the first six months, in percentages of annual sales, is as follows.

June	5%	September	12%
July	8	October	14
August	9	November	12

Richards has a policy of keeping inventory of finished product equal to budgeted sales for the next two months. Materials are bought and delivered daily, so no inventory is kept. The inventory of finished product at May 31 is expected to be 19,000 units.

Required
1. Prepare a budgeted income statement for the coming year.
2. Prepare a budgeted income statement for the first six months of the year.
3. Prepare a production budget by month for the first three months, in units.
4. Determine the firm's break-even point (in units) for a year. How might the managers of the firm interpret that information in light of their successful sales predictions using the given formula?

6-45 **Comprehensive budget (adapted from a problem prepared by Professor Maurice L. Hirsch, and continued in Chapter 7)** Banana City is a wholesaler of bananas and nuts. Mr. Bertram A. Nana, the president of the firm, has asked for your assistance in preparing budgets for fiscal year 19X7, which begins on September 1, 19X6. The following information has been gathered for your use.
1. Sales are expected to be $880,000 for the year, of which bananas are expected to be 50%, nuts 50%.
2. Sales are somewhat seasonal. Banana sales are expected to be $77,000 in November, with the rest spread evenly over the remaining eleven months. Sales of nuts are expected to be $40,000 per month except in October and November, when they are expected to be $25,000 per month, and in April and May, when they are expected to be $35,000 per month.
3. Cost of sales, the only variable cost, is 40% for both products.
4. Inventory of bananas is generally kept equal to a one-month supply. Inventory of nuts is usually held at a two-month supply.
5. Income taxes are 40% of income before taxes.
6. Fixed expenses for the year, all incurred evenly throughout the year, are expected to be as follows.

Rent	$ 24,000	Depreciation	$ 36,000
Insurance	12,000	Interest	6,000
Wages and salaries	120,000	Other fixed expenses	156,000

7. Inventories at August 31, 19X6, are expected to be bananas, $14,300; nuts, $27,500.
8. The firm expects to sell some land that it owns. The sale, which is expected to have a price of $6,000, will take place in October. The cost of the land on the balance sheet is $8,000.

Required
1. Prepare a budgeted income statement for the fiscal year ending August 31, 19X7.
2. Prepare a budgeted income statement for the first quarter of the fiscal year, by month, and in total.

3. Prepare a purchases budget by product for each month of the first quarter of the fiscal year and for the quarter as a whole.

Cases

6-46 ***Production budgeting with constraints*** Firms do not commonly hire and lay off workers when moderate changes in production are contemplated. Among the reasons for this are a feeling of responsibility to provide regular employment; the potential decline in the available work force if skilled workers left the community permanently because they were laid off; and union contracts providing for guaranteed employment. Under these conditions stable production becomes more desirable. For these same reasons, firms that have high degrees of seasonality may try to stabilize production to keep workers busy all year.

Robertson Company has the following sales forecast by month for the first eight months of 19X5 (in units): 3,000, 3,800, 4,200, 5,000, 5,400, 5,900, 4,800, 4,200.

The work force is now 100 men, who can produce 4,000 units per month. Overtime can be used to increase output by 10%. Since a five-man team works together, workers can be hired only in groups of five. The company's policy is to keep inventory equal to a two-month supply, and the beginning inventory is 6,800 units.

Required: Prepare a production budget for the first six months, including budgeted numbers of workers. Prepare to defend your answer.

6-47 ***Budgeting step-variable costs*** Corman Company manufactures several products using a great deal of machinery. Since it is critical to keep the machines running well, Corman pays a good deal of attention to maintenance. The chief engineer has determined that routine maintenance requires a complete shutdown and cleaning every 200 hours a machine has been running. This job costs $250. Excluding these major cleanings, maintenance costs for ten machines have been as follows for the past eight months. Each machine runs about the same amount of time each month as every other machine.

Month	Hours for Ten Machines	Maintenance Costs
1	2,200	$1,400
2	2,100	1,380
3	1,950	1,260
4	2,000	1,290
5	1,700	1,190
6	2,400	1,505
7	2,300	1,455
8	1,800	1,200

Required
1. Using the high-low method, prepare a flexible budget formula for maintenance costs, excluding the major cleaning at 200 hours.
2. Determine the budgeted cost levels for 1,600 hours and 100-hour intervals up to 2,500 hours, including the major cleaning costs. What can you say about the use of flexible budgets when such costs are present?

CHAPTER 7

FINANCIAL BUDGETING

Chapter 6 discussed comprehensive budgeting and illustrated the operating budgets of the total budget package. Financial budgets are equally important to the package. In this chapter we complete the illustration by developing the cash budget and pro forma balance sheet.

    We also show how financial statement data are used in the preparation of annual budgets and long-term budgets. Finally, we look at the special issues associated with budgeting in not-for-profit entities.

ILLUSTRATION OF CASH BUDGET

We prepared the budgeted income statement and purchases budget for Cross Company and can now proceed to the cash budget and pro forma balance sheet. Following are the balance sheet as of December 31, 19X3, and the budgeted income statement for the six-month period after that date (from Exhibit 6-3, page 227).

Cross Company
Balance Sheet as of December 31, 19X3

Assets		Equities	
Cash	$ 60	Accounts payable (merchandise)	$ 360
Accounts receivable	576	Accrued expenses	50
Inventory	600	Common stock	1,000
Plant and equipment, net	600	Retained earnings	426
Total	$1,836	Total	$1,836

Cross Company
Budgeted Income Statement, January 1, 19X4 to June 30, 19X4

Sales	$4,800
Cost of goods sold (all variable, at 60% of sales)	2,880
Gross profit	1,920
Other variable costs (15% of sales)	720
Contribution margin	1,200
Fixed costs (including $120 of depreciation)	240
Income	$ 960

We need the balance sheet at the beginning of the budget period because it shows both resources (assets) that are already available for use during the period and liabilities that must be paid during the period. For example, we used the inventory figure at December 31 in preparing the purchases budget.

Cash Receipts

To develop the budgeted income statement we relied on the sales forecast.

	Jan.	Feb.	Mar.	Apr.	May	June
Sales	$400	$600	$800	$1,000	$1,200	$800

To budget cash receipts we need more information. Does the company sell on credit or for cash only? How soon do credit customers pay their accounts? Assume that experience (adjusted for any *expected* changes in conditions) indicates that 20% of sales are collected in the month of sale, 48% in the month after sale, and the remainder (32%) in the second month after sale. The beginning Accounts Receivable consists of $400 of December sales and $176 of November sales.

We can now determine cash inflows for the six-month period. Exhibit 7-1 is a good general format for budgeting cash receipts from sales. The circled items

Exhibit 7-1
Cash Receipts

	Jan.	Feb.	Mar.	Apr.	May	June	Total
Sales for the month	$400	$600	$800	$1,000	$1,200	$ 800	$4,800
Collections from Sales							
20% of total sales for the month	$ 80	$120	$160	$200	$240	$ 160	$ 960
48% of prior month's sales	240	192	288	384	480	576	2,160
32% of second prior month's sales	176	160	128°	192	256	320	1,232
Total cash collections	$496	$472	$576	$776	$976	$1,056	$4,352

°$400 = total January sales, collected in January, February, and March ($80 + $192 + $128).

show the pattern of collection of January sales; the total is given below the schedule. Notice that an increase in cash receipts accompanies the increase in sales. But there is a lag. Except for January, the cash receipts for a month do not equal or exceed sales until June, when sales have already declined. By that time, collections are being made from the prior months in which sales were considerably higher. A firm can run out of cash while its sales are rapidly increasing, because it very likely pays cash to stock goods in advance of sales, but collects cash well after the point of sale. This situation will be more obvious when we examine cash disbursements.

Cash Disbursements

The major component of cash disbursements for the Cross Company is payments for purchases. To determine cash payments for purchases, we use the purchases budget developed in Chapter 6 (Exhibit 6-4, page 228) and the timing of payments for those purchases. If the company pays for goods on delivery, cash payments for purchases equal purchases in each month. Suppose, however, that Cross Company takes full advantage of the 30-day credit terms extended by its suppliers so that purchases are paid for in the month after purchase. (If Cross were granted 60-day credit, payments would be made in the second month after purchase, and so on.)

To derive cash payments it is necessary only to lag payments a month behind purchases, as in Exhibit 7-2. The January payment is for December purchases, which are Accounts Payable at December 31, 19X3. The other amounts come from the purchases budget developed in Chapter 6 and summarized here. Purchases are paid for in the month after purchase, so Accounts Payable at the end of any month equal that month's purchases. And cash disbursements for purchases in any month equal Accounts Payable at the end of the prior month.

Two parts of the cash budget are now complete: cash receipts from sales and cash disbursements for purchases. Other cash disbursements may be determined more easily than those for purchases. You will remember that variable expenses other than cost of sales are 15% of sales. Assume that one-third is paid in the month of incurrence, and two-thirds in the following month. (The portion paid in the month after incurrence could be for commissions to salespersons, who are paid in one month the commissions they earned in the previous month.) Thus, in each month, cash disbursements related to variable costs are 5% of that month's

Exhibit 7-2
Cash Disbursements for Purchases

	Jan.	Feb.	Mar.	Apr.	May	June	Total
Budgeted purchases	$480	$600	$720	$480	$420	$480	$3,180
Payments	$360	$480	$600	$720	$480	$420	$3,060

Exhibit 7-3
Cash Disbursements—Variable Costs

	Jan.	Feb.	Mar.	Apr.	May	June	Total
5% current month's sales	$20	$30	$ 40	$ 50	$ 60	$ 40	$240
10% previous month's sales	50[a]	40	60	80	100	120	450
Total	$70	$70	$100	$130	$160	$160	$690

[a] December accrued expenses, from December 31, 19X3, balance sheet, page 252.

sales, plus 10% of the sales of the previous month. A schedule of disbursements, by month, for those variable costs appears in Exhibit 7-3.

Total cash disbursements for variable costs ($690) do not correspond to variable costs on the income statement ($720) because of the timing of the payments. This difference is explained by considering accrued expenses. Of the January disbursements, $50 was accrued in December. This payment is not an expense in 19X4. At June 30, 19X4, $80 is owed for commissions on June sales of $800. The cash disbursement for June commissions is made in July. Thus, total disbursements of $690 include $50 for expenses of 19X3 and do not include $80 of June expense that will be paid in July ($690 − $50 + $80 = $720). The $80 appears as a liability on the balance sheet at June 30.

Suppose that the cash component of fixed costs is paid evenly over the six-month period. Depreciation, a noncash expense, is $120 out of the $240 fixed costs, so the cash portion is $120 ($240 − $120), or $20 per month. The complete cash disbursements budget is shown in Exhibit 7-4.

Cash Budget

With the data developed above, we can prepare a tentative cash budget. It is shown in Exhibit 7-5 on page 256. The budget is tentative because we will not know, until after preparing this schedule, whether revisions might be necessary because of potential cash shortages.

Exhibit 7-4
Cash Disbursements—All Costs

	Jan.	Feb.	Mar.	Apr.	May	June	Total
For purchases (Exhibit 7-2)	$360	$480	$600	$720	$480	$420	$3,060
Variable costs (Exhibit 7-3)	70	70	100	130	160	160	690
Fixed costs	20	20	20	20	20	20	120
Total	$450	$570	$720	$870	$660	$600	$3,870

Exhibit 7-5
Tentative Cash Budget

	Jan.	Feb.	Mar.	Apr.	May	June	Six Months
Beginning balance	$ 60ª	$106	$ 8	($136)	($230)	$ 86	$ 60
Collections (Exhibit 7-1)	496	472	576	776	976	1,056	4,352
Total available	556	578	584	640	746	1,142	4,412
Disbursements (Exhibit 7-4)	450	570	720	870	660	600	3,870
Ending balance (deficit)	$106	$ 8	($136)	($230)	$ 86	$ 542	$ 542

ª From December 31,19X3, balance sheet, page 252.

The total column in Exhibit 7-5 covers the six-month period, so the beginning balance is the balance at December 31, 19X3. Although the firm will complete the period with much more cash than it had at the start, the budget reveals that there will be cash deficits in March and April (and a balance of only $8 at the end of February) if all goes according to plan. If the firm had prepared a budget only for the entire six-month period, the managers would not have known in advance of the deficits, and would not have been on notice to make plans for dealing with the problem. Budgets should therefore be broken down into relatively short periods.

What could Cross do now? It could consider borrowing cash to tide it over the period during which the deficits appear. It could reconsider its inventory policy, reduce its purchases, and consequently reduce its needs for cash. It could also consider policy changes that would accelerate cash collections. But both types of policy changes might adversely affect sales.

Assume Cross can borrow cash at 12% interest, and that the firm decides to borrow to offset the expected cash deficits. The cash budget must be revised to incorporate the borrowings and the repayments (including interest). For simplicity, assume that borrowings must take place at the beginning of the month in which they are needed, and that repayments are made at the earliest possible time, which is at the end of a month with a budgeted surplus of cash. Under these circumstances, a loan must be outstanding for at least two months. Suppose that borrowings must be in multiples of $10 and that interest is paid at the time of repayment. Assume that the firm has a policy of maintaining a minimum cash balance of $50 at all times. (More about such policies later.) A revised cash budget appears in Exhibit 7-6.

Note that the revision of the cash budget requires us to revise the original budgeted income statement because that statement did not include interest expense.

Revised Financial Statements

A revised budgeted income statement for the six-month period is shown in Exhibit 7-7. The income statement shows the interest expense necessary to finance the budgeted level of operations. The exhibit includes a separate pro forma income

Exhibit 7-6
Revised Cash Budget

	Jan.	Feb.	Mar.	Apr.	May	June	Six Months
Beginning balance	$ 60	$ 106	$ 58	$ 54	$ 50	$ 78	$ 60
Collections	496	472	576	776	976	1,056	4,352
Total available	556	578	634	830	1,026	1,134	4,412
Disbursements	450	570	720	870	660	600	3,870
(1) Indicated balance	106	8	(86)	(40)	366	534	542
(2) Minimum required cash	50	50	50	50	50	50	50
1 − 2 = (3) Excess (deficit)	56	(42)	(136)	(90)	316	484	492
(4) Borrowings		50	140	90			280
(5) Repayments					(280)		(280)
Interest					(8)^a		(8)
4 + 1 − 5 = (6) Ending balance	$106	58	54	50	78	534	$ 534
Cumulative borrowings		$ 50	$190	$280	$—0—	$—0—	

^{a} 12% × 4/12 (four months) × $ 50 = $2.00
12% × 3/12 (three months)× $140 = 4.20
12% × 2/12 (two months) × $ 90 = 1.80
$8.00

statement for the first three months of the period so that you may check your understanding, and because a firm ordinarily prepares pro forma statements more frequently than once every six months.

A pro forma balance sheet for June 30 is shown in Exhibit 7-8. Here again, a pro forma balance sheet at an interim date—March 31—is included to facilitate your understanding and to recognize normal practice. In this instance, one impor-

Exhibit 7-7
Cross Company, Budgeted Income Statements

	Three Months Ending March 31, 19X4	Six Months Ending June 30, 19X4
Sales	$1,800	$4,800
Cost of goods sold (60% of sales)	1,080	2,880
Gross profit	720	1,920
Other variable costs (15% of sales)	270	720
Contribution margin	450	1,200
Fixed operating costs	120	240
Operating income	330	960
Interest expense	2.40^a	8
Income	$ 327.60	$ 952

^{a} At March 31, loans were outstanding for $190. Accrued interest was:
$ 50 × 2/12 × 12% = $1.00
$140 × 1/12 × 12% = 1.40
Total accrued interest and interest expense $2.40

Exhibit 7-8

Cross Company, Pro Forma Balance Sheets

Assets	As at March 31, 19X4	As at June 30, 19X4
Cash (from cash budget, Exhibit 7-6)	$ 54	$ 534
Accounts receivable (credit sales for month plus 32% of prior month's credit sales)	832	1,024
Inventory (from purchases budget, Exhibit 6-4)	1,320	900
Plant and equipment (beginning balance less depreciation for 3 and 6 months)	540	480
Total assets	$2,746	$2,938

Equities		
Accounts payable (from purchases budget, Exhibit 6-4)	$ 720	$ 480
Accrued expenses (10% of the month's sales)	80	80
Short-term loan (from cash budget, Exhibit 7-6)	190	0
Accrued interest on loan (Exhibit 7-7)	2.40	0
Common stock (beginning balance sheet, page 252)	1,000	1,000
Retained earnings (beginning balance plus income for period)	753.60	1,378
Total equities	$2,746	$2,938

tant reason for having pro forma statements (income statement and balance sheet) prior to the end of the six-month period is that the firm has to obtain a short-term loan. A potential lender will want information to help it decide whether the firm can repay the loan and will be interested in whether the management makes good use of budgets. The lender will want to see monthly cash budgets and pro forma statements at least each quarter, if not each month. Later, managers (and lenders) can compare the actual balance sheets at March 31 and June 30 with the pro forma ones to see whether operations are proceeding as planned. For example, suppose the sales forecast proves accurate, but Accounts Receivable are higher than budgeted. This could be a danger signal; if customers pay less quickly than anticipated, the firm could run into a cash shortage. Increasing receivables might also be a sign that the firm is extending credit to less worthy customers in order to meet its sales goals. This could be a costly move: bad debts might result, and the need for financing might increase as well.

Minimum-Cash-Balance Policies

Many companies adopt a policy of maintaining a minimum cash balance at all times. The minimum cash balance in our illustration ($50) is, of course, an assumed figure. In actual situations, the chief financial officer of the firm devotes considerable attention to determining this amount. As with almost all decisions, a tradeoff is involved, and two conflicting factors must be considered. First, the lower the minimum required balance, the greater the probability the firm will run out of cash. Remember we are budgeting—dealing with the future and with estimates. If customers pay more slowly than expected, or cash outflows are higher than expected, the firm could run out of cash.

Conflicting with the need to have sufficient cash to pay bills is the concern that idle cash earns no return. Keeping a high cash balance is costly because the firm *could* be investing the cash elsewhere to earn additional income or, perhaps, saving interest costs by retiring outstanding debt. The lost income (or savings foregone) that accompanies a high cash balance is an opportunity cost, and the manager must weigh carefully the conflicting objectives and decide on a reasonable compromise.

There are some sophisticated techniques, as well as some rules of thumb, for approaching the problem of determining an optimal minimum cash balance. For now it is enough to say that many firms just set a policy of carrying cash equal to, for example, budgeted cash disbursements for the coming two weeks or month. Under such a policy, the minimum required balances change, depending on budgeted disbursements. You will study closely the topic of determining minimum cash balances in your financial management course(s).

Concluding Comments

Now that we have presented all the statements and schedules that make up the comprehensive budget, we can point out other advantages of budgeting.

The cash budget and pro forma balance sheets are a basis for asset management. The managers can see that a large amount of cash becomes available at the end of June and they can begin to look for profitable uses for this cash. At the very least, the firm can buy marketable securities like government bonds and earn safe, though low, returns.

Knowing well in advance that extra cash will be needed, the firm is more likely to be able to find financing to carry it over the months in which deficits are budgeted. It will be able to explain to potential lenders why it needs the money and how a loan will be repaid. If the firm doesn't seek a loan until its cash balance is precariously low, it may have to pay a higher interest rate or it may not get a loan on any terms.

Our example is much simpler than is the case in practice. If a company's experience indicates that some portion of its credit sales will never be collected (become bad debts), the receipts budget reflects only the expected collections. There could, and probably would, be other receipts and disbursements. For example, many companies receive interest or dividends on investments, and, as was mentioned earlier, many expenses, such as taxes and insurance, are not paid monthly. In addition, a firm may be obligated to make periodic interest payments and repayments of outstanding long-term debt and perhaps to pay quarterly dividends.

Perhaps the single most commonly found item that is missing from the example budget is expenditures for new, long-lived assets. Because such expenditures are usually relatively large, their inclusion is critical if the budget is to fulfill its functions of identifying the timing of financial needs and providing a realistic picture of planned activities. Once managers have decided that certain major investments are to be made, it is simple to incorporate the expenditures into the cash budget. Making those decisions is not quite so simple, and the next two chapters consider the analyses that managers use to make them. At this point, you need only recognize that a firm's budget is not complete without including budgeted expenditures for new assets, as well as the means for financing those expenditures.

The firm in the illustration does not do any manufacturing. Chapter 6 shows that developing a budget for a manufacturer is more complex than for a nonmanufacturer, but that the principles are virtually the same. For example, as we showed in Chapter 6, the production budget for Brandon Company, a manufacturer, is very similar to the purchases budget for a retailer. If we know when the costs of production are paid, we can easily compute cash requirements for production. Let us continue the example started on page 229 with Brandon showing a production budget as follows.

Month	No. of Units Produced
January	340
February	280
March	336

The breakdown of production costs was as follows: materials at $4 per unit, other variable costs at $4 per unit, and fixed costs of $1,900.

Let us deal with the simplest of the assumed situations for Brandon Company, where materials are acquired as needed (no inventory is maintained). Adopting the just-in-time philosophy, and having zero inventory does *not* imply anything about the timing of payments for purchases. So, let us assume also that materials are paid for in the month after purchase and that all other production costs requiring cash are paid in the month incurred. Assume further that production in December was 300 units. (Why must we make some assumption about December production?) The budget for cash disbursements for manufacturing costs appears below.

	Jan.	Feb.	Mar.
Units produced	340	280	336
Cash disbursements:			
Materials ($4 × prior month's production)	$1,200	$1,360	$1,120
Other variable costs ($4 × current production)	1,360	1,120	1,344
Fixed costs	1,900	1,900	1,900
Total	$4,460	$4,380	$4,364

The totals will be included in the computation of total disbursements for the cash budget. The remainder of the budget package will be completed accordingly.

In principle there is little difference between the budgets for the retailer and the manufacturer. In practice, the manufacturer's budget is likely to be more complicated. For example, some production costs, such as depreciation, do not require cash outlay. Also, the materials used for production may be purchased in advance of production needs. In such a situation the cash disbursements for materials will be determined by a separate materials-purchases budget, as was the case in the example on page 231.

ANNUAL AND LONG-TERM BUDGETS

Managers use some of the techniques of financial statement analysis to assist them in budgeting for longer periods and in assessing long-term asset requirements and financing requirements—long-term debt and stockholders' equity. "Long term" usually means more than one year.

Asset Requirements

We have shown how operating and financing budgets relate to each other in the short term. Using budgeted sales and relationships of certain current assets to sales, we developed budgets of purchases and pro forma balance sheets showing budgeted amounts of cash, accounts receivable, and inventory. What was shown on the asset side of these balance sheets was essentially a statement of *asset requirements*—the amounts of various assets required to enable the firm to meet its goals of sales and income. We also suggested that the firm might have to reconsider its sales and profit goals if it could not obtain the financing needed to carry its planned levels of assets.

Managers make similar analyses when developing **long-term budgets.** If the firm forecasts increasing sales, it must also plan for the assets that will support those planned levels of sales. Sales can seldom be increased significantly without providing additional production capacity and allowing receivables to increase. In many situations, significantly higher sales cannot be achieved without stocking more inventory. In addition, the desired minimum cash balance will probably increase with higher sales volume.

In the long term, the planned levels of sales usually dictate the necessary levels of assets. Thus, we shall be using ratios of various assets to sales to determine the required amounts of those assets. Recognize, however, that the analyses undertaken and numbers used for long-term budgeting are less precise than when budgeting for the shorter term. Moreover, there is more opportunity for circumstances to change. When developing long-term plans, managers try to allow for changes in selling prices, purchase costs, and general economic conditions, but such changes are extremely hard to predict over relatively long periods. Hence, the predictions are fairly general, with managers trying to see what the firm's needs will be in broad terms. As time passes, managers refine their budgets of asset needs.

Financing Requirements

A firm requires financing, in the form of liabilities or stockholders' equity, because it needs assets to generate sales. The need for assets creates *financing require-ments*—the need for the items listed on the equity side of the balance sheet. The elements on the equities side of the balance sheet are often referred to as the *sources* of the assets. As the need for assets increases because of increased sales, so does the need for sources to finance them. A few sources of financing are available almost automatically. For example, few firms pay cash on delivery of merchandise; most buy on credit. When a vendor extends credit, it is, in effect, providing a short-term loan—a source of financing. Similarly, when a firm earns income and does not distribute assets to its owners in an amount equal to net income, retained earnings increase. Thus, increases in retained earnings are also sources of financing.

Few firms can meet all their financing needs through funds provided by operations and trade creditors. Cross Company used only short-term credit. How-ever, firms cannot use short-term loans too liberally. If working capital (current assets—current liabilities) and the current ratio (current assets/current liabilities) get too low, creditors will be reluctant to lend to the firm. Thus, firms will seek more permanent financing.

For more permanent financing, firms issue long-term debt or additional stock. A growing firm generally requires higher and higher levels of assets to support its increased sales and so needs more financing than a firm that is not growing. We have already noted that a firm not able to obtain the loan needed to support its short-term requirements might decide to scale down its purchases of goods, and that this could, in turn, reduce sales and profits. The same situation occurs in long-term budgeting. A firm might not be able to obtain the long-term financing to support the asset levels necessary to reach the projected levels of sales.

Managers know that advance planning is needed to obtain both short- and long-term financing. We noted that the balance of current assets and current liabilities was important to potential providers of short-term loans. The focus of interest for potential long-term lenders is the balance between long-term debt and equity capital. Those lenders are likely to expect a borrower to maintain some minimum ratio of long-term debt to equity, with the magnitude of the ratio depen-dent on various characteristics of the borrower. Hence, a firm must first study its long-term financing needs as a whole, and then plan its pursuit of specific types of long-term financing with those expectations in mind.

ILLUSTRATIONS OF ANNUAL AND LONG-TERM BUDGETS

Two types of procedures are used in budgeting for long periods: those that are used for a one-year period and those that are more appropriate for three- to five-year periods broken down into annual periods. Differences between the two types are primarily matters of detail; the composition of assets and equities for a one-year budget is more detailed than that for longer periods.

Annual Budgets

Strand Company, a manufacturer of electrical equipment, had the following income statement for 19X3.

Sales	$800,000
Variable costs at 60%	480,000
Contribution margin	320,000
Fixed costs	240,000
Income	$ 80,000

Strand's balance sheet at the end of 19X3 appears below. We include the percentages of current assets and current liabilities to sales because we will use them to develop the December 31, 19X4, pro forma balance sheet.

Assets			Percentage of Sales
Cash		$ 40,000	5.0%
Accounts receivable		120,000	15.0%
Inventory		60,000	7.5%
Total current assets		220,000	27.5%
Plant and equipment, net		600,000	
Total assets		$820,000	
Equities			
Current liabilities		$ 80,000	10.0%
Long-term debt		100,000	
Total liabilities		180,000	
Common stock	$500,000		
Retained earnings	140,000	640,000	
Total equities		$820,000	

Strand's managers forecast a 10% increase in sales for 19X4. They expect current assets and current liabilities at the end of 19X4 to bear the same percentage relationships to sales that they did at the end of 19X3. They also expect variable costs to be the same percentage of sales as they were in 19X3, and total fixed costs to increase to $260,000. They budget net plant and equipment at $720,000 at the end of 19X4. They do not expect to pay a dividend in 19X4.

The budgeted income statement for 19X4 is necessary for us to determine retained earnings, a significant source of financing, at the end of 19X4.

Sales ($800,000 × 110%)	$880,000
Variable costs at 60%	528,000
Contribution margin	352,000
Fixed costs	260,000
Income	$ 92,000

We now determine the asset requirements at the end of 19X4. The current assets are simply the percentages of sales from the 19X3 balance sheet multiplied by 19X4 budgeted sales.

Assets		Percentage of Sales
Cash	$ 44,000	5.0%
Accounts receivable	132,000	15.0%
Inventory	66,000	7.5%
Total current assets	242,000	27.5%
Plant and equipment, net	720,000	
Total asset requirements	$962,000	

The following schedule shows the available financing to support the asset requirements. Current liabilities are at the same percentage of sales as they were in 19X3. Long-term debt and common stock are at their 19X3 levels. Retained earnings is the $140,000 beginning balance plus the $92,000 income budgeted for 19X4.

Equities			Percentage of Sales
Current liabilities		$ 88,000	10.0%
Long-term debt		100,000	
Total liabilities		188,000	
Common stock	$500,000		
Retained earnings	232,000	732,000	
Total available equities		$920,000	

The $42,000 difference between Strand's asset requirements ($962,000) and its available equities ($920,000) is called a **financing gap.** What can Strand do about the gap?

Strand has several options. If it makes no plans to cover the gap, its cash at the end of 19X4 will be $2,000, rather than the budgeted $44,000. But $2,000 might be too low, and Strand might be, at some time, unable to pay a bill when due or to meet a payroll. Alternatively, Strand might plan some actions to reduce its current asset requirements, for example, by requiring speedier payment of receivables or carrying a smaller inventory. It might also decide to pay its current liabilities more slowly or to postpone some of its capital expenditures. Of course, Strand could also decide to cover all or part of the financing gap by using additional financing, either debt or equity.

Each of these actions has potential problems. Attempting to reduce asset requirements could hamper the company's ability to generate sales and profits. Slower payment of liabilities could harm the company's credit rating. Obtaining additional financing might be very costly because of unfavorable conditions in the economy. Strand's managers must evaluate all of the options and decide what risks they are willing to accept.

It is possible, of course, that an analysis of expectations and plans for asset requirements and available equities will reveal that available equities exceed asset requirements. In such cases, managers plan how to use the excess cash. Some possibilities are paying dividends, reducing long-term debt, and making other investments, perhaps in plant and equipment.

Long-Term Planning

In the previous section we prepared a pro forma balance sheet to see whether Strand could meet its objectives for the year. Doing the same for a longer term usually involves preparing a series of schedules containing summary information about asset requirements and available financing.

Long-term planning is mostly concerned with developing plans for expanding long-term debt and equity capital to meet financing requirements. The choice between debt and equity can be critical for the company, and most companies adopt some policy about how much debt they will allow. The policy is often stated as a maximum percentage of long-term debt to stockholders' equity, or to total long-term financing (long-term debt and stockholders' equity). The advantages and disadvantages of particular kinds of financing are studied in managerial finance. Here, we say only two things: (1) debt can be risky because failing to meet the periodic interest payments can cause bankruptcy; (2) equity financing is less risky but can lead to lower returns. (See Chapter 18 for a discussion of the risks and rewards of each type of financing.)

We illustrate long-term planning by using the following data, assumptions, and policies of the Klep Company. These data are the bases of Exhibits 7-9 and

Sales forecast in 19X4	$ 800,000	Current asset requirements are expected to be 30% of sales budgeted for the following year.
19X5	$1,000,000	
19X6	$1,300,000	
19X7	$1,700,000	Net fixed assets expected to be required to meet budgeted sales are 75% of sales budgeted for the following year.
19X8	$2,100,000	
Stockholders' equity		Desired current ratio of 3 to 1, so that current liabilities cannot exceed one-third of current assets.
12/31/X3	$ 412,000	
Net income is expected to be 10% of sales over the period of the forecast.		
Dividends of 40% of net income will be paid each year.		Desired ratio of long-term debt to equity of 0.5 to 1 (long-term debt cannot exceed 50% of stockholders' equity).

7-10, which determine year-by-year financing requirements. Exhibit 7-9 shows the analysis for 19X4 and 19X5 and how the numbers were derived. See if you can complete the rest of the table. (Answers appear in Exhibit 7-10.) Such a schedule gives the manager an idea of future financing needs.

Klep's managers can now direct their efforts to devising a plan for obtaining the financing to satisfy line (13), "additional requirements." For several reasons it is generally expensive and undesirable to obtain equity financing frequently. Therefore the firm might plan to obtain enough funds from issuing common stock in 19X4 to enable it to finance without additional debt until 19X8 or so. Funds received in excess of amounts currently needed might be invested or used to retire existing debt. As needs become more pressing, additional debt could be issued up to the limit prescribed by the 0.5 to 1 debt/equity ratio.

BUDGETING IN NOT-FOR-PROFIT ENTITIES

Not-for-profit entities, especially governmental units, make extensive use of budgeting, but the budgeting process is not usually of the type described earlier. First, such entities are likely to budget only for cash flows (expenditures and receipts), not for revenues and expenses. Second, the process is more likely to begin with expenditures as opposed to receipts. That is, in most cases, the problem is to determine what receipts are required to support the budgeted level of expenditures, as opposed to what costs will be incurred as a result of the budgeted level of revenues.

Budgets for not-for-profit entities are not usually as geared to activity levels as are budgets for businesses. Nevertheless, budget allowances for some cost categories can be determined by activity analysis. For example, a university might budget faculty positions by applying some formula based on student enrollment. Thus, an academic department might be given one position for each 300 credit hours expected to be taught. If the department is expected to teach 2,800 credit hours during the coming year, it will be authorized $9\frac{1}{3}$ positions (2,800/300). The one-third position would probably be filled by part-time instructors.

On the revenue (receipt) side, budgeting by not-for-profit entities could be relatively simple or quite complex. School districts and some municipalities like towns and cities rely chiefly on property taxes. Property taxes are levied based on the assessed valuation of real property (land and buildings) in the area. Once the entity has determined the total assessed valuation, it can set the tax rate simply by dividing the required revenues by the assessed valuation. If a school district requires $4,580,000 in revenues and the assessed valuation of property in the district is $54,000,000, the rate is 0.08482 ($4,580,000/$54,000,000), which is $84.82 per $1,000 of assessed value. Note that the required revenue is determined on the basis of the budgeted expenditures, which partially explains the need for careful planning and monitoring of budgeted expenditures in not-for-profit entities. A legal requirement that limits the increase in the tax rate in any year can

Exhibit 7-9

Financing Requirements for Klep Company
(in thousands of dollars)

		19X4	19X5	19X6	19X7
	(1) Sales	$800	$1,000	$1,300	$1,700
(1) × 10%	(2) Net income	80	100		
(2) × 40%	(3) Dividends	32	40		
(2) − (3)	(4) Add to stockholders' equity	$ 48	$ 60		
(1) for next year × 30%	(5) Current assets required	$300	$ 390		
(5) ÷ 3	(6) Permissible current liabilities	100	130		
(5) − (6)	(7) Working capital to be financed from long-term sources	200	260		
(1) for next year × 75%	(8) Net fixed assets required	750	975		
(7) + (8)	(9) Total long-term financing required	950	1,235		
	(10) Stockholders' equity [prior year plus (4)]	460	520		
(10) × 50%	(11) Permissible long-term debt	230	260		
(10) + (11)	(12) Total available long-term financing	690	780		
(9) − (12)	(13) Additional requirements	$260	$ 455		

Exhibit 7-10

Financing Requirements for Klep Company
(in thousands of dollars)

		19X4	19X5	19X6	19X7
	(1) Sales	$800	$1,000	$1,300	$1,700
(1) × 10%	(2) Net income	80	100	130	170
(2) × 40%	(3) Dividends	32	40	52	68
(2) − (3)	(4) Add to stockholders' equity	$ 48	$ 60	$ 78	$ 102
(1) for next year × 30%	(5) Current assets required	$300	$ 390	$ 510	$ 630
(5) ÷ 3	(6) Permissible current liabilities	100	130	170	210
(5) − (6)	(7) Working capital to be financed from long-term sources	200	260	340	420
(1) for next year × 75%	(8) Net fixed assets required	750	975	1,275	1,575
(7) + (8)	(9) Total long-term financing required	950	1,235	1,615	1,995
	(10) Stockholders' equity [prior year plus (4)]	460	520	598	700
(10) × 50%	(11) Permissible long-term debt	230	260	299	350
(10) + (11)	(12) Total available long-term financing	690	780	897	1,050
(9) − (12)	(13) Additional requirements	$260	$ 455	$ 718	$ 945

trigger the same reconsideration of plans forced on business enterprises whose asset requirements exceed available financing.

For government units that depend heavily on income and sales taxes, as do most states, determining required tax rates is more complex. Revenue estimates require estimates of total incomes subject to the income tax and of transactions subject to the sales tax. Forecasting methods such as those described in Chapter 6 may be used, and individual states have developed and used very sophisticated forecasting models.

The problems of developing receipts budgets for nongovernmental not-for-profit entities are more related to those of business entities. The variety of such entities rivals the variety of business entities, and the need for forecasts of revenue-related factors is at least as important. For example, tuition charges in a private school are set based on forecasts of enrollments and contributions, and the various service charges of a hospital are established by forecasting expected utilization. All the forecasting methods discussed in Chapter 6 are used in making such forecasts.

Government units like towns, states, school districts, and the federal government usually require voter or legislative approval of their budgets. Once adopted, the budget must be strictly adhered to; overspending may even be illegal. In addition, budget authorizations tend to be on a line-by-line basis. That is, specific amounts are authorized for specific categories of expenditures, such as salaries, equipment, supplies, travel, and postage. (The detail in such budgets can be overwhelming, with specified amounts for categories such as Grade II Typists and Grade IV Carpenters.) A budgeting process that includes a line-by-line approval procedure tends to have two major disadvantages in practice.

One problem with the line-by-line approval process is that individual managers often cannot exercise discretion in how they use the total budgeted funds to achieve the expected objectives. This inflexibility can lead to actions inconsistent with the objectives of the entity. For example, suppose that an accounting instructor in a public university is invited to a seminar on a contemporary accounting topic, that the dean and faculty are in favor of the trip, but that the travel budget is exhausted. Even if funds remain in the budget allowances for supplies, or telephone, or secretarial help, the trip cannot be authorized. The problem lies in the concentration on individual budget items rather than on the objectives to be accomplished.

A second problem that can result from line-by-line approval is that it tends to encourage the setting of current budget allowances based on prior year's (or an average of prior years') budget allowances or actual expenditures for each item. This general approach is called **incremental budgeting.** Under this approach, each department might be given a 5% increase (or decrease) in one or more of its line items. In a somewhat broader application of incremental budgeting, each department might be given a 5% increase (or decrease) and allowed to spread the total increase (or decrease) over whatever items are available. Either variation ignores the question of objectives. More important, either variation assumes that the increased (or decreased) benefits of changes in one segment of the total entity are equal to the increased (or decreased) benefits of any other segment. Further, when the current budget allowance is based on prior expenditures, there is a tendency for budget units to spend right up to the allowance in order to avoid cuts in the next period's budget. Occasionally, the media have reported particularly interesting examples of such actions, as an end-of-year purchase of a five-year supply of toilet tissue or wastebaskets.

We hasten to point out that the use of line budgeting and incremental budgeting is not limited to not-for-profit entities. Many businesses also use these techniques, especially in areas of discretionary spending, like employee training, and some general and administrative areas.

Recent years have seen increasing attention focused on the problems of budgeting in government and other not-for-profit entities. Two alternative budgeting approaches, zero-based budgeting and program budgeting, discussed in the next sections, have been suggested as possible means of alleviating some of the problems.

Zero-Based Budgeting

Strictly interpreted, **zero-based budgeting** means that a manager must justify every dollar that he or she requests in a budget proposal for any given year. Past budget allowances are irrelevant, and the manager must start from scratch to convince higher-level managers that the current request is necessary. In a strict but practical application of the zero-base concept, each budget unit develops its budget request as a series of **decision packages.** The most basic of the unit's services constitutes the first package, and incremental packages represent higher levels of service and/or additional services. A critical aspect of the decision packages is that each is associated with a *definable* level or quantity of services.

Higher-level managers perform cost-benefit analysis and, of course, exercise their judgment about the organization's needs, to evaluate and rank the packages from all units. The final budget, then, might include the basic packages from all budget units, plus some incremental packages. This approach helps to circumvent any assumption that increased (or decreased) expenditures in all units are equally beneficial (or harmful) to the entire organization. Moreover, forcing managerial review of even the most basic functions of a budget unit may help to show that some budget unit has outlived its usefulness. (That is, managers may conclude, after reviewing all the decision packages and considering the quantity of potentially available resources, that the most basic service level of a particular budget unit contributes less to achieving desired goals than do higher-than-basic service levels in other units.)

Because a full review of each and every budget request every year is very time-consuming, most organizations require such a review of some, or all, budget units only every few years. But the goals of these periodic reviews are the same as under the more strict application of the zero-base concept: to make sure that there is still a need to spend money for a particular service, and that the money being spent is being spent wisely. **Sunset legislation,** which requires that a program or regulatory agency approved by the legislature receive a full, regular review and be dropped if it has served its purpose, is a variation of this second approach to the implementation of zero-based budgeting.

Program Budgeting

Program budgeting requires that a budget indicate not only how the requested funds are to be spent, but also *why* the funds are to be spent. A program budget emphasizes the desired results of the unit's efforts and normally provides the unit's manager with considerable discretion in shifting expenditures from one category to another as long as the shift will increase the likelihood of achieving the desired results. For instance, a traditional budget for a school district shows the objects of the expenditures, such as teachers' salaries, textbooks, and supplies. A program budget for the district shows expenditures by such categories as reading, mathematics, remedial work, student activities, and support services. Similarly, a program budget for a police department might show amounts requested for crime prevention, juvenile work, and detection.

Budgeting by program should permit the people who supervise the spending (the citizens, the contributors, etc.) to make better decisions regarding the use of resources. One feature of program budgeting that should be particularly beneficial is that managers making budget requests are expected to be able to state clearly what would happen if their requests were cut by, say, 10%. Thus, the director of parks and recreation for a city should be in a position to say that such a cut would reduce the hours that a swimming pool would be open or require that grass be cut every ten days instead of once a week. This feature of program budgeting is, in its result, similar to what can be accomplished with zero-based budgeting, since different levels of service are associated with each level of requested funding.

The increasing interest in and use of program and zero-based budgeting probably owes much to an increasing public demand for accountability from not-for-profit organizations. Taxpayers appear to have become dissatisfied with the performance of some government units, and donors to charitable causes have expressed concern about the proportion of contributed funds devoted to administrative expenses. Program budgets that specify goals allow people to see where their money is going and, eventually, to see whether or not it was spent effectively. (If a school district requests money "to raise the average reading levels of its pupils," board members can later see whether the levels rose.)

Both program and zero-based budgeting are applicable to business entities as well as not-for-profit organizations. Corporate executives have, for example, adopted variations of these alternative approaches to budgeting for all or some portions of their organizations because of their increasing concern with the productivity of research and development, general administration, and other such activities. In the typical business use, however, program budgets are developed *in addition to,* rather than as a substitute for, the more traditional budgets.

SUMMARY

Σ

Comprehensive budgeting brings together and coordinates the plans of many managers and many levels of management. A comprehensive budget is the most conspicuous process of communication within a firm, and facilitates the coordination of major functional areas—production, sales, and finance.

Like operating budgets, financial budgets use forecasts and assumptions about the behavior of the various factors incorporated in them. Financial budgeting involves developing detailed budgets of cash receipts and cash disbursements and a pro forma balance sheet. The cash budgets use data from the purchases and expense budgets and from the pro forma income statement. Hence, effective financial budgeting depends on good operational budgeting.

Once the preliminary cash budget is completed, it may become apparent that additional financing is needed. Managers can then plan in advance to meet this need.

Financial budgets are often prepared for relatively long periods. Such budgets are less precise than those prepared for the short term, but they can still assist managers in assessing long-term asset and financing requirements.

Budgeting takes place in not-for-profit entities as well as businesses. Although many of the same principles apply, there are some differences, the most significant difference being that not-for-profit entities normally budget receipts based on budgeted expenditures, while business entities budget expenditures based on budgeted receipts. Two additional budgeting approaches, program and zero-based budgeting, have been introduced for government units, to help offset the tendency in not-for-profit budgeting to concentrate on detailed expenditures rather than on objectives. Variations of these approaches are also used by business entities.

KEY TERMS

cash budget
decision package
financial budget
financing gap
incremental budgeting

long-term budget
minimum cash balance
program budgeting
zero-based budgeting

REVIEW PROBLEM

This problem continues the review problem from Chapter 6. Using the following additional data, prepare a cash budget for January 19X4 and a pro forma balance sheet for January 31, 19X4. Prepare supporting budgets for cash receipts and cash disbursements.

Exempli Company
Balance Sheet at December 31, 19X3

Assets		Equities	
Cash	$ 20,000	Accounts payable	
Accounts receivable	30,000	(for merchandise)	$ 12,000
Inventory (6,000 units)	30,000	Common stock	200,000
Building and equipment, net	200,000	Retained earnings	68,000
Total	$280,000	Total	$280,000

1. Sales are collected 40% in month of sale, 60% in the following month.
2. Purchases are paid 40% in month of purchase, 60% in the following month.
3. All other expenses requiring cash are paid in the month incurred.

4. The board of directors plans to declare a $3,000 dividend on January 10, payable on January 25.

5. The budgeted income statement and purchases budget from the solution in Chapter 6 (page 233) are given below for convenience.

Exempli Company
Budgeted Income Statement for January 19X4

Sales		$100,000
Cost of sales		25,000
Gross profit		75,000
Variable costs:		
Commissions	$10,000	
Other variable expenses	5,000	15,000
Contribution margin		60,000
Fixed costs:		
Depreciation	2,000	
Other operating expenses	40,000	42,000
Budgeted income		$ 18,000

Purchases Budget for January 19X4

Cost of sales	$25,000
Desired ending inventory	45,000
Total requirements	70,000
Beginning inventory	30,000
Budgeted purchases	$40,000

Answer to Review Problem

Cash Budget

Beginning balance	$20,000
Receipts (see below)	70,000
Cash available	90,000
Disbursements	86,000
Ending balance	$ 4,000

Cash Receipts Budget

Collection from December sales	$30,000
Collection from January sales ($100,000 × 40%)	40,000
Total	$70,000

December sales will all be collected by the end of January. Because sales are collected in full by the end of the month following sale, all accounts receivable at the end of a month are expected to be collected in the coming month.

Cash Disbursements Budget

Merchandise ($40,000 × 40%) + $12,000	$28,000
Commissions	10,000
Various operating expenses	45,000
Dividend	3,000
Total	$86,000

Pro Forma Balance Sheet as of January 31, 19X4

Assets		Equities	
Cash (cash budget)	$ 4,000	Accounts payable[c]	$ 24,000
Accounts receivable[a]	60,000	Common stock	200,000
Inventory (purchases budget)	45,000	Retained earnings[d]	83,000
Building and equipment[b]	198,000		
Total	$307,000	Total	$307,000

[a] 60% of January sales of $100,000 (40% was collected in January).
[b] $200,000 beginning balance less $2,000 depreciation expense.
[c] 60% of January purchases of $40,000 (40% was paid in January).
[d] Beginning balance of $68,000 plus budgeted income of $18,000 minus dividend of $3,000.

Notice that cash declined by $16,000 (from $20,000 to $4,000), even though income was $18,000. The budgeted cash balance of $4,000 might be too low in management's judgment, and the firm might wish to seek a short-term bank loan.

ASSIGNMENT MATERIAL

Questions for Discussion

7-1 Cash budgeting — effects of external events You are controller of a large manufacturer and have recently completed your cash budget for the coming year. You now learn of each of the following events, which you are to consider independently. For each event, indicate (1) whether you expect it to influence your cash receipts or disbursements and (2) in which direction. Explain your answer.
1. The sales manager informs you that customers are not paying their bills as quickly as usual because of high interest rates.
2. The sales manager informs you that, due to a strike at the plant of a competitor, your firm's sales should be higher than budgeted.
3. Your suppliers, who have been giving you 45 days credit, are now requiring payment in 30 days.
4. Inventory policy is being changed from the carrying of the next two months' requirements to 150% of the next month's requirements.

7-2 Publication of budgets In financial accounting you studied the composition of the various financial statements usually distributed to persons outside the company. Included among these statements were the balance sheet and the income statement. This chapter states that a comprehensive budgeting program involves the preparation of the same statements using budgeted data. Budgeted financial statements are not normally made available to persons outside the organization. Do you see any advantages to publishing these budgeted statements as part of the annual reports? Do you see any disadvantages?

7-3   ***"Something is enough"***   The owner of a small chain of shoe stores has expressed dissatisfaction with the request from his budget director that he establish a policy regarding a minimum acceptable cash balance. "I see no reason for such a policy," he has said. "As long as the monthly budgets show that we can expect to have some cash on hand at the end of the month, why put still another assumption into the budget? There are far too many assumptions in the budget already." Comment on the owner's position.

7-4   ***Philanthropy or business sense?***   Many public utilities offer "level-payment plans" for their customers. For example, individuals purchasing natural gas for heating purposes from Consumers Power in Michigan, and individuals purchasing electricity from Texas Electric Service Companies, have the opportunity to spread the payments for their purchases over the entire year. The normal plan is for a given month's payment to be $\frac{1}{12}$ of the total cost of service provided in the 12 months ending with the current month.

Required: Discuss the reasons for a company to offer a level-payment plan.

7-5   ***Behavior of cash balances and profit***   Randolph Growing and Harry Declining were talking about the performances of their respective companies in recent months.

Growing: We have had rapid increases in monthly sales and are making profits hand over fist. We had expected this growth and have been keeping our inventories up to meet the increasing demand. However, our cash balances have been a problem. We have borrowed a lot of money lately.

Declining: Things have not been going as well for us. We have entered our slow season, and sales have been falling. Of course, we knew it would happen and planned accordingly. We are not making much profit, but do we have cash. Our balance has risen every month.

Required: Explain why cash is going in the opposite direction from profit for each of these companies.

Exercises

7-6   ***Cash receipts budget (continuation of 6-8 and 6-9)***   Gentry Company collects 40% of its sales in the month of sale and 60% in the following month. Receivables at the end of April were $102,000.

Required: Prepare cash receipts budgets for May and for June.

7-7   ***Cash budget (extension of 7-6)***   Gentry Company pays for its purchases in the month after purchase. Accounts payable for merchandise at the end of April were $160,000. Variable costs other than for cost of sales are paid as incurred, as are fixed costs requiring cash disbursement. The cash balance at the beginning of May is $30,000.

Required
1. Prepare cash disbursements budgets for May and for June.
2. Prepare cash budgets for May and for June.

7-8 *Cash receipts budget* Jasica Company expects the following sales for the first six months of 19X7. Figures are given in thousands of dollars.

	Jan.	Feb.	Mar.	Apr.	May	June
Budgeted sales	$1,200	$1,800	$1,900	$900	$2,200	$1,700

Cash collections expectations are as follows: 2% of sales become bad debts, 30% of sales are collected in the month of sale, 40% in the first month after sale, and 28% in the second month after sale. Sales in November 19X6 were $800,000, in December, $1,300,000.

Required: Prepare a schedule of budgeted cash receipts for the five-month period ending May 31, 19X7, by month.

7-9 *Production and cash disbursements budgets* The following data relate to Corr Company and its single product, a desk lamp.
  (a) Sales forecast, January through April, 19X9 (in units): 1,300; 1,600; 2,100; and 2,400.
  (b) Inventory policy: inventory is maintained at 150% of budgeted sales needs for the coming month.
  (c) Cost data: materials, $6 per unit; direct labor, $10 per unit; and variable overhead, $5 per unit. Monthly fixed costs are $15,000, including $3,000 depreciation.
  (d) Corr uses some JIT principles. It purchases materials daily and pays for them as delivered; all other costs requiring cash disbursements are also paid as incurred.
  (e) The beginning inventory for January is 1,800 units.

Required
1. Prepare a production budget for each of the first three months of 19X9.
2. Prepare a cash disbursements budget for each of the first three months of 19X9.

7-10 *Cash receipts and cash budget (continuation of 7-9)* The lamp sells for $40 per unit. All sales are on account with 30% collected in the month of sale, 70% in the month after sale. Receivables at December 31, 19X8 were $51,000.

Required
1. Prepare a schedule of budgeted cash receipts for each of the first three months of 19X9.
2. Prepare a cash budget for each of the first three months of 19X9. Cash at January 1 is $8,000.

7-11 *Cash budget (continuation of 6-10)* Jordan Clothing pays for its purchases in the month after purchase. Its accounts payable at December 31, 19X8, were $165,000. It collects 60% of its sales in the month of sale and 40% in the following month. Receivables at December 31, 19X8, to be collected in January, were $130,000. All of its fixed costs require cash disbursements and are paid as incurred. Its cash balance at December 31, 19X8, was $20,000.

Required
1. Prepare a cash receipts budget for each of the first three months of 19X9 and for the quarter as a whole.
2. Prepare a cash disbursements budget for each of the first three months of 19X9 and for the quarter as a whole.
3. Prepare a cash budget for each of the first three months of 19X9 and for the quarter as a whole.

7-12 Pro forma balance sheet (continuation of 7-11) Jordan Clothing's balance sheet at December 31, 19X8, appears below.

Assets		Equities	
Cash	$ 20,000	Accounts payable	$165,000
Receivables	130,000		
Inventory	220,000	Stockholders' equity	205,000
Total	$370,000	Total	$370,000

Jordan rents all of its fixed assets.

Required: Prepare a pro forma balance sheet as of March 31, 19X9.

7-13 Cash budget (continuation of 6-11) Thomas Company pays for its purchases in the month after purchase. Its accounts payable at December 31, 19X3, were $35,000. It collects 30% of its sales in the month of sale and 70% in the following month. Receivables at December 31, 19X3, to be collected in January, were $63,000. Depreciation is $5,000 per month. All of its other costs require cash disbursements and are paid as incurred. Its cash balance at December 31, 19X3, was $25,000.

Required
1. Prepare a cash receipts budget for each of the first three months of 19X4 and for the quarter as a whole.
2. Prepare a cash disbursements budget for each of the first three months of 19X4 and for the quarter as a whole.
3. Prepare a cash budget for each of the first three months of 19X4 and for the quarter as a whole.

7-14 Pro forma balance sheet (continuation of 7-13) Thomas Company had the following balance sheet at December 31, 19X3.

Assets		Equities	
Cash	$ 25,000	Accounts payable	$ 35,000
Receivables	63,000		
Inventory	64,000		
Fixed assets, net	150,000	Stockholders' equity	267,000
Total	$302,000	Total	$302,000

Required: Prepare a pro forma balance sheet as of March 31, 19X4.

7-15 *Cash budget – quarters* Walton Company expects the following results by quarters in 19X4 in thousands of dollars.

	1	2	3	4
Sales	$2,400	$3,000	$3,600	$2,100
Cash disbursements:				
Production costs	1,800	2,800	2,200	1,700
Selling and general	400	600	200	320
Purchases of fixed assets	0	400	600	400
Dividends	20	20	20	20

Accounts receivable at the end of a quarter are one-third of sales for the quarter. The beginning balance in accounts receivable is $700,000. Cash on hand at the beginning of the year is $120,000, and the desired minimum balance is $100,000. Any borrowings are made at the beginnings of quarters in which the need will occur, in $10,000 multiples, and are repaid at the ends of quarters. Ignore interest.

Required
1. Prepare a cash budget by quarters for the year.
2. What is the loan outstanding at the end of the year?
3. Can the firm be operating profitably in view of the heavy borrowing required?

7-16 *Pro forma balance sheet* The controller of Lamb Industries has been developing an analysis to see what financing requirements will be at the end of the current year. So far the controller has come up with the following data.

Budgeted Income Statement for Year
(in thousands of dollars)

Sales	$2,300
Cost of sales	1,100
Gross profit	1,200
Operating expenses	980
Income	$ 220

Outline of Pro Forma Balance Sheet
as of Year End (in thousands of dollars)

Assets		Equities	
Cash	$ 50	Current liabilities	$?
Accounts receivable	?		
Inventory	?	Stockholders' equity	2,590
Plant, net	2,400		
Total	$?	Total	$?

The firm's experience has been that accounts receivable are typically about 20% of sales, inventory about 40% of cost of sales. The firm expects to have about the same income-statement results for the next few years.

The controller would like to hold current liabilities to about one-half of current assets. The stockholders' equity figure given in the pro forma statement reflects expected profit and dividends for the year.

Required: Determine total asset requirements, total available equities, and the financing gap.

Problems

7-17 *Basic cash budget*   Before being called out of town on urgent company business, Sandy Banks, the controller of Zonar, Inc., had developed the following information for the company's cash budget for the next few months.

	Unit Sales	Unit Production	Material Purchases
January	1,000	1,400	$130,000
February	1,200	1,600	150,000
March	1,400	1,300	110,000

Zonar's one product, a stereo unit, sells for $600. Customers pay 40% in the month of sale, 60% in the following month. Material purchases are paid for in the month after purchase. Variable production costs, excluding materials, are $150 per unit of product. Fixed production costs are $150,000 per month, including $30,000 depreciation. Selling and administrative expenses are $40,000 per month, all cash, paid as incurred. Production costs other than those for materials are paid as incurred.

At January 1, the company had $360,000 in accounts receivable from December sales and owed suppliers of materials $500,000. Cash at January 1 was $35,000.

Required: Prepare budgets of cash receipts and disbursements and a cash budget for January and for February. If you show a negative cash balance, assume borrowing to bring it to zero. Ignore any interest.

7-18 *Comprehensive budget*   Borden Hardware Store is preparing its budgets for 19X7.

Forecasted Sales		Balance Sheet Data December 31, 19X6	
January	$60,000	Cash	$ 8,000
February	80,000	Accounts receivable	24,000
March	70,000	Inventory	54,000
April	90,000	Accounts payable (merchandise)	42,000

Other data are as follows:
(a)   Sales are on credit with 40% of sales collected in the month of sale and 60% in the month after sale.
(b)   Cost of sales is 60% of sales.

(c)   Other variable costs are 10% of sales, paid in the month incurred.
(d)   Inventories are to be 150% of next month's budgeted sales requirements.
(e)   Purchases are paid for in the month after purchase.
(f)   Fixed expenses are $3,000 per month; all require cash.

Required
1.   Prepare budgets of purchases for each of the first three months of 19X7.
2.   Prepare separate budgets of cash receipts and disbursements and a cash budget for each of the first three months of 19X7.
3.   Prepare a budgeted income statement for the three-month period ending March 31, 19X7.

7-19   *Cash budgeting – account analysis*   Using the following information, prepare cash budgets and supporting schedules for all months that you can. The beginning cash balance is $12,000.

	January	February	March	April
Sales	$90,000	$110,000	$100,000	$115,000
Accounts receivable, end of month	$36,000	$ 44,000	$ 45,000	$ 46,000
Purchases	$70,000	$ 60,000	$ 70,000	$ 50,000
Accounts payable, end of month	$21,000	$ 21,000	$ 28,000	$ 15,000

At the beginning of January, receivables were $28,000 and accounts payable were $20,000.

7-20   *Understanding budgets*   Below are the Blaisdel Company balance sheet at December 31, 19X0, and information regarding the company's policies and past experiences.

Balance Sheet Data, 12/31/X0

Cash	$ 35,000	Accounts payable	$ 12,000
Inventory	63,000	Income taxes payable	5,000
Receivables	16,000	Common stock	160,000
Fixed assets, net	96,000	Retained earnings	33,000
Total	$210,000	Total	$210,000

Additional information:
1.   All sales are on credit and are collected 70% in the month of sale and 30% in the month after sale.
2.   Expected sales for January, February, March, April, and May are $50,000, $60,000, $70,000, $66,000, and $65,000, respectively.
3.   Inventory is maintained at a level equivalent to the sales requirements for the following two months.
4.   Purchases are all on credit and are paid 80% in the month of purchase and 20% in the month after purchase.
5.   Other variable costs are 15% of sales and are paid in the month incurred.
6.   Fixed costs are $7,000 per month, including $1,000 of depreciation. Cash fixed costs are paid in the month incurred.

7. The firm's income tax rate is 40%, with taxes being paid in the month after they are accrued.
8. Cost of goods sold is expected to be 60% of sales.

Required
1. What are budgeted cash receipts for January 19X1?
2. What is the budgeted inventory at January 31, 19X1?
3. What are budgeted purchases for January 19X1?
4. What is budgeted net income for January 19X1?
5. What is the budgeted cash balance at the end of January 19X1?
6. What are budgeted accounts receivable at February 28, 19X1?
7. What is the budgeted book value of fixed assets at March 31, 19X1?
8. What are budgeted accounts payable at March 31, 19X1?
9. If the company declared a cash dividend of $1,200 during January, payable in February, what would be the balance reported for retained earnings in a pro forma balance sheet as of January 31, 19X1?
10. What amount would show as the liability for income taxes as of March 31, 19X1?

7-21   *Cash budget for a student*   Bo Phelps is a junior majoring in mathematics at a large university. At the beginning of the school year Bo wants to develop a cash budget for the fall term, which runs from September 1 through November 30. He has collected the following information.

Cash at September 1	$ 900
Tuition, due September 15	1,900
Room rent, due September 15 (for entire term)	600
Cost of meals, per month	250
Clothing expenditures, per month	50
Textbook purchases, due September 15	190

Bo has been awarded a scholarship of $2,000, the check for which should arrive by the end of the first week of September. He estimates that expenditures for dates and miscellaneous other items should total about $300 for the term, spread about evenly over each month. He also expects that he can get a part-time job that pays $8 per hour and that he will be able, for the most part, to set the hours he will work each month. The employer, a local business, must withhold 10% of Bo's earnings for income and social security taxes.

Required: Determine how many hours Bo must work each month to be able to maintain a $100 cash balance for emergencies.

7-22   *Comprehensive budget*   The following data pertain to Elgin's, a specialty store in a large shopping mall.

Sales Forecasts—19X8

January	$ 80,000
February	90,000
March	110,000
April	120,000
May	100,000

Balance Sheet at December 31, 19X7

Cash	$ 15,000	Accounts payable	$ 28,000
Accounts receivable	60,000	Accrued sales commissions	7,000
Inventory	102,000	Common stock	160,000
Net fixed assets	200,000	Retained earnings	182,000
Total	$377,000	Total	$377,000

Other data are as follows.

(a) All sales are on credit with 40% collected in the month of sale, and 60% in the month after sale.

(b) Cost of sales is 60% of sales.

(c) The only other variable cost is a 7% commission to salespeople that is paid in the month after it is earned. All sales are subject to the commission.

(d) Inventory is kept equal to sales requirements for the next two months' budgeted sales.

(e) Purchases are paid for in the month after purchase.

(f) Fixed costs are $10,000 per month, including $4,000 depreciation.

Required

1. Prepare a budgeted income statement for the three-month period ending March 31, 19X8.

2. Prepare a cash budget for each of the first three months of 19X8 and all necessary supporting budgets.

3. Prepare a pro forma balance sheet as of March 31, 19X8.

7-23 *Investing idle cash (extension of 7-22; adapted from a problem prepared by Professor Robert W. Koehler)* The president of Elgin's was pleased with the cash budget you prepared, but felt that the firm might be able to invest some of its available cash and thereby earn an additional return. He knows that if the funds are invested in a money market fund the firm will be able to earn 1% per month interest and to withdraw the money at any time. He believes that a $10,000 cash balance is sufficient and asks you to redo the cash budget to reflect the investing of excess cash at 1% per month. (Thus, you can invest $5,000 on January 1, because the $15,000 balance is $5,000 over the required minimum.) Assume that you invest at the ends of months (except for January 1).

Required: Respond to the president's request.

7-24 *Municipal budgeting – revenues* The City of Wentworth is preparing its budget for 19X9. Total required revenues are $36,000,000. The city has two major sources of revenue, sales taxes and property taxes. The sales tax is 2% of taxable retail sales, which includes virtually all sales except for food and medicine. The assessed valuation of taxable property is $560,000,000. An economist hired by the city has forecast total taxable retail sales at $860,000,000 for 19X9.

Required

1. Determine the property tax rate needed to meet the city's revenue objective, assuming that the estimate of retail sales is correct.

2. The city council is considering a proposal to reduce property taxes on homes owned by people over 65 years of age. It is proposed that the rate on such

homes be set at $30 per $1,000 assessed valuation. The total assessed valuation of homes owned by people over 65 is $45,000,000. Determine the rate that would have to be set on the remaining taxable property in order to meet the revenue objective if the proposal is adopted.

7-25 **Manufacturer's cash budget – three months** Tompkins Company produces a single product that sells for $15 per unit. Data are

(a) Variable manufacturing costs, all requiring cash, are $7 per unit.

(b) Variable selling and administrative expenses are $1 per unit.

(c) Fixed manufacturing costs requiring cash are $50,000 per month. Depreciation is $12,000 per month. Fixed selling and administrative expenses are $40,000 per month, all requiring cash.

(d) Tompkins maintains a two-month supply of finished goods. The beginning inventory (January 1) is 42,000 units.

(e) Tompkins has partially implemented JIT principles and so buys raw materials as needed, maintaining no inventory. The cost of raw materials is included in the variable manufacturing cost of $7.

(f) Tompkins makes all sales on credit, collecting 30% in the month of sale and 70% in the month after sale. The beginning balance in accounts receivable is $140,000.

(g) All cash manufacturing costs are paid for in the month of production.

(h) Tompkins pays 80% of selling and administrative expenses in the month of sale, 20% in the following month. At January 1 the firm owed $14,000 from December expenses.

(i) The minimum desired cash balance is $40,000, which is also the amount on hand at the beginning of January. If the firm needs to borrow, it does so in multiples of $10,000. It must borrow at the beginning of the month and repay at the end, if sufficient cash is available. The monthly interest rate is 1%, and Tompkins pays interest when it repays loans, or a portion of them.

(j) The sales budget for the first six months is, in units, January, 20,000; February, 26,000; March, 30,000; April, 32,000; May, 30,000; June, 28,000.

Required

1. Prepare a cash budget and any necessary supporting schedules for the first three months of the year, by month and in total.

2. Given your results in item 1, does the firm appear to be profitable? Explain.

3. Suppose that sales stabilized at 25,000 units per month. What will monthly cash collections be? What will monthly cash disbursements for manufacturing costs and for selling and administrative expenses be?

7-26 **Manufacturer's cash budget – changes in assumptions (continuation of 7-25)** The president of Tompkins Company is concerned about the budgeted financing requirements. He also believes that budgeted sales from March through May might be too high. He expects sales in each of those three months to be 2,000 units fewer than budgeted in 7-25.

Required

1. If you were to prepare new budgets based on the president's figures, do you think the financing requirements would be higher or lower than they were in 7-25? Why?

2. Prepare a new cash budget and supporting schedules using the president's estimates.

7-27 **One-month cash budget – discounts** Stony Acres Department Store makes about 20% of its sales for cash. Credit sales are collected 20%, 30%, 45% in the month of sale, month after, and second month after sale, respectively. The remaining 5% become bad debts. The store tries to purchase enough goods each month to maintain its inventory at 2½ times the following month's budgeted sales. All purchases are subject to a 2% discount if paid within ten days and the store takes all discounts. Accounts payable are then equal to one-third of that month's net purchases. Cost of goods sold, without considering the 2% discount, is 60% of selling prices. The firm records inventory net of the discount.

    The general manager of the store has asked you to prepare a cash budget for August and you have gathered the following data.

Sales:	
May (actual)	$220,000
June (actual)	260,000
July (actual)	300,000
August (budgeted)	340,000
September (budgeted)	300,000
Inventory at July 31, net of discount	455,700
Cash at July 31	65,000
Purchases in July (gross)	210,000
Selling, general, and administrative expenses budgeted for August	91,000 (includes $18,000 depreciation)

The firm pays all of its other expenses in the month incurred.

Required: Prepare a cash budget for August.

7-28 **Long-range financial budget** Millard Company has retained you to develop a financing plan for the next few years. You collect the following information about the firm's expectations, goals, and policies. All dollar amounts are in thousands.

Sales Forecasts	
19X4	$ 800
19X5	1,000
19X6	1,250
19X7	1,500

    Millard expects a return on sales of 12%. The directors of the firm would like to maintain the policy of distributing dividends in an amount equal to 60% of net income each year. The directors would also like to have a current ratio of at least 3 to 1 and do not want long-term debt to exceed 60% of stockholders' equity.

    Current asset requirements are 30% of expected sales in the coming year, and net fixed assets are 75% of budgeted sales for the coming year. At the end of 19X3, stockholders' equity is $500.

Required: Prepare a schedule showing financing requirements for 19X4, 19X5, and 19X6.

7-29 *Budgeting equations (CMA adapted)* Your firm has just acquired a new computer, and one of the first things that the president wants it to be used for is the preparation of the firm's comprehensive budget. He assigns you the task of formulating a set of equations that can be used to write a program to perform the computations required for the budgets. You consult with the chief programmer, and the two of you decide that the following notation should be used, which will make it easy for the programmer to prepare the necessary programs.

S_0 = sales in current month (units)

S_1 = sales in coming month (units)

S_{-1} = sales in prior month (units)

S_{-2} = sales in second prior month (units)

P = selling price per unit

CGS = cost of goods sold per unit (purchase price)

OVC = other variable costs per unit

FC = total fixed costs per month

FCC = fixed costs per month requiring cash disbursements

PUR = purchases in current month (units)

PUR_{-1} = purchases in prior month (units)

You examine the records of the firm and decide that the firm's policies or experienced relationships are as follows.
1. Collections on sales are 30% in the month of sale, 50% in the month after sale, and 20% in the second month after sale.
2. Inventory is maintained at twice the coming month's budgeted sales volume.
3. Purchases are paid for 60% in the month after purchase and 40% in the month of purchase.
4. All other costs are paid as incurred.

Required: Prepare equations that can be used to budget for the following.
1. Income for the current month.
2. Cash receipts in current month.
3. Purchases in current month in units.
4. Purchases in current month in dollars.
5. Cash disbursements in current month.

7-30 *Comprehensive budget (continuation of 6-45; adapted from a problem prepared by Professor Maurice L. Hirsch)* The following additional information about Banana City is available.
1. Sales of bananas are for cash only. Sales of nuts are on credit and are collected two months after sale.
2. Banana City's suppliers give terms of 30 days for payment of accounts payable. Banana City takes full advantage of the 30-day payments. (Assume that all months have 30 days.)
3. The firm must make quarterly payments on its income taxes. The payment for the first quarter of fiscal year 19X7 is due on January 15, 19X7. The liability for taxes payable shown on the balance sheet below is to be paid on October 15.

4. The fixed expenses of the firm that require cash disbursement are paid as incurred with the following exceptions: (a) insurance premiums are all paid on November 1 in advance for the next 12 months and (b) interest payments are all made on January 1. The $156,000 "other fixed expenses" shown in item 6 of 6-45 all require cash disbursements evenly over the year.
5. The balance sheet for August 31, 19X6 is given below.

Assets		Equities	
Cash	$ 15,000	Accounts payable (merchandise)	$ 26,000
Accounts receivable	75,000	Taxes payable	31,000
Inventories	41,800	Accrued interest	4,000
Prepaid insurance	2,000	Long-term debt, 6%	100,000
Land	8,000	Common stock	150,000
Equipment (net)	210,000	Retained earnings	40,800
Total	$351,800	Total	$351,800

6. Sales in the last part of fiscal year 19X6 are given below.

	June	July	August
Bananas	$31,000	$34,000	$32,500
Nuts	37,000	41,000	34,000

7. The firm expects to pay a dividend of $12,000 in October.

Required
1. Prepare budgets of cash receipts and disbursements for each of the first three months of fiscal year 19X7 and for the quarter as a whole.
2. Prepare a cash budget for the quarter by month, and in total.
3. Prepare a pro forma balance sheet for November 30, 19X6.

7-31 ***Pro forma balance sheet and financing requirements*** Jill Eyre, treasurer of Caldwell Company, has collected the following information as part of her planning. She believes that the company will have to issue long-term debt during the year, but she is unsure how much.

Budgeted Income Statement for 19X6	
Sales	$300,000
Cost of goods sold	210,000
Gross profit	90,000
Selling, general, and administrative expenses[a]	36,000
Income before taxes	54,000
Income taxes (40% rate)	21,600
Net income	$ 32,400

[a] Includes $10,000 depreciation expense.

Balance Sheet Data, December 31, 19X5

Plant and equipment—net	$150,000
Common stock	200,000
Retained earnings	83,000
Asset requirements:	
Cash—minimum desired balance	$ 25,000
Accounts receivable	30% of sales
Inventory	40% of cost of sales
Plant and equipment—net	$210,000
Equities available:	
Accounts payable	50% of inventory
Income taxes payable	50% of income tax expense

A dividend of $22,000 will be paid during 19X6.

Required: Prepare a statement of asset requirements and available equities as of the end of 19X6. Determine the amount of long-term debt that Caldwell will need at the end of 19X6.

7-32 *Financing growth*   The controller and treasurer of GlenCo Manufacturing have engaged you to assist them in long-term budgeting. GlenCo's board of directors has approved a long-term plan that envisions about a 15% annual rate of growth in sales, as reflected in the following sales forecasts, in millions of dollars.

Sales Forecasts

19X5	$40.0
19X6	46.0
19X7	52.9
19X8	60.8

The best information available indicates that net income will run at 10% of sales. The directors imposed some restrictions regarding financing. They wish to continue paying dividends of 40% of net income and want the current ratio to be at least 3 to 1. They believe that long-term debt should not exceed 30% of stockholders' equity.

Current asset requirements generally are about 40% of forecasted sales for the coming year, and net fixed assets are usually about 110% of forecasted sales for the coming year. Stockholders' equity is $32.0 million at the beginning of 19X5.

Required: Prepare a schedule to show the controller and treasurer the financing requirements that GlenCo faces from 19X5 through 19X7. Round to the nearest tenth of a million dollars.

7-33 *Comprehensive budget*   The balance sheet of your firm, Arcon Industries, at December 31, 19X5, is shown below. Also shown is a projected income statement for the first three months of 19X6, prepared by your chief accountant. You are happy with the projection and gloat about it to your banker. The banker, always eager to lend money, has asked if you will need any cash to get through the first quarter. "Of course not" is your reply. Later, back at your office, the chief accountant informs you of the following:

1. Sales are all on credit and are collected 50% in the month of sale, 50% in the month after sale.
2. It is company policy to build up inventory so that inventory is always equal to the next two months' sales in units. However, at December 31, 19X5, your inventory is depleted because of the dock strike.
3. You pay for purchases 50% in the month of purchase, 50% in the following month.
4. You are committed to paying the recorded cash dividend of $2,000 in March.
5. All cash expenses are paid in the month incurred, except for purchases.
6. The accounts receivable at December 31, 19X5 will be collected in January; the accounts payable at December 31, 19X5 will be paid in January.
7. The monthly breakdown of projected sales is as follows: January, $20,000; February, $30,000; and March, $50,000. In addition, April sales are expected to be $20,000, and May sales, $20,000.
8. Cash should not go below $5,000.

Balance Sheet at December 31, 19X5

Cash	$ 5,000		Accounts payable	$16,000	
Accounts receivable	10,000		Dividend payable	2,000	$18,000
Inventory	24,000	$39,000	Owners' equity		61,000
Plant and equipment, net of					
accumulated depreciation		40,000			
Total		$79,000			$79,000

Budgeted Income Statement
for the Three Months Ending March 31, 19X6

Sales (10,000 units × $10)		$100,000
Cost of sales (10,000 units × $6)		60,000
Gross profit		40,000
Operating expenses:		
Wages and salaries	$9,000	
Rent	3,000	
Depreciation	3,000	
Other expenses	1,500	16,500
Income		$ 23,500

Required: Do you regret your reply to your banker? Explain by preparing the appropriate schedules. (If borrowings are necessary, assume that they are in $1,000 multiples at the beginning of the month and that repayments are at the ends of months with 12% annual interest on the amount repaid.)

7-34 *Comprehensive budget (continuation of 6-32)* The managers of Calco Products Company have the following additional information.

Sales should be collected 30% in the month of sale, 70% in the following month. Purchases are paid 40% in the month of purchase, 60% in the following month. Fixed manufacturing costs include $20,000 per month depreciation. All manufacturing costs requiring cash disbursements are paid as incurred. All selling and administrative expenses require cash disbursements, with 80% paid as incurred, and the remaining 20% paid in the following month. The balance sheet at December 31 appears below.

Balance Sheet as of December 31, 19X5	
Assets	
Cash	$ 75,000
Accounts receivable	280,000
Finished goods (35,000 × $14)	490,000
Materials (66,000 × $8)	528,000
Net plant	1,200,000
Total assets	$2,573,000
Equities	
Accounts payable	$ 96,000
Accrued S, G, and A expenses	18,000*
Stockholders' equity	2,459,000
Total equities	$2,573,000

* $12,000 of the total relates to fixed costs.

Required
1. Prepare the following budgets for January and for February.
   (a) cash receipts
   (b) cash disbursements
   (c) cash
   The company desires a minimum cash balance of $60,000 at the end of each month. If operating projections show that borrowing is necessary to meet the minimum balance and cover a month's cash activity, such borrowings occur at the beginning of the month, in multiples of $10,000. Repayments, in multiples of $10,000, are made at the end of the month, as soon as cash balances permit them, and the bank charges interest at 1% per month. Interest payments are made only at the time a repayment occurs, and then only for the interest due on the amount being repaid.
2. Prepare a pro forma balance sheet as of the end of February. (Remember that interest accrues on loans outstanding, and that the income statement prepared for 6-32 does not yet reflect interest expense on any borrowed funds.)

7-35 Cash budget (continuation of 6-44) Richards Company collects its sales 30% in the month of sale, 30% in the next month, and 40% in the second month after sale. Fixed production costs not requiring cash are $40,000 per month. All selling, general, and administrative expenses require cash and are paid in the month incurred, except for sales commissions, which are paid in the month after incurrence.

All production costs requiring cash are paid 80% in the month of production, 20% in the month after production. This includes payments for materials, of which no inventory is kept since they are delivered daily.

Selected balance sheet data at May 30 are as follows.

Cash	$120,000 (equals the desired minimum balance)
Accounts receivable:	
From May sales	336,000
From April sales	120,000
Liabilities:	
Sales commissions	48,000
Production costs	66,000

Required: Prepare a cash budget for Richards Company for the first three months of the fiscal year, by month. If the need arises, show borrowings required to maintain the desired minimum balance of cash, in multiples of $10,000. Repayments are made at the ends of months and interest at 1% per month is paid when a repayment is made.

7-36 Analysis of budgets   Budgets for Simpson Company appear below for the first three months of 19X6. Answer the following questions about the assumptions and policies used in formulating them.

1. What are variable manufacturing costs per unit?
2. What are monthly fixed manufacturing costs requiring cash disbursements?
3. What are the firm's expectations about cash collections from receivables? (All sales are on account.)
4. What were sales in December 19X5?
5. What are accounts receivable at March 31, 19X6?
6. What proportion of variable selling and administrative expenses is paid in the month incurred, and what proportion is paid the following month? (*Hint:* Variable selling costs are 25% of sales.)
7. What are accrued expenses payable for selling and administrative expenses at March 31, 19X6?
8. How much cash does the firm expect to have at March 31, 19X6? (The balance at January 1 is $1,800.)
9. If the firm could sell 2,000 additional units in the three-month period, what would income be? (Ignore interest expense.)
10. Look at the production budget. From comparisons of inventories, sales, and so on, determine the firm's inventory policy.
11. Does the beginning inventory for January reflect the firm's policy? Show why or why not.
12. What are budgeted sales for April?

Budgeted Income Statement
for the Three Months Ending March 31, 19X6

Sales (10,000 units)		$30,000
Variable costs:		
Production	$8,000	
Selling and administrative	7,500	15,500
Contribution margin		14,500
Fixed costs:		
Production	1,800	
Selling and administrative	2,400	4,200
Income		$10,300

Production Budget (in units)

	January	February	March
Desired ending inventory	4,500	7,500	6,000
Units sold	2,000	3,000	5,000
Total requirements	6,500	10,500	11,000
Beginning inventory	2,500	4,500	7,500
Production	4,000	6,000	3,500

Cash Receipts Budget

	January	February	March
Collections:			
December sales	$ 750		
January sales	1,500	$4,500	
February sales		2,250	$ 6,750
March sales			3,750
Total collections	$2,250	$6,750	$10,500

Cash Disbursements Budget

	January	February	March
Production costs:			
Variable	$3,200	$4,800	$2,800
Fixed	600	600	600
Selling and administrative:			
Variable—current month	600	900	1,500
—prior month	150	900	1,350
Fixed	800	800	800
Totals	$5,350	$8,000	$7,050

7-37 Variable minimum cash balance   The chief financial officer of Bland Company has asked for your help in preparing a cash budget. He plans to maintain a minimum balance based on the budgeted disbursements for the coming month and is unsure how to proceed. He tells you the following about his policy. "If the coming month's budgeted receipts are greater than budgeted disbursements, I want to hold a balance equal to 10% of budgeted disbursements and invest any excess cash in short-term government notes. If budgeted disbursements are greater than budgeted receipts, I want to have enough cash to make up the budgeted deficit and have 20% of budgeted disbursements on hand to begin the month. We will borrow if the indicated balance is less than required."

The budgets for sales and purchases in the coming months are as follows.

	Sales	Purchases
April	$500,000	$470,000
May	780,000	550,000
June	900,000	560,000
July	600,000	480,000
August	650,000	600,000

Sales are collected 30% in the month of sale, 70% in the following month. Purchases are paid for 50% in the month of purchase, 50% in the following month. Sales in March were $450,000, and accounts payable for merchandise at March 31 were $185,000. Cash at March 31 was $140,000. Fixed expenses requiring cash disbursements are $110,000 per month.

Required
1. Prepare a schedule by month for the April–July period indicating the amounts that would have to be borrowed, or would be available for investment, in each month. Borrowings would be repaid as soon as possible and are not included in the determination of disbursements for the purpose of setting the desired balance. Borrowings would be repaid before investments were made and investments would be sold before borrowings are made. Ignore interest.
2. Discuss the policy. What advantages or disadvantages does it have in comparison to a policy of having a set number of dollars as the desired minimum balance?

Cases

7-38 Qualifying for a loan   The president of Stern's Department Store has requested your assistance. He will be seeking a large bank loan in a couple of months for the purpose of opening a new store and has been told by his banker that the March 31, 19X8 balance sheet should look good if the loan is to be granted. The banker said specifically that working capital should be at least $500,000 and that the current ratio should be at least 2.5 to 1.

The end of January is now approaching and the president is becoming anxious. He asks you to prepare a cash budget for February and March and a pro forma balance sheet as of March 31. The balance sheet at the end of January is expected to be about as follows, in thousands of dollars.

Assets		Equities	
Cash	$ 110	Accounts payable (merchandise)	$ 410
Accounts receivable	240	Notes payable	40
Inventory	680	Common stock	2,000
Building and equipment (net)	1,830	Retained earnings	410
Total	$2,860	Total	$2,860

The sales forecasts for the months of February, March, April, and May are, respectively, $780,000; $650,000; $600,000; and $820,000. Cost of sales averages 60% of sales. Receivables are collected 60% in the month of sale, 40% in the following month. Inventory is normally maintained at budgeted sales requirements for the following two months. Purchases are paid for in 30 days.

The notes payable shown in the balance sheet are due on March 15. Although the firm normally keeps a minimum cash balance of $80,000, the president asks you to disregard this for purposes of the budgets. He also informs you that monthly fixed costs are $265,000, of which $30,000 is depreciation. All fixed costs requiring cash are paid as incurred.

Required

1. Prepare the cash budget and pro forma balance sheet that the president wants. Use thousands of dollars.
2. Determine whether the firm will be likely to meet the criteria set by the bank.

7-39   *Financing requirements*   Larsen Company makes fertilizer in a midwestern state. The firm has nearly completed a new plant that will produce twice as much as the old plant, which is being scrapped. Swen Larsen, the owner, has consulted you about his financing requirements for the coming year. He knows that he will require additional financing because of the doubling of production, and he intends to obtain a loan as soon as possible. He is on good terms with local bankers and anticipates no difficulty in obtaining the loan, but he is anxious that it not be too large or too small.

The production process in the new plant is highly automated and can be carried out with a work force of the same size as that used last year in the old plant. The income statement for last year and the year-end balance sheet are as follows.

Income Statement for 19X4

Sales	$1,600,000
Cost of goods sold	1,040,000
Gross profit	560,000
Selling, general, and administrative expenses	390,000
Income	$ 170,000

Balance Sheet at December 31, 19X4

Assets		Liabilities and Owner's Equity	
Cash	$ 40,000	Accounts payable	$ 20,000
Accounts receivable	80,000	Common stock	900,000
Inventory of materials	250,000	Retained earnings	150,000
Plant and equipment—old plant	0		
—new plant	700,000		
Total	$1,070,000	Total	$1,070,000

You learn that depreciation expense on the old plant was $80,000 per year, all of which was included in cost of goods sold. The new plant will be depreciated at $120,000 per year. Wages paid last year to production workers were $280,000. Material purchases were $400,000, which is also the amount of material cost included in cost of goods sold (the beginning and ending inventories of materials were the same). Factory overhead, other than depreciation, was $280,000 last year. It is expected that factory overhead, other than depreciation, will be $360,000 in the coming year.

Selling, general, and administrative expenses are expected to be $430,000 during the coming year. Sales will be only 120% of last year's sales because it will take some time to reach the full output of the new plant. Mr. Larsen expects to spend $250,000 buying new equipment to complete the plant. This expenditure will be made as soon as he obtains the new loan. The factory will be operating at full capacity the last few months of the year, so ending requirements for current assets should be double the beginning amounts. Accounts payable are closely related to the amount of inventory carried. The firm ships its products on completion so that all inventory is raw materials.

Required: Prepare a budgeted income statement for 19X5 and a pro forma balance sheet (as far as possible) for December 31, 19X5. State any assumptions you have to make and indicate how much Mr. Larsen must borrow from the bank.

7-40 *Cash budgeting — a lender's viewpoint* You are the chief assistant to Mr. Barnes, the loan officer of Metropolitan National Bank. In December 19X4 Mr. Barnes discussed a loan with Mr. Johnson, manager-owner of a local dry goods store. Mr. Johnson has requested a loan of $250,000 to be repaid at June 30, 19X5. The store is being expanded and additional inventory is needed. From the proceeds of the loan, $200,000 will be spent on remodeling and new fixtures. The rest will be spent for additional inventory. At Mr. Barnes's request, Mr. Johnson submitted a budgeted income statement for the six months ending June 30, 19X5.

Sales	$900,000
Cost of goods sold	360,000
Gross profit	540,000
Selling, general, and administrative expenses, including $15,000 interest	310,000
Income	$230,000

Mr. Johnson said that, since $50,000 in depreciation was included in selling, general, and administrative expenses, the firm would generate more than enough cash to repay the loan with $15,000 in interest (12% annual rate). Mr. Barnes asks you to check out the forecast; you obtain the following information:

1. Sales are expected to be $100,000 in January, $140,000 in February, and $165,000 in each of the rest of the months of the entire year.
2. Merchandise is held equal to two months' budgeted sales.
3. Accounts payable are paid in 30 days.
4. About half of sales are for cash. The rest are collected in the second month after sale (60 days).
5. Cost of goods sold is variable, and 15% of sales is the variable portion of selling, general, and administrative expenses. All selling, general and administrative expenses, except depreciation, are paid in the month incurred.
6. At December 31, 19X4, the following balance sheet is expected.

Pro Forma Balance Sheet as of December 31, 19X4

Cash (desired minimum)	$ 20,000	Accounts payable	$ 30,000
Accounts receivable	40,000	Common stock	200,000
Inventory	60,000	Retained earnings	115,000
Building and equipment	375,000		
Accumulated depreciation	(150,000)		
Total	$ 345,000	Total	$345,000

Required: Determine whether the firm can repay the loan with interest at the end of the first six months of 19X5. If not, explain why in terms that will make Mr. Johnson understand where he made his mistakes.

7-41   ***Budgeting and industry data***   Ralph Robertson is considering opening a menswear store in a new shopping center. He has had a great deal of experience in men's stores and is convinced that he can make a success of his own store. He has asked you to develop a financing plan that he can take to a bank to obtain a loan. He knows that a bank manager will be more receptive to an applicant who has made careful plans of his needs. He gives you the following data obtained from a trade association's study of stores of the kind and size he plans to open (1,200 square feet of selling space).

Average sales per square foot	$70 per year
Average rent	$500 per month plus 5% of sales
Average gross profit	45% of sales
Average annual operating expenses (excluding rent and depreciation):	
At $60,000 sales annually	$19,200
At $90,000 sales annually	$26,700
Inventory requirements	four-month supply
Investment in fixtures and equipment (useful life of five years)	$22,000

Ralph plans to sell for cash only. He will have to pay cash for his first purchase of inventory, then he can get 30 days' credit from suppliers. His other operating expenses, including rent, will be paid in the month incurred.

Ralph expects to have a steady growth in sales for the first four months of operation (January–April 19X8) and to reach the monthly average for the industry in May. His projections for the first four months are as follows: $4,000; $4,500; $5,200; and $6,100.

Required
1. Prepare a budgeted income statement for the year 19X8.
2. Prepare a schedule showing his total financing requirements through April. Ralph will invest $10,000 of his own money.

CHAPTER **8**

CAPITAL BUDGETING, PART I

This chapter and the next require that you understand the principles of the time value of money. Before you begin this chapter, read the Appendix at the back of the book and work through the review problems to be sure that you understand these principles.

The comprehensive budget, the unifying topic of Chapters 6 and 7, reflects the results expected from a wide variety of planning decisions, such as those about product mix, cost structure, and pricing. Most of those decisions aim at achieving the best possible results given the firm's existing resources. That is, the decisions did not require large commitments of cash to investments in land, plant, machinery, or other long-lived assets. A comprehensive budget must also incorporate the planning decisions that *do* involve such long-term commitments, called **capital budgeting decisions.** Planned expenditures for new, long-lived assets are often the largest items in the cash disbursements budget.

Capital budgeting decisions are the subject of this and the next chapter. Such decisions entail sizable commitments of cash and generate returns—normally, income or cost savings—that will last for more than one year. Capital budgeting decisions are therefore also called *long-term decisions*.

As Chapter 5 pointed out, the usual rule for determining whether a decision is short-term or long-term is whether its effects will be complete within one year. This rule, while arbitrary, provides a good basis for distinguishing the two types of decisions. Capital budgeting decisions are like short-term decisions in that they both use differential revenues and costs. These concepts therefore remain relevant to capital budgeting decisions.

For two reasons, capital budgeting decisions are generally more risky than short-term ones. First, the firm will recoup its investment, if at all, over a longer period. That is, there is a longer waiting period between the time an expenditure is made and the time cash is received. Second, it is much more difficult to reverse a capital budgeting decision than a short-term decision. For example, suppose a firm raises its prices expecting to improve its profits, and sales fall so much that profits fall. Usually the firm can simply lower its prices. The firm may suffer a decline in profits for a short time, but it can recover fairly quickly once the managers see their error. But suppose a company buys land and constructs and equips a building especially to make a particular product. The plant may have little value in any other use (a low opportunity cost). If the product is unsuccessful, the firm will have made a large, nearly worthless investment.

Managers use the analytical techniques discussed in this and the following chapter to decide whether to undertake specific long-term projects. The expenditures on those projects selected by management are incorporated into short-term and long-term budgets such as those presented in the preceding chapter. We cover only briefly the issues surrounding decisions about how to *finance* long-term investments. In managerial finance you will study in more detail the problems of selecting from among financing alternatives.

CAPITAL BUDGETING AND RESOURCE ALLOCATION

In short-term decision making, considering only quantifiable factors, an action is desirable if incremental revenues exceed incremental costs. In capital budgeting decisions, the company must include as a relevant cost the **time value of money,** because capital budgeting decisions require investing money now to bring in more money in the future. The time value of money is an opportunity cost: by making a particular investment now, we give up the opportunity to make other investments.

Managers incorporate the time value of money into capital budgeting decisions by determining whether the expected rate of return on the incremental investment is greater than the rate that must be paid to suppliers of capital. The latter rate is called *cost of capital*. If the expected rate of return is greater than cost of capital, the investment is desirable; if the expected rate is less than cost of capital, the investment is not desirable. The study of cost of capital is the province of managerial finance. Thus, we include only a brief introduction to the concept.

Cost of Capital

Cost of capital is the cost, expressed as a percentage, of obtaining the capital resources to operate the firm. Capital is obtained from two sources, creditors and owners, corresponding to the divisions of liabilities and owners' equity on the balance sheet. The cost of capital supplied by creditors is the effective interest rate on borrowings. For example, if the firm has to make annual interest payments of $80,000 to obtain $1,000,000 from a sale of bonds with that face value, the effective interest rate is 8% ($80,000/$1,000,000).[1]

The cost of equity capital is more difficult to determine, for it is based on how much investors expect the firm to earn. In a simple situation this cost may be approximated by dividing the expected earnings by the market value of the stock. Thus, if a firm is expected to earn $3 per share and the market price of the stock is $30 per share, the cost of equity capital is 10% ($3/$30).

We are interested in cost of capital because it is the minimum acceptable rate of return on investment. It serves as a **cutoff rate of return.** Any project not expected to yield this rate should be rejected; projects expected to yield higher rates should be accepted.

Determining a firm's cost of capital is usually a complex task. Because of the practical difficulties of the task, managers might simply use their judgment to set a minimum acceptable rate. A rate so set is often called a **target rate of return,** and the firm will use this rate in deciding which projects to accept. In this and the next chapter we assume that cost of capital has been estimated and is to be used in the decision to accept or reject a project.

TYPES OF CAPITAL BUDGETING DECISIONS

This chapter considers two general types of capital budgeting decisions. One type involves making investments to increase volume, either by increasing the output of an existing product or by making a new product. The second type of decision relates primarily to costs, the goal being to find the least-cost way to accomplish some specific objective. The same basic analysis applies to both types of decisions, but circumstances surrounding them differ. Firms need not take advantage of opportunities to increase capacity; they can continue to operate with what they have. Investments made to reduce costs are different; here, the decision implies that the management has already decided to operate in a particular fashion and seeks the least costly way of doing so.

Cost minimization situations can be further subdivided into two basic types. First, in some situations, there is no choice because the operation must be performed if the firm is to remain in business. An automobile maker must assemble its cars; it cannot simply produce the parts and sell them to consumers. Given the decision that the firm will be an automobile maker, it must find the least expensive method of performing the essential assembly function. Should the firm use large amounts of labor or large amounts of machinery? Should the firm use existing machinery or replace it with more efficient equipment?

The second type of cost minimization situation covers projects unrelated to essential operations. For instance, top-level management may decide to provide a

---

[1] You may recall the determination of bond prices and effective interest rates from financial accounting. There are complications if bonds are issued at prices other than face value, but these problems are not important for our purposes.

cafeteria for employees. The firm will seek the least-cost method of providing this service. Although the firm may gain benefits from a cafeteria (through improved employee morale), future costs will increase rather than decrease. Nonessential investments do not increase the cash that will be available to the firm, but they are, nonetheless, important and should be scrutinized at least as carefully as other potential investments.

Capital Budgeting Techniques

In a typical investment situation, a manager authorizes an investment with the intention of receiving returns sufficient both to recoup the original investment and to reward the company adequately for the risk taken. But the returns come in the future, often over many years. That is, the manager must wait for both the return *of* the investment and the return *on* it. Hence, when making an investment decision, the manager tries to determine, considering the time value of money, whether the rate of return associated with the investment is greater or less than the minimum acceptable rate—cost of capital. There are two ways to do this: (1) find the rate of return associated with the project and compare that rate with the cost of capital, or (2) use the cost of capital to find the present value of the future returns and compare that value with the cost of the investment.

The second method is usually easier to apply. Using this approach, called the **net present value (NPV)** method, we compare the present value of future returns from an investment with the cost of obtaining those returns—the required investment. The alternative approach, finding the rate of return on a project and comparing it with a specified minimum acceptable rate, is usually called the **internal rate of return (IRR)** method. It uses the same basic concepts as the net present value approach. Later in this chapter, we consider two other commonly used techniques for analyzing long-term investments. These additional techniques are conceptually inferior to either the NPV or the IRR method because neither of the additional techniques considers the time value of money.

In three of the four analytical approaches to capital budgeting decisions discussed in this chapter, returns are defined as **cash flows,** not as income. Given the emphasis on income in prior chapters, and probably in your first course in accounting, we take some time to explain why cash flows are so important in capital budgeting.

Cash Flows and Book Income

In the short-term decisions covered in Chapter 5, the criterion for acceptance was whether the decision would increase the company's income. If incremental revenues exceeded incremental costs, income would increase and the decision would be wise. We did not speak of cash flows in Chapter 5 because, in short-term decisions, incremental revenues and incremental costs are also, respectively, incremental cash inflows and incremental cash outflows. In the short-term, those cash flows come in and go out within relatively short periods (during the year), so that the time value of money is not significant. Hence, the incremental profit of Chapter 5 was also incremental cash flow.

Capital budgeting decisions require investing cash now to get cash back later, sometimes much later. Moreover, if an investment is made in depreciable assets, the incremental incomes and the incremental cash flows will *differ* in the individual years of the life of the investment because of the accounting treatment of depreciation. When a depreciable asset is acquired, a cash outlay occurs in the year of acquisition. The cost of that asset is allocated over the years in which the asset is used, so the incomes of those years are reduced by the depreciation expense. But there is no associated outlay of cash in those years. Hence, the change in incomes of year 19X5 or 19X6 as a result of a long-term investment decision in 19X1 will not be the same as the change in cash flows of years 19X5 and 19X6 as a result of that same decision. The change in income will be smaller than the change in cash flow because income will be reduced by depreciation expense, which requires no cash flow. For this reason, we must be more specific in our analyses of decisions that involve depreciable assets and future incomes. We cannot use income as a substitute for cash flows (as we did in Chapter 5), because income will not be a good measure of cash flows.

Of course, depreciation is a legitimate expense for both accounting and tax purposes. And the income taxes to be paid in a given period *are* a cash outflow. While depreciation is not a cash flow, it does affect the cash outflow for income taxes. Hence, to determine the incremental cash flow from an investment for a particular year, we must know the depreciation expense for that year. Later in this chapter we show how to deal with the relationship between depreciation and income taxes.

As we proceed bear in mind one final and important point. As with all management decisions that deal with the future, the numbers used (for cash flows, useful lives, etc.) are *estimates*. They are almost never known with certainty at the time a decision must be made. In Chapter 9, we illustrate some techniques managers use to allow for this uncertainty.

BASIC EXAMPLE

As stated earlier, the principle introduced in Chapter 5—that the only relevant data for decisions are differential revenues and costs—also governs capital budgeting decisions. The relevant data for capital budgeting decisions are the incremental (or differential) cash flows expected from a decision. The following example illustrates the main points.

A firm with cost of capital of 12% has an opportunity to introduce a new product. The best available estimates are that the firm will be able to sell 3,000 units per year for the next five years at $14 each. Variable costs should be $5 per unit. To make the product, the firm will have to buy machinery that costs $60,000, has a five-year life with no salvage value, and requires annual fixed cash operating costs of $5,000 for maintenance, insurance, and property taxes. (Notice that we have not included depreciation as a cost because it does not require a cash payment. We also ignore income taxes for now.)

The annual incremental cash inflows appear below.[2]

	Annual Cash Flows Years 1–5
Revenues ($14 × 3,000)	$42,000
Variable costs ($5 × 3,000)	15,000
Contribution margin ($9 × 3,000)	27,000
Cash fixed costs	5,000
Expected increase in net cash inflows	$22,000

Using this information, we analyze the proposed investment in two basic ways.

Net Present Value (NPV) Method

When using the NPV method the question is whether it is wise to invest $60,000 today in order to receive $22,000 per year for five years. The investment is worthwhile if the present value of the $22,000 to be received each year for five years is greater than the $60,000 outlay required today (which, obviously, has a present value of $60,000). The present value of the future cash flows of $22,000 minus the $60,000 required investment is called the *NPV* or the *excess present value*. If it is positive (present value of the future cash flows exceeds the required investment), the investment is desirable. If it is negative, the investment is undesirable.

To determine the NPV we must first find the present value of $22,000 per year for five years at 12%. In an appropriate present value table (Table B in the Appendix, page 818), we see that the factor for a series of payments of $1 for five years at 12% is 3.605. Multiplying this factor by $22,000 we obtain $79,310 as the present value of the future cash flows. This means that if you desire a 12% return and expect annual payments of $22,000 for five years, you would be willing to pay up to $79,310 for this investment. Therefore, you are more than happy to pay only $60,000, and the investment is desirable. The NPV is $19,310 ($79,310 − $60,000). Below is a summary of the analysis.

Present value of future cash flows ($22,000 × 3.605)	$79,310
Investment required	60,000
Net present value	$19,310

---

[2] Notice that income, using straight-line depreciation of $12,000 per year ($60,000/5), would be $10,000 per year.

Internal Rate of Return (IRR) Method

Another approach to analyzing investment opportunities is to find the expected IRR. This method poses the question "What return are we earning if we invest $60,000 now and receive $22,000 annually for five years?" The investment is desirable if the IRR is higher than the cost of capital. The IRR is also called the **time-adjusted rate of return** or the **discount rate.**

If net cash flows are equal in each year, the IRR is not difficult to find. The rate *equates* the present value of the future cash flows with the amount to be invested now. Consider that the computation of the present value of the future flows is as follows:

$$\text{Present value of future flows} = \text{annual cash flows} \times \text{factor for the discount rate and the number of periods}$$

In computing the IRR, we use the cost of the investment as the present value, and try to determine the discount rate associated with the factor that, when multiplied by the annual flows, equals the cost of the investment.

The first step is to find the factor related to both the discount rate and number of periods. Rearranging the preceding equation yields

$$\frac{\text{Present value of future flows}}{\text{annual cash flows}} = \text{factor for the discount rate and the number of periods}$$

In our example

IRR = INVESTMENT / Cash flows

$$\frac{\$60,000}{\$22,000} = 2.727$$

We know that this factor, 2.727, relates to some discount rate and that the number of periods is five. Hence, we can find the discount rate by looking at the factors listed in the five-period row in Table B. In the five-period row under the 24% column, the factor is 2.745; in that row, under the 25% column, the factor is 2.689. Hence, the IRR on this project is between 24% and 25%. (You should have been able to tell that the IRR on this project was greater than 12% because the NPV computed in the previous section is positive.)

Although we could interpolate to find a more exact rate, it obviously falls between 24% and 25% and is higher than the cost of capital. Hence, the investment is desirable. Because we are dealing with estimates of future cash flows, greater precision is unwarranted.

Generality of the Analysis

Our example uses a new product, but the facts could just as well relate to expanding the productive capacity for an existing product. The facts could also relate to a case of reducing costs, a situation often encountered by companies responding to changes prompted by the new manufacturing environment. Suppose that instead of being for a new product, the investment is for labor-saving machinery that would cut $9 from the per-unit variable production costs of an existing product. (The change in variable costs increases the contribution margin on the old product by $9, which is equal to the contribution margin expected to result from the new product in the original example.) Assume further that the sales volume on the product is 3,000 units per year, and that the additional cash fixed costs for the new machinery are $5,000 (the same as in the original example). The incremental cash flows are then

Savings in variable costs ($9 × 3,000)	$27,000
Less incremental cash fixed costs	5,000
Net increase in annual cash flows (savings)	$22,000

Thus, the pattern of analysis is the same whether the cash flows result from selling new products, expanding output of existing products, or saving on operating expenses. Find the incremental cash flows and then apply one of the methods described. *How* the cash flows come about is irrelevant; the important thing is to estimate what the cash flows will be.

Not-for-profit entities often confront decisions involving the acquisition of long-lived assets. For example, a city might want to decide whether to build a new municipal building. Because such entities are not subject to income taxes, the analytical approaches we have illustrated are adequate. As we noted earlier, however, managers in for-profit entities must also consider that the cash outflow for income taxes can be affected by depreciation. The next section presents a refinement of the analytical process to recognize the effects of taxes.

TAXES AND DEPRECIATION

If income taxes are taken into account, the calculation of cash flows is slightly more complex. Continuing with the example of the new product, assume a 40% income tax rate and straight-line depreciation for income tax calculations.[3] The initial outlay is still $60,000, but the annual cash flows are different because the added income from the project is now subject to income taxes. The net cash inflow for each of the five years is computed opposite.

---

[3] Our purpose in discussing the tax effect of depreciation in this chapter is to emphasize that such an effect exists, not to explain the details of the tax law. Accordingly, in this chapter we do not consider such technical issues as the Accelerated Cost Recovery System or the requirement, if straight-line depreciation is chosen for tax purposes, to abide by the half-year, mid-quarter, or mid-month conventions.

Net Cash Flow for Each Year

	Tax Computation	Cash Flow
Revenues	$42,000	$42,000
Cash expenses (variable and fixed)	20,000	20,000
Cash inflow before taxes	22,000	22,000
Depreciation ($60,000/5)	12,000	
Increase in taxable income	$10,000	
Tax at 40% (cash outflow)	$ 4,000	4,000
Net annual cash inflow		$18,000

3,605

Depreciation on the asset reduces taxes. The $12,000 in depreciation expense saves $4,800 (40% × $12,000). This important saving is called the **tax shield,** or **tax effect of depreciation.**

We do not show net income in the above schedule because we want to emphasize that we are concerned with cash flows, not net income. However, you might find it easier, and more understandable, to develop an income statement and then add back depreciation to get net cash flow. (This is a calculation frequently used by both accountants and financial managers.) The income statement converted to a cash basis appears below, along with the determination of the NPV of the investment.

Revenues	$42,000
− Cash expenses	20,000
Cash inflow before taxes	22,000
− Depreciation	12,000
Income before taxes	10,000
− Tax at 40%	4,000
Increase in net income	6,000
Add back depreciation	12,000
Net increase in annual cash inflow	$18,000
Present value factor for 5 years at 12%	3.605
Present value of future cash inflows	$64,890
Investment required	60,000
Net present value	$ 4,890

Using either approach, annual cash inflows are now $18,000 per year (rather than $22,000), which, when discounted at 12%, have a present value of $64,890. The NPV is $4,890; the investment is still desirable. To compute the IRR, we find the present value factor that, when multiplied by $18,000, equals $60,000. The factor is 3.333 ($60,000/$18,000). The factor closest to this in the five-year row in Table B is 3.274, the factor for 16%. The IRR is therefore between 14% and 16%, but closer to 16%. (You should have expected an IRR greater than 12%, since the NPV is positive at a 12% cost of capital.)

UNEVEN CASH FLOWS

The basic example assumes that net cash inflows are equal each year, but it is not unusual for revenues, or cash expenses, or both, to vary from year to year. For example, revenues from a new product might grow in the early years and decline in later years, or might take several years to reach a particular, expected level. Too, if depreciation is not taken on a straight-line method for tax purposes, the tax paid each year (and hence the cash outflow for taxes) will vary. Or, the investment might have a salvage value that increases cash flow in the last year. We postpone to Chapter 9 a discussion of the somewhat more complex case of investments involving changes in inventory, which investments also involve uneven cash flows. (Remember that a goal of companies committed to the JIT philosophy is to reduce inventory levels to zero.)

Uneven cash flows complicate the mathematics of the analysis for a project but do not affect the basic principles of the analysis. We illustrate below two situations involving uneven cash flows.

Salvage Values

The cash flows from most projects involving the acquisition of depreciable assets could be uneven because of the salvage values of the assets at the ends of their useful lives. A simple way to incorporate this factor into the analysis is to find the after-tax cash flow from the salvage value and discount it separately.

Assume, for example, that the new asset purchased in the basic example has an expected salvage value of $5,000 at the end of its useful life. How would this expectation affect the analysis of the investment? Because of your knowledge of financial accounting, you might be inclined to suggest that the salvage value will change the depreciation of this asset. There are two important reasons why such is not likely to be the case. First, because salvage values are estimates of what will happen in the not-very-near future, they are commonly ignored in the calculation of depreciation. Second, the tax law specifies that salvage values be ignored. For these reasons, it is highly probable that any proceeds received from the sale of a depreciable asset at the end of its useful life will be taxed.

Using straight-line depreciation and incorporating the expected salvage value into the analysis, we get the following.

Cash Flows Years 1–5

	Tax Computation	Cash Flow
Revenues	$42,000	$42,000
Cash expenses	20,000	20,000
Cash inflow before taxes	22,000	22,000
Depreciation ($60,000/5)	12,000	
Increase in taxable income	$10,000	
Tax at 40%	$ 4,000	4,000
Net cash inflow per year, as before		$18,000

Summary of Present Value of Investment

Operating cash flows ($18,000 × 3.605)		$64,890
Salvage value:		
Total salvage value	$5,000	
Tax on salvage value at 40%	2,000	
After-tax cash inflow from salvage value	$3,000	
Times present value factor (Table A, page 818)		
for 5 years hence at 12%	0.567	
Present value of salvage value		1,701
Total present value		66,591
Investment required		60,000
Net present value		$ 6,591

The NPV when taxes were first considered was $4,890. The new NPV ($6,591) is higher by the $1,701 present value of the salvage value.

Variations in Revenues

We said earlier that cash flows vary if sales vary during the life of a project. The uneven flows change the analysis only in that we need to discount the flows individually, instead of as an annuity. To illustrate, let us change the example. Instead of sales of 3,000 units per year, suppose that sales are expected to be 2,000, 3,000, 3,000, 4,000, and 3,000 in years one through five, respectively. (Notice that the total is still 15,000 units for the five years.) *Before* any formal analysis, can you tell whether the investment will be more, or less, desirable than it was when sales were spread evenly over the five years? That is, will the NPV be higher or lower than the $4,890 determined earlier? If you decided that the investment will be less desirable (lower NPV) you are correct; sales will be later, so cash will be received later, and cash is worth less the longer you must wait to receive it.

The schedule on page 306 shows the calculations. For brevity, we use the original example (a new product) and use the $9 per-unit contribution margin instead of showing both revenues and variable costs. As expected, the NPV is now lower ($3,502 vs $4,890), but the investment is still desirable because the NPV is still positive. Notice that the totals are the same as they were before, which you can verify by multiplying the numbers in the previous schedule by five. Thus, total cash flow before taxes is $110,000 ($22,000 × 5), total income taxes are $20,000 ($4,000 × 5), and so on. The important point is that the sooner the flows come in, the more valuable they are.

Finding the IRR can be difficult when there are uneven cash flows. Trial-and-error and interpolation will give a close approximation of the rate, and many computers and hand-held calculators have programs to make such calculations. Because the NPV is positive, the IRR *must* be greater than the 12% discount rate used in calculating the present values. (The IRR is about 14.2%.)

Cash Flows and Present Values

	Year					
	1	2	3	4	5	Total
Unit sales	2,000	3,000	3,000	4,000	3,000	15,000
Contribution margin at $9	$18,000	$27,000	$27,000	$36,000	$27,000	$135,000
Less cash fixed costs	5,000	5,000	5,000	5,000	5,000	25,000
Pretax cash inflow	13,000	22,000	22,000	31,000	22,000	110,000
Less depreciation	12,000	12,000	12,000	12,000	12,000	60,000
Income before taxes	1,000	10,000	10,000	19,000	10,000	50,000
Income taxes at 40%	400	4,000	4,000	7,600	4,000	20,000
Net income	600	6,000	6,000	11,400	6,000	30,000
Add depreciation	12,000	12,000	12,000	12,000	12,000	60,000
Net cash flow	$12,600	$18,000	$18,000	$23,400	$18,000	$ 90,000
Present value factor (Table A)	0.893	0.797	0.712	0.636	0.567	
Present value	$11,252	$14,346	$12,816	$14,882	$10,206	$ 63,502
Less investment						60,000
Net present value						$ 3,502

DECISION RULES

The decision rules associated with the two methods of analysis we describe are simple. When the NPV method is used, a project having a positive NPV should be accepted; others should be rejected. When the IRR method is used, a project having an IRR greater than the firm's cost of capital should be accepted. The relationship of the two criteria is as follows.

1. If the IRR is less than cost of capital (or cutoff rate), the NPV is negative.
2. If the NPV is positive, the IRR is greater than cost of capital (or cutoff rate).

When analyzing any single project for acceptance or rejection, both methods lead to the same decision. The problem of multiple investment opportunities is discussed in Chapter 9.

As in other decision areas, managers could conclude that qualitative factors override the decision suggested by analyzing only quantifiable data. For example, a firm committed to producing high-quality, high-priced products might reject a project having a positive NPV if the proposed product is relatively cheap. Or a firm that manufactures toys might not make toy guns because of the personal convictions of its top managers. On the other hand, a firm might undertake an investment that showed a negative NPV if the project would bring the firm considerable prestige or perhaps enhance its image as an innovator. Where qualitative factors are important, managers should still perform quantitative analyses so they will have a better idea of the *cost* to the firm of accepting a particular qualitative goal as paramount.

Qualitative concerns are becoming increasingly important as companies adopt advanced manufacturing techniques. Some of the advantages of such techniques are difficult to quantify and might therefore be overlooked. For instance, while managers agree that increasing the quality of a product is desirable, the monetary effect is not easy to estimate. Similar considerations arise with such benefits as reducing cycle time.

OTHER METHODS
OF CAPITAL BUDGETING

Although the NPV and IRR methods are theoretically sound, some managers argue that they are not practical because of the many estimates involved (cost of capital, cash flows, useful lives, etc.). Interestingly, the methods advocated by these managers, which we cover now, require most of the same estimates as do the methods they object to.

Payback

One of the most commonly used methods of capital budgeting is the **payback** technique. This method poses the question "How long will it take to recover the investment?" If a project requires an outlay of $10,000 and will generate annual net cash inflows of $4,000, it has a payback period of 2.5 years ($10,000/$4,000). If the annual cash inflows are equal,

$$\frac{\text{Payback}}{\text{period}} = \frac{\text{investment required}}{\text{annual cash returns}}$$

Payback evaluates the rapidity with which an investment is recovered. But, it offers no information about the profitability of the project.

Decision rules when using the payback technique may be stated in different ways by different firms. Some firms set a limit on the payback period beyond which an investment will not be made. Others use payback to pick one of several investments, selecting the one with the shortest payback period.

The payback method has two very serious faults, the first of which is that it does not indicate the profitability of the investment. Payback emphasizes the return *of* the investment but ignores the return *on* the investment. The life of the project after the payback period is ignored altogether. Consider the two investment possibilities shown below.

	A	B
Cost	$10,000	$10,000
Useful life in years	5	10
Annual cash flows over the useful lives	$ 2,500	$ 2,000

Investment A has a payback period of four years ($10,000/$2,500), and B one of five years ($10,000/$2,000). Under the payback criterion, investment A would be better than investment B because its payback period is shorter. Yet it should be obvious that investment B is superior; the returns from A cease one year after the payback period, while B continues to return cash for five more years.

The second serious fault of payback method is that it ignores the *timing* of the expected future cash flows and so ignores the time value of money. This fault, like the method's failure to consider years after the payback period, can lead to poor decisions. Consider two investments, X and Y, as described below.

	X	Y
Cost	$10,000	$10,000
Cash inflows by year:		
1	$ 2,000	$ 6,000
2	6,000	3,000
3	2,000	1,000
4–8	3,000	3,000

Both X and Y have payback periods of three years; they also show equal total returns. But the equal payback periods are misleading because the investment in Y will be recovered much more quickly than that in X. For the same reason, even if the two investments promise equal *total* returns, the one that generates the returns more quickly is the more desirable. (The IRR on investment X is approximately 29%, whereas that on investment Y is about 31%.)

Despite its faults, payback can be useful. The payback period can be particularly important to a firm especially concerned about liquidity. Payback also can be used as a rough screening device for investment proposals, because a long payback period usually means a low rate of return. As a practical matter, the payback period is automatically computed in the process of calculating the IRR on an investment with equal annual cash flows. Consider the investment opportunity that was the basic example in this chapter. The investment required was $60,000, and annual cash inflows were $18,000 (page 303). When computing the IRR on this project, we determined that the investment divided by the annual cash inflows was 3.333, which is the payback period for the investment, as well as the present value factor for the discount rate and number of periods covered by the investment.

Some firms use payback as a measure of risk, because, in general, the longer it takes to get your money back, the greater the risk that the money will not be returned. As the time horizon lengthens, more uncertainties arise. Inflation might ease, or it might get worse; interest rates could rise, or they could fall; new techniques might be developed that would make the investment obsolete. Because of the increased uncertainty, a manager might prefer a project that pays back its investment in two years to one that takes ten years, even if the one with the ten-year payback period has a higher expected NPV and IRR.

Let us illustrate the point with an admittedly extreme example. Suppose that you have $1,000,000 to invest and are considering two possibilities, both of which involve buying a cargo of merchandise and shipping it to a distant country. One voyage will take a year to complete, the other five years. The expected after-tax cash returns at the ends of the periods are $1,160,000 for the one-year voyage and $3,713,000 for the five-year voyage. The expected IRRs on the voyages are 16% and 30%, respectively, and, when a cost of capital of 10% is used, the NPVs are $54,545 and $1,305,481.

A lot can happen to a ship on a long voyage—storms, piracy, or collisions with icebergs or rocks. Considering the hazards, who wouldn't feel that it was a lot safer tying up his or her money for one year rather than five despite the advantage of the longer voyage as determined under the normal techniques of analysis? Whether you would choose to invest in the one-year or the five-year opportunity would depend on your attitude about risk and return. Because of its emphasis on the rapidity of return *of* investment, the payback method of evaluation gives higher priority to the one-year voyage. There are other, more formal ways of dealing with the risk associated with investment opportunities, but payback is one of the most common.

Book Rate of Return

Another commonly used capital budgeting method that ignores the time value of money is the **book-rate-of-return** technique. Under this method, the average annual expected book income is divided by the average book investment in the project. That is,

$$\text{Average book rate of return} = \frac{\text{average annual expected book income}}{\text{average book investment}}$$

To illustrate, consider again the $60,000 investment opportunity in our basic example. The book net income for each of the five years of the project's life would be $6,000 (page 303). The average book investment in this project will be $30,000 ($60,000/2). With an annual net income of $6,000, and an average book investment of $30,000, the average book rate of return is 20% ($6,000/$30,000). This return is an *average* rate of return because we have used the average book investment. (The book rate of return will be different for each year because the average book investment in the project will change with each year's depreciation. For example, by using the average book investment in year one, the book rate of return would be $6,000/$54,000, or 11.1%; in the last year, the book rate of return would be $6,000/$6,000, or 100%.)

Let us compare these results with those obtained using the IRR method. The net annual cash inflows for the project are $18,000, for an IRR of something less than 16% (page 303). If the firm's cost of capital is 16% or more, the investment is unwise. Both the NPV and the IRR methods of analysis suggest that the investment should be rejected; use of the book rate of return as the criterion for evaluating investments would mislead managers to accept this investment opportunity.

To emphasize the deficiencies of the book-rate-of-return method, consider another, simpler example. Investments A and B require identical investments ($10,000) and produce identical total net incomes, and therefore identical average net incomes, and identical average rates of return of 26.7%. Investment A is clearly superior to investment B; the flows come in faster for A. (Assuming straight-line depreciation, the IRR on investment A is about 23%, whereas that on investment B is only about 15%.)

	A	B
Pretax cash flows by year:		
1	$10,000	$ 2,000
2	5,000	5,000
3	1,666	9,666
Totals	16,666	16,666
Depreciation	10,000	10,000
Income before taxes	6,666	6,666
Income taxes (40%)	2,666	2,666
Total net income	$ 4,000	$ 4,000
Average net income	$ 1,333	$ 1,333
Average book rate of return ($1,333/$5,000)	26.7%	26.7%

The book-rate-of-return method almost always misstates the internal rate of return because it ignores the timing of the cash flows. This flaw renders it an unsatisfactory method of capital budgeting.

SUMMARY EVALUATION OF METHODS

The critical difference between the NPV and IRR methods and the payback and book-rate-of-return methods is the attention given to the timing of the expected cash flows. The first two methods, called **discounted cash flow (DCF) techniques,** consider the timing of the cash flows; the last two methods do not. Because they recognize the time value of money, DCF techniques are conceptually superior, but payback is often used in conjunction with those techniques.

As stated earlier, some managers argue that DCF techniques are too complex or that they require too many estimates to make them useful in practice. We see little merit in these charges. All four methods require about the same estimates. DCF methods require estimates of future cash flows and the timing of those flows. The book-rate-of-return method requires estimates of future net incomes, which means making essentially the same estimates as those required to estimate cash flows. The payback method requires estimating cash flows but not useful lives. One point in favor of the payback method is that it emphasizes near-term cash flows, and near-term cash flows are usually easier to predict than flows in later years. However, as we pointed out, unless consideration is given to useful life, the payback method could lead to very poor decisions.

The NPV, the IRR, and the book-rate-of-return methods all require an estimate of the cost of capital, or at least a decision as to a minimum acceptable rate of return. The payback method requires a decision regarding the minimum acceptable payback period. In short, DCF techniques are no less realistic or practical than the other two approaches, and the conceptual superiority of the former argues strongly for their use.

INVESTING DECISIONS AND FINANCING DECISIONS

None of the examples in this chapter considered how the company will finance the project in question. That is, we did not say that the company plans to issue debt, common stock, some combination of the two, or finance the investment using cash flows from ongoing operations. The omission was deliberate. The investing decision should be kept separate from the financing decision.

It might be tempting to argue that if the firm plans to finance an investment with 9% debt, this rate should be used to discount the expected cash flows. It might also be tempting to subtract the interest payments as part of the cash flow computation. Resist these temptations!

A firm should not accept projects that will return less than the cost of capital, because it must earn a satisfactory return for *all* investors in the firm— both creditors and stockholders. Both types of capital suppliers are concerned about the safety of their investments and therefore monitor firm solvency by watching such factors as the ratio of debt to equity. If a firm makes too liberal use of debt and earns returns that exceed the interest rate but not cost of capital, it will find itself unable to raise *any* capital except at exorbitant rates. (Stockholders will sell their stock, which reduces the price and thus raises the cost of equity capital. Lenders will insist on higher interest rates, thus raising the cost of debt capital.)

Including interest payments as part of the cash flow computation reflects a misunderstanding of the concept of discounting. The use of cost of capital as the discount rate automatically provides for not only the recovery *of* the investment, but also a return *on* the investment at least equal to the cost of capital. If interest payments are subtracted to arrive at the net cash flow, the cost of debt is provided for twice—once by subtracting the interest payments, and again by using a discount rate that includes the cost of obtaining both the debt and equity capital.

SUMMARY

Decisions to commit resources for periods longer than a year are called capital budgeting decisions. Evaluating such decisions requires determining the investment and its resulting cash flows. Future cash flows may occur because of additional revenues and costs, or because of cost savings. Critical to capital budgeting is that most, if not all, of the numbers used in the analyses are estimates. The effects of depreciation on income taxes must also be recognized.

Effective evaluation of capital budgeting decisions requires consideration of the time value of money. The two approaches recommended are the net present value and the internal rate of return methods. Two other methods—payback and book rate of return—are often used, but are conceptually inferior because they fail to consider the time value of money. Nevertheless, such methods may be useful as rough screening devices for investment opportunities.

Discounted cash flow methods are used to decide on undertaking an investment. The solution is based on the firm's cost of capital. The interest rate that must be paid on borrowings for making the particular investment is not relevant to the analysis.

KEY TERMS

book rate of return	net present value (NPV)
capital budgeting decisions	payback period
cash flows	present value
cost of capital	target rate of return
cutoff rate of return	tax shield (effect) of depreciation
discounted cash flow (DCF) techniques	time-adjusted rate of return
discount rate	time value of money
internal rate of return (IRR)	

KEY FORMULAS

Present value of future flows = annual cash flows × present value factor

Net present value = present value of future flows − required current investment

$$\text{Payback period} = \frac{\text{investment required}}{\text{annual cash returns}}$$

$$\text{Average book rate of return} = \frac{\text{average annual expected book income}}{\text{average book investment}}$$

REVIEW PROBLEM

Dwyer Company has the opportunity to market a new product. The sales manager believes the firm could sell 5,000 units per year at $14 per unit for five years. The product requires machinery costing $60,000, having a five-year life and no salvage value. The machinery has fixed operating costs requiring cash disbursements of $4,000 annually. Variable costs per unit are $8. Straight-line depreciation will be used for both book and tax purposes. The tax rate is 40% and cost of capital is 14%.

Required
1. Determine the increase in annual net income and in annual cash inflows expected from the investment.
2. Determine the payback period.
3. Determine the book rate of return on the average investment.
4. Determine the NPV of the investment.
5. Determine the IRR of the investment.

6. Suppose the machinery has salvage value of $5,000 at the end of its useful life, which is not considered in determining depreciation expense. The tax rate on the gain at the end of the asset's life is 40%. How will your answer to item 4 change?

Answer to Review Problem

1.

	Tax Computation	Cash Flow
Sales (5,000 × $14)	$70,000	$70,000
Variable cost (5,000 × $8)	40,000	40,000
Contribution margin (5,000 × $6)	30,000	30,000
Fixed cash operating costs	4,000	4,000
Cash inflow before taxes	26,000	26,000
Depreciation ($60,000/5)	12,000	
Increase in taxable income	14,000	
Income tax at 40% rate	5,600	5,600
Increase in net income	8,400	
Add depreciation	12,000	
Net cash inflow per year	$20,400	$20,400

2. Payback period is about 2.941 years, which is $60,000 divided by $20,400.
3. The book rate of return on the average investment is 28%, which is annual net income of $8,400 divided by the average investment of $30,000 ($60,000/2).
4. $10,033, calculated as follows:

Net cash inflow per year	$20,400
Present value factor, 5-year annuity at 14% (Table B)	3.433
Present value of future net cash flows	$70,033
Less investment	60,000
Net present value	$10,033

5. The IRR is a little over 20%. The factor to seek is 2.941, which is the payback period calculated in item 2. The closest factor in the five-year row of Table B is 2.991, which is the 20% factor. Because 2.941 is less than 2.991, the rate is more than 20%. (Remember, the higher the rate, the lower the factor.)
6. The only change required is the determination of the present value of the salvage value less tax on the gain.

Salvage value	$ 5,000
Tax at 40%	2,000
Net cash inflow, end of year 5	$ 3,000
Present value factor for single payment, 5 years at 14% (Table A)	.519
Present value of salvage value	$ 1,557
Net present value from part 4	10,033
Net present value	$11,590

Notice that we did not have to recompute annual net cash flows. The firm still used $12,000 for depreciation expense. Therefore, at the end of five years, the machinery will have a book value of zero and the gain on disposal will equal the salvage value.

ASSIGNMENT MATERIAL

Questions for Discussion

8-1 **Rental payments and installment purchase** Is there any difference between the cost of (a) renting a car for $60 per month and (b) buying a car for $3,600, which you expect will have no value at the end of five years and for which you make payments of $60 per month for five years?

8-2 **Interest rates and economic activity** The federal government is concerned with regulating the level of economic activity—especially with encouraging production and investment to maintain high employment while not allowing excessive inflation. The government attempts to do this partly by changing interest rates through the Federal Reserve Board. How can the ability to influence interest rates be used to stimulate or discourage investment?

8-3 **Capital budgeting – effects of events** A capital expenditure proposal for a new machine has been analyzed. In what way(s) do each of the following events (not anticipated in the original analysis) affect the analysis? Consider each event independently.
1. The interest rate on long-term debt increases.
2. The company signs a new contract with its union. The negotiated wage rate for all categories of workers is higher than the prevailing rate.
3. The company raises the selling prices of its products.
4. Congress approves the use of a depreciation rate that provides much faster recognition of depreciation expense than was previously available.

Exercises

8-4 **Discounting**
1. Find the approximate IRR for each of the following investments.
   (a) Investment of $30,000 with annual cash flows of $6,000 for 14 years.
   (b) An investment of $90,000 with a single return of $150,000 at the end of four years.
2. Find the NPVs of the following investments at a 12% discount rate.
   (a) Annual flows of $30,000 for ten years are produced by an investment of $150,000.
   (b) An investment of $28,000 with annual flows of $8,000 for four years and a single return of $6,000 at the end of the fifth year.

8-5 **NPV and IRR methods** Jones Secretarial Service is thinking of buying some new word-processing equipment that promises to save $11,000 in cash operating costs per year. The equipment will cost $27,500. Its estimated useful life is four years. It will have no salvage value. (Ignore taxes.)

Required
1. Compute the NPV if the minimum desired rate of return is 10%.
2. Determine the IRR.

8-6 **Discounting** Solve each of the following independent problems.

1. Harry Smith starts college in one year. His father wishes to set up a fund for Harry to use for the $4,200 he will need each year for four years. Harry will make withdrawals at the beginning of each school year. If Mr. Smith can invest at 9%, how much must he invest today to provide for Harry's college expenses?

2. Brute McGurk is a senior in high school who weighs 450 pounds and runs the 100-yard dash in 8.7 seconds. He has been offered $250,000 per year to play professional football but would like to go to college. He believes that if he does go to college he will be able to earn $400,000 per year playing football after he graduates. In either case, his playing career will be over at 30, which gives him 12 years if he turns professional immediately. Assuming that going to college would cost him nothing and that his football salary would be paid at the end of each year, what should he do if the interest rate is 10%?

3. Henry Jackson is about to retire from his job. His pension benefits have accumulated to the point where he could receive a lump-sum payment of $120,000 or $20,000 per year for ten years, paid at the ends of years. Jackson has no dependents and fully expects to live ten years after he retires. If he can invest at 10%, which option should he take?

4. You have just won the $5,000,000 grand prize in a magazine sweepstakes. The prize will be paid in $167,000 installments for 30 years. If your interest rate is 10%, how much would you take now, instead of accepting the annuity?

8-7 **Time value of money relationships** Answer the following questions.

1. A person received a single payment of $8,050 as a result of having invested some money five years ago at an interest rate of 10%. How much did the person invest?

2. An investment of $2,000 returned a single payment of $5,000. The interest rate was 14%. How many years elapsed between the investment and the return?

3. A person received seven annual payments of $1,000 from an investment. The interest rate was 16%. What was the amount of the investment?

4. An investment of $1,000 returned $343 annually for some years. The rate of interest was 14%. How many payments were received?

5. A $12,000 investment made today will provide a 12% return. The returns will be paid in equal amounts over 12 years. What is the amount of the annual payment?

8-8 **Basic capital budgeting without taxes** Crestline Inc. produces custom paper boxes. Its managers have been trying to decide whether to buy a new folding machine for $100,000. It will last for five years, have no salvage value, and be depreciated using the straight-line method. The managers anticipate savings in cash operating costs of $35,000 in each of the five years. Cost of capital is 10%.

Required
1. Calculate the NPV of the investment.
2. Calculate the approximate IRR on the investment.
3. Determine the payback period for the investment.
4. Determine the book rate of return on the average investment.

8-9   Basic capital budgeting – taxes (extension of 8-8)   Redo 8-8 with Crest-line Inc. now being subject to a 30% income tax rate.

8-10   Basic cost savings   Grove City Pottery currently makes 200,000 large straw-berry jars per year at a variable cost of $11.40. Equipment is available for $600,000 that will reduce the variable cost by $1.80, while increasing cash fixed costs by $100,000. The equipment will have a $25,000 salvage value at the end of its four-year life and will be depreciated using the straight-line method. Norton faces a 40% income tax rate and a 12% cost of capital.

Required: Determine the NPV of the investment.

8-11   Basic capital budgeting   Boston Globes has an opportunity to reduce its an-nual cash operating costs by $20,000 by acquiring equipment that costs $60,000, has a five-year life, and has no salvage value. Boston uses straight-line deprecia-tion. Cost of capital is 14%. Ignore taxes.

Required
1. Determine the NPV of the investment.
2. Determine the approximate IRR.

8-12   Basic capital budgeting with taxes   Redo the previous assignment with a 40% income tax rate.

8-13   Comparison of methods (continued in Chapter 9)   Jason Company has three investment opportunities, summarized below.

	A	B	C
Cost	$70,000	$ 70,000	$ 70,000
Cash inflows by year:			
Year 1	35,000	35,000	4,000
Year 2	35,000	10,000	8,000
Year 3	0	45,000	10,000
Year 4	5,000	20,000	98,000
Total	$75,000	$110,000	$120,000
Average annual income	$ 1,250	$ 10,000	$ 12,500

Required
1. Rank the investment opportunities in order of desirability using (a) payback period, (b) average book rate of return (use average net book value of the investment as the denominator), and (c) NPV using a 16% discount rate.
2. Comment on the results.

8-14   NPV   Wilson Crocker owns a driving range. He presently pays several high school students $0.60 per bucket to pick up the golf balls that his customers hit. A salesman has shown him a machine that will pick up balls at an annual cash cost of $5,200 plus $0.05 per bucket. The machine costs $8,000 and has a four-year life. Crocker would use straight-line depreciation. Volume for the driving range is about

18,000 buckets per year. Crocker's combined state and federal tax rate is 30%. He believes that the appropriate discount rate is 16%.

Required: Determine whether Crocker should acquire the machine.

8-15 *Capital budgeting for a hospital* San Lucia Hospital has the opportunity to acquire a used CAT scanner for $200,000. It will last for ten years and have no salvage value. Estimated revenue is $110,000 per year, and estimated annual cash costs are $66,000. The hospital uses a 14% discount rate for capital budgeting decisions.

Required: For this project determine (a) the NPV, (b) the payback period, and (c) the approximate IRR.

8-16 *NPV and IRR* Morison Company makes high-quality wallpaper. Its managers believe that the company can increase productivity by acquiring some new machinery but are unsure whether it would be profitable.

The machinery costs $1,100,000, has a five-year life with no salvage value, and should save about $420,000 in cash operating costs annually. The company uses straight-line depreciation, has a 40% income tax rate, and a 14% cost of capital.

Required
1. Calculate the NPV of the investment.
2. Calculate the approximate IRR.

8-17 *Relationships* Fill in the blanks for each of the following independent cases. In all cases the investment has a useful life of ten years and no salvage value. Ignore income taxes.

	(a) Annual Cash Inflow	(b) Investment	(c) Cost of Capital	(d) Internal Rate of Return	(e) Net Present Value
1.	$ 45,000	$188,640	14%	____	$____
2.	$ 80,000	$____	12%	18%	$____
3.	$____	$300,000	____	16%	$ 81,440
4.	$____	$450,000	12%	____	$115,000
5.	$100,000	$____	____	14%	($ 38,300)

8-18 *Comparison of book return and NPV* Welton Company is introducing a product that will sell for $10 per unit. Annual volume for the next four years should be about 200,000 units. The company can use either a hand-fed or a semiautomatic machine to make the product. Data are as follows.

	Hand-fed Machine	Semiautomatic Machine
Per unit variable cost	$ 4	$ 2
Annual cash fixed costs	$725,000	$ 850,000
Cost of machine	$800,000	$1,400,000

Both machines have four-year lives and no anticipated salvage value. Welton uses straight-line depreciation, has a 40% income tax rate, and has a 14% cost of capital.

Required
1. Determine which machine has the higher book rate of return on average investment.
2. Determine which machine has the higher NPV.
3. Which machine should the firm acquire? Why?

Problems

8-19 *New product decision* Cavala Company has the opportunity to introduce a new radio with the following expected results.

Annual unit volume	250,000
Selling price	$ 60
Unit variable cost	$ 35
Annual cash fixed costs	$3,800,000

The product requires equipment costing $4,500,000 and having a three-year life with no salvage value. The company has a 12% cost of capital. The income tax rate is 40%, and straight-line depreciation will be used.

Required
1. Determine the NPV of the investment.
2. Determine the approximate IRR of the investment.
3. Suppose that the equipment has a $600,000 salvage value. Cavala will still depreciate the entire cost of the equipment. By how much will the NPV increase?

8-20 *Investing in JIT* Robson Industries operates several plants, one of which is moving toward JIT manufacturing. One of the first investments the plant will make is roughly $4 million to rearrange the factory into manufacturing cells. This cost is tax-deductible over five years using the straight-line method. The managers expect to save about $600,000 in annual manufacturing costs for the foreseeable future as a result of using cells. The tax rate is 40% and cost of capital is 10%.

Required: Determine the net present value of the investment. Use a 30-year period for the annual cost savings. It will be easier to discount the two types of flows separately.

8-21 *Installing a sprinkler system* Walton Company operates several factories, one of which was built some 30 years ago and is not in good condition. That factory has a fire insurance policy covering machinery, inventory, and the building itself. Premiums on the policy are $17,000 per year.

Recently, a fire inspector from the insurance company recommended that the premium be increased to $45,000 per year because the factory's fire protection has diminished. Its existing sprinkler system no longer works and cannot be repaired at a reasonable cost. The inspector told the plant manager that a new system, costing $120,000 and with a 10-year life and no salvage value, would be needed to continue the existing premium of $17,000 per year.

The system would be depreciated on a straight-line basis. The tax rate is 40% and Walton's cost of capital is 14%.

Required: Determine whether the sprinkler system should be bought.

8-22 ***Employment options*** Bob Wiblek is a college senior and an All-American football player. Drafted by the Bay City Beasts of the Tri-Continental League, he has been pondering two alternatives that the team has offered. The first is that Bob receives $500,000 per year for ten years, the second is that he receives $300,000 per year for 30 years. Either way, Bob and the team both expect his playing career to be over in ten years. Under either alternative, he would get the prescribed amounts whether or not he plays.

Bob would have an income tax rate of 30%. The team has a 40% income tax rate. Bob believes that a 10% discount rate is appropriate. The team has a 14% cost of capital.

Required
1. Which offer should Bob take?
2. Which offer is better for the team?
3. If your answers to items 1 and 2 differ, explain why. You need not make any calculations.

8-23 ***Importance of depreciation period*** Your company has the opportunity to buy machinery for $100,000. It will last for five years, be depreciated using the straight-line method, and save $30,000 in cash operating costs per year. Cost of capital is 10% and the tax rate is 40%.

Required
1. Determine the NPV of the investment.
2. Suppose now that you could depreciate the machinery over two years instead of five. Determine the NPV of the investment.

8-24 ***Meaning of IRR*** You want to withdraw $10,000 from a bank account at the end of each of the next three years. The interest rate is 10%.

Required
1. How much must you have in the bank at the beginning of the first year to be able to make the subsequent $10,000 withdrawals?
2. Schedule the activity in the bank account for the three years. Set up columns for Beginning Balance, Interest, Withdrawal, and Ending Balance. Interest is earned at 10% of the beginning balance of each year.

8-25 ***Manufacturing cells, JIT*** Some of the plant managers of Efron Manufacturing Company are trying to switch to JIT manufacturing. The manager of the Wilson Plant has developed the following data on the effects of introducing JIT, mainly from talks with managers whose plants have adopted JIT principles.

	(all amounts in thousand)	
	Current Cost	Estimated JIT Cost
Materials	$1,876.4	$1,692.0
Direct labor	2,845.2	2,312.0
Supervision	434.6	88.3
Maintenance	493.2	23.6*
Inspection, incoming		
and outgoing	256.3	32.8*
Other	673.9	569.5
Totals	$6,579.6	$4,718.2

* Most costs of maintenance and inspection will be carried out by workers
in their cells, thus greatly reducing the centrally administered amounts.

Moving to cellular manufacturing requires investments of $8 million for rearranging and for new machinery more suited to cellular manufacturing. All of these costs can be deducted for tax purposes over ten years. None of the depreciation and amortization of these costs is included in the figures above. The company has a 40% tax rate and a 12% cost of capital. The horizon for discounting the after-tax savings in operating flows is 20 years.

Required: Determine the net present value of the proposed change. You will find it easier to discount the two types of flows separately.

8-26 **Retirement options**   Mr. Ralph Mathews will retire in a few months, on reaching his 65th birthday. His firm provides a pension plan that offers two options: (1) a lump-sum payment of $150,000 on the day of retirement and (2) annual payments of $20,000 per year beginning on the date of retirement and ending at death. Mr. Mathews is not sure which option he should select and asks for your assistance. He tells you that he has no savings now, that he could earn a 14% return if he invested part of the lump-sum payment, and that he would like to spend $25,000 per year during his retirement. He has no relatives or other heirs and is not concerned about leaving an estate. He tells you that he could live on $20,000 per year but would much prefer to spend $25,000 and be more comfortable.

If he chooses the lump-sum payment, he will take out $25,000 to live on during the first year of retirement and invest the remainder. He will then draw $25,000 at the beginning of every year until the money runs out.

Required: Determine how long Mathews could afford to keep up a $25,000 per year standard of living.

8-27 **Expanding a product line**   Kiernan Company makes office equipment of various sorts, such as tables, desks, chairs, and lamps. The sales manager is trying to decide whether to introduce a new model of desk. The desk will sell for $500 and have variable costs of $260. Volume is expected to be 10,000 units per year for five years. To make the desks, the firm will have to buy additional machinery that will cost $3,000,000, have a five-year life, and no salvage value. Straight-line depreciation will be used. Fixed cash operating costs will be $1,500,000 per year.

The firm is in the 40% tax bracket and its cost of capital is 10%.

Required

1. Determine, using the NPV method, whether the new desk should be brought out.
2. Compute the payback period.
3. Determine the approximate IRR that the firm expects to earn on the investment.

8-28 **Buying air pumps** Magnum Mart is a chain of convenience stores that sell food, beverages, household products, and gasoline. Its managers are trying to decide how to acquire coin-operated air pumps that customers can use to fill their tires. One choice is to lease pumps for $850 per year, renewable annually. The other is to buy them for $1,500. Pumps have about a three-year life. For each pump, revenue should average $2,100 per year and operating costs, exclusive of lease payments or depreciation, $250 per year.

　　　　Magnum is in the 40% tax bracket, uses a 12% cutoff rate of return, and straight-line depreciation.

Required: Determine whether Magnum should lease or buy the pumps.

8-29 **Capital budgeting and reported earnings** The president of Wallco Industries has been disturbed by reports that the firm's stock is not considered a good buy. Wallco has been a rapidly growing company in a field that stresses swift technological advances. Wallco has an extensive research program and an ambitious building schedule, with $10 million plant and equipment expenditures planned for next year. The firm's stock is currently selling at $125, about 25 times earnings per share of $5 last year. Increased growth in earnings per share is viewed as necessary to sustain the price of the stock.

　　　　Wallco has a cutoff rate of return of 20% after taxes, using discounted cash flow techniques. The president wonders whether to institute another capital spending constraint: By the second year of operations a project must be expected to increase earnings per share by at least $0.40 for each $1,000,000 invested. He feels that such a requirement would help to keep the price of the stock from falling because of disenchantment of stockholders and financial analysts whose recommendations are often followed.

　　　　He shows you the following proposal.

Investment	$2,000,000
Cash inflows by year (before taxes):	
1	$ 600,000
2	800,000
3	1,050,000
4	1,110,000
5	1,500,000

The tax rate is 40%. There are 500,000 shares of common stock outstanding. Straight-line depreciation is used for both tax and book purposes.

Required

1. Determine whether the investment meets the 20% rate of return criterion.
2. Determine the effects of the investment on earnings per share.
3. What suggestions can you make to resolve the conflict?

8-30 ***Charitable donation*** Jan Williamson is a wealthy entrepreneur who wishes to make a substantial donation to her alma mater, Arkwright University. She is considering two alternatives, a $5,000,000 gift now or an equal annual amount in each of the next ten years.

In discussions with the president of Arkwright University, she has learned that the university earns a 10% return on its endowment fund and, of course, pays no income taxes. The president would be happy with either the $5,000,000 now or with equal annual amounts having a present value of $5,000,000. Mrs. Williamson is able to earn a 9% after-tax return investing in tax-free securities. She faces a combined state and federal tax rate of 35%.

Required
1. Determine the annuity that would yield a $5,000,000 present value to the university.
2. Should Mrs. Williamson make the lump-sum donation or pay the annuity that you determined in item 1?

8-31 ***When-to-sell decisions*** Smooth Scotch Company has a large quantity of Scotch whiskey that is approaching its sixth anniversary. When it reaches age six it can be sold for $700 per barrel. If it is held until it is ten years old it can be sold for $1,170 per barrel. Cost of capital is 12%.

Required
1. Determine the IRR that would be earned if the Scotch were held until it was ten years old.
2. Suppose that the price of six-year-old Scotch is $700 per barrel, but that the projected price of ten-year-old Scotch in four years is in doubt. What is the minimum price per barrel that the firm would have to receive four years hence to justify keeping the Scotch until it is ten years old?
3. Suppose now that the following schedule of prices is expected. Determine the point at which the Scotch should be sold using the criterion of highest IRR. (Assume that the cutoff rate of return is low enough so that all of the rates you compute would be acceptable. That is, the best decision is not to sell now.)

Years of Age	Expected Price
6	$ 700
7	800
8	950
9	1,200
10	1,400

4. Redo item 3 using the NPV criterion to make the decision.

8-32 ***Increasing capacity (continued in Chapter 9)*** Pitcairn Manufacturing Company has regularly been selling out its complete stock of its most popular style of men's socks, Heather. The production and marketing managers have been investigating ways to increase capacity and have determined that they could produce another 250,000 pairs annually if they bought equipment costing $1,200,000. The equipment has a five-year life with no salvage value. Pitcairn uses straight-line depreciation. The equipment would add $200,000 to annual cash fixed costs. The socks sell for $4 and have $1 per-pair variable cost. The variable cost would not be affected by using the equipment. The managers are confident of selling 200,000 more pairs annually. Cost of capital is 14% and the tax rate is 40%.

Required
1. Determine whether Pitcairn should acquire the equipment.
2. Suppose that additional volume is likely to be 250,000 pairs. Determine whether Pitcairn should acquire the equipment.

8-33 *Funding a pension plan*   Knowles Company has reached an agreement with the labor union that represents its workers. The agreement calls for the firm to pay $100,000 per year for the next ten years into a pension fund for the benefit of employees. Payments would begin one year from now.

Knowles has excess cash on hand from the sale of some of its assets, so the treasurer approaches the head of the union and asks if it would be all right to make a single, lump-sum payment to discharge the ten-year obligation. Before the head of the union gives a reply, the treasurer decides to determine the maximum amount that Knowles could pay right now. The company is in the 40% tax bracket and has cost of capital of 16%. The annual payments would be deductible for tax purposes in the years in which they were made and the single payment would be deductible in the current year.

Required: Determine the maximum amount that Knowles could pay in a lump-sum settlement of the obligation.

8-34 *Bond refunding*   Expost Company has outstanding a $1,000,000 (par value) issue of bonds bearing a 14% interest rate. The bonds mature in ten years. Interest rates are lower than they were when this issue was sold, and the firm can now raise cash on a ten-year bond at 10%. The directors of the firm are considering retiring the outstanding issue and replacing the old bonds with 10%, ten-year bonds. The firm would have to pay a premium of 12% over par value to buy back the currently outstanding issue. It would also have to spend $60,000 in legal fees and other costs to market the new issue. The premium is tax deductible in the year of refunding, but the costs of issuing the new bonds must be amortized evenly over ten years. The tax rate is 40%, and the company's cost of capital is 18%.

Required: Should the old issue be replaced?

8-35 *Capital budgeting by a municipality*   The City Council of Alton is considering the construction of a convention center in the downtown area. The city has been losing employment to surrounding suburbs, and tax revenues have been falling. The proposed center would cost $22,000,000 to build, and the city would incur annual cash operating costs of $500,000. The city controller has prepared the following estimate of receipts from the center over its estimated useful life of 30 years.

Rentals of space for trade shows, convention, etc.	$1,800,000

The controller states that the estimated revenues were based on total annual convention attendance of 200,000 persons. He reports that at 8% interest, the rate the city would have to pay on bonds to build the center, it would be a losing proposition. The present value of $1,300,000 ($1,800,000 − $500,000) annually for 30 years at 8% is $14,635,400, well below the cost of the center. (Assume this computation is correct.)

One member of the council comments that the rentals are not the only source of revenues to the city. To support this position, she offers studies showing that the average person attending a trade show or convention spends $500 in the city in which the event is being held. Because of the various taxes in effect, the city receives, on average, about 1% of all of the money spent in it.

Required
1. Prepare a new analysis, incorporating the additional tax receipts expected if the center is built.
2. Why is 8% used as the discount rate when it is the interest rate, not cost of capital? (Is the interest rate the same as the cost of capital to a city?)

8-36 Comparison of NPV and profit   Graham Auto Products is bringing out a new heavy-duty battery and has two choices with respect to the manufacturing process. No matter which choice it makes, it expects to sell 100,000 units per year for four years at $50 per unit. Data on the two processes are

	Labor-Intensive Process	Capital-Intensive Process
Per-unit variable cost	$ 20	$ 10
Annual fixed cash operating costs	$ 400,000	$ 600,000
Investment in equipment	$4,000,000	$6,000,000

Neither set of equipment is expected to have salvage value at the end of four years. The firm uses straight-line depreciation. Cost of capital is 16% and the tax rate is 40%.

Required
1. Which process will give the higher annual profit?
2. Which process will give the higher book rate of return on average investment?
3. Which process will give the higher NPV?
4. Which process would you select and why?

8-37 Capital budgeting for a computer service firm   Many firms are in the business of selling computer time to others. Customers include other business firms, universities, hospitals, and so on. One such computer service firm, Compuservice, Inc., currently has a Whizbang 85, a high-speed machine that it rents from the manufacturer for $18,000 per month. The firm is considering the purchase of a Zoom 125, which is the fastest machine of its type available. The Whizbang 85 would be kept even if the Zoom were bought. Cal Kulate, president of Compuservice, believes that a number of new customers would be attracted if the firm acquired the Zoom 125. He estimates additional revenues of $40,000 per month. Additional costs requiring cash would be $4,000 per month for maintenance and salaries for added operators. The Zoom sells for $1,200,000 and has a useful physical life of about 15 years. However, computer experts have estimated that the Zoom will probably be technologically obsolete in six years.

The firm would use straight-line depreciation of $225,000 per year in order to depreciate the computer to its estimated salvage value of $300,000 at the end of four years. The firm's tax rate is 40% and its cost of capital is 16%.

Required: Evaluate the proposed purchase.

8-38 *Investing in quality* Pellum Company manufactures a number of products in a relatively old plant. Parts of the manufacturing process are very outmoded. One result is that about 10 percent of output is spoiled in production. Spoiled output is scrapped. The manufacturing managers have been looking at new machinery and equipment that would reduce the rate of rejects to near zero. Outfitting the plant will cost about $6.5 million. The new machines have five-year lives and no salvage value. The company uses straight-line depreciation. The existing machinery is fully depreciated and has no sales value.

The total manufacturing costs of the plant under current conditions are about $94.6 million, with $58.0 million variable, the rest fixed. Cash fixed operating costs will increase by about $2.2 million annually if the new machinery were acquired. The tax rate is 40% and cost of capital is 12%.

Required
1. Determine the NPV of reducing spoiled output to zero while maintaining the current level of good output.
2. Annual revenue under existing conditions is $117.8 million. Suppose that demand is far above capacity so that the plant could increase sales by 10% if it acquired the new equipment. Determine the NPV of the investment.

8-39 *Reevaluating an investment* Ten years ago the Kramer Company, of which you are the controller, bought some machinery at a cost of $200,000. The purchase was made at the insistence of the production manager. The machinery is now worthless, and the production manager believes that it should be replaced. He gives you the following analysis, which he says verifies the correctness of the decision to buy the machinery ten years ago. He bases his statement on the 24.6% return he calculated, which is higher than the firm's cutoff rate of return of 20%.

Annual cost savings:	
Labor	$ 32,000
Overhead	29,000
Total	61,000
Less straight-line depreciation ($200,000/10)	20,000
Increase in pretax income	41,000
Income taxes at 40%	16,400
Increase in net income	$ 24,600
Average investment ($200,000/2)	$100,000
Return on investment	24.6%

Required: Do you agree that the investment was wise? Why or why not?

8-40 *Purchase commitment* Ralston Company buys copper from a number of suppliers, including the Boa Copper Company. The president of Boa has offered to sell Ralston up to 1,000,000 pounds of copper per year for five years at $0.80 per pound if Ralston will lend Boa $2,000,000 at 8% interest. The loan would be repaid at the end of five years, the interest would be paid annually.

Ralston uses at least 1,800,000 pounds of copper per year and expects the price to be $1.00 per pound over the next five years. The tax rate is 40% and Ralston's management considers the relevant discount rate to be 12%.

Required
1. Determine whether Ralston Company should accept the offer.
2. Determine the price at which copper would have to sell, per pound, over the next five years to make accepting the offer worthwhile.

8-41 ***New product – complementary effects*** Elmendorf Company makes a variety of cleaning products. The firm's research and development department has recently come up with a new glass cleaner that is superior to all of the products on the market, including the one that Elmendorf currently makes. The new cleaner would be priced at $6 per case and would have variable costs of $2 per case. Elmendorf would have to buy additional machinery costing $8,000,000 to make the new cleaner. The machinery would have a ten-year life. Expected volume of the new cleaner is 800,000 cases per year for ten years. In addition to the variable costs, there would be increased fixed costs of $200,000 per year requiring cash disbursements.

The machinery would be depreciated using the straight-line method with no provision for salvage value. There is about $100,000 expected salvage value at the end of ten years. The tax rate is 40% and cost of capital is 14%.

One problem with making the investment is that sales of the firm's existing cleaner would be affected. Volume of the existing cleaner is expected to fall by 300,000 cases per year. A case of the existing cleaner sells for $5 and has variable costs of $3.

Required: Determine the NPV of the proposed investment.

8-42 ***Uses of space (AICPA adapted)*** Lansdown Company manages large office buildings in the downtown area of a major city. One of the buildings it manages has a large, unused lobby area. A manager of the firm believes that a newsstand should be placed in the lobby. He has talked to managers of several other office buildings and has projected the following annual operating results if the company establishes a newsstand.

Sales	$49,000
Cost of sales	40,000
Salaries of clerks	7,000
Licenses and payroll taxes	200
Share of heat and light bills on the building	500
Share of building depreciation	1,000
Advertising for the newsstand	100
Share of Lansdown's administrative expense	400

The investment required would be $2,000, all for equipment that would be worthless in ten years. Before presenting the plan to his superiors, the manager learned that the space could be leased to an outside firm that would operate the same kind of newsstand. The other firm would pay $750 rent per year for each of the ten years. Because the lobby is heated and lighted anyway, Lansdown would supply heat and light at no additional cost. Lansdown's cost of capital is 12%. (Ignore taxes.)

Required
1. Determine the best course of action for Lansdown.
2. Determine how much annual rent Lansdown would have to receive to equalize the attractiveness of the alternatives.

8-43 **Magazine subscriptions** The managers of *PC Journal,* a magazine for computer users, are working on a campaign to get extended subscriptions. The magazine's base one-year rate is $23 for 12 issues. The rate for a two-year subscription is tentatively set at $40. Both amounts would be payable in advance. The variable cost per subscription per year is $10.00. Cost of capital is 12%. The company pays no income taxes.

Required
1. Suppose that all one-year subscribers will renew at the end of the year. Therefore, the company will either (a) collect $23 now and $23 in one year or (b) collect $40 now. Determine whether the magazine should offer the $40 rate for a two-year subscription.
2. Again, assuming that all subscribers taking one-year subscriptions would renew at the end of one year, determine the lowest two-year rate that the magazine should offer.
3. Suppose now that there is about a 40% attrition rate in subscriptions. That is, of every ten 1-year subscribers, four will not renew next year. Determine whether the magazine should offer the $40 rate. Assume that the variable costs are paid at the *beginning* of each year. You might find it convenient to work with a hypothetical batch of ten subscribers.
4. Using the facts from item 3, determine the lowest two-year rate that the magazine should offer.

8-44 **Long-term special order** Nova Company makes indoor television antennae that sell for $12 and have variable costs of $7. The firm has been selling 200,000 units per year and expects to continue at that rate unless it accepts a special order from the Acme Television Company. Acme has offered to buy 40,000 units per year at $9, provided that Nova agrees to make the sales for a five-year period. Acme will not take fewer than 40,000 units.

Nova's current capacity is 230,000 units per year. Capacity could be increased to 260,000 units per year if new equipment costing $100,000 were purchased. The equipment would have a useful life of five years, have no salvage value, and add $20,000 in annual fixed cash operating costs. Variable costs per unit would be unchanged.

Nova would use straight-line depreciation for tax purposes. The tax rate is 40% and cost of capital is 14%.

Required: Determine the best course of action for Nova Company. (Be sure to consider all of the available alternatives.)

Case

8-45 **Introduction of new product** Jerry Dollink, the controller of Radsiville Industries, Inc., tells you about a meeting of several top managers of the firm. The topic discussed was the introduction of a new product that had been undergoing extensive research and development. Jerry had thought that the product would be brought out in the coming year, but the managers decided to give it further study.

The product is expected to have a market life of ten years. Sales are expected to be 30,000 units annually at $90. The following unit costs were presented by James Barker, the manager of the division that would produce and sell the product.

Materials	$ 8
Direct labor	14
Overhead (manufacturing)	30
Selling and administrative expenses	12
Total costs	$64

Barker went on to point out that equipment costing $3,000,000 and having an expected salvage value of $100,000 at the end of ten years would have to be purchased. Adding the $900,000 that had already been spent on research and development brought the total outlay related to the new product to $3,900,000.

Depreciation of $300,000 per year would reduce taxes by $120,000 (40% rate). The $26 per-unit profit margin would produce $780,000 before taxes and $468,000 after taxes. The net return would then be $588,000 annually, which is a rate of return of about 8%, far below the firm's cost of capital at 14%. Barker concluded that the product should not be brought out.

Jerry tells you that Barker is a strong believer in "having every product pay its way." The calculation of the manufacturing overhead cost per unit includes existing fixed costs of $600,000 allocated to the new product. Additional cash fixed costs are $200,000 per year. Selling and administrative expenses were also allocated to the product on the basis of relative sales revenue. Commissions of $4 per unit will be the only incremental selling, general, and administrative expenses.

Required
1. Prepare a new analysis.
2. Explain the fallacies in Barker's analysis. Comment on why you might treat items differently from the way he did.

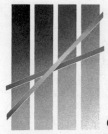

CHAPTER 9

CAPITAL BUDGETING, PART II

All the capital budgeting decisions discussed in Chapter 8 required the purchase of new productive assets. In this chapter we consider other kinds of decisions, but the basic principles remain the same. The new features require somewhat different methods of computing the net cash flows or the required investment, but the analyses still concentrate on cash flows and consider the time value of money.

Because of the importance of the many estimates in a capital budgeting decision, we introduce an analytical technique to help managers identify the most critical estimates. We also give attention to a few additional aspects of income tax law that affect capital budgeting decisions. Finally, because budgets reflect planning decisions and many of those decisions have social consequences, we conclude the chapter (and Part Two) with a discussion of the social consequences of decision making and a brief look at the special problem of decision making in the public sector.

COMPLEX INVESTMENTS

For many investment opportunities, the required investment is not a single cash payment for some new depreciable asset. Some opportunities require a change in the entity's investment in working capital or the replacement of existing assets. These features complicate the determination of the required investment.

Changes in Investment
in Working Capital

A capital budgeting decision involves an investment with a life of more than one year. Such investments usually involve noncurrent assets. It is not unusual, however, for such investment opportunities to also require a change in the entity's working capital (current assets–current liabilities). When a capital budgeting decision necessitates a change in working capital, that change must be incorporated in the analysis of the decision. The most common change is an increase in working capital, and we present that situation first. Later we discuss the less common and less analytically complex decisions requiring a decrease in working capital.

Unless all sales are for cash, an investment that involves increased sales is invariably accompanied by an increase in accounts receivable. Supporting a higher level of sales also requires a higher level of inventory for both retail firms and manufacturers who are not pursuing the zero-inventory goal of the JIT philosophy. (When you followed the development of a comprehensive budget for Cross Company in Chapter 6, you saw the impact on inventory levels of a short-term increase in sales.) Moreover, even if no increase in inventory is necessary, sales-increasing opportunities also increase the firm's current liabilities (payables for purchases of product, materials, labor, commissions, etc.).

The increase in payables is likely to be smaller than the increase in receivables, and most surely would be smaller than the combined increase in receivables and inventory. Hence, to undertake the sales-increasing opportunity the firm has to carry a higher level of working capital. Such an opportunity is said to require an investment in working capital. Investments in working capital are just as important as investments in noncurrent assets, and a capital budgeting opportunity must provide an acceptable return on *all* of the investment that it requires.

There is one difference between investments in working capital and in noncurrent assets. At the end of its useful life, a tangible asset often has a salvage value that is less than its cost. In contrast, working capital investments are typically recovered *in full,* or nearly so, because the larger receivables and inventory will be turned into cash during the final operating cycle in the life of the project. Remember the time lags, discussed in Chapters 6 and 7, between making a purchase and paying for it, and between making a sale and collecting for it. In the final year of a project, the expectation of reduced sales reduces the required inventory, thereby reducing the required purchases, which in turn reduces the amount of cash needed to pay for purchases and frees such cash for other uses. Similarly, cash collections in that final year should exceed sales related to the project, because of the delay in collecting for sales made in the previous year.[1]

---

[1] As a practical matter, the return of the net investment in current asset items may extend one or two months after the end of a project because of the lags in (1) collections for sales (through accounts receivable) and (2) payments for purchases (through accounts payable). When discounting cash flows several years hence, a difference of a month or two is not usually significant and can be ignored.

Dealing with projects that require investment in working capital is not particularly difficult. It is, however, important to recognize that *there are no tax effects* associated either with the initial increase in working capital or with its recovery at the end of the useful life of the project. (Remember that taxes are normally levied on income computed on the accrual basis.)

 ⁓ Consider an investment in a new product that is expected to have a useful life of five years. Revenues from the product are estimated to be $20,000 annually, with additional cash costs of $6,000. The investment is $30,000 in equipment and $35,000 in working capital. Straight-line depreciation is used, the equipment has no salvage value, cost of capital is 12%, and the tax rate is 40%. The cash flows and NPV of the project are computed below.

Cash Flows Years 1–5

	Tax Computation	Cash Flow
Revenues	$20,000	$20,000
Cash expenses	6,000	6,000
Pretax cash inflow	14,000	14,000
Depreciation ($30,000/5)	6,000	
Increase in taxable income	$ 8,000	
Tax at 40%	$ 3,200	3,200
Net cash inflow per year		$10,800

End of Year 5

Recovery of working capital investment	$35,000

Summary of Net Present Value of Investment

Operating cash inflows ($10,800 × 3.605)	$38,934
Recovery of working capital investment ($35,000 × 0.567)	19,845
Total present value	58,779
Investment required ($30,000 + $35,000)	65,000
Net present value	($ 6,221)

The investment is undesirable. If only the noncurrent asset investment is considered, the investment appears desirable because it shows a positive NPV of $8,934 ($38,934 − $30,000). Failure to consider the working capital requirements would lead to a bad decision.

In summary, when an investment requires an increase in working capital, the major change in the analysis involves the computation of the investment and of the cash flow in the project's final year. In contrast, the analytical change required by an investment involving a *decrease* in working capital relates only to the computation of the amount of investment that accompanies the project. The growing number of manufacturers adopting the JIT philosophy provide examples of the latter type of investment opportunity.

A manufacturer moving to implement the JIT philosophy looks for opportunities that enable it to reduce its inventory. In the first year of such an investment, the firm will draw units from existing inventory to meet its earliest sales needs, but will not purchase materials or incur other production costs to replace those units until the units are needed to meet sales delivery deadlines. Delaying purchases and production has the effect of freeing up, fairly early in that first year, cash that can be used for other purposes.

The cash flow implications of inventory-reducing projects are akin to those in projects requiring a build-up of inventory. But there is one important difference: A company committed to the JIT philosophy does not expect to return to its prior inventory levels at the end of the project's life. Hence, such a firm expects a cash saving in the first year of a project's life but does *not* expect an additional cash outflow in the project's final year. Accordingly, the only unusual aspect of the analysis of an inventory-reducing decision is that the cash saving from reducing inventory in the first year shows as a reduction of the investment required for the decision. (As an alternative, the cash saving could simply be added to the present value of the future cash flows.) The second case of a complex investment to be considered, the replacement decision, is different from investments involving working capital because it involves additional calculations to determine future cash flows.

Replacement Decisions

Businesses frequently face the problem of whether to replace an asset currently in use. Such a question is called a **replacement decision.** Replacement decisions are made when economic or technological factors make it possible to perform tasks at lower cost. Faster and more efficient machines and labor-saving devices enable the firm to earn higher returns. Typically, replacement decisions involve essential operations. The focus is on how to perform those operations.

Determining cash flows for replacement decisions is more complex than for decisions whether to purchase new assets because (1) there are tax differences if depreciation on the replacement is different from that on the existing assets, and (2) determining the net cost to purchase the replacement requires more steps. We illustrate two methods for evaluating replacement decisions: the incremental approach and the "total-project" approach.

The **incremental approach** focuses on the differences between the cash flows, given the alternatives of keeping the existing assets or replacing them. The **total-project approach** looks at the total cash flows and total present values under each alternative and compares the present values. As we shall see, the two approaches give the same results, so selecting one or the other is a matter of computational convenience.

Your firm now owns a machine for which it paid $100,000 five years ago. Other data relating to the machine are as follows.

Remaining useful life	5 years
Current book value	$50,000
Annual depreciation	$10,000
Expected sales value—now	$20,000
—in 5 yrs.	$10,000
Annual cash operating costs	$30,000

If you continue to use the machine for the next five years, there will be a tax (at an expected rate of 40%) on the expected salvage value, because that value was not included in the depreciation calculation. If the machine is sold now, the loss for tax purposes will be $30,000 ($50,000 book value − $20,000 sales price).

Suppose a new machine has come on the market that sells for $60,000, has an estimated useful life of five years with no salvage value, and costs only $15,000 per year to operate. The new machine can be depreciated over five years using the straight-line method. Suppose further that cost of capital is 16%. Is it wise to replace the old machine now?

As with any capital project, there are two considerations: initial investment and future cash flows. In a replacement decision, the computation of each of these is different from the computations we have made thus far. First we determine the initial investment as shown below.

	Tax Computation	Cash Outlay
Purchase price of new asset		$60,000
Book value of old machine	$50,000	
Sale price, which is a cash inflow	20,000	(20,000)
Loss for taxes, which can be offset against regular income	$30,000	
Tax saved (40%)	$12,000	(12,000)
Total cash benefit from sale		(32,000)
Net outlay for new asset		$28,000

The book value or cost of an existing asset is sunk and irrelevant to decisions. However, book value *does* affect taxes if the asset is sold and so must be considered in determining those taxes.[2] The sale of the old asset reduces the outlay for the new one by $32,000 because the firm will receive $20,000 from the sale and the loss on the sale produces a $12,000 saving in income taxes. Hence, a net outlay of only $28,000 is required to buy the new asset. Lest it appear that sales at a loss are desirable because they reduce taxes, consider that if the old

[2] In practice, the book value of an asset might not be the same as its carrying value for tax purposes (called its *tax basis*). For simplicity, in this section and in most of the assignment material, the book value and tax basis of the asset in question are equal. If there is a difference between the two, the tax effect of the gain or loss on disposition of an asset is computed using its tax basis. But the principles of the calculation remain unchanged: the carrying value of the asset is relevant only to the extent that it affects the cash flow for taxes.

asset could be sold for $60,000, creating a taxable gain of $10,000 and additional taxes of $4,000, the sale would bring in $56,000, substantially more than the $32,000 shown above.

Incremental Approach   Below is the computation of future cash flows, using the incremental approach.

Annual Cash Savings Years 1–5

		Tax Computations	Cash Flow
Pretax cash savings:			
Cash cost of using old asset		$30,000	
Cash cost of using new asset		15,000	
Difference in favor of replacement, cash inflow	(1)	15,000	$15,000
Additional depreciation:			
Depreciation on new asset ($60,000/5)		12,000	
Depreciation on old asset		10,000	
Additional tax deduction for depreciation	(2)	2,000	
Total increase in taxable income (1) − (2) =	(3)	$13,000	
Additional tax ($13,000 × 40%), cash outflow	(4)	$ 5,200	(5,200)
Additional net cash inflow favoring replacement (1) − (4)			$ 9,800

Salvage Values—End of Year 5

	Tax Computation	Cash Flow
Old asset	$10,000	
New asset	0	
Difference in favor of not replacing	$10,000	$10,000
Tax on difference, cash outflow	$ 4,000	(4,000)
Difference in favor of not replacing (decrease in cash flow)		$ 6,000

The $9,800 per year for five years is then discounted at 16%, yielding a present value of $32,085 ($9,800 × 3.274). The $6,000 difference in cash flows from salvage values is discounted at 16%, yielding $2,856 ($6,000 × 0.476). The difference is subtracted from the present value of the $9,800 annual flows because you must give up the salvage value of the old asset in order to obtain the increased annual flows.

Summary of Present Values of Investment—Incremental Approach

Present value of savings from using new machine (9800 × 3.274)	$32,085
Less: Present value of unfavorable difference in salvage values (6000 × .476)	2,856
Present value of future net savings	29,229
Required investment	28,000
Net present value of replacing machine	$ 1,229

The present value of future net savings from making a replacement now ($29,229) is greater than the net outlay required ($28,000), so the replacement is desirable. The decision rule, then, using the incremental approach, is to replace when the NPV of the replacement alternative is positive.

Total-Project Approach   A replacement decision can also be analyzed using a total-project approach. In the total-project approach we calculate, individually, the present values of the future outflows using the existing asset and using the replacement asset. The decision rule, using the total-project approach, is to accept the alternative with the *lower present value of future outflows*. This is because the analysis of both alternatives deals with costs (cash outflows), not revenues (cash inflows); the alternative with the lower present value minimizes costs.

For the example just given, the present value of the total outflows if the *existing* machine is used is calculated as follows.

Decision—Operate Existing Machine

	Tax Computation	Cash Flow
Annual operating costs	$30,000	$30,000
Depreciation	10,000	
Total tax-deductible expenses	$40,000	
Tax savings expected (40%)	$16,000	16,000
Net cash outflow expected per year		$14,000
Present value factor for 5 years at 16%		3.274 → *table B*
Present value of future operating outflows		$45,836
Less: Present value of salvage value ($6,000 × 0.476) *table A*		2,856
Present value of future cash outflows on existing machine		$42,980

Consider, now, the present value of the total cash flows if the new machine is purchased.

Decision—Sell Existing Machine, Buy New Machine

	Tax Computation	Cash Flow
Annual operating costs	$15,000	$15,000
Depreciation	12,000	
Total tax-deductible expenses	$27,000	
Tax savings expected (40%)	$10,800	10,800
Net cash outflow expected per year		$ 4,200
Present value factor for 5 years at 16%		3.274
Present value of future operating outflows		$13,751
Net outlay required for the new machine (page 333)		28,000
Present value of total cash outflows of buying new machine		$41,751

Comparing the two alternatives, we find

Present value of using existing machine	$42,980
Present value of buying and using new machine	41,751
Difference	$ 1,229

The present value of the total outlays associated with using the existing machine is greater than that of the total outlays associated with acquiring and using the new machine. Note that the $1,229 difference is equal to the NPV we computed using the incremental approach (page 334). The two approaches give the same results, and the choice between them is a matter of convenience.

In the replacement decision considered here, it was possible to continue using the currently owned asset. The same two analytical approaches can be used if an essential asset has reached the end of its useful life and alternatives exist as possible replacements. For example, suppose that a firm needs a new fork-lift truck because one of its existing trucks is about to be scrapped. Perhaps two different models are available as replacements, each with a different acquisition cost and associated annual operating costs. Because the firm is committed to replacing the old forklift, the decision becomes one of how to minimize the future costs and either the incremental or the total-project approach could be used.

MUTUALLY EXCLUSIVE ALTERNATIVES

The decision rules associated with analytical techniques presented in this and the preceding chapter identify investments that are wise without regard to whether the firm has funds available for investment. Recognize, however, that no firm has unlimited resources available to it. Investments that are wise under the decision rules already presented remain so even when resources are limited. But a limitation on resources means that all of the firm's investment opportunities are *competing* for the available resources. In some cases, the competition among opportunities is even more specific, as when the firm has two or more ways of accomplishing the same goal so that selecting one alternative precludes selecting the others. When this situation exists, we call the competing proposals **mutually exclusive alternatives.**

Some of the decisions already considered fit this definition—the replacement decision, for example. If the firm keeps its present equipment it does not buy the newer model or vice versa. Mutual exclusivity can also arise as a matter of policy. For example, a firm may have a policy of introducing no more than one new product in any one year.

Whether exclusivity is inherent in the proposals or is the result of management policy, it is not unusual for competing alternatives to have unequal lives. Some analysts suggest that another evaluation technique, the profitability index, can be particularly useful in ranking and deciding among alternatives. These two special topics are discussed in the next sections.

Unequal Lives

Alternative investment opportunities often have different useful lives. For example, both a conveyor belt and a fork-lift truck might meet the need to move semifinished units from one place to another, but the life of the former is likely to exceed that of the latter. Our techniques for evaluating investments can be used in such a case only if some way is found to make the alternatives comparable. One commonly used method of doing so is to assume a chain of replacements such that the analysis of each alternative covers the same number of years.

To illustrate this method, assume the following facts about two mutually exclusive investment opportunities, two versions (Model G-40 and Model G-70) of a machine that is essential to the firm's operations.

	Model G-40	Model G-70
Purchase price	$40,000	$70,000
Annual cash operating costs	$ 8,000	$ 6,000
Expected useful life	4 years	8 years

Neither machine has any expected salvage value at the end of its useful life. The firm's cost of capital is 14%. So as to concentrate on the specific problem at hand—the unequal lives of the alternatives—we ignore income taxes and so need not be concerned with depreciation.

The time period selected for use in the evaluation is eight years because that is the lowest common denominator for the lives of the two investments. (If the alternatives had lives of, say, four and six years, we would use a 12-year period to compare the two.) Evaluating first the alternative with the longer life (Model G-70), the present value of the expected cash outflows is $97,834, as shown below.

Annual operating costs	$ 6,000
Present value factor for 14% and 8 years	4.639 → Table B
Present value of operating costs	$27,834
Investment required	70,000
Present value of total cash outflows for G-70	$97,834

To provide comparable information about the alternative of using Model G-40, we assume replacement at the end of four years at a cost of $44,000 but with no change in annual operating costs. The present value of total cash outflows assuming a choice of Model G-40 is $103,168, as shown on the next page.

Annual operating costs, years 1–4	$ 8,000
Present value factor for 14% and 4 years	2.914
Present value of operating cash outflows, years 1–4	$ 23,312
Present value of purchase of replacement Model G-40 at the end of year 4 ($44,000 × .592)	26,048
Present values of cash outlays in years 5–8:	
Year 5 $8,000 × .519	4,152
Year 6 $8,000 × .456	3,648
Year 7 $8,000 × .400	3,200
Year 8 $8,000 × .351	2,808
Present value of future cash outlays	
Investment required now	40,000
Present value of total cash outflows for G-40	$103,168

Because we are dealing with cash outflows for the two alternatives we are interested in the lower present value, which is $97,834 for selecting Model G-70 (compared with $103,168 for selecting Model G-40). However, the firm's managers should consider how confident they are in the forecast of the replacement cost of the G-40 as well as the likelihood of a significant change in technology. These and other qualitative factors influence the final decision.

Ranking Investment Opportunities

In Chapter 8 we stated that the two discounted cash flow techniques (NPV and IRR) were conceptually superior to other methods presented in that chapter (payback period and book rate of return). It is possible, however, that if two or more proposals are *ranked* using each of the two conceptually superior methods, the *rankings* might not be the same. That is, the proposals ranking first and second using NPV might rank second and first using IRR. If the proposals are mutually exclusive there is now a conflict; the decision rule for NPV argues acceptance of one proposal, while the decision rule for IRR argues acceptance of the other.

To deal with such situations, some accountants and financial specialists prefer a third discounted cash flow technique, the profitability index, which, it is argued, is as useful as NPV and IRR in most situations but more useful than either of those approaches in evaluating mutually exclusive alternatives. The **profitability index (PI)** is the *ratio* of the present value of the future cash flows to the investment. In general terms,

$$\text{Profitability index} = \frac{\text{present value of future cash flows}}{\text{investment}}$$

Thus, a $100,000 investment with present value of future cash flows of $118,000 has a PI of 1.18. The decision rule for this third approach to evaluating investments is to accept projects with a PI greater than 1.0.

PI > 1

You should see that the decision rule for using PI will, in the case of acceptance/rejection decisions, produce the same results as the rules covering NPV and IRR. An investment with a positive NPV and an IRR greater than cost of capital also has a PI greater than 1.0. Also, unlike the payback period and book-rate-of-return approaches, PI considers the time value of money and is therefore conceptually superior to those methods.

However, except under very special circumstances, NPV is preferable to either IRR or PI when it comes to ranking competing alternatives. Let us see how the three criteria perform in an example, and explain those special circumstances.

Below are data for two mutually exclusive investment opportunities confronting a firm with a 10% cost of capital.

	Investment Opportunities	
	X	Y
Investment required	$50,000	$10,000
Life of investment	1 year	1 year
Cash flows, end of year 1	$55,991	$11,403
Present value of cash flows at 10% cost of capital (.909 × cash flow)	$50,896	$10,365
(NPV) Net present value of project	$ 896	$ 365
(IRR) Internal rate of return:		
Discount rate associated with factor .893 ($50,000/$55,991)	12%	
Discount rate associated with factor .877 ($10,000/$11,403)		14%
(P.I) Profitability index:		
$50,896/$50,000	1.018	
$10,365/$10,000		1.037

Project Y has both a higher IRR and a higher PI than does project X, which is higher using only the NPV criterion. *Provided that the 10% cost of capital is the rate at which alternative investments can be made,* project X should be selected. The simplest way to show this is as follows.

For both opportunities X and Y to be considered, at least $50,000 (the investment required for X) must be available for investment. If project Y is accepted (outlay of $10,000), $40,000 is available for other projects. Now assume that another, hypothetical project, Z, is available and that Z requires an investment of $40,000 and shows an expected return of 10%, the cost of capital. What cash would the firm have at the end of the year if it selected Y and invested the additional funds in Z? The firm's cash position is summarized below.

Cash provided by investment in project Y		$11,403
Cash provided by investment in Z:		
Investment returned	$40,000	
Earnings on the investment (10%)	4,000	44,000
Total cash available to firm at end of year		$55,403

At the end of the year, $55,403 is available to the firm from the two projects. But, had the firm invested the entire $50,000 in project X, it would have had $55,991 at the end of the year. Thus, accepting project Y and using the excess funds for another project produces less cash than results from accepting only project X.

The only time that the project with the higher PI or higher IRR should be chosen in preference to the one with the higher NPV is when investing in the former enables the firm to invest additional cash at a rate *greater* than the cost of capital *and* that opportunity is not available if the firm chooses the project with the higher NPV. Thus, in our example situation, we would choose project Y only if there were additional available investments with returns that were in excess of 10%, which investments would have to be foregone if the extra $40,000 were invested in project X.

SENSITIVITY ANALYSIS

In Chapter 5 we emphasized that decision analysis involves many estimates, errors in one or more of which could lead to an unwise decision. Because of the importance of estimates in decision making, managers analyze the sensitivity of decisions to changes in one or more variables. This testing of the estimates, called **sensitivity analysis,** involves trying to find out how much the value of a variable can rise or fall before a different decision is indicated. Although sensitivity analysis applies to all types of decisions, for several reasons it is especially beneficial when applied to capital budgeting decisions.

First, remember that the annual cash flow is multiplied by the present value factor. Hence, for a project with a ten-year life where cost of capital is 20% (present value factor of 4.192), a $1 drop in annual cash flow produces a drop of $4.192 in the present value of those flows.

A capital budgeting decision also involves the time value of money, which is not incorporated in short-term decision making. Suppose that an investment of $12,000 is expected to generate cash flows of $3,000 per year for ten years and that the discount rate is 12%. The project has a positive NPV; but considering the uncertainties surrounding estimates for years far into the future, a manager might wonder just how long the investment must continue producing an annual flow of $3,000 in order to earn at least the required 12% return. Dividing the investment by the annual cash flow gives a present value factor (also the payback period) of 4 ($12,000/$3,000). Knowing the discount rate (12%) and the present value factor (4.0) we can consult Table B, look down the 12% column, and see that 3.605 is the factor for five years, 4.111 for six years. Hence, the project must yield its annual flows of $3,000 for nearly six years in order to earn the required 12% return. In this case then, the estimated useful life of the project has to be in error by 40% (from ten to six years), a large error in the original estimate, before the decision changes, so the decision is not very sensitive to the estimate of useful life.

The outcome of analyzing a capital budgeting decision can also be affected significantly by differences in estimates of sales volumes, selling prices, and per-unit variable costs. (The effect of each such difference is magnified in the analysis, because each unit of volume is multiplied by contribution margin per unit.) Hence, managers might want to determine how sensitive a particular decision is to estimates of volume, selling price, or variable costs. For example, suppose that a firm with a cost of capital of 14% and in the 40% tax bracket can bring out a new product priced at $22. Variable costs of the product are expected to be $4 per unit; fixed costs requiring cash outlays are estimated at $100,000 annually, and the estimated annual sales volume is 10,000 units. Bringing out the new product requires an investment of $200,000, all for depreciable assets with a five-year life and no salvage value, and the firm uses straight-line depreciation. The initial analysis for this decision is shown below.

		Tax	*Cash Flow*
Expected contribution margin (10,000 × $18)		$180,000	$180,000
Fixed costs:			
Cash	$100,000		(100,000)
Depreciation	40,000		
		140,000	
Increase in taxable income		$ 40,000	
Tax at 40% (cash outflow)		$ 16,000	(16,000)
Net cash inflow per year			$ 64,000
Present value factor, 5-year annuity at 14%			3.433
Present value of annual cash inflows			$219,712
Investment required			200,000
Net present value			$ 19,712

Based on the available estimates, the project has a positive NPV and should be accepted. But how far can volume fall before the investment becomes only marginally desirable?

First, to achieve a present value *equal* to the investment the required after-tax cash inflow has to be $58,258 ($200,000/3.433). Because depreciation can be added back to net income to get cash flow, we can, instead, subtract depreciation from the *required* cash flow and obtain the required net income. We then divide the net income by (1 − tax rate) to get the required pretax income, just as we did in Chapter 2. From then on, ordinary VCP analysis is used to determine the required volume. The full computation is shown below.

Required after-tax cash inflow	$ 58,258
Less depreciation	40,000
Equals required after-tax income	$ 18,258
Divided by 60%, which is (1 − 40% tax rate), gives required profit before taxes	$ 30,430
Add fixed costs including depreciation	140,000
Equals required contribution margin	$170,430
Divided by $18 contribution margin per unit gives required sales volume	9,468 units

The above calculation is equivalent to preparing a cash flow schedule and tax computation schedule from the bottom up, a technique used in very early chapters. The required volume of 9,468 units is only 532 units less than the estimated volume, or 5.32% below the estimate. The margin for error here is small, and a relatively small decline in volume renders the investment undesirable even though it had a fairly high NPV when the 10,000 unit estimate was used.

An alternative method is to find the *change* in volume that will make the project yield just 14%. The NPV calculated before is $19,712. We can find the decrease in volume that will reduce NPV by $19,712 as follows.

Net present value	$19,712
Divided by 14% present value factor for 5 years	3.433
Equals change in annual net cash flows to make investment yield 14%	$ 5,742
Divided by (1 minus the tax rate) gives decrease in pretax cash flow	$ 9,570
Divided by $18 contribution margin gives decrease in sales	532 units

The alternative method is often more convenient. Managers can perform the same type of analysis to test the sensitivity of a decision to estimates of selling price and per-unit variable costs.

Sensitivity analysis gives managers an idea about how unfavorable occurrences like lower volumes, shorter useful lives, or higher costs affect the profitability of a project. It is used because of the uncertainty that prevails in almost any real-life situation. Some other ways to deal with uncertainty are introduced in Chapter 16.

MORE ON INCOME TAXES

Throughout this book we have treated income taxes rather generally. In particular, we have assumed that a single tax rate applies to all of a company's revenues and expenses, that only revenues and expenses of the current year affect taxes, and that the depreciation rules of financial accounting govern tax deductions for depreciation. None of these assumptions is always true. However, tax law is far too complex to be treated in depth in an introductory text in managerial accounting. We therefore point out only a few aspects of the law that bear on capital budgeting decisions.

First, no single tax rate applies to all incomes. Rates are graduated (progressively higher), and the rates depend on whether the business is incorporated. The federal tax rates for corporations begin at 15% for income up to $50,000 and increase to 34% for income over $75,000. However, above $100,000, the corporation loses the benefit of the lower rates, so that the rate on some incremental income can be as high as 39%. (The average rate never exceeds 34%.) The federal rates on incomes of unincorporated businesses depend on the incomes of their individual owners (including their incomes from sources other than the business).

These rates are 15% and 28%. Again, taxpayers lose the benefit of the lower rate at higher incomes, so that the rate on some incremental income can be 33%. Many states levy income taxes on individuals and on corporations, which can further increase the rates. Because large businesses are likely to be in the top brackets for both federal and state tax purposes, it is reasonable for them to use a single combined federal and state rate for analyzing capital budgeting decisions.

Second, income taxes do not depend solely on revenues and expenses for a given tax year. One feature of tax law, called the operating loss carryback/carryforward, allows businesses to offset losses in one year against profits in another. For example, if a qualifying company lost $200,000 in 19X4, then earned $50,000 in 19X5, it does not have to pay any taxes on the $50,000 because of the loss in 19X4. In fact, with some restrictions, the company does not have to pay income taxes until it earns over $200,000 cumulatively after 19X4.

The segment of the tax law that introduces the greatest difference between our general approach and the specifics of tax law relates to the treatment of depreciation. As pointed out in Chapter 8, determining the cash outflow for taxes requires considering the tax deduction for depreciation. Because the rules governing depreciation for tax purposes differ considerably from those governing depreciation for financial accounting purposes, we now consider, in some detail, the major factor in producing that difference, the Accelerated Cost Recovery System (ACRS).

ACRS

For many years prior to 1981, business entities were allowed to use a different, and faster, depreciation method for tax purposes than was used for financial accounting purposes. An entity could start using one of the accelerated methods of depreciation, and then switch to the straight-line method when that method would produce higher depreciation charges for tax purposes.

The life over which an asset could be depreciated for tax purposes was generally its *Asset Depreciation Range (ADR)* life. (ADR lives were developed by the Internal Revenue Service.) The schedule of ADR lives relieved a business from having to estimate useful lives for its assets for tax purposes.

The Economic Recovery Tax Act (ERTA) of 1981 continued to provide benefits from accelerated depreciation, but narrowed the options by introducing **ACRS.** ACRS specified much shorter depreciation periods than had previously been allowed. The Tax Reform Act of 1986 made some changes in ACRS. (Although both Acts allow businesses to use straight-line depreciation using the ADR lives, this is usually less advantageous than ACRS.) Under ACRS, the business places individual assets into various classes according to their ADRs. For most industrial and service companies, four classes of property are important:

5-Year Class: This class includes automobiles and light trucks, personal computers, typewriters, and certain other enumerated items.

7-Year Class: This class includes office furniture and equipment, most types of machinery, and other property with an ADR midpoint[3] of at least ten years and less than 16 years, plus certain enumerated items.

10-Year Class: This class contains property with an ADR midpoint of at least 16 years and less than 20 years, including certain types of transportation equipment.

31.5-Year Class: This class includes nonresidential real property such as factory buildings.

Exhibit 9-1 gives the percentages (rounded to the nearest 1%) of cost to be depreciated in each year for the three classes of most relevance to capital budgeting. Depreciation under ACRS reflects the 200% declining balance method, with a switch to straight-line depreciation when it benefits the business. Salvage value is not recognized under ACRS. ACRS also uses the "half-year convention," which means that assets are assumed to be put in service halfway through the year. Its practical effect is that, as the exhibit shows, assets are depreciated over one year more than their class lives; that is, 5-Year assets over six years, 7-Year assets over eight years, and so on. The half-year convention also applies to assets depreciated using the optional straight-line method under the 1986 Tax Reform Act.

ACRS is usually advantageous because it concentrates depreciation deductions in the earlier years of an asset's life. The ACRS class lives are much shorter than the ADR lives and so write-offs are considerably faster than they were previously. Tax payments in the early years are less than under the straight-line method. Payments in later years are higher, but remember that the present value of the tax payments is lower the later they are made.

Calculating depreciation under ACRS can be tedious. Exhibit 9-2 provides a shortcut method for finding the *present value of tax savings* for 5- and 7-Year

Exhibit 9-1
Percentages of Cost Depreciated Under ACRS

Year	5-Year Class	7-Year Class	10-Year Class
1	20%	14%	10%
2	32	25	18
3	19	18	14
4	12	12	12
5	12	9	9
6	5	9	7
7		9	7
8		4	7
9			7
10			6
11			3

[3] ADR lives were, as suggested by the term, given as a range of years. For example, the ADR for one type of asset might be stated as 11 to 15 years. Hence, the midpoint of the ADR life is 13 years.

Exhibit 9-2

Present Value of ACRS Tax Shields[a]

Discount Rate	5-Year Assets	7-Year Assets
.08	.811	.766
.10	.774	.722
.12	.738	.681
.14	.706	.645
.16	.675	.611
.18	.647	.580
.20	.621	.552
.22	.597	.526
.24	.574	.502

[a]Factors in this table are the sums of the percentages of depreciation for each period multiplied by the present value factors. For example, the factor for 10% for a 5-Year asset is (20% × .909) + (32% × .826) + (19% × .751) + (12% × .683) + (12% × .621) + (5% × .564). There is some rounding.

property at various discount rates. To use the table, multiply the cost of the asset by the factor for the life and discount rate, then multiply by the tax rate.

Let us look at an example to see how the table works. Suppose a company expects pretax cash flows of $3,000 per year from an asset costing $10,000. The asset is in the 5-Year class and, to reduce calculations, has a useful life of six years. The tax rate is 40% and cost of capital is 12%. A year-by-year analysis is below.

	Year					
	1	2	3	4	5	6
Pretax inflow	$ 3,000	$3,000	$3,000	$3,000	$3,000	$3,000
ACRS deduction	2,000	3,200	1,900	1,200	1,200	500
Taxable income	1,000	(200)	1,100	1,800	1,800	2,500
Tax at 40%	400	(80)	440	720	720	1,000
Net cash inflow	$2,600	$3,080	$2,560	$2,280	$2,280	$2,000
Present value factors	.893	.797	.712	.636	.567	.507
Present values	$ 2,322	$2,455	$1,823	$1,450	$1,293	$1,014
Total present value	$10,357					

It is much easier to determine this present value of the operating inflows net of tax, and *then* to add the present value of the ACRS tax shield.

Present value of operating flows	
$3,000 × (1 − .40) × 4.111 (from Table B)	$ 7,400
Present value of ACRS shield	
$10,000 × .40 × .738 (from Exhibit 9-2)	2,952
Total present value (rounding difference)	$10,352

We needed only two calculations. The operating flow, net of tax, is an annuity of $1,800 ($3,000 × [1 − .40]) for six years, and is discounted using the Table B factor for six years at 12%. Exhibit 9-2 gives the factor for a 5-Year asset at 12% as .738, which, when multiplied by the cost of the asset *and* by the tax rate, gives the present value of the tax shield.

On the whole, the depreciation deductions mandated under ACRS (or even the optional straight-line method) are more advantageous than those previously available, because of the relatively short lives now acceptable for tax purposes. Note, however, that the shorter lives are unlikely to be used to compute depreciation for financial reporting purposes because they are unlikely to coincide with the useful life of the property. An important result of ACRS is that the tax basis of an asset seldom equals its book value, which must be considered in calculating the taxable gain (or deductible loss) when the asset is sold. For capital budgeting decisions involving replacements of existing assets, the analysis of both current cash outlay and cash inflow from salvage value requires a calculation of the tax basis of the asset at the time of disposition.

SOCIAL CONSEQUENCES OF DECISION MAKING

Throughout most of this book we have assumed that the consequences of an action were limited to the entity taking that action. Such an assumption is not always warranted. The action of a single entity may have many effects, desirable or detrimental, for other entities.

For example, a company might find that using a machine that saves labor is justified on economic grounds. But the decision to use the machinery might put people out of work. The workers who lose their jobs will suffer if they cannot find other jobs fairly quickly. If they do not find work, they will receive unemployment compensation or some other type of payment that is borne by taxpayers. If they move away from the area to find work, they must incur moving costs, and there may be problems in uprooting their families. The reduced payroll of the plant may adversely affect the community through declines in economic activity such as retail sales. Other jobs may be lost as a result of the layoffs. Although some of these implications have been referred to in previous discussions of "qualitative considerations" of decision making, they were not specifically incorporated into the analyses. Costs that are not borne directly by the entity making a decision and taking an action are called **social costs,** or *externalities*.

Social benefits (also called externalities) are benefits not accruing directly to the entity making a decision. A company that hires workers who are currently unemployed (as opposed to hiring them away from other firms) provides benefits to the workers in the form of income and increased self-esteem, to the community in the form of increased economic activity and higher taxes, and to the taxpayers in the form of reduced expenditures for unemployment compensation. The firm does not benefit directly from these other benefits, even though its action caused them. It may not be possible for business managers to give direct and monetary recognition to externalities, but it should be possible to at least try to recognize their existence as individual decisions are studied.

Social benefits and costs are particularly critical in decisions made by government units like municipalities, states, and the federal government. Decision making in these and other not-for-profit entities is, like that in business firms, based on estimates of discounted benefits and costs. There are several major differences between the analyses used by business firms and government units. One difference is that government units do not pay income taxes, which makes their decision making somewhat simpler than that of businesses. But other factors in the government decision-making process make decisions much more difficult. These special factors fall into three general categories: (1) measurement problems; (2) problems in determining whether a particular effect is a benefit or a cost; and (3) problems in the distribution of benefits and costs.

Measurement problems arise in decisions of government units because, as we mentioned in Chapter 4, the benefits and costs are not just monetary. If an unemployed person obtains a job, the government benefits from additional taxes paid by the employed worker. But other benefits like the worker's increased self-esteem are not readily measurable. Cleaner air is economically beneficial because of fewer deaths from respiratory ailments, less sickness, and reduced cleaning bills for clothing and buildings. But the monetary value of the increased pleasantness that accompanies cleaner air is not readily measurable.

The second factor, determining whether an effect is beneficial or costly, often depends on one's point of view. The government has sanctioned actions to reduce the populations of wolves and coyotes in sheep and cattle-raising states. These programs have been favorably received by ranchers but deplored by conservationists. Programs that result in growth in population of a particular area may also receive mixed reviews. Some states and towns seek industrial development, while others discourage it.

The problem of the distribution of benefits and costs has been a difficult social question since the beginning of government. Suppose a city or town is considering the construction of a municipal golf course and analyses show that the fees received will be insufficient to earn the minimum desired rate of return. If the project is accepted the taxpayers will subsidize those who use the golf course. The town government might still decide to build the golf course because it feels that the people who would use it deserve some inexpensive recreation, even if the general taxpayers must pay some of the costs. Similar reasoning could apply to more widely used municipally owned facilities such as zoos, libraries, and parks.

The criterion that is most generally advocated for decision making by governmental units is the maximizing of "social welfare." Because of the many problems in identifying and quantifying social benefits and costs, this decision rule has generally meant the maximizing of economic benefits—those subject to monetary estimates. To the extent that this can be done, the same general analytical approaches proposed for business decision making can be used in the public sector. And, like the business manager, the decision maker in the public sector must make an effort to at least identify and consider the unquantified but relevant factors before reaching a final decision.

SUMMARY

Proper analysis of investment requirements and future cash flows is critical if a manager is to make good decisions about investing available funds. Required investment should include consideration of any required changes in the firm's working capital. Where the decision involves a replacement, the analysis may be particularly complex.

Mutually exclusive investment alternatives involve special problems. A third DCF technique, the profitability index, has been suggested to assist in choosing from among such alternatives. This technique can be useful, but the firm's circumstances in terms of available funds and investment opportunities should be considered before selecting a single capital budgeting technique for general use.

Whatever technique is used, managers find it helpful to perform sensitivity analysis. The use of sensitivity analysis is prompted by the number of estimates used in a typical capital budgeting situation.

Computations of cash flows for an investment opportunity require knowing the many special features of income tax laws, particularly the Accelerated Cost Recovery System (ACRS). But other factors, such as differing tax rates for different levels of income in different types and sizes of businesses, can influence both the amounts and the timing of cash flows from a particular investment opportunity.

Qualitative issues are associated with almost every investment opportunity. This is true in both the private and the public sectors. Decision makers in both sectors should make every effort to identify and quantify as many factors as possible and to consider factors that remain unquantified.

KEY TERMS

accelerated cost recovery system
incremental approach
mutually exclusive alternatives
profitability index (PI)

replacement decision
sensitivity analysis
total-project approach
working capital investment

KEY FORMULAS

$$\text{Profitability index} = \frac{\text{present value of future cash flows}}{\text{investment}}$$

$$\text{Working capital} = \text{current assets} - \text{current liabilities}$$

REVIEW PROBLEM – INVESTMENT IN WORKING CAPITAL

Chapman Products is considering a new product that will sell for $10 and have variable costs of $6. Expected sales volume is 22,000 units per year. Bringing out the new product requires a $30,000 increase in working capital as well as the purchase of new equipment costing $150,000 and having a five-year useful life and no salvage value. The new equipment has cash operating costs of $20,000 per year and will be depreciated using the straight-line method, ignoring the half-year convention. Chapman is in the 40% tax bracket and has 12% cost of capital.

Required: Determine the net present value of this investment opportunity.

Answer to Review Problem

The investment appears to be wise, as indicated by the following analysis.

Cash Flow, Years 1–5

	Tax Computation	Cash Flow
Additional contribution margin [22,000 × ($10 − $6)]	$88,000	$88,000
Cash operating costs of new machine	(20,000)	(20,000)
Additional pretax cash flow	68,000	
Depreciation ($150,000/5)	(30,000)	
Additional taxable income	$38,000	
Additional taxes, at 40%	$15,200	(15,200)
Net cash flow per year		$52,800

Cash Flow, End of Year 5

Recovery of working capital investment ($30,000 × .567)	$17,010

Summary of Net Present Value of Investment

Operating cash flows, years 1–5 ($52,800, from above, × 3.605)	$190,344
Recovery of working capital investment, as above	17,010
Total present value of future cash flows	207,354
Investment ($150,000 for machine + $30,000 for working capital)	180,000
Net present value of investment	$ 27,354

Note that the analysis shows the $30,000 increase in working capital as part of the investment required for the project, and then includes the recovery of that investment at the end of the project's life as part of the future cash flows. Note also that there is no tax effect of the working capital increase in either part of the analysis.

REVIEW PROBLEM – SENSITIVITY ANALYSIS, DETERMINING REQUIRED VOLUME

Refer to the facts in the first Review Problem. The managers of Chapman Products agree that of all the estimates required in their study of the new product, they are least certain about the annual volume of 22,000 units.

Required: Determine how many units per year the firm has to sell for the investment to earn 12%. Round calculations of required after-tax cash flow and required pretax profits to the nearest $100.

Answer to Review Problem

Annual sales have to be about 17,325 units. The first step is to calculate the after-tax cash flow per year that is required to meet the 12% rate of return. The required flow is $41,600 ($150,000 investment/3.605, the factor for an annuity of five years at 12%). From this amount we proceed to total required contribution margin and the required volume, as shown below.

Required after-tax cash flow per year	$41,600 (rounded)
Less depreciation ($150,000/5), which reduces income but does not affect cash flow	30,000
After-tax profit required	11,600
Divided by 1 − 40% tax rate	.60
Pretax profit required	$19,300 (rounded)
Fixed costs ($20,000 + $30,000)	50,000
Contribution margin required	$69,300
Contribution margin per unit ($10 − $6)	$4
Number of units of sales necessary to obtain required contribution margin ($69,300/$4)	17,325

REVIEW PROBLEM – REPLACEMENT DECISION AND REDUCTION IN WORKING CAPITAL

Eamon Company, which has a cost of capital of 14% and a tax rate of 40%, owns a machine with the following characteristics.

Book value	$55,000
Current market value	$40,000
Expected salvage value at end of its 5-year remaining useful life	0
Annual depreciation expense, straight-line method	$11,000
Annual cash operating costs	$18,000

Eamon's managers are looking for opportunities consistent with their desire to create a JIT manufacturing environment. The managers believe that by replacing the old machine and rearranging part of the production area, the company could reduce its investment in inventory as well as save on operating costs. The replacement machine has the following characteristics

Purchase price	$80,000
Useful life	5 years
Expected salvage value	$ 5,000
Annual cash operating costs	$ 3,000
Annual depreciation expense, straight-line, ignoring salvage value	$16,000

Rearrangement costs are expected to be $12,000 and can be expensed immediately for both book and tax purposes. By the end of the life of the new machine, Eamon's managers expect to be further advanced in their implementation of the JIT philosophy and so do not anticipate returning to the prior, higher level of inventory.

Required: Determine whether Eamon should purchase the new machine and undertake the plant rearrangement.

Answer to Review Problem

The project should be accepted. The incremental investment $26,200 is less than the present value of the future cash flows of $39,320.

Investment Required

	Tax	Cash Flow
Purchase price of new machine		$80,000
Selling price of existing machine	$40,000	(40,000)
Book value of existing machine	55,000	
Loss for tax purposes	$15,000	
Tax saving at 40%	$ 6,000	(6,000)
Cost of plant rearrangement	$12,000	12,000
Tax saving at 40%	$ 4,800	(4,800)
Reduction of working capital requirements		(15,000)
Net required investment		$26,200

Notice that the reduction in working capital is treated as a reduction of the required investment. Because the company does not expect to return to its prior inventory policies at the end of the life of this project, the calculation of cash flows from the project will *not* include a corresponding outflow in the project's final year. We calculate the annual cash flows and present values for this replacement decision using first the incremental approach and then the total-project approach.

Incremental Approach—Annual Cash Flows

	Tax	Cash Flow
Savings in cash operating costs ($18,000 − $3,000)	$15,000	$15,000
Additional depreciation ($16,000 − $11,000)	5,000	
Increase in taxable income	$10,000	
Increased tax at 40%	$ 4,000	4,000
Net annual cash inflow		$11,000
Present value factor for 5-year annuity at 14%		3.433
Present value of annual cash inflows		$37,763
Add present value of after-tax recovery of salvage value		
($5,000 × 60% × .519, factor from Table A)		1,557
Present value of future cash inflows		39,320
Required investment		26,200
Net present value		$13,120

Because depreciation was computed without regard to salvage value, the new asset will have no book value at the end of its life and the proceeds from its sale will be taxable.

Total-Project Approach—Keep Existing Machine

	Tax	Cash Flow
Cash operating costs	$18,000	$18,000
Depreciation	11,000	
Total expenses	$29,000	
Tax savings at 40%	$11,600	11,600
Net cash outflow		6,400
Present value factor for 5-year annuity at 14%		3.433
Present value of annual operating flows		$21,971

Buy New Machine

	Tax	Cash Flow
Cash operating costs	$ 3,000	$ 3,000
Depreciation	16,000	
Total expense	$19,000	
Tax saving at 40%	$ 7,600	7,600
Net cash *inflow*		4,600
Present value factor for 5-year annuity at 14%		3.433
Present value of annual inflows		15,792
Add present value of salvage value (above)		1,557
Net present value of future *inflows*		17,349
Net outlay required for machine		26,200
Net present value of future *outflows*		$ 8,851

The existing machine has a present value of outflows of $21,971, while the new machine has a present value of outflows of $8,851. The NPV in favor of replacing the existing machine is $13,120, as computed under the incremental approach.

Using the new machine will result in new annual cash inflows rather than outflows. This happens because depreciation is so high that the tax saving is greater than the annual cash operating costs. Do *not* conclude that if a replacement asset yields a positive cash flow, it is automatically a wise investment. In the example used here, if the project had not included the expectation of a reduction in inventory the replacement would not be wise.

REVIEW PROBLEM – ACRS

Strock Company is considering investing in a new machine that costs $100,000, has an eight-year expected life, and no salvage value. The machine is expected to save about $35,000 per year in cash operating costs and falls in the 7-Year ACRS class. Cost of capital is 14% and the tax rate is 40%.

Required: Determine the NPV of the investment, discounting the operating flows and the tax shield of depreciation separately. Use Exhibit 9-2 (page 345) to find the present value of the tax shield.

Answer to Review Problem

Operating flows $35,000 × (1 − 0.40) × 4.639	$ 97,419
Tax shield of depreciation ($100,000 × 0.40 × 0.645)	25,800
Total present value	123,219
Less investment	100,000
Net present value	$ 23,219

ASSIGNMENT MATERIAL

Questions for Discussion

9-1 Returns and income If all the forecasts for a capital project turn out as estimated, will the reported annual net income for the project equal the returns used in analyzing the project?

9-2 Factors in capital budgeting Governments frequently take actions that alter the economic climate. For each of the events listed below, state how it would change companies' capital spending, increase, decrease, or have no effect. Comment on what particular kinds of companies would be affected and how. Consider each independently.
1. Gasoline engines are outlawed for automobiles; electric cars only are approved.
2. For some years the price of cotton has been kept artificially high by government price supports. These supports are to be removed.
3. A high tariff is levied on foreign automobiles.
4. Federal corporate income taxes are raised from 34% to 40%.
5. All nations of the world sign a treaty to outlaw war, and they mean it.
6. Persons with low incomes are given cash grants for attending college.

9-3 Capital budgeting – effects of events A capital expenditure proposal for a new machine has been analyzed, based on then available information. How might each of the following events (not anticipated at the time the analysis was done) affect the analysis? Consider each event independently.
1. A proposal to increase taxes on real property (land and buildings) is approved by the voters of the city in which the firm has its manufacturing plant.
2. New tax law provides for a credit against income taxes; the credit is a specified percentage of the investment in new long-lived assets.
3. The *Wall Street Journal* carries a report of a new product that is likely to be a good substitute for the product made by the machine being considered.

Exercises

9-4 Comparison of methods (extension of 8-13) Determine the profitability index for each opportunity in 8-13 and rank the investments based on these values.

9-5 Basic investment analysis Cunningham Company can buy a machine that will reduce annual cash operating costs by $45,000. The cost of the machine is $200,000, and after its useful life of ten years it is expected to have no salvage value. The tax rate is 40% and cost of capital is 12%. The company uses straight-line depreciation.

Required
1. What is the NPV for the project?
2. What savings in annual cash-operating costs make this project return exactly 12%?
3. Assuming that operating savings are $45,000, as stated, what useful life must the machine have to make the investment worthwhile?
4. Suppose the project is not really a new investment but rather a replacement for a machine that has a remaining life of ten years and a current book value of $66,000. The old machine can be sold now for $12,000 and will have no residual value if retained to the end of its useful life. Annual depreciation is $6,600. Should the company replace the old machine with the new one?

9-6 Basic replacement decision Rohn Company manufactures gear assemblies and has the opportunity to replace one of its existing lathes with a new model. The existing lathe has a book value of $20,000 and a market value of $12,000. It has an estimated remaining useful life of four years, at which time it will have no salvage value. The firm uses straight-line depreciation of $5,000 per year on the lathe, and its annual cash operating costs are $75,000.

The new model costs $120,000 and has a four-year estimated life with no salvage value. Its annual cash operating costs are estimated at $32,000. The firm will use straight-line depreciation. The tax rate is 40% and cost of capital is 16%.

Required
1. Determine the investment required to obtain the new lathe.
2. Determine the present value of the net cash flows expected from the investment and the NPV of the investment.
3. Suppose that the new lathe has a salvage value of $5,000. The firm will ignore the salvage value in determining annual depreciation and so will have a gain that will be taxed at 40%. Determine the NPV of the investment.

9-7 Relationships Miller Company invested $180,000 in depreciable assets and earned a 14% internal rate of return. The life of the investment, which had no salvage value, was five years.

Required
1. Determine the net cash flow that Miller earned in each year, assuming that each year's flow was equal.
2. Assume that the tax rate is 40% and that Miller used straight-line depreciation for the investment. Determine the annual pretax cash flow that Miller earned.
3. The investment related to a new product that had a selling price of $10, variable costs of $4, and cash fixed costs of $25,000 per year. Assuming a 40% tax rate and straight-line depreciation, determine how many units had to be sold to earn an 18% internal rate of return.

9-8 Basic working capital investment Managers of DeCosmo Enterprises are considering a new high-performance videotape. They expect to be able to sell 40,000 units annually for the next five years at $10 each. Variable costs are expected to be $3 per unit, annual cash fixed costs $150,000. The product requires machinery costing $150,000 with a five-year life and no salvage value. The firm uses straight-line depreciation. Additionally, accounts receivable will increase about $90,000, inventory about $60,000. These amounts will be returned in full at the end of the five years. The tax rate is 40% and cost of capital is 16%.

Required: Determine the NPV of the investment.

9-9 *Replacement decision – working capital* Reynolds Company has the opportunity to replace a large drill press. Data on both presses appear below.

	Existing Press
Current book value and tax basis	$50,000
Annual cash operating costs	$80,000
Current market value	$30,000
Annual depreciation	$25,000
Remaining useful life	2 years
	Proposed Press
Price	$90,000
Annual cash operating costs	$20,000
Useful life	2 years

The company uses straight-line depreciation. Neither press is expected to have salvage value at the end of its useful life. Using the proposed press will require increased inventories of $40,000. The company has a 20% cost of capital and a 40% income tax rate.

Required: Determine the NPV of the proposed investment.

9-10 *Basic ACRS (continued in 9-27)* ORM Company has the opportunity to buy a machine for $1,500,000. It is expected to save $400,000 annually in cash operating costs over its ten-year life. For tax purposes, the company will use a 5-Year ACRS period. ORM has a 14% cost of capital and a 40% tax rate.

Required: Determine the NPV of the proposed investment.

9-11 *Investing to reduce inventory, JIT* Parkins Mills is a multiproduct manufacturer with a relatively modern factory. Parkins currently maintains considerable inventories of materials, purchased components, and work-in-process as buffer stock to offset slow incoming deliveries and production bottlenecks.

Manufacturing managers have been working on ways to reduce the investment in inventory and have plans that include working with suppliers to have deliveries made right to the production areas instead of to an outside loading dock, revamping the flow of goods through the plant, and coordinating production activities better. Rearranging and outfitting the plant will cost about $8.5 million. The new assets have five-year lives and no salvage value. The company uses straight-line depreciation.

The best estimates are that cash operating costs will increase by about $0.8 million per year if the investment is made, while inventories will be reduced from about $25.7 million to about $1.2 million. The tax rate is 40% and cost of capital is 12%.

Required: Determine the net present value of the proposed investment.

9-12 **Working capital**   The sales manager of Watlin Tools has received an offer from a company overseas. The overseas company offers to buy 10,000 power saws of Watlin's for $20 per unit, well below the usual $35 price. The sales manager believes that Watlin will not lose any domestic sales if it accepts the offer. Unit variable cost of the saw is $18. The only drawback the sales manager sees is that, while Watlin must make the units now, incurring $180,000 in cash costs, the customer will pay for the saws one year from now because of restrictions on taking money out of the foreign country. Watlin's cost of capital is 16%. Ignore taxes.

Required: Determine whether Watlin should accept the order.

9-13 **Mutually exclusive investments**   Miro Manufacturing Company needs additional productive capacity to meet greater demand for its products. Two alternatives are available. The firm can choose either one, but not both.

	Hand-Fed Machine	Semiautomatic Machine
Required investment in depreciable assets	$1,000,000	$2,000,000
Annual cash operating costs	$1,650,000	$1,280,000
Useful life	5 years	5 years

Under either alternative Miro expects additional revenues of $2.1 million. Additional variable costs are included in the cash costs given above. Straight-line depreciation will be used for either investment. Neither is expected to have any salvage value. The tax rate is 40% and cost of capital is 10%.

Required
1. For each alternative, compute: (a) NPV, (b) approximate IRR, (c) PI.
2. Make a recommendation on which alternative should be chosen.

9-14 **Sensitivity analysis (extension of 9-13)**   The cost behavior under each alternative in 9-13 is as follows.

	Hand-Fed Machine	Semiautomatic Machine
Variable cost as percentage of revenue	70%	30%
Fixed cash operating costs	$180,000	$650,000

Required: Determine the volume, in dollar sales, that will bring each alternative to an IRR of 10%. Does this new information affect the decision you made in 9-13?

9-15 **Basic ACRS**   Johnstone Manufacturing Company is considering a new machine that is expected to save $130,000 per year in scrap costs because of greater efficiency. The machine costs $500,000 and has a ten-year life with no expected salvage value. Johnstone has a 16% cost of capital and 40% tax rate.

Required
1. Determine the NPV of the investment using straight-line depreciation.
2. Determine the NPV of the investment using 5-Year ACRS depreciation. Use Exhibit 9-2 to determine the present value of the ACRS tax shield.

9-16 Review of Chapters 8 and 9 Bullmark Company is considering a new product, the Super Bull, that will sell for $8 per unit, have variable costs of $5 per unit, and annual cash fixed costs of $60,000. Equipment required to produce the Super Bull costs $210,000, is expected to last, and be depreciated on a straight-line basis, for six years, with no expected salvage value. Bullmark estimates that sales of the new product will be 50,000 units per year for six years. Bullmark is subject to an income tax rate of 40% and has cost of capital of 14%.

Required
1. What is the expected increase in future annual after-tax cash flows if the project is accepted?
2. What is the NPV of the project?
3. *For this question only,* suppose the project also involves an increase in inventories and receivables totaling $40,000. What is the NPV of the project?
4. What is the PI for the project? (Round to two decimal places.)
5. What is the payback period for the project? (Round to two decimal places.)
6. What is the approximate IRR for the project?
7. What is the total annual contribution margin the firm must show to earn a return equal to the 14% cost of capital?
8. Approximately how long must the life of the project be to earn a return of exactly 16%?

9-17 Relationships Fill in the blanks for each of the following independent cases. There are no salvage values for the investments. Ignore income taxes.

Case	(a) Years of Project Life	(b) Annual Cash Flows	(c) Initial Investment	(d) Cost of Capital	(e) Internal Rate of Return	(f) Net Present Value	(g) Profitability Index
1	15	$40,000	$____	__%	14%	$____	1.109
2	8	$____	$238,920	18%	16%	$____	____
3	12	$____	$215,292	16%	__%	$36,762	____
4	__	$80,000	$361,600	12%	__%	$____	1.25

9-18 Asset acquisition and ACRS Peyton Company is considering a new asset that costs $800,000 and that its managers expect to reduce cash operating costs by $250,000 per year over its ten-year estimated life. The asset qualifies for 5-Year recovery under ACRS. Cost of capital is 16% and the tax rate is 40%.

Required: Determine the NPV of the investment.

Problems

9-19   **Working capital investment**   The managers of Rawson-Harmon Company, a wholesaler of paper products, have been approached by managers of Clark Paper Products Company. Clark has offered Rawson-Harmon exclusive rights to distribute its products in the Denver area. The contract runs for three years, after which time either company can terminate the arrangement.

Rawson-Harmon's managers expect revenue from Clark's products to be about $200,000 per month, with variable costs (all cost of goods sold) about 85% of revenue. Incremental monthly fixed costs should be about $8,000. Additionally, Rawson-Harmon must carry inventory approximating a two-month supply and accounts receivable of about three months' sales. Rawson-Harmon will pay cash on delivery of Clark's products. Cost of capital is 20%. Ignore taxes.

Required: Determine whether Rawson-Harmon should accept Clark's offer.

9-20   **Replacement decision**   Charles Company, a maker of gardening products, is considering replacing a machine. Charles uses straight-line depreciation, has a 20% cost of capital, and a 40% income tax rate. Neither machine is expected to have salvage value at the end of its useful life. If the firm makes the replacement it will finance the investment with debt bearing 10% interest. The existing machine could be sold now for $25,000.

Existing Machine	
Book value	$60,000
Remaining useful life	3 years
Annual cash operating costs	$80,000
Annual depreciation	$20,000 each of next 3 years
Proposed Machine	
Price	$150,000
Useful life	3 years
Annual cash operating costs	$20,000

Required: Determine the NPV of the proposed investment.

9-21   **Comparison of alternatives**   Stanley Company must choose between two machines that will perform an essential function. Machine A costs $40,000, has a ten-year life with no salvage value, and costs $12,000 per year to operate (cash costs). Machine B costs $80,000, has a ten-year life with no salvage value, and costs $3,000 per year to operate. The tax rate is 40% and cost of capital is 10%. Straight-line depreciation will be used for either machine.

Required: Determine which machine should be bought and explain your answer.

9-22   **Unit costs**   Ramor Company manufactures running shoes. Its managers are considering entering the low-priced market and are looking at several alternatives. The model they wish to introduce will, they believe, sell 200,000 pairs annually at $22. Estimates of unit costs for two alternative production methods are as follows:

	Use Existing Facilities	Buy New Machinery
Materials	$ 3.50	$ 3.40
Direct labor	7.50	6.45
Variable overhead	2.50	2.15
Fixed overhead	3.75	4.225
Total unit costs	$17.25	$16.225

Company policy is to charge each product with both fixed and variable overhead. The basic charge for fixed overhead is $0.50 per direct labor dollar. The amount of fixed overhead shown for the new machinery includes $1.00 per unit for depreciation of $200,000 per year ($600,000 cost) on the new machinery, which has a three-year life. Thus, the $4.225 is $1.00 plus the normal overhead charge of $0.50 times $6.45 direct labor cost. One of the managers points out that the $1.025 difference in unit cost works out to $205,000 per year, a significant saving. He also points out that the after-tax saving is $123,000 (the tax rate is 40%), which gives a rate of return of 41% on the average investment of $300,000. Cost of capital is 18%.

Required
1. Determine the NPV of the investment.
2. Determine the approximate IRR on the investment.

9-23 **JIT, Inventory**   The Anderson Plant of Benson Industries is moving toward JIT principles. So far it has been setting up manufacturing cells and smoothing the flow of work. The next phase involves a multitude of changes related to reducing the number of vendors, ensuring the quality of the parts provided by the remaining vendors, opening walls so that trucks can make deliveries straight to the cell where the parts are used, and teaching new skills to workers.

All of these activities are estimated to cost about $4.5 million, of which $3.0 million can be expensed immediately for income tax purposes. The remaining $1.5 million is for changes in physical plant that must be depreciated over the next 10 years, using the straight-line method. The estimated annual cash savings before taxes over the next ten years are $200,000. Based on conversations with other plant managers, the Anderson Plant manager expects inventory to fall to about $80,000 from the current $2.6 million. The tax rate is 40% and cost of capital is 12%.

Required: Determine the net present value of the investment.

9-24 **Pollution control and capital budgeting**   Craft Paper Company operates a plant that produces a great deal of air pollution. The local government has ordered that the polluting be stopped or the plant will be closed. Craft does not wish to close the plant and so has sought to find satisfactory ways to remove pollutants. Two alternatives have been found, both of which will reduce the outflow of pollutants to levels satisfactory to the government. One, called Entrol, costs $1,000,000, has a ten-year life with no salvage value, and has annual cash operating costs of $180,000. The other, Polltrol, costs $2,000,000, has a ten-year life with no salvage value, and has cash operating costs of $210,000 annually. However, Polltrol compresses the particles it removes into solid blocks of material that can be sold to chemical companies. Annual sales of the material are estimated at $250,000.

Either device will be depreciated on a straight-line basis. Cost of capital is 16% and the tax rate is 40%.

Required: Determine which device the firm should buy.

9-25 ***Replacement decision and sensitivity analysis*** Hutson Company owns data processing equipment that cost $80,000 five years ago, now has a book value of $40,000, and a market value of $12,000. The equipment costs $35,000 per year to operate and will have no value at the end of five more years.

Hutson can buy equipment that costs $65,000, will last five years with no salvage value, and cost $18,000 per year to operate. It performs the same functions as the existing equipment.

The firm has a cost of capital of 14%. Ignore income taxes.

Required
1. Determine whether the new equipment should be purchased.
2. Determine the approximate IRR on the investment.
3. Suppose that the data processing manager knows that the new machine is more efficient than the old, but not how much more. What annual cash savings are necessary for the firm to earn 14%?
4. Suppose that the estimate of annual cash flows is reliable, but that the useful life of the new equipment is in question. About how long must the new equipment last in order that the firm earn 14%?

9-26 ***Alternative production method*** Lizmith Co. is considering a change in its manufacturing process, from a labor-intensive to a highly automated method. Information about the current method appears below.

Book value of existing equipment	$20,000
Remaining useful life of existing equipment	5 years
Annual tax depreciation of existing equipment	$ 4,000
Current market value of existing equipment	$25,000
Annual cash operating costs, existing method	$64,000

The alternative method requires a machine that costs $100,000 and has a useful life of five years with no salvage value. The new machine can accomplish the same task with annual cash operating costs of $40,000. Straight-line depreciation will be used for tax purposes for the new machine. The tax rate is 40% and cost of capital is 12%.

Required
1. What is the net investment associated with acquiring the new equipment?
2. What is the total present value of the future after-tax cash flows of a *switch* to the new equipment? Is the future cash flow negative or positive?
3. What is the NPV of the investment?

9-27 ***Sensitivity analysis and ACRS (extension of 9-10)*** The managers of ORM Company are not sure of the annual savings in cash operating costs that the machine will generate. One manager has asked how low the savings could be and the company still earn the 14% target rate of return.

Required: Determine the annual cash-operating savings that yield a 14% return.

9-28 **Sensitivity analysis**   The managers of Boston Products Company have been trying to decide whether or not to introduce a new deluxe birdfeeder. They expect it to sell for $30 and to have unit variable costs of $14. Fixed costs requiring cash disbursements should be about $500,000 per year. The feeder also requires machinery costing $400,000 with a four-year life and no salvage value. The company uses straight-line depreciation. Cost of capital is 16%.

The one point of which the managers are unsure is the annual unit volume. Estimates made by individual managers range from 40,000 to 65,000 units.

Required
1. Ignoring income taxes, determine the number of feeders per year the company must sell to make the investment yield just 16%.
2. Redo item 1 assuming a 40% income tax rate.

9-29 **Determining required cost savings**   Grunch Company can buy a machine that will reduce variable production costs of a product that sells 10,000 units annually. The machine costs $80,000, has no salvage value, and should last for five years. Annual fixed operating costs requiring cash are $20,000. Cost of capital is 16%.

Required
1. Ignoring taxes, what reduction in unit variable production costs is necessary to make the investment desirable?
2. Answer item 1 assuming a tax rate of 40% and straight-line depreciation.
3. Suppose now that the machine will reduce unit variable production costs by $4, but that annual volume is in doubt. What annual volume is needed to make the investment desirable? Consider income taxes.

9-30 **Benefit/cost analysis**   The Department of Health has made studies regarding treatment for two diseases, a type of kidney disease and a type of heart disease. The following data have been assembled.

	Kidney Disease	Heart Disease
Cost to save one life	$100,000	$150,000
Average age of victim at death	40 years	50 years
Average annual income of victims	$ 15,000	$ 25,000

The heart disease appears to be caused partly by stresses that affect higher-income people, which accounts in part for the difference in incomes between the two types of victims.

The department believes that a discount rate of 10% is appropriate. It also assumes that a person will work until age 70 (30 additional years for persons cured of kidney disease, 20 for those cured of heart disease).

Required
1. Compute the NPV of saving a single life from each disease. The cost to save the life is incurred immediately, and the annual incomes are assumed to be received at the ends of years.
2. Suppose that a lack of trained personnel makes it impossible to pursue treatment for both diseases. Whichever disease is selected for treatment, the same amount will be spent. Which disease do you prefer to see treated and why?

9-31 *Increased sales and working capital* Baker Company now makes several products in a labor-intensive fashion. The products average $4.50 in variable costs, of which labor is $2.25. Fixed costs are $100,000 annually. The firm has had difficulty in expanding production to meet increased demand and is considering a large machine that will enable a production increase to 105,000 with the same size work force. Sales are currently 80,000 units at $8 average selling price. The firm expects to sell all its production at $7 per unit if the machine is bought.

   Variable costs per unit other than labor will remain the same, and fixed costs will increase by the amount of depreciation on the new machine. The machine costs $80,000 and has a useful life of ten years. There will be increased working capital requirements of $80,000. Straight-line depreciation will be used for tax purposes; the tax rate is 40% and cost of capital is 14%.

Required: Determine whether Baker should buy the machine.

9-32 *Sensitivity analysis (extension of 8-32)* The managers of Pitcairn Company believe that volume will be 250,000 pairs, but are concerned about that estimate. They wish to know how many pairs of socks they must sell to earn an IRR of 14%.

Required
1. Determine the unit volume that will yield an IRR of 14%.
2. How does the calculation for item 1 change your attitude about the investment from your solution to 8-32?

9-33 *Backing a play* Kent Clark, a famous playwright, wants your company to back his forthcoming play, *I'll Fly Tomorrow*. He has prepared the following analysis.

Investment:	
Sets and other depreciable assets (straight-line basis)	$300,000
Working capital	100,000
Total investment	$400,000
Annual gross receipts, expected to continue for 4 years	$900,000
Annual salaries of actors and other personnel	$400,000
Rent, $20,000 + 5% of gross receipts	
Royalty to Clark, 10% of gross receipts	
Other cash expenses	$140,000

Your company has a cost of capital of 14% and a tax rate of 40%.

Required
1. Should your firm back the play on the basis of the information given?
2. At what level of annual gross receipts does the play yield a 14% IRR?

9-34 *Book values and tax bases* Your company owns two machines that are identical in all respects except that they have different book values and tax bases because of the use of different useful lives and methods of depreciation for book and tax purposes. Data summarizing the two machines follow.

	Machine A	Machine B
Net book value	$20,000	$40,000
Tax basis	$ 0	$30,000

The firm can depreciate $15,000 in each of the next two years for machine B for income taxes. It has no future tax depreciation available for machine A.

Your company needs only one machine now, and its managers are deciding which one to sell. Either machine will sell for $15,000. One manager has argued for the sale of machine A because it will then show a loss of only $5,000 ($15,000 − $20,000) while selling machine B gives a $25,000 loss ($15,000 − $40,000). The company has cost of capital of 20% and is in the 40% tax bracket.

Required: Use the NPV approach to determine which machine the firm should sell.

9-35   **Replacement decision**   The management of Bettel Metals Inc. is considering a new machine. The new machine is more efficient than the one currently in use and would save the firm $6,000 annually because of greater operating speed. To keep the old machine operating at the present level of efficiency requires immediate repairs costing $5,000. The repair cost is tax deductible this year. Annual depreciation on the old machine, which is expected to last ten years, is $1,800. No scrap value is expected at that time.

The new machine costs $37,300, including freight and installation charges. It has an expected useful life of ten years and no expected scrap value. Straight-line depreciation would be used on the new machine. The old machine has a book value of $18,000 and a market value of $12,000. The tax rate is 40%.

Required
1. Compute the net cash outlay if the new machine is purchased.
2. Evaluate the proposal, assuming a minimum required rate of return of 10%.

9-36   **Buying an athletic team**   A large portion of the purchase price of an athletic team is allocated to the value of the contracts of the players. This amount can be amortized for income tax purposes. Some have argued that the principal value of a franchise is the monopoly right to operate and earn revenues from television, ticket sales, and so on. The amount allocated to the monopoly right is not amortizable for tax purposes, much as the cost of land is not depreciable.

Suppose that you are in the 28% tax bracket and are considering buying the Midlands Maulers of the Transam Football League. You expect the operations of the team to generate pretax cash inflows of $4,000,000 annually. You also expect the league to fold in ten years, at which time your investment will be worthless. Your discount rate is 14%.

Required
1. Determine the maximum that you are willing to pay for the team assuming that the investment can be amortized evenly over ten years for tax purposes.
2. Determine the maximum that you are willing to pay for the team if you could not amortize the cost. (You then have a lump-sum tax deduction at the end of year 10 equal to your original investment.)

9-37   **Investing in quality, JIT**   Roush, Inc. manufactures a variety of products in a relatively old plant. Parts of the manufacturing process are very outmoded and the quality of the output is slipping. The company is coming to be viewed as a low-quality producer, which is expected to affect future sales adversely. The manufacturing managers have been looking at new machinery and equipment that would increase quality to the point where the company could enjoy a favorable reputation. They have also been looking at employing JIT principles. Outfitting the plant for the new machinery and to accommodate JIT will cost about $5.5 million. The entire investment can be depreciated over its ten-year useful life. It has no salvage value. The company uses straight-line depreciation. The new machinery will not affect variable costs, but will increase cash fixed costs by $0.8 million per year.

The managers do not expect sales to increase markedly if they fail to make the investment. Rather, they expect sales to fall by about $2 million per year if they do not make the investment. The contribution margin ratio is about 60% on the normal product mix. The managers also expect to reduce inventory by $4.4 million if they make the investment. The tax rate is 40% and cost of capital is 12%.

Required: Determine the net present value of the proposed investment.

9-38 ***Lease/purchase and obsolescence***   Some companies lease, rather than purchase, machinery and equipment. One reason is that leasing makes it easier to acquire newer equipment if technological progress is rapid. The user is usually not committed for as long a period in a lease as it is if the equipment were purchased. One type of equipment that is leased a great deal is computer hardware.

The controller of Stockton Company has been analyzing the firm's policy regarding computers, which are now being leased on a one-year basis. She is convinced that the firm is acting unwisely and should buy the equipment. Selected data related to currently leased equipment are as follows.

Cost of equipment	$1,500,000
Annual lease payment	$ 400,000
Physical life of computer	10 years
Tax rate	40%

Based upon these data, the controller calculates an NPV of purchasing the equipment at $64,800, using straight-line depreciation for tax purposes and a 14% discount rate. (The lease payments are fully deductible for tax purposes.)

The director of the computer center argues that the controller has not considered that Stockton has had to upgrade its equipment every three or four years, leasing newer, faster computers because of growth in their use. Anticipating that the growth will continue, the director suggests that a four-year economic life be used, rather than the ten-year physical life. He believes that purchased equipment could be sold at the end of four years for 20% of its purchase price.

Required
1. Verify the controller's computation of the NPV of purchasing the computer.
2. Prepare a new analysis based on the director's comments. Equipment should be depreciated down to salvage value over four years (no gain or loss on disposal).

9-39 ***Attracting industry***   Minerla is a small town with little industry and high unemployment. The mayor and members of the town council have been trying to interest businesses in locating factories in Minerla. Newman Industries has agreed to the following proposal of the town government. The town will build a $4,000,000 plant to Newman's specifications and rent it to Newman for its estimated useful life of 20 years at $100,000 per year provided that Newman employs at least 600 currently unemployed citizens of Minerla.

An economist from the state university has projected the following annual results if the plant is built.

Increases in retail sales in Minerla	$6,000,000
Increase in property tax base	$4,400,000

The mayor expects some increases in the cost of town government to result from the additional employees that Newman would transfer to the new factory.

Additional fire and police protection	$30,000
Additional school costs	50,000
Additional general governmental costs	15,000
Total additional annual costs	$95,000

The town levies a 1% tax on all retail sales and taxes property at a rate of $80 per $1,000. The relevant discount rate is 9%.

The state spends about $2,000 per year in direct support for each unemployed person. The economist said that total unemployment is likely to fall by about 1,500 persons because the factory would help to create other jobs.

The council feels that the factory should be built provided that the benefits to the town government do not exceed the costs.

Required
1. Determine whether the additional receipts to the town, less the additional costs, justify the building of the factory.
2. Assuming that your answer to item 1 is no, list and discuss other factors that might be considered and other actions that might be taken.

9-40 **Modification of equipment** Pride Company has several machines that have been used to make a product that the firm has phased out of its operations. The equipment has a book value of $600,000 and remaining useful life of four years. Depreciation is being taken using the straight-line method at $150,000 per year. No salvage value is expected at the end of the useful life.

Pride can sell the equipment for $320,000 now. The equipment can also be modified to produce another product at a cost of $400,000. The modifications will not affect the useful lives or salvage value and will be depreciated using the straight-line method. If the firm does not modify the existing equipment, it will have to buy new equipment at a cost of $800,000. The new equipment also has a useful life of four years with no salvage value, and would be depreciated using the straight-line method. The product to be made with the new equipment or modified existing equipment is essential to Pride's product line.

Cash operating costs of new equipment are $50,000 per year less than with the existing equipment. Cost of capital is 16% and the tax rate is 40%.

Required: Determine what Pride should do.

9-41 **Dropping a product** Stracke Company makes a variety of products in several factories throughout the country. The sales manager is unhappy with the results shown by Quickclean, a spray cleaner for household use. Quickclean is made in only one factory. A typical income statement appears on page 366.

Sales	$4,400,000
Variable costs	3,800,000
Contribution margin	600,000
Fixed costs	775,000
Loss	($ 175,000)

The production manager tells the sales manager that about $520,000 of the fixed costs shown above require cash disbursements. These are all avoidable. The remaining $255,000 in fixed costs consists of $100,000 in depreciation on equipment used only to make Quickclean and $155,000 in allocated costs. The equipment used to make Quickclean has a useful life of five more years, and no salvage value is expected at the end of five years. The book value is $500,000 and straight-line depreciation is being used.

Stracke has a cost of capital of 16% and the tax rate is 40%.

Required
1. Assume that the machinery used to make Quickclean has no resale value. If the product is dropped, the machinery will be scrapped. The loss is immediately tax deductible. Determine whether Quickclean should be dropped.
2. Assume that the machinery could be sold for $180,000. Redo item 1.

9-42 New product — complementary effects Ralph Berger, general manager of the McKeown Division of Standard Enterprises, Inc., is considering a new product. It will sell for $20 per unit and have variable costs of $9. Volume is estimated at 120,000 units per year. Fixed costs requiring cash disbursements will increase by $300,000 annually, mainly in connection with operating machinery that would be purchased for $2,000,000. The machinery has a useful life of ten years with no salvage value, and would be depreciated using the straight-line method.

The new product would be made in a section of the factory that is physically separate from the rest of the factory and is now leased to another firm for $120,000 per year. The other firm has expressed an interest in renewing the lease, which expires this month, for an additional ten years.

Berger expects inventories to increase by $500,000 if the new product is brought out. He also expects customers to pay for their purchases two months after purchase, but he is uncertain how to consider these factors.

Cost of capital is 20% and the tax rate is 40%.

Required
1. Determine whether the new product should be introduced.
2. Suppose that if the new product were brought out, the sales of an existing product would increase by 30,000 units per year. The existing product sells for $10 and has variable costs of $6. The increase in sales of this product will lead to increases in inventories and receivables of $60,000. Determine whether the new product should be brought out.

9-43 Sensitivity analysis Carter Pen Company makes several models of ballpoint and soft-tip pens. One model currently made is the Scribbler, which has been moderately successful. The machinery used to make the Scribbler requires replacement, and the firm is trying to decide whether to continue its manufacture.

The alternative to continuing to produce the Scribbler is to bring out a more expensive soft-tip pen, the Brush. Carter's managers believe that if both pens were produced, they would take sales from each other and so only one should be produced. Data on the two products are as follows.

	Scribbler	Brush
Selling price	$0.80	$2.20
Variable costs	$0.40	$0.90
Additional annual cash fixed costs	$300,000	$ 800,000
Required investment, all depreciable assets	$800,000	$1,500,000
Expected annual sales, in units	2,000,000	1,250,000

Neither investment will have salvage value at the end of the useful life, which is four years for both. Straight-line depreciation will be used for tax purposes. The tax rate is 40% and cost of capital is 16%.

Required
1. Use the NPV criterion to determine which product should be made.
2. The president is concerned about the effects on profitability of declines in volume from the expected figures. Determine the unit volume for each product that will give a 16% return. Determine the percentage decline from the original estimates that each volume represents. Does the new information affect your decision in item 1?

9-44 Closing a plant — externalities Fisher Manufacturing Company operates a plant in Vesalia, a small city on the Platte River. The firm has been notified that it must install pollution control equipment at the plant, at a cost of $4,000,000, or else close the plant. The plant employs 400 people, virtually all of whom will lose their jobs if the plant were to close. Fisher will make a lump-sum payment of $80,000 to the people put out of jobs if the plant closes.

A buyer is willing to purchase the plant for $400,000, which equals its book value. Fisher could shift production to the Montclair plant if it closed the Vesalia plant, with no increase in total cash production costs. (The increase in Montclair's cash production costs equals the cash operating costs of the Vasalia plant.) However, shipping costs will increase by $900,000 annually because the Montclair plant is much farther away from customers than the Vesalia plant.

The new equipment has a ten-year useful life with no salvage value. Straight-line depreciation is used for tax purposes.

The tax rate is 40% and cost of capital is 14%.

Required
1. Considering only monetary factors, determine whether Fisher should install the pollution control equipment or close the plant.
2. What other factors might be considered by those interested in the decision?

Cases

9-45 Replacement decision, ACRS (CMA adapted) Lamb Company manufactures several lines of machine products. One valve stem requires special tools that must soon be replaced. The tools are fully depreciated and have no resale value. Management has decided that the only alternative to replacing these tools is to buy the stem from an outside supplier at $20 per unit.

Lamb has been using 80,000 stems over the past few years and this volume is expected to continue, although there could be some decline over the next few years. Cost records show the following at 80,000 units.

Material	$ 3.80
Labor	3.70
Variable overhead	2.20
Fixed overhead	4.50
Total unit cost	$14.20

Replacing the specialized tools will cost $2,500,000. The new tools have a life of eight years and $100,000 residual value. Lamb will use ACRS. The tools qualify for a five-year recovery period. Cost of capital is 12%, the tax rate is 40%.

Lamb's managers have had discussions with the toolmaker's sales engineers and with another manufacturer that uses similar tools. Indications are that labor and variable overhead will drop, but that material cost will increase because the new tools require higher-quality material than the ones currently used. The best estimates appear below.

Material	$ 4.50
Labor	3.00
Variable overhead	1.80
Fixed overhead	5.00
Total unit cost	$14.30

Cash fixed costs associated with the new tools are $100,000 per year; with the existing tools these costs are $50,000 per year. There will be no such costs if Lamb buys the stem from the outside supplier.

Required
1. Determine whether Lamb should buy the stem or manufacture it using the new tools.
2. Lamb's managers are concerned about making such a large investment when there is a possibility that the volume of the part might drop. Determine the volume of parts that makes Lamb indifferent between making it and buying it.

9-46   Evaluating an investment proposal   Your new assistant has just brought you the following analysis of an investment you are considering. The investment relates to a new manufacturing process for making one of the firm's major products.

Required Investment	
New machinery (10-year life, no salvage value)	$350,000
Research and development	60,000
Administrative time	10,000
Total investment	$420,000

Annual Cash Flows (10 Years)	
Savings in cost over old process:	
Labor	$ 75,000
Materials	80,000
Variable overhead	40,000
Depreciation	(35,000)
Total operating savings	160,000
Less: Interest on debt to finance investment	35,000
Net savings before taxes	125,000
Less: Income taxes at 40% rate	50,000
Net cash flow after taxes	$ 75,000

Your assistant tells you that the new machinery would replace old machinery that has a ten-year remaining useful life with no salvage value. The old machinery will be scrapped if the new machinery is bought, and the salvage value equals the cost of having it removed. The old machinery has a book value of $110,000. The company uses straight-line depreciation for all machinery.

Your assistant also tells you that the listed costs for research and development and for administrative time relate solely to this project and contain no allocations. The costs have been incurred already, so their amounts are certain. The item in the analysis for interest on debt is for $350,000 at 10%, which will be borrowed if the new machinery is acquired.

Based on his analysis and the 16% cost of capital, he recommends that the project be rejected.

Required: Determine whether the investment should be made.

9-47 *Alternative uses of assets (AICPA adapted)* Miller Manufacturing Company has been producing toasters and blenders in its Syracuse plant for several years. The rent for the Syracuse factory building is $80,000 per year. When the lease expires at the end of four years, Miller intends to cease operations at that location and scrap the equipment.

Blender production is approximately 50,000 per year and the company expects to continue production at that level. However, because of intense competition and price erosion, the company has decided to stop making toasters.

Two areas of the Syracuse plant, making up about 30% of the total floor space, are devoted to toasters. The equipment used to make toasters has a book value of $140,000 and is depreciated at $35,000 per year. The company has received an offer of $20,000 for all the equipment now used in toaster production, and the buyer is not interested in anything less than all of it. If the equipment were sold, the space now used for toaster production could be subleased for $12,000 per year.

Because the production of blenders is to be continued, the production manager was asked if he needed the space and/or equipment now devoted to toaster production. He said that though he had no need for additional productive capacity for tasks currently undertaken at the plant, he is interested in using the space and equipment to manufacture a blender part now being purchased from an outside firm. The part is a blade assembly that the firm purchases for $5. The contract with the vendor runs for four more years and requires that Miller buy at least 5,000 assemblies per year.

Either of the two areas now used for toaster production could be converted to produce the blade assemblies. The production manager estimates the variable cost to produce an assembly at $3.60 and no additional fixed costs requiring cash would be incurred. However, the equipment now used has to be converted. He estimates the cost at $40,000 to convert enough of the equipment to make 35,000 assemblies per year and $80,000 to convert enough to make 60,000 assemblies. Because the prospective buyer of the equipment wants all or none of it, conversion of any of it means the company must forego the sale.

The company's tax rate is 40% and its cost of capital is 14%. Straight-line depreciation will be used on costs of converting equipment.

Required: Determine the best course of action.

9-48 ***Mutually exclusive investments***   Seagle Company requires machinery for an essential task that will be carried out for the next ten years. Two available machines meet the firm's needs.

	Rapidgo 350	Rapidgo 600
Purchase cost	$50,000	$90,000
Annual operating expenses, exclusive of depreciation	$12,000	$15,000
Useful life	5 years	10 years

Either machine will be depreciated using the straight-line method. The firm expects to have to pay $60,000 to replace the Rapidgo 350 at the end of five years, if that machine is selected. The other data applicable to the Rapidgo 350 given above are applicable to the replacement model as well.

Cost of capital is 16% and the tax rate is 40%.

Required: Determine the course of action the firm should take.

9-49 ***Expanding a factory***   Fisher Company needs more space and machinery to increase production. The production manager and president have been trying to decide which of two plans to accept.

	Plan A	Plan B
Investment required	$4,000,000	$5,500,000
Additional fixed cash operating costs per year	$ 600,000	$ 800,000
Additional capacity in machine-hours per year	200,000	280,000

The company uses straight-line depreciation. No salvage value is expected for either investment at the end of their ten-year useful lives.

The production manager prefers Plan B because the cost per machine-hour and investment per machine-hour are lower than those for Plan A. The president is unsure about this and asks the sales manager whether the capacity would be fully utilized. The sales manager provides the following data.

	Product		
	101-X	201-X	305-X
Potential increased sales, in units	30,000	40,000	30,000
Contribution margin per unit	$18	$24	$40
Machine-hours required per unit	2	4	5

Fisher pays income taxes at a 40% rate and has cost of capital of 12%.

Required: Determine which, if either, expansion plan should be accepted and how the increased capacity should be used (that is, how much of each product should be made).

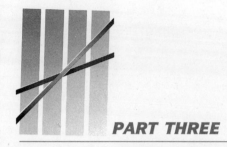

CONTROL AND PERFORMANCE EVALUATION

Part Three concentrates on the management functions of control and performance evaluation. To perform these functions more effectively, managers apply the principles and techniques of responsibility accounting. An essential step in the development of a responsibility accounting system is fixing responsibility for each cost. Fixing responsibility for costs is also important to derive the fullest advantage from comprehensive budgeting. In this part, the emphasis shifts from planning to control, and to evaluating actual results in relation to planned or budgeted results.

Human behavior and the ways in which accounting methods encourage particular kinds of behavior are treated extensively in the three chapters in this part. The major thrust of responsibility accounting is behavioral; the critical factor in its success is the extent to which the system encourages or discourages behavior consistent with the organization's best interests.

CHAPTER *10*

RESPONSIBILITY ACCOUNTING

Thus far we have concentrated on applying the concepts of managerial accounting to the management functions of planning and decision making. We now look more closely at managerial control, particularly performance evaluation. Managers exercise control through a management control system, a set of policies and procedures used to determine whether or not operations are going as planned, and if not, to suggest corrective action. **Responsibility accounting** is the gathering and reporting of information that is used to control operations and evaluate performance. The responsibility accounting system is the formal, financial communication system within the overall management control system.

Nonquantifiable factors are even more important to effective control and evaluation than they are to planning and decision making. Of particular concern is the potential for accounting reports to influence the actions of managers. The problem of cost allocation that we worked with in Chapters 5, 8, and 9 is also relevant here. We shall see later that there *are* good reasons for allocating costs— to encourage particular kinds of behavior and to assist in evaluating performance. But there are also good reasons *not* to allocate costs, so that the issue is less clear than it was in decision making, where allocation was undesirable.

GOAL CONGRUENCE AND MOTIVATION

Managers and other employees work to achieve their own goals, which can include salary, promotion, and recognition. In pursuit of those goals, they attempt to perform well on the measures by which they expect to be evaluated. The important question is whether, in so doing, they are also acting to achieve the goals of the firm. A major objective of management control is to encourage **goal congruence,** where people work to achieve the goals of the firm as *well* as their own goals. People must have *incentives* to work toward the firm's goals. The responsibility accounting system should assist managers in providing those incentives. Because reports generated by the responsibility accounting system influence behavior, they must be carefully designed and thoroughly understood.

A good responsibility accounting system reports only on factors that managers can, in a broad sense, control. Thus, uncontrollable costs either should not appear in performance reports or should be carefully segregated and labeled. Moreover, the system should give sufficient feedback for the manager to be aware of what has been happening, what trends might be expected, and, to the extent possible, why things happened the way they did.

Most of the major problems in developing an effective responsibility accounting system are behavioral. Managers must trust the system; they must believe that it accurately depicts performance. They must also believe the system is fair. Accordingly, the evaluation system should use performance evaluation criteria that are under the control of the managers. But if the system is to perform its function for the company as a whole, the feedback provided to the managers and the criteria used to evaluate them should also motivate them to act in such a way as to advance the goals of the firm.

The first step in implementing responsibility accounting is to establish responsibility centers.

RESPONSIBILITY CENTERS

To be held accountable for performance, managers must have clearly defined areas of responsibility—activities they control. A **responsibility center** is, as the words imply, an activity, such as a department, over which a manager exercises responsibility. It might appear to be relatively easy to identify activities with specific managers. A plant manager is in charge of a plant and is usually responsible for producing budgeted quantities of specific products within budgeted cost limits. A sales manager is responsible for getting orders from customers, and so on. In many cases, however, it is no simple task to isolate the responsibilities of managers.

The performance of one manager can be affected by the performance of others. The best salespeople in the world cannot sell poorly made products; by the same token, no production manager can minimize costs if production schedules change daily to accommodate rush orders. Such interdependencies cannot be eliminated entirely, but their effects can be minimized by careful selection of responsibility centers, appropriate use of rewards and penalties, and proper use of performance reports by managers who understand the information that they receive.

For example, to reduce the potential for conflict between sales and production because of the quality of the output produced, the production manager should be responsible for the quality of output as well as for production costs. Each situation where conflicts might arise must be considered by itself and appropriate procedures and responsibilities assigned to the managers potentially in conflict; there are few general rules to which one can turn for guidance.

There are three types of responsibility centers: cost centers, profit centers, and investment centers. The type of responsibility center depends on the breadth of control of the manager. Each type is considered in detail in this and the following chapter.

Cost Centers

A **cost center** is a segment whose manager is responsible for costs but not for revenues. A cost center can be relatively small, like a single department with a few people, but can also be quite large, such as an entire factory or the administrative area for a large firm. Some cost centers are composed of a number of smaller cost centers. For example, a factory may be segmented into many work stations, each of which is a cost center with several stations combined into departments that are also cost centers.

Profit Centers and Investment Centers

A **profit center** is a segment whose manager is responsible for both revenues and costs. For such a center, a type of profit figure is used to measure performance. In some cases, only direct costs are used to determine the center's profit figure; in others, the profit calculation includes some (or all) indirect costs. An **investment center** is a segment where the manager controls revenues, costs, and investment in assets. For such a center, it is possible to calculate return on investment as well as profit. In practice, both types of segments are often referred to as profit centers. Later in this chapter, and in parts of Chapter 11, we discuss various questions about how profit and investment might be measured.

Large companies usually have many profit/investment centers. Typically, managers of such segments have wider responsibilities than do managers of cost centers. Accordingly, managers of profit centers act, and are evaluated, much as if they were chief executives of autonomous companies.

A major reason for using profit and investment centers is that profit and return on investment are more comprehensive measures of success than is cost. To survive, a company must earn profits, not just control costs. Holding managers responsible for revenues and investment, as well as costs, permits a pinpointing of responsibility that is not possible when different managers are responsible for revenues, costs, and investment. Consider a company that is not earning satisfactory profits and does not use profit centers. Marketing managers, responsible only for revenue, can claim that manufacturing costs are too high. Production managers, responsible only for costs, can say that sales are too low. Who is right? If a manager is responsible for revenues *and* costs, he or she must generate sales *and* control costs, and it is easier to determine who is responsible for the poor profitability.

The idea that profit is a more comprehensive measure of performance than is cost has led some firms to create *artificial profit centers,* segments that do not deal with outsiders, but rather "sell" goods or services within the company. For instance, a data processing department might "charge" the segments that use its services. The department could then have an income statement, instead of just a statement of costs. The department's failure to show a profit—or to earn a satisfactory return on its investment—*might* indicate that it is inefficient. (A loss might even indicate that the company would be better off to buy the services from an outside company.) We emphasize *might* because factors outside the control of the data processing manager could affect the results and cause the department to appear inefficient. A common example of such a confounding factor occurs when a growing company acquires more computing equipment and personnel than it currently needs because of higher expected use in the future. (Current costs are higher than necessary, but it might have been a wise decision to acquire the higher capacity in anticipation of increased use in the future.) Decisions about whether to acquire services from inside or outside the company are make-or-buy decisions like those discussed in Chapters 5 and 8. Therefore, deciding whether to have a data processing department or to buy services from another company requires considering only incremental costs. We return to the question of charging users for services later in this chapter.

Criteria for Evaluation

Selecting criteria to measure and evaluate performance is important because the criteria influence managers' actions. The most common deficiencies in performance measurement are (1) using a *single* measure that emphasizes only one objective of the organization and (2) using measures that either misrepresent or fail to reflect the organization's objectives.

Managers want a single, comprehensive measure of performance, but the search for such a measure is seldom successful. Consider an example reported from the Soviet Union. Reportedly, the government was unhappy with the output of nails and decided to evaluate managers of nail factories by the weight of the nails produced. The managers could produce much greater weight by making only large spikes, and they did. Once the government saw that its performance measure was not working, it changed the basis of evaluation to the number of nails produced—and the factories began to pour out carpet tacks and small brads.

Although profit is a common measure of performance, it too can suffer from overemphasis. For example, managers *know* that emphasizing profits in the current period might be detrimental to profits in future periods. But a responsibility accounting system that emphasizes short-run profits can tempt managers to increase short-run profits at the expense of the long run. In recent years, many commentators have argued that U.S. companies concentrate too much on the short term. They have suggested that the failure to take a longer-term view was the principal factor in making U.S. businesses less competitive in world markets than, say, the Japanese.

Whether dealing with a cost, profit, or investment center, performance can only be evaluated by comparing results *with* something. Probably the best way to encourage managers to act in the firm's best interests is to measure their performance in relation to *budgeted* results. Managers of production departments are evaluated on whether they produce budgeted quantities of product at budgeted costs. Managers of nonmanufacturing departments, such as a computer center or market research group, could be evaluated on whether they performed their assigned tasks and met budgeted costs. Managers of profit centers are normally evaluated by comparisons of actual and budgeted profit, and investment centers might be evaluated on the basis of return on investment. (The special problems of evaluating investment centers are taken up in the next chapter, but most of the comments on profit centers are applicable to investment centers also.)

Of course, the legitimacy of evaluating a manager's performance by comparing budgeted and actual results depends on (1) how the budgeted amounts were determined and (2) to what extent the comparisons consider the controllability of differences. As discussed in Chapters 6 and 7, budgeted amounts must reflect *attainable* performance if managers are to take them seriously and strive to meet them. We also noted that managers tend to react more favorably to an evaluation based on a budget *they* helped to set. But even with budgets that are agreed upon in advance as attainable, an uncontrollable change in conditions can influence results, and managers do not react favorably to a reporting and evaluation system that fails to allow for variations due to circumstances beyond their control.

There are other bases for evaluating performance. Some companies evaluate managers on the basis of improvement over some prior period, or by comparison with other segments of the same firm. (Did the factory manager produce at a lower cost than he or she did last year? Did this division earn more profit this year than did the others?) Whatever bases are used for evaluation, both the evaluator and the evaluatee must understand the bases and the implications of using them.

Whatever the type of responsibility center, and whatever the basis used to compare with actual results, it is important to understand that evaluating a *segment* is different from evaluating its *manager*. A manager might be doing an excellent job even though the segment is performing poorly. For example, a segment doing business in a declining industry will not earn good profits. Similarly, a segment operating in a growing market might look healthy even if its manager is not doing as good a job as another manager could. The question in both cases is the standard for comparison: what *should* a segment be able to accomplish?

ORGANIZATIONAL STRUCTURE

The way a company is organized influences its reporting system. Different organizational structures result in different groupings of responsibilities. That is, the way the company is structured affects the areas controlled by individual managers. For instance, in one firm a factory manager might also have responsibility over the sales force that sells the products from that factory and so is in charge of a profit center. Another firm, similar to the first in product lines, factories, and other physical aspects, might assign the responsibility for the sales force to a corporate vice president of sales. The factory managers in such a firm manage cost centers. The reporting requirements for the two firms are quite different.

In general terms, an organization is characterized as *centralized* or *decentralized* depending on the extent of the responsibilities granted to its managers. If managers have a good deal of responsibility and authority and can make many types of decisions without the approval of higher levels of management, the organization is **decentralized.** Where managers can act less freely, the structure is **centralized.** We take up the question of decentralization more fully in Chapter 11. For now it is sufficient to note that, in general, profit and investment centers are more commonly associated with decentralization than are cost centers. This is because managers of profit and investment centers have broader responsibility than do managers of cost centers. As we explore the basics of responsibility accounting, the issue is not so much whether an organization is centralized or decentralized but how the structure affects the reports developed for whatever responsibility centers there may be.

The organizational structure depicted in Figure 10-1 shows a great many

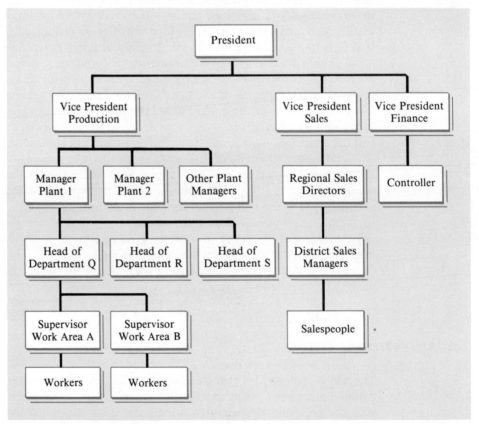

Figure 10-1   Sample of Organizational Structure

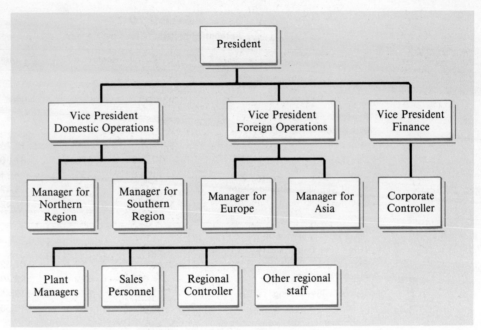

Figure 10-2   Sample of Organizational Structure

cost centers. The structure follows functional lines (production, marketing, administration, finance). Figure 10-2 shows an alternative organizational structure, with many profit or investment centers in which managers of each region are responsible for both production and sales. Note that the finance function is not delegated to individual operating managers in *either* structure. The responsibility for financing the entity rarely rests at other than the highest level of management. One reason for not delegating financing decisions to lower levels is a legal consideration: the issuance of bonds and/or stock commits the entire entity and so must be approved by managers with commensurate responsibilities. Legal issues aside, a firm's capital requirements can normally be met at less cost if the needs of its segments are consolidated and filled as a unit.

Responsibility Reporting for Cost Centers

Exhibit 10-1 (page 382) shows the interrelationships among reports for cost centers. The company whose reports are exhibited operates a factory that has three levels of supervision: (1) work stations, which are relatively small units under the control of foremen; (2) departments, which are collections of work stations under the control of a departmental supervisor; and (3) the factory as a whole, which is under the control of the factory manager. In addition, though not reflected in the reports, the factory managers are all subordinates of the vice president of manufacturing.

Exhibit 10-1

Responsibility Reports for Cost Centers

	Current Month		Year to Date	
	Budget	Over (Under)	Budget	Over (Under)
① Report to Foreman of Work Station 106—Drill Press				
Materials	$ 3,200	$ (80)	$ 12,760	$ 110
Direct labor	14,200	170	87,300	880
Supervision	1,100	(50)	4,140	(78)
Power, supplies, miscellaneous	910	24	3,420	92
Totals	$ 19,410	$ 64	$107,620	$1,004
② Report to Supervisor of Fabrication Department				
Station 106—Drill Press	$ 19,410	$ 64	$107,620	$1,004
Station 107—Grinding	17,832	122	98,430	(213)
Station 108—Cutting	23,456	876	112,456	1,227
Total work stations	60,698	1,062	318,506	2,018
Departmental costs (common to work stations):				
General supervision	12,634	0	71,234	0
Cleaning	6,125	324	32,415	762
Other	1,890	(67)	10,029	(108)
Totals	$ 81,347	$1,319	$432,184	$2,672
③ Report to Manager of Factory				
Fabrication department	$ 81,347	$1,319	$432,184	$2,672
Milling department	91,234	(2,034)	405,190	(4,231)
Assembly department	107,478	854	441,240	1,346
Casting department	78,245	(433)	367,110	689
Total departments	358,304	(294)	1,645,724	476
General factory costs (common to departments):				
Engineering	14,235	261	81,340	842
Heat and light	8,435	178	46,221	890
Building depreciation	3,400	0	20,400	0
General administration (includes accounting, travel, plant manager's office, etc.)	23,110	340	126,289	776
Total factory costs	$407,484	$ 485	$1,919,974	$2,984

As stated earlier, an important characteristic of good responsibility reporting is that reports include only controllable costs. Whether or not a particular cost is controllable—and hence includable in the report to a particular manager—depends on the manager's level in the hierarchy. For example, Exhibit 10-1 shows that the total cost reported to the department supervisor is greater than the sum of the costs reported to the foremen who are the supervisor's subordinates. The supervisor is responsible for all costs that are direct to the work stations under his or her supervision. But he or she is also responsible for those costs that are common (in the sense of not controllable by an individual work-station foreman) to the work stations within the group. In the exhibit, such common costs are general supervision (which probably includes the salary of the department supervisor), cleaning, and "other."

Similarly, the plant manager is responsible for some costs that the departmental supervisors are not: engineering, heat and light, building depreciation, and general administration. Reports for a real company show more detail, more itemizations of individual costs. We restricted the number of items for simplicity.

An important feature exhibited by the sample reports is that the amount of detail decreases as reports reach higher and higher levels of management. Managers cannot make effective use of information that is too detailed and voluminous. (Picture the president of IBM reading reports of several thousand cost centers.) Managers are usually concerned most with the performance of their immediate subordinates. Therefore, the reports they receive usually do not show performance details more than one level down. Departmental managers do not routinely receive reports detailing all of the costs of the work stations. Managers who want such detailed information can get it and might well seek it if they were concerned about some particular elements of cost. In general, regular—say, monthly—reports to departmental managers show only totals for work stations, just as regular reports to the factory manager show only totals for the departments.

One other aspect of the sample reports in Exhibit 10-1 deserves further discussion. Two of the three reports show some costs as common to work stations or to departments. There are always *some* costs that are common to two or more segments within an organization, but the managerial level at which a particular cost is controllable varies from firm to firm. For example, we show the costs of heating and lighting as common to departments, which suggests that individual departmental supervisors cannot control these costs. In another firm, each department might have a meter to monitor the consumption of utilities, in which case the cost might well be controllable at the departmental level. Similarly, one company might require that requests for operating supplies identify the work station at which they are to be used, while another might require only that the operating department be noted on the request. Thus, a cost is not always common by its nature, but may be so because the organization does not produce information by segments below a certain level.

Large amounts of costs that cannot be assigned (and, of course, controlled) at lower levels can be frustrating to managers who evaluate the performance of subordinates. Remember that reports to subordinates are likely to include only those costs assignable to them, though their *actions* could influence common costs that appear only on reports to higher levels of management. (To use the earlier example, the use of operating supplies may be controllable by the manager of a work station, even if existing procedures do not identify costs at that level.) Whether it is worthwhile to adopt procedures to assign responsibility for a particular cost to lower levels of management depends not only on the significance of the cost but also on the benefits to be gained by doing so. Benefits might include savings from lower-level managers being more careful in using particular items (supplies, repair services, whatever). But the benefits must be weighed against the cost of obtaining the additional information (meters, time required to fill out more detailed requisition forms and to produce more detailed reports, etc.). In any case, the facts in a particular case determine whether a cost is controllable at a given level of management, and the responsibility reporting system should follow, as closely as possible, the principle of including only controllable items.

Exhibit 10-2
Responsibility Reports for Profit Centers (thousands of dollars)

	Current Month		Year to Date	
	Budget	Over (Under)	Budget	Over (Under)
Report to Product Manager—Appliances, European Region				
Sales	$122.0	$1.5	$ 387.0	$ 3.2
Variable costs:				
Production	47.5	2.8	150.7	5.9
Selling and administrative	12.2	1.8	38.7	1.9
Total variable costs	59.7	4.6	189.4	7.8
Contribution margin	62.3	(3.1)	197.6	(4.6)
Direct fixed costs	36.0	(1.2)	98.5	(3.1)
Product margin	$ 26.3	($1.9)	$ 99.1	($ 1.5)
Report to Manager—European Region				
Product margins:				
Appliances	$ 26.3	($1.9)	$ 99.1	($ 1.5)
Industrial equipment	37.4	3.2	134.5	7.3
Tools	18.3	1.1	59.1	(2.0)
Total product margins	82.0	2.4	292.7	3.8
Regional expenses (common to all product lines)	18.5	0.8	61.2	(1.3)
Regional margin	$ 63.5	$1.6	$ 231.5	$ 5.1
Report to Executive Vice President				
Regional margins:				
European	$ 63.5	$1.6	$ 231.5	$ 5.1
Asian	78.1	(4.3)	289.4	(8.2)
North American	211.8	(3.2)	612.4	(9.6)
Total regional margins	353.4	(5.9)	1,133.3	(12.7)
Corporate expenses (common to all regions)	87.1	1.4	268.5	3.1
Corporate profit	$266.3	($7.3)	$ 864.8	($15.8)

Responsibility Reporting
for Profit Centers

The principle of controllability also applies to responsibility reporting for profit centers (and for investment centers, which we consider in more detail in Chapter 11). Exhibit 10-2 (opposite) provides sample reports for a firm that organizes profit centers around product lines and geographical areas. Managers at the lowest level of profit center are responsible for product lines. They are subordinate to the managers of the geographical areas, who are in turn, responsible to the executive vice president.

The unallocated costs—regional expenses common to product lines, or corporate expenses common to regions—consist of many items. For instance, regional expenses include the salaries of people at regional headquarters, including those in accounting, personnel, finance, and other functions administered from regional headquarters. These costs are not direct to product lines, and product managers cannot control them. In addition, "image-building" advertising not aimed at particular product lines, could also be under the control of a regional manager. At the total-firm level there are similar kinds of common costs.

For simplicity, the report for the regional manager includes only product margins for each of the product groups. In some companies, such managers receive more detail, such as sales and costs, and some firms also report expenses of special concern, such as advertising and promotion. Similarly, reports could also show critical percentages, such as contribution margin or profit to sales.

Exhibit 10-3 shows an approach that provides more detail on individual components of the appliance segment in the European region. This approach draws attention to costs that are common to the different categories of appliances. To focus attention on the format, we have omitted budgeted figures. The critical

Exhibit 10-3
Alternative Responsibility Reporting Format
Report to Product Manager—Appliances, European Region (thousands of dollars)

	Total	Small Home Appliances	Large Home Appliances	Commercial Appliances
Sales	$390.2	$126.3	$109.5	$154.4
Variable costs:				
Production	156.6	41.1	31.2	84.3
Selling and administrative	40.6	14.2	18.1	8.3
Total variable costs	197.2	55.3	49.3	92.6
Contribution margin	193.0	71.0	60.2	61.8
Direct fixed costs	27.4	9.5	11.2	6.7
Margin	165.6	$ 61.5	$ 49.0	$ 55.1
Costs common to products in the appliance line	68.0			
Product margin	$ 97.6			

point in responsibility reporting is conveying the best information; the selections of the elements to include and the format are secondary. Notice that the amount of detail is greater in the alternative format and that some costs shown as direct to product lines in Exhibit 10-2 are shown as common to the individual products in the line in Exhibit 10-3.

In both Exhibit 10-2 and Exhibit 10-3, the sample reports to the manager of appliance sales for the European region include production costs. The implication is that the manager for the region can control, and is responsible for, production costs. Control of production is not necessary to justify this type of reporting. From earlier chapters you know that decisions about individual products or product lines are based on profitability. For decision-making purposes, then, regional sales managers must be *aware* of the costs of manufacturing the products being sold. Accordingly, reports to managers who are responsible only for sales and regional selling costs very often include some charge for the products, even though such reporting does not follow strictly the principle of controllability.

Choosing an Organizational Structure

Should a firm organize into profit and investment centers or into cost centers? Should it centralize or decentralize decision making? The answers to these questions depend on many factors, not least of which are the attitudes and philosophies of top managers. Company presidents who are uncomfortable with having subordinates make many critical decisions tend to centralize decision making; others, who prefer to give subordinates a great deal of responsibility and emphasize accountability, tend to decentralize.

Even after a firm has decided to use profit centers, there remains the question of how to make the separations. The segmentation could be along product lines, geographical areas, types of customers (industrial, government), or markets (leisure, household products, mining). The choice should be influenced by whether the segmentation facilitates evaluation; and that depends to some extent on the amount of common costs associated with each alternative structure. If each factory serves a particular geographical region and makes many products, it is more reasonable to segment by region than by product line. If each factory produces a single product or product line and serves all regions, it is more reasonable to segment by product or line. (Of course there could be sales managers in each region, but the profit centers are the product lines, not the regions.)

Setting up an organizational structure is difficult. Rarely does only one structure make sense for a given firm. Moreover, a structure found useful at one time, by one set of managers, will not remain useful forever. Managers, including top managers, change; products and product lines are dropped, added, or regrouped; manufacturing activities are transferred among plants or otherwise changed, perhaps because of technological innovations. Hence, the structure of the organization, for responsibility reporting as for operating purposes, requires regular review and reconsideration.

CONTROL, EVALUATION, AND COST ALLOCATION

Virtually all responsibility centers use services provided by other centers. The terms **service department** and **service center** are used to describe centers that do not work on the company's products, but rather provide services to other service departments and to operating departments. (Centers that work on the company's products are usually called **operating departments.**) Examples of service departments are personnel, accounting, building security, and data processing.

In Chapter 3 we introduced the term *direct cost* (or *separable cost*) to describe a cost that is specifically identifiable with a particular activity. Managerial accountants also use that term to refer to a cost that is controlled by the manager receiving the report. Still another term that refers to the same concept is **traceable cost.** In contrast, then, the term *indirect cost* refers to a cost that the manager receiving a report cannot control directly. Such costs are *common* or *joint* to several responsibility centers. Many such costs are incurred by service departments for the benefit of other departments. (Of course, there are indirect costs that are *not* incurred in service departments, as, for example, depreciation on a factory building that houses both operating and service departments.)

A compelling reason for companies to establish a service department that incurs costs for the benefit of several responsibility centers is that having such a department is cheaper than having each center perform or acquire the service on its own. (If there is no personnel department, each department must screen and hire its employees, maintain their records, and do all the other tasks that a personnel department performs.) In addition, companies sometimes establish a service department because their managers believe that a qualitative issue, such as a need for confidentiality, makes it wise to perform a particular service inside rather than have outsiders do it.

Because the responsibility centers that use the services of a service department benefit from those services, it seems natural that the users should "pay" for those services. The method most commonly used to reflect a "payment" for such services in reports to managers of service-using departments is to *allocate* the costs of the service department to the using departments. You have encountered allocations throughout this book. In Chapter 2 you saw that a total cost per unit gives misleading information because it requires allocating fixed costs to units of product. In Chapters 5, 8, and 9 you saw that the only costs relevant for decision making are incremental costs and that allocated costs are not incremental and therefore not relevant.

Virtually all managerial accountants reject the use of cost allocations for decision making. But they disagree about whether to allocate indirect costs for control and performance evaluation. (The allocation issue has become increasingly important because the indirect costs of operating modern factories are growing rapidly as direct laborers are replaced by robots and the corresponding need for computer operators and maintenance workers.) Thus, while users unquestionably benefit from the activities of service departments, there are serious questions about whether to charge using departments for the services and, if so, how.

Reasons for Not Allocating Costs

There is general agreement that the variable costs of a service center should be allocated to service-using departments because the managers of those departments can cause an increase in such costs. For example, a manager who orders 1,000 copies of a document from the Central Copying Center should pay for, perhaps in the form of an allocation, at least the incremental cost of the copies, which probably approximates their variable cost. Where managerial accountants disagree is on the matter of allocating indirect *fixed* costs. There are two principal arguments against allocating indirect fixed costs, both of which stress the potentially adverse behavioral consequences.

First, because indirect fixed costs are not controllable by the users, allocating them violates the principle of controllability. Managers charged with costs they cannot control might come to distrust the whole system of control and evaluation. They might attempt to "beat the system" and so take actions not congruent with the company's objectives. Even with *variable* indirect costs, while the using manager controls the use of the service, he or she does not control the cost of providing the service. For instance, in a variation of an earlier example, a firm might establish its own power-generating department to provide electricity to the factory. Managers of power-using departments might be able to influence the volume of power generated, thus influencing *total* variable costs in the service department. But such managers cannot control the per-unit variable cost.

The second reason has to do with making decisions. Because indirect fixed costs are common to several users, they are not differential to those users. As shown in Chapter 5, making sound decisions requires using differential revenues and costs. Managerial accountants who oppose including cost allocations in reports prepared for control and evaluation purposes argue that showing allocations in such reports could lead managers to make poor decisions.

Reasons for Allocating Costs

There are several reasons to allocate fixed indirect costs for control and performance evaluation. We have already mentioned one reason: users benefit from the costs incurred by service departments and should have to pay for them. Failing to allocate also understates the full cost of operating the using centers. As we show in later chapters, the full-cost idea is important in product costing—determining the unit cost of products so as to determine inventory and cost of goods sold for financial reporting and income tax purposes. Because allocations *must* be made for financial reporting, there is a tendency also to use them in internal reporting.

Another reason for allocating is to remind managers of the existence of indirect costs and the need to cover them. If the company as a whole is to make a profit, its revenues must cover not only the direct costs of its profit centers, but also the indirect costs of the company as a whole.

Probably the most appealing reasons for showing allocated costs in reports are behavioral. For one, proponents of allocations argue that if indirect costs are not allocated, managers might overuse services because they view the services as "free." For example, if a company does not allocate its computer costs, managers might use more computer time than is economically justified, thus straining capacity and perhaps leading to an unwise purchase of additional capacity. Allocating computer costs could discourage overuse and help prevent incurring unnecessary costs. For a somewhat different example of using cost allocation to control costs, consider the situation of a sales manager who controls credit terms offered to customers and the level of inventory maintained. The sales manager normally wants to carry a high inventory and offer liberal credit terms, with the firm incurring costs to carry the investment in inventory and receivables. The sales manager is less likely to allow those assets to increase excessively if he or she is charged a financing cost based on the investments in those assets. (Note, however, that if the major objective of a relatively new firm is to establish a strong demand for its products by getting as much market penetration as possible, allocating financing costs to the sales manager works against achieving the firm's objective.)

Interestingly, some proponents of using cost allocations on performance reports offer a conflicting argument, also behavioral. They suggest that allocations are helpful when a service is, in the opinion of upper-level managers, *underused*. The reasoning behind this suggestion is that managers will use the service more because they are already paying for it through the cost allocation. For proponents of cost allocations, resolution of the apparent contradiction about how managers will respond to allocations lies in the *way* the costs are allocated, which we discuss shortly, not in the *fact* of allocation.

Another behavior-oriented reason for allocating indirect costs is that the managers to whom costs are allocated will encourage the managers of service departments to keep the cost of the service under control. For example, suppose the manager of computer services wants to buy newer, faster equipment. He or she first has to convince the users that it is economically sound for them. In the absence of allocations, users have no reason to object to decisions that increase computer costs.[1]

The behavior-influencing aspects of cost allocations can be significant in a number of ways. An interesting realistic example was reported by the Portables Group of Tektronics Company.[2] The Group had been allocating overhead based on direct labor, but its design and process engineers had driven direct labor costs down to less than 7% of total manufacturing cost (just over 3% on some of its newer products). Because overhead costs were high and rising, the overhead allocation rate per direct labor hour was extremely high. Thus, though direct labor cost was fairly low, the high overhead cost allocated on the basis of direct labor

---

[1] A major study found that the most common reasons for allocating corporate indirect service costs to profit centers for purposes of evaluating performance are: (1) to remind managers of the existence of indirect costs; (2) to make the sum of profit-center profits equal total company-wide profit; (3) to fairly reflect each center's use of services; (4) to encourage profit-center managers to pressure service managers to control costs; (5) to encourage use of services. See James M. Fremgen and Shu S. Liao, *The Allocation of Corporate Indirect Costs,* New York: National Association of Accountants, 1981.

[2] John W. Jonez and Michael A. Wright, "Material Burdening," *Management Accounting* (August 1987), 27–31.

made the total cost that *seemed* to be labor-related very high, and many managers interpreted the situation as requiring efforts to further reduce direct labor. (Note that labor-reducing efforts that also increased overhead simply raised the overhead allocation rate.) Fortunately, the Group undertook an internal study that showed that costs related to materials and components—purchasing, receiving, inspecting, storage, and recordkeeping—constituted roughly half of overhead costs. Follow-up of this study showed that design and process engineers often recommended using more parts when their use reduced direct labor because, there being no overhead charge on parts, there was no incentive either to reduce the number of components or to standardize those in use.

After its study of overhead costs, the division began to allocate its material-related overhead based on the number of component parts needed and their annual use. A sample calculation of the two-step allocation process is shown below.

Total material-related overhead	$5,000,000
Total number of parts needed, all types	6,250
Annual cost to carry a part	$800
Cost per part (example):	
Part A, annual use, 20,000 units	$800/20,000 = $0.04
Part B, annual use, 500 units	$800/500 = $1.60

The first step in the allocation process is to determine a cost per part, regardless of the annual volume of use of that part. The next step uses the annual volume of the part to determine a cost per unit, which cost is *then* allocated to the product based on the quantity of each part used in the product. Adopting the new cost-allocation plan influenced behavior in three important ways. First, it encouraged engineers to reduce the number of parts in existing products. Second, it encouraged standardization of parts for use in several products. Third, it encouraged use of fewer, and more standardized, parts in new products.

Whatever the reasons for allocating, remember that virtually all allocations are arbitrary. By *arbitrary* we mean that there is no way to prove that a particular allocation method is better than another. Nevertheless, some allocation methods are more reasonable than others, and, as stated earlier, different allocation methods might influence managers differently. We shall, therefore, discuss further how allocations are made and the potential behavioral effects of various allocation methods.

Allocation Methods and Effects

Once managers decide to allocate indirect costs, they must select a basis for making the allocations. The basis is usually some measure of activity or use of the service. For instance, some companies use the number of employees in each department as the basis for allocating the costs of its personnel department. Similarly, costs related to a building (such as depreciation, property taxes, and insurance) are probably allocated on the basis of the space occupied by the departments.

The best allocation basis is one that reflects the causal relationship of use to cost. That is, if the users' actions cause the cost to increase, then the costs should be charged accordingly. The next best basis is one that reflects the benefits that the user receives. For instance, it is reasonable to allocate heating expense based on the space that each department occupies—a measure of the benefits received. Even if the managers of using departments cannot control heating expense, they must have heated space to operate.

When neither a use nor a benefit basis is available, allocations are often made on the basis of a department's "ability to bear" indirect costs. For example, there is no reasonable measure of how much each segment benefits from costs such as the salary of the president or the annual audit fee. Therefore such costs are often allocated based on sales or assets, with the idea that these measures reflect the segment's ability to bear them. (Or they might not be allocated at all.) Finally, sales is often used as the allocation basis when no measure of benefits received is available. (Of course, sales is a *reasonable* basis only if it reflects benefits received.)

Even if we assume some effort is made to allocate on the basis of use, there are still several approaches to allocating indirect costs (both fixed and variable) and it is not easy to select a method that will work, in the sense of accomplishing goal congruence. Using the following information, we shall illustrate and comment on a few common methods.

 Raleigh Company has one service department, the Maintenance Department, and two operating departments: Fabrication and Assembly. Data for the departments follow.

Operating Department	Hours of Maintenance Service Used
Fabrication	20,000
Assembly	10,000
Total	30,000

Maintenance Department Costs for Year	Budgeted	Actual
Fixed	$ 75,000	$ 79,500
Variable:		
$5 per hour ✗ (30,000)	150,000	
$5.10 per hour		153,000
Total	$225,000	$232,500

Allocating Actual Costs Based on Use

The simplest (and worst) allocation method is to allocate the *actual* total cost of the Maintenance Department based on the operating departments' relative use of the service. We can make the necessary calculations in two ways, both of which give the same result. First, we can calculate the actual per-hour rate of providing the service, which is $7.75 ($232,500 actual cost divided by 30,000 hours). The allocations are below.

Fabrication (20,000 × $7.75)	$155,000
Assembly (10,000 × $7.75)	77,500
Total maintenance cost allocated	$232,500

The other calculation uses the relative shares of the two operating departments. The Fabrication Department used two thirds of the maintenance time (20,000/30,000), so it is allocated two thirds of the total cost, or $155,000. The Assembly Department used one third (10,000/30,000) and is allocated $77,500.

This method is poor for two reasons: (1) it allocates actual costs rather than budgeted costs and (2) it allocates fixed costs based on use. Because the method allocates actual costs, it passes the inefficiencies (or efficiencies, if actual costs are less than budgeted costs) of the Maintenance Department on to the operating departments. The operating managers are responsible for the *use* of the service, but not for the cost. The maintenance manager is responsible for maintenance costs.

Allocating fixed costs based on use is bad because the amount allocated to one department is affected by the actions of managers in other departments. To see this, suppose that each of Raleigh's operating departments *budgeted* 20,000 hours of maintenance for the year. The budgeted rate is $6,875, computed as below.

Variable rate	$5.000
Fixed rate ($75,000/40,000)	1.875
Total rate (per hour)	$6.875

Budgeted total maintenance costs would have been $275,000 [$75,000 + ($5.00 × 40,000)], and each operating manager would have budgeted $137,500 in maintenance cost. Allocating on the basis of actual use, the manager of the Assembly Department looks good because he is charged $60,000 less than budget ($137,500 budget minus $77,500 actual). But the manager of Fabrication looks bad. The Fabrication Department is charged $155,000, $17,500 over budget, *even though it used exactly the budgeted amount for this service*. The additional charge arose partly because the Maintenance Department was over its budget, but more importantly because the Assembly Department used less of the service than it had budgeted. If an allocation is to be used in evaluation, the allocation to a given department should not be affected by the actions of other departments. In general, allocating fixed costs based on use encourages managers to underuse the service because the allocation depends not only on how much service a particular manager uses, but also on how much the other managers use.

This allocation method is equivalent to a static budget allowance, which we discussed in Chapter 6. Operating managers are encouraged to overbudget their use of service, because if they use less of the service than budgeted, they will *appear* to have controlled the cost well. If the concept of flexible budgeting is applied, the budget allowance for each department is based on the fixed and variable components of the maintenance cost, so that the operating departments are charged a flat amount (a share of budgeted fixed costs) plus an amount based on use (at the budgeted variable rate).

Another serious problem of allocating fixed costs based on actual use is that an operating manager might interpret allocated amounts as incremental costs and use these irrelevant costs in making decisions. Suppose the manager of the Assembly Department is considering a decision requiring an additional ten hours of maintenance service. Seeing the $7.75 per hour rate used in the final allocation for the most recent period, he or she might estimate the amount to be charged at about $77.50 (10 × $7.75). Yet the *incremental* cost to Raleigh is the variable cost for ten hours, and only incremental costs are relevant to the decision. Note that this problem is independent of the difference between budgeted and actual use. If actual use and costs had been as budgeted, so that the actual allocation rate equalled the budgeted rate of $6.875, the manager of the Assembly Department would still be led to overstate the incremental cost of the decision.

Allocating Budgeted Costs Using Dual Rates   A better allocation method is to allocate only *budgeted* costs, which prevents passing the efficiencies (or inefficiencies) of the service department on to operating departments. In addition, this method employs the concept of flexible budgeting by treating fixed and variable costs separately. Budgeted variable costs are allocated based on use (because total variable costs change as use changes); fixed costs are allocated based on long-term expected use. The term *dual rates* refers to allocating fixed costs and variable costs differently.

The use of dual rates overcomes the problems associated with allocating fixed costs based on use because each department's allocated fixed cost is a lump sum determined before the year begins. The idea supporting this approach is that fixed costs are incurred to provide the capacity to serve, and the decisions that determined the capacity of the Maintenance Department were based, at least in part, on estimates made earlier by the managers of the operating departments. The argument is that if the manager of the Assembly Department has *requested* some amount of capacity, he or she should pay for it.

Suppose the estimated long-term use is 60% for the Fabrication Department and 40% for the Assembly Department. We then have the following allocations, which assign variable costs at the budgeted rate of $5 per hour of use.

		Fixed	Variable	Total
Fabrication	(60% × $75,000)	$45,000	$100,000	$145,000
Assembly	(40% × $75,000)	30,000	50,000	80,000
Total		$75,000	$150,000	$225,000

This method has several advantages. One is that operating managers do not absorb the inefficiencies of the Maintenance Department because only budgeted costs ($225,000) are allocated. Consistent with the concept of flexible budgeting, operating managers are charged a budgeted lump sum and a budgeted variable rate. Because there is a charge for use, operating managers probably will not overuse the service. Because the hourly charge and the lump-sum charge are known in advance, the managers probably will not underuse the service. Notice also that the amount charged to a department depends only on that department's use, not on the use made by other departments. Moreover, operating managers are not likely to consider the allocated fixed costs in making decisions because the amount of allocated fixed cost is independent of the actual use of the service.

Allocating Through Transfer Prices   An entirely different approach to allocating the costs of a service department to using departments is to use a transfer price. A **transfer price** is a charge for services (or for goods) that one segment renders to another.[3] As mentioned earlier, the use of transfer prices makes the service departments into artificial profit centers. Transfer prices are not cost allocations in the strict sense of the term because the charge is not necessarily related to the costs of the service department. Often, the transfer price approximates the market price for the services, which is the price that operating departments have to pay to obtain the services from an outside company. Because the transfer price is set in advance, the using manager knows exactly how much he or she will be charged to, say, employ another ten hours of maintenance time. In this respect, the transfer price shares the advantage of the dual-rate method of allocation.

Suppose that in our example the transfer price for maintenance services was set at $8 per hour—a price management considered to be the best estimate of the cost to acquire maintenance services from another company. The amounts charged to each department are as below.

Fabrication	(20,000 × $8)	$160,000
Assembly	(10,000 × $8)	80,000
Total maintenance cost charged		$240,000

The Maintenance Department will show revenues of $240,000, costs of $232,500, and therefore a profit of $7,500. It is important for you to understand that using *a transfer price does not change the actual cost incurred*. The total cost was $232,500. Operating departments show maintenance costs of $240,000, and the Maintenance Department a $7,500 profit. The net, $232,500, is the actual cost incurred.

Using transfer prices to create artificial profit centers is not a simple task, as evidenced by the experience of Weyerhauser Company, reported in 1987.[4] All

---

[3] Transfer prices are also commonly used when profit centers "sell" goods to sister segments within the company. Chapter 11 discusses this use of transfer prices.
[4] H. Thomas Johnson and Dennis A. Loewe, "How Weyerhauser Manages Corporate Overhead Costs," *Management Accounting* (August 1987), 20–26.

corporate-level service departments of that company are required to charge for their services. The Financial Services Department provides general accounting and payroll services, and its charges are based on a variety of factors. For example, charges to account for receivables are based on invoice volume and number of customers and are adjusted for situations that require hand-processing. In developing its charges for general accounting work, the Department used separate rates for employees of three types: analytical, clerical, and systems. A critical factor in Weyerhauser's system is that users were free to acquire services from outside the company. Consistent with comments made earlier, one result of the transfer-pricing system (called "charge-backs" at Weyerhauser) was that service department managers became profit-conscious, seeking to provide better services to the company *and* seeking outside customers for their services.

There is another important advantage to using transfer prices. The transfer price can be increased or decreased to encourage less or more use of the service, respectively. It is probably easier to encourage or discourage use through transfer pricing than it is by using the cost-allocation methods described earlier.

One difficulty with trying to use a transfer price that approximates the outside cost for the service is that the outside cost for an equivalent service is often very difficult to determine. But if reliable outside prices are available, there is a significant advantage to using that price as a transfer price and treating a service department as a profit center. If a department consistently shows losses under such a pricing system, upper-level managers are alerted to the possibility that the firm could benefit from shutting down the department and buying outside. Such a decision must consider the structure of fixed costs (avoidable and unavoidable) and would be made along the lines described in Chapter 5 in connection with make-or-buy decisions.

What to Do?

Managers should be charged with at least the incremental costs associated with carrying out their functions. Thus, if some amount of cost of a service department, or portion of cost of a joint activity, is attributable to a particular department, it should be charged to it.

If allocations are to be made, amounts allocated should, if feasible, reflect budgeted rather than actual costs. Charges should be for the quantity of the service received based on budgeted variable costs of providing the services. Budgeted fixed costs could be allocated in lump-sum amounts based on the long-run percentages of the service capacity required by each operating department. Thus, budgeted fixed costs of the personnel department could be allocated based on expected numbers of employees in the operating departments, the costs of the accounting department by the expected volume of transactions originating in the operating departments, and the costs of maintenance by the expected number of machine-hours in each department. The allocation to a particular department should not be affected by the actions of other departments.

Compromises are possible. Performance reports can show controllable and uncontrollable (allocated) costs separately. If higher-level managers, the ones evaluating the performance reports, recognize the distinction, there is less likelihood of misunderstanding and complaining from the lower-level managers.

One further alternative should be considered when trying to develop a reasonable and acceptable transfer price or allocation scheme for performance reporting. The firm can try to increase the extent to which a manager can control the costs for which he or she will be held responsible. We mentioned this point earlier, using the examples of separate utility meters and more detailed requisition forms and reporting of supplies use. The higher the total amount of a cost that might be brought under better control by additional efforts, the more likely it is that the firm will benefit from such efforts. JIT companies, through use of manufacturing cells, are especially effective at making costs direct to cells. Such costs as maintenance and quality control, which are likely to be common to operating departments in conventional companies, are usually direct to JIT cells.

We emphasize that performance reports and their content are specific to the circumstances that a particular company faces and to the preferences of its managers. No set of simple rules governs all conceivable situations or leads to reports that satisfy all managers.

Effects on Firm Income

One final point bears remembering. Allocations and transfer prices are managerial accounting devices, not economic activities. Hence, changes in allocations and transfer prices cannot, by themselves, change the firm's total income. Changes in the firm's income *can* occur if a change in an allocation or transfer price induces managers to act differently. But so long as the managers of the individual segments continue to operate as they have, the firm's total income will not be affected. We can illustrate this with an example.

Suppose a firm is organized into two segments, manufacturing and selling, and each segment is a profit center. The manufacturing segment "sells" to the marketing segment, which in turn, sells to outsiders. Data for the two segments are as follows.

	Manufacturing	Marketing
Selling price	$20	$30
Variable costs:		
Manufacturing costs	$12	
Selling costs		$3
Fixed costs	$100,000	$50,000

The variable costs for the marketing division are the $3 selling costs plus the $20 the segment is charged by the manufacturing division. If the firm produces and sells 20,000 units, an income statement by segment shows the following.

↷ sells to .

	Manufacturing	Marketing
Sales 20,000 × $20	$400,000	
20,000 × $30		$600,000
Variable costs at $12 per unit	240,000	
($20 + 3) at $23 per unit		460,000
Contribution margin	160,000	140,000
Fixed costs	100,000	50,000
Income	$ 60,000	$ 90,000

Total income is $150,000 ($60,000 + $90,000). Suppose now that the transfer price is lowered to $15 per unit. This reduces the revenues of the manufacturing segment and the costs of the marketing segment, but does not affect the company's income. An income statement for 20,000 units with the $15 transfer price is given below.

	Manufacturing	Marketing
Sales 20,000 × $15	$300,000	
20,000 × $30		$600,000
Variable costs at $12 per unit	240,000	
at $18 per unit ($15 + $3)		360,000
Contribution margin	60,000	240,000
Fixed costs	100,000	50,000
Income (loss)	($ 40,000)	$190,000

Total income is still $150,000 ($190,000 − $40,000), even though the incomes for the segments have changed. The $100,000 reduction in revenues to the manufacturing division ($400,000 − $300,000) is exactly offset by the reduction in variable costs of the marketing division ($460,000 − $360,000 = $100,000). Because a transfer price is revenue to one segment and a cost to the other segment, the price does not affect total income for the firm *unless* a change in the transfer price induces the manager of some segment to make some change in the operations of the segment.

OTHER USES OF ALLOCATIONS

In discussing why allocations might appear on performance reports, we pointed out that allocations are needed for product costing (for financial reporting and income tax purposes). Allocations are also necessary for other purposes. For instance, public utilities like electric and telephone companies are required to justify price increases to state commissions. Part of the justification for an increase is increases in costs, and these costs must be allocated among different classes of customers (residential, commercial, industrial) to determine the increases that each will bear. Reimbursements to hospitals under Medicaid are based on costs that include allocations, as are payments to cities, counties, and states under some federal grants.

The Cost Accounting Standards Board (CASB) was a potent force in support of making allocations. The CASB specified rules for allocating costs by firms that do certain kinds of business with the federal government. The Board issued a number of regulations regarding many aspects of allocation, including the bases to use for allocations and the costs to include in or exclude from the pool of costs to be allocated. (CASB pronouncements use the terms *allowable* and *not allowable* to indicate which types of costs—direct or allocated—may be included in reports for reimbursement.)

When organizations allocate costs for one or more of the purposes that demand such allocations, they are, as we stated previously, trying to develop a "full cost," with each activity or segment bearing its "fair share" of the indirect costs. The allocations may have to be made for the purpose of reporting on a particular contract, for preparing external financial statements, or in order to abide by some law. For example, society's interests may be served by reimbursing a hospital for an operation on the basis of the full cost of the operation (including the costs to provide and maintain an operating room). But just because a contract, generally accepted accounting principles, some regulatory agency, or a legislative mandate demands the allocation of joint costs does not make that allocation any the less arbitrary.

SUMMARY

Managers need accounting information to control operations, and their efforts must be evaluated on bases that are consistent with the goals of the firm. Responsibility accounting should assist in achieving goal congruence and in motivating managers. No single responsibility accounting system is appropriate for all firms, or for the same firm over its lifetime. The responsibility accounting system must parallel the structure of the organization. The structure of the organization depends on the nature of its operations and on the attitudes and management styles of top managers.

The reporting segments of a responsibility accounting system may be cost centers, profit centers, or investment centers. Most firms use all three types of responsibility centers. Whatever the plan for segmenting the firm for reporting purposes, the individual managers can be held responsible for only that which they can control.

Cost allocations can be troublesome in responsibility accounting, as they have been shown to be in decision making. Conflicting objectives of cost allocation are charging managers for benefits they receive and reporting on the controllable aspects of the managers' operations in order to increase their motivation. Transfer prices, the selling prices established for artificial profit centers, can alleviate some of the problems of cost allocations. The pervasive behavioral considerations in responsibility accounting make it difficult to draw general conclusions about the best or most useful approaches to follow.

KEY TERMS

centralized organization structure
cost center
decentralized organization structure

goal congruence
investment center
profit center

responsibility accounting
responsibility center
service department

traceable cost
transfer price

REVIEW PROBLEM

Wolfert Company makes and sells air conditioners and operates in three regions: the Northeast, Southeast, and Southwest. Data for 19X5 are given below, in thousands of dollars.

	Northeast	Southeast	Southwest
Sales	$2,400	$5,600	$3,800
Variable cost of sales	1,220	2,200	1,700
Variable selling costs	170	330	240
Direct fixed costs:			
Production	310	810	440
Selling	240	400	280
Administrative	320	440	380

Common fixed costs were $450,000 for administration and $110,000 for selling.

Required: Prepare a performance report by region, showing contribution margin and regional profit. Show common costs as lump-sum deductions in the total column.

Answer to Review Problem

Performance Report for 19X5
(in thousands of dollars)

	Northeast	Southeast	Southwest	Total
Sales	$2,400	$5,600	$3,800	$11,800
Variable costs:				
Production	1,220	2,200	1,700	5,120
Selling	170	330	240	740
Total variable costs	1,390	2,530	1,940	5,860
Contribution margin	1,010	3,070	1,860	5,940
Direct fixed costs:				
Production	310	810	440	1,560
Selling	240	400	280	920
Administration	320	440	380	1,140
Total direct traceable fixed costs	870	1,650	1,100	3,620
Regional profit	$ 140	$1,420	$ 760	$ 2,320
Common fixed costs:				
Selling				110
Administration				450
Total joint costs				560
Income				$1,760

APPENDIX: OTHER ALLOCATION SCHEMES

As indicated in the chapter, allocations of common costs *must* be made for some purposes and can be useful for influencing behavior. Allocation schemes are, therefore, of considerable interest. This appendix describes two techniques that many managerial accountants believe to be superior to the basic methods described in the chapter. The first is the **step-down method,** the second the **reciprocal method.** The chapter illustrated the **direct method.**

Step-Down Method

A distinguishing feature of many allocation schemes, particularly those specified under cost-reimbursement contracts, is the use of a multistep allocation. The process is called **step-down allocation,** the **step method,** or simply, **step-down.** It is seen in the legislated or regulated methods for determining how much to reimburse hospitals for services performed for citizens.

Basically, the step-down method allocates the costs of service departments *one department at a time.* The idea behind the method is to recognize that service departments provide services for other service departments as well as for operating departments. The costs of all service departments, except the first to be allocated, will reflect their shares of the costs of *some* of the other service departments. In contrast, the direct method does not recognize services that service departments provide to other service departments. An example should make this clear.

Consider GNL Manufacturing Company, which has, for simplicity, two operating departments and two service departments. The operating departments, Forging and Machining, receive services from Personnel and Administration. Personnel keeps all employee records and handles payrolls; Administration handles all other administrative tasks. Each service department provides services to the other service department as well as to the two operating departments. Data for the most recent month follow.

Department	Direct Costs	Number of Employees
Personnel	$ 200,000	10
Administration	500,000	30
Forging	1,800,000	100
Machining	3,000,000	300
Total costs	$5,500,000	440

As with any allocation situation, we must select the bases for making the allocations. Suppose that GNL's managers decide to allocate Administration costs based on the direct costs of the departments and Personnel costs based on the number of employees.

Because the step-down method allocates the costs of one service department at a time, we must decide which service department's costs to allocate first. Several guidelines can be used to determine the sequence. One is to start with the department that serves the most other service departments. Another is to order the departments based on the percentage of their services that go to other service departments. Suppose GNL's managers decide to allocate Administration costs first.

The following schedule shows the allocation of Administration costs, using direct costs as the basis.

	Personnel	Forging	Machining	Total
Direct costs	$200,000	$1,800,000	$3,000,000	$5,000,000
Percentage of total	4%	36%	60%	100%
Allocation	$ 20,000	$ 180,000	$ 300,000	$ 500,000
Previous totals	200,000	1,800,000	3,000,000	5,000,000
New total cost	$220,000	$1,980,000	$3,300,000	$5,500,000

Total costs are still $5,500,000, the total direct costs before allocation. But the total is now spread differently, with the $500,000 from Administration now in the other three departments.

We're now ready to allocate the costs for Personnel, and we use the number of employees as the basis. Notice that we allocate $220,000, the *new* total of costs in Personnel. Under the step-down method, a service department's costs build up through successive allocations to it. Note also that no Personnel costs are allocated to Administration. Once you allocate costs *from* a department, you do not allocate any back *to* the department. Below is the allocation of the Personnel costs and the final totals allocated to the operating departments.

	Forging	Machining	Total
Number of employees	100	300	400
Percentage of total	25%	75%	100%
Allocation of personnel	$ 55,000	$ 165,000	$ 220,000
Previous totals	1,980,000	3,300,000	5,280,000
New total cost	$2,035,000	$3,465,000	$5,500,000

How will managers react when presented with a report that shows all costs assigned to the two operating departments? Some will be tempted to compute a unit cost for each department, based perhaps on the number of direct labor hours worked in each. Such temptations should be avoided. By their nature, allocations are arbitrary no matter how sophisticated the method used to calculate them. The results are always influenced by the allocation basis chosen. Had we selected different bases for allocating the costs of either of the service departments, the final results would be different. Also, the results are influenced by the order in which allocations were made. That is, had we chosen to allocate Personnel first, the final total costs for each operating department would have been different. In summary, the allocation process succeeds in *assigning* the costs of service departments to the operating departments, but does not change the fact that the costs of service departments are common to the departments serviced.

The following schedule summarizes the procedures and explicitly shows the step-down feature as each department's costs are allocated.

	Administration	Personnel	Forging	Machining	Total
Direct costs	$500,000	$200,000	$1,800,000	$3,000,000	$5,500,000
Administration	(500,000)	20,000	180,000	300,000	
Personnel		(220,000)	55,000	165,000	
Total			$2,035,000	$3,465,000	$5,500,000

The total costs of the two operating departments ($5,500,000) are, of course, the same as the total costs of all departments before the allocation procedure began. As stated many times, allocations do not, by themselves, change total costs.

Reciprocal Method

The reciprocal, or **simultaneous,** method of allocation recognizes, more fully than does the step method, the services that each service department renders to other service departments. This means, in terms of the example used above, that not only are Administration costs allocated to Personnel, but Personnel costs are also allocated to Administration. To accomplish this reciprocal allocation we first find the percentages that each service department *receives* from the other. The original data from the example are presented below, in somewhat modified form, to facilitate the calculations.

Services Provided By	Services Provided To				
	Personnel	Administration	Forging	Machining	Total
Administration:					
Direct Costs	$200,000		$1,800,000	$3,000,000	$5,000,000
Percentages	4%		36%	60%	100%
Personnel:					
No. of employees		30	100	300	430
Percentages		6.98%	23.25%	69.77%	100%

The next step in the reciprocal method is to calculate what are called the **adjusted costs** of the service departments, to recognize that the departments provide services to each other. To accomplish this we set up simultaneous equations, letting P = the adjusted costs for Personnel and A = the adjusted costs for Administration. The equations are

$$P = \$200,000 + 0.04A$$

$$A = \$500,000 + 0.0698P$$

One approach to solving these equations is to substitute the equation for A in that for P, as below. (You could use other approaches, of course.)

$$P = \$200,000 + 0.04(\$500,000 + 0.0698P)$$

Simplifying and rearranging this equation yields

$$P = \$220,616$$

and substituting for P in the equation for A yields

$$A = \$515,399$$

The final step is to allocate these adjusted costs to the two operating departments using the percentages computed above. (That is, we do *not* adjust the percentages as was done using the step-down method.)

Service Departments	*Operating Departments*		Total Costs
	Forging	Machining	
Personnel			$220,616
$220,616 × 0.2325	$ 51,293		
$220,616 × 0.6977		$153,924	
Administration			515,399
$515,399 × 0.36	185,544		
$515,399 × 0.60		309,239	
Totals	$236,837	$463,163	$700,000

Notice that the total costs allocated equal the direct costs of the two service departments ($500,000 for Administration and $200,000 for Personnel).

Using the reciprocal method of allocation, we obtain the final total costs of the two operating departments.

	Forging	Machining	Total
Direct costs	$1,800,000	$3,000,000	$4,800,000
Allocations, from above	236,837	463,163	700,000
Totals	$2,036,837	$3,463,163	$5,500,000

The final total cost is still $5,500,000, the sum of the direct costs of the four departments, showing once again that the method of allocating costs does not, by itself, change the total cost incurred.

Those who favor the reciprocal method claim it is more "accurate" than other methods (including step-down). That is true in the sense that the reciprocal method recognizes all reciprocal services. But the method is subject to the same objection as is any other allocation method. It is arbitrary and so cannot be said to yield a "true" or "correct" cost for an operating department (especially if the costs of one or more of the service departments are largely fixed).

In this case, the choice between the step-down and reciprocal methods does not produce a significant difference in the total costs finally assigned to individual operating departments. (The difference is $1,837, which is less than 1% of the final total cost for each department.) In other cases, the difference could be much larger, and the need for managers to understand the potential impact of alternative allocation methods much greater.

ASSIGNMENT MATERIAL

Questions for Discussion

10-1   Relationships with previous material   What similarities are there between (a) the material in this chapter and (b) the emphasis on cost behavior in Chapters 2, 3, and 4 and the material in Chapters 5 and 8 on the data used in short-term and long-term decision making?

10-2   Responsibility versus control   The manager of a store of a large chain of supermarkets said the following to the controller of that chain.

> My son, who is taking a managerial accounting course at CU, has been telling me about something called responsibility accounting and how it can help to motivate employees. How come we don't have responsibility accounting in our stores? I've got a meat manager who pretty much keeps that department in my store going. My son says the meat department would be a good candidate for what he calls a profit center. What do you think?

What do you think?

10-3   Responsibility centers – universities   What problems do you see in establishing and evaluating responsibility centers in the following: (a) universities, (b) colleges or schools within universities, and (c) departments within colleges?

10-4   Responsibility reporting   The annual report of a major manufacturer carried the following paragraph (paraphrased).

> Specialization also continues within each marketing force as we increase the number of personnel. We are experiencing a steady rise in the number of customers as well as in the variety and complexity of products and equipment. As a result, an increasing proportion of our salespeople concentrate on just one or a few industries—or on certain product categories.

Suppose that in the past the salespeople sold all products to all kinds of customers in different industries. What effects will the new method of directing the efforts of the individual salespeople have on the responsibility reporting system?

10-5 *Organizational structure* The letter from the chief executive officer in an annual report of Genesco Inc. included the following paragraphs and chart.

NEW ORGANIZATION STRUCTURE

In many ways the most significant internal change has been Genesco's new management organization structure. At the Board meeting at the end of February, the Directors designated me the chief executive officer of the corporation. I then designed and implemented a new management structure. As shown in the chart below, the chief operating officers and the chief administrative officer report directly to me. Each officer is responsible for a major area of Genesco's operations.

Reporting to the chief operating officers are the group presidents, each of whom is responsible for a number of related operating companies. Reporting to the group presidents are the presidents of the operating companies.

In this chain of command, each executive knows his responsibilities, has the authority to take the action necessary to produce results, and knows that he is accountable for those results. This organization permits the rapid, decentralized decision making necessary in the apparel industry.

Which of the group presidents is likely to be responsible for an investment center? a profit center? a cost center?

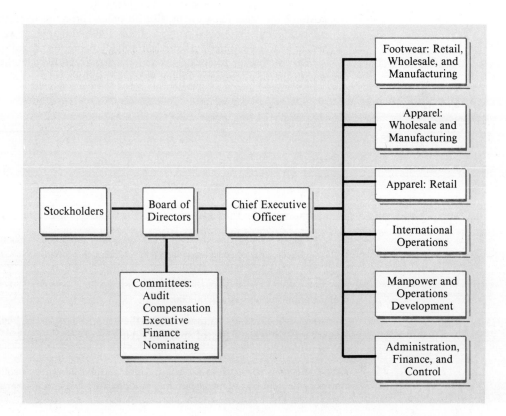

10-6 ***Pricing, timing, allocations, and public relations*** For many years telephone companies did not charge for directory assistance (calling an operator to get a number). When they did begin to charge (usually 20 cents per request after three free requests per month), a commentator said: "This is ridiculous. They have operators on duty anyway, so there is no additional cost for their giving out a number. Ma Bell has just found another way to get into our pockets."

Required: Comment on the quotation.

10-7 ***Artificial profit centers*** A national trade association held a seminar for chief executives where one of the topics discussed was responsibility accounting and the profit-center concept as a means of "correctly evaluating departments." Two executives who attended the conference made the following statements to their respective chief accounting officers.

1. "I want you to set up as many profit centers as possible, beginning with the legal department. From now on, departments using the services of the legal department will be charged at $40 per hour. That's about twice the average lawyer's salary and ought to cover the nonsalary costs of the legal department. We haven't even allocated the costs of the legal department up to now, and we might as well do something to let our managers know that when they ask for legal advice they can expect to pay for it."

2. "Well, you accountants have done it again. Like all the other high-priced professionals you insist on coming up with special names for something that everyone already understands. For years now we've been allocating the costs of the legal department, like all other corporate departments, to the operating units in our company, and now I'm told that what we need to do is set up a 'transfer price.' That's just a fancy name for allocating the costs."

   Do you foresee any problems with the first executive's intentions? Do you agree with the position taken by the second executive?

Exercises

10-8 ***Alternative allocation bases*** The following data refer to the three departments of ABC Company.

	A	B	C
Sales	$800,000	$400,000	$800,000
Square feet of space occupied	4,000	4,000	2,000

Total common costs are $200,000.

Required: Allocate the common costs to the departments on the bases of (a) sales dollars and (b) square feet of space occupied.

10-9 ***Basic allocation methods*** Mighty Mart Stores has three profit centers and one service center, a central purchasing department. Data appear below.

	Profit Centers		
	Groceries	Meat	Canned Goods
Percentage of central purchasing services used in current year	20%	40%	40%
Expected long-term use of central purchasing services	30%	30%	40%

Budgeted central purchasing costs were $600,000 fixed and $300,000 variable. Actual fixed costs were $620,000, and actual variable costs were $290,000.

Required
1. Allocate the actual central purchasing costs to the profit centers based on actual use of the services.
2. Allocate the budgeted variable central purchasing costs to the profit centers based on actual use of the services and the budgeted fixed costs based on expected long-term use.
3. Which of the two methods do you prefer? Why?

10-10 **Performance report** York Tool Company operates six departments in its main plant. Each department manager is responsible for materials, direct and indirect labor, supplies, small tools, and equipment maintenance. The factory manager is responsible for buying equipment and for all other costs. The manager of the Stamping Department received the following performance report last month. The costs of building occupancy have been allocated to the department.

	Budget	Actual	Over (Under)
Materials	$ 32,800	$ 31,900	($900)
Direct labor	36,200	36,500	300
Indirect labor	13,350	14,120	770
Supplies	6,600	6,450	(150)
Small tools	4,200	4,340	140
Equipment:			
Depreciation	12,800	12,800	0
Maintenance	5,700	4,950	(750)
Building:			
Depreciation	2,200	2,200	0
Maintenance	980	950	(30)
Property taxes	760	770	10
Total	$115,590	$114,980	($610)

Required: Prepare a new performance report that shows only the costs for which the manager of the Stamping Department is responsible.

10-11 **Step-down allocation method (related to Appendix)** Mott Company has two service departments, Personnel and Administration, and two operating departments, Foundry and Assembly. The schedule below shows the percentages of activity that each service department provides each of the other departments, both service and operating.

Department Providing Service	Department Receiving Service			
	Personnel	Administration	Foundry	Assembly
Personnel	0%	60%	10%	30%
Administration	20%	0%	60%	20%

The costs of Personnel and Administration were $200,000 and $300,000 respectively. One of the staff made the following allocations.

	Foundry	Assembly
Personnel:		
$200,000 × (.10/.40)	$50,000	
$200,000 × (.30/.40)		$150,000
Administration:		
$300,000 × (.60/.80)	225,000	
$300,000 × (.20/.80)		75,000
Total	$275,000	$225,000

The controller is wondering whether it would make any difference to use the step-down method, instead of the direct method shown above.

Required: Allocate the service department costs using the step-down method, beginning with Personnel costs.

10-12 *Reciprocal allocation (continuation of 10-11)*

Required: Do the allocation in 10-11 using the reciprocal method.

10-13 *Allocations—actual versus budgeted costs* Merion Turf Products produces lawn fertilizers and grass seed. The company's Research Department, which works to improve both types of products, had budgeted costs, virtually all fixed, of $450,000. These costs were to be allocated to the two product lines based on the relative amounts of time spent on each. All of the scientists keep time sheets showing which projects they work on each month.

At year end the Research Department had actually spent $496,000 as a result of unanticipated cost increases and some inefficiencies in the department. The manager of the Fertilizer Department had budgeted $225,000 for allocated research costs but found that he was actually charged with $276,760. The final allocation was based on actual costs and actual relative time spent on work for his department. He was not happy with the situation, especially when he learned that the manager of the Grass Seed Department had canceled a major project, resulting in lower-than-budgeted research on grass seed.

Required: Suggest a way to allocate research costs that will not unduly penalize the managers of the Fertilizer and Grass Seed Departments.

10-14 **Hospital allocations and decisions** Blake Memorial Hospital is a full-service hospital with several departments. Departments that perform services directly for patients are called *revenue centers* and include the Medical, Surgical, and Emergency Departments. Other departments, such as Admissions, Patient Records, Laundry, and Housekeeping, are called *service centers*. Costs of service centers are allocated to revenue centers. Below is a schedule showing the percentages of costs allocated from two service centers to two revenue centers, together with the direct costs of each of the service centers.

		Revenue Center	
Service Center	Costs	Medical	Surgical
Admissions	$300,000	70%	30%
Records	$400,000	20%	80%

The hospital receives reimbursements from Blue Cross, Medicaid, and other third parties for services performed for some patients. The reimbursement contracts typically allow recovery of both direct and indirect costs. Such reimbursements amount to about 30% of total Medical Department costs and about 90% for surgical costs. Thus, at the present time, the hospital is reimbursed for $144,000 of its Admissions costs, calculated as follows:

Through medical reimbursements ($300,000 × 70% × 30%)	$ 63,000
Through surgical reimbursements ($300,000 × 30% × 90%)	81,000
Total	$144,000

The hospital administrator is considering some different procedures that will increase the cost of Records by $10,000, while reducing Admissions costs by $6,000. Although the change is obviously not beneficial on cost grounds, the administrator is well aware of the differing reimbursement rates.

Required
1. Calculate the total reimbursement that the hospital now receives for the indirect costs of Admissions and Records.
2. Calculate the total reimbursement that the hospital will receive if the new procedures are adopted.

10-15 **Transfer prices and goal congruence** The controller of Calvert Company has set transfer prices for service departments, all of which used to be cost centers. One is for stenographic services. The charge is $13 per hour, based on total budgeted hours of available service and total budgeted costs for the stenographic pool. The manager of one operating department, a profit center, has obtained a price of $10 per hour for stenographers' time from an outside agency for a task that will take about 50 hours. The manager informs the controller and the manager of the stenographic pool of the outside price and is told to take it if he wishes; the transfer price will not be lowered.

Required: Comment on the position taken by the controller and the manager of the stenographic pool. (Budgeted costs for the pool are about 90% fixed.) Make a recommendation.

10-16 **Set of performance reports** Arcon, Inc., manufactures office equipment. The Raleigh Plant produces several models of copiers. The following schedule shows year-to-date controllable costs for the Assembly Department and for all others as a whole, in thousands of dollars.

	Assembly		All Others	
	Budget	Over (Under)	Budget	Over (Under)
Materials	$13.3	$1.1	$ 81.3	$3.2
Direct labor	26.4	(2.2)	247.1	4.3
Other controllable costs	16.6	1.8	108.4	(1.5)

There were $74,000 in budgeted costs controllable by the plant manager, but not by any of the department managers. Actual costs were $1,200 over budget. The Raleigh Plant is part of the Southeast region. Regions, like plants, and departments, are cost centers. Budgeted costs of the other plants in the region totaled $3,265,200, actual costs were $12,300 over budget. Budgeted costs of $120,600 (actual were $1,300 over budget) were controllable by the regional manager, but not by the plant managers.

Required: Prepare a set of responsibility reports for the Assembly Department, the Raleigh Plant, and the Southeast region using the format of Exhibit 10-1.

10-17 **Development of performance report** Stratton Company is organized by functional areas: sales, production, finance, and administration. The Sales Department has product managers who are responsible for a particular product and who are evaluated based on the following typical performance report.

Product Zee Activity Report
May 19X4—Manager, J. Harrison

Sales (30,000 units)		$300,000
Cost of goods sold		172,000
Gross profit		128,000
Other expenses:		
Advertising	$28,000	
Travel	17,000	
Depreciation	6,000	
Office expenses	19,000	
Administrative expense	23,000	93,000
Product profit		$ 35,000

The following additional information about the report is available.
(a) Because of problems in the production process, cost of goods sold is $11,000 higher than budgeted.
(b) The product manager spent $16,000 on product advertising. The remainder is an allocated share of general advertising costs incurred by the firm.

(c) Depreciation charges consist of the following: 20% on furniture and fixtures in the product manager's office and 80% for the building where all the firm's activities take place.

(d) Office expenses include $3,000 allocated from the expenses of the vice president for sales (salaries, data processing, etc.).

(e) Administrative expenses are allocated based on relative sales.

Required: Revise the performance report for product Zee to reflect the principle of controllability.

Problems

10-18 *Where did the income come from?* The income statement in the 1982 annual report for Pitney Bowes, Inc. shows total revenues of $1,455 million and net income of $83 million. The report also shows the following information, in millions of dollars.

	Operating Profit
Industry segments:	
Business equipment	$122.3
Retail systems	18.6
Business supplies	8.1
Total	$149.0
Geographical areas:	
United States	$125.2
Europe	7.3
Other (principally Canada)	14.6
Total	$147.1

Another table in the report shows revenues, using the same categories (segments and areas), but the breakdowns in both parts of that table add up to $1,455 million.

Required: Explain why the segments' revenues add up to the amount shown in the income statement, while neither of the totals in the two categories agrees with the total net income in the income statement.

10-19 *Step-down allocation (related to Appendix)* Walker Company has two operating departments, Machining and Assembly. It also has the following service departments: Personnel, Data Processing, and General Administration. The controller wishes to allocate the service department costs using the step-down method, beginning with Data Processing, then Personnel, and lastly, General Administration. She wants to use the following bases: Data Processing, number of transactions; Personnel, number of employees; General Administration, total direct costs (before any allocation of service department costs).

The controller has assembled the following data.

Department	Total Direct Costs	Number of Employees	Number of Data Processing Transactions
Data processing	$ 200,000	20	0
Personnel	150,000	30	20,000
General administration	300,000	100	30,000
Machining	2,000,000	300	40,000
Assembly	3,000,000	600	10,000

Required: Prepare a step-down allocation.

10-20 Performance reporting and allocations Clark Company, a furniture outlet, allocates indirect costs to its two departments based on sales. The income statement for 19X5 appears below.

	Indoor Furniture	Outdoor Furniture	Total
Sales	$350,000	$350,000	$700,000
Direct costs	180,000	180,000	360,000
Controllable profit	170,000	170,000	340,000
Indirect costs	150,000	150,000	300,000
Income	$ 20,000	$ 20,000	$ 40,000

In 19X6, the Indoor Department increased its prices and its sales increased to $400,000, while those of the Outdoor Department remained at $350,000. Direct costs of each department were again $180,000, and total indirect costs were again $300,000.

Required
1. Prepare a departmental income statement for 19X6 allocating indirect costs based on sales.
2. Comment on the results. Are they logical? Did the manager of outdoor furniture do a better job in 19X6 than in 19X5?

10-21 Responsibility for rush orders Howard Company's sales manager often requests rush orders from the production department. Howard's production process requires a great deal of setup time whenever changes in the production mix are made. The production manager has complained about these rush orders, arguing that costs are much lower when the process runs smoothly. The sales manager argues that the paramount consideration is to keep the customer's goodwill and that therefore all sales orders should be made up as quickly as possible.

Required
1. Identify the issues creating the conflict.
2. What steps might be taken to effect a satisfactory solution?

10-22 ***Performance measurement*** The sales manager of Warner Company is evaluated on the basis of total sales. Exceeding the sales budget is considered good performance. The sales budget and cost data for 19X3 are shown below.

	Product			
	Alpha	Beta	Gamma	Total
Sales budget	$150,000	$300,000	$550,000	$1,000,000
Variable costs	75,000	135,000	165,000	375,000
Contribution margin	$ 75,000	$165,000	$385,000	$ 625,000

Actual sales for the year were

Alpha	Beta	Gamma	Total
$500,000	$400,000	$200,000	$1,100,000

Actual prices were equal to budgeted prices, and variable costs were incurred as budgeted (per unit).

Required
1. Did the sales manager perform well? Support your answer with calculations.
2. What suggestions do you have regarding the performance measurement criterion used by the firm?

10-23 ***Behavioral problem*** Watson Company recently bought a copier with a capacity of 10,000 copies per day. The annual fixed costs of the copier are $24,000, the variable cost is $0.01 per copy. Previously, Watson had leased a similar copier with annual fixed costs of $14,000 and variable cost of $0.06 per copy. Watson allocates the fixed costs of the copier based on expected long-term use of the copier and the variable costs based on actual use.

Total copying had run about 8,000 per day with the old machine. The new copier is nearly always running at capacity, and people have complained that they cannot get copies within a reasonable time. Some managers have been forced to send material to outside copying services, which charge about $0.08 per copy.

Required: What seems to be happening, and what do you recommend, if anything?

10-24 ***Cost allocation – direct method*** The schedule below shows the percentages of service that the service departments of Winston Inc. provide to each other and to the operating departments.

Department Providing Service	Department Receiving Service			
	Purchasing	Administration	Trimming	Cutting
Purchasing		20%	50%	30%
Administration	30%		10%	60%

The direct costs of the Purchasing Department are $280,000, of the Administration Department $300,000.

Required: Use the direct method to allocate the service department costs to the operating departments. Assignment 10-11 shows how to calculate the percentages.

10-25 ***Cost allocation—step-down method*** Use the information from the previous assignment to do a step-down allocation, beginning with the Administration Department.

10-26 ***Cost allocation—reciprocal method*** Use the information from 10-24 to do a reciprocal allocation.

10-27 ***Allocations and expense reimbursement*** You need to take a business trip from your office in Atlanta to a branch in Los Angeles sometime in the next few weeks. You have also planned to play in a golf tournament near San Francisco. You manage to combine the trips so that you fly to Los Angeles, finish your business, then go to the tournament. Some airfares are

Atlanta–Los Angeles each way	$380
Los Angeles–San Francisco each way	$105
Atlanta–San Francisco each way	$420

Because you will be staying over a weekend, you get a special excursion ticket that allows you to make the entire trip for $740. You spend three days working, two days playing golf. Your company reimburses your business expenses.

Required
1. How much airfare will you show on your expense account?
2. Suppose that you were your boss. How much airfare would you allow the company to reimburse?

10-28 ***Responsibility for factory costs*** It is usually not possible to tell whether a cost is the responsibility of a specific manager simply by knowing its object classification (rent, wages, salaries, shipping, etc.). For each of the following costs, indicate some circumstances under which it would, or would not, be the responsibility of the following: (a) foreman, (b) department manager, and (c) plant manager.
1. Wages of factory workers
2. Rent on equipment
3. Electricity for machinery
4. Cost of materials
5. Cost of forms used for reporting hours worked by laborers, production results in each area, and performance reports for those areas.

10-29 ***Allocations and performance reporting*** Koehler Company allocates common costs to product lines. Before the beginning of each fiscal year, it develops budgeted rates for both manufacturing and selling costs based on budgeted common costs and budgeted company-wide revenues. At year-end, it reallocates common costs based on the actual results for the year. For 19X6, the budgeted rates were: manufacturing, 30% of revenue; selling, 10% of revenue. The actual rates turned out to be 35% for manufacturing, 12% for selling.

Budgeted and actual results reflecting these rates as well as the controllable costs for the Jensin line of apparel appear below, in thousands of dollars.

	Budget	Actual
Sales	$100.0	$110.0
Cost of sales	65.0	76.0
Gross margin	35.0	34.0
Selling expenses	20.0	23.7
Product line margin	$ 15.0	$ 10.3

The manager of the Jensin line was puzzled by the results. He was fairly sure that most controllable costs, fixed or variable, were reasonably on target, given the higher sales volume. He would have to explain the results to his superior in a few days and was concerned about what to say.

Required: Prepare a new report that separates controllable costs from allocated costs. Give the manager of the Jensin line some comments to make to his superior.

10-30 *Performance report for a cost center* Stan Porter, the manager of the Casting Department of Western Foundries, was disturbed by the report that he received last month.

Monthly Cost Report—Casting Department

	July, 19X6
Materials	$ 31,900
Direct labor	67,400
Indirect labor	2,410
Power	19,250
Maintenance	5,360
Other	10,210
Total	$136,530

Porter's superior had commented unfavorably on power and maintenance costs, both of which were higher than in previous months. Both costs are mixed, with the variable portions relatively controllable by the department managers, the fixed portions not controllable at the departmental level. The amounts shown are allocations based on the department's use of the services each month. The Casting Department used 9,200 kilowatt-hours of power and 800 hours of maintenance service in July. The budgeted monthly costs of the two services are

Power cost = $130,000 + $0.05 per kilowatt-hour

Maintenance cost = $24,000 + $0.80 per maintenance-hour

The Casting Department's long-term shares of the services are estimated at 10% for power and 15% for maintenance. All other costs on the report are controllable by the department manager.

Required: Prepare a new performance report for the Casting Department showing controllable costs and noncontrollable costs separately. Allocate fixed power and maintenance costs based on the department's long-term use of the services.

10-31 ***Performance report in a service company***   Bill Wardlaw is the partner in charge of the Tax Department at Bryan & Cummings, a large firm of Certified Public Accountants. The firm also has an Audit Department and a Management Services Department. Bill recently received the following performance report.

	February	March
Revenues	$140,600	$148,400
Costs:		
Staff salaries	76,800	77,400
Travel and supplies	7,800	8,100
Occupancy and utilities	9,800	10,900
General office expense	15,400	21,800
Total costs	109,800	118,200
Income	$ 30,800	$ 30,200

Wardlaw thought that the department had done much better in March than in February and was surprised by the report. He talked to the firm's internal accountant, who had prepared the report, to gather additional information. Staff salaries, travel, and supplies are all direct to the department. Occupancy and utilities are allocated based on space occupied. In March, the lease on the firm's office had run out and was renewed at a higher rent. General office expense is allocated to departments based on revenue. The Audit and Management Services Departments both experienced drops in revenue in March, resulting in a higher share going to the Tax Department.

Required: Revise the preceding report to show revenue, direct costs, controllable profit, allocated indirect costs, and income. Do you believe that the Tax Department performed better in February than in March? Why or why not?

10-32 ***Compensation plan (CMA adapted)***   Parsons Company compensates its salespersons with commissions and a year-end bonus. The commission is 20% of a "net profit," which is computed as the normal selling price less manufacturing costs. (Such costs contain some allocated fixed overhead.) The profit is also reduced by any bad debts on sales written by individual salespersons. The granting of credit is the responsibility of the firm's credit department, and credit approval is required before sales are made.

Salespeople can give price reductions, which must be approved by the sales vice president. Commissions are not affected by such price concessions.

The year-end bonus is 15% of commissions earned during the year provided that the individual salesperson has achieved the target sales volume. If the target is not reached, there is no bonus. The annual target volume is generally set at 105% of the previous year's sales.

Required

1. Identify the features of the compensation plan that are likely to motivate the salespeople to work in the best interests of the firm. Explain your answers.
2. Identify the features of the plan that are likely to be ineffective or even counterproductive in motivating salespeople to work in the firm's interests. Explain your answers.

10-33 *Selecting an allocation base*   Carter Brothers Discount Mart has just begun to allocate indirect costs to its departments. The controller has decided to allocate annual building rent of $2,000,000 based on the floor space that each department occupies. Jennifer Bynum, the manager of the Children's Department, has objected to this basis. She contends that the basis should be the relative value of the space. Her department is on the second floor. Comparable second floor space rents for about $10 per square foot, while first floor space rents for about $15 per square foot.

The Children's Department occupies 20,000 square feet of the total 100,000 square feet on the second floor. The first floor also has 100,000 square feet.

Required

1. Determine the amount of cost that the Children's Department would be allocated using the controller's method.
2. Determine the amount of cost that the Children's Department would be allocated using Jennifer's method.
3. Which method seems better to you? Why?

10-34 *Promotion decision*   Food Miser is a chain of grocery stores that pays its managers monthly bonuses based on the performance of their departments. All indirect costs are allocated to departments, and all department managers believe the allocations to be fair. The Lakewood Store recently ran a month-long half-price promotion on canned goods, giving the following results, in thousands of dollars.

	Canned Goods	All Other	Total
Sales	$46.5	$246.0	$292.5
Variable costs	32.4	94.0	126.4
Contribution margin	14.1	152.0	166.1
Fixed costs	12.8	105.2	118.0
Income	$ 1.3	$ 46.8	$ 48.1

All managers acknowledged the promotion to be successful. Without it, the Lakewood Store had shown results similar to those below.

	Canned Goods	All Other	Total
Sales	$40.6	$231.6	$272.2
Variable costs	22.4	90.2	112.6
Contribution margin	18.2	141.4	159.6
Fixed costs	11.8	106.2	118.0
Income	$ 6.4	$ 35.2	$ 41.6

Required

1. Did the manager of the Canned Goods Department receive a better-than-normal bonus for the month of the promotion?
2. Should the manager of the Canned Goods Department have received a better-than-normal bonus? Why or why not?

10-35 *Allocations and decisions*   Cramer Company has several product lines, each under the control of a different manager. Each manager is evaluated partly on profit. The expenses charged to each line are the direct costs of the line plus 15% of sales. (The 15% covers costs not directly associated with the lines, such as salaries of the corporate staff, interest on corporate debt, and service functions like personnel, building security, and cafeteria. These costs are virtually all fixed.) The president of the company estimated that 15% would cover these expenses at budgeted sales of $6,000,000 for the coming year. Each year the percentage is adjusted based on budgeted costs and budgeted sales for the entire company.

The manager of the small appliances line has the opportunity to sell 20,000 units to a chain store at $30 each. Per-unit variable costs are $27, ignoring the 15% charge. There would be no incremental fixed costs associated with the order, and there is sufficient capacity to make the additional units.

Required

1. Given the existing plan for evaluating performance, will the manager of small appliances accept the order? Why or why not?
2. Is it in the company's best interests for the manager to accept the order? Why or why not?

10-36 *Performance measures*   Below are six job titles and the measure by which performance in that job is judged. Comment on each.

Job or Job Title	Performance Measure
(a) Director of the county's mental health program.	The number of patients released from treatment.
(b) Director of a program to reduce unemployment.	The number of jobs found for persons on the unemployment rolls, as a percentage of the total unemployed persons.
(c) Director of a regional program to rehabilitate substandard housing.	The number of homes now meeting local building codes that had previously been classified substandard.
(d) The operator of a particular machine.	The number of hours the machine is running.
(e) A salesperson.	The dollars of sales orders written divided by the number of customers visited.
(f) A college professor.	The enrollment in the professor's classes.

10-37 *Evaluation of compensation plans (AICPA adapted)*   Gibson Company was established some years ago to bring several new products to the market. Its founders believed that once customers tried their products, they would become well accepted. For the first several years, Gibson grew at a rate the founders considered to be satisfactory. In recent years some problems have developed both in the firm's profitability and in the morale of and harmonious relationships among the firm's salespeople. Since the company began, salespeople have been paid a base salary plus an 8% commission. The following data are available for two salespeople for the most recent year.

	Ronald McTavish	James Christy
Gross sales orders written	$250,000	$180,000
Commissions	20,000	14,400
Sales returns	17,500	9,000
Cost of goods sold—all variable	139,500	68,400
Discretionary expenses of salesmen (travel, entertainment, etc.)	19,200	21,500

Required
1. Determine which salesperson contributed more to the company's profit by preparing a performance report for each.
2. What changes, if any, do you recommend be made in the company's compensation method?

10-38 **Allocation and behavior**   Brenner Company allocates common production costs such as depreciation, property taxes, payroll office, and factory accounting on the basis of the cost of materials used on jobs in each production department. Budgeted material costs for the coming year are $300,000, common production costs $750,000.

The manager of the Fabricating Department has developed a new process that requires 10% more materials than the old process, but 20% less labor time. Without the new process, she expects to incur materials costs of $60,000 and labor costs of $50,000 during the coming year.

Required: Is it desirable to introduce the new process? Consider the viewpoints of both the firm and the manager of the Fabricating Department. If your answers conflict, suggest a solution.

10-39 **Cost allocations and performance measurement**   Edwards Company allocates indirect costs to its three products, each of which is the responsibility of a different manager. The three managers are evaluated based on the pretax incomes generated by their respective products. Income statements for a typical month are as follows, in thousands of dollars.

	Product			
	Toasters	Ovens	Dishwashers	Total
Sales	$1,200	$800	$400	$2,400
Variable costs	720	420	150	1,290
Contribution margin	480	380	250	1,110
Indirect costs—allocated	450	300	150	900
Income	$ 30	$ 80	$100	$ 210

The manager for toasters believes that if he reduces his price from $20 per unit to $18 per unit, sales will rise from 60,000 to 85,000 units. Variable costs per unit will remain the same. Sales of the other products will not be affected.

Required
1. Determine whether the price decrease benefits the firm.
2. Prepare a new set of income statements based on the manager's estimates. Be sure to reallocate the indirect costs based on the new sales figures. Is it in the manager's best interest to reduce the price? Comment on the advisability of allocating indirect costs this way.

10-40 Assignment of responsibility   The controller of Baldwin Company is authorized to charge sales departments with overtime premium paid to production workers when a sales manager requests an order that requires overtime. (Overtime premium is the difference between the wage rate paid when workers are on overtime and their regular rate.) There are four sales managers, each responsible for a different product.

During March budgeted production totaled 20,000 units; capacity production, without overtime, is 22,000 units. Because demand for all the company's products increased early in the month, on March 10, each of the four sales managers requested additional production of 1,000 units. The production manager reported that the extra 1,000 units of products A and B were made during regular working hours while the extra production of C and D was carried out during hours when overtime rates were paid. Each unit of any product takes one hour to produce, and overtime premium is $2 per hour.

Required: Which sales manager(s) should be charged with the overtime premium and how much?

10-41 Performance reporting—alternative organizational structure (CMA adapted)   Cranwell Company sells three products in a foreign market and a domestic market. An income statement for the first month of 19X2 shows the following.

Sales		$1,300,000
Cost of goods sold		1,010,000
Gross profit		290,000
Selling expenses	$105,000	
Administrative expenses	72,000	177,000
Income		$ 113,000

Data regarding the two markets and three products are given below.

	Products		
	A	B	C
Sales:			
Domestic	$400,000	$300,000	$300,000
Foreign	100,000	100,000	100,000
Total sales	$500,000	$400,000	$400,000
Variable production costs (percentage of sales)	60%	70%	60%
Variable selling costs (percentage of sales)	3%	2%	2%

Product A is made in a single factory that incurs fixed costs (included in cost of goods sold) of $48,000 per month. Products B and C are made in a single factory and require the same machinery. Monthly fixed production costs at that factory are $142,000.

Fixed selling expenses are joint to the three products, but $36,000 is direct to the domestic market and $38,000 to the foreign market. All administrative expenses are fixed. About $25,000 is traceable to the foreign market, $35,000 to the domestic market.

Required

1. Assume that Cranwell has separate managers responsible for each market. Prepare performance reports for the domestic and foreign markets.
2. Assume that Cranwell has separate managers responsible for each product. Prepare performance reports for the three products.

10-42 *Cost allocations, transfer prices, and behavior* Several top executives of Millard Company are discussing problems they perceive in the company's methods of cost allocation. For each of the costs discussed below, indicate what changes will help accomplish the stated objectives.

(a) Computer cost, which is 95% fixed, is allocated using a transfer price of $100 per hour of use. The executives believe that lower-level managers do not use the computer enough.

(b) Maintenance costs, which are budgeted at $10 per hour variable and $200,000 per year fixed, are allocated by dividing total incurred cost by total maintenance hours worked and distributing the resulting per-hour cost to operating departments according to the number of hours of maintenance work done. The executives believe that operating managers request maintenance work only in emergencies (i.e., when machinery is about to break down). Production has halted while repairs were made on critical machines. Operating managers have complained that the per-hour cost is too high.

(c) Millard has a consulting department that advises operating managers on various aspects of production and marketing. The costs of the department are fixed but discretionary and have been rising in recent years because of heavy demand for its services. The costs are not allocated because it was felt that managers should be encouraged to use the service. One executive commented that operating managers call the department to find out where to go for lunch.

10-43 *Allocations and behavior* R. A. Shore is a large mail-order company dealing in men's and women's clothing and accessories. Shore operates its six regional distribution centers as profit centers. Until now, each distribution center handled its own trucking requirements. Shore has just acquired a fleet of trucks, which are under the control of the traffic manager, who is based at central headquarters.

The traffic manager anticipates having to hire outside truckers because Shore's fleet is insufficient to meet peak demands. He wants the managers of the distribution centers to provide monthly estimates of their trucking needs, from which he will decide how much, if any, outside trucking to hire. There are two potential problems with the estimates. If they are either too high or too low, costs will be higher than necessary.

First, the typical agreement with an outside trucker provides for a payment of $1.20 per mile, but with a guarantee of 2,000 miles for a month. Thus, the trucker will be paid $2,400 even if he drives only 1,000 miles. The guarantees can add up to a substantial amount if the estimates are too high. Second, if the estimates are too low, the traffic manager must scramble to find additional truckers in the middle of the month, also adding to costs. Therefore, accurate estimates of trucking needs are desirable. The controller wants a cost allocation scheme that will encourage accuracy.

Required
1. Suppose that the controller decides not to allocate trucking costs. Do you expect the managers of the distribution centers to pay much attention to their monthly estimates of needs?
2. Answer the question in item 1 assuming that the controller decides to allocate all trucking costs, both for the owned fleet and for outsiders, based on mileage used by each center.
3. What would you do to encourage the managers of the distribution centers to act in Shore's best interests?

10-44 Allocations and managers' bonuses   Walter Grove, the owner of Grove-Mart, wants to pay his department managers bonuses totaling $7,500. Grove wants the $7,500 allocated based on the profit each department earns. In the following income statement, all indirect costs are allocated based on sales.

	Dry Goods	Housewares	Total
Sales	$250,000	$500,000	$750,000
Total direct costs	166,000	437,000	603,000
Controllable profit	84,000	63,000	147,000
Indirect costs (all fixed):			
Sales salaries	16,000	32,000	48,000
Other	8,000	16,000	24,000
Total indirect costs	24,000	48,000	72,000
Profit	$ 60,000	$ 15,000	$ 75,000

Some salespeople work in one department or the other, while some cover both departments. The manager of Housewares argues that the allocation of indirect sales salaries is inappropriate. He believes that the allocation should be based on the relative direct sales salaries of $60,000 for Dry Goods and $20,000 for Housewares. (These amounts are included in direct costs.) He says that the work of the salespeople is related to the total sales effort.

Required
1. Compute each manager's bonus given the existing allocations.
2. Prepare a new income statement allocating indirect sales salaries as suggested by the manager of Housewares. Compute each manager's bonus.
3. Comment on the results. Which method of allocation gives the better result?
4. How might Grove distribute the $7,500 to the managers in a reasonable way without getting into arguments over allocations?

10-45 Performance report   The controller of Caldwell Department Store is developing performance analyses for the managers of the store's three major lines—housewares, clothing, and sporting goods. He has prepared the following income statement, in thousands of dollars.

	Housewares	Clothing	Sporting Goods	Total
Sales	$900	$1,200	$400	$2,500
Cost of goods sold	500	680	180	1,360
Gross profit	400	520	220	1,140
Other expenses:				
Salaries	60	90	40	190
Advertising	45	60	20	125
Rent	40	40	20	100
Depreciation	20	16	12	48
General and administrative	90	120	40	250
Miscellaneous	60	85	32	177
Total expenses	315	411	164	890
Profit	$ 85	$ 109	$ 56	$ 250

You learn the following about the data in the above statements:

(a) Cost of goods sold is direct.

(b) Salaries expense includes allocated salaries of $75,000 for employees whose work takes them into different departments. The controller used relative sales to make the allocations.

(c) Advertising is partly allocated. Each department is charged at standard market rates for newspaper space, radio time, and television time that its manager requests. The $50,000 cost of general advertising ordered by the sales vice president was allocated based on sales dollars.

(d) The rent allocation is based on floor space occupied. The three departments occupy 100,000 square feet. Sporting Goods is in the basement, the others on the first floor. Similar property in the city rents for $1.05 per square foot for first floor space, $0.80 for basement space. Rent on space occupied by the administrative offices is included in general and administrative expenses.

(e) Depreciation is all for furniture and fixtures within the departments.

(f) General and administrative expenses are allocated based on sales dollars.

(g) Miscellaneous expenses are partly separable, partly allocated. The allocated amounts by department are as follows: Housewares, $28,000; Clothing, $36,000; and Sporting Goods, $16,000.

Required: Prepare a new performance report using the principle of controllability. Include a column for unallocated costs, as well as one for each department.

10-46   Transfer prices and behavior   All operating departments of Jacson Company are profit or investment centers, and some service departments are artificial profit centers. The Maintenance Department is an artificial profit center that charges $10 per man-hour for work that it does for operating departments. The variable cost per man-hour is $4, and fixed costs are $40,000 per month.

The manager of Department A, an operating department, has just determined that some changes in the production process can be made. If the changes are made, maintenance requirements will drop from 2,100 man-hours per month to 1,600. However, the variable cost to produce a unit of product will increase from $6 to $7. Department A produces 4,000 units of product per month.

Required
1. Determine the change in monthly profit for Department A if the production process is changed.
2. Determine the change in profit of the Maintenance Department if Department A changes its production process.
3. Determine the effect on the firm's monthly profit of the change in Department A's production process.
4. Suppose that the manager of Department A was prompted to study possible changes in the production process because he had heard that the transfer price for maintenance work was to be raised to $12 per hour. The higher price was proposed by the Maintenance Department manager because he expected a $1 increase in variable cost per man-hour and had approved other expenditures that will raise fixed costs by $8,000 per month. For the last several months, the Maintenance Department has shown a profit of $8,000, and the proposed new transfer price was designed to maintain that profit level.
    (a) How many hours of maintenance work per month are currently done by the Maintenance Department?
    (b) If the manager of Department A makes the change in the production process, what profit will Maintenance show for a month?

10-47 Cost allocation   Galco Industries allocates indirect costs to departments and product lines using direct labor hours as the basis. The allocations for 19X5 are based on 400,000 direct labor hours and $1,910,000 indirect costs. Data related to one product line, cleaners, and to all others as a group, for 19X5 follow.

	Totals	Cleaners	All Others
Direct labor hours	400,000	50,000	350,000

Required: Allocate the indirect costs to cleaners and to the others using direct labor hours as the basis.

10-48 Multiple activity allocation bases (continuation of 10-47)   The managers of Galco have become convinced that they need several bases to reflect the activities that drive their indirect costs. After careful study, the controller developed the following information regarding cost pools and activities that drive the pools.

Cost Driver	Amount of Activity	Amount of Related Indirect Costs
Labor hours	400,000 hours	$1,580,000
Recordkeeping	150,000 entries	180,000
Number of parts	4,000 parts	150,000
Total indirect costs		$1,910,000

Data related to one product line, cleaners, and to all others as a group, for 19X5 follow.

	Totals	Cleaners	All Others
Direct labor hours	400,000	50,000	350,000
Recordkeeping entries	150,000	6,000	144,000
Number of parts	4,000	100	3,900

Required
1. Allocate each group of costs separately to cleaners and to the group of others using the separate bases.
2. The company sells 30,000 cases of cleaners annually. Its direct costs are $16.50 per unit. Calculate the total per-case costs using your results from this assignment and those from the previous assignment. Comment on the difference.

10-49 **Performance report** Budgeted and actual results for the carpet line of Glenn Products appear below, along with selected other data. Glenn makes a wide variety of products, with each line under a single manager.

Carpet Line, January 19X6 (in thousands of dollars)

	Budget	Actual	Over (Under)
Sales	$434.0	$446.4	$12.4
Cost of sales	262.0	279.1	17.1
Gross margin	172.0	167.3	(4.7)
Operating expenses	97.0	100.0	3.0
Profit	$ 75.0	$ 67.3	($ 7.7)

Other data:
1. The carpet line is manufactured in several plants, all of which make other products using fabric and other materials that go into carpets. The fixed costs of all of these factories, totaling about $8 million per month, are allocated to product lines based on relative variable manufacturing costs. Budgeted variable manufacturing costs for the carpet line were about 38% of sales, while actual costs were about 39% of sales because of some price reductions.
2. The carpet line had budgeted and actual fixed operating expenses traceable to its operations of $32,600. Variable operating expenses, both budgeted and actual, were 6% of sales. The remaining costs shown in the statement were allocated expenses common to the entire business of the firm. These costs are allocated based on relative sales.

Required: Prepare a report on the carpet line that identifies the responsibility of the manager in charge. Use the format of Exhibit 10-2 but include a column for actual results as well as for budgeted results and amounts over or under.

10-50 **Assignment of responsibility** Peckman Company has one manager in charge of purchasing and another in charge of production. The purchasing manager is responsible for acquiring raw materials at the lowest possible cost consistent with quality standards. The production manager is responsible for meeting production quotas at the least possible cost. Prices of the materials fluctuate, and the purchasing manager attempts to take advantage of these fluctuations by buying large quantities when he believes that prices will rise in the near future and holding off on purchases when he believes that prices will fall. The production manager complains that these buying habits adversely affect his performance. He cites the following reasons:

(a) Bottlenecks frequently develop because materials are unavailable when the purchasing manager is waiting for better prices.

(b) Efficiency is reduced when large purchases are made because it is difficult to find the needed materials when there is so much stored in a limited space.

The production manager suggests that limits be placed on the quantities of materials that can be bought at any one time and that minimum levels be set for each type of material so that sufficient quantities will always be available. The purchasing manager feels that these limitations will adversely affect profits because purchases will often have to be made at unfavorable times.

Required

1. Discuss the issues involved.
2. How can their responsibilities be separated?
3. What recommendations do you have?

10-51 Cost allocations in a university Ed Cranston, the new dean of the School of Business at Midstate University, is concerned. It is only early February, and he has just received a report from the university's printing and duplicating service showing that the school has exceeded its budget for duplicating for the academic year. The report appears as follows.

Printing and Duplicating Department Statement of Budget and
Charges for the School of Business, September–January

Annual Budget	Actual Charges	Over (Under)
$4,200	$4,350	$150

An enclosed note states that Ed must either stop using the service or obtain approval of a supplemental budget request from the chief fiscal officer of the university. Ed pulls out his latest statement, from December, and finds that actual charges at that time were $1,830. Since the school was on vacation during a good part of January, he wonders how $2,520 could have been incurred in January.

He finds out that costs for the Printing and Duplicating Department in January were $6,300, of which $700 was for paper, $2,000 for salaries, $2,000 for machine rentals, and $1,600 general overhead (allocated share of all university utilities, depreciation, etc.). A total of 35,000 copies was made in January, a relatively low number because of the vacation. However, several faculty members in the School of Business had a substantial amount of printing done for scholarly papers that they were circulating to other professors throughout the country. The School of Business was responsible for 14,000 of the 35,000 copies. The $2,520 charge was computed by dividing total department costs for the month by the number of copies ($6,300/35,000) to arrive at a charge of $0.18 per copy. Ed also learns that during a typical month about $8,600 in cost is incurred and 150,000 copies are processed. Paper is the only variable cost.

Required: Evaluate the cost allocation system used and recommend changes if you think any are necessary.

10-52 *Allocation of costs—distribution channels* Weisner Company sells its products through wholesalers and retailers. Eric Stern is in charge of wholesale sales, and Ralph Pike manages retail sales. Frederick Weisner, president of the firm, has ordered an analysis of the relative profitability of the two channels of distribution to determine where emphasis should be placed. The following data show the operations for the last six months.

	Wholesalers	Retailers
Sales	$2,000,000	$3,000,000
Cost of sales—all variable	1,600,000	2,000,000
Sales commissions (3% of sales)	60,000	90,000
Managers' salaries	18,000	18,000
Advertising (allocated as a percentage of sales dollars)	12,000	18,000
Selling expenses—salespeople's expenses, delivery, order processing, credit checking (allocated on the basis of number of orders from each group)	80,000	160,000
General expenses (allocated as a percentage of sales dollars)	40,000	60,000
Total expenses	1,810,000	2,346,000
Income	$ 190,000	$ 654,000

The same products are sold to both wholesalers and retailers, but prices to wholesalers are about 20% less than those to retailers.

Required
1. Comment on the reasonableness of the allocation methods used.
2. Recast the statement based on the principle of controllability.
3. What further information would help in assigning costs to the responsible managers?

Cases

10-53 *Performance measurement* Tenspeed Company has been in the business of repairing bicycles for many years. Average profits had been $60,000 annually, with revenues of $150,000. The firm recently began to sell bicycles and to provide free repairs for one year after sale. As a result, total profits have increased as shown in the income statement below for a typical year.

	Bicycle Sales	Repairs	Total
Revenues	$400,000	$100,000	$500,000
Variable costs	160,000	75,000	235,000
Contribution margin	240,000	25,000	265,000
Separable fixed costs	80,000	15,000	95,000
Income	$160,000	$ 10,000	$170,000

The manager of the Repair Department has complained that his performance looks bad solely because he is charged with the costs of repairing bicycles sold by the firm, while not being credited with any revenue for this work. He contends that he should be credited with revenue of 200% of variable costs of the repair work on sold bicycles, which is consistent with the revenue on regular repair work.

The bicycle sales manager says that such a markup is too much, but that he is willing to accept a transfer price equal to variable cost of work done on bicycles sold. The mix of work in the Repair Department is two-thirds regular repairs, one-third repairs on bicycles sold by the firm.

Required
1. Recast the income statement to reflect the Repair Department manager's position. (Add the revenues credited to the Repair Department to variable costs of the Bicycle Sales Department.)
2. Recast the income statement to show results if the Repair Department were credited with revenue equal to the variable cost of repair work done on bicycles sold.
3. What recommendations can you make? Give reasons.

10-54 *Allocations and behavior*   Clifford Electronics operates a single plant. Clifford allocates indirect costs to departments and then to product lines based on their direct labor content. Each department concentrates on one product line. The cost of an average unit of one of its major lines, made in Department Z, appears below. The data relate to a recent month when the company made 50,000 units of the product line.

Materials and components	$ 90
Direct labor at $12 per hour	24
Indirect costs at 500% of direct labor	120
Total cost	$234

The indirect cost rate of 500% of direct labor cost is based on actual total indirect costs divided by the $4,000,000 total company-wide labor cost for the most recent month. Because of the high combined labor and indirect costs, the department manager urged the Design Engineering Department to work on reducing the labor time in the product. The engineers did a great deal of redesigning that resulted in a 25% reduction in labor time over a six month period, largely by using costlier parts and components that required less time to assemble. The department manager was then surprised to see the following analysis for the sixth month of the program, when production was 50,000 units.

Materials and components	$ 95
Direct labor at $12	18
Indirect at 650% of direct labor	117
Total cost	$230

The manager was aghast at the results and could not understand why such a concentrated effort had shown so little payoff. The manager of engineering was also distressed at the results. The most disappointing aspect was the sharp increase in the indirect cost rate, and the manager decided to determine its cause. He learned that total labor hours for the company decreased about 10% over the six month period because other departments were also trying to reduce labor costs.

Required
1. Determine total indirect costs allocated to the product line in each month.
2. What reasons might there be for the disappointing results?

10-55 *Allocations and behavior (continuation of 10-54)* The controller of Clifford Electronics was well aware of the problems created by its use of direct labor to allocate all indirect costs. She did considerable analysis and developed the following plant-wide pools of average monthly indirect costs, as they related to particular cost drivers.

Activity	Amount of Activity	Amount of Related Indirect Costs
Labor cost	$ 3,480,000	$ 9,880,000
Recordkeeping	2,400,000 entries	840,000
Materials	$48,000,000 cost of materials	11,350,000
Engineering hours	4,000 hours	770,000
Total indirect costs		$22,840,000

The controller noted that using direct labor cost to allocate the indirect costs gave a rate of about 650%, as Department Z experienced in a previous month. That is, $22,840,000/$3,480,000 = 656\%$. She wanted to see how the allocations would change using these four bases, instead of just direct labor. She collected the following data for the line described in the preceding assignment.

Labor cost	$ 900,000
Recordkeeping	400,000 entries
Cost of materials used	$4,750,000
Engineering hours	300 hours

Required
1. Calculate the rate per unit of activity for each group of indirect costs.
2. Use the rates calculated in part 1 to allocate indirect costs to Department Z, and determine the unit cost of the average product in Z's line using the new allocation.
3. Comment on the differences between this allocation scheme and the one that uses only direct labor cost.

10-56 *Performance measurement in an automobile dealership* In automobile dealerships the sales managers of new and used cars are commonly evaluated according to the profits on sales of new and used cars, respectively. A new-car sales agreement may include some allowance for a traded-in used car. The trade-in allowance is often based on what the used-car manager is willing to pay the new-car manager for the car. For example, suppose that a customer wants to buy a new car that has a list price of $12,000 and trade in a used car. If there were no trade-in, the price of the car would be $11,200. If the used-car manager will give

$3,500 for the used car to be traded in, the new-car salesperson could allow up to $4,300 to the customer, because the net price would still be satisfactory. The $7,700 cash paid ($12,000 list price—$4,300 allowed on the old car) is the same as the difference between the $11,200 desired price and the $3,500 that the used-car manager will pay for the car.

Sometimes the used-car manager will offer lower prices than at other times, say, if his lot is full and sales are slow. If the used-car manager will pay only $2,800 for the car, the salesperson could give only a $3,600 trade-in allowance to obtain $11,200.

Required

1. Assuming that each manager is evaluated on profits in his respective area, what is the disadvantage of the system to the new-car manager? Is there a disadvantage to the used-car manager?
2. Suppose that the dealership's policy provides that if the new-car manager is unhappy with the price offered by the used-car manager, the former can try to sell the car to another used-car dealer. In the second example, suppose the new-car manager believed that the trade-in automobile could be sold to another used-car dealer for $3,500. The $11,200 deemed acceptable for the new car would be obtained ($7,700 from the customer plus $3,500 from selling the trade-in), so this deal for the new car would be accepted despite the lower bid from the used-car manager. What conflicts could arise under this system? Does the system encourage the managers to act in the best interests of the total firm?

10-57 **Home office allocations and decisions** Worcester Manufacturing Company has 14 sales offices throughout the United States and Canada. Each sales office is a profit center, with the local manager able to set prices and offer special discounts to obtain customers. Many functions like checking creditworthiness of customers, billing, and others are centralized in the home office. A few years ago, the president decided to charge the sales offices for these functions. After some thought, he set the charge at 8% of revenue. Home office costs are almost all fixed.

The firm's factories bill the sales offices for goods at prices established annually. The charge includes both variable manufacturing costs and a margin to cover fixed costs. Variable manufacturing costs average about 40% of revenue at current prices.

Lee Mott, manager of the Miami office, has come to you for advice. He is considering a price reduction that he expects to add considerably to unit volume but is unsure of the effects on profit. He begins by showing you an income statement that reflects his expectations for the coming year without the price reduction.

Miami Office Budgeted Income Statement for 19X2

Sales		$2,400,000
Cost of sales		1,200,000
Gross margin		1,200,000
Salaries and commissions	$490,000	
Rent, utilities, insurance	86,000	
Home office charge	192,000	768,000
Profit		$ 432,000

Mott believes that it is possible to obtain the following increases in unit volume given the associated decreases in selling prices.

Decrease in Price	Increase in Unit Volume
5%	20%
10%	35%

Mott tells you that the only variable costs of running the office are the 15% commissions that salespeople earn. Of course, his "cost of sales" is variable also because it depends on unit volume, as is the home office charge because it depends on total revenue. Mott is evaluated on the profit that his office generates.

Required
1. Determine whether or not Mott should reduce prices, and if so, by how much.
2. Determine which action (hold prices, reduce by 5%, reduce by 10%) is in the firm's best interests.

10-58 *Incurred costs and performance*   Weldon Oil Company operates a refinery in the northeastern United States. During the winter about 200 workers are employed as drivers of fuel-oil trucks to deliver oil for heating purposes. Drivers are paid $10 per hour. During the summer there is no need for their services as fuel-oil truck drivers, and they are given jobs in the refinery. These refinery jobs pay only $7 per hour. However, company policy is to pay the drivers their usual $10 rate.

The refinery manager is charged with the $10 wage paid to the drivers while they work in the refinery. The manager of fuel-oil distribution bears no charge except when the workers are delivering fuel oil. The refinery manager does not object to employing the drivers during the summer. Even with this addition to his regular work force he must hire students and other temporary employees in the summer. He does, however, object to the $10 charge in the summer, because he can obtain equally qualified (for those jobs) workers at $7 per hour and he must use the drivers as a matter of company policy.

Required: Discuss the issues involved and make a recommendation about the charges for the drivers' wages during the summer.

CHAPTER 11

DIVISIONAL PERFORMANCE MEASUREMENT

Responsibility accounting systems provide information that helps managers control operations and also help higher-level managers evaluate performance. This chapter studies control and evaluation in investment centers, though much of the discussion also applies to profit centers. Investment centers are often large enough to be divisions[1] of a large firm. They are often relatively autonomous and act almost as independent firms. The use of investment centers allows their managers to be evaluated almost as if they were chief executive officers of firms.

Investment centers control all the major components of financial performance (revenues, costs, and investments). They can therefore be evaluated by more complete measures of performance than can cost centers or profit centers, which do not control all these elements. The more complete the performance measure the better, and the measures described in this chapter are more complete than cost or profit measures.

DECENTRALIZATION

The term **decentralized** refers to companies that give managers broad authority. Companies that use investment centers are usually highly decentralized. Man-

[1] The term *division* can refer to any large operating unit of a firm, but in this chapter it refers to an investment center.

agers of such centers are responsible for and control revenues, expenses, and investment. In highly decentralized firms, operating units (usually called *divisions*) are almost autonomous; division managers are responsible for both production and marketing, as well as for functions such as personnel and accounting. Division managers also prepare and submit capital budgets to central headquarters for approval. However, division managers usually have no control over long-term financing, which is administered by central headquarters.

Benefits of Decentralization

Proponents of decentralizing argue that it promotes better decision making. They believe that managers who are closest to an operation can make better decisions because they are better able to gather and evaluate information than are centrally located corporate managers. Managers at the scene can also act more quickly because they do not need to report to headquarters and wait for approval of their proposed actions.

In a modern business of any complexity, it is impossible to operate without delegating some authority to lower-level managers. Because of the interdependence of functional areas, conflicts between functional managers are inevitable. Hence, it is often wise to make some managers responsible for both revenues and costs. Then, when conflicts occur, one of those managers becomes responsible for resolving them. When the firm's chief executive is the only manager whose span of responsibility includes both conflicting functions, arbitration and settlement of disputes must necessarily take place at the top. Decentralization allows conflicts among managers of functional areas to be resolved at a lower level. Top management can also make better evaluations of managerial performance if the interdependencies and conflicts are resolved by managers responsible for profit and return on investment.

One benefit that flows from the increased ability to evaluate performance and fix responsibility is that top management need not make day-to-day decisions. With decentralization, top management can use the principle of management by exception when monitoring the activities of subordinate managers.

Decentralization is also advantageous to firms that operate in different industries. Over the past few decades, firms have greatly widened their range of products, and this diversification increases the need to give broad responsibility to division managers. A president or other chief operating officer of a corporation cannot be expected to be knowledgeable about a great many product lines, such as textiles, furniture, appliances, automobile supplies, movies, and sporting goods.

There is considerable evidence that the broader responsibility that accompanies decentralization increases motivation. Studies have shown that workers and managers alike tend to perform better as their responsibilities increase. In general, the least-motivated people are those who perform a single task again and again throughout the day. The term *job enlargement* is often applied to giving increased responsibility. People who do much of the work on a product, as opposed to doing only one small operation, and managers who control most of the factors that affect profitability, become more committed to their jobs—viewing their jobs as sources of satisfaction, not just as sources of income.

Managers of nearly autonomous divisions are well prepared for higher positions. Such managers appreciate all aspects of a company's operations, instead of only one. The chief executive of Container Corporation of America, in an annual report, commented on the advantages of decentralization:

> The corporate organization consists of over 21,000 men and women, working in plants and offices, laboratories, forests and paperboard mills in the U.S. and six other countries. Its 140 plants and mills operate as relatively independent businesses, under a management system that delegates authority and responsibility to local managers. This decentralized organization, which provides for successful development of local markets, also constitutes an environment which encourages individual self-development. One measure of its success, over the years, is that virtually all of the company's present senior management team is a product of this system.

Problems of Decentralization

Decentralization has its problems. The major one is that managers operating in nearly autonomous fashion might make decisions that harm the firm. Indeed, perhaps the most formidable problem of decentralization is achieving goal congruence while at the same time promoting and maintaining divisional autonomy. Two managerial accounting issues are related to this important problem of decentralization. First, there is the need to develop methods of evaluating performance that work to the benefit of the firm as a whole. Second, there is a need to develop transfer prices that, as far as possible, produce decisions that are in the best interests of the firm. We turn first to the problem of selecting performance measures for divisions.

MEASURES OF PERFORMANCE

Income

Although income, the "bottom line," is the most widely examined (and least understood) financial datum, it is unsatisfactory for measuring the performance of divisions. First, net income includes expenses such as interest and taxes that are not normally under the control of divisional managers. Second, any income figure, be it pretax or before interest and taxes, tells only part of the story. A division that earns $10 million might be far less successful than one earning $3 million. The other part of the story is the investment that the manager uses to generate the income.

Although income is not the most useful performance measure, neither is it irrelevant. Indeed, the widely used performance measures that are discussed in this chapter all consider income. But the importance of income is as a part of other measures rather than as a measure in itself.

Return on Investment

Return on investment (ROI) is the general term used to describe a ratio of some measure of income to some measure of investment. In financial accounting you may have seen the ratio: net income divided by stockholders' equity, usually called *return on equity* (ROE). ROE is one type of ROI. Another is *return on assets* (ROA), usually measured as income before interest and taxes divided by total assets. Some firms use the term *return on capital employed,* or just *return on capital,* to designate the same ratio. Corporate managers generally use an ROI measure of the following form.

$$\text{ROI} = \frac{\text{divisional income}}{\text{divisional investment}}$$

There are many variations in practice, with firms defining and measuring **divisional income** and **divisional investment** in different ways. We examine some of these ways shortly.

ROI is the most frequently used criterion for divisional performance measurement. It has a distinct advantage over divisional profit because companies usually have divisions of different sizes. A division earning $100,000 on an investment of $1,000,000 is more efficient than one earning the same profit on an investment of $5,000,000. ROI makes it possible to compare the *efficiency* of different-size divisions by relating output (*income*) to input (*investment*).

Some managers find it helpful to restate the ROI formula when they are analyzing operating performance and looking for ways to improve it. The restatement expands the basic formula, income ÷ investment:

$$\text{ROI} = \frac{\text{income}}{\text{sales}} \times \frac{\text{sales}}{\text{investment}}$$

As you can see, the expanded version gives the same final answer because "sales" appears in the numerator of one factor and the denominator of the other and thus cancels out.

The expanded form helps to focus the manager's attention on the two components of ROI. The first, income ÷ sales, is the familiar **return on sales (ROS)** ratio. The second, sales ÷ investment, is **investment turnover.** This expanded version clearly shows that an increase in sales, by itself, will not increase ROI because sales cancels out. But a decrease in investment, with other factors remaining the same, will increase ROI (as will an increase in income with other factors held constant).

A manager can also determine the effect on ROI of a decision expected to change two factors. Suppose that ROS is now 15% and investment turnover is 2 times; ROI is 30% (15% × 2). If the manager is considering changing the product mix to items with lower margins and faster turnover, which will increase turnover to 2½ times while reducing ROS to 10%, he or she could see that ROI will fall to 25% (10% × 2½).

The values of the two components of ROI often give clues to the strategies used by companies or divisions. For example, a single company might operate both conventional department stores and discount stores. Both kinds of stores might earn the same ROI, but do so using very different strategies.

Assume the following data.

	Conventional Department Store Division	Discount Division
Sales	$2,000,000	$2,400,000
Divisional profit	240,000	192,000
Divisional investment	1,000,000	800,000
Return on sales	12%	8%
Investment turnover	2	3
Return on investment	24%	24%

The discount operations have a lower return on sales but a higher turnover.

While the advantages of ROI in considering relative sizes and alternative strategies are obvious, absolute size still matters. Recall from Chapter 8 that a company is wise to accept all proposed investments with expected returns greater than cost of capital. The same general principle is used in evaluating divisions by residual income.

Residual Income

Residual income (RI) is the income a division produces in excess of the **minimum required (desired, target) rate of return.** Top management establishes the minimum rate of return, which should be greater than cost of capital, as described in Chapter 8. Some companies set different minimum rates of return for different divisions to reflect differences in the risks associated with their businesses. A division in a risky industry such as fashion merchandise should earn higher returns than one in a more stable industry such as paper.

RI is computed as follows.

$$RI = \text{income} - (\text{investment} \times \text{target ROI})$$

min.

The parenthetical term is the profit that must be earned to satisfy the minimum requirements. It is the minimum required *dollar* return. Anything over that amount benefits the company. (Of course, *any* income benefits the company, but the minimum required ROI is needed simply to keep it going.) If the firm earns less than investors demand, they will invest their capital elsewhere and the firm will go out of business. The argument for using RI to evaluate divisional performance is that it measures the profit that the division provides to the firm over and above the minimum profit required for the amount invested.

RI has an important advantage over ROI as a measure of divisional performance. Applying it could show that a division with a higher ROI is less valuable *to the firm as a whole* than one with a lower ROI. Suppose that Division A produces a $200,000 income on an investment of $1,000,000, an ROI of 20%, while Division B earns $1,500,000 on an investment of $10,000,000, an ROI of 15%. Depending on the required ROI for the firm, the contributions of the divisions to the firm as a whole will appear quite different. Let us consider two possibilities: (1) required ROI is 10% and (2) required ROI is 18%. The RIs for each division are

| | 1 | | 2 | |
| | Required ROI is 10% | | Required ROI is 18% | |
	Division A	Division B	Division A	Division B
Investment	$1,000,000	$10,000,000	$1,000,000	$10,000,000
Divisional income	$ 200,000	$ 1,500,000	$ 200,000	$ 1,500,000
Required minimum return (investment × minimum return)	100,000	1,000,000	180,000	1,800,000
Residual income	$ 100,000	$ 500,000	$ 20,000	($ 300,000)

If the minimum required ROI is 10%, Division B makes a greater contribution to the firm than does Division A despite Division B's lower ROI. In this situation we could say that Division B was more valuable to the firm. On the other hand, if the firm has an 18% minimum ROI, Division A contributes more and is more valuable under the RI criterion.

When RI is used as the criterion for evaluating divisional performance, the division rated highest is the one with the highest RI. In some ways RI is similar to net present value used as the criterion for evaluating capital expenditures. Under that criterion, the most desirable capital project is the one with the highest net present value after discounting future returns at the cost of capital (or the minimum required rate of return).

Because RI uses the same factors that ROI does (namely, divisional income and divisional investment), the same questions arise as to what should be included in those numbers and how to measure the components. These questions are discussed later in the chapter.

BEHAVIORAL PROBLEMS

ROI Versus RI

Despite the reservations stated in Chapter 8, in this chapter we accept the use of book values for "investment," and book income for "return" in the computation of ROI. We *know* that using book amounts for investment and income can create problems. But ROI is the most commonly used measure for evaluating divisional performance, and most users calculate ROI based on book amounts. Moreover, over relatively long periods, book ROI may well approximate the internal rate of return computed using cash flows. Admitting the drawbacks of using book ROI, we can still say that a firm should expand if it can earn an ROI in excess of cost of capital.

Unfortunately, using ROI as the criterion for divisional performance evaluation can encourage managers to pass up projects that promise returns in excess of the minimum required return if the expected return is lower than the division's current ROI. Consider a division manager who expects an income of $300,000 on investment of $1,000,000 (ROI of 30%) and has an opportunity offering a $75,000 incremental profit on an incremental investment of $300,000 (ROI of 25% on the investment). Suppose further that the firm's required rate of return is 20%, and that the proposed new investment is in receivables and inventory and is recoverable at the end of the life of the investment. (Under these circumstances, the internal rate of return on the new investment equals the book rate of return.)

If the performance of the division (and its manager) is evaluated on the basis of ROI, the manager will be inclined to reject the new investment because ROI (now 30%) will fall, as can be seen in the following computations.

Investment before new project		$1,000,000
Additional investment for the project		300,000
Total investment		$1,300,000
Divisional profit:		
Current	$300,000	
From new project	75,000	
Total divisional profit		$ 375,000
Divisional ROI after new investment	$\frac{375\,000}{1\,300\,000} =$	28.8%

From the firm's viewpoint, the proposed investment should be undertaken because it promises an ROI in excess of the minimum required (20%). To encourage the division manager to make the decision that benefits the firm as well as the division, the evaluation criterion must take into account the minimum required return. The residual income approach to evaluation does just this.

Using RI in the situation just described shows the following.

	Without New Project	With New Project
Divisional investment	$1,000,000	$1,300,000
Minimum required ROI	20%	20%
Divisional profit	$ 300,000	$ 375,000
Less minimum required	200,000	260,000
Residual income	$ 100,000	$ 115,000

A division manager evaluated on the basis of RI will undertake this project because performance improves. This should not be surprising because the 25% ROI on the investment exceeds the required 20%. The ROI criterion encourages maximization of the *ratio* of profit to investment. The RI criterion encourages maximization of total *dollars* of profit in excess of the minimum required dollar return.

Using ROI as the performance measure might also encourage a manager to make an investment that is poor from the standpoint of the firm, but desirable from the view of the division because it raises a currently low ROI. Suppose a firm has a minimum required ROI of 20% and that a divisional manager currently expects income of $200,000 on an investment of $2,000,000, for a 10% ROI. How would the manager respond to an opportunity to increase income $15,000 by investing $100,000 in receivables and inventory? Divisional ROI increases to 10.2%.

$$\text{New ROI} = \frac{\$200,000 + \$15,000}{\$2,000,000 + \$100,000} = \frac{\$215,000}{\$2,100,000} = 10.2\%$$

Yet the proposed action actually generates negative residual income of $5,000 because a $100,000 investment requires income of $20,000 to meet the 20% minimum required rate of return. If the manager is evaluated on the basis of ROI, he or she is encouraged to accept the investment, but that is not the case if RI is the evaluation criterion. The current negative RI of $200,000 [$200,000 − ($2,000,000 × 20%)] would be $5,000 lower if the investment proposal were accepted.

Book Results and Discounted Cash Flows

In the examples for the previous section, book ROI equaled the internal rate of return on the proposed investment. That is seldom the case, especially with investments in plant and equipment. Very few divisional managers have the authority to make large capital investments without getting approval from officers at the corporate level. Therefore, a divisional manager earning a low ROI probably could not make a capital investment that would raise divisional ROI if its internal rate of return was below cost of capital. But because they use *book* income and investment, both ROI and RI can produce results that lead managers to avoid investments that would benefit the firm.

Consider the following example. A manager is considering a project that requires a $100,000 investment and provides pretax cash flows of $40,000 per year for five years. The company requires a pretax return of 25% on investment. The present value of the $40,000 stream of payments discounted at 25% is $107,560 ($40,000 × 2.689). Under the decision rules developed in Chapter 8, the investment is desirable because it promises a return of $107,560 for an investment of $100,000 (a positive NPV of $7,560). The book rates of return and RIs for the first two years of the investment are as follows, using the straight-line method of depreciation.

Year	Additional Cash Flow	Additional Depreciation	Increase in Book Income	Average Additional Investment[a]	ROI on Additional Investment	RI[b]
1	$40,000	$20,000	$20,000	$90,000	22.2%	($2,500)
2	$40,000	$20,000	$20,000	$70,000	28.6%	$2,500

[a] Book value of investment at beginning of year plus book value at end of year, divided by two.
[b] Income of $20,000 minus 25% required return on average additional investment.

Book ROI is below the minimum required in the first year, and RI for that year is negative. The division manager, seeing that undertaking the project will penalize performance in the first year, is not encouraged to accept the project.

Both ROI and RI rise over time unless income from the investment declines sharply. The falling book investment (resulting from depreciation) causes this pattern of returns, and the pattern is more extreme if the firm uses an accelerated method of depreciation. Even if cash flows, and therefore book income, decline, the pattern of increasing ROI is likely to occur.

The rise in ROI based on book values is even more pronounced in more realistic situations where returns do not begin immediately or do not reach their peaks in the early years. Ordinarily some lead time is required—to build a plant, install machinery, test the operation, remove "bugs," and generally get the operation going. It is also not uncommon to incur heavy startup costs in the opening of a new plant or even the remodeling of an existing one. The returns are likely to increase over the first few years as the plant gains efficiency. If a new product is involved, its sales in the first year or two may well be substantially lower than those in later years.

Thus, two factors work against the manager—lower income in early years and the natural tendency of ROI to rise as the book value of the investment falls because of depreciation charges. What can be done to encourage the manager to pursue worthwhile investments?

One way to avoid the first-year drop in ROI and thereby encourage managers to accept desirable investments is to leave the new investment out of the base for calculating ROI until the project is on-stream and running well. A version of this approach has been used by Burlington Industries, Inc., basing ROI calculations on investment at the end of the previous six months; this mitigates the effects of large amounts of construction in progress.[2] Of course, many major projects will take a relatively long time before they are running well.

Another approach is to amortize startup costs over several years instead of reporting them all in the income statement in the first year of an investment's life. A third possibility, seldom observed in practice, is to base depreciation charges on budgeted income to be earned over several years; this results in lower depreciation in early years and higher charges in later years. Although top-level corporate managers might not object to leaving assets out of the base or to amortizing

[2] As reported by Donald R. Hughes, then assistant controller of Burlington Industries, Inc., in Thomas J. Burns, ed., *The Behavioral Aspects of Accounting Data for Performance Evaluation* (Columbus, Ohio: College of Administrative Science, Ohio State University, 1970), 56.

startup costs, there is not much support for increasing-charge depreciation. Perhaps the main reason for lack of interest in such depreciation methods is that they are almost never used in financial accounting.

Essentially, the problem just described is a conflict between the long and the short terms. As has been stated many times in this book, many actions that can help meet short-term goals are harmful in the long run. Such actions could reduce profits, ROI, and RI in the long term, but by then the manager might have been promoted to another job. Conversely, a manager who takes actions that benefit the division and firm in the long run, while hurting short-term performance, could be fired. The manager who takes over could well reap the benefits of the predecessor's good decisions. Obviously, then, it is unwise to evaluate divisions and their managers simply by reference to ROI, RI, or any other single quantitative measure. Qualitative factors must enter the evaluation process.

PROBLEMS IN MEASUREMENT

Whether ROI or RI is used as the evaluation criterion, we still must determine what revenues, costs, and investments are to be included in the calculations. The determinations should be made along the lines of responsibility, with controllability as the principal criterion for including costs and investment. If a division manager is held responsible for earning returns (income) on investment, he or she should control the elements of both income and investment.

To compute the income for which the division's manager is responsible, we must identify variable costs and direct fixed costs. As discussed in Chapter 10, some companies also allocate common, indirect fixed costs for several reasons. If common fixed costs are allocated to divisions, they should be separated from direct fixed costs and clearly labeled as allocated. Opinions differ as to what to include in and how to measure divisional investment. As a start, investment includes at least those assets that are used only by a particular division.

Investment

Under normal circumstances, most assets can readily be identified with specific divisions. Virtually all plant and equipment, for example, are under the control of divisions. Inventory and receivables, which are also investments, are generally under divisional control because the divisional manager controls production and credit terms. Cash may or may not be under divisional control. Division managers usually control some cash, but in many cases central headquarters receives payments directly from customers and pays bills submitted by the divisions.

Some assets are controlled only at the highest level of management. Central headquarters controls the headquarters building and equipment, investments in the securities of other firms, and such intangible assets as goodwill and organization costs.

Suppose we have analyzed the revenues, costs, and assets of Multiproducts, Inc., and have identified these by divisions as shown in Exhibit 11-1.

The firm has three operating divisions, A, B, and C, and a central corporate office. The minimum required ROI for the firm is 10%.

Exhibit 11-1

Multiproducts, Inc. (in millions of dollars)

| | Division | | | | |
	A	B	C	Unallocated	Total
Investment					
Cash	$ 20	$ 30	$ 60	$ 30	$ 140
Accounts receivable, net	60	80	90		230
Inventory	100	180	240		520
Prepaid expenses	10	10	20	20	60
Plant and equipment—net of depreciation	200	320	440	60	1,020
Investments	10	—	—	100	110
Total assets	$400	$620	$850	$210	$2,080
Income					
Sales	$100	$400	$700		$1,200
Variable costs	30	220	400		650
Contribution margin	70	180	300		550
Direct fixed costs	30	90	140		260
Divisional profit	$ 40	$ 90	$160		290
Common fixed costs					60
Income					$ 230

From the data in Exhibit 11-1 we can compute ROI and RI for each division and for the firm as a whole. The latter computation should be based on an investment defined as the total assets of the firm. Note that no performance measurement is given for unallocated assets.

| | Division | | | Firm as |
	A	B	C	a Whole
Computation of ROI				
Profit of the segment	$ 40	$ 90	$160	$ 230
Investment for the segment	400	620	850	2,080
ROI (profit/investment)	10%	14.5%	18.8%	11.1%
Computation of RI:				
Profit of the segment	$ 40	$ 90	$160	$ 230
Required return (investment × minimum return of 10%)	40	62	85	208
RI (profit − required return)	$ —	$ 28	$ 75	$ 22

Amounts shown are in millions of dollars.

Although the firm earns an 11.1% ROI, only one division earns so low a rate. Because of unallocated costs and assets, the divisions must earn more, perhaps considerably more, than the minimum required ROI, if the company as a whole is to earn the required minimum of 10%. Note also that the combined RI of the divisions is partly consumed by the unallocated costs and assets, so that, although the divisions earn residual income of $103 million ($0 + $28 + $75), the firm earns only $22 million in excess of a 10% return on total assets.

When top management establishes an overall target ROI for the firm, it has two strategies available to encourage division managers to help achieve that target. One approach is to set divisional target ROI higher than the overall desired rate. Another is to allocate as much cost and investment as possible to divisions. Managers favoring the second strategy argue that divisional managers should be made aware of the substantial costs and investment involved in running the firm as a whole, which each of the divisions must work to offset. This argument was described in Chapter 10.

Another and perhaps more persuasive justification for following the strategy of allocating common costs and common assets to divisions is available. Corporate managers are interested in whether a division is earning returns comparable to those of independent firms in the same industry. If the division is to be treated more or less as an independent, autonomous entity, corporate managers argue that it should bear the costs and assets that an independent company requires. An independent firm must incur many costs, and maintain many assets, that a division often does not. For example, an independent firm performs research and development, while a division can rely on a centrally administered R&D organization. Similarly, an independent firm must maintain some cash, while a division may rely on a centralized cash management function to meet its needs. To make reasonable comparisons between the division and an outside firm, then, corporate management might allocate central costs and assets to divisions (also reminding divisional managers of the needs met by the central administration).

Firms that allocate corporate costs among divisions do so in many ways. In some firms, central headquarters charges each division a management fee for services provided. For instance, divisions need financing, just as if they were separate firms, and the charge reflects that service. The fee might be a percentage of revenue, total investment in the division, or some other base. One large firm charges each division 2% of gross sales.

The effort to make division managers realize that they must consider the performance of the entire firm may be worthwhile, but the allocation of central costs and assets to divisions must be understood for what it is—an allocation. Whatever the allocation methods used, managers at both the divisional and corporate levels must be aware that allocations in no way change the nature of the costs or assets as indirect to the divisions and not controllable by the divisional managers.

Liabilities

There usually is no satisfactory way to assign *all* liabilities to divisions. Some current liabilities (payables, accrued expenses) are readily associated with particular divisions. As a rule, divisions cannot issue long-term debt, and their managers are not responsible for it. That is, managers of divisions are operating managers, not financial managers. Long-term debt results from financing decisions made at the highest level of management on the basis of the organization's overall needs and problems. Long-term debt could be allocated to divisions on the basis of relative investments in fixed assets and working capital, but there is little interest in doing so in practice. For performance measurement purposes, many firms include only those liabilities that are definitely (not arbitrarily) related to divisions, and define divisional investment as controlled assets minus divisional liabilities.

✳ Using *any* liabilities in determining divisional investment naturally increases ROI, because the denominator (the investment base) decreases while the numerator (profit) remains the same. If we were to include liabilities in measuring investment in the example on page 442, the computations of ROI and RI are as follows, using assumed values for liabilities.

	Divisions			Firm as a Whole
	A	B	C	
Computation of ROI				
Profit of the segment	$ 40	$ 90	$160	$ 230
Total assets	400	620	850	2,080
Divisional liabilities (assumed)	60	170	310	540
Divisional investment	340	450	540	1,540
Unallocated liabilities (assumed)				730
Total investment	$340	$450	$540	$ 810
ROI	11.8%	20.0%	29.6%	28.4%
Computation of RI:				
Profit of the segment	$ 40	$ 90	$160	$ 230
Required return (investment above × minimum return of 10%)	34	45	54	81
RI	$ 6	$ 45	$106	$ 149

Amounts shown are in millions of dollars.

 Both RI and ROI are higher for all divisions and for the firm as a whole when liabilities are included in the computations.

From a behavioral standpoint, the question whether to include liabilities is undecided. In favor of their inclusion is that most current liabilities are related to the operating level of the division and provide financing to it and to the firm. On the negative side, divisional managers could be encouraged to allow liabilities to rise too high in order to reduce investment and increase ROI. If divisional managers, say, delay payments to suppliers, the credit rating of the firm as a whole might suffer. A reasonable compromise might be a corporate policy that allows managers to carry, say, trade payables up to the length of time specified by suppliers. Then, if a division had 40 days' purchases in accounts payable and suppliers offered 30-day credit, the division could not deduct the extra 10 days'

worth of liabilities to determine divisional investment. Under this policy, the manager has no incentive to allow payables to extend beyond the suppliers' credit terms. (Note that divisional managers have no opportunity for delaying payments if cash disbursements are handled at the central headquarters.)

Fixed Assets

For all computations to this point, you have been given the amount of the investment in assets. In Exhibit 11-1, for example, the investments in cash, inventory, and fixed assets were given, but there was no mention of how these amounts were determined. There are many views about which valuation method to use for fixed assets. Some of the valuation bases used are original (gross) cost, original cost less accumulated depreciation (often called *net cost,* or *net book value*), and current replacement cost. The method used can have a significant effect on ROI and RI, and each valuation basis has advantages and disadvantages.

The most popular basis by far is net book value. Its principal advantages are that it conforms to financial accounting practice and that it recognizes the decline in productivity that usually accompanies increasing age. Many believe it to be the most reasonable basis given that divisional income includes depreciation expense. (It is argued that, if depreciation is recognized for determining income, it should also be recognized in computing investment.) The major disadvantage of net book value is that it gives, as shown earlier, rising ROI and RI over time.

Using gross (original) cost for valuing fixed assets overcomes the objection about rising ROI and RI. DuPont has stated its views in the following manner.

> Since plant facilities are maintained in virtually top condition during their working life, we believe it would be inappropriate to consider that operating management was responsible for earning a return on only the net operating investment. Furthermore, if depreciable assets were stated at net depreciated values, earnings in each succeeding period would be related to an ever-decreasing investment.[3]

Yet virtually all assets do lose productivity as they age, and the use of gross cost does not consider that decline. Moreover, the investment in a fixed asset *does* decline over time, as the firm recovers it through the cash flows it produces.

Both gross and net book values suffer from the defect that they reflect costs that the firm has already incurred, perhaps many years ago. Managers who have older assets generally have lower investment bases (either gross or net) than managers using similar assets that are newer and, in all likelihood, costlier. For

[3] Frank R. Rayburn and Michael M. Brown, "Measuring and Using Return on Investment Information," in James Don Edwards and Homer A. Black, eds., *The Managerial and Cost Accountant's Handbook* (Homewood, Illinois: Dow Jones-Irwin, 1979), 331. The authors were quoting from D. Solomons, *Divisional Performance: Measurement and Control* (Homewood, Illinois: Richard D. Irwin, 1965), 134–135, as modified by letter from E. I. DuPont dated August 8, 1978.

this reason, many accountants and managers advocate the use of replacement costs.

There are at least two ways to define replacement cost. Some consider replacement cost to be the current cost of assets now being used. Under this interpretation, current cost is measured as the acquisition cost of new assets just like those currently in use or as the cost of acquiring assets of the same age and condition as those being used. Others consider replacement cost to be the current cost of obtaining similar productive capacity or service. Under this interpretation, the emphasis is on how the firm currently would choose to accomplish a particular task. For example, suppose a company has a fleet of fork-lift trucks to move material within its factory. Under the second interpretation, the replacement cost of the fleet is the cost of an automated conveyor system if the division would replace the fleet with such a system. Because managers should continuously evaluate the alternatives available for accomplishing tasks, we believe the second interpretation (equivalent productive capacity) to be more appropriate for evaluating divisional performance. There is, however, much disagreement on this point.

Whatever definition of replacement cost is adopted, its use eliminates the problems of different depreciation methods and also allows for changes in prices. Thus, managers are not penalized or rewarded simply because of the depreciation methods used or the respective ages of their assets. The normal accounting system does not automatically provide information about current replacement costs, and the practical difficulties and associated costs of determining replacement costs were long thought to be too great to warrant their development.[4] Despite the disadvantages, original cost less accumulated depreciation remains the most popular approach for determining the value of fixed assets.

THE SUBJECT OF EVALUATION – DIVISION OR MANAGER

There is an important distinction between using ROI and RI as diagnostic tools and as performance measures for divisional managers. ROI and RI give clues to where the firm might be wise to increase, maintain, or reduce investment, and other things being equal, higher ROI and RI are desirable. However, for evaluating *managers* of divisions, both ROI and RI have drawbacks, depending on how the results for a division are interpreted. The critical issue is the standard used for comparison. With what should we compare a division's results?

---

[4] Beginning in 1979, the Securities and Exchange Commission and the Financial Accounting Standards Board required certain companies to report some replacement cost information in their external financial statements. As such information became available to those companies for *internal* purposes at no additional cost, some firms might have elected to use the information for internal reporting. These requirements to provide replacement cost information were removed in 1986, and no evidence yet exists regarding the extent to which the affected companies used the information for internal purposes or continued to produce the information when it was no longer required.

There are several bases for comparison, including comparisons among divisions within the firm, with historical results in the same division, with industry averages, and with budgets. Divisions within the firm can be ranked in terms of relative profitability. The ranking also might provide some insight into the relative contributions of the divisions. But such a ranking should *not* be used to rank the managers of the respective divisions, because different kinds of divisions should be *expected* to have different ROIs. For example, ROI is generally higher for units (divisions or firms) operating in consumer markets than for those selling mostly to other industrial firms. Both ROI and RI should be higher for divisions taking on high risks. (For example, a division in plant genetics, a very risky field, should do better than one making clothing.) The performance of a particular division manager must not be obscured by intrafirm comparisons that ignore the nature of the division. A mediocre manager might be able to earn a respectable ROI in a division operating in a growing industry. On the other hand, an excellent manager might be doing a great job to maintain an ROI of 5% in a division operating in a declining industry.

Comparing current results with historical results in the same division overcomes differences in results stemming from divisions being in different industries. If there is a change in managers, the relative performance of two managers can also be compared. On the other hand, historical comparisons suffer from the same objections as do intrafirm comparisons and should be interpreted carefully. That is, there is no way to tell whether historical experience is good or bad. Nevertheless, historical comparisons indicate relative improvement or decay.

Comparing divisional results with industry averages can be useful because differences among divisions resulting from differences in industry do not influence the comparison. A division (and its manager) can be seen as better or worse than the firms with which it compe...s. Such comparisons present their own problems, however, because, as noted earlier, a division should be expected to earn a higher ROI than an entire firm operating in the same industry. A division benefits from being part of a larger organization. As the trend to diversification continues, it becomes increasingly difficult to find companies to which the performance of a single division can be compared.[5]

Budgets that are developed with participation by divisional managers are valuable tools for assessing the performance of division managers. When managers participate and commit themselves to meeting budgeted goals, comparisons of actual and budgeted results are usually thought to be the best possible comparisons for evaluation purposes.

Exhibit 11-2 shows budgeted and actual statements of income and financial position for a division.

---

[5] Even if there are independent firms in essentially the same industry, it is no simple matter to compare them with a division. As Chapter 18 shows, comparisons among independent firms are not easy because of such factors as different accounting methods (first-in-first-out versus last-in-first-out is one example), different degrees of diversification, and different ages of plant assets.

Exhibit 11-2
Divisional Performance Report (in millions of dollars)

	Budget	Actual	Variance
Sales	$573.0	$591.0	$18.0
Variable costs (perhaps detailed)	246.0	251.2	5.2
Contribution margin	327.0	339.8	12.8
Direct fixed costs	140.0	141.4	1.4
Divisional profit	187.0	198.4	11.4
Allocated costs	12.0	15.0	3.0
Profit	$175.0	$183.4	$ 8.4
Assets employed:			
Cash	$ 15.5	$ 17.0	$ 1.5
Receivables	110.0	141.0	31.0
Inventory	90.0	122.5	32.5
Fixed assets, net	450.0	453.4	3.4
Total assets employed	$665.5	$733.9	$68.4
ROI	26.3%	25.0%	1.3%

Controllable costs are shown separately from allocated costs. There are no allocations of assets; all assets shown are controlled by the division's manager. The exhibit also shows why budgeted and actual ROI were not the same. The division earned more profit than budgeted, but its receivables and inventories climbed much higher than budgeted, resulting in a reduced ROI. This type of report gives more information than simple comparisons of ROI, RI, or both.

TRANSFER PRICES

A great deal of intrafirm buying and selling can occur in decentralized firms, which necessitates the setting of transfer prices. Some firms in the food industry have farming operations that supply their own processing plants as well as those of other firms. A textile mill might sell some of its cloth to divisions within the same firm for further processing and some to outsiders.

Pricing Policies

Transfer prices are important in evaluating performance because they are revenues to the selling division and costs to the buying division. We know from Chapter 10 that changes in transfer prices do not, in themselves, affect the firm's total profits. Total profits are affected only if individual managers change their operations because of a change in transfer prices. Because of their *potential* for promoting actions that might not be consistent with the interests of the total firm, transfer prices are important factors in divisional performance measurement. The following examples explore some implications of several transfer-pricing policies.

1. *Actual cost with or without a markup for the selling division.* This pricing scheme offers the selling manager no incentive to keep costs down. With a percentage markup, the selling manager makes more profit by allowing costs to rise. The manager of the buying division would naturally object that his or her costs (and hence reported performance) are adversely affected.

2. *Budgeted cost, with or without a markup.* This method encourages the selling manager to keep costs down. If there is a markup, the selling division can earn a profit. The buying manager appreciates not having cost inefficiencies passed on from the selling division but prefers no markup at all. Thus, discussions center on budgeted cost and markup percentages.

3. *Market prices.* This method is generally considered the best. It puts both the buying and selling managers on an independent basis, provided that they are free to buy or sell on the outside as well as within the firm. Given this freedom, the managers are in the position of the chief executives of autonomous firms. One difficulty in implementing this policy is that there might not be outside market prices available for the division's products, or the prices that are available might not be representative. For instance, available prices might reflect relatively small transactions, whereas the divisions deal in very large quantities. Under such circumstances, the buying manager might contend that the outside prices are artificially high and that he or she should pay less because of the quantities bought. In many cases, the transfer price is less than the market price to reflect cost savings from dealing internally. For instance, suppose a division pays a 15% commission on outside sales, none on inside sales. The transfer price should be 85% of the market price to reflect that saving. Market prices might not be a good choice as a transfer price if the selling division is operating below capacity.

4. *Incremental cost.* Such prices are best, theoretically, when the selling division is operating below capacity. The manager of the selling division will object to this approach because it yields no profit to that division.

5. *Negotiated prices.* This method allows managers to bargain with each other and alleviates some problems that arise with other methods. If there are outside markets, a manager who is dissatisfied with the offered price can buy or sell in the outside market.

Despite our suggestion that market-based transfer prices are generally best, we hasten to point out that the autonomous division manager who is setting a transfer price must use judgment *and understand the information available*. Like the managers involved in making decisions discussed in earlier chapters, division managers must understand the concepts of contribution margin and incremental cost, and the implications of those concepts in light of the available alternatives.

For example, in Chapter 5 you read of the analysis underlying a decision whether to accept a special order at less than the normal price. Critical to that analysis was whether the firm had an alternative use for the facilities and whether the contribution margin covered any incremental fixed costs.

The same principles apply when a division manager has to propose a selling price for an order from another division. When the selling division has excess capacity, its results (and the manager's reported performance) will be improved if the price covers variable costs and incremental fixed costs, and the manager should offer a transfer price accordingly. When the division's capacity can be fully used without taking the order, the selling manager should demand the market price, less any costs saved by dealing internally. (An order might cause a division operating below capacity to lose regular sales. If the division is 4,000 units under capacity, an order for 5,000 will result in a loss of 1,000 at the regular price. The minimum acceptable transfer price is incremental cost for the first 4,000, market price for the last 1,000.)

In summary, if treated as the heads of autonomous units, division managers should be free to develop offers of transfer prices that reflect the cost structures of their divisions and the available alternatives. When the division is operating at full capacity, with some sales being made to customers outside the firm, a market-based transfer price is nearly always best. When the division is operating below capacity, a transfer price that falls between incremental cost and market price is usually best. Hence, division managers must understand the cost structures of their divisions and use that knowledge in setting transfer prices. If they have the freedom to negotiate prices, the resulting actions are likely to be in the firm's best interests. To see why this is true, let us consider an example.

Illustrations

Division A buys a component for its major product from an outside supplier for $13 per unit. The component is exactly like the product made by Division B, another division of the same firm, and the manager of A has asked B to supply the item at $10. Division B now sells its output to outside customers. The budgeted income statement for the coming year for Division B is shown below.

Budgeted Income Statement, Division B	
Sales, 10,000 × $15	$150,000
Variable costs, 10,000 × $7	70,000
Contribution margin	80,000
Fixed costs	30,000
Income	$ 50,000

Let us assume, for simplicity, that Division B could make the component needed by A with no change in fixed costs and with the same variable cost per unit that it has now. How should the manager of B respond to the requested price? What price serves the best interests of the divisions and of the firm? The answer depends on the alternatives available to the manager of Division B, and on his understanding of those alternatives and costs.

Suppose that Division B has a capacity of 11,000 units. If it accepts Division A's business, it loses 5,000 units of outside sales. (Capacity of 11,000 less 6,000 to Division A leaves 5,000 units available for sales to outsiders, a reduction of 5,000 from present sales of 10,000 units.) Below is a budgeted income statement for the division if a transfer takes place at $13, the price that A now pays to an outside supplier.

Budgeted Income Statement, Division B
(Component Purchased Internally for $13)

Sales to outsiders, 5,000 × $15	$ 75,000
Sales to A, 6,000 × $13	78,000
Total sales	153,000
Variable costs, 11,000 × $7	77,000
Contribution margin	76,000
Fixed costs	30,000
Income	$ 46,000

Because Division A is *already* paying $13 to an outside supplier, purchasing the component internally for that price would not change the division's income and its manager would be indifferent to the source of supply. The manager of Division B would not accept the $13 price, because the profit of the division would decline by $4,000 (from $50,000 to $46,000). Is the decision that the sale is not in the best interest of the manager of Division B also in the best interest of the firm as a whole?

From the standpoint of the firm, the decision is a make-or-buy decision such as you studied in Chapter 5. That is, if Division B makes the component and sells it to Division A, the component is made by the firm; alternatively, the component could be bought from an outside supplier. We can, therefore, look at the decision from the point of view of the firm as we did in Chapter 5.

Lost contribution margin from outside sales by Division B (5,000 × [$15 − $7])	$40,000
Savings of variable costs paid to outside supplier (6,000 × [$13 − $7])	36,000
Loss to firm	($ 4,000)

The change in the firm's income (a $4,000 decline) equals the combined changes in the incomes of its divisions (no change for A, a $4,000 decline for B).

Suppose now that Division B can produce 20,000 (rather than 11,000 units) but that it can sell only 10,000 units to outsiders. If fixed costs will not be affected by producing additional units for sale to Division A, Division B's results will improve by selling to A at any price greater than B's variable cost of $7 per unit. For example, a budgeted income statement for Division B if the transfer takes place at as little as $8 per unit is on page 452.

Budgeted Income Statement, Division B
(Component Purchased Internally for $8)

Sales to outsiders, 10,000 × $15	$150,000
Sales to A, 6,000 × $8	48,000
Total sales	198,000
Variable costs, 16,000 × $7	112,000
Contribution margin	86,000
Fixed costs	30,000
Income	$ 56,000

The manager of Division A will be happy to accept an $8 price, for that division's income will increase by $30,000 (6,000 units × [$15 − $8]). The manager of Division B *should* accept the $8 price because that division's income would improve by $6,000, the $1 contribution margin ($8 − $7) on the 6,000 additional units. If you understood the previous example, you should see that the firm's top managers also want the transfer to take place. The firm's total income would increase by $36,000, the combined changes in the incomes of its divisions ($30,000 + $6,000). Analyzing the situation as a make-or-buy decision, the company saves $36,000 in variable costs [6,000 × ($13 − $7)] by making the unit rather than buying it outside.

It would be unfortunate if the manager of Division B didn't understand the division's cost structure and considered a price of $8 to be unacceptable. For example, suppose the manager had reviewed the original budgeted income statement and concluded that the cost was $10 per unit (variable costs of $70,000 plus fixed costs of $30,000, divided by the 10,000 units of planned production). The decision not to sell at $8 would, as indicated earlier, have been detrimental to Division A, to the firm, and to Division B.

✳ As a matter of fact, as long as Division B has excess capacity, *any* price less than the market price of $13 and greater than B's variable costs of $7 is advantageous to both divisions and to the firm as a whole. Division A acquires the component at a lower price than it would have to pay to an outside supplier. Division B gains some contribution margin. And the firm benefits from having a lower total cost of the product (the $7 variable cost from Division B rather than the $13 outside price). Indeed, even a transfer price of $7 should be acceptable. Division B loses nothing and could gain by being able to retain good workers who might otherwise have left the area for other jobs, or by keeping good relations with suppliers who might be concerned about the low levels of B's orders for materials.

In summary, the major issue from the standpoint of the company as a whole is not the choice of a transfer price but whether the transfer should take place at all. For the company, the decision is a make-or-buy decision. For the buying division, the question is simply which supplier (sister division or outside firm) offers the lower price (assuming equal quality, delivery schedules, etc.). For the selling division, the decision is a special order decision, as in Chapter 5, and the concern is whether the contribution margin from selling inside offsets the loss, if any, of contribution margin from lost outside sales. If the transfer is profitable from the standpoint of the company as a whole, the best transfer-pricing system is one that prompts the managers to make a decision in the best interests of the firm as a whole. Thus, the establishment of transfer prices requires judgment and a full understanding of the circumstances and of the managerial accounting information available.

MULTINATIONAL COMPANIES – SPECIAL PROBLEMS

Companies that operate in many countries are usually called *multinationals*. Some multinationals operate divisions in foreign countries, others set up separate, legal corporations. A division, or subsidiary corporation, that operates in France does business in French francs, not in dollars, and reports its financial results in francs. It pays French taxes and tariffs. Many U.S. companies are multinationals, as are many foreign companies such as British Petroleum, Toyota, and Unilever. Multinationals face special problems related both to evaluating performance and to transfer pricing.

With respect to evaluation, multinationals must cope with changes in exchange rates, which are the relationships of foreign currencies to dollars. For instance, the British pound sterling has over some periods been worth anywhere from $1.50 to $1.90 or so. One problem for performance evaluation is that the local manager—the one in the foreign country—does business in the foreign currency, but the multinational cares about the results in its home currency (dollars for U.S. multinationals). The trouble is that the local manager and the division can look good or bad in U.S. dollars simply because of changes in exchange rates, even though he or she is not responsible for exchange rate fluctuations.

Consider the following division's monthly income statement in Xs, the currency of a foreign country.

	Division X
Sales	X3,000
Expenses	2,000
Income in local currency	X1,000

If an X was worth $10 during the month, the division would show $10,000 income for the month. But suppose that next month the division does exactly the same business and has the same income statement, but that the value of an X drops to $8. The division then shows $8,000 income, a 20% drop from last month even though it did the same business. Evaluating the manager's (or the division's) performance on the basis of reports using the currency of the home country penalizes him or her for a decline in the exchange rate (and gives undue credit when the rate rises, of course). The question of translating foreign currency also vexes financial accounting.

The transfer pricing problem for multinationals is equally troublesome. Because different countries have different income tax rates, it is desirable, from the overall corporate point of view, to show higher profits in low-tax countries, lower profits in high-tax countries. One way to do so is through transfer prices. For example, suppose that Division A buys a product from Division B. The divisions are in different countries, but both use the same currency, denoted as T. Data appear below.

Selling price of Division A's product	T100
Variable cost, excluding transfer price	T20
Tax rate in Division A's country	20%
Variable cost of Division B's product	T30
Tax rate in Division B's country	60%

Income statements below show the effects, including income taxes, of transferring 1,000 units of Division B's product at T30 and at T60.

	Transfer at T30	
	Division A	Division B
Sales (1,000 × T100)	T100,000	
(1,000 × T30)		T30,000
Variable cost [1,000 × (T20 + T30)]	T50,000	
(1,000 × T30)		T30,000
Contribution margin	50,000	0
Income tax at 20% and 60%	T 10,000	0

Better off

	Transfer at T60	
	Division A	Division B
Sales (1,000 × T100)	T100,000	
(1,000 × T60)		T60,000
Variable cost [1,000 × (T20 + T60)]	80,000	
(1,000 × T30)		30,000
Contribution margin	20,000	30,000
Income tax at 20% and 60%	T 4,000	T18,000

worse

Total income taxes are only T10,000 at the lower price, T22,000 at the higher price. (The corporation minimizes its total taxes if Division B *gives* the product to Division A, but the authorities in Division B's country would certainly not permit that.) If the corporation forces Division B to sell at a low price, it saves considerable taxes, but penalizes the performance of Division B and its manager. Of course, dictating the low transfer price also enhances the reported performance of Division A and its manager.

Similar problems arise with import duties, or tariffs, which are typically based on values reported for incoming goods. If a division is transferring goods to another that is located in a high-tariff country, a low transfer price reduces the tariff. Some countries also have export duties, though they are much less common than import duties. With high export duties, it is, of course, best to have a low transfer price.

Another area where income-shifting is tempting is in management fees and allocations of corporate costs. A corporation can shift income from a division (foreign country) to itself (home country) by charging a management fee. If the fee is based on sales or assets, it is really just a cost allocation. But the more cost charged to a division or subsidiary in a high-tax country and the less charged to those in low-tax countries, the lower the multinational's total tax bill. Here again, the reported performance of the local managers is influenced by corporate policies.

Besides the problems associated with portraying performance, some of the practices described above, if arbitrarily imposed, are unethical and in some countries illegal. Various authorities such as those responsible for collecting income taxes in the various countries will try to ensure that artificially high or low transfer prices are disallowed and that corporate charges reflect the services provided at the corporate level.

SUMMARY

The evaluation of investment centers requires determining which revenues, costs, and investment the manager can control. Commonly used performance measures are return on investment (ROI) and residual income (RI). ROI is the most popular measure, but RI is advantageous from a behavioral point of view. Use of either criterion requires answering difficult questions about which items to include in divisional income and investment and involves different opinions about how some items should be measured.

Intrafirm sales and purchases introduce the problem of transfer prices. Such prices can encourage managers to take actions that harm the firm as a whole. However, managers who are free to negotiate transfer prices are likely to make decisions that benefit both the divisions and the firm. Companies with divisions in countries using a different currency have special problems in evaluating the performance of those divisions. Such companies also have problems in setting transfer prices that take into consideration the different tax structures of the countries in which their divisions operate.

KEY TERMS

allocated costs
decentralization
divisional investment
divisional profit (income)
investment turnover

minimum required (desired target) rate of
   return
residual income (RI)
return on investment (ROI)
transfer price

KEY FORMULAS

Return on investment (ROI) = $\dfrac{\text{divisional income}}{\text{divisional investment}}$

$$\text{Return on investment (ROI)} = \frac{\text{income}}{\text{sales}} \times \frac{\text{sales}}{\text{investment}}$$

$$\text{Return on sales (ROS)} = \frac{\text{income}}{\text{sales}}$$

$$\text{Investment turnover} = \frac{\text{sales}}{\text{investment}}$$

$$\text{Residual income (RI)} = \text{income} - (\text{investment} \times \text{desired ROI})$$

REVIEW PROBLEM

The manager of the Bartram Division of United Products Company has given you the following information related to budgeted operations for the coming year, 19X5.

Sales (100,000 units at $5)	$500,000
Variable costs at $2 per unit	200,000
Contribution margin at $3 per unit	300,000
Fixed costs	120,000
Divisional profit	$180,000
Divisional investment	$800,000

The minimum required ROI is 20%.

Required: Consider each part independently.
1. Determine the division's expected ROI using the second formula on page 435.
2. Determine the division's expected RI.
3. The manager has the opportunity to sell an additional 10,000 units at $4.50. Variable cost per unit would be the same as budgeted, but fixed costs would increase by $10,000. Additional investment of $50,000 would also be required. If the manager accepted the special order, by how much and in what direction would his RI change?
4. Of its total budgeted volume of 100,000 units, Bartram expects to sell 20,000 units to the Jeffers Division of United Products. However, the manager of Jeffers Division has received an offer from an outside firm. The outside firm would supply the 20,000 units at $4.20. If Bartram Division does not meet the $4.20 price, Jeffers will buy from the outside firm. Bartram could save $25,000 in fixed costs if it dropped its volume from 100,000 to 80,000 units.
   (a) Determine Bartram's profit assuming that it meets the $4.20 price.
   (b) Determine Bartram's profit if it fails to meet the price and loses the sales.
   (c) Determine the effect on the firm's total profit if Bartram meets the $4.20 price.
   (d) Determine the effect on the firm's total profit if Bartram does not meet the price.

Answer to Review Problem

1. 22.5%

$$\frac{\text{income}}{\text{sales}} \times \frac{\text{sales}}{\text{investment}} = \frac{\$180,000}{\$500,000} \times \frac{\$500,000}{\$800,000} = 0.36 \times 0.625 = 0.225 = 22.5\%$$

2. $20,000

Profit budgeted	$180,000
Minimum required return ($800,000 × 20%)	160,000
Residual income budgeted	$ 20,000

3. RI would increase by $5,000. This can be determined either by considering the changes in the variables or by preparing new data for total operations. Considering only the changes

Increase in sales (10,000 × $4.50)	$45,000
Increase in variable costs (10,000 × $2)	20,000
Increase in contribution margin	25,000
Increase in fixed costs	10,000
Increase in profit	15,000
Increase in minimum required return ($50,000 × 20%)	10,000
Increase in RI	$ 5,000

A new income statement and calculation of new total RI would show the following.

Sales ($500,000 + $45,000)	$545,000
Variable costs (110,000 × $2)	220,000
Contribution margin	325,000
Fixed costs ($120,000 + $10,000)	130,000
Divisional profit	195,000
Minimum required return ($850,000 × 20%)	170,000
Residual income	$ 25,000

The new $25,000 RI is $5,000 more than RI based on budgeted operations without the special order.

4. (a) $164,000. If Bartram accepts the lower price, revenue (and hence contribution margin) will be reduced by $0.80 per unit for 20,000 units. With no change in fixed costs, the $16,000 drop in contribution margin means a similar drop in profit. An income statement under the new assumption would show the following.

Sales [($5 × 80,000) + ($4.20 × 20,000)]	$484,000
Variable costs ($2 × 100,000)	200,000
Contribution margin	284,000
Fixed costs	120,000
Divisional profit	$164,000

(b) $145,000. If Bartram does not accept the lower price, the *full* contribution margin from sales to Jeffers will be lost. The avoidable fixed costs will be saved. The contribution margin lost would be $60,000 (20,000 units at $3), and the fixed costs saved would be $25,000. Hence, divisional profit would drop $35,000 ($60,000 − $25,000) to $145,000 ($180,000 budgeted profit − $35,000).

The answer could also be arrived at by reference to the income statement prepared in item a. The contribution margin lost would be $44,000 (20,000 × the lower contribution margin of $2.20), with fixed costs savings of $25,000. The net decline in profits would be $19,000 ($44,000 − $25,000), which, when subtracted from the $164,000 total profit shown in the income statement in item a, equals $145,000.

A third, somewhat longer, approach to the problem would be to prepare an income statement assuming the sales to Jeffers are not made. This approach, too, shows a new divisional profit of $145,000.

Sales ($5 × 80,000)	$400,000
Variable costs ($2 × 80,000)	160,000
Contribution margin	240,000
Fixed costs ($120,000 − $25,000)	95,000
Divisional profit	$145,000

(c) If you concluded that the firm's total profit would change as a result of the change in the transfer price, you have forgotten a very important point made in Chapter 10. Changes in transfer prices do not, in themselves, change total profits. Only if changes in transfer prices cause managers to change their operations and actions can change in total profits occur. In this situation, the manager of Bartram Division had planned to sell to Jeffers Division and his income statement was budgeted accordingly. If he accepts the lower price, he will still be selling to Jeffers. Similarly, the manager of Jeffers Division had planned to buy from Bartram Division. He will still buy from Bartram Division, but at a lower price. The only thing that has changed is the transfer price. The reduction in the profit of the Bartram Division (because of the lower contribution margin) will be exactly offset by the increase in the profits of the Jeffers Division (because of that division's lower costs). Hence, the firm's total profit will not change.

(d) The firm would lose $19,000 if Jeffers bought its units from an outside supplier. You should see that from the point of view of the firm as a whole, the decision is basically a make-or-buy decision such as was discussed in Chapter 5. Consider, therefore, the two possible decisions, from the total firm's point of view.

	Decision	
	Buy from Outside Supplier	*Make Product Inside (Bartram)*
Purchase price (20,000 × $4.20)	$84,000	
Variable cost to produce (20,000 × $2)		$40,000
Avoidable fixed costs		25,000
Costs of each decision	$84,000	$65,000

As this analysis indicates, the decision to produce internally carries a $19,000 advantage.

Another approach to this problem is to consider the profits of the individual divisions and how those profits would differ from originally budgeted profits if a purchase were made from an outside supplier. If Jeffers is able to purchase from either Bartram or an outside supplier at a price of $4.20, *its* profits will increase $16,000 (20,000 units × $0.80 saved) over what has been budgeted with an original transfer price of $5.00. For this reason, the manager of Jeffers would be eager to obtain the lower price, however this can be accomplished. Now consider the position of the manager of Bartram Division, who has budgeted profits of $180,000. The profit of *his* division will decline $35,000 (budgeted profits of $180,000 − $145,000 profits, computed in item b), if he does not get the order from Jeffers. For this reason, the manager of Bartram should not want to lose the order from Jeffers. Putting these two changes in divisional profits together, we see that there will be a $19,000 loss (a gain of $16,000 by Jeffers and a loss of $35,000 by Bartram).

The important factor in this second approach is that if each division's manager evaluates his own situation properly, each will make a decision consistent with the good of the firm as a whole. The manager of Jeffers Division will wisely seek the lower price because it will increase his profits. The manager of Bartram Division will wisely consider the lower price because failing to do so will decrease his profits.

ASSIGNMENT MATERIAL

Questions for Discussion

11-1 *Alternative accounting methods* Explain how various inventory cost flow assumptions (last-in-first-out, first-in-first-out, weighted average) can affect the measurement of return on investment for a division.

11-2 *Product-line reporting* Financial analysts often express the desire that companies publish annual reports broken down by division or principal lines of activity. They have said they would like to see financial statements broken down by products, or perhaps separated into wholesale and retail business, or maybe separated into government and commercial business. What problems might arise from attempting to fulfill this desire for additional information? What recommendations might you make?

11-3 *Types of responsibility centers* Assume that the following multiple-choice question appeared on an examination covering this chapter and that the instructions were to select the single best answer.
Which of the following is true?
(a) All investment centers qualify as profit centers, but not all profit centers qualify as investment centers.
(b) All profit centers qualify as investment centers, but not all investment centers qualify as profit centers.
(c) All cost centers qualify as profit centers, but not all profit centers qualify as cost centers.

(d)   All cost centers qualify as investment centers, but not all investment centers qualify as cost centers.

Forced to make a choice, most students would correctly select answer (a). If, however, only the first alternative were presented and the instructions were to indicate whether the statement was true or false, some of those same students might decide that the statement was false. What line of reasoning would those students present to justify their answer and how would you respond to their position?

Exercises

11-4   RI, ROI, and VCP analysis   The following data refer to the DCB division of Mega Corporation. DCB sells one product.

Selling price	$8
Variable cost	$2
Total fixed costs	$400,000
Investment	$1,000,000

Required: Answer the following questions, considering each independently.
1.   If the manager of DCB desires a 20% ROI, how many units must she sell?
2.   If the division sells 120,000 units, what will ROI be?
3.   The minimum desired ROI is 15%. If the division sells 120,000 units, what is RI?
4.   The manager desires a 25% ROI and wishes to sell 100,000 units. What price must be charged?
5.   The minimum desired ROI is 20% and RI is $30,000. What are sales, in units?

11-5   Comparison of ROI and RI, investment decisions   The manager of Technic Division of Microprod, Inc., has developed the following schedule of investment opportunities. The schedule shows the amount to be invested and the expected annual profit. Currently, investment is $10,000,000 and profits are $2,500,000.

Investment Opportunity	Amount of Investment	Annual Profit
A	$ 500,000	$ 85,000
B	700,000	170,000
C	1,000,000	240,000
D	1,100,000	310,000
E	1,200,000	170,000

Required
1.   The division manager wishes to maximize ROI. (a) Which projects will he select? (b) What ROI will he earn?
2.   The manager wishes to maximize RI. Determine which projects he will select and the RI he will earn if the minimum desired ROI is (a) 15% and (b) 20%.

3. Assuming that the ROI on each project approximates the internal rate of return discussed in this chapter and in Chapter 8, which policy (maximizing ROI or maximizing RI) is better for the firm? Assume that the minimum desired ROI equals cost of capital.

11-6 Basic transfer pricing Burns Division of Arnett Industries manufactures batteries. Princess Division makes toys and has been buying 100,000 batteries per year from an outside supplier at $1.40 each. The manager of Princess Division recently asked the manager of Burns Division whether he would be interested in supplying the batteries, and at what price. Burns Division expects the following results in the coming year without considering a sale to Princess Division.

Sales (2,000,000 at $1.90)	$3,800,000
Variable costs at $0.90	1,800,000
Contribution margin	2,000,000
Fixed costs	1,200,000
Profit	$ 800,000

Burns has the capacity to produce 2,500,000 batteries.

Required
1. Suppose that Burns sold the batteries to Princess at $1.20 each. What would Burns Division's income be?
2. By how much, and in what direction, would income for Arnett Industries change if Burns supplied the batteries to Princess?
3. Repeat items 1 and 2 assuming that Burns can produce only 2,000,000 batteries and must therefore lose regular sales to supply Princess.

11-7 Basic transfer pricing Wharton Division of Tunney Industries manufactures furniture. Data on a sofa that Wharton makes appear below.

Selling price		$800
Variable costs:		
Fabric	$150	
Other variable costs	350	
Total variable costs		500
Contribution margin		$300
Expected volume		2,000 units

Wharton buys the fabric from an outside supplier. The manager of Wharton learns that Seagrave Division of Tunney makes a fabric that meets his requirements. Seagrave sells the fabric to outside customers for $180. Variable cost to Seagrave is $100. The manager of Wharton offers to buy the fabric at $120.

Required
1. Seagrave has plenty of capacity to serve its outside customers and meet Wharton's needs. If Wharton buys 2,000 units from Seagrave at $120:
   (a) What will happen to Seagrave's income?

(b) What will happen to Wharton's income?

(c) What will happen to Tunney Industries' income?

2. Redo item 1 assuming that Seagrave has no excess capacity and will lose outside sales if it supplies Wharton.

11-8 Product line evaluation "My division as a whole is evaluated on ROI and RI, so why shouldn't I use those measures to evaluate my product lines?" The speaker was Lynn Cathcart, manager of the Household Products Division of General Enterprises, Inc. Cathcart provided the following data regarding the three major lines that the division handles.

	Cleaners	Disinfectants	Insect Sprays
Margin	30%	25%	25%
Turnover	2.5 times	2 times	2.2 times
Annual revenues, millions	$30	$20	$44

Required

1. For each product line, determine ROI, total investment, and annual profit.

2. The minimum required ROI is 30%. Determine RI for each product line.

11-9 Components of ROI The following data refer to the three divisions of International Enterprises, Inc.

	Huge Division	Giant Division	Colossal Division
Sales	$3,000	$5,000	$10,000
Profit	600	500	1,600
Investment	2,400	2,500	4,000

Required

1. Compute ROI for each division, using the ratios of ROS and investment turnover.

2. Assume that each division could increase its ROS by one percentage point with the same sales as are currently shown. Recompute ROI for each division and comment on the differences between the results here and those in item 1.

11-10 ROI and VCP analysis The following data refer to the operations of Martin Division of LND Enterprises.

Selling price per unit	$30
Variable cost per unit	$18
Fixed costs per year	$300,000
Investment	$900,000

Required
1. Determine the number of units that must be sold to achieve a 25% ROI.
2. The manager has been approached by a firm that wishes to buy 10,000 units per year at a reduced price. Current volume is 43,000 units. Accepting the special order will increase fixed costs by $30,000 and investment by $80,000.
   (a) Determine ROI without the special order.
   (b) Determine the lowest price at which the manager can sell the additional 10,000 units without reducing ROI.

11-11 **Performance evaluation criteria** Foster Company has four divisions. Operating data for 19X7 are, in thousands of dollars, as follows.

	A	B	C	D
Divisional profit	$ 3,000	$ 2,500	$ 6,000	$1,700
Assets employed	$18,000	$14,000	$42,000	$8,000

Required
1. Rank the divisions according to (a) ROI, (b) RI if the minimum required ROI is 10%, and (c) RI if the minimum required ROI is 15%.
2. What other information might be helpful in evaluating the divisions?

11-12 **Transfer prices for service work** The service department of an automobile dealership does two general kinds of work: (1) work on cars brought in by customers and (2) work on used cars purchased by the dealership for resale. The service manager is often evaluated on the basis of gross profit or some other dollar measure. Because of the evaluation measure, the prices to be charged to the used-car manager for reconditioning and repair work on cars bought for resale are particularly important. The used-car manager is also likely to be evaluated by his profits. Thus, he wants service work done as cheaply as possible. The service manager naturally wants the prices to be the same as those he charges outside customers.

Required
1. What possible transfer prices could be used, and what are their advantages and disadvantages?
2. What do you recommend?

11-13 **Basic RI relationships** Grendel Division had RI of $2 million, investment of $25 million, and asset turnover of two times. The minimum required ROI was 20%.

Required
1. Determine Grendel's sales, profit, and ROS.
2. Determine the ROS that Grendel needs to raise its RI to $3 million, holding sales and investment constant.
3. With the ROS calculated in part 1, determine the sales required to earn $3 million RI, holding investment constant.

11-14 Transfer prices and decisions   Armonk Division of Green Industries sells its one product, a chemical compound, to outside firms and to Braser Division. Braser pays Armonk $4 per gallon for the compound, processes it into an industrial cleaner at an additional variable cost of $2 per gallon, and sells it for $9 per gallon. Budgeted income statements for the two divisions appear below. Green has no other divisions.

	Armonk	Braser	Total
Sales to outsiders:			
200,000 gallons	$1,000,000		$1,000,000
60,000 gallons		$540,000	540,000
Sales to Braser:			
60,000 gallons	240,000		240,000
Total sales	1,240,000	540,000	1,780,000
Variable costs:			
$2.50 per gallon	650,000		650,000
$4 transfer price plus $2		360,000	360,000
Total variable costs	650,000	360,000	1,010,000
Contribution margin	590,000	180,000	770,000
Fixed costs	400,000	80,000	480,000
Income	$ 190,000	$100,000	$ 290,000

Required
1. Braser Division has found an outside supplier who will sell the compound at $3.50 per gallon. The supplier insists on providing all 60,000 gallons that Braser needs. If Armonk reduces the transfer price to $3.50 and keeps Braser's business, what will the income for the firm as a whole be? What will each division's income be?
2. If Armonk refuses to meet the price and Braser buys outside, what will the income for the firm and for each division be? Armonk cannot increase its outside sales.
3. Suppose that if Braser buys outside, Armonk could increase its outside sales by 45,000 gallons. Armonk's capacity is 260,000 gallons, so it cannot meet Braser's needs and also increase its outside sales. If Braser buys outside and Armonk increases its outside sales, what incomes will the firm and each of the divisions earn?

11-15 Range of transfer price   Microtec Division of CR Industries makes a microchip that it now sells only to outside companies. The Consumer Products Division of CR is bringing out a new oven that requires a sophisticated chip and has approached Microtec for a quotation. Microtec sells the chip for $47 and incurs variable costs of $12. It has excess capacity. The Consumer Products Division can acquire a suitable chip from outside the company for $41.

Required
1. Determine the advantage to CR Industries as a whole for the Consumer Products Division to buy the chip from Microtec, as opposed to buying it outside.

2. Determine the minimum price that Microtec would accept for the chip.
3. Determine the maximum price that Consumer Products would pay Microtec for the chip.
4. How would your answers to each of the preceding items change if Microtec were working at capacity?

11-16 Basic ROI relationships Gandolf Division of Nationwide Motors had sales of $40 million, ROI of 30%, and asset turnover of 2.5 times.

Required
1. Determine Gandolf's (a) investment, (b) profit, (c) ROS.
2. Suppose that by reducing its investment Gandolf could increase its asset turnover to three without affecting sales or income. What will its ROI be?

11-17 ROI and RI relationships Fill in the blanks in the following schedule. Each case is independent of the others. In all cases, the minimum desired ROI is 20%.

		Case		
	A	B	C	D
Sales	$400	$___	$400	$700
Income	$___	$___	$___	$___
Investment	$___	$300	$200	$___
Margin	15%	8%	___%	6%
Turnover	___ times	3 times	___ times	___ times
ROI	30%	___%	___%	___%
RI	$___	$___	$ 15	$ 22

11-18 Relationships Fill in the blanks for each of the following independent situations. In all cases the minimum required ROI is 20%.

	(a) Income	(b) Investment	(c) ROI	(d) RI
1.	$2,000	$10,000	___	___
2.	$3,000	___	30%	___
3.	___	$20,000	30%	___
4.	___	$30,000	___	$1,000
5.	$4,000	___	___	$ 500
6.	___	___	30%	$3,000

11-19 Transfer prices—pushing capacity For several years, ABC Division of Slavic Corp. has been selling some (currently 8,000 units) of its product to XYZ Division of the same company at a price slightly below that charged to outside customers. Current income statements for the two divisions are as follows.

	ABC Division	XYZ Division
Sales of ABC:		
To outsiders (80,000 at $5.50)	$440,000	
To XYZ (8,000 at $5.00)	40,000	
Sales of XYZ:		
To outsiders (8,000 at $65.00)		$520,000
Total sales	480,000	520,000
Variable costs:		
ABC (88,000 at $2.00)	$176,000	
XYZ (8,000 at $5.00)		$ 40,000
XYZ (8,000 at $35)		280,000
Total variable costs	176,000	320,000
Contribution margin	304,000	200,000
Direct fixed costs	230,000	95,000
Divisional profit	$ 74,000	$105,000

XYZ Division has received an offer from an outside supplier to sell 8,000 units such as those currently being purchased from ABC for $4.50.

Required

1. Assume that ABC's manager refuses to meet the outside supplier's price and cannot increase outside sales.
   (a) How will ABC's profit be affected if XYZ purchases the units from the outside supplier?
   (b) How will total profit of Slavic Corp. be affected if XYZ buys the units from the outside supplier?
2. Assume now that ABC's manager doesn't want to meet the price offered by the outside supplier because she feels she's already giving XYZ a bargain. She says that meeting XYZ's needs is stretching her factory's capacity and that, while she couldn't make outside sales beyond the current level (80,000), her per-unit variable cost would drop to $1.85 for *all* units and her fixed costs would drop by $18,000 if she didn't sell to XYZ. How will total profit of Slavic Corp. be affected if XYZ accepts the offer from the outside supplier to provide 8,000 units at $4.50?

11-20   *Review of Chapters 10 and 11* Tschebert Company has only two divisions, Tschett and Bert. Selected information about each follows.

	Tschett	Bert
Divisional sales	$1,600,000	$2,400,000
Divisional income	240,000	160,000
Divisional investment	1,000,000	800,000

Unallocated costs that are common to both divisions are $70,000 per year, and assets (net of liabilities) that are not associated with either division are $400,000.

Required: Answer the following questions. (Note: The answers to most questions do not depend on the answers to previous questions.)
1. What is the ROS for Tschett Division?
2. What is the investment turnover for Tschett Division?
3. What is the ROI for Tschett Division?
4. What is the ROI for the firm as a whole?
5. What is RI for Bert Division if Tschebert's minimum required ROI is 12%?
6. Suppose Tschebert's top managers decide to allocate common costs to its divisions on the basis of divisional sales.
   a. Determine Bert Division's ROI.
   b. Determine the ROI for the firm as a whole.
7. If Tschebert's top managers decide to allocate common costs on the basis of divisional investment, what will ROI be for the firm as a whole?

Problems

11-21 *Performance evaluation criteria* Hawthorne Company has two divisions, Hi and Lo. The firm evaluates divisional managers based on ROI. Budgeted data for the coming year are as follows.

	Hi	Lo	Total
Sales	$ 600,000	$ 300,000	$ 900,000
Expenses	300,000	200,000	500,000
Divisional profit	$ 300,000	$ 100,000	$ 400,000
Investment	$1,200,000	$1,000,000	$2,200,000

An investment opportunity is available to both divisions. It is expected to return $40,000 annually and requires an investment of $200,000.

Required
1. Given that the divisional managers are evaluated based on ROI, which, if either, of the managers will accept the project? Explain.
2. Assume that the managers are evaluated on residual income. If the minimum required ROI is 18%, which, if either, of the managers will accept the project? Explain.
3. If the minimum required ROI is 18%, is it in the firm's best interest for a division to accept the project? Explain.

11-22 *Components of ROI* The managers of two divisions of Diversified Company were recently discussing their operations. Frank Margin commented, "I get a good return on sales, about 20%, but my investment is a drag. Turnover last year was only 0.80 times." Flo Turns said, "My problem is margins; turnover is about four times, but return on sales is only 4%."

Required
1. Compute ROI for each division.
2. (a) Assume that Frank Margin's division will maintain the same ROS. Determine the investment turnover he must achieve to obtain a 20% ROI.

(b) Assume that Flo Turns' division will maintain its turnover. Determine the ROS she must achieve to obtain a 20% ROI.

11-23 Transfer prices and required profit margins John Roberts, the used-car manager of the Snappy Wheels automobile dealership, is distressed by the firm's transfer pricing policy. Roberts is expected to earn a gross profit of 25% of sales in the used-car operation. He is charged with the trade-in price he sets for a used car plus any reconditioning work. The charge for reconditioning is based on actual costs by the service department plus a one-third markup over cost (25% on sales). Roberts feels that he is being unduly penalized by the one-third markup. Alan Black, the service manager, is held responsible for earning a 25% gross profit on sales and he argues that it would not be fair to force him to do reconditioning work any cheaper than the work he does on customers' cars.

Roberts has recently been approached by Joe Sharp, the owner of Sharp's Garage, an independent repair shop. Sharp offers to do reconditioning work for Roberts at 20% over cost, the work to be done during Sharp's slack periods. The work will generally take about four days longer than work done by the service department, which has no excess capacity.

Required: Should Roberts take his reconditioning business to Sharp?

11-24 Appropriate transfer prices The Rohn Division of BLQ Industries expects the following results in 19X6, selling its product only to outside customers.

Sales (100,000 units at $8)	$800,000
Variable costs at $5	500,000
Contribution margin	300,000
Fixed costs	150,000
Profit	$150,000

Early in 19X6, the manager of Betts Division of BLQ asked the manager of Rohn to supply 20,000 units to Betts. Betts would modify the units at a variable cost of $4 and sell the resulting product for $11. Rohn Division has capacity of 110,000 units and will therefore lose 10,000 units in outside sales if it supplies the 20,000 to Betts. Rohn's fixed costs remain constant up to capacity.

Required
1. If Rohn does transfer 20,000 units to Betts, which modifies and sells them as described, what will happen to the profit of BLQ Industries as a whole?
2. What is the minimum transfer price that Rohn will accept from Betts for the 20,000 units?
3. What is the maximum transfer price that Betts will pay?
4. Suppose that Rohn's capacity is 150,000 units. Its outside sales cannot increase over 100,000 units. Redo item 1.

11-25 ROI and RI on a special order The Appliance Division of TVM Industries has the opportunity to sell 250,000 units of one of its principal lines to a large chain store at $24 per unit. Selected data follow.

Annual unit volume	1,700,000
Normal selling price	$40
Unit variable cost	$18
Annual fixed costs	$30,000,000
Divisional investment	$25,000,000

The manager of the Appliance Division expects a 50,000 unit decline in sales at the normal price if he supplies the chain. He also expects fixed costs to increase by $100,000 and investment to increase by $1,200,000 if he accepts the order.

Required
1. Determine whether the manager of the Appliance Division should accept the order, assuming that he is evaluated based on ROI.
2. Determine whether the manager of the Appliance Division should accept the order, assuming that he is evaluated based on RI and that the minimum required ROI is 20%.

11-26 Make-or-buy and transfer pricing Lansing Enterprises, Inc. has three divisions, A, B, and C. One of the firm's products uses components made by A and B, with the final assembly done by C. One unit from A and one from B are required.

Data for the product are as follows.

Selling price (C division)	$100
Variable costs:	
A division	$32
B division	16
C division	14
Total variable costs	$62
Volume	1,000 units

Divisions A and B charge Division C $40 and $24, respectively, for each unit. Division C has been approached by an outside supplier who will sell the component now made by Division A at $35 per unit.

Required
1. Prepare partial income statements, down to contribution margin, for A, B, and C based on current operations.
2. Determine whether the offer from the outside supplier should be accepted. If A meets the outside price, C will continue to buy from A.
3. Suppose that A can sell its entire output of 1,000 units per year at $44 if it performs additional work on the component. The additional work will add $5 to variable cost per unit; fixed costs will be unchanged. Capacity of Division A is 1,000 units. Should A meet the outside supplier's price or allow C to buy from the outside supplier? Support with calculations. Is A's decision good for the company?

11-27 Goal congruence and motivation Rex Company manufactures furniture and related products. The manager of Redfern Division has been seeking bids on a particular type of chair to be used in a new living room suite she wants to market. No division within the firm can supply the chair.

The lowest outside bid is $120 from Dorfman Chair Company. Wisner Chair Company has bid $130 and would purchase some of the materials from the Ronson Upholstery Division of Rex Company. The Ronson Division, which has excess capacity, would incur variable costs of $25 for the amount of material needed for one chair and would be paid $46 by Wisner. The manager of the Redfern Division knows that Wisner would buy the materials from Ronson and that Dorfman would not. Each division manager is evaluated on the basis of ROI.

Required
1. As manager of the Redfern Division, which bid would you accept, Dorfman's or Wisner's? Explain.
2. As president of the firm, which bid do you want to see accepted? Explain.
3. What recommendation can you make?

11-28 *Divisional performance – interactions*   Acme Camera Company has two divisions, film and cameras. The manager of the Film Division, John Kretzmar, has just received a report from his laboratory indicating a breakthrough in a new type of film that produces much clearer pictures. The film can only be used in the X-40, a low-priced camera made by the Camera Division. The film currently sold for the X-40 has a variable cost per roll of $0.90 and sells for $3.00 per roll. The film currently sells 2 million rolls per year.

Kretzmar is confident that if he devoted his efforts and facilities to the production and sale of the new film he could sell 2.5 million rolls at $2.80 each. Additionally, he believes, on the basis of several market research studies, that if the Camera Division sold 200,000 more X-40s per year, sales of the new film could reach 4.8 million rolls. The variable cost of the new film is $0.80 per roll, additional fixed costs to produce it are $250,000 per year, and additional required investment totals $600,000.

Sam Brewer, manager of the Camera Division, is not happy with the proposal that he increase production of X-40s. He argues that the camera has a contribution margin of only $6 and that he would have to increase his investment by $4,000,000 and his fixed costs by $500,000 in order to increase production by 200,000 units. He is virtually certain, as is Kretzmar, that the extra units could be sold, but he is also well aware that the firm's minimum required ROI is 20%.

Required
1. Compute the change in RI for the Camera Division if production and sales of X-40s are increased by 200,000 units to show why Brewer is not eager to expand its production.
2. If the manager of the Camera Division will not increase production, what is the best action for the Film Division?
3. What is the best action for the firm as a whole?

11-29 *RI, ROI, VCP analysis, and effects of decisions*   The following data refer to the Pratt Division of Standard National Company.

Selling price	$40
Variable costs	$24
Total fixed costs	$200,000
Investment	$800,000
Planned sales in 19X9	30,000 units

Required: Answer the following questions, considering each one independently.

1. What is planned ROI for 19X9?

2. The minimum required ROI is 20% and the division manager wishes to maximize RI. A new customer wants to buy 10,000 units at $32 each. If the order is accepted, the division will incur additional fixed costs of $40,000 and will have to invest an additional $160,000 in various assets. Should the order be accepted?

3. The minimum desired ROI is 20% and the manager wishes to maximize RI. The division makes components for its product at a variable cost of $4. An outside supplier has offered to supply the 30,000 units needed at a cost of $5 per unit. The units that the supplier would provide are equivalent to the ones now being made and the supplier is reliable. If the component is purchased, fixed costs will decline by $20,000 and investment will drop by $40,000. Should the component be bought or made?

4. Again, minimum required ROI is 20% and the goal is maximizing RI. The manager is considering a new product. It will sell for $20, variable costs are $12, fixed costs will increase by $80,000, and sales are expected to be 15,000 units. What is the most additional investment that can be made without reducing RI?

5. Assume the same facts as in item 4 except that investment in the new product is $400,000 and that introducing the product will increase sales of the existing product by 2,000 units.
    (a) Should the new product be introduced?
    (b) Determine the increase in unit sales of the existing product needed to justify introducing the new product.

11-30 ***Corporate charges and behavior*** MST Company charges its operating divisions a percentage of sales to cover corporate expenses, which are virtually all fixed. The percentage is based on budgeted sales and budgeted corporate expenses and is predetermined for each year. In 19X6 the charge is 3%. The charge is included in calculating the profit of each division and its ROI, which is the basis for evaluating the performance of divisional managers.

Calco Division makes electronic equipment and has some excess capacity. Its manager has found a customer who will pay $10 million for a batch of product that has variable costs of $8.8 million. No incremental fixed costs are associated with the order. Accepting the order will require increased investment in receivables and inventories of about $5.1 million. The 3% charge is not included in the $8.8 million.

The divisional manager expects to earn $15.5 million on an investment of $70.5 million without the order.

Required

1. Should the divisional manager accept the order, acting in his own best interests?

2. Assuming that the minimum required ROI is 20%, is it to the firm's advantage to accept the order?

11-31 ***Performance measurement – athletic programs*** Haltom University is a medium-sized private university with a religious affiliation. Perhaps prompted by the prospect of declining college enrollment, a number of faculty members at Haltom have become increasingly concerned about the costs of the school's athletic program. The football program has been subjected to particular scrutiny. One professor has assembled the following data and argues, based on these data, that football is clearly a drain on funds needed elsewhere in the university.

19X4 Football Program

Revenue from ticket sales		$300,000
Revenue from concessions		25,000
Total revenue		325,000
Associated costs:		
Tuition for players on scholarship	$120,000	
Room rent in dormitories for players	22,000	
Board and incidentals for players	110,000	
Coaches' salaries	90,000	
Portion of salaries of athletic director, ticket office		
personnel, attendants, etc.	17,000	
Uniforms, equipment, etc.	10,000	
Total costs		369,000
Net loss on football program		($ 44,000)

Required
1. Comment on each item. Should it be included? If you are uncertain, state the conditions under which it should be included or excluded.
2. What other information do you want before reaching a decision on the desirability of the football program?

11-32 Transfer prices   Below is a budgeted income statement for Superdivision of Weaver, Inc. The division sells both to outsiders and to a sister division.

	Intercompany Sales to Subdivision	Sales to Outsiders
Sales:		
100,000 units at $10		$1,000,000
50,000 units at $8	$400,000	
Variable costs ($4 per unit)	200,000	400,000
Contribution margin	200,000	600,000
Fixed costs ($300,000, allocated at $2 per unit)	100,000	200,000
Profit	$100,000	$ 400,000

Required
1. Subdivision can buy all of its requirements from an outside supplier at $7 per unit and will do so unless Superdivision meets the $7 price. The manager of Superdivision knows that if he loses the business of Subdivision, he will not be able to increase his sales to outsiders and his fixed costs will not change. Should Superdivision meet the $7 price from the standpoint of (a) the firm and (b) Superdivision?
2. Superdivision meets the $7 price. It then is offered the opportunity to sell 60,000 units to a chain store at $7 each. The price of the 100,000 units now

sold to outsiders will not be affected. However, Superdivision has capacity of 190,000 units and if it cannot fill all of the requirements of Subdivision then Subdivision will have to buy all the units outside at $7. Should Superdivision accept the order, considering (a) the firm and (b) Superdivision?

3. Suppose now that Subdivision has received the offer from the outside supplier, who will provide as many units as Subdivision wants to buy at $7. Superdivision no longer has the opportunity to sell the 60,000 units to the chain store. The manager of Superdivision believes that if he reduces his prices to outsiders he can increase those sales greatly. His best estimates are that if he reduces the price to $9.20 he can sell 120,000 units, to $8.40, 150,000 units, and to $7.80, 170,000 units. Capacity is 190,000 units. Superdivision can sell any amount up to 50,000 units to Subdivision. Subdivision will buy units from the outside supplier as necessary. What should be done? How many units should Superdivision sell to outsiders, and how many units should it sell to Subdivision at $7.

11-33 ROI, RI, and investment decisions The manager of Brandon Division of Greene Industries has been analyzing her investment opportunities. The division currently has profits of $1,250,000 and investment of $5,000,000.

Investment Opportunity	Annual Profit	Amount of Investment
A	$300,000	$ 900,000
B	300,000	1,600,000
C	240,000	1,200,000
D	280,000	800,000
E	260,000	1,000,000

Required

1. Assume that the manager wishes to earn the highest ROI possible. Determine which projects she will select and the ROI that she will earn.
2. Assume that the division manager wishes to maximize RI. Determine which projects she will select and the total RI that she will earn if the minimum required return is (a) 20% and (b) 28%.
3. Assuming that the ROI on each project approximates the internal rate of return discussed in Chapter 8, determine which policy is better for the firm: maximizing ROI or maximizing RI. Assume that the minimum desired ROI approximates cost of capital.

11-34 Transfer pricing The Macron Division of 2M Company expects the following results in 19X6.

Sales (100,000 at $3)		$300,000
Variable costs	$120,000	
Fixed costs	150,000	270,000
Profit		$ 30,000

Sparkman Division of 2M Company wants to buy 30,000 units of Macron's product. Sparkman will incur an additional $0.80 per unit and sell the resultant new product for $4.50. Macron has capacity for 120,000 units.

Required
1. What will happen to the profit of the firm as a whole if the transaction takes place at a transfer price of $1.50?
2. What will happen to the profit of each division if the transaction takes place at the $1.50 transfer price?
3. What is the minimum transfer price Macron will accept for the 30,000 units?

11-35   ***ROI and RI — capitalizing human resources***   Business Products Division of Data Systems Company develops software for business applications for mainframe computers and microcomputers. The division employs 350 people, of whom 320 are accounting and data processing professionals, the remainder clerks, secretaries, and editors. Because the division does no manufacturing, it has very low assets—about $500,000, consisting of microcomputers, office equipment, and an extensive library. The division earned $1,500,000 last year. The company controller believes that the 300% ROI ($1,500,000/$500,000) misstates the division's results because the asset base omits the costs of training professional employees. The division spent $750,000 last year (19X5) on such training, including sending employees to seminars and the startup time for new employees.

The controller realizes that generally accepted accounting principles do not condone capitalizing the costs of human assets, but she nonetheless thinks it would be interesting to see how the division would look were it to capitalize these costs and amortize them over five years. She develops the following data for the past four years (the division's entire life), in thousands of dollars.

Year	Book Profit	Training Cost	Book Assets
19X2	$ 110	$400	$220
19X3	520	500	270
19X4	960	600	420
19X5	1,500	750	500

Training costs are included as expenses in the book profit figures.

Required
1. Determine ROI for each year using the data given and applying generally accepted accounting principles.
2. Determine profit, investment, and ROI for each year using the controller's method. That is, capitalize training costs and amortize them over five years, beginning with the year of the expenditure.
3. Compare the results in items 1 and 2. Comment, including statements about the advantages and disadvantages of the controller's approach.

11-36   ***Transfer prices and goal congruence (CMA adapted)***   A. R. Oma Company manufactures a line of men's perfumes and aftershave lotions. The manufacturing process is a series of mixing operations with the adding of aromatic and coloring ingredients. The finished product is bottled and packed in cases of six bottles each.

The bottles are made by one division, which was bought several years ago. Management believed that the appeal of the product was partly due to the attractiveness of the bottles and so has spent a great deal of time and effort developing new types of bottles and new processes for making them.

The bottle division has been selling all of its output to the manufacturing division at market-based transfer prices. The price has been determined by asking other bottle manufacturers for bids on bottles of the appropriate size and in the required quantities. At present, the firm has the following bids.

Quantity, Cases of 6 Bottles	Price per Case	Total Price
2,000,000	$2.00	$ 4,000,000
4,000,000	1.75	7,000,000
6,000,000	1.6666	10,000,000

The bottle division has fixed costs of $1,200,000 per year and variable costs of $1 per case. Both divisions are investment centers, and their managers receive significant bonuses based on profitability, so the transfer price is of great interest to both of them.

The perfume manufacturing division has variable costs, excluding the cost of bottles, of $8 per case and fixed costs of $4,000,000 annually. The market research group has determined that the following price-volume relationships are likely to prevail during the coming year.

Sales Volume in Cases	Selling Price per Case	Total Revenue
2,000,000	$12.50	$25,000,000
4,000,000	11.40	45,600,000
6,000,000	10.65	63,900,000

The president believes that the market-based transfer price should be used in pricing transfers. The bottle division has no outside sales potential because the firm does not wish to supply its highly appealing bottles to competitors.

Required
1. Of the three levels of volume given, determine which will provide the highest profit to the (a) bottle division, (b) perfume division, (c) firm as a whole.
2. Do the results in item 1 contradict your understanding of the effectiveness of market-based transfer prices? Explain why or why not.
3. Make a recommendation to the president of the firm.

11-37 Transfer pricing (CMA adapted) The manager of the Arjay Division of National Industries, Inc. has the opportunity to supply a brake assembly to an aircraft manufacturer for $50. The manager is willing to accept the order if he can break even on it because he has excess capacity and will be able to keep skilled workers busy who would otherwise have to be laid off. Additionally, he believes there is a good chance of getting more business from the same firm at better prices.

Bradley Division of National Industries makes a part that is used in the brake assembly. Bradley is operating at capacity and producing the part at a variable cost of $4.25. Its selling price is $7.50 to outsiders. None of its output is currently being sold internally.

The manager of Arjay decides to offer Bradley a price that will result in breaking even on the order. He determines that the other costs involved in filling the order are as follows, per unit.

Parts purchased outside	$23
Other variable costs	14
Fixed overhead and administration	8
Total, before fitting	$45

He decides to offer the manager of Bradley $5 per fitting, which brings the total cost per unit to $50, the selling price of the assembly. The firm is decentralized and the managers are evaluated based on ROI.

Required
1. Determine whether the manager of Bradley is likely to accept the $5 offer.
2. Determine whether it is to the firm's advantage for Bradley to supply the part at $5.
3. As the controller of National Industries, what do you advise be done?

11-38 **Budgeted and actual results**   Managers of divisions of Wycliff Company receive bonuses based on ROI. The bonuses constitute about 30% of total compensation of the average manager. Part of the bonus depends on whether the manager meets budgeted ROI.

F. C. Smith took over as general manager of the Poursh Division in late 19X1. Budgeted and actual results for 19X6 appear below, in thousands of dollars.

	Budget	Actual
Sales	$2,500	$2,480
Cost of sales	(1,250)	(1,310)
Operating expenses	(750)	(610)
Profit	$ 500	$ 560
Investment		
Current assets (50% of sales)	$1,250	$1,280
Current liabilities (40% of current assets)	(500)	(580)
Plant and equipment, net	1,800	1,770
Total investment	$2,550	$2,470
ROI	19.6%	22.6%

Smith received a sizable bonus. Commenting on the results, he said that once he saw that sales would not meet budget, he began to cut costs, especially in discretionary areas such as maintenance, employee training, and engineering (engineers were responsible for improving the quality of products and methods of manufacturing). He also held off payments to suppliers, letting them finance more of the division's asset requirements.

Required: Comment on Smith's performance. Refer to specific items above.

11-39 **Divisional performance, cost allocations, and dropping a product line** Randy Rathman is the manager in charge of two product lines for Kingston Company. He has just received the following income statement for the three months ended March 31, 19X7. The statement shows Randy's two product lines and the total results for the firm. There are 10 product lines in the firm.

	Product Line		
	A	B	Total Firm
Sales	$100,000	$200,000	$2,000,000
Separable expenses:			
Cost of sales	60,000	100,000	1,050,000
Selling and general	29,000	50,000	450,000
Total separable expenses	89,000	150,000	1,500,000
Common costs (allocated on basis of sales dollars)	15,000	30,000	300,000
Total expenses	104,000	180,000	1,800,000
Income (loss)	($ 4,000)	$ 20,000	$ 200,000

Randy is disturbed by the showing of product line A. He believes that the line is contributing to the common costs of the firm and should be kept, but he is worried about the effect on his performance.

Required
1. Prepare an income statement assuming that product line A is dropped. Show the effects on both Randy's and the firm's performance. All separable costs are avoidable. Be sure to reallocate common costs to product line B based on its relative percentage of the new sales for the firm. Round to the nearest $500.
2. Comment on the results. Does Randy's performance look better if product line A is dropped? Is it better? Is the decision good for the firm?

11-40 **Developing divisional performance data** Dixon Company has three divisions, X, Y, and Z. The following data regarding operations and selected balance sheet elements have been prepared by the firm's accountant (in thousands of dollars).

	X	Y	Z
Sales	$2,000	$3,000	$5,000
Cost of goods sold	1,000	1,400	3,300
Gross profit	1,000	1,600	1,700
Selling and administrative expense	400	900	800
Income	$ 600	$ 700	$ 900
Current assets	$ 400	$ 700	$ 600
Current liabilities	$ 300	$ 200	$ 100
Fixed assets (net)	$2,250	$3,000	$3,750

After determining costs and assets directly traceable to the divisions, the accountant allocated the remainder in the following way.

(a) Common cost of goods sold of $1,800 was allocated based on sales dollars.
(b) Common selling and administrative costs of $1,000 were allocated on the basis of relative sales dollars.
(c) Common fixed assets of $3,000 were allocated on the basis of relative shares of directly assignable fixed assets of $1,500, $2,000, and $2,500, for X, Y, and Z, respectively.
(d) All current assets except cash (which is held and managed by corporate headquarters) are directly assignable. Cash of $200 is allocated based on sales.

Required

1. On the basis of the data developed by the firm, rank the divisions according to ROI on net assets and RI, with a 15% minimum required ROI.
2. Recast the statements, computing divisional profit and assets employed without allocations. Rank the divisions on the same bases as in item 1. Comment on the differences between your rankings.

11-41 **Performance evaluation and behavior** The manager of the Croydan Division of General Goods, Inc. has been evaluating a proposed investment. His analysis indicates that the project will show an internal rate of return of 23% before taxes, well above the 16% required by the firm. He is, however, concerned with the effect the investment will have on the book rate of return for his division based on beginning-of-year book value—the basis on which his bonus is computed. The following results are budgeted for the next three years without considering the effects of the proposed investment (in thousands of dollars).

	19X1	19X2	19X3
Sales	$2,600	$2,900	$3,500
Costs	1,600	1,650	2,000
Divisional profit	$1,000	$1,250	$1,500
Invested capital (beginning of year)	$4,000	$4,400	$5,000
ROI	25%	28.4%	30%

Data on the proposed project are as follows.

Investment	$600
Revenues (annually for three years)	500
Costs before depreciation (annually for three years)	200

Straight-line depreciation will be used, and a staff member has prepared the following analysis.

	Pro Forma Data		
	19X1	*19X2*	*19X3*
Revenues (prior + $500)	$3,100	$3,400	$4,000
Costs (prior + $400)	2,000	2,050	2,400
Divisional profit	$1,100	$1,350	$1,600
Invested capital	$4,600	$4,800	$5,200
ROI	23.9%	28.1%	30.7%

Required
1. Is the investment desirable if the pretax rate of return required is 16%?
2. Is it desirable from the standpoint of the manager of the Croydan Division?
3. If your answers to items 1 and 2 conflict, can you suggest a reconciliation?

11-42 Transfer pricing Westfall Division of Bailey Enterprises makes stereophonic speakers and sells them to other firms for use in complete systems. The division can make 45,000 speakers per year and cannot increase production because of shortages of specialized skilled labor. Data for the division's product follow.

Selling price		$80
Variable manufacturing costs	$48	
Variable selling costs	8	56
Contribution margin		$24

Westfall has just lost a customer and volume is projected at 40,000 speakers per year for the next several years. Another division of Bailey, Leakes Division, is interested in buying speakers from Westfall and putting them in sets to be sold through retail outlets. Leakes now buys speakers of somewhat higher quality than those made by Westfall at $84 each. The speakers are of better quality than the rest of the components of the set, so the manager of Leakes intends to reduce prices and predicts higher volume if she changes to the lower-quality speakers. Volume of the set in which the speakers are to be used is currently 3,500 per year. If the price were reduced from $680 to $600, volume is expected to be 4,500 units per year. Variable costs are currently $460 per set, including the $168 for two speakers now purchased outside. Leakes Division wants 9,000 speakers per year from Westfall and has offered $62 per speaker. Westfall will not incur variable selling expenses on speakers sold to Leakes.

Required
1. Determine whether it is in the firm's best interests if Westfall sold speakers to Leakes.
2. At the suggested transfer price, is it in the interests of each of the managers to have Westfall sell to Leakes?
3. Determine the limits on the transfer price—that is, the highest price that Leakes is willing to pay and the lowest price that Westfall will accept.

11-43   ***Problems of market-based transfer prices***   Planton Division of Borgan Industries has developed an electronic measuring system that requires a sophisticated microprocessor. CLI Division makes such a microprocessor and currently sells it for $200 on the outside market. CLI incurs variable costs of $50 per unit. CLI has a lot of excess capacity. It now sells 30,000 units of the microprocessor per year and could make close to 40,000 units. However, if it tried to increase outside sales to 36,000 units, it would have to reduce its selling price on all units to $160. Accordingly, it has been restricting output.

   The manager of Planton received a bid of $200, the current market price, from CLI for the microprocessor and then analyzed data regarding expected volume at different selling prices. He intended to set the price of the measuring system at either $600 or $550. His analysis follows.

	Selling Price	
	$600	*$550*
Expected variable costs, per unit:		
Materials	$ 90	$ 90
Microprocessor from CLI	200	200
Labor and variable overhead	110	110
Total variable costs	400	400
Contribution margin	$ 200	$ 150
Expected volume	5,000 units	6,000 units

Required

1. At the $200 transfer price, what price will the manager of Planton Division set for the measuring system?
2. From the standpoint of the firm, which price is better, $600 or $550?
3. The manager of CLI Division knows that Planton will buy 5,000 microprocessors at the $200 price. What is the minimum price he will accept for 6,000 units—the price that gives him the same total contribution margin he could earn selling 5,000 at $200?
4. Will the transfer price you calculated in item 3 induce the manager of the Planton Division to try to sell 6,000 units of the measuring system at $550? Assume that the two managers have to agree on both the transfer price and the quantity to be taken. That is, the alternatives that the Platon manager faces are to (1) buy 5,000 microprocessors at $200 and (2) buy 6,000 at $175.

Cases

11-44   ***Divisional performance and accounting methods***   A division manager for McKy Company has been criticized for allowing ROI to fall in the past two years. He has explained that the division has made some large investments on which a 30% before-tax ROI is expected. He complains that the use of straight-line depreciation is hurting ROI, on which his performance is evaluated. Below are comparative income statements and other data for the past three years.

	19X1	19X2	19X3
Sales	$2,200	$2,900	$3,800
Variable costs	1,200	1,500	1,800
Contribution margin	1,000	1,400	2,000
Discretionary costs	300	500	700
Committed costs (largely depreciation)	300	450	700
Total fixed costs	600	950	1,400
Divisional profit	$ 400	$ 450	$ 600
Invested capital			
(principally plant and equipment)	$1,000	$1,600	$2,400
ROI	40%	28%	25%
Capital expenditures	$ 200	$ 900	$1,500

Required

1. Explain why the falling ROI (in the years indicated) may not indicate poor performance.
2. What possible solutions are there?

11-45   Capital budgeting and performance evaluation   Arnold Donald, manager of the Western Division of Global Enterprises, Inc., is considering an investment. He can save $10,000 in cash operating costs per year using a machine that costs $40,000 and has a ten-year life with no salvage value. Arnold calculates the book rate of return in the first year as 15% [($10,000 − $4,000 depreciation)/$40,000]. He therefore decides that the machine is not a wise investment because his current rate of return is 20% and he is evaluated based on ROI. (His current income is $40,000 and investment is $200,000.)

The seller of the machine offers to lease it at $8,500 per year if Arnold will accept a noncancellable lease for ten years. Arnold asks your advice and specifically requests that you consider the effect of the lease on book ROI.

Arnold further informs you that the firm's minimum desired ROI before taxes is 12%, which approximates cost of capital.

Required: Advise Arnold regarding his choices. Comment on whether the lease or purchase alternative is better from his standpoint and from the firm's.

11-46   National Automobile Company — A; introduction of a new model   National Auto Company consists of four relatively autonomous divisions. In the past each division has concentrated on a relatively limited range of models designed to appeal to a particular segment of the automobile market. The Kalicak Division has been producing midsized cars for many years. They range in price (to dealers) from $4,000 to $5,200.

One day last August, Noel Mack, general manager of the Kalicak Division, was studying some reports prepared by the firm's Market Research Department at central headquarters. Mack had been considering for some time the possibility of bringing out a stripped-down version of the division's most popular model, the Panther. He had been hesitant to do so because he feared that sales of the higher-priced Panthers would suffer. The market research indicated, however, that lost sales of higher-priced versions would be negligible if a new Panther were introduced and priced to sell to the customer for about $4,100. The lowest price at retail now charged for a Panther is $4,550.

Mack was pleased at the results of the study and instructed his production manager to determine the costs of producing 80,000 units of the new model per year—the number of units that the study indicated could be sold. Mack also asked for information about additional investment in equipment, inventories, and receivables necessitated by the higher volume.

A few days later Mack had the additional information. The production manager estimated the cost per unit to be $3,600, composed of the following basic categories.

Variable costs	$3,000
Fixed costs	600
Total	$3,600

The fixed cost per unit included $10,000,000 in existing fixed costs that would be reallocated to the new model under a complicated formula used by the division's cost accounting department. The additional investment in equipment was $80,000,000 and in receivables and inventories about $30,000,000.

Mack was reasonably certain that the information he had gathered was as accurate as estimates are likely to be. He consulted with several large dealers and concluded that the model could be priced at $3,800 to dealers. Any higher price would force the dealers to charge more than $4,100, with a consequent decline in volume below the 80,000 per year target.

Like the other divisional managers, Mack is evaluated based on the residual income earned by his division. The minimum required return is 18%. Income taxes are ignored in determining residual income for the divisions.

Required: Determine whether the new Panther should be brought out.

11-47 *National Automobile Company – B; interaction effects of decisions*

While mulling over his decision whether to introduce the new Panther model, Noel Mack was eating lunch with Bob Tibbit, general manager of the Hatfield Division, which specializes in compact and subcompact cars. Mack told Tibbit about the study he had ordered and gave a general picture of the results, including the projection of 80,000 units of volume of the new model.

After lunch, Tibbit called Wallace Richards, the chief of market research for the firm, and requested more information about the study. Richards said that the study indicated a potential decline in volume of 30,000 units of one of the Hatfield Division's best-selling higher-priced models if Kalicak brought out the new lower-priced model. Tibbit asked why that datum had not been included in the report given to Mack and was told that Mack had only asked for estimates in declines in volume of Kalicak Division cars. Tibbit slammed down the telephone and called his production manager and sales manager. He informed them of the situation and demanded that they quickly collect information.

Several days later, the production manager informed Tibbit that the model in question, which sold to retail dealers for $3,400, had unit costs of $2,900 at the division's current volume of 160,000 units per year. Fixed costs of $500 were included in the $2,900 figure. Tibbit asked what savings in fixed costs might be expected if volume were to fall by 30,000 units and was told that the fixed cost per unit would rise to about $560, even though some fixed costs could be eliminated. Conversations with other managers revealed that the division's investment could be reduced by about $70,000,000 if volume fell as stated.

Tibbit was visibly distressed by what he had heard. He was concerned with his division's interests, but realized that Mack had the right to operate in accordance with his best interests. He pondered the possibility of going to the firm's executive vice president for advice.

Required
1. Determine the effect on Hatfield of the introduction of the new Panther.
2. Determine the effect on the firm of the introduction of the new Panther.

11-48 ***ROI at Burlington Industries, Inc.***[6] Burlington Industries, Inc. is a very large and widely diversified manufacturer of textiles and associated products. The organization consists of several largely autonomous divisions, the performances of which have been evaluated using, among other measures, ROI and dollar profit. Profit measures are before tax but after a special deduction called the Use of Capital Charge (UOCC). The minimum required ROI for a division is the weighted average of the minimum required ROIs for three different types or classes of assets. The three classes are (1) accounts receivable less accounts payable, (2) inventories, and (3) fixed assets.

The central managers at Burlington have stated that the use of different required ROIs recognizes the different risks of the different types of investment. They feel that fixed assets, which are committed for relatively long periods and lack liquidity, should earn a higher ROI than assets committed for a shorter time. Receivables, which are turned into cash more quickly than are inventories, require a lower ROI. The minimum required ROIs for the three classes are 7% for receivables-less-payables, 14% for inventories, and 22% for fixed assets. These minimums are based on estimates of cost of capital and of relative investment in each class of assets for the firm as a whole.

The following data relate to a hypothetical division of Burlington, stated in thousands of dollars.

Sales	$23,450
Cost of sales	16,418
Selling and administrative expense	1,678
Other expenses, not including UOCC	1,025
Accounts receivable less accounts payable	2,540
Inventories	3,136
Net fixed assets	3,560

[6] This problem was adapted from material in a paper presented by Donald R. Hughes, then assistant controller of Burlington Industries, Inc., at a symposium at Ohio State University. The symposium's papers, and discussions of them, are in Thomas J. Burns, ed., *The Behavioral Aspects of Accounting Data for Performance Evaluation* (Columbus, Ohio: College of Administrative Science, Ohio State University, 1970). We acknowledge gratefully the permission of Professor Burns to adapt the material.

Required
1. Prepare an income statement for the hypothetical division. Use the same basis as is used by Burlington.
2. Compute ROI for the division and the weighted-average minimum required ROI.
3. Comment on the method used by Burlington. Does it seem to encourage desirable behavior on the part of managers? Is the use of different minimum ROIs a good idea?

CHAPTER 12

CONTROL AND EVALUATION OF COST CENTERS

This chapter applies the concepts of responsibility accounting to cost centers in manufacturing firms. We explain how managers set performance standards, how they use standards for performance evaluation, and what problems they encounter in using standards. We examine the role of standard costs for planning, with a major emphasis on developing standards for variable costs and interpreting variances from those standards.

PERFORMANCE CONCEPTS

There are two ways of measuring performance: effectiveness and efficiency. *Effectiveness* relates to whether a particular job was done or objective achieved. *Efficiency* is a more complex concept of performance because it relates output to input, incorporating in the measure the cost required to accomplish a task. Burning your house down is an effective way to rid it of mice but is not a very efficient method because you lose your house. Setting out traps should keep the mice down to a manageable number; it is not totally effective but is relatively efficient.

Total effectiveness and maximum efficiency (least cost) rarely are attainable in the same situation. Most situations require trade-offs that depend on the relative importance of the two objectives. Suppose a firm receives a rush order. Filling the order within the specified time might require incurring more cost than normal because of overtime premium and disruption of production schedules. The decision to accept or reject the order depends on an analysis of incremental revenues and costs as shown in Chapter 5. If the company accepts the order, it sacrifices efficiency to achieve effectiveness (filling the order).

This chapter is concerned primarily with measures of efficiency. We describe techniques for analyzing how well managers have controlled the *acquisition* and *use* of resources.

STANDARDS AND STANDARD COSTS

A standard is a norm, a criterion by which performance is judged. One standard for effectiveness is producing a specified amount of product. One standard for efficiency, the focus of this chapter, is whether a given output was produced at budgeted cost. A **standard cost** is a per-unit cost that a company should incur to make a unit of product. Companies use standard costs for materials, direct labor, and variable overhead.[1]

Standard Prices and Standard Quantities

A standard cost has two components: a standard price, or rate, and a standard quantity. Both standards relate to the input factor (materials, direct labor, variable overhead). The standard price, or rate, is the amount that *should* be paid for one unit of the input factor: $2 per pound of material, $8 per hour of direct labor, $4 variable overhead per machine hour. The standard quantity is the amount of the input factor that *should* be used to make a unit of product: three pounds of material, four direct labor hours. Thus, if a unit of product should require four direct labor hours and the standard labor rate is $8 per hour, the standard direct labor cost per unit is $32 (4 hours × $8).

Standard Costs and Budgets

As early as Chapter 1 we described budgeting as the process of relating required resources (inputs) to planned results (outputs). Chapter 6 developed the principles of flexible budgets and flexible budget allowances. Recall that a flexible budget

[1] Note that no standard for fixed overhead per unit of output is listed. Since total fixed costs are, by definition, unaffected by changes in volume, the fixed cost per unit depends on the number of units produced. Hence, an expected fixed cost per unit can serve as a standard only if the volume of production on which it is based is the volume actually achieved. Standards for evaluating the performance of managers responsible for fixed costs are discussed later in this chapter.

allowance is the amount of cost that should be incurred *given the actual level of activity*. Activity could have been output (number of units produced) or input (number of labor or machine hours). The difference between the actual cost and the flexible budget allowance is called a *variance*.

The relationship of standard costs to flexible budgets is simple and direct: a standard cost is a per-unit expression of a flexible budget allowance *based on actual output*. Thus, with the standard quantity of labor of four hours per unit of product and the standard labor rate is $8 per hour, the standard cost for labor is $32 per unit of product. The flexible budget allowance for one unit is also $32. If the company makes 2,000 units, the flexible budget allowance for labor is $64,000 ($32 × 2,000). (Notice also that the total standard time to make 2,000 units is 8,000 hours: 4 hours per unit × 2,000 units. Multiplying 8,000 total standard hours by the $8 standard rate gives the same $64,000 flexible budget allowance.) Now, if actual direct labor cost was $66,200, there was a variance of $2,200 ($66,200 minus the flexible budget allowance of $64,000). In the pages that follow we show how to analyze that variance.

It is also possible to establish a flexible budget allowance that considers inputs rather than outputs. Remember that for any of the required input factors (for example, labor), two factors determine total cost: the quantity of the input used (the number of hours worked by laborers) and the cost of a unit of such input (the hourly wage paid to laborers). In the situation described above, if 8,100 hours of labor were used, the flexible budget allowance based on *input* is $64,800 ($8 per hour × 8,100 hours worked).

In this chapter, we use the term *total standard cost* to refer to the flexible budget allowances based on *output*. As we shall see, however, flexible budgets based on inputs are useful in fixing responsibility, evaluating performance, and controlling operations.

Illustration of Standard Variable Cost

Coulter, Inc., a manufacturer of wooden packing crates, uses standard variable costs to aid in planning and control. Careful study has determined that if workers are producing at normal efficiency the direct labor time per crate is one-half hour. Also given normal efficiency, 20 feet of lumber should be used per crate. Direct laborers are normally paid $6 per hour, and lumber costs $0.10 per foot. Additionally, variable overhead is expected to be incurred at the rate of $2 per direct labor hour. Using these data, we compute the standard variable cost of a crate as shown in Exhibit 12-1 on page 488. The Exhibit also shows actual results for a recent month.

In practice, there might be several materials besides lumber; there also might be several kinds of direct labor at different rates. We use a single type of each factor to focus on the general concepts. The same reason prompts our use of variable overhead based on hours of direct labor. Measures of activity other than labor hours could be used for variable overhead. The selection of a measure for overhead requires identifying the causal factor most closely associated with over-

Exhibit 12-1
Standard Variable Costs

Cost Factor	Standard Quantity × Standard Price = Standard Cost		
Materials	20 feet	$0.10	$2.00
Direct labor	½ hour	$6.00	3.00
Variable overhead	½ hour	$2.00	1.00
Total standard variable cost per crate			$6.00

Actual results:

Crates produced	1,000
Materials purchased (23,000 feet)	$2,415
Direct labor (480 hours at $6.10)	$2,928
Variable overhead incurred	$ 980

head incurrence (see Chapter 3). In a highly automated plant, variable overhead is probably related to machine-hours or processing time, rather than to labor hours. In complex situations, the rate might be based on several factors and determined by the use of multiple regression analysis, as in the appendix to Chapter 3. The important thing is to find some reasonable way to develop an overhead rate that can be translated into a variable overhead per unit of product. For simplicity we use a single figure for variable overhead. Many costs are included in this category, such as the variable portions of utilities, supplies, and payroll fringe benefits.

A standard variable cost per unit is a tool a manufacturer can use for planning, control, and performance evaluation. The standards can be used to plan for variable production costs at any level of production. When actual production is known, the standard cost per unit can be multiplied by the number of units produced to give the flexible budget allowance for that production level. Managers can compare actual costs with expected costs to evaluate performance. The differences between standard and actual costs are called **variances.**

VARIANCES

We begin the illustration of variance analysis with direct labor costs. With a single exception, the analysis to be shown here is the same for the other cost factors.

Labor Variances

Given that in one month 1,000 crates are made, what *should* direct labor cost be? The total standard direct labor cost, or flexible budget allowance, for 1,000 crates is $3,000, computed as follows, from data in Exhibit 12-1.

$$
\begin{array}{ccccc}
\text{Total} & \text{actual} & \text{standard} & \text{standard} & \text{standard} \\
\text{standard} = \text{production} \times & \text{hours} & = & \text{hours} & \times \text{rate per} \\
\text{cost} & \text{(units)} & \text{per unit} & \text{allowed} & \text{hour}
\end{array}
$$

$$
\$3{,}000 = 1{,}000 \times \tfrac{1}{2}\text{ hour} = 500 \text{ hours} \times \$6.00
$$

The term *standard hours allowed* describes the physical quantity of direct labor that should have been used to produce 1,000 units. We could also have computed the flexible budget allowance for 1,000 crates by simply multiplying the 1,000 crates by the $3.00 standard direct labor cost per crate. The calculation to be used is largely a matter of convenience.

Direct laborers actually worked 480 hours during the month and earned $6.10 per hour, for $2,928 total actual cost. Actual costs were $72 less than standard (standard cost of $3,000 − $2,928 actual cost), producing a total variance of $72. But why? And who is responsible for the difference?

In some types of performance reporting (as in Chapter 10, for example), no distinction is made between variances in prices paid and in quantities purchased. However, in a large organization some managers control either prices or quantities, but not both. A foreman is likely to be responsible only for the quantities of labor and material used, not for wage rates or material prices.

We want to isolate the type of variance so that we can identify the manager responsible for it. Here, we want to separate our $72 total variance into two components: (1) the difference due to price; and (2) the difference due to quantity. Many terms are used to describe such variances. Price variances are sometimes called *rate, budget,* or *spending variances.* Quantity variances are sometimes called *use* or *efficiency variances.* The particular term you use is not important so long as you know which kind of variance is being referred to.

There are two common approaches to separating a total variance into its components. The first deals with total costs. We hold one of the factors constant (either price or quantity), and see what portion of the total variance is due to the effects of the other factor. The actual total labor cost can be separated as follows.

$$
\begin{array}{ccc}
\text{Actual} & \text{actual rate} & \text{actual cost} \\
\text{input} & \times \text{ for input } = & \text{of input} \\
\text{quantity} & \text{factor} & \text{factor} \\
480 \text{ hours} & \times \quad \$6.10 \quad = & \$2{,}928
\end{array}
$$

To accomplish our objective we need a flexible budget allowance based on our *input* factor, labor. The budget allowance is computed below as $2,880—the number of hours actually worked times the standard wage rate.

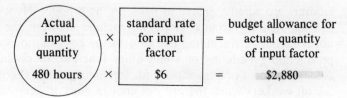

The only difference between the two calculations is the rate used for the input factor. The input factor, circled in the calculations, is the same for both, 480 hours. Hence, the difference between the actual cost incurred ($2,928) and the flexible budget allowance ($2,880) is due to the difference between the standard wage rate and the actual wage rate. That $48 difference ($2,928 − $2,880) is the **labor rate variance,** and is _unfavorable_ because the actual cost is greater than the flexible budget allowance for that quantity of input (480 hours).

The variance due to quantity is calculated in much the same way. We calculate the flexible budget allowance based on the actual *output* (1,000 units) as opposed to the actual input (480 hours). That budget allowance is $3,000.

Standard input quantity	×	standard rate for input factor	=	budget allowance for actual quantity of output
1,000 units × ½ hour per unit = 500 hours ×		$6	=	$3,000

Compare this formulation with the one immediately preceding it, where a budget allowance was computed for the *actual* quantity of the input factor, labor hours. Note that both calculations use the standard rate for the input factor, boxed in the calculations. The only difference between the two calculations is the quantity of input, labor hours. Hence, the $120 difference between the two budget allowances ($3,000 − $2,880) is due to the difference in the quantity of labor used. This difference is called the **labor efficiency variance** and is *favorable* because workers worked fewer than the 500 standard hours allowed for 1,000 units of output. Our analysis shows that the $72 total variance can be explained as follows.

Labor rate variance	$ 48 unfavorable
Labor efficiency variance	120 favorable
Total labor variance	$ 72 favorable

These relationships are diagramed in Exhibit 12-2. The leftmost figure is actual cost, the middle figure is a flexible budget allowance based on input, and the right-hand figure is the budget allowance based on output. The chart can be used to determine the variance for any adjacent numbers: if the number to the right is larger than the one to the left, the variance is favorable; the variance is unfavorable if the opposite is true.

The labor efficiency variance is intended to indicate how efficient direct laborers are when assigned to work on the product. Hence, the labor hours used to compute that variance should not include *idle time,* the time when laborers are not so assigned. Including idle time in the computation could mask problems in production scheduling or some other function, or could label, as labor inefficiency, the cost of a manager's (or top management's) conscious decision not to lay off workers when there is not enough work to keep them busy. Moreover, if

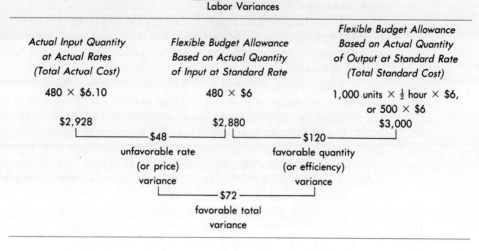

Exhibit 12-2
Labor Variances

Actual Input Quantity at Actual Rates (Total Actual Cost)	Flexible Budget Allowance Based on Actual Quantity of Input at Standard Rate	Flexible Budget Allowance Based on Actual Quantity of Output at Standard Rate (Total Standard Cost)
480 × $6.10	480 × $6	1,000 units × ½ hour × $6, or 500 × $6
$2,928	$2,880	$3,000

└────── $48 ──────┘ └────── $120 ──────┘
unfavorable rate   favorable quantity
(or price)   (or efficiency)
variance   variance

└────────────── $72 ──────────────┘
favorable total
variance

idle time is included in the computation, a supervisor whose performance is evaluated by the size and direction of the efficiency variance could be prompted to take actions that are not in the firm's best interest. For example, the supervisor of workers who would otherwise have idle time might assign them to making units and components not required by production schedules, which means that the firm will incur unnecessary costs for storage, financing, insurance, taxes, etc. Such an action is obviously contrary to the efforts of many manufacturing companies today who are, as we have noted throughout this book, adopting just-in-time and other modern techniques that imply smaller (or no) inventory.

Alternative Computation Methods

We can also calculate variances by dealing directly with the differences between the standard and actual figures for rate and quantity. The labor rate variance could be computed as follows.

$$\frac{\text{Labor rate}}{\text{variance}} = \frac{\text{actual}}{\text{hours}} \times \left(\frac{\text{standard}}{\text{rate}} - \frac{\text{actual}}{\text{rate}}\right)$$

$$-\$48 \quad = \quad 480 \quad \times (\$6 - \$6.10)$$

Direct laborers were paid $0.10 per hour more than standard (an unfavorable occurrence) and earned this amount over 480 hours.

The same approach could be used to calculate the labor efficiency variance.

$$\frac{\text{Labor}}{\text{efficiency}} = \frac{\text{standard}}{\text{rate}} \times \left(\frac{\text{standard}}{\text{hours}} - \frac{\text{actual}}{\text{hours}}\right)$$

$$\$120 \quad = \quad \$6 \quad \times (500 \text{ hours} - 480 \text{ hours})$$

Employees worked 20 fewer hours than the standard required to produce 1,000 units (a favorable occurrence).

When the number inside the parentheses (using these alternative formulations) is negative, as in the rate variance, the variance is unfavorable. When the number inside the parentheses is positive, as in the efficiency variance, the variance is favorable.

You may use either or both methods. A minor difficulty with the alternative method is that sometimes the actual rate may be a number with several digits after the decimal point. For example, if workers were paid $2,920 for 480 hours of work, the actual rate is $6.083333. . . . You would then have a small difference between the rate variance computed in this way and that computed using the method described earlier. Multiplying the standard rate by actual quantity and subtracting this value from actual total cost (or vice versa, depending on which is larger) always yields a precise answer.

Variable Overhead Variances

We used labor variances to illustrate the computations, but we could as easily have used variable overhead. The computations are the same, extending to the use of direct labor hours *if* variable overhead is budgeted according to labor hours (as they are in our example).

As shown in Exhibit 12-1, variable overhead costs for the month are $980. What are the variable overhead variances? Total standard variable overhead cost for 1,000 units of output is $1,000 ($1 standard cost per crate × 1,000 crates, or 500 standard direct labor hours at $2 standard rate per hour). Hence, we know that the total variance is $20 favorable (actual cost of $980 compared with a standard of $1,000).

Exhibit 12-3 shows that actual direct labor hours are used to determine the middle term (the flexible budget based on the actual quantity of input), and that standard labor hours are used to determine the right-hand term. (The right-hand term is also given by $1 standard variable overhead per unit × 1,000 units.) Both variable overhead variances, the **variable overhead budget variance** (or **spending variance**) and the **variable overhead efficiency variance,** are calculated in the same fashion as are the labor variances. Exhibit 12-3 shows the calculations.

Although the variable overhead budget variance is calculated in much the same way as the labor rate variance, it is not a rate variance in the sense of being the result of the prices paid for the input factor (overhead). For example, using more factory supplies than standard will show up in the variable overhead budget variance, not in the variable overhead efficiency variance.

The $20 budget variance can be computed using the alternative calculation method described earlier. However, because we were given only total overhead incurred, we must divide the total cost of $980 by the actual hours of 480 to determine the actual rate at which the variable overhead was incurred. That rate is about $2.0416 ($980/480). The format of the calculation is the same as for the computation of the direct labor variance.

Exhibit 12-3
Variable Overhead Variances

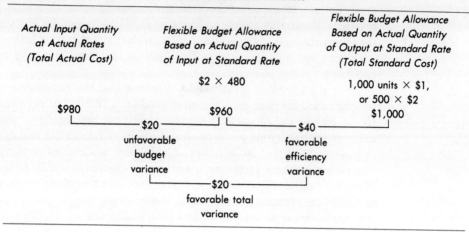

Actual Input Quantity at Actual Rates (Total Actual Cost)	Flexible Budget Allowance Based on Actual Quantity of Input at Standard Rate	Flexible Budget Allowance Based on Actual Quantity of Output at Standard Rate (Total Standard Cost)
	$2 × 480	1,000 units × $1, or 500 × $2
$980	$960	$1,000

⌊———— $20 ————⌋ ⌊———— $40 ————⌋
unfavorable   favorable
budget   efficiency
variance   variance

⌊———— $20 ————⌋
favorable total
variance

$$\text{Budget variance} = 480 × (\$2.00 - \$2.0416) = -\$19.97 \text{ (difference due to rounding)}$$

The $40 variable overhead efficiency variance can also be calculated using the standard rate per direct labor hour of $2 and the difference between the actual and standard hours.

$$\text{Efficiency variance} = \$2 × (500 - 480) = \$40$$

When variable overhead standards are based on direct labor hours, the only difference in calculating labor and overhead variances is in the rates; that is, actual and standard direct labor hours are used both for labor and overhead. In fact, the variable overhead efficiency variance is the result of using more or less labor than standard. Consider some of the costs that might be included in variable overhead. Payroll taxes, pensions, other fringe benefits, and many other costs will be incurred whenever employees work and regardless of whether they work efficiently or inefficiently. If the employee puts in an hour, the other costs follow. Hence, if there are inefficient labor hours (an unfavorable labor efficiency variance), there will be an unfavorable variable overhead variance, and vice versa. *As long as variable overhead is related to labor hours,* overhead efficiency variances do not indicate efficient (or inefficient) use of variable overhead but rather the efficient (or inefficient) use of direct labor. Moreover, in a situation where variable overhead is related to some *other* measure of activity, such as labor cost, machine time, or cycle time (the time a product spends in the manufacturing process), the variable overhead efficiency variance will reflect the efficient or inefficient use of the related factor.

Of course, some elements of variable overhead may be related directly to the number of units produced, rather than to an input factor such as labor hours. For example, costs such as packaging materials (boxes, padding, lining) are directly related to units produced. Workers who pack the products should use standard quantities of these materials for each packaged product even if they work more or less efficiently than standard (take more or less time to package the product). If variable overhead contains significant amounts of such cost elements, the conventional calculations of variable overhead efficiency *and* budget variances are not appropriate for analysis and may give rise to interpretation problems.

Let us look at an example. Suppose that the per-pound standard cost of supplies used for packing a carton of product is $0.60, that each carton is expected to use one pound of packing supplies, and that the standard packing time is six minutes, or 10 cartons per hour. If the company relates the variable-overhead cost of packing to direct labor hours, it will show a standard packing cost of $6 per labor hour, because each hour a worker is expected to use 10 pounds of material at $0.60 per pound. Now, suppose that in one month workers packed 10,000 cartons in 1,000 hours (exactly at standard), that packing supplies were purchased at $0.60 per pound (also at standard), but that workers used 11,000 pounds of packing supplies. The total actual cost of supplies that month is $6,600 (11,000 pounds × $0.60 per pound). The conventional calculations of the variances, using unit costs, are shown in the following diagram.

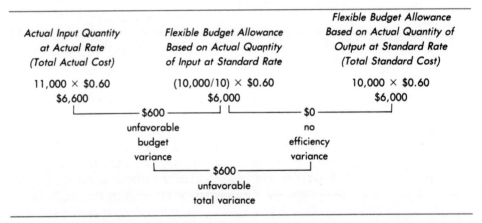

Actual Input Quantity at Actual Rate (Total Actual Cost)	Flexible Budget Allowance Based on Actual Quantity of Input at Standard Rate	Flexible Budget Allowance Based on Actual Quantity of Output at Standard Rate (Total Standard Cost)
11,000 × $0.60	(10,000/10) × $0.60	10,000 × $0.60
$6,600	$6,000	$6,000

$600 unfavorable budget variance

$0 no efficiency variance

$600 unfavorable total variance

Does the analysis reflect the facts as we know them? No. The budget variance is not caused by paying a price different from the $0.60 standard. It arises because workers used more pounds of packing supplies than standard for the number of cartons packed. The budget variance for this overhead item is actually an efficiency variance because it results from the inefficient use of the input factor (packing supplies) by the laborers.

In a practical situation, analyses of variable overhead variances include the computation of variances for each cost element classified as variable overhead. When there are significant costs of the type just described—ones related to units of output rather than strictly to direct labor hours, or other input factor—it is wise to analyze these costs separately, in a fashion similar to the analysis of materials variances, which we cover in the next section.

Materials Variances

The material price variance is slightly different from its counterparts in labor and variable overhead because material, unlike labor, can be stored. What is purchased in one period is not necessarily used in that period, but the economic effect of paying more or less than standard price for materials occurs at the time of purchase. Consequently, the **material price variance** is calculated based on the quantity of material *purchased,* not the quantity *used.* (The earlier that managers are aware of variances, the sooner they can take corrective action, so it makes sense to isolate the variance at the time of purchase rather than at the time of use.) The **material use variance** is calculated in the same way as are the labor and overhead efficiency variances.

The firm in our example bought 23,000 feet of lumber for $2,415 (see Exhibit 12-1). The average price was $0.105 ($2,415 ÷ 23,000). The standard price per foot of lumber is $0.10 (also from Exhibit 12-1). In calculating the material price variance, the flexible budget allowance is based on what you expect to pay for the quantity *purchased:* $2,300 (23,000 feet × $0.10 per foot). The material price variance is diagramed in Exhibit 12-4.

Exhibit 12-4
Material Price Variance

Actual Quantity of Input Purchased, at Actual Prices	Flexible Budget Allowance for Actual Quantity of Input Purchased, at Standard Rate
	23,000 × $0.10
$2,415	$2,300

└────────────── $115 ──────────────┘
unfavorable material
price variance

If we use the alternative formula, we must remember to use the actual quantity purchased, as follows.

$$\begin{matrix} \text{Material} \\ \text{price} \\ \text{variance} \end{matrix} = \begin{matrix} \text{actual} \\ \text{quantity} \\ \text{purchased} \end{matrix} \times \left(\begin{matrix} \text{standard} \\ \text{price} \end{matrix} - \begin{matrix} \text{actual} \\ \text{price} \end{matrix} \right)$$

$$-\$115 = 23{,}000 \times (\$0.10 - \$0.105)$$

The material use variance is calculated the same as the direct labor and variable overhead efficiency variances. The firm used 19,500 feet of lumber to make 1,000 crates. The standard quantity of lumber per crate is 20 feet (see Exhibit 12-1), so the total standard quantity for 1,000 crates is 20,000 feet. The standard cost of lumber for 1,000 crates is $2,000 (20,000 feet at $0.10 per foot, or 1,000 crates multiplied by the standard material cost per crate of $2, as shown in Exhibit 12-1). The material use variance is diagramed in Exhibit 12-5 on page 496.

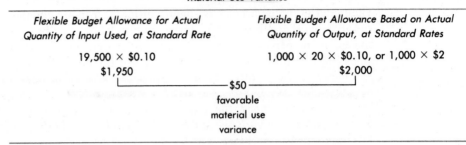

Exhibit 12-5

Material Use Variance

Flexible Budget Allowance for Actual Quantity of Input Used, at Standard Rate	Flexible Budget Allowance Based on Actual Quantity of Output, at Standard Rates
19,500 × $0.10	1,000 × 20 × $0.10, or 1,000 × $2
$1,950	$2,000

$50
favorable
material use
variance

Alternatively, we can calculate the material use variance by using the following formula.

$$\frac{\text{Material use}}{\text{variance}} = \text{standard price} \times \left(\begin{array}{l} \text{standard} \\ \text{quantity} \\ \text{for output} \\ \text{achieved} \end{array} - \text{actual quantity} \right)$$

$$\$50 \quad = \quad \$0.10 \quad \times (20,000 - 19,500)$$

We were able to show labor and variable overhead variances in one schedule for each (see Exhibits 12-2 and 12-3, respectively). We cannot do that with materials variances because there are two middle terms, one based on units purchased, the other on units used. This is the only difference between materials variances and the other types of variance.

Interaction Effects

Strictly speaking, the methods illustrated do not correctly show the effects on performance due to price differences alone. The price variances are computed using actual quantities. Hence, the managers responsible for acquiring resources (materials, labor, overhead) are assigned responsibility for some of the efficiency or inefficiency of the managers who control the use of resources.

In the example, standard direct labor hours for 1,000 crates are 500, actual hours are 480, and there is a $0.10 per hour unfavorable wage rate variance. We showed the rate variance as $48 ($0.10 × 480). One could argue that the manager responsible for wage rates should be charged with a $50 variance ($0.10 × 500 standard hours). That manager cannot control hours worked, and it is unfair to give him or her credit for the efficient (or inefficient) use of workers' time.

The $2 difference between $48 and $50 is due to interaction of rate and efficiency and is not properly chargeable to either manager. It is a joint variance. The variance due to use of labor is assigned correctly to the manager of resource use; the efficiency variance is calculated based on the standard wage rate. In the earlier computations with this example on page 491, the effects of interaction were assigned to the manager responsible for acquiring labor, even though some of the variance was caused by variances from standard hours. In practice, the interaction effect is rarely large, so it is included in the rate variance as we have done.

VARIANCES AND PERFORMANCE EVALUATION

Isolating variances is the first step toward providing information for performance evaluation. As we pointed out in Chapter 10, the relevant factors in evaluating the performance of an individual manager are those that the manager is responsible for and can control. Quantifying the effects of price and quantity differences is not the same thing as identifying the *causes* of, and the responsibility for, the differences. Knowing that workers were paid more or less than the standard rate, or worked more or less than the standard hours, does not explain *why* these variances occurred.

Two issues complicate the interpretation of variances. First, variances signal nonstandard performance only if they are based on up-to-date standards that reflect current production methods and factor prices. Suppose that changing production methods to increase quality results in using more labor time. If the company does not change the standard labor time, it will have unfavorable labor efficiency variances. These variances are not the fault of the managers responsible for using labor; the fault lies with the standard. It can be costly to issue new standards every time a minor change occurs, and frequent revisions of standards might even cause the standards to lose their meaning. Accordingly, the decision to revise standards must compare the cost of making the revision with the expected benefits in the form of better control and performance evaluation.

The second issue that clouds the interpretation of variances is that they are not independent of one another. One variance may be directly related to others, either in the same or a different department. (We confronted a similar situation in Chapter 10, where the use of a particular cost-allocation scheme could cause one manager's actions to affect the reported performance of another.) For example, suppose the purchasing manager buys lower-quality materials that cause increases in labor time. Unfavorable labor and variable overhead efficiency variances in processing departments are traceable to, and should be considered with, the favorable materials price variance from the purchase of the materials. Thus, knowing that there was a variance for some element of cost (material, labor or overhead) is not the same as knowing why the variance occurred or which manager was responsible for it.

INVESTIGATING VARIANCES

When variances occur, managers must decide whether (1) the amount of the variance is sufficient to warrant investigation; (2) there is a reasonable probability that finding the cause of the variance will lead to corrective action (some variances are not correctable); and (3) the cost of investigating the cause of the variance and correcting the problem will be less than the cost of a recurrence of the variance. As a general rule, a variance should be investigated if the inquiry is expected to lead to corrective action that will reduce costs by an amount greater than the cost of the inquiry.

Managers want to investigate only significant variances. Two criteria are generally used to evaluate significance: absolute size and percentage of standard cost. A variance of $5 is almost certainly not worth investigating, whereas a variance of $100 might be. If actual cost is $500 and standard cost is $400, the $100 variance is 25% of standard. This large a percentage variance might well be worth investigating, whereas a $100 variance from a standard cost of $85,000 is almost certainly not. Thus, absolute size of a variance is probably less important than its percentage of standard cost.

The cost of investigating variances is difficult to determine. If there are personnel whose job it is to make these investigations, there is likely to be no additional cost because their salaries must be paid in any event. However, with a fixed amount of time to spend on various tasks, it is wise to concentrate on variances that are likely to be correctable and whose correction may be expected to yield large savings. (There is an opportunity cost of managerial time, so investigation always has *some* cost.)

Many companies use **control charts** to decide when a particular variance should be investigated. These charts show past cost behavior patterns so that efforts will not be wasted investigating costs that normally show wide fluctuations. A control chart is shown in Figure 12-1.

The dots represent actual costs. The dotted lines represent the limits within which variances are not investigated. The lines could be set closer to or farther away from total standard cost. The closer the limits, the more variances will be investigated, and vice versa. The wide scattering of costs suggests high variances. A manager who believes that the production process is under adequate control and that the variances are unavoidable will set wide limits. A manager who thinks that most variances are caused by correctable factors will set narrow limits. There are many sophisticated ways of developing control charts; you are likely to study some of these in statistics courses.

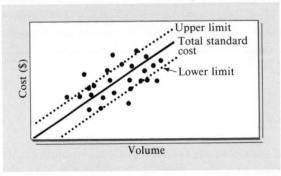

Figure 12-1   Sample Control Chart

One fact that should *not* be important in deciding whether to investigate a variance is whether the variance is favorable or unfavorable. That is, managers should avoid the tendency to believe that favorable variances can be left uninvestigated because they indicate that things are going better than expected and should not be changed. As we pointed out in the previous section, variances are not independent, so that a favorable variance in one responsibility area might have unfavorable effects on another area. Moreover, favorable variances can be caused by actions that could harm the firm in the long run. For example, favorable variances in material prices or labor efficiency could come from a lessened concern for the quality of the finished products. When customers recognize the reduced quality, the reputation and subsequent sales of the firm will be hurt. Short-run profits might increase because of lower costs (favorable variances), but long-run profits may suffer.

Because, as we suggested early in the chapter, standards can be useful for planning, one of the most important reasons for investigating variances is simply to detect bad standards. Variances can occur just because of out-of-date standards. Variances can also result if standards are set at levels that are initially either too tight or too loose. If standards are used for planning and decision making, they must reflect current information about attainable performance.

SETTING STANDARDS — A BEHAVIORAL PROBLEM

Like any managerial tool, standards should be used when they contribute to achieving the firm's objectives, and the setting of standards should take into consideration the potential for influencing behavior.

Some managers believe that there are circumstances under which using standard costs could obscure, or even conflict with, the firm's objectives. For example, consider that an important part of the philosophy of advanced manufacturing environments is continual improvement. Many managers in companies committed to advanced manufacturing techniques believe that using standard costs encourages people to focus on meeting the standard rather than on continuing to improve performance. Some managers in such firms also believe that calculating variances is counterproductive because variances direct attention to a single aspect of performance while the firm is emphasizing overall performance. Despite the potential for conflicts, some prominent companies that use advanced manufacturing techniques use standards. The standards are updated frequently so that meeting them is a dynamic process.

Another factor affecting how useful standard costs are likely to be in advancing the firm towards its objectives is the life-cycle stage of the firm's product. The cycle for most products begins with a period of rapid sales growth, followed by a period of maturity (stable sales), and finally a period of sales decline. In the growth stage, products are often highly differentiated and subject to rapidly changing technology. They compete on the basis of style or function, not price, and the critical success factors (and major objectives of the firm) are increasing sales and achieving a high market-share. Some managers believe that using standard costs during the growth stage directs undue attention to cost control at a time when margins are likely to be high and being a low-cost producer contributes little to overall profitability. Even those managers agree, however, that using standard costs is likely to be very helpful in achieving the firm's goals in the mature stage of a product's life, when price competition is pervasive and cost control is one of the firm's principal competitive weapons.

When the circumstances suggest, and managers recognize, that using standard costs helps to achieve the firm's objectives, several ways are available for setting standards. The most common are engineering methods and managerial estimates based on experience and knowledge of the production process. These methods are most relevant to determining quantity standards.

Engineering Methods

Some companies develop standard quantities for materials and labor by carefully examining production methods and determining how much of an input factor is necessary to obtain a finished unit. In time-and-motion studies, which are often used to set labor standards, an industrial engineer analyzes the movements necessary to perform each task. For example, a worker might have to reach into a bin, pick up a part, place it on the workbench, drill two holes in specified places, then place the part into another bin. Each movement is timed. The total time required to perform the entire task becomes the standard time allowed. Similarly, with materials, industrial engineers study the characteristics of the product and its materials to determine how much material is required per unit. (Such determinations consider material wasted through cutting and trimming.)

Engineering methods are also used to set standards for some overhead items, such as maintenance. The industrial engineer will identify the necessary components of a desirable maintenance program and estimate the costs of each component. A standard is then established that allows for specified maintenance expense per machine-hour used, with an allowance for other maintenance that occurs because parts break or wear out.

Although some overhead items can be analyzed using engineering methods, it is usually difficult to analyze overhead by starting with a unit of product. Unlike materials and labor, most overhead costs are not directly related to single units of product. Large amounts of overhead are more likely to be related to large quantities of product, labor hours, or machine hours. Therefore, standards for elements of variable overhead are more often developed using methods that are illustrated in Chapter 3: high-low, scatter diagram, and regression analysis.

Managerial Estimates

Some firms rely on the judgment of the managers most closely associated with a task to determine quantities of input needed to produce a unit of product. Such managers understand current production conditions and specifications. This approach to setting standards is advantageous because, as we noted in Chapter 6, when managers participate in setting standards and budgets, they are more likely to commit to meeting them. There is, however, some reluctance to allow the responsible managers to set standards without guidance, as some higher-level managers believe that standards set in this way will include unnecessary slack (that is, standards will be too loose). Hence, when standards are initially determined by managerial estimates, a careful review of the standards usually follows at higher levels of management.

What Standard – Ideal, Attainable, or Historical?

What level of performance ought to be considered in developing a standard? Should the standard be based on what can be done under the best possible conditions? Should it include allowances for waste, fatigue, and bottlenecks—that is, currently attainable performance? Should it be based on past performance, an historical measure?

An **ideal standard** can be attained only under *perfect* conditions. It assumes that laborers continuously work at the peak of their abilities; that materials always arrive at work stations on time; that tools never break; that maintenance on machines never stops production; that no one makes mistakes. In short, an ideal standard is not likely to be achieved under anything like normal working conditions.

Some argue that ideal standards are the best because the resulting variances alert managers to deviations from the ideal and motivate workers to do the best possible job. Whether ideal standards really do assist managers in these ways is questionable. Some evidence from the behavioral sciences suggests that motivation is reduced rather than increased by the use of ideal standards. Being unattainable goals, ideal standards can foster discouragement, lack of commitment to the goal, and distrust of higher levels of management. Frustrated managers and workers might even ignore standards they know to be unattainable.

Currently attainable performance as a standard is based on expectations about efficiency under *normal* working conditions. Such a standard allows for unavoidable losses of efficiency due to recurring problems that can never be eliminated. But currently attainable standards are not lax. Performance requirements are high, but they are attainable if everything goes reasonably well.

Research in the behavioral sciences indicates that managers and workers respond well to standards as goals when they have participated in setting the standards *and* when the standards are attainable. Such standards can also be useful for planning, whereas ideal standards cannot. (A management that uses ideal standards must make adjustments to *plan* accurately for expenses, pro forma financial statements, and cash flows.) Additionally, currently attainable standard costs are of more value than ideal standard costs for decision-making purposes. Acceptance of special orders, price reductions or increases, promotional campaigns, and other special decisions must be based on *expected* variable costs, not those that could be obtained only under ideal conditions.

Historical standards are based on experience. The use of historical performance as a standard has serious drawbacks. Past inefficiencies are perpetuated as they become built into the standard. Changes in product design and work methods that drastically affect labor and material requirements might be ignored. Historical achievements have no particular significance *except as they may aid in predicting the future*. (Compare this reservation with those expressed earlier—particularly in Chapters 5, 6, 7, and 11—about the usefulness of historical information for predicting the future.)

VARIANCES AND COST CENTERS

Managers of cost centers typically receive reports like the one in Exhibit 12-6. Here, the number of units produced is less than the number budgeted, which could indicate that the manager was ineffective because he or she failed to meet the production goal. But failure to meet the production goal could have been caused by a problem in a department that had previously worked on the product, in which case *this* manager cannot be held responsible for the shortfall in production. If the production shortfall is the manager's fault, then shortfalls also are likely to appear in any departments that subsequently work on the product. In any case, the cause of the production shortfall must be determined before this manager's performance can be evaluated.

The "actual" costs reported to the manager on the sample report in Exhibit 12-6 have been adjusted to eliminate price variances. That is, the amounts in the *Actual* column for materials, labor, and supplies are actual quantities multiplied by standard prices. This approach is used when the manager controls only the quantities of each factor used.

Because, as we noted earlier, calculating a variance does not explain its cause, performance reports usually contain a section for comments and explanations of variances. The department manager can then concentrate on those variances that need explanation and, if the cause of the variance is in that department, comment on the prospects for improvement. The sample performance report shows some noncontrollable costs clearly labeled as such and shown separately. Chapter 10 pointed out reasons for doing this.

In general, variable costs are controllable whereas many fixed costs are not, at least over short periods. Allocated costs are not controllable by the department to which they are allocated. Thus, depreciation on equipment in the machining department is direct to the department, but not controllable in the short run.

VARIANCES
AND INCOME STATEMENTS

Typically, managers of profit or investment centers receive performance reports that show both revenues and expenses—that is, they receive some type of income statement. A manager responsible for both revenues and costs is concerned with variances related to both aspects of profit. The sample income statement in Exhibit 12-7 (page 504) shows one format for reporting variances.

Exhibit 12-6

Departmental Performance Report

Month __May 19X7__

Department __Machining__   Manager __R. Jones__
Date Delivered __6/4__   Date Returned __6/6__

	Budgeted	Actual	Variance
Production, in units (original budget 11,000 units)		9,000	2,000
Controllable costs, for actual production of 9,000 units:			
Materials, standard of __$2__ *	$18,000	$18,800	$800U ①
Labor, standard of __$3__ *	27,000	28,800	1,800U ①
Supplies, standard of __$0.10__ *	900	880	20F
Repairs	$1,100	$1,200	$100U
Indirect labor	900	900	0
Total controllable costs	$47,900	$50,580	$2,680U
Noncontrollable costs:			
Depreciation __Machinery used in__ __department__	$1,500	$1,500	0
Heat and light (allocated)	200	220	20U
Other allocated costs	800	860	60U
Total noncontrollable costs	$2,500	$2,580	$80U
Total costs	$50,400	$53,160	$2,760U

*Actual costs are at standard prices.

Comments and Explanations
① *Faulty materials required more time and created more waste.*

Exhibit 12-7

Sample Income Statement (thousands of dollars)

Sales		$14,345
Standard variable cost of sales		11,112
Standard variable manufacturing margin		3,233
Variances:		
Materials	$ 89U	
Direct labor	109U	
Variable overhead	6F	
Total		192U
Actual variable manufacturing margin		3,041
Variable selling and administrative expenses		871
Contribution margin		2,170
Fixed costs:		
Budgeted fixed manufacturing costs	1,045	
Budget variance—fixed manufacturing costs	15U	
Selling and administrative expenses	554	
Total fixed costs		1,614
Income		$ 556

Note that the sample report does not show price and use variances separately. This particular income statement is a summary report and would be supported by one or more schedules showing the details of the variances. The number of supporting schedules, and the details on them, depend on the level of the manager receiving the report: the higher the level, the less supporting detail. The general manager of a large division of a large company does not need to know about labor variances by cost center, only by plant. Note that we did include in the sample report a budget variance relating to fixed manufacturing costs. Such variances are, as shown in the next section, identified for reporting purposes and analyzed for possible managerial action.

One point that might not be obvious from the sample income statement is the difference in the quantity measures used for cost of sales and for calculating variances. The standard variable cost of sales is based on the number of units sold. On the other hand, variances are computed, as you know, on the basis of the number of units produced. We shall see more income statements of this type in Chapter 14.

CONTROL OF FIXED COSTS

We know from earlier discussions that total cost per unit of product changes with a change in production because there is a fixed component in the total cost. For product costing purposes, discussed in Chapter 14, a standard fixed cost per unit is sometimes computed. But for *control* purposes, the notion of a standard fixed cost per unit has little meaning. Only the total cost incurred for each element of fixed overhead is relevant.

Fixed overhead is made up of several components, such as depreciation, property taxes, supervisory and managerial salaries, and the fixed components of mixed costs, such as maintenance and power. Each item is budgeted separately for the department that controls it.

There are two fixed cost variances. For the current purpose, the question of cost control, only the budget variance requires comment. The other variance is described in Chapters 13 and 14.

Budget Variance

The **fixed overhead budget variance** is the difference between actual and budgeted fixed cost and is computed for each element of cost for a particular department. Budget variances occur for many reasons. There may have been changes in the prices for resources (a raise in salaries, an increase in property taxes); some discretionary costs, such as employee training or travel, might have been increased or decreased by managerial action; and quantities of resources used might have been greater or less than budgeted, as when more or fewer janitors were hired than were budgeted.

The major considerations in analyzing budget variances related to fixed costs are behavioral. A manager who is worried about exceeding his or her budget might postpone discretionary costs (such as employee training). On the other hand, a manager might incur unnecessary costs if he or she fears that being below budget this period will lead to a budget cut for the next period.

A manager can manipulate some discretionary costs to achieve a low *total* budget variance (total fixed costs incurred less total fixed costs budgeted). Focusing only on totals can obscure critical problems. The manager who scrimps on employee training or maintenance is improving short-run performance to the detriment of the long run. This type of undesirable action might escape notice if only the totals were considered.

There are different philosophies about budgeting fixed costs. There are advocates of tight budgets, loose budgets, and budgets based on currently attainable performance levels. Our preference is for the use of currently attainable budgets, with the persons whose budgets are being set participating in the determination of what is currently attainable. Likewise, the methods used in setting standard variable costs—historical analysis, engineering methods, and managerial judgment—can also be applied to the budgeting of fixed costs.

Fixed Costs on Performance Reports

The cost-center performance report shown in Exhibit 12-6 does not distinguish between controllable variable costs and controllable fixed costs. Whereas materials and direct labor are usually variable, the other controllable items could be variable, fixed, or mixed. Such a report can easily be revised to show the fixed and variable components of controllable costs as shown in Exhibit 12-8 on page 506.

Exhibit 12-8
Departmental Performance Report

Month __May 19X7__

Department __Machining__   Manager __R. Jones__

Date Delivered __6/4__   Date Returned __6/6__

	Budgeted	Actual	Variance
Production, in units (original budget 11,000 units)		9,000	2,000
Controllable costs, for actual production of 9,000 units:			
Variable:			
Materials, standard of __$2__ *	$18,000	$18,800	$800U ❶
Labor, standard of __$3__ *	27,000	28,800	1,800U ❷
Supplies, standard of __$0.10__ *	900	880	20F
Total variable costs	$45,900	$48,480	$2,580U
Fixed:			
Repairs	$1,100	$1,200	$100U
Indirect labor	900	900	0
Total fixed costs	$2,000	$2,100	$100U
Total controllable costs	$47,900	$50,580	$2,680U
Noncontrollable costs:			
Depreciation __Machinery used in department__	$1,500	$1,500	0
Heat and light (allocated)	200	220	20U
Other allocated costs	800	860	60U
Total noncontrollable costs	$2,500	$2,580	$80U
Total costs	$50,400	$53,160	$2,760U

*Actual costs are at standard prices.

Comments and Explanations

① *Faulty materials required more time and created more waste.*

This report differs from Exhibit 12-6 in only one respect: it separates the fixed and variable components of controllable costs. For planning, the manager wants to know whether a variance is likely to recur. It might be easier to plan for future variances if the fixed and variable controllable costs are separated. If a fixed cost is running $1,000 per month more or less than budgeted, and this variance is expected to continue, the manager can count on the variance being $1,000 per month. A direct labor efficiency variance of 10% of standard cost will be a different dollar amount in each month, depending on production. Thus, planning for future operations requires different analyses for the two kinds of costs—fixed and variable.

A PROBLEM AREA: SEPARATING FIXED AND VARIABLE COSTS

In some situations the firm might not be able to isolate the variable overhead and the fixed overhead budget variances because it cannot determine how much of the *actual* overhead cost incurred is fixed and how much is variable. For example, a cost like electricity usually has both a fixed and a variable component. But it might not be possible to determine how much of the actual cost relates to the fixed component and how much to the variable component.

Suppose that electricity is budgeted using the following formula: Total cost = $2,450 + ($0.80 × machine hours). The fixed portion is for lighting; the variable portion is for machinery that is operated only when products are being made. Assume that the standard and actual cost per kilowatt-hour is $0.03. Any difference between actual electricity cost and the flexible budget amount must then be caused by the quantity of electricity used. At the end of the month, the firm's managers cannot tell how much electricity was used for machinery (the variable portion) and how much for other purposes (the fixed portion) unless there are separate meters for the machinery.

For a particular month, suppose that the standard machine hours per unit are two, that production was 4,000 units, that 8,100 machine hours were used (100 hours over standard), and that actual electricity cost was $9,210. The total standard hours allowed for production of 4,000 units are 8,000 (4,000 × 2). The total budgeted cost for electricity is $8,850 ($2,450 + [$0.80 × 8,000 standard machine hours]). Because we cannot, in the absence of separate meters, analyze the actual cost into its fixed and variable components, we cannot calculate separately the budget variances for the fixed and variable elements. In such cases, most firms calculate a single budget variance for the mixed cost as a whole. If we use the data in our example, the budget variance is

$$\text{Total budget variance} = \text{actual cost} - \text{flexible budget based on input}$$
$$= \quad \$9,210 \quad - [(\$0.80 \times 8,100) + \$2,450]$$
$$= \quad \$9,210 \quad - \$8,930$$
$$= \$280 \text{ unfavorable variance}$$

The variance is unfavorable because actual cost exceeds the budget allow-ance. We also know that actual machine hours were 100 over standard, so we know there is an $80 unfavorable variable overhead efficiency variance.

Why might a firm not isolate the fixed and variable components of the actual cost? Why, for example, wouldn't the firm in the preceding example install meters on its machines in order to determine how much electricity is related to machines and how much to lighting the factory? The answer, as stated in Chapter 10, is usually that the cost to obtain the additional information is greater than the benefits. In this instance, the cost to install and maintain the meters might exceed the savings that could be achieved through better control. A fundamental principle of managerial accounting is that obtaining additional information is desirable only if the benefits exceed the costs.

STANDARDS AND MULTIPRODUCT COMPANIES

So far we have dealt with companies making a single product. Multiproduct companies can also use standard costs. No conceptual problems are introduced simply because a company makes more than one product, but a practical question arises about the extent to which detailed information should be produced and the cost of obtaining the additional information.

Although it is seldom a problem for a multiproduct firm to develop standard costs, it can be difficult, even impossible, to isolate variances by product. This is true if the several products are manufactured using the same facilities and the same workers, and the company cannot determine the *actual* use of materials and labor or machine time for *each* product. That is, the costs of materials and labor are traceable to production as a whole, but it might be very costly or impossible to keep track of material use and direct labor time on the production of each product. In such cases, variances relate to all products as a group. It is desirable to keep track of materials and direct labor by product if the cost of obtaining the informa-tion is less than the potential benefits of having that information.

Despite the difficulties of obtaining information about the actual costs of individual products, managers are interested in knowing such costs for planning and decision making. As a practical matter, a firm might occasionally keep track of materials and labor by product as a check on the standards. In addition, man-agers might suspect inappropriate standards and undertake an investigation if efficiency variances appeared to be influenced by product mix.

STANDARD COSTS FOR NONMANUFACTURING ACTIVITIES

Some firms have developed standard costs for nonmanufacturing activities. These activities have certain traits that render the development of standard costs diffi-cult. Measuring output in nonmanufacturing activities is difficult. Rarely do homo-geneous physical units flow out of the work done by the product design, legal, accounting, marketing, and general administration departments. There is seldom a definable measure of output because there is no standard product.

Costs associated with administrative work also tend to be more fixed than those of manufacturing. Consequently, it might be impossible to develop standard variable costs per unit of output even if an appropriate unit of output could be found. Therefore, administrative activities are usually controlled by static budgets, rather than by standard variable costs. Thus, the earlier material on control of fixed costs is applicable to nonmanufacturing activities, but the material on standard variable costs usually is not.

The difficulties notwithstanding, there have been and will continue to be attempts to develop standards for nonmanufacturing activities. For example, the number of typing strokes per page has been standardized by some organizations, as have the number of files processed and the number of books shelved. This is a challenging and important area of managerial accounting.

SUMMARY

Standard costs are a tool for planning, control, and evaluation of cost centers. The manager of a cost center, and his or her superiors, receive information showing the efficiency of the operation. Comparisons of planned production with actual production indicate whether the manager was effective.

The standard for each major element of product cost (material, labor, and overhead) is a combination of two separate standards: one for the quantity of the factor used in the product, the other for the price of a unit of that factor. The total variance between budgeted and actual cost can be analyzed into one related to a difference in price and another related to a difference in the quantity of the factor used. Since a single manager is not usually responsible for both prices of resources and the quantity of resources used, separating total variances into price and use components assists in assigning responsibility. The separation is also helpful in planning future operations.

Because interdependencies exist among managerial functions, variances shown on the performance report for a manager cannot automatically be attributed to the good or bad performance of that manager. The causes of variances are not always easy to determine and include not only poor management in the department showing the variance but also, though certainly not limited to, poor management in an entirely different department. The cause could also be a bad standard.

KEY TERMS

control chart	labor rate variance
currently attainable performance	material price variance
engineered standards	material use variance
fixed overhead budget variance	standard cost
flexible budget allowance	variable overhead efficiency variance
historical standards	variable overhead budget (spending)
ideal standard	variance
labor efficiency variance	variances

KEY FORMULAS

$$\text{Total standard cost for input factor} = \text{actual production} \times \text{standard quantity of input factor per unit of production} \times \text{standard rate for input factor per unit of input}$$

$$\text{Total actual cost for input factor} = \text{actual input quantity} \times \text{actual price for input factor}$$

$$\text{Price variance} = \text{actual quantity of input acquired} \times \left(\text{standard price per unit of input} - \text{actual price per unit of input} \right)$$

$$\text{Quantity variance} = \text{standard price per unit of input} \times \left(\text{standard quantity of input required} - \text{actual quantity of input used} \right)$$

REVIEW PROBLEM

Baldwin Company makes cabinets. One model, the Deluxe, has the following requirements.

Materials	44 feet of wood at $0.20 per foot
Direct labor	4 hours at $7 per hour
Variable overhead	$5 per direct labor hour

During June 19X4 the firm made 1,200 Deluxe cabinets. Operating results were

Material purchases	58,000 feet at $0.19	$11,020
Material used	53,200 feet	
Direct labor	4,750 hours at $7.10	$33,725
Variable overhead		$23,900

Required: Compute the standard variable cost per Deluxe cabinet and the variances for June 19X4.

Answer to Review Problem

Standard Variable Cost	
Material (44 feet of wood at $0.20)	$ 8.80
Direct labor (4 hours at $7 per hour)	28.00
Variable overhead at $5 per direct labor hour	20.00
Total standard variable cost	$56.80

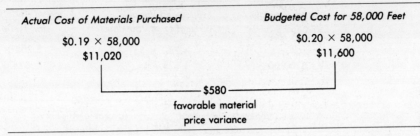

Alternatively, $58,000 \times (\$0.20 - \$0.19) = \$580$ favorable

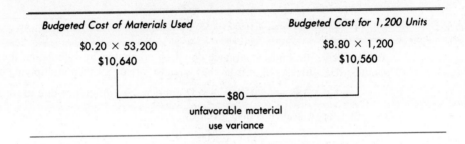

Alternatively, $\$0.20 \times [(1,200 \times 44) - 53,200] = \$80$ unfavorable

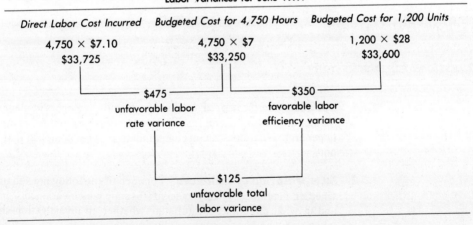

Alternatively, the labor rate variance is

$$4,750 \times (\$7 - \$7.10) = -\$475 \text{ unfavorable}$$

The labor efficiency variance is

$$\$7 \times [(1,200 \times 4) - 4,750] = \$7 \times (4,800 - 4,750) = \$350 \text{ favorable}$$

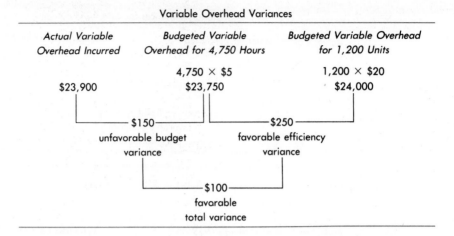

Alternatively, the budget variance could be computed by calculating the actual rate of about $5.032, subtracting it from the standard rate of $5, then multiplying by 4,750 hours.

$$4,750 \times (\$5 - \$5.032) = -\$152 \text{ unfavorable (difference due to rounding)}$$

The efficiency variance is also given by

$$\$5 \times (4,800 - 4,750) = \$250 \text{ favorable}$$

Note that because the variable overhead standard is based on direct labor hours, the only difference between the computation of the labor efficiency variance and the variable overhead efficiency variance is the rate used.

ASSIGNMENT MATERIAL

Questions for Discussion

12-1 **Budgeting and standards**   Budgeting aids managers in planning and control. Standard costs are useful for assisting in budgeting and for planning and control in general. What does the use of standard costs accomplish that budgeting does not?

12-2 **Interpretation of variances**   For each of the following situations (a) indicate whether a variance is likely to occur; (b) state which variance(s) might be affected and in what direction; and (c) state whether an investigation should be undertaken and whether corrective action could be taken.
1. Wage rates have risen because a new union contract has been signed.
2. To increase safety, the plant manager has reduced the speeds at which forklifts carrying materials and semifinished products can be driven.
3. The firm sells its waste materials, chiefly metals, to a scrap dealer. Lately, revenue from waste sales has increased, while production has been steady.
4. Exceptionally heavy rainfall necessitates the drying out of materials that are stored outside.

5. The electric utility that supplies the company has been having difficulty with its generators. There are frequent blackouts and brownouts.

6. Many part-time workers are hired because of increases in production.

12-3 ***Revising standards*** State whether each of the following events calls for revising standards and, if so, which standard(s). If possible, state the direction of the revision. Assume that currently attainable performance is the basis for all standards.

1. Complaints from customers about dullness of a metallic finish on the product have induced the production manager to assign a worker to buff the surface.

2. The labor efficiency variance has consistently been unfavorable by 2% to 4%.

3. A new material that is more expensive than the old is being used. However, there is less waste and it is easier to handle.

4. The product is a wooden cabinet. Previously, a number of parts of the cabinet had been nailed together. Now those parts are being screwed together.

5. A strike at a supplier's plant has forced the purchase of some materials at higher prices from other sources.

6. Electricity rates have increased. The plant uses a great deal of electricity for machinery.

7. An overhead crane has been installed to speed the movement of semifinished product from one work station to another.

12-4 ***Effects of changed conditions*** Each of the following describes a change that occurred after standards had been set for the period and then lists three of the variances that were discussed in the chapter. For each item, select the variance most likely to be affected by the change and explain your choice.

1. To meet a shortage of workers in the face of a steady demand for the product, the firm decided to hire less experienced workers than it hired in the past.
Variances: Material price variance, labor rate variance, labor efficiency variance.

2. Faced with the prospect of a shortage of the firm's normal materials, the firm decides to use a new, more expensive material that produces less waste and is easier to handle.
Variances: Labor rate variance, variable overhead budget variance, variable overhead efficiency variance.

3. Based on a suggestion from a worker, the process for assembling certain parts of the final product has been changed so that a single employee assembles six components. Before the change, two employees of the same department worked independently to assemble three components each and a third employee in that department put together the subassemblies produced by those two employees.
Variances: Material use variance, labor efficiency variance, variable overhead spending variance.

12-5 ***Setting standards*** The controller of a large manufacturing company said: "In our company the standard cost is the true cost; actual cost is simply an aberration from true cost." Speculate on how the standards might have been set.

12-6 ***Responsibility for variances (CMA adapted)*** Phillips Company uses a standard cost system. Variances for each department are calculated and reported to the department manager. Reporting has two major purposes: for use by superiors in evaluating performance, and for use by managers in improving their operations.

Jack Smith was recently appointed manager of the Assembly Department. He has complained that the system does not work properly and discriminates against his department because of the current practice of calculating a variance for rejected units. The procedures for making this calculation are as follows: (1) all units are inspected at the end of the assembly operation; (2) rejected units are examined to see if the cause of rejection can be assigned to a particular department; (3) units that are rejected but cannot be identified with a particular department are totaled; (4) the unidentifiable rejects are apportioned to each department on the basis of the identifiable rejects. Thus, if a department had 20% of the identified rejects, it will also be charged with 20% of the unidentified rejects. The variance, then, is the sum of the identifiable rejects and the apportioned share of unidentified rejects. Evaluate the validity of Smith's claim and make a recommendation for resolving the problem.

12-7 ***Significance of variances*** Ann Jackson, controller of Stone Company, was recently told by several production managers that "as long as total costs do not exceed budgeted costs, based on standard prices and quantities, there is no reason to do any investigating or analysis."

Required: Comment critically on the statement. Cite at least two reasons for rejecting it.

Exercises

12-8 ***Standard cost computations*** Blivet Company makes a plastic deck chair. It has established the standard prices and quantities for a finished unit as follows:

Material	4 pounds at $1 per pound
Direct labor	3 hours at $8 per hour
Variable overhead	$6 per direct labor hour (DLH)

Blivet also has fixed overhead of $100,000 per year.

Required: Fill in the blanks in the following items.
1. The standard cost per unit of finished product is
   (a) _____ for material.
   (b) _____ for direct labor.
   (c) _____ for variable overhead.
2. At 70,000 direct labor hours, total variable overhead cost should be _____ .
3. At 90,000 direct labor hours, production should be _____ units.
4. If 100,000 pounds of material are used, production should be _____ units.
5. At 60,000 direct labor hours, total material used should be _____ pounds.
6. If 66,000 pounds of material are used, total variable overhead cost should be _____ and total labor cost should be _____ .

12-9 ***Fundamentals of standard costs and variances*** Bryant Company manufactures decorative statues. Each statue requires 20 pounds of special clay and two labor hours. The standard price of clay is $3 per pound. The standard direct labor rate is $9 per hour and the standard variable overhead rate is $6 per direct labor hour.

During November, Bryant manufactured 1,000 statues. It bought 25,000 pounds of clay for $71,800 and used 22,000 pounds. Bryant paid direct laborers $17,200 for 1,900 hours and incurred $12,500 in variable overhead.

Required
1. Determine the standard variable cost of a statue.
2. Determine all variable cost variances.

12-10 Basic material and labor variances Fergon Company makes a lamp shade and had the following budgeted and actual results in December.

	Budget	Actual
Unit production	10,000	11,000
Direct labor hours	20,000	21,700
Materials used, yards	40,000	43,200

The standard labor rate is $10 per hour, standard material price $2 per yard.

Required: Calculate the direct labor efficiency variance and the material use variance.

12-11 Basic variance relationships, materials Fill in the blanks below. You can work them in order, but you do not have to.

Standard material cost per unit of product	$ 20
Material use variance	$ 2,000F
Standard material use for quantity produced, in pounds	23,600
Number of pounds of material purchased	30,000
Material price variance	$ 3,000U
Standard price per pound of materials	$ 5
Standard pounds of materials per unit of product	_____
Units produced	_____
Number of pounds of materials used	_____
Amount paid for materials purchased	_____

12-12 Basic variance relationships, direct labor Fill in the blanks below. You can work them in order, but you do not have to.

Direct labor rate variance	$ 5,200F
Amount paid to direct laborers	$306,800
Excess of actual labor hours over standard labor hours for quantity produced	1,000
Direct labor efficiency variance	$ 6,000U
Standard direct labor hours per unit	3
Standard direct labor rate per hour	_____
Flexible budget allowance for actual hours worked	_____
Actual direct labor hours worked	_____
Total standard cost of direct labor for quantity produced	_____
Total standard direct labor hours for quantity produced	_____
Units produced	_____

12-13 **Variance computations** Below are the standard variable costs for one of Halsey Knitting sweaters, the Highlander.

Material, 2 pounds of yarn at $6 per pound	$12
Labor, 2 hours of labor at $8 per hour	16
Variable overhead, $3 per labor hour	6
	$34

Actual results in March were as follows.

Production	1,000 sweaters
Materials purchased and used	1,900 pounds for $12,100
Hours of labor worked	2,100 hours
Cost of labor	$16,300
Variable overhead incurred	$ 6,500

Required: Compute all variable cost variances.

12-14 **Comprehensive variance analysis** 4N Company makes industrial cleaners. Standard costs for Scumaway appear below, along with actual results for March.

Materials, 3 pounds at $4 per pound	$12
Direct labor at $10 per hour	30
Variable overhead at $6 per DLH	18
Total standard variable cost	$60

Actual results for March:
1. Production was 1,200 units.
2. Material purchases were 3,200 pounds at $3.90 per pound.
3. The firm used 3,620 pounds of material in production.
4. Direct laborers worked 3,800 hours at $10.10, earning $38,380.
5. Variable overhead was $22,000.

Required: Compute all variable cost variances.

12-15 **Variance computations** Trivet Company makes after-shave lotion and has developed the following standard cost per case of finished product.

Material	4 gallons at $1	$ 4
Direct labor	2 hours at $7	14
Variable overhead	$4 per DLH	8
Total standard variable cost per unit		$26

In 19X5, actual results were

Direct labor hours worked	21,500
Number of units produced	11,000
Rate paid to direct laborers	$7.20 per hour
Materials purchased	50,000 gallons
Price paid for materials	$0.96 per gallon
Materials used in production	45,000 gallons
Variable overhead incurred	$85,800

Required: Compute all variable cost variances.

12-16 ***Revision of standard costs*** Clarkson Company manufactures toys. One group of toys consists of small cars, each of which requires the same quantities of materials and direct labor. The cars are packaged and sold in batches of 50. The standard variable cost of a batch is given below.

Materials	$10.00
Direct labor (4 hours)	16.00
Variable overhead	12.00
Total standard variable cost	$38.00

The production supervisor is uncertain how to prepare the budget for the coming year. He tells you the following.
(a) Material costs will be an average of 20% higher because of price increases.
(b) Laborers will get a 5% raise at the beginning of the year.
(c) Increased efficiency will reduce direct labor hours by 10%.
(d) The variable overhead rate will increase to $3.40 per direct labor hour.

Required: Prepare revised standard variable costs.

12-17 ***Relationships — labor variances*** Each of the situations given below is independent. The only element of cost being considered is direct labor. Fill in the blanks.

	a	b	c	d
Units produced	2,000	8200	3,000	2000
Actual hours worked	4,800	4,200	5850 AQ	6200
Standard hours for production achieved	5,000	4100	6000	6,000
Standard hours per unit	2.5	0.5	2	3
Standard rate per hour	$ 6	$ 10	$ 4	4
Actual labor cost	29110	$41,800	23700	$24,500
Rate variance	$ 310U	200F	$ 300U	$ 300F
Efficiency variance	1200 F	$ 1,000U	$ 600F	$ 800U

(handwritten row labels: AQ = Actual hours worked; SQ = Standard hours for production achieved; SR = Standard rate per hour)

12-18 *Variance analysis*   Kuhn Car Products makes automobile antifreeze. Kuhn has developed the following formula for budgeting monthly factory overhead costs. Total overhead cost = $140,000 + ($10 × direct labor hours). Other data relating to the cost of a case of the product are given below.

Materials	4 gallons at $1.50 per gallon
Direct labor	20 minutes at $10 per hour

Last month Kuhn produced 12,000 cases and had the following costs.

Materials purchased	49,000 gallons	$ 73,000
Materials used	51,200 gallons	
Direct labor	3,920 hours	$ 38,750
Overhead		$188,500

Required: Compute the price and quantity variances for materials and direct labor and the total variance for overhead.

12-19 *Performance reporting*   The president of your company has asked you to investigate some unfavorable variances that occurred in one of the departments last month. You were given the following summary of the department's performance report.

	Budget	Actual	Variance
Production (in units)	2,000	2,500	500F
Costs (based on budgeted production):			
Direct labor	$6,000	$7,000	$1,000U
Supplies	400	650	250U
Repairs	1,000	1,200	200U
Power	800	1,100	300U
Total costs (all variable)	$8,200	$9,950	$1,750U

Required
1. Was performance poor?
2. What suggestions do you have?

12-20 *Variances – relationships among costs*   Read the following in its entirety and then fill in the blanks.

1. Standard variable costs per unit:		
(a) Materials	4 pounds @ $____	$____
(b) Direct labor	____ hours @ $6.00	$12.00
(c) Variable overhead	$3 per DLH	$____
2. Production		8,000 units
3. Material purchases	33,000 pounds	$62,000
4. Material used, at standard prices	31,200 pounds	$____

5. Direct labor, actual	_____ hours	$80,800
6. Material price variance		$ 4,000F
7. Material use variance		$
8. Direct labor rate variance		$ 3,200F
9. Direct labor efficiency variance		$
10. Variable overhead spending variance		$ 1,200U
11. Variable overhead efficiency variance		$
12. Variable overhead, actual		$

12-21 Standards — machine-hour basis Wilkens Company is highly automated and uses machine-hours to set standard variable costs. A unit requires two pounds of material costing $6 per pound and 12 minutes of machine time. The standard variable overhead rate is $10 per machine-hour. There is no direct labor; all workers are classified as indirect labor, and their wages are considered part of variable overhead.

During June, 23,000 units were produced using 5,200 machine-hours. Variable overhead costs were $50,300. Purchases of materials were 54,000 pounds for $318,000 and 45,000 pounds were used.

Required
1. Compute the standard variable cost of a unit of product.
2. Compute the variances for June.

Problems

12-22 Standards in a service function Graham Labs performs blood tests for local physicians. Dr. Graham, head of the company, has instituted a standard cost system to help control costs and measure employee efficiency. After extensive consultations with his employees, he developed the following standards for some high-volume tests.

Test	Standard Time (in minutes)
Blood sugar	12
Cell count	10
Others	6

The company's 12 lab technicians earn an average of $11 per hour, with a range of $10.25 to $11.50. During July, the first month the system was in effect, the lab had the following results.

Test	Number Performed
Blood sugar	4,500
Cell count	2,300
Others	5,400

Lab technicians earned $20,300 for 1,780 hours.

Required: Determine the labor rate variance and labor efficiency variance.

12-23 ***Investigation of variances*** The production manager of Knowles Company tells you that he exercises management by exception. He examines a performance report and calls for further analysis and investigation if a variance is greater than 10% of total standard cost or is more than $1,000. He is not responsible for any rate or price variances and is therefore concerned only with efficiency variances. During April, the following occurred.

1. Materials used: 4,520 gallons
2. Direct labor hours: 7,850
3. Production: 2,000 units

The standard cost of a unit is as follows.

Materials (2 gallons at $4)	$ 8
Direct labor (4 hours at $8)	32
Variable overhead ($6 per DLH)	24
Total standard variable cost	$64

Required

1. Compute the variances for which the production manager should be held responsible.
2. Determine which variances should be investigated according to his criteria.

12-24 ***Determining a base for cost standards*** The production manager of Wingate Company recently performed a study to see how many units of product could be made by a worker who had no interruptions, always had materials available as needed, made no errors, and worked at peak speed. He found that a worker could make 20 units in an hour under these ideal conditions. In the past, about 15 units per hour was the actual average output. However, some new materials handling equipment had recently been purchased and the manager is confident that an average of 18 units per hour could be achieved by nearly all workers.

All workers are paid $12 per hour. A month after the study was made, workers were paid $960,000 for 80,000 hours. Production was 1,410,000 units.

Required

1. Compute the standard labor cost per unit to the nearest $0.001 based on
   (a) historical performance
   (b) ideal performance
   (c) currently attainable performance
2. Compute the labor efficiency variance under each of the standards in item 1 and comment on the results. Which method of setting the standard would you choose for planning purposes? For control purposes? Explain.

12-25 ***Investigation of variances*** The supervisor of the Stamping Department is pleased with her performance this past month, which showed a favorable material use variance of $1,000. The following data relate to the stamping operation.

Units produced	2,000
Standard costs for materials:	
Libidinum, 3 pounds at $3	$ 9
Larezium, 2 pounds at $4	8
Total standard material cost	$ 17

The operation used 5,000 pounds of libidinum and 4,500 pounds of larezium.

Required
1. Verify the amount of the material use variance.
2. Did the supervisor do a good job this month? What questions must be answered before coming to a conclusion about the manager's performance?

12-26 **Determination of standard costs** Vernon Company makes its single product, Shine, in the following way: Materials Dull and Buff are mixed in 500-pound batches in a 3 : 2 ratio: (three pounds of Dull for each two pounds of Buff). The mixing is done by two laborers and takes three hours. The resulting mixture is boiled for four hours, which requires four workers. The mixture that comes out of the boiler yields four pounds of finished product for each five pounds of raw material, so that the 500 pounds of material mixed become 400 pounds of final product. (Evaporation during boiling reduces the volume.)

All laborers earn $6 per hour. Variable overhead is $3 per direct labor hour. Dull costs $2.80 per pound; Buff costs $2 per pound.

Required: Determine the standard variable cost per pound of Shine.

12-27 **Standards and variances, two products** Bascomb Company makes two coffee tables. Both go through essentially the same process, and the company does not keep records regarding the amounts of material and labor used in making each model, only for the two models as a whole. Standard cost data are

	Harcombe	Exeter
Materials:		
2 pounds at $4 per pound	$ 8	
3 pounds at $4 per pound		$12
Direct labor	16	24
Variable overhead	12	18
Total standard costs	$36	$54

All direct laborers earn $8 per hour, and the variable overhead rate is $6 per direct labor hour. The same material is used in both models.
During March, the company had the following results.

Production	2,000 Harcombe, 1,500 Exeter
Material purchases	9,000 pounds at $4.15 per pound
Material used	8,900 pounds
Direct labor	8,750 hours at $7.95 per hour
Variable overhead	$55,500

Required

1. Compute all variable cost variances for production as a whole.
2. Can you compute variances for each model? If not, why not? Explain why you might want to isolate variances to the individual models?

12-28 **Input standards versus output standards** Cassidy Company manufactures an industrial solvent. The company budgets manufacturing costs based on direct labor hours. The production manager is unable to interpret the report he has just received and asks for your assistance. The report contains the following data.

	Actual Cost at 10,000 Direct Labor Hours	Budgeted Cost for 10,000 Hours
Materials used at standard prices	$ 25,800	$ 24,000
Direct labor	68,300	68,000
Indirect labor	27,200	26,500
Other variable overhead	27,400	27,300
Total variable costs	$148,700	$145,800

Cassidy budgeted 50,000 gallons of production. Actual production was 51,000 gallons, which requires 10,200 direct labor hours at standard performance.

Required: For each component of cost, determine the variance due to efficiency (or inefficiency) and that due to spending or price.

12-29 **Bases for standard costs and decisions** Sewell Company uses very tight standards for determining standard costs. The production manager believes that the use of standards achievable only under ideal conditions helps to motivate employees by showing them how much improvement is possible and therefore giving them goals to achieve.

The sales manager has criticized the use of such high standards for performance and correspondingly low standard costs because it increases his difficulty in determining whether business at lower than normal prices should be accepted. In one specific instance, the sales manager was offered the opportunity to sell 4,000 units at $8.50, which is $4 below the normal selling price. He rejected the offer. The standard variable cost per unit of product is as follows.

Materials (3 pounds at $0.50)	$1.50
Direct labor ($\frac{1}{2}$ hour at $6 per hour)	3.00
Variable overhead ($4 per direct labor hour)	2.00
Total standard variable cost	$6.50

The sales manager was uncertain whether the order should have been accepted. He knew that the standards were never met. What bothered him was the extent to which they were not met. He asked his assistant to try to determine whether the order would have been profitable. The assistant developed the following information: Material price and labor rate variances are negligible. However, during a normal month, when 10,000 units are produced, the material use variance, direct labor efficiency variance, and total variable overhead variance are about $2,000, $6,000, and $5,200, respectively, all unfavorable.

Required
1. Assuming that the experience of the month presented would have applied when the special order was being made up, should the order have been accepted?
2. Develop new standard variable costs based on currently attainable performance, assuming that the month described reflected currently attainable performance. Be sure to include both prices and quantities for each input factor.

12-30 **Multiple products** Cross Company manufactures three models of small plastic chairs. The standard material cost is $0.80 per pound, standard labor rate is $8.00 per hour, and standard variable overhead rate is $3.00 per direct labor hour. The standard quantities of each cost factor for each model appear below.

	Model 1	Model 2	Model 3
Materials, pounds	24	24	42
Direct labor hours	5	5	2

Actual results for March were

Production:	
Model 1	12,000
Model 2	16,000
Model 3	14,000
Materials purchased	1,400,000 pounds at $0.78
Materials used	1,275,000 pounds
Direct labor	173,000 hours for $1,365,200
Variable overhead	$497,000

Required: Determine the variable cost variances.

12-31 **Standards and idle time** Prescott Textiles manufactures a single kind of cloth in its Petzel Mill. The standard labor cost per 100 yards of cloth is $14.00, which is two standard labor hours at $7 per hour. In August, orders were slow and the mill turned out only 1,200,000 yards, well below the usual volume. Workers were paid for 29,000 hours. The company guarantees a 40-hour workweek to employees with five years of service. About 5,500 of the 29,000 hours were idle time, when eligible employees were paid, but had no work to do.

Required
1. Calculate the labor efficiency variance using the 29,000 hours actually worked.
2. Can you conclude from your answer to item 1 that the work force was inefficient in August? Why or why not? What do you recommend?

12-32 *Analyzing results — sales and cost variances* Managers of Reed Blanket Company were disappointed at the shortfall in profit for 19X7, as shown in the income statements below, in millions.

	Budgeted	Actual
Unit sales	10.0	10.8
Sales	$120.0	$122.1
Variable manufacturing costs:		
Materials	20.0	21.8
Direct labor	15.0	17.0
Variable overhead	5.0	5.2
Total variable costs	40.0	44.0
Contribution margin	80.0	78.1
Fixed costs:		
Manufacturing	50.0	50.8
Selling and administrative	20.0	19.9
Total fixed costs	70.0	70.7
Profit before taxes	$ 10.0	$ 7.4

Required: The president wants an analysis showing why profit fell short of budget. He wants you to determine the effects of the difference between budgeted and actual unit volume, budgeted and actual selling prices, and budgeted and actual costs for the volume achieved. Production equalled sales. Prepare such an analysis and be sure that it fully accounts for the difference between budgeted and actual profit.

12-33 *Flexible and static budgets* Marvel Manufacturing Company is managed by a family, none of whose members understand accounting. Ralph Marvel, one of the managers, was elated at the following performance report.

	Budget	Actual	Variance
Production	30,000	26,000	
Materials	$ 75,000	$ 72,000	$ 3,000F
Direct labor	45,000	40,000	5,000F
Variable overhead	90,000	86,000	4,000F
Fixed overhead	60,000	60,000	
Total	$270,000	$258,000	$12,000F

Ralph showed the report to Susan Roberts, the newly hired assistant controller, saying that one did not need to understand accounting to see that coming in under budget was a good thing.

Required: As Ms. Roberts, what would you say to Mr. Marvel?

12-34 Variance analysis — changed conditions Your firm makes a warm-up outfit with the following standard costs.

Materials (3 pounds at $4)	$12
Direct labor (2 hours at $8)	16
Variable overhead ($4 per DLH)	8
Total standard variable cost	$36

The standards have proved to be currently attainable and are generally met within small variances each month. In August the manufacturing vice president brought in a glowing report from the purchasing department. The company bought materials for $3.50 per pound. The new materials were different from the old but were of equal quality for the finished product. The materials bought during August were used in September with the following results.

Production scheduled	4,000 units
Actual production	3,700 units
Direct labor (8,350 hours)	$66,100
Variable overhead	$34,200
Materials used	12,300 pounds

Required

1. Compute all variances that you can.
2. Why might the variances have occurred?
3. Assuming that the experience of September will continue, should the company continue buying the new material?

12-35 Economic cost of labor inefficiency Columbia Windows makes high-quality bay windows for houses. It sells to wholesalers who in turn sell to building contractors or homeowners. Some months of the year the company has trouble keeping up with demand and loses sales because customers are generally unwilling to wait and buy from a competitor. Direct labor time is constrained by the production process, so that the company can obtain a maximum of 280,000 direct labor hours per month. The typical product mix results in an average standard labor time of 14 hours per unit. The standard labor rate is $10 per hour, and the standard variable overhead rate is $8 per direct labor hour. Average material cost is $82 per unit, and average selling price $620 per unit. Results for two recent months appear below. January is typically a slow month, June a busy one, with orders for over 22,000 units.

	January	June
Units produced	12,500	19,200
Actual labor hours	179,400	280,000

Material costs were at standard. The actual labor rate equalled the standard rate, and variable overhead was incurred as budgeted for actual direct labor hours.

Required
1. Compute the labor efficiency variance and variable overhead efficiency variance for each month.
2. Do the variances for both months reflect the true cost to the firm of labor inefficiency? Why or why not?

12-36 *Unit costs and total costs* Wilton Matthews, the production manager of KRL Industries, was disturbed at the results for November (shown below). Budgeted production was 90,000 units, and actual production was 100,000 units.

	Budget for 90,000 Units	Actual for 100,000 Units
Materials	$ 288,000	$ 341,800
Direct labor	679,500	773,800
Variable overhead	339,750	391,300
Fixed overhead	850,000	860,700
Total costs	$2,157,250	$2,367,600
Cost per unit	$ 23.969	$ 23.676

Purchases of materials were about equal to use and were at 5% over standard prices. Labor rates were 2% over standard.

Matthews tells you that the 5% material price variance and 2% labor rate variance were the source of the unfavorable results, offering the following calculations to support his case.

Adjust budgeted costs to 100,000 units ($2,157,250 × 100/90)	$2,396,944
Materials price variance ($288,000 × 100/90 × .05)	16,000
Labor rate variance ($679,500 × 100/90 × .02)	15,100
Total allowable costs	$2,428,044

"Look, these guys who prepare the reports can't hold me to a budget for 90,000 units when I put out 100,000. Besides, they charged me with variances that I am not responsible for, so I actually came in way under budget. Even with the stupid way they made up the report, you can see that my unit cost was below budget, but I *should* look even better."

Required: Matthews is responsible for material and labor use and for all overhead costs. Determine whether his claim of good cost control is correct by calculating the total variances for which he is responsible. Calculate as many individual variances as you can.

12-37 *Design change variances* Grogan Company manufactures machine tools and often changes the design of a tool during the year to make it more suitable for customers. Grogan does not change the standards when it changes the design, which has caused some grumbling by production managers. The controller wants to be able to reconcile the year's actual results with the original budget and argues that changing standards during the year makes it virtually impossible to do so.

As a compromise, a production manager has suggested dividing the efficiency variances into two parts, one that captures the effects of design changes, the other to reflect efficiency in meeting the standard created by the revised design. The total efficiency variance will still be the difference between actual inputs at standard prices and the original standard inputs at standard prices. The following data are representative of design changes.

	Original	Redesigned
Materials:		
6 feet at $3 per foot	$18.00	
7 feet at $3 per foot		$21.00
Direct labor:		
.60 hours at $10 per hour	6.00	
.55 hours at $10 per hour		5.50
Variable overhead at $7 per DLH	4.20	3.85
Totals	$28.20	$30.35

Production of the tool was 2,000 units, requiring 13,700 feet of material and 1,180 direct labor hours.

Required
1. Determine the material, direct labor, and variable overhead efficiency variables, ignoring the redesign.
2. For each variance, determine how much resulted from the design change and how much from efficient or inefficient use of input factors.

12-38 Use of unit costs The foreman of the machining department of Glenmills Company has just received the following performance report, which was prepared by the new cost accountant.

	Costs per Unit		
	Budget	Actual	Variance
Materials	$ 3.00	$ 2.96	($0.04)
Direct labor (1.5 hours per unit at standard)	6.00	6.084	0.084
Variable overhead:			
Indirect labor	2.40	2.48	0.08
Power	0.90	0.93	0.03
Fixed overhead	4.00	4.95[a]	0.95
Totals	$16.30	$17.404	$1.104

[a] Actual cost incurred divided by actual production in units.

Budgeted production was 12,000 units, actual production was 10,000 units. Budgeted fixed overhead per unit is based on budgeted production. You learn that actual material cost in the report is based on standard prices and that all other actual cost figures are based on actual prices and quantities.

The foreman is not responsible for direct labor rates, which were $3.90 at actual cost. He is also not responsible for variable overhead spending variances, but he is responsible for fixed overhead budget variances.

Required: Prepare a new report including only those items for which the foreman is responsible. (You may wish to use a different type of presentation from that shown above.)

12-39 ***Analysis of income statement*** The controller of Taylors Company has given you the following income statement.

Sales 20,000 × $20		$400,000
Standard variable cost of sales		240,000
Standard variable manufacturing margin		160,000
Variances:		
Materials	$ 6,000F	
Direct labor	4,000U	
Variable overhead	3,000U	1,000U
Actual variable manufacturing margin		159,000
Fixed costs:		
Budgeted manufacturing costs	75,000	
Fixed cost budget variance	2,000U	
Selling and administrative costs	40,000	117,000
Income before taxes		$ 42,000

The controller gives you additional data. Production was 22,000 units. Material purchases were all made at standard price. Direct laborers averaged 0.85 hours per unit, which was 0.05 hours above the standard time. Actual direct labor cost was $144,800. The standard variable overhead rate is $2 per direct labor hour.

Required: Answer the following questions.
1. What was the direct labor efficiency variance?
2. What was the direct labor rate variance?
3. What was the standard material cost per unit?
4. What was actual total variable overhead?
5. What was the variable overhead efficiency variance?
6. What was the variable overhead budget variance?
7. What was actual total fixed manufacturing cost?
8. If the standard material price is $2 per pound, how many pounds are needed at standard to make a unit of product?
9. How many pounds of material did the firm use?

12-40 ***Forecasting income*** Robyn Company had the following income statement in 19X7.

Sales (110,000 × $20)		$2,200,000
Standard variable cost of sales		880,000
Standard variable manufacturing margin		1,320,000
Variances:		
Materials	$ 2,400U	
Direct labor	1,800F	
Variable overhead	1,600F	1,000F
Actual variable manufacturing margin		1,321,000
Fixed costs:		
Manufacturing	560,000	
Selling and administrative	470,000	1,030,000
Income		$ 291,000

The details of standard cost were

Materials (0.50 pounds at $4 per pound)	$2.00
Direct labor (0.40 hours at $10 per hour)	4.00
Variable overhead at $5 per direct labor hour	2.00
Total standard variable cost	$8.00

The company's industrial engineers have redesigned the product so that (1) material requirements should be 0.45 pounds and (2) direct labor hours should be 0.35. The company expects to produce 120,000 units in 19X8 and to sell 115,000. Material costs will increase to $4.20 per pound. Each element of fixed cost should increase by 5%.

The managers and engineers expect to see material use about 2% over the 0.45 pounds standard because it will take some time for workers to learn the new production methods. They also expect direct labor for the year to be 6% or so above standard for the same reason. They do want to use the 0.45 pounds and 0.35 hours as the standards, however, because they expect workers to operate at standard by mid-year. The standard variable overhead rate will increase by $0.20 per hour because of rising prices for input factors such as supplies and power. All elements not mentioned should be about the same as they were in 19X7.

Required

1. Determine the standard cost for the product for 19X8.
2. Prepare an income statement for 19X8 reflecting the manager's expectations, using the same format as the one for 19X7.

12-41 *Relationships among data* Dempsey Company uses standard variable costs. Variable overhead rate is based on direct labor hours. The following data are available for operations during April 19X4.

Total production	_____
Actual labor cost	$61,600
Actual materials used	5,900 pounds
Actual variable overhead	$37,150
Standard labor cost per unit	$_____
Standard material cost per unit	$ 4.50
Standard variable overhead cost per unit	$_____
Materials purchased (8,200 pounds)	$12,800
Material price variance	$ 500U
Labor rate variance	$ 2,500U
Variable overhead spending variance	$_____ F or U
Material use variance	$_____ F or U
Labor efficiency variance	$ 900F
Variable overhead efficiency variance	$_____ F or U
Direct labor hours worked	9,850 hours
Standard labor rate	$_____
Standard direct labor hours per unit	5 hours
Variable overhead rate per DLH	$ 4

Required: Fill in the blanks. (*Hint:* You cannot do the parts in the order given.)

Cases

12-42   *Standard costs — alternative raw materials*   Visodane, Inc. manufactures a household cleaner called Kleenall that is sold in 32-ounce (¼-gallon) plastic bottles. The cleaner can be made using either of two basic raw materials—anaxohyde or ferodoxin. Their respective costs are $10 and $8 per pound. Whichever material is used is mixed with water and other chemical agents and is then cooked. The product is then bottled, and the bottles are packed into cartons of 20 bottles each.

Each batch is made with 1,200 gallons of water, costing $0.30 per 100 gallons. Chemical agents other than raw materials cost $120 per batch. If anaxohyde is used, 100 pounds are mixed with the water and chemical agents. If ferodoxin is used, 110 pounds are needed. Mixing takes three hours and requires three laborers.

The mixture is then cooked, for 80 minutes if anaxohyde is used and 90 minutes if ferodoxin is used. One worker is needed for the cooking process. With either raw material, the output of the cooking process is 1,000 gallons because of evaporation. Bottling and packing requires one laborer working two hours.

All laborers are paid $6 per hour. Variable overhead is based on the time required in each process because the high degree of mechanization makes direct labor a poor measure of activity for variable overhead. Overhead per hour is $30 for the mixing process, $120 for the cooking process, and $60 for the bottling and packing process. Bottles cost $0.04 each and the cartons cost $0.20 each.

Required
1. Compute the standard cost of a carton of 20 bottles of Kleenall, assuming (a) anaxohyde is used and (b) ferodoxin is used.
2. Suppose that each carton sells for $20 and that cooking time available each month is 1,000 hours. Which material should be used?

12-43 **Developing standard costs (CMA adapted)** The controller of Berman Detergents has asked for your help in preparing standard variable costs for its major product, Sudsaway. Berman has never used standard costs, and the controller believes that better control will be achieved if standards are used. He wants the standards to be based on currently attainable performance.

The following data are available for operations in 19X6.

Materials used (1,350,000 gallons at $0.80 per gallon)		$1,080,000
Direct labor (160,000 hours at $5.50 per hour)		880,000
Variable overhead:		
Indirect labor	$240,000	
Maintenance and repairs	80,000	
Packaging materials	370,000	
Other variable overhead	480,000	1,170,000
Total variable production costs		$3,130,000

During 19X6, 740,000 cases of Sudsaway were produced. Each case contains 12 bottles of 16 ounces each, a total of 1.5 gallons per case. During 19X6 the firm used an inferior raw material. During 19X7 the firm expects to pay $0.90 per gallon for a better material. Even with the better material, some shrinkage will occur during production. The controller expects that output of Sudsaway in gallons will be 90% of the raw material put into process.

The firm employed a number of inexperienced workers in 19X6. They worked about 48,000 of the total direct labor hours, which is about 12,000 more than standard hours. During 19X7 the controller expects all workers to be normally productive and to earn an average wage of $5.80.

According to the controller, variable overhead costs were under control during 19X6, given the excessive labor hours worked. Packaging materials were not affected by the excessive labor hours, being related to cases actually produced. Indirect laborers will receive a 10% wage increase early in 19X7.

Required: Prepare standard variable costs, by category of cost, for a case of Sudsaway.

12-44 **Standard costs – joint products** Sigmund Company buys a single raw material and processes it into two intermediate products, guild and stern. Both guild and stern are further processed into final products; neither can be sold at split-off.

The joint process is supervised by one manager; the additional processing of each product is supervised by separate managers. Based on currently attainable performance, it takes six workers three hours to process a one-ton batch of raw material into 800 pounds of guild and 1,000 pounds of stern. The remainder is worthless waste. The raw material costs $360 per ton. All laborers are paid $6 per hour, and variable overhead is $4 per direct labor hour.

Still based on currently attainable performance, it takes three workers five hours to complete the processing of an 800-pound batch of guild, and four workers three hours to complete a 1,000-pound batch of stern. When completed, guild sells for $0.75 per pound, stern for $0.90.

Required: Compute whatever standard costs you think might be helpful. Explain why you computed the ones you did.

12-45 *Standard costs, variances, and evaluation (CMA adapted)* Bergen Company manufactures a single product. Standard variable cost of a unit is given below.

Material (1 pound plastic at $2)	$ 2.00
Direct labor (1.6 hours at $4)	6.40
Variable overhead	3.00
Total standard variable cost	$11.40

The variable overhead cost is not related to direct labor hours, but rather to units of product because production is thought to be the causal factor in the incurrence of the variable overhead elements. The elements of variable overhead, based on a yearly volume of 60,000 units of production, are as follows.

Indirect labor (30,000 hours at $4)	$120,000
Supplies, oil (60,000 gallons at $0.50)	30,000
Maintenance costs, variable portion (6,000 hours at $5 per hour)	30,000
Total budgeted variable overhead	$180,000

Fixed overhead is budgeted as follows, based on 60,000 units of product.

Supervision	$ 27,000
Depreciation	45,000
Other fixed overhead (includes fixed maintenance costs of $12,000)	45,000
Total budgeted fixed overhead	$117,000

During November, 5,000 units were produced and actual costs were as follows.

Material (5,300 pounds used at $2)	$10,600
Direct labor (8,200 hours at $4.10)	33,620
Indirect labor (2,400 hours at $4.10)	9,840
Supplies (6,000 gallons of oil at $0.55)	3,300
Variable maintenance costs (490 hours at $5.30)	2,597
Supervision	2,475
Depreciation	3,750
Other fixed overhead (includes maintenance of $1,100)	3,600
Total	$69,782

Purchases of materials were 5,200 pounds at $2.10 per pound. The firm has divided responsibilities so that the purchasing manager is responsible for price variances for material and oil and the production manager is responsible for all quantities of materials, labor (direct and indirect), supplies, and maintenance. The personnel manager is responsible for wage rate variances and the manager of the maintenance department is responsible for spending variances.

Required

1. Calculate the following variances.
   (a) material price
   (b) material use
   (c) direct labor rate
   (d) direct labor efficiency
   (e) total variable overhead
   (f) total fixed overhead
2. Prepare a report that details the overhead variances of each element by responsibility. (A convenient method is to list the managers across the top, and under each show the variances for which they are responsible.) You should account for all variable and fixed overhead variances. That is, the total of your answers to item 1 should be distributed to individual managers.

PART FOUR

PRODUCT COSTING

Part Four deals with product costing—determining unit costs of manufactured products. Knowledge of product costing is important to nonaccounting managers because they receive reports that use one or another of the methods considered in Part Four.

An understanding of cost behavior and of the significance of unit costs is particularly important in interpreting reports of manufacturing firms. Cost allocation is further considered, together with its effects—how it can obscure information necessary for planning and decision making. The discussion of product costing methods also covers some of the potential behavioral problems associated with such methods. Thus, product costing also has implications for control and performance evaluation.

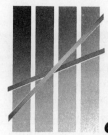

CHAPTER 13

INTRODUCTION TO PRODUCT COSTING: JOB-ORDER COSTING

This chapter begins a sequence of three chapters devoted to **product costing**—determining costs of inventory and of goods sold—for manufacturing firms. This and the next two chapters deal only with highlights of the subject, providing an introduction to the basic approaches to product costing and cost accumulation methods.

GENERAL APPROACHES

The most common approach to product costing is **absorption costing,** or full costing. Under absorption costing, inventory cost includes fixed manufacturing costs. As indicated in earlier chapters, stating fixed costs as per-unit amounts is unwise for planning, control, and decision making. An alternative approach, **direct costing,** or **variable costing,** follows the principle advocated throughout this book—that managers should consider fixed costs only in total, not per unit. Variable costing is illustrated in Chapter 14.

Given the emphasis in managerial accounting on *not* using per-unit fixed costs, why should a manager understand absorption costing? To answer this you have to understand that accounting systems serve several purposes. They provide information for managers, but they must also produce information for financial reporting and taxation purposes. As pointed out in Chapter 1, users of financial accounting reports are different from those of managerial accounting reports. Financial accounting reports are subject to generally accepted accounting principles. Generally accepted accounting principles (as well as income tax law) require that the unit cost of manufactured products include *all* manufacturing costs, both variable and fixed. Therefore, inventories on the balance sheet and cost of goods sold on the income statement of a manufacturer must include both variable and fixed manufacturing costs. This means that the behavioral classification of costs used in VCP analysis is not acceptable for external reporting. The accounting system must produce absorption costing information to satisfy these requirements.

Companies often use data required for external purposes for internal purposes, so managers are likely to encounter absorption costing in some reports. Managers in nonmanufacturing firms are not affected by the carryover of financial accounting rules to managerial reports, because in such firms the only cost normally associated with a unit of product (sold or in inventory) is a variable cost—the purchase cost of the unit. But managers in a manufacturing firm who receive reports based on the rules of external reporting must remember that per-unit costs in those reports include both variable and fixed manufacturing costs. As we know from earlier chapters, per-unit total costs can be misleading. Accordingly, managers in manufacturing firms must understand how the information was developed and, more importantly, how to interpret that information in performing their functions of planning and control.

This chapter will help you understand and use absorption-costing information. But first, you need to understand the cost flows in a manufacturing firm.

COST FLOWS

Every firm incurs a variety of costs. A merchandiser incurs the cost of purchasing a ready-for-sale product, plus the costs of selling the product and administering the firm. A manufacturer incurs costs for the purchase of materials and components, the labor performed to turn them into finished products, the facilities needed for the manufacturing process, and, of course, its selling and administrative efforts.

The selling and administrative costs of either type of firm are expensed in the period incurred and are called **period costs.** They are not affected by absorption costing. Manufacturing costs are not expensed until the product is sold and are called **product costs.** The accounting path followed by a product cost, from the time it is incurred to the time it becomes an expense, is called the **flow of costs.**

From your study of financial accounting you are familiar with the flow of product costs for a merchandiser. The cost of purchased products flows into inventory and then into cost of goods sold. For a manufacturer, the flow is basically the same—costs flow into inventory and then to cost of goods sold. But the situation is complicated by two factors noted in Chapters 3 and 6: (1) manufacturers typically have not one but three types of inventory and (2) the cost of a manufacturer's inventories includes more than the purchase price of materials.

At any given time, a manufacturer might have three different inventories.

1. **Finished goods inventory,** consisting of units of product that are ready for sale. This inventory is equivalent to what is called *inventory* by a merchandising concern.
2. **Work in process inventory,** consisting of semifinished units of product (such as automobiles without windshields, doors, or engines). Reaching this semifinished state requires not only materials but also labor and machinery. This inventory has no equivalent in a merchandising concern.
3. **Materials inventory,** consisting of the various materials and purchased components that go into a finished product but on which no work has yet been done. Here, again, there is no equivalent in a merchandising concern. We use the term *materials* to refer also to purchased components.

Thus, although the product costs of a manufacturing concern flow into inventory and eventually to cost of goods sold, as with a merchandising concern, the process is more complicated because the flow involves more than one type of inventory and costs other than purchase costs.

The flow of product costs in a manufacturer is shown in Figure 13-1. The costs of materials are first collected in the Materials Inventory account.[1] As materials are requisitioned for use in production, their costs flow to the Work in Process Inventory.[2] The cost of labor is first collected in Direct Labor and then

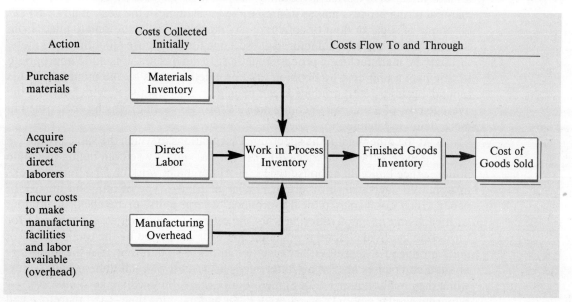

Figure 13-1   Flow of Costs in a Manufacturing Firm

[1] Many titles are used in practice to designate the same things. For instance, some companies use the title "Stores" to refer to the account that contains the cost of materials and purchased components.
[2] To make it easier to follow the discussion, we capitalize the names of accounts, while using lowercase to denote the items themselves. Thus, "Work in Process Inventory" refers to the account, while "work in process" refers to the physical, semifinished product.

flows to Work in Process, reflecting work done to bring products to a semifinished state. Manufacturing overhead costs are collected in Manufacturing Overhead and then flow to Work in Process to reflect the role of such items as supervision, utilities, and depreciation in transforming materials into salable product. Thus, Work in Process collects the costs of materials, labor, and manufacturing overhead.

The costs accumulated in Work in Process are transferred to Finished Goods, to reflect the cost of units completed and ready for sale. Finally, the costs of units sold are transferred from Finished Goods to Cost of Goods Sold. Generally speaking, then, *all* manufacturing costs flow through Work in Process to Finished Goods and, finally, to Cost of Goods Sold.

The approach to collecting information about the production process differs depending on whether the company makes a single product or a variety of dissimilar products. The next section explains the significance of this distinction.

MANUFACTURING PROCESSES

Some companies make only one product over and over again, in a more or less continuous process. Every pound of sugar or flour or coffee, every gallon of tomato juice, every brick is virtually the same as any other. The nature of the manufacturing process makes it impossible to distinguish the cost of any *particular* pound of sugar or flour or coffee, or any *particular* gallon of tomato juice, from the cost of any other manufactured at the same time, because all of the units move through the manufacturing process together. In such cases, it is quite appropriate to calculate a unit cost by dividing total production costs by the number of units (pounds, gallons, etc.) produced, and managers can be satisfied with knowing the average cost of a unit. Such companies use **process costing,** which is discussed in more detail in Chapter 15.

At the other end of the spectrum are situations in which the same product is rarely, if ever, produced twice. A construction company seldom builds the same bridge, office building, or house twice. A printer might work on 50 different books in a month, each with a different number of pages, type of ink, and quality of paper. Such companies typically produce several units, or batches, of product with each unit or batch differing from the others. Calculating an average cost for the period by dividing total production costs for the period by the total number of units produced is senseless, because the units are so different. Yet the managers of such companies are keenly interested in the cost of each unit or batch. For, while they might not make the same product again, they will make similar ones— requiring similar amounts of material, labor and machine time—and therefore will want to use the costs of current jobs to estimate costs of future jobs. Such companies use **job-order costing,** which is the focus of this chapter.

Along the spectrum are many hybrids, including many companies best described as mass producers or *repetitive manufacturers*. These companies produce relatively standard products but so many different ones that they cannot use the simple averaging procedure described above for process costing. We discuss these companies in Chapter 14.

JOB-ORDER COSTING

A job-order costing system keeps track of the materials and labor used on a particular job and then *applies, absorbs,* or *assigns* manufacturing overhead to it. Tracing materials, labor and machine time to specific jobs is not a big problem; workers simply keep track of their time and of the materials and machine time they use on each job, and report them on forms designed for that purpose. But it is impossible to trace manufacturing overhead costs to jobs; manufacturing overhead costs—such as heat, light, power, and machinery depreciation—are not direct to specific jobs. Hence, the overhead costs are applied (assigned) to specific jobs indirectly, by determining an *overhead rate per unit of some input factor* (such as labor hours, machine hours, material content, or whatever) with which overhead costs vary most closely. Managers use the techniques described in Chapter 3 to determine the input measure with which total overhead is most closely associated.

Assigning overhead costs to one activity (a job) based on the level of some other activity (like labor hours) is not a new concept. We did this in Chapter 12, where we noted that variable overhead is often related to labor or machine time. In this chapter we relate overhead costs to some input factor such as labor. Roughly speaking, when we assign overhead based on an input factor, we are saying that if a particular job requires, say 10% of total direct labor time, that job should also bear 10% of total overhead.

Exhibit 13-1 contains the basic information we shall use to illustrate job-order costing. (For now, ignore the lower part of the exhibit, which deals with budget information.) Farr Company manufactures electronic sensing devices to customer order. Three jobs (J-1, J-2, and J-3) were worked on in July. Farr uses machine hours to apply overhead.

The material and direct labor costs in Exhibit 13-1 were accumulated through records prepared by employees showing how much material and how much labor and machine time were used. All that remains is to apply overhead to the jobs. There are two commonly used methods for doing so: actual costing and

Exhibit 13-1
Farr Company Data for July

Total overhead costs			$140,000	
Total machine hours			7,000	

	Job Number			
Job Data	J-1	J-2	J-3	Total
Machine hours	2,000	1,000	4,000	7,000
Materials used	$20,000	$62,000	$30,000	$112,000
Direct labor cost	$20,000	$20,000	$30,000	$ 70,000

Budgeted data for year:		
Machine hours	100,000	
Overhead costs, $1,200,000 + ($5 per machine hour)	$1,700,000	

normal costing. We shall illustrate both methods, and then discuss the impact of those procedures on the financial statements, particularly on the income statement.

Actual Costing

Under **actual costing,** all of the overhead incurred during a period is applied to the jobs worked on in that period. To assign all the overhead costs to the jobs, we calculate the overhead *rate* by dividing total actual overhead by the total amount of the relevant input factor—machine hours. In general form

$$\text{Overhead rate} = \frac{\text{total manufacturing overhead}}{\text{total manufacturing activity}}$$

In the specific situation here we have

$$\text{Overhead rate} = \frac{\$140,000}{7,000}$$

$$= \$20 \text{ per machine hour}$$

The total costs of the three jobs can now be summarized as below.

| | Job Number | | |
	J-1	J-2	J-3
Overhead ($140,000):			
2,000 hrs. at $20	$40,000		
1,000 hrs. at $20		$20,000	
4,000 hrs. at $20			$ 80,000
Materials	20,000	62,000	30,000
Direct labor	20,000	20,000	30,000
Total cost of job	$80,000	$102,000	$140,000

Notice that all $140,000 of overhead cost is assigned to the three jobs ($40,000 + $20,000 + $80,000 = $140,000).

Suppose that job J-1 was the only one sold in July. Its cost would appear in the July income statement as Cost of Goods Sold. If job J-2 was finished but not sold, then its cost would appear in the July 31 balance sheet as Finished Goods Inventory. And if job J-3 was still incomplete at the end of July, its cost would appear on the balance sheet as Work in Process Inventory.

Actual job-order costing is simple but is not commonly used because it can produce misleading results. The reason is that overhead rates can fluctuate significantly from month to month, so that similar jobs done in different months might have quite different amounts of overhead and, hence, total cost. Perceiving the jobs as similar, managers might sell the products at about the same price, and the different gross profits (because of the differing total costs) could lead to incorrect conclusions about profitability.

You may have already guessed, after having seen how the rates were computed, that there are two reasons for fluctuations in overhead rates. First, activity (machine hours in our example) can differ from month to month because of seasonality or changes in the economy. Second, overhead costs can fluctuate for reasons other than changes in operating activity. Heating is an obvious example. Although heating costs are higher in winter, it is of doubtful value to say that products made in the winter "cost more." Consider the following example.

Farr Company normally incurs variable overhead at $5 per machine hour and fixed overhead averages $100,000 per month (see Exhibit 13-1). In May its fixed overhead is $100,000, but in December, because of seasonal factors, it is $110,000. Machine hours are 10,000 in May, but 5,000 in December, because of seasonal factors in the demand for its products. Under actual job-order costing, the overhead rates for the two months are computed below.

	May	December
Total overhead costs:		
$100,000 + (10,000 × $5)	$150,000	
$110,000 + (5,000 × $5)		$135,000
Machine hours	10,000	5,000
Overhead rate per machine hour	$ 15	$ 27

Suppose, now, that Farr makes two similar jobs in May and December, each requiring 100 machine hours, $1,000 direct labor, and $800 in materials. The total costs of the jobs are

	Job Done in	
	May	December
Materials	$ 800	$ 800
Labor	1,000	1,000
Overhead, at $15 and $27	1,500	2,700
Total	$3,300	$4,500

Does the job done in December really cost $1,200 more than the one done in May? Is it likely that a customer would be willing to pay more for a product just because it was made in one of the company's slow months? In fact, customers can usually get lower, not higher, prices in slow months, because companies need the business to keep their workers busy. Yet the profitability of the two jobs will *appear* different if they were sold at the same price, and this appearance could mislead a manager who is trying to develop a price quotation on a similar job. Most companies avoid this problem by using *normal costing*.

Normal Costing

Normal costing smooths overhead rates over the year. The vehicle used to accomplish this smoothing is a **predetermined overhead rate.** That is, the firm uses a single overhead rate throughout the year, rather than an actual rate for each month. A predetermined overhead rate is just what the term suggests: an overhead rate calculated in advance. It is not based on actual costs and activity, but rather on budgeted results.

$$\frac{\text{Predetermined}}{\text{overhead rate}} = \frac{\text{budgeted manufacturing overhead for year}}{\text{budgeted production activity for year}}$$

Again, budgeted production activity can be expressed as direct labor hours, machine hours, or some other measure that managers think appropriate. The activity measures used in normal costing are the same as those used in actual costing; the difference is in the use of budgeted rather than actual figures.

Let us illustrate normal job-order costing with Farr Company, using July activity and the budgeted data at the bottom of Exhibit 13-1 (page 541). The budget formula for overhead costs has the same form we saw in several earlier chapters.

$$\frac{\text{Total budgeted}}{\text{overhead}} = \frac{\text{budgeted}}{\text{fixed costs}} + \left(\frac{\text{budgeted variable cost}}{\text{per unit of activity}} \times \frac{\text{budgeted}}{\text{activity}}\right)$$

Total budgeted overhead for the year is $1,700,000, which includes budgeted fixed costs of $1,200,000, plus $5 of variable cost per machine hour (MH) times 100,000 budgeted machine hours. The *predetermined* overhead rate is $17 per MH ($1,700,000/100,000). This rate, multiplied by the number of hours worked on each job, gives the overhead costs of the jobs worked on in July.

	Job Number		
	J-1	J-2	J-3
Overhead:			
2,000 hrs. at $17	$34,000		
1,000 hrs. at $17		$17,000	
4,000 hrs. at $17			$ 68,000
Materials, as before	20,000	62,000	30,000
Direct labor, as before	20,000	20,000	30,000
Total cost of job	$74,000	$99,000	$128,000

Notice that material cost and direct labor cost are the same for each job as they were under actual costing (schedule on page 542), but the overhead cost assignments are different. This difference marks the distinction between actual costing and normal costing. The following analysis should help you understand the different treatments of overhead under the two costing methods.

Under actual costing, the overhead cost assigned to a particular job is:

$$\frac{\text{Overhead assigned}}{\text{to job}} = \frac{\text{actual hours}}{\text{worked on job}} \times \frac{\text{total actual overhead}}{\text{total actual hours}}$$

Under normal costing, the overhead assigned to a job is

$$\begin{array}{c}\text{Overhead assigned} \\ \text{to job}\end{array} = \begin{array}{c}\text{actual hours} \\ \text{worked on job}\end{array} \times \frac{\text{total budgeted overhead}}{\text{total budgeted hours}}$$

Thus, under actual costing, total actual overhead is assigned to jobs. Under normal costing, the total overhead assigned to jobs equals actual overhead only if total budgeted overhead equals total actual overhead *and* total actual hours equal total budgeted hours. (Offsetting differences could make the assignment come out even, but that is unlikely.) The difference between actual overhead and applied overhead under normal costing is called **misapplied overhead.**

For the specific jobs worked on in July, which set of costs—actual or normal—is "correct"? There is no answer to this question, much as there is no answer to the question whether first-in-first-out or last-in-first-out is the "correct" inventory cost flow assumption. What matters is that managers know which alternative is used and understand how it affects the reports they receive.

Misapplied Overhead

To explore the implications of using normal versus actual costing, let us look at the total overhead costs assigned under the two methods to jobs worked on in July.

	Overhead Applied to Jobs Using	
	Actual Costing (page 542)	*Normal Costing* (page 544)
Job J-1	$ 40,000	$ 34,000
Job J-2	20,000	17,000
Job J-3	80,000	68,000
Total	$140,000	$119,000*ᵃ*

ᵃ Note that you can also calculate total applied overhead by multiplying the predetermined overhead rate of $17 by the 7,000 total machine hours: $17 × 7,000 = $119,000.

We show a $21,000 difference in overhead applied for the two methods ($140,000 − $119,000), actual being greater than applied under normal costing. Misapplied overhead is the difference between actual overhead and applied overhead (and cannot occur when actual costing is used). If actual overhead is greater than applied overhead, the difference is called **underapplied (underabsorbed) overhead.** If applied overhead is greater than actual overhead, we call it **overapplied (overabsorbed) overhead.** In July, Farr has underapplied overhead of $21,000. What is the significance of overapplied or underapplied overhead?

At first glance, misapplied overhead looks like the variances studied in Chapter 12. That is, if one views applied overhead as the "standard," any overapplication or underapplication might appear to be analogous to favorable and unfavorable variable cost variances. But the analogy must not be carried too far. Remember that the predetermined overhead rate is based on both budgeted costs *and* budgeted production activity. True, the overapplied or underapplied overhead could result because actual costs are lower (a favorable variance) or higher (an unfavorable variance) than budgeted. But it is also true that overapplied or underapplied overhead can result from a difference between the actual level of production activity and the activity level used to calculate the predetermined overhead rate.

To illustrate these two points, let us look more closely at the July results for Farr Company, when machine time used totaled 7,000 hours. The budget formula for the annual overhead cost is $1,200,000 of fixed costs plus $5 per machine hour for variable cost. With monthly fixed overhead budgeted at the average of $100,000 (one twelfth of the annual amount), July's budgeted and actual costs can be compared as below.

Actual costs, fixed and variable	$140,000
Budgeted costs [$100,000 + ($5 × 7,000 hours)]	135,000
Budget variance, unfavorable	$ 5,000

Farr incurred $5,000 more overhead cost than budgeted, an unfavorable budget variance. The calculation of a **budget variance** is not new with this chapter. In this case, we cannot determine how much of this variance relates to fixed cost and how much to variable cost because we do not know the *actual* amounts of fixed and variable costs. This point was discussed in Chapter 12. But we *do* know now that $5,000 of the $21,000 underapplied overhead represents an unfavorable budget variance because actual costs were higher than budgeted costs.

Let us look at the other factor affecting the predetermined rate and, therefore, the amount of overhead applied. We know (again from Exhibit 13-1) that Farr planned to use 100,000 machine hours for the year, for a monthly average of $8,333\frac{1}{3}$ hours. But only 7,000 hours of machine time was used in July. The variance caused by a difference between actual hours of machine time and the budgeted hours used in the calculation of the rate that is used to apply overhead is called the **volume variance,** or the **idle capacity variance** and is computed as follows.

Budgeted cost, as computed above	$135,000
Applied cost ($17 × 7,000 actual hours)	119,000
Volume variance, unfavorable	$ 16,000

Note that using budgeted cost in the calculation eliminates the effect of any budget variance. When applied overhead exceeds budgeted overhead, the volume variance is *said to be* favorable; when the opposite is true, the variance is *said to be* unfavorable. Hence, we have now identified two unfavorable variances that add up to the $21,000 difference between actual and applied overhead for the month.

The meaning of a budget variance is clear, but what does the volume variance mean? Does it have any economic significance? Very little, if any. Whether it is favorable or unfavorable is not good or bad per se, because it relates solely to the smoothing of fixed overhead and arises *only* because actual hours do not equal the monthly average of budgeted hours. To demonstrate this point more clearly, let us look further at the $17 predetermined overhead rate.

The budgeted overhead cost used in the calculation of the $17 predetermined overhead rate has both a fixed and a variable component. The variable portion of the rate is $5 per hour, so the fixed portion is $12. (Alternatively, budgeted fixed overhead is $1,200,000 and budgeted hours are 100,000, also giving a $12 fixed portion.) Now, look at the difference between actual hours (7,000) and the 8,333⅓ monthly share of the hours budgeted for the year. The $16,000 volume variance is exactly that 1,333⅓ hour difference multiplied by the $12 rate for fixed overhead. Perhaps this point is more easily seen if you recast the calculation of the volume variance and separate budgeted and applied costs into their variable and fixed components, as below.

	Variable Portion	Fixed Portion
Budgeted cost (7,000 hours × $5)	$35,000	$100,000
Applied cost:		
7,000 hours × $5	35,000	
7,000 hours × $12		84,000
Volume variance (1,333⅓ hours × $12)	—	$ 16,000

The flexible budget allowance for variable costs depends on the actual level of activity. But because fixed costs are not expected to change with the level of activity, the budgeted amount is not affected when more (or fewer) hours are worked than were budgeted. Thus, what produces the volume variance is the difference between budgeted and actual production activity, the 1,333⅓ hours.

We now have three different, but equivalent, formulas for calculating the volume variance.

$$\begin{aligned}\text{Volume variance} &= \frac{\text{total budgeted}}{\text{manufacturing overhead}} - \frac{\text{total applied}}{\text{manufacturing overhead}} \\[2mm] &= \frac{\text{total budgeted fixed}}{\text{manufacturing overhead}} - \frac{\text{total applied fixed}}{\text{manufacturing overhead}} \\[2mm] &= \frac{\text{predetermined overhead}}{\text{rate for fixed costs}} \times \left(\frac{\text{budgeted}}{\text{production volume}} - \frac{\text{actual}}{\text{production volume}}\right)\end{aligned}$$

You should use whichever formula is most convenient in a given situation; they all give the same answer.

We can also use the graphical format shown in Chapter 12 to compute the overhead budget variance and volume variance.

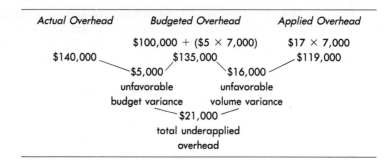

Before leaving this topic we want to remind you that applying overhead is an accounting device. Managers should not expect to incur overhead at the rate used to apply it. Rather, they should expect to incur overhead according to the budget formula.

Combining Overhead Rates

We began the illustration of normal costing by computing a predetermined overhead rate based on budgeted total manufacturing overhead. Seeing that the budget formula for overhead has both a fixed and a variable component, and that two of the three formulas for computing volume variance use a separate overhead rate for the fixed component, you may be wondering why we compute only a *total* budget variance.

To determine separate budget variances for variable and fixed overhead, a firm must be able to separate *actual* costs into their fixed and variable components. Many elements of manufacturing overhead are mixed costs. From Chapter 3 you know that the analytical techniques for estimating the variable and fixed components of such costs—high-low, regression, scatter diagrams—rely on past observations of the total cost for the element being analyzed. As we discussed in Chapter 12, the ability to develop a formula for predicting the total amount of some cost for budgeting purposes does not imply the ability to recognize the fixed and variable portions of that cost *as it is incurred*. A combined overhead rate, such as we used in the example, is appropriate when a firm cannot classify actual costs as either variable or fixed and so cannot compute separate overhead budget variances.

INCOME STATEMENTS, ACTUAL AND NORMAL COSTING

We began this chapter by stating that absorption costing, which requires that fixed manufacturing cost be included in the total cost for a product, is the most commonly followed approach to product costing and is required in annual reports. We have also illustrated, using a job-order company, two methods for assigning overhead costs to product. We now look at how the costing methods affect the income statement.

Exhibit 13-2 shows the July income statement for Farr Company under the two methods. We have assumed that Farr had $40,000 of selling and administrative expenses and that, as stated earlier, job J-1 was completed and sold for $150,000. Costs accumulated on jobs J-2 and J-3 remain in inventory at the end of the month.

The most obvious and critical difference is the amount of income ($30,000 under actual costing and $15,000 under normal costing). What caused the $15,000 difference?

The difference between actual absorption costing and normal absorption costing lies in the treatment given to overhead. So, you were quite right if you identified the income difference as related to the difference in overhead treatment. You were wrong, however, if you thought the income difference was because normal costing *ignored* some of the overhead actually incurred. Total manufacturing overhead under both methods is the actual amount of $140,000. The actual-costing income statement shows the actual overhead in a single amount; the normal-costing income statement shows the actual overhead in two amounts, $119,000 assigned to production, and $21,000 as a separate deduction.

Exhibit 13-2
Farr Company, Income Statements for July

		Normal Costing	Actual Costing
Sales		$150,000	$150,000
Normal cost of sales	$74,000[a]		
Plus underapplied overhead	21,000		
Cost of sales		95,000	80,000[b]
Gross profit		55,000	70,000
Selling and administrative expenses		40,000	40,000
Income		$ 15,000	$ 30,000
Details of cost of sales			
Cost of sales:			
Beginning inventories		$ 0	$ 0
Materials		112,000	112,000
Labor		70,000	70,000
Overhead		119,000	140,000
Total costs		301,000	322,000
Less ending inventory		227,000[c]	242,000[d]
Normal cost of sales		74,000	
Underapplied overhead		21,000	
Cost of sales		$ 95,000	$ 80,000

[a] Cost of job J-1 from page 544.
[b] Cost of job J-1 from page 542.
[c] Job J-2 ($99,000) + job J-3 ($128,000) = $227,000.
[d] Job J-2 ($102,000) + job J-3 ($140,000) = $242,000.

If you look closely at the statements you will see that the source of the $15,000 difference in income is the $15,000 difference in the ending inventories. Specifically, the cost of job J-2 is $3,000 greater and that of J-3 is $12,000 greater under actual costing than under normal costing, and that difference occurs because more overhead was assigned to those jobs under actual costing. Remember that overhead was assigned at the actual rate under actual costing, but at a predetermined rate for normal costing, so that for a single period within the year such differences are not uncommon. Most companies using normal costing convert to actual costing if they have significant amounts of overapplied or underapplied overhead after a full year's activity. In so doing, the overhead assigned to unfinished jobs is adjusted to the actual rate, and the difference in inventory disappears.

Although we showed underapplied overhead as an addition to normal cost of sales, there is another possibility. We could also have shown a figure called *normal gross margin*, which is sales minus normal cost of sales. We would then have subtracted underapplied overhead from normal gross margin. Either approach can be used and the income figure will be the same. The choice is a matter of preference. The income statement in Exhibit 13-3 shows the alternative format and also separates underapplied overhead into the budget variance and volume variance.

One final observation on how operating results for an interim (part of a year) period can differ under actual and normal costing. In the illustration there were no unfinished jobs at the beginning of July, so the entire difference in incomes between the two methods could be identified with the different assignments of overhead to jobs in inventory at the end of the month. Had there been a beginning inventory, July incomes would also have been affected by different assignments of overhead to jobs in that inventory.

Exhibit 13-3
Farr Company, Normal Costing Income Statement for July

Sales		$150,000
Normal cost of goods sold		74,000
Normal gross margin		76,000
Variances:		
Budget variance	$ 5,000U	
Volume variance	16,000U	21,000
Gross margin		55,000
Selling and administrative expenses		40,000
Income		$ 15,000

SEPARATE OVERHEAD RATES

Our example used a single overhead rate for an entire plant, and related overhead to the use of machine time. Most companies use different overhead rates for different cost pools. A **cost pool** is a group of overhead costs driven by the same activity.

The most common example of a cost pool is the costs of a department where the elements of overhead are related to a single departmental activity, such as labor hours or machine time. Companies could also ignore departmental lines and apply different cost pools by developing separate overhead rates based on different activities. For example, a pool of overhead costs associated with materials—purchasing, receiving, inspecting, storing—could be applied to jobs based on the material cost incurred on each job. A separate rate could apply labor-driven costs—training, personnel and payroll functions, payroll taxes, etc.—to jobs on the basis of labor hours worked, or perhaps labor cost. Similarly, a pool of overhead costs driven by the presence and use of machinery could be applied based on the machine hours used on a job. If a company could clearly establish the cost-to-activity relationships, it might use different rates for labor time and for machine time in a single department, or even separate rates for every machine in the plant.

For brevity we use the term *separate rates* to refer to any rates other than a single, plant-wide rate. Separate rates should be considered whenever different input factors drive different pools of cost. Of course, it is more costly to operate a system where separate rates are used. Hence, such rates should be adopted only when the expected benefits exceed the additional costs of developing the rates and keeping the necessary records. The following sections offer examples of possible benefits through improved decision making and cost management.

Overhead Application and Pricing

One area of decision making that might be improved through the use of separate rates is pricing. The data given below relate to Reinhart Company, a maker of electrical equipment all of which must be worked on, though to a varying extent, in its two departments, Fabrication and Assembly.

| | Department | | |
	Fabrication	Assembly	Totals
Variable overhead rate per DLH	$8	$2	
Budgeted direct labor hours	25,000	25,000	50,000
Total budgeted variable overhead	$200,000	$ 50,000	$250,000
Budgeted departmental fixed overhead	200,000	100,000	300,000
Total budgeted overhead	$400,000	$150,000	$550,000
Direct labor hours, budgeted	25,000	25,000	50,000
Predetermined overhead rates	$16	$6	$11

Reinhart has been applying overhead to jobs using its plant-wide rate of $11 per direct labor hour, which rate it also used to develop price quotations. Reinhart's managers consider profits to be unsatisfactory. After careful study they traced all variable and fixed costs to the departments, and then computed the separate (departmental) rates also shown above. As you can see, the $11 rate does not capture the differences between the departments; it is only $3 higher than the *variable overhead rate alone* in Fabrication.

To see how using the single rate could have affected pricing, and profits, suppose Reinhart sets its prices at 120% of expected manufacturing costs, including overhead. Quoted prices will include $13.20 ($11 × 120%) of overhead for each hour of work required in either department. If the company gets the budgeted 25,000 hours of fabrication work, it will be charging customers $330,000 ($13.20 × 25,000) for overhead in that department. The charges are less than the department's total overhead ($400,000). Of course, charging $13.20 per hour for overhead for assembly work would bring contribution margin to help offset the shortfall, but only if Reinhart is successful in its bids on jobs requiring assembly labor. Will Reinhart get that business?

Remember that not all jobs require equal time in each department, and assume Reinhart has a competitor that uses departmental rates but has a similar cost structure and pricing policy. The competitor's prices will include a charge for overhead of only $7.20 ($6 × 120%) per hour of assembly work, $6 less than Reinhart's charge. For every hour of fabrication work, the competitor would charge $19.20 ($16 × 120%), $6 more than Reinhart. By using the single rate to develop its price quotations, Reinhart might be getting most of the business requiring a high proportion of fabrication time; but we've already seen that reaching the budgeted activity of 25,000 hours for that department will not cover the department's total overhead. Unfortunately, the competitor would probably be getting most of the jobs requiring a great deal of assembly labor, thereby reducing Reinhart's prospects for making a profit.

In this case, using departmental rates improves decision making. The key to improvement was recognizing that, while the activity driving overhead was labor hours in both cost pools, the relationships were different for the two pools. In another situation, improved decision making might come from separate rates that used different activities for each pool. In all cases, the important first step toward possible improvement is carefully studying and classifying overhead costs into their pools.

Overhead Application and Cost Management

In recent years, many manufacturers have observed changes in the composition of their costs. In particular, companies adopting new manufacturing techniques such as just-in-time, flexible manufacturing, and computer-integrated manufacturing, are finding that material and labor costs are declining significantly as percentages of total manufacturing cost, while overhead is climbing, both in absolute dollars and as a percentage of total cost. Increased overhead is a natural consequence of the greater need, in the new manufacturing environment, for support personnel such as engineers, computer experts, highly skilled maintenance workers, and other employees that are not direct laborers. The changes taking place are not only increasing overhead, they are increasing its fixed component.

With overhead rising and direct labor falling, companies that applied overhead based on direct labor saw application rates rise, sometimes astronomically (perhaps to hundreds of dollars per labor hour). Managers increased their efforts to control costs, but some of their actions seemed to aggravate the situation by further increasing overhead rates. After careful study of their costs, some companies found that separate rates could better direct attention to areas where cost control actions would be effective.

An instructive example comes from the managers of the Portables Group of Tektronix Company, some of whose experiences were discussed briefly in Chapter 10 (page 389).[3] Direct labor had declined to less than 7% of total manufacturing cost (to just over 3% on some of its newer products). Simultaneously, overhead costs were rising because the Group was introducing new manufacturing methods and the manufacturing operation had become increasingly dependent on technology. Overhead rates, which were based on direct labor, became extremely high. Although labor cost per se was low, coupling the cost of direct labor time with the large overhead charge produced a *total* labor-based cost that was very high. Unfortunately, some managers directed their cost control efforts to finding ways to reduce labor time. Of course, simply reducing labor time further increased overhead rates, because so much of overhead was now fixed; and the increase was even greater when labor-time savings were achieved through more use of technology.

As we reported in Chapter 10, the Group conducted an extensive study of overhead costs and determined that costs of materials-related activities, such as purchasing, receiving, etc., were significant. The Group changed its procedures for assigning overhead. It began to use both materials and conversion activities (labor and machine time) to apply the costs in different pools. The new overhead assignments have helped managers to better understand the effects of their actions and also helped to focus their attention on areas offering significant potential for cost reduction.

In this case, using separate overhead rates improved cost management. The keys to the improvement were recognizing that overhead was driven by more than one factor and, again, carefully classifying costs into their pools.

SUMMARY

Σ Product costing is the determination of costs of inventory and of cost of goods sold for manufacturing firms. For financial reporting and income tax purposes, manufacturers must use absorption costing, which requires all manufacturing costs, variable and fixed, to be included in the calculation of unit cost.

In a manufacturing firm, costs flow through inventory accounts to cost of goods sold. Data regarding cost flows are accumulated in various ways, depending on the manufacturing process. Companies that produce essentially identical products accumulate costs using process

[3] John W. Jonez and Michael A. Wright, "Material Burdening," *Management Accounting* (August 1987), 27–31.

costing. Companies that seldom produce the same product accumulate costs using job-order costing.

Some firms compute product costs based on actual costs. Others use a normal costing system, under which they apply overhead to products using predetermined overhead rates based on budgeted manufacturing overhead and budgeted production activity. The rate is usually stated as a cost per unit of some input measure such as direct labor hours. Separate overhead rates can be calculated for each department or other cost pool, or for a factory as a whole.

When normal costing is used, there will virtually always be a difference between actual overhead and applied overhead. The difference, called *underapplied or overapplied overhead,* can be reported in an income statement as an adjustment to either normal cost of sales or normal gross margin. Underapplied or overapplied overhead can be analyzed into a budget variance and a volume variance. The latter variance has little, if any, economic significance.

KEY TERMS

absorption (or full) costing	materials inventory
actual costing	normal costing
applied (absorbed) overhead	overapplied (overabsorbed) overhead
budget variance	period costs
cost pool	predetermined overhead rate
finished goods inventory	product costs
flow of costs	underapplied (underabsorbed) overhead
idle capacity variance	volume variance
job-order costing	work in process inventory

KEY FORMULAS

$$\text{Predetermined overhead rate} = \frac{\text{budgeted manufacturing overhead for year}}{\text{budgeted production activity for year}}$$

$$\begin{matrix}\text{Variable overhead} \\ \text{budget variance}\end{matrix} = \begin{matrix}\text{actual} \\ \text{variable} \\ \text{overhead}\end{matrix} - \begin{matrix}\text{flexible budget} \\ \text{allowance for actual} \\ \text{production activity}\end{matrix}$$

$$\begin{matrix}\text{Underabsorbed} \\ \text{(overabsorbed)} \\ \text{overhead}\end{matrix} = \begin{matrix}\text{actual} \\ \text{manufacturing} \\ \text{overhead}\end{matrix} - \begin{matrix}\text{applied} \\ \text{manufacturing} \\ \text{overhead}\end{matrix}$$

$$\begin{matrix}\text{Fixed overhead} \\ \text{budget} \\ \text{variance}\end{matrix} = \begin{matrix}\text{actual} \\ \text{fixed} \\ \text{overhead}\end{matrix} - \begin{matrix}\text{budgeted} \\ \text{fixed} \\ \text{overhead}\end{matrix}$$

$$\text{Volume variance} = \begin{matrix}\text{budgeted (fixed)} \\ \text{manufacturing} \\ \text{overhead}\end{matrix} - \begin{matrix}\text{applied (fixed)} \\ \text{manufacturing} \\ \text{overhead}\end{matrix}$$

$$\text{Volume variance} = \begin{array}{c} \text{predetermined} \\ \text{overhead rate for} \\ \text{fixed overhead} \end{array} \times \left(\begin{array}{c} \text{budgeted} \\ \text{volume} \end{array} - \begin{array}{c} \text{actual} \\ \text{volume} \end{array} \right)$$

Total overhead budget variance = actual total overhead − budgeted total overhead

REVIEW PROBLEM

Boulder Company makes drill presses to customer order and uses job-order costing. The firm began the month of March with no inventories. During March, it worked on two jobs, for which data appear below.

	Job #15	Job #16
Materials used	$69,000	$45,000
Direct labor at $10 per hour	$35,000	$60,000

Boulder incurred factory overhead costs of $209,000. Budgeted monthly factory overhead is $150,000 + ($5 × direct labor hours). The firm uses a predetermined overhead rate based on 10,000 direct labor hours per month. Activity does not usually fluctuate much from one month to another.

Required
1. Calculate the predetermined overhead rate per direct labor hour.
2. Determine the amounts of overhead to apply to each job.
3. Determine the overhead budget variance and volume variance.
4. Suppose that job #15 was sold for $240,000 and job #16 remained in inventory. Selling and administrative expenses for March were $24,000. Prepare an income statement for March. Treat variances as adjustments to normal cost of sales.
5. Suppose now that the firm used actual costing, allocating overhead to jobs based on the actual overhead rate per direct labor hour. Determine the amounts of overhead applied to each job and prepare an income statement assuming the relevant data from item 4.

Answer to Review Problem

1. $20.00 per direct labor hour, calculated as follows.

$$\text{Predetermined rate} = \frac{\text{total budgeted overhead}}{\text{total budgeted activity}}$$

$$= \frac{\$150,000 + (\$5 \times 10,000)}{10,000}$$

$$= \$20$$

The rate consists of $15 fixed and $5 variable. Because there is no significant fluctuation in activity during the year, it is reasonable to use the monthly rather than the annual figures to calculate the rate. In fact, with annual fixed overhead of $1,800,000 ($150,000 × 12) and 120,000 direct labor hours (10,000 × 12), we would have exactly the same result.

2.

	Job #15	Job #16	Total
Direct labor hours:			
$35,000/$10	3,500		
$60,000/$10		6,000	9,500
Overhead at $20 per hour	$70,000	$120,000	$190,000

3.

Actual Overhead	Budgeted Overhead	Applied Overhead
	$150,000 + ($5 × 9,500)	9,500 × $20
$209,000	$197,500	$190,000

$11,500
unfavorable budget
variance

$7,500
unfavorable volume
variance

$19,000
total underapplied overhead

4.

Sales		$240,000
Cost of sales:		
Normal cost of sales[a]	$174,000	
Variances:		
Budget variance	11,500 U	
Volume variance	7,500 U	
Cost of sales		193,000
Gross profit		47,000
Selling and administrative expenses		24,000
Income		$ 23,000

[a] Job #15, materials + direct labor + applied overhead = $69,000 + $35,000 + $70,000 = $174,000.

5. The problem here is simply to determine the actual overhead rate.

$$\text{Actual rate} = \frac{\text{actual overhead}}{\text{actual activity}}$$

$$= \frac{\$209,000}{9,500 \text{ hours}}$$

$$= \$22.00 \text{ per hour}$$

The applied amounts are

	Job #15	Job #16	Total
Direct labor hours	3,500	6,000	9,500
Overhead applied at $22 per hour	$77,000	$132,000	$209,000

Thus, all overhead goes to individual jobs, so there are no variances. The income statement would show the following, with job #15 costing $181,000 ($69,000 + $35,000 + $77,000).

Sales	$240,000
Cost of sales	181,000
Gross margin	59,000
Selling and administrative expense	24,000
Income	$ 35,000

The difference in incomes ($23,000 versus $35,000) arises from the differences in inventory. Under normal costing, as in item 2, overhead of $120,000 is applied to job #16, which is still in inventory. Under actual costing, as shown above, overhead of $132,000 is applied to job #16. The $12,000 difference in income under the two methods is explained by the $12,000 difference in the overhead assigned to the job remaining in inventory (job #16).

ASSIGNMENT MATERIAL

Questions for Discussion

13-1 ***Interrelationships with earlier chapters*** What similarities and differences do you see between predetermined overhead rates and flexible expense budgets?

13-2 ***Absorbing overhead*** Business people sometimes make statements like: "Our overhead rates allow us to absorb overhead costs at 80% of capacity."

Required: What do you think this statement means?

13-3 ***Overhead application*** "Underapplied overhead is a bad sign because the more overhead you apply, the lower your fixed cost per unit." Discuss this statement critically.

13-4 ***Actual and normal costing*** Suppose a company begins and ends a year with no inventories. Will there be any difference between its income computed using actual costing and using normal costing? Why or why not?

13-5 ***"What's normal about it?"*** A student sitting near you in class just asked this question. The student does not see how you can apply overhead using a predetermined rate, and went on to say: "If overhead cost per hour is $15 in one month and $6 the next, that's the way it goes. All this 'applying' business is a bookkeeping trick, but it doesn't make any sense in the real world."

Required: Comment on the statements.

13-6 ***Are cost accountants the villains?*** Mr. Robert Fox, executive vice president of Creative Output, a management consulting firm in Connecticut, was quoted as arguing that allowing cost accounting "to dictate the way a factory floor is organized and run" is harmful. Fox was further quoted as saying that

The cost accounting system assigns part of overall costs of running the factory to each step in the manufacturing process. Each hour a machine is running, for instance, may be costed at a given amount. A foreman will then try to get as much material as he can through that machine . . . to keep the costs assigned to his particular work stations as low as possible.

Required: Discuss the quotation. If the quotation is correct, what kinds of allocations must the manufacturer be making?

Exercises

13-7 Basic actual job-order costing Brindley Furniture uses actual job-order costing, applying overhead to jobs based on direct labor hours. Brindley worked on two large orders in March.

	Job	
	M-1	*M-2*
Material cost	$80,000	$115,000
Direct labor cost	$70,000	$ 85,000
Direct labor hours	9,000	11,000

Actual overhead in March was $180,000.

Required
1. Determine the actual overhead rate for March.
2. Determine the amount of overhead to be applied to each job.
3. Determine the total cost of each job.

13-8 Basic normal job-order costing (extension of 13-7) Suppose now that Brindley uses normal costing, with a predetermined overhead rate of $10 per direct labor hour.

Required
1. Determine the amount of overhead to be applied to each job.
2. Determine the total cost of each job.
3. Determine the amount of overapplied or underapplied overhead for March.
4. Suppose that Brindley budgeted annual overhead using the formula: $1,500,000 + ($4 × direct labor hours). The predetermined overhead rate was based on 250,000 budgeted direct labor hours. Assuming that budgeted monthly fixed overhead is $125,000, what were the budget variance and volume variance?

13-9 Job-order costing income statements (extension of 13-7 and 13-8) Brindley Furniture's job M-1 was incomplete at the end of March, while job M-2 was sold for $600,000. Selling and administrative expenses were $150,000.

Required
1. Prepare an income statement for March using the results from 13-7.
2. Prepare an income statement for March using the results from 13-8. Show any misapplied overhead as an adjustment to normal cost of sales.

13-10 *Job-order costing — income statement* SBO Company uses normal job-order costing. Its predetermined overhead rate is based on the following data.

Variable overhead per direct labor hour	$ 2
Total budgeted fixed overhead	$600,000
Total budgeted direct labor hours	200,000

The company began 19X5 with no inventories. A summary of material and direct labor cost for 19X5 appears below.

	Total	Jobs Sold	Jobs in Ending Inventories
Material costs	$ 800,000	$ 700,000	$100,000
Direct labor cost	$1,800,000	$1,600,000	$200,000
Direct labor hours	180,000	160,000	20,000

Total sales were $6,000,000; selling and administrative expenses were $2,600,000. Total actual manufacturing overhead was $840,000.

Required
1. Compute the predetermined overhead rate for 19X5.
2. Prepare an income statement for 19X5 with overapplied or underapplied overhead shown as an adjustment to cost of sales.

13-11 *Predetermined overhead rates* For each of the following situations, fill in the missing data. The predetermined overhead rates are based on budgeted fixed costs and budgeted machine hours for the year. There is no variable overhead.

	(a) Fixed Overhead Rate	(b) Budgeted Fixed Overhead	(c) Budgeted Hours	(d) Actual Hours	(e) Fixed Overhead Applied
1.	_____	$180,000	30,000	31,000	_____
2.	$8	_____	20,000	22,000	_____
3.	_____	$ 70,000	_____	11,000	$ 77,000
4.	$4	$160,000	_____	_____	$172,000

13-12 *Selecting an overhead base* Pruess Company does not now use predetermined overhead rates for applying fixed overhead to jobs. The controller wishes to begin doing so and has developed the following information for one department: Budgeted fixed manufacturing overhead for the coming year is $560,000; budgeted direct labor hours are 80,000; budgeted machine hours are 70,000.

Required
1. Compute predetermined rates based on (a) direct labor hours and (b) machine hours.

2.   The results for the year were as follows: fixed manufacturing overhead, $565,000; direct labor hours, 81,000; machine hours, 68,000. For each of the rates determined in item 1, determine (a) the amount of overhead applied to jobs and (b) the amount of overapplied or underapplied overhead.

13-13   Overhead relationships — variances   Each of the following cases is independent. Fill in the blanks, being sure to indicate whether a variance is favorable or unfavorable. The amounts for "total budgeted overhead" are the flexible budget allowances for the actual level of activity for the period. In each case, the firm uses a single rate to apply both fixed and variable overhead.

Case	(a) Total Budgeted Overhead	(b) Total Actual Overhead	(c) Total Applied Overhead	(d) Budget Variance	(e) Volume Variance
1	$400,000	$402,000	$403,000	_____	_____
2	$600,000	_____	$585,000	$6,000U	_____
3	_____	$310,000	_____	$6,000U	$18,000F
4	$400,000	_____	_____	$6,000F	$10,000U

13-14   Job-order costing — assigning overhead   Marquette Boatworks uses normal costing and its predetermined overhead rate is based on the following information. Monthly budgeted overhead = $800,000 + ($0.60 × direct labor cost). Monthly budgeted direct labor cost is $1,000,000. At the end of March, the following information was available.

	Total	Jobs Sold	Jobs in Ending Inventory of Work in Process	Jobs in Ending Inventory of Finished Goods
Material cost	$ 630,000	$500,000	$ 70,000	$60,000
Direct labor cost	$1,010,000	$820,000	$100,000	$90,000

Actual overhead for the month was $1,388,000.

Required
1.   Compute the predetermined overhead rate based on direct labor cost.
2.   Determine cost of goods sold for the month.
3.   Determine ending inventory of work in process.
4.   Determine ending inventory of finished goods.
5.   Determine overapplied or underapplied overhead.
6.   Determine the volume variance.

13-15   Predetermined overhead rates — job-order costing   Walton Company uses predetermined rates for fixed overhead, based on machine hours. The following data are available relating to 19X5.

Budgeted fixed factory overhead cost	$240,000
Budgeted machine hours	40,000
Actual fixed factory overhead cost incurred	$242,000
Actual machine hours used	39,000
Actual machine hours by job	

Job No.	Machine Hours Used on Job
12	8,000
13	14,000
14	7,000
15	10,000

Required

1. Compute the predetermined overhead rate.
2. Determine the overhead to be applied to each job.
3. Determine the budget variance and the volume variance.

3-16 Job order costing – two overhead rates MFG Industries applies overhead to jobs using two rates—one based on material cost of each job, the other based on machine hours for each job. Because of the high amounts of overhead associated with purchasing, receiving, storing, and issuing materials, the managers believe that simply using machine hours to allocate this overhead is inappropriate. Summary data for 19X5 follow.

	Budget	Actual
Material-related overhead	$ 240,000	$ 234,000
Machine-related overhead	$ 700,000	$ 697,000
Cost of materials used on jobs	$1,600,000	$1,582,000
Direct labor cost	$ 900,000	$ 869,000
Machine hours	100,000	98,000

Data related to jobs worked on in 19X5 follow.

			Jobs in Ending Inventory	
	Totals	Jobs Sold	Work-in-Process	Finished Goods
Material cost	$1,582,000	$1,321,000	$82,000	$179,000
Direct labor cost	$ 869,000	$ 788,000	$33,000	$ 48,000
Machine hours	98,000	77,000	7,000	14,000

Sales were $3,890,000 and administrative expenses were $356,000.

Required

1. Compute the predetermined overhead rates for materials and for machine hours.

2. Determine the cost of jobs sold and the cost of each type of ending inventory.
3. Prepare an income statement showing misapplied overhead as an adjustment to normal cost of sales.

13-17 Basic job order costing   Rehman Machinery, Inc. manufactures large custom drills. It uses a predetermined overhead rate of $4.20 per machine hour. During August, Rehman worked on three jobs. Data appear below.

	Z-101	K-221	K-341
Machine hours	2,280	930	2,910
Direct labor cost	$23,400	$14,200	$36,320
Material cost	$24,570	$ 9,220	$26,245

Job Z-101 was completed and sold. The other jobs remained in inventory. Actual overhead for August was $25,210.

Required
1. Determine the overhead to be applied to each job.
2. Determine normal cost of sales and ending inventory.
3. Determine overapplied or underapplied overhead.

13-18 Comparison of actual and normal costing   Riopelle Company uses actual job-order costing, assigning overhead to jobs based on direct labor cost. During March, Riopelle had the following activity.

	Jobs Worked on in March		
	M-1	M-2	M-3
Material cost	$28,000	$41,000	$32,000
Direct labor cost	$24,000	$18,000	$28,000

Total actual overhead was $196,000; selling and administrative expenses were $28,000. Job M-1 was sold for $160,000. Jobs M-2 and M-3 were incomplete at the end of March.

Required
1. Determine the actual overhead rate per direct labor dollar.
2. Determine the overhead assigned to each job and the total cost of each job.
3. Prepare an income statement for March.
4. Suppose now that Riopelle uses normal costing. Its predetermined overhead rate is based on $2,100,000 budgeted overhead and $700,000 budgeted direct labor cost for the year. Calculate the predetermined overhead rate and redo items 2 and 3 using normal costing. Show any misapplied overhead as an adjustment to normal gross margin.

13-19 Graphical analysis of overhead   The graph below shows the budgeted manufacturing overhead for Minich Company.

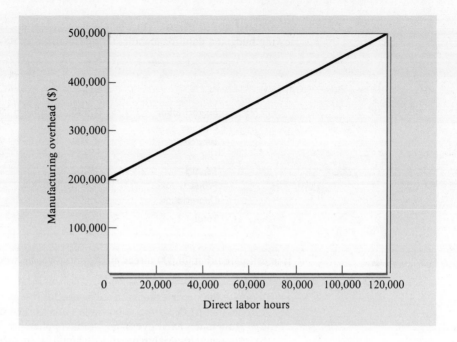

Required
1. Draw in the line that represents applied overhead for each of these two cases.
   (a) The predetermined overhead rate is $5 per direct labor hour.
   (b) The predetermined overhead rate is based on 100,000 direct labor hours.
2. Suppose that actual overhead equals budgeted overhead and that volume is 90,000 direct labor hours. What are the volume variances under each of the two cases from item 1?

13-20 ***Basic job-order costing*** Kelton Company makes a wide variety of gear assemblies for industrial applications. The firm uses normal costing, with a predetermined overhead rate of $3.70 per machine hour. During March 19X6 Kelton worked on the jobs listed below.

	Job Number		
	311	*312*	*313*
Materials used on job	$15,260	$21,340	$ 8,890
Direct labor cost	$17,250	$13,550	$10,100
Machine hours	1,480	1,230	860

Required
1. Compute the amounts of overhead to be applied to each job and the total cost of each job.
2. Actual overhead for March was $12,980. What was overapplied or underapplied overhead?

13-21 *Overhead application* The controller of Williams Company received the following budgeted data for manufacturing overhead costs of 19X7.

	Fixed Amount	Variable Cost per Direct Labor Hour
Indirect labor	$ 47,800	$0.40
Supplies	25,300	0.15
Lubricants	7,700	0.10
Utilities	46,400	0.48
Repairs	21,000	0.17
Property taxes	6,000	0
Depreciation	32,000	0
Total	$186,200	$1.30

It is estimated that 70,000 direct labor hours will be worked in 19X7.

Required
1. Compute the predetermined fixed overhead rate per direct labor hour.
2. Assume that 67,000 direct labor hours are worked on jobs in 19X7.
   (a) How much fixed overhead will be applied?
   (b) How much variable overhead should be incurred? How much applied?
   (c) If actual overhead costs are $274,800, what are the budget variance and volume variance?

13-22 *Overhead application* Vavasour Company is a highly automated operation that measures its activity by machine hours. Its managers have budgeted machine hours for the coming year, 19X2, at 300,000. They budget annual manufacturing overhead as: total budgeted overhead = $600,000 + ($3 × machine hours).

Required
1. Compute the predetermined overhead rate for 19X2.
2. At the end of 19X2, the controller collected the following information. There were no beginning inventories.

Total manufacturing overhead incurred		$1,585,000
Total machine hours:		315,000
Machine hours on jobs sold	275,000	
Machine hours on jobs in ending inventories	40,000	

Determine the amounts of applied overhead in costs of goods sold and in ending inventories. Determine the amount of overapplied or underapplied overhead and break it down into the budget variance and volume variance.

Problems

13-23 *Job order costing – two overhead rates* Billings Machines uses two rates to apply overhead to jobs even though it does not have two departments. One rate is based on material cost, the other on machine time. Billings has relatively high overhead that is related to buying, receiving, storing, and issuing materials; hence the managers believe that applying this overhead through the relative material cost of jobs is appropriate. The data below relate to 19X4.

	Budget
Material-related overhead	$ 640,000
Machine-related overhead	$1,100,000
Cost of materials used on jobs	$1,600,000
Machine hours	200,000

Data related to three jobs worked on in March follow.

	Job XT-56	Job XR-23	Job XY-67
Material cost	$21,000	$82,000	$39,000
Direct labor cost	$16,000	$13,000	$18,000
Machine hours	8,500	4,500	2,900

Actual material-related overhead was $59,200 and actual machine-related overhead was $92,800.

Required
1. Compute the predetermined overhead rates for materials and for machine hours.
2. Determine the amount of overhead to be applied to each job and the total cost of each job.
3. Determine overapplied or underapplied overhead for each type of overhead.

13-24 ***Job-order costing – two departments***   Barton Machinery Company makes industrial robots to customer order. There are two departments, Machining and Assembly. The Machining Department is highly mechanized, and the Assembly Department is labor intensive. Accordingly, the firm applies overhead using machine hours in the Machining Department, direct labor hours in the Assembly Department. Budgeted data for 19X6 appear below.

	Machining Department	Assembly Department
Total budgeted overhead	$720,000	$120,000
Machine hours	120,000	
Direct labor hours		60,000

During March Barton worked on two jobs.

	Job #1029	Job #1030
Materials used	$21,000	$32,000
Direct labor, Assembly Department, at $6 per hour	$12,000	$19,200
Machine hours in Machining Department	4,000	5,000

Required

1. Calculate the predetermined overhead rate for each department.
2. Calculate the overhead applied to each job and the total cost of each job.
3. Actual overhead in the Machining Department was $55,500 and in the Assembly Department was $10,200. Calculate overapplied or underapplied overhead for each department.

13-25 **Basic job-order costing** Walker Company manufactures precision optical instruments that its customers need made to order. Walker uses normal costing, setting its predetermined overhead rate based on machine hours. For 19X4, the rate is $11.40 per hour, which is based on $3,192,000 budgeted overhead and 280,000 budgeted hours.

During January, the firm worked on three jobs.

	Job Number		
	M-101	R-12	Z-610
Materials used	$ 36,800	$ 74,200	$41,600
Direct labor cost	$122,200	$119,200	$77,300
Machine hours	8,800	8,200	7,200

Job M-101 was completed and sold while the other two remained in inventory at the end of January. Actual overhead incurred in January was $271,300.

Required

1. Determine the amount of overhead that should be applied to each job.
2. Determine normal cost of goods sold for January and ending inventory.
3. Determine overapplied or underapplied overhead for January.

13-26 **Job costing in a service firm** Russell and Morrison is a firm of architectural engineers operating in a single office in a medium-sized city. The firm charges clients for the time that each person on the staff spends on the client's business, using a rate of $2\frac{1}{2}$ times the person's salary, based on an 1,800-hour working year. Thus, an architectural draftsman earning a salary of $15,000 is charged out to clients at $21 per hour [($15,000/1,800) × 2.5 = $20.83, rounded to $21]. The rate is intended to cover all costs and to yield a profit.

Budgeted results for 19X9 follow.

Salaries of professional staff	$ 700,000
Salaries of support personnel (clerks, typists, etc.)	78,000
Other costs	680,000
Total expected costs	$1,458,000

The listed costs do not include salaries for Russell and Morrison. Each partner expects to work about 1,200 chargeable hours at a rate of $60 per hour. About 80% of the time of professional staff is chargeable to clients, about 40% of the time of support personnel. Nonchargeable time is for general firm business, professional activities (attending seminars and continuing-education programs), and business development.

Required

1. What total income will the partners earn if their estimates prove correct?
2. Suppose that two professional employees work on a design for a particular client. One earns $18,000 per year, the other $21,000, and each works 12 hours on this particular project. How much will the firm charge the client for the project assuming that neither the partners nor the support staff is involved in this project? (Round hourly rates to the nearest dollar.)

13-27 Overhead costs and pricing policy HortonWorks is a medium-sized machine shop that does custom work for industrial customers. Business is seasonal, with about four busy months, three slack months, and the rest about average. HortonWorks uses an actual job-order costing system, assigning overhead to jobs at the end of each month based on the labor cost of each job. Ray Horton, the owner, sets prices using the following format, with hypothetical data.

Estimated material cost	$32.50
Estimated labor cost	16.80
Subtotal	49.30
Allowance for overhead at 60%	29.58
Subtotal	78.88
Allowance for profit at 10%	7.89
Price	$86.77

Horton developed the formula based on experience and on the financial results of the past few years. Overhead has averaged about 60% of the sum of material and labor costs, and a 10% profit is reasonable in the industry.

Horton has found that similar jobs seem to be more or less profitable depending on the month in which they are done. This bothers him, and he has begun to wonder whether his pricing policy is sensible.

Required

1. In which months, busy or slack, will jobs *appear* more profitable? Why?
2. Should Horton modify his pricing policy? What should he do?

13-28 Job-order costing The data below pertain to the March operations of Covera Machine Tool Company. The company ships jobs as it completes them, keeping no inventory of finished goods.

Jobs in beginning work in process:	
Materials	$237,670
Direct labor	$322,200
Factory overhead	$467,190
Materials put into process in March:	
To jobs in ending inventory	$228,310
To jobs finished and sold in March	$881,480
Direct labor for March:	
To jobs in ending work in process	$452,400
To jobs finished and sold in March	$892,880

The company uses normal costing and applies overhead at $1.50 per direct labor dollar. The material and labor costs for jobs finished and sold include the cost to finish the beginning inventory of work in process.

The company had sales of $4,680,000 in March, selling and administrative expenses of $453,650.

Required
1. Determine the overhead cost in ending inventory of work in process and in cost of goods sold.
2. Overhead was overapplied by $18,430 in March. What was actual overhead?
3. Prepare an income statement for March, treating overapplied overhead as an adjustment to normal cost of sales.

13-29 *Job order costing – comparison of overhead rates* Walton Machines uses a single overhead rate based on machine hours. One of its managers believes that the company could benefit from using two rates, one based on material cost, the other on machine time. The manager believes that because Walton has relatively high overhead related to buying, receiving, storing, and issuing materials, applying this overhead through the relative material cost of jobs is appropriate. The data below relate to 19X4.

	Budget
Material-related overhead	$ 480,000
Machine-related overhead	1,300,000
Total overhead	$1,780,000
Cost of materials used on jobs	$1,600,000
Machine hours	200,000

Data related to three jobs worked on in March follow.

	Job XT-56	Job XR-23	Job XY-67
Material cost	$21,000	$82,000	$39,000
Direct labor cost	$16,000	$13,000	$18,000
Machine hours used	8,500	4,500	2,900

Actual material-related overhead was $39,800 and actual machine-related overhead was $105,800.

Required
1. Compute the predetermined overhead rate per machine hour assuming that Walton uses only machine hours to apply overhead, as it has been doing.
2. Determine the amount of overhead to be applied to each job and the total cost of each job.
3. Redo parts 1 and 2 using the two rates as suggested by the manager. Comment on the differences in job costs here and in part 2.

13-30 **_Job-order costing, beginning inventory_** Wisconsin Machinery Company makes large industrial machines. It uses a job-order costing system applying overhead at $15 per direct labor hour. Direct laborers are paid $8 per hour. The following data relate to jobs worked on in March 19X4.

	4-22	4-23	4-24	4-25
Costs in beginning inventory:				
Materials	$ 34,000	$10,000	0	0
Direct labor	48,000	8,000	0	0
Overhead	90,000	15,000	0	0
Total	$172,000	$33,000	0	0
Costs incurred in March:				
Materials	$11,000	$46,000	$60,000	$ 9,000
Direct labor	$16,000	$32,000	$52,000	$12,000

Jobs 4-22, 4-23, and 4-24 were completed and sold. Job 4-25 was not finished at the end of March. Total overhead incurred during March was $212,000.

Required
1. Compute the amounts of overhead to be applied to each job.
2. Compute the amount of overapplied or underapplied overhead for March.
3. Compute cost of goods sold for March and the inventory at March 31.
4. Revenue from the three jobs sold was $860,000. Selling and administrative expenses for March were $180,000. Prepare an income statement for March.

13-31 **_VCP analysis for a job order company_** Brill Optics manufactures special lenses to customer order. Kim Brill, the owner, is trying to develop a profit plan and has collected the following budgeted data for 19X7.

Material cost	$200,000
Labor cost (40,000 hours at $9 per hour)	360,000
Variable overhead	160,000
Fixed overhead	240,000
Selling and administrative expenses, all fixed	120,000

Brill has set a predetermined overhead rate of $10 per direct labor hour. He sets prices at 120% of total manufacturing cost, including applied overhead.

Required
1. What profit will Brill earn if operations meet his expectations?
2. Suppose that Brill is able to generate only 35,000 direct labor hours worth of work, a 12.5% decline. Materials and variable overhead also decline by 12.5%. Brill treats underapplied overhead as an adjustment to normal cost of sales. What profit will he earn, again setting prices using applied overhead?
3. What pricing policy, stated as a percentage of total manufacturing cost, will give Brill a $100,000 profit working 40,000 direct labor hours?

13-32 **_Costing and pricing in a hospital_**   The controller of Prairie Memorial Hospital has recently decided to set prices for laboratory tests using a formula based on costs. She has analyzed each type of test as follows.

Class of Test	Time Required (minutes)	Number Performed in Average Year
I	12	38,000
II	15	17,000
III	30	9,000

Variable costs are negligible. The controller believes that because all lab technicians are salaried, it is best to treat their salaries as overhead costs. Total annual overhead costs are $960,000.

Required
1. Calculate a predetermined overhead rate per minute. Round to the nearest $0.001.
2. Determine the price for each class of test that will make the laboratory break even. Round prices to the nearest cent.
3. Suppose that the laboratory performs 37,000 Class I; 17,000 Class II; and 10,000 Class III tests. Total costs are $965,000. Determine profit or loss.

13-33 **_Overhead application and pricing decisions_**   Grendel Company makes high-quality furniture. The company has just received an offer from a large wholesaler for a single batch of goods. The price is $25,000, which is about $10,000 less than normal. The sales manager is sure that existing sales would be unaffected by the special order and wants to accept the order if any profit can be made. The production manager provided the following estimates of cost for the order.

Materials	$ 6,000
Direct labor (3,000 hours)	9,000
Overhead	15,000
Total	$30,000

The production manager informed you that the overhead cost is based on the overhead application rate of $5 per direct labor hour. The rate includes both fixed and variable overhead and was based on 60,000 expected direct labor hours and $300,000 budgeted total overhead costs. The rate last year was $5.50, based on 50,000 direct labor hours and $275,000 total overhead costs. The production manager told you that the difference in rates is due to the difference in budgeted direct labor hours—the cost structure is the same this year as last year.

Required
1. Determine the incremental cost of the order. Should it be accepted?
2. What other factors should be considered in deciding whether to accept this special order?

13-34 ***Overhead rates and cost analysis*** Walton Machinery Company makes industrial machines. The firm has been operating well below capacity, and the sales manager has been trying to increase orders. She recently received an offer to bid on a large press and submitted the specifications to Walton's cost estimators. Their estimate appears below.

Materials	$29,600
Direct labor at $9 per hour	19,800
Overhead at $12 per direct labor hour	26,400
Total manufacturing cost	75,800
Standard allowance for selling and administrative expenses,	
10% of manufacturing cost	7,580
Total cost	83,380
Standard allowance for profit at 15% of total cost	12,507
Suggested price	$95,887

The sales manager told the executive vice president that this suggested price is not low enough to get the job. She said that the customer expected a price in the neighborhood of $75,000, which another company had already bid. The vice president called in the controller, who said that the overhead rate was about 60% variable, 40% fixed, and that variable selling and administrative expenses were negligible. The vice president was reluctant to meet the $75,000 price but agreed to think it over and get back to the sales manager.

Required: Advise the managers. Should they meet the $75,000 price?

13-35 ***Pricing policy and profits*** Sumter Milling is a job-order firm. It uses material supplied by its customers, so that virtually all of its manufacturing costs are direct labor and overhead. Jackie Wiggins, the controller, prepared the following data for use in establishing the company's pricing policy for the coming year.

Total budgeted direct labor hours	240,000
Total budgeted manufacturing costs	$4,800,000

Total budgeted manufacturing costs were developed using the formula:

Total manufacturing costs = $1,200,000 + ($15 × direct labor hours)

Total selling and administrative expenses are budgeted as: $800,000 + ($0.10 × revenue). The management of the company seeks an $880,000 profit.

Required
1. Determine the revenue Sumter must earn to achieve its profit objective.
2. Determine the price per direct labor hour Sumter must charge to achieve the objective.
3. Suppose that the company uses the pricing policy you developed and actually works 230,000 direct labor hours. What will its profit be?
4. Suppose that the company uses your pricing policy and works 250,000 hours. What will its profit be?

13-36 *Changing overhead rates* Benson Electronics has been on a cost-cutting program designed to help it meet foreign competition. The cost of a typical unit of Benson's major product appears below.

Materials and components	$180
Direct labor	44
Overhead at 400% of direct labor	176
Total cost	$400

The overhead cost reflects actual overhead divided by actual labor hours at 50,000 units, the expected production level of the product. Benson's engineers did considerable redesigning of the product line to reduce labor cost. They introduced some custom-made components, which, though costlier than the existing components, were easier to assemble into the units. They also changed some job descriptions and rerouted product flow. The head of engineering understood that the changes would raise material/component costs by about $16, but would reduce labor cost by roughly $16 and therefore reduce overhead by about $64 at the 400% rate. The results in the first six months were not encouraging as the following unit cost calculation, which as before is based on actual overhead costs and direct labor for 50,000 units, shows.

Materials and components	$190
Direct labor	29
Overhead at 600% of direct labor	174
Total cost	$393

The heads of production and engineering, as well as the controller, were not happy with the results. A great deal of work had resulted in little net decrease in unit cost. The most disappointing aspect was the sharp increase in the overhead rate occasioned by the drop in direct labor.

Required
1. Determine total overhead before and after the cost-cutting program.
2. Suppose that the entire difference you found in part 1 is attributable to the component of overhead that varies with direct labor. Determine the variable component of overhead, with respect to direct labor. Can you now explain why costs did not fall as much as one might have thought?
3. What do you recommend?

13-37 *Normal costing* Boardman Company manufactures equipment used to cap bottles. The following data summarize 19X3 activities.

Beginning inventories of work in process and finished goods	$ 360,000
Materials put into process	2,240,000
Direct labor	1,780,000
Manufacturing overhead incurred	2,520,000
Selling and administrative expenses	880,000
Sales	7,960,000

The firm uses an overhead application rate of $1.40 per direct labor dollar, based on budgeted direct labor cost of $1,800,000 and the following formula for budgeting manufacturing overhead:

Manufacturing overhead = $1,440,000 + ($0.60 × direct labor cost)

At the end of the year, the controller determined that the following costs were in the indicated places.

| | | | Ending Inventory of | |
	Total	Jobs Sold	Incomplete Jobs	Finished Jobs
Materials	$2,240,000	$1,890,000	$120,000	$230,000
Direct labor	$1,780,000	$1,480,000	$100,000	$200,000

Required: Prepare an income statement for the year, using normal costing and showing the budget variance and volume variance as separate adjustments to gross margin.

13-38 **Comparison of actual and normal costing** Wharton Company began 19X5 with no inventories. It experienced the following results in that year.

| | | Amounts Included in | |
	Total	Cost of Goods Sold	Inventories
Materials used	$ 500,000	$450,000	$ 50,000
Direct labor	$1,000,000	$900,000	$100,000

The company had actual overhead costs of $2,200,000 and selling and administrative expenses of $700,000. Revenue was $4,500,000.

Required
1. Assume that the firm allocates actual overhead to jobs using direct labor cost. (a) Determine the amount of overhead that will appear in cost of goods sold and in the ending inventories. (b) Prepare an income statement for the year.
2. Assume that Wharton uses a predetermined overhead rate of $2 per direct labor dollar and treats any underapplied or overapplied overhead as a separate item on the income statement. (a) Determine the amounts of applied overhead that would appear in cost of sales and in ending inventories. (b) Prepare an income statement for the year.

13-39 **Overhead rate behavior** Ned Clinton, controller of Walcott Industries, has been puzzled by the behavior of overhead rates. The company has been engaged in a program to reduce costs and the focus has been on direct labor and associated overhead costs. Because the average cost per direct labor hour (DLH) was in the $10.20–$10.40 range and the average overhead rate around $39 per DLH, Clinton expected savings in the area of $50 for reductions in DLH.

Clinton has been collecting data (see below) for the past few quarters to track the progress of the program. Output was about the same in each quarter, so the decreased labor hours represent improved performance.

Quarter	Direct Labor Hours	Direct Labor Cost	Overhead Cost	Overhead Rate per DLH
3rd 19X1	62,000	$634,500	$2,432,000	$39.23
4th 19X1	61,100	629,450	2,431,900	39.80
1st 19X2	61,200	630,180	2,431,200	39.74
2nd 19X2	58,300	601,100	2,428,800	41.66
3rd 19X2	55,400	569,900	2,427,200	43.81

Clinton was puzzled at the behavior of the overhead rate. He knew that overhead was not totally variable with direct labor, but thought that there surely should have been a considerable drop in overhead as direct labor hours declined.

Required
1. Using the high-low method, determine the component of overhead costs that varies with direct labor hours.
2. State why you think Clinton might have been incorrect in his estimates of the effects of reducing labor time and what he might do now.

13-40 *Overhead application and levels of activity* The managers of LeVine Window Company have been discussing the overhead application rate for the coming year. They agree that total manufacturing overhead should be budgeted at $1,200,000 plus $1.50 times direct labor hours, but are not sure what they should budget for direct labor hours. One manager has argued that 300,000 hours is as good an estimate as any, another that 360,000 hours is better.

Required
1. Compute the predetermined overhead rate using (a) 300,000 hours and (b) 360,000 hours.
2. Suppose that the firm actually works 320,000 direct labor hours and incurs total manufacturing overhead costs of $1,710,000. (a) What would the budget variance and volume variance be if the firm had selected 300,000 hours to set the predetermined rate? (b) What would the same two variances be if the firm had used 360,000 hours to set the rate?

13-41 *Job-order costing and decisions* Last month, Marchmont Furniture Company began work on custom-made chairs ordered by a retail store. When the work was nearly complete, the retailer went bankrupt and was not able to pay for the chairs. The sales manager of Marchmont immediately called other stores in an effort to sell the chairs. The original price was $210,000, but the best price the sales manager could get if the chairs were finished according to the original specifications was $140,000. This offer was from the Z-Store chain. Randle Company, which also operates a chain of stores, offered $158,000 for the chairs provided that different upholstery and trim were used. The sales manager talked to the production manager about the order and got the following information.

	Costs Accumulated to Date
Materials	$ 31,500
Direct labor (7,000 hours at $5)	35,000
Factory overhead at $10 per hour	70,000
Total accumulated costs	$136,500

The factory overhead rate includes $4 variable overhead and $6 fixed overhead. The additional work required to complete the chairs was estimated as follows by the production manager.

	Original Specifications	Randle's Specifications
Materials	$4,100	$9,000
Direct labor hours	800 hours	1,800 hours

Required
1. Using the firm's costing method, determine the total costs to be charged to the job assuming (a) the work is completed based on the original specifications and (b) the chairs are modified as required by Randle Company.
2. Determine which offer Marchmont should accept.

13-42 ***Job-order costing – service business*** Sofdat Inc. develops computer programs for businesses, hospitals, local governments, and other organizations. The company has been having difficulty analyzing the profitability of jobs and estimating costs for use in bidding.

The company has hired you to develop a job-order costing system. So far, you have decided that production costs should include the costs listed below.

Programmers' salaries	$480,000
Supervisors' salaries	120,000
Other costs of programming	240,000

You decide that the company should use normal costing, treating programmers' salaries as direct labor with each programmer having an hourly rate equaling his or her salary divided by the normal 2,000-hour working year. You also decide to treat the other two elements of cost as manufacturing overhead. You intend to use programming hours to set the predetermined overhead rate because programmers earn different salaries. Finally, you intend to treat the cost of idle programming time (actual salaries paid less salaries charged to jobs) and "excess cost" (amounts charged to jobs in excess of actual salaries paid) as part of overhead.

The president expects selling and administrative expenses to be $180,000. She also expects programmers to work about 24,000 hours, and you decide to use this figure to compute the predetermined overhead rate.

The president is interested in seeing how the system will operate and gives you the following information for a hypothetical month. There was no beginning inventory. Sales were $170,000. All costs incurred were one twelfth of the estimated annual amounts given above. Jobs sold had a total of 1,350 programming hours and jobs in process at the end of the month had 450 programming hours, so that actual charged hours for the month were 1,800 (1,350 + 450). Information on programmers' salaries follows.

Salaries on jobs sold	$27,000
Salaries in ending inventory	$ 9,200

Idle time was $3,800 ($40,000 incurred − $27,000 − $9,200).

Required
1. Calculate the predetermined overhead rate per hour of programmer's time.
2. Determine the cost of ending inventory of jobs in process.
3. Determine overapplied or underapplied overhead cost for the month, including idle time.
4. Prepare an income statement for the month showing overapplied or underapplied overhead as a separate expense or negative expense.

13-43 ***Comparing actual and normal costing — seasonal business*** Barnett Company has used actual job-order costing for several years. At the end of each month, a clerk divides total manufacturing overhead cost incurred during the month by total direct labor cost for the month to get an overhead rate per labor dollar. He then applies overhead at this rate to each job worked on during the month. Because the company uses actual costing, there is no underapplied or overapplied overhead.

The president has been unhappy with this method because it results in widely differing overhead costs in different months. The work is highly seasonal, with the summer months very heavy and the winter months light. The president has asked you to show how normal costing differs from actual costing and has given you the following data regarding two similar jobs done in the past year.

	Job J-12	Job A-16
Material cost	$10,410	$10,310
Direct labor	16,900	16,400
Overhead	40,560	29,520
Total	$67,870	$56,230

Job J-12 was done in January, when total overhead was $528,000 and total labor cost was $220,000. Job A-16 was done in August, when total overhead was $1,179,000 and total labor cost was $655,000. The firm budgets annual overhead using the formula:

Total annual overhead = $3,200,000 + ($1.20 × direct labor cost)

Total budgeted labor cost for the current year is $4,000,000.

Required

1. Develop the predetermined overhead rate based on total budgeted overhead and labor cost.
2. Determine the costs of the two jobs using the rate calculated in item 1.
3. Comment on the advantages of using predetermined overhead rates.

13-44 Multiple overhead rates   Percan Industries has been using a single overhead rate, but its managers have become convinced that they need several rates to reflect the activities with which overhead costs are associated. After careful study, the controller developed the following budgeted information regarding cost pools and activities that drive the pools.

Activity	Amount of Activity	Overhead Costs in Pool
Labor hours	400,000 hours	$1,580,000
Machine set-ups	1,600 set-ups	$ 128,000
Recordkeeping	150,000 entries	$ 90,000

Data related to jobs worked on in 19X5 follow.

	Totals	Jobs Sold	Jobs in Ending Inventories
Material cost	$2,582,000	$2,321,000	$261,000
Direct labor cost	$4,169,000	$3,788,000	$381,000
Direct labor hours	410,000	371,000	39,000
Machine set-ups	1,640	1,560	80
Entries	152,000	136,000	16,000

Actual overhead costs were, by pool: labor hour-based, $1,610,000; machine set-up-based, $131,780; and recordkeeping, $92,600.

Required

1. Compute the predetermined overhead rates for each activity.
2. Determine the amount of each type of overhead to apply to jobs sold and jobs still in inventory.
3. Determine the total cost of jobs sold and the cost of ending inventory.
4. Determine the amount of misapplied overhead for each cost pool.

13-45 Effects of separate overhead rates (extension of 13-44)   One of the managers of Percan Industries says that the new system with its three overhead cost pools is more elaborate and costly than the company needs. He proposes to go back to the old basis, where all overhead was applied using labor hours. In trying to convince him of the wisdom of the separate rates, you pull out the following information about two products that the company manufactures regularly. The data are for typical-sized batches of each product. The company makes several models of each product, but they are all roughly the same.

	Product XT-12	Product JY-09
Material costs	$260	$1,240
Labor cost	280	2,880
Direct labor hours	20	200
Machine set-ups	6	1
Recordkeeping entries	200	80

Required

1. Determine the cost of each product using the overhead rates you developed in the previous assignment.
2. Determine the cost of each product using a single overhead rate based on labor hours. Use the budgeted data from the previous assignment and remember to include all of the overhead cost, not just the labor-driven cost.
3. Comment on the results.

13-46 *Analyzing overhead* The president of your company has asked you some questions about overhead. You recently changed the accounting system from actual to normal costing, with some opposition from other managers who could not see the advantages. Although the president was not happy with the actual costing system, he is not convinced that normal costing is a significant improvement.

The specific questions he wants you to answer relate to determining whether or not costs are under control and what information he can get from the figures for underapplied and overapplied overhead. He gives you the following results from the most recent three months.

	March	April	May
Direct labor hours worked on jobs	14,000	8,000	5,000
Total overhead incurred	$71,000	$52,000	$51,000
Total overhead applied at $6 per direct labor hour	84,000	48,000	30,000
Underapplied (overapplied) overhead	($13,000)	$ 4,000	$21,000

The predetermined rate of $6 per hour was calculated using budgeted direct labor hours for the year of 120,000 and budgeted overhead of $480,000 fixed and $2.00 variable per direct labor hour. Budgeted fixed overhead is $40,000 for each of the three months shown above.

Required: Making any calculations you consider relevant, tell the president what he can learn using the above data.

13-47 *Departmental versus plant-wide overhead rates* Caldwell Company operates two departments, Grinding and Assembly, in a plant that makes optical devices such as binoculars and telescopes. Because nearly all of its products are made to customer order, Caldwell uses job-order costing. In the past, it has used a single overhead application rate based on total budgeted direct labor hours and total budgeted overhead. The rate for 19X8 was computed using the data opposite.

	Grinding Department	Assembly Department	Total
Total budgeted overhead	$1,200,000	$800,000	$2,000,000
Budgeted direct labor hours	200,000	50,000	250,000
Rate ($2,000,000/250,000)			$8

Budgeted overhead was based on the following formulas.

Grinding Department	$800,000 + ($2 × direct labor hours)
Assembly Department	$500,000 + ($6 × direct labor hours)

The firm bases its bid prices on total estimated cost including direct labor, materials, and overhead at $8 per direct labor hour. The controller has been thinking about changing to departmental rates and has collected the following data regarding two jobs recently completed. All direct laborers earn $10 per hour.

	Job 391	Job 547
Direct labor hours:		
Grinding	330	80
Assembly	30	180
Material cost	$3,000	$2,500
Direct labor cost	3,600	2,600

The policy is to bid a price that is 150% of the total estimated manufacturing cost.

Required

1. Determine the overhead that the firm will apply to each job using the $8 plantwide rate. Determine the total cost of each job. Assuming that the actual results for each job were also the estimated results that the firm used to set the bid prices, determine the price that the firm bid for each job.
2. Compute the predetermined overhead rate for each department.
3. Determine the amounts of overhead applied to each job, the total cost of each job, and the bid price for each job using the predetermined departmental overhead rates that you computed in item 2.
4. Comment on the differences in your results for the two jobs using the plantwide rate and departmental rates. Do you recommend that the firm switch to departmental rates?

13-48 Departmental overhead rates Jurgenson Electric makes electric motors. The motors go through three departments: Fabrication, Machining, and Assembly. The company has been using a predetermined rate for variable overhead, but the results have not been satisfactory. Jurgenson prices its motors at 250% of variable cost and has been finding that some models sell poorly, some well.

The variable overhead rate was calculated in the following way: The chief cost accountant determined total variable overhead and total direct labor hours in the three departments and calculated the weighted average. The schedule below shows the derivation of the rate, based on an average month.

Department	Direct Labor Hours Worked	Total Variable Overhead
Fabrication	6,000	$ 48,000
Machining	10,000	60,000
Assembly	14,000	42,000
Total	30,000	$150,000

Weighted average variable overhead rate = $5 per direct labor hour
($150,000/30,000).

The following schedule shows the determination of prices for two models, the 136 and the 260, for lots of 100 motors.

	Model 136	Model 260
Materials	$ 350	$ 410
Direct labor ($4 per hour)	320	260
Variable overhead ($5 per hour)	400	325
Total variable cost	$1,070	$ 995
Multiplied by 2.5 (250%) equals price per 100	$2,675	$2,487.50

Direct labor hours for each model, by department, are given below.

	Model 136	Model 260
Fabrication	40	5
Machining	25	10
Assembly	15	50
Total direct labor hours	80	65

The chief cost accountant realizes that the variable rates per direct labor hour are different among the departments. But he believes that it is simpler to use the weighted-average rate.

Required
1. Compute the variable costs of each model using variable overhead rates based on the individual departmental rates.
2. Compute the selling prices that the firm will charge using the data given in item 1.
3. Do you think the firm is wise to use the weighted-average variable overhead rate? Why or why not?

13-49 **VCP analysis in a job-order firm** Carthage Machine Works manufactures industrial machinery, principally small cutting equipment. Virtually all machines are custom made and Carthage uses job-order costing. The president has developed the following estimates for the coming year, 19X8.

Material cost	$280,000
Direct labor hours	20,000
Direct labor wage rate	$9 per hour
Variable manufacturing overhead	80% of direct labor cost
Fixed manufacturing overhead	$200,000
Selling and administrative expenses	$ 70,000

The president tells you that her pricing policy is to charge the customer 125% of material cost plus a per-hour amount for direct labor. She wants to earn a profit of $60,000 before taxes in 19X8.

Required
1. Determine the price per direct labor hour the firm must charge to meet the target profit.
2. Suppose that the company adopts the per-hour charge you computed in item 1 and has the following results: material costs, $300,000; direct labor hours, 18,000. All overhead costs are incurred as expected (variable per unit of activity and fixed in total). Determine the profit that the company will earn.

13-50 *Actual and normal costing – large inventory changes* OH Company manufactures a product out of air. The plant is completely automated so that there is no direct labor. In fact, the only manufacturing cost is $300,000 annual depreciation. Selling and administrative expenses are all fixed at $100,000 per year.

The firm began 19X6 with no inventories. During the first six months it made 150,000 units and sold 100,000. During the last six months it made 50,000 units and sold 100,000. The selling price is $3 per unit.

Required
1. Prepare income statements for each six-month period assuming that the firm uses actual costing and incurs all costs evenly over the year.
2. Prepare income statements for each six-month period assuming that the firm uses normal costing with the predetermined overhead rate per unit of product being $1.50, based on budgeted annual production of 200,000 units. The volume variances should appear as adjustments to gross margin.

13-51 *Overhead application and cost control* Tucker Print Shop had the following results in three recent months.

	April	May	June
Actual overhead costs	$25,000	$28,000	$34,000
Applied overhead costs	18,000	27,000	36,000

Walter Tucker, the owner, said that cost control was poor in April, better in May, and excellent in June. "We really need to overapply overhead because that reflects good cost control," he said.

Tucker budgets overhead as $2 variable per direct labor hour and $240,000 fixed per year. Monthly fixed overhead is budgeted at $20,000. Tucker uses 60,000 direct labor hours per year to set its predetermined overhead rate.

Required

1. Determine Tucker's predetermined overhead rate.
2. Determine the number of direct labor hours Tucker worked in each month.
3. Determine whether Tucker controlled overhead costs in each month by computing the budget variance for each month.
4. Explain to Mr. Tucker why his conclusions about cost control were, or were not, correct.

Cases

13-52 **Cost Justification**   The following material is taken from a column by Rowland Evans and Robert Novak that appeared in the July 8, 1976 *Knickerbocker News* (Albany, New York). At that time, the federal election laws required that candidates for the presidency limit spending before their parties' conventions to $13 million.

> When Treasury Secretary William Simon traveled to Raleigh, N.C., last Jan. 20 to address the state Chamber of Commerce and then a President Ford Committee (PFC) reception, the taxpayers' bill was $2,310. The reimbursement to Uncle Sam for the PFC for political expenses: $17.44. . . .
>
> The method used for Simon's Jan. 20 journey to North Carolina, an important primary state, is the model. The Air Force charged $2,310 for a Jetstar carrying Simon and seven others (including aides and Secret Service agents) to North Carolina. Since Simon occupied only one of eight seats, his share of the cost is $288.75. The 30 minutes spent at the PFC reception amounted to only 5 per cent of the portal-to-portal time from Washington. So, 5 percent of $288.75 is $14.44. Add $3 for the share of meals, and the cost to the PFC is $17.44.

Required

1. Suppose that you had been engaged as a consultant to former President Ronald Reagan, who was President Ford's opponent in that campaign for the Republican nomination. What would you say about the method used to determine the cost billed to the PFC? What other information would you seek?
2. Suppose that you were engaged as a consultant to the PFC. How would you defend the $17.44 charge?

13-53 **What is cost? — consumer action**   Easy Ed Johnson's Belchfire Auto Agency advertises that it will sell cars at $50 over cost and that anyone who can prove that Ed is making more than $50 on a sale will get a $5,000 prize. Phyllis Henley decides to disprove Ed's claim. She obtains the following information from a consumer magazine.

Cost Data from *Consumer Scoop*—
Belchfire 8 with Standard Equipment

Invoice cost to dealer	$3,400
Commission to salesman, basic rate per car	100
Variable cost of make-ready services (lubrication, washing, etc.)	40
Total cost to dealer	$3,540

Since Phyllis knows that Ed has been selling this particular model for $3,900, she marches into the showroom and demands a $5,000 prize because she can "prove" that Ed is selling this model at $360 over his cost. Ed, with considerable aplomb, summons his accountant, who presents the following information to Phyllis.

Invoice cost to dealer	$3,400
Commission to salesman, basic rate per car	100
Cost of make-ready services	120
General overhead	230
Total cost	$3,850

The accountant points out that Phyllis failed to consider the "real" costs of running a large automobile dealership. He states that the make-ready and general overhead costs are based on the total service department cost and total overhead costs divided by the number of cars sold last year (500). General overhead costs are virtually all fixed. Ed pleasantly and politely offers his condolences to Phyllis for having failed to win the $5,000 and invites her back any time she wants to buy a car at $50 over cost.

Phyllis is not at all happy with her reception at Ed's or the data provided by his accountant, and she decides to sue for the $5,000.

Required: Assume that Phyllis loses the case at the local level and appeals the decision to a higher court. The trial judge (original decision) agreed with the explanation of Easy Ed's accountant. Nevertheless, Phyllis argues that Easy Ed is defrauding the populace and owes her $5,000. Her lawyer has asked you to serve as an expert witness. What will your testimony be?

13-54 *Budgeting, cash flow, product costing, motivation* After almost two decades of profitable operations, Pennywise Company experienced its first loss in 19X6, and all internal reports during the first 11 months of 19X7 indicated a second losing year. At the meeting of the board of directors at the end of December 19X7, the members were given the first draft of the basic operating data for 19X7. (Exhibit 1 shows the basic data available to the directors at the meeting.) Public announcement of the data is made shortly after the directors' meeting.

The directors had maintained the dividend so as not to antagonize the stockholders or give the impression that the recent losses were any more than a temporary setback. Most of the directors had come to realize, by the end of 19X7, that future dividends were advisable only if the company returned to profitable operations. Consequently, the board members were willing to consider any plans which might help minimize inefficiencies, reduce costs, and build a profitable operation once again.

The chairman of the board (and principal stockholder), Mr. Ira Hayes, had recently attended a conference sponsored by the National Association of Manufacturers on motivating personnel to better performance. Mr. Hayes was not particularly impressed with most of the discussions. He told the personnel manager, Mr. Gray: "Those speakers all seemed to concentrate on qualitative and nonquantifiable issues like working conditions and improving the general atmosphere to promote creativity and individuality. There was the usual lot of noise about implementing methods of 'participatory management,' and the like,

Exhibit 1
Pennywise Company—Operating Data for 19X7

Part A: Condensed Statement of Income

Sales (1,200,000 units at $12 per unit)	$14,400,000
Cost of goods sold	11,760,000
Gross margin on sales	2,640,000
Selling and administrative expenses	3,630,000
Net operating loss for the year 19X7	($ 990,000)

Part B: Miscellaneous Operating Data

Normal operating capacity, in units		1,875,000
Fixed costs:		
Manufacturing		$ 6,000,000
Selling and administrative		750,000
Variable costs, per unit:		
Manufacturing	$4.80	
Selling and administrative	$2.40	

and coordinating the efforts of the management team. But really, there wasn't much in the way of concrete suggestions.''

Having been closely associated with the company since its founding by Mr. Hayes 16 years before, Mr. Gray was well acquainted with Mr. Hayes' feelings on the matter of motivation. As Mr. Hayes had said on many occasions, he was convinced that the surest (and easiest) way to really motivate people was to provide monetary incentives of some kind and then let them know exactly what measures would be used to assess their performance. In keeping with this philosophy, Mr. Hayes proposed, at the first board meeting in 19X8, that the company adopt a profit-sharing plan in which all employees could participate. The other members of the board were receptive to the idea and a committee was appointed to draw up a plan.

According to the plan devised by the committee, the company would set aside cash equal to a certain percentage of before-tax profits. The cash would be distributed to all employees on the basis of a preestablished formula. Or, more correctly, a set of such formulas was needed because the performances of employees in different areas of the company had to be measured in different ways. Mr. Ira Hayes Jr., the president, wanted to provide his own incentives to encourage better performance by sales and production personnel. He gave the sales and production manager, individually, several long and enthusiastic pep talks on expanding their respective areas to higher levels. He further authorized an expenditure for $450,000 on a national advertising program.

Production in the plant reached the normal capacity of 1,875,000 units for the year 19X8. At the board meeting in early 19X9, the president remarked: "Back in the black again. The field people did a great job pushing sales up by almost 17%." (Exhibit 2 shows the data presented to the board at that meeting.)

The board was pleased with the results of their new plan and with its apparent immediate effectiveness. There was, in fact, much optimistic talk at the meeting about the effect that the new plan would have on 19X9 operations, especially because the special sales campaign would probably not be repeated regularly. The board voted to continue the plan for at least one more year. After

Exhibit 2
Pennywise Company—Operating Data for 19X8

Sales (1,406,250 units at $12)		$16,875,000
Cost of goods sold:		
Fixed costs	$ 6,000,000	
Variable costs (1,875,000 @ $4.80)	9,000,000	
	15,000,000	
Less: Ending inventory (468,750 units @ $8.00)	3,750,000	
		11,250,000
Gross margin on sales		5,625,000
Selling and administrative expenses:		
Fixed costs	1,200,000	
Variable costs (1,406,250 @ $2.40)	3,375,000	
		4,575,000
Operating profit before taxes and allowance for profit-sharing pool		1,050,000
Provision for profit-sharing pool		210,000
Operating profit before taxes		840,000
Provision for federal income taxes		420,000
Net income for the year 19X8		$ 420,000
Dividends to common stockholders ($0.20 per share)		$ 200,000

the vote, Mr. Hayes Jr. suggested that it would probably be good for employee relations if the board would announce soon when the pool for profit sharing would be distributed in cash to the employees because the dividend announcement had already been widely publicized. In an outer room, the sales manager, the production manager, and the controller were discussing the advantages and disadvantages of nepotism and of nonoperating management on the board of directors.

The questions following this paragraph are not designed to limit your discussion or specifically direct your analysis. Nor is there any particular significance to the order in which they are listed. You will find it worthwhile to answer the first one first because it may provide some clue as to how you might proceed. It is probably inefficient to answer each of the questions directly and in order because some are interrelated, but you may want to incorporate some comments about each of them in your answer.

1. What is the company's break-even point?
2. What is the company's system for implementing the management functions of planning and control?
3. Are profits likely to continue?
4. Has the profit-sharing plan contributed to efficiency? to cost reduction? to a return to profitable operations?
5. Should the board announce a cash distribution to employees relatively soon?

13-55 Determining product costs Renata Tomato Company processes and cans tomato paste. The company has the capability to can whole tomatoes as well, but has not done so for about a year because of lack of profitability. The production manager and controller were recently discussing the production budget for the next several months. They agreed, on the basis of the information in the schedule on page 586, that the firm should continue to process only tomato paste. The firm has the capacity to process 5,000,000 pounds of tomatoes per month, whether for canning whole or making into paste.

	Whole Tomatoes	Tomato Paste
Selling price per case	$6.00	$5.80
Variable costs:		
Tomatoes[a]	3.10	2.00
Direct labor	0.90	1.00
Variable overhead	1.80	2.00
Packaging	0.52	0.60
Total variable costs	6.32	5.60
Contribution margin	($0.32)	$0.20

[a] Whole tomatoes must be grade A tomatoes, which cost 15.5¢ per pound.

Paste is made from grade B tomatoes, which cost $0.08 per pound. There are 20 pounds of tomatoes in a case of whole tomatoes, 25 pounds in a case of paste.

A few days after the decision had been made to process only paste, the president received a call from a large tomato grower who offered to sell Renata as many pounds of tomatoes as it could use for the next six months. The price was to be $0.095 per pound, and the batches would be mixed A and B grades. The grower guaranteed that at least 40% of the tomatoes would be grade A.

The president told the production manager about the offer. The latter replied that it should cost $0.005 per pound to sort the tomatoes into the two grades, but that there would be no other additional costs if the offer were accepted. The firm's capacity to process 5,000,000 pounds per month would not be affected. The firm can sell all it can produce of either product.

The production and sales managers decided to investigate the probable effects of taking the offer. They agreed that it was profitable to can whole tomatoes if the price were much less than the current $0.155 per pound, but they were uncertain of the effects on the contribution margin of paste. They agreed to ask the controller to prepare a new analysis of relative profitability of the two products. The controller's analysis showed that paste was now a losing proposition, while whole tomatoes were extremely profitable. The controller's analysis showed the cost of tomatoes for both products at $0.10 per pound, the purchase price and additional sorting costs.

	Whole Tomatoes	Tomato Paste
Selling price per case	$6.00	$5.80
Variable costs:		
Tomatoes	2.00	2.50
Other variable costs	3.22	3.60
Total variable costs	5.22	6.10
Contribution margin	$0.78	($0.30)

The production manager and sales manager wondered about the wisdom of using the $0.10 per pound cost of tomatoes for both products. "After all," said the sales manager, "aren't we paying more for the grade A tomatoes and less for the grade B? It seems unreasonable to say that they cost the same." The controller said that other methods were possible, suggesting that the costs could also be assigned based on the ratios of costs of buying tomatoes already sorted. "If we did it that way," he said, "buying 2,000,000 pounds of grade A tomatoes at $0.155 would cost $310,000. The 3,000,000 grade B tomatoes would cost $240,000 at $0.08. The total cost is $550,000. The cost of grade B is thus about 43.6% of the total. So we could assign $218,000 ($500,000 × 43.6%) to the grade B tomatoes in the package deal. That gives a cost per pound of $0.07267. Doing the same with the grade A produce gives $0.141 per pound."

At this point the president entered the room and commented that it seemed to him that the firm was buying $240,000 worth of grade B tomatoes at $0.08 per pound and the rest of the purchase and sorting costs should be assigned to the grade A tomatoes. "That gives $260,000 to the grade A ($500,000 − $240,000), which is $0.13 per pound. Isn't that best?"

Required
1. Determine whether the firm should buy the unsorted tomatoes.
2. Discuss the appropriateness of the methods of determining the cost of tomatoes suggested by each of the managers and make a recommendation.

CHAPTER **14**

STANDARD COSTING: ABSORPTION AND VARIABLE

Chapter 12 showed how standards are used to help control costs. Chapter 13 introduced two product-costing methods: actual costing and normal costing. This chapter shows how standard costs are used in product costing. Under **standard costing,** inventories are valued at standard cost and variances appear on the income statement as expenses (or as negative expenses, if favorable). Large and medium-sized manufacturers use standard costing much more than actual or normal costing. An important reason is that standard costing integrates standard costs and variances into the company's records, so that variances are calculated as a normal part of the record-keeping process. It is wise to have as much information as possible captured directly in the accounts, because it is then easier to retrieve and more likely to be accurate.

Chapter 13 also introduced absorption costing—the product costing method required for external reporting. The per-unit cost under absorption costing includes a per-unit fixed cost, which earlier chapters have consistently shown to be unwise for planning and decision making. This chapter introduces an alternative to absorption costing, called **variable costing,** or **direct costing.** Variable costing excludes fixed production costs from inventory calculations and uses the familiar contribution margin format of the income statement. Variable costing is widely used for internal reporting.

STANDARD ABSORPTION COSTING

As described in Chapter 12, companies establish standard costs for materials, direct labor, and variable overhead. Under standard absorption costing, the firm also determines a **standard fixed overhead cost** per unit of product. The resulting *total* standard cost per unit is used to determine the cost of inventory and the cost of goods sold. Variances from standard, including the volume variance, are treated as expenses (or negative expenses, if favorable).

Let us begin with a simple situation where the company makes a single product. Later in this section we give an example of the additional step required to use standard absorption costing in a multiproduct firm that uses a single basis for applying its overhead costs. In a brief but separate section we illustrate the relevant differences in procedures when standard absorption costing is used by a multiproduct firm that also uses more than one basis to apply its overhead costs.

Chapter 12 covered the determination of standards for variable production costs, so the only new task in the simplest example is to develop a standard for fixed overhead. The concept of a predetermined overhead rate is useful here. Because it makes only one product, the company in this example can determine a standard fixed cost per unit by dividing total budgeted fixed manufacturing overhead by some number of units of product. (There is no need to use an *input* factor, such as labor hours or machine hours, because *all* hours are worked on the same kind of product.) Thus, if managers budget fixed manufacturing overhead of $4,000,000 for the year and production of 200,000 units, the standard fixed cost per unit is

$$\text{Standard fixed cost per unit} = \frac{\text{budgeted fixed overhead}}{\text{budgeted units of production}}$$

$$= \$4,000,000/200,000 = \$20$$

Exhibit 14-1 presents data for the SMP Company, which produces an automobile part. The company has standards for labor, material, and variable over-

Exhibit 14-1

SMP Company, Operating Data for 19X5

Production in units	110,000
Sales in units, at $80 each	90,000
Ending inventory in units	20,000
Actual production costs:	
Variable at $20 per unit	$2,200,000
Fixed	$3,200,000
Selling and administrative expenses:	
Variable at $5 per unit	$ 450,000
Fixed	$1,400,000
Standards and budgets:	
Budgeted fixed production costs	$3,000,000
Standard variable production costs	$20 per unit

(handwritten annotation: 200 000 unfav.)

head. To simplify the situation, we will group all the standard variable costs into a single per-unit variable cost. Because you have already learned to analyze variances in variable costs, we will further assume that variable costs were incurred as budgeted (that is, that there were no variances).

Notice that the variable selling and administrative expenses are incurred based on units sold, not units produced. To analyze the year's activity and prepare an income statement, we need to know the budget variance and volume variance for fixed overhead. There is a $200,000 unfavorable budget variance because actual fixed overhead ($3,200,000) exceeded the budget ($3,000,000). (Recall from Chapter 12 that some companies cannot separate actual fixed overhead from actual variable overhead and so cannot calculate the fixed overhead budget variance.) But to determine the volume variance, we must first decide upon a standard cost.

Calculating a Standard Fixed Cost

The standard fixed cost per unit depends, as does the predetermined overhead rate, on two things: (1) the choice of a *measure* of activity (number of units, direct labor hours, or machine hours, for example) and (2) a *level* of activity (budgeted units or hours, for example). Since we are dealing with a single-product firm, the most obvious measure of activity is units of product, but a level of activity to be used in the calculation must also be chosen.

Under normal costing, the predetermined overhead rate is based on budgeted activity for the coming year. That same level of activity could be used to establish the standard cost per unit, but two other levels are commonly used: normal activity (or normal capacity) and practical capacity.

Normal activity (normal capacity) is the average expected activity over the coming two or more years. Two years is the minimum, four or five years the maximum. The objective of using this activity level is to have a standard fixed cost that reflects the firm's expected long-term fixed costs, not the costs for a single year.

Practical capacity is the maximum level of activity the company can achieve given the usual interruptions. Events such as strikes or severe shortages of materials are not considered "usual." As with budgeted and normal activity, the measure of volume might be units of product, direct labor hours, or something else. Standard costs based on practical capacity reflect the lowest reasonable long-term average fixed cost.

Let's assume that late in 19X4 the managers of SMP decided to set the standard per-unit fixed cost using normal capacity of 100,000 units. The standard is $30 per unit.

$$\frac{\text{Standard fixed}}{\text{cost per unit}} = \frac{\text{budgeted fixed overhead}}{\text{normal capacity}}$$

$$= \$3,000,000/100,000 = \$30 \text{ per unit}$$

The total standard cost per unit is $50, consisting of the $20 standard variable cost per unit and the $30 standard fixed cost per unit. We shall use this standard fixed cost to determine variances, and, if variances are not significant, the standard will also be used in external financial statements.

Fixed Overhead Variances

The *total* fixed overhead variance (misapplied overhead) is $100,000, computed as follows.

Total actual fixed overhead	$3,200,000
Applied fixed overhead (110,000 × $30)	3,300,000
Misapplied overhead, overapplied	$ 100,000

Since SMP Company incurred variable production costs equal to standard costs for 19X5, there are no other variances.

As with normal costing, the volume variance under standard costing is budgeted fixed overhead minus applied fixed overhead, and the budget variance is actual fixed overhead minus budgeted fixed overhead Below is an analysis of the fixed overhead variances using the diagram format introduced in Chapter 12.

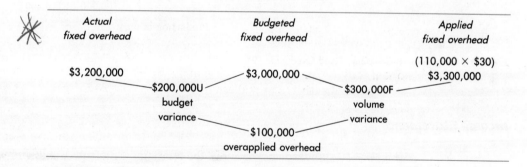

You already knew there was a $200,000 unfavorable budget variance. You should have expected a favorable volume variance because actual production was greater than the production level used to establish the standard fixed cost per unit. The favorable volume variance of $300,000 could also be calculated as follows.

$$\text{Volume variance} = \begin{pmatrix} \text{actual} \\ \text{units} \\ \text{produced} \end{pmatrix} - \begin{pmatrix} \text{units at} \\ \text{normal} \\ \text{capacity} \end{pmatrix} \times \begin{array}{c} \text{standard} \\ \text{fixed cost} \\ \text{per unit} \end{array}$$

$$= (110,000 - 100,000) \times \$30$$

$$= \$300,000 \text{ favorable}$$

Figure 14-1 provides a graphical analysis of the facts in the example.

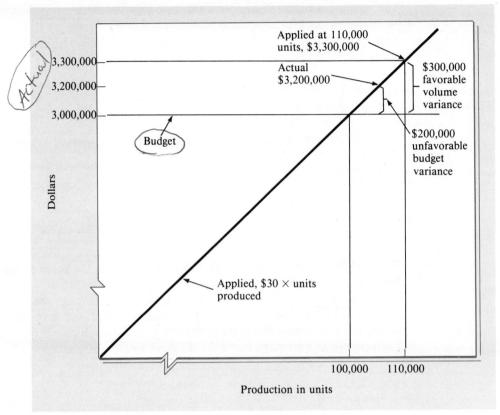

Figure 14-1   SMP Company, Fixed Overhead, 19X5

Income Statements

Using the $50 standard cost per unit, the operating data from Exhibit 14-1, and the fixed overhead variances calculated above, we can prepare an income statement for SMP Company for 19X5. Exhibit 14-2 shows the statement. As you can see, the format is similar to those used for actual and normal absorption costing in Chapter 13, which in turn were based on the typical presentation used in financial accounting. That is, cost of sales is computed by adding the beginning inventory and the additional costs for the year, and then subtracting the ending inventory.

Notice that the variable production costs and fixed production costs added to the beginning inventory are at standard cost per unit multiplied by unit production. *Under standard costing, all amounts in the calculation of standard cost of goods are the standard cost per unit multiplied by the number of units.* This is true for the beginning inventory, applied production costs, cost of goods available for sale, and standard cost of goods sold. Therefore, if the standard cost of units in the beginning inventory is the same as the standard cost for the current year, *standard cost of sales is simply the per-unit standard cost multiplied by the number of units*

Exhibit 14-2
SMP Company, Income Statement for 19X5

Sales (90,000 × $80)		$7,200,000
Standard cost of sales:		
Beginning inventory	$ 0	
Variable production costs (110,000 × $20)	2,200,000	
Applied fixed production costs (110,000 × $30)	3,300,000	
Cost of goods available (110,000 × $50)	5,500,000	
Ending inventory (20,000 × $50)	1,000,000	
Standard cost of goods sold (90,000 × $50)		4,500,000
Standard gross margin		2,700,000
Variances:		
Fixed manufacturing cost budget variance	200,000U	
Volume variance	300,000F	100,000F
Actual gross margin		2,800,000
Selling and administrative expenses		1,850,000[a]
Income		$ 950,000

[a] Fixed costs of $1,400,000 plus variable costs of $450,000 (90,000 × $5).

sold. When this is the case, as it is in our example, there is no need to show the details of the section for the standard cost of sales, and an income statement such as the one in Exhibit 14-3 could also be used. The placement of variances is a matter of choice. Some prefer to show them as adjustments to standard cost of goods sold, others as adjustments to standard gross margin. You should see that the final results for actual gross margin and income will be the same regardless of where the variances appear in the statement.

Before we show how standard fixed costs are used in a multiproduct firm, complete the review problem on page 594 to make sure you understand the basics of standard absorption costing in a single-product firm.

Variances are Negative if favourable

Exhibit 14-3
SMP Company, Income Statement for 19X5 (Alternative)

Sales		$7,200,000
Cost of sales:		
Standard cost of sales (90,000 × $50)	$4,500,000	
Variances:		
Fixed manufacturing cost budget variance	200,000U	
Volume variance	300,000F	
Cost of sales		4,400,000
Actual gross margin		2,800,000
Selling and administrative expenses		1,850,000
Income		$ 950,000

If F decrease cost of sales if U inc. CoS.

Review Problem

Assume that SMP Company continued to use the same standard costs for 19X6. Its operating data for 19X6 were as follows.

Production, in units	95,000
Sales, in units, at $80 each	100,000
Ending inventory, in units	15,000
Actual production costs:	
Variable at $20 per unit	$1,900,000
Fixed	$2,950,000
Selling and administrative expenses:	
Variable at $5 per unit	$ 500,000
Fixed	$1,400,000
Standard variable production cost	$20 per unit
Budgeted fixed production costs	$3,000,000

Prepare income statements for 19X6, using the formats shown in Exhibits 14-2 and 14-3. The solution appears in Exhibit 14-4.

Multiple Products

Standard costing is especially popular with firms that make several similar products. It can also be used by companies that make several products of different design. So long as the products are relatively standard, even a job-order firm can use standard costs. The prerequisite for using standard costs is the ability to develop reasonable standards for each input factor. Consider Richards Company, which makes two models of tables, Model 345 and Model 788. Through engineering studies the company has determined that the standard material and labor costs for making each model are as follows.

	Model 345	Model 788
Standard material cost	$20	$60
Standard labor cost, at a standard rate of $10 per hour:		
3 hours × $10	$30	
5 hours × $10		$50

Richards budgets factory overhead with a formula that was developed using regression analysis (see Chapter 3). The equation is

$$\text{Annual factory overhead} = \$2,000,000 + (\$8 \times \text{direct labor hours})$$

Richards can establish the standard variable overhead cost per unit of *each model* simply by multiplying the $8 variable overhead rate by the number of labor hours per unit for that model—a standard of $24 ($8 × 3 hours) for Model 345, and of

Exhibit 14-4

SMP Company, Income Statement for 19X6

Sales (100,000 × $80)		$8,000,000
Standard cost of sales:		
Beginning inventory (from Exhibit 14-2)	$1,000,000	
Variable production costs (95,000 × $20)	1,900,000	
Applied fixed production costs (95,000 × $30)	2,850,000	
Cost of goods available (115,000 × $50)	5,750,000	
Ending inventory (15,000 × $50)	750,000	
Standard cost of goods sold (100,000 × $50)		5,000,000
Standard gross margin		3,000,000
Variances:		
Fixed manufacturing cost budget variance	50,000F	
Volume variance	150,000U	100,000U
Actual gross margin		2,900,000
Selling and administrative expenses		1,900,000[a]
Income		$1,000,000

Income Statement for 19X6, Alternative Format

Sales (100,000 × $80)		$8,000,000
Cost of sales:		
Standard cost of sales (100,000 × $50)	$5,000,000	
Variances:		
Fixed manufacturing cost budget variance	50,000F	
Volume variance	150,000U	
Cost of sales		5,100,000
Actual gross margin		2,900,000
Selling and administrative expenses		1,900,000
Income		$1,000,000

Calculation of Variances

Actual fixed overhead	Budgeted fixed overhead	Applied fixed overhead
		(95,000 × $30)
$2,950,000	$3,000,000	$2,850,000

$50,000F budget variance $150,000U volume variance

$100,000 underapplied overhead

[a] Fixed costs of $1,400,000 plus variable costs of $500,000 (100,000 × $5).

$40 ($8 × 5 hours) for Model 788. Establishing a standard *fixed* overhead cost for each model of table requires not only a knowledge of the number of labor hours worked on each table but also a predetermined overhead rate per labor hour.

Suppose that, in this case, Richards uses its normal capacity of 500,000 labor hours to set the predetermined overhead rate. The predetermined overhead rate for fixed overhead is $4 ($2,000,000/500,000). Using the $4 rate per direct labor hour, the total standard cost for each model is

	Model 345	Model 788
Standard material cost	$20	$ 60
Standard labor cost, at the standard labor rate of $10 per hour		
3 hours × $10	30	
5 hours × $10		50
Standard variable overhead, at the standard rate of $8 per hour		
3 hours × $8	24	
5 hours × $8		40
Standard fixed overhead, at the standard rate of $4 per hour		
3 hours × $4	12	
5 hours × $4	—	20
Total standard cost per unit	$86	$170

Richards will use these standard costs for reporting inventory and cost of goods sold, as well as for analyzing variances. Suppose the firm makes 90,000 units of Model 345 and 42,000 units of Model 788. Total fixed overhead applied and the volume variance are

Total fixed overhead applied:	
Model 345 (90,000 units × $12 standard fixed cost per unit)	$1,080,000
Model 788 (42,000 units × $20 standard fixed cost per unit)	840,000
Total applied fixed overhead	1,920,000
Budgeted fixed overhead	2,000,000
Volume variance, unfavorable	$ 80,000

Whether Richards could also determine a budget variance for fixed overhead depends on whether it can separate fixed and variable costs as they are incurred.

Comparison of Standard and Normal Costing

Although the normal-costing concept of a predetermined overhead rate is related to the idea of a standard fixed cost per unit, the results reported under the two types of costing systems are not the same. Remember that, under normal costing, overhead is applied on the basis of the actual use of the input factor. In a standard costing system, overhead is applied on the basis of the number of units produced. Let us see how the results would differ in the case of Richards Company, using as an example the production activity given in the preceding section.

In the prior analysis, the volume variance was calculated by applying the standard fixed overhead cost per unit: this cost was based on the standard number of labor hours per unit. The actual number of hours worked on each type of product was not needed. But assume that to achieve the production given above the firm had to work 280,000 hours making Model 345 tables and 205,000 hours making Model 788 tables, for a total of 485,000 hours. If the firm had been using normal costing with a predetermined fixed overhead rate of $4 per hour (the same as the rate used to determine the standard cost per unit), the total fixed overhead applied for the year would have been $1,940,000 (485,000 actual hours × $4 per hour), or $20,000 more than the overhead applied under standard costing ($1,920,000). Exhibit 14-5 shows these differences in overhead application and how they affect the reported volume variance.

Exhibit 14-5
Comparison of Normal and Standard Costing

Normal Costing	
Total *actual* hours worked:	
Model 345	280,000
Model 788	205,000
Total actual hours	485,000
Predetermined overhead rate	$4
Total fixed overhead applied	$1,940,000
Budgeted fixed overhead	2,000,000
Volume variance—unfavorable	$ 60,000
Standard Costing	
Total *standard* hours for output level achieved:	
Model 345 (90,000 units × 3 hours per unit)	270,000
Model 788 (42,000 units × 5 hours per unit)	210,000
Total standard hours	480,000
Predetermined overhead rate	$4
Total fixed overhead applied equals the amount determined using units of product (see page 596)	$1,920,000
Budgeted fixed overhead	2,000,000
Volume variance—unfavorable	$ 80,000

Unless standard hours equal actual hours, normal costing and standard costing give different volume variances. The two systems will always give the same *budget* variance, because the budget variance is simply actual cost minus budgeted cost. But different volume variances arise because different amounts of fixed overhead are *applied* under the two methods. The difference in volume variances serves to remind you of what we said when the concept of a volume variance was introduced in Chapter 13: the variance has little or no economic significance and reflects only the effect of using some activity level other than the actual to determine the overhead application rate.

We have presented several costing methods in this and previous chapters. The table below summarizes the similarities and differences among the three methods, actual costing, normal costing, and standard costing, showing the basis for determining *inventoriable* cost of a unit of product.

Cost Element	Actual Costing	Normal Costing	Standard Costing
Materials	actual cost	actual cost	standard cost
Direct labor	actual cost	actual cost	standard cost
Overhead	actual cost	applied cost	standard cost
	(actual input ×	(actual input ×	(standard input ×
	actual rate)	predetermined rate)	predetermined rate)

The table shows that actual costing and normal costing differ only in the treatment of overhead, as explained in Chapter 13. Standard costing differs from both of the other methods in using standard rather than actual costs. As shown earlier, the only difference between standard costing and normal costing with respect to overhead is that applied overhead under standard costing is based on standard quantities of the input factor (or, what amounts to the same thing, on actual unit production), while overhead applied under normal costing is based on the actual quantities of input factors.

Multiple Overhead Application Bases

As discussed in Chapter 13, a firm can sometimes benefit from using different bases to apply different pools of overhead costs. Multiple application bases can be used with standard absorption costing. Suppose Tronix Company makes two models of electronic instruments and has two major types of overhead. The pool of overhead costs related to direct labor is budgeted at $3,000,000; that related to materials is budgeted at $500,000. Using the procedures illustrated earlier (pages 594–600) Tronix determined a rate of $4 per direct labor hour for applying its labor-based overhead pool. It wants to apply material-related overhead on the basis of the number of component parts in its products.

As when using labor or machine time to apply overhead, the first step in determining the application rate is to select some level of the activity—in this case, use of component parts. Tronix bases its rate on the total number of component parts budgeted for use during a year and computes its application rate as below.

	Portable Model	Table Model
Number of component parts	100	200
Budgeted production	6,000	2,000
Total budgeted use of components	600,000	400,000
Overhead rate per component used on either model	$500,000/1,000,000 = $0.50	

Assuming that the portable and table models require eight and 12 hours of direct labor, respectively, the standard *overhead* cost per unit of each model is

	Portable Model	Table Model
Material-related overhead:		
100 components at $0.50	$50	
200 components at $0.50		$100
Labor-related overhead:		
8 hours at $4 per hour	32	
12 hours at $4 per hour		48
Total standard overhead cost	$82	$148

Tronix will combine the standard overhead costs of $82 and $148 with the standard costs of other inputs for each model to get a total standard cost per unit. Its accounting system will collect data on actual and applied overhead for each overhead pool, and Tronix will calculate misapplied overhead and budget and volume variances for each pool.

VARIABLE COSTING

Thus far, we have discussed only absorption costing systems. Such systems are required for financial reporting and for income tax purposes and are often used, as we mentioned earlier, for internal purposes also. However, throughout this book we have recommended internal reports using the contribution margin format, which treats all fixed costs as period costs. When this approach is applied to product costing, the result is called *variable costing*.

Variable costing excludes fixed production costs from the unit costs of inventories, and treats *all* fixed costs as expenses in the period incurred. It is possible—and we think preferable—to use variable costing for internal reports. The flow of manufacturing costs using variable costing can easily be shown by a slight variation of the cost-flow figure presented in Chapter 13. Figure 14-2 (page 600) depicts the difference in cost flows under variable and absorption costing systems.

Exhibit 14-6 (page 600) shows how the same operating data for 19X5 and 19X6 that were presented earlier for SMP Company would show in income statements using standard variable costing. Because there are no variable cost variances, the results using standard variable costing are the same as they would be if the firm used actual variable costing.

If you had been given exactly the same information about SMP Company in an earlier chapter, say Chapter 3, you would probably have prepared income statements like those in Exhibit 14-7 on page 601.

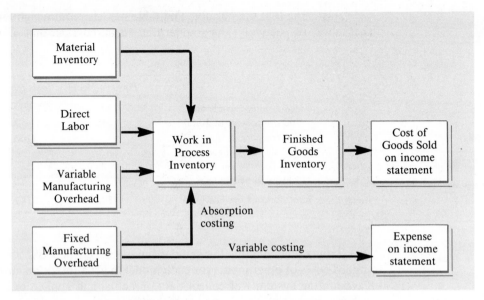

Figure 14-2   Flow of Costs in a Manufacturing Firm

Exhibit 14-6
SMP Company, Income Statements—Standard Variable Costing

	19X5	19X6
Sales	$7,200,000	$8,000,000
Standard variable cost of sales:		
Beginning inventory (0 × $20, 20,000 × $20)	0	400,000
Variable production costs:		
110,000 × $20	2,200,000	
95,000 × $20		1,900,000
Cost of goods available	2,200,000	2,300,000
Ending inventory:		
20,000 × $20	400,000	
15,000 × $20		300,000
Standard variable cost of sales:		
90,000 × $20	1,800,000	
100,000 × $20		2,000,000
Standard variable manufacturing margin at $60	5,400,000	6,000,000
Variable selling and administrative expenses ($5 per unit sold)	450,000	500,000
Contribution margin at $55	4,950,000	5,500,000
Fixed costs:		
Budgeted fixed production costs	3,000,000	3,000,000
Fixed production cost budget variance	200,000U	50,000F
Selling and administrative expenses	1,400,000	1,400,000
Total fixed costs	4,600,000	4,350,000
Profit	$ 350,000	$1,150,000

Exhibit 14-7

SMP Company, Income Statements—Variable Costing

	19X5	19X6
Sales:		
90,000 × $80	$7,200,000	
100,000 × $80		$8,000,000
Variable costs:		
Manufacturing costs:		
90,000 × $20	1,800,000	
100,000 × $20		2,000,000
Selling and administrative:		
90,000 × $5	450,000	
100,000 × $5		500,000
Total variable costs at $25	2,250,000	2,500,000
Contribution margin	4,950,000	5,500,000
Fixed costs:		
Production	3,200,000	2,950,000
Selling and administrative	1,400,000	1,400,000
Total fixed costs	4,600,000	4,350,000
Profit	$ 350,000	$1,150,000

The income statements in Exhibit 14-6 only *appear* to be different from and more complex than statements you have seen in earlier chapters, but the only real difference is in the amount of detail on cost of sales. Whether you use the shortened format of Exhibit 14-7 or the expanded format of Exhibit 14-6, the incomes for the two years are the same and reflect an expensing of fixed costs in the year incurred. Without knowing it, you have been preparing variable costing income statements since Chapter 3.

Comparing Variable and Absorption Costing Results

Compare the results under variable costing with the results under absorption costing for the same economic activity (see Exhibits 14-2 and 14-4). Absorption costing income is higher than variable costing income for 19X5 and lower for 19X6. Can you explain why this is so? Of course you can! Absorption costing income in 19X5 is higher because absorption costing transfers some of the fixed costs of 19X5 into 19X6 as part of the cost of the ending inventory of 20,000 units. Absorption costing income in 19X6 is lower because a similar shift of 19X6 costs (to 19X7) was smaller (fixed costs in an ending inventory of only 15,000 units) than the amount of fixed costs transferred in from 19X5.

In more general terms, the differences are traceable to the relationship between production and sales. Subject to a few technicalities, *when production exceeds sales, so that ending inventory is greater than beginning inventory, ab-*

sorption costing gives a higher income than variable costing. When sales exceed production, absorption costing gives a lower income than variable costing. The difference in incomes is due entirely to the fixed costs that are carried forward in inventory under absorption costing. Such costs are shown on the balance sheet as inventory and are expensed when the goods are sold. Exhibit 14-8 shows the amounts of fixed production costs expensed in each year under the two approaches, along with a reconciliation of the incomes.

Exhibit 14-8
Reconciliation of Incomes—Variable and Absorption Costing

	19X5	19X6
Comparison of reported income:		
Variable costing (Exhibit 14-6)	$ 350,000	$1,150,000
Absorption costing (Exhibits 14-2 and 14-4)	950,000	1,000,000
Difference to be explained	($ 600,000)	$ 150,000
Explanation of income difference:		
Fixed production costs in beginning inventory		
(transferred from prior year):		
0 units × $30	$ 0	
20,000 units × $30		$ 600,000
Fixed production costs incurred during the year	3,200,000	2,950,000
	3,200,000	3,550,000
Less fixed production costs in ending inventory		
(being transferred to a future year):		
20,000 units × $30	600,000	
15,000 units × $30		450,000
Total fixed costs expensed under absorption costing for the year	2,600,000	3,100,000
Total fixed costs expensed under variable costing— equal to total fixed costs incurred	3,200,000	2,950,000
Difference between fixed costs incurred and expensed for the year	($ 600,000)	$ 150,000

If the standard fixed cost *per unit* does not change from year to year, the difference between absorption costing income and income under variable costing can be computed directly by multiplying the standard fixed cost per unit by the change in units in inventory. Thus, we could have made the reconciliation shown in Exhibit 14-8 simply by using the formula

$$
\begin{array}{c}
\text{Difference} \\
\text{in} \\
\text{incomes}
\end{array}
=
\left(
\begin{array}{c}
\text{units in} \\
\text{beginning} \\
\text{inventory}
\end{array}
-
\begin{array}{c}
\text{units in} \\
\text{ending} \\
\text{inventory}
\end{array}
\right)
\times
\begin{array}{c}
\text{standard} \\
\text{fixed cost} \\
\text{per unit}
\end{array}
$$

$$
\begin{array}{c}
\text{19X5} \\
\text{Difference}
\end{array}
= \quad (0 \quad - \quad 20{,}000) \quad \times \quad \$30 = (\$600{,}000)
$$

$$
\begin{array}{c}
\text{19X6} \\
\text{Difference}
\end{array}
= \quad (20{,}000 \quad - \quad 15{,}000) \quad \times \quad \$30 = \$150{,}000
$$

Variable Cost Variances

Under variable costing, the only fixed cost variance is the budget variance. Variable cost variances are reported in essentially the same way we have reported fixed cost variances. Suppose that SMP had actually incurred $1,950,000 variable production costs in 19X6, which is $50,000 over the standard for 95,000 units. The variable costing income statement for 19X6 appears as follows, using the data from Exhibit 14-6.

Sales	$8,000,000
Standard variable cost of sales	2,000,000
Standard variable manufacturing margin	6,000,000
Less *variable* cost variances	50,000U
Actual variable manufacturing margin	5,950,000
Variable selling and administrative expenses	500,000
Contribution margin	5,450,000
Fixed costs:	
Budgeted fixed production costs	3,000,000
Fixed production cost budget variance	50,000F
Selling and administrative expenses	1,400,000
Total fixed costs	4,350,000
Income	$1,100,000

Income here is $50,000 less than in Exhibit 14-6 only because we have assumed $50,000 unfavorable variable cost variances.

EVALUATION OF METHODS

We have already stated our belief that variable costing is superior to absorption costing for internal reporting purposes. Not all managers, whether accountants or others, agree with our position. It seems evident, however, that absorption costing is used for internal reporting primarily because it is required for external reporting, so that preparing other reports has some incremental cost.

External Reporting

Although arguments about the suitability of either method for external reporting are not germane to internal reporting, we mention some here to alert you to the principal justifications offered for absorption costing.[1]

[1] For income tax reporting, the tax law, which can be extraordinarily complex, governs the determination of inventory and related costs of sales. We might point out that in a growing economy, inventories and costs will rise. Companies probably pay more taxes under absorption costing than they would under variable costing, which could be one reason why the government requires absorption costing.

The *matching concept,* to which you were introduced in financial accounting, holds that costs must be matched against related revenues or against the revenues of the periods that have benefited from the costs. As an example, under this concept, the cost of fixed assets is assigned, through depreciation, to the years of the life of the fixed asset.

Fixed production costs "benefit" the firm in the sense that few modern firms could produce anything at all without the resources that give rise to such costs. For example, *having* a factory building and equipment entails depreciation, property taxes, some level of maintenance, and other fixed costs. Similarly, many salaried factory personnel (such as managers and supervisors) are essential to producing goods. Thus, one could argue, based on the matching concept, that fixed production costs should not be expensed until goods are sold. This argument is made by those favoring absorption costing.

Advocates of variable costing for financial reporting purposes offer a counterargument. They say that fixed production costs benefit production, but production *as a whole,* rather than the production of any single unit. In other words, fixed costs prove the *capacity* to produce, regardless of whether, or to what extent, the capacity is used. Thus, once the firm is in business and able to produce goods, fixed production costs are not needed for *this* or *that* unit in one or another period, only for production as a whole. Accordingly, the argument continues, considering fixed costs on a per-unit basis is inappropriate because fixed costs cannot be identified with individual units; they are *common* to all units produced. Controversy about the most appropriate method for external reporting purposes has continued for many years, and we do not expect it to stop in the foreseeable future.

Internal Reporting

Variable costing has an important advantage for internal reporting. It presents information in the form that is most useful for managers—the form needed for VCP analysis.

Separating fixed and variable costs and reporting contribution margin enable managers to perform the VCP analysis that cannot be done working directly with absorption costing statements. Managers cannot predict income for future periods using an absorption costing income statement. There are two reasons: (1) they must predict not only sales for the future period, but also production, and (2) they must break down the cost figures into their fixed and variable components (i.e., managers must *develop* the information that is already *provided* by variable costing).

With variable costing, production has no influence on income. Managers can concentrate on the effects of changes in sales without having to allow for production. If sales fall from one period to another, variable costing income will also fall. Using absorption costing, income might well rise in a period of falling sales if production is a good deal higher than sales. Most managers are accustomed to thinking of sales, not production, as the income-generating activity of the firm. Therefore, variable costing is more in tune with a manager's basic understanding of income than is absorption costing.

Variable costing offers another significant advantage because its income figure is not affected by production. Variable costing income represents an equilibrium in the sense that it shows what the company would earn, per period, in the long run if sales continue at the same level. Absorption costing income can be misleadingly high when production exceeds sales because the income level cannot be maintained at the same level of sales. (You should not produce indefinitely in excess of sales unless sales are rising.)

A conversation reported in a symposium graphically illustrates this point. One of the speakers, a manager of a large international CPA firm, told the group about a conversation with the vice president of manufacturing of a client company. The vice president had said that the factory was running full tilt even though sales were bad. When the speaker asked why, the vice president stated that the factory had underabsorbed overhead for the first part of the year and received a directive from corporate headquarters to absorb more overhead and "have a profitable year." The speaker inquired what was being done with the unsold goods and the vice president responded, "Oh, we rented a warehouse down the street. . . ."[2]

Of course, absorption costing requires allocating fixed costs to units of product. We have consistently argued that allocations are unwise for managerial purposes because they obscure VCP relationships, can lead to poor decisions, and are not helpful in control and performance evaluation. Absorption costing can therefore be criticized because it requires allocations.

In summary, the information that *managers* need is provided much more directly by variable costing statements. Where absorption costing is used, managers must recast statements in order to perform many of the analyses needed to plan, make decisions, control, and evaluate performance.

Advocates of absorption costing argue that variable costing might prompt managers to take a short-run approach to problems when a long-run approach is more desirable. They acknowledge the usefulness of variable costing information for specific short-run decisions (like accepting special orders), but argue that, in the long run, concentrating on variable costs can be harmful. One major objection is that if fixed costs are not considered to be costs of product, managers might set prices too low to cover fixed costs and earn profits. They argue that managers who become accustomed to variable costing reports could come to ignore the fixed costs that might be the great bulk of production costs. In short, advocates of absorption costing argue that it is useful because it alerts managers to the need to cover both fixed and variable costs.

There are two counterarguments to the position just described. One is that even absorption costing does not include *all* costs as product costs. Selling and administrative costs are excluded from inventory under both costing methods, and in many cases these costs exceed production costs. The other counterargu-

---

[2] Robert D'Amore, "Just-in-Time Systems," in *Cost Accounting, Robotics, and the New Manufacturing Environment,* ed. Robert Capettini and Donald K. Clancy (Sarasota, FL: American Accounting Association, 1987), 8.4.

ment is that it is unnecessary to allocate fixed costs to units in setting prices when the firm faces competition and cannot charge any price it chooses. For example, suppose a firm *could* analyze the expected volume-price relationships as suggested in Chapter 4 and select the best combination of price and expected volume. If a firm has discretion over prices and can expect to sell about the same volume no matter what price is charged, there is no harm in using a total cost per unit to set prices. However, firms in these circumstances are much less common than firms that face competition and therefore cannot charge any price they wish.

If absorption costing is to be used, it seems better to use a standard fixed cost per unit rather than an actual fixed cost per unit. When a standard fixed cost is used, the income effects of production's being different from sales are isolated in the volume variance. Moreover, the use of standard fixed costs per unit would help to reduce the likelihood of a manager's changing prices at frequent intervals just because total cost per unit is changing as production changes.

SUMMARY

Standard costing is a method of product costing that uses standard costs instead of actual or normal costs. One major benefit of standard costing is that it ties the accounting records to the variances that are used for control purposes. Another benefit is that it simplifies recordkeeping for a firm that makes several products.

Standard absorption costing requires the calculation of a standard fixed cost per unit. Like normal costing, standard absorption costing permits calculation of volume and overhead budget variances. But the volume variance, under either approach, is of little economic significance. Setting a standard fixed cost per unit requires selecting a level of activity, the most common of which are normal activity and practical capacity. The magnitude, and direction of the volume variance depend on the activity level chosen for setting the standard. Standard absorption costing can be used by multiproduct firms, including those that use more than one basis to apply overhead costs.

The required use of absorption costing for external reporting has contributed to the internal distribution of, and the need for managers to understand, absorption costing reports. For internal purposes, some firms use standard variable costing or actual variable costing, both of which consider only variable production costs as product costs and treat fixed manufacturing costs as expenses. Variable costing is compatible with both VCP analysis and the contribution margin format of the income statement.

KEY TERMS

normal activity (capacity)
practical capacity
standard costing

standard fixed overhead cost per unit
variable (direct) costing

KEY FORMULAS

$$\text{Standard fixed cost per unit} = \frac{\text{budgeted fixed overhead}}{\text{units of production}}$$

$$\text{Volume variance—standard costing} = \left(\begin{array}{c}\text{actual} \\ \text{units} \\ \text{produced}\end{array} - \begin{array}{c}\text{units at} \\ \text{selected} \\ \text{capacity}\end{array}\right) \times \begin{array}{c}\text{standard} \\ \text{fixed cost} \\ \text{per unit}\end{array}$$

REVIEW PROBLEM

In 19X7, SMP Company again used a $20 standard variable cost and $30 standard fixed cost based on $3,000,000 and 100,000 units. SMP produced 112,000 units and sold 102,000. It incurred all manufacturing costs as expected. Selling and administrative expenses were again $5 variable per unit and $1,400,000 fixed.

Required
1. Prepare an income statement using absorption costing.
2. Prepare an income statement using variable costing.

Answer to Review Problem

1.

SMP Company, 19X7 Income Statement—Absorption Costing

Sales (102,000 × $80)		$8,160,000
Standard cost of sales:		
Beginning inventory (15,000 × $50)	$ 750,000	
Variable production costs (112,000 × $20)	2,240,000	
Fixed production costs (112,000 × $30)	3,360,000	
Cost of goods available (127,000 × $50)	6,350,000	
Ending inventory (25,000 × $50)	1,250,000	
Standard cost of goods sold (102,000 × $50)		5,100,000
Standard gross margin		3,060,000
Fixed cost volume variance, favorable		360,000
Actual gross margin		3,420,000
Selling and administrative expenses		1,910,000
Profit		$1,510,000

The volume variance can be computed in either of two ways. It is the difference between budgeted fixed production costs of $3,000,000 and applied fixed production costs of $3,360,000. Because applied costs exceeded budgeted costs, the variance is favorable. It is also the difference between the 112,000 units produced and the 100,000 units used to set the standard fixed cost, multiplied by the standard fixed cost (12,000 units × $30 = $360,000).

2.

SMP Company, 19X7 Income Statement—Variable Costing

Sales (102,000 × $80)		$8,160,000
Standard variable cost of sales:		
Beginning inventory (15,000 × $20)	$ 300,000	
Variable production costs (112,000 × $20)	2,240,000	
Cost of goods available (127,000 × $20)	2,540,000	
Ending inventory (25,000 × $20)	500,000	
Standard variable cost of sales (102,000 × $20)		2,040,000
Standard variable manufacturing margin		6,120,000
Variable selling and administrative expenses		510,000
Contribution margin		5,610,000
Fixed costs:		
Production	$3,000,000	
Selling and administrative expenses	1,400,000	4,400,000
Profit		$1,210,000

As explained in the chapter, the $300,000 difference in income under the two methods results because of the fixed overhead costs in the beginning and ending inventories under absorption costing. The beginning inventory of 15,000 units included fixed overhead costs of $450,000 (15,000 × $30 standard fixed cost per unit) carried forward from 19X6. The ending inventory of 25,000 units includes fixed overhead costs of $750,000 (25,000 × $30) being carried forward to 19X8. The $300,000 difference in income occurs because the fixed costs being carried forward *from* 19X7 ($750,000) are greater than those carried forward *to* 19X7 ($400,000). That is, the income difference results from the *increase in inventory* or, described another way, because 19X7 production (112,000 units) was greater than 19X7 sales (102,000 units).

ASSIGNMENT MATERIAL

Questions for Discussion

14-1 Variable and absorption costing "The trouble with variable costing is that I have to put all of the fixed costs on the income statement right away. With absorption costing I can put some of them into inventory where they belong and take care of them later when the products are sold." Discuss these statements critically.

14-2 Period costs – product costs The distinction between product costs and period costs is a major point of contention between the advocates of variable costing and those of absorption costing. Is the distinction important for decision making?

Exercises

14-3 Basic standard costing – absorption and variable Rath Company makes Zuds, a household cleaning product. Zuds sells for $15 per case and has a standard variable manufacturing cost of $5 per case. Fixed production costs are

$600,000 per month; fixed selling and administrative expenses $350,000 per month. The firm began March 19X1 with no inventories and had the following activity in March and April.

	March	April
Production in cases	120,000	90,000
Sales in cases	100,000	100,000

The president wants two sets of monthly income statements: one showing monthly income using variable costing, the other showing monthly income using absorption costing with normal activity of 100,000 cases per month used to set the standard fixed cost.

Required: Prepare income statements by month as the president requested. Use the format that shows the details of beginning and ending inventories and of production costs in the cost of goods sold section.

14-4 ***Standard costing income statements*** The following data pertain to the operations of Lindsey Corporation for 19X8.

Normal capacity	200 units
Practical capacity	300 units
Budgeted production	240 units
Actual production	250 units
Actual sales ($25 per unit)	240 units
Standard variable production cost per unit	$10
Fixed production costs—budgeted	$2,400

During 19X8 there were no variable cost variances and fixed costs incurred were equal to the budgeted amount. There were no beginning inventories and no selling, general, or administrative expenses.

Required
1. Determine the standard cost per unit assuming that standard fixed cost is based on (a) normal capacity, (b) practical capacity, and (c) budgeted production.
2. Prepare income statements for each of the three bases computed in item 1.

14-5 ***Basic absorption costing*** Perry Industries manufactures disk drives for microcomputers. Data related to its best-selling model, which is the only one made in its Bristol plant, appear below.

Production:	
April	12,000 units
May	8,000 units
Sales:	
April	8,000 units
May	11,000 units
Standard variable manufacturing cost	$125
Standard fixed manufacturing cost	75
Total standard manufacturing cost	$200

Perry has set its standard fixed manufacturing cost based on normal activity of 10,000 drives per month and budgeted fixed manufacturing costs of $750,000 per month. There was no inventory at the beginning of April. The drive sells for $300. Selling and general expenses are $350,000 per month. All manufacturing costs were incurred as expected (variable per unit and total fixed) in both months.

Required: Prepare standard absorption costing income statements for April and for May.

14-6 *Basic variable costing (continuation of 14-5)*   Using the data in the previous assignment, prepare standard variable costing income statements for Perry Industries for April and for May.

14-7 *Effect of measure of activity (extension of 14-5)*   The president of Perry Industries has heard that some companies use practical capacity as the basis for determining standard fixed manufacturing costs. He asks you to show him how using Perry's practical capacity of 15,000 drives per month would affect the income statements you prepared for 14-5.

Required: Prepare the income statements that the president wants. Comment on the differences between these statements and the ones you prepared for 14-5.

14-8 *Absorption costing*   TRS Company makes a cabinet that sells for $50. The standard variable manufacturing cost is $20, and the standard fixed manufacturing cost is $10, based on budgeted fixed costs of $1,000,000 and budgeted production of 100,000 units. During 19X6, the company produced 96,000 units and sold 90,000. All manufacturing costs were incurred as budgeted, variable per unit and fixed in total. Selling and administrative expenses were $1,350,000, all fixed. There were no beginning inventories.

Required: Prepare a standard absorption costing income statement.

14-9 *Variable costing (extension of 14-8)*   Prepare an income statement for TRS using variable costing.

14-10 *Standard fixed cost and volume variance*   The following data refer to the operations of Hinson Company for 19X8.

Normal capacity	240,000 units
Practical capacity	300,000 units
Actual production	250,000 units
Fixed costs—budgeted and actual	$600,000

Required
1. Compute the standard fixed cost per unit based on (a) normal capacity and (b) practical capacity.
2. Compute the volume variances for each of the methods given in item 1.

14-11 *Relationships*   For each of the following independent situations, fill in the missing data. In all cases, the standard fixed cost per unit is based on normal capacity of 10,000 units.

	(a) Standard Fixed Cost per Unit	(b) Total Budgeted Fixed Costs	(c) Actual Production	(d) Volume Variance (Favorable)
1.	$__	$____	8,000	$8,000
2.	$3	$____	____	$6,000
3.	$__	$40,000	8,000	$____
4.	$__	$30,000	____	($7,500)

14-12 **Effects of changes in production – standard variable costing** The following data relate to Elliot Pencil Company's best-selling model.

Sales (30,000 cases at $10)	$300,000
Production costs:	
Variable costs, standard and actual	$4 per case
Fixed, budgeted and actual	$150,000

The company has no beginning inventories and no selling and administrative expenses.

Required: Prepare income statements using standard variable costing assuming the firm produced (a) 30,000 cases and (b) 31,000 cases. Show the details of the cost of sales section of the income statements.

14-13 **Effects of change in production – standard absorption costing (extension of 14-12)**

Required: Assume that Elliot Pencil company uses standard absorption costing with a standard fixed cost per case of $5 based on normal activity of 30,000 cases. Prepare income statements assuming that production is (a) 30,000 cases and (b) 31,000 cases. Show details of cost of sales.

14-14 **"Now wait a minute here."** The title of this problem is the statement your boss made when you showed him the results of completing item 1 of this assignment.

Hownet makes panes for greenhouse windows, selling them for $10 each. Standard variable manufacturing cost is $2 and total fixed manufacturing costs are $60,000. Normal volume is 10,000 units, so that the standard fixed cost per unit is $6. Your boss had asked you to determine the firm's gross profit (after any production variances) from selling 10,000 units. The company treats all variances as adjustments to standard gross margin. Being conscientious, you decided to check your results by preparing income statements down to actual gross margin under each of the following cases. There are no beginning inventories.
1. Sales are 10,000 units, production is 10,000 units.
2. Sales are 10,000 units, production is 10,001 units.
3. Sales are 10,001 units, production is 10,001 units.
4. Sales are 9,999 units, production is 10,001 units.

Required
1. Prepare the income statements.
2. Explain why your boss gave the response he did.
3. Tell your boss why the results came out as they did.

14-15   Basics of absorption and variable costing   Fixed Company was organized on January 1, 19X5, and began operations immediately. The balance sheet immediately after organization showed plant and equipment of $2,400,000 and common stock of $2,400,000. The plant is completely automated and makes its one product out of air. Its only cost is $240,000 depreciation, based on a ten-year life and the straight-line method. During the first two years of operation the company had the following results.

	19X5	19X6
Units produced	140,000	100,000
Units sold	120,000	120,000

All sales were at $5 per unit and were for cash. The company uses a standard fixed cost of $2 per unit based on normal volume of 120,000 units. There were no cash disbursements in either year so that cash at the end of each year was $5 multiplied by cumulative sales.

Required
1. Prepare income statements for each year.
2. Prepare a balance sheet as of the end of each year.
3. Repeat items 1 and 2 using variable costing.

14-16   Interpreting results   The president of Stockley Jellies, Inc. has been reviewing the income statements of the two most recent months. She is puzzled because sales rose and profits fell in March, and she asks you, the controller, to explain.

	February	March
Sales ($30 per case)	$540,000	$660,000
Standard cost of sales	270,000	330,000
Standard gross profit	270,000	330,000
Volume variance	40,000	(50,000)
Selling and administrative expenses	(150,000)	(150,000)
Income	$160,000	$130,000

The standard fixed cost per case is $10, based on normal capacity of 20,000 cases per month.

Required
1. Determine production in each month.
2. Explain the results to the president.
3. Prepare income statements using variable costing.

14-17   Income determination – absorption costing   The following data apply to Ronsen Company's 19X4 operation.

Sales (80,000 units)	$1,600,000
Production	90,000 units
Variable costs of production, standard and actual	$ 900,000
Fixed production costs, budgeted and actual	$ 360,000
Selling, general, and administrative costs	$ 250,000

Required: Prepare income statements for 19X4 using standard absorption costing with (1) 90,000 units and (2) with 100,000 units used to set the standard fixed cost.

14-18 *Income determination — variable costing (extension of 14-17)*

Required: Prepare an income statement for Ronsen for 19X4, using standard variable costing.

14-19 *Relationships* Fill in the blanks for each of the following independent situations. In all situations, selling price is $10, standard and actual variable manufacturing cost is $6, fixed production costs, budgeted and actual, are $100,000, and the volume used to set the standard fixed cost per unit is 50,000 units. There are no selling and administrative expenses.

	(a)	(b)	(c)	(d)
			Income—	Income—
	Unit	Unit	Variable	Absorption
Case	Sales	Production	Costing	Costing
1	70,000	_____	$_____	$170,000
2	_____	_____	$90,000	$110,000
3	50,000	55,000	$_____	$_____

14-20 *All-fixed company* Fixed, Inc., manufactures a single product from garbage. It sells for $3 per unit. The production process is automated and there are no variable costs. Fixed production costs are $10,000 per month. Normal activity is 10,000 units per month, and the standard fixed cost per unit is $1. Fixed has no selling and administrative expenses. Fixed began May with no inventory. Its activity for May, June, and July is summarized below, in units.

	May	June	July
Production	11,000	10,000	9,000
Sales	9,000	10,000	11,000

Required
1. Prepare income statements for each of the three months using standard absorption costing. Show the details of the cost of sales calculations.
2. Prepare income statements for each of the three months using standard variable costing.

Problems

14-21 *Standard costing — absorption and variable* Corson Company makes shaving lotion and uses standard absorption costing. Standard labor and materials per case are

Materials (3 gallons at $4 per gallon)	$12
Direct labor (0.50 hour at $10 per hour)	5

Total annual manufacturing overhead is budgeted according to the formula: $500,000 + ($2 × direct labor hours). The company uses normal capacity of 25,000 direct labor hours (50,000 cases) to set the standard fixed cost.

Corson began 19X7 with no inventories. It produced 45,000 cases and sold 40,000 at $40 each. Selling and administrative expenses were $200,000. There were no variable cost variances, and fixed production costs were incurred as budgeted ($500,000).

Required
1. Determine the total standard cost per case.
2. Prepare an income statement for 19X7.
3. Prepare an income statement for 19X7 using variable costing.

14-22 ***Absorption costing and variable costing*** Gordon Soups, Inc. makes a variety of soups. Data related to its chicken gumbo appear below.

Selling price per case	$50
Variable manufacturing costs per case	$15
Fixed manufacturing costs per month	$300,000
Selling and general expenses, all fixed, per month	$ 80,000

Gordon uses standard absorption costing, basing its unit fixed cost on normal activity of 15,000 cases per month. In July, Gordon produced 16,000 cases and sold 14,000. There were 3,000 cases in beginning inventory at standard cost. All costs were incurred as expected.

Required
1. Determine the standard fixed cost per unit.
2. Prepare an income statement for July. Use the short form of the income statement but calculate cost of goods sold separately.
3. Prepare an income statement for July assuming that Gordon uses variable costing. Remember that inventory at the beginning of July will be at standard variable cost.

14-23 ***Budgeted income statements*** Morrison WinterSports manufactures several lines of skiing equipment. Its Riverdale Plant makes a single model, the M-80 ski. Budgeted data for 19X7 appear below.

Sales (36,000 pairs at $70)	$2,520,000
Production	38,000 pairs
Standard variable cost	$15
Standard fixed cost	25
Total standard cost	$40
Selling and administrative expenses:	
Fixed	$600,000
Variable	$8 per pair

Morrison uses normal activity of 40,000 pairs per year and budgeted fixed manufacturing costs of $1,000,000 to set its standard fixed cost. There were no beginning inventories.

Required
1. Prepare a budgeted income statement using standard absorption costing.
2. Prepare a budgeted income statement using standard variable costing.

14-24 **Analysis of results (extension of 14-23)** The Riverdale Plant of Morrison WinterSports actually produced 42,000 pairs and sold 40,000. All costs were incurred as expected—fixed in total and variable per unit.

Required
1. Prepare an income statement using standard absorption costing.
2. Prepare an income statement using standard variable costing.
3. Which set of statements from this and the previous assignment, the absorption or the variable, gives better information for analyzing results?

14-25 **Analysis of income statement – standard costs** The income statement for Bourque Manufacturing Company for 19X6 appears below. The company has established the following standards for a unit of finished product.

Materials (10 pounds at $1)	$10
Direct labor (2 hours at $8)	16
Variable overhead ($1 per direct labor hour)	2
Fixed overhead	2
Total	$30

The fixed overhead standard is based on normal capacity of 20,000 units. During 19X6, 49,000 direct labor hours were worked and 238,000 pounds of material used.

Bourque Manufacturing Company, Income Statement for 19X6

Sales (20,000 units at $40)		$800,000
Cost of goods sold—at standard		600,000
Standard gross profit		200,000
Variances:		
Materials	$3,000U	
Labor	3,000U	
Variable overhead	3,000U	
Fixed overhead:		
Spending variance	5,000F	
Volume variance	8,000F	4,000F
Gross profit		204,000
Selling, general, and administrative expenses		130,000
Income		$ 74,000

Required
1. Based on the information provided, determine the following:
   (a) Number of units produced.
   (b) Material use variance.
   (c) Material price variance.

    (d) Direct labor efficiency variance.
    (e) Direct labor rate variance.
    (f) Variable overhead efficiency variance.
    (g) Variable overhead spending variance.
    (h) Fixed overhead incurred.
2. Prepare an income statement using standard variable costing.

14-26 **Conversion of absorption-costing income statement from normal to practical capacity (extension of 14-25)** The standard costs and the income statement for Bourque Manufacturing Company use a standard fixed cost per unit based on normal capacity of 20,000 units. Assume, instead, that Bourque bases its standard fixed cost per unit on its practical capacity of 25,000 units.

Required
1. Determine the standard fixed cost per unit.
2. Prepare an income statement for 19X6.

14-27 **Absorption costing and variable costing** VCX Company uses standard absorption costing, basing its standard fixed cost on 200,000 units of product per year, and $600,000 annual budgeted fixed manufacturing overhead. Standard variable manufacturing cost is $6 per unit. Results for 19X6 appear below. There were no beginning inventories.

Unit production	190,000
Unit sales (at $20 per-unit price)	185,000
Actual variable manufacturing costs	$1,140,000
Actual fixed manufacturing costs	$ 600,000
Actual selling and administrative expenses, all fixed	$ 800,000

Required
1. Determine the standard fixed cost per unit and the total standard cost per unit.
2. Compute all variances.
3. Prepare an income statement for 19X6. Show any variances as adjustments to standard cost of sales.
4. Prepare an income statement using variable costing.

14-28 **Reconciling incomes – absorption costing** AFT Industries had the following budgeted income statement for March, 19X5, in thousands of dollars.

Sales	$4,210.0
Standard cost of sales	1,894.5
Standard gross margin	2,315.5
Selling and administrative expenses (all fixed)	1,800.0
Income	$ 515.5

The budgeted volume was 210.5 thousand units at a selling price of $20. Standard cost of sales was $9, of which $4 was fixed. The assistant who prepared the statement had no information about budgeted production, so assumed that it would be equal to normal activity of 220 thousand units per month, eliminating the volume variance.

AFT actually sold 212 thousand units and produced 215 thousand; actual fixed production costs were $880 thousand, actual variable production costs $1,075 thousand. Selling and administrative expenses were as budgeted.

Required
1. Prepare an income statement reflecting the actual results.
2. Does it make sense that actual income is less than budgeted income when actual sales were higher than budgeted sales? Explain as best you can why the actual results were different from budget.

14-29 Reconciling incomes – variable costing

Required
1. Use the information from the previous assignment to prepare budgeted and actual income statements for AFT Industries using variable costing.
2. Explain the difference between budgeted and actual income.

14-30 Costing methods and product profitability
Forman Company makes three products in the same plant. Fixed costs are applied to products based on the number of direct labor hours required to make the product. The rate of application is based on budgeted fixed costs of $900,000 and budgeted direct labor hours of 150,000. Per-unit data for the products are as follows.

	A	B	C
Selling price	$160	$64	$90
Production costs, including applied fixed cost based on predetermined rate	$150	$56	$81
Direct labor hours required for one unit of product	9	4	3

Required
1. Determine variable production costs per unit for each product.
2. Assuming that variable costs of production are the only variable costs, determine which product yields (a) the highest contribution margin per unit; (b) the highest contribution margin percentage; and (c) the highest contribution margin per direct labor hour.
3. If a manager asked you which product is the most profitable, what would you answer?

14-31 Analysis of income statements
As chief financial analyst of Markem Enterprises, Inc., you have been asked by the president to explain the difference between the two income statements prepared for his consideration. One was prepared by the controller, the other by the sales manager. Both used the same data from last year's operations.

	Statement A	Statement B
Sales (10,000 units)	$1,000,000	$1,000,000
Cost of goods sold:		
Beginning inventory	0	0
Production costs	600,000	900,000
Ending inventory	(200,000)	(300,000)
Cost of goods sold	400,000	600,000
Gross profit	600,000	400,000
Other costs	500,000	200,000
Income	$ 100,000	$ 200,000

Variable costs of production, the only variable costs, are $40 per unit.

Required
1. Determine which statement was prepared using variable costing, which using absorption costing.
2. Determine (a) fixed production costs; (b) selling and administrative costs; (c) production in units; and (d) cost per unit of inventory for both statements.
3. Which statement do you think was prepared by which manager and why do you think so?

14-32 Conversion of income statement The manager of the Morgan Division of Rorshoot Industries has been on the job only a short time. The income statement below, for the third quarter of 19X7, is the first report he has received. He is having some difficulty understanding it because he is familiar only with variable costing, and he has asked you to convert the statement to a variable costing basis.

Sales		$1,324,000
Cost of sales		893,700
Gross profit		430,300
Operating expenses:		
Selling and administrative	$276,300	
Unabsorbed fixed overhead	21,600	297,900
Income		$ 132,400

From reviewing internal records you have determined the following:
1. Selling and administrative costs are all fixed.
2. The division sells its one product at $40 per unit.
3. Fixed manufacturing overhead is applied at $12 per unit.
4. There was no fixed overhead budget variance.
5. Production during the quarter was 38,200 units.

Required: Prepare an income statement using standard variable costing.

14-33 Effects of costing methods on balance sheet McPherson Company has a loan with a large bank. Among the provisions of the loan agreement are (a) the current ratio must be at least 3 to 1 and (b) the ratio of debt to stockholders' equity must be no higher than 75%. The balance sheet at December 31, 19X4 follows.

Assets		Equities	
Cash and receivables	$ 460,000	Current liabilities	$ 200,000
Inventory (40,000 units at variable cost)	200,000	Long-term bank loan	300,000
Total current assets	660,000	Stockholders' equity	760,000
Fixed assets (net)	600,000		
Total assets	$1,260,000	Total equities	$1,260,000

Current ratio $660,000/$200,000 = 3.3/1
Debt/stockholders' equity $500,000/$760,000 = 65%

The budgeted income statement for 19X5 follows.

Sales (100,000 units)		$1,000,000
Variable cost of sales		500,000
Variable manufacturing margin		500,000
Other variable costs (variable with sales)		50,000
Contribution margin		450,000
Fixed costs:		
Manufacturing	$300,000	
Other	50,000	350,000
Income		$ 100,000

Budgeted production is 100,000 units. The company's president foresees substantial expenditures for fixed assets and intends to obtain a loan to finance these expenditures. He projects the following pro forma balance sheet for December 31, 19X5.

Assets		Equities	
Cash and receivables	$ 400,000	Current liabilities	$ 240,000
Inventory (40,000 units at variable cost)	200,000	Long-term bank loans	460,000
Total current assets	600,000	Stockholders' equity	860,000
Fixed assets (net)	960,000		
Total assets	$1,560,000	Total equities	$1,560,000

He sees that the firm will be in default on both provisions of the loan agreement. (Compute the current ratio and debt/stockholders' equity ratio to verify his finding.) Trying to resolve the problem, he lists the following points.
(a) Practical capacity is 150,000 units.
(b) The company might benefit by using absorption costing.

Required
1. Prepare the income statement and balance sheet using standard absorption costing, with production of 150,000 units used to set the standard fixed cost. Also assume production of 150,000 units. Assume that all increased production costs are paid in cash.
2. Is the company safely within the limits of the loan agreement?
3. Is the company better off using absorption costing?

14-34 **VCP analysis and absorption costing**   The Baltic Division of Kramer Industries manufactures large drill bits. The division had the following plans for the first quarter of 19X5.

Unit sales	80,000
Selling price	$40
Variable cost	$24
Fixed costs	$800,000

The divisional manager expected profit of $480,000 from these results. The actual income statement for the quarter appears below. The divisional manager was surprised to see that the targets for volume, price, and costs were met or exceeded, but that profit was less than anticipated.

Sales (82,000 units at $40)	$3,280,000
Standard cost of sales at $30	2,460,000
Standard gross margin	820,000
Production variances	(180,000)
Actual gross margin	640,000
Selling and administrative expenses	200,000
Profit	$ 440,000

The divisional manager was informed that all variable costs and 75% of fixed costs were for manufacturing. The division uses standard costing, with practical capacity of 100,000 units per quarter used to set the standard. Actual production was only 70,000 units in the first quarter of 19X5 because of a large supply of inventory left over from the previous period.

Required
1. Prepare an income statement using variable costing.
2. Tell the divisional manager how your income statement would be of more help to him than the one shown above.

14-35 **Standard costing – two overhead rates**   Cannon Industries applies overhead to products using two rates—one based on machine hours, the other on the number of component parts. The latter rate is used because of the high amounts of overhead associated with purchasing, receiving, storing, and issuing parts. The company does not classify any employees as direct labor because production is highly automated. Summary data for 19X5 follow.

	Budget
Parts-related overhead	$1,200,000
Machine-related overhead	$6,480,000
Machine hours	100,000
Total number of parts to be used	8,000,000

The overhead costs given above are largely fixed with respect to output. Data for product GT-1029 appear below.

Component parts, 11 parts at average $2.50 price	$27.50
Machine time, 0.15 hours	

During March, 19X6, the company made 60,000 of model GT-1029, and no other products. Parts-related overhead was $105,300, machine-related overhead was $542,230. The managers expect both of these categories of cost to be incurred evenly throughout the year. Use of parts was at standard.

Required
1. Calculate the predetermined overhead rates for parts and for machine hours.
2. Determine the standard cost of product GT-1029.
3. Determine whatever variances you can.

14-36   **Preparing income statements**   Bob Cransk, the president of BC Company, has been receiving monthly reports like the one below since he founded the company 10 years ago. As BC's newly hired controller, you have been discussing the reports with Cransk, trying to decide whether to make any changes. (All numbers are in thousands of dollars.)

	March	February
Sales	$1,256.8	$1,452.4
Standard cost of sales	769.3	879.7
Production variances	7.3U	29.8U
Cost of sales	776.6	909.5
Gross margin	489.2	542.9
Selling and administrative expenses	406.4	412.6
Profit before taxes	$ 82.8	$ 130.3
Summary of variances:		
Materials	$8.4U	$ 7.1U
Direct labor	7.8U	6.9U
Overhead	8.9F	15.8U
Total	$7.3U	$29.8U

Cransk has told you that he is generally satisfied with the reports, but he is sometimes surprised because they seem to contradict what he believes from his knowledge of operations. He attributes some of his surprise to his lack of understanding of accounting principles.

"For example," he said, "February is a good month. March starts our slow season. I expected February to be a little better than it was, but it seemed okay. March showed better than I had thought it would. I know that our production affects income, so I sort of make mental adjustments for it, but I'd rather not have to."

A review of the records reveals that standard variable cost of sales was $580.5 in February, $510.3 in March. Total fixed manufacturing overhead was $305.2 in February, $299.8 in March. Budgeted fixed manufacturing overhead was $304.5 in both months. Variable overhead variances were $3.2 unfavorable in February, $2.3 unfavorable in March. Although there is some variation in selling and administrative expenses, they can be considered fixed.

Required
1. Prepare income statements for February and March using standard variable costing.
2. Tell Cransk how much of the variances in the income statements above are attributable to the use of absorption costing.

14-37 *Incorporating variances into budgets* Viner Company is developing its budgets for the coming year. The firm uses the standard costs shown below for its final product.

Materials (3 gallons at $3)	$ 9
Labor (4 hours at $5)	20
Variable overhead, ($6 per DLH)	24
Total standard variable cost	$53

Budgeted fixed manufacturing costs are $300,000. Selling, general, and administrative expenses, all fixed, are budgeted at $400,000. Generally, there is about a 10% variance over standard quantity for materials, but the materials usually cost 5% less than the standard price. Direct laborers will receive a 6% wage increase at the beginning of the year, and labor efficiency is expected to be 4% better than standard. An unfavorable variable overhead spending variance of 5% is expected. Sales for the year are budgeted at 20,000 units at $100; production schedules indicate planned production of 24,000 units. There are no beginning inventories. The purchases of raw material are budgeted to be equal to expected material use.

Required
1. Determine the expected variable cost variances for the year.
2. Prepare a budgeted income statement for the coming year using standard variable costing.

14-38 *Costs and decisions* "You're fired!!" was the way your boss, the controller of Saran Bathing Suit Company, greeted you this morning. His ire was based on the two income statements shown below. A few months ago you recommended accepting an offer from a national chain for 10,000 suits at $12 each. At that time, inventories were getting too high because of slow sales. Things have not improved noticeably since then. Your recommendation was based on the variable production costs of $10 per unit, which are the only variable costs. The total standard cost of $16 per suit includes $6 in fixed costs, based on normal production of 130,000 units.

Income Statements for 19X4

	If Special Order Had Not Been Accepted	Actual, with Special Order
Sales: 100,000 × $25	$2,500,000	$2,500,000
10,000 × $12		120,000
Total sales	2,500,000	2,620,000
Cost of sales at standard cost of $16	1,600,000	1,760,000
Standard gross profit	900,000	860,000
Volume variance (20,000 × $6)	120,000U	120,000U
Actual gross profit	780,000	740,000
Selling and administrative expenses	710,000	710,000
Income	$ 70,000	$ 30,000

"Your stupidity cost us $40,000, you jerk!! Now clean out your desk and scram."

Required: Prepare an argument that will get your job back.

14-39 **Actual versus standard costs — multiple products** Brennan Company makes luggage. For some time, its managers have been dissatisfied with the firm's cost information. Unit costs have fluctuated greatly and have not been useful for planning and control purposes.

Under the present system, unit costs are computed at the end of each month. The costs are determined by allocating all actual production costs for the month to the various models produced, with the allocation based on the relative material costs of the various models.

The controller has decided to develop standard costs for product costing purposes. He has analyzed the material and labor requirements for each model, based on what he believes to be currently attainable performance. The results of his analysis follow. (For simplicity, the problem is limited to three models.)

	Briefcase #108	Cosmetic Case #380	Two-Suiter #460
Material costs	$12.00	$14.00	$18.00
Labor hours required	0.5	0.8	1.5

Workers all earn $8 per hour, and the firm usually works about 6,000 labor hours per month. The controller intends to use 6,000 hours to set the standard fixed cost per unit. His analysis of monthly manufacturing overhead yielded the formula: $90,000 + ($7 × direct labor hours).

During April the firm had the following results. There were no inventories at April 1.

	#108	#380	#460
Production in units	3,000	2,500	1,200
Sales in units	2,400	1,800	1,000
Sales in dollars	$84,000	$90,000	$85,000

There were no variable cost variances and fixed production costs were $92,000.

Required
1. Compute the standard cost for each model.
2. Compute the ending inventory of finished goods.
3. Prepare an income statement for April. Selling and administrative expenses were $28,000.

14-40 **Interim results, costing methods, and evaluation of performance**
Kleffman Company sells a product with a highly seasonal demand. The budgeted income statement for 19X7 is given below.

Sales (240,000 units)		$2,400,000
Cost of goods sold—at standard:		
Materials	$420,000	
Direct labor	540,000	
Manufacturing overhead	600,000	1,560,000
Gross profit—at standard		840,000
Selling, general, and administrative expenses		420,000
Income before taxes		$ 420,000

Budgeted production is 240,000 units, the number used to set the standard fixed cost per unit. The controller has determined that materials, labor, 40% of manufacturing overhead ($240,000), and $120,000 of the selling, general, and administrative expenses are variable. All fixed costs are incurred evenly throughout the year.

January and February are relatively slow months, each with only about 5% of annual sales. March is the first month of a busy period, and production in February is generally high in order to stock up for the anticipated increase in demand. The actual income statements for January and February 19X7 appear below.

	January	February
Sales (12,000 units)	$120,000	$120,000
Cost of goods sold—at standard	78,000	78,000
Gross profit—at standard	42,000	42,000
Manufacturing variances:		
Variable costs	3,000F	4,000U
Fixed cost—budget	2,000F	3,000U
Fixed cost—volume	9,000U	7,500F
Gross profit—actual	38,000	42,500
Selling, general, and administrative expenses	31,000	31,000
Income	$ 7,000	$ 11,500

Although the president is pleased that performance improved in February, he has asked the controller why the two months showed different profits, since sales were the same. He also wonders why profits were not about 5% of the $420,000 budget, as each month's sales were 5% of the annual budget.

Required
1. Explain to the president why profits in January and February would be expected to be less than 5% of the budgeted annual profit, even though each month's sales were 5% of the budgeted annual amount.
2. Explain to the president why profits differed in the two months. Comment on the president's being pleased that "performance improved in February."

14-41   ***Income statements and balance sheets***   Arens Company makes a single product, a microwave oven that sells for $300. Standard variable cost of production is $180 per unit, and the only other variable cost is a 10% sales commission. Fixed production costs are $3,600,000 per year, incurred evenly throughout the year. Of that amount, $800,000 is depreciation and the remainder all require cash disbursements. Fixed selling and administrative expenses of $200,000 per month all require cash disbursements.

For inventory costing Arens uses a standard fixed cost of $45 per unit, based on expected annual production of 80,000 units. However, during 19X6 the firm experienced the following results, by six-month periods.

	January–June	July–December
Sales in units	30,000	40,000
Production in units	32,000	42,000

The firm sells for cash only and pays all of its obligations as they are incurred. Its balance sheet at December 31, 19X5, in thousands of dollars was as follows.

Assets		Equities	
Cash	$ 400		
Inventory (1,000 units)	225	Common stock	$3,000
Plant and equipment (net)	3,000	Retained earnings	625
Total assets	$3,625	Total equities	$3,625

During 19X6, all costs were incurred as expected, variable costs per unit and fixed costs in total.

Required
1. Prepare income statements (in thousands of dollars) for each of the two six-month periods and the year as a whole.
2. Prepare balance sheets as of June 30 and December 31, 19X6, in thousands of dollars.

14-42   ***Pricing dispute***   Calligeris Company manufactures brake linings for automobiles. Late in 19X2 the firm received an offer for 10,000 linings from Phelan Company. Phelan was unwilling to pay the usual price of $5 per lining but offered to buy at a price that would give Calligeris a $0.50 gross profit per lining.

Without consideration of the order, Calligeris expected the following income statement for the year.

Sales (100,000 linings at $5)		$500,000
Cost of goods sold at standard:		
Beginning inventory (20,000 at $4)	$ 80,000	
Variable production costs (100,000 units at $2.50)	250,000	
Fixed production costs at $1.50 per unit	150,000	
Cost of goods available for sale	480,000	
Ending inventory (20,000 at $4)	80,000	
Cost of goods sold at standard		400,000
Standard gross profit		100,000
Volume variance (20,000 at $1.50)	30,000F	
Selling and administrative expenses	50,000	20,000
Income		$ 80,000

The production manager decided that the order could be filled from inventory, so no additional production was planned. The firm shipped 10,000 linings to Phelan Company, billing that firm for 10,000 units at $4.50 per lining. No additional costs were incurred in connection with this order.

Required
1. Prepare an income statement for 19X2 assuming that the actual results for the year were as planned except that the additional sale was made to Phelan company. Do the results show that the firm earned the agreed gross profit?
2. Suppose that you were the controller of Phelan Company. Would you dispute the $4.50 price? If so, why? What price would you propose and why?

14-43 Predetermined overhead rates – multiple products The controller of Salmon Company has been developing a new costing system. He believes that the use of standard costs would reduce the cost of recordkeeping and simplify the firm's internal reporting to managers. He has asked your assistance and you have collected the following information relating to the firm's three products.

	Model 84	Model 204	Model 340
Variable production costs	$4	$7	$11
Direct labor hours required	0.50	0.80	1.50

The firm works 50,000 direct labor hours per year at its normal operating level, and the controller uses that figure to set the predetermined overhead rate. Budgeted fixed production costs are $300,000. Operating results for 19X4 appear below. There were no beginning inventories.

	Production in Units	Sales in Units	Sales in Dollars
Model 84	30,000	25,000	$250,000
Model 204	24,000	20,000	$280,000
Model 340	20,000	18,000	$450,000

All production costs were incurred as expected, variable costs per unit and total fixed costs. Selling and administrative expenses were $140,000.

Required
1. Compute standard fixed costs per unit for each model.
2. Compute the ending inventory in dollars for each model.
3. Prepare an income statement for 19X4.

14-44 Standard costs and pricing   The controller of Carolina Mills has been discussing costs and prices with the treasurer. The controller wants to use 2,400,000 machine hours to set standard fixed costs, while the treasurer prefers to use 3,000,000 hours. The controller feels that the lower base will make it easier for the company to absorb its fixed overhead, but the treasurer is concerned that the company might set its prices too high to be competitive with other companies.

"Look," the treasurer said, "suppose we use our formula for budgeting total manufacturing costs, materials, labor, and overhead."

Total manufacturing cost = $7,680,000 + $4.25 per machine hour

"Now," he went on, "if we use your basis of 2,400,000 hours and our usual pricing formula, setting prices at 150% of total manufacturing cost, we will have higher prices than competition will permit, with consequent loss of volume."

The controller replied, "I can't agree with you. Your basis of 3,000,000 hours is very close to practical capacity, and we'd be taking the risk of having a significant amount of underabsorbed overhead that would really hurt our profits."

Required
1. Suppose that selling and administrative expenses are $6,200,000, all fixed. What profit will the company earn if it uses 2,400,000 hours to set standard fixed costs, sets prices using the formula given above, and sells output requiring 2,400,000 machine hours? (Assume no inventories.)
2. Repeat item 1 substituting 3,000,000 machine hours for 2,400,000 hours.
3. Is the real issue here the selection of the base for applying fixed overhead? Why or why not? What is the real concern?

14-45 Product costing methods and VCP analysis   Tollgate Company expects to produce 190,000 units in 19X6. The firm uses a predetermined overhead rate for fixed overhead based on 210,000 units, which is normal capacity. Overabsorbed or underabsorbed overhead is shown separately in the income statement. The selling price is $16 per unit. At the expected level of production Tollgate expects the following costs.

Variable production costs	$1,330,000
Fixed production costs	630,000
Fixed selling and administrative costs	434,000

In addition, there are variable selling costs of $2 per unit. The firm had no inventory at the end of 19X5.

Required
1. Determine the break-even point assuming that variable costing is used.
2. Determine the number of units that must be sold to break even given that production will be 190,000 units. Assume absorption costing.

3. If your answers to the first two items differ, explain the difference, showing calculations.
4. Would your answer to item 2 be different if the firm had had a beginning inventory of 10,000 units costed at the same per-unit amount that the firm will use in 19X6? Explain why or why not, with calculations.

14-46 ***Comprehensive review, budgeting, overhead application*** Ruland Company makes and sells a single product. The product sells for $20, and Ruland expects sales of 880,000 units in 19X5. The distribution of sales by quarters is expected to be 20%, 25%, 25%, and 30%. The firm expects the following costs in 19X6.

Manufacturing Costs

	Fixed	Variable per Unit
Materials (4 pounds at $0.80)	—	$3.20
Direct labor (0.5 hour at $5)	—	2.50
Maintenance	$ 46,000	0.20
Indirect labor	422,000	0.40
Supplies	316,000	0.05
Power	186,000	0.10
Depreciation	1,900,000	—
Supervision	310,000	—
Miscellaneous	320,000	0.05
Totals	$3,500,000	$6.50

Selling, General, and Administrative Expenses

	Fixed	Variable per Unit
Sales commissions		$2.00
Salaries and wages	$1,200,000	—
Other expenses, including interest	4,350,000	
Total	$5,550,000	$2.00

Budgeted production and purchases are

Quarter	Production (units)	Raw Material Purchases (pounds)
1	210,000	733,000
2	220,000	950,000
3	260,000	904,000
4	210,000	795,000
Total	900,000	3,382,000

Other information relating to Ruland's operation follows.
1. The firm uses a standard fixed cost of $3.50 per unit.
2. Sales are collected 60 days after sale.

3. Purchases of raw materials are paid for in the month after purchase.
4. Direct labor costs unpaid at the end of a quarter are about 10% of the cost incurred in that quarter. All other manufacturing costs requiring cash disbursements (all but depreciation) are paid as incurred, except for raw material purchases.
5. All selling, general, and administrative expenses require cash disbursements and are paid as incurred except for salesperson's commissions. These are paid in the month after incurrence.
6. The firm has a 40% income tax rate. At year end, the amount of unpaid taxes is about 25% of the total expense for the year.
7. A dividend of $300,000 will be paid in 19X5.
8. Purchases of plant assets, all for cash, will total $2,100,000 in 19X5.
9. Assume that sales, production, and purchases of raw materials are spread evenly over the months of each quarter (one-third of quarter in each month of the quarter).

The balance sheet at the end of 19X4 appears as follows, in thousands of dollars.

Assets		Equities	
Cash	$ 840	Accounts payable (materials)	$ 240
Accounts receivable	2,800	Accrued commissions	120
Inventory—finished goods (146,000 units)	1,460	Accrued payroll (direct labor)	64
Inventory—materials (530,000 pounds)	424	Income taxes payable	80
Plant and equipment	16,200	Long-term debt	4,000
Accumulated depreciation	(8,400)	Common stock	7,000
		Retained earnings	1,820
Total	$13,324	Total	$13,324

Required

1. Prepare a budgeted income statement for 19X5.
2. Prepare a cash budget for 19X5 for the year as a whole, not by quarter.
3. Prepare a pro forma balance sheet for the end of 19X5.
4. Without preparing new statements, describe the differences that would occur in your prepared statements if the firm were using variable costing.

Cases

14-47 *Costing methods and evaluation of performance* Ralph Sampson is the manager of the Wallace Division of Fizer Industries, Inc. He is one of several managers being considered for the presidency of the firm, as the current president is retiring in a year.

All divisions use standard absorption costing; normal capacity is the basis for application of fixed overhead. Normal capacity in the Wallace Division is 40,000 units per quarter, and quarterly fixed overhead is $500,000. Variable production cost is $50 per unit. Ralph has been looking at the report for the first three months of the year and is not happy with the results.

Wallace Division Income Statement for First Quarter

Sales (25,000 units)		$2,500,000
Cost of goods sold:		
Beginning inventory (10,000 units)	$ 625,000	
Production costs applied	1,562,500	
Total	$2,187,500	
Less ending inventory	625,000	1,562,500
Gross profit		937,500
Volume variance		(187,500)
Selling and general expenses		(500,000)
Income		$ 250,000

The sales forecast for the second quarter is 25,000 units. Ralph had budgeted second-quarter production at 25,000 units but changes it to 50,000 units, which is practical capacity for a quarter. The sales forecasts for each of the last two quarters of the year are also 25,000 units. Costs incurred in the second quarter are the same as budgeted, based on 50,000 units of production.

Required
1. Prepare an income statement for the second quarter.
2. Does the statement for the second quarter reflect Ralph's performance better than that for the first quarter? Can you make any suggestions for reporting in the future? Do you think Ralph should be seriously considered for the presidency of the firm? Why or why not?

14-48 Costing methods and performance evaluation Warren Progman, the new manager of the Oliver Division of General Products Company, was greatly displeased at the income statements that his controller, Hal Gannon, had been giving him. Progman had recently been placed in charge of the division because it had not been showing satisfactory results. Progman was upset because, although sales had risen in each of the last two months, profits had not kept pace. Income statements for the last three months are given below.

	March	April	May
Sales	$360,000	$440,000	$560,000
Cost of sales	198,000	264,000	381,000
Gross profit	162,000	176,000	179,000
Other expenses	142,000	150,000	162,000
Profit before taxes	$ 20,000	$ 26,000	$ 17,000

Progman asked Gannon why profits had declined when sales had increased and why a substantial increase in sales from March to April had produced only a small increase in profits. Gannon's reply was simply that operations had gone according to plans that Progman had set, and that the problems that Progman wanted to know about were due to the method of accounting for product costs and the relationships of sales to production.

Progman was unimpressed with this explanation and rather testily pointed out that he had been put in charge of the division to "turn it around," and he was not about to let accounting conventions give corporate management second thoughts about placing him in charge. Gannon, who was fully aware of the claims Progman had made when being considered for the manager's job, had not liked Progman from the start. To the suggestion that accounting conventions were standing in the way of Progman's performance, Gannon replied only that the reports for all divisions were prepared from the same uniform accounting system and in the form required for corporate reporting. He told Progman that the reports were prepared using generally accepted accounting principles, which was necessary because the corporation was publicly held and had to issue reports to shareholders. He did not tell Progman that he believed the methods used by the firm for external reporting were inappropriate for internal purposes.

Later, at lunch with Frank Holloway, the division's sales manager, Gannon related the conversation that he had had with Progman. Holloway, who had also wondered about the firm's accounting methods, asked Gannon why he didn't just explain the statements to Progman. "Not on your life," said Gannon. "I see no reason to help that braggart. Let *him* explain to the top brass why things aren't going the way he said they would if he were put in charge instead of me."

"Actually," Gannon continued, "what he's worried about just isn't a difficult problem. Cost of sales included both standard cost and the adjustment needed when production for the month did not equal the 25,000-unit volume that was used to set the standard fixed cost of $9 per unit. In fact, things have gone very well. We had no variances at all except for volume. Selling prices held very well at $20 per unit, and the division is doing much better now. But would I like to be there when the brass asks Progman why things are not going so well! Why, even production in April was right on target at 25,000 units budgeted."

Required

1. Explain the results in the three-month period. You may wish to compute standard fixed costs per unit and production in each month.
2. Prepare income statements for the three months using variable costing.

14-49 Costing methods and product profitability   At a recent meeting, several of the managers of Cornwall Valve Company were discussing the firm's costing and pricing methods. Although there was general agreement that the methods should be helpful to managers in determining which products to emphasize, there was considerably less agreement on which methods would accomplish this.

The sales manager, Ralph Stokes, expressed his preference for product costs based on variable costs only. "I see no reason to charge a product with fixed costs. Contribution margin is, after all, the critical question in selecting the products to push."

"I just can't agree with you," said Bill Rollo, the production manager. "If you'd just take a walk through the plant you'd be reminded that men and materials aren't the only things needed to produce one of our valves. There are tons of machinery that cost money too. Ignoring those costs can only get you into trouble, and it sure isn't very realistic anyway. You've *got* to consider the machine time required for each product, and that can only be accomplished by allocating the fixed production costs to products. Machine time is critical, and production costs should be allocated on a machine-hour basis."

To make this point, Bill put an example on the conference room blackboard. "Look, let me show you. Let's take just three of our basic products that all require time in the grinding department. That department has a capacity of 1,000 machine hours a month, and the monthly fixed costs of the department are $10,000.'' Below is the schedule Bill put on the board.

	101-27	101-34	101-56
Selling price	$9.00	$12.00	$17.40
Variable costs	5.00	6.00	8.40
Contribution margin	4.00	6.00	9.00
Fixed costs	1.00	1.25	2.50
Profit per unit	$3.00	$ 4.75	$ 6.50
Number of valves processed per hour	10	8	4

Bill continued, ''Now what I've done is compute a fixed cost per unit by dividing the $10 per hour fixed cost by the number of valves of each type that we can process in one hour. You can see that what I use the grinding machinery for *does* make a difference. It seems to me that this approach is much better at showing which products to emphasize. This shows that the 56 is the best bet and the 27 is the worst.''

''But Bill,'' said Ralph, ''we don't disagree. The 56 is a winner because it has the highest contribution margin, and we wouldn't push the 27 because it contributes the least. What are we arguing about?''

Bill was not too happy about having his own example used to counter his argument. He admitted that, in the case he used, the relative rankings of the products were the same as they would be using the contribution margin approach. But he still felt that his method would be more valuable to the sales manager than a simple contribution margin approach, and he looked around the room for support.

''Well, now, it's nice to hear that you two are so interested in the information my staff has to offer,'' commented Joe Anderson, the controller. ''But if you want to be realistic, let's consider something else. We're committed to making some of each of these valves, though not nearly enough to keep the grinding department operating at capacity. So the big decision isn't really which valve to produce and sell. What we really need to know is which one to produce after we've met the commitments we made. And the kicker is that we could probably sell all of whatever we produce. The way I see it, we have about 600 hours of grinding time available for discretionary production. So what do we do?''

Bill continued to argue for his approach, and he specifically attacked the question of pricing. ''The way we price our products just isn't rational; I know we could do better if we considered the fixed costs the way I said. We should be selling the 27s for $12.50 if we want to make them as profitable as the 56s, and we'd have to jack the price of 34s by $1.75 to equal the profit on the 56s. Okay, okay, I can see you're getting upset about the idea of such increases, Ralph. I know the customers would be unhappy. But if we cater to their needs by producing these models, we ought to get a fair return for doing it.''

Required: Determine which valve should be produced once the committed demand is satisfied. Criticize the analyses of the sales manager and the production manager, including their comments about pricing.

CHAPTER *15*

PROCESS COSTING AND THE COST ACCOUNTING CYCLE

Chapter 13 introduced product costing—determining a total per-unit cost of a manufactured product. While the emphasis was on job-order costing, the concepts introduced (such as cost flows, application of overhead) apply to all types of manufacturing situations. Companies that manufacture a single, homogeneous product or a group of such products use a cost accumulation method called process costing. The first part of this chapter discusses process costing.

We continue our study of product costing, placing the flow of manufacturing costs in an *accounting* framework and illustrating the cost accounting cycle. The illustrations cover the journal entries and accounts employed in job-order costing and process costing. In addition, we illustrate the accounting cycle for a standard costing system. The cost control benefits of using standard costs are significant, and standard costs can be used by some job-order firms and by all process-costing firms. Finally, we briefly describe how the cost accounting cycle might differ in a JIT company.

PROCESS COSTING

Some examples of companies that can use process costing are producers of sugar, bricks, cement, and bulk chemicals. Although the production of such a product may include several phases, each unit of product proceeds through each phase with many other units.

The essence of process costing is the accumulation of costs by process (phase in the production operation) for a period. The firm calculates per-unit costs for goods passing through a process by dividing costs for the process by the number of units generating those costs. Hence, the result is an average cost per unit. Such an averaging is necessary because all units are worked on together.

For internal reporting, a process-costing firm, like a job-order firm, can determine unit costs using either variable or absorption costing, as described in Chapter 14. We know, however, that for financial reporting and tax purposes, all firms must use absorption costing, so we shall concentrate on that approach for process costing. All three of the illustrated absorption-costing options—actual, normal, and standard—are available to a firm using process costing.

The only new problems introduced by process costing have to do with units started in one period and completed in another. The calculation of per-unit cost for a period takes the general form

$$\frac{\text{Unit}}{\text{cost}} = \frac{\text{Production costs}}{\text{Units}}$$

Because production costs are incurred in two different periods when units are only partially finished at the end of one period, applying the general formula requires that both its numerator and denominator be more clearly defined. The clarification comes by selecting a cost-flow assumption (weighted-average or first-in-first-out) such as you learned about in financial accounting. Combining the costs from two different periods is a *weighted-average* approach; maintaining a separate identity for the costs in the beginning inventory is a *first-in-first-out* (FIFO) approach. In this chapter we use the weighted-average cost flow. (The appendix to this chapter describes the calculation of unit costs using the FIFO method.)

To illustrate process costing, we use Ronn Company. Exhibit 15-1 shows the relevant data for its operations in August and September. The goal is to compute the cost of a unit produced in each of those months and, of course, the cost of any ending inventory.

Exhibit 15-1
Data for Ronn Company

	August	September
Production costs	$206,000	$191,400
Unit data:		
In process at beginning of month	0	5,000
Completed during month	100,000	90,000
In process at end of month	5,000	10,000
Percentage of completion for end-of-period work	60%	40%

While 100,000 units were completed in August, another 5,000 units were still in process and only 60% complete at the end of that month. Similarly, Ronn finished 90,000 units in September (including the 5,000 started in August) and ended the month with 10,000 units that were only 40% complete. Because there were no partially finished units on hand at the beginning of August, we know that the numerator of the unit-cost calculation is the $206,000 of production costs for that month. Because we are using the weighted-average cost flow, we also know that the numerator of the unit-cost calculation for September is the total of that month's production costs of $191,400 and whatever costs are carried over from August for the 5,000 units in the beginning inventory. The denominators of both unit-cost calculations must reflect the units whose costs are included in the numerators. Determining the appropriate denominators requires an understanding of the concept of equivalent production.

Equivalent Production

Total production costs for a given month relate to the work done on units both finished and in process at month end. Therefore, we cannot calculate the cost of a finished unit simply by dividing total costs incurred by the number of units *finished*. For example, while Ronn Company incurred *some* of its August production costs to start and finish 100,000 units in that month, it also incurred some of those costs to do 60% of the work on the 5,000 units still in process at the end of the month. Hence, you cannot compute a per-unit cost for the 100,000 units completed simply by dividing the total costs of $206,000 by those 100,000 units. The denominator in the unit-cost calculation must give some consideration to the work done on units still in inventory.

The situation in September has still another dimension because that month's production costs were incurred for three types of work: (1) work to finish the units in process at the beginning of the month; (2) work to start and finish some units within the month; and (3) work on the units in process at the end of the month. Here, the denominator in the calculation of a per-unit cost must consider not only the work on the ending inventory, but also the work done to finish the units started in August (the beginning inventory). To see how ending and beginning in-process inventories are handled in computing per-unit costs, let us begin with August, when the only complication is units in process at the end of the period. (Determining a unit cost for August is also important because, as we stated earlier, the numerator of the unit-cost calculation for September includes the costs carried over to that month for the beginning inventory.)

Ending Inventory   To determine the cost of a unit of product when some partially completed units are on hand at the end of the period, the denominator of the unit-cost calculation must include the amount of work done during that period on those partially finished units. Ronn Company completed 100,000 units and did 60% of the work on another 5,000 units. The denominator in the unit-cost calculation is the **equivalent production** of complete units.

Units completed during August	100,000
Completed units *equivalent* to the work done on partially completed units (5,000 units × 60% complete)	3,000
Total equivalent production	103,000

What this calculation says is that 5,000 units that are 60% complete are the *equivalent* of 3,000 units that are 100% complete.

The formula for equivalent production using the weighted-average method is

$$\text{Equivalent production—weighted average} = \text{units completed} + \left(\text{units in ending inventory} \times \text{percentage complete}\right)$$

Knowing the equivalent production of 103,000 units and the relevant production costs, we can compute the unit cost of a completed unit in August as follows:

$$\frac{\text{Production costs}}{\text{Equivalent production}} = \frac{\$206,000}{103,000 \text{ units}} = \$2.00 \text{ per unit}$$

We can account for the total production costs of $206,000 as follows.

Cost of finished units transferred to finished goods (100,000 × $2 per unit)	$200,000
Cost of ending inventory (5,000 units × 60% × $2 unit cost)	6,000
Total production costs accounted for	$206,000

The $6,000 of cost assigned to the partially completed units in the ending inventory is important because it becomes part of the numerator for determining the unit cost for September.

Beginning Inventory   We already know that, because we are using the weighted-average cost flow, the numerator for calculating per-unit cost for September is the total of September production costs ($191,400) and the costs carried over for units started in August ($6,000 computed immediately above). Once again, the denominator in the unit-cost calculation is equivalent production, which is determined using the formula given earlier.

$$\text{Equivalent production—weighted average} = \text{units completed} + \left(\text{units in ending inventory} \times \text{percentage complete}\right)$$
$$= 90,000 + (10,000 \times 40\%)$$
$$= 94,000$$

There is no need to consider the percentage of the work that was done each month on the beginning inventory because the numerator of the per-unit cost calculation combines the costs of the incomplete work from August with the costs of completing the work in September. Thus, the cost of completing a unit in September is:

$$\text{Cost per unit—weighted average} = \frac{\text{cost of beginning inventory} + \text{costs incurred during the period}}{\text{equivalent production—weighted average}}$$

For Ronn Company, the unit cost for September is

$$\text{Unit cost—} \atop \text{weighted average} = \frac{(\$6,000 + \$191,400) = \$197,400}{94,000} = \$2.10$$

All this means is that, on average, it took $2.10 to make a unit of product in September. The total costs (remember we are merging the costs from the beginning inventory with the production costs in September) of $197,400 are accounted for as follows.

Costs of finished units transferred to finished goods (90,000 × $2.10)	$189,000
Cost of ending inventory (10,000 units × 40% × $2.10 unit cost)	8,400
Total cost accounted for	$197,400

Notice that the total costs incurred in August and September were accounted for by the costs transferred out of the process plus the costs remaining in process. Because it uses the computed unit cost, this calculation offers a check on your work. If the total costs accounted for as either transferred out or still in process do not agree with beginning inventory plus current period cost, you have made an error.

Although no other conceptual problems arise with the use of process costing, one very common, practical situation increases the number of calculations, and another common, practical situation requires special care in computing the cost of ending inventory. The first situation is where the basic components of manufacturing cost (material, labor, and overhead) are not equally complete (or incomplete) at a given time. The second situation is where, as is the case for the majority of manufacturing companies, there is more than one department, phase, or process. The next two sections discuss these common situations.

Materials and Conversion Costs

Our example with Ronn Company assumed that the percentage-of-completion figure applied to all productive factors alike—material, labor, and overhead. Such a situation is quite unlikely. Materials are usually put into a process at an early stage, so that work-in-process inventories usually include all, or nearly all, the materials but significantly less than the total labor and overhead. Consider a company that manufactures sugar from sugar beets. Although grinding beets into sugar takes a certain amount of time and certain types of facilities, all the beets are added at the start of production. Hence, at any given time, 100% of the cost of materials has been incurred, though until the beets are completely processed, less than 100% of the costs of labor and overhead have been incurred.

Labor is usually needed to convert materials into a product, and manufacturing overhead is usually incurred throughout a process. Hence, labor and overhead are called conversion costs. In a heavily automated process, direct labor may be relatively insignificant and included in overhead, so that the only conversion cost is overhead. In any case, labor and overhead are often assumed to have the same completion percentage.

Although differing degrees of completion for materials and conversion costs do not change the general formula for computing unit costs, they do necessitate separating total costs and determining separate equivalent production for materials and for conversion costs. We illustrate this computational difference using the data from Exhibit 15-2.

Exhibit 15-2
Production Data for Borne Company for May

		Materials	Conversion Costs
Costs for beginning inventory		$ 4,000	$ 5,600
Production costs incurred in May		$36,000	$52,000
Unit data:			
Units completed	45,000		
Units in process	5,000		
Percentage of work complete		100%	60%

First, equivalent production must be computed for the two types of costs.

	Materials	Conversion Costs
Units completed during the period	45,000	45,000
Completed units *equivalent* to the work done on partially completed units:		
5,000 units × 100%	5,000	
5,000 units × 60%		3,000
Equivalent production	50,000	48,000

The unit cost calculations are

$$\frac{\text{Unit cost}}{\text{for materials}} = \frac{\$4{,}000 + \$36{,}000}{50{,}000} = \$0.80 \text{ per unit}$$

$$\frac{\text{Unit cost for}}{\text{conversion costs}} = \frac{\$5{,}600 + \$52{,}000}{48{,}000} = \$1.20 \text{ per unit}$$

Using these unit costs, we compute the cost of a unit transferred to finished goods as $2.00 (the $0.80 cost of materials, plus the $1.20 labor and overhead cost to complete each unit). The cost of the ending inventory of work in process is computed as follows.

Material cost (5,000 units × 100% × $0.80)	$4,000
Conversion cost (5,000 units × 60% × $1.20)	3,600
Total cost of ending work in process inventory	$7,600

Taking advantage of the checkpoint presented in earlier sections, we can confirm that the total costs are fully accounted for through the transfer of completed units and the costs assigned to the ending inventory.

Total costs to be accounted for:	
Costs in beginning inventory ($4,000 + $5,600)	$ 9,600
Costs for current month ($36,000 + $52,000)	88,000
Total	$97,600
Total costs accounted for as:	
Cost of finished units transferred to finished goods	
(45,000 × $2.00)	$90,000
Cost of ending inventory, computed above	7,600
Total	$97,600

Thus, the different percentages of completion for materials and conversion costs require only that we compute different amounts of equivalent production and separate total costs by type. Normally, the accounting process separates the costs of each of the cost elements, and people in charge of a particular process are well aware of the differing degrees of completion for the cost elements, so the complications posed by the different completion percentages are usually easy to resolve.

The only other computational problem that warrants mention in this introduction to process costing arises when the manufacturing operation requires more than one process. As you will see, that complication is really a special case of the situation in which units are complete to differing degrees for some types of costs.

Multiple Processes

If a product goes through more than one process, its *total* cost obviously includes the costs of all the processes. Suppose the manufacture of a particular product includes first a forming operation cutting large blocks of some raw material into smaller blocks and then a sanding phase (refining the shapes to common specifications). The cost of a finished unit includes the cost of both the forming and the sanding processes. The cost of a unit in process in the sanding department includes not only the cost of that department but also the total per-unit cost of the forming phase.

To illustrate the computation of unit costs with multiple processes, let us extend the example of Borne Company, for whom the basic production data for

May are provided in Exhibit 15-2 (page 638). Suppose the 45,000 units completed in May, at a unit cost determined earlier to be $2, are actually transferred to the finishing department. No materials are added during the finishing process, and overhead in that department is closely associated with labor hours. Operating data for June for the finishing process are

Unit Data:	
On hand at beginning of June	0
Transferred in from prior department	45,000
Transferred to finished goods	40,000
On hand at end of period (70% complete)	5,000
Cost Data:	
Beginning inventory	0
Transferred in from prior department (45,000 × $2 per unit)	$ 90,000
Department's conversion costs for June	$156,600

What is the cost of a unit transferred in June from the finishing process?

The first step, of course, is to calculate the equivalent production for the finishing process.

Units completed during the period	40,000
Completed units equivalent to the work done on partially completed units (5,000 × 70%)	3,500
Equivalent production	43,500

Dividing equivalent production into the conversion costs for the month ($156,600) yields a unit cost for the finishing process of $3.60. The cost of a unit transferred to finished goods is the $2.00 from the prior department plus the $3.60 cost from the finishing department, or $5.60. The cost of the ending in-process inventory is

Prior department costs (5,000 × 100% × $2.00)	$10,000
Conversion cost for finishing (5,000 × 70% × $3.60)	12,600
Total cost of ending inventory	$22,600

The total cost to be accounted for by the finishing department consists of the costs transferred in ($90,000), the costs in the beginning inventory (none), and the department's production costs for the month ($156,600), or $246,600. That total is accounted for as follows.

Cost of units transferred to finished goods (40,000 × $5.60)	$224,000
Cost of ending in process inventory, computed above	22,600
Total cost accounted for	$246,600

Thus, transferring in units from an earlier manufacturing process does *not* affect the calculation of equivalent production or of the unit cost for the department.

The rest of this chapter is devoted to illustrating the *accounting framework* not only for process costing but also for the other product-costing options.

THE COST ACCOUNTING CYCLE

Chapter 13 presented an overview of the flow of manufacturing costs (Figure 13-1, page 539), noting that costs are first accumulated by object (materials, labor, and overhead) and are then passed on, through Work in Process, to Finished Goods and, ultimately, to Cost of Goods Sold.[1] In Chapter 14 we noted that the choice between absorption and variable costing determines whether fixed manufacturing costs pass through Work in Process or are assigned directly to expense for the period. At no time, however, have we described these cost flows using accounts and journal entries. The transition from a set of ideas to an accounting flow is not difficult. Figure 15-1 (page 642), which is but a minor variation of similar figures in Chapters 13 and 14, translates cost flows to changes in specific accounts.

The two major cost accumulation systems are *process* and *job-order costing*. Actual or normal costing can be used under either system, and standard costs can often be used under either system. Despite the differences among the various combinations, the general form of the journal entries to formalize the flow of costs does not differ much from one system to another, because, as Figure 15-1 shows, there is a limited number of places for costs to be collected or transferred. The first illustration is of actual process costing, the second of normal job-order costing. We shall also illustrate standard costing. Because it is relatively easy to see what steps are *not* necessary under variable costing, all of the illustrations use absorption costing.

Illustration of Actual Process Costing

Mason Company produces a special type of plywood. The manufacturing process requires sequential applications of layers of wood until the plywood reaches the required thickness. For simplicity, we assume that there were no beginning inventories of work in process. (The implications of beginning work-in-process inventories for the calculation of equivalent production were discussed on pages 636–37.) The firm had the following transactions in 19X5. (We omit explanations of the journal entries because the descriptions of the transactions serve that purpose.)

---

[1] Following the pattern introduced in Chapter 13, we indicate the names of accounts by using capital letters, while using lowercase letters to denote the objects themselves. Thus, "Work in Process" refers to an account, while "work in process" refers to the physical, semifinished product.

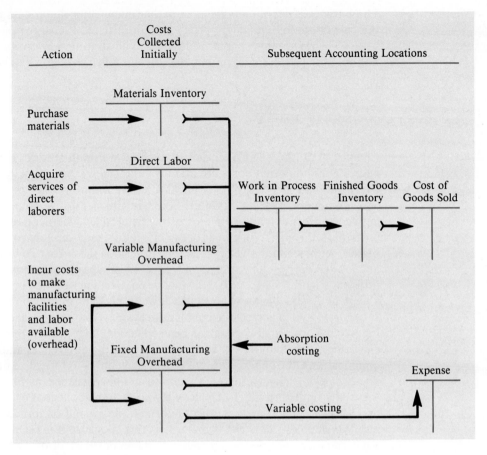

Figure 15-1   Cost Accounting Cycle

Purchase of materials: Mason bought 1,400,000 feet of wood at $0.095 per foot.

1.	Materials Inventory (1,400,000 × $0.095)	$133,000	
	Cash or Accounts Payable		$133,000

Materials put into process: Mason used 1,300,000 feet of wood.

2.	Works in Process (1,300,000 × $0.095)	$123,500	
	Materials Inventory		$123,500

Direct labor incurred: Direct laborers earned $344,400 for 41,000 hours of work at $8.40 per hour. The cost was charged to Work in Process.

3a.	Direct Labor	$344,400	
	Cash or Accrued Payroll		$344,400
3b.	Work in Process Inventory	$344,400	
	Direct Labor		$344,400

Overhead costs incurred: Mason incurred the following overhead costs. For brevity we list only a few individual items and lump the bulk of overhead costs into the "Other" category.

Variable overhead:	
Indirect labor	$ 84,000
Supplies	12,000
Other	155,300
Total variable overhead	$251,300
Fixed overhead:	
Supervision	$ 74,000
Depreciation	96,000
Other	291,000
Total fixed overhead	$461,000

Overhead costs are seldom put directly into Work in Process Inventory. Instead, a firm usually gathers the costs in an account called *Manufacturing Overhead* (or into two such accounts: one for variable overhead and one for fixed overhead), and keeps additional records of the types of costs incurred.

4a.	Variable Manufacturing Overhead	$251,300	
	Cash, Accrued Payables		$251,300
4b.	Fixed Manufacturing Overhead	$461,000	
	Accumulated Depreciation		$ 96,000
	Cash, Accrued Payables		$365,000

The manufacturing overhead accounts are for convenience and are especially helpful when standard costing is used, as we shall show shortly. The amounts put into the manufacturing overhead accounts are now transferred to Work in Process Inventory.

5.	Work in Process Inventory	$712,300	
	Variable Manufacturing Overhead		$251,300
	Fixed Manufacturing Overhead		$461,000

Production: Mason finished 40,000 square yards of plywood. Another 3,000 square yards were still in process at the end of 19X5. These 3,000 square yards were two-thirds finished. That is, on the average, the plywood remaining in process had two thirds of the materials and two thirds of the labor required to make a finished square yard.

To transfer the cost of finished units to Finished Goods Inventory, we need to know the per-unit cost of those units finished. Therefore, we need equivalent production, which is calculated as follows.

$$\frac{\text{Equivalent}}{\text{production}} = 40,000 + (3,000 \times 2/3) = 42,000 \text{ square yards}$$

The 42,000 equivalent production figure is used to determine the cost per unit. At this point we have $1,180,200 in Work in Process Inventory, composed of the following costs. The numbers in parentheses refer to journal entries.

Materials (2)	$ 123,500
Direct labor (3b)	344,400
Variable overhead (5)	251,300
Fixed overhead (5)	461,000
Total	$1,180,200
Divided by equivalent production	42,000
Equals cost per unit	$28.10

The $28.10 cost per unit is used for the transfer to Finished Goods Inventory.

6.	Finished Goods Inventory (40,000 × $28.10)	$1,124,000	
	Work in Process Inventory		$1,124,000

Sales: Mason sold 35,000 square yards at $40 each.

7a.	Cash or Accounts Receivable (35,000 × $40)	$1,400,000	
	Sales		$1,400,000
7b.	Cost of Goods Sold (35,000 × $28.10)	$ 983,500	
	Finished Goods Inventory		$ 983,500

Selling and administrative expenses: Mason incurred $340,000 in selling and administrative expenses.

8.	Selling and Administrative Expenses	$340,000	
	Cash, Accrued Payables		$340,000

At this point the accounts for direct labor, variable overhead, and fixed overhead all have zero balances. The other key accounts show the following.

Work in Process Inventory						Finished Goods Inventory			
(2)	$ 123,500					(6)	$1,124,000	$983,500	(7b)
(3b)	344,400					Bal.	$ 140,500		
(5)	712,300	$1,124,000	(6)						
	1,180,200	1,124,000							
Bal.	$ 56,200								

Cost of Goods Sold		
(7b)	$ 983,500	

Materials Inventory			
(1)	$ 133,000	$123,500	(2)
Bal.	$ 9,500		

An income statement for Mason Company is given in Exhibit 15-3.

Exhibit 15-3
Income Statement for Mason Company—Actual Process Costing

Sales (7a)[a]	$1,400,000
Cost of goods sold (7b)	983,500
Gross profit	416,500
Selling and administrative expenses (8)	340,000
Income	$ 76,500

[a] Figures in parentheses indicate journal entry numbers from the earlier illustrations.

Illustration of Job-Order Costing

Portland Mill Works makes various industrial products that require work in two departments, stamping and assembly. The Stamping Department uses costly machinery and relatively little direct labor. Accordingly, the managers believe that machine hours is the appropriate measure of activity for applying overhead in that department. The Assembly Department is relatively labor intensive, with machinery limited to small devices. The managers use direct labor hours as the measure of activity for applying overhead in that department.

The company has established predetermined overhead rates as shown below.

	Stamping Department	Assembly Department
Total budgeted overhead	$600,000	$250,000
Divided by budgeted levels of activity	200,000 machine hours	100,000 direct labor hours
Equals predetermined overhead rates	$3.00 per MH	$2.50 per DLH

Exhibit 15-4 (page 646) presents the actual results for the year, including the overhead applied for each department.

We can calculate misapplied overhead as follows.

Total actual overhead ($608,000 + $244,000)	$852,000
Total applied overhead ($630,000 + $237,500)	867,500
Total overapplied overhead	$ 15,500

The journal entries and accounts of a job-order firm are similar in form to those of a process costing firm (or one that uses standard costs). Essentially, job-

Exhibit 15-4
Portland Mill Works, Results for 19X6

Activity Data	Totals	Jobs Sold	Jobs in Ending Work in Process Inventory	Jobs in Ending Finished Goods Inventory
Machine hours in Stamping Department	210,000	190,000	7,000	13,000
Direct labor hours in Assembly Department	95,000	80,000	5,000	10,000
Cost Data				
Materials used	$ 650,000	$ 580,000	$30,000	$ 40,000
Direct labor	800,000	720,000	20,000	60,000
Applied overhead:				
Stamping Department at $3.00[a]	630,000	570,000	21,000	39,000
Assembly Department at $2.50[b]	237,500	200,000	12,500	25,000
Total costs	$2,317,500	$2,070,000	$83,500	$164,000
Actual Overhead				
Stamping	$ 608,000			
Assembly	244,000			
Total	$ 852,000			

[a] Total, 210,000 × $3.00 = $630,000; jobs sold, 190,000 × $3.00 = $570,000, etc.
[b] Total, 95,000 × $2.50 = $237,500; jobs sold, 80,000 × $2.50 = $200,000, etc.

order costing is a specific identification method, so that transfers from Work in Process Inventory to Finished Goods Inventory and to Cost of Goods Sold are based on the particular jobs finished and sold. For Portland Mill Works, the following entries summarize our knowledge of the flows. All of the information comes from Exhibit 15-4.

Materials used

1.	Work in Process Inventory		$ 650,000	
	Materials Inventory			$ 650,000

Direct labor

2a.	Direct Labor		$ 800,000	
	Cash or Accrued Payroll			$ 800,000
2b.	Work in Process Inventory		$ 800,000	
	Direct Labor			$ 800,000

Overhead incurrence and application

3a.	Factory Overhead—Stamping Department		$ 608,000	
	Factory Overhead—Assembly Department		244,000	
	Various Credits, Cash, Accrued Expenses,			
	Accumulated Depreciation			$ 852,000
3b.	Work in Process Inventory		$ 867,500	
	Factory Overhead—Stamping Department			$ 630,000
	Factory Overhead—Assembly Department			237,500

Completion of jobs

4.	Finished Goods Inventory	$2,234,000	
	Work in Process Inventory		$2,234,000

This entry is the total cost of all jobs completed during the year, which consists of the $2,070,000 cost of jobs sold plus the $164,000 cost of jobs still in Finished Goods Inventory at year end.

Cost of sales

5.	Cost of Goods Sold	$2,070,000	
	Finished Goods Inventory		$2,070,000

At this point, the various manufacturing overhead and inventory accounts appear as follows.

Factory Overhead—Stamping				Factory Overhead—Assembly			
(3a)	$ 608,000	$ 630,000	(3b)	(3a)	$ 244,000	$ 237,500	(3b)
		22,000	Bal.	Bal.	6,500		

Work in Process Inventory				Finished Goods Inventory			
(1)	$ 650,000			(4)	$2,234,000	$2,070,000	(5)
(2)	800,000			Bal.	$ 164,000		
(3b)	867,500	$2,234,000	(4)				
	2,317,500	2,234,000					
Bal.	$ 83,500						

Cost of Goods Sold		
(5)	$2,070,000	

The amounts shown as ending balances in Cost of Good Sold and the two inventory accounts agree with the amounts shown in Exhibit 15-4. The balances of the factory overhead accounts represent the overapplied or underapplied overhead for the departments. The net overapplied overhead of $15,500 ($22,000 overapplied in stamping minus $6,500 underapplied in assembly) agrees with the misapplied overhead computed on page 645.

What happens to the balances representing misapplication (actual different from applied) of overhead? As Chapter 13 stated, there are two possibilities. The $15,500 can be shown in the income statement, as an adjustment either to cost of goods sold or to gross margin, or the company could convert to an actual costing basis by allocating the misapplied overhead to all the work done during the year.

Illustration of Standard Costing

Our final illustration of the cost accounting cycle is a standard costing system. Virtually all such systems transfer costs *from* Work in Process Inventory to Finished Goods Inventory at the total standard cost of units completed and transferred. But costs can be put *into* Work in Process Inventory in two ways: (1) put in actual quantities of inputs at standard prices or (2) put in standard quantities of inputs at standard prices. We shall illustrate the latter technique.

Data for one of DMV Company's products appear in Exhibit 15-5. For simplicity, we shall assume that the firm has no inventories of work in process—that it finishes the units it starts each day. With the information given, we can calculate the several variances as shown in the table on page 649.

Exhibit 15-5
DMV Company
Data for Illustration

Standard Costs

Materials (3 pounds at $3 per pound)	$ 9
Direct labor (2 hours at $8 per hour)	16
Variable overhead at $6 per DLH	12
Fixed overhead[a]	20
Total standard cost	$ 57

Results for March 19X6

Beginning inventory of finished units at standard cost	
(500 units × $57)	$ 28,500
Units produced in March	9,000
Units sold in March	9,200
Ending inventory of finished units	300

Costs in March

Materials purchased (no beginning inventory)	$ 92,000
Materials used, 26,000 pounds	
Direct labor (19,000 hours × $8.20)	$155,800
Variable overhead	$112,000
Fixed overhead	$198,000

[a] Budgeted fixed overhead $200,000 per month/normal capacity of 10,000 units.

Materials Variances

Price variance [($3 × 30,000 pounds) − $92,000]	$ 2,000 unfavorable
Use variance [(9,000 × 3 × $3) − (26,000 × $3)]	3,000 favorable

Labor Variances

Rate variance [($8.00 − $8.20) × 19,000 hours]	3,800 unfavorable
Efficiency variance [(9,000 × 2 × $8) − (19,000 × $8)]	8,000 unfavorable

Variable Overhead Variances

Budget variance [($6 × 19,000) − $112,000]	2,000 favorable
Efficiency variance [(18,000 − 19,000) × $6]	6,000 unfavorable

Fixed Overhead Variances

Budget variance ($200,000 − $198,000)	2,000 favorable
Volume variance [(10,000 − 9,000) × $20]	20,000 unfavorable

The journal entries describing the events of March appear below. One objective of a standard costing system is to isolate variances in the accounts as quickly as possible, instead of just making separate calculations outside of the accounting system. Timely determination of variances helps in control because the sooner the managers know about variances, the sooner they can decide whether or not to investigate and possibly act. Hence, in the entries shown below, *price* variances are isolated when the cost is incurred, which is when the variance first becomes known, and *quantity* variances are isolated when costs are put into process. Thus, the entries putting costs into process are made at the end of the period, when production is known, because you must know production to determine the efficiency variances and fixed overhead volume variance. As we have said, there are other possible patterns, but they all share the essential characteristic of standard costing: all inventories appear at standard cost at the ends of periods.

Material purchases

1.	Materials Inventory (30,000 pounds × $3)	$ 90,000	
	Material Price Variance	2,000	
	Cash or Accounts Payable		$ 92,000

Material use

2.	Work in Process Inventory (27,000 pounds × $3)	$ 81,000	
	Material Use Variance		$ 3,000
	Materials Inventory (26,000 pounds × $3)		78,000

Direct labor

3a.	Direct Labor (19,000 × $8)	$152,000	
	Direct Labor Rate Variance	3,800	
	Cash or Accrued Payroll		$155,800

3b.	Work in Process Inventory (18,000 × $8)	$144,000	
	Direct Labor Efficiency Variance	8,000	
	Direct Labor		$152,000

Variable overhead

4a.	Variable Manufacturing Overhead (19,000 × $6)	$114,000	
	Variable Overhead Spending Variance		$ 2,000
	Various Credits, Cash, Accrued Expenses		112,000
4b.	Work in Process Inventory (18,000 × $6)	$108,000	
	Variable Overhead Efficiency Variance	6,000	
	Variable Manufacturing Overhead		$114,000

Fixed overhead

5a.	Fixed Manufacturing Overhead	$200,000	
	Fixed Overhead Budget Variance		$ 2,000
	Various Credits, Cash, Accumulated		
	Depreciation		198,000
5b.	Work in Process Inventory (9,000 × $20)	$180,000	
	Fixed Overhead Volume Variance	20,000	
	Fixed Manufacturing Overhead		$200,000

Completion of goods

| 6. | Finished Goods Inventory (9,000 × $57) | $513,000 | |
| | Work in Process Inventory | | $513,000 |

Cost of sales

| 7. | Cost of Goods Sold (9,200 × $57) | $524,400 | |
| | Finished Goods Inventory | | $524,400 |

The T-accounts for each type of inventory and for Cost of Goods Sold appear below. The beginning balance in Finished Goods Inventory is the standard cost of the 500 units on hand at the beginning of March (from Exhibit 15-5). The ending balance reflects the standard cost of the remaining 300 units (300 × $57 = $17,100). Materials Inventory shows the standard price of the 4,000 pounds in the ending inventory, which is the 30,000 pounds bought less the 26,000 used.

	Work in Process Inventory				Finished Goods Inventory			
(2)	$ 81,000			3-1 Bal.	$ 28,500			
(3b)	144,000			(6)	513,000	$524,400	(7)	
(4b)	108,000				$541,500	$524,400		
(5b)	180,000	$513,000	(6)	3-31 Bal.	$ 17,100			
	$513,000	$513,000						

	Materials Inventory				Cost of Goods Sold		
(1)	$ 90,000	$ 78,000	(2)	(7)	$524,400		
3-31 Bal.	$ 12,000						

At this point, all of the variances have been isolated in separate accounts. What is the disposition of variances? There are usually two alternatives. They can be carried to the income statement as adjustments to either cost of goods sold or to gross margin. Or, they can be prorated among those accounts still containing the cost elements that gave rise to the variances. Thus, variances other than the material price variance would be prorated among Cost of Goods Sold, Finished Goods Inventory, and Work in Process Inventory. The proration of a material price variance would also involve Material Inventory if materials were still on hand at the end of the period. As stated earlier, the need for proration depends on the magnitude of the variances and the ending inventories, since generally accepted accounting principles accept standard costs for financial reporting purposes as long as the income-statement results of using such costs do not differ materially from the results under actual costing. Unfortunately, what constitutes a "material" difference has never been defined.

Illustration of Product Costing in a JIT Environment

Because just-in-time inventory policies are characteristic of advanced manufacturing systems, firms using such systems have no significant work in process inventory and so have relatively few problems in accounting for that type of inventory. Some JIT companies might, however, have significant finished goods inventories, in which case product costing is still a concern. One technique used by such companies is **backflushing,** or **backflush costing.**

With backflushing, there are relatively few entries during a period. There is no effort to keep Materials Inventory, Work-in-Process Inventory, or Finished Goods Inventory at their "correct" balances. Rather, companies using this technique maintain two inventory accounts, one for finished goods, and the other for both materials and work in process.

The following example shows one way to record events using a backflush system. Data for the example appear below.

Beginning inventories	None
Materials and components purchased and put into process	$250,000
Labor and overhead costs incurred	$180,000
Units completed	40,000
Units sold	35,000

Because materials are put into process almost immediately after being received, there is no need for separate accounts for materials and work in process and material purchases are recorded in the following manner.

Materials and In-Process Inventory	$250,000	
Cash or Accounts Payable		$250,000

Conversion costs are collected in a single account as below.

Conversion Costs	$180,000	
Cash, Accounts Payable, Accumulated Depreciation, etc.		$180,000

Because there is relatively little direct labor, there is no need for detailed labor reporting. The above two entries are made throughout the period as events require.

The average cost of production for the period is $10.75 [($250,000 + $180,000)/40,000]. At the end of the period, an entry is made to record the cost of the ending inventory of finished units and the cost of units sold.

Cost of Sales (35,000 × $10.75)	$376,250	
Finished Goods Inventory (5,000 × $10.75)	53,750	
Materials and In-Process Inventory		$250,000
Conversion Costs		180,000

The recording could also be done using standard costs, though JIT companies typically use actual rather than standard costs.

The pattern of entries shown above is not the only possibility. Some companies charge all costs to Finished Goods Inventory on the basis of reports of the number of units completed, and make a transfer of Cost of Sales only at month-end. Because backflush costing has the potential for reducing the information provided to managers during an accounting period, it is best suited to a firm with relatively stable levels of production activity and few in-process units.

Final Comparative Comments

We have illustrated the cost accounting cycle in four situations. First, we showed a company that used actual process costing; next, a job-order firm that used normal costing; then, an operation that used standard costs; and finally, actual costing in a JIT environment. At this point it is desirable to review briefly not only the illustrations but also the many topics covered as part of our three-chapter discussion of product costing.

Any cost accounting system can be classified as either variable costing or absorption costing, the difference being that only the latter assigns fixed manufacturing overhead to units of product. Any system will use actual, normal, or standard costs. The nature of the manufacturing operation tends to separate cost accumulation systems into job order and process. Both types of firms could use either absorption or variable costing, and actual, normal, or standard costs. (Most job order systems do not use standard costs because of the differences among the products produced on the various jobs.)

Yet, with all these possibilities, the only real differences among the various methods, systems, and techniques relate to the valuation of inventories. That is, since the costs incurred by a firm in a given period are whatever they are, the different techniques that have been discussed are simply different ways of assigning those costs to two different sets of units: those sold and those still on hand. If a company has no inventories, all of the various approaches and combinations thereof will produce the same amount of income on the income statement.

Thus, managers, who must use accounting reports to help them in decision making, must know the basis of the reports and must comprehend the effects that any given approach or technique will have on those reports. Since any of the approaches and techniques affect the valuation of inventories, a manager's first concern should be about what constitutes *inventoriable cost*.

SUMMARY

The nature of a manufacturing operation determines whether a company uses job-order or process costing. Calculating unit costs under process costing is complicated by the existence of incomplete units of inventory at the beginning and/or end of a period. The concept of equivalent production was developed to overcome this complication, but the existence of beginning inventories requires adopting a cost-flow assumption (weighted average or first-in-first-out).

The flow of costs through a manufacturing firm can be accounted for using several methods or systems regardless of whether a company uses job-order or process costing. Specifically, a firm can use either actual or normal costing in the assignment of manufacturing overhead, or it can use standard costs for some or all components of manufacturing cost. (In addition, of course, a firm could use either variable or absorption costing, but the latter is required for external reporting and therefore is likely to be used for internal reports.)

The journal entries to record cost flows are, in general form, quite similar for job-order and process costing. They are somewhat more complex when standard costs are used, because entries in that situation must isolate variances into separate accounts, but they can be somewhat less complex in an advanced manufacturing environment.

KEY TERMS

backflushing
conversion costs

equivalent production
process costing

KEY FORMULAS

$$\text{Equivalent production—weighted average} = \text{units completed} + \left(\text{units in ending inventory} \times \text{percentage complete} \right)$$

$$\text{Equivalent production—first-in-first-out} = \text{units completed} + \left(\begin{array}{c} \text{units in} \\ \text{ending} \\ \text{inventory} \end{array} \times \begin{array}{c} \text{percentage} \\ \text{complete} \end{array} \right) - \left(\begin{array}{c} \text{units in} \\ \text{beginning} \\ \text{inventory} \end{array} \times \begin{array}{c} \text{percentage} \\ \text{complete} \\ \text{in prior} \\ \text{period} \end{array} \right)$$

$$\text{Cost per unit—weighted average} = \frac{\text{cost of beginning inventory} + \text{costs incurred during the period}}{\text{equivalent production—weighted average}}$$

REVIEW PROBLEM – PROCESS COSTING

Stambol Manufacturing Company makes a chemical solvent and uses weighted-average process costing. Data for April 19X8 are as follows.

Beginning inventory of work in process	$ 6,000
Materials used	$485,000
Direct labor incurred	$648,000
Overhead incurred	$604,000
Gallons completed and sent to finished goods	800,000
Gallons in ending inventory (75% complete)	40,000

Required

1. Determine equivalent production and cost per unit.
2. Determine the cost of the ending inventory of work in process.
3. Prepare a T-account for Work in Process Inventory. Check the ending balance with your answer to item 2.
4. There was no inventory of finished product at the beginning of April. During April, 730,000 gallons were sold and 70,000 gallons remained in ending finished goods inventory. Determine the cost of goods sold and the cost of the ending inventory of finished product.

Answer to Review Problem

1. Equivalent production and cost per unit.

Equivalent Production	
Gallons completed	800,000
Equivalent production in ending inventory (40,000 × 75%)	30,000
Equivalent production for April	830,000

Cost per Unit—Weighted Average	
Beginning inventory of work in progress	$ 6,000
Costs incurred:	
Materials	485,000
Direct labor	648,000
Overhead	604,000
Total	$1,743,000
Divided by equivalent production	830,000
Equals cost per unit	$2.10

2. Ending inventory of work in process is $63,000 (30,000 equivalent units × $2.10).

3.   Work in Process Inventory

Beginning balance	$ 6,000		
Materials	485,000		
Direct labor	648,000		
Overhead	604,000	$1,680,000 transferred out (800,000 × $2.10)	
	1,743,000	1,680,000	
Ending balance	$ 63,000		

The $63,000 balance equals the answer to item 2.

4. Cost of goods sold is $1,533,000, 730,000 gallons multiplied by $2.10. Ending inventory of finished goods is $147,000, which is 70,000 gallons (800,000 − 730,000) multiplied by $2.10.

REVIEW PROBLEM—STANDARD COSTING

Mason Company, whose actual operations were accounted for in the chapter (pages 641–45), has changed to standard costing. It developed the following standards per square yard of plywood.

Materials (30 feet of wood at $0.10 per foot)	$ 3
Direct labor (1 hour at $8 per hour)	8
Variable overhead ($6 per direct labor hour)	6
Fixed overhead*	9
Total standard cost	$26

*Based on budgeted fixed overhead of $450,000 and normal capacity of 50,000 square yards ($450,000/50,000 = $9 per square yard).

Required
1. Using the actual results detailed in the chapter, calculate the variances from standard cost.
2. Prepare journal entries to record the events.
3. Prepare T-accounts for Work in Process Inventory, Finished Goods Inventory, Materials Inventory, and Cost of Goods Sold at standard.
4. Prepare an income statement for the year and contrast it with the one shown in Exhibit 15-3 that uses actual costing.

Answer to Review Problem

1.   *Materials Variances*

Price variance [1,400,000 feet × $0.005 ($0.10 − $0.095)]	$ 7,000	favorable
Use variance [1,300,000 − (42,000 × 30 feet) × $0.10]	4,000	unfavorable
	Direct Labor Variances	
Rate variance [41,000 hours × ($8.40 − $8)]	$16,400	unfavorable
Efficiency variance [41,000 hours − (42,000 × 1)] × $8	8,000	favorable

Variable Overhead Variances

Spending variance [$251,300 − (41,000 × $6)]	$ 5,300 unfavorable
Efficiency variance [41,000 hours − (42,000 × 1)] × $6	6,000 favorable

Fixed Overhead Variances

Budget variance ($461,000 − $450,000)	$11,000 unfavorable
Volume variance [(50,000 − 42,000) × $9]	72,000 unfavorable

2.

1.	Materials Inventory (1,400,000 × $0.10)	$ 140,000	
	Material Price Variance		$ 7,000
	Cash or Accounts Payable		133,000
2.	Work in Process (1,260,000 × $0.10)	$ 126,000	
	Material Use Variance	4,000	
	Materials Inventory		$ 130,000
3a.	Direct Labor (41,000 × $8)	$ 328,000	
	Direct Labor Rate Variance	16,400	
	Cash		$ 344,400
3b.	Work in Process Inventory (42,000 × 1 × $8)	$ 336,000	
	Direct Labor Efficiency Variance		$ 8,000
	Direct Labor		328,000
4a.	Variable Manufacturing Overhead (41,000 hours × $6)	$ 246,000	
	Variable Overhead Spending Variance	5,300	
	Cash, Accrued Payables		$ 251,300
4b.	Fixed Manufacturing Overhead (budget of $450,000)	$ 450,000	
	Fixed Overhead Budget Variance	11,000	
	Accumulated Depreciation		$ 96,000
	Cash, Accrued Payables		365,000
5a.	Work in Process Inventory (42,000 × $6)	$ 252,000	
	Variable Overhead Efficiency Variance		$ 6,000
	Variable Manufacturing Overhead		246,000
5b.	Work in Process Inventory (42,000 × $9)	$ 378,000	
	Fixed Overhead Volume Variance (8,000 × $9)	72,000	
	Fixed Manufacturing Overhead		$ 450,000
6.	Finished Goods Inventory (40,000 × $26)	$1,040,000	
	Work in Process Inventory		$1,040,000
7a.	Cash or Accounts Receivable (35,000 × $40 selling price)	$1,400,000	
	Sales		$1,400,000
7b.	Cost of Goods Sold (35,000 × $26)	$ 910,000	
	Finished Goods Inventory		$ 910,000
8.	Selling and Administrative Expenses	$ 340,000	
	Cash, Accrued Payables		$ 340,000

3.

	Work in Process Inventory		
(2)	$ 126,000		
(3b)	336,000		
(5a)	252,000		
(5b)	378,000	$1,040,000	(6)
	1,092,000	1,040,000	
Bal.	$ 52,000		

	Finished Goods Inventory		
(6)	$1,040,000	$910,000	(7b)
Bal.	$ 130,000		

Materials Inventory				Cost of Goods Sold	
(1)	$ 140,000	$ 130,000	(2)	(7b)	$ 910,000
Bal.	$ 10,000				

Income Statements for Mason Company—Absorption Costing

	Actual Process Costing		Standard Process Costing
Sales (7a)[a]	$1,400,000		$1,400,000
Cost of goods sold (7b)	983,500		910,000
Gross profit	416,500		490,000
Manufacturing variances:			
Material price (1)		$ 7,000F	
Material use (2)		4,000U	
Direct labor rate (3a)		16,400U	
Direct labor efficiency (3b)		8,000F	
Variable overhead spending (4a)		5,300U	
Variable overhead efficiency (5a)		6,000F	
Fixed overhead budget (4b)		11,000U	
Fixed overhead volume (5b)		72,000U	87,700U
Actual gross profit			402,300
Less: Selling and administrative			
expenses (8)	340,000		340,000
Income	$ 76,500		$ 62,300

[a]Figures in parentheses indicate journal entry numbers.

APPENDIX: PROCESS COSTING – THE FIFO METHOD

We stated in this chapter that there is a need to choose a cost-flow assumption (weighted average or first-in-first-out) when units are worked on in two periods. The need arises because the cost to work on a unit of product might change from one period to the next.

The illustration in the chapter used the weighted-average method. It is just as reasonable—and intuitively more appealing—to argue that the costs incurred in the current period apply only to that portion of the work done in the current period. This alternative leads to the use of the **first-in-first-out (FIFO)** method. Adopting this method changes the calculation of the unit cost for the current period, because it affects both the numerator and the denominator of the calculation of current-period unit cost. The numerator includes (1) only the production costs of the current period, and the denominator includes only the work done during the current period.

Illustration of FIFO

To illustrate FIFO, let us return to the data used in this chapter to illustrate the weighted-average method. For your convenience, the data in Exhibit 15-1 are reproduced in Exhibit 15-6.

Exhibit 15-6
Data for Ronn Company

	August	September
Production costs	$206,000	$191,400
Unit data:		
In process at beginning of month	0	5,000
Completed during month	100,000	90,000
In process at end of month	5,000	10,000
Percentage of completion for end-of-period work in process	60%	40%

The company starts the month of August with no units in process. Hence, there is no need to know the cost flow assumption. The unit cost for August is computed, as shown in the chapter, by dividing the total manufacturing costs in August ($206,000) by the equivalent production in that month (103,000), for a unit cost of $2.00. That is, whatever work was done on whatever units were processed in August (started and finished during the month, or still unfinished at the end of the month), the total costs were $206,000. The cost of processing a *full* unit was $2.00 ($206,000/103,000).

The situation in September is different. In September, 90,000 units were completed and 10,000 were on hand, 40% complete. But of the 90,000 units completed, 5,000 units were 60% complete at the beginning of the period, so that the production costs for September apply to those beginning inventory units *only* to the extent of the 40% of the work done in September. Therefore, we calculate the cost of processing a unit of product in September by using *only* September's costs and an equivalent production figure that reflects *only* September's work. We already know that production costs in September were $191,400, so the task is to calculate an equivalent production related only to the September work. What we need is an equivalent production number that relates only to the work done in September. We can determine that number simply by backing out the work done in August from the weighted-average equivalent production computed for September. That is, if we start with the number of finished units (90,000 in September, in the present example), we need only subtract the amount of work done on some of those units *prior* to September. Thus, the calculation of equivalent production for September using the FIFO assumption is

Units completed in September (90,000 × 100%)	90,000
Work done on units partially complete at the end of September (10,000 × 40%)	4,000
Weighted-average equivalent production (page 636)	94,000
Less work done in August on units completed in September (5,000 units × 60%)	3,000
Equivalent production, FIFO	91,000

We can generalize this calculation in this way.

$$\begin{matrix} \text{Equivalent} \\ \text{production} \\ \text{—first-in-} \\ \text{first-out} \end{matrix} = \begin{matrix} \text{units} \\ \text{com-} \\ \text{pleted} \end{matrix} + \left(\begin{matrix} \text{units in} \\ \text{ending} \\ \text{inventory} \end{matrix} \times \begin{matrix} \text{percent} \\ \text{complete} \end{matrix} \right) - \left(\begin{matrix} \text{units in} \\ \text{beginning} \\ \text{inventory} \end{matrix} \times \begin{matrix} \text{percent} \\ \text{complete} \\ \text{in prior} \\ \text{period} \end{matrix} \right)$$

Under FIFO, equivalent production reflects only work done during the current period. Thus, the calculation of FIFO unit cost uses only the production costs for the period. The formula under FIFO is

$$\text{Unit cost—FIFO} = \frac{\text{production costs for the period}}{\text{equivalent production—FIFO}}$$

In the example, the unit cost is $2.1033, September production costs of $191,400 divided by equivalent production of 91,000 units. Because the unit cost determined for August was the same regardless of the cost-flow method, the total costs to be accounted for in September are the same as they were in the Chapter (page 637) and consist of

Costs of beginning inventory (5,000 units × 60% × $2)	$ 6,000
Production costs for September	191,400
Total cost to be accounted for	$197,400

These costs either have been transferred to finished goods (for the completed units) or are associated with the units still in process. With the FIFO assumption, the cost relevant to the units in process at the end of the period is the unit cost for work done in September, or $2.1033. The cost assigned to the ending inventory of 10,000 units that are 40% complete would be $8,413 (10,000 × 40% × $2.1033).

The costs transferred to finished goods can be determined by analyzing the units transferred.

Transfer of units that were in process at the beginning of the month:	
Cost from prior period, beginning inventory (5,000 × 60% × $2)	$ 6,000
Completion costs (5,000 × 40% × $2.1033)	4,207
Total	10,207
Transfer of units started and completed in September (90,000 − 5,000) × $2.1033	178,780
Total	$188,987

Thus, the total cost of $197,400 can be accounted for as

Costs transferred to finished goods	$188,987
Costs in ending inventory	8,413
Total cost accounted for	$197,400

If you compare the FIFO results with the weighted-average results shown in the chapter, you will see that the unit cost for September under FIFO ($2.1033) is slightly higher than that under weighted average ($2.10, page 637). Hence, the total cost of the ending work in process under FIFO ($8,413) is slightly higher than that under weighted average ($8,400, page 637). The magnitude of the difference is a function of the illustrative data; you should not assume that the difference will always be so small.

Why Choose FIFO?

At the start of this appendix, we suggested that FIFO is intuitively appealing. This is so because the costs incurred in a given period are applicable only to the work done during that period. The method is also appealing because it supports a manager's interest in controlling costs. The per-unit cost given by the weighted-average method is not suitable for control purposes because it mixes performance of the current period with performance in prior periods.

Because the unit-cost calculation under FIFO uses (1) an equivalent production that includes only current work and (2) only the current period production costs, managers obtain performance data for different periods. From Chapter 12 we know that some companies establish *standard* costs for certain aspects of the manufacturing process, and that comparisons of actual costs with standards give managers useful information for control and performance evaluation. For a company that uses standard costs and process costing, FIFO is particularly useful because it does not intermingle actual costs from two periods.

ASSIGNMENT MATERIAL

Questions for Discussion

15-1 **"True" fixed cost** Is there any meaning to the statement that there is a "true" fixed cost per unit of product? Discuss.

15-2 **Kinds of standards** If you were president of a manufacturing firm, which of the following income statements would you prefer to receive and why?
(a) One showing actual costs only.
(b) One showing standard costs and variances, with standard costs based on ideal standards.
(c) One showing standard costs and variances, with standard costs based on currently attainable standards.

Exercises

15-3 **Basic process costing** TUV Company uses weighted-average process costing. It makes its product from garbage and so has no material costs. The data opposite relate to July.

Beginning inventory	$3,200
Units completed in July	20,000 units
Units in ending work in process, 60% complete	4,000 units

Conversion costs incurred in July were $24,800.

Required
1. Determine equivalent production for July.
2. Determine the unit cost.
3. Determine the cost of the ending inventory of work in process.
4. Determine the cost of goods transferred to finished goods.

15-4   ***Job-order costing – journal entries***   Grimes Machine Shop had the following activity in March. Grimes uses actual job-order costing.
(a) The company used $4,960 in materials on jobs.
(b) Direct labor was $7,280.
(c) Factory overhead was $4,710.
(d) The cost of jobs finished was $12,500.
(e) The cost of jobs sold was $9,600.

Required: Prepare journal entries to record these events.

15-5   ***Basic process costing – weighted average***   The data below relate to the operations of Houston Milling Company for March. The company puts materials, labor, and overhead into process evenly throughout.

Beginning inventory, (5,000 units, 80% complete)	$4,400
Units completed in March	71,000 units
Ending inventory, 60% complete	15,000 units

Production costs incurred in March were $235,600. The company uses the weighted-average method.

Required
1. Compute equivalent production.
2. Compute unit cost.
3. Compute the cost of the ending inventory.
4. Compute the cost of units finished and transferred to finished goods inventory.

15-6   ***Basic process costing – FIFO (extension of 15-5, related to Appendix)***   Redo the previous assignment using the first-in-first-out method.   •

15-7   ***Relationships, volume variances, and production***   Ayres Inc. began 19X8 with 20,000 units of product on hand. During the year, it sold 110,000 units, and had 15,000 units in inventory at year end. Standard fixed cost per unit is $5 based on budgeted fixed overhead of $500,000 for the year.

Required
1. Compute the volume variance for 19X8.
2. Determine what would have happened to Ayres's total income if production had increased by 1,000 units but sales had remained the same.

15-8   ***Relationships – income, production, and volume variance***   Fosheim
Company sells a single product at $10 per unit. There are no variable manufactur-
ing costs, and fixed manufacturing costs are budgeted at $300,000. In 19X5 the
company had a standard gross profit of $160,000, income of $58,000, and sales of
40,000 units. Selling and administrative expenses in 19X5 were $90,000, and fixed
manufacturing costs were incurred as budgeted.

Required
1.   Compute the standard fixed cost per unit.
2.   Compute the volume variance for 19X5.
3.   Determine how many units were produced in 19X5.
4.   Determine what Fosheim would have shown as income in 19X5 if the com-
     pany had used variable costing.

15-9   ***Relationships – income, sales, and volume variance***   In 19X3 Bishop
Company sold 98,000 units of product. Variable cost per unit was $6, both stan-
dard and actual. The standard fixed manufacturing cost per unit is $8 and selling
and administrative expenses were $200,000. Fixed manufacturing costs were
incurred as budgeted. Income for 19X3 was $176,000 after considering an unfa-
vorable volume variance of $16,000. There was no change in inventories over the
year 19X3.

Required
1.   Determine the selling price of a unit of product.
2.   Determine the level of volume used to set the standard fixed cost per unit.
3.   Determine the budgeted amount of fixed manufacturing costs.

15-10   ***Process costing – unit costs***   Valley Manufacturing Company uses a process
costing system. The following data apply to July 19X9. Percentages of completion are the same for materials and for conversion costs.

		Units
Beginning inventory, 20% complete		3,000
Finished during July		35,000
Ending inventory, 60% complete		5,000
Production costs:		
Cost in beginning inventory	$ 23,700	
Incurred during July	$766,700	

Required
1.   Compute the cost per unit of the units finished during the period, using the
     weighted-average method.
2.   Compute the amount of ending work in process inventory and transfers to
     finished goods.
3.   Prepare a T-account for Work in Process Inven.ory.

15-11   ***Process costing (extension of 15-10, related to Appendix)***   Redo 15-10,
using first-in-first-out.

15-12   ***Backflush costing***   Timmins Company has completed the transition to just-in-
time manufacturing and is attempting to simplify its recordkeeping. The controller has given you the following data for January and asked what is the simplest,
most direct way to record the events.

Beginning inventories	none
Units finished	100,000
Units sold	90,000
Materials purchased and used	$410,000
Direct labor and manufacturing overhead	$350,000

There was no ending inventory of materials or of work-in-process.

Required: Determine ending inventory and cost of goods sold.

15-13   *Backflush costing, journal entries – continuation of 15-12*

Required: Prepare journal entries for Timmins Company's January activity.

15-14   *Process costing – two departments* Berke Manufacturing Company makes a single product, a chemical called Argot. The product is made in two processes, mixing and boiling. The following data apply to May 19X7. There were no beginning inventories. Percentages of completion are the same for materials and for conversion costs.

	Mixing	Boiling
Barrels completed during May	70,000	70,000
Barrels on hand at May 31	9,000	
Percentage complete	60%	
Production costs incurred	$52,780	$42,000

Required
1. Compute the cost per barrel for each process.
2. Compute the amount of ending work in process inventory in the Mixing Department.
3. The firm had no finished product on hand at the beginning of May. Of the 70,000 gallons finished during May, 60,000 were sold. Compute cost of goods sold and ending inventory of finished goods.

15-15   *Process costing* Hittite Company makes a water-soluble paint. All materials are put into process and are then mixed for several hours. Data for July are

Unit Data

Gallons completed in July	180,000
Gallons in ending inventory	30,000
Percentages complete:	
Materials	100%
Conversion costs	80%

Cost Data

	Materials	Conversion Costs
Beginning inventory	$ 3,240	$ 9,620
Incurred during July	$42,960	$127,060

Required
1. Using the weighted-average method, compute equivalent production for (a) materials and (b) conversion costs for the month of July.
2. Compute unit costs for each cost factor using the weighted-average method.
3. Prepare the journal entry to transfer the cost of finished gallons to Finished Goods Inventory.
4. Prepare a T-account for Work in Process Inventory.
5. Prove that your ending balance in Work in Process, from item 4, is correct.

Problems

15-16   *Equivalent production and unit costs* Borr Company manufactures a single type of fertilizer in a single process. Data for April are as follows.

Beginning inventory of work in process	5,000 pounds
Completed in April	150,000 pounds
Ending inventory of work in process	20,000 pounds
Cost of materials used in production	$366,150
Conversion costs incurred	$571,900
Costs in beginning inventory:	
Materials	$ 14,650
Conversion costs	$ 19,400

The inventories were 100% complete for materials. The beginning inventory was 75% complete for conversion costs, and the ending inventory was 60% complete. The company uses the weighted-average method.

Required
1. Determine equivalent production for materials and for conversion costs.
2. Determine unit costs for materials and for conversion costs.
3. Determine the cost of the ending inventory of work in process and the cost transferred to finished goods inventory.

15-17   *Equivalent units and standard costs (related to Appendix)* The production manager of Kneehi Company has just received his performance report for June 19X9. Among the data included are the following.

	Costs		
	Budgeted	*Actual*	*Variance*
Material	$10,000	$11,500	$1,500U
Direct labor	20,000	21,300	1,300U
Variable overhead	15,000	15,400	400U
Fixed overhead	18,000	18,800	800U
Total	$63,000	$67,000	$4,000U

The budgeted amounts are based on 2,000 units, the number actually completed during June. The production manager is upset because 800 half-finished units are still in process at the end of June and are not counted as part of production for the month. However, at the beginning of June, 300 units were one-third complete.

Required
1. Compute equivalent unit production on a first-in-first-out basis.
2. Prepare a new performance report.

15-18 *Costing methods and pricing* The sales manager and the controller of Emerson Company were discussing the price to be set for a new product. They had accumulated the following data.

Variable costs	$8 per unit
Fixed costs	$80,000 per year

The sales manager had set a target volume of 10,000 units per year. He determined average fixed cost to be $8 per unit, bringing average total cost per unit to $16. The firm follows a policy of setting prices at 200% of cost, so the sales manager stated that the price should be $32 per unit.

The controller said that $32 seemed high, especially as competitors were charging only $30 for essentially the same product. The sales manager agreed, stating that perhaps only 8,000 units per year could be sold at $32. However, he was convinced that the price should be set at 200% of cost. He added that it was unfortunate that fixed costs were so high, because he felt that 10,000 units could definitely be sold if the price were $30, and probably 12,000 at $28. However, it would not be possible to achieve the desired markup at those prices.

Required
1. Point out the fallacies in the reasoning of the sales manager. (You might wish to show what would happen at the $32 price. Would the firm achieve the desired markup?)
2. Determine which price ($32, $30, $28) will give the highest profit.

15-19 *Overhead rates, standard cost income statement* The following data pertain to the operations of Dickson Company for 19X5.

Budgeted production		100,000 units
Actual production		90,000 units
Budgeted costs for 100,000 units:		
Materials	$ 400,000	
Direct labor	300,000	
Variable overhead	200,000	
Fixed overhead	300,000	
Actual costs:		
Materials	$ 350,000	
Direct labor	280,000	
Variable overhead	190,000	
Fixed overhead	320,000	
Administrative	400,000	
Actual sales (80,000 units)	$1,600,000	

There were no beginning inventories. Dickson uses a standard fixed cost based on budgeted production.

Required: Prepare a standard cost income statement. Show variances separately for each category of manufacturing cost.

15-20 **Standard cost system — journal entries** Watson Company makes a single product. Its standard cost is given below.

Materials (2 pounds at $4)	$ 8
Direct labor (3 hours at $5)	15
Variable overhead ($6 per direct labor hour)	18
Fixed overhead (based on normal capacity of 50,000 units)	10
Total standard cost	$51

At the beginning of 19X9 there were no inventories. During 19X9 the following events occurred.
(a) Material purchases were 120,000 pounds for $455,000.
(b) Direct laborers were paid $790,000 for 151,000 hours of work.
(c) Variable overhead of $895,000 was incurred.
(d) Fixed overhead incurred was $490,000.
(e) Materials used were 95,000 pounds.
(f) Production was 48,000 units. All units started were finished.
(g) Sales were 45,000 units at $100 each.

Required: Prepare journal entries to record these events. Isolate variances as early as possible.

15-21 **Process costing — journal entries** Swanson Company makes a single type of pump on an assembly line. The firm uses process costing and applies manufacturing overhead at the rate of $12 per direct labor hour. Inventories at the beginning of 19X6 were as follows.

Raw material	$ 34,000
Work in process	67,000
Finished goods	125,000

During 19X6 the following transactions took place.
1. Material purchases were $286,000.
2. Wages earned by direct laborers for 35,000 hours were $289,000.
3. Raw materials costing $271,000 were put into process.
4. Other manufacturing costs incurred were

(a) Indirect labor	$ 46,000
(b) Supervision and other salaries	182,000
(c) Utilities and insurance	23,500
(d) Depreciation	72,000
(e) Other miscellaneous costs	112,000

5. Transfers from Work in Process to Finished Goods were $863,000.
6. Sales were $1,314,000.

7. Cost of goods sold was $818,000.
8. Selling and administrative expenses were $387,000.

Required
1. Prepare journal entries to record these events.
2. Determine the ending balance in each inventory account.
3. Prepare an income statement for 19X6.

15-22 **Product costing and VCP analysis** The president of Landry Company asked for your assistance in analyzing the firm's revenue and cost behavior. You gathered the following data relating to the firm's only product.

Selling price		$10
Variable costs:		
Production	$4	
Selling	2	6
Contribution margin		$ 4
Fixed production costs	$120,000 per month	
Fixed selling and administrative expenses	$ 30,000 per month	

You calculated the monthly break-even point as 37,500 units and the monthly sales required to earn the president's $8,000 target profit as 39,500 units.

Three months after you provided the analysis, the president called you. On your arrival at his office he gave you the following income statements.

	April	May	June
Sales	$380,000	$395,000	$420,000
Cost of goods sold	243,200	269,300	316,125
Gross profit	136,800	125,700	103,875
Selling and administrative costs	106,000	109,000	114,000
Profit (loss) before taxes	$ 30,800	$ 16,700	($ 10,125)

The president is extremely upset. He asks why your analysis does not hold, particularly because the production manager assured him that variable costs per unit and fixed costs in total were incurred as budgeted during the three months. The sales manager has also assured the president that selling prices were as expected.

After a few minutes you talk to the controller, who tells you the firm uses actual absorption costing and produced the following quantities of product during the three months: April, 50,000 units; May, 40,000 units; June, 32,000 units. There were no inventories on hand at the beginning of April.

Required: Explain the results to the president. Show calculations of the determination of cost of goods sold for each month.

15-23 **Process costing** Stockton Company makes a chemical spray that goes through two processes. Data for February are as follows.

	Mixing Department	Boiling Department
Gallons transferred to Boiling Department	75,000	
Gallons transferred to finished goods		68,000
Gallons on hand at end of month	9,000	15,000
Percent complete:		
Prior department costs	—	100%
Materials	100%	—ᵃ
Labor and overhead	60%	40%
Costs incurred during February:		
Materials	$18,480	—
Labor and overhead	$32,160	$25,900
Beginning inventories:		
Gallons	8,000	8,000
Costs:		
Materials	$ 1,680	—
Prior department costs	—	$ 6,350
Labor and overhead	$ 4,020	$ 2,220

ᵃNo material is added in this department.

Required
1. Determine the weighted-average equivalent production by cost category for each department.
2. Determine the per-unit cost by category for the Mixing Department.
3. Prepare the journal entry to record the transfer from the Mixing Department to the Boiling Department.
4. Determine the cost per unit by cost category for the Boiling Department.
5. Prepare the journal entry to record the transfer of product from the Boiling Department to Finished Goods.
6. Prepare the T-accounts for Work in Process for each department. Verify the ending inventory balances.

15-24 **_Process costing (related to Appendix, extension of 15-23)_**   Assume that Stockton Company uses FIFO and that the beginning inventory in the Mixing Department was 60% complete as to materials and 70% complete as to conversion costs.

Required
1. Determine the FIFO equivalent production by cost category for the Mixing Department and the unit cost for each category.
2. Determine the total cost to be transferred to the Boiling Department.
3. Prepare a T-account for Work in Process in the Mixing Department and verify the ending inventory balance.

15-25 **_Standard costs – performance evaluation_**   Topham Company is opening a new division to make and sell a single product. The product is to be made in a factory that has a practical capacity of 150,000 units per year. Production is expected to average 120,000 units after the first two years of operation. During the first two years, sales are expected to be 80,000 and 100,000, respectively, with production being 100,000 and 110,000 in those years.

The product is to sell for $20, with variable manufacturing costs of $8. Fixed production costs are expected to be $360,000 annually for the first several years. Selling and administrative costs, all fixed, are budgeted at $300,000 annually.

Ronald Yost, controller of the firm, has suggested that the normal capacity of 120,000 units be used to set the standard fixed cost per unit. The other managers agree that Ron's idea is sound, and Bill Roberts, the controller of the new division, is given the task of developing budgeted income statements based on the data given.

The operations of the first year are summarized as follows.

Sales (78,000 units)	$1,560,000
Production	115,000 units
Costs incurred:	
Variable production costs	$ 930,000
Fixed production costs	370,000
Selling and administrative costs	300,000

Required
1. Prepare a budgeted income statement based on the expected results in the first year of operations.
2. Prepare an income statement based on actual results.
3. Comment on the results. Was performance better than expected or worse? Explain.

15-26 Standard cost income statement – relationships and variances The income statement for Rider Company for 19X6 appears on page 670. Other data are as follows.
(a) There were no beginning inventories.
(b) Fixed overhead absorbed per unit is $2, based on budgeted production of 250,000 units, and budgeted fixed costs of $500,000.
(c) The standard direct labor rate is $4 per hour.
(d) Variable overhead standard cost is based on a rate of $2 per direct labor hour.
(e) Direct laborers worked 116,000 hours.
(f) The standard price for materials is $0.50 per pound.
(g) Material purchases were 800,000 pounds at $3,000 over standard price.

Required: Determine the following:
1. Standard cost per unit, including standard prices and quantities for each element of cost.
2. Standard variable cost per unit.
3. Production for the year.
4. Ending inventory at standard cost.
5. Fixed overhead costs incurred.

Sales (200,000 units)		$2,000,000
Cost of sales:		
Materials	$300,000	
Direct labor	400,000	
Overhead	600,000	1,300,000
Standard gross profit		700,000
Manufacturing variances:		
Materials	$ 12,000U	
Direct labor	18,000F	
Variable overhead spending	4,000U	
Variable overhead efficiency	8,000F	
Fixed overhead budget	7,000F	
Other underabsorbed overhead	20,000U	3,000U
Actual gross profit		697,000
Selling and administrative expenses		600,000
Income		$ 97,000

6. Cost of materials purchased.
7. Material use variance.
8. Pounds of material used in production.
9. Direct labor efficiency variance.
10. Direct labor rate variance.
11. Direct labor costs incurred.
12. Variable overhead costs incurred.
13. Amount by which income would have increased if one more unit had been sold, no more produced.
14. Amount by which income would have increased had one more unit been produced and sold.

15-27 Interpretation of standard cost statement The following income statement represents the operations of Thomas Company for June. Variable manufacturing costs at standard are 50% of total standard manufacturing cost. Standard fixed cost per unit is based on normal activity of 30,000 units per month.

Thomas Company
Income Statement for June. 19X4

Sales (20,000 units)		$200,000
Standard cost of sales		120,000
Standard gross profit		80,000
Manufacturing variances:		
Materials	$2,000U	
Direct labor	1,000F	
Overhead budget	1,000U	
		2,000U
		78,000
Volume variance		24,000U
Gross profit, actual		54,000
Selling, general, and administrative costs		48,000
Income		$ 6,000

Required: Answer the following questions.
1. What are fixed and variable standard costs per unit?
2. What are monthly fixed manufacturing costs?
3. How many units were produced in June?
4. If beginning inventory of finished goods was $60,000 at standard cost, how much is ending inventory at standard cost? (*Hint:* Prepare an expanded cost-of-goods-sold section.)

15-28 **Income statement for standard costing, practical capacity (extension of 15-27)**   Assume the same facts as in 15-27, except for the following.
(a) Production is 22,000 units.
(b) Total fixed production costs are $90,000.
(c) Thomas bases its standard fixed cost per unit on its practical capacity of 40,000 units per month.
(d) There were no beginning inventories.

Required: Prepare a new income statement. (*Hint:* The standard fixed cost per unit will not be the same as that determined in 15-27.)

15-29 **Standard costs, budgets, variances, journal entries**   The following data relate to the operations of Warner Company for 19X2.

Budgeted sales (100,000 units)	$1,000,000
Budgeted production	140,000 units
Budgeted costs:	
Materials (2 pounds per unit)	$ 210,000
Direct labor (1 hour per unit)	420,000
Variable overhead ($1 per direct labor hour)	140,000
Fixed overhead—manufacturing	300,000
Selling and administrative (all fixed)	180,000

The firm uses a standard cost system; the preceding production costs are based on standard cost per unit. Standard fixed cost per unit is based on 150,000 units of production at practical capacity. The inventory of finished goods at December 31, 19X1, is 13,000 units. There were no other inventories at December 31, 19X1.
Actual results for 19X2 are

Sales (95,000 units)	$950,000
Production	130,000 units
Materials purchased (250,000 pounds)	$192,500
Materials used	236,000 pounds
Direct labor (133,000 hours)	$402,000
Variable overhead	128,000
Fixed overhead	285,000
Selling and administrative expenses	175,000

Required
1. Prepare a budgeted income statement for 19X2.
2. Prepare all necessary journal entries to record events in 19X2. The produc-

tion manager is responsible for all variances except material price and labor rate.

3. Prepare an income statement for 19X2.

15-30 ***Actual process costing, journal entries, and income statement***   Wilberforce Company uses actual process costing. The following data relate to its operations in July 19X7. There were no beginning inventories.

1. Material purchases were $39,600 for 12,000 pounds ($3.30 per pound).
2. Payments to direct laborers were $28,850 for 7,300 hours of work.
3. Variable overhead costs incurred were $58,510.
4. Fixed overhead costs incurred were $86,500.
5. Material use was 11,000 pounds.
6. Units completed totaled 7,200. At the end of July 19X7, units in process totaled 500 and were 40% complete.
7. Sales were 6,500 units at $50 per unit.
8. Selling and administrative expenses were $106,000.

Required

1. Prepare journal entries for July.
2. Prepare an income statement for July.

15-31 ***Standard process costing, journal entries, and income statement (extension of 15-30)***   The president of Wilberforce Company needs your assistance. He wants to know whether his firm could use standard costing and how it works. He believes that the following standards are appropriate.

Materials (1.5 pounds at $3.20)	$ 4.80
Direct labor (1 hour at $4)	4.00
Variable overhead at $8 per direct labor hour	8.00
Fixed overhead at $12 per direct labor hour	12.00
	$28.80

The president tells you that the per-unit fixed overhead figure of $12 is based on normal capacity of 7,000 direct labor hours per month.

Required

1. Prepare journal entries for July using standard process costing.
2. Prepare an income statement for July using standard process costing.

15-32 ***Special order***   Western Corn Oil Company has found that its sales forecast for 19X6 was too high by about 40,000 cases of oil. Because the production budget was not revised, inventory is expected to be about 40,000 cases above normal at year end. In early December the sales manager was offered the opportunity to sell 25,000 cases at $4.80, well below the normal price of $8. Regular sales would not be affected by the order. He asked the controller for an analysis of the order and was given the partial income statement shown below. The controller said that because general and administrative expenses would not be affected, it was only necessary to determine the effect on gross profit.

Expected Income Statements

	Without Order	With Order
Sales	$2,400,000	$2,520,000
Standard costs of sales, $6 per case	1,800,000	1,950,000
Standard gross profit	600,000	570,000
Volume variance	(120,000)	(120,000)
Actual gross profit	$ 480,000	$ 450,000

The sales manager was puzzled and asked the controller about the volume variance. The controller replied that the volume variance related to production, not sales, and that production would not be increased because inventory was already too high. She said that the volume variance resulted because the firm used 400,000 cases on which to base the standard fixed cost, and actual production was expected to be only 340,000 cases.

Required
1. Determine whether the order should be accepted.
2. Prepare new partial income statements, using variable costing.
3. Prepare a new partial income statement assuming that production would be increased by 25,000 cases if the order were accepted.

15-33 Job-order costing – standards and variances Carlson Company makes a variety of furniture. The company has established the following standard variable costs for some of its high-volume models.

	Chair Model 803	Sofa Model 407
Materials:		
Wood	$ 24	$ 58
Fabric	46	92
Other	13	21
Total materials	83	171
Direct labor at $5 standard rate per hour	65	90
Variable overhead at $8 per direct labor hour	104	144
Total standard variable cost	$252	$405

During June the firm worked on two jobs. Order 82 was for 80 units of Model 803, and order 83 was for 50 units of Model 407. Both jobs were finished and sold for a total of $97,000.
Cost data are as follows.

Materials used, at standard prices:	
Wood	$ 4,855
Fabric	8,360
Other	2,090
Direct labor (2,050 hours × $5 per hour)	10,250
Variable overhead incurred	16,850

Fixed production costs were incurred as budgeted, $24,600. Selling and administrative expenses were $18,700. There were no material price variances.

Required
1. Determine the standard cost of each job order, by individual cost category.
2. Determine the following variances: material use, by type of material; direct labor efficiency; variable overhead spending; variable overhead efficiency.
3. Prepare an income statement for June using standard variable costing. Show the variances calculated in item 2 as a lump sum.

15-34 Comprehensive problem in costing methods The following data relate to Gagner Company operations for 19X5.

	Budgeted	Actual
Production (units)	200,000	180,000
Sales (units)	190,000	160,000
Direct materials	$400,000	$375,000
Direct labor	$600,000	$580,000
Variable overhead	$400,000	$395,000
Fixed overhead	$200,000	$208,000
Selling, general, and administrative expenses	$700,000	$700,000

There were no beginning inventories; sales prices averaged $15 per unit; practical capacity is 250,000 units.

Required
1. Prepare income statements based on the following costing methods:
   (a) actual absorption costing.
   (b) standard absorption costing—fixed overhead based on budgeted production (show the total variance for each element of cost).
   (c) standard absorption costing using practical capacity as the fixed overhead allocation base.
   (d) standard variable costing.
   (e) actual variable costing.
2. Compare and contrast the results obtained in item 1.

15-35 Comprehensive problem in costing methods (extension of 15-34)
Gagner Company now has data regarding operations for 19X6, during which selling prices again averaged $15 per unit. The following data relate to 19X6 activity.

	Budgeted	Actual
Production (units)	150,000	190,000
Sales (units)	140,000	200,000
Direct materials	$300,000	$400,000
Direct labor	$450,000	$590,000
Variable manufacturing overhead	$300,000	$410,000
Fixed manufacturing overhead	$200,000	$215,000
Selling, general, and administrative expenses	$700,000	$720,000

Required: Prepare income statements for 19X6, using each of the methods listed in the previous assignment.

15-36 ***Standard costs and product profitability***   Tucumcary Office Products Company makes three sizes of file folders. The company has practical capacity of 50,000 machine hours per year and uses that figure to set standard fixed costs for each size of folder. At the beginning of 19X6 the controller had prepared the following data regarding the three sizes of folders (all data per carton of 50 folders).

	Two-Inch	Three-Inch	Four-Inch
Selling price	$17.00	$24.00	$31.00
Standard variable costs	8.00	11.00	16.00
Standard fixed costs	4.80	6.40	9.80
Total standard costs	12.80	17.40	25.60
Standard gross profit	$ 4.20	$ 6.60	$ 5.40
Expected sales in cartons	44,000	25,000	30,000
Machine hours required per carton	0.3	0.4	0.6

The sales manager has informed the controller that he has been approached by a large office supplies chain. The chain wants to buy 24,000 cartons of a six-inch folder and is willing to pay $40 per carton. The sales manager had discussed the offer with the production manager who stated that the folders could be made using the existing equipment. Variable costs per carton should be $19, and 0.8 machine hours should be required per carton.

Because the chain will take not fewer than 24,000 cartons, the sales manager was fairly sure that the firm did not have the capacity to fill the special order and still manufacture its other products in the volumes required by the expected sales. He therefore asked the controller to develop data on the proposed order and to decide which of the existing products should be partially curtailed. The controller then prepared the following analysis, which is incomplete because he was called away before finishing it. The sales manager was not sure how to proceed from this point and asked you to help him make the decision.

	Six-Inch Folder
Selling price	$40.00
Standard variable cost	19.00
Standard fixed cost	12.80
Total standard cost	$31.80
Standard gross profit	$ 8.20

The controller also prepared the following analysis of budgeted profit for the year.

	Two-Inch	Three-Inch	Four-Inch	Total
Standard gross profit per carton	$4.20	$6.60	$5.40	
Expected volume	44,000	25,000	30,000	
Total expected gross profit—standard	$184,800	$165,000	$162,000	$511,800
Expected volume variance				140,800
Expected actual gross profit				371,000
Budgeted selling and administrative expenses, all fixed				327,000
Budgeted profit before taxes				$ 44,000

The firm generally manufactures about as many cartons of each size of folder as it sells. Because it rarely experiences differences between standard and actual machine hours for given levels of production, it computes its volume variance based on the difference between 50,000 hours and actual hours worked.

Required: Prepare an analysis for the sales manager showing him whether the special order should be accepted and for which products, if any, production and sales should be reduced.

15-37 **Review problem**   Sally Ann Frocks is a manufacturer of dresses. Its relevant range is 1,500 to 5,000 dresses per month. For the month of May 19X5, it has prepared the following forecast.

Sales (2,500 dresses @ $30 each)
Variable manufacturing costs per dress:
   Materials (3 yards @ $2 per yard)
   Direct labor (2 hours @ $0.50 per hour)
   Variable overhead ($1 per DLH)
Fixed manufacturing overhead ($3,000)
Variable selling costs (commissions at 10% of sales)
Fixed selling and administrative costs ($6,000)
Inventories:
   May 1, 19X5   none
   May 31, 19X5   materials 500 yards, finished dresses 500

Normal capacity is 3,000 dresses per month, which is the basis for overhead application.

Required: Answer the following questions.
1. What is practical capacity?
2. What is budgeted production for May?
3. How many yards of materials should be purchased during May?
4. How many hours does it take to produce a dress?
5. What are total variable manufacturing costs per dress?
6. What are total manufacturing costs per dress?
7. What is contribution margin per dress?
8. What is the cost per dress if variable costing is used?
9. What is the cost per dress if actual absorption costing is used?

10. What is the cost to produce one additional dress?
11. What is the cost to produce and sell an additional dress?
12. What is the predetermined fixed overhead rate per direct labor hour?
13. What are total budgeted manufacturing costs for May?
14. Give a formula for total manufacturing costs in the range of 1,500 to 5,000 dresses per month.
15. What would the predetermined fixed overhead rate be per direct labor hour if practical capacity were used as the base?
16. What is budgeted income for May?
17. What is the break-even point, in dresses?
18. By how much could budgeted sales fall before a loss was incurred?
19. By how much would income increase for each unit sold above budgeted volume?

15-38 Process costing, second department (related to Appendix, extension of 15-24) The beginning inventory in the Boiling Department of Stockton Company was 50% complete as to conversion costs.

Required: Using the data from 15-23 and 15-24 and the above information, do the following.
1. Determine the FIFO equivalent production for conversion costs in the Boiling Department and the per-unit conversion cost.
2. Determine the total cost to be transferred from the Boiling Department to Finished Goods.
3. Prepare a T-account for Work in Process in the Boiling Department and verify the ending inventory balance.

15-39 Review of Chapters 12, 13, 14, and 15 ARC Industries makes fiberglass insulation, selling it for $20 per roll. The standard variable cost per roll is as follows.

Material (25 pounds at $0.20 per pound)	$5
Direct labor (0.20 hour at $10 per hour)	2
Variable overhead at $5 per direct labor hour	1
Total standard variable cost per roll	$8

Budgeted fixed production costs are $1,500,000 per year.
ARC began 19X3 with no inventories. Actual results for 19X3 follow.

Sales (230,000 rolls)	$4,600,000
Production	260,000 rolls
Production costs:	
Materials purchased (7,000,000 pounds)	$1,425,000
Materials used	6,450,000 pounds
Direct labor (53,000 hours)	$ 520,000
Variable manufacturing overhead	$ 270,000
Fixed production overhead	$1,480,000
Selling and administrative costs, all fixed	$ 800,000

The firm uses actual absorption costing for most purposes, though it has established standard variable production costs. The treasurer wants to see how standard costing works for income determination and asks you to prepare income statements using the two approaches. One statement is to be a standard variable costing statement, the other a standard absorption costing statement, with 250,000 rolls used to set the standard fixed cost.

Required
1. Determine all variances from standard costs, including the fixed overhead budget and volume variances.
2. Prepare the income statements that the treasurer requested. On each, show the variances as a lump sum subtracted from the standard gross margin or contribution margin.

15-40   *Review of Chapters 12, 13, 14, and 15 (extension of 15-39)*   During 19X4 ARC Industries produced 240,000 rolls and sold 250,000. The same standards and budgets in effect in 19X3 applied to 19X4, and the selling price remained at $20 per roll. Actual costs follow.

Materials purchased (6,200,000 pounds)	$1,210,000
Materials used	5,900,000 pounds
Direct labor (47,000 hours)	$ 475,000
Variable overhead	$ 240,000
Fixed production overhead	$1,510,000
Selling and administrative costs	$ 810,000

Required: Prepare income statements using the same bases as for 15-39. Again, calculate all variances and show the appropriate total as a lump sum on each statement.

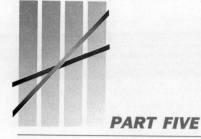

PART FIVE

SPECIAL TOPICS

The last part of this book covers three topics that are often treated in managerial accounting courses, but that are also frequently included as parts of other courses. Chapter 16 introduces several quantitative decision-making techniques that are commonly employed in approaching real-world problems. Chapter 17 covers the cash flow statement. Chapter 18 introduces financial statement analysis and is geared primarily to the uses of financial statements by managers, creditors, and stockholders.

CHAPTER *16*

QUANTITATIVE METHODS AND MANAGERIAL ACCOUNTING

We have stressed throughout this book that making decisions requires considering both quantitative and qualitative factors. Because of the increasing mathematical sophistication of managers and the availability of computers, much attention has been given in recent years to refining the uses of quantifiable data in decision making. These refinements have usually been applied to determine the best course of action in complex situations. But the principles of the techniques are equally applicable in less complex cases.

Many managers do not fully understand all of the mathematics that underlie some of these quantitative techniques. Nevertheless, any manager, and most certainly a managerial accountant, should be familiar with these techniques, their uses, and their limitations. First, managers must be able to describe the problems and to specify the relevant information to the specialist who sets up and solves them. Second, managers must be able to comprehend what the specialist is saying and grasp the basics of the proposed solution. Third, managers must know and understand the limitations of a given technique, so that they can evaluate the applicability of a proposed technique to the problem at hand and suggest changes if the solution appears to be ineffective.

QUANTITATIVE METHODS – AN OVERVIEW

The term *quantitative methods* describes sophisticated mathematical techniques for solving managerial problems. Other terms are *operations research, model building,* and *quantitative analysis.* You have used quantitative methods throughout this book. VCP analysis uses simple algebra; budgeting uses mathematically stated relationships among variables (collections on receivables are 40% of the current month's sales, 60% of the preceding month's sales); and capital budgeting uses present values.

Almost all of the quantitative techniques in this book require that managers state their expectations about the future. They predict prices, costs, demand, and so on. Often, the quantifiable factors are stated in equations [income = (sales price × units sold) – (variable costs × units sold) – fixed costs]. Operations research techniques and models work the same way. We determine which quantifiable factors are relevant to a decision, express relationships among those factors in equations, and solve the equations to obtain the answers. One major difference between operations research models and the techniques you have been using is the level of complexity. In one respect all quantitative methods are the same: a solution is only as good as the predictions about future conditions. If these predictions do not turn out to be true, the best result will probably not be realized.

STATISTICAL DECISION THEORY

We applied the **expected value** concept to sales forecasting in Chapter 6 when managers believed that several outcomes were possible and assigned probabilities to each of these outcomes. The concept is applicable to many other situations.

Suppose your company is considering alternative methods of acquiring computer time. There are three feasible choices.

(a) You can rent a computer for a flat rate of $5,500 per month, using as much time as you need.
(b) You can rent a computer for $2,000 per month plus $40 per hour of use.
(c) You can use a service bureau (a firm that rents computer time to others) for $80 per hour.

You have assessed the likelihood of your needs as follows.

(1) Event (Estimated Hours of Computer Time Needed per Month)	×	(2) Estimated Probability of Occurrence	=	(1) × (2) Expected Value
60		.25		15
100		.45		45
150		.30		45
		1.00		105

The expected value of required time is 105 hours. You can now compare the costs related to the three choices at 105 hours as follows.

Alternative	Cost
(a) Rent for $5,500 per month	$5,500
(b) Rent for $2,000 plus $40 per hour	
(105 hours at $40 per hour = $4,200) + $2,000	$6,200
(c) Buy time from the service bureau at $80 per hour	
(105 hours × $80 per hour)	$8,400

Renting the computer for $5,500 per month is the least-cost choice.

The costs of choices can also be directly associated with the probabilities of occurrence. You compute the **conditional values,** which are the monetary results of the events—computer costs in this example, then multiply these values by the probabilities. You could compute the expected value of the cost for choice (b) as follows.

(1) *Hours Required*	*(2)* *Probability*	×	*(3)* *Conditional Value[a]*	=	*(2) × (3)* *Expected Value*
60	.25		$ 4,400		$1,100
100	.45		6,000		2,700
150	.30		8,000		2,400
	1.00				$6,200

[a] For example, $4,400 = $2,000 + ($40 × 60 hours).

The expected cost for choice (c) is computed as below.

Hours Required	*Probability*	×	*Conditional Value*	=	*Expected Value*
60	.25		$ 4,800		$1,200
100	.45		8,000		3,600
150	.30		12,000		3,600
	1.00				$8,400

Choice (a) has the same cost no matter what the required hours. Therefore, the cost is 100% certain to be $5,500.

Variance Investigation

As stated in Chapter 12, a variance should be investigated when the expected savings from investigation exceed the cost of the investigation. The expected value framework is often helpful here as well.

Suppose a $300 variance has occurred and is expected to continue for six months if not corrected. An investigation to find its cause will cost nothing. The chances are about 80% that even after identifying the cause, the variance cannot be corrected. The expected values of the costs of investigating and not investigating are summarized below.

Choice 1—Do Not Investigate

Expected cost of $300 for six months	$1,800

Choice 2—Investigate

Event	Probability of Outcome	×	Conditional Value	=	Expected Value
Cause is correctable	.20		0		0
Cause is not correctable	.80		$1,800		$1,440
Total	1.00				$1,440

It is worthwhile to investigate the variance; it costs nothing to investigate, and there are potential savings of $1,800. The $360 ($1,800 − $1,440) difference between expected values has special significance. It is the maximum amount you would be willing to spend to investigate whether the variance can be corrected. This amount is called the **value of perfect information,** which is the difference between (1) the expected value of the best alternative, given the existing information, and (2) the expected value of alternatives when you know in advance what event will occur.

To confirm that $360 is the maximum you would pay to investigate the variance, suppose that it will cost $360 to investigate. What are the expected values (costs) of the two choices?

Choice 1—Do Not Investigate

Cost of $300 for six months	$1,800

Choice 2—Investigate

Event	Probability of Outcome	×	Conditional Value	=	Expected Value
Cause is correctable	.20		$ 360[a]		$ 72
Cause is not correctable	.80		2,160[b]		1,728
Total	1.00				$1,800

[a] The cost to investigate will be incurred.
[b] The cost to investigate plus the cost of the continued variance will be incurred.

Thus, the expected cost of both choices is the same.

Let us modify the circumstances. The cost to investigate a variance is $200 and there is a 30% probability that the variance was caused by a random disturbance and will not continue beyond the first period. The usual expected value approach can be used under these circumstances also. The analysis follows.

Choice 1—Do Not Investigate

Event	Probability of Outcome	×	Conditional Value	=	Expected Value
Variance is random, will stop without action	.30		0		$ 0
Variance will continue	.70		$1,800		1,260
Total	1.00				$1,260

Choice 2—Investigate

Event	Probability of Outcome	×	Conditional Value	=	Expected Value
Variance is random, will stop without action	.30		$ 200		$ 60
A problem exists that can be corrected	.14[a]		200		28
A problem exists that cannot be corrected	.56[b]		2,000		1,120
Total	1.00				$1,208

[a] The 20% chance of being able to take corrective action now applies to only 70% of the cases. The probability thus becomes 70% × 20%, or 14%. (Remember the total probabilities must be 1.0.)
[b] Same reasoning as in above note except that the probability of there being an uncorrectable problem is 70% × 80%, or 56%.

Under the new conditions, the expected cost of investigating ($1,208) is still less than the expected cost of not investigating ($1,260). But the difference between the two choices is less ($52 as opposed to $360). This makes sense because not only is there a cost to investigate, but now there is a 30% chance that you do not have to do anything and the variance will stop.

Another approach to solving the problem is the **decision tree,** a commonly used device that offers a graphical representation of the problem. The decision tree for this decision, shown in Figure 16-1 (page 686), works in essentially the same way as the tabular format but has the advantage of allowing a step-by-step determination of probabilities when there are several possible events within other events (the 80%–20% probabilities within the 70% probability). Both approaches show that the expected cost of investigating is less than the expected cost of *not* investigating.

Capital Budgeting Application

Firms frequently have opportunities that could bring either high rewards (high net present values) or large losses (high negative net present values). Such opportunities are risky because they involve potential loss, but they can also be rewarding. (Chapter 3 discussed cost structure and risk; the substitution of fixed costs for variable costs could be either beneficial or disastrous, depending on the future

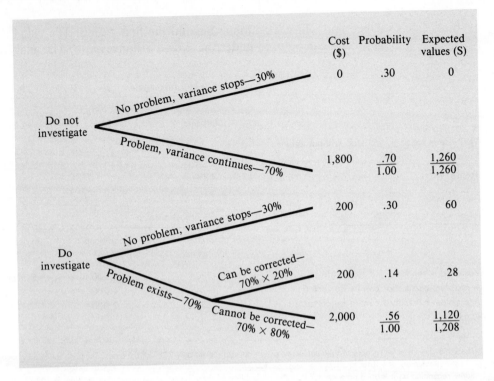

Figure 16-1   Decision Tree

levels of sales.) Consider a manufacturer who is trying to decide whether to market a new toy.

Assume the following possibilities for annual after-tax cash flows in two circumstances: the toy sells well; the toy is a flop.

	Sells Well	Flops
Years 1–5	$15,000	$1,000

Suppose the marketing group believes there is a 60% chance of the toy's being a big seller and a 40% chance of its being a flop. What is the expected value?

	Cash Flow	×	Probability of Occurrence	=	Expected Value
Sells well	$15,000		.60		$9,000
Flops	1,000		.40		400
Total			1.00		$9,400

The cash flows are now expressed as an expected value of $9,400. The $9,400 can then be discounted at cost of capital to determine whether the net present value is positive.

At times it may be unwise to rely solely on expected values. Suppose you were given the following choices: (1) take $10,000 now or (2) flip a coin, heads you get $40,000, tails you lose $20,000. Compute the expected values (assuming an honest coin, of course).

Choice 1—A certain gain of $10,000.
Choice 2—An expected value of $10,000, as indicated below.

Event	Probability	×	Conditional Value	=	Expected Value
Heads	.50		$40,000		$20,000
Tails	.50		−20,000		−10,000
	1.00				$10,000

The two choices appear equally valuable, since both have an expected value of $10,000. But unless you have a great deal of money, you probably would not select choice 2. As with most decisions, nonquantifiable factors are important. The difficulty with relying solely on the expected value is this: the expected value concept is based on probabilities, and probability theory is based on mathematical laws that assume large numbers of occurrences. If you had 1,000 chances to play the coin flip game just described, it would not matter much whether you took the $10,000 or tossed the coin. You could expect to win about 500 times, lose about 500 times. But with only one try, you do not have the laws of large numbers on your side.

Operations researchers have tried to incorporate such considerations into the simple expected value model by attaching *utilities* to the various outcomes. (Utility represents the degree of "better-offness" or "worse-offness" associated with the events.) By using utilities, operations researchers try to recognize that generally it detracts more from your well-offness to lose $20,000 than is added by winning $20,000. But assigning values to utilities is a matter of judgment, and assigned values differ markedly depending on who is doing the choosing. Different managers make different decisions, even if they all use the same data. Some are more willing than others to accept risks. We consider this point in more detail in the following section.

Payoff Tables

Managers use the expected value concept most often when they must make the same decision several times and have several available strategies with probabilities attached to the possible outcomes of each. A typical application is deciding how many units of a product to buy (or make) when there are given probabilities for sales and the unsold units are discarded or sold at substantial losses.

Suppose a florist must decide how many corsages to buy each week. All units must be bought in advance and no additional purchases are possible once the week has begun. Unsold corsages are discarded. The florist has estimated the demand as given below. (For computational simplicity we assume only three possible outcomes. Computers make it possible to analyze more realistic situations quickly.)

Demand in Units	Probability of Demand
4,000	20%
8,000	50%
12,000	30%

The variable cost per corsage is $6, and the selling price is $10.

Because the corsages are purchased in advance and discarded if unsold, the florist loses $6 on each unsold corsage. This is the trouble with a perishable good: buying (or making) more than can be sold brings a penalty of the variable cost of the unsold units (less any salvage value). *Perishability* is an economic concept, not a physical one. Corsages deteriorate rapidly; newspapers do not. But day-old newspapers do not sell any better than wilted flowers. High-fashion goods are another example of a perishable good in the economic sense.[1]

The approach to analyzing the purchasing decision for perishable goods is to prepare **payoff tables.** For each purchasing strategy, prepare a table of *conditional values* for each possible level of demand, without regard to the probabilities of such experience. Then prepare a second table that shows the expected values (that is, considering the probabilities) of each strategy. (We could combine the tables, but that makes it much harder to follow the logic.) Exhibit 16-1 shows the conditional values.

Exhibit 16-1
Conditional Values of Strategies

	Strategy: Purchases of		
Event: Demand	4,000	8,000	12,000
4,000	$16,000	($ 8,000)	($32,000)
8,000	16,000	32,000	8,000
12,000	16,000	32,000	48,000

Each entry in the table is the contribution margin, or loss, from that particular combination of demand and purchases. Thus, if the firm *bought* 4,000 units, it would sell 4,000 units no matter what the demand because it could not buy any more even if it learned that buyers would demand 8,000 or 12,000 units. Hence, if purchases are 4,000 units, the firm will earn $16,000 contribution margin by selling

---

[1] Almost all goods are perishable to some extent, because a company can rarely guarantee that it can sell all that it makes or buys. The question is one of degree, and a florist is surely more vulnerable than a car dealer.

4,000 units ($4 per unit × 4,000 units) and will lose nothing by having to discard units bought but not sold.

If the firm buys 8,000 units and can only sell 4,000, costs will be $48,000 (8,000 × $6) and revenues only $40,000 (4,000 × $10), for a loss of $8,000. Put another way, the firm would earn $16,000 contribution margin on the 4,000 units sold but would lose $6 per unit for the 4,000 unsold units discarded. If the firm did sell 8,000 units, it would earn revenues of $80,000, have costs of $48,000, and a contribution margin of $32,000 ($4 × 8,000). The same contribution margin would be earned if the firm could have sold 12,000 units but only sold 8,000, because only 8,000 were purchased.

The next step is to compute the expected value of each possible outcome, using the probabilities of demand. Exhibit 16-2 summarizes the expected values.

Exhibit 16-2
Expected Values of Strategies

| | | Strategy: Purchases of | | | | | |
| | | 4,000 | | 8,000 | | 12,000 | |
Demand	Probability	CV[a]	EV[b]	CV[a]	EV[b]	CV[a]	EV[b]
4,000	.20	$16,000	$ 3,200	($ 8,000)	($ 1,600)	($32,000)	($ 6,400)
8,000	.50	16,000	8,000	32,000	16,000	8,000	4,000
12,000	.30	16,000	4,800	32,000	9,600	48,000	14,400
Expected values			$16,000		$24,000		$12,000

[a] Conditional values from Exhibit 16-1.
[b] Conditional value multiplied by probability.

Notice that the expected value of the strategy of purchasing 4,000 units ($16,000) is equal to the conditional value of each outcome: demand of 4,000, 8,000, and 12,000. This should not be surprising, because the firm can sell only 4,000 units if it buys only that many. The problem with that strategy is that the firm foregoes contribution margin if it could have sold more than 4,000 units.

Notice also that the outcomes, both conditional and expected values, of buying 12,000 units are more widely dispersed than the others. We would expect this because the more you buy *and* sell, the higher the profit, the more you buy and do *not* sell, the lower the profit or higher the loss. Buying 12,000 is the riskiest strategy.

Using the expected value criterion, the florist would buy 8,000 units, the strategy with the highest expected value ($24,000). But remember that we are dealing with expectations: the actual values might be different from the ones expected. Most managers recognize how important the estimated probabilities are to the results and will perform "what if" analysis (the sensitivity analysis discussed in earlier chapters). For example, the manager might compute what happens if the probability of selling 12,000 units increases to 40%, with an offsetting decrease in the probability of selling 8,000 units, or might try several plausible combinations of probabilities. Using a microcomputer and one of the many available software packages, the manager could obtain information about many such combinations in just a few minutes.

Again, we stress the point that no quantitative method, from VCP analysis through expected value calculations, *tells* you what to do. It tells you only what will happen *if*—and "if" is a big word—all your predictions are correct. Accordingly, firms that continually make decisions about producing or purchasing perishable goods do this type of analysis often.

The value of perfect information can also be computed from payoff tables. In this application, it equals the difference between the contribution margin that would be earned if the firm knew how many units would be demanded and therefore purchased exactly that many, and the expected value of the strategy it would follow using only probabilities.

If the firm knew in advance how many corsages would be demanded, it would buy exactly that many and would have the following expected value of contribution margin, selling 4,000 units in 20% of the weeks, 8,000 units in 50% of the weeks, and 12,000 units in 30% of the weeks.

Sales	Contribution Margin, Conditional Value (Exhibit 16-1)	Probability	Expected Value
4,000	$16,000	.20	$ 3,200
8,000	32,000	.50	16,000
12,000	48,000	.30	14,400
Expected value			$33,600

Notice that the expected values correspond to those in Exhibit 16-2 for the entries in the same row and same column. That is, the entry in the row for 4,000 here is $3,200 as in the 4,000 row and column in Exhibit 16-2. In the 8,000 row, 8,000 column is $16,000; and in the 12,000 row 12,000 column is $14,400. The same is true of the conditional values.

In this case, then, the value of perfect information is $9,600 ($33,600 − $24,000, the expected value of the strategy of buying 8,000 units each week). We can confirm the $9,600 value of knowing the level of demand by showing the expected sales for a ten-week period, following the strategy of buying 8,000 units each week and following the optimal strategy when the florist knows in advance what the week's demand will be.

During the ten-week period, the firm should sell 4,000 corsages twice (20% × 10 weeks); 8,000 corsages five times; and 12,000 corsages three times. Following the strategy of buying 8,000 each week, it would have losses of $8,000 twice and gains of $32,000 eight times. (As shown in Exhibit 16-1, the company loses $8,000 when demand is 4,000 units and gains $32,000 when demand is 8,000.) Total contribution margin for the ten-week period is $240,000 [($32,000 × 8) − ($8,000 × 2)]. With perfect information, the florist buys and sells 4,000 corsages twice, 8,000 corsages five times, and 12,000 corsages three times. The contribution margin for the period is

Sales	Number of Weeks	×	Contribution Margin per Week	=	Total
4,000	2		$16,000		$ 32,000
8,000	5		32,000		160,000
12,000	3		48,000		144,000
Total					$336,000

The difference between the expected contribution margin with perfect information ($336,000) and using the optimal strategy without such information ($240,000) is $96,000 that is ten times—for ten weeks—the $9,600 calculated earlier as the value of perfect information.

In the real world it is impossible to obtain *perfect* information, but the concept is still valuable. *Some* additional information is almost always obtainable at a cost; test-marketing new products is an example of an effort to obtain more information. The questions are whether the information gained would result in a change in strategy, whether decisions would be better if the information were available, and whether the cost of obtaining the information is less than the benefits.

Developing Probabilities

The probabilities used to compute expected values can be intuitive and judgmental, or they can be developed using more objective, sophisticated statistical techniques.

At one extreme, probabilities might be "best estimates" of experienced managers. There might be some historical basis for the estimates, as when managers develop rules of thumb through experience and believe that the current situation is similar to previous situations. For example, if a machine is not operating at peak efficiency, the manager might rely on several years of experience with similar machines to estimate a probability of about 60% that an internal part is wearing out, and 40% that some random factor is at work that will not continue.

In some cases, managers' estimates of probabilities are based on the presence or absence of external factors. Good examples are provided by firms whose business depends greatly on the weather. A firm that sells hot dogs and soft drinks at baseball parks might develop its sales probabilities based on weather forecasts. The hotter the day is expected to be, the more soft drinks the firm can expect to sell. Of course, the validity of the manager's estimates depends on the accuracy of the weather forecasts.

Managers will often try to narrow the range of estimates by getting additional information and using statistical techniques to evaluate the information. Market research is one commonly used way to obtain additional information. A firm might be considering a new product that will require a nationwide advertising and promotional campaign. Because such campaigns can be very costly, the company might test-market the product using a regional campaign. After the small-scale campaign is underway, the managers can analyze the information and gain a better perspective on probable nationwide sales. You might study some of these techniques in courses in marketing and statistics.

Because probabilities are estimates, some managers react negatively to quantitative techniques that use them. Such managers argue that "sound business judgment" is better than quantitative analysis because the former does not require a lot of assumptions. But when a manager makes a decision, with or without the help of quantitative analysis, the decision *implies* some beliefs about the future. Consider a decision to set a production level without first examining the probable demand for the product. Such a decision implies *some* expectation about demand. Any manager who selects a particular course of action—say, ordering 4,000 corsages—is making assumptions about the future, whether or not those assumptions (expectations) are specifically stated.

INVENTORY CONTROL MODELS

Chapters 6 and 7 showed that inventory policy is important and that a conflict exists between having too much inventory and having too little. Merchandising companies must stock inventory to attract customers; manufacturers that do not use just-in-time methods must do likewise in that they must stock materials and components so as to avoid shutting down production. (We except JIT companies because, as you will recall, part of the JIT philosophy is the virtual elimination of all inventories.) Significant costs are incurred in carrying inventory, such as the opportunity cost of the money invested in it. Accordingly, managers try to minimize the investment in inventory, while at the same time keeping customers satisfied and production lines running smoothly. Inventory control models have been the subject of considerable research, and entire journals are devoted to them.

Inventory Costs

Three kinds of costs are associated with inventory: (1) the costs of ordering and receiving inventory, called **ordering costs;** (2) the costs of having inventory on hand, called **carrying costs;** and (3) the costs of *not* having enough inventory, called **stockout costs.** Examples of costs in each of these categories appear in Exhibit 16-3.

We want to minimize total inventory costs. A major difficulty is that the three types of costs are not independent. The more you order at one time, the lower the ordering costs. But the more you order, the higher your average inventory, thus increasing carrying costs. On the other hand, the higher your inventory, the less likely you are to lose sales (incur stockout costs).

Only incremental costs are relevant in determining the desired level of inventory. Hence, in any particular situation one or more of the costs listed in Exhibit 16-3 might not be relevant. For example, a firm with large amounts of space for which there are no alternative uses, has no incremental storage cost. If

Exhibit 16-3
Inventory Costs

Costs of Ordering (including Receiving)

1. Processing the order
2. Forms used
3. Time spent (opportunity cost)
4. Order follow-up time
5. Unloading and inspection

Costs of Carrying Inventory

1. Cost of capital on investment
2. Space used
3. Wages of storage personnel section
4. Personal property taxes
5. Fire and theft insurance
6. Recordkeeping
7. Risks of obsolescence and deterioration

Costs of Not Having Enough Inventory

1. Lost contribution margin from sales
    (a) Current sales are lost because customers could not get what they wanted.
    (b) Later sales might be lost because the dissatisfied customers do not return and other customers do not come because of word-of-mouth notification that your selection is inadequate.
2. Bottlenecks in production because of lack of materials or components.

insurance premiums are based on the quantity of goods carried, they are relevant; if the premium is a flat amount no matter how much inventory is carried (unlikely, but possible), it is irrelevant.

Determining stockout costs can be especially difficult. These costs are opportunity costs and do not appear in accounting records. For this reason, they might be inadvertently ignored or their significance downplayed, even though they are as real as, and might be far greater than costs that are recorded. When goods have a relatively high contribution margin, the cost of stockouts could well exceed, by several times, the total costs of carrying inventory sufficient to ensure against stockouts.

Managers deal with the problem of minimizing costs in two stages: (1) they determine *when* to order, that is, how low to allow inventory to fall before ordering a new supply, and (2) they determine *how much* to order at a time. Ordering only as much as you need and at the right time minimizes costs.

When to Order — The Reorder Point

How low should we allow inventory to fall before we order more? The answer to this question is the **reorder point** and can be expressed in either units or dollars. In determining the reorder point, the goal is to minimize the total of stockout and carrying costs.

The reorder point depends on three things: lead time, safety stock, and the expected daily use of inventory. **Lead time** is the number of working days between placing and receiving an order. **Safety stock** is the quantity of inventory that serves as a cushion in case an order comes in late or use is greater than expected during the lead time. The reorder point is computed as follows.

Reorder point = safety stock + (daily use × lead time)

Suppose that the lead time is ten days, daily use is 20 units, and no safety stock is considered necessary. The reorder point is 200 units (20 units × 10 days). *If* your predictions are accurate, you will not run out of inventory. As you use the last unit, the new units will have just come in. If the manager believes that a safety stock of 100 units is desirable, the reorder point will be 300 units (200 + 100). Then, if the order arrives late or there is an unexpected need for more than 20 units on one or more days, there will be enough stock to last until the order is received. The behavior of inventory for this situation is depicted in Figure 16-2. It is assumed in that graph that 800 units are ordered at a time.

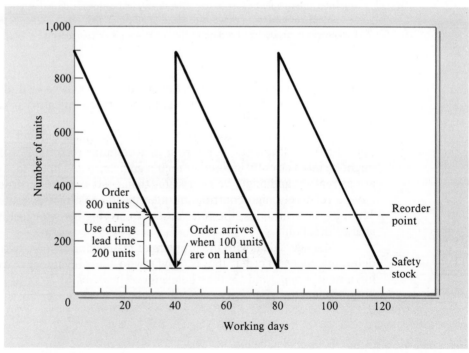

Figure 16-2   Behavior of Inventory Level

Expected daily use is annual use divided by the number of working days a year. Suppose that records reveal the annual use to be $60,000, that there are 200 working days in the year, that lead time is 15 days, and that a safety stock of $5,000 is desired. The reorder point in dollars is $9,500, computed as below.

$$\text{Reorder point} = \$5,000 + (\$300 \times 15) = \$9,500$$

Determining Safety Stock

One of the most critical aspects of inventory management is determining the level of safety stock. Stockout costs are most closely related to the amount of safety stock carried. Companies carry safety stock because of the uncertainties associated with the two factors that affect inventory use during the time between placing and receiving an order, namely, lead time and daily use. If both these factors are known, there is no reason to carry safety stock and the first term in the reorder-point formula drops out. (If lead time can then be driven down to a few hours, or minutes, rather than days, the company can carry only trivial amounts of inventory.)

Suppose normal lead time is ten days but can be as long as 15 days. Suppose also average daily use is $300 but can be as high as $420. Based only on the averages, the reorder point before considering safety stock is $3,000 (10 days × $300). Using the extreme possibilities for lead time and daily use, and no safety stock, the reorder point is $6,300 (15 days × $420). If we reorder when inventory is $6,300, we are virtually certain never to run out. But the cost of carrying so much inventory might be prohibitive. Moreover, while we might expect occasionally to experience 15-day lead time or daily use of $420, seldom would we encounter both at the same time. So, a compromise is in order. We would select a reorder point between $3,000 (no safety stock) and $6,300 ($3,300 safety stock). To arrive at a compromise, a manager might investigate not only how *often* the lead time exceeds ten days and daily use exceeds $300, but also the importance of the item in the sales or production picture. For example, because stockout costs are high, a higher safety stock is warranted for a high-volume, high-contribution-margin item. For the same reason, a higher safety stock would be set for a part used in several of the firm's major products than for one used in only a few, slow-moving products.

Because analyzing the flow of inventory items can be very expensive, managers usually make detailed analyses for only a few items of especial importance. Low-cost, nonessential items might be given reorder points based solely on an experienced manager's intuition.

How Much to Order —
The Economic Order Quantity

The answer to the question "how much to order at a time?" is the **economic order quantity (EOQ).** Our examples use firms that do not manufacture the item but order it from a supplier. The analysis is the same for manufactured items, but the term *economic lot size* is then used.

In determining how much to order at a time, the goal is to minimize the sum of the costs of ordering and of carrying inventory. Suppose a firm uses 12,000 units of product during a year. ("Uses" can mean either sells or uses in some other way. Supplies and raw materials are used, but not sold.) The estimated incremental costs of carrying inventory are $0.60 per unit per year. The incremental cost of placing an order is estimated at $225 (including incremental clerical costs, forms, data processing, delivery, etc.).[2] If use is even throughout the year, we can calculate the EOQ by using the formula that appears below. (The assumption that use is even throughout the year is critical to the EOQ model. The solution provided by the model will not produce the desired results if use varies significantly from month to month or week to week.)

$$EOQ = \sqrt{\frac{2CD}{k}}$$

where

C = the incremental order cost;

D = the number of units used in a year (annual demand);

k = the annual carrying cost per unit.

Applying the formula to the example gives

$$EOQ = \sqrt{\frac{2 \times \$225 \times 12,000}{\$0.60}}$$

= 3,000 units
or 4 orders per year (12,000/3,000)

The formula can also be used when the annual demand and the carrying costs are stated in dollars, instead of units. In our example, suppose that the cost of a unit is $5, so that annual demand is $60,000 (12,000 × $5). Carrying costs are 12% of cost ($0.60/$5). The formula is

$$EOQ = \sqrt{\frac{2 \times \$225 \times \$60,000}{12\%}}$$

= $15,000 (which is 3,000 units at $5)

Exhibit 16-4 shows the costs associated with three order quantities. It should help you to understand the behavior of the two types of costs affected by the size of the order. The annual carrying cost is the per-unit amount multiplied by the average inventory. The average inventory here means the amount in excess of safety stock. (Remember that the carrying costs of safety stock are the same

---

[2] If we were dealing with a manufactured item, the costs to be considered would be those of setting up to make a batch of the product (for example, the idle time during the setup).

Exhibit 16-4

Annual Incremental Inventory Costs for Selected Order Quantities

(a)	(b)	(c)	(d)	(e)	(f)
			Annual	Annual	Total
	Average	Orders	Carrying	Ordering	Annual
Order	Inventory	per Year	Costs	Costs	Costs
Quantity	(a)/2	12,000/(a)	$0.60 × (b)	$225 × (c)	(d) + (e)
2,000	1,000	6	$ 600	$1,350	$1,950
3,000	1,500	4	900	900	1,800
4,000	2,000	3	1,200	775	1,975

regardless of the order quantity.) The average inventory is half of the order size because we assume even use throughout the year.

Notice that at the EOQ, computed earlier to be 3,000 units, total carrying costs equal total ordering costs. This is always true because of the relationships of these costs to order size.

Figure 16-3 is a graphic presentation of the cost behavior reflected in Exhibit 16-4. It shows the behavior of each group of costs and of total cost. Notice that the total-cost curve is relatively flat over the range near the EOQ. This means that modest errors in calculating the EOQ do not cost a great deal. Notice that, again, the EOQ is the point at which total carrying costs equal total ordering costs.

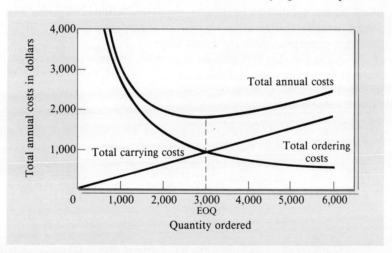

Figure 16-3   Behavior of Annual Inventory Costs

There is a relationship between the EOQ and JIT. If a company can reduce its set-up (or ordering) cost to near-zero, then the EOQ approaches zero. This means that the company should make or buy one unit at a time, not large batches, so that average inventory is negligible. Thus, a very simplified way of looking at a JIT company is that it has near-zero lead time, as mentioned earlier, which eliminates the need for safety stock, and near-zero set-up costs, which makes the EOQ very small. Inventory control models therefore give a theoretical justification of how JIT companies are able to operate.

LINEAR PROGRAMMING

Chapter 5 noted that profits are maximized when the firm makes the combination of products that maximizes the contribution margin per unit of a fixed resource. The example in that chapter involved only one fixed resource, machine-time; it is more likely that several resources will be fixed.

When a multiproduct company faces several constraints it can use **linear programming** to determine the combination of products that will maximize profits. Linear programming can also be used to find the combination of input factors that minimizes the cost of an activity. A cattle feeder can determine the least-cost mix of various feeds to provide a specific level of nourishment. Or, a firm with several factories and warehouses can determine the least-cost way to move the required quantities of finished product from factories to warehouses.

The mathematics involved in linear programming is complex and will not be detailed in this book. However, you should be able to recognize the kinds of problems that can be solved with linear programming, understand the formulation of the problem, and see what is being done when the problem is solved.

Essentially, linear programming is the solving of a system of simultaneous linear equations that includes an **objective function** specifying what is to be maximized (usually contribution margin) or minimized (usually cost). The rest of the system's equations state the **constraints.**

A firm makes two products, X and Y. Both products require time in the Assembly Department and the Finishing Department. Data on the two products appear below.

	X	Y
Hours required in Assembly Department	2	4
Hours required in Finishing Department	3	2
Selling price	$65	$100
Variable cost	40	60
Contribution margin	$25	$ 40

Each week, 100 hours are available in the Assembly Department, and 90 hours in the Finishing Department. Using these data we can formulate the linear program in the following four steps.

Step 1. Formulate the objective function, which in this case is to maximize total contribution margin per week.

$$\text{Maximize: contribution margin} = \$25X + \$40Y$$

where X and Y stand for the numbers of units of each product that will be produced.

Step 2. Formulate the constraints as inequalities.

$$2X + 4Y \leq 100$$

$$3X + 2Y \leq 90$$

Each inequality describes the constraint of available time in a department. The first states that the hours spent assembling X (2 hours per unit) plus those spent assembling Y (4 hours per unit) cannot exceed (must be equal to or less than) 100, the available capacity of the Assembly Department. Similarly, the second inequality states that the hours used in finishing X (3 hours per unit) plus those spent in finishing Y (2 hours per unit) cannot exceed 90, the number of hours available in the Finishing Department.

Two other constraints are required—nonnegativity constraints.

$$X \geq 0$$

$$Y \geq 0$$

These constraints eliminate a solution that is mathematically possible but calls for negative production of a product.

The entire set of equations and inequalities appears below.

Maximize: contribution margin $= \$25X + \$40Y$

Subject to the constraints:

$$2X + 4Y \leq 100$$

$$3X + 2Y \leq 90$$

$$X \qquad \geq 0$$

$$Y \geq 0$$

Step 3. Graph the lines representing constraints. The constraints on the capacities of the two departments are shown in Figure 16-4 (page 700). The nonnegativity constraints are implicit because we show only the upper right-hand quadrant of the graph, where production of both products is zero or positive.

The lines representing the capacity constraints can be drawn intuitively. For example, the assembly constraint is $2X + 4Y \leq 100$. Thus, if only product X is made, maximum production is 50 units, which is 100/2. If only Y is made, maximum production is 25 units (100/4). Hence, the points on the axes are determined and the line is drawn to connect them. Each point on the line represents a possible combination of production. For example, assembling 30 units of X requires 60 hours of assembly time. There would be 40 hours left (100 − 60) to assemble units of Y. In that time, 10 units of Y could be assembled.

Notice on the graph that the point $30X, 10Y$ is not inside the shaded area, the area of feasible, possible solutions. The firm can *assemble* that combination of units, but it cannot *finish* the combination because the point $30X, 10Y$ lies above the line representing the Finishing Department constraint. All points within the area of feasible solutions are achievable combinations of production, all points outside the area are unachievable.

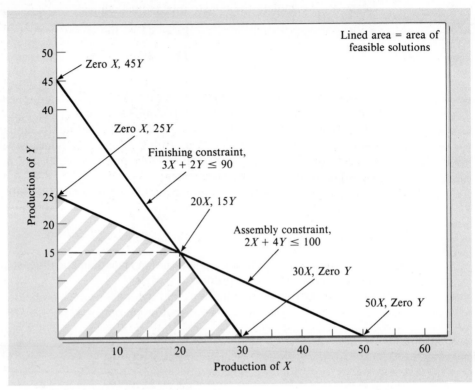

Figure 16-4   Graphic Solution of Constraints on Capacity

Step 4.   Determine the contribution margin at each of the corners in the area of feasible solutions. In linear programming an optimal solution always occurs at a corner, an intersection of two lines.[3] (The axes are considered to be lines.)

Corner		Contribution Margin		Total Contribution
X	Y	X	Y	Margin
0	0	$ 0	$ 0	$ 0
30	0	750	0	750
20	15	500	600	1,100
0	25	0	1,000	1,000

The corner *20X, 15Y* produces the best solution.

It is often possible to solve for the intersections of constraints using simultaneous equations.[4] This enables you to find the intersection of two constraints

---

[3] Other solutions may also yield the best possible result, but none yields a better result than is achieved at an intersection.

[4] The most widely used technique for solving large linear programming problems is called the *simplex method.* It requires finding solutions to a set of simultaneous equations until the optimal solution is found.

without having to draw an accurate graph. Using our illustration, we turn the inequalities into equations.

$$(1)\ 2X + 4Y = 100$$

$$(2)\ 3X + 2Y = \ \ 90$$

Multiplying equation (2) by 2 and subtracting equation (1) we obtain

$$4X = 80$$

$$X = 20$$

Substituting 20 for X in equation (1) gives

$$40 + 4Y = 100$$

$$4Y = \ \ 60$$

$$Y = \ \ 15$$

Many other types of constraints are possible. Figure 16-5 shows the graph when market conditions limit the sales of product X to 16 units per week. The formerly optimal solution of $20X, 15Y$ is no longer feasible. Two new corners have been created: $16X$, zero Y and $16X$, $17Y$. Clearly, $16X$ and $17Y$ must be more desirable than $16X$ and zero Y. The question is now whether $16X, 17Y$ is better

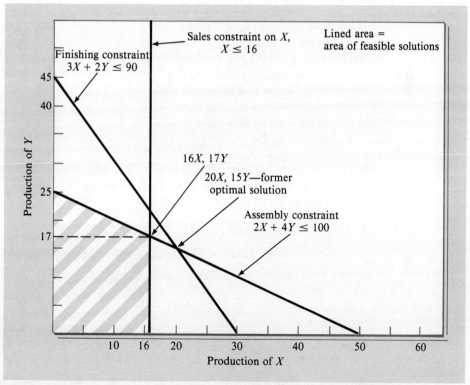

Figure 16-5   Linear Programming: Graphic Solution of Constraints on Capacity and on Sales of X

than zero *X*, 25*Y*, which was the second best solution in the original problem. At *16X*, 17*Y*, total contribution margin per week is $1,080 [($25 × 16) + ($40 × 17)]. This is better than the $1,000 earned producing only 25 units of *Y*.

The constraint of the Finishing Department is no longer critical. It now lies completely outside the area of feasible solutions; therefore, the time in the Finishing Department will not be fully used. The Finishing Department will have eight hours of unused capacity because 16 units of *X* and 17 of *Y* can be finished in 82 hours.

$$3X + 2Y \leq 90$$
$$3 \times 16 = 48$$
$$2 \times 17 = \underline{34}$$
$$\text{Total} \qquad 82$$

Managers would consider reducing the available capacity of the Finishing Department if it expected the constraint on sales of *X* to continue. They might also do finishing work for another company to use the capacity.

Sensitivity Analysis

Sensitivity analysis, the testing of a solution to see how much it changes if one or more variables were to change, is an important part of decision making. Let us consider the original situation when there was no constraint on the sales of product *X*. The sales manager might expect the price of *X* to fall, which would lower its contribution margin. Total contribution margin would also fall so long as the firm stayed with its original plan to produce 20 units of *X* and 15 of *Y*. At some point the drop in contribution margin would make it more profitable for the firm to produce 25 units of *Y*, none of *X*, than to continue with the original plan. That point is an indifference point, as described in Chapter 3.

The manager is interested in knowing how far the contribution margin of *X* has to fall before he should stop producing it. He can determine that by finding what contribution margin from *X* in the *20X*, 15*Y* combination would equal the total contribution margin from zero *X*, 25*Y*. Using *C* to denote the contribution margin from a unit of *X*, the manager can frame the following equation.

$$\begin{array}{cc} \text{Produce } 25Y & \text{Produce } 20X,\ 15Y \\ \$40 \times 25 \ = (C \times 20) + (\$40 \times 15) \\ \$1,000 \ = 20C + \$600 \\ C = \$20 \end{array}$$

Consequently, if the contribution margin per unit of *X* went below $20, the firm would stop producing *X* and devote its facilities solely to making *Y*.

Similarly, a rise in the price and contribution margin per unit of *Y* would make the firm more likely to stop producing *X* and produce more of *Y*. The equation below states that when the contribution margin of 25 units of *Y* equals that of 15 units of Y plus 20 units of X, the firm would earn the same with either production mix. Here, C represents contribution margin per unit of Y.

$$C \times 25 = (C \times 15) + (\$25 \times 20)$$
$$C \times 25 = (C \times 15) + \$500$$
$$C \times 10 = \$500$$
$$C = \$50$$

If contribution margin of Y goes above $50 per unit, the firm will earn more total contribution margin producing $25Y$, zero X, than $15Y$, $20X$.

Sensitivity analysis, essentially, is repeatedly performing calculations that differ only in the values used for some of the variables. The availability of computers has significantly reduced the time required for such analyses.

Shadow Prices

A manager who has solved a linear programming problem often wishes to know whether it would be beneficial to add capacity in a particular department. He or she is interested in the value of adding, say, an hour per week of assembly time. The value of adding an hour of capacity is the additional contribution margin that could be earned. This amount is the **shadow price** of the resource.[5] A shadow price is an opportunity cost—the cost of *not* having an additional unit of capacity.

We shall calculate the shadow price of the assembly constraint using our original illustration in which there was no constraint on the sales of product X. To make it easier to show graphically, we shall add eight hours of capacity to the Assembly Department, rather than one hour. Figure 16-6 (page 704) shows the new assembly constraint. It also shows the former optimal solution, where the assembly constraint and finishing constraint lines intersected when capacity in the Assembly Department was 100 hours per week. Notice that the new corner, $18X$, $18Y$ shows the firm making fewer units of X than before, but more units of Y.

Checking the new corners for the optimal solution, we have

Corner		Contribution Margin		Total Contribution
X	Y	X	Y	Margin
18	18	$450	$ 720	$1,170
0	27	0	1,080	1,080

[5] Stated generally, a shadow price is the value of being able to relax a constraint by one unit. A unit could be an hour, or a unit of product. For example, in the illustration in which sales of X were limited to 16 units per week, a shadow price could be computed for that constraint. It would be the difference between contribution margin at $16X$, $17Y$ and at the optimal solution if 17 units of X could be sold.

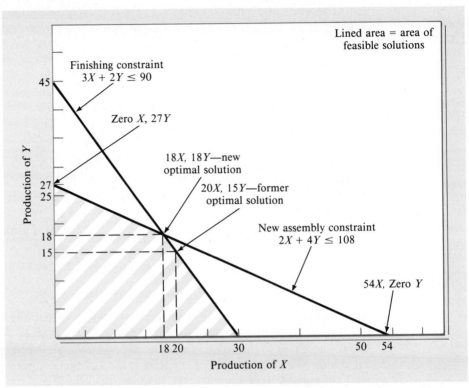

Figure 16-6 Linear Programming: Graphic Solution of Increased Assembly Capacity

The new optimal solution of *18X, 18Y* has total contribution margin of $1,170 per week. That is $70 higher than the $1,100 earned under the optimal solution of *20X, 15Y* when the Assembly Department had 100 available hours. Therefore the firm would be willing to pay up to $70 per week to get an additional eight hours of assembly capacity. The shadow price is $8.75, which is $70/8 hours. If we had used 101 hours, we would have had contribution margin of $1,108.75. We would also have had a noninteger solution, with fractional units of both products being made. In linear programming, capacity is fixed for the planning period (a week, day, month, or year). In the long run the firm can add to capacity or reduce it. Shadow prices give an idea of the value of adding capacity and are important information for long-run planning.

LEARNING CURVES

American companies have paid a great deal of attention to improving employee productivity, both in manufacturing and nonmanufacturing functions. People generally improve performance (that is, reduce the time needed to do a task) as they become more familiar with the task. For instance, airplane manufacturers have determined that the labor time required for each airplane of a given model declines as the workers learn. Companies incorporate the expectation of improved performance in their planning in many ways.

The **learning curve** is a measure of increases in efficiency. The rate of performance improvement, expressed as a percentage, is called the *learning rate*. The most common form of the learning curve is expressed as follows: as output doubles, the *average* time to make a unit or batch of units drops to the learning rate percentage multiplied by the average time at the previous point. An example will clarify this relationship.

Northern Manufacturing is about to begin making a new product. The expected labor time for the first batch is 10 hours, and the expected learning rate is 80%. Exhibit 16-5 illustrates the learning curve for Northern. The exhibit shows, for selected numbers of batches, both the average time per batch and the total time.

Exhibit 16-5

Examples of Expected Average and Total Times—80% Learning Curve

Total Output in Batches	Expected Average Time per Batch (hours)	Expected Total Time (hours)[a]
1	10 (given)	10
2	8 (10 × 80%)	16 (2 × 8)
4	6.4 (8 × 80%)	25.6 (4 × 6.4)
8	5.12 (6.4 × 80%)	40.96 (8 × 5.12)

[a] Number of batches x average time per batch.

Notice that the exhibit shows results only at doubling points (2 is double 1, 4 is double 2, 8 is double 4). To determine the average time for some other number of batches, we can use the following formula.

$$Y = aX^b$$

where

Y = average time for X number of batches;

a = the time required for the first batch (or unit);

X = total output (number of batches);

b = the learning exponent.

The value of b is the logarithm of the learning rate (expressed as a decimal) divided by the logarithm of 2. (Because many calculators include both logarithm and exponentiation functions, using the formula is not difficult.) With the formula you can find the average time for any output level. For instance, in the above example, the value of b is about $-.322$. Thus, the per-batch average time for seven batches is

$$Y = 10 \times 7^{-.322}$$

$$= 10 \times .5344$$

$$= 5.344$$

We stress that the learning curve is expressed in terms of the per-batch *average time* for some total number of batches, not the *incremental time* to produce some number of additional batches. Thus, if we refer to Exhibit 16-5, the second batch does not require eight hours; rather eight hours is the per-batch average time to produce both the two batches. To find the incremental time for a batch, you must first find the total times for that number of batches and for one batch fewer. For Northern, we know from Exhibit 16-5 that eight batches require 40.96 hours. Seven batches require 37.408 hours (7 × 5.344, the average time computed above using the formula). Hence, the eighth batch requires 3.552 hours (40.96 − 37.408).

You can also apply the learning curve directly to cost, rather than to time. For example, we could have said that labor and variable overhead costs were $10 for the first batch. In that case, the answers derived in the exhibit or from the formula would be expressed in dollars.

The learning curve is useful in planning and controlling. Managers can estimate labor time, and therefore labor and labor-related variable overhead costs, for specific quantities of output. They can then determine, by comparing actual time or cost with the estimated values, whether learning is as expected.

Let us look at how this quantitative method might be useful in decision making. Suppose that CompuCom is considering a customer's offer to buy eight batches of a specialized microprocessor. (A batch could be 500, 1,000, or any other number of units, so long as all batches are the same size.) The customer has offered to pay $80,000 for the entire order. No incremental fixed costs are associated with the order. Materials and purchased components will cost $3,500 for each batch. (Recognize that this portion of the cost is not subject to a learning curve.) CompuCom estimates the cost of direct labor and labor-related variable overhead for the first batch at $3,000 and has usually experienced an 80% learning rate.

CompuCom's managers will not accept the order unless they expect more than $35,000 in contribution margin, because the company could earn about that amount doing other business if the order were not accepted. If no learning were involved, or if the managers were unaware of the potential for efficiency, the order would be rejected on the basis of the following analysis.

Revenues		$80,000
Variable costs:		
Materials and components (8 × $3,500)	$28,000	
Labor and related overhead (8 × $3,000)	24,000	52,000
Expected contribution margin		$28,000

However, the order does have the desired profit potential if the learning factor is considered. The following schedule shows the expected costs of labor and related variable overhead, based on the 80% learning rate and expected costs of the first batch.

Total Output in Batches	Expected Average Cost per Batch	Expected Total Cost[a]
1	$3,000 (given)	$ 3,000
2	2,400 ($3,000 × 80%)	4,800 (2 × $2,400)
4	1,920 ($2,400 × 80%)	7,680 (4 × $1,920)
8	1,536 ($1,920 × 80%)	12,288 (8 × $1,536)

[a] Number of batches × average cost per batch.

With this cost information, the order would be analyzed as below.

Revenues		$80,000
Variable costs:		
Materials and components (8 × $3,500)	$28,000	
Labor and related overhead, as above	12,288	40,288
Expected contribution margin		$39,712

The total expected contribution margin from the order is nearly $12,000 more than that shown by the analysis that did not consider the cost reduction expected to result from learning. The order now appears to be more profitable than the available alternative (contribution margin of $35,000) and would be accepted. Thus, managers must study their firms' experiences for evidence of potential cost reductions as a result of learning and incorporate that potential into decision making.

SUMMARY

Managers use a variety of quantitative techniques to help them make decisions. Statistical decision theory enables managers to incorporate the effects of uncertainty into their analyses. Inventory control models offer rational ways of evaluating inventory policies, including the associated purchasing decisions. Linear programming helps managers decide how best to use existing resources. Shadow prices help managers to understand the significance of existing constraints and the potential gains from capacity expansion. Learning curves are useful in planning and controlling labor and labor-related costs.

Much of the information needed for using these techniques is supplied by managerial accountants. Therefore, they must be aware of the objectives and information requirements of such techniques. The managerial accountant will sometimes have to assist in formulating the problem and must therefore understand the capabilities and limitations of the techniques available.

KEY TERMS

decision tree

carrying costs

conditional value

economic order quantity (EOQ)

expected value

lead time

learning curve

linear programming

ordering costs

payoff table

reorder point

safety stock

shadow price

stockout costs

value of perfect information

KEY FORMULAS

$$\text{Economic order quantity} = \sqrt{\frac{(2 \times \text{incremental ordering cost} \times \text{annual demand})}{\text{annual carrying cost}}}$$

Reorder point = safety stock + (daily use × lead time)

REVIEW PROBLEM – EXPECTED VALUES

In March, Grauger Company experienced an unfavorable cost variance of $2,000. Based on experience and judgment, the production manager believes there is a 40% probability that the variance was due to random causes and will not continue. A 60% probability exists that there is some difficulty in the production process and that the variance will continue at $2,000 per month for the next two months. Investigating the variance would cost $800. If the variance is investigated and something is wrong with the process, there is a 70% probability that corrective action could be taken and a 30% probability that nothing can be done.

Required: Determine the expected costs of investigating and of not investigating the variance.

Answer to Review Problem

1.   Expected Cost of Investigating

Event	Cost	Probability	Expected Value
Variance is random and will not continue	$ 800	.40	$ 320
Variance is caused by problem in process that can be corrected	800	.42[a]	336
Variance is caused by problem that cannot be corrected	4,800[b]	.18[c]	864
Expected cost of investigating		1.00	$1,520

[a] 60% × 70%.
[b] $800 + (2 × $2,000).
[c] 60% × 30%.

2.   Expected Cost of Not Investigating

Event	Cost	Probability	Expected Value
Variance is random	0	.40	0
Variance is caused by problem in process and will continue	$4,000	.60	$2,400
Expected cost of not investigating		1.00	$2,400

The variance should be investigated because the expected cost to investigate is less than that of not investigating.

REVIEW PROBLEM – INVENTORY CONTROL

The following data apply to one of Tebbetts Company's products.

Annual use	12,000 units
Annual carrying cost	$0.80 per unit
Order cost	$300 per order
Safety stock	500 units

There are 200 working days per year, and the lead time is 12 days.

Required
1. Determine the reorder point.
2. Determine the EOQ.

Answer to Review Problem

1.

Safety stock	500
Use during lead time [12 × (12,000/200)]	720
Reorder point	1,220

2. 3,000 units.

$$\text{EOQ} = \sqrt{\frac{2 \times \$300 \times 12,000}{\$0.80}} = \sqrt{\frac{\$7,200,000}{\$0.80}} = \sqrt{9,000,000} = 3,000 \text{ units}$$

ASSIGNMENT MATERIAL

Questions for Discussion

16-1 *Optimum order size – changing conditions* Explain the effect that each of the following tends to have on the optimum order size for a product.
(a) Leading banks have announced a reduction in the prime interest rate.
(b) The selling price of the product declines with no change in its purchase cost.
(c) The company moves to a high-crime, inner-city area.
(d) The city increases the personal property tax rate.
(e) There is a substantial increase in the demand for the product.
(f) The company changes from the straight-line method of depreciating its warehouse to the sum-of-the-years'-digits method.

16-2 *Reorder point* Indicate how each of the following factors, considered independently, influences the reorder point for inventory (relatively high, relatively low, or no effect). Explain your answers.
1. The company has low fixed costs and high variable costs (85% of sales).
2. A product is stored in expensive, custom-made freezers.

3. The product is ice cream, sold from a store in a large shopping center.
4. Your suppliers have had falling profits because of intense competition.
5. Your major supplier is having difficulties because two stockholder factions have been fighting for control.

Exercises

16-3 *Inventory control*   Ridley Company uses 60,000 units of a particular raw material per year. The material is used evenly throughout the year. Order costs are $1,600 per order, and carrying costs are $12 per unit. The firm carries a safety stock of 2,000 units, has a lead time of 8 days, and works 200 days per year.

Required
1. Determine the reorder point.
2. Determine the EOQ.

16-4 *Variance investigation*   Cole Company's controller has determined that it costs $800 to investigate a variance and that corrective action is possible in one out of four cases investigated. An unfavorable variance of $1,800 has occurred. The production process will be changed after next month, so that any savings will be for only one month if corrective action can be taken. Should the variance be investigated?

16-5 *Inventory control*   Using the following data, determine the EOQ and the reorder point for Part No. 368. Round your computations to even units and dollars.

Cost per unit	$40
Use per year	12,000 units
Carrying costs	15% of cost
Order costs	$1,000 per order
Lead time	10 days
Safety stock	1,000 units
Working days per year	200

16-6 *Basic learning curve*   Industrial engineers at Kemp Inc., a manufacturer of industrial presses, expect the first unit of a new model, the XZ-18, to require 2,000 direct labor hours. They also expect an 80% learning curve.

Required
1. Determine the average direct labor time and the total direct labor time to make four units of the XZ-18.
2. Determine the average direct labor time and the total direct labor time to make eight units of the XZ-18.

16-7 *New products – expected values and risk*   The sales manager of Happy Toy Company is considering two new toys, a doll and a game. On the basis of market research and experience, she has formulated the following table.

	Doll		Game	
Event	Cash Flow	Probability	Cash Flow	Probability
Big success	$60,000	.2	$90,000	.3
Fair success	40,000	.5	50,000	.4
Flop	10,000	.3	(20,000)	.3

Required

1. Determine the expected value of cash flows associated with each new toy.
2. Which one would you select, and why?

16-8 ***Linear programming – formulation of problem*** Garson Company makes three products, A, B, and C. Their respective contribution margins are $60, $70, and $80. Each product goes through three processes: cutting, shaping, and painting. The numbers of hours required by each process for each product are as follows.

Hours Required in Each Process

Product	Cutting	Shaping	Painting
A	4	2	4
B	3	5	3
C	5	2	2

The following numbers of hours are available per month in each process: cutting, 8,000; shaping, 6,000; and painting, 4,000.

Required: Formulate the objective function and constraints to determine the optimal production policy.

16-9 ***Linear programming*** PQ Company makes two products.

	P	Q
Selling price	$50	$30
Variable costs	$25	$20
Labor hours required per unit:		
Grinding Department	3	1
Assembly Department	2	2

The firm has 900 hours of labor time available in the Grinding Department and 800 available in the Assembly Department.

Required: Determine the optimal product mix.

16-10 ***Learning curve*** Tallman Industries is bidding on a contract to make eight batches of landing gear assemblies for an aircraft company. Tallman's engineers expect direct labor and variable overhead for the first batch to be $50,000. Variable overhead is related to direct labor. Tallman usually achieves an 85% learning rate.

Required

1. Determine the expected average cost for direct labor and variable overhead for the eight batches.
2. Determine the expected total cost for direct labor and variable overhead for the eight batches.

16-11 Learning curve (extension of 16-10)   Tallman's managers expect the cost of materials and purchased components to be $25,000 per batch (not subject to learning). They also want an average contribution margin of $15,000 per batch.

Required

1. Determine the price that Tallman must bid to earn $15,000 average contribution margin per batch for eight batches.
2. Suppose now that the contract is for 16 batches. Redo item 1.
3. Suppose that the contract is still for eight batches, but that Tallman's managers believe that the learning rate will actually be 80%. Redo item 1.

16-12 Cost structure and probabilities   The production manager of Omega Company is considering modifying one of his machines. The modification will add $10,000 per month to the cost of running the machine but will reduce variable operating costs by $0.20 per unit produced. The modification itself costs nothing, and the machine can be returned to its current operating method at any time.

The product made on the machine has an uncertain demand; the best estimates available are as follows.

Monthly Demand	Probability
25,000	.20
40,000	.40
60,000	.20
70,000	.20

Required

1. Determine the number of units that must be produced to justify the modification.
2. Determine the expected value of making the modification. Should it be made?

16-13 Payoff table   Campus Program Company sells programs for football games. The owner has collected the following data regarding the pattern of sales.

Quantity Sold (cases)	Probability
400	.20
600	.60
700	.20

The owner is uncertain of the number of cases of programs to order. He must order one of the quantities given above. A case of programs sells for $300, and the purchase price is $100. Unsold programs are thrown away.

Required: Construct a payoff table to determine the number of cases of programs the firm should order.

16-14 *Linear programming, formulation of problem* Carter Company makes two models of its basic product. Data are

	X	Y
Selling price	$80	$100
Material requirements, pounds	2	1
Labor time, hours	2	3

Materials cost $8 per pound and the combined labor and variable overhead rate is $12 per labor hour. The company has 400 pounds of material and 500 hours of labor available. It can sell all of either model that it can make. Fixed costs are $2,000, of which $700 is depreciation. All fixed costs are unavoidable.

Required: Formulate the objective function and constraints.

16-15 *Linear programming (extension of 16-14)* Refer to 16-14.

Required
1. Determine the optimal mix.
2. Determine the shadow price of the labor constraint. Assume the addition of 20 hours of labor.

16-16 *Sensitivity analysis* The florist for whom you prepared the payoff table on page 689 is not impressed. He has decided to order 4,000 corsages per week because he does not want to be stuck with unsold goods. Because you own a share of the business, you would like him to order 8,000 per week. In an effort to show him that he is being unduly conservative, you decide to show him how low the risk is by using more pessimistic probabilities. Because you would not order 12,000 corsages, you can lump together the probabilities of selling 8,000 and 12,000. (The contribution margin from ordering 8,000 corsages is the same whether demand is 8,000 or 12,000.)

Required: Determine the expected values of ordering 8,000 corsages with the following probabilities.

Case	Demand in Units	Probability of Demand
1	4,000	.30
	8,000	.70
2	4,000	.40
	8,000	.60
3	4,000	.50
	8,000	.50

16-17 *Inventory control – sensitivity* Morton Company sells a product with the following attributes.

Annual demand	10,000 units
Annual carrying cost per unit	$2
Order cost	$400

Required
1. Determine the EOQ. Determine the annual cost associated with this policy.
2. Suppose that the firm halves the order quantity, doubling the number of orders from the one you calculated in item 1. What is the cost of following the nonoptimal policy?

Problems

16-18   *Expected values — a law firm*   The firm of Smith, Jones, and Jankowski has been approached by Hirt, a victim of a whiplash injury suffered in an automobile accident. He wants the firm to represent him in a court suit, with the firm's fee being one third of the total judgment given by the court.

Jankowski estimates that 2,000 hours are needed to prepare and try the case, with the opportunity cost being $80 per hour. Based on experience with similar cases, he believes that the following judgments and associated probabilities are reasonable estimates on which to decide whether to accept the case.

Judgment for Hirt	Probability of Judgment
0	.40
$180,000	.20
$300,000	.30
$420,000	.10

Required: Determine whether the firm should accept the case.

16-19   *Inventory control*   Blitzen Industries makes products in individual production runs, because all its products must go through one particular machine. Each time a new production run is set up, the firm incurs incremental costs of $1,500.

The cost to carry a unit of product A is $4 per year, including taxes, insurance, spoilage, and return on investment. Sales of product A are 24,000 units per year.

Required
1. Determine the number of units of A that should be made each run.
2. The company carries a safety stock of 800 units of A, the working year is 300 days, and production of a batch requires ten days. At what inventory level should a production run be made?

16-20   *Learning curve in administrative work*   The Dean of Admissions at Mid-State University needs student help to process 12,000 application forms. She has found that a new student helper can process 30 forms the first day. The helpers usually achieve a 80% learning rate. The Dean plans to hire 25 helpers, so each will process 480 forms. You may consider 30 forms to be a batch.

Required: Determine how many days it will take 25 new helpers to process the 12,000 forms.

16-21 Variance investigation Edwards Company has just experienced a $3,000 unfavorable variance. The production supervisor believes that there is a 30% chance that the variance was a one-time thing and will not continue. He believes that if an investigation is made, the chance of correcting the variance is 60% and of not correcting it is 40%. It costs $800 to investigate a variance. The most that will be lost if the variance continues is $4,000.

Required: Determine whether to investigate the variance.

16-22 Linear programming Fast Class Company makes two products, the Fast and the Class. Fasts sell for $12 and have variable costs of $5. Classes sell for $14 and have variable costs of $6. Both products are put through two processes—cutting and forming. Each unit of Fast requires two hours of cutting and four hours of forming. Each unit of Class requires three hours of cutting and two of forming. The company has available 3,000 hours of cutting time and 2,400 hours of forming time per month. Fixed costs in cutting are $400, in forming are $300, all unavoidable.

Required: Determine the number of Fasts and Classes that should be produced each month.

16-23 Shadow prices and sensitivity analysis (extension of 16-22) Refer to 16-22.

Required: Consider each item independently.
1. Determine the shadow price of the forming constraint.
2. Determine the price of Fasts that would make the company indifferent between the current optimal mix (from 16-22) and making all Fasts.
3. Determine the price of Classes that would make the company indifferent between the current optimal mix (from 16-22) and making all Classes.

16-24 Product selection Henson Electronics is trying to decide which of three products to introduce. The managers think that only one should be brought out in order to concentrate promotional effort. Information about the products follows.

	Radio	Toaster	Coffee Maker
Selling price	$22	$37	$45
Variable cost	13	20	25
Contribution margin	$ 9	$17	$20
Sales forecasts, in units, with	25,000 (20%)	12,000 (10%)	15,000 (60%)
probabilities in parentheses	40,000 (40%)	19,000 (25%)	20,000 (20%)
	50,000 (30%)	25,000 (50%)	25,000 (20%)
	75,000 (10%)	38,000 (15%)	

Required
1. Compute the expected values of contribution margins for the three products.
2. Which product would you select, and why?

16-25 *Expected value of hole-in-one*   The sponsors of the Eastern Open, a major golf tournament, have decided to give a new automobile to any player who gets a hole-in-one during the tournament. The car they have selected costs $22,000. One of the sponsors owns an insurance agency and offers to insure the tournament against a hole-in-one for $800. If the sponsors buy the policy and someone does get a hole-in-one, the insurance company will buy the car. Statistics show that a hole-in-one occurs about every 75 tournaments.

Required: Determine the expected value of *not* buying the insurance. Would you buy the insurance if you were a sponsor?

16-26 *Learning curve in make-or-buy decision*   Barfield Company currently buys a component for one of its products at $22 per unit. Barfield needs 32,000 units of the component in the coming year. The product will be redesigned, so that the component will not be needed beyond the coming year. The production manager believes that Barfield could make the component with the following costs for the first batch of 1,000 units.

Materials	$13,000
Direct labor and variable overhead	15,000
Total variable cost	$28,000

There are no incremental fixed costs because Barfield could use existing equipment. The production manager expects an 85% learning rate on direct labor and variable overhead. Consider a batch to be 1,000 units.

Required: Determine whether Barfield should make or buy the component.

16-27 *Make or buy*   Walters Company manufactures ceramic figurines. Sometimes the company subcontracts production of its designs to other companies, paying a set amount per piece. The chief designer has come up with a new item that most of the managers expect to be a best seller. Some of the managers are less sure and want to be as cautious as possible.

If Walters manufactures the item, it must lease additional space and machinery at a cost of $80,000 for the coming year. The lease could not be canceled for one year. Unit variable cost is $14, and the selling price is $36. Alternatively, the company could subcontract production. A local outlet has agreed to produce the item and sell it to Walters Company at $23.

Based on her experience with other, similar items, the company's sales manager has developed the following estimates of demand and probabilities for the new figurine.

Demand	Probability
7,000	.20
9,000	.30
12,000	.30
14,000	.20

Required: Determine the expected value of the profit on the figurine if Walters (a) makes it internally and (b) subcontracts it.

16-28   *Inventory control — effects of errors in policy*   The purchasing manager of Kensington Company buys one of its principal products in batches of 2,000, basing the amount of the purchase on his judgment. Data for the product are

Order cost	$800
Carrying cost, annual per unit	$2
Annual demand	20,000

Required
1. Determine the EOQ.
2. Determine the cost to the firm of not following the optimal purchasing policy. That is, determine the difference between total costs under the existing policy and under the optimal policy.
3. Determine how high carrying costs must go to make the EOQ 2,000 units.
4. Determine the order costs that will make the EOQ 2,000 units, assuming that the carrying costs are $2.

16-29   *Inventory control — determination of incremental costs*   Rankin Company currently has no stated inventory policy. The sales manager and controller have asked you to assist in preparing a policy. Two of the factors to be determined are the cost of carrying inventory and the cost of ordering. The following information pertains to the company's only product.

Cost per unit	$90
Sales per year	15,000 units
Required return on investment	15%
Insurance	$500 per year plus $1.70 per unit of average inventory
Taxes	$2 per unit of average inventory
Storage	The firm leases a warehouse that can hold 20,000 units. Rent is $1,000 per year
Costs of purchasing department:	
Salaries	$12,000 per year fixed, plus $50 per order
Forms, postage	$10 per order

In addition, each time an order is received, the company hires men from a local employment service to unload the order. On any size order, three men are hired at $30 each.

Required: Determine the EOQ. Be sure to determine which costs shown above are relevant to the analysis, which are not.

16-30   *Special order decision — probabilities*   The sales manager of Schieren Company has been approached by a chain store that would like to buy 10,000

units of the firm's product. The sales manager believes that the order should be accepted because the price offered is $6 and variable costs of production are $5.

In a conversation with the production manager, the sales manager extracted the following information: (1) Sufficient capacity exists to meet the special order; (2) prices for materials and wage rates are expected to increase by the time the order would be manufactured, but the amounts of the increases are not certain. The best estimates follow.

New Variable Cost	Probability
$5.20	.30
5.70	.40
6.60	.30

Required
1. Determine the expected contribution margin on the special order.
2. What other factors should be considered in reaching a decision?

16-31 Cost of investigating a variance Chapman Company's production manager has been trying to decide whether a particular variable overhead variance should be investigated. The variance was $300 unfavorable this past month, and is expected to continue at the rate of $300 for five more months if nothing is done. The estimated cost to investigate the variance is $600, and the chances are four out of five that nothing can be done to correct the variance even if its cause can be isolated. If the variance is found to be correctable, the total savings, not considering the cost of the investigation, will be $1,500 (the total cost of the variance over the next five months).

Required: Determine whether the variance should be investigated.

16-32 Expected values and utilities The sales manager of Winston Toy Company has been studying a report prepared by a consultant. The company had asked the consultant to study the advisability of bringing out a new doll that would be quite different from anything on the market. The report indicated that there was considerable variation in sales expectations. The consultant concluded that there was about a 60% chance of selling 50,000 dolls and a 40% chance of selling only 10,000.

The doll's price is to be $24, with variable costs of $20. Incremental fixed costs, primarily for advertising, are $120,000.

The sales manager decided, on the basis of the expected value of profit, that the doll should be introduced, but the president of the firm was leery. The president felt that the doll was apt to lose money and that the company had had too many duds in recent years. After some discussion, the president decided that losing a dollar was twice as bad as earning a dollar was good. He instructed the sales manager to prepare a new analysis incorporating his utility, although he did not call it that.

Required
1. Prepare a schedule showing the expected value of profit without consideration of the president's views.

2. Prepare a new schedule in which the president's views are incorporated. Determine whether the doll should be brought out.

16-33 *Variance investigation* Richter Company experienced an unfavorable variance of $2,000 in May. The production manager found, from past data, that 30% of the time a variance of this size is experienced, nothing is wrong with the process and the variance stops. When there is a problem, 60% of the time the variance continues for two additional months, at $2,000 per month, and 40% of the time it continues for three additional months, also at $2,000 per month.

Investigating the variance costs $800. If there is a problem with the production process, it can be corrected 40% of the time. The other 60% of the time nothing can be done. The 40% and 60% probabilities apply both to variances that would continue for two additional months and to those that would continue for three additional months. If the investigation has been done and the cause of the variance found to be correctable, correcting it costs an additional $600.

Required
1. Determine the expected cost of not investigating the variance.
2. Determine the expected cost of investigating the variance.

16-34 *Variance investigation (CMA adapted)* Cilla Company manufactures a line of women's handbags. A summary of Cilla's cutting department operations for May 19X5 showed a $16,000 unfavorable materials use variance.

Donna Cook, the supervisor of the department, gathered the following information to assist her in deciding whether to investigate the variance.

Estimated cost to investigate the variance	$ 4,000
Estimated cost to make changes if the department is operating incorrectly	$ 8,000
Estimated savings if changes are made	$40,000
Estimated probability that department is operating incorrectly	10%

Required: Determine whether Ms. Cook should investigate the variance.

16-35 *Capital budgeting probabilities* The following estimates have been prepared by the production manager of Hector Company. They relate to a proposed $60,000 investment in a machine that will reduce the cost of materials used by the firm. Cost of capital is 16%. Ignore taxes.

Annual Cash Savings		Useful Life	
Event	Probability	Event	Probability
$20,000	.30	9 years	.40
14,000	.30	8 years	.40
12,000	.40	6 years	.20

Required
1. Compute the expected values of annual cash savings and useful life. Determine whether the machine should be purchased.

2. The production manager wishes to see whether the machine would be a good investment if each of his most pessimistic estimates, but not both at the same time, came true. Determine whether the investment would be desirable if (a) the useful life is the expected value computed in item 1 and annual cash flows are only $12,000; (b) the annual cash flows are equal to the expected value computed in item 1 and the useful life is only six years.

16-36 **Expected values**   The managers of Hawkins Company are trying to decide how to operate in the coming year. The company rents a machine that performs essential operations on the product; the rental period is one year. The product sells for $10 per unit and has variable costs of $1.

Three machines are available; operating and other data are

Machine	Productive Capacity	Annual Rent
Standard	11,000 units	$50,000
DeLuxe	12,000	54,000
Super	13,000	55,500

The sales forecast for the coming year has been based on the 10,000 units sold the prior year; demand for the product is expected to increase, but the size of the increase is uncertain. The best estimates follow.

Sales in Units	Probability
11,000	.30
12,000	.50
13,000	.20

Required: Determine the best course of action for the company.

16-37 **Inventory control – quantity discounts**   Alexander Company buys one of its principal products from Zephyr Company in batches of 2,000. The product costs Alexander $10, and annual demand is 20,000 units. Annual carrying costs are $1.60 per unit, which includes a required rate of return of 10% (all other carrying costs are related to units, not cost), and incremental ordering costs are $160 per order. The current batch size is the EOQ for this product.

Zephyr sells this product only to Alexander and has to set up a production run every time an order is received. There are no carrying costs because Zephyr maintains no inventory, and setup costs are $1,000 per production run. The production manager of Zephyr asked the sales manager whether it might not be a good idea to offer Alexander a price reduction if Alexander agreed to buy half as often, and double the usual quantity. After some discussion, they agreed to offer Alexander a $0.20 price reduction for buying in batches of 4,000 units or more.

Required
1. Compute the annual gain or loss to both Alexander and Zephyr if the price reduction is granted.

2. Suppose that Zephyr offers to supply all 20,000 units at a single time. Determine the lowest price per unit that Zephyr could charge and not reduce its income below the level it would earn supplying the product in batches of 4,000.

3. Determine whether Alexander should buy all of its annual requirements at once, at the price you computed in item 2. (Assume that Alexander would still get the $0.20 reduction if it decided to buy 4,000 units at a time.)

16-38 **Payoff table**   The Evening News is a large metropolitan newspaper. The paper is sold through dealers who are charged $0.20 per copy that they sell. Unsold copies are returned to *The News* and full credit is given. The unsold copies are sold as wastepaper for $0.02 each. The variable cost of producing a paper is $0.10.

The News currently prints 500,000 papers each day. Management is considering a change and has asked for your help. A recent study showed the following results.

Papers Returned	Percentage of Time
100,000	20%
50,000	20%
0	60%

The study also indicated that when 500,000 copies were all sold, there were often more papers demanded. The best estimates are that 25% of the time 500,000 copies are demanded, 25% of the time 550,000 are demanded, and 10% of the time 600,000 papers could be sold if they were available.

Required
1. Determine the best strategy for *The Evening News*.
2. Determine the value of perfect information.

16-39 **Linear programming, graphical solution**   Salinas Furniture Company makes two types of sofas, traditional and modern. Because of their different types of construction they require different amounts of machine time and skilled labor time. The company has available, per week, 1,000 hours of skilled labor and 1,200 hours of machine time. The variable costs associated with skilled labor, including both wages and variable overhead, are $7 per hour; for machine time, the variable costs are $6 per hour. The firm can sell all of the modern sofas it can make, but only 200 traditional sofas per week.

Additional data on the two sofas are as follows.

	Traditional	Modern
Selling price	$240	$180
Material costs (the only other variable cost)	$ 80	$ 60
Labor hours required, per unit	4	2
Machine hours required, per unit	3	4

The following figure plots the above constraints.

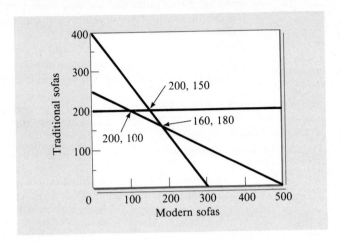

Required
1. Determine the number of each sofa that should be produced each week.
2. Assuming that the price of modern sofas remains constant, at what price for traditional sofas should the firm increase its production of traditional sofas and reduce that of modern sofas?

16-40 *Expected values – capital budgeting*   Fleming Company plans to build a factory to manufacture a new product. The product and the factory are expected to have useful lives of ten years. No salvage value is expected for any of the components of the factory. The firm's marketing research staff has studied the potential demand for the product and has provided the following information.

Expected Annual Demand	Probability of Demand
200,000 units	60%
250,000 units	40%

The firm can build a factory with capacity of either 200,000 or 250,000 units. Data on the two possible factories are given below.

Capacity	Total Cost, All Depreciable Assets	Annual Fixed Costs Requiring Cash
200,000	$1,500,000	$300,000
250,000	1,800,000	380,000

The product will sell for $5 and have variable costs of $1. The tax rate is 40% and cost of capital is 16%. Straight-line depreciation is used for tax purposes.

Management has decided to base its decision on net present value. Whichever factory shows the greater favorable difference between the present value of the expected value of future cash flows and the required investment will be built.

Required: Prepare analyses of the expected values of future cash flows under the two investment possibilities. Determine which factory should be built.

16-41   *Expected values (AICPA adapted)*   Wing Manufacturing Company makes a chemical compound, product X, that deteriorates rapidly. Any left unsold at the end of the month in which the firm makes it becomes worthless. The variable cost of manufacturing the product is $50 per pound and the selling price $80 per pound. The demand for the product, with associated probabilities, appears below.

Monthly Demand	Probability
8,000	.25
9,000	.60
10,000	.15

The management of Wing believes that it is necessary to supply all customers who order product X. Failing to do so would result, in the managers' judgment, in losing not only sales of product X, but also sales of other products. Wing has found a company that will sell product X to it at $80, plus $10 freight per pound. The managers want to develop a policy regarding production. Some argue that the high cost of obtaining additional amounts from the outside supplier makes it desirable to produce 10,000 pounds per month. Others argue that it is safer to produce less and to buy from the supplier as needed.

Required: Determine what production strategy maximizes the expected value of profit.

CHAPTER *17*

STATEMENT OF CASH FLOWS

An accounting information system must serve the needs of both financial and managerial accounting. Much of the information prepared for distribution outside the firm is used by the firm's managers. For example, data from income statements and balance sheets are used for performance measurement and budgeting.

A third statement commonly used in financial accounting is the statement of cash flows. This chapter discusses its content and development.

INTEREST IN CASH FLOWS

Profitability is but one of the factors important for the survival and growth of the firm. Also important are the current and future inflows and outflows of cash. From Chapter 7 we know that managers develop cash budgets to help them anticipate potential shortages of cash needed for carrying out the firm's plans. (Will cash be available for planned operating levels? for capital expenditures? for dividends? for repaying debt?)

Managers are responsible for planning how and when cash will be obtained and used. When planned cash outflows are more than the inflows that planned activities are likely to produce, managers must decide what to do. At times, they obtain financing (through borrowing or the issuance of stock) or dispose of some existing investment (by selling some asset, or perhaps an entire segment of the business). At other times, they curtail planned activities by revising their plans for operations (e.g., dropping a special advertising campaign) or new investments

724

(e.g., delaying acquisition of new machinery). Or, they might revise planned payments to financing sources (e.g., delay debt repayment or reduce dividends). Whatever they do, the managers' goal is to balance the cash available and the needs for cash.

Lenders, stockholders, suppliers, and other outsiders are also aware of the importance of planning and of decisions for balancing available cash and cash needs. They know that cash flows into the firm from operations, financing sources, and sales of fixed assets and other investments. They know that cash is used for operations, dividends and repayment of debt, and expansion. They are interested in cash flows and changes in cash position because these reflect the firm's decisions for implementing its short-term and long-term plans for operations, investment, and financing. Stated more generally, outsiders are interested in information about the firm's **operating, investing,** and **financing activities** and the cash flows associated with those activities.

The year-end balance sheet shows the *cumulative* effects of past operating, investing, and financing decisions—the firm's assets, unpaid borrowings, equity capital raised, and results of past operations. The income statement shows some of the current effects of these past decisions. The cash flow statement is needed because neither of the other statements directly addresses the firm's *current activities* in these three important areas and the balancing of the cash flows associated with them. The cash flow statement is, like the other statements, after-the-fact (or historical). But it provides the interested reader with further information to assess managerial decisions and performance and prospects for future profit, payments to financing sources, and growth.

FORMAL CASH FLOW STATEMENT

Because the cash flow statement is distributed outside the firm, its form and content are governed by official pronouncements on generally accepted accounting principles (GAAP).[1] As you might have guessed from the preceding discussion, the **cash flow statement** has three basic parts, which classify the firm's cash inflows and outflows as related to operating, investing, or financing activities. The following lists provide examples.

Operating flows: Inflows include cash received from customers, and perhaps for interest and dividends on investments. Outflows include cash paid for inventory, salaries and wages, taxes, and other expenses, including interest.

Investing flows: Inflows include receipts from sales of long-lived operating assets, such as property, plant, equipment, and patents, from repayments on loans made to others, and from sales of investments. Cash outlays to acquire

---

[1] The official pronouncement governing cash flow statements is Statement of Financial Accounting Standards, No. 95 (Stamford, Conn., Financial Accounting Standards Board, 1987). That pronouncement is the source of statements in the chapter about GAAP requirements.

these same types of assets, or to make loans to others, are examples of investing outflows.

Financing flows: Inflows include cash received from long-term or short-term borrowing and from issuing stock. Dividends, purchases of treasury stock, and repayments of borrowings are examples of financing outflows.

As you can see from the examples, most cash flows are easy to classify. An important exception is interest payments. These cash outflows to providers of one type of financing, debt capital, are included among the operating flows. Dividend payments to providers of equity capital are, however, reported among the financing flows. A major, though not entirely satisfactory, reason for this exception appears to be a desire to go as far as possible to include items affecting net income among operating cash flows. To accommodate readers with a different view, the Financial Accounting Standards Board (FASB) requires that cash paid for interest be reported separately.[2]

Beyond the basic classification scheme, other, mostly practical, considerations affect the content and format of a cash flow statement. Before we present an example of a typical statement and illustrate its development, we discuss the three most important of these considerations.

Defining Cash

Cash is an extremely important asset, one the firm cannot get along without. On the other hand, for short periods financial managers often invest cash in excess of immediate needs in highly liquid, income-producing securities such as government notes. In such cases, the firm's *immediately usable* funds include not only cash but also those highly liquid securities (called **cash equivalents**).

To recognize the nature of the firm's short-term investments, GAAP require that the cash flow statement be based on the combination of cash *and* cash equivalents. That is, the amount reported as the net change in cash resulting from all types of activities will equal the change in the sum of cash and cash equivalents. The practical implications of using the sum are that the cash relating to the purchases and sales of such securities will not be reported among the investing activities, and that the net gain or loss from sales of the securities will be included among the operating cash flows.

Reporting Operating Cash Flows

As stated above, both internal and external users of financial statements normally view the income statement as a report of a firm's operating activities. Now, reread

---

[2] The same reasoning applies to interest and dividend revenues. However, the FASB required separate disclosure of these revenues only if a firm presents its operating cash flows using the "direct method." This method is discussed later.

the examples of operating cash flows provided earlier. Does the income statement report these inflows and outflows? Does reported net income equal the net cash flow from operating activities? The answer to both questions is "no."

From your study of financial accounting you know that the income statement is prepared using the accrual basis of accounting and does not necessarily reflect cash transactions relating to operations. (Studying comprehensive budgeting reinforces the distinction between accrual accounting, which is the basis for pro forma financial statements, and cash flows, which are reflected in separate budgets.) Thus, desired information about operating cash flows is not available directly from an income statement.

To meet the need for information about cash flows relating to operating activities, two reporting approaches have achieved general acceptance and are permitted by the FASB. The first approach, called the **direct method,** separately reports operating cash inflows and outflows as described earlier. A reporting of operating cash flows under this approach resembles a cash budget showing receipts and disbursements for operations. The second approach, called the **indirect method,** reports only the *net* cash flow from operations, but does so by presenting reported net income and then adjusting that amount for the effects of *noncash* items that affected net income. Thus, the indirect approach neither reports inflows and outflows separately nor describes the major outflows. Rather, it reconciles (explains the difference between) reported income and net cash flow from operations. The calculation of operating cash flows in this manner is often called a **reconciliation of net income and cash flow from operations.** Because many external users of financial statements are also interested in an explanation of the differences between reported income and cash flow, a firm using the direct method is also required to provide such a reconciliation. We use the indirect method in the sample format and the illustration to be presented shortly, because you will have to understand the reconciliation approach whether or not the cash flow statement uses that method of presentation. The direct method will be illustrated later.

Noncash Transactions

A firm can engage in significant operating, investing, and financing activities without affecting either cash or cash equivalents. For example, suppose a firm issues a ten-year note to buy machinery. Acquiring machinery is an investment; issuing the note is a financing activity. Alternatively, suppose the firm settles some of its long-term debt by issuing common stock. Both the issuance of stock and the reduction of debt affect the financing of the firm, but do not affect cash.

Although flows of cash (and cash equivalents) are important, a statement of operating, investing, and financing activities should not ignore such transactions. Accordingly, *significant activities not involving cash flows must also be reported,* either in a separate schedule or in narrative form. Whichever alternative is adopted, great care must be taken to report these noncash transactions in a way that clearly reflects the *net cash flow* for each of the three major types of activities. For simplicity, we use the first (separate schedule) approach in the sample format and basic illustration.

Format of the Statement

Exhibit 17-1 shows a skeleton outline of a cash flow statement. The sample uses the indirect method of presenting operating cash flows and reports important noncash transactions in a separate schedule.

Exhibit 17-1
Example Company, Statement of Cash Flows for 19X8

Net cash flow from operating activities:		
Net income	xxx	
Adjustments for noncash expenses, revenues, losses, and gains included in income:		
	xxx	
	(xxx)	
	xxx	
Net cash flow from (for) operating activities		xxx
Cash flows from investing activities:		
	xxx	
	(xxx)	
	xxx	
Net cash provided (used) by investing activities		xxx
Cash flows from financing activities:		
	xxx	
	(xxx)	
	xxx	
Net cash provided (used) by financing activities		xxx
Net increase (decrease) in cash		xxx
Cash balance, beginning of year		xx
Cash balance, end of year		xxx
Schedule of Noncash Investing and Financing Activities:		
	xxx	
	xxx	
	xxx	

Note the descriptions of the *net* cash flow in each of the three major sections. Depending on the transactions during the year, the net flow in any section could be an inflow or an outflow and the description would be worded accordingly.

With this outline in mind, we shall illustrate the development of a cash flow statement.

ILLUSTRATION

The basis for our illustration is the USL Corporation, a retailer whose financial statements are provided in Exhibits 17-2 (opposite) and 17-3 (page 730). For convenience, in Exhibit 17-3 we have shown the increase or decrease in each balance-sheet item.

ILLUSTRATION   729

Exhibit 17-2

USL Corporation

Combined Statement of Income and Retained Earnings for 19X5

Sales		$1,000,000
Cost of goods sold:		
Beginning inventory	$100,000	
Purchases	540,000	
Cost of goods available for sale	640,000	
Less ending inventory	190,000	
Cost of goods sold		450,000
Gross profit		550,000
Expenses:		
Depreciation	56,000	
Interest	12,000	
Income taxes	123,700	
Other	128,800	
Total expenses		320,500
Net income		229,500
Retained earnings at the beginning of the year		190,000
		419,500
Dividends declared and paid during the year		30,000
Retained earnings at the end of the year		$ 389,500

From the comparative balance sheets we can see that USL's cash decreased $174,500 and that there are no short-term investments that might qualify as cash equivalents. Our objective, then, is to develop a statement that shows how USL's operating, investing, and financing activities combined to produce that decrease. Remember now that the balance sheet shows the cumulative effects of all past operating, investing, and financing activities. If the net result of all such activities during the current year was to decrease cash by $174,500, the changes in the *other* items in the balance sheet must also reflect the effects of such activities during the year. We will refer to these other changes as we proceed to develop the cash flow statement. Let us begin by determining cash flow from operations.

Cash from Operations

We want to know net cash flow from operating activities. Using the indirect method, we must begin with net income, which was $229,500. (Note that in analyzing net income we are dealing with one of the two factors contributing to the net change in Retained Earnings.) Deriving net operating cash flow from net income is not difficult if you keep in mind the makeup of the income statement and the balance sheet. Look at Exhibit 17-2 and ask yourself the following questions. *Why* might revenues on the income statement differ from cash collected from customers? *Why* would cost of goods sold and the various expenses differ from

Exhibit 17-3

USL Corporation

Balance Sheets as of December 31

Assets	19X5	19X4	Increase (Decrease)
Current assets:			
Cash	$ 185,500	$ 360,000	($174,500)
Accounts receivable, net	272,000	130,000	142,000
Inventory	190,000	100,000	90,000
Prepaid expenses	8,000	20,000	(12,000)
Total current assets	655,500	610,000	
Noncurrent assets:			
Plant and equipment, at cost	928,000	600,000	328,000
Less accumulated depreciation	215,000	160,000	55,000
Total noncurrent assets	713,000	440,000	
Total assets	$1,368,500	$1,050,000	
Equities			
Current liabilities:			
Short-term bank loan	$ 34,000	$ 50,000	(16,000)
Accounts payable	135,000	105,000	30,000
Accrued expenses—taxes	38,000	2,000	36,000
—wages	12,000	3,000	9,000
Total current liabilities	219,000	160,000	
Bonds payable, due 19X9	100,000	100,000	—
Total liabilities	319,000	260,000	
Owners' equity:			
Common stock	660,000	600,000	60,000
Retained earnings	389,500	190,000	199,500
Total owners' equity	1,049,500	790,000	
Total equities	$1,368,500	$1,050,000	

the cash disbursed for purchases and expenses? The answers to these questions give the content of the adjustments section of the cash flow statement.

Revenues Versus Cash Inflows   Differences between sales and cash receipts occur for two reasons. First, early in the year cash was received from customers for sales made last year and included in last year's income statement. (This amount was the beginning balance of accounts receivable.) Second, for some sales made late in the year, cash will not be collected until next year. (Amounts still due at year's end constitute accounts receivable at the end of the year.) Thus, net income reflects sales made this year regardless of the period in which cash was collected, while cash receipts reflect cash collected this year regardless of the period in which the sales were made. *Hence, to move from the amount of net income to the cash flow for the year, we must (1) add the accounts receivable at*

ILLUSTRATION **731**

the beginning of the year, and (2) subtract the accounts receivable at the end of the year. In the case of USL Corporation, we add $130,000 and subtract $272,000, or we can simply subtract the $142,000 increase in Accounts Receivable. This is the first adjustment on the statement. (You may want to look briefly now at the completed statement shown in Exhibit 17-4 on page 735.)

Cost of Sales Versus Cash Outflows Consider next why there would be a difference between cost of goods sold ($450,000) on the income statement and the amount of cash actually paid for merchandise. Two factors create a difference.

First, the beginning and ending inventories affect cost of goods sold for the year regardless of the year in which the firm pays for inventory. The beginning inventory increased cost of goods sold and so decreased net income; the ending inventory decreased cost of goods sold and so increased net income. Thus, net income reflects the effects of inventories, while cash payments for merchandise have no relationship to whether the items were or are on hand. *Hence, to remove from net income the effect of inventories, which have no direct relationship to cash flows, we must (1) add the beginning inventory, and (2) subtract the ending inventory.* In USL's case, we add $100,000 and subtract $190,000, or we can simply subtract the $90,000 increase. This is the second adjustment in the statement on page 735.

The second reason for a difference between the cost of goods sold and the cash outflows for merchandise is that cost of goods sold shows the merchandise purchases made this year regardless of when the purchased merchandise was paid for. From your knowledge of financial accounting you know two things. First, early in the year cash was paid for purchases made in the prior year. (This amount was the beginning balance in accounts payable.) Second, some purchases made late in the year will not be paid for until the next year. (Unpaid amounts at the year's end constitute the ending balance in accounts payable). Thus, cost of goods sold, as shown in this year's income statement, may be higher or lower than cash payments for merchandise, depending on the relationship between the beginning and ending balances in Accounts Payable. *Hence, to move from net income to the cash flow for the year, we must (1) subtract the accounts payable at the beginning of the year and (2) add the accounts payable at the end of the year.* In the case of USL, we subtract $105,000 and add $135,000, or we can simply add the $30,000 increase. This is the third adjustment in the completed statement on page 735.

Operating Expenses and Cash Outflows Finally, let us consider why the expenses shown on the income statement do not equal the actual cash disbursements for such expenses. One reason for a difference is well known to you. The first expense listed, depreciation, requires *no* current disbursement of cash.[3] De-

---

[3] Expenses for depletion of natural resources and amortization of intangible assets are like depreciation in that they are allocations of previously incurred costs, with no requirement for current cash outlays. Accordingly, these expenses would give rise to adjustments such as the one for depreciation. Those familiar with the accounting for bonds payable will recognize that the amortization of bond premium and discount would also qualify as adjustments. (Amortization of bond discount would be an addition to income, like depreciation; amortization of bond premium would be a deduction.)

preciation expense reduced net income without having any effect on cash flows this period. *Hence, to remove from net income the effect of depreciation expense, we must add depreciation* (in USL's case, $56,000) *to reported net income*. This is the fourth adjustment on the statement on page 735.

There are two other reasons for the difference between the amounts shown in the income statement for various expenses and the cash payments for such expenses: accruals and prepayments. Let us consider accruals first.

In the early part of the year cash is paid to liquidate liabilities for expenses of the prior year (accrued expenses at the beginning of the year); in the latter part of the year expenses are incurred for which cash will not be disbursed until the next year (the beginning balance of accrued expenses). Thus, the current year's income is reduced by this year's expenses regardless of the year in which the expenses were paid for, while disbursements for the year cover cash payments for expenses regardless of the year in which the expense is incurred. *Hence, to move from net income to cash flow for the year, we must (1) subtract the accrued expenses at the beginning of the year and (2) add the expenses accrued but unpaid at the end of the year*. In the case of USL, we subtract $2,000 and $3,000, the beginning balances in the two accrued expense accounts (for taxes and wages); then, we add $38,000 and $12,000, the ending balances of the same two accruals. For simplicity, we will add $36,000 and $9,000, the increases in the two accounts. These are the fifth and sixth adjustments in the completed cash flow statement on page 735.[4]

Prepayments of expenses are similar to expense accruals in that the year in which cash is paid is not the year in which the expense affects net income. With prepayments, however, the cash flow occurs *before* the item appears in the income statement. Thus, the current year's income is reduced by some expenses paid for in the previous year (the beginning balance of prepaid expenses), but cash was paid this year for expenses that do *not* reduce income until next year (the ending balance of prepaid expenses). *Thus, to move from net income to the cash flow for the year, we must (1) add the beginning-of-the-year prepayments and (2) subtract the end-of-year prepayments*. USL will subtract $20,000 and add $8,000, or simply subtract the $12,000 decrease in Prepaid Expenses. This is the seventh and final adjustment in the cash flow statement and completes the explanation of the difference between USL's net income and its cash flow from operations.

Investing and Financing Activities

Look again at the comparative balance sheets in Exhibit 17-3. Every item on the balance sheet, except Bonds Payable, shows a change between the two years. We

---

[4] Companies differ in the number of accrued expenses that are reported separately in the balance sheet, but the adjustment calculation is the same for all accrued expenses. The cash flow statement can show a separate adjustment for each accrual, or a single adjustment that covers all accruals.

ILLUSTRATION **733**

know already that the changes in Accounts Receivable, Inventory, Prepaid Expenses, Accounts Payable, two expense accruals, and part of the changes in Accumulated Depreciation and in Retained Earnings relate to operating activities. What brought about the other changes? Unless our investigation of these changes reveals some way in which they affected net income, they must be related to financing and investing activities.

By applying a little common sense, we can reach tentative conclusions about the reasons for those changes; then, with a few inquiries, we can complete the cash flow statement. Below is a summary of the changes in balance-sheet items other than those we already know to be related only to operations.

Item	Change Increase (Decrease)	Change Already Explained, Increase (Decrease)
Retained earnings	$199,500	$229,500
Common stock	60,000	
Short-term bank loan payable	(16,000)	
Accumulated depreciation	55,000	56,000
Plant and equipment	328,000	

The combined statement of income and retained earnings (Exhibit 17-2) shows that the net change in Retained Earnings is due to the net income *and* the payment of dividends. Thus, we know that there was a $30,000 cash outflow for dividends, a financing activity to be reported in the statement on page 735.[5]

The $60,000 increase in Common Stock must have come from issuing additional stock. Whether the stock was issued for cash can be determined by inquiry. If issued for cash, the issuance would be an inflow among the financing activities in the cash flow statement. If the stock was issued in return for, say, plant and equipment, we would have a noncash financing and investing activity to be disclosed in the separate schedule with the cash flow statement. Let us assume that $22,000 of the stock was issued for cash and the remaining $38,000 was issued to acquire new equipment. We list the $22,000 inflow among the financing flows in the statement. Because the $38,000 transaction involved no cash, it does not appear in any of the three basic sections of our statement; rather, it is included in the separate schedule devoted to noncash investing and financing activities.

Short-term bank loans decreased by $16,000. Let us assume that the decrease resulted from a new loan of $80,000 and repayments of old loans of $96,000.

---

[5] Note that, in the example, the change in Retained Earnings related to dividends equals the amount of dividends paid in cash. On occasion, a liability will exist at the beginning or the end of the period, or both, for dividends declared but not paid. In such cases, the formal cash flow statement would still report only the cash dividends paid during the period. To determine the cash paid for dividends, you must start with the change in Retained Earnings caused by dividend declarations and then adjust for the change in the reported liability for dividends.

The formal cash flow statement shows both the new borrowing and the repayment as financing activities.

The increase in Accumulated Depreciation requires a little more analysis. We already know that depreciation for the year was $56,000, which increased Accumulated Depreciation by the same amount. Since the net increase is only $55,000, something must have happened during the year to decrease Accumulated Depreciation by $1,000. From your knowledge of financial accounting you know that Accumulated Depreciation decreases when a depreciable asset is sold.[6] You could then conclude that some asset was sold and determine its cost and selling price. Suppose we learn that equipment that had cost $10,000 and had accumulated depreciation of $1,000 was sold for $9,000, its book value. The $9,000 is reported as a cash inflow from investing activities.

We just determined that Plant and Equipment decreased by $10,000 when some equipment was sold. Yet over the year, Plant and Equipment increased by $328,000, so there must have been additions to plant and equipment of $338,000. We already know that $38,000 of that increase related to equipment acquired through the issuance of common stock, and we have included this information on the schedule of noncash activities. The remainder of the difference, $300,000, must have been for other additions. If only cash was involved (as we shall assume), this outflow would show as an investing activity.

To summarize briefly, we started with comparative balance sheets for USL and noted that cash had decreased by $174,500. To *explain* that change, we analyzed the changes in all the other balance sheet accounts. The results of that analysis appear in the formal cash flow statement shown in Exhibit 17-4, which is further discussed in the next section.

Cash Flow Statement

The illustrative cash flow statement in Exhibit 17-4 provides a basis for further discussion. Consider first the adjustments to net income. If you reflect for a moment about the adjustments, you will recognize that the fourth, for depreciation, is quite different from the others.

The depreciation adjustment, required because depreciation expense appears on the income statement, has *no* relation to the operating cash inflows or outflows for the current period. The other six adjustments are needed because of short-term timing differences between cash flows and appearance on the income statement. Once you understand the reasoning for the treatment of these other adjustments, you may find the following rules helpful.

1. Add to net income a decrease in an asset (or an increase in a liability) resulting from operating activities.

---

[6] The cost of an asset is removed from the asset account, and the accumulated depreciation on that asset is removed from the Accumulated Depreciation account.

ILLUSTRATION   735

2. Subtract from net income an increase in an asset (or a decrease in a liability) resulting from operating activities.

Exhibit 17-4
USL Corporation, Statement of Cash Flows for 19X8

Net cash flow from operating activities:		
Net income	$229,500	
Adjustments for noncash expenses and revenues included in income:		
Increase in accounts receivable	(142,000)	
Increase in inventory	(90,000)	
Increase in accounts payable	30,000	
Depreciation for the year	56,000	
Increase in accrued taxes	36,000	
Increase in accrued wages	9,000	
Decrease in prepaid expense	12,000	
Net cash provided by operating activities		$140,500
Cash flows from investing activities:		
Purchase of plant and equipment	300,000	
Sales of equipment	(9,000)	
Net cash used by investing activities		(291,000)
Cash flows from financing activities:		
New short-term borrowing	80,000	
Repayment of short-term debt	(96,000)	
Proceeds from issuance of common stock	22,000	
Dividends on common stock	(30,000)	
Net cash used by financing activities		(24,000)
Net change (decrease) in cash		(174,500)
Cash balance, beginning of year		360,000
Cash balance, end of year		$185,500
Schedule of Noncash Investing and Financing Activities:		
Issuance of common stock to acquire new equipment	$38,000	

Note that the net change in cash, a decrease of $174,500, agrees with the decrease shown in the comparative balance sheets (see Exhibit 17-3). The two statements are thus linked, with the cash flow statement describing the cash inflows and outflows that contributed to the decline in cash, a balance sheet item. A link with the income statement is provided by using the indirect method to present cash flow from operations.

As we have shown, the information for a cash flow statement can be developed by analyzing the other financial statements and asking a few questions. Because the managers of the firm have access to information about its actual cash flows, the task is relatively easy. Without access to information about actual flows, the task is more difficult but not impossible. But for anyone—manager, stockholder, or creditor—presented with a cash flow statement, what is important is to understand its contents and implications; and that understanding begins with an understanding of how the statement is developed.

OPERATING FLOWS — SPECIAL CONSIDERATIONS

In developing USL's cash flow statement, we used the indirect method of presenting operating cash flows. We also used fairly common transactions. In this section we discuss and illustrate two important variations of these basic circumstances.

The Direct Method, Inflows and Outflows

Although the indirect method of reporting the cash flow from operating activities is acceptable, the FASB and a majority of financial statement users prefer the direct method. Supporters of the direct method stress their interest in its separate disclosure of inflows and outflows. Of course, the *net* operating cash flow is the same regardless of the method used to present information about it. Hence, the same items that reconcile the net income with net operating cash flow under the indirect method also explain the differences between cash inflows and outflows for specific items included in the income statement.

Consider the three major income-statement categories that affected net income for USL Corporation: sales, cost of goods sold, and expenses. What is the difference between sales reported in the year's income statement and cash received during the year from customers? You answered that question already (page 730): the beginning and ending balances in Accounts Receivable. What is the difference between reported cost of goods sold and cash payments to acquire merchandise? The beginning and ending balances in Inventory and Accounts Payable (page 731). Finally, why are the expenses shown on the income statement different from the year's cash payments for operating expenses? Accruals, prepayments, and the noncash expense of depreciation (page 732).

Thus, the same type of analysis that produced the information needed to reconcile reported net income with net operating cash flow provides the information needed to present net operating cash flow under the direct method. The only difference is that, to develop the information about inflows and outflows separately, adjustments must be made to individual items in the income statement, rather than to the net result of those items (net income). Let us determine the separate operating cash flows for USL using the information developed earlier. In each case we begin with the amount reported on the income statement (see Exhibit 17-2) and compute the cash flow for that item.

Cash Receipts from Customers   Reported sales were $1,000,000, but Accounts Receivable increased by $142,000. We can compute the cash received from customers as follows.

Sales		$1,000,000
Add Accounts Receivable, beginning of year		
(additional current cash collections)	$130,000	
Deduct Accounts Receivable, end of year		
(uncollected sales)	(272,000)	
Increase in Accounts Receivable		(142,000)
Cash receipts from customers		$ 858,000

Cash Payments to Merchandise Suppliers   Cost of goods sold reported for the year was $450,000, but we know that this amount differed from cash payments to suppliers because of changes in Inventory and in Accounts Payable. To convert Cost of Goods Sold to cash payments to suppliers, we adjust for changes in these two balance-sheet items, as follows.

Cost of goods sold		$450,000
Eliminate effect of change in Inventory:		
Add Inventory, end of year	$190,000	
Deduct Inventory, beginning of year	(100,000)	
Increase in Inventory		90,000
Eliminate effect of change in Accounts Payable:		
Add Accounts Payable, beginning of year	55,000	
Deduct Accounts Payable, end of year	(85,000)	
Increase in Accounts Payable		(30,000)
Cash payments to merchandise suppliers		$510,000

If you have trouble seeing why an increase in Inventory should be added to cost of goods sold to arrive at cash payments while an increase in Accounts Payable is subtracted, consider again how these items affect cost of goods sold and review the explanation on page 731.

Cash Payments for Expenses   From the earlier analysis we know that depreciation and the changes in Prepaid Expenses and two accrued expense accounts explain the difference between reported expenses and the cash flows for expenses. In response to the strongly expressed preferences of financial statement users, the FASB requires separate reporting of the cash paid for two expense items, interest and income taxes. (This requirement applies whether the direct or the indirect method is used to present operating cash flows.) Hence, although the same calculations apply to all the expenses, we have to separate these two items from other expenses. Accordingly, we can calculate the cash payments for expenses as on page 738.

	Total	Interest	Income Taxes	Other
Expenses for the year	$320,500	$12,000	$123,700	$184,800
Eliminate effect of depreciation	(56,000)			(56,000)
Eliminate effect of change in Prepaid Expenses:				
Add beginning Prepaid Expenses	$ 8,000			8,000
Deduct ending Prepaid Expenses	20,000			(20,000)
Increase in Prepaid Expenses	(12,000)			
Eliminate effect of change in accrued expenses:				
Add beginning accrued expenses:	5,000		2,000	3,000
Deduct ending accrued expenses	50,000		(38,000)	(12,000)
Increase in accrued expenses	(45,000)			
Cash payments for expenses	$207,500	$12,000	$ 87,700	$107,800

Formal Presentation   Exhibit 17-5 shows the cash flow statement for USL Corporation as it would appear under the direct method of presenting cash flow from operations. As you can see, the net cash flow from operations is the same as that shown in Exhibit 17-4 when the indirect method was used. Note that, with the use of the direct method, the details of the *computations* (i.e., the descriptions of the adjustments) are not part of the presentation. Remember, however, that a reconciliation of net income and net cash flow from operations must also be provided.

Firms differ in the number and types of items reported separately. For example, some choose to highlight amounts paid for wages and fringe benefits, rent, or some other expense of major significance. USL's statement shows one item more than the required minimum detail for cash outflows, because it is acceptable to combine payments for merchandise with payments for other expenses.

In the next section we discuss a not uncommon circumstance that affects both the computation and the reporting of operating cash flows regardless of which reporting approach is followed.

Nonoperating Gains and Losses

One transaction that we included in the example is unlikely. We assumed that the sale of plant and equipment was at book value. Given that assumption, there was no gain or loss on the sale to appear in the income statement, and we had only to report the proceeds as an inflow from investing activities. It is highly unlikely,

Exhibit 17-5

USL Corporation, Statement of Cash Flows for 19X8

Net cash flow from operating activities:		
Cash receipts from customers	$858,000	
Cash payments to merchandise suppliers	(510,000)	
Interest paid	(12,000)	
Income taxes paid	(87,700)	
Cash paid for other expenses	(107,800)	
Net cash provided by operating activities		$140,500
Cash flows from investing activities:		
Purchase of plant and equipment	300,000	
Sales of equipment	(9,000)	
Net cash used by investing activities		(291,000)
Cash flows from financing activities:		
New short-term borrowing	80,000	
Repayment of short-term debt	(96,000)	
Proceeds from issuance of common stock	22,000	
Dividends on common stock	(30,000)	
Net cash used by financing activities		(24,000)
Net change (decrease) in cash		(174,500)
Cash balance, beginning of year		360,000
Cash balance, end of year		$185,500
Schedule of Noncash Investing and Financing Activities:		
Issuance of common stock to acquire new equipment	$38,000	

however, that a noncurrent asset will be sold at exactly its book value. Thus, when a sale occurs, the resulting gain or loss will be included in net income.

Reporting a gain or loss on the sale of an investment in no way changes the fact that the sale is an investing activity. The proceeds from the sale are still an inflow to be reported under investing activities. The primary complication presented by such sales is that the resulting gains or losses must be properly handled when calculating cash flow from operating activities, and the concern exists whether the firm uses the direct or the indirect method.

For example, suppose a long-term investment that had cost $30,000 was sold for $45,000. Cash of $45,000 was provided by the sale, and that amount should be shown on the cash flow statement as an inflow from investing activities. But the income statement for the year will have included the $15,000 gain on the sale. Hence, net income increased by $15,000 as a result of a nonoperating activity. Under either the direct or the indirect method of presenting operating cash flows, the $15,000 income effect of the sale will have to be eliminated. (If the book value of the investment had been $60,000, so that a $15,000 loss, rather than a $15,000 gain, occurred on the sale, the cash inflow would still be $45,000, and the $15,000 loss on the sale would also have to be eliminated to arrive at the cash flow from operating activities.)

Thus, gains and losses from investing activities are adjustments in deriving operating cash flows from amounts reported in an income statement. In a cash flow statement that uses the indirect method of reporting flows from operating activities, losses appear as additions to net income and gains as subtractions. Exhibit 17-6 contains a cash flow statement for a company (not USL Corporation) that follows the indirect method and sustained both a loss and a gain as a result of sales of investments. You should recognize that, if the firm had used the direct method, the gain and loss would not appear separately but would have been considered (and eliminated) when the firm converted the detailed items in its income statement into cash flows.

Exhibit 17-6
Lenseth Company, Statement of Cash Flows for 19X8

Net cash flow from operating activities:		
Net income	$203,000	
Adjustments for noncash expenses, revenues, losses, and gains included in income:		
Increase in accounts receivable	(98,000)	
Decrease in inventory	29,500	
Increase in accounts payable	54,000	
Depreciation for the year	103,000	
Decrease in accrued expenses	(24,200)	
Gain on sale of investment in stock of Sky Co.	(262,000)	
Loss on sale of equipment	13,600	
Net cash provided by operating activities		$ 18,900
Cash flows from investing activities:		
Purchase of plant and equipment	(152,500)	
Sale of equipment	12,700	
Sale of stock investment in Sky Co.	392,000	
Net cash provided by investing activities		252,200
Cash flows from financing activities:		
Proceeds from new long-term debt	286,300	
Dividends on common stock	(52,000)	
Acquisition of treasury stock	(123,700)	
Net cash provided by financing activities		110,600
Net increase in cash		381,700
Cash balance, beginning of year		562,100
Cash balance, end of year		$943,800
Schedule of Noncash Investing and Financing Activities:		
Conversion of long-term debt to common stock		$254,000

CONCLUDING COMMENTS

Over the years, a common misconception has arisen that depreciation and similar expenses represent inflows of cash. This misconception is understandable if we recognize that (1) the indirect method of computing operating cash flows has predominated in practice and (2) under that method depreciation is added to net income to arrive at cash flow from operations. As you know, depreciation neither increases nor decreases cash. It requires no current outlay of cash; rather, an outflow of cash occurs at the time the asset is acquired, and that outflow is reported as an investing activity.

In one sense, however, depreciation *influences* cash flows. Because depreciation is deductible for tax purposes, a firm's income tax payment—which *is* an operating cash flow—is lower than it would have been had there been no depreciation to deduct. Hence, the net cash inflow from operations is higher than would be the case had there been no depreciation. But if the firm had no revenues and still had depreciation, there would be no cash from operations. Thus, depreciation can help the firm *retain* cash, by decreasing taxes, but only when some revenue produces an inflow of cash to be retained.

We should also point out that the cash flow statement provides information beyond a classified listing of the firm's cash flows. As we note in the next chapter, an understanding and evaluation of a firm's activities requires review of more than one year's financial statements. At this point we comment only briefly on insights that might be provided by review of the cash flow statements.

Consider the companies whose cash flow statements are provided in the chapter. Exhibits 17-4 and 17-5 show that USL Corporation spent more cash on investments than was made available from normal operations and traditional financing sources. Exhibit 17-6, for Lenseth Company, shows that the major source of cash to fund its new investments in plant and equipment was the sale of another investment. Are these good or bad signs? As you might expect, the answer is that it depends. A substantial net new investment in plant and equipment suggests expansion and the potential for growth in earnings. True, normal operating activities and financing sources didn't provide enough cash for USL's new investment. But USL's cash balance at the beginning of 19X8 was relatively large (about 34% of total assets), which might indicate that significant new financing was obtained in the preceding year. (Remember that a firm must plan in advance to meet cash needs for long-term capital investments.) And because one *expects* managers to make profitable investments, one cannot automatically question Lenseth's financing of new investments through a sale of a previously profitable one. Thus, review of the prior year's financial statements, particularly the cash flow statement, is necessary before drawing conclusions. To return to the ideas presented at the beginning of this chapter, perhaps the primary value of a cash flow statement is that it shows managers' current responses to planned short-term and long-term needs for cash.

SUMMARY

Information about flows of cash is important to both managers and external parties. Generally accepted accounting principles require a cash flow statement as part of a typical financial statement package. Some short-term investments qualify as cash equivalents.

A firm's activities can generally be classified as operating, investing, or financing activities. A formal cash flow statement reports a firm's cash flows under these three headings. Significant activities having no effect on current cash flows are also reported, either in narrative form or in a separate schedule of the cash flow statement.

Two approaches are acceptable for presenting information about cash flows relating to operating activities. One approach, the indirect method, reconciles net income with the net cash flow from operations. The indirect method does not report operating inflows and outflows separately. The preferred approach, the direct method, reports inflows and outflows separately but does not offer a direct link between the cash flow statement and reported net income. Cash flow statements prepared using either the direct or the indirect method will report the same *net* cash flow from operations, the same cash flows relating to investing and financing activities, and the same net change in cash, and will disclose the cash paid for interest and for income taxes. Statements using the direct method must also provide a reconciliation of net income to net cash flow from operations.

KEY TERMS

cash equivalents

cash flow statement

cash flow from operations

direct method

financing activities

indirect method

investing activities

operating activities

REVIEW PROBLEM

Comparative balance sheets and a combined statement of income and retained earnings for Harold Company are given in Exhibits 17-7 and 17-8.

The following additional information is also available to you.

1. Common stock was issued for $200 cash.
2. Investments costing $40 were sold at a gain of $30.
3. Equipment costing $30 and with accumulated depreciation of $20 was sold for $10.

Required
1. Determine cash flow from operations using the indirect method.
2. Prepare a cash flow statement for 19X7.
3. Show the cash flow from operations using the direct method. Show separately the cash inflow from sales and the cash outflows for merchandise purchases, operating expenses, interest, and income taxes.

Answer to Review Problem

1. To compute cash flow from operations we must determine the adjustments to net income. Review of the company's income statement reveals the need for three adjustments:
   (a) Depreciation, a noncash expense, has reduced income.
   (b) The sale of a long-term investment, a *nonoperating* transaction, has increased income.
   (c) The change in Inventory, which is not directly related to cash flows, has increased net income.
   The change in Inventory (an increase) produced higher net income because the ending inventory (which reduced cost of goods sold and hence increased income) was greater

Exhibit 17-7
Harold Company, Balance Sheets at December 31

Assets	19X7	19X6	Change Increase (Decrease)
Current assets:			
Cash	$ 205	$ 190	$ 15
Accounts receivable, net	420	430	(10)
Inventory	350	310	40
Total current assets	975	930	
Investments	120	160	(40)
Plant and equipment	2,500	2,250	250
Accumulated depreciation	(800)	(720)	80
Total assets	$2,795	$2,620	
Equities			
Current liabilities:			
Accounts payable	$ 210	$ 220	(10)
Accrued expenses—taxes	28	22	6
—interest	6	16	(10)
—other	31	32	(1)
Total current liabilities	275	290	
Long-term debt	100	250	(150)
Total liabilities	375	540	
Owners' equity:			
Common stock, no par value	1,800	1,600	200
Retained earnings	620	480	140
Total owners' equity	2,420	2,080	
Total equities	$2,795	$2,620	

than the beginning inventory (which increased cost of goods sold and hence decreased income).

We can then turn to the comparative balance sheets for any other facts that might cause the reported components of net income (revenues, cost of goods sold, and operating expenses and other income and expense) to differ from cash flows relating to operations. Review of the comparative balance sheets reveals the need for three additional adjustments:

(d) The change in Accounts Receivable means there is a difference between cash inflows from operations and reported revenues.

(e) The change in Accounts Payable means there is a difference between cash outflows for operations and the reported cost of goods sold because there is a difference between cash outflows for purchases and reported purchases.

(f) The change in various accrued expenses means that there is a difference between operating cash outflows for expenses and reported operating expenses, interest, and taxes.

Exhibit 17-8

Harold Company

Combined Statement of Income and Retained Earnings for 19X7

Sales		$2,350
Cost of goods sold:		
Beginning inventory	$ 310	
Purchases	890	
Cost of goods available for sale	1,200	
Less ending inventory	350	
Cost of goods sold		850
Gross profit on sales		1,500
Operating expenses:		
Depreciation	100	
Other operating expenses	359	
Total operating expenses		459
Operating income		1,041
Other income and expense:		
Gain on sale of investment	30	
Interest expense	21	
Net other income		9
Income before taxes		1,050
Income tax expense		320
Net income		730
Retained earnings at December 31, 19X6		480
		1,210
Dividends declared and paid		590
Retained earnings at December 31, 19X7		$ 620

Changes in the other balance-sheet items, though they may have affected cash, would not have given rise to operating cash flows. If such changes affected net income, their effect should be eliminated from net income as we compute the cash flow from operating activities. Let us look at the other balance-sheet changes.

A change in noncurrent investments is normally from an investing activity, a sale or purchase. A cash flow from such a change does not result from operations. We have already recognized that net income must be adjusted to remove the effect of the sale of investments on net income (adjustment (b) above). A change in plant and equipment is also an investing activity, a sale or purchase. The income statement shows no evidence that either type of investing activity affected net income. The only operations-related change in Accumulated Depreciation is the depreciation for the year, which has no effect on cash flow from operations. We have already identified an adjustment (a) to remove the effect of the depreciation expense from the net income.

The changes in long-term debt and common stock, whatever their causes, give rise to financing flows. Again, there is no evidence (such as a gain from retirement of debt) in the income statement that financing activities affected net income. The change in Retained Earnings is explained by net income, which we have already considered, and the payment of dividends, which is a financing activity.

Thus, we can compute the cash flow from operations by starting with net income and making the six adjustments (a) through (f).

Reconciliation of Net Income and Cash from Operations	
Net income	$730
Adjustments for noncash expenses, revenues, and gains:	
(a) Depreciation for the year	100
(b) Gain on sale of long-term investment	(30)
(c) Increase in inventory	(40)
(d) Decrease in various accounts receivable	10
(e) Decrease in accounts payable	(10)
(f) Decrease in various accrued expenses	(5)
Cash flow from operations	$755

2. In item 1, the information needed for one section of the statement, cash flow from operations, was developed. Our objective now is to find any nonoperating inflows or outflows of cash. For this information we refer again to the balance-sheet changes that did not affect cash flow from operations. The changes, already discussed briefly, are summarized below.

Item	Change Increase (Decrease)	Change Already Explained Increase (Decrease)
Investments	($40)	Sold item for $30 gain
Plant and equipment	250	($30)
Accumulated depreciation	80	80
Long-term debt	(150)	
Common stock	200	
Retained earnings	140	730

Let us examine each of these changes carefully.

The $40 decrease in Investments was the result of a sale that produced a gain of $30. Since the investments that were sold cost $40 (the amount of the balance-sheet decrease in Investments), the *proceeds* from the sale must have been $70. Hence, we have an investing cash inflow of $70 to be reported on the statement.

The normal reason for an increase in Plant and Equipment is a purchase of new equipment. But, we already know that during the year the company sold equipment that originally cost $30, thus reducing Plant and Equipment by $30. Thus, the purchases of new plant and equipment must have been enough to offset this decrease and produce a net increase in Plant and Equipment of $250, or $280 ($250 + $30). So we have two transactions: sale of equipment and purchase of equipment, both of which involve investing cash flows. The old equipment was sold for $10, and this amount should be reported as an investing cash inflow. The new equipment must have cost $280 and should be reported as an investing use of cash.

As we know, depreciation neither produces nor uses cash. Hence, the change in Accumulated Depreciation is not a cash inflow or outflow. We have already explained the $80 increase for the year. Accumulated Depreciation increased by $100 because of the current year's depreciation expense, as shown on the income statement. Accumulated Depreciation decreased by $20 because an asset on which depreciation of

$20 had accumulated was sold. The net change is an increase of $80 (an increase of $100 offset by a decrease of $20). In our analysis of Plant and Equipment, we determined that an investing cash inflow of $10 should be reported in connection with the sale of equipment.

The normal reason for a decline in long-term debt is that some of the debt was repaid. Such a repayment is a financing outflow. Since we have no evidence to indicate some other reason for the decrease, we shall report the decline as a financing outflow in the amount of $150.

Common Stock increased by $200; the usual explanation for such an increase is that additional shares of stock were issued. This conclusion is confirmed by the information obtained at the beginning of the problem, and so we include among the financing inflows of cash the issuance of additional stock for $200.

The lower portion of Exhibit 17-8 reports that the net change in Retained Earnings resulted from an increase because of net income and a decrease because of dividends. Net income is an operating source of cash, and we have already dealt with cash from operations. The payment of dividends should be reported on our statement as a $590 financing outflow of cash.

Having analyzed and explained all the changes in balance sheet accounts during the year, we now incorporate our conclusions into the cash flow statement, as shown in Exhibit 17-9.

Exhibit 17-9
Harold Company, Cash Flow Statement for 19X7

Net cash flow from operating activities:		
Net income	$730	
Adjustments for noncash expenses, revenues, and gains:		
Decrease in accounts receivable	10	
Increase in inventory	(40)	
Decrease in accounts payable	(10)	
Depreciation for the year	100	
Decrease in various accrued expenses	(5)	
Gain on sale of long-term investment	(30)	
Net cash provided by operating activities		$755
Cash flows from investing activities:		
Acquisition of plant and equipment	(280)	
Sale of equipment	10	
Sale of investments	70	
Net cash used by investing activities		(200)
Cash flows from financing activities:		
Retirement of long-term debt	(150)	
Proceeds from issuance of common stock	200	
Dividends on common stock	(590)	
Net cash used by financing activities		(540)
Net increase in cash		15
Cash balance, beginning of year		190
Cash balance, end of year		$205

3. Calculating cash flow from operations under the direct method requires you to look at the individual sections of the income statement and apply the adjustments determined

in item 1 to specific sections. Below are the calculations of specific operating cash inflows or outflows.

Computation of Cash Receipts from Customers

Sales		$2,350
Add Accounts Receivable, beginning of year (additional current cash collections)	$430	
Deduct Accounts Receivable, end of year (uncollected sales)	(420)	
Decrease in Accounts Receivable		(10)
Cash receipts from customers		$2,360

Cash Payments to Merchandise Suppliers

Cost of goods sold		$ 850
Eliminate effect of change in Inventory:		
Add Inventory, end of year	$350	
Deduct Inventory, beginning of year	(310)	
Increase in Inventory		40
Eliminate effect of change in Accounts Payable:		
Add Accounts Payable, beginning of year	220	
Deduct Accounts Payable, end of year	(210)	
Decrease in Accounts Payable		10
Cash payments to merchandise suppliers		$ 900

Cash Payments for Operating Expenses

	Operating	Interest	Taxes
Expenses for the year	$459	$21	$320
Eliminate effect of depreciation (noncash expense)	(100)		
Eliminate effect of change in accrued expenses:			
Add accrued expenses, beginning of year	32	16	22
Deduct accrued expenses, end of year	(31)	(6)	(28)
Cash payments for expenses	$360	$31	$314

We already know that the only other item to affect net income, the gain on sale of investments, resulted from an investing, rather than operating, activity. Hence, neither the gain nor the proceeds from the sale would be reported as part of the cash flow from operations. If Harold Company used the direct method of reporting its cash flow from operations, that segment of its cash flow statement would appear as below.

Net cash flow from operating activities:	
Cash receipts from customers	$2,360
Cash payments to merchandise suppliers	(900)
Cash paid for interest	(31)
Cash paid for income taxes	(314)
Cash payments for operating expenses	(360)
Net cash provided by operating activities	$ 755

Note that the $755,000 cash provided by operating activities agrees with the amount shown in Exhibit 17-9, where the indirect method of reporting was used.

ASSIGNMENT MATERIAL

Questions for Discussion

17-1   **Depreciation and cash**   It is often said that cash generated by operations consists of net income and depreciation. Explain why this statement is or is not true.

17-2   **Net income and cash flow**   Walter Bryant started Bryant Machine Shop five years ago. The shop has been profitable and Mr. Bryant has been withdrawing cash in an amount equal to net income each year. He has taken out an amount equal to nearly half of his original investment of $80,000, most of which was used originally to purchase machinery. Mr. Bryant's customers pay cash on completion of work. He keeps very little inventory and pays his bills promptly, and he is puzzled because the cash balance keeps growing despite his withdrawals. Can you explain the increase in cash?

17-3   **Net income and cash**   Suppose that a large retail chain and a railroad earned the same net income. Which firm would you expect to show the higher cash provided by operations? Explain your answer.

17-4   **Explanation of a cash flow statement**   You have provided the president of Ralston Company with a full set of financial statements, including a statement of cash flows. He understands everything except some of the adjustments in the operations section of the statement. He has three specific questions:
1.   "Why do you subtract the increase in accounts receivable? We don't pay out cash for our accounts receivable, we collect it."
2.   "You show the decrease in inventory as an addition. We sure didn't get any cash because our inventory decreased. In fact, the decrease means that we have less to sell next year and will have to spend more cash to replenish our supply. So why add it back to net income?"
3.   "Our accrued expenses increased, and you showed this as an addition? Look, we had especially heavy payroll costs at the end of the year, and we paid them the third day of the new year. So it seems to me that we had to use more cash because of the increase, not less."

Required: Explain each of the items to the president.

17-5   **"How am I doing?"**   Clyde Mackey, president of Mackey Enterprises has just received a copy of the company's 19X8 financial statements from the company's controller. "I give up," Mr. Mackey says. "For years you've been telling me that if I want to know how the business is doing I should look at the income statement, not our cash balance. Now you give me an income statement, but you also give me a statement that tells me what happened in the company's cash account. So which statement do I look at to find out how I'm doing?"

Required: Respond to Mr. Mackey's question.

Exercises

17-6 Cash receipts from customers Fill in the blanks in the following schedule.

Sales (shown in 19X8 income statement)	$800,000	$1,000,000	$_____	$910,000
Net Accounts Receivable:				
At beginning of 19X8	42,000	37,000	18,000	31,000
At end of 19X8	25,000	45,000	25,000	$_____
Cash collected from customers in 19X8	$_____	$_____	853,000	925,000

17-7 Cash payments to merchandise suppliers For each of the three cases given below, compute the cash paid in 19X7 to merchandise suppliers.

	Case A	Case B	Case C
Cost of goods sold (as reported in the 19X7 income statement)	$831,000	$595,000	$3,316,000
Merchandise inventory:			
Beginning of 19X7	215,000	142,000	846,000
End of 19X7	193,000	91,000	872,000
Accounts payable:			
Beginning of 19X7	21,000	22,000	78,000
End of 19X7	32,000	18,000	64,000
Cash paid to merchandise suppliers during 19X7	$_____	$_____	$_____

17-8 Relationships Fill in the blanks in the following schedule.

	Case A	Case B	Case C
Cost of goods sold (as reported in the 19X3 income statement)	$659,000	$431,000	$_____
Merchandise inventory:			
Beginning of 19X3	91,000	57,000	262,000
End of 19X3	84,000	71,000	245,000
Accounts payable:			
Beginning of 19X3	32,000	68,000	93,000
End of 19X3	41,000	$_____	85,000
Cash paid to merchandise suppliers during 19X3	$_____	423,000	2,824,000

17-9 Components of cash flow from operating activities Which of the following items would appear in the operations section of the cash flow statement for Washburn Company? Washburn uses the indirect method of presenting the cash flow from operations.
1. Depreciation expense for the year.
2. Increase in Dividends Payable.
3. Decrease in Income Taxes Payable.

4. Loss from sale of long-term investments.
5. Decrease in Prepaid Insurance.
6. Increase in Inventory.
7. Proceeds from sale of long-term investments.
8. Increase in Accounts Receivable.
9. Amortization of patents covering Washburn's major product.
10. Payment for machinery to be used to produce Washburn's major product.

17-10 Classifying activities State how each of the following transactions is classified, as an operating, investing, or financing activity.
1. Sale of merchandise (an inventory item) for cash.
2. Sale of merchandise (an inventory item) on account.
3. Sale of a fully depreciated machine for cash.
4. Declaration of a cash dividend on common stock.
5. Payment of a previously declared cash dividend on common stock.
6. Purchase of merchandise (for resale) on credit.
7. Payment of cash for purchase made in item 6.
8. Payment of the premium on a three-year policy for theft insurance on the firm's inventory.
9. Acquisition of land by issuing a long-term note payable.
10. Payment of wages.
11. Purchase of 10,000 shares of the firm's common stock from some of its stockholders. The price paid is less than that at which the shares were originally issued.
12. Sale of 5,000 shares of treasury stock at a price in excess of that paid to acquire the stock.
13. Accrual of interest due on a 20-year mortgage note payable.
14. Conversion of some 20-year convertible bonds to common stock.
15. Payment of previously accrued wages and salaries for employees.

17-11 Reconciliation of net income and cash from operations Select from the following list those items that are relevant to a reconciliation of net income and cash from operations and prepare such a reconciliation.

Loss on sale of long-term investment	$ 43,000
Increase in accounts receivable	52,500
Increase in land	48,000
Increase in accrued expenses payable	6,800
Decrease in inventory	26,500
Decrease in accounts payable	112,000
Decrease in prepaid insurance	1,500
Increase in common stock	85,000
Net income	174,000
Depreciation expense	61,000
Decrease in cash	14,000
Cash received from sale of long-term investment	228,800
Cash provided by operations	148,300

17-12 Cash payments for operating expenses For each of the three cases given below, compute the cash paid in 19X7 for operating expenses.

	Case A	Case B	Case C
Operating expenses (according to the 19X7 income statement)	$476,900	$31,425	$4,150,000
Prepaid expenses:			
Beginning of 19X7	12,000	1,863	97,100
End of 19X7	9,300	1,541	105,400
Accrued expenses:			
Beginning of 19X7	21,200	3,260	57,800
End of 19X7	25,100	2,045	53,400
Cash paid in 19X7 for operating expenses	$_____	$_____	$_____

17-13 Relationships Fill in the blanks in the following schedule.

	Case A	Case B	Case C
Operating expenses (according to the 19X7 income statement)	$927,400	$123,865	$_____
Prepaid expenses:			
Beginning of 19X7	25,400	12,500	103,000
End of 19X7	19,300	$_____	81,000
Accrued expenses:			
Beginning of 19X7	48,800	21,426	193,000
End of 19X7	51,100	24,382	242,000
Cash paid in 19X7 for operating expenses	$_____	$118,416	4,250,000

17-14 Cash from operations – indirect method In 19X9, Drew Company reported net income of $28,000. You also have the following information about 19X9.
1. Depreciation expense for the year was $109,000.
2. Increase in Accounts Receivable from 19X8 to 19X9 was $17,000.
3. Decrease in Inventory from 19X8 to 19X9 was $9,000.
4. Decrease in Accounts Payable from 19X8 to 19X9 was $14,000.
5. Increase in Accrued Expenses from 19X8 to 19X9 was $6,000.

Required: Compute cash flow from operations.

17-15 Effects of transactions Determine the effect, if any, of each transaction listed below on (a) net income and (b) cash. Show the amount of the change and its direction (+ or −).
1. Common stock was issued in exchange for equipment. The agreed price was $300,000.
2. A dividend payable in cash of $120,000 was declared, but not paid.
3. The dividend in item 2 was paid.
4. An account receivable of $10,000 was written off against the Allowance for Doubtful Accounts.
5. A customer who owed the firm $12,000 on account receivable gave the firm equipment with a fair market value of $12,000 in settlement of the receivable.
6. Interest payable was accrued in the amount of $14,000.

7. The interest payable in item 6 was paid.
8. The firm bought 100 shares of its own stock for the treasury. The cost was $4,600, paid in cash.
9. Inventory with a cost of $18,000 was written off as obsolete.
10. Plant assets that had cost $45,000 and were one third depreciated were sold for $12,000 cash.

17-16 Classifying activities   Indicate whether each of the following transactions would be classified as an operating, investing, or financing activity.
1. Cash collected on previously recorded credit sale of merchandise.
2. Sale of factory machinery for an amount of cash that exceeds the machine's book value.
3. Sale of factory machinery for an amount of cash that is less than the machine's book value.
4. Payment of cash for previously recorded credit purchase.
5. Payment of the premium on a three-year policy for theft insurance on the firm's inventory.
6. Acquisition of land by issuing common stock having a market value in excess of par.
7. Payment of wages.
8. Purchase of 10,000 shares of the firm's common stock from some of its stockholders. The price paid is in excess of the price at which the shares were originally issued.
9. Sale of 5,000 shares of treasury stock at a price in excess of that paid to acquire the stock.
10. Payment of previously accrued interest on a 5-year note payable.
11. Declaration and issuance of a 5% stock dividend on common stock.
12. Receipt of insurance proceeds as a result of destruction of company's factory buildings and machinery because of an earthquake. (The proceeds exceeded the book value of buildings and machinery destroyed.)

17-17 Analysis of noncurrent accounts   The following data were taken from the records of Miller Mining Company.

	End of Year	
	19X6	*19X5*
Plant and equipment	$2,240,000	$1,980,000
Accumulated depreciation	(980,000)	(740,000)
Mineral properties, net of depletion	3,750,000	2,950,000

You have also determined that plant and equipment costing $240,000 and with accumulated depreciation of $90,000 was sold for $80,000 and that depletion expense related to mineral properties was $440,000. The only other transactions affecting the accounts shown were depreciation expense, purchases of plant and equipment, and purchases of mineral properties.

Required
1. Determine the amount of cash provided by sales of plant and equipment.
2. Determine the gain or loss to be added or subtracted in the reconciliation of net income to cash flow from operations.
3. Determine the amount of depreciation expense to be added to net income in the reconciliation of net income to cash flow from operations.
4. Determine the amount of cash paid to buy plant and equipment.
5. Determine the amount of cash paid to buy mineral properties.

17-18   Cash flow from operations – special situations (continuation of 17-14)   After more careful study of Drew Company's income statement for 19X9, you determine that the following items also affected net income.
1. Amortization of intangible assets, $22,000.
2. Loss of sale of plant assets, $3,000.
3. On one sale, for $24,000, the customer gave Drew Company a five-year note bearing interest at 9%.

Required: Recompute the cash provided by operations considering this additional information.

17-19   Statement preparation   Below is a list of items that would appear in the cash flow statement for Collins Company for the year 19X8.

Net income for the year	$346,000
Dividends paid during the year	140,000
Proceeds from sale of a 10-year bond issue	350,000
Amortization of the company's patents	47,000
Depreciation expense	153,000
Cash received on sale of land	106,000
Decrease in inventory	17,000
Increase in accounts receivable	74,000
Gain on the sale of land	20,000
Decrease in accrued expenses	12,000
Cash purchase of new equipment	400,000
Cash purchase of a long-term investment	265,000
Increase in income taxes payable	6,000
Decrease in accounts payable	48,000
Purchase of land and buildings by giving a 20-year note	350,000

Required: Prepare a cash flow statement for 19X8 using all the items given. (*Hint:* The change in cash was an increase of $66,000.)

17-20   Converting cash flow to income   Boyd Company uses the direct method of reporting cash flow from operations. Below is the operations sections of its cash flow statement for 19X7.

Cash receipts from customers		$917,000
Cash payments for:		
Merchandise for resale	$470,000	
Wages and salaries	160,000	
Income taxes	25,000	
Other operating expenses	120,000	
Total cash payments for operating activities		775,000
Cash provided by operations		$142,000

Other data taken from Boyd's records for 19X7 show the following.
1. Accounts receivable increased by $20,000.
2. Accounts payable decreased by $8,000.
3. Inventory remained constant at $50,000.
4. Accrued wages and salaries (the only accrued expense) increased by $3,000.
5. Depreciation expense was $55,000.

Required: Determine Boyd Company's reported net income for 19X7.

17-21 **Reconciliation of net income and cash flow from operations (continuation of 17-20)**   Using the data provided in 17-20, prepare a reconciliation of net income and cash flow from operations.

17-22 **Cash flow statement from comparative balance sheets**   Below are the balances of certain balance-sheet items for Lorelei Company at December 31, 19X5, and 19X6.

	December 31	
	19X5	19X6
Cash	$ 4,000	$23,000
Accounts receivable, net	5,000	9,000
Inventory	12,000	10,000
Long-term investments	2,000	—
Property, plant, and equipment	30,000	47,000
Totals	$53,000	$89,000
Accumulated depreciation on plant		
and equipment	$ 5,000	$ 8,000
Accounts payable	3,000	5,000
Notes payable, due in 1 year	4,000	3,000
Long-term notes payable	10,000	18,000
Common stock	25,000	29,000
Retained earnings	6,000	26,000
Totals	$53,000	$89,000

The following information is also available about the firm's transactions in 19X6.

1. Net income for the year was $27,000.
2. Depreciation on plant and equipment for the year was $3,000.
3. Long-term investments were sold during the year for $8,000.
4. Property, plant, and equipment costing $5,000 was purchased for cash.
5. Dividends of $7,000 were declared and paid.
6. Some equipment was purchased by giving a $12,000 long-term note.
7. The company liquidated a $4,000 long-term note payable by issuing capital stock to the holder of the note.

Required: Prepare a cash flow statement for 19X6. Use the indirect method to present operating cash flows.

Problems

17-23 ***Determining cash flow from operations***   With the information provided for each of the following cases, determine the cash provided (used) by operations.

	Case A	Case B
From the income statement:		
Sales	$1,850,000	$851,850
Cost of goods sold	925,000	436,200
Operating expenses, total	683,000	428,500
Depreciation expense (included in expense total)	73,000	128,000
From the balance sheet:		
Increase (decrease) in Accounts Receivable	25,000	(32,000)
Increase (decrease) in Prepaid Expenses	(12,000)	8,300
Decrease in Inventory	37,000	24,500
Increase (decrease) in Accounts Payable	(68,000)	41,000
Increase in Accrued Expenses	17,000	6,400

17-24 ***Cash from operations – direct method (continuation of 17-23)***   For each case in 17-23, prepare the operations section of the cash flow statement using the direct method of presenting operating cash flows.

17-25 ***Distinguishing operating cash flows***   In 19X5, Bard Company reported net income of $168,600. The following facts are also known about the year's activities.

Increase in Inventory	$ 5,000
Decrease in Prepaid Expenses	400
Depreciation expense—company cars	31,000
Increase in Accounts Receivable	12,000
New short-term bank borrowings	45,000
Decrease in Dividends Payable	32,000
Amortization expense—patents	9,000
Decrease in Accounts Payable	4,000

Required

1. Compute the cash flow from operations for 19X5.
2. Explain how your answer in item 1 would change if you also knew that during 19X5 Bard sold some machinery for $2,800 cash, incurring a loss of $1,300.

17-26 **Selecting relevant information**   Use the following information as necessary to compute cash flow from operations for the year.

Net income	$ 80
Increase in Accounts Receivable	12
Increase in Inventory	40
Decrease in Accrued Interest Receivable	3
Increase in Long-term Investments	135
Depreciation and amortization expense	161
Gain on sale of machinery and equipment	27
Proceeds from sale of machinery and equipment	198
Increase in Accounts Payable	74

17-27 **Cash flow statement from transaction information**   Fisher Company began 19X4 with $18,000 cash. The following information is available for 19X4 activities.

1. Net income was $115,000.
2. Depreciation expense was $70,000.
3. Fisher retired bonds payable that were due in 19X9. The cash paid to retire the bonds was equal to their $60,000 book value.
4. Fisher paid $90,000 cash for new plant and equipment.
5. Fisher declared dividends of $18,000 to be paid in January of 19X5. Dividends payable at the end of 19X3 were $3,000.
6. One of Fisher's long-term investments in stock was written off as a loss in 19X4 because the company in which Fisher had invested went bankrupt. The book value of the investment was $30,000.
7. Accounts Receivable increased by $15,000 during the year.
8. Inventory increased by $26,000 during the year.
9. Prepaid Expenses decreased by $8,000 during the year.
10. During 19X4 Fisher sold, for $54,000 cash, a patent with a $38,000 book value.

Required: Prepare a cash flow statement for Fisher Company for 19X4.

17-28 **Cash flows from transactions**   Transactions of Martin Company for 19X6 and other selected data are given below.

1. Sales, all on account, were $800,000.
2. Cost of goods sold was $360,000.
3. Depreciation expense was $60,000.
4. Other operating expenses, all paid in cash, were $210,000.
5. Equipment was purchased for $220,000 cash.
6. Long-term investments were sold at an $8,000 gain. They had cost $57,000.
7. Common stock was issued for cash of $150,000.

8. A building that had cost $80,000 and had accumulated depreciation of $72,000 was destroyed by fire. There was no insurance coverage.

9. Over the year, the following changes occurred in the current accounts.

Cash	+$ 17,000
Accounts receivable, net	+ 128,000
Prepaid expense	+ 12,000
Inventory	+ 82,000
Accounts payable	+ 14,000

Required

1. Determine net income for 19X6.
2. Prepare a cash flow statement for 19X6.

17-29 **Effects of transactions** Explain how each of the following affects the 19X9 cash flow statement of Gray Company.

1. A long-term investment in the common stock of Black Company was sold for $183,000, which was $42,000 less than its book value at the date of sale.

2. At the beginning of 19X9, Gray had a patent with a book value of $180,000. On November 15, 19X9, Gray sold the patent for $98,000. Amortization expense (for 19X9) to the date of sale was $45,000.

3. On October 31, 19X9, Gray sold some of its equipment for $18,000. The book value of the equipment at the beginning of 19X9 was $13,000, and 19X9 depreciation on the equipment to the date of sale was $2,200.

4. On July 3, 19X9, when the market value of its common stock was $28 per share, Gray declared a 10% stock dividend on its 100,000 shares of outstanding $20 par-value stock. The dividend was distributed on October 1, 19X9.

5. On April 1, 19X9, Gray retired an outstanding issue of bonds, paying $103,500 in cash. The bonds had a book value at the date of retirement of $98,300. Amortization of discount on these bonds between January 1 and April 1 of 19X9 was $200.

6. On March 19, 19X9, Gray acquired new machinery valued at $460,000. Gray paid $85,000 in cash for this machinery and gave a five-year, 10% note for the difference.

17-30 **Cash flow** As you were walking down the hall to your office at Complan Company, you met the president of the firm. She was disturbed at the latest financial statements and wanted your help. She explained that the firm was faced with a serious shortage of cash even though profits were high and working capital increased. She showed you the following condensed financial statements. (All data are in thousands of dollars.)

Complan Company, Income Statement for 19X7	
Sales	$6,720
Cost of sales	3,850
Gross profit	2,870
Operating expenses	2,140
Net income	$ 730

Complan Company, Balance Sheets as of December 31			
Assets	19X7	19X6	Change
Cash	$ 25	$ 380	($355)
Accounts receivable, net	990	860	130
Inventory	1,445	1,200	245
Plant and equipment, net	3,850	3,370	480
Total	$6,310	$5,810	
Equities			
Accounts payable	$ 190	$ 280	($90)
Accrued expenses	110	200	(90)
Long-term debt	2,250	2,200	50
Common stock	2,080	2,080	0
Retained earnings	1,680	1,050	630
Total	$6,310	$5,810	

The president told you that it had been touch-and-go whether the firm would have enough cash to pay a $100,000 dividend that had been declared when the directors realized that the firm was having an excellent year. To pay the dividend, the firm had to increase its long-term borrowings by $50,000. "We made $730,000 and had depreciation expense of $150,000. We did buy $630,000 worth of plant assets, but I figured that our cash would stay about the same as it was last year. Look at this stuff and tell me what happened."

Required: Explain the results to the president.

17-31 ***Cash flow statement from comparative trial balances*** Below are the beginning and ending balances of the balance sheet accounts for Truitt Company for 19X3.

	Beginning of Year		End of Year	
	Dr.	Cr.	Dr.	Cr.
Cash	$ 36,000		$ 26,000	
Accounts receivable	50,000		60,000	
Allowance for bad debts		$ 10,000		$ 12,000
Inventory	70,000		85,000	
Buildings and equipment	190,000		240,000	
Patents	26,000		20,000	
Accounts payable		30,000		40,000
Accrued wages payable		4,000		5,000
Accumulated depreciation on buildings and equipment		96,000		100,000
10-year bonds payable		80,000		104,000
Premium on bonds payable		—		1,000
Treasury stock	—		4,000	
Common stock		100,000		135,000
Retained earnings		52,000		38,000
Total	$372,000	$372,000	$435,000	$435,000

The following information is also available about the firm's activities in 19X3.
1. Net income was $14,000.
2. Dividends of $8,000 were declared and paid.
3. A stock dividend was declared and distributed, and for this reason $20,000 was charged to Retained Earnings, which amount represented the par and market value of the stock issued in connection with the dividend.
4. Depreciation in the amount of $8,000 was recorded as expense this year.
5. Machinery costing $6,000 and having a book value of $2,000 was sold for $3,000 cash in 19X3.

Required: Prepare a cash flow statement for Truitt Company for 19X3. You may assume that any changes other than those described above are attributable to reasonable transactions with which you should be familiar.

17-32 **Treatment of transactions**   Explain how each of the following transactions is reflected on a cash flow statement. Be specific.
1. Depreciation expense was $340,000.
2. A $110,000 dividend was declared late in the year and will be paid early next year.
3. Fixed assets costing $380,000 with accumulated depreciation of $170,000 were sold for $80,000 cash.
4. Long-term investments were written off because the firms issuing the securities went bankrupt. The write-off was $220,000.
5. The firm issued long-term debt in exchange for land. The value of the land was $640,000, which equaled the value of the debt.
6. Near the end of the year the firm sold a parcel of land for $300,000, which was $60,000 more than its cost. The buyer gave the firm a 5-year, 8% note for $300,000.
7. The firm paid $50,000 in settlement of a dispute relating to its income tax return of three years ago. The firm debited Retained Earnings for $50,000.

17-33 **Statements from limited data**   The following *changes* in the balance sheet accounts for Rohmer Company occurred during 19X8.

	Change	
Account	Debit	Credit
Cash	$120	
Accounts receivable, net		$180
Inventory	120	
Plant and equipment	350	
Accumulated depreciation		90
Accounts payable	80	
Accrued expenses		30
Long-term debt	15	
Common stock		200
Retained earnings		185
Totals	$685	$685

The firm had net income of $225 and paid dividends of $40. No plant assets were sold or retired.

Required: Prepare a cash flow statement. In the absence of available information, make the most reasonable assumption about the cause of a change.

17-34   *Classification of items in the cash flow statement*   A list of items follows, most of which appear on a cash flow statement for Brillan Company for 19X8. During the current year, cash increased by $101,000.
1. Dividends declared during the year were $125,000, but dividends actually paid in cash were $103,000.
2. An issue of 10-year bonds payable was sold for $275,000 cash.
3. Amortization of the company's franchise cost was $6,000.
4. Depreciation on the company's tangible fixed assets was $159,000.
5. Land was sold at a loss of $14,000; cash received for the sale was $74,000.
6. Decrease in Inventory was $6,000.
7. Increase in Accounts Receivable was $81,000.
8. Increase in Accrued Expenses Payable was $11,000.
9. Decrease in Income Taxes Payable was $24,000.
10. Increase in Accounts Payable was $51,000.
11. Decrease in Prepaid Expenses was $1,000.
12. Increase in Allowance to Reduce Short-term Investments to Lower-of-Cost-or-Market was $3,000.
13. Decrease in short-term bank borrowings (debt) was $13,000.
14. Cash paid for new equipment was $500,000.
15. Cash paid for a long-term investment was $158,000.
16. A ten-year note payable for $200,000 was given to acquire land and buildings.
17. Amortization of discount on the 10-year bond issue mentioned in item 2 was $2,000.
18. Cash received as dividend on stock held as a long-term investment and accounted for on the equity basis was $25,000.
19. Amortization of discount on a long-term investment in bonds was $3,000.
20. Cash received from sale of treasury stock was $6,000; the stock had cost the company $4,000.
21. Increase in credit balance of Deferred Taxes account was $4,000.
22. Brillan's portion of net income of company whose stock is mentioned in item 18 was $56,000.
23. Net income for the year was $402,000.

Required: Prepare a cash flow statement for Brillan Company for 19X8.

17-35   *Comprehensive problem*   Comparative balance sheets and an income statement for RJM Company are given below. All data are in millions of dollars.

RJM Company, Balance Sheets as of June 30

Assets	19X7	19X6
Cash	$ 9.5	$ 28.7
Accounts receivable, net	125.8	88.6
Inventories	311.4	307.0
Prepayments	12.6	11.4
Total current assets	459.3	435.7
Investments	68.3	71.8
Plant and equipment	1,313.9	1,240.6
Accumulated depreciation	(753.1)	(687.4)
Intangible assets	42.5	46.2
Total assets	$1,130.9	$1,106.9
Equities		
Accounts payable	$ 62.6	$ 59.8
Taxes payable	32.4	29.6
Accrued expenses	38.9	52.6
Total current liabilities	133.9	142.0
Long-term debt	505.3	496.2
Common stock, no par value	384.2	377.4
Retained earnings	107.5	91.3
Total equities	$1,130.9	$1,106.9

RJM Company, Income Statement for 19X7

Sales and other revenue		$896.3
Expenses:		
Cost of goods sold	$493.2	
Depreciation	69.3	
Amortization	3.7	
Income taxes	85.0	
Other expenses	203.5	854.7
Net income		$ 41.6

Sales and other revenue includes a gain of $0.8 million on sale of investments. Amortization expense is related to intangible assets. Other expenses include losses of $1.3 million on sales and other disposals of equipment. These assets had cost $9.6 million and had accumulated depreciation of $3.6 million. Long-term debt and common stock were issued for cash.

Required: Prepare a cash flow statement for the year ended June 30, 19X7.

17-36 *Cash flow statement from comparative trial balances – comprehensive problem* Below are the trial balances for Mesmer Company at the beginning and the end of 19X5.

	Beginning of Year		End of Year	
	Dr.	Cr.	Dr.	Cr.
Cash	$ 50,000		$ 60,000	
Accounts receivable	150,000		200,000	
Inventory	250,000		270,000	
Prepaid expenses	50,000		70,000	
Land	250,000		307,000	
Buildings and equipment	700,000		838,000	
Bond discount—5% bonds	—		8,000	
Allowance for bad debts		25,000		35,000
Accumulated depreciation		300,000		421,000
Accounts payable		170,000		220,000
Accrued expenses		105,000		115,000
Bonds payable:				
5% bonds		—		200,000
6% bonds		175,000		—
Bond premium—6% bonds		4,000		—
Long-term notes payable		—		80,000
Capital stock—par value		450,000		475,000
Paid-in capital in excess of par		81,000		83,500
Retained earnings		140,000		123,500
	$1,450,000	$1,450,000	$1,753,000	$1,753,000

The following data are available regarding Mesmer Company's 19X5 activities.

1. Net income was $70,000 including gains and losses on transactions relating to fixed assets and bond retirements.

2. Land costing $100,000 was purchased, paying 20% in cash and giving long-term notes payable for the remainder of the purchase price. The only other transaction related to land was a sale that produced a gain of $12,000.

3. Equipment that had originally cost $82,000 and had a book value of $23,000 was sold for $8,000 cash. Additional equipment was purchased for cash.

4. At the beginning of the year, bonds payable carrying an interest rate of 5% and a maturity value of $200,000 were sold for $190,000 cash. Very shortly thereafter, the 6% bonds were purchased on the open market for $159,000 and retired.

5. During the year, a stock dividend was declared and issued and was appropriately accounted for by a charge against Retained Earnings for $27,500, the market value of the stock distributed in connection with the dividend. The market value was 10% higher than the par value for the shares issued. Cash dividends were declared and paid as usual.

Required: Prepare a cash flow statement for 19X5.

CHAPTER *18*

ANALYZING FINANCIAL STATEMENTS

From Chapter 2 we already know that managers often express target profits as a ratio of income to sales (return on sales). We have also seen that the ratio of income to total assets (or some other measure of return on investment) is commonly used in measuring divisional performance. The chapters on comprehensive budgeting stressed the development of pro forma financial statements and the cash squeeze that can accompany buildups of inventories and receivables. This chapter addresses the analysis of financial statements, including the calculation, interpretation, and evaluation of ratios of one element of the financial statements to another.

Many people and organizations outside a company, such as suppliers and investors in debt or equity securities, are interested in a firm's activities. Banks that provide short-term loans, insurance companies that buy long-term bonds, brokerage firms that give (or sell) investment advice to their customers, mutual funds that buy stocks or bonds—all of these, and many other institutions, employ financial analysts to help them make decisions about individual firms. Individual investors also perform financial analyses in making investment decisions. Our approach to analyzing financial statements is that of a financial analyst, who makes recommendations to potential investors after studying financial statements and other sources of information about a business. Because the analyst's conclusions and recommendations can affect a firm's ability to obtain credit, sell stock, and secure new contracts, its managers must be aware of what concerns the financial analyst. But as we proceed, it should become obvious that managers and analysts share many of the same concerns.

PURPOSE AND APPROACH
OF THE ANALYST

Financial analysts, like company managers, base their decisions on expectations about the future. Thus, just as a manager's analysis focuses on forecasts, that of the financial analyst concentrates on what the future holds. Analysts want to know what to expect from a firm—whether it will be able to pay its bills, repay loans with interest, pay dividends on stock, or expand into new areas. The financial analyst, like the firm's managers, is concerned with the past only insofar as it can be considered a reliable guide to the future. For example, an impressive history of growth in net income and sales, financial stability, and capable management is irrelevant to the firm's future if its major product becomes virtually illegal (e.g., asbestos, the insecticide DDT) or obsolete (e.g., early types of computers and calculators). Nevertheless, like managers who use information such as a cost prediction formula based on past experience, analysts assume that what has held true in the past is likely to continue *unless* they have information that indicates otherwise. Hence, both analysts and the firm's managers must be continually alert for signs that the future will differ from the past.

In addition to having a common focus on the future, the firm's managers and the financial analyst use many of the same analytical approaches. Because a firm's well-being often depends on investors' continued willingness to supply capital at reasonable rates, internal managers try to duplicate the analyses made by outsiders (especially financial analysts) so they can see the firm as outsiders do. Managers review these analyses to see whether the firm's ratios are out of line with those of other firms in the industry or with what the managers believe to be the expectations of outsiders.

For obvious reasons, the internal manager has access to more information than the external analyst and can study ratios, and their underlying components, in more depth. For example, by using a technique described later in this chapter, an outsider might calculate the *average* age of a firm's accounts receivable. The internal manager could, however, obtain a more precise picture of the age of receivables by requesting a schedule of receivables that shows exactly how much of the total receivables are under 30 days old, 31 to 60 days old, and so on. In effect, the external analyst obtains a general picture of the firm's operations and financial position, while the internal analyst is interested in, and can obtain information about, the details of that picture. This difference is consistent with the interests of the two analysts. The external analyst is interested in the firm as a whole, its prospects for the future, and the decisions by management as a team. The internal analyst is interested also in what specific actions can be taken by individual managers.

GENERAL METHODS OF ANALYSIS

Financial analysis consists of a number of interrelated activities. Among the most important are considerations of ratios and trends and the comparison of ratios and trends against some norms. (A *norm* is a standard for comparison, which could be an average value for a particular industry or for all firms in the economy.) Trends are of interest as clues to the future.

Areas of Analysis

Different types of investors are interested in different aspects of a firm. Short-term creditors, such as suppliers and banks considering loans of relatively short duration (90 days or six months), are concerned primarily with the firm's short-term prospects. They want to know whether the firm will be able to pay its obligations in the near future. Banks, insurance companies, pension funds, and other investors considering relatively long-term commitments (e.g., ten-year loans) cannot ignore short-term prospects, but are more concerned with the long-term outlook. Even if such investors are satisfied that the firm has no short-term problems, they want to be reasonably sure that the firm has good prospects for long-term financial stability and can be expected to repay its longer-term loans with interest.

Stockholders, current and potential, are also interested in both the short-term and long-term prospects of the firm. But their interest goes beyond the company's ability to repay loans and make interest payments. Their concern is with potential profitability—the ability to earn satisfactory profits and pay dividends—and the likelihood that the market price of the stock will increase.

We have divided the discussion of these aspects of a firm's prospects into three major areas: liquidity, solvency, and profitability. For the most part we work with ratios. Apart from expressing relationships between two factors, ratios are useful because they facilitate comparisons among firms of different sizes.

Sample Financial Statements

We shall use the comparative financial statements and additional financial information about Graham Company (shown in Exhibit 18-1 on pages 766–67). We include the cash flow statements because they are part of the typical financial statement package.

The analysis has actually begun in the exhibit because it shows the percentages of sales for each item on the income statement and the percentage of total assets or total equities for each balance sheet item. These percentage statements, or **common size statements,** can sometimes help an analyst to spot trends.

Two of the more important percentages on the income statement are the **gross profit ratio,** which is gross profit divided by sales, and **return on sales (ROS),** which is net income divided by sales. These ratios for Graham in 19X6 are 38.5% and 7.9%, respectively. The gross profit ratio improved in 19X6 over 19X5, but ROS declined.

Financial analysts and internal managers are interested in ROS and the gross profit ratio because these ratios indicate how valuable a dollar of sales is to the firm. These ratios are not the same as the contribution margin ratio, but they do give a rough idea of the profit/sales relationship. A relatively low ROS, com-

Exhibit 18-1

Graham Company, Balance Sheets as of December 31

	19X6		19X5	
	Dollars	Percent	Dollars	Percent
Current assets:				
Cash	$ 80,000	5.2%	$ 50,000	3.6%
Accounts receivable, net	180,000	11.6	120,000	8.7
Inventory	190,000	12.2	230,000	16.7
Total current assets	450,000	29.0	400,000	29.0
Plant and equipment—cost	1,350,000	87.1	1,150,000	83.3
Accumulated depreciation	(340,000)	(21.9)	(250,000)	(18.1)
Net plant and equipment	1,010,000	65.2	900,000	65.2
Other assets	90,000	5.8	80,000	5.8
Total assets	$1,550,000	100.0	$1,380,000	100.0
Current liabilities:				
Accounts payable	$ 110,000	7.1%	$ 105,000	7.6%
Accrued expenses	40,000	2.6	15,000	1.1
Total current liabilities	150,000	9.7	120,000	8.7
Long-term debt	600,000	38.7	490,000	35.5
Total liabilities	750,000	48.4	610,000	44.2
Common stock, 22,000 shares	220,000	14.2	220,000	15.9
Paid-in capital	350,000	22.6	350,000	25.4
Retained earnings	230,000	14.8	200,000	14.5
Total stockholders' equity	800,000	51.6	770,000	55.8
Total equities	$1,550,000	100.0	$1,380,000	100.0

Graham Company, Income Statements for the Years Ended December 31

	19X6		19X5	
	Dollars	Percent	Dollars	Percent
Sales	$1,300,000	100.0%	$1,080,000	100.0%
Cost of goods sold	800,000	61.5	670,000	62.0
Gross profit	500,000	38.5	410,000	38.0
Operating expenses[a]	280,000	21.6	210,000	19.4
Income before interest and taxes	220,000	16.9	200,000	18.6
Interest expense	48,000	3.7	42,000	3.9
Income before taxes	172,000	13.2	158,000	14.7
Income taxes at 40% rate	68,800	5.3	63,200	5.9
Net income	$ 103,200	7.9	$ 94,800	8.8

[a] Including depreciation of $90,000 in 19X6 and $75,000 in 19X5.

Graham Company, Cash Flow Statements for the Years ended December 31

	19X6	19X5
Net cash flow from operating activities:		
Collections from customers	$1,240,000	$1,075,000
Payments to suppliers	(755,000)	(656,400)
Payments for operating expenses	(182,000)	(143,600)
Interest paid	(44,000)	(39,000)
Taxes paid	(55,800)	(58,400)
Net cash provided by operating activities	203,200	177,600
Cash flows for investing activities:		
Purchase of plant and equipment	(200,000)	(97,000)
Sale of plant and equipment		12,000
Purchase of other assets	(10,000)	
Net cash used by investing activities	(210,000)	(85,000)
Cash flows from (for) financing activities:		
Proceeds from bond issue	110,000	
Repayment of short-term loans		(42,000)
Payment of dividends	(73,200)	(63,000)
Net cash from (for) financing activities	36,800	(105,000)
Increase (decrease) in cash	30,000	(12,400)
Cash balance, beginning of year	50,000	62,400
Cash balance, end of year	$ 80,000	$ 50,000

bined with a gross profit ratio that is normal for the industry, could indicate that operating expenses are out of line with those of other firms. As we mention several times in this chapter, ratios provide clues or indicators, but they do not tell you that a firm is acting wisely or unwisely.

Balance-sheet ratios are used to see whether the proportions of particular assets or liabilities are increasing or decreasing, and whether they are within reasonable bounds. We shall explore balance-sheet ratios in more detail later in the chapter.

LIQUIDITY

Liquidity is a firm's ability to meet obligations due in the near future. The more liquid a firm, the more likely it is to be able to pay its employees, suppliers, and holders of its short-term notes payable. A company with excellent long-term prospects could fail to realize them because it was forced into bankruptcy when it could not pay its debts in the near term. Hence, while liquidity is most important to short-term creditors, it is also of concern to long-term creditors and stockholders.

Working Capital and the Current Ratio

Working capital, the difference between current assets and current liabilities, is a very rough measure of liquidity. Graham had the following amounts of working capital at the ends of 19X5 and 19X6.

	19X6	19X5
Current assets	$450,000	$400,000
Current liabilities	150,000	120,000
Working capital	$300,000	$280,000

Working capital is positive and increased. But this does not necessarily mean that the firm has adequate liquidity or became more liquid. Most analysts consider changes in working capital as only a very rough indication of changes in liquidity and supplement their analysis with several other calculations. Working capital is stated in absolute dollar terms and hence is greatly influenced by the size of the firm.

The **current ratio** is a measure of relative liquidity that takes into account differences in absolute size. It is used to compare firms with different total current assets and liabilities as well as to compare the same firm's liquidity from year to year.

$$\text{Current ratio} = \frac{\text{current assets}}{\text{current liabilities}}$$

Graham has current ratios of 3.33 to 1 in 19X5 ($400,000/$120,000) and 3 to 1 in 19X6 ($450,000/$150,000). Therefore, we would say that, on the basis of the current ratio, the firm seemed to be less liquid at the end of 19X6. There is a very good reason for saying "seemed to be less liquid." One major problem that arises with any ratio, but especially the current ratio, is that of composition. The **composition problem** arises when one uses a total, such as total current assets (or current liabilities), that might mask information about the individual components. How soon will the current assets be converted into cash so that they can be used to pay current liabilities? How soon are the current liabilities due for payment? You already know that current assets normally are listed in the order of their liquidity, from cash, the most liquid, to prepaid expenses. The analyst obtains a general idea of the potential magnitude of the composition problem by reviewing the common size balance sheet to see the extent to which current assets are composed of relatively liquid items.

Quick Ratio (Acid-Test Ratio)

The **quick ratio,** or **acid-test ratio,** is cash plus accounts receivable plus marketable securities divided by current liabilities. It is similar to the current ratio, but includes only those assets that are cash or "near cash" (called **quick assets**). Hence, the ratio gives a stricter indication of short-term debt-paying ability than does the current ratio.

$$\text{Quick ratio} = \frac{\text{cash + marketable securities + receivables}}{\text{current liabilities}}$$

Graham had no marketable securities at the end of either year, so its quick ratios are as follows.

$$19X5 \quad \frac{\$50,000 + \$120,000}{\$120,000} = 1.42$$

$$19X6 \quad \frac{\$80,000 + \$180,000}{\$150,000} = 1.73$$

Graham seems to have increased its liquidity because its quick ratio increased. We could say that the firm was better able to meet current liabilities at the end of 19X6 but we would still like to know how soon its current liabilities have to be paid and how rapidly the firm can expect to turn its receivables and inventory into cash.

Working Capital Activity Ratios

Two commonly used ratios provide information about the time within which the firm expects to realize cash from its receivables and inventories. And, although we cannot tell the time within which the firm must pay its various current liabilities simply by examining the financial statements, one commonly used ratio offers some insight into the company's bill-paying practices.

Accounts Receivable Turnover   Accounts receivable turnover is a measure of how rapidly the firm collects its receivables; in general, the higher the turnover the better.

$$\text{Accounts receivable turnover} = \frac{\text{credit sales}}{\text{average receivables}}$$

In general, average receivables are defined as the beginning balance plus the ending balance, divided by 2. This simple averaging procedure is satisfactory so long as there are no extremely high or low points during the year (including the end of the year). If a firm has widely fluctuating receivable balances, it is better to use a monthly average. For illustrative purposes we assume that all of Graham's sales are on credit. Because we do not have the beginning balance for 19X5, we can only calculate the turnover of average receivables for 19X6 for Graham Company. (Some analysts do compute turnovers using end-of-year values.)

$$\frac{\$1,300,000}{(\$120,000 + \$180,000)/2} = \frac{\$1,300,000}{\$150,000} = 8.67 \text{ times}$$

Some analysts make a related calculation called number of **days' sales in accounts receivable.** This figure indicates the average age of ending accounts receivable.

$$\text{Days' sales in accounts receivable} = \frac{\text{ending accounts receivable}}{\text{average daily credit sales}}$$

Average daily sales is simply credit sales for the year divided by 365. For Graham Company, we have average daily credit sales of about $2,959 ($1,080,000/365) for 19X5 and about $3,562 ($1,300,000/365) for 19X6. Hence, days' sales in accounts receivable are

$$19X5 \quad \frac{\$120,000}{\$2,959} = 41 \text{ days}$$

$$19X6 \quad \frac{\$180,000}{\$3,562} = 51 \text{ days}$$

On the average, then, Graham's accounts receivable were 41 days old at the end of 19X5 and 51 days old at the end of 19X6. The collection period has lengthened considerably in one year, but the period must be interpreted in light of the credit terms offered to customers. The faster customers pay, the better. But there are always trade-offs. If the firm loses sales because of tight credit policies, the advantage of faster collection might be more than offset by the loss of profits because of lower total sales. The increase in the average collection period might well be the result of a management decision to offer more liberal terms to stimulate sales.

We used Graham's total sales to compute the two receivables-related ratios because we assumed that all sales were on credit. An outside analyst seldom knows what portion of sales is on credit and uses total sales for lack of better information. The ratios so computed are not misleading as long as the proportions of cash and credit sales did not change significantly (another instance of "the composition problem"). An internal manager, of course, has access to information about the composition of total sales and could make a more precise calculation of the receivables ratios. Moreover, the internal manager is extremely interested in the precise patterns of customer payments, for cash budgeting and control purposes. Nevertheless, as a first step in the analysis, the internal manager is likely to use the same general ratios as the external analyst.

Inventory Turnover   The same type of analysis applies to the firm's inventory. Inventory turnover is calculated as follows.

$$\text{Inventory turnover} = \frac{\text{cost of goods sold}}{\text{average inventory}}$$

Again, average inventory is usually considered to be the sum of the beginning and ending balances divided by 2. If the firm has higher inventories and lower inventories for significant portions of the year because of seasonal business, it is better to use monthly figures to determine the average.

Graham's inventory turnover for 19X6 is about 3.8 times, calculated as follows.

$$\frac{\$800,000}{(\$230,000 + \$190,000)/2} = \frac{\$800,000}{\$210,000} = 3.8$$

We cannot compute the 19X5 turnover of average inventory because we do not know the beginning balance, but using the year-end inventory, turnover is 2.9 ($670,000/$230,000).

This measure indicates the efficiency with which the firm uses its inventory. High inventory turnover is critical for many businesses, especially those that sell at relatively low markup (ratio of gross profit to cost) and depend on high sales volumes to earn satisfactory profits. For example, discount stores and food stores rely heavily on quick turnover for their profitability. Firms with very high markups, such as jewelry stores, do not need such rapid turnovers to be profitable.

Investment in inventory can be very expensive. Some costs—insurance, personal property taxes, interest on the funds tied up in inventory, and obsolescence—can be very high. Therefore, managers prefer to keep inventory as low as possible. The problem is that if inventory is too low, particularly in firms such as retail stores, sales might be lost because customers cannot find what they want.

Analysts will also sometimes calculate the number of **days' sales in inventory,** which is a measure of the supply that the firm maintains.

$$\text{Days' sales in inventory} = \frac{\text{ending inventory}}{\text{average daily cost of goods sold}}$$

Average daily cost of goods sold is simply cost of goods sold for the year divided by 365. For Graham, this is $1,836 ($670,000/365) for 19X5 and $2,192 ($800,000/365) for 19X6. Days' sales in inventory are as follows.

$$19X5 \quad \frac{\$230,000}{\$1,836} = 125 \text{ days}$$

$$19X6 \quad \frac{\$190,000}{\$2,192} = 87 \text{ days}$$

The decline in days' sales in inventory could indicate a deliberate change in inventory policy, or perhaps just a temporary reduction of inventory because of heavier than expected sales near the end of the year.

As you may remember from your study of financial accounting, generally accepted accounting principles (GAAP) allow several different formats for the income statement. Some formats do not show cost of goods sold, so that the outside analyst cannot compute inventory turnover using the approach just presented. In such cases, the analyst will use total sales as a substitute for cost of goods sold, even though sales and inventory are not measured in the same way. (Sales is measured in selling prices, while inventory is measured in cost prices.) The inventory turnover so derived is, of course, overstated—a unit costing $1 and sold for $2 will reflect two inventory turnovers when only one unit has been sold. If analysts recognize the automatic overstatement in the calculation, they will not be misled by the results.

As you will recall from Chapter 13, a manufacturing firm has not one but three types of inventory: raw materials, work in process, and finished goods. The calculation of inventory turnover, as described above, relates to the finished goods inventory of a manufacturing firm, since only that inventory is measured on the same basis (full cost of a completed unit) as cost of goods sold. An internal analyst also should be able to compute the turnover for the firm's inventory of raw materials.

$$\frac{\text{Turnover of}}{\text{inventory of}} = \frac{\text{raw materials used in production}}{\text{average raw materials inventory}}$$

An external analyst is seldom able to compute this second inventory turnover because externally available financial statements seldom provide sufficient information to determine the value of the numerator of the ratio.

Days' Purchases in Accounts Payable   This ratio is of special concern to both creditors and the firm's managers.

$$\frac{\text{Days' purchases in}}{\text{accounts payable}} = \frac{\text{ending accounts payable}}{\text{average daily purchases}}$$

The calculation of this ratio by an internal analyst in a merchandising firm is relatively easy because such an analyst can determine total purchases for the year and can readily compute average daily purchases (total purchases/365). The external analyst could compute total purchases as follows.

$$\text{Purchases} = \frac{\text{cost of}}{\text{goods sold}} + \frac{\text{ending}}{\text{inventory}} - \frac{\text{beginning}}{\text{inventory}}$$

For Graham, days' purchases in accounts payable is about 53 days.

$$\frac{\text{Days' purchases}}{\text{in accounts payable}} = \frac{\$110,000}{(\$800,000 + \$190,000 - \$230,000)/365}$$

$$= \frac{\$110,000}{\$2,082} = 52.8 \text{ days}$$

We cannot compute the ratio for 19X5 because we do not know the beginning inventory for that year.

The value for 19X6, about 53 days, must be interpreted in light of the normal credit terms offered by suppliers. If the normal terms require payment in 60 days, the ratio indicates no significant problem; if normal credit terms are cash in 30 days, the ratio suggests that a problem may exist. Of course, it pays a firm to take as long as possible to pay its suppliers, so long as it does not incur high interest charges or damage its credit rating.

PROFITABILITY

Profitability can be measured in absolute dollar terms, such as net income, or by using ratios. The most commonly used measures of profitability fall under the general heading of **return on investment (ROI).** As described in Chapter 11, ROI is actually a family of ratios having the general form

$$\frac{\text{Return on}}{\text{investment}} = \frac{\text{income}}{\text{investment}}$$

External investors, especially stockholders and potential stockholders, are interested in the return that they can expect from their investments. Managers within the firm are concerned with earning satisfactory returns on the investments that they control. As a practical matter, then, different analysts and managers will define both income and investment differently when trying to measure the same basic relationship. In this section, we present some of the most often used alternative ways of looking at this basic relationship of accomplishment (return, income) to effort (investment).

Return on Assets (ROA)

ROA is a measure of operating efficiency, of how well the firm's managers have used the assets under their control to generate income. The following ratio is one way to make the calculation.

$$\frac{\text{Return on}}{\text{assets}} = \frac{\text{net income} + \text{interest} + \text{income taxes}}{\text{average total assets}}$$

For Graham, ROA was about 15% for 19X6, calculated as follows.

$$\frac{\text{Return on}}{\text{assets}} = \frac{\$103,200 + \$48,000 + \$68,800}{(\$1,380,000 + \$1,550,000)/2}$$

$$= \frac{\$220,000}{\$1,465,000} = 15.0\%$$

We add interest and income taxes back to net income, which is equivalent to using income before interest and income taxes. Remember that we are concerned with operations; interest and, to some extent, income taxes depend on how the company finances its assets—how much debt it uses. Moreover, income taxes are affected by many matters not related to operations, which provides another reason for adding them back. (Some of these nonoperating factors are the company's investments in securities and its use of tax benefits such as percentage depletion.) Some analysts add back only interest; others add back only the after-tax effect of interest. There is an argument to support almost any definition of the numerator in the ROA calculation. Choosing one alternative over another is largely a matter of personal preference.

Average total assets is normally the sum of the beginning and ending balance-sheet amounts divided by 2, although if significant fluctuations occur from month to month, it is better to use monthly data to determine the average. Some analysts use end-of-year assets in the denominator, some use beginning-of-year amounts, and still others use total assets minus current liabilities. (Analysts in the latter group argue that current liabilities are "automatic" sources of financing and typically relate to operating, rather than financing, decisions.) In this chapter, we use average total assets, with no consideration of current liabilities, but we caution you that this is a matter of choice and preference.

Both internal and external analysts can obtain the information for this ratio directly from publicly available financial statements, and can make direct comparisons with firms in the same industry.

Return on Common Equity (ROE)

ROA is a measure of operating efficiency. Common stockholders are also concerned with the return on *their* investment, which is affected not only by operations but also by the amount of debt and preferred stock in the firm's capital structure. Graham Company has no preferred stock, but it does have debt.

ROE is computed as follows.

$$\text{Return on common equity (ROE)} = \frac{\text{net income}}{\text{average common stockholders' equity}}$$

In the absence of preferred stock, average common stockholders' equity is simply the sum of the beginning and ending amounts of stockholders' equity divided by 2. If there is preferred stock, preferred dividends must be subtracted from net income in the numerator, and the amount of total stockholders' equity attributable to preferred stock is subtracted in the denominator to obtain common stockholders' equity.

ROE for Graham in 19X6 is a bit over 13%.

$$\frac{\$103,200}{(\$770,000 + \$800,000)/2} = \frac{\$103,200}{\$785,000} = 13.1\%$$

Notice that Graham's ROE is less than its ROA. If a firm finances its assets solely with common stock, such a relationship will hold between ROE and ROA because ROE is computed using after-tax income. But debtholders do not participate in the earnings of the firm; they receive a stipulated, constant amount of interest. Hence, the firm can increase its ROE if it uses debt, provided that ROA is greater than the interest rate it must pay to debtholders. This method of using debt (or preferred stock) to increase ROE is called **leverage** or **trading on the equity.** It involves risk as well as the potential for greater return.

The Effects of Leverage

Suppose that a firm requires total assets of $1,000,000 to earn $180,000 per year before interest and income taxes, for an ROA of 18%. The tax rate is 40%. Three alternative financing plans are possible: (1) all common stock; (2) $400,000 common stock and $600,000 in 7% bonds (interest expense of $42,000); and (3) $400,000 in common stock and $600,000 in 8% preferred stock (dividends of

$48,000). The schedule below shows the differing effects of the three alternatives on ROE.

	(1) All Common Stock	(2) Debt and Common Stock	(3) Preferred Stock and Common Stock
Income before interest and taxes	$ 180,000	$180,000	$180,000
Interest expense at 7%	0	42,000	0
Income before taxes	180,000	138,000	180,000
Income taxes at 40%	72,000	55,200	72,000
Net income	108,000	82,800	108,000
Less preferred stock dividends	0	0	48,000
Earnings available for common stock	$ 108,000	$ 82,800	$ 60,000
Divided by common equity invested	$1,000,000	$400,000	$400,000
Equals return on common equity	10.8%	20.7%	15%

Note that dividends on preferred stock must be subtracted from net income to reach earnings available for common stockholders because the preferred shareholders have a prior claim on the firm's earnings. Note also that, though the plans that include debt or preferred stock both result in lower earnings available for common equity, both produce a higher ROE than would be achieved if all common equity were used. That is, these two plans provide the benefits of leverage.

Unfortunately, leverage works both ways. It is good for the common stockholder when earnings are high and bad when they are low. If the firm earns only $60,000 before interest and taxes, it has the following results.

	(1) All Common	(2) $600,000 Debt	(3) $600,000 Preferred
Income before interest and taxes	$60,000	$60,000	$60,000
Interest expense	0	42,000	0
Income before taxes	60,000	18,000	60,000
Income taxes at 40%	24,000	7,200	24,000
Net income	36,000	10,800	36,000
Preferred stock dividends	0	0	42,000
Earnings available for common	$36,000	$10,800	($6,000)
Common equity invested	$1,000,000	$400,000	$400,000
Return on common equity	3.6%	2.7%	negative

As you can see, ROE is highest if all common equity is used, but the return is very low. Firms that have relatively stable revenues and expenses, like public utilities, can use considerable leverage. Leverage is very risky for firms in cyclical businesses like automobiles, aircraft, and construction, where income fluctuates greatly from year to year. A couple of bad years in a row could bring a heavily leveraged firm into bankruptcy. During the 1980's, leverage was so important in the acquisition of entire companies that the term *leveraged buyout,* or LBO, became a standard part of financial discussions. Often such acquisitions were financed with high-yield bonds, called *junk bonds* by many because of their high risk.

Earnings per Share (EPS)

An investor in common stock is less concerned with the total income of the firm than with his or her share of that income. That share is his or her proportional interest in the firm. Publicly owned companies must present earnings per share (EPS) data. EPS is the most widely cited statistic in the financial press, business section of newspapers, and recommendations by brokerage firms and other investment advisers. In relatively simple cases, EPS is calculated as follows:

$$\text{Earnings per share (EPS)} = \frac{\text{net income} - \text{dividends on preferred stock}}{\text{weighted-average common shares outstanding}}$$

The weighted average of common shares outstanding is used because it is the best measure of the shares outstanding throughout the period when the income is earned. If we assume that Graham Company had 22,000 shares outstanding all through 19X5 and 19X6, as well as at the ends of those years, its EPS figures are

$$19X5 \quad \frac{\$94,800 - 0}{22,000} = \frac{\$94,800}{22,000} = \$4.31$$

$$19X6 \quad \frac{\$103,200 - 0}{22,000} = \frac{\$103,200}{22,000} = \$4.69$$

EPS in 19X6 was $0.38 higher than in 19X5. This is an 8.8% growth rate, which can be calculated as follows.

$$\text{Growth rate of EPS} = \frac{\text{EPS current year} - \text{EPS prior year}}{\text{EPS prior year}}$$

For Graham

$$\frac{\$4.69 - \$4.31}{\$4.31} = 8.8\%$$

In general, the higher the growth rate the investing public as a whole expects from a firm, the more it is willing to pay for the common stock. Of course, an increase in EPS does not mean that the firm is growing. It might simply reflect a rebound from a particularly poor year. Hence, growth rates should be calculated over a number of years, rather than for a single year as we have done here.

Some companies take on commitments that, under certain circumstances, obligate them to issue additional common stock in the future. The most common of these commitments are **convertible securities,** bonds and preferred stock that can be converted into common stock at the option of the owner. These securities can be converted into common shares, which poses the problem of potential

dilution (decreases) in EPS, because earnings have to be spread over a greater number of shares. The calculation of EPS when dilution is possible can be incredibly complex.[1] We shall show a single illustration, which is necessarily quite simple. Assume that a firm has net income of $200,000, 80,000 common shares outstanding, and an issue of convertible preferred stock. The preferred stock pays dividends of $20,000 per year and is convertible into 30,000 common shares. Using the basic formula, EPS is $2.25.

$$\text{EPS} = \frac{\$200,000 - \$20,000}{80,000} = \frac{\$180,000}{80,000} = \$2.25$$

In some cases the $2.25 is presented on the income statement and called *primary earnings per share.* Then, another EPS calculation, called *fully diluted earnings per share,* is made. Fully diluted EPS is calculated assuming that the convertible securities had been converted into common stock at the beginning of the year.[2] Had this occurred, there would have been no preferred dividends, but an additional 30,000 common shares would have been outstanding for the entire year. We calculate fully diluted EPS by adding back the preferred dividends on the convertible stock to the $180,000 earnings available for common stock and adding 30,000 shares to the denominator.

$$\text{Fully diluted EPS} = \frac{\$180,000 + \$20,000}{80,000 + 30,000} = \frac{\$200,000}{110,000} = \$1.82$$

Price-Earnings Ratio (PE)

The PE ratio is the ratio of the market price of a share of common stock to its earnings per share. The ratio indicates the amount an investor is paying to buy a dollar of earnings. PE ratios of high-growth companies are often very high, while those of low-growth or declining firms tend to be low. Assume that Graham's common stock sold at $60 per share at the end of 19X5 and $70 at the end of 19X6. The PE ratios are

$$\frac{\text{Price-}}{\text{earnings}} = \frac{\text{market price per share}}{\text{earnings per share}}$$
$$\text{ratio}$$

$$19\text{X}5 \quad \frac{\$60.00}{\$4.31} = 14$$

$$19\text{X}6 \quad \frac{\$70.00}{\$4.69} = 14.9$$

[1] The computation of EPS is governed by *Accounting Principles Board Opinion No. 15* (New York: American Institute of Certified Public Accountants, 1969) and *Unofficial Accounting Interpretations of APB Opinion No. 15* (New York: American Institute of Certified Public Accountants, 1970). Together, these two documents contain about 100 pages.

[2] Under certain circumstances, some convertible securities are included in the computation of primary EPS.

The PE ratio increased from 19X5 to 19X6. This could have happened because EPS had been growing rather slowly until 19X6 and investors believed the rate would increase in the future. Such a situation justifies a higher PE ratio. It is also possible that PE ratios for most firms increased because of good economic news and expectations of good business conditions.

Dividend Yield and Payout Ratio

We have been viewing earnings available for common stockholders as the major return accruing to owners of common stock. However, investors do not "get" EPS. They receive dividends and, they hope, increases in the market value of their shares. The **dividend yield** is a measure of the current cash income that an investor can obtain per dollar of investment.

$$\text{Dividend yield} = \frac{\text{dividend per share}}{\text{market price per share}}$$

Graham declared and paid dividends of $63,000 in 19X5 and $73,200 in 19X6 on 22,000 shares, giving dividends per share of $2.86 and $3.33 for 19X5 and 19X6, respectively. Given per-share market prices of $60 and $70 at the ends of 19X5 and 19X6, dividend yields are

$$19X5 \quad \frac{\$2.86}{\$60} = 4.77\%$$

$$19X6 \quad \frac{\$3.33}{\$70} = 4.76\%$$

The **payout ratio** is the ratio of dividends per share to earnings per share. For Graham, the payout ratio in 19X6 is 71% ($3.33/$4.69) and in 19X5 was 66% ($2.86/$4.31). In general, companies with high growth rates have relatively low dividend yields and payout ratios. Such companies are investing the cash that could be used for dividends. Investors who favor high-growth companies are not looking for dividends so much as increases in the market price of the common stock. Because such hoped-for increases may or may not occur, investing in high-growth companies is generally riskier than investing in companies that pay relatively high, stable dividends.

SOLVENCY

Solvency refers to long-term safety, to the likelihood that the firm will be able to pay its long-term liabilities. It is similar to liquidity but has a much longer time horizon. Both long-term creditors and stockholders are interested in solvency—the long-term creditors, because of a concern about receiving interest payments and a return of principal; the stockholders, because they cannot receive dividends and benefit from increased market prices unless the firm survives.

Debt Ratio

One common measure of solvency is the debt ratio, which is calculated as follows.

$$\text{Debt ratio} = \frac{\text{total liabilities}}{\text{total assets}}$$

This ratio measures the proportion of debt in the firm's capital structure. It is also called the *debt-to-assets ratio*. As with some other ratios, variations provide much the same information. For example, some analysts calculate a debt-to-equity ratio, dividing total liabilities by stockholders' equity; others calculate a ratio of long-term liabilities to total assets or of long-term liabilities to fixed assets, such as property, plant, and equipment. The basic objective is the same with all of these ratios: to determine the firm's degree of debt. The higher the proportion of debt in the capital structure, the riskier the firm. Firms in different industries can handle different percentages of debt. For example, public utilities typically have very high percentages of debt, manufacturing firms somewhat less.

The debt ratios for Graham Company for 19X5 and 19X6 are

$$19X5 \quad \frac{\$610,000}{\$1,380,000} = 44.2\%$$

$$19X6 \quad \frac{\$750,000}{\$1,550,000} = 48.4\%$$

Notice that if we subtract the debt ratio from 1, we get the proportion of stockholders' equity in the capital structure. This is usually called the *equity ratio*. Like the debt ratio, it is a way of measuring solvency, but from a different standpoint.

Graham's debt ratio increased from 19X5 to 19X6, but we cannot tell whether it is near a dangerous level without knowing a good deal more. We can obtain some additional information by calculating the burden that interest expense places on the firm.

Times Interest Earned

Times interest earned, or interest coverage, measures the extent to which operations cover interest expense. The higher the ratio, the more likely the firm will be able to continue meeting the interest payments.

$$\text{Times interest earned} = \frac{\text{income before interest and taxes}}{\text{interest expense}}$$

Graham had interest coverage of 4.8 times in 19X5, but slipped to 4.6 times in 19X7.

$$19X5 \quad \frac{\$200,000}{\$42,000} = 4.8 \text{ times}$$

$$19X6 \quad \frac{\$220,000}{\$48,000} = 4.6 \text{ times}$$

We use income before interest and taxes because interest is a tax-deductible expense. Some analysts also add depreciation in the numerator. Reasoning that depreciation does not require cash payments, these analysts believe that the numerator in their ratio approximates the total amount of cash available to pay interest.

Cash Flow to Total Debt

A major study of ratios computed for actual companies showed that the single best ratio for predicting a firm's failure was the ratio of cash flow to total debt.[3] In that study, cash flow was defined as net income plus depreciation, amortization, and depletion, and total debt was defined as total liabilities plus preferred stock.

$$\frac{\text{Cash flow to}}{\text{total debt}} = \frac{\text{net income + depreciation + amortization + depletion}}{\text{total liabilities + preferred stock}}$$

Graham has no amortization or depletion and no preferred stock. Therefore, the values of the ratio are

$$19X5 \quad \frac{\$94,800 + \$75,000}{\$610,000} = \frac{\$169,800}{\$610,000} = 27.8\%$$

$$19X6 \quad \frac{\$103,200 + \$90,000}{\$750,000} = \frac{\$193,200}{\$750,000} = 25.8\%$$

The research study drawing attention to this ratio was conducted before companies were required to provide a cash flow statement as part of the financial-statement package. Using the operating cash flow taken directly from Graham's cash flow statement, the ratios are

$$19X5 \quad \frac{\$177,600}{\$610,000} = 29.1\%$$

$$19X6 \quad \frac{\$203,200}{\$750,000} = 27.1\%$$

Though both versions of this solvency ratio show a decline, the decline does not seem serious. Nevertheless, comparison of the ratio with the industry average might indicate a potential problem.

RATIOS AND EVALUATION

Calculating ratios for the current year is only the starting point in analyzing a firm's operations and prospects. Comparisons are critical and many factors besides the magnitudes of the ratios must be considered.

[3] See William H. Beaver, "Financial Ratios as Predictors of Failure," Empirical Research in Accounting, Selected Studies, 1966, *Journal of Accounting Research*, 1967, 71–111.

The firm's ratios should be compared with those from prior years, trends must be evaluated, and interrelated ratios explored. (Is the company becoming more or less liquid? More or less profitable? Were changes in sales and ROA consistent with changes in turnovers of receivables and inventory?) Whenever possible, ratios should also be compared with those of similar firms and with those for the industry as a whole. (Are the firm's ratios consistent with, and moving in the same direction as, those for the industry? Are out-of-line ratios or trends explainable?)

Several factors make both interfirm and industry comparisons difficult. Comparisons become more difficult as more and more companies diversify their operations. Some highly diversified companies operate in 15 or more different industries. A welcome trend in financial reporting is increased public disclosure of data about the major segments that make up diversified companies. Such additional disclosure allows analysts to make comparisons that were not possible when only overall results were available.

Even comparisons with fairly similar companies must be made with care because ratios can differ considerably when companies use different accounting methods. For example, differences in the accounting methods used to value inventory (e.g. FIFO and LIFO) can influence many ratios. If purchase prices have generally been rising, a LIFO firm will show a lower inventory, current ratio, ROS, and EPS, and a higher inventory turnover than a FIFO firm. The longer the price trend has continued and the longer the firm has used LIFO, the more marked the effects of the difference in inventory method. Consider too the effects of different depreciation methods on ratios. A firm using the sum-of-the-years'-digits method will show lower book values for its fixed assets than one using the straight-line method; and the differences will affect all ratios involving total assets, net income, or both.

Until 1977, profitability measures were significantly influenced by whether a firm acquired the use of fixed assets by issuing long-term debt or stock or by arranging long-term leases. To a great extent, the effects of this particular difference in financing arrangements were eliminated by the issuance of *Financial Accounting Standard No. 13*,[4] but some differences still remain.

Even comparisons among similar companies using similar accounting methods can be misleading in the sense that a firm that shows up better than another in several measures of liquidity, profitability, or solvency might not be more successful, better, or stronger than another. For example, a company might be *too* liquid. Too much cash is not as bad as too little cash, but having excessive cash is unwise, because cash does not earn profits unless it is used for something. Faster turnover of inventory could be the result of unnecessarily low selling prices. A shorter collection period on receivables could result from highly restrictive credit policies. Hence, turnovers must be studied in relation to ROS and gross profit ratios, and to trends in the industry. In short, no single ratio, or group of ratios, should be considered in a vacuum.

---

[4] Financial Accounting Standards Board, *Statement of Financial Accounting Standards No. 13, Accounting for Leases* (Stamford, Connecticut: Financial Accounting Standards Board, 1976).

Another factor to consider in evaluating a firm is the extent to which one or more ratios can be affected by a single transaction. For example, consider the effect of a large cash payment for a current liability. Such a payment reduces both cash and current liabilities, and has no effect on total working capital. Yet it can improve the current ratio. To illustrate, look at the ratios for Graham Company at the end of 19X6 and assume that it paid current liabilities of $30,000 just before the end of the year. Its current assets before the payment would have been $480,000 ($450,000 + $30,000), and its current liabilities would have been $180,000 ($150,000 + $30,000), giving a current ratio of 2.67 to 1. This ratio is lower than the 3 to 1 we calculated earlier. Before the payment the acid-test ratio would have been 1.6 to 1 [($80,000 + $180,000 + $30,000)/($150,000 + $30,000)]. This is also lower than the ratio calculated earlier (1.73 to 1). Actions taken to improve ratios are called **window dressing.** This particular type of window dressing is possible if the current ratio and acid-test ratio are greater than 1 to 1. If those ratios are less than 1 to 1, paying a current liability will reduce them, but window dressing is then possible by delaying payments of current liabilities.

Any evaluation based on ratios and comparisons of them must recognize the relative importance of the ratio to the particular industry. The nature of the product and of the production process, the degree of competition in the industry, and many other industry-related factors are relevant in interpreting a particular firm's liquidity, profitability, and solvency ratios. For example, consider the utility industry. Because a utility is a monopoly, the government unit granting the monopoly right also regulates many of the utility's actions. In most cases, the regulating authority both ensures and limits the profitability of the utility. Liquidity problems are unlikely for a utility because their cash flows are relatively stable, they need not build up inventories in advance because they sell a service, and because their uncollectible accounts are limited by the ability to close off a necessary service. For the same reasons, the investing public tolerates a more leverage and a lower, but more stable, level of profitability in a utility.

All of the preceding considerations point out the need for understanding (1) the company being analyzed and (2) the industry in which the company operates. That a company's ratios differ from those in the past, or are in line or out of line with those of other companies in the industry, is not, *per se,* good or bad. (Knowing that, between 1980 and 1982, Chrysler Corporation improved its liquidity, profitability, and prospects for solvency, in relation to both its prior performance and to the average for the industry, does not change the fact that the entire industry performed poorly during that period.)

SUMMARY

Σ

Ratio analysis is used in making investment decisions. Analysts are concerned with trends in ratios and with whether a firm's ratios are in line with those of other firms in the same industry. Ratios can be classified into three major types: liquidity, profitability, and solvency.

Which ratios to use and which to emphasize depend on the type of decision to be made. Short-term creditors are primarily concerned with liquidity. Long-term creditors are concerned more with solvency than with liquidity and profitability, but the latter aspects are still important. Current and potential common stockholders are most concerned with profitability, but liquidity and solvency are still significant.

Ratio analysis must be used with care. Ratios provide information only in the context of a comparison. Comparisons must be made with other firms and with norms for the industry. Different accounting methods, such as LIFO and FIFO, sum-of-the-years'-digits depreciation and straight-line depreciation, can cause similar firms to show quite different ratios.

KEY TERMS

common size statements
composition problem
convertible securities
dilution (of earnings per share)
leverage
liquidity

quick assets
return on investment
solvency
window dressing
working capital

KEY FORMULAS

Liquidity Ratios

$$\text{Current ratio} = \frac{\text{current assets}}{\text{current liabilities}}$$

$$\text{Quick ratio (acid-test ratio)} = \frac{\text{cash} + \text{marketable securities} + \text{receivables}}{\text{current liabilities}}$$

$$\text{Accounts receivable turnover} = \frac{\text{credit sales}}{\text{average accounts receivable}}$$

$$\text{Days' sales in accounts receivable} = \frac{\text{ending accounts receivable}}{\text{average daily credit sales}}$$

$$\text{Inventory turnover} = \frac{\text{cost of goods sold}}{\text{average inventory}}$$

$$\text{Days' sales in inventory} = \frac{\text{ending inventory}}{\text{average daily cost of goods sold}}$$

$$\text{Inventory turnover (raw materials)} = \frac{\text{raw materials used in production}}{\text{average raw materials inventory}}$$

$$\text{Days' purchases in accounts payable} = \frac{\text{ending accounts payable}}{\text{average daily purchases}}$$

Profitability Ratios

$$\text{Return on assets (ROA)} = \frac{\text{net income} + \text{interest} + \text{income taxes}}{\text{average total assets}}$$

$$\text{Return on common equity (ROE)} = \frac{\text{net income}}{\text{average common stockholders' equity}}$$

$$\text{Earnings per share (EPS)} = \frac{\text{net income} - \text{preferred stock dividends}}{\text{weighted-average common shares outstanding}}$$

$$\text{Price-earnings ratio (PE)} = \frac{\text{market price per share}}{\text{earnings per share}}$$

$$\text{Dividend yield} = \frac{\text{dividend per share}}{\text{market price per share}}$$

$$\text{Gross profit ratio} = \frac{\text{gross profit}}{\text{sales}}$$

$$\text{Return on sales (ROS)} = \frac{\text{net income}}{\text{sales}}$$

$$\text{Payout ratio} = \frac{\text{dividends per share}}{\text{earnings per share}}$$

Solvency Ratios

$$\text{Debt ratio} = \frac{\text{total liabilities}}{\text{total assets}}$$

$$\text{Times interest earned} = \frac{\text{income before interest and taxes}}{\text{interest expense}}$$

$$\text{Cash flow to debt} = \frac{\text{net income} + \text{depreciation} + \text{amortization} + \text{depletion}}{\text{total liabilities} + \text{preferred stock}}$$

REVIEW PROBLEM

Financial statements for Quinn Company are given below.

Quinn Company, Balance Sheets as of December 31

Assets	19X7	19X6
Cash	$ 180,000	$ 200,000
Accounts receivable, net	850,000	830,000
Inventory	620,000	560,000
Total current assets	1,650,000	1,590,000
Plant and equipment	7,540,000	6,650,000
Accumulated depreciation	(1,920,000)	(1,500,000)
Total assets	$7,270,000	$6,740,000
Equities		
Accounts payable	$ 220,000	$ 190,000
Accrued expenses	450,000	440,000
Total current liabilities	670,000	630,000
Long-term debt	1,000,000	950,000
Total liabilities	1,670,000	1,580,000
Common stock, no par value	4,000,000	4,000,000
Retained earnings	1,600,000	1,160,000
Total equities	$7,270,000	$6,740,000

Quinn Company, Income Statement for 19X7

Sales		$8,650,000
Cost of goods sold		4,825,000
Gross profit		3,825,000
Operating expenses:		
Depreciation	$ 420,000	
Other operating expenses	2,135,000	2,555,000
Income before interest and taxes		1,270,000
Interest expense		70,000
Income before taxes		1,200,000
Income taxes at 30% rate		360,000
Net income		$ 840,000

Quinn Company, Cash Flow Statement for 19X7

Net cash flow from operating activities:		
Collections from customers		$8,630,000
Payments to suppliers		(4,855,000)
Payments for operating expenses		(2,163,000)
Interest paid		(72,000)
Taxes paid		(320,000)
Net cash provided by operating activities		1,220,000
Cash flows for investing activities–purchase		
of plant and equipment		(890,000)
Cash flows from (for) financing activities:		
Payment of dividends	($400,000)	
Proceeds from new long-term debt issue	50,000	
Net cash from (for) financing activities		(350,000)
Change in cash (decrease)		(20,000)
Cash balance, beginning of year		200,000
Cash balance, end of year		$ 180,000

There were 200,000 shares of common stock outstanding throughout the year. The market price of the stock at year end was $65. All sales are on credit.

Required: Compute the following ratios as of the end of 19X7 or for the year ended December 31, 19X7, whichever is appropriate.
1. Current ratio.
2. Quick ratio.
3. Accounts receivable turnover.
4. Days' credit sales in accounts receivable.
5. Inventory turnover.
6. Days' sales in inventory.
7. Days' purchases in accounts payable.
8. Gross profit ratio.

9. Return on sales (ROS).
10. Return on assets (ROA).
11. Return on equity (ROE).
12. Earnings per share (EPS).
13. Price-earnings ratio (PE).
14. Dividend yield.
15. Payout ratio.
16. Debt ratio.
17. Times interest earned.
18. Cash flow to debt ratio.

Answers to Review Problem

1. Current ratio

$$\frac{\$1,650,000}{\$670,000} = 2.46 \text{ to } 1$$

2. Quick ratio

$$\frac{\$180,000 + \$850,000}{\$670,000} = 1.54 \text{ to } 1$$

3. Accounts receivable turnover

$$\frac{\$8,650,000}{(\$850,000 + \$830,000)/2} = 10.3 \text{ times}$$

4. Days' sales in accounts receivable

$$\frac{\$850,000}{\$8,650,000/365} = 36 \text{ days}$$

5. Inventory turnover

$$\frac{\$4,825,000}{(\$620,000 + \$560,000)/2} = 8.2 \text{ times}$$

6. Days' sales in inventory

$$\frac{\$620,000}{\$4,825,000/365} = 47 \text{ days}$$

7. Days' purchases in accounts payable

$$\frac{\$220,000}{(\$4,825,000 + \$620,000 - \$560,000)/365} = 16.4 \text{ days}$$

8. Gross profit ratio

$$\frac{\$3,825,000}{\$8,650,000} = 44.2\%$$

9. ROS

$$\frac{\$840,000}{\$8,650,000} = 9.7\%$$

10. ROA

$$\frac{\$840,000 + \$70,000 + \$360,000}{(\$7,270,000 + \$6,740,000)/2} = 18.1\%$$

11. ROE

$$\frac{\$840,000}{(\$5,600,000 + \$5,160,000)/2} = 15.6\%$$

12. EPS

$$\frac{\$840,000}{200,000} = \$4.20$$

13. PE ratio

$$\frac{\$65}{\$4.20} = 15.5 \text{ times}$$

14. Dividend yield

$$\frac{\$2}{\$65} = 3.1\%$$

15. Payout ratio

$$\frac{\$2}{\$4.20} = 47.6\%$$

16. Debt ratio

$$\frac{\$1,670,000}{\$7,270,000} = 23.0\%$$

17. Times interest earned

$$\frac{\$1,270,000}{\$70,000} = 18 \text{ times}$$

18. Cash flow to debt ratio

$$\frac{\$840,000 + \$420,000}{\$1,670,000} = 75.5\%$$

ASSIGNMENT MATERIAL

Questions for Discussion

18-1 **Dividend yield** Your friend bought stock in NMC Corporation five years ago for $20 per share. NMC is now paying a $5 dividend per share and the stock sells for $100. He says that the 25% dividend yield is an excellent return. How did he calculate the dividend yield? Is he correct?

18-2 ***Ratios and accounting methods***   LIFO Company uses the last-in-first-out method of inventory determination; FIFO Company uses first-in-first-out. They have virtually identical operations, physical quantities of inventory, sales, and fixed assets. What differences would you expect to find in ratios of the firms?

18-3 ***Ratios and operating decisions***   Bronson Company and Corman Company are in the same industry and have virtually identical operations. The only difference between them is that Bronson rents 60% of its plant and equipment on short-term leases, while Corman owns all of its fixed assets. Corman has long-term debt of 60% of the book value of its fixed assets. Bronson has none. The two firms show the same net income because Bronson's rent and depreciation are the same as Corman's depreciation and interest. What differences would you expect to find in the ratios of the two firms?

18-4 ***Ratios and accounting methods***   SYD Company uses sum-of-the-years'-digits depreciation. SL Company uses straight-line depreciation. Both firms have the same original cost of fixed assets. Their operations are also about the same. They are both growing rapidly, in sales, profits, and assets. What differences would you expect to find between the ratios of the two firms?

18-5 ***Liquidity***   You are the chief loan officer of a medium-sized bank. Two firms have applied for short-term loans, but you can only grant one because of limited funds. Both firms have the same working capital and the same current ratio. They are in the same industry and their current ratios are well above the industry average. What additional information about their current positions would you seek?

18-6 ***Seasonality and ratios***   The following independent questions deal with seasonality in ratio analysis.
1. The inventory turnover of Robertson Toy Store, which does about half of its business in November and December, was computed at 22 times, based on the average of the beginning and ending inventories. The firm's fiscal year ends January 31. Does the turnover figure reflect the firm's activity?
2. The president of Skimpy Bathing Suit Company was bragging that his current ratio was 5 to 1 and his acid-test ratio 4 to 1. The ratios were computed on October 31. Do you expect the firm to have such ratios throughout the year?
3. The accounts receivable turnover for Long Golf Ball Company, which sells golf balls only in the northeastern United States, was only 2 times. The computation was based on the receivables at June 30, 19X7, and June 30, 19X8. Does the firm seem to have problems collecting its accounts?

18-7 ***Price-earnings ratio***   Your friend says that his investment strategy is simple. He buys stocks with very low PE ratios. He reasons that he is getting the most for his money that way. Do you agree that this is a good strategy?

18-8 ***Relevance of ratios to industry*** The annual report of GTE (General Telephone and Electronics) Corporation for 1982 contained the normal complement of financial statements. The major sections and amounts in its balance sheet follow (listed in the order, and with the same major headings, as in the statement).

| | December 31 | |
| | 1982 | 1981 |
Assets	(in millions of dollars)	
Property, plant, and equipment	$18,236	$16,927
Investments and other assets	561	506
Current assets	3,497	3,532
Totals	$22,294	$20,965
Shareholders' Equity and Liabilities		
Shareholders' equity	$ 5,816	$ 5,071
Minority interests in equity of subsidiaries	597	592
Preferred stock	744	701
Long-term debt	8,304	7,979
Reserves and deferred credits	3,251	2,912
Current liabilities	3,582	3,710
Totals	$22,294	$20,965

Required: Discuss the relevance of the three ratio groups to the analysis of a firm such as GTE.

18-9 ***Ratio variations*** The Financial Highlights section of the 1986 annual report of Motorola Inc. includes the values of the following ratios for 1985 and 1986.
(1) Return on average invested capital (stockholders' equity) plus long-term and short-term debt, net of marketable securities.
(2) Percent of total debt less marketable securities to total debt less marketable securities plus equity.
To which of the three general categories of ratios does each of these ratios belong? How would you explain why the components of these ratios differ from those given in the chapter?

Exercises

18-10 ***Effects of transactions*** Indicate the effects of each of the following transactions on the firm's (a) current ratio and (b) acid-test ratio. There are three possible answers: (+) increase, (−) decrease, and (0) no effect. Before each transaction takes place, both ratios are greater than 1 to 1.

Transaction	Effects on	
	(a) Current Ratio	(b) Acid-Test Ratio
Example: Purchase inventory for cash	0	—
1. Purchase inventory on account	——	——
2. Pay a current account payable	——	——
3. Borrow cash on a short-term loan	——	——
4. Sell, at a loss, marketable securities held as a temporary investment	——	——
5. Borrow cash on a long-term loan	——	——
6. Collect an account receivable	——	——
7. Record accrued expenses payable	——	——
8. Sell a plant asset for cash at a profit	——	——
9. Sell a plant asset for cash at a loss	——	——
10. Buy marketable securities, for cash, for a short-term investment	——	——
11. Purchase inventory for cash	——	——

18-11 Relationships Answer the questions for each of the following independent situations.

1. The current ratio is 2.5 to 1. Current liabilities are $120,000. What are current assets?
2. ROA is 18%; ROE is 20%. There is no preferred stock. Net income is $2 million, and average total assets are $16 million. What is average total stockholders' equity?
3. The current ratio is 3 to 1; the acid-test ratio is 1.8 to 1; and cash and receivables are $360,000. The only current assets are cash, receivables, and inventory.
   (a) What are current liabilities?
   (b) What is inventory?
4. Accounts receivable turnover is 6 times; inventory turnover is 5 times. Both accounts receivable and inventory have remained constant for several years. All sales are on credit. On January 1, 19X8, the firm bought inventory.
   (a) On the average, how long will it be before the new inventory is sold?
   (b) On the average, how long after the inventory is sold will cash be collected?
5. A firm had current assets of $200,000. It then paid a current liability of $40,000. After the payment, the current ratio was 2 to 1. What were current liabilities before the payment was made?
6. A firm normally has accounts receivable equal to 35 days' credit sales. During the coming year it expects credit sales of $730,000 spread evenly over the year. What should its accounts receivable be at the end of the year?

18-12 Leverage Balance Company is considering the retirement of $600,000 in 10% bonds payable. These bonds are the company's only interest-bearing debt. The retirement plan calls for the firm to issue 20,000 shares of common stock at a total price of $600,000 and use the proceeds to buy back the bonds. Stockholders' equity is now $1,000,000, with 25,000 shares of common stock outstanding (no preferred stock). The firm expects to earn $300,000 before interest and taxes in the coming year. The tax rate is 40%.

Required
1. Determine net income, EPS, and ROE for the coming year, assuming that the bonds are retired before the beginning of the coming year. Assume no change in stockholders' equity except for the new stock issue.
2. Determine net income, EPS, and ROE for the coming year, assuming that the bonds are not retired. Again, assume that year-end stockholders' equity will be the same as at the beginning of the year.
3. Is the proposed retirement wise? Why or why not?

18-13 **Return on assets and return on equity** Travis Toys, Inc., has annual sales of $22 million, and ROS of 6%. Interest expense is $0.8 million; total assets are $16 million; and the debt ratio is 60%. There is no preferred stock. Ignore taxes.

Required
1. Determine income, ROA, and ROE.
2. Suppose the firm could increase its ROS to 6.5% and keep the same level of sales. What would net income, ROA, and ROE be?
3. Suppose that Travis reduced its debt ratio to 40% by retiring debt. New common stock was issued to finance the retirement, keeping total assets at $16 million. Net income is $1.72 million because of lower interest expense that now totals $0.40 million. What are ROA and ROE?

18-14 **Financing alternatives** The founders of Marmex Company are trying to decide how to finance the firm. They have three choices:
1. Issue $2,000,000 in common stock.
2. Issue $1,200,000 in common stock and $800,000 in 10% bonds.
3. Issue $1,200,000 in common stock and $800,000 in 12% preferred stock.
Income before interest and taxes is expected to be $500,000. The tax rate is 40%.

Required
1. Compute net income, earnings available for common stock, and ROE for each financing choice.
2. Suppose that the tax rate increases to 60%. Redo item 1. Can you draw any conclusions about the effects of tax rates on the relative desirability of the three choices?

18-15 **Effects of transactions** Indicate the effects of each of the following transactions on the firm's (a) receivables turnover; (b) inventory turnover; (c) gross profit ratio. The possible answers are (+) increase, (−) decrease, and (0) no effect. Before each transaction takes place, the ratios are as follows: (a) receivable turnover of 8 times; (b) inventory turnover of 6 times; (c) gross profit ratio of 25%.

	Effects on		
	(a)	(b)	(c)
	Receivables	Inventory	Gross Profit
Transaction	Turnover	Turnover	Ratio
1. Purchase inventory on account	——	——	——
2. Sell merchandise, for cash, at the normal price	——	——	——
3. Sell a plant asset, at a profit, for some cash and a short-term note	——	——	——
4. Sell merchandise, on account, at a bargain (lower than normal) price	——	——	——
5. Receive merchandise returned by a customer for credit	——	——	——

18-16 *Return on assets and equity* Randolph Company has average total assets of $4,000,000 and a debt ratio of 30%. Interest expense is $120,000, and return on average total assets is 12%. The firm has no preferred stock. Ignore taxes.

Required
1. Determine income, average stockholders' equity, and ROE.
2. Suppose that sales have been $3,600,000 annually and are expected to continue at this level. If the firm could increase its ROS by one percentage point, what would be its income, ROA, and ROE?
3. Refer to the original data and your answers to item 1. Suppose that Randolph retires $600,000 in debt and therefore saves interest expense of $60,000 annually. The firm would issue additional common stock in the amount of $600,000 to finance the retirement. Total assets would remain at $4,000,000. What would be the income, ROA, and ROE?

18-17 *Effects of transactions – returns ratios* Indicate the effects of each of the following transactions on the firm's (a) ROS, (b) ROA, and (c) EPS. There are three possible answers: (+) increase, (−) decrease, and (0) no effect. Before each transaction takes place, the ratios are as follows: (a) ROS, 10%; (b) ROA, 5%; (c) EPS, $0.25.

	Effects on		
	(a)	(b)	(c)
	ROS	ROA	EPS
1. Sell a plant asset for cash, at twice the asset's book value	——	——	——
2. Declare and issue a stock dividend	——	——	——
3. Purchase inventory on account	——	——	——
4. Purchase treasury stock for cash	——	——	——
5. Acquire land by issuing common stock	——	——	——

18-18 *Ratios* The financial statements for Massin Company, a merchandising firm, appear opposite. The company has 200,000 common shares outstanding. The price of the stock is $21. Dividends of $0.80 per share were declared. The balance sheet at the end of 19X5 showed approximately the same amounts as that at the end of 19X6.

Massin Company, Income Statement for 19X6 (in thousands of dollars)

Sales		$3,200
Cost of goods sold		1,400
Gross profit		1,800
Operating expenses:		
Depreciation	$ 240	
Other	1,060	1,300
Income before interest and taxes		500
Interest expense		60
Income before taxes		440
Income taxes at 40% rate		176
Net income		$ 264

Massin Company, Balance Sheet as of December 31, 19X6 (in thousands of dollars)

Assets			Equities	
Cash		$ 200	Accounts payable	$ 210
Accounts receivable		400	Accrued expenses	280
Inventory		350		
Total current assets		950	Total current liabilities	490
Plant and equipment	$3,200		Long-term debt	680
Accumulated			Common stock	920
depreciation	1,200	2,000	Retained earnings	860
Total assets		$2,950	Total equities	$2,950

Required: Calculate the following ratios.
1. Current ratio.
2. Acid-test ratio.
3. Accounts receivable turnover.
4. Inventory turnover.
5. Days' purchases in accounts payable.
6. Gross profit ratio.
7. ROS.
8. ROA.
9. ROE.
10. EPS.
11. PE ratio.
12. Dividend yield.
13. Payout ratio.
14. Debt ratio.
15. Times interest earned.
16. Cash flow to debt.

Problems

18-19 Analyzing ROE (adapted from a paper by Professor William E. Ferrara) Chapter 11 introduced the idea of separating the components of ROI as follows.

$$\text{ROI} = \frac{\text{net income}}{\text{sales}} \times \frac{\text{sales}}{\text{investment}}$$

Applying this separation to the calculation of return on stockholders' equity, we could express ROE as

$$\text{ROE} = \frac{\text{net income}}{\text{sales}} \times \frac{\text{sales}}{\text{stockholders' equity}}$$

This separation is less enlightening than it might be, however, because net income combines the effects of financing choices (leverage) with the operating results. Letting total assets/stockholders' equity stand as a measure of financial leverage, we can also express return on stockholders' equity as follows.

$$\text{ROE} = \frac{\text{net income}}{\text{sales}} \times \frac{\text{sales}}{\text{total assets}} \times \frac{\text{total assets}}{\text{stockholders' equity}}$$

Sales and total assets cancel out, leaving the ratio net income/stockholders' equity. The three-factor expression allows the analyst to look at operations (margin × turnover, the first two terms) separately from financing (the last term).

The separation is not perfect because interest (financing expense) is included in calculating net income, but the expansion is adequate for many purposes. Thus, the product of the first two terms is a measure of operating efficiency, while the third is a measure of leverage and therefore of financial risk.

The following data summarize results for three companies.

Company Results (in thousands of dollars)			
	A	B	C
Sales	$4,500	$6,000	$5,000
Net income	$ 450	$ 400	$ 480
Total assets	$4,500	$4,500	$4,400
Stockholders' equity	$3,000	$2,000	$4,000
ROE	15%	20%	12%

Required: Calculate ROE for each company using the three-factor expression and comment on the results. You should be able to draw tentative conclusions about the relative operating and financing results of the companies.

18-20 Current asset activity The treasurer of Billingsgate Company has asked for your assistance in analyzing the firm's liquidity. She provides the following data.

	19X6	19X5	19X4
Total sales (all credit)	$480,000	$440,000	$395,000
Cost of goods sold	320,000	290,000	245,000
Accounts receivable at year end	64,000	48,000	31,000
Inventory at year end	50,000	44,000	38,000
Accounts payable at year end	37,000	29,000	28,000

Required
1. Compute accounts receivable turnover for 19X5 and 19X6.
2. Compute days' credit sales in accounts receivable at the ends of 19X5 and 19X6.
3. Compute inventory turnover for 19X5 and 19X6.
4. Compute days' sales in inventory at the end of 19X5 and 19X6.
5. Compute days' purchases in accounts payable at the ends of 19X5 and 19X6.
6. Comment on the trends in the ratios. Do the trends seem to be favorable or unfavorable?

18-21 Constructing financial statements from ratios The following information is available concerning the Warnock Company's expected results in 19X7 (in thousands of dollars). Turnovers are based on year-end values.

Required: Fill in the blanks.

Return on sales	8%
Gross profit percentage	30%
Inventory turnover	4 times
Receivables turnover	5 times
Current ratio	3 to 1
Ratio of total debt to total assets	40%

Condensed Income Statement

Sales	$800
Cost of sales	____
Gross profit	____
Operating expenses	____
Net income	$____

Condensed Balance Sheet

Cash	$ 30	Current liabilities	$____
Receivables	____	Long-term debt	
Inventory	____	Stockholders' equity	600
Plant and equipment			
Total	$____	Total	$____

18-22 **Effects of transactions on ratios** Indicate the effects of each of the following transactions on the firm's current ratio, acid-test ratio, and debt ratio. There are three possible answers: increase (+), decrease (−), and no effect (0). Before each transaction takes place, the current ratio is greater than 1 to 1 and the acid-test ratio is less than 1 to 1.

	Effects		
	Current Ratio	Acid-Test Ratio	Debt Ratio
Example: An account payable is paid.	+	−	−
1. Inventory is bought for cash.	——	——	——
2. A sale is made on account, with cost of sales being less than the selling price.	——	——	——
3. Long-term bonds are issued for cash.	——	——	——
4. Land is sold for cash at its book value.	——	——	——
5. Marketable securities being held as temporary investments are sold at a gain.	——	——	——
6. Common stock is issued in exchange for plant assets.	——	——	——
7. An account receivable is collected.	——	——	——
8. Long-term debt is issued for plant assets.	——	——	——
9. A dividend payable in cash is declared, but not paid.	——	——	——
10. The dividend in item 9 is paid.	——	——	——
11. A short-term bank loan is paid.	——	——	——
12. Depreciation expense is recorded.	——	——	——
13. Obsolete inventory is written off, with the debit to a loss account.	——	——	——

18-23 **Comparison of firms** Condensed financial statements for Amex Company and Corex Company appear below. Both companies are in the same industry and use the same accounting methods. Balance-sheet data for both companies were the same at the end of 19X4 as at the end of 19X5.

Balance Sheets, End of 19X5 (in thousands of dollars)

Assets	Amex Company	Corex Company
Cash	$ 185	$ 90
Accounts receivable	215	170
Inventory	340	220
Plant and equipment (net)	850	810
Total assets	$1,590	$1,290
Equities		
Accounts payable	$ 150	$ 140
Other current liabilities	80	90
Long-term debt	300	500
Common stock	700	300
Retained earnings	360	260
Total equities	$1,590	$1,290

Income Statements for 19X5

		Amex Company		Corex Company
Sales		$3,050		$2,800
Cost of goods sold		1,400		1,350
Gross profit		1,650		1,450
Operating expenses:				
Depreciation	$ 280		$240	
Other	1,040	1,320	900	1,140
Income before interest and taxes		330		310
Interest expense		30		55
Income before taxes		300		255
Income taxes at 40% rate		120		102
Net income		$ 180		$ 153
Earnings per share		$ 0.90		$ 0.77
Dividends per share		$ 0.40		$ 0.20
Market price of common stock		$12.00		$11.50

Required: On the basis of the data given, answer the following questions.
1. Which company seems to be more liquid?
2. Which company seems to be more profitable?
3. Which company seems to be more solvent?
4. Which stock seems to be a better buy?
Support your answers with whatever calculations you believe appropriate.

18-24 **Effects of transactions – selected ratios** In the following exhibit, several transactions or events are listed in the left-hand column and the names of various ratios and the value of that ratio before the associated transaction are listed in the right-hand column. Indicate the effect of the transaction on the specified ratio. There are three possible answers: (+) increase, (−) decrease, and (0) no effect.

Transaction	Effect on Ratio	Ratio of Concern
1. Write off an uncollectible account receivable	_____	Current ratio of 3 to 1
2. Sell merchandise, on account, at less than normal price	_____	42 days' sales in accounts receivable
3. Borrow cash on a short-term loan	_____	Acid-test ratio of 0.9 to 1
4. Write off an uncollectible account receivable	_____	Return on sales of 18%
5. Sell treasury stock at a price greater than its cost	_____	Return on equity of 20%
6. Acquire plant asset by issuance of long-term note	_____	Debt ratio of 40%
7. Record accrued salaries payable	_____	Times interest earned of 3.2
8. Record depreciation on plant assets	_____	Cash flow to debt ratio of 60%

Transaction	Effect on Ratio	Ratio of Concern
9. Return inventory items to supplier, for credit	——	Inventory turnover of 8 times
10. Acquire plant asset by issuance of common stock	——	Debt ratio of 60%

18-25 ***Construction of financial statements using ratios***   The following data are available for Wasserman Pharmaceutical Company as of December 31, 19X4, and for the year then ended.

Current ratio	3 to 1
Days' sales in accounts receivable	60 days
Inventory turnover	3 times
Debt ratio	40%
Current liabilities	$300,000
Stockholders' equity, all common stock	$1,200,000
Return on sales	8%
Return on common equity	15%
Gross profit ratio	40%

Wasserman has no preferred stock, no marketable securities, and no prepaid expenses. Beginning-of-year balance-sheet figures are the same as end-of-year figures. All sales are on credit and the only noncurrent assets are plant and equipment.

Required: Prepare a balance sheet as of December 31, 19X4, and an income statement for 19X4 in as much detail as you can with the available information. Round the calculation of average daily credit sales to the nearest dollar.

18-26 ***Dilution of EPS***   Boston Tarrier Company has been very successful in recent years, as shown by the income statement data given below. The treasurer of the firm is concerned because he expects holders of the firm's convertible preferred stock to exchange their shares for common shares early in the coming year. All of the company's preferred stock is convertible, and the number of common shares issuable on conversion is 300,000.

Boston Tarrier Company, Selected Income Statement Data

	19X6	19X5
Net income	$3,400,000	$2,600,000
Preferred stock dividends	800,000	800,000
Earnings available for common	$2,600,000	$1,800,000

Throughout 19X6 and 19X5 the firm had 500,000 shares of common stock outstanding.

Required
1. Compute primary EPS for 19X5 and 19X6.
2. Compute fully diluted EPS for 19X5 and 19X6.

18-27 *Inventory turnover and return on equity* Timmons Company is presently earning net income of $300,000 per year, which gives a 10% ROE. The president believes that inventory can be reduced with tighter controls on buying. Any reduction of inventory frees cash, which would be used to pay a dividend to stockholders. Thus, stockholders' equity would drop by the same amount as inventory.

Inventory turnover is 3 times per year. Cost of goods sold is running at $2,700,000 annually. The president hopes that turnover can be increased to 5 times. He also believes that sales, cost of goods sold, and net income will remain at their current levels.

Required

1. Determine the average inventory that the firm currently holds.
2. Determine the average inventory that would be held if turnover could be increased to 5 times per year.
3. Determine ROE if Timmons can increase turnover and reduce stockholders' equity by the amount of the reduction in investment in inventory.

18-28 *Ratios – industry averages* The president of Brewster Company has been concerned about its operating performance and financial strength. She has obtained, from a trade association, the averages of certain ratios for the industry. She gives you these ratios and the most recent financial statements of the firm. The balance-sheet amounts were all about the same at the beginning of the year as they are now.

Brewster Company, Balance Sheet as of December 31, 19X6 (in thousands of dollars)

Assets		Equities	
Cash	$ 860	Accounts payable	$ 975
Accounts receivable	3,210	Accrued expenses	120
Inventory	2,840	Taxes payable	468
Total current assets	6,910	Total current liabilities	1,563
Plant and equipment (net)	7,090	Bonds payable, due 19X9	6,300
		Common stock, no par	4,287
		Retained earnings	1,850
Total assets	$14,000	Total equities	$14,000

Brewster Company, Income Statement for 19X6

Sales	$11,800
Cost of goods sold	7,350
Gross profit	4,450
Operating expenses, including $650 depreciation	2,110
Operating profit	2,340
Interest expense	485
Income before taxes	1,855
Income taxes at 40% rate	742
Net income	$ 1,113

Brewster has 95,000 shares of common stock outstanding, which gives earnings per share of $11.72 ($1,113,000/95,000). Dividends are $5 per share and the market price of the stock is $120. Average ratios for the industry are

Current ratio	3.8 to 1	Return on equity	17.5%
Quick ratio	1.9 to 1	Price-earnings ratio	12.3
Accounts receivable turnover	4.8 times	Dividend yield	3.9%
Inventory turnover	3.6 times	Payout ratio	38.0%
Return on sales	7.6%	Debt ratio	50.0%
Return on assets	17.6%	Times interest earned	6 times
		Cash flow to debt	25.0%

Required

1. Compute the ratios shown above for Brewster Company.
2. Prepare comments to the president indicating areas of apparent strength and weakness for Brewster Company in relation to the industry.

18-29 Generation of cash flows Humbert Company must make a $600,000 payment on a bank loan at the end of March 19X9. At December 31, 19X8 Humbert had cash of $95,000 and accounts receivable of $355,000.

Estimated cash payments required during the first three months of 19X9, exclusive of the payment to the bank, are $315,000. Humbert expects sales to be $810,000 in the three-month period, all on credit. Accounts receivable are normally equal to 40 days' credit sales.

Required

1. Determine the expected balance in accounts receivable at the end of March 19X9. Assume that the three-month period has 90 days.
2. Determine whether the firm will have enough cash to pay the bank loan on March 31, 19X9.

18-30 Evaluation of trends and comparison with industry Comparative balance sheets and income statements for Marcus Manufacturing Company appear below. Your boss, the chief financial analyst for Hanmattan Bank, has asked you to analyze trends in the firm's operations and financing and to make some comparisons with the averages for the same industry. The bank is considering the purchase of some shares of Marcus for one of its trust funds.

Marcus Manufacturing Company Balance Sheets
as of December 31 (in thousands of dollars)

Assets	19X7	19X6
Cash	$ 170	$ 180
Accounts receivable	850	580
Inventory (finished goods)	900	760
Total current assets	1,920	1,520
Plant and equipment (net)	2,050	1,800
Total assets	$3,970	$3,320

Equities	19X7	19X6
Current liabilities	$ 812	$ 620
Long-term debt	1,640	1,300
Common stock	1,000	1,000
Retained earnings	518	400
Total equities	$3,970	$3,320

Marcus Manufacturing Company, Income Statements (in thousands of dollars)

	19X7	19X6
Sales, all on credit	$4,700	$4,350
Cost of goods sold	2,670	2,460
Gross profit	2,030	1,890
Operating expenses	1,470	1,440
Income before interest and taxes	560	450
Interest expense	130	100
Income before taxes	430	350
Income taxes at 40% rate	172	140
Net income	$ 258	$ 210
Earnings per share	$2.58	$2.10
Market price of stock at year end	$32	$28
Dividends per share	$0.96	$0.80

Selected data from the 19X5 balance sheet include the following.

Accounts receivable	$ 510
Inventory (finished goods)	620
Total assets	2,940
Stockholders' equity	1,320

The following are averages for Marcus's industry.

Current ratio	2.7 to 1	Receivable turnover	8.5 times
Quick ratio	1.4 to 1	Inventory turnover	4.2 times
Debt ratio	52%	Return on assets	15%
Price-earnings ratio	11.5	Return on equity	13.5%
Dividend yield	4.5%	Return on sales	5.0%
Payout ratio	48.0%		

Required: Compute the above ratios for Marcus for 19X6 and 19X7 and comment on the trends in the ratios and on relationships to industry averages.

18-31 **_Trends in ratios_** As the chief investment officer of a large pension fund, you must make many investing decisions. One of your assistants has prepared the following ratios for MBI Corporation, a large multinational manufacturer.

	Industry Average All Years	Year 19X7	19X6	19X5
Current ratio	2.4	2.6	2.4	2.5
Quick ratio	1.6	1.55	1.6	1.65
Receivable turnover	8.1	7.5	7.9	8.3
Inventory turnover	4.0	4.3	4.2	4.0
Debt ratio	43.0%	38.0%	41.3%	44.6%
Return on assets	17.8%	19.1%	19.4%	19.5%
Return on equity	15.3%	15.1%	15.6%	15.9%
Price-earnings ratio	14.3	13.5	13.3	13.4
Times interest earned	8.3	9.7	9.5	8.9
Earnings per share growth rate	8.4%	7.1%	6.9%	7.0%

Required: What is your decision in the following cases? Give your reasons.
1. Granting a short-term loan to MBI.
2. Buying long-term bonds of MBI on the open market. The bonds yield 7%, which is slightly less than the average for bonds in the industry.
3. Buying MBI common stock.

18-32 *Financial planning with ratios*   The treasurer of MaxiMart, Inc., a large chain of stores, has been trying to develop a financial plan. In conjunction with other managers, she has developed the following estimates, in millions of dollars.

	19X3	19X4	19X5	19X6
Sales	$100	$120	$150	$210
Fixed assets, net	80	95	110	125

In addition, for planning purposes she is willing to make the following estimates and assumptions about other results.

Cost of goods sold as a percentage of sales	60%
Return on sales	10%
Dividend payout ratio	30%
Turnovers based on year-end values:	
Cash and accounts receivable	4 times
Inventory	3 times
Required current ratio	3 to 1
Required ratio of long-term debt to stockholders' equity	50%

At the beginning of 19X3 the treasurer expects stockholders' equity to be $60 million and long-term debt to be $30 million.

Required: Prepare pro forma balance sheets and any supporting schedules you need for the end of each of the next four years. Determine how much additional common stock, if any, the firm will have to issue each year if the treasurer's estimates and assumptions are correct.

18-33 **Leverage** Mr. Harmon, treasurer of Stokes Company, has been considering two plans for raising $2,000,000 for plant expansion and modernization. One choice is to issue 9% bonds. The other is to issue 25,000 shares of common stock at $80 per share.

  The modernization and expansion is expected to increase operating profit, before interest and taxes, by $320,000 annually. Depreciation of $200,000 is included in the $320,000. Condensed financial statements for 19X4 are given below.

Stokes Company Balance Sheet
as of December 31, 19X4

Assets		Equities	
Current assets	$ 3,200,000	Current liabilities	$ 1,200,000
Plant and equipment (net)	7,420,000	Long-term debt, 7%	3,000,000
Other assets	870,000	Stockholders' equity	7,290,000
Total assets	$11,490,000	Total equities	$11,490,000

Stokes Company Condensed Income
Statement for 19X4

Sales		$8,310,000
Cost of sales	$5,800,000	
Operating expenses	1,200,000	7,000,000
Operating profit		1,310,000
Interest expense		210,000
Income before taxes		1,100,000
Income taxes at 40% rate		440,000
Net income		$ 660,000
Earnings per share, based on 100,000 outstanding shares		$6.60
Dividends per share		$3.30

  Mr. Harmon is concerned about the effects of issuing debt. The average debt ratio for companies in the industry is 42%. He believes that if this ratio is exceeded, the PE ratio of the stock will fall to 11 because of the potentially greater risk. If Stokes increases its common equity substantially by issuing new shares, he expects the PE ratio to increase to 12.5. He also wonders what will happen to the dividend yield under each plan. The firm follows the practice of paying dividends equal to 50% of net income.

Required

1. For each financing plan, calculate the debt ratio that the company would have after the securities (bonds or stock) are issued.
2. For each financing plan, determine the expected net income in 19X5, expected EPS, and the expected market price of the common stock.
3. Calculate, for each financing plan, the dividend per share that Stokes would pay following its usual practice and the yield that would be obtained at the market prices from your answer to item 2.
4. Suppose that you now own 100 shares of Stokes Company. Which alternative would you prefer the firm to use? Why?

TIME VALUE
OF MONEY

Suppose you had the choice between receiving $10,000 now and receiving $10,000 at some specified time in the future? Suppose you are absolutely sure to receive $10,000 at the specified later time. Under these conditions, virtually everyone would choose the first alternative. A dollar now is worth more than a dollar to be received later. This statement sums up an important principle: **money has a time value.** The reason that a dollar now is worth more than the certainty of a dollar to be received in the future is that you could invest the dollar now and have more than a dollar at the specified later date. It does not matter whether you expect inflation or deflation to change the purchasing power of money; you always prefer money now to the promise of *the same amount* of money later.

Many economic decisions involve investing money now in the hope of receiving *more* money later on. Any analysis of such decisions must consider the time value of money. Suppose you can invest $10,000 today with a promise that you will receive $10,800 at the end of one year. Should you make the investment? You know that to justify waiting for the money the amount to be received should be larger than the amount available to you now. But how much larger? It depends on what else you could do with the cash you have to make the investment—the opportunities that are available.

Suppose your best alternative is to earn 10% interest per year in another investment. If you invest $10,000 at 10% per year, you have $11,000 at the end of one year [$10,000 + ($10,000 × 10%)]. Comparing the two alternatives, you could have $11,000 at the end of the year as a result of a $10,000 investment now, or you could have $10,800 at the end of the year for a $10,000 investment now. You should choose the first alternative.

What happens when the time horizon is extended beyond one period? Suppose you can invest $10,000 today and receive $12,000 at the end of two years. Should you make the investment if the interest rate on another alternative is 10%? First determine how much you would have at the end of two years if you invested at a rate of 10%, as follows.

Now	You have $10,000
At the end of year 1	You have $11,000 [$10,000 + ($10,000 × 10%)]
At the end of year 2	You have $12,100 [$11,000 + ($11,000 × 10%)]

The interest earned in the second year is 10% of the total amount you have at the end of the first year, *not* 10% of the $10,000 you originally invested. This is the unique feature of **compound interest:** you earn the quoted interest rate both on the original amount invested and on the interest that you subsequently earn. Thus, at the end of two years, you have $12,100. The $12,100 is the **future value** of the $10,000 at a 10% interest rate. The $10,000 is the **present value** of $12,100 at a 10% interest rate.

By comparing the values of each available alternative at the end of the two years, you can see that it is not desirable to invest $10,000 now to receive $12,000 at the end of the two years. You could have $12,100 by investing elsewhere. We show this by comparing the two values at the *end* of the investment term. It is more common practice to compare present values.

PRESENT VALUE
OF A SINGLE AMOUNT

To evaluate an opportunity to receive a single payment at some date in the future at some interest rate, we must determine the present value of that choice. Instead of determining how much we would have at some future date if we invested $1 now, we want to know how much we would have to invest now to receive $1 at some future date. The preceding example showed that, at a 10% interest rate, an investment of $10,000 will accumulate to $12,100 at the end of two years. The present value of $12,100 two years from now is thus $10,000. The procedure to determine present values is called **discounting**, and the interest rate used is also called the **discount rate.** The specified amount of money to be received later is always a combination of the original investment (sometimes called *principal*) and the interest on that investment. The higher the interest rate, the more interest included in the total and so the smaller the amount of the total that constitutes principal.

Formulas are available for determining the present value of a sum of money to be received in the future. Some computer spreadsheets have functions to find present and future values. You can also use tables to determine present values without the formulas. Suppose we wanted to find the present value of $1.21 to be received two years from now when we know that the interest rate is 10%. (We know already that the present value is $1, and this is the answer the table should give us.) Table A on page 818 shows the present value of $1 to be received at various times in the future and at various interest rates. Referring to the 10% column and the row for two periods, we find the factor .826. This means that the present value of $1 to be received two years from now is $0.826 when the interest rate is 10%. Because we expect to get $1.21, not $1, we must multiply the factor by 1.21. This multiplication produces a present value of $0.99946, which is not significantly different from $1. (The slight difference is due to rounding in preparing the table.) The factors in Table A are generated by the formula,

$$(1 + i)^{-n}$$

where i = the interest rate and n = the number of periods.

Two characteristics of Table A are significant and should be understood. First, as you move down any column in Table A, the factors become smaller. You should expect this because the longer you must wait for a payment, the less it is worth now. If a dollar now is worth more than a dollar to be received in one year, then surely a dollar to be received one year later is worth more than one to come two years later. Second, the factors become smaller as you move across the table in any row. As the interest rate increases, the present value of the amount to be received in the future decreases. This should also be expected. The higher interest rate you can expect to earn on the sum invested now, the less you need to invest now to accumulate a given amount at the end of some number of years. In summary, the longer you have to wait for your money and the higher the interest rate you can earn, the less it is worth to you now to receive some specified amount at a future date.

PRESENT VALUE OF A STREAM OF EQUAL RECEIPTS

Sometimes it is necessary to compute the present value of a *series* of equal amounts to be received at the ends of a series of years. Such a stream is an **annuity** and describes, for example, bond interest received annually for a number of years. It is possible to find the present value of an annuity by finding the present values of each component of the stream and adding them. For example, what is the present value of an annuity of $1 per year for four years at 10%?

Received at End of Year	Amount to Be Received	Present Value Factor (from Table A)	Present Value of Future Receipt
1	$1	.909	$0.909
2	$1	.826	0.826
3	$1	.751	0.751
4	$1	.683	0.683
Present value of this annuity			$3.169

This procedure is cumbersome, especially if the annuity is to last for many years. You are multiplying the same number ($1) by several different numbers (the present value factors). From your study of mathematics, you know that the sum of these multiplications is equal to the product of the constant number ($1) and the sum of the different numbers. If you add up the present value factors (3.169) and multiply that sum by $1, you will get the same answer. (This can be verified at a glance because we are using an annuity of $1.)

Many practical situations deal with a series of equal receipts over several periods. These could be analyzed by using Table A and the lengthy procedure described above. But the task is made simpler by using a table like Table B on page 818, which adds the present value factors for you. Look at Table B in the column for 10% and the row for four periods. The factor is 3.170. This is the present value of a series of four $1 receipts when the interest rate is 10%. (The factor, 3.170, is rounded up from the sum of the factors given in Table A.)

The values shown in Table B are the cumulative sums of the factors from Table A (with an occasional rounding difference). The factor for an annuity for one period in Table B is the same as the factor for a single receipt in Table A, at the same interest rate. Try adding down Table A and checking each successive sum with the factor in Table B. The factors are generated by the formula,

$$\frac{1 - (1 + i)^{-n}}{i}$$

where i = the interest rate, and n = the number of periods.

All the factors in both tables relate to future receipts (or payments) of $1. When dealing with amounts other than $1, you must multiply the factor by the number of dollars involved to compute the present values. But remember that you can use Table B only when the individual payments in the stream are equal.

STREAMS OF UNEQUAL AMOUNTS

What if the payments to be received in the future are *not* equal? You could use the factors from Table A, but that can be cumbersome.

If *most* of the payments are equal, you can find the present value of the equal portions of each payment using Table B, then discount the remainder separately. We shall illustrate this method by modifying the previous example. Instead of receiving $1 per year for four years, you will receive $1 at the end of each of the first three years and $2 at the end of the fourth year.

From Table B we know that $1 per year for four years has a present value of $3.170 at 10%. That is the present value of the stream *except* for the extra $1 to be received at the end of year 4. Looking in Table A (for the present value of $1 to be received at the end of four years) we find that the extra $1 has a present value of $0.683. Adding the $0.683 to the $3.170, we obtain $3.853. We can check this by discounting each receipt separately.

Received at End of Year	Amount to Be Received	Present Value Factor (from Table A)	Present Value of Future Receipt
1	$1	.909	$0.909
2	$1	.826	0.826
3	$1	.751	0.751
4	$2	.683	1.366
Present value of this series of payments			$3.852

The difference ($0.001) is due to rounding.

Suppose that only $0.60 is to be received at the end of the fourth year. We now have a stream of equal payments of $1 for three years, then a $0.60 payment at the end of the fourth year. Use Table B to find the present value of a stream of $1 payments for three years, then add to it the present value of $0.60 to be received at the end of four years (from Table A). The solution is as follows.

Present value of $1 per year for 3 years at 10% ($1 × 2.487)	$2.4870
Present value of $0.60 at end of year 4 at 10% ($0.60 × .683)	0.4098
Present value of this series of payments	$2.8968

COMPUTATIONS FOR PERIODS OTHER THAN YEARS

In many instances, payments are made more than once a year. For example, a savings bank might credit interest quarterly or even daily, and interest on most bonds is paid semiannually. Nevertheless, it is common practice to quote an annual interest rate.

If interest is *compounded* more often than annually, the rate of interest actually earned is higher than the quoted interest rate. Suppose a savings bank pays 6% annual interest compounded semiannually. How much will you have at the end of a year if you deposit $1,000 today? You earn $30 for the first six months ($1,000 × 0.06 × ½). For the second six months, you earn interest on $1,030 ($1,000 + $30) and the interest earned is $30.90 ($1,030 × 0.06 × ½). Hence, at the end of the year you have $1,060.90. In effect, you earned at the rate of 6.09% per year, because the interest of $60.90 for one year is 6.09% of the $1,000 invested for that year. The 6.09% is called the **effective interest rate** and must be distinguished from the quoted, or **nominal interest rate** of 6%. We could say that the investment is earning 3% *per period* (6% divided by the two compoundings per year). Each period you are earning 3% on whatever sum is invested during that period. For any particular nominal interest rate, the effective interest rate rises as the number of compoundings per year increases.

Compound interest tables are constructed on the basis of an interest rate *per period*. Therefore, you must be careful to determine the interest rate you should use in any given situation. If you want the present value of an amount to be received ten years from now using an *effective* rate of 10%, you look in Table A in the 10% column and the row for ten periods. (Remember that an effective rate is a rate per year.) If, on the other hand, you want the present value of an amount to be received ten years from now using a nominal interest rate of 10% compounded semiannually, you look in Table A in the *5% column* (10% divided by the number of compoundings per year) and the row for *20 periods* (10 years × the number of compoundings per year).

In most situations you know the nominal interest rate. Therefore, to complete the desired computation you must convert the nominal rate to a rate per compounding period and revise the number of periods to take into account the compoundings. *When consulting the tables, you use for the number of periods, the number of years times the number of compoundings per year, and the interest rate is the nominal annual rate divided by the number of compoundings per year.* Doing this you are stating the interest rate per compounding period.

One practical example involves applying almost every technique in this appendix. Suppose you can buy a bond that will mature (be retired) in ten years. The bond carries a nominal interest rate of 6%, and interest is paid semiannually. You *want* to earn 10% compounded semiannually. How much would you be willing to pay for a bond with a face (maturity) value of $10,000?

First, you must recognize that your investment has two components. If you buy the bond you contract to receive (1) $10,000 ten years from now and (2) payments of $300 ($10,000 × 0.06 × ½) every six months for ten years. What is each of these components worth to you now? The price you would be willing to pay for the bond is the sum of the present values of the components.

To compute the price you would pay for the bond, you need the following.

1. The present value of $10,000 to be received ten years from now. You want to earn 10% compounded semiannually, so you refer to Table A for the present value factor for 20 periods (10 years × 2 compoundings) at 5% (10% divided by 2 compoundings). The factor is .377, so the present value you are looking for is $3,770 ($10,000 × .377).
2. The present value of an annuity of $300 to be received each six months for ten years. You want to earn 10% compounded semiannually, so you refer to Table B for the present value factor for 20 periods (10 years × 2 compoundings) at 5% (10% divided by 2 compoundings). The factor is 12.462, so the present value you are looking for is $3,739 ($300 × 12.462).

Thus, the price you would pay for this $10,000, 6% bond is $7,509 ($3,770 + $3,739). Note that the interest rate per period (5%) and the number of periods (20) are the same for both calculations. The bond is a single investment and earns a single rate of interest even though it provides both a single payment and an annuity.

USES AND SIGNIFICANCE
OF PRESENT VALUES

Should you invest a sum of money now in order to receive a larger amount later (whether the amount comes in a single payment, a stream of payments or both)?

Your decision should be based on the amounts of the cash to be invested and received later, the length of time over which the inflows are received, and the interest rate.

Where the dollars to be received in the future are known, you can refer to the tables for an appropriate factor, multiply by the number of dollars to be received in the future, and compare that amount with the money that must be invested now to receive the amount or amounts in the future. If the result of the multiplication is greater than the amount to be invested now, the present value of the future returns is greater than the investment and the investment is desirable. Such an investment has a positive *net present value*. If the result of the multiplication is smaller than the required investment, the opportunity is not desirable. (It has a negative net present value.)

The use of present values is not limited to accounting. You may apply your knowledge of present values in the study of economics, finance, and statistics. Some specific applications of present values in accounting are discussed in Chapters 8, 9, and 16.

The most common use of present value is to find values of future payments. In some situations, however, you want to find the interest rate from investing so many dollars now and receiving so many in the future. The procedures are discussed in the next section.

DETERMINING INTEREST RATES

When you wish to know the interest rate on a given investment with known future receipts, you also use present value tables. The interest rate so determined is called the **discount rate,** the **time-adjusted rate of return,** or the **internal rate of return.** The last term is the most common.

To find the present value of a stream of equal future receipts, you multiplied the amount of the regular receipt by a factor that incorporated both the length of the series of receipts and the interest rate being earned. This can be shown mathematically.

$$\begin{array}{c} \text{Present value of} \\ \text{future receipt(s)} \end{array} = \begin{array}{c} \text{amount of each} \\ \text{future receipt} \end{array} \times \begin{array}{c} \text{factor for discount} \\ \text{rate and waiting period} \\ \text{(present value factor)} \end{array}$$

In previous examples, you were looking for the value to the left of the equal sign. In trying to find the interest rate on a given investment when you know the future receipts, you are looking for the interest rate that *equates* the present value of the future receipts with the investment required to produce those receipts. Using the preceding equation, you are stating that the value to the left of the equal sign is the investment required now. You know the amount of the future receipts, and you know one element in determining the factor required—the waiting period. You want the missing element in our equation—the interest rate, or internal rate of return.

Suppose you can invest $3,791 today and receive $1,000 per year for five years beginning one year from now, and you want to know the interest rate you would be earning. Substituting in the preceding equation yields

$3,791 = $1,000 × (the factor for the interest rate for five periods)

The factor is 3.791, which is obtained by rearranging the equation to show

Present value factor for five periods = $3,791/$1,000 = 3.791

The $1,000 payments are an annuity, so you can look in Table B for the factor in the five-period *row* that is closest to 3.791. That exact factor is found in the 10% column, so the investment yields a rate of return of 10%. (We can check this by multiplying $1,000 by 3.791, giving $3,791 as the present value.) In general terms, this basic equation can also be shown as

$$\text{Present value factor} = \frac{\text{present value of receipts (required investment)}}{\text{periodic receipts}}$$

The formula can also be used with a single payment. Suppose you could receive $1,450 at the end of four years if you invested $1,000 today. The factor to look for in Table A is 0.690 (rounded), which is $1,000/$1,450. Looking across the four-period row in Table A, we come to .683 in the 10% column. The rate of return is therefore a bit less than 10%.

You can also use this modification of the basic equation if you know the receipts, the amount of investment (which is the present value), and the interest rate, but you want to know the length of time. Suppose you could invest $1,000 now and receive $300 per year, but the number of years is uncertain. If you want a 14% rate of return, you can compute the number of years over which you would have to receive the $300 payments.

$$\text{Present value factor} = \frac{\$1,000}{\$300} = 3.333$$

This factor is for 14% and an unknown number of years. Therefore you look down the 14% column in Table B and find that 3.433 is the factor for five years. If you received five $300 annual payments you would earn slightly more than the desired 14%.

DETERMINING REQUIRED RECEIPTS

In some decision-making situations you want to know the receipts, either single payment or annuity, needed to earn a particular interest rate (or internal rate of return), given the necessary investment and the life of the receipts. The basic formula can be rearranged as follows.

$$\text{Periodic receipt} = \frac{\text{present value of receipts (required investment)}}{\text{present value factor}}$$

Suppose you can invest $10,000 now and hope to receive $3,000 per year for six years. You would like to earn a 12% return. If you *do* receive $3,000 per year your rate of return will be about 20% ($10,000/$3,000 = 3.33, which is close to the factor for 20% and six years). However, you are uncertain whether you *will* actually receive $3,000 and want to know the minimum annual receipt for six years that will give a 12% return.

$$\text{Periodic receipt} = \frac{\$10,000}{4.111 \text{ (the factor for six years and 12\%)}} = \$2,432$$

Thus, if you receive at least $2,432 each year for the next six years you will earn at least a 12% return.

This method can also be applied to single payments; the only difference is the table to be used. Suppose you can invest $1,000 and receive a single payment at the end of five years. If you wish to earn a 14% return, you would have to receive $1,927 (rounded), which is $1,000/.519, the factor for a single payment at 14% at the end of five periods.

SUMMARY

Many situations or decisions involve cash inflows and outflows at different times. Such situations require recognizing the time value of money. To evaluate a situation that involves cash flows occurring at different times, it is necessary to use the values of those flows at the same point in time.

Almost all managerial accounting decisions involving cash flows at different times use the *present value* of those flows as the point of analysis. The present value of a single cash flow at some time in the future can be computed manually or determined with the help of tables such as Table A. When several future cash flows are involved, it is usually easier to compute their present value by using tables such as Table B. Although tables such as Table B apply only when the individual amounts in the series of cash flows are equal, it is possible to deal with uneven cash flows by using Tables A and B.

The present value of a future cash flow (or a series of future cash flows) depends on the amount of the flow(s), the interest (discount) rate, and the length of the waiting period. In some situations, the present value is known, but one of the other elements is not. The tables can also be used to determine the value of the unknown element.

Applications of the concept of present values include the computation of bond prices and the evaluation of other long-term investment opportunities. Chapters 8, 9, and 16 of this book all include managerial problems that must be analyzed using present values.

KEY TERMS

annuity	future value
compound interest	internal rate of return
discounting	nominal interest rate
discount rate	present value
effective interest rate	time value of money

KEY FORMULAS

$$\text{Present value of future receipts(s)} = \text{amount of each future receipt} \times \text{factor for discount rate and waiting period (present value factor)}$$

$$\text{Present value factor} = \frac{\text{present value of receipts (required investment)}}{\text{periodic receipts}}$$

$$\text{Periodic receipt} = \frac{\text{present value of receipts (required investment)}}{\text{present value factor}}$$

REVIEW PROBLEMS

1. Find the present value of the following sets of payments if the discount rate is (a) 10% and (b) 16%.

Received at End of Year	Amount				
	i	*ii*	*iii*	*iv*	*v*
1	$1,000	$1,000	$2,000	$1,500	$ 0
2	1,000	1,000	2,000	2,000	3,000
3	1,000	1,000	2,000	2,000	3,000
4	1,000		2,000	2,000	3,000
5			5,000		4,000

2. Find the discount rates for the following situations.

Case	Investment Required Now	Periodic Receipts	Number of Years for Receipts
i	$ 3,605	$1,000	5
ii	$12,300	$2,000	10
iii	$ 9,380	$3,000	5

3. Fill in the blanks for each of the following situations. All involve a single payment to be received at the end of the number of years given.

Case	Investment	Year in Which Payment to Be Received	Payment to Be Received	Interest Rate
i	$_____	4	$4,000	14%
ii	$1,000	5	$1,464	_____
iii	$3,000	—	$5,290	10%
iv	$5,000	7	_____	14%

4. Fill in the blanks for each of the following situations. All involve streams of equal annual payments. Round dollar calculations to the nearest $1.

Case	Investment	Annual Cash Payments	Number of Years Payments to be Received	Interest Rate
i	$_____	$1,000	10	14%
ii	$10,000	_____	8	10%
iii	$20,000	$5,000	—	8%
iv	$10,000	$2,000	8	_____

Answers to Review Problems

1. i. Stream of equal payments of $1,000 per year for four years.
    (a) At 10%—3.170 × $1,000 = $3,170
    (b) At 16%—2.798 × $1,000 = $2,798

    ii. Stream of equal payments of $1,000 per year for three years.
    (a) At 10%—2.487 × $1,000 = $2,487
    (b) At 16%—2.246 × $1,000 = $2,246

    iii. Stream of four equal payments and larger amount at end of fifth year. We will discount the four equal payments and add the present value of the fifth one.

    (a) At 10%—3.170 × $2,000 $6,340
        (Table A, five years, 10%) .621 × $5,000   3,105
                                                              $9,445

    (b) At 16%—2.798 × $2,000 $5,596
        (Table A, five years, 16%) .476 × $5,000   2,380
                                                              $7,976

    iv. Stream of unequal payments for four years. The easiest method is to find the present value of a $2,000 stream of payments for four years and subtract the present value of $500 at the end of one year.

    (a) At 10%—3.170 × $2,000 $6,340.00
        (Table A, one year, 10%) .909 × $500   (454.50)
                                                              $5,885.50

    (b) At 16%—2.798 × $2,000 $5,596.00
        (Table A, one year, 16%) .862 × $500   (431.00)
                                                              $5,165.00

    v. Stream of unequal payments beginning at the end of year two. Although there are shortcuts, it is probably simplest to discount separately.
    (a) At 10%

    (b) At 16% the present value is $7,712. Computations are similar to those for (a), except that the factors for 16% are used.

Received at End of Year	Amount to Be Received	Present Value Factor (From Table A)	Present Value of Future Receipt
1	0		
2	$3,000	.826	$2,478
3	$3,000	.751	2,253
4	$3,000	.683	2,049
5	$4,000	.621	2,484
Present value of this series			$9,264

2.

$$\frac{\text{Investment required}}{\text{periodic receipt}} = \text{the factor}$$

  i. $\dfrac{\$3,605}{\$1,000} = 3.605$ for five years $= 12\%$ in Table B

  ii. $\dfrac{\$12,300}{\$2,000} = 6.15$ for ten years; 6.145 for 10% is the closest factor

  iii. $\dfrac{\$9,380}{\$3,000} = 3.126$ for five years; closest factor is 3.127 for 18%

3. All of these problems require the use of Table A.
  i. $2,368. $4,000 × .592 (the factor for 14% for four years)
  ii. About 8%. $1,000/$1,464 = .683, which is very close to .681, the factor for a single payment in five years at 8%.
  iii. About six years. $3,000/$5,290 = .567, which is very close to the 6-year factor at 10% (.564). In this case, you know the interest rate, so you are looking for the factor in the column that is closest to .567.
  iv. $12,500. $5,000/.400 (the factor for seven years at 14%)

4. All of these problems can be solved by using the equation

$$\text{Present value} = \text{annual payment} \times \text{present value factor}$$

The present value, in each case, is the amount of the investment.
  i. $5,216. $1,000 × 5.216 (the factor for ten periods at 14%)
  ii. $1,874. $10,000/5.335 (the factor for eight periods at 10%)
  iii. About five years. $20,000/$5,000 = 4.0, which is the factor for 8% and an unknown number of years. Moving down the 8% column in Table B, we find 3.993, which is the closest factor to 4.0 under 8%.
  iv. About 12%. $10,000/$2,000 = 5.0, which is the factor for eight years and an unknown interest rate. The closest factor in the 8-period row is 4.968, which is the factor for 12%. The true rate is slightly less than 12%.

ASSIGNMENT MATERIAL

1. Computations – present values Find the present value of the following sets of payments if the discount rate is as noted for each set.

Received at End of Year	Set A at 8%	Set B at 10%	Set C at 20%
1		$2,000	($3,000)
2		2,000	$4,000
3		2,000	$4,000
4		2,000	$4,000
5		2,000	$4,000
8	$10,000		

2. **Missing factors**   Fill in the blanks for each of the following independent investment opportunities.

Case	Investment Required Now	Periodic Receipt	Number of Years of Receipt	Interest (Discount) Rate
A	$16,950	$3,000	10	__%
B	$16,775	_____	10	8%
C	$_____	$5,000	13	18%
D	$10,000	$2,500	—	24%

3. **Computation of bond prices**   You are considering investing in some corporate bonds. Each bond is different, and because the companies are different, you believe you should earn a different rate of interest (effective interest rate) on each investment. The relevant data for each bond are provided below.

	Bond of Company		
	A	B	C
Face value	$10,000	$5,000	$20,000
Nominal (stated) interest rate	10%	8%	6%
Years to maturity	7	8	7
Interest paid	Annually	Annually	Semiannually
Desired interest rate	12%	10%	10%

Required: Compute the price you would pay for each bond.

4. **Present values and rates of return**   The following information is available about two investments.

	A	B
Required investment now	$10,000	$20,000
Cash flows, annually for 7 years	$ 2,500	$ 4,700

Required
1. Compute the approximate internal rate of return that each investment yields.
2. Compute the present value of each investment if the desired rate of return is 10%.

3. Determine the annual cash flows that would have to be received for each year in the 7-year period to make each investment provide a 16% return.

4. For each investment, determine the number of years that the stated annual cash flows would have to be received to make the investment provide a 20% return.

5. **Present values – unusual timing** Many situations involve cash flows occurring at or near the end of a period. Still others involve flows at or near the beginning of a period. Tables A and B can be used to deal with both types of situations. For each of the following situations, compute the present value of the cash flows described.

(a) A receipt of $5,000 four years from today; the interest rate is 9%.

(b) A receipt of $1,000 per year at the beginning of each of five years beginning today; the interest rate is 8%.

(c) A receipt of $10,000 per year for seven years, the first receipt to arrive exactly six years from today; the interest rate is 12%.

6. **Relationships** Fill in the blanks for each of the following investments.

Item	Case 1	2	3	4
a. Investment required now	———	$416,250	$32,280	———
b. Present value at desired rate of return	———	———	$31,080	$358,000
c. Annual cash receipt	$9,000	$125,000	———	$ 50,000
d. No. of years cash to be received	16	8	4	———
e. Desired rate of return	16%	14%	———	9%
f. Rate of return yielded	20%	———	18%	14%

Table A
Present Value of $1

one time cash flow

Number of Periods	5%	6%	8%	9%	10%	12%	14%	16%	18%	20%	22%	24%	25%
							Interest Rates						
1	.952	.943	.926	.917	.909	.893	.877	.862	.847	.833	.820	.806	.800
2	.907	.890	.857	.842	.826	.797	.769	.743	.718	.694	.672	.650	.640
3	.864	.840	.794	.772	.751	.712	.675	.641	.609	.579	.551	.524	.512
4	.823	.792	.735	.708	.683	.636	.592	.552	.516	.482	.451	.423	.410
5	.784	.747	.681	.650	.621	.567	.519	.476	.437	.402	.370	.341	.328
6	.746	.705	.630	.596	.564	.507	.456	.410	.370	.335	.303	.275	.262
7	.711	.665	.583	.547	.513	.452	.400	.354	.314	.279	.249	.222	.210
8	.677	.628	.541	.502	.467	.404	.351	.305	.266	.233	.204	.179	.168
9	.645	.592	.500	.460	.424	.361	.308	.263	.225	.194	.167	.144	.134
10	.614	.558	.463	.422	.386	.322	.270	.227	.191	.162	.137	.116	.107
11	.585	.527	.429	.387	.350	.287	.237	.195	.162	.135	.112	.094	.086
12	.557	.497	.397	.355	.319	.257	.208	.168	.137	.112	.092	.076	.069
13	.530	.469	.368	.326	.290	.229	.183	.145	.116	.093	.075	.061	.055
14	.505	.442	.340	.299	.263	.205	.160	.125	.099	.078	.062	.049	.044
15	.481	.417	.315	.274	.239	.183	.140	.108	.084	.065	.051	.040	.035
16	.458	.394	.292	.251	.218	.163	.123	.093	.071	.054	.042	.032	.028
20	.377	.312	.215	.178	.149	.104	.073	.051	.037	.026	.019	.014	.012
30	.231	.174	.099	.075	.057	.033	.020	.012	.007	.004	.003	.002	.001

Table B
Present Value of $1 Annuity

Annual Cash flows.

Number of Periods	5%	6%	8%	9%	10%	12%	14%	16%	18%	20%	22%	24%	25%
							Interest Rates						
1	.952	.943	.926	.917	.909	.893	.877	.862	.847	.833	.820	.806	.800
2	1.859	1.833	1.783	1.759	1.736	1.690	1.647	1.605	1.566	1.528	1.492	1.457	1.440
3	2.723	2.673	2.577	2.531	2.487	2.402	2.322	2.246	2.174	2.106	2.042	1.981	1.952
4	3.546	3.465	3.312	3.240	3.170	3.037	2.914	2.798	2.690	2.589	2.494	2.404	2.362
5	4.329	4.212	3.993	3.890	3.791	3.605	3.433	3.274	3.127	2.991	2.864	2.745	2.689
6	5.076	4.917	4.623	4.486	4.355	4.111	3.889	3.685	3.498	3.326	3.167	3.020	2.951
7	5.786	5.582	5.206	5.033	4.868	4.564	4.288	4.039	3.812	3.605	3.416	3.242	3.161
8	6.463	6.210	5.747	5.535	5.335	4.968	4.639	4.344	4.077	3.837	3.619	3.421	3.329
9	7.108	6.802	6.247	5.996	5.759	5.328	4.946	4.607	4.303	4.031	3.786	3.566	3.463
10	7.722	7.360	6.710	6.418	6.145	5.650	5.216	4.833	4.494	4.192	3.923	3.682	3.571
11	8.306	7.887	7.139	6.805	6.495	5.988	5.453	5.029	4.656	4.327	4.035	3.776	3.656
12	8.863	8.384	7.536	7.160	6.814	6.194	5.660	5.197	4.793	4.439	4.127	3.851	3.725
13	9.394	8.853	7.904	7.487	7.103	6.424	5.842	5.342	4.910	4.533	4.203	3.912	3.780
14	9.899	9.295	8.244	7.786	7.367	6.628	6.002	5.468	5.008	4.611	4.265	3.962	3.824
15	10.380	9.712	8.559	8.061	7.606	6.811	6.142	5.575	5.092	4.675	4.315	4.001	3.859
16	10.838	10.106	8.851	8.313	7.824	6.974	6.265	5.669	5.162	4.730	4.357	4.033	3.887
20	12.462	11.470	9.818	9.129	8.514	7.469	6.623	5.929	5.353	4.870	4.460	4.110	3.954
30	15.372	13.765	11.258	10.274	9.427	8.055	7.003	6.177	5.517	4.979	4.534	4.160	3.995

INDEX